MARKETING Principles & Strategy

Second Edition

Henry Assael
Stern School of Business
New York University

The Dryden Press
Harcourt Brace College Publishers
Fort Worth Philadelphia San Diego
New York Orlando Austin San Antonio
Toronto Montreal London Sydney Tokyo

Editor in Chief: **Robert A. Pawlik**
Acquisitions Editor: **Lyn Keeney Hastert**
Developmental Editor: **Paul Stewart**
Project Editor: **Jim Patterson**
Production Manager: **Jacqueline Parker**
Designer: **Brian Salisbury**

Address for Editorial Correspondence
The Dryden Press, 301 Commerce Street, Suite 3700, Fort Worth, TX 76102

Address for Orders
The Dryden Press, 6277 Sea Harbor Drive, Orlando, FL 32887
1-800-782-4479, or 1-800-433-0001 (in Florida)

ISBN: 0-03-076708-3

Library of Congress Catalogue Number: 92-70670

Credits appear on page CR-1, which constitutes a continuation of the copyright page.

Printed in the United States of America

3 4 5 6 7 8 9 0 1 2 048 9 8 7 6 5 4 3 2

The Dryden Press
Harcourt Brace & Company

To Alyce

The Dryden Press Series in Marketing

Assael
Marketing: Principles and Strategy
Second Edition

Bateson
Managing Services Marketing: Text and Readings
Second Edition

Blackwell, Blackwell, and Talarzyk
Contemporary Cases in Consumer Behavior
Fourth Edition

Boone and Kurtz
Contemporary Marketing
Seventh Edition

Churchill
Basic Marketing Research
Second Edition

Churchill
Marketing Research: Methodological Foundations
Fifth Edition

Czinkota and Ronkainen
International Marketing
Third Edition

Dunn, Barban, Krugman, and Reid
Advertising: Its Role in Modern Marketing
Seventh Edition

Engel, Blackwell, and Miniard
Consumer Behavior
Seventh Edition

Futrell
Sales Management
Third Edition

Ghosh
Retail Management

Hutt and Speh
Business Marketing Management: A Strategic View of Industrial and Organizational Markets
Fourth Edition

Ingram and LaForge
Sales Management: Analysis and Decision Making
Second Edition

Kurtz and Boone
Marketing
Third Edition

Murphy and Cunningham
Advertising and Marketing Communications Management: Cases and Applications

Oberhaus, Ratliffe, and Stauble
Professional Selling: A Relationship Process

Park and Zaltman
Marketing Management

Patti and Frazer
Advertising: A Decision-Making Approach

Rachman
Marketing Today
Second Edition

Rogers, Gamans, and Grassi
Retailing: New Perspectives
Second Edition

Rosenbloom
Marketing Channels: A Management View
Fourth Edition

Schellinck and Maddox
Marketing Research: A Computer-Assisted Approach

Schnaars
MICROSIM
Marketing simulation available for IBM PC and Apple

Sellars
Role Playing: The Principles of Selling
Second Edition

Shimp
Promotion Management and Marketing Communications
Third Edition

Talarzyk
Cases and Exercises in Marketing

Terpstra and Sarathy
International Marketing
Fifth Edition

Tootelian and Gaedeke
Cases and Classics in Marketing Management

Weitz and Wensley
Readings in Strategic Marketing Analysis, Planning, and Implementation

Zikmund
Exploring Marketing Research
Fourth Edition

PREFACE

It is generally recognized that marketing is central to all business functions because of its role in defining customer needs and directing the firm's resources to meet these needs. The rapid changes in the environment of the 1980s and 1990s has heightened awareness of the importance of this role as firms have had to face increasing foreign competition, economic discontinuities, and the need to become more ecologically conscious. As the 21st century approaches, the successful marketers will be those who can best define customer needs in the context of even more rapid changes in the business environment.

As a result of these changes, the study of marketing has become more fascinating and more complex. It is essential for any basic marketing text to *(1) give students an understanding of marketing concepts, (2) describe these concepts in the context of current applications, and (3) develop the concept to application links in the context of a rapidly changing environment.* These three needs have guided the development of this text.

THE BASIC APPROACH

The positive reception to the first edition of *Marketing: Principles and Strategy* was based primarily on the effective integration of marketing concepts and applications. This integration is a hallmark of the second edition as well. Marketing concepts are introduced in a *process approach* in which marketing is described as a series of processes—market segmentation, new product development, marketing research, and so forth. Most chapters start out by describing the marketing process in question in a series of steps that become the major headings for the chapter. The student is thus given a conceptual road map to the chapter.

The concept to applications link is accomplished in two ways. First, an opening vignette focuses on a specific company example that is often carried through the rest of the chapter to illustrate key applications of marketing concepts. For example, Gillette's plans and strategies in introducing the Sensor razor is used to introduce the subject of marketing planning in Chapter 3, and to illustrate key aspects of this process throughout the chapter. Second, stand-alone examples are used to reinforce key points. For example, the chapter on market segmentation cites examples of alternative approaches in identifying and targeting market segments, and in positioning products to these segments.

The concept to application link is framed in the context of a changing marketing environment. The dynamic nature of the marketing environment is established early, in Part 2, with chapters citing changes in the international, social, ecological, economic, and competitive dimensions of marketing. Subsequent chapters show how these environmental changes directly impact on various components of marketing strategy.

ORGANIZATION OF THE BOOK

The emphasis on concepts and applications in a changing environment provides the basis for organizing this book. Part 1 provides an introduction to marketing, explains the role of marketing in the business organization, and describes the process of marketing planning.

The remainder of the book is organized based on the four steps required to develop marketing plans as follows:

Part 2, *Identifying marketing opportunities,* describes the various components of the marketing environment. A chapter on the international environment emphasizes the globalization of marketing and the growing importance of foreign competition. A separate chapter devoted to competitive advantage provides additional focus on competitive forces that impact on marketing strategy, and is a distinctive signature of this book.

Part 3, *Defining the target market*, focuses on the need to target marketing effort to customer segments based on their needs. Marketers must understand their customers and obtain information on their needs if they are to effectively target marketing effort. Chapters in this section deal with the process of collecting marketing information, the nature of consumers and organizational buyers, and the process of market segmentation.

Part 4, *Developing the marketing mix*, describes how a mix of marketing strategies is developed and implemented. The basic components of the marketing mix are considered—product, distribution, advertising, sales promotion, and pricing strategies. A distinctive aspect of the book is the inclusion of services marketing as part of the marketing mix. Although the primary focus is on planning at the product level, components of the marketing mix are tied back to the firm's broader directions spelled out in the corporate strategic plan.

Part 5, *Strategic planning, evaluation, and control* considers the broader corporate dimensions of marketing by focusing on strategic planning. It then describes how managers evaluate and control their marketing operations at both the product and corporate level. The last chapter emphasizes marketing productivity in the context of control of marketing operations, reflecting the attempts of American companies to counteract the productivity advantages established by foreign competitors.

CHANGES IN THE SECOND EDITION

The second edition has been substantially revised in several respects. Most important is the greater emphasis on international marketing and ecological issues. These areas are likely to represent the most significant changes in the marketing environment of the 1990s and beyond. Additional changes are a focus on ethical issues in every aspect of marketing, greater emphasis on services marketing, and an earlier introduction of the marketing planning process to provide an organizational framework for the rest of the book. A further addition in the second edition is the inclusion of video cases for each chapter (found at the end of the book) that provide information in addition to that in the video to give students a more comprehensive perspective on the case.

Each of these changes is described more fully below.

INTERNATIONAL

American companies are realizing that global communications and modes of transportation have produced greater similarities in needs and tastes among consumers across national boundaries. As a result, they see foreign markets as areas of opportunity, particularly when many industries are maturing at home. Adding to the increasing importance of an international perspective is the decrease in trade barriers in the 1990s.

American companies are adopting a more international perspective because of threats as well as opportunities. Foreign competition continues to dominate many industries, putting domestic companies at a competitive disadvantage based on quality and cost. It is only in the 1990s that domestic companies in industries such as automobiles and electronics are beginning to be competitive with foreign producers.

These issues are treated in the second edition in three ways. First, the international marketing chapter has been moved to the front of the book (now Chapter 5) to better provide a framework for focusing on international issues. Second, a new box entitled *Global Marketing Strategies* has been introduced that provides a forum for discussing international marketing strategies in each chapter. Third and most important, international marketing examples are integrated into the discussion of marketing concepts in each chapter.

ECOLOGICAL ISSUES

Ecological concerns are becoming more prevalent both in the boardrooms of corporate America and among consumers in the 1990s. Among many companies, planning groups are devoting significant time and resources to solving problems in the areas of recycling, packaging, pollution control, and waste disposal. Consumers are becoming increasingly concerned about company actions in these areas. In a 1990 survey, 84 percent of respondents said they were changing their shopping habits as a result of environmental concerns.

This edition makes frequent references to ecological issues by integrating examples throughout, the first being a reference to Arm & Hammer's environmental positioning of its product line in Chapter 1. A new feature is a box in each chapter entitled *Ethical and Environmental Issues in Marketing* which treats either an ethical or environmental issue, or both (given the frequent interaction between the two). For example, the box in Chapter 2 cites DuPont's actions in the area of environmental controls and asks whether it has been sufficiently responsive to ecological issues.

ETHICAL ISSUES

There has been an increasing consciousness of ethical issues in marketing as reflected by the greater focus on such issues in both marketing curricula and management programs. The second edition reinforces the approach taken in the first edition by treating ethical issues in each area of the marketing mix—product safety, packaging, advertising, sales promotions, personal selling, pricing, and distribution. Ethical issues are also discussed in the context of strategies in the international arena, and more generally in marketing planning.

As noted, a new feature is the box in each chapter on *Ethical and Environmental Issues in Marketing.* For example, the boxed item in the international marketing chapter deals with Nestle's sale of infant formula to third world consumers and the ethical issues involved. The ethics box in the chapter on market segmentation deals with the ethical issues created when RJR targeted Uptown cigarettes to African-American consumers.

SERVICES MARKETING

With the service sector accounting for over half of the GNP and three out of four jobs in the American economy, services marketing continues to receive special attention in this edition. The prior edition was the first marketing text to incorporate service into the marketing mix rather than treat it as an appendage at the end of the book. This treatment reflects the central role of services and its equal stature to products in the development of marketing strategies.

This emphasis is reinforced in this edition with additional examples of services throughout the text in key areas such as segmentation, advertising, distribution, and pricing strategies. The attempt is to integrate services throughout the book rather than rely on one chapter on services.

INTEGRATION OF MARKETING PLANNING

Another important change in the second edition is an earlier introduction of marketing planning as Chapter 3. As noted, the book is organized based on the marketing planning process with subsequent chapters dealing with the key phases of this process. Placing marketing planning at the front of the book provides a good integrative focus for students and an organizing framework that is more comprehensible.

VIDEO CASES

A new feature of this edition is the video case and accompanying videotape for each chapter. These 23 video cases supplement the information in the text by providing students with additional insights on the company and industry. They also provide a thought provoking look at specific aspects not otherwise discussed. For example, the case on Federal Express in Chapter 2 provides additional information on FedEx's international strategy which enhances the concepts and examples given within the chapter.

ADDITIONAL FEATURES

The first edition was cited for several strengths that are maintained in the second edition. One is a student-friendly writing style that engages rather than talks down to the student. The frequent, up-to-date examples serve to keep marketing concepts alive for students and provide a further motive for student involvement.

Several pedagogical features in the first edition are maintained in the second, namely:

- *Learning objectives* at the beginning of each chapter that also serve as a framework for a chapter summary.
- *End-of-chapter questions* designed to involve the student and encourage a better understanding of marketing concepts. The questions are often framed in an applications context to ask the students to apply concepts to the examples cited.
- A *listing of key terms* in each chapter with a full *glossary* in the back of the book.
- *Additional readings* for each chapter found at the end of the book.
- *Appendixes* on marketing math and on careers in marketing.

A new pedagogical item in the second edition is an end-of-chapter section titled *You are the Decision Maker* which presents situations and mini-cases, often in the form of quotes by managers, and asks students to react. These questions allow students to more fully explore and apply marketing concepts cited in the chapter.

TEACHING AND LEARNING SUPPLEMENTS

A full range of teaching and learning supplements are included in support of the text. All components have been reviewed by existing and potential adopters and have been thoroughly tested. The package includes the following:

INSTRUCTOR'S MANUAL

Changes and new information to this edition's instructor's manual are provided by the author and by Judy Keeley of Northern Illinois University. The manual is organized by chapter and is designed to provide additional, up-to-date examples of marketing concepts that can provide a useful context for class discussion. It also provides suggested projects by chapter, should course requirements include a term project. Answers to end-of-chapter questions are also included. The manual is organized as follows:

- Objectives
- Chapter outline
- Lecture guide
- Term projects
- Answers to end-of-chapter questions
- Answers to section on "You are the Decision Maker"
- Answers to questions for the two boxed items per chapter

TEST BANK

The author and Robert M. Cosenza, of California State University at Fresno, prepared the test bank, which has been fully reviewed to ensure relevance and an appropriate range of difficulty. It includes over 2,000 questions organized by chapter and by sections within the chapter. Each question is rated for difficulty. The test bank includes true/false, multiple choice, and essay questions for each chapter.

In addition to the printed version of the test bank, *computerized test banks for IBM and Apple PCs* are also provided. The computerized test bank provides the same questions as in the printed version and allows the instructor to preview, edit, and add test questions as well as print "scrambled" forms of tests.

TRANSPARENCY ACETATES AND TEACHING NOTES

Robert F. Gwinner of Arizona State University created or hand picked over 175 transparency acetates (also available in slide form). These include carefully selected ads and other examples that extend the text discussion, as well as a reproduction of 26 of the figures in the text. Additional text figures are included as transparency masters in the media instructors manual.

VIDEO PACKAGE

Twenty-three professionally produced videos were selected for this edition, one for each chapter, to illustrate the real-world dynamics and applications of marketing principles. Each video was chosen to support the major marketing concepts of the related chapter. The combination of the case writeup in the text and the videos provide a rich and comprehensive case example for each chapter.

MEDIA INSTRUCTOR'S MANUAL

The media instructor's manual was developed by the author and provides answers to questions for the video cases for each chapter. In most cases, further questions and answers are provided in addition to those in the video case in the text.

The media manual is organized as follows:

- A repeat of the case writeup and an expanded set of questions
- Concepts discussed
- Teaching objectives
- Central problems
- Outline of the video
- Answers to case questions

COMPUTER SIMULATION

The media manual includes a description of the *MICROSIM-PC game.* This is a computer program that simulates the consumer market for microwave ovens over a three year period. Students assume they are marketing managers for a major company in this industry. Their objective is to maximize profits for the firm.

STUDY GUIDE

The study guide, by Thomas J. Quirk of Webster University, is designed to help students apply marketing concepts in the text rather than rely on rote memorization. The study guide contains the following for each chapter:

- Learning objectives recap
- Detailed chapter outline
- Key terms
- "Fill-in-the-blank" exercises
- Applications problems
- Additional cases for analysis

TEXT DEVELOPMENT

Both the first and second editions of the text were treated as a new product and have gone through most of the early steps in new product development—idea generation, concept testing, product development, and product testing. Focus groups were run to get reactions to the first edition and guide development of the second. In addition, a full review of the first edition was conducted to obtain specific reactions on a chapter-by-chapter basis.

In developing the second edition, the text was thoroughly reviewed by both adopters and non-adopters and class tested. Comparative reviews with other texts were also conducted. A complete photo research program insured that the exhibits were closely tied to the examples in the case.

ACKNOWLEDGMENTS

The review process for the second edition involved 19 reviewers. The reviews proved invaluable in providing suggestions for changes in the second edition and improvements in each chapter. I am indebted to the following reviewers for their help and insights in shaping the final product:

Becky Beasley, *University of Texas at Arlington*
Roger Blackwell, *The Ohio State University*
Robert Cosenza, *California State University—Fresno*
Bernice Dandridge, *Diablo Valley College*
Daniel P. Darrow, *Ferris State University*
Dayle Dietz, *North Dakota State College*
Douglas M. Egan, *Lewis & Clark College*
Sharon Galbraith, *Seattle University*
Joyce Guthrie, *James Madison University*
Robert F. Gwinner, *Arizona State University*
Denise Johnson, *University of Louisville*
Judy Keeley, *Northern Illinois University*
Hal Koenig, *Oregon State University*
Thomas R. Mahaffey, *Sienna College*
Richard Nordstrom, *California State University—Fresno*

Thomas J. Quirk, *Webster College*
Robert D. Reid, *James Madison University*
Larry Rogers, *Ohio University*
Richard Shreve, *University of Wisconsin—Superior*
Jerry E. Wheat, *Indiana University—Southeast*

I am also indebted to the following people for their role in developing the ancillary materials:

- Judy Keeley, who helped me develop the *Instructor's Manual.*
- Robert Cosenza, who helped me develop the *Test Bank.*
- Robert Gwinner, who prepared the transparency acetates.
- Peter Kaminski, of Northern Illinois University, who prepared the Marketing Mathematics appendix.
- Edward Golden, of Central Washington University, who developed the Careers Guide appendix.

A number of colleagues at the Stern School of Business at New York University were also very helpful in reviewing portions of the manuscript. These included Bruce Buchanan, who helped on the pricing chapters; Richard Colombo, on marketing research; Sam Craig, on the promotional mix; Arieh Goldman, on distribution and international marketing; Avijit Ghosh, on strategic planning; Eric Greenleaf, on new-product development and sales management; Priscilla La Barbera, on advertising; and Robert Shoaf, on organizational buyer behavior.

An excellent group at The Dryden Press provided strong support for this effort. Special thanks are due to two individuals, Lyn Keeney Hastert, my marketing editor, and Paul Stewart, my developmental editor. Lyn was supportive at every step in the development of the second edition. Her advice regarding ways to strengthen the text and ancillaries was invaluable. Paul oversaw every detail in the developmental process, from chapter development to photo research. The level of assistance he provided on a day-to-day basis helped ensure that the second edition would be a strong offering. Thanks are also due to Jim Patterson, the project editor, for overseeing the final stages of product development and ensuring that all the stages in the critical path were completed. Several other people at Dryden deserve mention. Brian Salisbury, the art and design director, has developed the art program to ensure that design supports content. Jacqueline Parker, the production manager, has organized the details of the production process and helped maintain a rigorous schedule. Lise Webb, marketing manager, has taken the principles in this book to heart by producing a well-integrated marketing plan.

I am also grateful to my research assistants at the Stern School, Elko Swaak, Janet Wheeler, and Beth Fainberg. They supplied much of the research material used, as well as assisting in gathering background material for the video cases.

Final thanks go to my wife Alyce for being my foremost consultant and research assistant. Her support in this process cannot be justly measured in words.

Henry Assael
November, 1992

CONTENTS IN BRIEF

CONTENTS

004320
PRODUCT
PROMOTION
PLACE
PRICE
$

PART I

The Marketing Pro

Marketing has been recognized as an increasingly important area in business operations because it deals with understanding and identifying customers, and directing the firm's resources to meet their needs. The rapid changes in the world economy in the 1980s and 1990s have made marketing more central, more complex, and more exciting. No matter what career path you follow, you will probably have to consider issues directly or partially related to marketing. It is also more likely that these issues will involve international as well as domestic markets.

The three introductory chapters in this section attempt to explain what marketing is (Chapter 1), the role of marketing in the business firm (Chapter 2), and the nature of marketing planning (Chapter 3). In so doing, these chapters explain why marketing is central to all business operations, and the relation of marketing to other business functions such as finance, accounting, and manufacturing. They also set the stage for considering how marketing operates in the broader social, economic, ecologic, competitive, and legal environment.

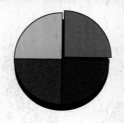

CHA 1

What is Marketing?

YOUR FOCUS IN CHAPTER 1

To learn:

- *What marketing is.*
- *The environmental dimensions of marketing.*
- *The relationship of marketing to other business functions.*
- *The role of marketing in the past and its role in the present.*
- *The broader role of marketing.*
- *The ethical and social responsibilities of marketers.*

Harley-Davidson: Back on the Road to Profitability with Marketing Savvy

After a long detour, Harley-Davidson, the only domestic manufacturer of motorcycles, is back on the road to profitability. For years Harley-Davidson's problem was that it long relied on a mystique of big bikes ridden by the black leather crowd to sell motocycles. But by the early 1980s, that traditional market for large motorcycles was shrinking, and the company was facing bankruptcy.[1] To get the company back on track, Harley followed a set of sound marketing principles: (1) Identify a customer group, (2) find out what they want, and (3) position the products accordingly.

With its traditional customer base dwindling, Harley first needed to identify a customer group that would represent a new segment of bike riders. The company eyed the growing number of baby boomers (those born in the post–World War II baby boom) as a potential target, a group very different from its traditional market. The second step was finding out what "baby boomers" wanted. Could the maturing, increasingly conservative baby boomer be a target for motorcycles? After researching this group, Harley came out with the answer—a definite "yes." By the late 1980s, many baby boomers were past forty and heading for midlife crises. They were looking for the escape and the fantasy that Harley Davidson's big bikes offered.

In order to successfully tap the baby boom market, Harley had to accomplish the third step: positioning its product to the needs of the target group. This meant making the motorcycle a vehicle to satisfy the baby boomer's fantasies. How could Harley do it? By "smoothing its rougher edges." Smoothing its rougher edges did not mean changing the basic product. Baby boomers wanted to satisfy their fantasies with big bikes, so Harley knew it had to keep its bikes "looking big, mean and American."[2] It kept big doses of chrome and heavy iron—and an engine that sounded like thunder. The problem was that, to appeal to a higher-income market, Harley had to increase the reliability of its machines and change its image.

Increasing reliability was easy. Harley knew that its new generation of bike riders would not put up with frequent repairs, so it introduced a new engine, an improvement on its then-familiar V-twin. Bikers no longer had to get their hands dirty to fix their machines. Image was more of a problem. Many of Harley's dealerships looked dark and menacing until Harley stepped in and insisted the dealers clean up their stores. Now dealers not only sell motorcycles, but motorcycle fashion clothing in a clean, neon-lit atmosphere. The tie-in with motorcycle garb even included a fashion night at Bloomingdale's.

Harley went further to attract the higher-income baby boomer. It featured celebrities such as Kurt Russell and Elizabeth Taylor on Harley-Davidsons in its advertising. It also changed its ads from a "heavy-metal" approach to a softer look. One ad even featured a baby in a Harley T-shirt asking "When did it start for you"; that is, wanting a Harley.[3] To further soften its image, Harley even put the company name on products like cologne and wine coolers. It is also offering options such as stereo systems and intercoms built into helmets to attract baby boomers.

Harley's success in appealing to baby boomers is reflected in the profile of its current owners: Over 60 percent have attended college, one in three is a professional or manager, and median income is $45,000—hardly a profile of a dropout from society. Harley's success is also reflected in its current sales and profits. By 1990, the company was selling 41,000 motorcycles a year, up by 50 percent from the early 1980s. Revenues and earnings more than tripled from 1985 to 1989.[4]

Harley is following a fourth key principle of marketing: Try to keep customers happy after they buy. It established Harley Owners Groups, or HOGs, to bring new owners together and to reinforce the joys of biking. HOGs give riders instant companionship through organized rides, rallies, and charity runs. HOG rallies are popular with baby boomers who avoid the tough biker rallies of the black leather jacket set.

Harley is not satisfied with its new thrust. It is looking for additional markets for future expansion. For example, biking has traditionally been a male-dominated activity, so Harley is trying to encourage more women to become riders by establishing a "Ladies' Harley" club. Harley is also looking abroad for more sales. Over one-third of its sales are abroad and foreign sales are expanding faster than those in the United States. Whereas other companies have suffered at the hands of foreign competitors—most notably domestic auto and electronic companies—Harley has fared well with about 60 percent of the U.S. market for heavy motorcycles.

Harley's long detour is over. It is clearly on track to profitability, both in the United States and abroad, because it is following sound marketing principles.

WHAT IS MARKETING?

As the experience of Harley-Davidson shows, the most important objective in any business is to identify and satisfy customers, thus creating profitability for the firm. As a result, marketing is central to any business firm, and any business executive must understand its role in his or her organization. Whether you are going into investment banking, financial services, accounting, management, or production, you will never be far from a firm's customers and a firm's competition. Knowing what marketing is and how marketing strategies are developed will help you deal with your customers and competitors.

Marketing* *can be defined as all activities directed toward identifying and satisfying customer needs and wants through a process of exchange.*[5] To understand this definition, we must understand the meaning of

1. the customer
2. the process of exchange
3. the marketing management process required to satisfy customer needs

THE CUSTOMER

The customer is an individual who is a prospective buyer of a product or service. We can refer to a customer for autos, a customer for pollution-control equipment, or a customer for financial services. The customer for an auto or for financial services is the *final consumer. The* **final consumer** *purchases and consumes the product or service.* The customer for pollution-control equipment is an *organizational buyer.* **Organizational buyers** *purchase products and services to help in the manufacture, servicing, or distribution of other products.*

MARKETS

In most cases, marketing activities are designed to meet the needs of groups of customers rather than just one customer. *A* **market** *is composed of actual or potential buyers of a product, and the sellers who offer goods to meet buyers' needs.* We can refer to a market for heavy motorcycles composed of existing owners and prospective buyers of these products and manufacturers such as Harley, Kawasaki, and Suzuki, who market them to the public. It makes sense that the word *marketing* is derived from *markets,* because a market requires a process of exchange between buyers and sellers.

MARKET SEGMENTS

Market segments *are groups of customers with similar needs and characteristics.* Companies divide the market into segments, then target specific segments with specific product offerings.

Market segmentation is distinct from mass marketing, which offers a single product to as wide a market as possible. The advantage of market segmentation is the ability to design product offerings to better meet customer needs. For example, Kellogg segments the adult cereal market into those who emphasize nutrition,

*Terms in bold face and their definition can be found in the glossary at the end of the book.

EXHIBIT 1.1

Kellogg Segments the Adult Cereal Market

Health-Conscious Segment

Nutrition-Conscious Segment

Calorie-Conscious Segment

health, or weight watching. It targets consumers in the nutritional segment with cereals which have natural ingredients and high vitamin content such as Just Right. It targets consumers in the health segment with high fiber cereals such as All-Bran, and it targets calorie watchers with low-calorie cereals such as Product 19 (see Exhibit 1.1). The alternative would be to offer one cereal in an attempt to appeal to all three segments, a strategy that is unlikely to meet the needs of these segments and attract as many consumers as a segmentation approach.

The market segment Harley-Davidson originally targeted was the tough, hard-riding black leather set. Harley then sought to broaden its market by targeting baby boomers. In so doing, it was appealing to another market segment—baby boomers seeking fantasy as they approach middle age. Consumers in this group are a market segment, because they have similar needs for motorcycles that are distinct from other segments such as the Hell's Angels component of the market. Appealing to the baby boomer segment required a set of marketing strategies totally different from those appealing to the Hell's Angel segment.

THE EXCHANGE PROCESS

Marketing activities require a process of *exchange. The* **exchange process** *is a dynamic process in which a seller requires payment to satisfy a buyer's need for a valued object or service.* The process requires three conditions to come together: 1) an agreed object of value; 2) communication between buyer and seller; and 3) a delivery of value (see Figure 1.1). The key component of exchange in most advanced economies is a price mechanism that reflects the value of the good to the buyer,

FIGURE 1.1

The Components of Exchange

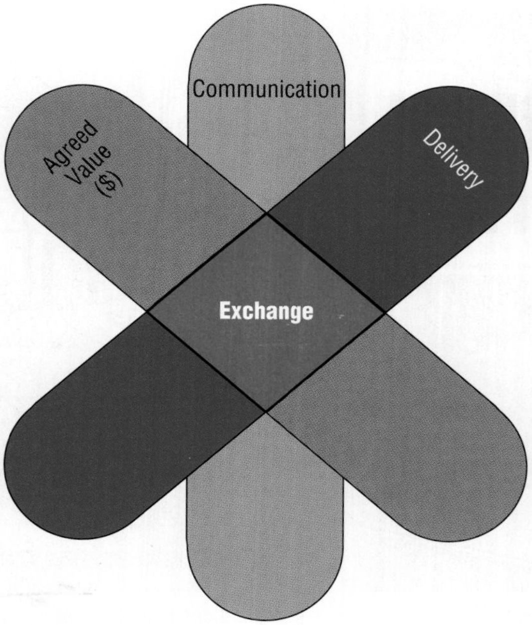

although barter is possible in some cases. As we will see later in the book, there are many methods for establishing the price of a good or service, and companies sometimes fail to correctly estimate the value of their goods and services to buyers. But in most cases, prices do a reasonable job of reflecting value.

A price tag of $15,000 on the upper end of Harley's motorcycle line posed no problem for many baby boomers, indicating the value some put on living out a fantasy. What buyers often get in the process of exchange is not so much the functional benefits of a product, such as a smooth ride or quick acceleration, but the psychic benefits—for example, a middle-aged federal government administrator who dons a leather vest on weekends and rides his Harley, claiming "This is the real me."[6]

The second condition for exchange to take place is *communication from seller to buyer* to inform buyers of product characteristics, price, and availability. Such communication is achieved on a face-to-face basis through personal selling and impersonally through advertising. Harley advertises its product line primarily in specialty magazines read by motorcycle enthusiasts. But it also relies on face-to-face contacts through its dealers to inform prospective buyers of price and product features.

The third requirement of exchange is *delivery of value*. Delivery of value from buyer to seller involves the payment for goods and services. Delivery from seller to buyer involves transfer of goods and services. An efficient process of exchange also assumes that the buyer obtains the goods and services that will provide the expected value. If a buyer obtains defective merchandise that is not replaced, or if a seller fails to receive payment for goods delivered, an inefficient process of exchange occurs because the value expected by each party is not delivered.

FIGURE 1.2

The Marketing Process

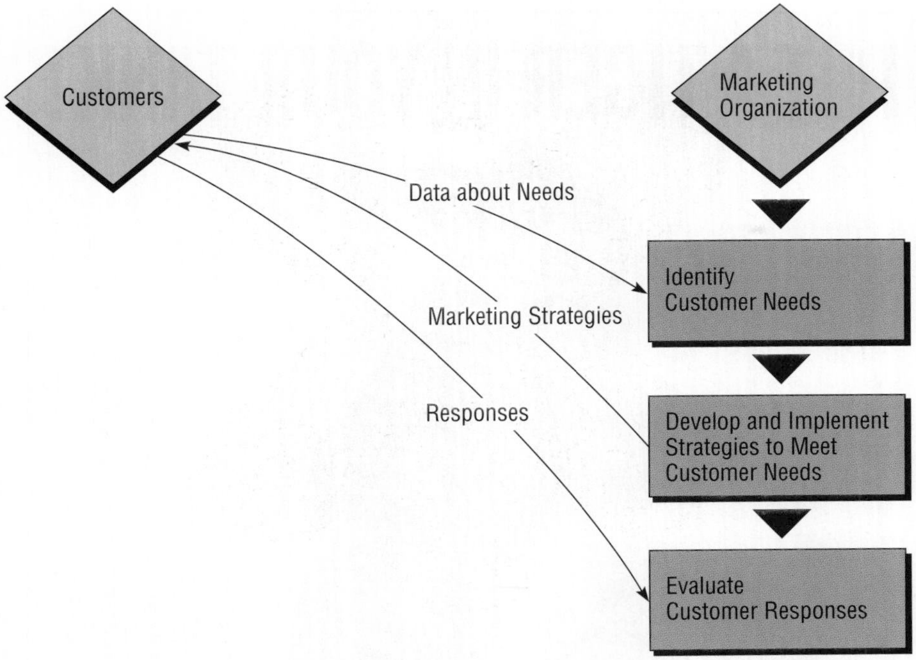

THE MARKETING MANAGEMENT PROCESS

The **marketing management process** *is the mechanism by which the marketing organization interacts with its customers* (see Figure 1.2). The marketing manager's responsibility is to initiate and monitor these activities. First, the marketing organization *identifies customer needs.* It then *develops and implements marketing strategies* to meet these needs. Finally, the *customer's response* is analyzed to determine how well customer needs were met.

IDENTIFY CUSTOMER NEEDS

The marketing manager's first task is to obtain information relating to customer needs. Once such information is collected, marketers can develop products and formulate marketing strategies to meet these needs.

Customer needs are often identified in open-ended discussions among small groups of consumers moderated by a professional researcher. This method is known as *focus group interviews.* A number of years ago, a study conducted by Esso (now Exxon) analyzed attitudes toward driving and through in-depth interviews found that many drivers want a sense of freedom and power, a surge of acceleration to free themselves from the mundane aspects of everyday life. This finding was the basis for Esso's long-standing advertising theme "Put a tiger in your tank" (see Exhibit 1.2).

Researchers conduct surveys in person, by phone, or by mail and ask specific questions regarding consumer preferences, product usage, and consumer characteristics. PepsiCo was given the idea of a fruit-based soft drink—eventually introduced as Slice—when consumer surveys showed that 75 percent of regular users

EXHIBIT 1.2

Appealing to Consumer Needs in Driving

of lemon–lime soft drinks said they would prefer a carbonated beverage that contained fruit juice.[7] Because lemon–lime beverages accounted for about 13 percent of soft drink sales, a fruit-based drink represented significant potential. A survey identified an important consumer need.

One company that has been sensitive to consumer needs is Church & Dwight, makers of Arm & Hammer products including the well-known baking soda. The company was one of the first to anticipate consumers' growing ecological concerns. Greater ecological consciousness dates to the first "Earth Day" in 1970. At the time, Church & Dwight introduced its first Arm & Hammer product other than baking soda: a phosphate-free detergent that uses sodium bicarbonate, the ingredient in baking soda. It also established a new use for baking soda, deodorizing refrigerators.[8] Since 1970, the company has had one underlying theme in its new product introductions: Bring out products that are ecologically sound. In so doing, it caught the growing wave of concern for environmental protection among most American consumers in the 1980s.

Once a company identifies a need, like the desire for environmentally safe products, it must determine what group of consumers have that need. This group is known as the target market. *The* **target market** *is a market segment that the company tries to reach with its products and services.* A firm cannot appeal to all segments in a market, so it must target one or a few segments. Companies define a target segment by identifying consumers with a common set of needs, determining their characteristics, and assessing the likelihood they will purchase the company's products.

Church & Dwight identified ecologically conscious consumers as a target market. It found that most of these consumers are younger, better educated, and more likely to influence the opinions and actions of others. In introducing phosphate-free detergents, the most logical strategy for Church & Dwight was to try to get this group to buy the product first, in the expectation they would influence others to buy. Such a strategy encourages a diffusion of purchases from the target group to the general population as environmental concerns grow.

DEVELOP MARKET STRATEGIES

The second responsibility of marketing management in Figure 1.2 is to develop and implement marketing strategies. **Marketing strategies** *are the means by which firms attempt to influence their customers.* Marketing strategies require: 1) developing products to meet customer needs, 2) positioning products to target segments, and 3) formulating an effective marketing mix.

DEVELOPING PRODUCTS TO MEET CUSTOMER NEEDS Firms develop new products and maintain existing ones to meet customer needs. *New products* are essential to generate profits on an ongoing basis. Ongoing new-product activity is possible only if an effective new-product development process exists. Such a process requires a mechanism for identifying customer needs, generating new product ideas, developing products, testing them in selected markets for a period of time to see how well they sell, and, finally, introducing them nationally.

Church & Dwight's success since the 1970s has been built on its ability to introduce new products such as deodorants, shampoos, skin-care items, and mouthwash. These products, under the Arm & Hammer name, were marketed with the common theme that they are environmentally friendly. Its deodorants were some of the first to be advertised as being unharmful to the ozone layer.

The company also introduced a series of industrial products to protect the environment. It developed a new paint stripper with no toxic solvents that was used to help restore the Statue of Liberty in 1986 (see Exhibit 1.3). It also discovered that baking soda, when fed into smokestacks, can absorb chemicals causing acid rain before they are emitted. And, it introduced a system for removing lead from water systems. The company's chief executive reflected Church & Dwight's main focus on customer need-identification when he said, "the environmental movement . . . fits so much of what we do."[9]

EXHIBIT 1.3

A Non-Toxic Paint Stripper Made by Arm & Hammer Helped Restore the Statue of Liberty

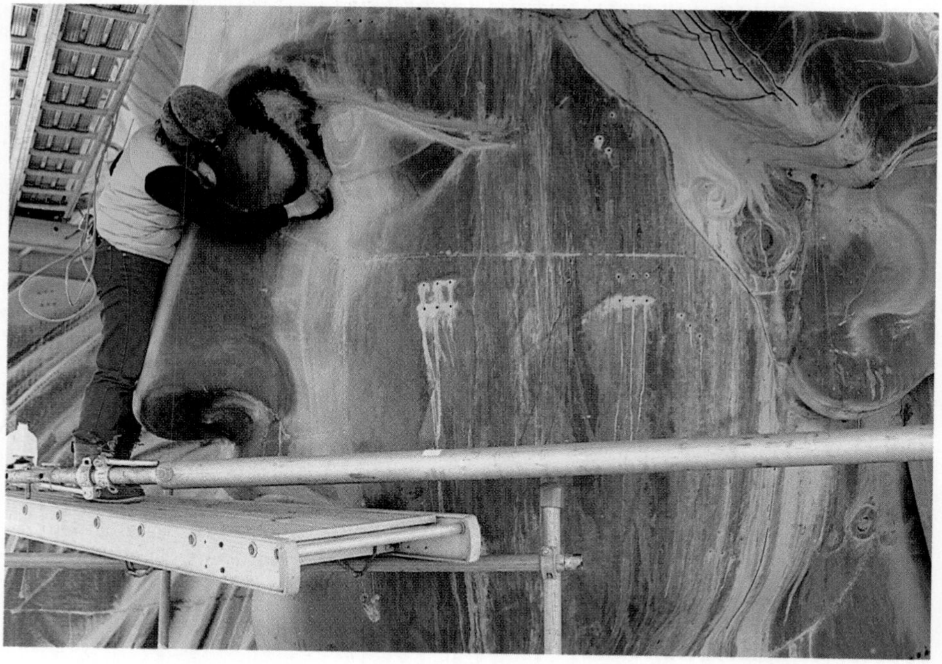

Marketers do not rely only on new products to satisfy customer needs. They must constantly manage *existing products* to ensure they continue to meet needs. It took fifteen years for Church & Dwight's detergent brand to be one of the market leaders and the company's most profitable product. Such success is the result of perseverance borne of constant advertising and the use of in-store price incentives to induce consumers to try the product. A key component of managing existing products is to add variations. Once Church & Dwight's detergent was established, it then introduced other laundry and household cleaning products to trade off the strength of the detergent brand. It introduced Arm & Hammer powdered and liquid bleaches and Arm & Hammer carpet deodorizer.

POSITIONING PRODUCTS TO TARGET MARKETS The benefits of new and existing products must be communicated to a target market. The main product benefits to be communicated define the product's positioning. **Product positioning** *is the way the marketing organization communicates the benefits and features of a product to consumers.*

Church & Dwight positions its products on two dimensions. First, it communicates the functional benefits of the brand—the cleaning benefits of its detergents, the whitening advantages of its bleaches, the freshening abilities of its deodorizers. But these benefits do not give the company's products an advantage over better-known and more-powerful competitors such as Procter & Gamble's Tide detergent or Lever Brothers' Wisk. The second dimension positions Church & Dwight's products on environmental and health concerns; for example, phosphate-free detergents and ozone-friendly deodorizers. These claims have led to more-distinctive positioning of Church & Dwight's products and have permitted a relatively small company to compete with giants.

FORMULATING AN EFFECTIVE MARKETING MIX Companies must develop a **marketing mix,** *that is a mix of marketing strategies, to influence customers to buy their products and services.* This mix is frequently referred to as the **four Ps of marketing**: *product, promotion, place, and price.*

The *product* component of the marketing mix ensures that product characteristics provide benefits to the consumer; the *promotional* component communicates through advertising, personal selling, and sales promotions, the product's ability to satisfy the customer. The *place*, or *distribution*, component distributes the product to the right place at the right time to meet customer needs; and the *price* component ensures the product is priced at a level that reflects consumer value. Together, the four P's work in a single, integrated plan determined by the product's positioning (see Figure 1.3).

The marketing mix for Arm & Hammer detergent can be used as an example. The basic advantage of the *product* is its phosphate-free quality. Church & Dwight identifies environmental safety as the feature that distinguishes Arm & Hammer detergents from competitors and effectively communicates this benefit to consumers through *promotional* strategies, primarily advertising.

Price is also an important part of the marketing mix for Arm & Hammer detergent. One of the reasons that it took fifteen years for the brand to become an established competitor was that, for many years, Church & Dwight insisted on pricing its detergent at parity with the giants. In 1985, the company began pricing

FIGURE 1.3

The Four Ps of Marketing

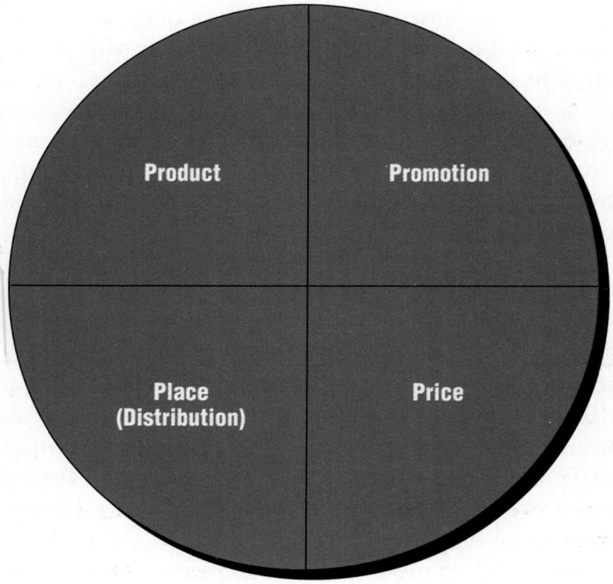

its detergents 20 percent below Tide, the market leader.[10] This strategy encouraged consumers to try the product and was instrumental in more than doubling sales from 1984 to 1990.

One aspect of the marketing mix with which the company had a problem was *distribution*. Church & Dwight obtained distribution for its new detergent brand in supermarkets primarily because of its well-established baking soda. But as its product line grew, its distribution facilities were no longer adequate. Church & Dwight had to improve its transportation facilities, increase its warehouses, and enlarge its sales force to ensure on-time delivery.

Once Church & Dwight solved its distribution problems and arrived at a proper pricing strategy, all the elements of a well-coordinated marketing mix were in place for its detergent brand—a product with an important competitive advantage, an advertising campaign based on the effective positioning of the product, a price incentive to induce consumers to try the brand, and wide-spread distribution.

EVALUATE CUSTOMER RESPONSES TO COMPANY STRATEGIES

The third responsibility of marketing management, shown in Figure 1.2, is to evaluate customer responses. Church & Dwight tracks customer purchases by determining sales and market share for each brand. **Market share** *is the amount consumers spend on a brand as a percent of total expenditures on all brands in the product category.*

Sales and market share figures do not fully measure the success of marketing strategies. Companies must know what is going on in the customer's mind—that is, attitudes toward the offerings of the company and its competitors, reactions to proposed new products, awareness of the company's advertising, intention to buy, and so forth. Companies obtain this type of information from product tests and from consumer surveys. Such research has two objectives: first, to learn consumer reactions to new product offerings and to marketing strategies before they are introduced; second, to determine how consumers react to product offerings once they are introduced.

Church & Dwight first asks consumers to try its new products in product tests and then introduces the products into test markets to evaluate sales before introducing them on a national basis. Church & Dwight also conducts consumer surveys to determine how products are used and consumer attitudes toward its products. One such survey produced a surprising finding: Consumers who use baking soda as a deodorizer in their refrigerator think they change the box every *four* months, but actually change it every *fourteen* months. This finding led Church & Dwight to introduce a new advertising campaign using a series of seasonal reminders to replace the box.[11]

MARKETING IS ALSO A CORPORATE GAME PLAN

Our description of marketing has focused primarily on product strategies. There is another dimension of marketing: corporate strategies. Corporate strategies are designed to determine the total set of products the firm will offer and in so doing to identify the business or businesses the firm should be in. Corporate strategies are much broader than product strategies because they determine the general direction of the firm, leading to issues such as whether the firm should develop or acquire new businesses and whether the firm should divest itself of poorly performing businesses.

The corporate dimension of marketing requires asking "Where is the company heading in the next five years?" In answer to this question, Church & Dwight is looking abroad for growth. The environmental movement took hold in Europe before it did in the United States. The potential market for the Arm & Hammer line of products in Western Europe is largely untapped. Church & Dwight is also actively marketing its industrial products in Europe, working with leading European chemical companies in Britain, Germany, and Belgium to establish a market for products such as its industrial paint stripper. The severe environmental problems of the former Communist nations of Eastern Europe also represent an opportunity for Arm & Hammer. The company is well-positioned to market pollution-control products to these countries.

The extension of the Arm & Hammer line, the decision to market it to environmentally conscious consumers, and the strategy to look for opportunity abroad all suggest that marketing is more than developing strategies for an individual product. It is also a corporate game plan for future growth.

THE MARKETING ENVIRONMENT

A company's ability to meet customer needs is influenced by the marketing environment. *The* **marketing environment** *is composed of the influences and trends outside the firm that affect its ability to meet customer need.* Such influences include competition, the economy, technology, ecology, government regulations, and demographic and life-style trends. Managers identify changes in customer needs, competitive actions, and other environmental factors such as technology, the economy, and legal and regulatory trends. Generally, the two most important external influences on a company are its customers and its competitors. Marketing organizations develop strategies to meet customer needs and to establish an advantage over their competitors. Marketing strategies are then evaluated based on customer and competitive responses to these strategies.

Figure 1.4 expands the marketing process shown in Figure 1.2 to include both customer and competitive influences in the marketing environment. Customer needs caused the increasing emphasis on ecology, creating the opportunity for Church & Dwight to expand the Arm & Hammer line beyond baking soda. This opportunity was reinforced by two other environmental factors: first, the initial absence of any competition in introducing ecologically safe household products; second, the technology that allowed Church & Dwight to develop from baking soda such industrial products as a paint-stripping compound or a pollution-control product that absorbs toxic chemicals.

The second environmental influence shown in Figure 1.4 is competition. Marketers try to establish **competitive advantage,** *that is, superiority over competition based on product quality, better distribution and services, and/or lower costs and selling price.* Pepsi-Cola attempted to exploit competitive advantage when Coca-Cola introduced New Coke. Roger Enrico, president of Pepsi-Cola USA, made the famous statement, "After 87 years of going at it eyeball to eyeball, the other guy just blinked."[12] The implication was that Coke felt impelled to change its formula to be more like Pepsi-Cola in order to strengthen its hand in the teenage market. Pepsi-Cola quickly mounted an advertising campaign to take advantage of apparent competitive weakness. In one ad, a young girl, Coke in hand, asks "Why did

FIGURE 1.4

The Expanded Marketing Process

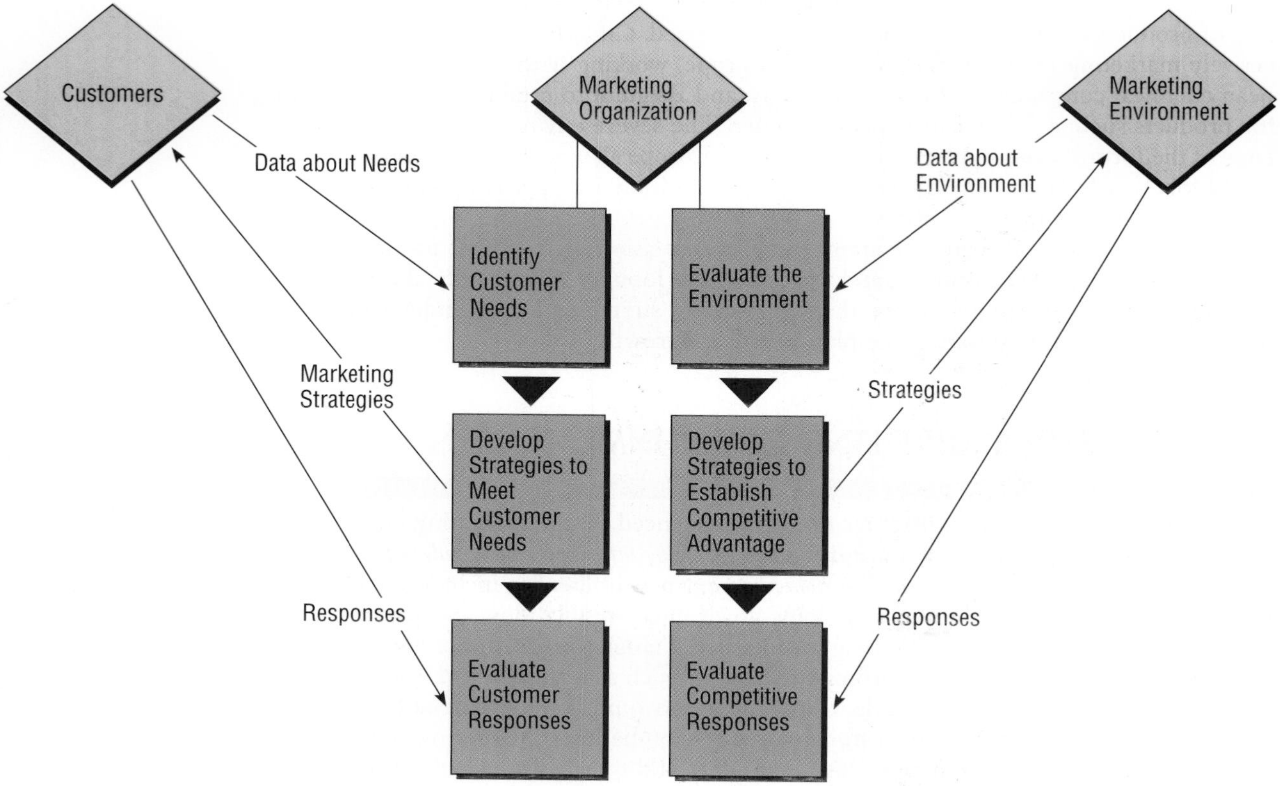

they do it to me? I liked it (Coke) the way it was." Ultimately, the introduction of New Coke did not create a competitive advantage for Pepsi-Cola. Coke reintroduced the old formula and the outcome was, if anything, a net increase in Coca-Cola's market share.

THE GLOBAL MARKETING ENVIRONMENT

The marketing environment influences a company's marketing strategy in both domestic and international operations. Since international operations have expanded greatly, global influences are increasingly important. Today, three out of four manufacturing jobs are linked to products sold abroad.[13] On a worldwide basis, more than half of new products are developed for foreign markets.[14] Many American firms such as Coca-Cola, IBM, Polaroid, Gillette, Johnson & Johnson, and Colgate–Palmolive earn more than half their revenue abroad (see Exhibit 1.4). Also, foreign firms such as Nestlé, Unilever, and Shell Oil are often mistaken for American companies because they have substantial operations in the United States.

EXHIBIT 1.4

IBM Looks for Growth Abroad

American firms are increasingly likely to look abroad for marketing opportunities in the 1990s. Demand in many domestic industries is stagnant; while foreign markets are opening up. The elimination of trade barriers among the countries in the European Economic Community (better known as the Common Market) in 1992 means that for trading purposes, Europe will be one country rather than many. This poses both opportunity for, and threats to, American firms: opportunity in making it easier to market products across national boundaries; threats in that larger European companies might emerge and create more competition for American firms.

The attempted shift of Eastern European countries and the countries of the former Soviet Union from a centralized to a market economy also presents opportunities for American firms. As a free-market mechanism develops and consumers gain purchasing power, markets will be open for American goods. Further, trade barriers are being reduced in the Pacific Rim countries—Japan, Korea, Taiwan, Singapore—providing additional markets for American goods.

When multinational companies market abroad, they prefer to market their products on a standardized basis across countries. Introducing one standardized brand is much less costly to produce than several differentiated brands. Also, by reinforcing the same theme in their advertising, companies can build a world

GLOBAL MARKETING STRATEGIES

Harley-Davidson Goes Global

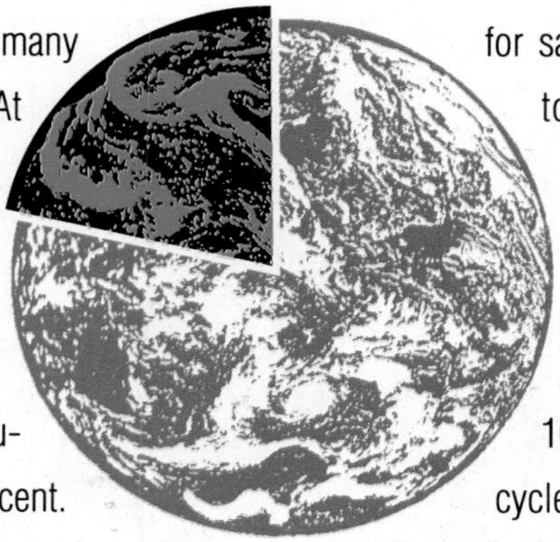

Harley Davidson is winning the competitive wars with foreign producers, both at home and abroad, at a time when many American companies are losing. At home, Harley has regained market share from Kawasaki, Yamaha, Suzuki, and Honda. In 1985, its share of the heavy motorcycle market was 28 percent, with the Japanese manufacturers claiming the other 72 percent. By 1990, it reversed the tide, claiming 66 percent of the market with Japanese motorcycles representing only 34 percent. As we have seen, Harley accomplished this feat by positioning its bikes to a new target group, baby boomers.

Even more impressive is Harley's showing abroad. The company was motivated to look abroad for sales because demand for heavy motorcycles in the United States was rapidly declining. With over 60 percent of a declining market, the company had little room for growth. Overseas, Harley has only 10 to 20 percent of the heavy motorcycle market, and according to a company spokesperson, future growth will come from international operations. Overseas sales totalled 15,000 in 1990 and would have been more except that the company was operating at full production capacity.

image. Coca-Cola communicates a single unifying message in 155 countries plus the South Pole. It advertises and packages with "one look, one sight, one sound," constantly reinforcing what the consumer sees at home and abroad.

But there is a basic danger in such standardized strategies. Standardization may be achieved at the cost of gearing products and strategies to the particular needs of customers in various countries. Although Coca-Cola strives for standardization, it recognizes the need to adapt to local environments. In Germany, where the use of TV commercials is tightly restricted by the government, Coke uses a lot of magazine advertising. In Japan, the company found the distribution system so complex that it established its own network of bottlers. In China, Coca-Cola agreed to buy local cashmere wool and wine to help the government raise foreign exchange as part of the deal to introduce its flagship brand. And, when the Berlin Wall came down, the company was one of the first into East Germany, selling Coke off its trucks until a distribution system could be established.

This diversity of regulations and customs across countries means that international marketing operations tend to be riskier. Moreover, requirements set by foreign governments to enter their markets, and differences in language, customs, media, and distribution, make international marketing more complicated than domestic marketing.

GLOBAL MARKETING STRATEGIES

Through its advertising, Harley tries to maintain a uniform image around the world, one of ruggedness and power. Although the image is uniform, the bikes are not. Harley modifies its products to meet the requirements of overseas markets, changing its speedometers, for instance, to read in kilometers. In the past, the company left it up to its overseas dealers to make such changes. In the process of adapting to foreign markets, Harley went from 250 variations of its motorcycles to 1,053. That increases production and marketing costs; but, as the company's director of international operations says, "If you are going to deal internationally, you have to have the right products."

Question: Harley's advertising strategy is fairly standardized across countries, whereas its motorcycles are adapted to local conditions. What is the rationale behind this strategy?

Source: "How Harley Outfoxed Japan With Exports," *The New York Times*, August 12, 1990, p. F5.

Given the increasing importance of international marketing, global applications of marketing strategies will be cited in each chapter.

MARKETING SYSTEMS

In evaluating and meeting customer needs, marketers must establish the facilities for an exchange process to take place. **Facilitating marketing systems** *provides the means for an exchange process whereby goods are transferred from manufacturers to customers, and a reverse transfer of payments is made from customers to manufacturers.* This process of exchange requires three distinct systems: (1) *a* **marketing information system** *that allows management to determine what products to offer to meet customer needs so exchange can take place*; (2) *a* **communications system** *that informs customers of products and influences them to buy*; and (3) *a* **distribution system** *that delivers what the customer wants, when and where the customer wants it.*

Facilitating systems are depicted as part of a total marketing system in Figure 1.5. The customer is at the center. The role of the marketing organization (the next circle in the figure) is to provide an exchange with the customer, facilitated by information, communications, and distribution systems. These facilitating systems operate in a broader marketing environment composed of competitive, social, technological, legal and regulatory, and economic forces.

THE MARKETING INFORMATION SYSTEM

Management relies on a marketing information system to identify marketing opportunities, test products and strategies, and evaluate customer responses. The system generates information from three sources: the environment, the marketing organization, and marketing research agencies. Environmental information is provided by government agencies, trade associations, the company's management and sales personnel, its distributors, and its competitors. The marketing organization also provides its management important information such as sales data, market share, and costs. Also, research firms are called on to evaluate marketing opportunities and strategies by conducting customer surveys and running various experiments to test components of the marketing mix.

THE COMMUNICATIONS SYSTEM

The marketing communications process involves three types of organizations: the marketing organization, advertising agencies, and the mass-communication media. The marketing organization—that is, the manufacturer of the brand being advertised—is responsible for developing the product, positioning it, and paying for the communications process. The company and its advertising agency develop a campaign to inform and influence consumers. They also develop an overall communications mix which can be composed of direct mailings, in-store displays, sales promotions, public relations, and a media plan that might involve TV, radio, magazine, and newspaper ads. The advertising agency purchases time and space in these various media according to strict goals formulated to reach specific target markets.

THE DISTRIBUTION SYSTEM

The networks through which marketing organizations move their products to their customers are known as **channels of distribution**. The simplest channel is selling directly to the customer. This form of selling is most common for industrial goods such as generators or automation systems, because the cost and complexity of such industrial goods often requires direct contact between buyer and seller. Most consumer goods are sold through intermediaries. Companies using intermediaries frequently sell to wholesalers who then sell to retailers. Selling to a few wholesalers is more economical than selling to thousands of small retailers.

Some national marketers sell directly to retailers despite the greater costs. Frito-Lay maintains a competitive advantage by delivering products directly to supermarkets, as well as to small retail outlets, from 1,800 warehouses through a sales force of more than 10,000 people. In this way, it can ensure fresh products, shelf space for its brands, and favorable promotions at the point of sale.

FACILITATING SYSTEMS IN FOREIGN MARKETS

Because the United States has one of the most advanced economies in the world, its information, communications, and distribution networks are far more developed than those in most other countries. It is important for American marketers operating abroad to recognize the nature and limitations of the facilities of the host country.

The Eastern European countries and those in the former Soviet Union are a

FIGURE 1.5

The Total Marketing System

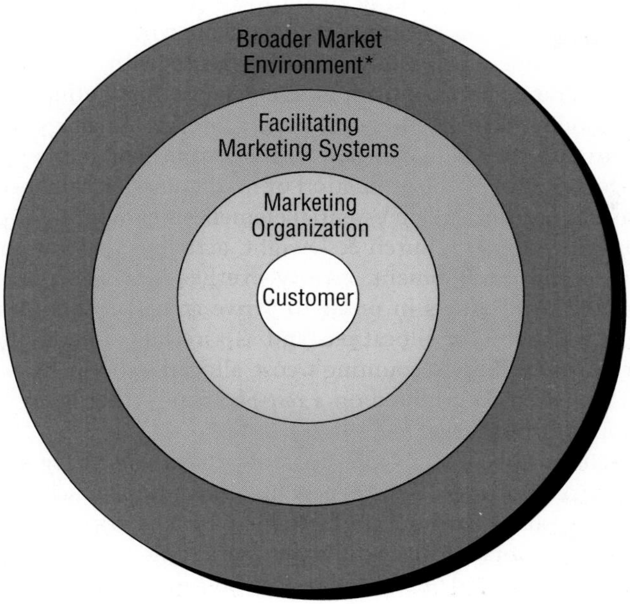

* Competitive, social, technological, legal, regulatory, and economic forces.

good example of the shortcomings of facilitating systems abroad. Distribution in these countries is primitive by U.S. standards because of poor road networks. Phone systems are inefficient and, since not all consumers own a phone, consumer telephone surveys cannot be used. Supplies of raw materials can also be spotty. It was these limitations in the facilitating systems that led McDonald's to become almost totally self-sufficient when it opened its Moscow restaurant. McDonald's had to make its own beef patties and buns and developed its own potato-growing facilities for its french fries.

The lack of convertible currencies in these countries has further complicated the marketing process. Companies such as Coca-Cola and PepsiCo have had to accept local products that can be sold in the West in exchange for their goods. In Hungary, Coca-Cola trades its soft drinks for glass bottles that it can use in bottling plants. In Poland, Pepsi trades its products for furniture it uses in its Pizza Hut subsidiaries.[15]

MARKETING'S RELATIONSHIP TO OTHER BUSINESS FUNCTIONS

Because of its central role, marketing must be performed in coordination with other business activities. Therefore, it is essential to understand the relationship of marketing to other business functions in the firm, namely: finance, accounting, manufacturing, and research and development (R&D).

Finance is essential to evaluating marketing performance because it determines the profitability of individual products such as Arm & Hammer detergents or Harley motorcycles. Managers responsible for products must develop budgets, control costs, and estimate the profitability of the product. If a product is performing poorly, a financial analysis is necessary to determine whether it should be retained or deleted from the line. H. J. Heinz seeks marketers with a financial background to manage their brands because of the importance of budgeting and cost control in developing product plans.[16] At the corporate level, top management must assess alternative sources of financing for new products and new markets.

Accounting contributes to the evaluation of marketing performance by allocating costs. Such cost allocations are an essential element in computing profits. In multiproduct companies such as Church & Dwight, activities that cut across products, such as research and development, factory overhead, and corporate advertising, must be allocated to products in order to arrive at net profits. Accounting procedures determine such cost allocations and as a result, directly affect evaluation of a product's profitability. Accounting's cost allocations also help marketers set prices. Prices are often determined on a *cost-plus basis*—that is, by using cost as a base and adding a profit target.

Marketing must also be closely coordinated with *manufacturing*. Production runs are based on marketers' forecasts for new and existing products. Schedules must be developed to ensure distribution of products by a certain date. Failure to correctly coordinate manufacturing within the marketing effort can be devastating. Apple underestimated the demand for its Macintosh Classic Computer. While a $40 million global advertising campaign sparked tremendous demand for the computer, customers ready to make a purchase were being told they would have to wait several months for delivery. These shortages cost Apple an estimated $100 million in the last quarter of 1990.[17]

Coordination between marketing and *research and development* (R&D) is particularly important in the development of new products. Marketing provides R&D with information relating to consumers' needs in order to help scientists and engineers formulate product ingredients and designs that will meet those needs. R&D must then communicate the product's physical properties and performance capabilities to marketing.

Smooth integration between marketing and other business functions is not always easy to achieve. For example, manufacturing characteristically strives for efficient production, which requires longer runs and fewer and simpler products. Marketing prefers shorter production runs to facilitate quick distribution and wants more models to meet varying consumer needs. Similarly, R&D tends to develop products that may have more features and design elements than consumers need. Marketing prefers to eliminate unnecessary design features to keep prices competitive.

MARKETING: PAST, PRESENT, AND FUTURE

Figure 1.4 shows that the environmental factors which most influence marketers are customers and the competition. It is only since the 1950s that marketing has been characterized by a *customer orientation* and only since the 1980s that it has been characterized by a *competitor orientation*. Before 1950, marketing was driven first by a *production orientation* and then by a *sales orientation*.

FIGURE 1.6

Marketing's Past and Present Orientation

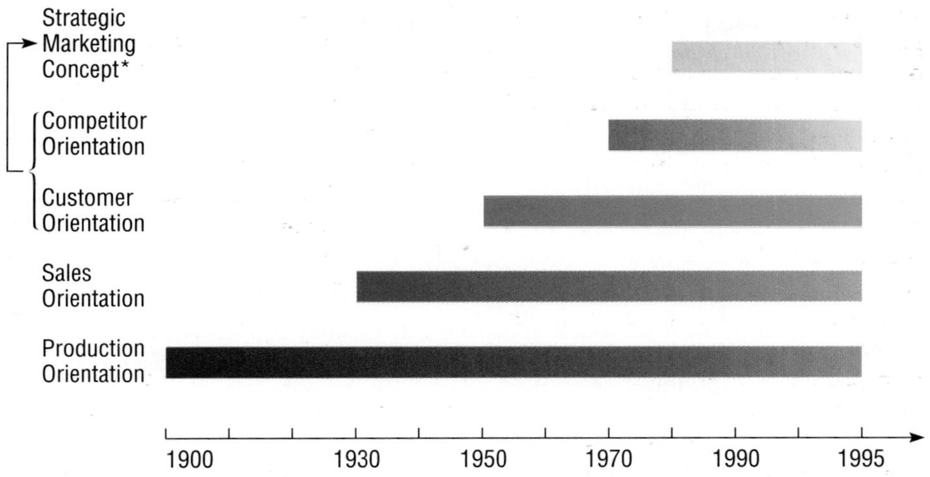

* Strategic marketing concept = customer orientation + competitor orientation.

PRODUCTION ORIENTATION

When marketing was first recognized as a business activity at the turn of the century, it was essentially an adjunct of production and agriculture. It was seen as a means of exchanging farm commodities and of bringing manufactured products to market. Management concentrated on increasing output and production efficiencies. Selling was secondary because, in most cases, high-quality products were scarce and could "sell themselves."

Firms that focus primarily on production efficiency and product availability, with little regard for the needs of consumers, have a **production orientation.** This orientation is most likely to succeed in a seller's market—that is, where demand exceeds supply. In these conditions, the manufacturer does not have to be concerned with selling the product and focuses on increasing production through improvements in manufacturing capabilities.

Production-oriented firms have sometimes become so focused on bringing out the highest quality product that they lose sight of customer needs. Assuming that "customers will beat a path to the door of the manufacturer that builds a better mousetrap," they have allowed their focus on research and development (R&D) and production to blind them to the fact that customers are not always willing to pay more for higher quality.

Figure 1.6 suggests that a production orientation was prevalent before 1930. But many firms are production-oriented even today. When RCA introduced SelectaVision, its entry into the videodisc market, it was convinced the product would be widely accepted. It failed to take into account the importance to consumers of a recording capability. The general acceptance of videocassette recorders forced RCA to withdraw the product in the mid 1980s. Had RCA been more attuned to customer needs, it would have withdrawn from videodiscs and begun marketing VCRs much earlier.

SALES ORIENTATION

Many companies shifted from a production orientation to a sales orientation during the Great Depression of the 1930s. Overcapacity spurred management to institute a *hard-sell approach* that sometimes antagonized customers. The philosophy of a **sales orientation** *was to sell what the company made rather than to make what it could sell based on customer needs.* Most firms had sales departments; few had marketing departments. The predominant factor in the marketing mix was the sales force.

This sales orientation continued until the 1950s, encouraged by a post–World War II seller's market caused by shortages. Companies did not have to define customer needs. They could continue to sell what they made.

Even today, many firms use a hard-sell approach characteristic of a sales rather than a marketing orientation. Such an approach is typical of products that consumers do not generally seek out—insurance or magazine subscriptions, for example. The visibility of a hard-sell approach has created problems for marketing's image. The most effective selling is need-oriented; that is, the salesperson assesses customer needs and directs the sales message accordingly.

CUSTOMER ORIENTATION: THE MARKETING CONCEPT

The **marketing concept** *is the philosophy that marketing strategies must be based on known customer needs.* This philosophy characterizes a **customer orientation.** It began to win wide acceptance in the mid 1950s. Pent-up demand for consumer goods after World War II had been met. Consumers had stocked up on durable goods at the onset of the Korean War, and by the mid 1950s demand for these products was decreasing. Consumers became more selective in their purchases. As a result, supply exceeded demand, yet consumers had plenty of purchasing power. The economy experienced its first true buyer's market—consumers had the money but were not buying.

Some marketers reacted by continuing to be sales oriented—pushing the existing lines, heightening selling efforts, repeating selling themes, and unloading excess inventories. These firms continued to sell on a mass-market basis with little thought of targeting products to the needs of particular customer segments. Firms with more foresight reacted by developing a greater diversity of products directed to segments of customers having similar needs. They became customer-oriented.

One of the first companies to recognize the need for a customer orientation was General Electric. A GE executive clearly stated the marketing concept that emerged from this period:

> The principal task of the marketing function . . . is not so much to be skillful in making the customer do what suits the interests of the business as to be skillful in conceiving and then making the business do what suits the interests of the customer.[18]

As a result of its new, customer-oriented perspective, GE redefined the meaning of marketing in its 1952 annual report and was the first to use the term marketing concept.

> The marketing concept . . . integrates marketing into each phase of the business. Thus marketing, through its studies and research, will establish for the engineer, the design and manufacturing person, what the customer wants in a given product, what price he or she is willing to pay, and where and when it will be wanted.[19]

The development of the marketing concept changed the nature of marketing activities by:

- *Spurring new product development.* A greater diversity of products was required to meet customer needs.
- *Emphasizing market segmentation.* Customers with similar needs were identified (for example, taste, convenience, and decaffeinated segments in the coffee market), and strategies were directed to these segments.
- *Focusing on marketing communications.* Product benefits had to be communicated to customer segments. Advertising became more diverse and informative.
- *Creating greater selectivity in personal selling.* Sales personnel had to determine customer needs and develop their sales messages accordingly. Standardized sales approaches were no longer as effective.
- *Creating more selective media and distributive outlets.* Specialized magazines began to appear, direct mail was used to reach customer segments, and specialty wholesalers and retailers became more prominent.
- *Encouraging marketing research.* Information relating to customer needs was required. Consumer surveys were used more frequently to identify opportunities, and new products underwent more rigorous consumer testing.

The shift from a sales orientation to a customer orientation did not occur overnight. Companies like General Electric were quick to recognize the changes in marketing strategy required by the acceptance of the marketing concept. Other companies are still operating on the basis of a production or sales orientation.

COMPETITOR ORIENTATION: THE STRATEGIC MARKETING CONCEPT

Although the marketing concept seems perfectly plausible as a basis for developing marketing strategy, some companies began to realize that there was something lacking. A company could be perfectly customer oriented and do all the right things—good marketing research, strong new-product development, products positioned to customer needs and targeted to market segments—yet sustain heavy losses because it was outmaneuvered by competitors.

What was lacking was a focus on both customers and competition known as the strategic marketing concept (see Figure 1.6). *The* **strategic marketing concept** *states that the firm must satisfy customer needs while sustaining a competitive advantage to ensure long term profitability.* As a result, this concept reflects a customer and a competitor orientation.[20] As an example, even before its acquisition by Chrysler, American Motors had decided to produce only Jeeps. It stopped producing passenger cars, not because it was ineffective in defining customer needs, but because it did not have the resources to compete head-on with Ford, Chrysler, and General Motors. American Motors was able to achieve a *competitive advantage* by satisfying the needs of a segment of the auto market that the Big Three regarded as too small to enter—jeep owners.

A competitor orientation began to be accepted in the mid 1970s. It has been a more recent marketing focus for several reasons. First, economic conditions such as the rapid inflation in the 1970s, the steep recession in the early 1980s, and the sluggish economic recovery afterward heightened the cost consciousness of many domestic firms. Renewed recession in the 1990s created continued pressures to reduce costs. Firms that operated in industries where products were relatively undifferentiated began to realize that they had to gain some advantage over their competitors to make a profit. The only recourse seemed to be to reduce costs by increasing productivity or to find some technological breakthrough to gain product superiority. Competition from lower-cost foreign manufacturers heightened the need to find some sustainable advantage as a basis for long-term profitability.

Second, many firms embarked on a rash of acquisitions of high-growth companies in the 1960s and 1970s to increase short-term earnings. In so doing, they strayed from their areas of expertise. These firms then divested themselves of these acquisitions so they could concentrate on the core businesses in which they had a competitive advantage. PepsiCo—owners of Pepsi-Cola beverages and Frito-Lay snack foods—acquired Wilson Sporting Goods and North American Van Lines, then divested itself of these companies because of a lack of marketing expertise in sporting goods and transportation. On the other hand, it kept its acquisitions in fast foods—Pizza Hut, Taco Bell, and KFC, formerly Kentucky Fried Chicken—because of its expertise in the food business.

Taking a competitor orientation may not seem new. The concept of competition has been at the center of economic thought for the last 200 years. In general, though, business firms did not adequately evaluate competition in developing marketing strategies before 1975. Most companies would embark on a certain course of action and then react to competitors' responses. A competitor orientation requires a more *proactive* stance—evaluating the strengths and weaknesses of competitors and anticipating their responses to the company's actions before a particular strategic alternative is selected.

An example of a failure to project competitive responses was Bristol-Myers' introduction of Datril, a nonaspirin pain reliever designed to compete with Tylenol. Bristol-Myers introduced an undifferentiated product at a lower price, not realizing that Tylenol could easily cut its price below Datril's and maintain an acceptable profit margin. It did, and Datril languishes with a tiny share of the market.

A competitor orientation does not displace a customer orientation, it reinforces it. The more competitive the market, the more attuned a company must be to customer needs. In the absence of a competitor orientation, a firm may successfully satisfy customer needs but at a loss.

THE BROADER ROLE OF MARKETING

Marketing is concerned not only with consumer products (products for final consumption). Strategies must be developed to market goods sold to *businesses* (referred to as business-to-business marketing) as well. Strategies must also be developed to market *services* as well as products. Marketing strategies can also be developed by *not-for-profit firms* as well as companies run for profit. Finally, marketing activities can be conducted by *intermediaries* such as retail and wholesale firms as well as by manufacturing firms.

There is one additional element in this broader concept of marketing: Marketing must extend beyond the business sphere to consider the societal concerns of its customers if marketing organizations are to fulfill their social responsibilities.

BUSINESS-TO-BUSINESS MARKETING

Business-to-business marketing *involves the sale of products to firms so that they can manufacture or process other products* (machine tools, generators), *or to support such activities* (business computers, order forms, copiers) (see Exhibit 1.5). *The prod-*

EXHIBIT 1.5

An Example of Business-to-Business Marketing

ucts marketed on a business-to-business basis are called **industrial products** and actually represent a higher sales volume than consumer goods. They are purchased by organizational buyers, whereas consumer products are purchased by final consumers. The term *customers* refers to all buyers, industrial and consumer. The term *consumers* refers only to final consumers of the product.

The principles in marketing industrial products are usually the same as those that apply to consumer goods. But there are some important differences. Organizational buyers often deal with products that are more technically complex than consumer goods. They need to negotiate with a salesperson who can describe product performance and service support. As a result, personal selling plays a more important part in marketing industrial products than consumer goods. For example, when AT&T sells a telecommunications system to IBM, specifications for the system and terms of sale will be negotiated by a team of salespeople and engineers who must become intimately familiar with IBM's communications needs.

The new-product development process is also likely to differ. Technological development is likely to be more rapid for industrial products. The development process is likely to be longer and capital expenditures on new products greater. Another difference is that, compared to consumer goods, postpurchase service is more likely to be important for industrial goods. As a result, service capabilities are an important factor in influencing the customer to buy.

In general, the business-to-business sector has lagged behind consumer marketers in adopting a strategic marketing concept. The focus in industrial firms tends to be more on internal factors such as company resources and capabilities than on external factors such as customer needs and competitor reactions. But this focus is slowly changing. For example, Dun and Bradstreet, one of the foremost purveyors of information services to corporate America, operated with little regard for customer needs for almost 140 years. Its "take it or leave it" attitude was profitable until the computer and electronic revolution created competition. The company then began to change its focus to develop new services geared to the needs of industrial users. It expanded its staff to include computer experts and marketing researchers so that it was no longer dominated by salespeople. The new philosophy is summarized by D&B's chairman:

> Instead of concentrating on new ways to package and sell information we happen to have on hand, we are beginning to look at the changing needs of the marketplace and to devise ways to fill those needs.[21]

SERVICES MARKETING

The American economy is increasingly service-oriented. Services produce about half of the U.S. gross national product. As a result, service marketing is receiving increasing attention. Airlines, hotel chains, and financial services companies are becoming more marketing-oriented (see Exhibit 1.6). Some of these companies are beginning to hire product managers from such staunch consumer-goods companies as General Foods and Procter & Gamble to apply marketing skills to services.

Any product manager moving from consumer products to services encounters a drastic change in environment. Services are intangible, whereas products are tangible. Services are produced by people, products by machines. As a result, services tend to be more variable in quality, while products are more standardized. A consumer buying a box of corn flakes knows what is in the box. A consumer boarding a flight or going into a restaurant is less assured of the consistency of what he or she is buying. Another difference between products and services is that unused services cannot be stored. An airline cannot store empty seats, whereas an auto manufacturer can keep unsold cars in inventory. Compared to products, the perishability of services creates more risks for services marketers.

Much of the recent attention to services marketing is due to the greater marketing orientation of the financial community. Banks, brokerage houses, and insurance companies have become more marketing-oriented, because many of the restraints on competition have been lifted. As a result, Merrill Lynch is offering banking services, Citicorp is going into the brokerage and insurance business, and companies such as Sears, J. C. Penney, and General Electric have subsidiaries in financial services. These companies are seeking a competitive advantage by better serving customer needs.

NOT-FOR-PROFIT MARKETING

Not-for-profit institutions such as hospitals, museums, charities, and educational institutions are also beginning to market their activities. (The ad for the San Diego Zoo in Exhibit 1.7 is an example of a not-for-profit institution marketing its ser-

EXHIBIT 1.6

An Example of Services Marketing

© 1991 American Express Travel Related Services Company, Inc.
You're not about to wear your financial savvy and stability on your sleeve.
There are other places.
THE CARD.
THE AMERICAN EXPRESS® CARD.

vices.) This is a significant sector of the economy. Few people realize that not-for-profit organizations account for 20 percent of all economic activity in the United States.

Not-for-profit companies have a more difficult task in marketing their activities than companies in the profit sector, because they must influence both donors of funds as well as their own customers. These organizations have recently begun to use marketing tools to help them to influence their constituents. Charitable organizations such as the Heart Fund and the American Cancer Society advertise with a dual message—to influence people to stop smoking and to ask for contributions. Colleges and private schools use direct mail and personal selling to ask for contributions and to attract students.

The U.S. government is also using marketing techniques to sell ideas and services. The Environmental Protection Agency is advertising to increase public awareness of environmental issues. The Department of Agriculture uses marketing techniques to sell ideas such as improving children's eating habits. And, the U.S. Army has advertised extensively to attract recruits to sustain an all volunteer army.

EXHIBIT 1.7

An Example of Not-for-Profit Marketing

Celebrate the San Diego Zoo's 70th birthday.

MARKETING BY INTERMEDIARIES

The examples in this chapter have described marketing by the producers of goods and services. Intermediaries between manufacturers and customers, primarily wholesalers and retailers, also engage in marketing. These firms identify opportunities, develop marketing strategies to satisfy customer needs, and seek competitive advantages. The difference is that they are providing a specific set of services to consumers—time, place, and possession utilities (or values) in the exchange of goods. They provide **time utility** *by ensuring products are distributed so consumers can buy and consume them when they are needed.* They provide **place utility** *by ensuring consumers can buy these products in convenient locations.* And they provide **possession utility** *by giving consumers the means to exchange money for product ownership.*

Wholesalers and retailers gain competitive advantage by providing superior store facilities and services. For example, 7-Eleven stores established a competitive advantage by offering late-hour and weekend shopping in convenient locations. Retailers and wholesalers also define target segments and position their offerings to these segments. J. C. Penney has tried to appeal to a more affluent segment by upgrading its image and repositioning its line to higher-quality merchandise.

THE ETHICAL AND SOCIETAL DIMENSIONS OF MARKETING

The nature of marketing has changed significantly in the 1980s because of a greater awareness among both marketers and customers that marketing organizations have an ethical responsibility to their customers and an even broader responsibility to society as a whole. This ethical and societal responsibility of marketing goes well beyond the marketing concept of satisfying customer needs through sound marketing strategies.

There are two problems with the marketing concept. First, subscribing to the marketing concept does not always ensure ethical behavior. Marketers may *appear* to be satisfying customer needs when, in fact, the needs are being subverted. Advertising cooking oil as low in cholesterol may be a true claim; but when the fat content of the product is high, the company cannot really claim to be satisfying consumer needs for healthier products. Similarly, advertising packaging as recyclable may be true. But when there are no facilities for recycling, and packages are left to decompose at a slow rate in landfills, the consumer's need for environmentally safe products is not being met. In each of these cases, the marketer is deceiving the consumer, purposefully or not.

Second, even when marketers legitimately satisfy the needs of their customers, such satisfaction may infringe on the needs of others. Satisfying one target segment's need for a spray deodorant may affect the rights of other consumers by depleting the ozone barrier and heightening the risk of skin cancer. Introducing disposable diapers with greater absorbency may satisfy the needs of parents for a more comfortable baby, but it also creates bulkier diapers which aggravate landfill problems. Cigarette companies may satisfy the needs of smokers, but in so doing they also increase passive smoking and heighten the risk of lung cancer for nonsmokers as well. In each case, satisfying the needs of one group infringes on the rights of others.

The first set of issues concern the ethics of marketers in meeting their responsibilities to their customers. The second set of issues go beyond the company's customers and concern marketing's broader responsibilities to society as a whole.

ETHICAL RESPONSIBILITIES OF MARKETERS TO THEIR CONSUMERS

There is no easy definition of what constitutes unethical marketing practices. Ultimately, each marketer must rely on his or her own value system to determine what is ethical. That value system should recognize consumer rights to safety, to full information, and to value for the price paid. The American Marketing Association (AMA) has established a code of ethics to provide guidelines for ethical conduct. It says, in part, that:

> Marketers shall uphold and advance the integrity, honor and dignity of the marketing profession by being honest in serving consumers, clients, employees, suppliers, distributors, and the public.[22]

The code then outlines responsibilities for each component of the marketing mix. For *products and services*, it says that marketers have the responsibility to ensure product safety, to disclose all product risks, and to identify any factor that might change product performance. Did General Motors fulfill these responsibilities when it was sued to recall 1.1 million X-body cars for faulty brakes?[23] Probably not.

For *advertising*, the code states that marketers must avoid deceptive and misleading communications, must reject high-pressure sales tactics, and must avoid manipulating consumers to buy. Did Warner Lambert fulfill these responsibilities when it advertised Listerine as preventing colds despite the fact that no evidence for the truthfulness of the claim existed? Probably not.

For *distribution*, the code says that suppliers should not coerce their intermediaries into taking unwanted products and that they should not create false shortages to drive up the prices of their products. Did Chrysler fulfill these responsibilities in the early 1960s when it forced its dealers to take unwanted cars during an economic downturn? Probably not.

For *pricing*, the code stipulates that marketers must not engage in price fixing or predatory pricing and must fully disclose all prices associated with the purchase including service, installation, and delivery. Did several pharmaceutical companies fulfill these responsibilities in 1992 when they conspired to fix prices for infant formula? Probably not.

As further insurance of consumer rights, the AMA code states that marketers should provide the means to hear consumer complaints and to adjust them equitably. Some companies have made a concerted effort to hear consumer complaints. Whirlpool has a "cool line" to provide a 24-hour-a-day facility for consumers to make complaints and inquiries directly to company headquarters. Johnson & Johnson's 22 subsidiaries each have consumer-affairs departments with representatives on call 24 hours a day to receive consumer complaints.[24] Procter & Gamble has an 800 number on each of its packages should consumers want information or have a complaint.

A more important consideration is that products be produced and marketed to avoid these complaints in the first place. Marketers must make sure consumers get what they pay for and must, above all, guarantee product safety. In addition, concern for consumer welfare would dictate providing fuller information on product ingredients and company safeguards against polluting the environment. Ultimately, the issue is whether marketing organizations are willing to support a philosophy of social consciousness, one that attempts to resolve the potential conflict between profit maximization and social welfare.

Although the AMA code is helpful in highlighting ethical issues, it is not sufficient to provide guidelines for ethical action. Should an individual work for a cigarette company if he or she believes that cigarettes cause cancer? Should an international marketer subscribe to the practice of offering bribes if all the company's competitors are doing it? Should a manager approve of the practice of buying a competitor's product, analyzing it, and then duplicating it? Should an advertiser go along with a strategy of promoting a brand as new and improved when there have been only minor changes in the product? These areas are not covered by the law or by the AMA code.

ETHICAL RESPONSIBILITIES OF MARKETERS TO SOCIETY

Marketing companies have become more conscious of their responsibilities to society, both from the standpoint of public health and preservation of the environment. From the standpoint of health, companies are offering more nutritional alternatives to traditional foods, from low fat sour creams to non-caffeinated soft drinks. But these companies also have a responsibility to verify their health claims. There is also the question of marketing products such as liquor and cigarettes that could be harmful. Some marketers of beer have attempted to fulfill a societal

EXHIBIT 1.8

A Miller Brewing Company Ad Discourages Teen Drinking

responsibility by advertising that underage persons should not drink (see the Miller ad in Exhibit 1.8) and that beer drinkers should not drive.

By far the most pervasive societal issue of the last ten years has been the environment. Most companies see the environment as *the* societal issue of the 1990s. One study found that 86 percent of chief executive officers of major companies felt that environmental issues will be in the forefront of future ethical concerns.[25] This recognition of the importance of the environment is also reflected in company actions. Consider the following:

- Wal-Mart, the nation's largest retailer, places hang tags in its stores to identify products that are environmentally friendly.
- Both Procter & Gamble and Lever Brothers have introduced concentrated detergents in smaller packages advertised as taking up less space in overburdened landfills.
- Monsanto organized a task force of scientists and engineers to analyze the effects of any new materials and chemicals on the environment and on users. It views the task force as an "early warning system" intended to blow the whistle on any new product concept that may introduce unacceptable hazards to users.[26]
- McDonald's agreed to eliminate its plastic "clamshell" packaging in 1990 to ensure more environmentally sensitive packaging. The company also

ETHICAL AND ENVIRONMENTAL ISSUES IN MARKETING

Getting on the Environmental Bandwagon with Misleading Claims

Some companies have gotten on the environmental bandwagon by making claims to be environmentally conscious that are dubious at best. Questionable environmental claims relate primarily to two areas: biodegradability and recycling. Biodegradability of products is an issue because if products (particularly plastics) do not decompose, they will remain pollutants for years. Hefty, Glad, and Handi-Wrap trash bags have added chemicals to promote decomposition of their bags and have advertised these products as biodegradable. The problem is that to be biodegradable, products must be exposed to sunlight; yet most products wind up as landfill, preventing decomposition.

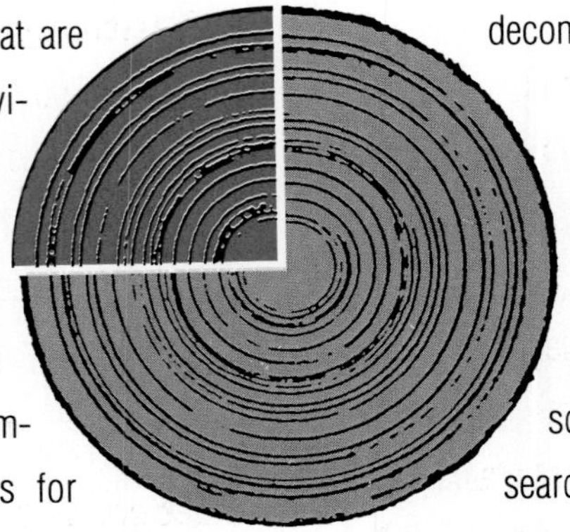

Procter & Gamble took a novel approach to the problem of biodegradability by promoting research into composting—a method of turning garbage into humus, a rich soil-like material. Based on this research, it found that it could develop diapers so that 80 percent of the material could be turned into compost. To bring this development to public attention, P&G began advertising that it could turn disposable diapers into the material needed by

announced that it intends to use only recycled materials in building new restaurants.[27]

Given the likely dominance of ethical and societal issues in marketing in the 1990s, we will deal with these issues in every chapter in the book.

SUMMARY

1. **What is marketing?**
   Marketing is a dynamic set of activities directed toward identifying and satisfying customer needs through a process of exchange. It requires an exchange process and a marketing management process. Exchange allows buyers and sellers to obtain something of value from each other. The marketing management process defines customer needs, develops new products to meet these needs, positions a product to a defined target segment; develops a mix of advertising, price, and distribution strategies to market the product nationally; and evaluates customer reactions once the product is introduced.
2. **What are the environmental dimensions of marketing?**
   Managers must evaluate customer needs in a broad marketing environment that

ETHICAL AND ENVIRONMENTAL ISSUES IN MARKETING

nurseries to grow trees. Unfortunately, by 1992 only ten U.S. communities had solid waste composting plants.

Companies producing food wraps, cups, and foam containers have also claimed that these products can be recycled. The problem here is that such claims assume that consumers can bring products to recycling facilities, and few such facilities exist.

These claims have led the Federal Trade Commission and attorneys general for eight states to investigate whether they constitute deceptive advertising. The Environmental Protection Agency is trying to resolve the issue of what constitutes a justifiable environmental claim by developing guidelines for the use of terms such as biodegradable and recyclable.

Pressure from government and environmental groups has led some companies to change their policies. Mobil decided to withdraw any reference to biodegradability from its Hefty trash bags because of "mounting confusion over the meaning and value of such claims."

Question: Was Mobil's claim that Hefty trash bags are biodegradable an unethical action?

Source: "Mobile Ends Environmental Claim," *The New York Times*, March 30, 1990, p. D1.

includes competition, the economy, technology, government regulations, and demographic and life-style trends. Another important component of the environment is the operation of marketing systems that facilitate the exchange of goods and services in the economy. A communications system informs consumers about products and influences them to buy. A distribution system delivers what consumers want, when and where they want it. An information system enables management to develop marketing strategies aimed at introducing products fitted to consumer needs.

3. **What is the relationship of marketing to other business functions?** Marketing plays a central role in the firm in conjunction with other business functions. Finance provides marketing managers the profit criteria for evaluating product performance. Accounting allocates costs to products to permit determination of profits. Manufacturing ensures that the product is ready to be distributed when promised. Research and development formulates and designs new products.
4. **What was marketing's role in the past, and what is its role at present?** In the past, marketing was production- and sales-oriented. A production orientation meant that marketers were more concerned with developing products based on their production and research and development capabilities rather than on customer needs. A sales orientation meant that marketers were willing

to sell what the company made rather than to determine what should be made to meet customer needs.

Marketing's current role provides strategic direction to the business firm by ensuring that all marketing strategies are developed based on known customer needs. Marketing also recognizes the importance of developing a sustainable advantage over competitors to prevent the firm from losing ground to competitors. The focus on both customer needs and competitive advantage is called the strategic marketing concept.

5. **What is the broader role of marketing?**
The broader role of marketing encompasses business-to-business, international, service, and not-for-profit marketing in both the manufacturing and distribution sectors. It also recognizes the social responsibilities of the marketing firm to ensure product safety, product quality, and adequate environmental protection.

6. **What are the ethical and societal responsibilities of marketers?**
Marketers have a responsibility to their customers to ensure product safety, to provide full information, and to ensure value for the price paid. Marketers have a broader responsibility to society to ensure that products sold to one group do not harm another and to work toward a safe environment. These responsibilities reflect the ethical standards of marketers. To the degree that they are fulfilled, marketers are operating ethically in selling their goods and services.

KEY TERMS

Marketing (p. 4)
Final consumer (p. 4)
Organizational buyer (p. 4)
Market (p. 4)
Market segment (p. 4)
Exchange process (p. 5)
Marketing management process (p. 7)
Target market (p. 9)
Marketing strageties (p. 9)
Product positioning (p. 10)
Marketing mix (p. 11)
Four Ps of marketing (p. 11)
Market share (p. 12)
Competitive advantage (p. 13)
Facilitating marketing systems (p. 17)
Marketing information system (p. 17)
Communications system (p. 17)
Distribution system (p. 17)
Channels of distribution (p. 18)
Production orientation (p. 21)
Sales orientation (p. 22)
Marketing concept (p. 22)
Customer orientation (p. 22)
Strategic marketing concept (p. 23)
Business-to-business marketing (p. 24)
Industrial products (p. 25)
Time utility (p. 28)
Place utility (p. 28)
Possession utility (p. 28)

QUESTIONS

1. Why is marketing central to all business functions?
2. What is a market segment? What is the importance of identifying a market segment in developing marketing strategies?
3. What are the necessary conditions for a process of exchange to take place? How do these conditions apply to Harley-Davidson's recent success in the heavy motorcycle market?
4. What is the marketing management process? How did Church & Dwight apply the marketing management process in expanding Arm & Hammer's product line?
5. What developments are encouraging American firms to look abroad for new opportunities?
6. What are the pros and cons of introducing a standardized product on a global basis?
7. What are the roles of the three facilitating systems described in this chapter?
8. A pharmaceutical company is considering developing a three-in-one hair care product—a shampoo, conditioner, and rinse all in one. The marketing manager for the project wants to make sure that (1) the right ingredients are developed to make a safe and effective product that will provide shampoo,

conditioning, and rinse benefits; (2) financial criteria will be established for product performance; (3) costs will be fairly allocated to the new product; and (4) the product will be available before the advertising campaign is introduced. How can nonmarketing business functions contribute to each of these areas?

9. Consider the statement, "Marketing strategies must be based on known customer needs." In what ways did acceptance of this statement in the 1950s represent a marked departure from the past? What are the implications of the statement for
   a. advertising strategies?
   b. product strategies?
   c. marketing research?
   d. strategies to gain competitive advantage?
10. What is the difference between the marketing concept and the strategic marketing concept? Why does the strategic marketing concept give a business firm a sounder basis for developing marketing strategies?
11. What were the reasons companies began to focus more on competition in developing marketing plans and strategies in the 1980s?
12. A product manager for a deodorant line accepts a job at Citicorp as product manager of its new line of cash management accounts. What differences is the manager likely to find in developing marketing strategies for a financial service such as cash management accounts as opposed to a consumer product such as deodorants?
13. What are the responsibilities of marketers to their customers? How would these responsibilities apply to Harley-Davidson? To Church & Dwight?
14. What are the marketing implications of the growing consumer concerns regarding the environment?

QUESTIONS: YOU ARE THE DECISION MAKER

1. The owner of a small business producing costume jewelry read the introduction to this chapter. She then made the following comment:

   It is all well and good to talk about firms like Harley-Davidson and Church & Dwight as having marketing savvy and being successful. They have the resources and the clout. But what about us small firms? We can't spend millions on new product development and advertising. I really wonder how relevant your description of marketing is to our operations.

   a. What is the relevance of the definition of marketing in this chapter to a small producer of costume jewelry?
   b. What is the relevance of the three-step description of the marketing process in Figure 1.1 to this firm?
2. A manager of a medium-sized industrial firm producing electrical cable also read the chapter. His reaction was somewhat different than that of the small business owner in the previous question. He said:

   A company like Church & Dwight relies mostly on advertising to sell its products. We are very different. We rely on our sales force, not advertising, as the main contact with customers. Occasionally we will develop new products, but our products are pretty much like our competitors'. So we really do not need marketing as you describe it. We need an effective sales force. We fit into your description of being a sales-oriented company. And that's pretty much where we should be.

   a. Do you agree with this view?
   b. What might cause the company to shift from a sales orientation to a customer orientation?
   c. What might cause it to shift to a strategic marketing orientation?
3. The chairman of the board of a large oil company states:

   The marketing concept is fine for companies providing packaged goods. These are differentiated products in highly competitive industries that need to advertise to stimulate demand. But we are producing standardized products in a situation of scarcity. Our main concern is not satisfying consumer needs, but trying to discover and exploit scarce resources.

   a. As executive vice-president for marketing, you take exception to the chairman's statement. On what grounds?
   b. Under what environmental conditions might the chairman become more concerned with satisfying customer needs?

CHAPTER 2

Marketing in Business Organizations

YOUR FOCUS IN CHAPTER 2

To learn:

- *The role of marketing management within the firm.*
- *The dual role of marketing in the firm, from both the product and corporate perspective.*
- *The importance of the strategic business unit in the marketing planning process.*
- *The nature of product marketing planning and strategic marketing planning.*
- *The strategy alternatives that are available to marketing managers at the product level and at the SBU or corporate level.*

Kodak: Facing Marketing Threats at Home and Abroad

When Kodak sponsored the men's and women's doubles matches at a major U.S. tennis tournament in 1989, a Kodak vice president stepped out to make the awards. Just then, a big green Fuji blimp came into sight. Everyone laughed, including the Kodak VP.

But Fuji is no laughing matter at Kodak. The Japanese company took the lead in introducing high-speed film into the American market, reducing Kodak's share of the amateur film market from almost 100 percent to 75 percent.[1] Fuji was also the innovator in disposable cameras. And another foreign competitor, Sony, has taken the lead in developing perhaps the greatest threat to Kodak, electronic cameras that may eventually make film obsolete.[2]

For a company that was the darling of Wall Street, with a reputation for producing technically superb, easy-to-use cameras, Kodak's reversal was startling. Kodak's problems started in the 1970s, when it decided to leave development and mass-marketing of two highly profitable products, 35 millimeter and VCR cameras, to Japanese companies. The 1980s then saw a series of stinging setbacks—consumer rejection of its disc camera and 8 millimeter VCR entry, loss of a patent infringement suit to Polaroid for introducing Kodak instant cameras, and erosion of its dominance in color film. Most painful of all, the company cut back marketing its highly touted alkaline and lithium battery line with losses of close to $200 million, realizing it could not go head-to-head with established competitors such as Duracell and Eveready.[3]

Kodak reacted with a great deal of soul-searching. It realized that its near-monopoly position in film often led the company to ignore customers and competitors. Worse, the company became so risk averse that management often strangled new product ideas. As the company's chairman quipped, "It's time to make this elephant dance."[4] Kodak "started dancing" by reorganizing the company into 17 business units focused on specific markets such as electronic photography, office automation, and health care. Managers in each unit were responsible for identifying new product opportunities to meet customer needs and for targeting existing products to defined customer segments.

The reorganization resulted in a marketing-oriented Kodak capable of developing products more attuned to customer needs. New products such as Ektar, a highly successful film for sophisticated amateurs, took only two years from development to introduction. In contrast, it took eighteen years for Kodachrome film to reach the marketplace.[5] Product introductions were also gaining a beat on competition. Kodak's disposable cameras were introduced in 1989 in Japan and quickly gained an advantage over Fuji's disposables, because they had a wide-angle lens.

Kodak is also meeting its most significant threat head-on, electronic cameras capable of storing images on discs and displaying pictures on disc players hooked up to TV sets. Although Sony has taken the lead in developing these cameras, Kodak is not sitting still. In 1991, it announced development of a photo compact disc system capable of giving photographers the option of using film or storing images on CDs.[6] The company realizes that if future photography is indeed filmless, Kodak could go the way of the streetcar and the record player.

Kodak's greater customer orientation led to another major change. The company realizes it is no longer in the film business but in the imaging business. This perspective is preparing Kodak to eventually cut its emotional and historic ties to its most basic business, film. The company is now saying that it makes products that process and convert images, whether they are photographs, hospital x-rays, or data transmissions.[7] This focus on imaging is allowing Kodak to look beyond photography to related businesses such as electronic publishing, factory machine vision systems, digital scanning, and microfilm management. The glue holding these diverse businesses together is imaging processes.

Kodak is now a company that seems to be in focus. It is better prepared to meet competitive threats at home. And, its newfound innovativeness is leading it to challenge Fuji on its home turf. Kodak's turnaround is reflected in profit performance: 1990 earnings of over $1 billion compared to a 1989 loss of $360 million.[8] Whereas in the late 1980s, many analysts were wondering whether Kodak would survive the battering it was taking, today, the company is well positioned to grow into the twenty-first century—with or without film.

THIS PICTURE WAS TAKEN BY SOMEONE WHO DIDN'T BRING A CAMERA.
It was taken with the film that's a camera: the Kodak Fun Saver panoramic 35 camera. Pre-loaded with Kodak Gold 200 film for true, accurate color prints. So affordable. So easy to use. After you've taken 12 pictures, you return the camera…film and all…for processing. You'll get back remarkable 10" wide prints.
THE FILM THAT'S A CAMERA™
Kodak
FunSaver
Panoramic
35
KODAK COMMITMENT: As part of our environmental action program, film processors are encouraged to return the cameras to Kodak for recycling.
© Eastman Kodak Company, 1991.

THE ROLE OF MARKETING MANAGEMENT IN THE FIRM

Marketing managers at Kodak and in other companies are responsible for developing marketing plans and strategies. *A* **marketing plan** *is a document developed by marketing managers that (1) identifies marketing opportunities, (2) defines the target market that represents opportunity, (3) develops a mix of marketing strategies directed to this target, and (4) guides the evaluation and control of the marketing effort.* Figure 2.1 shows that this textbook is organized based on these steps.

DEVELOP MARKETING PLANS AND STRATEGIES

The overall role of marketing management in the firm is to develop marketing plans and strategies, both for new products and existing ones. A set of integrated strategies (the marketing mix) is necessary to exploit opportunities.

Marketing strategies must be developed in some organized way. The vehicle for developing marketing strategies is the marketing plan. There are two kinds of marketing plans: a product marketing plan and a strategic marketing plan. *The* **product marketing plan** *charts the marketing strategy for an individual product or service, generally over a one-year period. The* **strategic marketing plan** *establishes guidelines for long-term corporate growth and develops the total mix of products the company will offer (the company's product mix), usually over a five-year period.* Both the product and strategic plan must define:

- What a firm wants to accomplish. This must be expressed as specific objectives based on management's assessment of marketing opportunities.
- How the firm plans to accomplish its objectives as defined by the marketing strategies management selects.
- What resources management requires to implement the plan.
- How management should implement the specific strategies.

THE PRODUCT MARKETING PLAN

The product marketing plan is designed to implement the four steps in Figure 2.1 for an individual product. The next chapter is devoted to describing in more detail the marketing planning process for an individual product.

When Kodak developed its product plan for Ektar, the company's film for advanced amateurs, it followed the four steps in Figure 2.1 closely. First, Kodak identified an opportunity to produce a new film for an emerging market. Kodak then identified a segment of amateur photographers who were more involved in picture-taking than the typical amateur as the target market. This group wanted a finer-grained film with better resolution, particularly in enlargements. Third, Kodak developed a marketing mix to introduce Ektar through its established network of film retailers at a premium price. Given the interest of the target group in photography, advertising was placed primarily in specialty magazines geared to the advanced amateur and in more-general-circulation magazines targeted to *upscale* (that is, higher income and better educated) consumers (see Exhibit 2.1). Fourth, Kodak is evaluating sales results and monitoring advertising, price, and distribution strategies for the product. Kodak's initial evaluation based on sales is that Ektar is a success.

FIGURE 2.1

Role of Marketing Management in the Business Organization

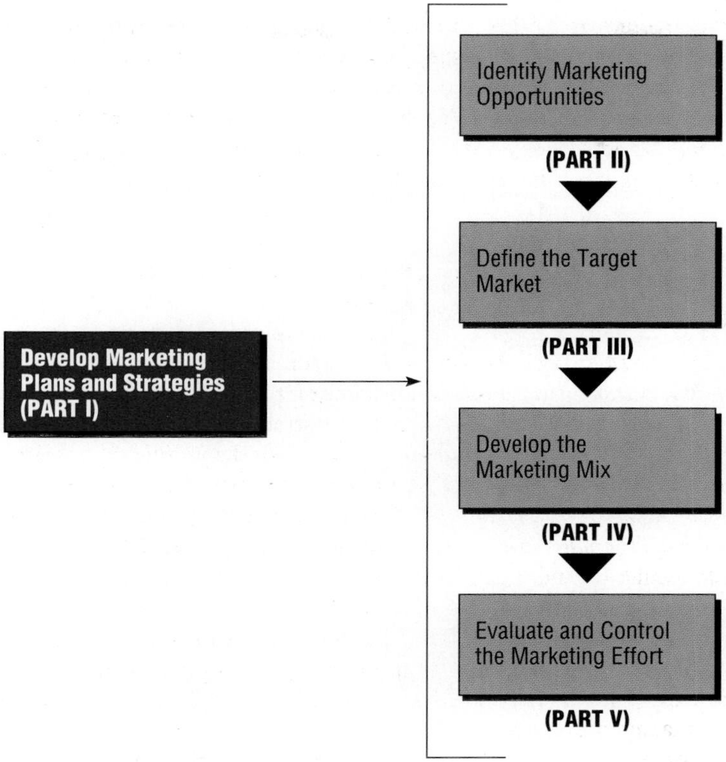

THE STRATEGIC MARKETING PLAN

A strategic marketing plan also implements the four steps in Figure 2.1 but in the context of the firm's product mix. *A* **product mix** *is all the products offered by a firm or business unit.* The most important step is the first, evaluating longer term opportunities. In the case of Kodak, this was the projected increase in the demand for higher resolution film. Management then identifies targets for its mix of products and develops longer term strategies to exploit opportunities. It then allocates resources to various business units and product lines based on this assessment. For example, the strategic plan would recommend the amount of resources the Consumer Products Business Unit (the unit at Kodak responsible for film) should get to market the new Ektar line.

Companies that develop strategic marketing plans are frequently organized based on *strategic business units (SBUs).* **SBUs** *are units within the company that are organized around markets with similar demand.* The SBU organization encourages a planning focus directed to meeting customer needs and gaining competitive advantage. Kodak has seventeen SBUs in all. Electronic publishing is one of the SBUs at Kodak, because the business unit directs a product line to a group of customers with similar needs, quality in-house publishing capabilities.

EXHIBIT 2.1

Kodak Targets the Advanced Amateur Photographer with Ektar

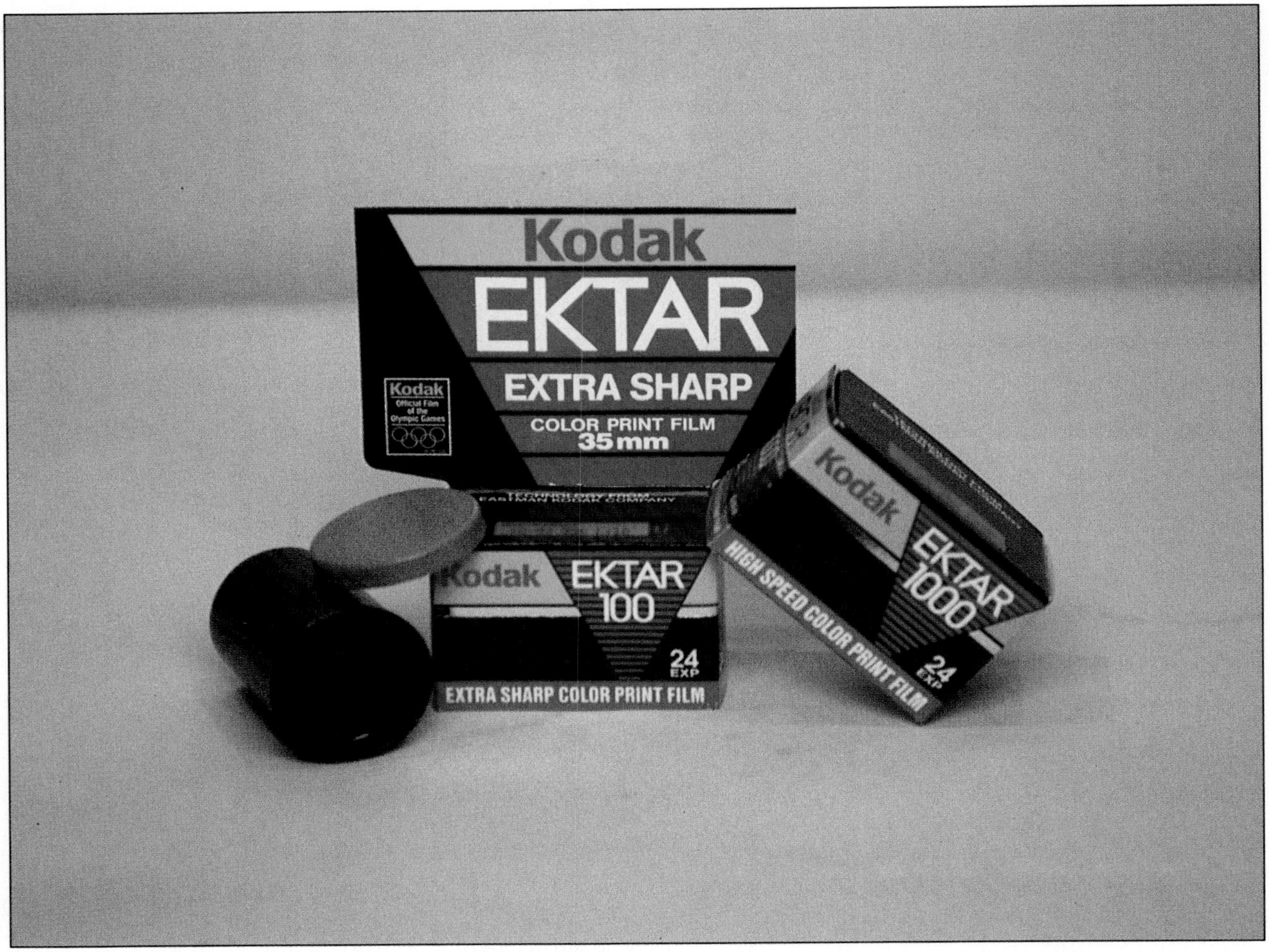

For firms operating in many markets such as Kodak, strategic plans are usually developed at each business unit and then coordinated at headquarters. For one-market companies (for instance, Michelin Tires) or medium-to-small companies, there are no SBUs. The strategic plan is usually formulated encompassing all the corporation's products.

MARKETING MANAGERS

Two types of marketing managers are responsible for marketing planning within the firm. *A* **product manager** *is responsible for developing the product marketing plan and for marketing the individual product.* The product manager must formulate a mix of marketing strategies, develop a budget to implement these strategies, and ensure the strategies are carried out. The product manager has profit responsibility for the product.

FIGURE 2.2

The Marketing Planning Matrix

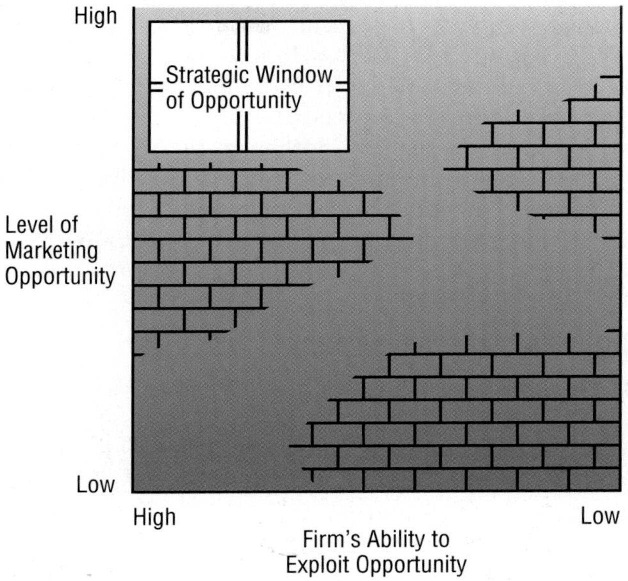

A **business manager** *has responsibility for developing the strategic marketing plan within a business unit.* The business manager identifies opportunities that can be exploited by the business unit, determines whether such opportunities should be exploited by developing new products or repositioning existing products, and allocates resources to individual products within the business unit. The business manager has profit responsibility for the SBU.

To better understand the product and strategic marketing planning processes, we will consider each of the four steps in Figure 2.1.

IDENTIFY MARKETING OPPORTUNITIES

In order to develop marketing plans and strategies, marketing managers must identify opportunities in the marketplace. This is accomplished by analyzing customer needs and other environmental conditions.

The environment the firm faces is the external component in identifying marketing opportunity. The internal component is the firm's ability to exploit these opportunities with its resources. These two dimensions are shown in Figure 2.2. The level of opportunity identified by the firm is on the vertical axis. Opportunity depends on factors such as unmet customer needs, competitors' weaknesses, new technologies, emerging life-style and demographic trends, the regulatory climate, and economic conditions.

The firm's ability to exploit such opportunities is on the horizontal axis. A company can better exploit a defined opportunity if it has some previous managerial and marketing experience, distribution facilities and a sales force, production capabilities, technological know-how, and financial resources. If one or more of these capabilities is lacking, the question management must answer is whether to acquire it in order to exploit a given opportunity. The combination of the level of opportunity and the firm's ability to exploit it is titled the *marketing planning matrix*. All marketing plans are formulated based on the two key dimensions shown in Figure 2.2.

For example, Fuji saw an opportunity to introduce disposable cameras in Japan in 1987, and quickly captured 10 percent of the camera market. (In the United States they only have a 1 percent share.)[9] Kodak saw a 30 percent growth rate for disposables in Japan and realized that if it did not come out with an entry, Fuji would have the market to itself. But Kodak could not come out with a "me-too" product; it needed some competitive advantage that it could translate into an opportunity relative to Fuji's offerings. The competitive advantage was introducing disposables with special features—a wide-angle lens in one model, a waterproof camera in another. The Japanese consumer's penchant for novelty products made the cameras an immediate success.

THE STRATEGIC WINDOW OF OPPORTUNITY

The combination of an opportunity and the firm's ability to exploit it is called the **strategic window of opportunity** (see the upper left-hand corner of Figure 2.2).[10] If the strategic window is "open," this means that the firm has the ability to meet marketing opportunities. A window of opportunity occurs because the firm has identified changes in the environment that create opportunity and is willing to allocate its resources to exploit this opportunity.

Sony saw an opportunity to take a device used by newspaper reporters—a mobile audio-cassette recorder—and make it into a product that would eventually become the Sony Walkman. The company saw a generation of youth raised on TV and immediate gratification who wanted to carry their entertainment with them. Sony had the resources to exploit this opportunity with a ready-made product that required minor modifications, the financial clout to establish manufacturing facilities, an intense advertising campaign, and worldwide distribution. Sony saw the strategic window and opened it.

Sometimes firms mistakenly think the strategic window is open, because they do not evaluate their ability to exploit an opportunity carefully enough. Kodak's experience in the battery market is a good case in point. The company thought it had a natural market because (a) 90 percent of Kodak's photo retailers sell batteries, (b) before Kodak ever entered the market, a survey showed that 15 percent of consumers thought the company already sold batteries, (c) Kodak's newly developed lithium batteries had a longer life than competitors (see Exhibit 2.2), and (d) demand for batteries was increasing with the growing popularity of electronic toys, laptop computers, and portable music and video products.[11]

The problem was that Kodak first entered the battery market with an alkaline battery that had no advantage over competitive products. It forgot a basic principle: If a company challenges established leaders like Duracell or Eveready, it must offer consumers some advantage. Kodak followed this prescription with disposable cameras in Japan, but not with batteries in the United States. Further, although its new lithium battery held the promise of longer shelf life, its entry was delayed by technological problems. What sealed Kodak's fate in batteries is that it underestimated the durability and strength of the market leaders. Duracell and Eveready countered Kodak's entry with heavy advertising campaigns. With only a 7 percent share of the battery market, Kodak could not justify heavy ad expenditures. Finally, in 1990 Kodak decided that it could not be a viable factor in batteries and began cutting back on advertising and distribution.[12]

EXHIBIT 2.2

An Attempt to Exploit Opportunity that Failed

DEFINE THE TARGET MARKET

The next responsibility of marketing managers, as shown in Figure 2.1, is to define the target market. Both product and business managers must identify segments of the market based on consumer needs and the characteristics of each segment. Companies often conduct marketing surveys for this purpose. The first objective in such a survey is to identify customer needs. Once individual customer needs are identified, customers can be grouped into segments by similar needs. The survey would then identify the characteristics of customers in each segment.

For example, the key in introducing Ektar was to distinguish between two segments, the typical amateur photographer and the advanced amateur. Kodak's research found that the typical amateur generally gets involved with photography with the arrival of the first child. As the children grow older, interest in photography generally wanes. As a result, Kodak is projecting a long-term decrease in demand for film among typical amateurs because fewer individuals will be in their child-bearing years as baby boomers get older. But some "typical" amateurs maintain their interest in photography. This "advanced" amateur group increases its purchase of film over time. Surveys showed that this group is composed primarily of upscale, older baby boomers past their prime child-bearing years.

Defining the market as upscale and older baby boomers guides marketing managers in media selection and advertising. Television ads should be slotted into shows that this group is most likely to watch. Print ads should be in magazines read by higher-income people aged 35 to 45. Because this group is interested in quality film, ads should emphasize the performance of Ektar.

Kodak thus targeted its marketing effort by first identifying a market segment with similar photographic needs and then determining its characteristics. Knowing the characteristics of the segment allowed Kodak to target promotional efforts to reach this group.

Targets in international markets must be identified on the same basis. Kodak was successful in introducing disposable cameras in Japan, because it identified a significant segment of Japanese consumers that had a penchant for gadgets such as a waterproof disposable camera. Kodak determined that this gadget-prone segment was made up mostly of upscale Japanese baby boomers, allowing it to better target its promotional efforts to this group.

The definition of the target market is typically addressed in the product marketing plan. But the strategic marketing plan must also consider the target market. For instance, definition of a new target for film, such as advanced amateurs, may moderate projections of a decrease in demand for film in the five-year strategic plan. Beyond five years, the key question is when electronic cameras might start making film obsolete.

DEVELOP THE MARKETING MIX

The central component of the product marketing plan is a mix of marketing strategies designed to develop, price, promote, and distribute the product. The strategies in a marketing mix must be coordinated to ensure that they work together to meet the needs of target consumers. Advertising must communicate product features designed to meet customer needs. The ad in Exhibit 2.3 may be eye-catching and may attract attention, but strawberries hardly communicate the product benefits of UBS's brake blocks. The ad is not coordinated with product benefits.

Distribution should be coordinated with advertising so when advertising for a product starts, the product is on the store shelves in sufficient supply to meet consumer demand. When Gillette introduced its Sensor razor in 1990, consumers quickly bought out supplies in many stores, leaving disgruntled consumers who could not buy the product and disgruntled retailers who wanted more. Price must also be coordinated with advertising and product quality. High priced products must be able to deliver quality and performance, and such quality should be communicated in the advertising.

Although Kodak's entry into batteries failed, its development of a marketing mix for its alkaline batteries is instructive. Kodak introduced Supralife, its alkaline battery, with a $20 million national advertising campaign that focused on product performance. An additional $22 million effort encouraged people to try the product by offering discounts off battery purchases plus rebates on purchases of Kodak cameras and film.[13] Distribution support was already strong with 200,000 stores selling Kodak film, and Kodak expanded this network to supermarkets and drugstores.

The advertising and distribution strategies developed for the alkaline line made it easier for Kodak to subsequently introduce Ultralife, its lithium entry. Kodak introduced Ultralife at a premium price of $5 a battery. The advertising campaign focused on the benefit of twice as much power and twice as much life. The product was also advertised to electronics manufacturers as having a ten-year shelf life, an

EXHIBIT 2.3

An Example of a Lack of Coordination in the Marketing Mix

important benefit for companies whose battery-powered products sometimes sit on retail shelves for months.[14]

The weakness in the plan was not in the mix of marketing strategies but in the assumption that the company could come out with a product with no inherent competitive advantages (alkaline batteries) so as to pave the way for a product that had such advantages (lithium). By the time lithium batteries came out, Kodak had lost its initiative in the battery market.

Whereas the product manager is responsible for implementing the marketing mix for a product, the business manager (for Kodak's Consumer Products Business Unit) is concerned with integrating the marketing efforts of all the products within the SBU—films, cameras, and batteries. The manager's prime responsibility is allocating resources to these products to allow implementation of the various product plans.

Coordination of the marketing mix is likely to be more difficult for international marketers. Traditionally, companies operating abroad have left development of the marketing mix to local managers to take account of local needs and customs. But as the world has grown smaller, and consumers are exposed to similar TV images, there is more opportunity to market the same product with the same advertising themes globally. Such an approach would require coordinating conflicting local needs—for example, viewing a detergent as a source of pride in getting clothes clean in Italy versus viewing the same detergent as a time-saver in Germany. The integration of the European Economic Community in 1992 is likely to spur the need for such coordination. As trade barriers come down, products will be marketed across Europe on a more standardized basis.

GLOBAL MARKETING STRATEGIES

Kodak versus Fuji: Battling on Each Other's Home Turf

When Kodak balked at being an official sponsor of the 1984 Summer Olympics in Los Angeles, Fuji jumped at the chance. Not only did it fill the skies with green Fuji blimps, but it also filled the airwaves with advertising for Fuji film. That effort helped the company capture 12 percent of the U.S. film market, the equivalent of about 90 million rolls of film.

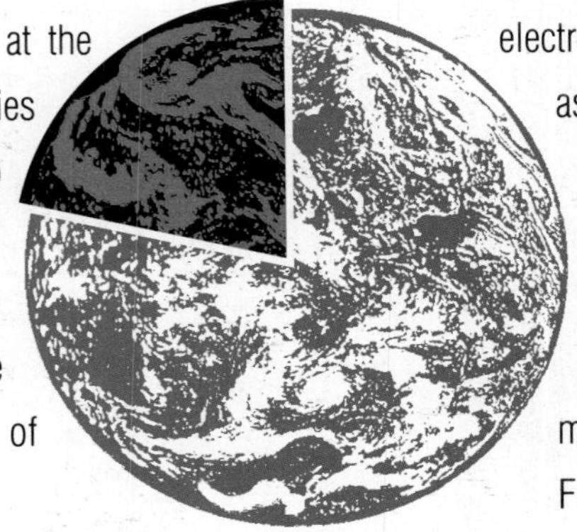

Fuji did not stop at film, however. It set its sights on the broad-based imaging line on which Kodak is relying for future growth. In 1989 it began manufacturing floppy disks in Massachusetts. The same year, it opened a plant in South Carolina to make videotapes. And, it plans to start producing film in the United States as well. Equally disturbing to Kodak is Fuji's potential to get the jump on competitors in new-product development. The company got an early lead in electronic photography with an electronic camera on the market as early as 1985. It was a year ahead of Kodak in disposable cameras. And, in 1990 it introduced a new super-saturated color film targeted to professional photographers a few months before Kodak's entry.

Fuji's reach is not limited to the United States and Japan. As sales for its film in the United States levelled off, Fuji looked to Western Europe and captured 20 percent of the film market, primarily from Kodak and Agfa, the leading European film producer.

But Kodak is not sitting still. It is bringing the battle to the world's second largest photography market, Japan. It captured the same market share

EVALUATE AND CONTROL THE MARKETING EFFORT

The final responsibility of marketing managers, as shown in Figure 2.1, is to evaluate and control performance based on the marketing plan. For product managers, this means tracking sales and comparing revenues and costs to those projected in the product marketing plan. If sales are lower than expected, the product may have to be withdrawn or adjustments made in the marketing mix. If advertising, distribution, or sales costs are significantly over budget, the product manager must either bring these costs into line or justify why the budget should be increased. Competitive activity must also be evaluated. The product manager will need to adjust the marketing plan if a competitor comes in with a superior product or a lower price.

A product manager also relies on data from surveys to determine how consumers evaluate the product and competitive offerings as well as their awareness of

GLOBAL MARKETING STRATEGIES

from Fuji in Japan—12 percent—as Fuji captured from Kodak in the United States. Kodak is also willing to discount its film in Japan to gain more market share, something it would never consider in the United States. The company gained a rare advantage over Fuji with its introduction of wide-angle and waterproof disposable cameras, a boon to the Japanese consumer's desire for novelty. And, to ensure it is matching Fuji's technological capabilities in the United States, Kodak is spending $500 million to build a research and development lab in Japan. Kodak is also beating out Fuji in new markets. Kodak was the first to enter Iran, for example, as that country softened its policies toward the West.

This give and take between the two companies on the global battlefield is becoming legendary. Kodak's clear objective is to encroach on Fuji's home turf so as to divert Fuji's attention from the U.S. market. Ironically, if Kodak is successful, Fuji may redouble its efforts in the United States to divert Kodak from Japan.

Question: Would Kodak be better off concentrating its resources in the United States to ward off competition from Fuji rather than attempting to compete in Japan?

Sources: "Sharply Focused," *Forbes*, December 24, 1990, pp. 50 and 53; and "Kodak Remains Out of Focus in Japan When It Comes to Key Color Film Market," *The Wall Street Journal*, 1990, pp. B1 and B7; and "Iran's Warm Front Reaches All the Way to the U.S.," *Business Week*, June 17, 1991, p. 47.

advertising and their intention to buy. If adjustments have to be made in the marketing mix, these surveys indicate what these adjustments should be.

Business managers evaluate marketing performance of each product in the SBU's mix. Resources are allocated on this basis. Because battery sales did not meet expectations, the business manager for Kodak's Consumer Products Unit decided to cut back on marketing expenditures for the battery line and shift resources elsewhere. Increased expenditures in developing Kodak's electronic camera or in expanding distribution of disposables abroad might have been facilitated by a cutback in expenditures for batteries.

International companies face a more difficult problem in controlling marketing operations because of a greater diversity of factors beyond their control. A domestic marketer does not need to worry about trade regulations and does not have the same level of uncertainty about the political environment. Tariffs (taxes on imported goods), quotas, and restrictions on foreign investments can inhibit a firm's attempt to implement its marketing strategies abroad. For example, some Third World countries such as Egypt encourage foreign investment, while others such as Nigeria insist on government participation in any foreign operations. Political events such as the Gulf War also introduce uncertainties that make it difficult to control foreign operations.

THE ORGANIZATIONAL FRAMEWORK FOR MARKETING

In the previous section, we mentioned two types of marketing managers—a product manager responsible for marketing strategies for a product, and a business manager responsible for marketing strategies for the business unit.

A third type of executive is also responsible for marketing in the firm—*a* **corporate marketing manager**, *who is part of the top management of the company and evaluates the marketing performance of all the business units within the firm.* At Kodak this means evaluating not only the Consumers Product Unit but the 16 other

FIGURE 2.3

Three Levels of Marketing Management and Planning

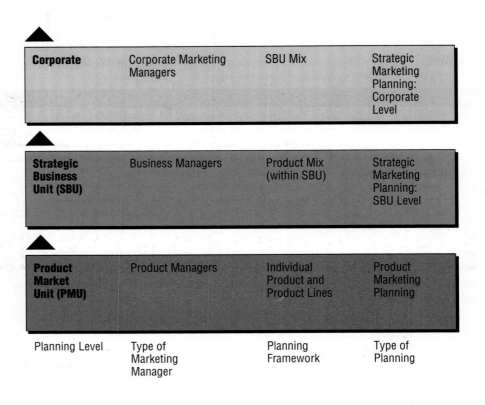

Planning Level	Type of Marketing Manager	Planning Framework	Type of Planning
Corporate	Corporate Marketing Managers	SBU Mix	Strategic Marketing Planning: Corporate Level
Strategic Business Unit (SBU)	Business Managers	Product Mix (within SBU)	Strategic Marketing Planning: SBU Level
Product Market Unit (PMU)	Product Managers	Individual Product and Product Lines	Product Marketing Planning

SBUs such as photo-finishing, electronic photography, health care, and office automation. Using this evaluation, a top management group will decide on the amount of resources the company should allocate to each of its business units. The marketing management and planning responsibilities for these three marketing levels are summarized in Figure 2.3.

THE PRODUCT MARKET UNIT (PMU)

The key planning unit at the product level is the product market unit (PMU). A **product market unit** *is responsible for marketing a set of products within a product category. A* **product category** *is a grouping of products that serve similar functional needs and that can be substituted for each other*. Batteries are a product category since they serve the same basic function—a portable power source—and can generally be substituted for one another. A firm usually offers several brands within a product category, each managed by a product manager.

Figure 2.4 shows the organization of the product, business-unit, and corporate levels at Kodak. It focuses on the Consumer Products Unit as an example of these levels. There are at least three PMUs within the consumer products SBU: cameras, film, and batteries. Individual products within each PMU are shown. The camera PMU has 35 millimeter, Instamatic, and VCR cameras. The film unit has the Ektar line as well as Ektachrome, Kodachrome, and black and white films. The battery PMU has alkaline (Supralife) and lithium (Ultralife) batteries.

FIGURE 2.4

Example of Organizational Structure for Marketing Planning at Kodak

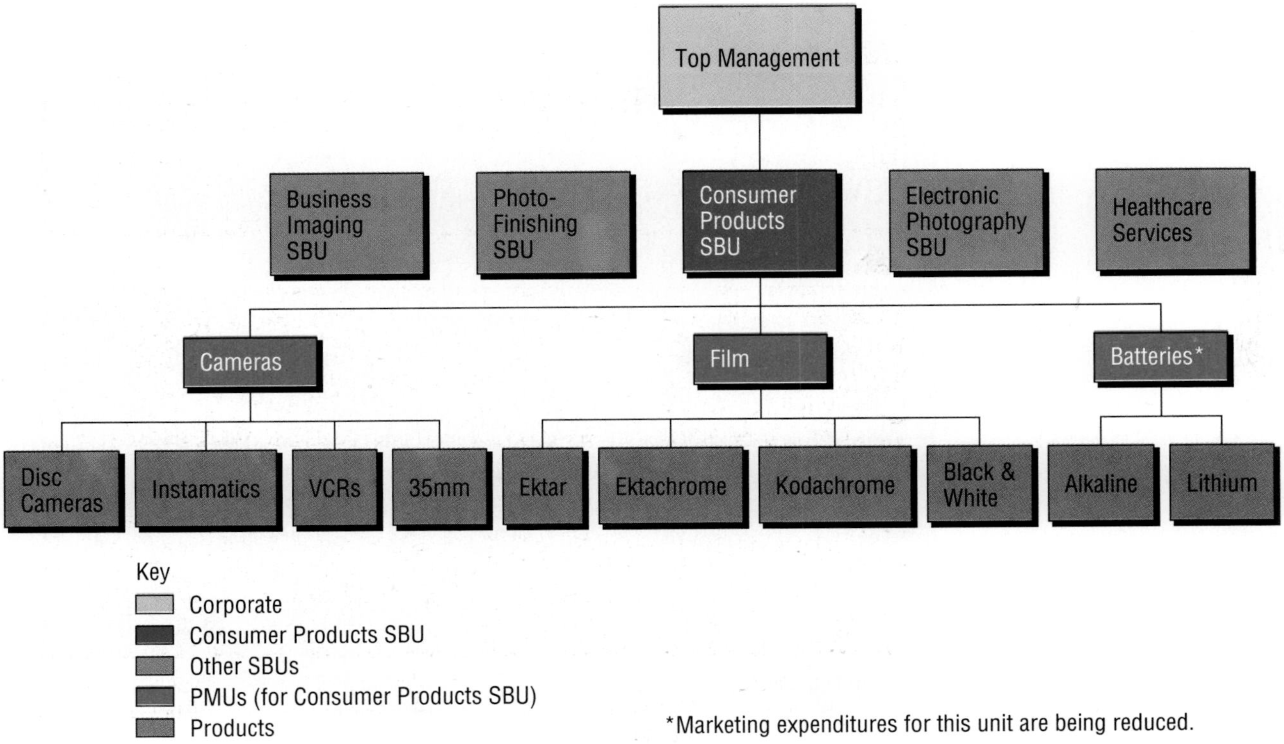

THE STRATEGIC BUSINESS UNIT (SBU)

The next level up in the marketing management hierarchy in Figure 2.3 is the strategic business unit. The planning focus of the business manager in an SBU is the unit's product mix (see Figure 2.3). The business manager reviews the plans submitted by the product managers and develops an overall strategy that defines where the SBU is heading for the next five years (the strategic marketing plan). Thus, the business manager for Kodak's Consumer Products Unit might develop a five-year plan that projects substantial growth in high-resolution film, moderate growth in regular 35 millimeter film, flat sales for cameras, and declining sales for batteries. Resource allocations to these product market units would be made based on this assessment. The business manager then submits the strategic marketing plan to top management for approval.

The SBU framework we have been discussing assumes a multi-unit company such as Kodak. Small to medium-sized companies, and some large companies serving single markets, do not have an SBU organization. In these cases the company operates essentially like a single strategic business unit.

THE CORPORATE LEVEL

The third, and highest, level of marketing management within the firm is at the corporate level. Figure 2.3 shows that top management's responsibility is to evaluate the company's mix of business units through a strategic marketing plan at the corporate level. The plan allocates resources to each business unit based on corporate management's evaluation of SBU plans and will chart a five-year course for the company. For example, top management at Kodak had to give approval to the development of electronic cameras based on projections that they will begin displacing regular cameras by the turn of the century.

FIGURE 2.5

An SBU/Market Matrix for Kodak

	Markets			
SBUs	Consumer	Commercial/ Industrial	International	Government
Business Imaging	✗	✓	✓	?
Photo Finishing	✗	✓	✓	?
Consumer Products	✓	✗	✓	✗
Electronic Photography	✗	✓	✓	?
Health Services	✗	✓	?	?

A useful tool for assessing new business areas is an SBU/market matrix. The SBU/market matrix is designed to provide an overall view of the businesses the firm is in and the targets of these businesses. Figure 2.5 lists five of Kodak's SBUs (shown in Figure 2.4) down the side and its basic market areas across the top. Checks indicate areas now served by Kodak products. Crosses indicate areas that are not relevant (for instance, industrial or government markets for the Consumer Products Unit). Question marks indicate areas of potential entry, such as government markets for the business-imaging and health-care SBUs. The SBU/market matrix provides a good summary of top management's evaluation of areas for future growth. This overall view of the company also provides an important perspective that is beyond the scope of any single SBU's strategic plan.

MARKETING AT THE PRODUCT LEVEL

Whether it takes place at the product level or at the SBU and corporate level, the steps in the marketing planning process are very similar. Figure 2.6 summarizes and compares these steps for both the product marketing plan and the strategic marketing plan. However, the plans differ significantly in *scope* (opportunity identification and strategies are more broadly focused in the strategic plan compared to the product plan); in *level of planning* (plans are formulated at a higher level in

FIGURE 2.6

The Product Marketing Plan and the Strategic Marketing Plan

the strategic plan); and also in *the time horizon* (the strategic plan is generally developed with a five-year horizon and is revised yearly; the product plan is a one-year document).

In this section we discuss the product marketing plan, using the example of planning for what has been called the brand of the decade—the 1982 introduction of Diet Coke. In the next section we describe the strategic marketing plan using the example of Toyota's long-term strategy for marketing its cars in the United States.

PRODUCT MARKETING PLANNING

In 1982 Coca-Cola introduced Diet Coke, the first product with the Coke name other than the company's flagship brand. The brand quickly became the leading diet soft drink, outselling 14-year-old Diet Pepsi and Coca-Cola's own Tab. The brand grew at an annual rate of over 30 percent, and by 1990 it held over 11 percent of the soft drink market—in an industry where each share point is worth $250 million.[15] That made Diet Coke close to a $3 billion-a-year brand.

Diet Coke's amazing performance led some marketers to dub it the brand of the decade. How did the brand achieve this record? By following each of the basic steps for a product marketing plan in Figure 2.6.

FORMULATING MARKETING OBJECTIVES

Marketing objectives are performance criteria set by management for a product, a business unit, or the company as a whole. Marketing objectives at the corporate and business unit level are stated as broad goals for exploiting opportunity and as more specific profit objectives for the next five years. Marketing objectives for individual products are stated in terms of sales, market share, and profits for the coming year. Coca-Cola's management saw that the diet cola market had grown steadily at 10 percent a year for the previous ten years while sales of sugar-based colas were leveling off. Although its diet cola, Tab, was growing with the market, the drink appealed almost exclusively to women. But many diet cola drinkers were men, and Diet Pepsi was getting most of them. As a result, Pepsi had a larger share of diet cola drinkers.

Coca-Cola's management established a singular marketing objective—to introduce a brand that would capture leadership of the diet cola market from Pepsi by attracting male diet cola drinkers. A secondary objective was to ensure that such a brand did not steal a substantial amount of sales from Tab.

IDENTIFYING MARKETING OPPORTUNITY

The product plan evaluates opportunities in specific markets. Coca-Cola's assessment of opportunity in the diet cola market was positive. Management saw that 30 percent of diet cola drinkers were males and that this segment was growing three times as fast as female diet cola drinkers.[16] Although Pepsi had leadership in the diet cola market, it was not directing its appeals specifically to men. Male diet cola drinkers were being ignored and Coca-Cola saw a significant opportunity to appeal to them.

Coca-Cola's management saw another opportunity: to use the Coke name on a product other than the company's leading brand for the first time in Coca-Cola's 90-year history. Putting the Coke name on a diet cola would be the primary means

FIGURE 2.7

The Product-Planning Focus

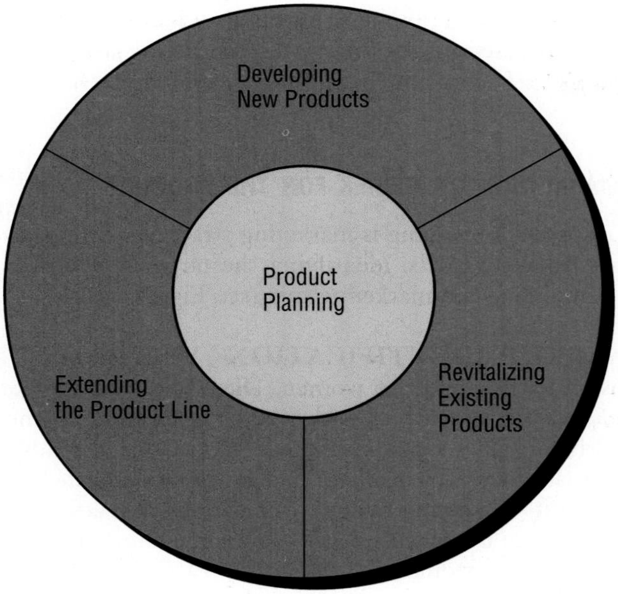

of propelling the new brand into a leadership position in diet colas, and what better name than Diet Coke?

DEFINING THE PRODUCT PLANNING FOCUS

The focus in a product marketing plan can be directed to developing new products, to revitalizing existing products, or to extending a product line (see Figure 2.7).

NEW-PRODUCT DEVELOPMENT The area of opportunity identified by Coca-Cola required developing and testing a new product. Consumers of diet colas were generally dissatisfied with the taste, feeling that they were giving up the taste benefits of regular colas for the benefit of a lower calorie drink. Coca-Cola began testing alternative formulations in an attempt to improve the taste. By 1982, after thousands of consumer taste tests, the company felt it had a winning formulation, one worthy enough to carry the Coca-Cola name.[17]

REVITALIZING EXISTING PRODUCTS Product plans can also be developed to revitalize existing products. Revitalization strategies might involve introducing a new and improved formulation, reducing the price, or repositioning the product to better appeal to the target segment. Coca-Cola attempted to revitalize its flagship brand in 1985 by changing the formula. The objective was to increase Coke's appeal to teenagers by formulating a sweeter tasting cola. The company

FIGURE 2.8

Components of Marketing Strategy

alienated many of its loyal buyers with the change and quickly reverted to the original formula.

EXTENDING THE PRODUCT LINE The marketing plan can also focus on extending the product line by building on a successful new-product introduction. **Product-line extensions** *are variations of an existing product.* Once Diet Coke was introduced, Coca-Cola planned to offer a caffeine-free version as a product line extension.

DEVELOPING MARKETING STRATEGIES FOR THE PRODUCT

The outcome of product planning is marketing strategies. Strategies for a product are directed toward three goals: identifying the target segment, positioning the product, and formulating the marketing mix (see Figure 2.8).

TARGET MARKET IDENTIFICATION Whereas both Tab and Diet Pepsi were positioned to appeal to women, Diet Coke also targeted men. It did so by showing sports figures such as hockey star Wayne Gretzky and football great Marcus Allen drinking Diet Coke in TV ads. Diet Coke also advertised in print ads in primarily male-focused magazines such as *Sports Illustrated* (see Exhibit 2.4). The company split its marketing budget to males and females roughly in proportion to their numbers in the marketplace—about one-third of the budget targeted to men and two-thirds to women.

PRODUCT POSITIONING Once the target market is identified, the product must be positioned to meet its needs. One of Coca-Cola's early decisions was to position Diet Coke based on taste rather than calories. The low-calorie benefit was conveyed through the name of the brand and did not constitute any competitive advantage. Management felt that the brand's advantage relative to Diet Pepsi was in its taste.

MARKETING MIX Establishing a positioning for the product sets the stage for developing a marketing mix to deliver the product to the target market. The company introduced Diet Coke with a $20 million advertising campaign based on the theme "Just for the taste of it" to reflect the positioning on taste rather than weight control. A bevy of celebrities—ranging from the Pointer Sisters to Jessica Rabbit, "star" of the movie *Who Framed Roger Rabbit*—were used to sing Diet Coke's theme. The company also promoted the brand by distributing millions of price-off coupons and by offering periodic sweepstakes. More recently, Coca-Cola introduced a novel promotion to counter Pepsi: In some stores, every time a Pepsi sale is rung up at the cash register, a coupon-dispensing machine offers the consumer a coupon for a free Diet Coke.[18]

So far we have cited three components of the marketing mix—a new *product* formulation, a strong *advertising* campaign, and *price* incentives such as coupons. Coca-Cola did not forget the fourth component, *distribution*. It was assured of strong distribution through supermarkets and food stores because of its leading position in soft drinks. But distribution also requires a bottler network to process syrup into soft drinks, bottle the product, and distribute it to retailers. Coca-Cola made sure that its bottlers were fully behind the brand and had the capacity to bottle and distribute it.

EXHIBIT 2.4

A Recent Diet Coke Ad Appearing in Sports Illustrated

EVALUATION AND CONTROL

Once a product plan is implemented, it continues to serve an important function as the basis for evaluating product performance and controlling costs. The product manager will track sales and market share (that is, a product's sales as a percent of total sales in a market) on a monthly basis to determine if revenue objectives are being met. Advertising, sales promotion, and distribution costs will also be tracked to make sure they do not go over budget.

If performance goals are not being met or if environmental factors change, the product manager will change components of the marketing plan to more effectively direct the product to the target market. This may involve a change in the product's positioning, a decrease in price, or a change in allocations to TV and print advertising.

Diet Coke acheived an 11 percent share of the soft-drink market with a two front appeal to men and women as separate target markets. Once these buyers were in the Diet Coke camp, however, the competitive environment of the diet cola market had changed. Diet Coke's advertising goal in the early 1990s changed accordingly. The campaign was redirected to target baby boomers rather than focusing on male-female differences because baby boomers now represented the highest consumption of diet soft drinks. In Diet Coke's case, the marketing effort meant redefining the target market.

PRODUCT STRATEGY ALTERNATIVES

New products are not the only strategic avenue open to the product manager. An alternative to new products is to spend more money reinforcing existing products. Further, both existing and new products can be directed to a company's existing customers or to new customers. These two dimensions produce the four product strategy alternatives in Figure 2.9: market penetration, market expansion, product line extensions, and new-product development.

STRATEGIES FOR EXISTING PRODUCTS

Companies use market-penetration strategies to try to increase sales of existing products in existing markets. *A* **market penetration strategy** *is a strategy aimed at maintaining a competitive advantage already gained by strong product performance.* Increasing advertising, reducing prices, expanding distribution, or modifying a product may all be used to strengthen a product's position.

Once Diet Coke became established, it began to follow a strategy of market penetration. It initially tried to attract Diet Pepsi users. But as sales began to reach a plateau, the company began appealing to cola drinkers in general. It kicked off a campaign in the 1989 Super Bowl to attract Pepsi rather than Diet Pepsi drinkers with the claim that half a million Pepsi drinkers switched to Diet Coke. Companies like Coca-Cola also use coupons and price reduction to induce consumers of competitive brands to switch, hoping that once they try the company's brand, many will continue to buy it.

A second product strategy used by companies for existing products, **market expansion,** *targets existing products to new markets.* This can involve geographic expansion, targeting of new demographic and life-style segments, or expanding demand by attracting nonusers to the product. Converse provides a good example

FIGURE 2.9

Product Strategy Alternatives

	Existing Products	**New Products**
Existing Customers	Market Penetration	Product Line Extension or New Product Development
New Customers	Market Expansion	New Product Development

EXHIBIT 2.5

An Example of a Market Expansion Strategy

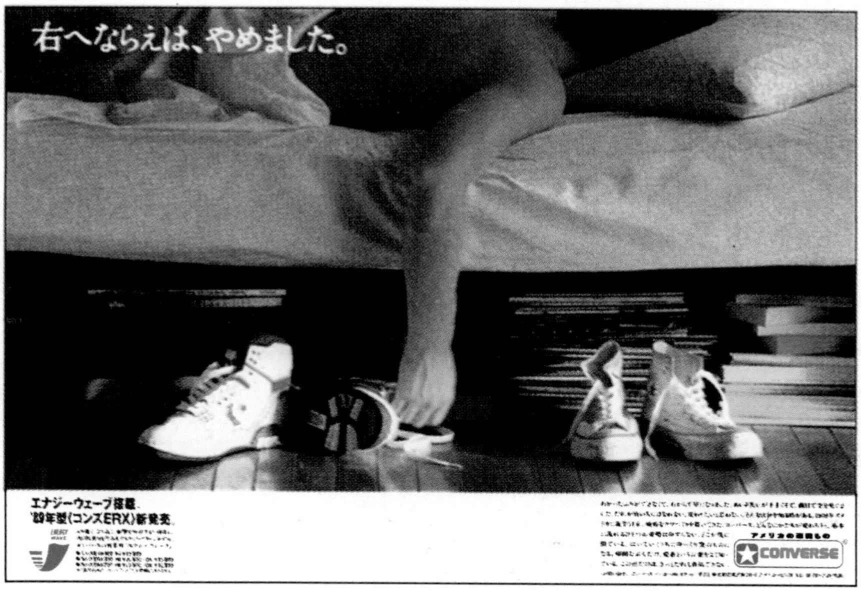

of geographic expansion. Riding the increasing popularity of basketball abroad from Spain to Japan, the company decided to expand its overseas efforts (see Exhibit 2.5). As a result, it sold over $50 million worth of basketball shoes abroad, tripling international sales since 1986.[19]

A company can also seek to expand markets for existing products by appealing to new target segments. As we saw in the last chapter, Harley-Davidson expanded its market by appealing to a new segment—baby boomers entering their forties. Market expansion can also be achieved by influencing nonusers of a product category to become users. Arm & Hammer, for instance, developed an effective advertising campaign to get nonusers to use baking soda by emphasizing new uses as a toothpaste, a refrigerator deoderizer, and so on.

STRATEGIES FOR NEW PRODUCTS

Strategies for new products require a company to either extend existing product lines or to develop totally new products. As examples of *product line extensions,* Procter & Gamble expanded Crest toothpaste to include gels and a tartar-control formula in a variety of packaging options, and Häagen Dazs capitalized on its strong market position in ice cream by expanding into frozen yogurt (see Exhibit 2.6).

A **new product development strategy** *creates new products to serve both existing and new customers* (see Figure 2.9). Kodak's introduction of its VR-G film with improved color quality was intended to keep its existing film users from switching to Fuji film. Its introduction of Ektar was targeted to a new segment, sophisticated amateurs who wanted high-resolution film.

EXHIBIT 2.6

An Example of a Product-Line Extension (From Ice Cream to Frozen Yogurt)

MARKETING AT THE SBU AND CORPORATE LEVEL

While the product marketing plan guides the targeting, positioning, and delivery of a product, the strategic marketing plan guides the overall direction of the company and its business units. The key in guiding the SBUs and the company over a five-year period is to identify strategic windows—that is, opportunities in the environment that can be exploited and sustained for competitive advantage.

We will describe Toyota's successful entry into the U.S. car market as an example of the strategic planning process in Figure 2.6. The difference between the Toyota example and that of Diet Coke is that Toyota's entry into the U.S. market determined its future corporate growth, whereas Diet Coke's introduction did not in itself define Coca-Cola's future.

THE STRATEGIC PLANNING PROCESS

In 1958 Toyota sold 288 cars in the United States.[20] Its first imported car, the Toyopet, was a flop. Its block shape made it look like a truck, its engine made it sound like a truck, and the rough and uncomfortable interior made it feel like a truck. But by 1988 the company was selling 630,000 cars—nearly a 25 percent share of foreign car sales in the United States—with star performers like the Toyota Corona and Corolla.[21] How did Toyota manage this remarkable turnaround? It used a strategic marketing plan to enter the U.S. market by identifying unmet customer needs and exploiting Detroit's weaknesses. Toyota followed the five planning steps in Figure 2.6 with a single-minded devotion that ensured success.

DEFINE CORPORATE OBJECTIVES

Toyota's failure in the U.S. market in the late 1950s led it to reanalyze its market-entry strategy. Its corporate objectives, supported by the Japanese government, were to look for markets that might provide superior investment returns and international trade benefits over the long term. The U.S. auto market was a prime candidate for fulfilling these objectives—a market that Toyota was not about to give up on.

Toyota also recognized that its long-term survival would depend on establishing a presence abroad. Its forecasters saw tremendous growth in the worldwide demand for automobiles. Toyota's foremost corporate goal was to get a share of that demand. With the help of the Japanese government, Toyota was prepared to invest heavily to fulfill this goal.

IDENTIFY MARKETING OPPORTUNITIES

Just as identifying marketing opportunities is crucial to marketing at the product level, it is critically important at the SBU and corporate level. After the failure of the Toyopet, Toyota conducted a complete study of U.S. auto dealers and owners. It identified a substantial gap between what many customers wanted and what Detroit was giving them. By the 1960s, attitudes toward cars were changing. Instead of looking on cars as status symbols, many Americans were looking for fuel economy, durability, easy maintenance, and service reliability. All this added up to a substantial segment of car buyers that wanted a smaller car. At the time, Volkswagen was the only manufacturer that was giving it to them.

Instead of filling this gap, American car manufacturers were continuing to build larger and more expensive cars in a production-oriented mode. The strategic window of opportunity was open. Toyota entered it with the introduction of the Corona in 1965, the first viable alternative to the Volkswagen.

Toyota's willingness to stay in the American market for seven years and invest in research and distribution facilities demonstrates one important difference between Japanese and American car makers. The Japanese companies were willing to take a long-range view of profitability by absorbing losses in the short term to sustain themselves in the American marketplace for the long term. This long-term view could work only if the Japanese companies brought some sustainable competitive advantage to the American marketplace. And they did, in the form of high-quality products at lower prices, made possible by higher productivity levels in Japanese factories. Without these competitve advantages, no amount of Japanese governmental support would have helped.

DEFINE THE STRATEGIC PLANNING FOCUS

The strategic focus for Toyota's entry into the American car market was clearly corporate. The company gave virtually total attention, as well as a good portion of its resources, to entry into the American market. By 1965 a series of successful new-car introductions in Japan provided Toyota with the means to finance its overseas expansion. But Toyota did not just import its successful domestic cars into the United States; it developed cars like the Corona, with the American consumer in mind.

DEVELOP CORPORATE (OR SBU) GROWTH STRATEGY

A **corporate growth strategy** *is the means by which a company plans to exploit marketing opportunities, usually over the following five years.* Growth strategies deal with decisions regarding businesses rather than individual products. For example, Toyota's growth strategy was to further its international business by fueling entry into the U.S. car market. It did so with superior products at reasonable prices.

Toyota's success with the Corona paved the way for the next phase in its growth strategy; to consolidate its competitive advantage over American car manufacturers. Toyota introduced the Corolla series as an additional compact alternative. In 1974 it offered an enlarged version of the Corolla to appeal to mid-sized car buyers. In the process, Toyota continuously invested in plant and equipment to maintain product quality.

These efforts paid off. The central element in Toyota's corporate growth strategy—establishing itself in the U.S. car market with a superior line of compacts—was a clear success.

EXHIBIT 2.7

Workers in the General Motors/Toyota Plant: A Joint Venture in SPC

American workers build Toyota Corolla and Geo Prizm passenger cars as well as Toyota compact pickup trucks at New United Motor Manufacturing, Inc., the Toyota-General Motors joint venture in Fremont, California. Workers practice *Jidoka,* the principle which calls for guaranteeing quality in the manufacture process itself and fixing problems as they occur rather than depending upon a final inspection and rework.

EVALUATION AND CONTROL

As at the product level, the fifth step in strategic marketing planning is evaluation and control. Toyota constantly evaluated sales results as it adapted its strategic plan to a changing environment.

Toyota also exerted tight cost controls that enabled it to produce many more cars per employee than American manufacturers. Toyota was able to achieve higher productivity by following quality control procedures, adopted by most Japanese manufacturers, known as statistical process control (SPC). **Statistical process control** *seeks to control production defects at the time they occur rather than after the fact*. It does so by encouraging workers to be responsible for quality control on the production line as a group. SPC conforms well to the Japanese emphasis on the individual's responsibility to the group. SPC resulted in lower costs, allowing lower prices. Toyota's product superiority and lower costs thus permitted the company to sustain its competitive advantage over American car manufacturers.

General Motors attempted to learn Toyota's approach to quality control by a simple expedient, entering into a joint venture with Toyota to produce pickup trucks in a California assembly plant. GM's objective is to implement Japanese methods of quality control to improve its productivity (see Exhibit 2.7).

ALTERNATIVE CORPORATE GROWTH STRATEGIES

At both the corporate and the business unit levels, the company's strategy for growth is the key element in the strategic marketing plan. Figure 2.10 shows some alternative growth strategies. These alternatives are determined by two key questions: First, does the company seek growth in businesses related to its core markets, or does it seek growth in new business areas? Kodak is sustaining its core market in film in the short term while seeking growth in new imaging businesses and in electronic photography for the long term.

The second question, applicable both to core markets and to new businesses, is whether growth is attained through internal development of products (as in Toyota's case), or through external acquisition (a strategy used by Chrysler when it acquired American Motors in 1987). These strategies will be explored in Chapter 22, where we more fully discuss strategic marketing planning and corporate growth strategies.

FIGURE 2.10

Alternative Corporate Growth Strategies

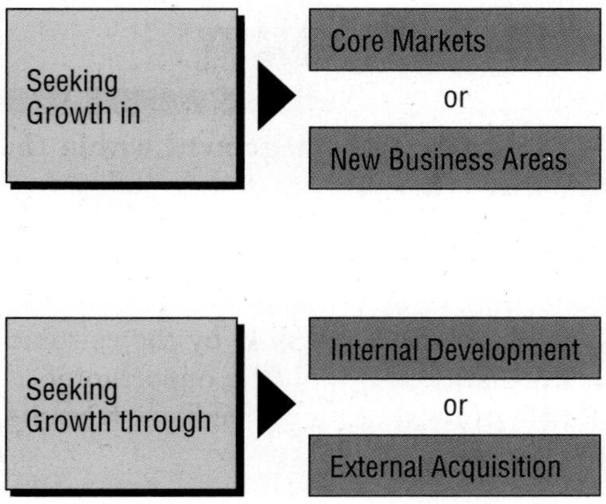

ETHICAL AND ENVIRONMENTAL ISSUES IN MARKETING

DuPont: Incorporating Environmental Issues into Its Strategic Plans

It took the Bhopal gas leak in India, the Exxon Valdez spill in Alaska, the picture of devastating pollution in Eastern Europe, and a good dose of environmental terrorism during the Persian Gulf War to get business leaders to sit up and take notice of environmental issues. But most telling of all is the fact that their own customers, the American public, overwhelmingly favor increased regulation of business to reduce pollution.

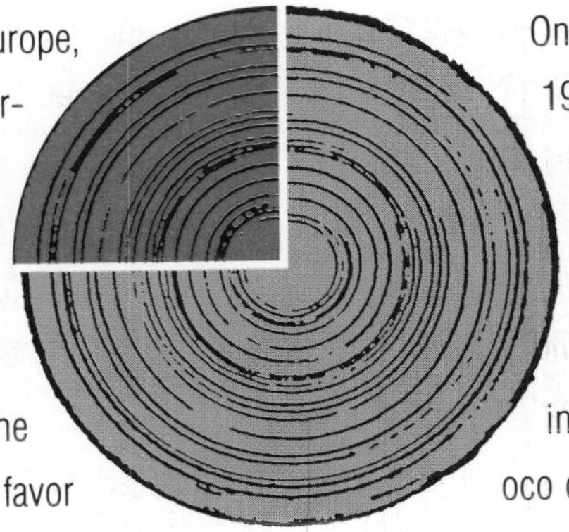

Some companies have reacted by seeing the issue as "us versus them," us being corporate America and them being environmentalists. The reaction of Exxon to its oil spill, for example, was not a model of environmental concern as it fought further court-imposed fines for polluting Prince William sound. Other companies have recognized the need to plan ahead for environmental controls to avoid further damaging the environment.

One of these companies is DuPont. In 1988, DuPont decided to phase out all chemicals that damage the earth's protective ozone layer. In 1989, the company reacted to the Exxon Valdez oil spill by announcing that all tankers built for its Conoco oil subsidiary will have double hulls, a feature that would reduce the danger of any future oil spill. DuPont also established a goal of reducing chemical emissions from its factories by 60 percent by 1993 even though it was not required to do so.

DuPont's actions are part of a process that incorporates environmental assessment in its strategic plans. All departmental heads are directly responsible for issues relating to the environment, such as

SUMMARY

1. **What is the role of marketing management within the firm?**
   Marketing managers have the primary responsibility to fulfill the marketing function within the firm. They identify marketing opportunities, develop strategies to use the firm's resources to exploit these opportunities, implement these strategies, and evaluate them. A key factor is the existence of a *strategic window of opportunity*, which is identified not only by the existence of an opportunity, but also by the firm's ability to exploit the opportunity.
2. **What is the dual role of marketing in the firm, from both the product and corporate perspective?**
   There are two types of marketing managers in most multi-unit firms, a product manager and a business manager. The responsibilities of these individuals

ETHICAL AND ENVIRONMENTAL ISSUES IN MARKETING

control of pollution emissions, product safety management, and disposal of toxic wastes. Plans for ensuring environmental controls in the manufacture of chemicals must be stipulated. The adequacy of these environmental controls are reviewed by a corporate-wide environmental quality committee chaired by DuPont's second highest ranking executive, the vice-chairman of the board of directors. And, DuPont has tied its managers' environmental record to their pay, creating a monetary incentive to ensure environmental consciousness.

Will DuPont's attempt to account for environmental issues in its planning process work? There are skeptics. Some say that a directive from top management to departmental heads is not enough; that a belief in a company's responsibility for the environment must exist and that such a belief has not permeated the ranks of middle management. Others point to the existence of an environmental committee headed by a vice-chairman as window dressing. Still others say that although it took only ten days to issue the directive to eliminate ozone-depleting chemicals, the company knew about the problem 14 years earlier.

The skeptics may or may not be right, but there is no question that DuPont is a more environmentally conscious company.

Question: Is DuPont's planning process enough to insure future environmental responsibility?

Sources: "Color Them Green," *Wharton Alumni Magazine*, Winter 1991, pp. 17–19; and "Turn Exxon Into a Model Environmental Citizen," *Business Week*, May 20, 1991, p. 44.

reflect their dual role. The product manager for a particular product is responsible for developing, implementing, and evaluating strategies for the product. The business manager is in charge of a strategic business unit (SBU)—that is, a division of a company organized to reflect market demand. The business manager evaluates the SBU's product mix, charts a course for the SBU by allocating resources to individual products, and submits a plan for approval to top management.

3. **What is the importance of the strategic business unit in the marketing planning process?**
Since the strategic business unit is organized on the basis of market demand, it encourages a more marketing-oriented view of company operations. Before the SBU organization was introduced, most companies were organized on functional lines (for example, marketing, manufacturing, R&D) or on the basis

of similarities in technology. The reorganization at Kodak on SBU lines—as an example—resulted in improving the ability of the company to meet customer needs and gain a competitive advantage, because it focused on markets rather than functions. The various functional areas were brought together under one roof and coordinated to better serve market needs.

4. **What is the nature of product marketing planning and strategic marketing planning?**
The product marketing plan charts the marketing strategy for an individual product. It is the responsibility of the product manager. The plan identifies the opportunities for marketing the product, sets performance objectives, identifies a target segment, positions the product to meet customer needs, and develops a mix of pricing, distribution, and advertising elements to market the product. Cost estimates and revenue goals in the plan serve as bases for evaluating the performance of the product.
The strategic marketing plan for a business unit evaluates its product mix and charts a course for the SBU by allocating resources to individual products. SBU plans are submitted to corporate managers, who then evaluate the company's business mix and allocate resources to the business units in the context of a corporate strategic plan.

5. **What strategy alternatives are available to marketing managers at the product level and at the SBU or corporate level?**
Strategic alternatives available to product managers are to strengthen existing products among current customers, to extend existing products to new market segments, or to develop new products to appeal to the company's current customer base. In each case the strategic focus is on individual products.
Strategic alternatives available to business or corporate managers deal with entering new businesses. Management can consider entering new businesses in its core markets, or it can consider acquiring companies outside its areas of core competency. It can move into these new business areas through a process of internal new-product development or external acquisition of companies.

KEY TERMS

Marketing plan (p. 38)
Product marketing plan (p. 38)
Strategic marketing plan (p. 38)
Product mix (p. 39)
Stategic business unit (SBU) (p. 39)
Product manager (p. 40)
Business manager (p. 41)
Strategic window of opportunity (p. 42)
Corporate marketing manager (p. 48)
Product market unit (PMU) (p. 49)
Product category (p. 49)
Product-line extension (p. 54)
Market penetration strategy (p. 56)
Market expansion strategy (p. 56)
New product development strategy (p. 57)
Corporate growth strategy (p. 60)
Statistical Process Control (p. 61)

QUESTIONS

1. What do we mean by a strategic window of opportunity? Was the strategic window open for the introduction of Diet Coke in 1982? Why?
2. What is the difference between a product marketing plan and a strategic marketing plan? Specify differences in (a) objectives, (b) opportunity identification, (c) strategies, and (d) the nature of evaluation and control.
3. What are the purposes of a marketing plan?
4. Why is Kodak a more marketing-oriented company today than it was before 1984? Specify (a) organizational changes and (b) strategies that suggest a greater marketing orientation.
5. What factors prompted Kodak to enter the battery market? Why did sales fail to meet expectations?

6. What is the importance of defining a target market in the product marketing plan? How does the definition of the target market for the Ektar film line as "upscale older baby boomers" affect the marketing plan for the product?
7. What is the distinction between a product marketing unit and a strategic business unit?
8. What is the purpose of developing an SBU/market matrix such as that in Figure 2.5? What strategic decisions might be made based on this matrix?
9. How do the marketing responsibilities of the product manager for lithium batteries at Kodak differ from those of the business manager for the Consumer Products SBU?
10. How do the marketing responsibilities of the business manager for the Consumer Products SBU differ from those of the corporate marketing manager at Kodak?
11. The product marketing plan can be directed toward developing new products, revitalizing existing products, and extending the product line. Explain and provide examples.
12. What are the components of a marketing mix? Describe the components of Diet Coke's marketing mix.
13. What are the differences between strategies of new-product development, market penetration, and market expansion? When is a company most likely to follow each of these strategies?

QUESTIONS: YOU ARE THE DECISION MAKER

1. A marketing manager for a large consumer-goods company read the description of Kodak's turnaround in the beginning of this chapter and made the following comment:

   You don't turn a company around by just reorganizing. An SBU structure is fine, but it doesn't necessarily change the way you think. Kodak still has a lot of old-line managers. Don't forget they rarely brought fresh blood into the company before 1984. What Kodak needs is not just a reorganization, but a change in corporate culture. As far as I'm concerned, the jury is still out as to whether Kodak has really shifted from a production to a marketing orientation.

   a. Do you agree with this statement?
   b. What do you suppose the marketing manager meant by a "corporate culture"?
2. How might Kodak apply strategies of (a) market expansion and (b) market penetration to its line of disposable cameras? What actions would each type of strategy require? Which strategy would Kodak be most likely to use first: market penetration or market expansion? When would it switch from one strategy to another?
3. Why did Toyota's re-entry into the U.S. market after the Toyopet failure represent a strategic window of opportunity for the company?

CHAPTER 3

Marketing Planning

YOUR FOCUS IN CHAPTER 3

To learn:

- *How a firm develops a marketing plan for a new or existing product.*
- *How the market for the product should be evaluated.*
- *The strategic issues in identifying a target market and positioning the product.*
- *The mix of marketing elements—advertising, distribution, and price—that should be used to implement the strategy for the product.*
- *How a firm can estimate future sales.*

Gillette: A Global Marketing Plan for the Sensor Razor

In 1987, Gillette was at a key juncture. It had just successfully fought a takeover bid by Revlon and was about to face another one. Even more threatening, profits from its core business, razors, were shrinking because more men were using disposable razors, a product with much lower profit margins than cartridge-type razors such as Gillette's Trac II and Atra. Ironically, it was Gillette that created the disposable razor market in 1975, thinking that the throwaways were a logical extension of its regular razor line. It never dreamed that two-thirds of all shavers would someday use disposables. Adding to a sinking feeling among Gillete's management was the fact that the company's toiletry and hair-care line was stagnant. Even though it had leading brand names like Right Guard deodorant and Silkience shampoo, profits from these brands were disappointing.[1]

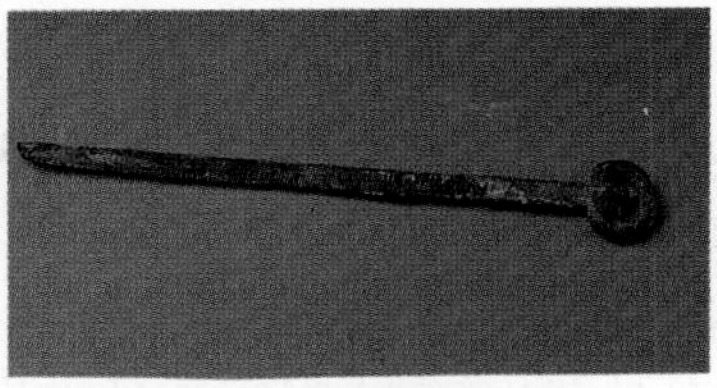

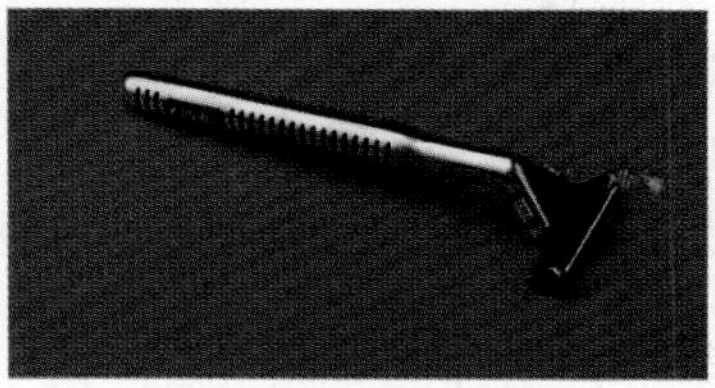

But the company had an ace up its sleeve that could spell salvation, a new razor that by 1987 had been in development for seven years. The last new razor Gillette had introduced was the Atra in 1977. It immediately began seeking an improvement. By 1980, research and development came up with an answer: Whereas the Atra system had a pivoting head to adjust to a man's face, the new razor would have a much more sensitive system—twin razors suspended on springs that would glide over the contours of a man's face much like a car with a good suspension system glides over potholes.[2]

It took seven years for the company to solve a succession of technical problems, chief of which was the need to develop new laser technology that could make 93 precise welds a second to join the twin razors to tiny springs.[3] By 1987, Gillette's R&D group was confident the company could mass produce the new razor.

Management then got into high gear and started formulating the key requirement to make the product a success, a sound *marketing plan.* Called the Sensor to convey the razor's ability to sense and glide over the contours of the skin, management made two early decisions that would shape the marketing plan and eventually ensure success. First, it decided to introduce the Sensor as a cartridge system only. There was strong sentiment within Gillette that with two-thirds of the market using disposables, there should be a disposable version of the Sensor as well. But Gillette's top management decided that introducing a disposable version would be defeating its objectives of trying to increase profit margins by shifting consumers from disposables to cartridge systems.

The second decision was even more important. For the first time, Gillette would introduce a new product on a worldwide basis rather than in stages. Sensor would be introduced in January 1990 simultaneously in 19 countries in both North America and Europe. With 70 percent of its profits coming from overseas sales, Gillette's decision was not surprising.[4] Further, disposables had not caught on abroad as they had in the United States because most foreign countries could not accept the "throwaway" ethic that was acceptable to U.S. consumers. If anything, Sensor would have less of an uphill struggle abroad than in the United States.

Management also made another decision that spelled a departure from the past: Sensor would be introduced with a global marketing strategy. Whereas in the past, marketing strategies were varied to meet the needs of consumers in individual countries, Sensor would be introduced with no product modifications across countries and with the same global advertising theme. In the words of one executive, "For the first time, we were going to take a truly global approach with one product, one brand name, one advertising campaign, and one marketing strategy."[5]

Sensor was introduced to the world on January 28, 1990, with three commercials on Super Bowl XXIV at a cost of $3 million, part of a first-year $110 million promotional campaign.[6] Advertising cited the advance in razor technology with a basic theme line introduced earlier for the Atra—"Gillette. The best a man can get." The marketing plan was designed to convince Atra and Trac II users to trade up to the Sensor *and* to convince users of disposables to switch to an advanced system providing a better shave. If the product was profitable, Gillette planned to introduce a line of toiletries under the Sensor umbrella. An underlying objective was to get back to the company's original image of providing quality shaving systems, an image that was tarnished by the introduction of Gillette's disposable razors.

What happened? Sensor was the most successful new product introduction in Gillette's history. In 1990, the company sold 24 million razors and 350 million cartridges, figures that were 20 percent higher than its original objective. Its advertising and public-relations campaign reached 500 million people worldwide. The product was clearly the turnaround that Gillette was looking for. Sensor's success was based on a sound product, a sound marketing plan, and a global reach.[7]

THE MARKETING PLANNING PROCESS

A company needs a plan for each product it markets. Such a **marketing plan** *specifies strategies to be used and resources required.* The process of developing such plans is called *marketing planning* and involves the eight steps listed in Figure 3.1.

Step 1. The product manager first conducts a **situation analysis,** *which is a preliminary evaluation of the market for the product.* The situation analysis will define the market (what products are likely to compete with the company's brand); determine the market's key characteristics such as competitive intensity, required capital investment, means of distributing the product, and stability of demand; and estimate its size to determine its potential.

Step 2. The product manager evaluates marketing opportunity for the company's product based on an assessment of customer needs, competitive strengths and weaknesses, and other factors. This involves a marketing analysis of both the opportunities and threats facing a product and its strengths and weaknesses. An **opportunity/threat analysis** *requires information on the competition, customers, and other aspects of the environment to identify opportunities to meet customer needs and threats the product might face* (these are factors *external* to the company that are generally beyond its control). An evaluation of the company's strengths and weaknesses determines whether it has the ability to exploit the opportunities identified by management. Such a **strength/weakness analysis** *requires information on company resources and capabilities to market a product.* These are factors *internal* to the company that are generally within its control.

Step 3. The product manager uses the marketing opportunity evaluation to develop product objectives in the form of sales and profit goals. Gillette's management felt that a reasonable goal for Sensor was to capture 7 percent of the shaver market in the first year. Actually, the brand captured 9 percent of the market.

Step 4. The product manager formulates marketing strategies to fulfill product objectives. Two key elements are to determine the target market, which is the market segment or segments the firm is aiming at with its marketing effort, and the product positioning, which is the way product features and benefits are communicated to this target.

Market leaders generally target a wide number of segments that encompass the total market. For example, Gillette has offerings in the three key segments of the shaver market: disposables, with its line of Good News disposable razors; cartridge systems, with its Trac II, Atra, and now Sensor razors; and electric shavers, with its German-based Braun line. Smaller firms or later entrants into the market may target one segment. For example, Bic targets the disposable segment only.

Product positioning strategies convey the benefits of the product in a way that distinguishes it from competition. This requires an integrated advertising and sales strategy that focuses on a few key customer benefits. Sensor was positioned as a revolutionary new shaving system that would provide a closer and more comfortable shave. But more than that, the imagery was designed to convey quality and value so as to convince users that the new system was worth the extra cost relative to disposables and other cartridge-type systems.

FIGURE 3.1

The Marketing Planning Process

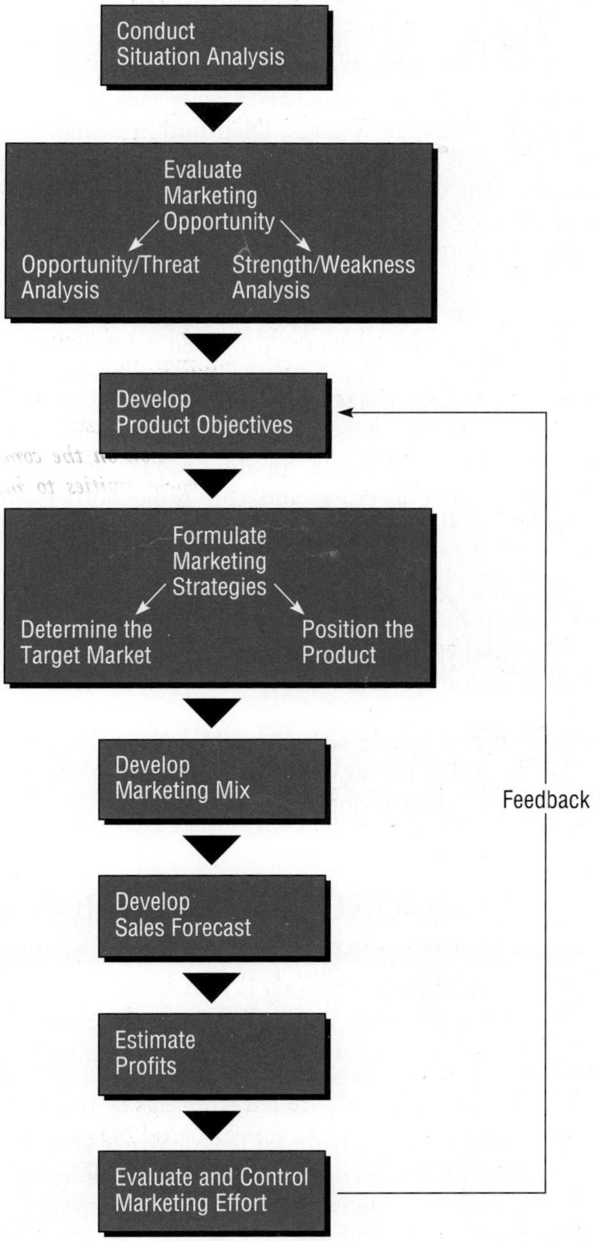

Step 5. Once the target market has been identified and the positioning decided upon, the next step is to develop a marketing mix, which is composed of advertising, pricing, and distribution elements that work together to implement the product's positioning. One of the product manager's important responsibilities is to develop a budget for the various elements of the marketing mix. From this budget, profits can be projected for the product.

Sensor's marketing mix involved heavy advertising spending on a global basis in the first year. The company was anxious to get as many razors sold as possible, even at a discount, because it makes its money primarily on the cartridges, not the razors. As a result, part of the promotional plan was to provide discount coupons on the razors and to distribute a number of free samples in key market areas to encourage trial. After an introductory period, the razor would be sold at retail at $3.75 and cartridges at an average of 75 cents each, a price about 25 percent higher than most other cartridge systems. Distribution would be through the company's established channels for shaving products both in the United States and abroad. A key requirement would be to ensure that enough of the product was sent to retailers in advance of the January 1990 introduction to ensure that demand created by the company's promotional efforts could be met.

Step 6. When the marketing mix has been developed, the product manager develops a *sales forecast* based on the proposed marketing strategy. While sales forecasts are developed at various times in the process of marketing planning, they are more reliable at later stages.

Step 7. Next, estimated profits for the product are calculated based on revenue projections from sales forecasts and cost projections from marketing and other expenditures.

Step 8. The final step is to evaluate and control the marketing effort. Product managers track product performance and make adjustments in positioning strategies and the marketing mix to ensure that product objectives are met. Feedback to management on product performance may lead to changes in product objectives.

In the rest of this chapter, we will explore each of the steps shown in Figure 3.1 in more detail, using the example of Gillette developing a marketing plan for Sensor's entry into the shaving market.

CONDUCTING THE SITUATION ANALYSIS

The first step in marketing planning is to conduct a situation analysis, which consists of four steps: *defining the market* for a certain product, *identifying market characteristics*, *estimating market potential*, and *conducting a preliminary market assessment.*

DEFINING THE MARKET

A firm must evaluate an opportunity for a particular market. Therefore, the first step in marketing planning is to gain an understanding of the composition of the market. In Chapter 1, we defined a *market* as a group of actual or potential buyers of a product category. In this respect, we can identify a market for cellular telephones, for video-cassette recorders, or for razors. But there is a problem in defining a market in this way: It does not reflect consumer needs. Buyers identified as a market generally have a common set of needs for a product category. The common need for cellular telephones is mobile communications; the common need for video-cassette recorders is in-home entertainment; the common need for razors is shaving.

Therefore, it would be more appropriate to identify a market by needs such as mobile communications, in-home entertainment, or shaving rather than by product category. If Gillette identified the market as razors (the product) rather than shaving (the process that reflects consumer needs) it would tie itself to a product category that could eventually become obsolete. Suppose that 20 years from now a company invents a low-intensity laser device that can take the stubble off a man's face or a woman's legs on a day-to-day basis with no risk, effort, or discomfort. A company that identified its market as razors would soon be out of business.

Kodak's method of market definition goes to the very question of its survival. It defines its markets based on the imaging needs of its customers (medical imaging, photo imaging, data imaging, and so forth). It does not identify its markets by film type. If it did, it would be wedded to film technology. Given the emergence of filmless electronic photography, Kodak is positioned to shift from film to filmless technology, because it is defining markets by consumer needs rather than by products.

A key question for a product manager is how broadly or narrowly to define the market. Consumers can satisfy their shaving needs with cartridge-type razors, with disposables, or with electric razors. In investigating an opportunity like the introduction of the Sensor razor, should management consider customers for all three products as part of the market, or should management define the market more narrowly? Gillette identified the market as the *wet* shaving market encompassing users of disposables and cartridge-type razors but excluding users of electric razors. Management felt that the needs of the wet- and dry-shaving market were very different. Disposable users could be won over to a new type of cartridge razor, but users of electric shavers probably could not be won over to wet shaving.

Management's thinking on the shaving market is reflected in Figure 3.2. Assume Gillette asks consumers to position shaving products by their substitutability to

FIGURE 3.2

A Perceptual Map of the Shaving Market

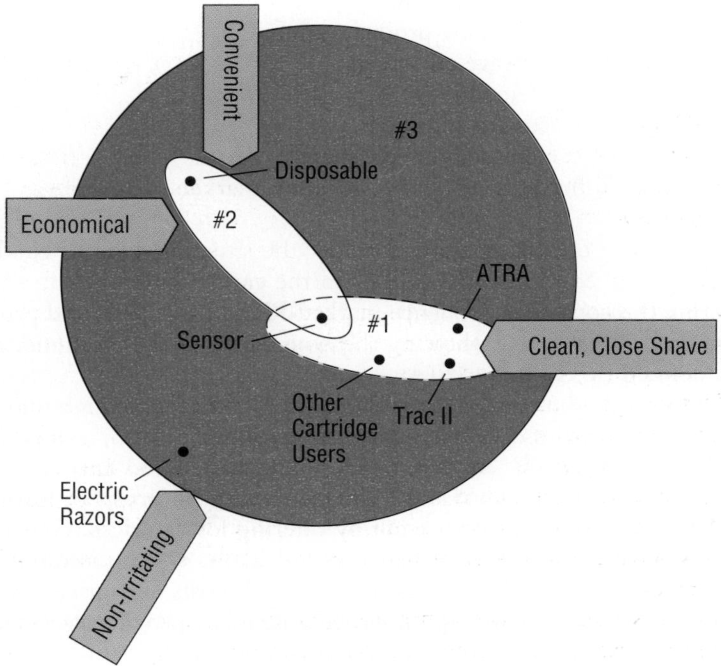

each other and to identify the benefits they see in each product. The results of such a survey can be portrayed in a perceptual map such as in Figure 3.2. *A* **perceptual map** *is a visual representation of the similarity between products and the benefits consumers associate with each product.* The Trac II and Atra systems are seen as most similar. Other cartridge-type systems are seen as somewhat similar to Trac II and Atra. Disposables and electric razors are seen as different, but disposables are much closer to cartridge-type razors than are electric razors.

When consumers are asked to link benefits to products, cartridge systems are associated with a close, clean shave; disposables with convenience and economy; and electric razors with a lack of irritation. The three key segments in the shaver market are composed of consumers who identify one of these benefits as their primary need in shaving.

The circles represent three ways to define the market. One would be to focus solely on cartridge-type users, meaning that Sensor would be competing with Trac II, Atra, and competitive shavers (area 1 in the map). There are two problems with this market definition. First, Gillette would be competing with itself since it owns most of the cartridge market. Second, the definition ignores the potential substitutability between disposables and cartridge-type razors.

The second definition would identify the market as wet shaving—that is, disposables and cartridge systems (area 2). The third definition would be all shavers (area 3). The problem here is that it would be difficult to attract users of electric shavers because they regard wet shaving as irritating to their skin.

Gillette chose to identify the market for Sensor as wet shaving (area 2). Management's intention was to position Sensor in the area that intersects both the disposable and cartridge markets as indicated in Figure 3.2.

IDENTIFYING MARKET CHARACTERISTICS

A firm must identify market characteristics for a new product entry or for intensified effort by an existing product. Seven desirable market characteristics include:[8]

1. Good potential for market growth
2. Few barriers to entry (for new product only)
3. Opportunity for competitive advantage
4. Stability in customer demand
5. No large capital investment required
6. Good prospects for increased market share
7. A high return on investment relative to other markets

To see how these criteria operate, consider the situation analysis conducted by General Telephone & Electronics (GTE) in the early 1980s when it was considering entering the consumer appliance market. Market segments and products are listed at the top of Table 3.1, showing the boundaries of the consumer appliance market as defined by GTE.

As presented at the bottom of the table, barriers to entry are high due to strong competition and a necessarily large capital investment. Also, competition was intense. Had it entered this market, GTE would have faced entrenched market leaders such as General Electric and Whirlpool, with no prospect for effectively competing with these companies except by offering lower prices. Given the high cost of entry, such a low price strategy was not likely. Other discouraging characteristics were that the industry was mature; both costs and prices were rising; and potential for market growth was poor, because many products were stagnating.

TABLE 3.1

GTE's Situation Analysis of the Consumer Appliance Market

MARKET DEFINITION

MARKET SEGMENTS

Dealers
Housing contractors
Commercial laundries and laundromats
Final consumers

PRODUCTS

Laundry appliances
Dishwashers
Disposal units
Ranges
Refrigerators

MARKET CHARACTERISTICS

Barriers to entry: High, because of large capital investment required to achieve economies of scale.
Competition: Intense, with an increase in private-label brands creating more competition.
Industry leaders: Large, with integrated operations.
Products: Mature, with little difference among products.
Price: Increasing, to keep pace with inflation of labor and raw material costs.
Industrial growth: Slow; e.g., laundry products at 2 percent growth per year.
Demand: Cyclical. Tied to housing starts.

Source: Private communication from General Telephone & Electronics

Further, customer demand was cyclical, tied primarily to housing starts. Not surprisingly, GTE decided against market entry.

Just as GTE's situation analysis discouraged it from entering the appliance market, Gillette's situation analysis encouraged introduction of the Sensor. The prospects for market growth were good, based on the potential to attract disposable users and to get Atra and Trac II users to trade up. Gillette could establish a competitive advantage based on the superior shave that Sensor provided. There were good prospects for increasing Gillette's market share by getting Bic disposable and Schick cartridge users to switch to Sensor. Sensor would also provide a higher return on investment than disposables or other cartridge systems. The only negative was the large investment required in R&D and manufacturing facilities, but this could also be regarded as a positive because it inhibited entry by competition.

ESTIMATING MARKET POTENTIAL

The third element in a situation analysis, **market potential,** *represents the total demand for the product category. Demand for the product category is known as* **primary demand**—for example, demand for all shaving products. *Demand for a brand is known as* **selective demand**—for example, demand for the Sensor razor. Market potential measures primary demand.

There are two ways of measuring market potential: by direct derivation or by market estimation. **Direct derivation** *requires deriving estimates of primary demand* *from factors in the marketplace that are directly related to consumer purchases.* For example, the number of marriages can be used as an estimate of demand for engagement rings. **Market estimation** *requires estimating the number of buyers in the marketplace and the quantity purchased from past sales data or from surveys.* No market factors exist which are closely related to primary demand.

When GTE evaluated the market for large appliances, it used a direct derivation approach by linking new purchases to a logical market factor, housing starts. Assume that GTE estimates 4 million housing starts in the coming year, each of which will require a washing machine. In addition, based on past purchasing patterns, GTE estimates that 2 million existing households that do not own a washing machine will buy one. Finally, GTE must estimate the replacement market for washing machines. Assume that based on past purchasing patterns, 10 percent of households with washing machines will replace them in any given year. If 60 million households own a washing machine, the replacement market would be 6 million units. Total (primary) demand will therefore be 12 million units. If the average price of a washing machine is $400, then total market potential for washing machines is $4.8 billion (12,000,000 × $400).

Gillette used market estimation to determine the market potential for blades (cartridges and disposables). When a market factor is not related to demand, a company can use the following formula to estimate potential:

$D = n \times q \times p$

where

D = total market demand
n = number of buyers in the market
q = average quantity purchased per year
p = price.

Applying the formula to demand for blades, assume Gillette estimates that 600 million men and 100 million women use razor blades *worldwide*. On average, men use about 12 blades per year (about one a month) and spend 50 cents per blade. As shown in Table 3.2, total demand for blades among men is $3.6 billion. Women also use an average of 12 blades per year and spend less than men (40 cents on

TABLE 3.2

Estimate of Worldwide Market Potential for Blades and Shavers (In Billions of Dollars)

	# CONSUMERS (In Millions) (n)	×	AVG. QUANTITY PER YEAR (q)	×	AVG. PRICE PAID (p)	=	MARKET POTENTIAL (In Millions) (D)
Men's Blades	600	×	12	×	.50	=	$3.60
Women's Blades	100	×	12	×	.40	=	.48
Razors	50 (Replacement) 20 (New)	×	1	×	3.30	=	.23
		TOTAL BLADE AND RAZOR POTENTIAL				=	$4.31

average) because they use more disposables. Therefore, market potential for the women's market in Table 3.2 is $480 million.

Estimates for cartridge-type razors are based primarily on replacements. Gillette estimates that approximately 50 million razors are replaced each year, and an additional 20 million are sold to new shavers or to those switching from disposables. Because the average price of a cartridge-type razor is $3.30, market potential for razors is about $230 million (see Table 3.2). The total blade and razor market is therefore about $4.3 billion. Because more than 95 percent of this amount represents blades, it is clear that most profits in the shaving market are derived from the sale of blades, not razors.

After market potential is determined, the product manager can use an estimate of a product's expected market share to calculate a preliminary sales forecast for a brand (selective demand). Gillette expected that Sensor would capture 7 percent of the razor and blade market, translating into a sales forecast of $301 million in the first year ($4.3 billion × .07). But this forecast is based on the retail price. Assuming that Gillette sells to intermediaries at about 50 percent of the retail price, its revenue based on a 7 percent market share would be about $150 million ($301 million × .5).

CONDUCTING A PRELIMINARY MARKET ASSESSMENT

Having identified the market and estimated market potential, the product manager next evaluates the market on a preliminary basis to pave the way for a more formal analysis of market opportunities. Gillette's preliminary evaluation of the razor market was fairly dismal. The disposable market was growing, rising from almost zero in 1975 to 60 percent of revenues by 1990. The average disposable razor costs about 40 cents, whereas an individual cartridge for a Trac II or Atra razor costs about 65 cents. Gillette was operating on a narrower profit base because of the shift to disposables. Further, sales of Trac II began declining when the Atra was introduced, as a result of cannibalization. **Cannibalization** *is a switch by a consumer from one of a company's products to another with no net gain in sales.* Further, sales of Atra were starting to decline by 1988 in the face of increasing sales of disposables (see Figure 3.3).

FIGURE 3.3

Sales Trends of TRAC II and ATRA Showed Need to Revitalize the Shaver Market

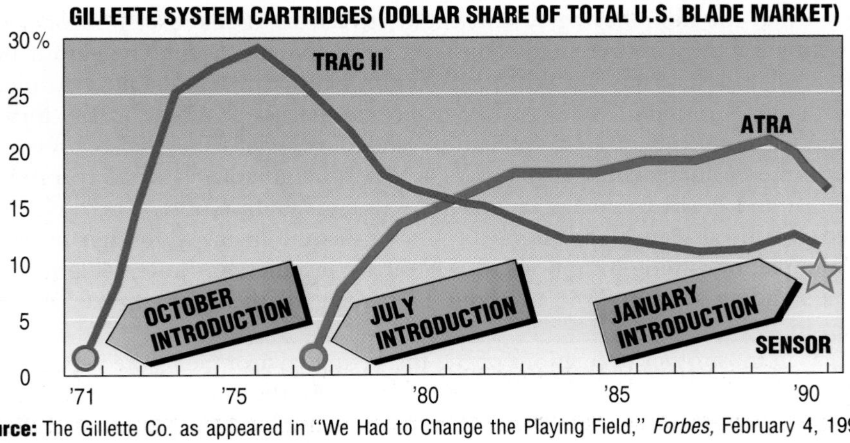

Source: The Gillette Co. as appeared in "We Had to Change the Playing Field," *Forbes,* February 4, 1991, p. 86.

These circumstances created an urgency in Gillette's search for opportunity in the shaver market. The company had to introduce a product to attract disposable users and to stem the decrease in sales for Trac II and Atra. As we know, the company did have a new product waiting in the wings.

EVALUATING MARKETING OPPORTUNITY

With the situation analysis completed, the next step in the marketing planning process is to evaluate marketing opportunities and to prepare a preliminary sales forecast. There are two components to evaluating marketing opportunities: an *opportunity/threat* analysis and an analysis of company *strengths and weaknesses.*

OPPORTUNITY/THREAT ANALYSIS

The opportunity/threat analysis is designed to evaluate the environment, to identify areas where the firm should allocate resources, and to evaluate the risks of pursuing such opportunities. Marketing opportunities are generally identified based on unmet customer needs, competitive weaknesses, new technologies, and other environmental trends such as a more favorable regulatory climate and improved economic conditions. Any opportunity also brings with it threats such as a lack of customer demand, competitive retaliation, competing technologies that might make the firm's innovation obsolete, or an economic downturn. These areas will be reviewed in greater depth when the marketing environment is presented as a source of opportunity and threat in Chapter 4.

Gillette conducted an opportunity/threat analysis on the Sensor razor and discovered opportunities in three major environmental components cited above: consumer needs, competition, and technology. It was technology that initiated the opportunity assessment when Gillette engineers developed a method for independently suspending twin blades on springs. The only remaining question was whether the new technology would provide a closer shave. Extensive tests were positive: consumers rated the Sensor system as providing a superior shave. The company also determined that competition was unlikely to duplicate the technology because of its complexity and expense. Gillette's 17 patents on the design and production of the Sensor, and the expense of establishing a complex laser-guided assembly line, protected the company from immediate competitive entry.

Two other factors spelled opportunity for Sensor. First, management strongly believed that the new shaving system could attract disposable users. Second, the international market represented significant profit potential with the elimination in 1992 of trade barriers within the 12-nation European Community (formerly known as the Common Market). The emerging market economy in the former Communist countries of Eastern Europe and the Soviet Union also presented opportunities. Gillette could also look to an emerging middle class in Latin America, India, and Asian countries such as Taiwan and South Korea. These changes spelled greater affluence and more disposable income in many foreign markets. For example, by aiming its appeals to wealthier consumers in India, Gillette went from a standing start in 1986 to about 17 percent of the urban Indian shaving market in 1990.[9]

Yet, as in most other evaluations of the marketing environment, the very factors that spell opportunity can also represent threat. At the time Gillette was conducting its opportunity/threat analysis, its new technology was untested. A $200

TABLE 3.3

Opportunity/Threat and Strength/Weakness Analysis For Sensor (Ratings on a ten-point scale)

OPPORTUNITY/THREAT ANALYSIS RATING*		STRENGTH/WEAKNESS ANALYSIS RATING**	
1. Barriers to competition	10	1. Management Know-How	10
2. Customer Needs	8	2. Distribution Network	10
3. Domestic Growth Rate	8	3. Research and Development	9
4. Foreign Growth Rate	5	4. Manufacturing Facilities	9
5. Patent Protection	4	5. Financial Resources	3
AVG. ON TEN-POINT SCALE	7.0	AVG. ON TEN-POINT SCALE	8.2
AVG. FOR PAST OPPORTUNITY/THREAT ANALYSES AT GILLETTE	5.5	AVG. FOR PAST STRENGTH/WEAKNESS ANALYSES AT GILLETTE	6.0

*Higher number means greater opportunity
**Higher number means stronger position

million price tag on research and development was threatening to make the project economically unfeasible. There was the threat of cannibalization; that is, many of Gillette's new customers would be former Atra and Trac II users rather than disposable users or users of competitive cartridge systems. In addition, the company had no solid evidence that users of disposable razors would switch to a new cartridge system in the numbers required to make the Sensor profitable. Further, although Gillette's patents afforded some protection, there was no assurance that a competitor could not come along and duplicate key elements of the technology, but with sufficient differences to circumvent patent protection. For example, Schick's parent, Warner Lambert, had already spent $50 million developing a new razor called the Tracer that was a relative unknown to Gillette's management.

These opportunities and threats are summarized on the left-hand side of Table 3.3. The table reflects a more formal opportunity/threat analysis in which management identified the common environmental factors that define opportunities and threats—customer needs, competitive entry, new technologies, and so forth—and rated each. The objective was to come up with an overall assessment of the opportunity and determine whether to pursue it.

Management rated barriers to competitive entry very high (a ten on a ten-point scale) because it believed that competition could not duplicate Gillette's complex technology. Management also rated unmet consumer needs high (an eight) because it believed the new Sensor system would meet the needs of a large part of the market for a closer shave.

Further, management rated the growth rate abroad as high (an eight) and rated the growth rate in the United States as moderate (a five) primarily because disposables were not as entrenched abroad.

Gillette recognized that much of its growth rate would come from cannibalizing its existing products. It was willing to accept such cannibalization for two reasons: First, the profits on the Sensor were higher than those on either the Trac II or the Atra, so a switch from one of these products to the Sensor would still produce more profits for Gillette. Second, Schick was readying a new product, the Tracer. If Gillette did not come out with the Sensor, users of the Atra or Trac II might switch to Schick. It is always better for an existing customer to switch to another company product rather than to a competitor, even if the switch does represent cannibalization.

The last factor in the opportunity/threat analysis, patent protection, was rated relatively low (a four) because of the threat that competition could duplicate components of Gillette's technology.

The average market opportunity score is 7.0 on a ten-point scale, which compares favorably to a corporate norm of 5.5 when the same criteria were used to evaluate other opportunities such as introducing a disposable version of the Sensor. Therefore, the opportunity/ threat analysis would indicate the Sensor razor should be introduced.

STRENGTH/WEAKNESS ANALYSIS

Before recommending market entry, a product manager must evaluate the company's strengths and weaknesses to determine its ability to exploit the defined opportunity. Such an analysis is most important when a company (1) enters the market for the first time, (2) faces rapid environmental changes that may require reevaluating its resource needs for an existing product, or (3) faces the threat of competitive entry.

Such an analysis for the Sensor razor is shown on the right-hand side of Table 3.3. The five factors listed represent the necessary resources and skills to successfully introduce Sensor. Because of its leadership in the shaving market, with a market share of over 60 percent, the company is rated strong on know-how. It has an established distribution network. Further, it has strong research and development capabilities and well-established manufacturing facilities, resulting in a rating of nine or ten for each of these factors. The only uncertainty is financial resources. Having engaged in a buyback of its stock because of a takeover threat and having already spent $200 million on development of the Sensor, Gillette was in a relatively weak financial position, resulting in a rating of three on this factor. The average resource assessment score is 8.2, which compares favorably with an average score of 6.0 when the company's strengths and weaknesses were matched to other opportunities.

We can now place Sensor in the strategic planning matrix shown in Figure 3.4, which is a duplicate of the matrix in the previous chapter. The results of the opportunity/threat and strength/weakness analysis show that Sensor is positioned in the area defined as a strategic window of opportunity and should be introduced.

PRELIMINARY SALES FORECAST

The product manager for Sensor had to take one more step before recommending market entry: development of a preliminary sales forecast based on the opportunity/threat and strength/weakness analysis. Management's judgment of Sensor's sales potential was positive, based on the assessment shown in Table 3.3. As a result, it would be realistic to expect Sensor to attain a market share of 7 percent in the first year of introduction. A 7 percent market share would result in sales of $300 million and revenues of approximately $150 million in the first year. On this basis, the product manager recommended that Sensor be introduced worldwide and that planning for such an introduction begin immediately.

FIGURE 3.4

Sensor's Strategic Window of Opportunity

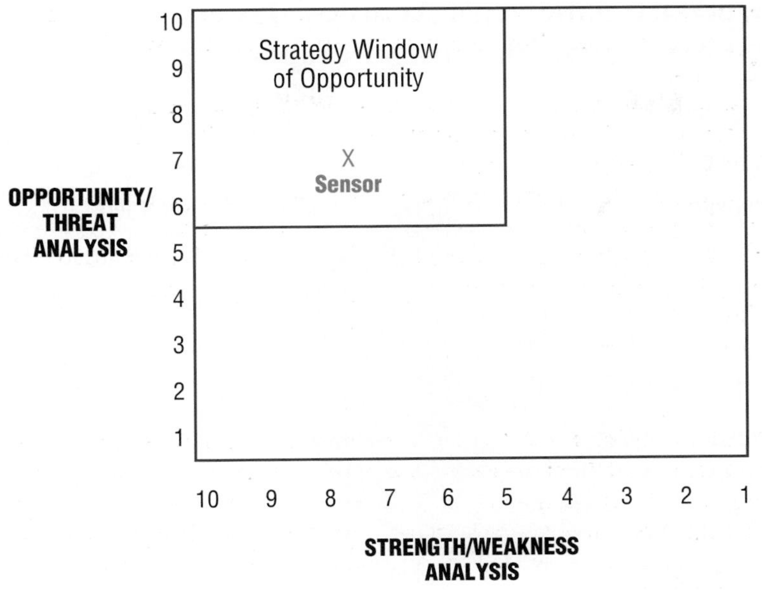

DEVELOPING PRODUCT OBJECTIVES

Conducting a situation analysis and evaluating marketing opportunities gives the product manager a basis for the next step in marketing planning: developing realistic objectives for the product. A marketing plan can list three types of marketing objectives for product performance: sales volume, market share, and profitability. Additional marketing objectives might be stated in terms of the components of the marketing mix, that is, advertising or distribution levels required to achieve sales, market-share, and profit objectives.

SALES VOLUME

Sales-volume objectives will depend on a company's opportunity assessment. Based on Gillette's positive assessment of Sensor's potential for trading up Trac II and Atra users and for attracting disposable users, management felt a reasonable sales goal would be to sell 20 million razors and 300 million blades in the first year of operation. The company was planning on selling the Sensor razor at $3.75 retail and the cartridges at about 75 cents each. This would translate into a dollar goal of $300 million at retail ($3.75 × 20 million + .75 × 300 million) which would represent revenue to Gillette of approximately $150 million because the company gets 50 percent of the retail price.

MARKET SHARE

Market-share goals are closely tied to sales objectives. Some firms first establish a sales goal and determine if the resultant market share places it in a viable competitive position. A sales goal of $300 million at retail would represent about a 7

ETHICAL AND ENVIRONMENTAL ISSUES IN MARKETING

Corporate America's Achilles' Heel: A Short-Term Planning Perspective

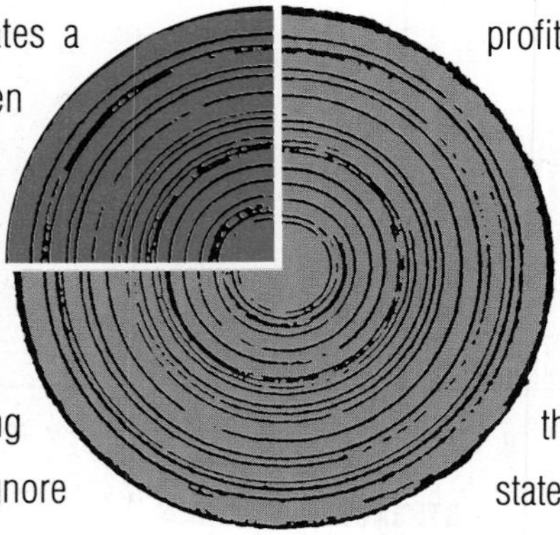

Gillette's willingness to pour $200 million into research and development for Sensor over a ten-year period demonstrates a long-term perspective that is often lacking in American companies. One of the major criticisms of marketing planners is that they often take a short-term view that tends to focus on quarterly results for existing products or services and that they ignore identifying longer term opportunities.

Before 1980, for example, product managers of Avon's perfume and toiletry lines emphasized short-term returns by buttressing the existing door-to-door distribution system. Few were willing to stick their necks out and recommend a total revamping of the system that might lead to more of a focus on sales at the workplace so as to follow the increasing proportion of working women. Such a recommendation would have required a longer term perspective to adjust to a changing environment. Top management was more focused on maintaining revenues and profits for the short term.

There is good reason why corporate America often takes a short-term focus. Many large companies are publicly held, and management must answer to its stockholders through quarterly revenue and profit statements. There is often a conflict between investing in research and development for the long term and accounting to company stockholders for the short term. Most stockholders do not invest in companies for the long haul and would prefer to see immediate results. Sometimes this short-term view creates perverse and possibly unethical behavior by top management. For instance, a former chief executive at Standard Brands boasted of a 20-year string of earnings increases. What he did not divulge was that he made certain that earnings went

percent share of the shaver market (total potential is $4.3 billion). Alternatively, firms might establish market-share objectives first, then estimate sales. Gillette might have established a market-share goal of 7 percent as a requirement for success, then determined the sales level required to achieve this market-share goal.

PROFITABILITY The third category of product goals, profitability objectives, are most frequently stated in terms of **return on investment (ROI)**, *which equals net profits divided by total investment*. A reasonable basis for establishing an ROI objective might be to compare ROI for a product to an alternative investment.

Assume that Gillette determines it could take the money it plans to use to introduce Sensor, invest it in high-yield bonds and gain a 9 percent return. Then a

ETHICAL AND ENVIRONMENTAL ISSUES IN MARKETING

up each year by only a certain amount to ensure they could be topped the following year. His strategy made stockholders happy and drove up Standard Brand's stock price.

What is the solution to conflicting long- and short-term planning goals? No one has come up with a ready answer. Gillete's experience is instructive. The company was willing to spend money in research and development because it needed to revitalize the shaver market and strongly felt Sensor was the answer. But Gillette's staying power—a ten-year development process—almost cost the company its independence. The large investment, coupled with weakness in the shaver market due to the growth of disposables, left the company financially weak and a target of two takeover bids supported by disgruntled shareholders. Gillette survived only by buying back large blocks of its own stock. As a result, current management could stay on course with Sensor.

Gillette's experience shows that perhaps the best way to overcome corporate America's Achilles' heel is to have a planning process in place that ensures the company can identify future opportunities. But in so doing, management must also ensure sufficient short-term earnings or, like Gillette, run the risk of becoming a takeover target.

Questions: Is it ethical for a company to manipulate its earnings to satisfy its stockholders? What is the conflict between a long- and short-term focus in marketing planning? How did Gillette's investment in the Sensor reflect this conflict?

Sources: *The New American Century,* (New York: Fortune magazine, 1991), pp. 12–28; Bryan Burroughs and John Helyar, *Barbarians at the Gates* (New York: Harper Perennial, 1990), p. 17; and "Is Short-Term Really the American Way," *Industry Week,* June 5, 1989, pp. 12–15 and 18.

reasonable ROI objective for Sensor might be 10 percent. Can the company's sales goal of $300 million at retail and market-share goal of 7 percent produce this ROI level? If not, sales and profit goals are out of line. Gillette would have to determine whether it should settle for the lower ROI produced by $300 million in sales, or whether it can realistically increase its sales goal to achieve the required ROI.

MARKETING MIX

The marketing plan should also set goals for the components of the marketing mix, including distribution, advertising, and price. These goals establish the requirements for meeting sales, market share, and profit objectives. For example, Gillette might establish a goal of making 80 percent of all men over 18 aware of Sensor six months after introduction. It establishes this goal as a minimum requirement if it is to reach $300 million in sales in the first year. Further, it might establish a distribution goal of 95 percent of all drugstores and 80 percent of all supermarkets.

FORMULATING MARKETING STRATEGIES

Once product objectives have been developed, the next step in the marketing planning process is to formulate a **marketing strategy,** which is the basic approach a company will take in trying to influence customers to buy the product. Formulating marketing strategy requires identifying a target market and positioning the product to the target. The target market and positioning strategy will determine the marketing-mix elements designed to implement this strategy.

IDENTIFYING THE TARGET MARKET

A **target market** *is the market segment the firm is trying to attract with its marketing effort.* As we have seen in Chapter 1, a market segment is a group of consumers with similar needs that can be identified and appealed to by a specific product or product line. Marketing strategy is designed to communicate a product's benefits to the target market.

Figure 3.5 presents the three market segments of the shaver market originally presented in Figure 3.2: One segment emphasizes a clean, close shave; another convenience and economy; and another a non-irritating shave. These three segments are identified as part of the men's shaving market, with the women's shaving market listed separately. Each target segment is broken out by domestic and international markets, reflecting possible variations in targeting for Sensor depending on whether consumers are in the United States or abroad. For example, given that there are fewer disposable users abroad, this segment would not be considered a primary target of opportunity for Sensor.

There are also two demographic segments identified in Figure 3.5. The "clean/close shave" segment in the United States is divided into those 45 and over and those under 45, because Gillette's research shows that the 45-and-over group in this segment are much more loyal to Gillette products.[10] This group is more likely to equate Gillette with quality and value than the under 45 group. Gillette regards both segments as targets but realizes it has more of a selling job to do with the under-45 segment. This same split does not seem to exist abroad, because Gillette is the market leader regardless of age.

The segments in Figure 3.5 represent the total shaver market. The first question management must answer is what portion of the total market it will target. Gillette decided to target cartridge users at home and abroad and disposable users primarily in the North American market. Because the primary target was the "clean, close shave" segment, it was apparent that this benefit would have to be a strong appeal in Sensor's promotional campaign. One key question Gillette would have to consider is whether to vary its promotional campaign to the 45-and-over versus the under-45 segments in the United States.

A second strategic issue raised by a product/market matrix is whether the company should expand its market coverage beyond the primary target. Figure 3.5 identifies disposable users abroad as a possible secondary target, since disposables are popular in a few European countries. Women might also be a secondary target, both at home and abroad. Although most use disposables, some could be attracted to a new shaving system that promises smoother legs.

FIGURE 3.5

Market Segments for Shaving Products: A Product-Market Matrix

PRODUCTS	MARKET SEGMENTS								
	MEN							WOMEN	
	Clean, Close Shave			Economy, Convenience		Non Irritating		U.S.	Foreign
	U.S.		Foreign	U.S.	Foreign	U.S.	Foreign		
	45 & Over	Under 45							
Cartridges	*	*	*						
Disposables				*	#			#	#
Electric									

* = Primary Market
\# = Secondary Market

A third strategic issue is whether the company should market one product to the total market, offer one product marketed to individual segments, or offer separate products, each targeted to specific segments. If Gillette begins targeting women shavers, it would probably follow the latter strategy—developing a separate product for this segment. A logical product-line extension of Sensor would be the same shaving head mounted on a razor with a slimmer handle for women's shaving needs. Such an extension would target women who use cartridge systems. Prodigy, a home computer information linkup introduced by Sears, offers one system to all consumers, but advertises to target different segments. Exhibit 3.1 shows ads targeted to baby boomers with children, dual income households, and affluent households.

If the company decides on line extensions like a razor for women, a fourth issue is whether to immediately target many segments with a full line or to target primary segments with a basic product first, then direct line extensions to secondary markets later. Gillette is targeting Sensor to the primary markets first and considering line extensions to secondary markets after.

PRODUCT POSITIONING

Once the target market has been identified, the product manager must develop a strategy to communicate product benefits to the target. The link between identifying a target and positioning a product to that target is illustrated by the light-beer market. The first light beer was a brand called Gablingers, introduced by Rheingold. The target was weight-conscious consumers, and the beer was positioned as a low-calorie alternative to regular beer. The positioning as a diet beer

EXHIBIT 3.1

Differing Segments Targeted for a Single Product

FIGURE 3.6

Product Positioning Strategies

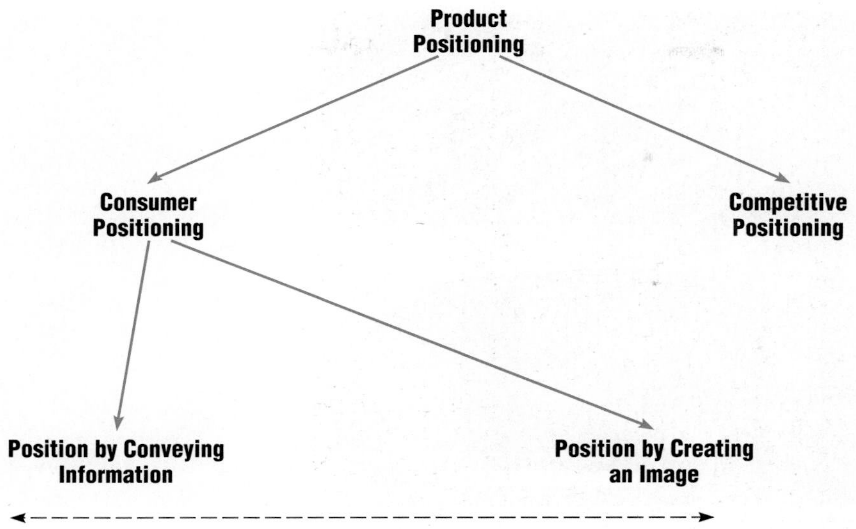

caused Gablingers to fail, because most beer drinkers shunned the diet connotation.

Miller saw an opportunity to introduce a beer as light rather than low calorie. It defined its target as heavier-beer-drinking, blue collar workers, many of whom wanted to watch their weight but did not want to be reminded they were doing it. Miller won this group over to light beer by showing tough athletes such as Dick Butkus drinking light beer. The definition of the target market and the product's positioning were closely linked since a substantial segment of heavier-beer drinkers wanted a lighter alternative to regular beer.

Managers can use two broad approaches to positioning a product, as shown in Figure 3.6, consumer versus competitive positioning. Consumer positioning links the product to consumer benefits and product features. Competitive positioning communicates the product's benefits by comparing it to competitive products.

CONSUMER POSITIONING

Figure 3.6 shows that product benefits can be communicated by conveying information, by creating an image, or by a combination of both. Pure informational positioning cites detailed product information. Positioning by image allows the consumer to "read in" almost any desired benefit by using ambiguous themes that can mean many different things to different people.

Car manufacturers have used both information- and image-based approaches. The ad for Lincoln in Exhibit 3.2 is primarily informational. It positions the Continental as a performance car for the family, and cites specific features in the copy such as anti-lock brakes and fuel-injected engine. Toyota uses an image approach. The ad for the Corolla in Exhibit 3.2 says little about the car's features. The

EXHIBIT 3.2

Positioning by Information versus Imagery

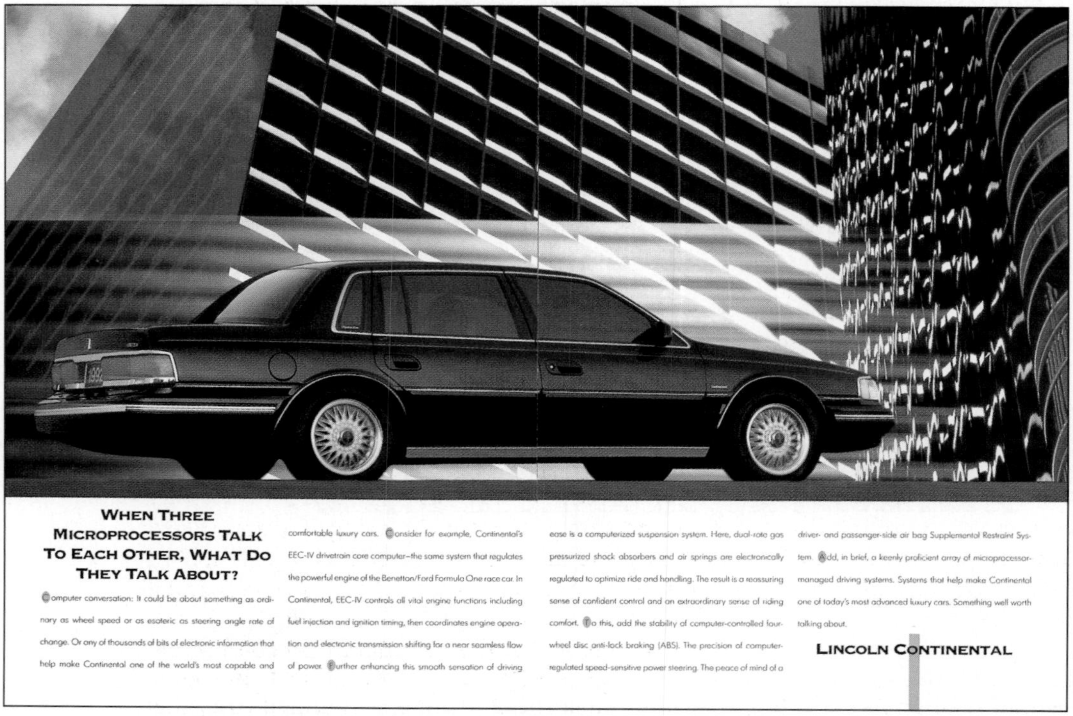
WHEN THREE MICROPROCESSORS TALK TO EACH OTHER, WHAT DO THEY TALK ABOUT?
Computer conversation: It could be about something as ordinary as wheel speed or as esoteric as steering angle rate of change. Or any of thousands of bits of electronic information that help make Continental one of the world's most capable and comfortable luxury cars. Consider for example, Continental's EEC-IV drivetrain core computer–the same system that regulates the powerful engine of the Benetton/Ford Formula One race car. In Continental, EEC-IV controls all vital engine functions including fuel injection and ignition timing, then coordinates engine operation and electronic transmission shifting for a near seamless flow of power. Further enhancing this smooth sensation of driving ease is a computerized suspension system. Here, dual-rate gas pressurized shock absorbers and air springs are electronically regulated to optimize ride and handling. The result is a reassuring sense of confident control and an extraordinary sense of riding comfort. To this, add the stability of computer-controlled four-wheel disc anti-lock braking (ABS). The precision of computer-regulated speed-sensitive power steering. The peace of mind of a driver- and passenger-side air bag Supplemental Restraint System. Add, in brief, a keenly proficient array of microprocessor-managed driving systems. Systems that help make Continental one of today's most advanced luxury cars. Something well worth talking about.
LINCOLN CONTINENTAL

COROLLA
Corolla. Over 15 million happy memories, and still counting.
Your parents' car. Your first car. The car you learned to drive in. Millions of people have fond memories of a Toyota Corolla. And though we've made lots of changes to the Corolla over the years, the soul of the car has always stayed the same. It's still known as reliable. Practical. And economical.*
Which may be why, over the last 25 years, we've made more than just 15 million† Corollas.
We've also built lots of lasting relationships.
"I love what you do for me."
TOYOTA
26 33

theme, "Over 15 million happy memories," can be interpreted in many different ways. Regardless of the interpretation, the intent is to create positive feelings about the car.

Gillette's positioning of Sensor was primarily image-oriented but had an informational base. The brand name, the product design, the package, and the advertising were meant to convey an image of value and quality. The Gillette name on the package became bolder, and the razor had a sleek, stylish design to reinforce a quality image. Advertising showed various vignettes in men's lives—men with women, dads with kids, men playing sports, and so forth. In the words of the advertising executive responsible for the campaign, "Each man can choose what he responds to,"[11] meaning that the ads can be interpreted in various ways, but the common denominator—a quality product—is always conveyed. Advertising communicated information as well as imagery by informing consumers about the nature of the new shaving system. Gillette's positioning strategy was the same worldwide, with a simultaneous introduction in 19 countries.

COMPETITIVE POSITIONING

As a product is established, and as competition intensifies, many companies shift to a more competitive positioning approach by advertising product superiority compared to competitors or by using comparative advertising. **Comparative advertising** *directly names a competitor in an advertisement.* MCI names AT&T in its ads for long-distance calls, citing the advantages of MCI's service compared with the market leader (see Exhibit 3.3).

A danger in such competitive positioning is that the consumer may confuse the brand with the competitor being cited. When SOS compares itself to Brillo, consumers may be more likely to remember Brillo and associate the benefits cited to Brillo rather than to SOS.

REPOSITIONING STRATEGIES

Occasionally, the market position originally developed for a product becomes weakened due to competition, technological developments, or some other factor, and the product must be repositioned. For example, 7-Up positioned its flagship brand as the soft drink with no caffeine, using the theme "Never had it, never will." The company's objective was to capture a niche ignored by the cola giants, health-conscious soft-drink buyers. The speed with which Pepsi and Coke came out with caffeine-free line extensions surprised 7-Up. The company's unique positioning was lost. As a result, it combined the no caffeine appeal with a prior theme, The Uncola, an attempt to position 7-Up as the non-cola alternative to Pepsi and Coke (see Exhibit 3.4).

DEVELOPING THE MARKETING MIX

Once the marketing strategy has been formulated, the next step is to develop a marketing mix, including product, advertising, distribution, and pricing strategies that can effectively position the product to the target market.

Three steps are required. The first step is to determine the components of the marketing mix. The second step is to determine consumer responses to the marketing mix—that is, assess responses to proposed price levels, sales promotions,

EXHIBIT 3.3

An Example of Competitive Positioning

EXHIBIT 3.4

An Example of a Repositioning Strategy

personal-selling strategies, and advertising executions. The third step is to determine the budget for marketing-mix components—the amount of money to spend on advertising, sales promotion, personal selling, and distribution.

DETERMINING THE COMPONENTS OF THE MARKETING MIX

We have seen in Chapter 1 that the marketing-mix components are often referred to as *The Four Ps:* product, place, promotion, and price.

PRODUCT

Product is the most basic component of the marketing mix. It represents the product features, the package, the brand name, and post-sales service support. In the case of Sensor, critical product decisions dealt with the ability to mount twin blades on tiny springs, the design of the product, and the package housing for the razor (see Exhibit 3.5).

PLACE

Place represents the actions the company takes to make sure the product gets to the right target group at the right location and at the right time. Gillette used its own sales force to sell to large food and drugstore chains. The sales force also sold to wholesalers who then sold to smaller food and drugstores. These wholesalers are an indispensable part of Gillette's distribution system since it would be uneconomical for the company to sell direct to small retailers.

An important component of distribution strategy is the trade support and allowances the company gives its retailers and wholesalers to induce them to stock and actively sell the product. Many food companies give large chains cash payments known as *slotting allowances* to induce them to put a new product on the shelf.

EXHIBIT 3.5

Product—One of the Four Ps: Gillette Stresses Sensor's Product Design

Manufacturers will also give retailers advertising allowances to support local advertising of their products. For example, an auto manufacturer like Ford will agree to pay a percentage of its dealers' local advertising costs.

PROMOTION

The tactics the company uses to communicate the product's positioning are collectively called *promotion. The four key promitional elements: advertising, sales promotions, public relations, and personal selling are often referred to as a* **promotional mix** within the broader context of the marketing mix.

While each of these components must be individually developed, it is also important that they be integrated within the marketing plan. For instance, the plan must ensure that the product is available to customers before the advertising campaign begins. Advertising a product before it is distributed will result in consumer ill-will. It is also critical that the advertising be in tune with the price level. A number of years ago, an attempt was made to create a quality image for a low-priced beer by using status symbols such as a fox hunt. The imagery was lost on the blue-collar target market for the beer. Similarly, the price level must be consistent with product quality. Generally, higher prices connote higher quality. But if consumers pay a higher price and quality expectations are not met, sales are likely to suffer.

Gillette's promotional mix for Sensor was centered on a worldwide advertising campaign that cost $100 million in 1990. The basic theme, "Gillette. The best a man can get," was designed to convey the value of the razor and was coupled with highly emotional images of a man's moments in his everyday life. Exhibit 3.6 shows excerpts from the Gillette Worldwide campaign produced by its ad agency BBDO. Advertising was coordinated with a public-relations campaign that won mention for the Sensor on TV shows ranging from "The CBS Evening News" to "The Tonight Show."[12] An $8 million sales promotional campaign resulted in coupons being mailed to five million men and free samples being mailed to users of competitive products.[13] The campaign was timed to be coordinated with advertising.

PRICE

The fourth component of the marketing mix is *price*. Should Sensor be introduced at a higher price than other cartridge systems on the assumption that consumers will see Sensor as an improved shaving system and will be willing to pay more? This pricing approach is known as a *skimming strategy*. It produces high operating margins, but it also encourages competitive entry. Alternatively, should Sensor be introduced at parity with other cartridge systems or at an even lower price? Such an approach, known as a *penetration strategy*, would be instituted to try to get the greatest share of market possible and to discourage competitive entry. Although this tactic might preempt competition, it might not bring in enough revenue to recoup the high developmental costs during a product's introduction.

Gillette chose a skimming strategy, pricing the razor at $3.75 and blades at about 75 cents each in retail stores. These prices were about 20 percent higher than other cartridge systems. Management felt that consumers would see the value in buying a Sensor and would be willing to pay a higher price. There was little risk of quick competitive entry given the $200 million price tag for development.

EXHIBIT 3.6

Promotion—One of the Four Ps: BBDO's Worldwide TV Campaign for Gillette Sensor

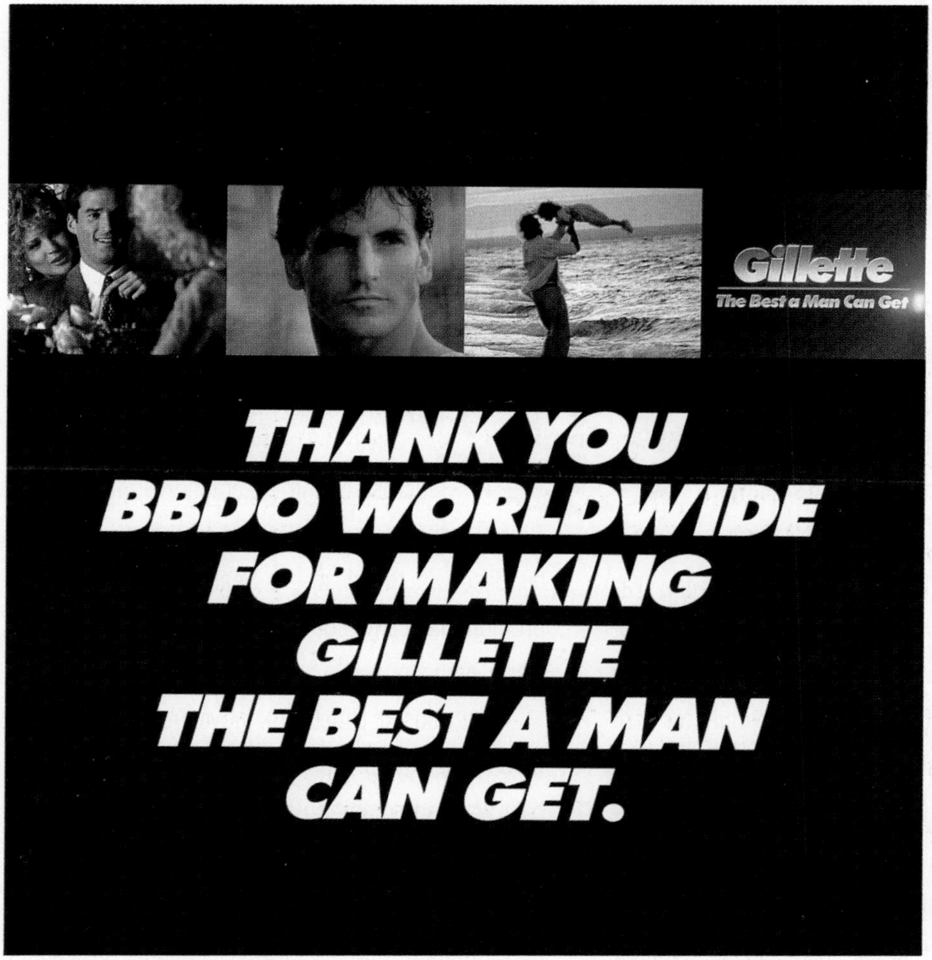

Further, Gillette could not hope to recoup this sum within a reasonable time if it used a penetration strategy.

DETERMINING CONSUMER RESPONSES TO THE MARKETING MIX

The marketing plan must provide for testing alternative marketing-mix strategies to determine which will be the most effective. Products must be tested to determine the final form of the product offering. Managers can test the product idea, before incurring production costs, by asking consumers to react to a description of the product. The company can then produce prototypes and test customer reactions to them. For packaged goods, in-home use tests or controlled tests in company facilities can be conducted. When product features are close to being finalized, product alternatives can be evaluated in test markets before being introduced nationally.

GLOBAL MARKETING STRATEGIES

Sensor's Marketing Mix: Going From a Local to a Global Strategy

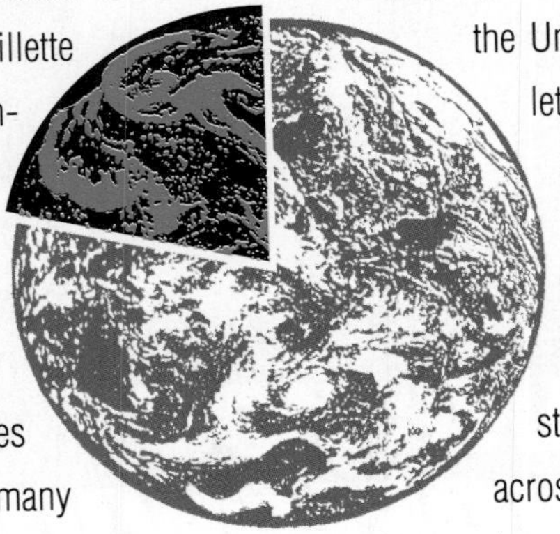

The introduction of Sensor represented a departure in Gillette's approach to its international markets. Until 1990, Gillette had marketed its products on a country-by-country basis. For example, in marketing Atra abroad, the company would let product managers in each country develop an advertising plan to account for local tastes and customs. A campaign in Germany might emphasize the efficiency of Atra's pivoting head in fitting to the contours of a man's face, whereas a campaign in Italy might portray the reaction of the man's wife or girlfriend to a smoother face. Packaging might also differ to account for variations in customs, taste, and usage, but all strategies had to be approved by corporate headquarters in the United States.

Sensor was a total reversal of this localized approach. It was going to be marketed as a global brand with a standardized strategy. Advertising was introduced simultaneously in 19 countries using 26 different languages. Minor variations acknowledged the need for some differences; for example, showing men playing soccer in European ads and football in the United States. The basic theme, "Gillette. The best a man can get" was the same, with minor modifications to adjust to language differences. (A literal translation of the French theme would be "perfection, malestyle.") The positioning was the same across countries: emotional vignettes out of a man's everyday life tied to the message that he deserves the best—a Sensor. A $110 million promotional campaign made the introduction of a world brand possible.

What caused Gillette to move from a local to a global strategy for Sensor? In the mid 1980s, a debate was raging among international marketers as to whether brands should be marketed on a more standardized basis worldwide. Until then, the conventional wisdom was that greater consumer orientation meant adjusting brands to the needs and customs of consumers in different countries. But local strategies were expensive, and developing separate marketing

Other components of the marketing mix must also be tested before they are introduced to the marketplace. For example, Gillette might have tested alternative campaigns—a purely informational campaign that cites product features; a strictly image-oriented campaign that links positive feelings to the product; or a combination of the two. Prices should also be tested to determine sales results at various price levels. Similarly, sales promotion devices should be tested in various markets to determine how consumers respond.

GLOBAL MARKETING STRATEGIES

campaigns for individual countries could prove economically unfeasible. Global strategies provided economies of scale in production and advertising because of uniform manufacturing requirements and the development of the same commercials worldwide.

Marketers cited greater similarity in consumer needs as the basic reason global strategies were more feasible. Television has encouraged greater similarity across countries by exposing consumers the world over to the same brands, fads, and fashions. More economical modes of transportation have made many consumers world travelers, further exposing them to a variety of products. Today, teenagers in Paris, Tokyo, and New York may have more in common with each other than with older fellow citizens.

Gillette's management began the same debate: "Should we begin marketing world brands or continue to subscribe to local adaptation of marketing strategies?" Sensor was a good test case. They took a closer look at the shaver market and found that men around the globe who shave relate to it in very much the same ways. Few men like scraping their face in the morning, but most do because, in the words of a senior Gillette executive, they figure "If I'm not clean shaven, I look like a bum." Further, men are emotionally tied to shaving because it relates to their self-esteem.

The argument that shaving is a universal task viewed similarly across countries was sufficient to convince management to launch its first world brand—Sensor. The brand's performance has more than justified Gillette's global outlook.

Questions: What was the basis for Gillette's local approach in international markets before 1990? What was its rationale in introducing Sensor as a world brand?

Sources: "Gillette Sensor: Global Innovation in Technology and Marketing," *Marketing Review,* March 1991, pp. 16 and 29; and "Global Lather," *Forbes,* February 5, 1990, pp. 146 and 148.

DETERMINING THE BUDGET FOR THE MARKETING MIX

The third step in developing the marketing mix is to determine a budget, specifying both the total marketing expenditures and the expenditures for each component of the marketing mix. For example, a firm that plans multimedia advertising must establish an advertising budget as part of the marketing budget and allocate expenditures to various media such as television, newspapers, and magazines. It must also determine a sales promotion budget, allocating money for coupons, in-store displays, and trade promotions. And budgets must be established for personal selling, distribution, and product development.

In general, two types of approaches are used: a top-down and a bottom-up approach. In the *top-down approach*, the product manager first establishes an overall budget by determining the amount of marketing expenditures necessary to meet sales goals. This amount is then allocated among the various marketing-mix components. The product manager for Sensor might have determined that a $120 million marketing budget would be required to introduce the product and achieve the sales goal of $150 million in revenues in 1990. This $120 million would then be divided among product, promotion, and distribution efforts. The $120 million figure is determined by estimating the expenditure levels necessary to achieve sales and profitability objectives.

In contrast to the top-down approach, the *bottom-up approach* first determines what marketing-mix elements are required to implement product strategy, then estimates the marketing budget as the sum of expenditures required for product development, advertising, sales promotion, and distribution. The required marketing expenditures are then subtracted from estimated sales revenues to determine whether profit goals will be met. If goals are not met, management must either scale down the marketing mix or consider withdrawing the product.

The bottom-up approach is more widely used because it is easier to estimate a marketing budget. However, it could result in an excessively high estimate of marketing expenditures because each component of the marketing mix is estimated separately. Advertising, distribution, and sales managers might have a vested interest in setting a high estimate for their respective functions. Further, integration between components of the marketing mix might be more difficult. The advantage of a top-down approach is that it starts with an overall budget figure derived from estimated sales and is thus more likely to avoid overestimating of marketing requirements.

FORECASTING SALES

The next step in the marketing planning process is sales forecasting. Whereas market potential estimates total demand for the product category (primary demand), a **sales forecast** *estimates demand for an individual brand (selective demand)*. The sales forecast depends on the marketing effort the firm plans for the coming year. Sales forecasts can be stated in dollars or in units and provide the revenue base for estimating profits from marketing strategies.

Approaches to sales forecasting vary in complexity from the simplest approach (forecasts based on executive judgment) to the most complex (forecasts based on statistical models). Sales forecasts are also based on composites of sales-force opinion, past sales data, surveys of consumer buying intentions, and test marketing.

EXECUTIVE JUDGMENT

Sales forecasts often rely on executive judgment. One study found that 96 percent of the companies interviewed used some form of judgment method in forecasting sales.[14] Yet few of these companies relied only on managerial judgment; most used historical analysis or customer surveys as well.

An example of sales forecasting by executive judgment is the **Delphi method** *in which a panel of experts is used to try to reach a consensus on expected sales.* A number of experts are asked to make individual forecasts, stating their reasoning in writing. Forecasts are pooled and sent back to the panel of experts, who are then asked to make a second forecast. Generally, a consensus emerges after three or four rounds based on a free exchange of information.

Another judgment technique is the **expected-value approach** *which asks managers to estimate the probability of various scenarios occurring* (for example, the introduction of new technology, entry into the market by the company's chief rival within one year, or shortages in raw materials) *and to predict the sales results as a consequence.* Managers then weight the estimated sales by the probability of occurrence to arrive at a forecast for the product.

COMPOSITE OF SALES-FORCE OPINIONS

Sometimes management bases judgment forecasts on salespeople's estimates of product sales for their territories and then adds these estimates to get a forecast of total sales. This approach is used most frequently in industries where a salesperson's expertise is important in influencing the customer. A salesperson selling complex industrial goods or consumer durables must have a more-intimate knowledge of his or her customers and is better equipped to make an accurate estimate of future sales.

However, many salespeople are likely to be biased in their estimates, and few have the time or inclination to do the research required to come up with an accurate estimate. As a result, firms usually buttress sales-force estimates with other forecasting methods.

PAST SALES DATA

When products have been on the market long enough to establish a sales trend, one of the most practical approaches to forecasting sales is to extrapolate a sales trend into the future. This assumes, however, that changes in the environment will not alter these trends.

That assumption may be warranted in a stable industry, but environmental changes could occur to alter these trends. Until the health craze, demand for corn oil was fairly static. Then, the American public discovered the value of using unsaturated oils, and suddenly the sales of a lackluster product took off way beyond its projected trend line.

The simplest approach in using past sales data is to project a constant percentage if sales have been growing at a steady rate. For example, if the average growth rate in sales per year has been 10 percent in the last five years, then next year's sales forecast will be 1.10 times this year's sales. A more complex approach is to use **time series analyses** *in which a mathematical growth rate in sales is determined by statistical techniques and projected to future years.*

Another approach to forecasting using past trends is the use of **historical analogy,** *in which past sales results of one product are used to forecast sales of a similar new product.* For example, past sales of car telephones might be used to estimate the sales growth for cellular telephones. Or, the past sales curves for the Trac II and Atra razors could be used to forecast the growth in sales for the Sensor (see Figure 3.2). This technique is most reliable when the new product is very similar to past products. But there may be differences between the new and the old product. For instance, relying entirely on data about car phones to project sales of cellular phones could be misleading because of differences in ease of use, clarity of reception, and price.

Despite the weakness of historical methods of forecasting, a survey found that 60 percent of the companies reported using them.[15]

SURVEYS OF CONSUMER BUYING INTENTIONS

Surveys of consumer intentions to buy a company's products are also commonly used in developing sales forecasts. A company might test product prototypes, before market introduction, by asking consumers their intention to buy. Research has shown that the proportion of consumers who say they will definitely buy is a good predictor of the product's market share.

Some firms with multiple product lines have maintained a panel of consumers who periodically fill out questionnaires regarding buying intent. General Electric maintained such a panel for many years. Consumers were asked their intention to buy large appliances such as refrigerators, washing machines, and so forth. GE could then forecast demand for its brands based on an estimate of its market share in each appliance category.

The problem with forecasts based on buying intentions is that consumers do not always fulfill them. Intentions are a less reliable predictor of future sales for higher-priced items because a variety of factors may cause the consumer to delay or change purchasing plans. One survey conducted in the 1950s measured purchase intentions for cars, then followed up to see whether consumers bought. Among those who said they planned to buy, 63 percent bought a new car. Among those who said they did not plan to buy, 29 percent bought a new car. Today, intentions might be an even less reliable predictor of future behavior, particularly for higher-priced items, because of the economic uncertainties created by recessions in the early 1980s and 1990s.

TEST MARKETING

The risks in relying on consumer intentions to forecast sales leads many companies to take the additional step of introducing a product into test markets prior to national introduction. In this way, managers rely on actual, rather than intended, behavior to derive sales forecasts.

Test areas are selected to reflect national market conditions. If test-market areas could be guaranteed to be representative of the national market, an accurate sales projection could be obtained simply by multiplying the sales results in the test market by a factor equal to the national population. Thus, if the market size in the test areas is one-twentieth of the national market, sales results multiplied by 20 would yield the sales forecast. Yet, rarely do test areas adequately represent the national market. Therefore, some adjustments must be made to sales results in test areas before projecting to the national market.

Assume for example, that Gillette selected five markets to test Sensor—Seattle, San Diego, Minneapolis, Dallas, and Boston. Yet Gillette's share in these markets is 55 percent compared to a national market share of 63 percent. Gillette would then adjust the sales estimates for Sensor upward in these five markets to better reflect national shaving preferences.

STATISTICAL MODELS

The weakness of historical forecasts and managerial judgment has led some companies to develop statistical models to forecast sales. There are two types of statistical models: probabilistic and deterministic. **Probabilistic models** *rely on past consumer purchasing behavior to estimate the probability that consumers will purchase.* For example, if a consumer bought the same brand four times in a row, the model might estimate a 95 percent chance the consumer will buy the same brand again. While probabilistic models are useful, they do not take into account environmental factors such as new technology or aggressive pricing by competitors, which may change even long-standing consumer purchase behavior.

Deterministic models *use marketing variables such as advertising expenditures, price level, couponing, and so forth as their basis for predicting sales or market share.* A deterministic model might forecast that a product will attain a certain market share or sales level if a specified amount is spent on advertising and sales promotions, if a certain price level is established, and if the company attains a certain level of distribution. As these marketing-mix components change, the model will forecast different market-share and sales levels.

Deterministic models are important because they are the only sales forecasting technique to provide diagnostic as well as predictive information to management.

PROFIT ESTIMATES

Sales forecasts provide the revenue base for the next step in marketing planning: estimating a product's profits. Profit estimates must also take into account the costs of marketing a product. *Cost estimates* are derived from the estimated costs to develop, produce, and market the product. Revenues for the Sensor were estimated at $150 million for the first year (1990) based on projected sales of 20 million razors and 300 million cartridges. But management estimated total costs at $198 million, resulting in an expected loss of $48 million in 1990. A loss of that magnitude is not unusual for a new product with high research-and-development costs. By the second year, (1991) Gillette forecast a 20 percent increase in revenues and decreases in marketing and manufacturing costs, resulting in an expected profit of $40 million. Gillette expects Sensor to remain profitable after 1991 until a new shaving system is introduced.

EVALUATION AND CONTROL

The final step in marketing planning is ongoing evaluation and control. Once a marketing plan is implemented, the product manager will evaluate actual product performance—particularly the effectiveness of the marketing mix—during the first year, and these data then serve as input into the planning cycle for the following year. This is represented by the feedback loop in Figure 3.1 from evaluation and control back to product objectives.

If sales are below estimate, the product manager must determine what steps are necessary to remedy the situation. Often, changes in advertising, promotion, price, or distribution are required. Before being implemented, though, such changes must be supported by data indicating how they would improve sales performance.

Sometimes, a failure to meet sales or profitability objectives requires more basic changes than an adjustment in the marketing mix. For instance, management might have miscalculated consumer needs or competitive reaction. In such cases, it may be necessary to make basic changes in the positioning of the brand or in the definition of the target market. Management must also be prepared to consider withdrawing the product, painful as this action might be.

Control is maintained by the product manager monitoring marketing costs to ensure they are within budget. There must be enough flexibility to allow advertising and promotional costs to be increased if necessary—for instance, if competitive activity requires an increase in coupons or if greater trade promotion expenditures are needed to convince the trade to accept the new product—without bringing the total amount significantly above budget.

As noted earlier, Sensor performed well above expectations in 1990, selling 24 million razors and 350 million cartridges.[16] These figures produced revenues 20 percent higher than expected, meaning that Sensor was almost profitable in its first year.

Interestingly, Sensor's success created some control problems. Gillette could not meet the unexpected demand for the product. Initial advertising and news coverage generated such a high level of awareness and interest that most stores reported quickly running out of stock for the brand. The company reacted by increasing its production capacity and delaying the introduction of Sensor into Spain and Italy so as to increase inventory in the United States.[17] It also delayed further advertising expenditures because of the high level of awareness that had been created by the January 1990 launch.

Gillette's experience shows that control is necessary not only if sales are below expectation but if they are above as well. The company had to quickly adjust to its lack of preparation for a surge in demand for the new product.

SUMMARY

1. **How does a firm develop a marketing plan for a new or existing product?**
A process must be established under the direction of the product manager that involves the following:
   - Conducting a situation analysis to evaluate the market for the product
   - Evaluating the opportunities and threats in marketing the product and assessing the company's strengths and weaknesses in the market
   - Developing product objectives on the basis of the opportunity/threat and strength/weakness analyses
   - Identifying the target market for the product and establishing a strategy to position the product to meet the needs of the target
   - Developing a marketing mix to implement product strategy
   - Forecasting sales and establishing initial profit projections
   - Evaluating and controlling the marketing effort
2. **How should the market for the product be evaluated?**
The product manager should first identify the market for the product, which would entail identifying customer needs and the products customers perceive as filling these needs. Next, the characteristics of the market should be evaluated on criteria such as growth in demand, capital investment, and potential profitability in order to determine market attractiveness. The total potential for the market should then be estimated. Market potential can be estimated by direct derivation if market factors are closely related to demand. If not, potential can be estimated by market estimation based on the projected number of buyers, the average number of units they purchase, and price.
3. **What are the strategic issues in identifying a target market and positioning the product?**
The plan should indicate whether the target for the product is the total market or specific segments. Further, it should indicate if an expansion of the target market is feasible and, if so, what segments should be targets for future effort.

The plan should also indicate the strategy for positioning—that is, whether the product should be positioned based on consumer benefits by utilizing imagery and/or communicating information, or on comparisons with competitive products.

4. **What mix of marketing elements—advertising, distribution, and price—should be used to implement the strategy for the product?**
The marketing plan must specify the components of the marketing mix, namely: product features; a promotional mix that includes advertising, promotion, and sales plans; a distribution plan to identify distribution channels and trade support; and strategies for setting and changing prices. The product manager must specify a budget for the marketing effort and the amount allocated to each component of the marketing mix.

5. **How can a firm estimate future sales?**
Future sales will be based on market potential and the firm's planned marketing strategy. Methods for sales forecasting include (1) relying on past sales data, (2) managerial judgment, (3) basing forecasts on consumer responses, and (4) marketing models.

KEY TERMS

Marketing plan (p. 68)
Situation analysis (p. 68)
Perceptual map (p. 72)
Market potential (p. 73)
Primary demand (p. 73)
Selective demand (p. 73)
Direct derivation method (p. 73)
Market estimation method (p. 74)
Cannibalization (p. 75)
Return on investment (ROI) (p. 80)
Marketing strategy (p. 82)
Target market (p. 82)
Comparative advertising (p. 87)
Promotional mix (p. 90)
Sales forecast (p. 94)
Delphi method (p. 94)
Expected-value approach (p. 95)
Time series analyses (p. 95)
Historical analogy (p. 95)
Probabilistic models (p. 96)
Deterministic models (p. 97)

QUESTIONS

1. What are the key steps in the marketing planning process for a product? Why do you suppose
   a. the situation analysis is the first step in the process?
   b. the situation analysis and identification of opportunity precede establishing product objectives?
2. Apply the marketing planning model in Figure 3.1 to:
   a. Harley-Davidson's repositioning of its heavy motorcycles (Chapter 1).
   b. Kodak's decision to introduce disposable cameras in Japan (Chapter 2).

   In each case, what were (a) the environmental opportunities and threats, (b) the company's capabilities to enter the market, (c) the target market for the product, (d) the general positioning strategy, and (e) key components of the marketing mix?
3. Two companies producing cellular telephones define the market differently. One defines it as "mobile communications," whereas the other defines it as "cellular telephones."
   a. What is the difference in these market definitions?
   b. What are the implications of each definition for identifying marketing opportunity, competition, and a target market?
   c. Which definition do you find more useful for marketing planning? Why?
4. Where should Gillette establish the market boundaries for Sensor based on Figure 3.2? Why?
5. Use the seven criteria on page 72 to rate the market attractiveness of the introduction of Sensor.
6. How can Procter & Gamble use *direct derivation* to estimate market potential for disposable diapers? How can Eagle Snack Foods use *market estimation* to estimate the market potential for potato chips? Provide examples of each.

7. What is meant by product cannibalization? One could argue that Sensor should not be introduced because most sales will come from users of Trac II and Atra, and these sales will not represent a net increase for Gillette. What is the fallacy in this argument?
8. What might be the differences in an opportunity/threat analysis for a product marketed in the United States compared to a product marketed on a global basis?
9. The chapter identifies four strategic issues regarding target-market identification. How do these issues apply to Sensor's introduction?
10. What are the objectives of positioning a product by information, by imagery, by competition? Provide examples of each.
11. In each of the following instances, a company wants to forecast sales for one or more of its products. Which of the sales forecasting methods cited in the chapter would you recommend in each case? Why?
    a. A firm that has experienced a steady rate of sales growth in the last ten years.
    b. A company in a highly volatile industrial market that is controlled by a few large producers.
    c. A consumer-goods company that frequently tests new hair-care and toiletry items.
    d. An industrial products company that finds a predictable relationship between its price and promotional activities and its sales results.
    e. A company that is introducing a new diet drink similar to one it introduced several years ago.

QUESTIONS: YOU ARE THE DECISION MAKER

1. An executive for a small electronics firm was asked for a general reaction to this chapter. In part, he said:

   You know, we do most of what you say here—situation analysis, opportunity/threat analysis, strength/weakness analysis, identifying target markets, and so forth. But a couple of things you should know: First, we don't call it that. A "situation analysis" is our baseline review to assess the market potential for a new product. The "opportunity/threat analysis" is looking at the pros and cons for introducing the product. The "strength/weakness analysis" is our way of asking "What do we need to go into the market?" Second, and as you probably gather, we are not nearly as formalized as you indicate in your chapter. Sometimes I'm a one-man planning operation, walking around with the opportunity/threat analysis in my head.

   a. Do the executive's comments suggest that the marketing planning process in Figure 3.1 is not useful for small businesses?
   b. Is there a problem with the executive "walking around with the opportunity/threat analysis in his head"?

2. The executive made another point:

   If you take this formalized planning process too far, it can shackle the more entrepreneurial and innovative part of your business. And that's the part that's going to ensure a company's survival for the next 50 years!

   a. Do you agree with the statement?
   b. Is there a danger of making the marketing planning process too structured and formalized?

PART II

Identifying Marketing Opportunities

Identifying marketing opportunities is one of the most important tasks of the marketing manager because opportunity defines the products the company will market and the businesses it will pursue. The ability of a firm to assess the environment and identify opportunities largely determines its profitability. Since identifying marketing opportunities requires an analysis of the marketing environment, Chapter 4 describes the social, technological, ecological, and legal environment of marketing. In Chapter 5, we consider opportunity identification in international markets. American companies are facing greater foreign competition at home, while looking to foreign markets as areas of increasing opportunity. Finally, in Chapter 6 we focus on one of the most important sources of marketing opportunity, competitive advantage. Most marketing firms operate in a competitive environment and must consider how to gain advantages over competitors by better meeting customer needs.

CHAPTER 4

Marketing Opportunity in a Dynamic Environment

YOUR FOCUS IN CHAPTER 4

To learn:

- *What creates opportunities and threats in the marketing environment.*
- *How marketers systematically analyze environmental changes to better shape marketing strategies.*
- *The basic environmental trends—social, technological, economic, and legal and regulatory—that will shape marketing opportunities in the 1990s.*

McDonald's—Can It Cope with a Changing Environment?

The early 1990s saw McDonald's facing the beginnings of a fall from dominance. With its average restaurant suffering a 3 percent sales loss and a 7 percent drop in operating income, the chain was forced to hike menu prices to stay marginally profitable.[1] Why? Because the company found itself caught in a consumer revolt against its menu and corporate mentality.

Long the barometer of America's penchant for fast foods, McDonald's allowed itself to ignore its aging customers, who were becoming more health conscious and ecologically concerned. As a result, those who grew up eating beneath the Golden Arches began turning elsewhere while McDonald's once-proud image became tarnished by environmental groups. By the late 1980s, McDonald's was under attack for its plastic packaging, its fatty hamburgers, and its low-nutrition menu. For example, the Environmental Defense Fund, a consumer advocacy group, was a vocal critic of company policy. As one analyst said of the company's situation, "The theme for the next few years is going to be McStruggle."[2] What an ironic predicament for a company whose founder, Ray Kroc, was a litter fanatic who told his first franchisees to pick up garbage in a two-block radius of their restaurants.

McDonald's, never known for quick responses, is turning threat into opportunity. The chain that pulls in $7.30 of each $100 Americans spend on fast-food is repositioning itself as a champion of nutrition and the environment.[3] McDonald's began the change in 1987, when it ordered its suppliers to reduce the weight of such things as its foam containers. It made concern for the environment the theme of its 1989 annual report, adding emphasis by printing it on recycled paper. And for the coup de grace, it launched a $100 million annual campaign to buy recycled materials for use in building and remodeling its restaurants. (The figure was in addition to the $60 million McDonald's had already budgeted for recycling.)

Timing the announcement to coincide with Earth Day 1990, McDonald's labeled the program McRecycle USA and took out ads in business publications touting an 800 number that suppliers of recycled materials could call.[4] It also switched from fatty beef tallow to 100 percent vegetable oil, added bran muffins and low-fat yogurt to its stable,[5] posted product information in its stores, and began test marketing health-conscious entries such as fettucini.[6] Yet despite all this, as of the early 1990s McDonald's still failed to change the perceptions of the core customers it had lost and continued to be viewed as ecologically and nutritionally unfriendly.

Then McDonald's counterattacked with a decisive one-two public relations combination. In November 1990, it announced it was eliminating polystyrene packaging, long the bane of critics who claimed the bulky plastic containers clogged precious landfill space.[7] Just days later, the chain unveiled a 91 percent low-fat burger, later named McLean Deluxe.[8] Suddenly, McDonald's was viewed as being in the vanguard of corporate environmentalism.

What happened? McDonald's turned threat into opportunity. Its USA President, Edward Rensi, created an environmental affairs unit that he charged with reshaping public perceptions about the chain. Its first actions included joining the Environmental Defense Fund in a task force to study the polystyrene issue and adding ecological education to McDonald's training school, Hamburger University.[9] A New York ad agency was employed to trumpet the philosophical change.[10]

By 1991, all these moves were beginning to pay dividends. An *Advertising Age*/Gallup Organization survey found that 67 percent of respondents found McDonald's either "very concerned" or "somewhat concerned" about the environment. Burger King's rating was 10 percentage points behind.[11]

But don't look for McDonald's to abandon its roots entirely. Even though it withdrew its 500-calorie, 57 percent-fat McDLT, it continued promoting the McJordan, a 520-calorie, 50 percent-fat quarter-pound burger with cheese, barbecue sauce and smoked bacon.[12]

As one executive said, "We've got ketchup in our blood."[13]

OPPORTUNITY AND THREAT IN THE MARKETING ENVIRONMENT

Chapter 1 described the marketing environment as those external forces that are the source of marketing opportunities and profits. As the McDonald's example shows, those forces can also be threatening. Yet, environmental forces are generally beyond a company's control. Marketing organizations try to *adapt* to changing environmental conditions, they rarely can *control* them. McDonald's could not stop the aging of its customer base and the greater health consciousness of American consumers. But it is adapting by becoming more conscious of health and ecological issues. In so doing, McDonald's is trying to change an environmental threat into an opportunity.

Opportunities are not always defined by dealing with threats. Most of the time, firms identify windows of opportunity based on some environmental trend. Although the trend toward greater health and nutritional consciousness spelled trouble for McDonald's, it created an opportunity for Kellogg to develop nutritional cereals targeted to adults. In cases such as these, the marketing organization either tries to change a threat into an opportunity (McDonald's) or tries to exploit an opportunity (Kellogg) through forces it *can* control—marketing strategies.

The interaction between controllable marketing strategies and uncontrollable environmental forces is illustrated in Figure 4.1. The marketing organization must evaluate key environmental trends, namely: social, competitive, technological, ecological, economic, and legal and regulatory. The result of these trends is the creation of environmental opportunities and threats. The marketing organization then responds to these opportunities and threats by developing a mix of product, distribution, promotional, and pricing strategies to satisfy customer needs.

Companies need information to evaluate environmental trends. Many have established **environmental scanning** *units that are responsible for collecting information on the environment and evaluating it*. Such units might obtain demographic information from the Census Bureau, life-style information from consumer surveys, and technological information from trade publications and professional journals. Environmental scanning units then uncover trends based on this information and report them to management.

In this chapter, we will consider specific trends in the environment that define marketing opportunities and threats for managers in many industries. These trends represent changes in five of the seven components of the marketing environment shown in Figure 4.1: social, technological, ecological, economic, and legal and regulatory. The remaining two components, international influences and competition, will be considered in Chapters 5 and 6.

SOCIAL TRENDS

Social trends in American society directly affect marketing strategies since they help determine consumer needs and purchasing decisions. Social trends represent changes in four factors: demographics, life-styles, cultural values, and subcultural influences. The first, **demographics,** *describes the objective characteristics of an individual—age, education, occupation, income, marital status, location, and so forth.* The second, **life-styles,** *is defined by consumers' activities, interests, and opinions.* We can talk of an active and outgoing life-style, a health-oriented life-style, and a conservative life-style. The third social factor, **cultural values,** *are beliefs shared by a large number of people in a society leading to common patterns of behavior.* Common values in American culture are materialism, youthfulness, and personal achievement. The fourth, **subcultural influences,** *involves the values and behavior that distinguish subcultures from society as a whole.* We will explore trends in each of these social factors in more detail.

CHANGING DEMOGRAPHIC CHARACTERISTICS

Marketers closely track changes in demographic characteristics because they help determine customer needs and purchases. Three demographic trends will have the most direct impact on marketing strategies in the 1990s: (1) changes in the age composition of the American market, (2) changes in family composition; and (3) the increasing proportion of working women.

FIGURE 4.1

Marketing Strategies and the Marketing Environment

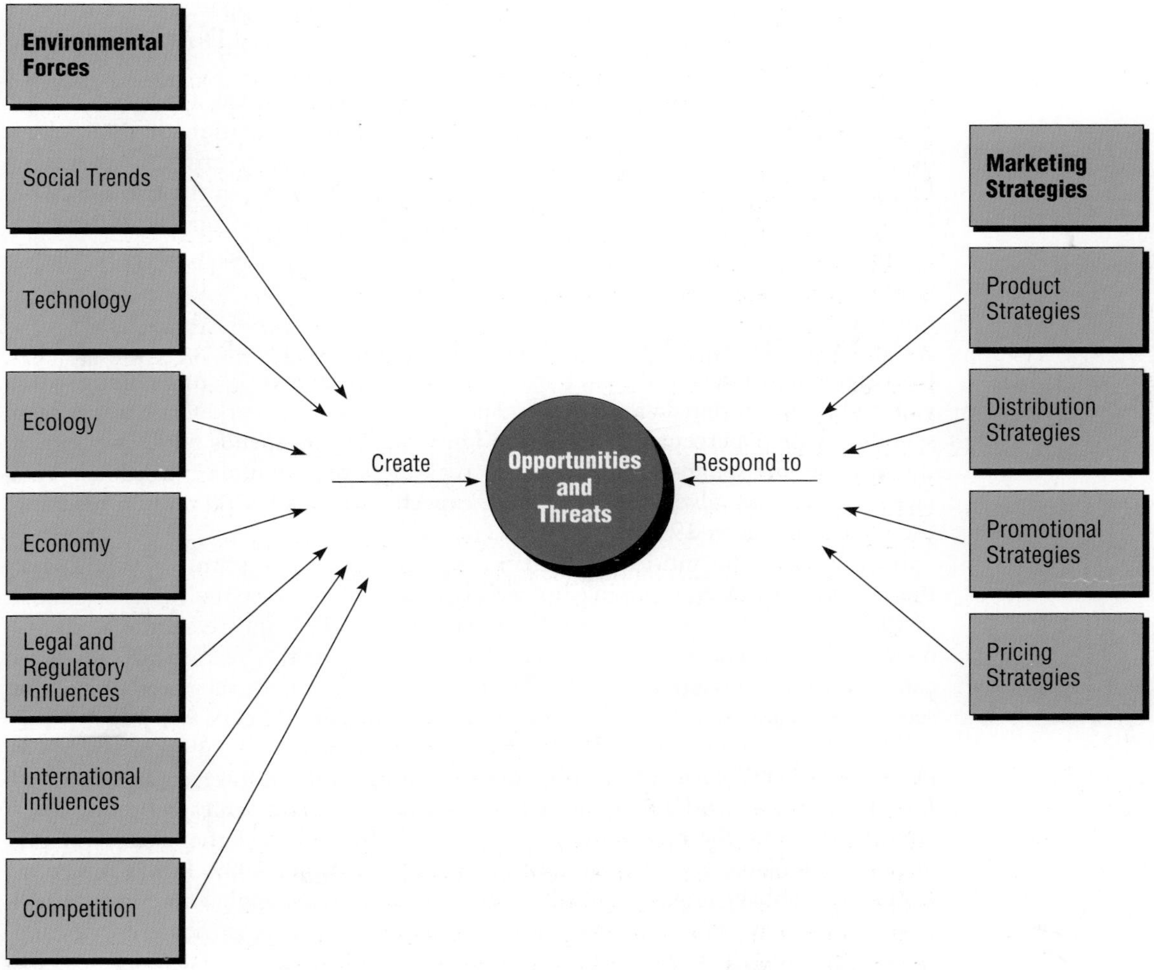

CHANGING AGE COMPOSITION

A long-term demographic trend has been a change in the age composition of American society. Changes in the birth rate and in life expectancy account for changes in age composition. The post–World War II years saw a 50 percent increase in the birth rate. As a result, those born from 1946 to 1964 are known as the *baby-boom generation.* From 1965 on, there was a steady decrease in the birth rate, except for a small increase from 1977 to 1983. Because of this decrease, teenagers (known as the *youth market*) have represented a decreasing proportion of the population. The second factor, life expectancy, has been increasing due to improved medical care and greater health consciousness. The result is an expected increase in the *mature market* (those 50 and over). Marketers will be focusing on these three age groups in coming years.

BABY BOOMERS Baby boomers, 77 million strong, account for one-third of the population and significantly more than one-fourth of the economy's purchasing power. Most are in their prime spending years and have $985 billion in income, a figure that is expected to double by the year 2000.[14]

Since marketers cannot assume boomers will act as their parents did, they are testing ways of selling to a generation that thinks young but is grappling with the realities of mid-life. Levi Strauss recognized that the expanding waist line of aging baby boomers might cut into its sales of jeans and introduced Docker slacks with a fuller cut to appeal to this group.[15]

Often overlooked are the younger boomers (born between 1955 and 1964). Since they did not belong to the anti-establishment generation of their older brothers and sisters, younger boomers tend to be more conservative. As marketers fine-tune their approach, they will begin distinguishing between the two sets. The Chivas Regal and Gitano advertisements in Exhibit 4.1 point up one distinction in approach. The former is geared to couples with older children, while the latter targets parents with newborns.

THE YOUTH MARKET Although the number of people age 12 to 19 fell by 5 percent between 1986 and 1989—and is expected to keep declining—the youth market will remain a particularly desirable target for marketers because teen spending rose 4 percent in the 1980s. The average boy spends $49 a week, and the average girl spends more than $55, regardless of economic conditions. This fact is not lost on advertisers, who were expected to spend $700 million reaching the youth market in 1991.[16]

In contrast to the anti-establishment teenagers of the 1960s and 1970s, those of the 1990s are more conservative, materialistic, and fitness-oriented, spending most of their money on clothing, entertainment, automobiles, and recreational equipment. Nike has reflected the latter emphasis in print ads that feature athletes associated with various sports (see Exhibit 4.2). College students voted them the second best campaign to reflect their interests. The first? Levi's 501 jeans.[17]

The youth market may be the first truly global market.[18] The presence of MTV in 33 countries suggests the youth market's commonality of interest, and PepsiCo Inc., Levi Strauss, and The Gillette Co. are among the companies designing marketing programs for one generic teen. Coca-Cola reflected the trend when it unveiled its "You can't beat the feeling" ads in December 1989. It was the company's first global campaign aimed at teens. Interest in the global teen market will probably increase as the economies of Eastern European countries improve, and teens there find themselves with more disposable income.[19]

EXHIBIT 4.1

Ads Targeted to Older and Younger Baby Boomers

They don't brag about their kids,
or make you watch slides of their vacations.
What are you saving the Chivas for?

Ad campaign geared to older baby boomers

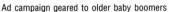

GITANO
A New American Tradition For Today's Spirited Family.™

Ad campaign geared to younger baby boomers

THE MATURE MARKET The mature market is also expanding in both numbers and purchasing power. This group now controls half of the country's discretionary income and 77 percent of its assets. While one in every four Americans is now age 50 or older, a third of all Americans will belong to this group within 30 years,[20] and they will have more money because of better pension and retirement plans.

Despite the purchasing power of this group, one advertising agency estimates that only 6 or 7 percent of TV commercials are targeted to the mature market. Marketers have found it difficult to position products to this market for the simple reason that people do not like to be reminded they are getting older. Wendy's famous "Where's the beef?" commercial may have temporarily boosted sales, but it drove away legions of older customers who resented its portrayal of an elderly woman as crotchety. A life insurance commercial featuring Danny Thomas was roundly attacked for suggesting viewers shouldn't wait "until it's too late."[21] There have been dozens of similar gaffes.

Marketers who hit the mark stress vitality over age. On its pleasure cruises, Royal Viking Cruise Lines has begun promoting seminars on financial planning,

EXHIBIT 4.2

Nike Appeals to the Youth Market

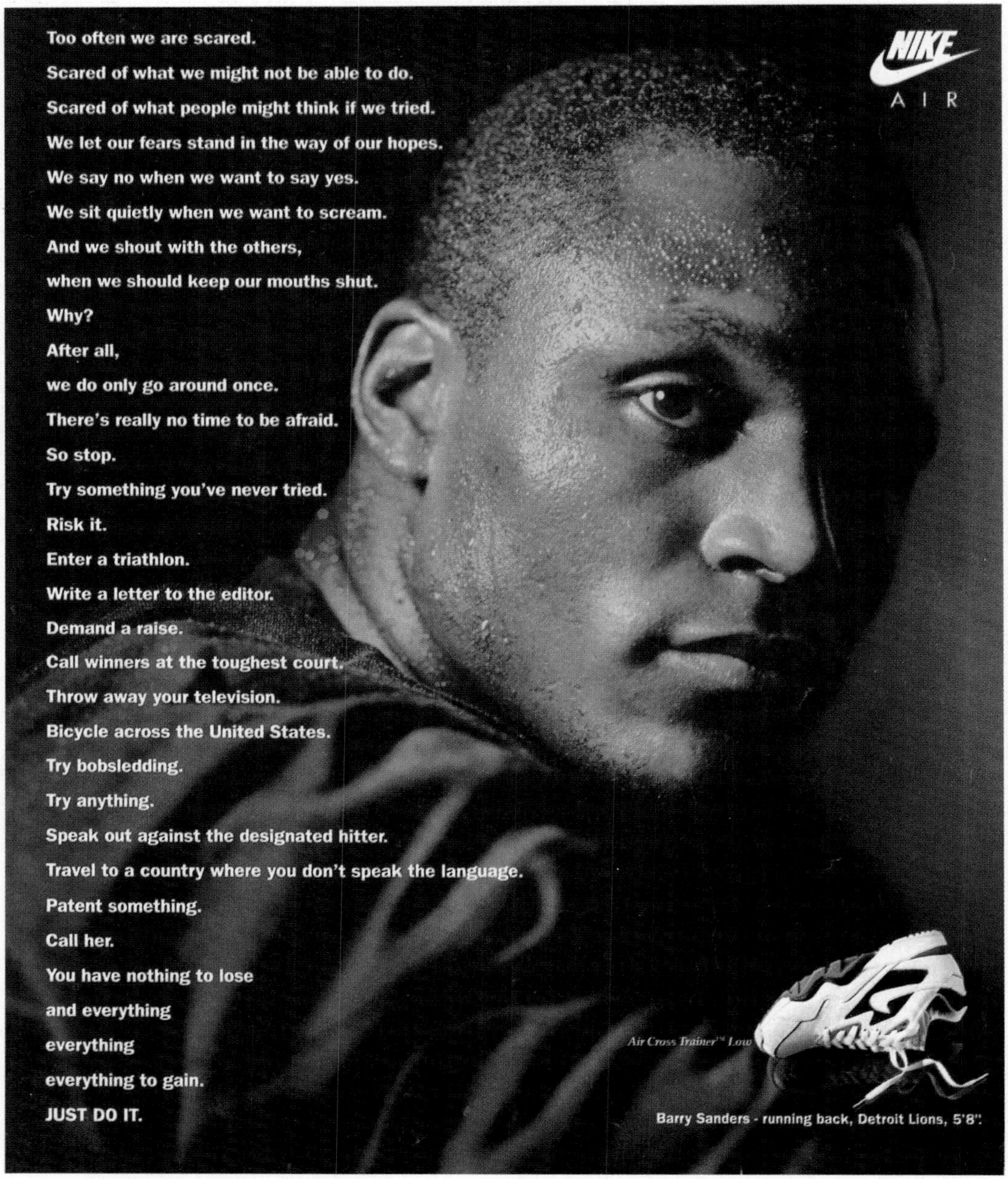

computers, writing, and foreign policy (see Exhibit 4.3).[22] General Foods positioned Bran Flakes to the health concerns of older consumers by using 71-year-old Lena Horn in a spot whose theme was "Getting the best out of life." And while Procter & Gamble is planning a global launch of its Metamucil laxative brand, it is testing Metamucil fiber wafers in the United States with ads that say "Fiber therapy for busy people."[23]

EXHIBIT 4.3

Ad Targeting Older Consumers

CHANGING FAMILY COMPOSITION

The American family is becoming smaller and less cohesive. In 1950, 70 percent of families were composed of a working father, a mother at home, and at least one school-age child. In 1987, only 17 percent could be so classified.[24] By 1989, for the first time, there were more families without children at home than with children.

Why this dramatic change? We already noted one reason—more career-oriented women. Two other factors are a decrease in the birthrate after 1960 and a doubling in the divorce rate. (Today, 50 percent of marriages end in divorce, triple the 1970 rate.) As a result, there are more single-person households (one fourth of the population lives alone);[25] more single-parent homes (more than half the children will live in one by the year 2000);[26] smaller families in married households; and a steady decrease in the proportion of teenagers, a decline which will not end until 1997.

While smaller, or more-fractured, families could be threatening to many marketers, several are trying to turn these trends into opportunity. The Hyatt hotel

GLOBAL MARKETING STRATEGIES

Looking for Opportunity Abroad: McDonald's in Moscow

While McDonald's is facing threats at home, it is aggressively looking for opportunities abroad. McDonald's in Moscow is a good example. George Cohon spent 14 years dreaming about opening the first McDonald's in the former Soviet Union. The president of McDonald's Restaurants of Canada saw 290 million Russian citizens whose principal diet consisted of meat, bread, and potatoes and thought: "This is what we sell. This has to be an unbelievable market for us." In the beginning, he did not know how right he would be.

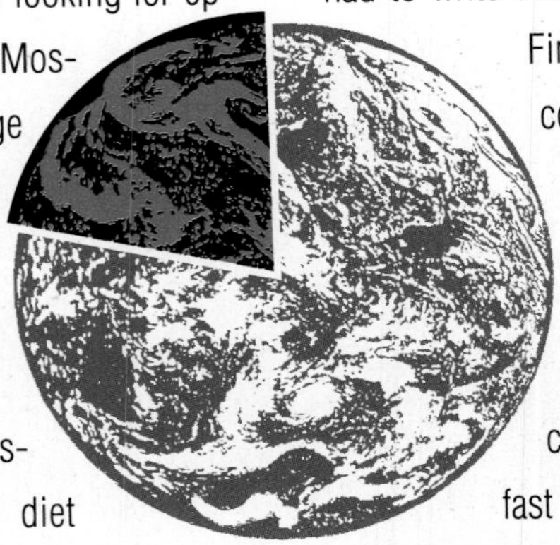

With domestic sales decreasing because of a change in America's eating habits, by 1991 soaring sales from its 2,600 foreign units were the only thing boosting McDonald's net income. When McDonald's finally opened a restaurant in Moscow in 1990, it was more than a fulfillment of Cohon's dream; it was an act of necessity for the stagnating chain. There was only one problem: Russia was unlike any foreign country where McDonald's had outlets. So Cohon had to write the marketing rules from scratch.

First, he decided that since he had no competition, employing media buys and billboards would be wasted effort. Instead of defining or segmenting his market, he decided to introduce McDonald's as a broad concept by educating Russians about fast foods. That involved McDonaldizing Moscow, whose city council has a 51 percent stake in the operation. Reasoning that Russians ate with utensils, never with their hands, he spent his ad budget on brochures and tray liners explaining how to eat a Big Mac, not why to buy one. He also stayed away from using the company's mascot, Ronald McDonald, figuring it would merely confuse potential customers. McDonald's Muscovite teen employees, meanwhile, were instructed in the ways of being unrelentingly cheerful and clean, characteristics that Soviet consumers were not used to. Customers were similarly taught how to stand in line,

chain, for instance, is considering countering the threat of fewer traveling families by luring single-parents with discounted rates.[27] Candy bar companies such as Nestlé and Hershey turned the threat of declining consumption due to fewer children and teenagers into opportunity by importing high-quality chocolates from Europe for adults.[28]

Some marketers are also looking at changes in family composition abroad. Heinz has been eyeing the potentially lucrative Chinese market. With 22 million babies born in China each year (six times the number in the United States), Heinz saw an opportunity for introducing baby products. In 1990, it began marketing

GLOBAL MARKETING STRATEGIES

American style.

Cohon's audience was more than receptive. After all they had spent a year hearing awe-struck reports on Soviet TV about McDonald's work ethic, quality control systems, and Big Mac economics.

"I don't think you can rush off helter-skelter and say, 'OK, it's open, let's go in.' You have to do your homework. You have to be very targeted about what you want to do once you get in there," Cohon said of his strategy.

That logic led him to forgo some of McDonald's more off-beat entries and stick only to hamburgers. To do it just right, he struck pacts with Russian agronomists to raise cattle similar to American livestock and arranged for the planting of the first crop of Russet Burbank potatoes in Russia. The Russians could not handle everything, however, so seeds were imported from the company's farms in the Netherlands, tomato paste from Portugal, and apples from Bulgaria.

If Cohon is keeping things simple for now, that does not mean he is ignoring ways to expand the market later. For instance, plans are already afoot to introduce chicken once Big Mac's take hold. "What a nice shot in the market that's going to be," he says.

Questions: Why did McDonald's decide to open restaurants in Russia? What problems did McDonald's confront which were particular to the Russian marketplace?

Source: "An Icon Wakes Up To a Troubled Future," *The New York Times*, May 12, 1991, p. F1; "How Big Mac Made It To Moscow," *Advertising Age*, January 22, 1990, p. 16; and "Of Famous Arches, Beeg Meks and Rubles," *New York Times*, January 28, 1990, pp. 1 and 12.

rice cereal for babies and almost immediately saw a profit. The cereal is precooked and instant, appealing to the 70 percent of Chinese women who work outside the home.[29]

INCREASING PROPORTION OF WORKING WOMEN

One of the most significant changes in American society has been the increasing proportion of women in the work force. As Figure 4.2 shows, the proportion of working women increased from one-third in 1950 to 58 percent in 1990 and is

FIGURE 4.2

Women in Labor Force as a Percentage of all Women

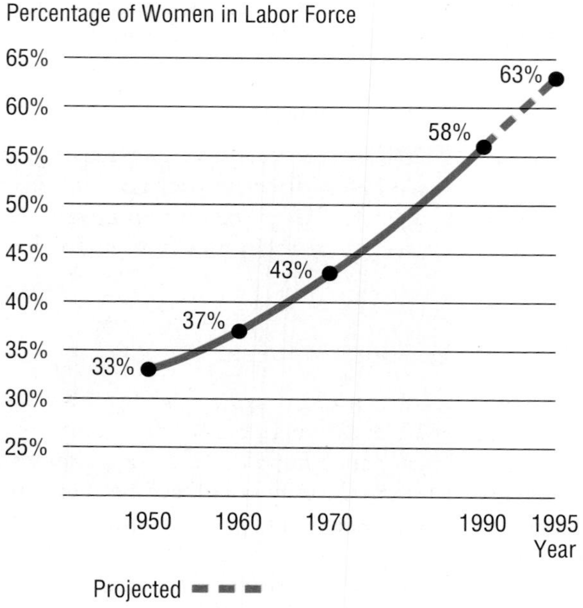

Source: "Employed Persons with Single and Multiple Jobs by Sex," *Monthly Labor Review,* Department of Labor, May 1982, p. 48, Table 1; "A Portrait of the American Worker," *American Demographics,* March 1984, p. 19; *Handbook of Labor Statistics,* June 1985. Tables 1, 6, and 50; and *Monthly Labor Review,* February 1986, Table 1. Bureau of Labor Statistics, *Monthly Labor Review,* July 1988, Table 5, p. 60. Projections to 1995 from *Statistical Abstracts of the United States,* 1991, p. 386.

projected to rise to 63 percent by 1995. Not only are more women working, but they are entering the work force earlier. Among women in their twenties and thirties, 70 percent are employed. They hold the majority of jobs as insurance adjustors, real estate agents, and bill collectors. In addition, the number of women judges, lawyers, and scientists has more than tripled since 1971.[30]

The increasing proportion of working women has posed both threat and opportunity for many marketers. An opportunity has been created by the time crunch faced by working women. In 1975, 45 percent of working women felt they had enough leisure time. By 1990, only 35 percent felt they had enough time. As a result, working women are fueling a boom in catalog shopping, telephone shopping, and direct mail because they do not have time to shop. L'Eggs now sells 60 percent of all its panty hose by direct mail.[31]

Some food marketers have viewed the trend as a threat, particularly those whose products are directed to the traditional homemaker. Yet many food companies created opportunity from threat by developing new, more convenient categories or by refocusing existing products as easy-to-prepare meals. Campbell repositioned its Chunky soups as the perfect light meal that even a husband can fix for his working wife. As a hedge, food companies have further exploited the emphasis on time-saving convenience by buying fast-food outlets. With working wives averaging 7.4 meals out per week, it is not surprising to see General Mills, General Foods, Quaker Oats, and Pepsi-Cola all buying established fast-food companies.[32]

Marketers have also begun segmenting the working woman market. After one study that found 75 percent of women reported playing a role in buying office computer equipment, Toshiba created an ad showing a woman directing an otherwise all-male meeting as a Toshiba laptop sits on the conference table. Clearly, Toshiba saw a neglected niche in women business leaders.

CHANGING LIFE-STYLE TRENDS

A second social trend that is important to marketers is changing life-styles. Three recent, broad changes that have had a direct impact on consumer purchases are (1) a change in male and female roles, (2) an interest in a healthier life-style, and (3) a more conservative life-style, especially in the youth and baby-boom markets.

A CHANGE IN MALE–FEMALE ROLES

The increase in the number of working women and the decrease in family size have significantly changed male and female purchasing roles. Men are assuming more of the burdens of child care and shopping (they now account for 40 percent of food shopping dollars). As a result, they have become more involved in traditionally female purchases such as cereal, soap, and toothpaste.[33] Marketers of food and household products have begun to pay more attention to men. Cascade dishwasher detergent used to show two women worried about spots on their glasses. Now the ad features two men fretting about the same spots before their female dinner dates arrive.[34] General Foods, meanwhile, has shifted many package designs from pink backgrounds with script print to darker hues and bolder print to appeal to males.[35]

Women's purchasing roles have changed as dramatically as men's. Their greater independence has resulted in a shift toward more personal goals, leading them to spend more on travel, dining out, entertainment, services, and luxury products. As a result, companies selling credit cards, financial services, life insurance, and cars are portraying women in more-realistic, professional ways. American Express showed early sensitivity to this portrayal in its "interesting lives" series of vignette ads in the mid-1980s. One showed a wife taking her husband out to dinner with the American Express card as he recited her accomplishments.

A HEALTHIER LIFE-STYLE

Another life-style trend with an important impact on marketing strategies is the greater emphasis on health and nutrition. While barely a third of grocery shoppers read labels in 1985, by 1990 half did. A 1989 study found that almost half of consumers surveyed reported buying a food product promoting good health in the previous 30 days.[36]

Americans are quitting smoking, drinking less liquor and coffee, and avoiding red meats. Americans are also embracing fat-free diets. When Kraft General Food's Entenmann's division introduced a line of 30 cakes, cookies, and pastries in 1990 that were fat-free and low in sodium, it earned $164 million in nine months, leading analysts to project the company's revenues would grow about 16 percent.[37] Entenmann's is just one of seven no-fat categories at Kraft, which is banking on the category for sustained growth.[38] Little wonder then that "light"

EXHIBIT 4.4

Repositioning Timex Watches to Fitness-Oriented Consumers

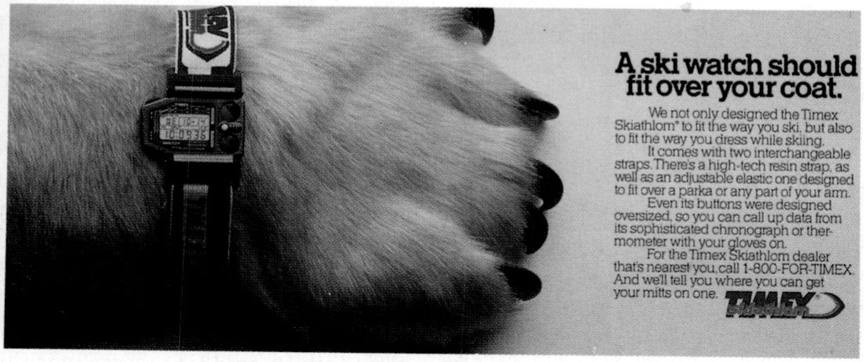

and "natural" foods are now the fastest-growing category on supermarket shelves. Many are even backed by innovations such as telephone nutrition centers that provide consumers with nutritional information.

A related life-style trend is greater emphasis on fitness. More Americans are jogging, doing aerobics, and engaging in sports activities than ever before. One company that has followed this trend is Timex watches. The company used to market plain, low-priced, durable watches. As consumers became more style conscious, sales fell. Timex then decided to change its image and reposition its watches to younger, sports-oriented consumers. It came out with watches for aerobic fans that can measure pulse rates, for racing fans that can track car speeds, and for skiers that can measure low temperatures[39] (see Exhibit 4.4). As a result of its repositioning to the fitness market, Timex's sales soared.

Companies for whom the health and fitness trend poses a potential environmental threat (for instance, liquor, cigarette, and coffee companies) have gone with the trend by diversifying or adapting their product line. Cigarette companies have diversified into foods and beverages. Philip Morris, for example, has become the second largest food company in the world by acquiring General Foods in 1985 and Kraft in 1988. Coffee companies have responded similarly. Rather than continue to rely on a declining coffee market, Nestlé acquired Stouffer's Foods and got on the nutritional bandwagon with the introduction of Lean Cuisine. Liquor companies have been expanding their product lines into lower-proof products.

A MORE CONSERVATIVE LIFE-STYLE

The 1980s saw the youth market become increasingly conservative. Young people today are more concerned with their careers and are more style and fashion conscious. As a result, they are spending more money on clothing, personal grooming products, and automobiles.

Teenagers and college students are also more involved with food and household products than were their predecessors. Many who come from divorced households are already accustomed to the role of family purchasing agent, and they carry their awareness of food and household products to college. As a result, General Foods, Castle & Cooke, Kraft, and Lipton all have started running ads in teen magazines. At *Seventeen* magazine, food ads skyrocketed by 30 percent in 1990.[40]

Marketers have begun to adapt to the greater family orientation of baby boomers. Canada Dry developed a campaign in 1988 to appeal to "couch potatoes." One commercial shows a bunch of friends lounging at home reminiscing about the 1970s. Another shows a young career couple who decide to relax at home with Chinese food and Canada Dry rather than go out.[41]

CHANGING CULTURAL VALUES

We have seen how demographic and life-style trends pose both opportunity and threat in the marketing environment. A third significant social trend is cultural change. Most cultural values such as the emphasis on individualism, personal achievement, and youth and vitality are fairly enduring parts of the American landscape. Significant changes in values do occur, however.

One such cultural trend is a current shift toward traditionalism, representing greater emphasis on family and patriotic values. Until the mid 1980s, a "me" orientation was fairly pervasive, especially among baby boomers and the youth segment. It reflected a need to live life "my way," a fierce desire to live for today without concern for the more-restrictive values that might be imposed by society or family. The resulting search for immediate gratification—fueled by the boom years in the mid-80s—led to an increase in spending on travel, entertainment, clothing, and personal grooming products. Ads such as Prudential Insurance's advertisement, "I need me," and Miss Clairol's "This, I do for me," were symbolic of cultural values.

The 1990s are seeing a reemergence of a "we" orientation, reflecting a more traditional focus on family values and the work ethic. As consumers harken back to the family—saving more and investing in furniture, housing, and education—they develop a heightened appreciation of community. These values have given rise to greater concern for the environment, homelessness, and drugs. At the same time, greater traditionalism is also resulting in more emphasis on patriotism and religious values. Marketers have captured these values with themes such as Chevrolet's "Heartbeat of America" (see Exhibit 4.5) and Miller's "Made the American way."

SUBCULTURAL INFLUENCES

A fourth broad social influence important to marketers involves the values and behavior in the United States of **subcultures**—*broad groups that have similar values distinguishing them from society as a whole.* American society is so diverse that many subcultures exist defined by region, national origin, religion, or ethnic identification. The three most important are African Americans (representing 12 percent of the population), Hispanic Americans (representing 8 to 10 percent), and Asian Americans (representing 3 percent). Together, these three groups represent almost one-fourth of American consumers. The key question for marketers is how they differ from other consumers, and what marketing opportunities these differences might represent.

EXHIBIT 4.5

Appealing to Traditionalism

THE AFRICAN-AMERICAN MARKET

African-American consumers are as diverse as white consumers, so to refer to them as a homogeneous group is misleading. Yet a few distinctions remain. African Americans are more likely to try new products—particularly clothing—while staying brand loyal when they have found something they like.[42] Their spending power is on the rise. Since on average, African-American consumers are six years younger than whites, a larger proportion of them will be entering their prime spending years in the 1990s.[43] It stands to reason, therefore, that marketers are paying more attention to this important group, which boasts $250 billion in purchasing power.[44]

African Americans are targeted by the same demographic and life-style criteria as whites. Carmakers increasingly have directed ads to an emerging African-American middle class in much the same way they target whites. The Ford ad in Exhibit 4.6 for its LX line is an example.

When products are targeted correctly to African Americans, the targeting can be interpreted as a recognition of the community's buying power and importance. But when targeted wrongly, a significant cultural backlash can be generated. This happened to R.J. Reynolds Tobacco Co. in 1989 when it launched Uptown, a brand aimed squarely at African Americans. Uptown was the first *name brand* designed specifically for African Americans. As such, it came under immediate fire from the U.S. secretary of health and human services, religious leaders, and the medical profession, all of whom decried the company's targeted approach of an unhealthy product to a specific racial group. As a result, R.J. Reynolds was forced to withdraw Uptown from tests and scrap the project.[45]

THE HISPANIC-AMERICAN MARKET

Hispanic Americans are a more distinct subculture than African Americans because more than two-thirds of Hispanic Americans speak Spanish at home.[46] Further, Hispanic Americans tend to be more traditional and conservative than most other groups. This orientation is reflected in the dominant role of the man, as well as in the view of four-fifths of Hispanic women that having a child is the most important event in their lives.[47]

Like African Americans, Hispanics tend to be brand loyal, showing more faith in the quality of nationally advertised products than most other consumers. They are also more likely to be influenced by advertising than are other market segments.

EXHIBIT 4.6

Targeting Middle-Class African Americans

Since the Hispanic market grew 34 percent in the 1980s (four times faster than the general population), more companies began paying attention to it.[48] All has not gone smoothly, however, especially where manufacturers have tried to use all-purpose marketing. When Tropicana advertised its orange juice in Miami as *jugo de china*, it assumed Miami's Cubans would read *china* as orange, because that's the way it translated to Puerto Ricans. Tropicana was wrong. Miami's Cubans thought Tropicana was advertising juice from the Orient.[49]

Polaroid managed to get it right when it advertised its Spectra instant camera to Hispanics by showing a father's picture of his wife and newborn baby. The focus is on an emotional family moment, a moment that would have a great deal of appeal for Hispanics. In contrast, the company focuses more on the camera and its features when advertising to the general market. From this success, Polaroid has gone deeper into the Hispanic market by advertising on Univision, a Spanish-language cable network (see Exhibit 4.7).

THE ASIAN-AMERICAN MARKET

Asian Americans are the most highly educated and affluent subculture. Like African Americans and Hispanics, they have a strong ethnic identity and a great cultural diversity, with Chinese Americans representing the largest group, followed

EXHIBIT 4.7

Targeting Hispanic-American Consumers

WE'VE HELPED POLAROID® DEVELOP A WHOLE NEW MARKET.
In 1984, Polaroid took its first modest steps into the Hispanic market. The company spent a grand total of $100,000 in Spanish-language media.
But that was enough to convince them that they were onto something big.
In 1988, Polaroid spent more than ten times that amount in Hispanic media. And they're planning another 50% increase in 1989.
The vast majority of those dollars are going to be spent on UNIVISION. Because Polaroid has learned that there's no better way to reach America's Hispanics. We can put you in touch with 85% of U.S. Hispanic households. Nobody else comes close to that. Most important, we talk their language. Spanish is the first language of 94% of Hispanics in this country.
But it isn't just the sheer numbers we deliver that has made UNIVISION so popular with Polaroid. The quality of our audience is equally attractive. The fact is, Polaroid has discovered that not only are Hispanics buying the company's products, they're buying the costlier, top-of-the-line Spectra® cameras.
Today, there are nearly 20 million Hispanics in the U.S. with some $134 billion in purchasing power. It's a market no savvy advertiser can afford to ignore. Let us help put you in the picture. Call your UNIVISION sales representative.
For the best in Spanish-language news, entertainment, children's, sports and variety programming, there *is* only one television network.
UNIVISION IS HISPANIC-AMERICA'S TELEVISION NETWORK.™
New York (212) 826-5200; Chicago (312) 944-2199; Los Angeles (213) 859-7200; San Francisco (415) 392-2006;
Dallas (214) 869-0202; Detroit (313) 540-5705; Miami (305) 444-0800; Orange County (714) 474-8585

by Filipinos, Japanese Americans, Vietnamese, and Koreans. Because of their high rate of immigration (70 percent of America's Asians immigrated in the past two decades), this group is growing 14 times faster than the general population.[50]

Generally, marketers have ignored Asian Americans and used general marketing campaigns to attract them. It is difficult to target all Asian Americans simultaneously because of the diversity in nationalities and the lack of a single market (there is no national Asian cable TV network, for instance). But target marketing for Asians has worked in a regional context. For example, the heavy concentration of Chinese Americans in California made it possible for the Bank of America to dub its English ads and run them on the local Chinese language cable stations.[51]

OBTAINING INFORMATION ON SOCIAL TRENDS

Companies must obtain information on shifts in demographics, life-styles, and cultural values. Information on demographic trends is available from government sources. The Bureau of Census provides information on changes in age, income, education, and regional distributions in the United States. The Bureau of Labor Statistics provides similar information on employment, such as the proportion of working women.

Trends in life-styles and cultural values are harder to determine because there are no standard definitions for these variables, and government agencies do not track them. In the 1980s, several private agencies began filling an important need by tracking such social trends.

The Value and Life Style Program (VALS) of the Stanford Research Institute has surveyed American consumers since the early 1980s to identify groups with similar values and life-styles. It has identified eight groups with labels such as actualizers, achievers, strivers, and strugglers.[52] Each group is identified by its life-styles, values, and demographics. Actualizers have the highest income and self-esteem of any group, have a wide range of interests, and are open to change.

Avon subscribed to the VALS program because it was facing a particular threat based on its reliance on door-to-door selling. The increasing proportion of working women resulted in a "double whammy," fewer women at home to buy and fewer part-timers available to serve as Avon salesladies. In the late 1970s, the company gave its blessing to the natural reaction of its salespeople, to sell at the workplace rather than at home. But it was reacting to events in a knee-jerk fashion rather than anticipating them. One of the first things a new management team did in 1983 was to establish an environmental scanning unit. The group subscribed to VALS to better determine how to change Avon's image. One consumer segment identified by VALS, the *strivers*, was of particular interest. This group was status oriented and focused on style in an attempt to emulate more-upscale consumers. Women in this group were described as wanting to maintain their personal appearance, improve their feelings about themselves, and accept themselves more. They view fragrances and beauty products as a means to this goal. Partly as a result of the VALS research, Avon introduced a campaign to this life-style group based on the theme, "We're going to make you feel beautiful."[53]

TECHNOLOGICAL TRENDS

We have been exploring how companies have adapted their marketing strategies to a variety of social trends. But such trends represent only one dimension of the marketing environment. Technological trends are also critically important in identifying marketing opportunities. These trends include new directions in research and development (R&D) that might lead to new products or even to new industries. They also include new technologies that change the way consumers or marketers do things.

RESEARCH AND DEVELOPMENT

Companies rely on their research and development facilities to create new products and technologies. The pace of technological change has increased in the 1980s, putting greater pressure on marketers to maintain adequate research and development facilities.[54]

For many companies, new technology has been the road to marketing opportunity. For example, in 1991 Apple and IBM, once fierce rivals in the home-computer market, agreed to join ranks to create a new computer operating system that will be commonly used in both companies' future products, thereby establishing a new market for each.[55] Polaroid's development of the instant camera, Sony's introduction of the Walkman, RCA's role in developing color television, and

Du Pont's development of synthetic fibers all illustrate how technological breakthroughs can give a company a competitive advantage for many years.

The link between R&D and marketing opportunity is shown in one study that found a high correlation between R&D expenditures and corporate profitability.[56] That is why many companies try to maintain research and development facilities that can give them an edge in technology. It is especially important to have an edge in industries such as telecommunications, computers, electronics, chemicals, and pharmaceuticals, where the pace of technological change is rapid. In industries such as paper, furniture, and textiles, the technological pace is slower, and R&D expenditures are low. Here, technology is unlikely to be so critical in creating marketing opportunity and competitive advantage.

Just as new technologies can present marketing opportunities, they can also present environmental threats to companies whose current technology could be undermined. Railroads were brought close to extinction by the airlines and the automobile, the steel industry was threatened by the development of aluminum, and the wool industry declined as a result of the development of synthetic fibers.

But new technologies can also pose a threat to the companies that develop them. A company that pursues new technologies in order to maintain technological leadership may end up developing products the consumer does not need. In the 1980s, Kraft General Foods tried twice to introduce a line of prepackaged microwaveable meat dinners that could sit on shelves for months. What Kraft didn't bank on was the consumer's perception that meat dinners which can be stored at room-temperature must be loaded with unsavory chemicals. As a result, its A La Carte and Impromptu lines went nowhere.[57]

NEW MARKETING TECHNOLOGIES

A dramatic change that has had a pronounced influence on the marketing environment has been the development of technologies that provide consumers with new shopping and entertainment options, both inside and outside the home. New technologies also give marketers options for dealing with information that have improved the way they implement strategies.

IN-HOME SHOPPING AND INFORMATION SERVICES

Many consumers have changed their shopping habits because of new technologies. One of the most important innovations has been to provide consumers with a greater facility for in-home shopping through cable TV networks. Over 56 percent of U.S. households subscribed to cable TV channels in 1990, and satellites have permitted cable companies to move from local to national programming.[58] The largest cable channel devoted to shopping, the Home Shopping Network (HSN), operates by offering items on its cable TV network to consumers who then phone in their orders. It has been estimated that 35 percent of all U.S. households regularly watch a home-shopping TV station.[59]

Another home-shopping technology—**videotex**—*is an interactive system that permits subscribers to access product information, news services, electronic "chat" networks, and even telephone directories on their TV screens via a small computer terminal that is attached to the home's cable TV converter.* Consumers order the products or services directly through the terminal.

Once thought to be a marketing breakthrough, the videotex audience has remained quite small, with only 1.5 million homes equipped to use it.[60] Companies such as Warner Communications, Knight-Ridder, American Express, and AT&T have invested in videotex with poor results. Videotex should not be counted out, however. The prime users are computer-literate young people, and as they age and gain more disposable income, they may aid videotex expansion.

A main entry into videotex is called Prodigy, which requires a home computer equipped with a modem using telephone lines for the two-way transmission of information through the computer.[61] Jointly backed by IBM and Sears, Prodigy's offerings range from airline tickets to clothing. Users complain about slow response, frequent advertisements, and the shallowness of its offerings. But IBM and Sears are showing no signs of backing off their investment and recently took the service national.[62]

Overall, manufacturers see in-home shopping as an area of opportunity since it affords another outlet for their goods. But there are constraints. The main one is the reluctance of consumers to shop at home, because they prefer to see the merchandise and interact with salespeople. At the same time, many retailers view home shopping as a threat—an alternative purchasing channel that may lower their sales.

HOME ENTERTAINMENT TECHNOLOGIES

A revolution in technology in the 1980s was the introduction of integrated in-home entertainment systems. VCRs have led the way and are projected to be adopted as widely as TV. In 1990, over 68 percent of U.S. households had VCRs,[63] a remarkably rapid rate of adoption considering the figure was only 10 percent in the early 1980s.

In-home entertainment is viewed as an opportunity by the electronics and computer industry, but it is viewed as a potential threat by the advertising industry, because commercials on programs recorded at home can be "zapped"—that is, bypassed so that only the program is seen. Advertisers have tried to adapt to the threat by placing commercials on VCR tapes. Such advertising would open up a new, if limited, media channel.

NEW CONSUMER TECHNOLOGIES OUTSIDE THE HOME

The last decade has seen the emergence of an important shopping technology outside the home, **electronic retailing,** *which permits consumers to gain product information and make purchases through computer terminals in various locales.* Such electronic retailing affords manufacturers yet another channel for distributing their products.

One form of electronic retailing is the kiosk. In several Southern supermarket chains, kiosks feature terminals with touch-screens that allow consumers to get free coupons by typing their phone numbers on keypads. A database compiled from requests helps manufacturers target their customers more effectively.[64]

Other manufacturers cut out the middleman and run their own kiosks. For instance, Murjani International, a manufacturer of jeans, introduced electronic kiosks outside many retail stores in 1986, giving shoppers the opportunity to make purchases 24 hours a day and guaranteeing delivery in two days.[65]

Among other innovations are videoscreens on shopping carts that carry product ads (the ads get "triggered" by infrared signals transmitted as shoppers pass certain products);[66] TV monitors placed throughout stores that carry computer-animated ads (the concept is being backed by Nynex);[67] and video signs that supermarkets such as A&P carry aisle by aisle[68] (see Exhibit 4.8).

EXHIBIT 4.8

New Shopping Technologies

7
Pet Needs
Cleansers
Detergents
Bath Soap
Look! Spend Less.
A&P employs a variety of techniques to reach today's time-pressed consumer with messages about our own services as well as specific product and price information. Along with traditional print ads, colorful direct mail distributions and high-impact radio and television spots, electronic technology is making point-of-sale promotion more dynamic. Standing below one of our digital LED aisle signs are Michael Larkin, Executive Vice President, Operations (left) and James Madden, Senior Vice President, Operations.
Andrew Fuchs
Vice President
Metro New York
Group
Paul Gallant
President
Compass Foods

NEW INFORMATION TECHNOLOGIES

New information technologies make marketing more efficient not only for consumers, but also for companies. The widespread proliferation of personal computers and microprocessing capabilities has given marketers instant access to sales trends, cost data, competitive data, and statistical analyses. Such information is stored in a central computer, but it can be easily accessed through personal computers. As a result, the past decade has seen an increasing reliance by managers on PCs for marketing and financial analysis.

One important advance in technology is the placement of scanners in retail stores. The use of laser scanners to scan bar codes on products and record items at checkout counters has provided a wealth of information to manufacturers and retailers. In some markets, consumers use magnetically coded cards, allowing manufacturers to determine the characteristics of buyers of their products. Scanners also provide retailers with up-to-the-minute sales data, giving them the ability to better control inventory. We will consider these advances in data collection in Chapter 7.

ECOLOGICAL TRENDS IN MARKETING

In the late 1980s, marketers were faced with an entirely new influence—the "Green" movement. As suburban homeowners picketed incinerator plants, cities passed new antidumping statutes, and teenagers began refusing to use foam trays in school cafeterias, "environmentalism" became a front-line political issue in the United States. This was reflected in consumer responses to old ways of packaging and selling. A 1990 study found 84 percent of the shoppers surveyed said they were concerned about environmental issues and were changing their shopping habits because of it.[69] We saw how McDonald's changed its corporate posture to align itself with the movement. It is by no means alone. Most manufacturers are developing new products or repositioning old ones to catch up with the trend, which thus far has centered on pollution and recycling.

POLLUTION

Consumer awareness about the hazards of pollution has grown significantly. In 1990, for instance, one survey found that 62 percent of Americans considered pollution a very serious problem, up from 44 percent in 1984.[70] With this new-found support, environmental groups and politicians began targeting manufacturers that they believed produced needless pollutants that clogged precious landfill space. Because 3.6 billion pounds of discarded disposable diapers are delivered to landfills annually, environmentalists started targeting Procter & Gamble, the market leader.

P&G fought on two fronts. First, it attempted to satisfy environmentalists by reducing the weight of its diaper packaging and by contributing $20 million to develop ways to turn its disposables into compost for tree nurseries.[71] But the company also tried to convince consumers its products were not as bad as Green activists claimed. Toward that end, it produced two brochures and mailed them to more than 14 million households, pressing the point that its diapers made up less than 2 percent of the solid waste in municipal landfills. It also attached coupons for Luvs and Pampers.[72] Despite P&G's efforts, legislation proposing bans on disposables is pending in several states.[73]

General Motors, on the other hand, has found opportunity, not risk, in the Green movement. The company has invested heavily in a pollution-free electric car called the Impact. Still in test production, the Impact has been clocked as having a 120-mile range, enough power to reach 60 miles-per-hour in eight seconds, and a top speed of 100 miles-per-hour. Some analysts expect it to be available in the mid 1990s. GM is also positioning itself as an environmentally friendly company by developing "intelligent vehicle" highway systems that give drivers up-to-date traffic information in the hopes they can avoid congestion and wasteful mileage.[74]

EXHIBIT 4.9

A Consumer Organization Promotes Recycling

IF YOU'RE NOT RECYCLING
YOU'RE THROWING IT ALL AWAY.
SM
A little reminder from the Environmental Defense Fund that if you're not recycling, you're throwing away a lot more than just your trash.
You and your community can recycle. Please write the Environmental Defense Fund at: EDF-Recycling, 257 Park Avenue South, New York, NY 10010, for a free brochure that will tell you virtually everything you need to know about recycling.
EDF
TM
Ad Council
© 1988 EDF

RECYCLING The drive to recycle grew out of the antipollution movement. Consumer groups such as the Environmental Defense Fund have mounted publicity campaigns to heighten recycling awareness (see Exhibit 4.9). There is evidence these campaigns are taking hold. One survey found that 41 percent of newspaper buyers said they would cancel their subscriptions if they knew the company did not use recycled paper.[75]

As a result, many companies have begun using recycling as a promotional mechanism. Coca-Cola and PepsiCo have announced they are going to market their brands in recycled plastic bottles.[76] To help promote its microwave entrees, Kraft General Foods advertised the fact that its meals were served on recycled plastic trays. Fuji Photo Film, Bristol Myers Squibb, Calvin Klein, and Estee Lauder all are working on environmentally friendly packaging.[77]

Manufacturers and retailers run the risk of overloading consumers with their claims. But in the short term, Green marketing has become a potent force.

ECONOMIC TRENDS

A fourth environmental influence on marketing opportunity is economic conditions. Economic stagnation inhibits marketers from seeking new opportunities, while a boom in spending may encourage them to increase R&D budgets and accelerate the pace of new-product introductions.

The 1980s began with a severe recession that had a lasting effect on consumer purchasing habits. The subsequent recovery was rich and enduring. Then, the recession of 1990–92 again wreaked havoc with consumer markets. Predictably, the three periods affected assessments of environmental opportunity and threat.

THE EARLY-1980s RECESSION AND MID-1980s RECOVERY

Rampant inflation in the late 1970s and deep recession in the early 1980s reduced real income for many consumers and led to a sharp reduction of **discretionary income** *(the amount left after paying for necessities and taxes)*. As a result, consumers reduced spending and became more price sensitive. They were more likely to buy low-priced **private brands** *(store-owned brands sold at lower prices than national brands)* or **generic products** *(unbranded products identified by product category only)*.[78] Consumers were also more likely to hunt for bargains and to use coupons to save money.

Although the subsequent recovery increased discretionary income and produced a greater willingness by consumers to spend for services, electronics, and time-saving products, a vestige of the recession remained in that consumers stayed price sensitive and less loyal to nationally advertised brands than before.

The American economy grew at an average rate of only 2 percent after 1984. The stock market crash of October 1987 put a temporary damper on consumer spending by undermining confidence in the economy. But spending quickly rebounded to pre-crash levels.

THE 1990–92 RECESSION

The 1990–92 recession was steep and enduring. It differed from the one ten years before in one key respect: Instead of relying on generic or no-name brands, manufacturers relied on a strategy of **value pricing** *(providing less expensive versions of brand-name products)*. With manufacturers putting the name of major brands on less-expensive "clones," consumers were given far more choices than ten years before.[79] In the midst of the recession, Wilkinson Sword launched an economy line of razors designed to compete with private brands. Similarly, McDonald's instituted a value pricing policy by marking down some of its menu items to below a dollar. The chain is reacting to reduced consumer discretionary income and similar cuts by Wendy's and Burger King.[80]

Companies are also aiming value-price advertising campaigns at the recession. One motel chain ran an ad for $29 rooms saying "You don't need any more bad news about the economy"[81] (see Exhibit 4.10). If the recession accomplished anything for marketers, it let many turn risk into opportunity by recognizing a previously untapped category, the price-sensitive consumer.

A LOOK TO THE FUTURE

More enduring changes in the economy have caused some marketers to sound a note of caution in assessing future opportunity. Intensified foreign competition has increased expenditures by American consumers on foreign goods. Imports are sub-

EXHIBIT 4.10

Advertising to Price-Sensitive Consumers in a Recession

stantially higher than exports, resulting in a trade gap that has weakened the economy. Finding it difficult to compete with the lower labor costs and higher productivity of foreign competitors, many American manufacturers are scaling back their manufacturing facilities and are buying parts and assembled products from foreign countries, particularly Japan. Corporate America's weakened manufacturing base has led to a greater emphasis on service, and less on production in our economy.[82]

The shift to a service economy and the cutback in America's industrial base may lead to long-term problems that have not yet played out. If America's manufacturing base continues to shrink, the economy of the 1990s will suffer.

On the brighter side, there is evidence that American industry is becoming more effective in competing with foreign manufacturers. Many American companies have become more sensitive to consumer needs and have adopted the quality control methods that gave Japanese companies an edge in productivity, allowing them to achieve greater efficiencies in production and marketing. Further, a weakened American dollar has made foreign goods more expensive in the United States and American goods less expensive abroad. As a result, the trade gap is decreasing. Perhaps the best economic assessment for the 1990s is cautious optimism, an upbeat view of marketing opportunity—but not too upbeat.

THE LEGAL CONTEXT OF MARKETING

If we are to understand how marketing strategies operate, we must first have some awareness of the laws that affect marketing actions. There are three basic purposes for enacting marketing legislation. The first is to ensure fair competition. Before the turn of the century, large monopolies in oil, banking, and the railroads were eliminating competition and charging consumers high prices as a result. The Sherman Antitrust Act, passed in 1890, prohibits monopolies or collusive practices by competitors that restrain trade. The act attempts to ensure that smaller competitors will not be driven from the marketplace and that consumers will have a reasonable set of alternatives from which to choose.

The second objective is to protect consumers from unfair business practices. Consumers have the right to safe products, to honest advertising, and to full disclosure of product contents and terms of sale. Laws have been passed ensuring consumers of these rights. For example, the Truth in Lending Act, passed in 1968, requires lenders to fully disclose all finance charges in consumer credit agreements.

The third objective is to protect the interests of society. Businesses must have a responsibility to protect the environment. Yet society can not rely on the good will of corporations to fulfill these responsibilities. Laws have been passed to protect the environment, such as the Clean Air Act that requires companies to conform to strict controls to avoid air pollution and acid-rain emissions.

Table 4.1 groups various laws affecting marketing strategy according to which component of the marketing mix they affect—the company's product, distribution, advertising, or pricing. The product-related laws are designed to protect the consumer by guaranteeing product safety and disclosure of product contents. The Consumer Product Safety Commission Act, for instance, created a commission with the power to test and recall unsafe products. Laws (namely the Lanham Act) are also designed to protect a company's **trademarks** (that is, *the names and symbols used to identify brands and companies*) by registering them.

Distribution-related laws are designed to restrict three types of practices: (1) establishing an **exclusive sales territory** *wherein a territory is granted by a manufacturer to an intermediary* (a wholesaler or retailer), giving it sole rights to sell the company's product in the area; (2) **exclusive-dealing contracts** *requiring an intermediary to buy only the company's lines;* and (3) **tying contracts** *requiring an intermediary to take other products in the company's line in order to obtain the desired product.* These restrictions apply only if a court judges the actions by the manufacturer to be in restraint of trade.

Advertising laws have empowered the Federal Trade Commission to eliminate deceptive and misleading advertising. For example, the FTC forced Warner Lambert to stop advertising that Listerine mouthwash helps prevent colds and, further, required the company to advertise that the former claim was not true.[83] The FTC also monitors and controls advertising to children. As an example, it prohibited advertisements for Spiderman vitamins that could have encouraged children to consume harmful amounts of vitamins.[84]

In the pricing area, government regulations restrict three pricing practices. In **price fixing,** *competitors agree to maintain fixed price levels to avoid competition.* In **predatory pricing,** *a company attempts to establish market dominance by pricing below cost to drive other competitors out of the market,* then raises prices once it has established market dominance. Both practices are considered anti-competitive and are outlawed by the Sherman Antitrust Act. In **price discrimination,** *a seller charges different prices to intermediaries for the same product.* The Robinson–Patman Act prohibits this practice unless there is some cost justification to charge a lower price to one buyer than another (for example, savings in transportation costs or for large purchase quantities).

REGULATION

Regulatory trends affect marketing opportunity because they define the constraints that government places on marketing actions. Regulation is closely tied to the legal environment since laws have established regulatory agencies such as the Federal

TABLE 4.1

Selected Laws Affecting Marketing Actions

PRODUCT RELATED	PROVISIONS OF LEGISLATION
Lanham Act (1946)	Provides trademark protection for brand names on goods shipped in interstate or foreign commerce.
Fair Packaging and Labeling Act (1966)	Requires manufacturers to disclose ingredients and volume on the package.
Truth in Lending Act (1968)	Requires full disclosure of all finance charges in consumer credit agreements.
Child Protection Act (1969)	Allows the Food and Drug Administration to remove dangerous children's products from the market.
Consumer Product Safety Commission Act (1972)	Established the Consumer Product Safety Commission to identify, ban, and recall unsafe products.
DISTRIBUTION RELATED	
Sherman Antitrust Act (1890)	Limits right of seller to award an intermediary exclusive rights to a territory if such an exclusive arrangement restricts competition.
Clayton Act (1914)	Prohibits exclusive dealing wherein a seller requires a customer to buy only the company's line. Also prohibits *tying contracts* wherein a seller requires a customer to take other products in the seller's line.
ADVERTISING RELATED	
Federal Trade Commission Act (1914)	Established the Federal Trade Commission to monitor unfair practices, including advertising.
Wheeler–Lea Amendment to FTC Act (1938)	Enlarged the powers of the Federal Trade Commission to prevent deceptive and misleading advertising.
PRICING RELATED	
Sherman Antitrust Act (1890)	Outlaws price fixing and predatory pricing in restraint of trade.
Robinson–Patman Act (1936)	Prohibits price discrimination wherein the same product is sold to intermediaries at different prices without cost justification.

Trade Commission and the Food and Drug Administration. These and other regulatory agencies are responsible for ensuring that products are safe, that advertising is truthful, and that full information is provided to consumers.

The Federal Trade Commission (FTC) and the Food and Drug Administration (FDA) exert the most control over marketing actions. The *Federal Trade Commission* was established in 1914 to curb the monopoly powers of big business and unfair trade practices. Since then, it has also taken on a watchdog role to discourage unfair and deceptive advertising. The *Food and Drug Administration* was created in 1906 largely as a result of the outcry produced by Upton Sinclair's book *The Jungle*, which exposed unsanitary conditions in Chicago's meat-packing houses. The FDA is empowered to set product standards to ensure consumer safety and to require disclosure of product contents. The basic issue is the extent to which government regulatory agencies should become involved in ensuring consumer welfare and fair competition. The alternative to government regulation is to let an industry regulate itself.

The Reagan administration strongly favored industry self-regulation and began to dismantle some of the regulatory apparatus put in place in the 1960s and 1970s. When the Reagan Administration arrived in Washington, the new president made his views on regulation known by saying, "Unnecessary regulation simply adds to the costs to business and consumers alike without commensurate benefits."[85] The result was the dismantling of a torrent of rules and standards enacted in the 1970s governing industry.[86] The FTC, the FDA, the Environmental Protection Agency, and the Consumer Product Safety Commission scaled back regulatory actions. For example, in the 1970s, the FTC would bring action against an advertiser if an advertisement had the *potential* to deceive. In the 1980s, advertising had to be *clearly* deceptive to *most* consumers before the FTC would take action.

The Bush Administration has slowed this process of deregulation by putting more teeth into the agencies neglected by the Reagan Administration. One reason for this reversal is that surveys showed a majority of American consumers believe that deregulation has hurt them.[87] The greatest activity has come from the Food and Drug Administration under a newly appointed chairman, David Kessler. In a two-week period during the summer of 1991, Kessler's FDA promulgated dozens of proposals that were designed to end the confusion over food-labeling that had confounded the agency for 25 years (see Ethical and Environmental Issues in Marketing box). A mix of Congressional mandates and FDA initiatives, the proposals sought to force manufacturers to disclose such things as waxes used to coat produce and the percentage of fruit in juices. The sudden flurry was described by one FDA official as "the largest amount of food labeling activity since the early 1970s."[88]

The FTC also began taking a more activist stand, although less uniformly. In 1990, its new chairman announced the advertising industry would be held accountable for ads or practices regarded as unfair and deceptive.[89] Even the Federal Communications Commission—long a hallmark of Reagan deregulation—grew more aggressive, adopting rules in 1991 that limited the number of commercials on children's programs.[90]

SUMMARY

1. **What creates opportunities and threats in the marketing environment?** Opportunities and threats are created by social, technological, economic, and regulatory trends in the environment. Trends such as the increasing proportion of women employed outside the home, a decrease in family size, and more emphasis on health and fitness are opportunities for some companies and threats for other companies.
2. **How can marketers systematically analyze environmental changes to better shape marketing strategies?**

ETHICAL AND ENVIRONMENTAL ISSUES IN MARKETING

Ethics and Nutritional Labeling: Are Marketers Helping or Hurting Consumers

When Food and Drug Administration agents swept into a Minnesota warehouse in April 1991 and seized 2,400 cases of Citrus Hill Fresh Choice orange juice, the marketing industry was left speechless. There had been seizures before, but no one could remember any this aggressively waged. The same day, federal prosecutors acting on the FDA's behalf filed suit against Procter & Gamble, the juice's manufacturer, alleging misrepresentation on grounds Citrus Hill was made from concentrate. The suit was more than a message to P&G, which quickly agreed to arop the word "fresh" from the labels. It was an alert to the marketing industry that new FDA chief David Kessler meant to rewrite—or more literally, write—the rules on food labeling.

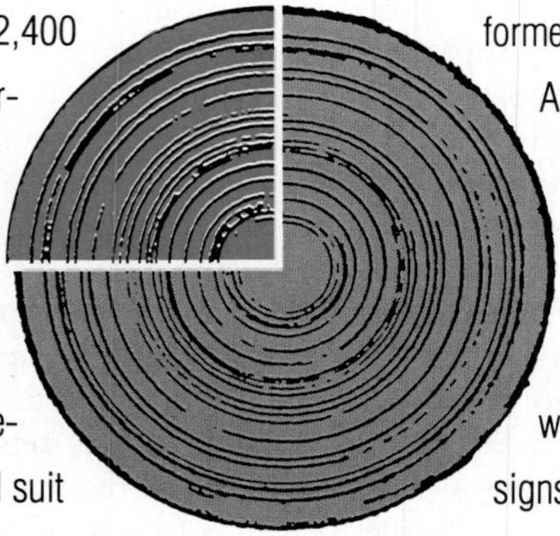

Advertising Age called the Citrus Hill incident a "regulatory milestone," but it will not likely be the only one on Kessler's watch. In mid-1991, the lawyer and former director of medicine at New York's Albert Einstein College of Medicine began turning his attention to cholesterol and fat-free claims.

A month after the juice seizure, several food makers were ordered to wipe "no cholesterol" claims and heart signs off their vegetable oil labels or face similar actions. Since all vegetable oils are cholesterol free, the FDA maintained that using the 100-percent free claim wrongly implied differences existed. P&G immediately took the claim off its Crisco and Puritan oils, but companies such as CPC Best Foods—makers of Mazola—were less eager to admit defeat, insisting instead that they were really helping consumers. The claim "is intended to correct a common conception that all fats and oils contain choles-

Marketers systematically analyze the environment through a process of environmental scanning. This process requires teams of specialists to collect environmental information and assess its potential impact on the company. Such information is available through a variety of sources including marketing research surveys, the business press, industry sources, and research companies that specialize in assessing environmental trends.

3. **What are the basic environmental trends—social, technological, economic, and legal and regulatory—that will shape marketing opportunities in the 1990s?**

   Four types of *social trends* directly influence opportunity: changes in consumer demographic characteristics, life-styles, cultural values and subcultural influ-

ETHICAL AND ENVIRONMENTAL ISSUES IN MARKETING

terol," one CPC statement said.

For the FDA, the ethical issue was whether food marketers were misleading consumers who trusted their nutritional claims. The agency maintained that the 100-percent cholesterol-free claims merely deflected attention from the high-fat contents of products that could contribute to heart ailments. As evidence of the potential harm, the agency referred to studies showing 40 percent of shoppers believe cholesterol-free products are low in fat. To heighten consumer awareness, Kessler's agency began working on a series of prototype labels that would compare a product's fat, cholesterol, fiber and sodium content with "daily reference values," or the recommended maximum amount of each that a consumer should have each day.

The proposed labels raise the issue of how much consumers need to know and how much of it must be reflected on labels. The simple answer is that any information which helps consumers make reasoned choices about how to protect their health is good for them.

Question: Was Citrus Hill misleading consumers in using the word "fresh" on its labels? Do marketers mislead consumers in using fat-free and cholesterol-free claims? How can marketers ensure such claims do not mislead consumers?

Sources: "P&G Gives in, Axes Its 'Fresh' Label," *Advertising Age,* April 29, 1991, p. 1; "Washington Cracks Another Whip Against Misleading Claims," *Adweek's Marketing Week*, May 20, 1991. p. 7; "The FDA is Swinging a Sufficiently Large Two-By-Four," *Business Week,* May 27, 1991, p. 44; "Cholesterol Crackdown," *Advertising Age*, May 20, 1991, pp. 1 and 56; "FDA Orders Vegetable Oil Makers to Drop No Cholesterol Claim," *Marketing News*, June 10, 1991, p. 8; and "Juice Label Rule Asked by FDA," *New York Times*, July 2, 1991, p. D1.

ences. Demographically, the most significant trends in the 1980s were the greater numbers of baby boomers and elderly consumers in the marketplace, the changing character of the American family as a result of smaller families and more singles, and the increasing proportion of working women.

The 1980s saw significant life-style changes, too. Male and female roles have begun to shift, as more women have entered the workforce. In addition, consumers are placing greater emphasis on health and nutrition. Baby boomers and youth are showing greater conservatism. The American consumer of the 1980s displayed different cultural values from consumers of earlier years, emphasizing personal enhancement while also emphasizing greater traditionalism through family values and the work ethic. Subcultures are also receiving more attention, with marketers targeting particular segments of African Americans, Hispanic Americans, and Asian Americans.

Important changes in the *technological environment* have provided consumers with new shopping and entertainment options and have given businesses more-powerful data-gathering and analysis capabilities.

Ecological trends have also had an impact on defining marketing opportunity. Greater awareness of the importance of environmental protection has placed more emphasis on creating a pollution-free environment and recycling products.

Economic trends such as steep recessions in the 1980s and 1990s had a lasting effect on consumers, making them more price conscious and less brand loyal. Slow growth in the late 1980s, more-intense foreign competition, and the reduced manufacturing base of many U.S. companies may be grounds for concern well into the 1990s.

The most significant *regulatory trend* of the 1980s was the Reagan administration's dismantling of much of the regulatory apparatus designed to protect consumers. The result has been reduced powers of the FTC to control advertising practices and the weakened regulatory roles of the Consumer Product Safety Commission, the Food and Drug Administration, and the Environmental Protection Agency. The Bush administration has strengthened the regulatory role of many of these agencies.

KEY TERMS

Environmental scanning (p. 106)
Demographics (p. 106)
Life-styles (p. 106)
Cultural values (p. 107)
Subcultural influences (p. 107)
Subcultures (p. 117)
Videotex systems (p. 122)
Electronic retailing (p. 123)
Discretionary income (p. 127)
Private brands (p. 127)
Generic products (p. 127)
Value pricing (p. 127)
Trademarks (p. 129)
Exclusive sales territory (p. 129)
Exclusive-dealing contracts (p. 129)
Tying contracts (p. 129)
Price fixing (p. 129)
Predatory pricing (p. 129)
Price discrimination (p. 129)

QUESTIONS

1. What are the key sources of marketing opportunity? Provide examples.
2. Firms try to create opportunity from potential threat. In turn, opportunity almost always leads to threat. Why? Provide examples of each of these two circumstances.
3. What is the purpose of environmental scanning? How can McDonald's apply environmental scanning in assessing the marketing environment of the 1990s?
4. What are the implications of changes in birth rate and life expectancy for marketing strategy? Cite examples.
5. What are the most significant changes in the composition of the American family? What are the causes for these changes? What are the marketing implications?
6. Social changes in the 1980s created environmental threats for the following companies and industries:
   a. Avon: faced with an increasing proportion of working women
   b. Pepsi: faced with a decreasing proportion of teenagers
   c. the liquor industry: faced with an increasing proportion of baby boomers

   In each case, what was the threat? How did each company/industry try to turn threat into opportunity?
7. What are the marketing implications of changing male–female roles for:
   a. a financial-service company
   b. an automobile manufacturer
   c. a producer of packaged foods

8. What types of companies might regard the increasing emphasis on health and nutrition as a threat? What types of companies are most likely to regard these trends as an opportunity? How have companies threatened by these trends tried to turn them into opportunities?
9. The chapter suggested that youth and baby boomers were becoming more conservative. What are the marketing implications of such a trend for:
   a. clothing manufacturers
   b. producers of personal grooming products
10. Consider the following technological trends: (a) in-home shopping through cable TV, (b) electronic retailing, (c) widespread adoption of VCRs for in-home entertainment.
    What kind of businesses have considered each of the preceding a threat? Why?
11. The chapter cited an increase in concern on the part of consumers for environmental protection, particularly in ensuring a pollution-free environment. Cite examples of firms adjusting their strategies to address these environmental concerns.
12. What has been the position of the Food and Drug Administration toward product labeling? What are the implications for marketing strategy?

QUESTIONS: YOU ARE THE DECISION MAKER

1. An executive for a large industrial firm producing standardized items was asked about the need for environmental scanning in his company. He made the following comment:

   You know, we sell a commodity product in a stable environment. Even in the 1990–92 recession, we did not hurt much. I don't see the need for us to be concerned about environmental change. When you're in a stable business without too much product change, you don't have to be that concerned about environmental scanning.

   Do you agree with this assessment? Under what circumstances might environmental changes represent a threat to this company?
2. A manufacturer of home cleaning products introduces a new floor cleaner and wax combination. The advantage of the product is that it removes dirt more quickly and effectively while protecting the floor. The company decides to advertise with a theme of a wife using the product, then guests coming in and marveling at the floor. The final scene shows the husband extolling the wife's homemaking abilities.
   a. In what ways does this advertising approach contradict basic demographic, life-style, and cultural changes described in this chapter? (Be specific in citing these trends.)
   b. What type of an advertising approach could be used to better conform to the trends you cited above? What are the advantages of your suggested approach?
3. One automobile industry executive, commenting on the advisability of designing ads for the African-American market, said

   We develop one campaign for the total market based on the performance advantages of our cars. Yes, we could spend money developing a different advertising campaign for African Americans. But why should we, when African Americans use pretty much the same reasons for buying as whites?

   What are the pros and cons of developing an advertising campaign specifically directed to the African-American market?
4. One marketing executive, commenting on the deregulation during the Reagan administration, said

   Deregulation was overdue. Regulatory agencies were starting to be a real problem for us. Take the FTC. We had to worry about substantiating claims we would ordinarily regard as typical advertising pitches, like "Gets clothes cleaner than most other leading detergents." Now, we don't have that problem. The FTC leaves us alone unless a claim is clearly misleading.

   Do you feel that marketing executives should regard deregulation as favorable and government regulation as unfavorable? Under what circumstances might government regulation help a marketer?

CHAPTER 5

Opportunity in the International Marketplace

YOUR FOCUS IN CHAPTER 5

To learn:

- *The reasons firms enter international markets.*
- *The pros and cons of global versus local international marketing strategies.*
- *The steps involved in developing an international marketing plan.*
- *The environmental factors most likely to influence a firm's decision to enter foreign markets.*
- *The strategies firms use to enter foreign markets.*

Procter & Gamble: Experiencing the Ups and Downs of International Marketing

Procter & Gamble (P&G) may be the number one marketer of consumer packaged goods in the United States, with leading brands such as Tide detergent, Crest toothpaste, Folgers coffee, and Pampers disposable diapers. But until recently, when it came to competing abroad, P&G was often humbled. It frequently misread consumer needs and competitive intentions. It was often beaten to the punch by tough competitors like Unilever in Europe and Kao in Japan. And, it has had a tendency to fritter away its resources on the second, third, or fourth position in a foreign market rather than concentrating its resources to be number one. As a result, P&G was not the feared giant abroad that it is at home.

All that is slowly changing as P&G learns to be an effective global marketer. Much of the change is due to Edwin Artzt, P&G's current CEO and former head of international operations. Artzt is spearheading a drive to be a major player in the newly opened markets of Eastern Europe with the 1990 acquisition of the leading detergent company in Czechoslovakia and possible deals in Poland and Hungary.[1] He made P&G a world player in cosmetics with the acquisitions of Noxell (makers of Cover Girl) in 1989, Old Spice in 1990, and Max Factor and Betrix in 1991, all companies with a strong international presence.[2] In addition, he has strengthened P&G's position in Japan to a point where losses were turned into profits by the late 1980s, and the country is now P&G's second most profitable foreign market.[3] These efforts are reflected in the increased importance of international markets to P&G: Overseas operations represented only 12 percent of company profits in 1984; by 1990 they represented well over one-third.

The reason for P&G's increasing success in foreign markets is no secret. The company has simply shed its philosophy that what works in the United States is likely to work abroad and is now more attuned to the needs and customs of foreign consumers.

Japan is a good microcosm of P&G's transition to effective international marketer. As Artzt said, P&G "stormed into the Japanese market [in 1972] with American products, American managers, American advertising, and American sales methods and promotional strategies."[4] As a result of this all-American strategy, P&G failed to take account of two critical components of Japan's marketing environment: consumer customs and habits and Japan's distribution system.

The lack of understanding of the Japanese consumer was most telling. P&G created the disposable diaper market in Japan by introducing Pampers in 1977. The product was relatively thick and bulky, designed for mothers who intended to leave diapers on their babies for long periods. P&G failed to realize that Japanese women are among the most tidy and fastidious in the world, doing twice as many washloads and changing diapers twice as often as the average American family. The bulky diaper encouraged Japanese companies such as Kao and Uni-Charm to come in with a thinner, leak-resistant diaper geared to the needs of Japanese mothers. Pampers share of disposable diapers went from 90 percent in 1977 to 7 percent in 1985.[5]

In another example of the company's lack of understanding of the Japanese consumer, P&G introduced Camay Soap with a commercial showing a man meeting a woman and complimenting her on her skin. But in Japanese culture, it is bad manners for a man to impose his opinion on the choice of a woman's toiletry articles. As a result, Camay's market share did not rise above 2 percent.

P&G also stumbled in failing to take into account the differences in distribution between the United States and Japan. In the United States, most large packaged-goods manufacturers sell directly to supermarket chains such as A&P or Kroger. But Japan is dominated by 325,000 small retail stores serviced by a large number of wholesalers. These wholesalers are essential in reaching small retailers. Further, Japanese culture requires establishing personal relationships to cement the loyalty of wholesalers. Yet P&G chose to follow its domestic distribution strategy by going directly to retailers—alienating wholesalers and leaving P&G at a disadvantage to companies like Kao, who has excellent, long-standing relations with wholesalers.[6]

Under Artzt, P&G recognized the fallacy of its all-American approach and began orienting its marketing strategies toward local tastes and customs. It created an improved diaper with one-third the thickness of the original model. As a result, Pampers' share went from 7 percent in 1985 to 28 percent by 1988. The new diaper also became the prototype for Ultra Pampers, now sold worldwide. The company also changed its advertising focus to account for Japanese sensitivities, eliminating the man in the Camay ad, for example, and linking the product to a beautiful complexion. And, P&G began establishing long-term relationships with wholesalers to ensure reaching small retail stores.

P&G has had its ups and downs in international markets, but now things are looking up because of a greater willingness to adapt marketing strategies to local needs and customs.

THE IMPORTANCE OF INTERNATIONAL MARKETING

Procter & Gamble's experiences show that international marketing is likely to increase in importance as more U.S. firms look for opportunity abroad. **International marketing** *is the development of marketing strategies to sell products across national boundaries.* From the perspective of the United States, this includes marketing our goods abroad (exports) and marketing foreign goods here (imports). Exhibit 5.1 shows both the export and import side of international marketing with a Chevrolet ad directed toward a German audience and a Honda ad directed toward an American audience.

The importance of international marketing is reflected in the fact that three-fourths of manufacturing jobs in the United States are linked to exports.[7] In 1990, exports were $394 billion, representing almost 15 percent of the country's gross national product. Imports of foreign goods were even higher, $495 billion, reflecting the United States' increasing trade gap.[8]

International marketing tends to be big business. About 80 percent of exports are sold by the 250 largest companies in the United States. Coca-Cola gets 77 percent of its revenue from selling in 155 countries;[9] it makes more money in Japan than in the United States. Colgate-Palmolive relies more on foreign sales than its larger archrival, P&G, with 60 percent of sales coming from overseas markets compared to 40 percent for P&G. In 1990 Kellogg's sales abroad exceeded those in the United States for the first time.[10] Other companies that earn more revenue abroad than in the United States are IBM, Digital Equipment, Gillette, Johnson & Johnson, and Pfizer.

On the other side of the coin, foreign companies like Sony, Hitachi, Toyota, and Mercedes have established a major presence in the United States. Many foreign-owned companies such as Nestlé, Lever, Lipton, and Shell Oil are often mistaken for American companies, because they earn a significant percentage of their revenues in the United States. Swiss-based Nestlé generates only 5 percent of its earnings in its domestic market.

The data cited above may show the importance of international marketing in the American economy, but they do not reflect the growing importance of international operations. The proportion of our gross national product represented by sales abroad will continue to grow into the next century. Yet there is little sign that the trade deficit resulting from greater imports than exports will diminish, meaning that sales by foreign competitors in the United States will increase. This means that *anyone entering the field of marketing must be aware of how to meet customer needs abroad and how to compete with foreign marketers at home.*

REASONS FOR ENTERING INTERNATIONAL MARKETS

Why are U.S. marketers increasingly looking abroad for opportunity? Four key reasons are cited: stagnant domestic markets, govenment regulations at home, decreasing trade barriers abroad, and globalization of the marketplace.

STAGNANT DOMESTIC MARKETS

One of the most important reasons cited for entering foreign markets is that they offer a greater potential for faster growth than domestic markets. The sharp 1990–92 recession, the decrease in the value of the American dollar (making American goods cheaper abroad), and a leveling off in demand in key categories like autos

EXHIBIT 5.1

Ad for an American Car Maker Selling Abroad and a Foreign Car Maker Selling in the United States

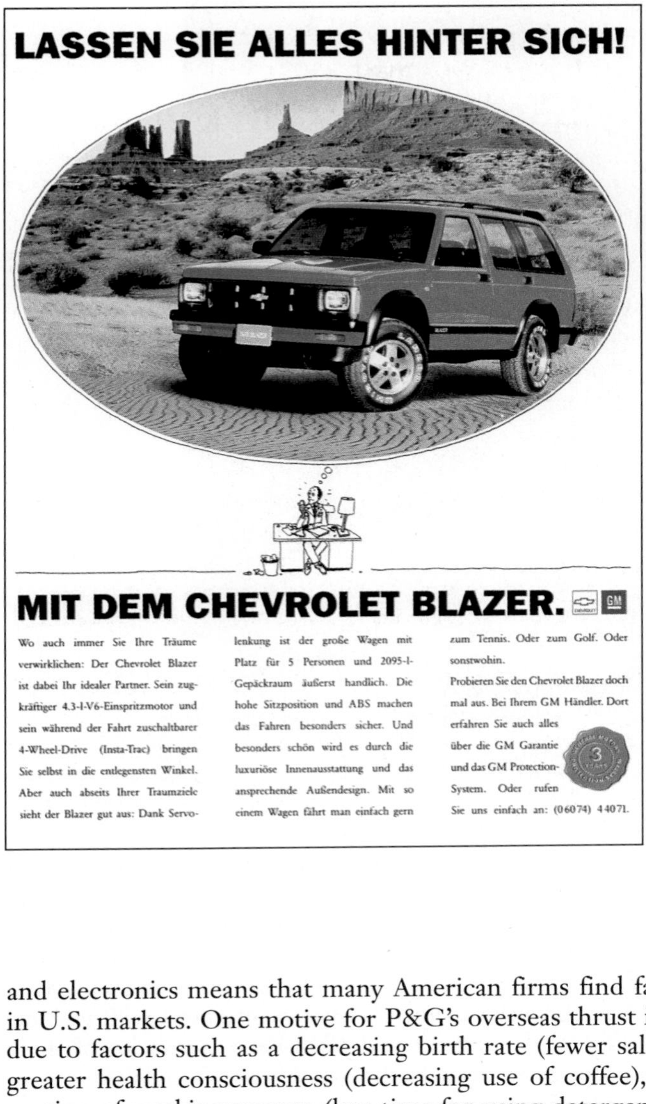

and electronics means that many American firms find faster growth abroad than in U.S. markets. One motive for P&G's overseas thrust is stagnant domestic sales due to factors such as a decreasing birth rate (fewer sales of disposable diapers), greater health consciousness (decreasing use of coffee), and the increasing proportion of working women (less time for using detergents).

Whirlpool is another company expanding its global operations due to a lack of opportunity at home. The company saw an eight percent decrease in sales of its major appliances in early 1991 due to a saturated market for kitchen appliances, a lack of new housing construction, and increased competition from General Electric and Maytag. On the other hand, in Europe only 14 percent of households own clothes dryers and only 19 percent have dishwashers. This adds up to an expected growth rate for kitchen appliances that will be twice as high as in the American market.

Whirlpool reacted by buying a controlling interest in Philips, a major producer of appliances in Europe. It is also establishing markets in Asia and Latin America. It entered a joint venture with Acros to sell its appliances to an emerging middle

EXHIBIT 5.2

Whirlpool Seeks Opportunity Abroad

class in Mexico (see Exhibit 5.2). It identified a growing market of young professionals who wanted Western-style appliances in India and adapted its washing machines for that country so that agitators would not snarl flowing Indian saris.[11]

In addition to appliances, other industries with low growth in the United States have also looked abroad. For example, Kellogg has increased its European presence because several Western European countries have experienced a 20 percent growth rate for cereals.[12] Digital Equipment and IBM have seen sales of their mainframe computers in Europe grow at twice the rate of the United States. And Anheuser Busch is increasing foreign operations, because beer consumption in the United States is stagnant.

GOVERNMENT REGULATIONS AT HOME

Another reason companies seek marketing opportunities abroad is due to government regulations at home. For example, when AT&T divested itself of its affiliates, known as the Baby Bells, part of the agreement was that the affiliates would not manufacture telephone equipment, provide long-distance service, or expand into cable television so as to ensure they would not compete with AT&T. But these restrictions did not apply to foreign markets. As a result, the Baby Bells, such as Nynex, US West, and Pacific Telesis, have begun looking to Europe for opportunities. As the head of international operations at Nynex said, "We are simply recognizing that the opportunities for growth are greater outside the United States than within."[13] As a result, Nynex (which serves New York and New England) is negotiating with Poland and Hungary to restructure their primitive telephone service, is providing computer software to the British financial-service industry, and is providing facsimile transmission (FAX) capabilities to the Scandinavian Telecommunications Service.

US West, based in Denver, is building Eastern Europe's first cellular telephone system in Hungary. It is also laying a 12,000-mile fiber-optic cable across Russia to improve long-distance service in that vast country. Pacific Telesis is also actively seeking opportunities in Europe with a $6 billion contract to build a cellular network in Germany and cable television networks in England.[14]

Government regulations may also encourage foreign competitors to seek opportunity in the United States. The high interest rates maintained by the Japanese government to cool off a highly charged economy have had the desired effect of decreasing spending on luxury items by Japanese consumers. Decreased spending at home and recession in the United States have prompted many Japanese companies to look to other foreign markets, primarily Europe and the Far East for opportunity. In 1990, Japanese companies invested $14.4 billion in Europe, a 74 percent increase from the previous year.[15]

DECREASING TRADE BARRIERS ABROAD

Trade barriers abroad are decreasing, prompting firms to look to foreign markets for investment opportunities. In the past, many countries put up trade barriers to protect domestic industries. Currently, many of these barriers are falling in the interest of free global competition. Historically, Japan followed a strict policy of protecting its industries. In the late 1980s, it began opening many of its markets to foreign competitors, particularly in computers and electronics. The world's two closest trading partners, the United States and Canada, have also loosened trade regulations with the North American Free Trade Agreement concluded in 1992 that includes Mexico as well. The agreement will encourage many American companies to look to their neighbor to the north for opportunity and will increase trade between the two countries well beyond the current $150 billion. It is also projected to increase trade with Mexico by $16.7 billion by 1995. The demise of communism in Eastern Europe has also loosened trade restrictions imposed by central planners and opened up these markets to foreign competition.

A further spur to defining marketing opportunity abroad was the elimination of trade barriers in 1992 by the twelve countries in the European Community (better known as the Common Market). The EC plans to introduce a common currency and to coordinate all economic policies. This economic unification will create a market of 320 million people, 25 percent larger than the United States.[16] This will be the largest economic entity in the world, making it a highly attractive marketing opportunity for American companies.

GLOBALIZATION OF THE MARKETPLACE

Another factor encouraging marketers to look abroad for opportunity is the globalization of the marketplace as a result of the convergence of tastes and preferences across many countries. The world is getting smaller because of greater travel and improved communications. Teenagers the world over are exposed to similar fads,

EXHIBIT 5.3

Targeting the Global Teenager

tastes, and peer pressures. Thai, French, and Brazilian teenagers might wear the same brand of jeans. A Sony Walkman is a common sight in the streets of Jakarta, Amsterdam, Tel Aviv, and Shanghai. Swatch watch recognized this trend by targeting its advertising campaign to the global teenager (see Exhibit 5.3). Rock culture is helping fuel this global trend because of the expansion of satellite TV stations. MTV, the rock video channel, aired its first global show in 1989 because it "bet that teens tastes and attitudes are now sufficiently similar to warrant a global assault."[17]

As a result, the opportunity for developing world brands such as Coca-Cola, Marlboro cigarettes, and Swatch watches is greater. Marketers can now introduce brands targeted to global similarities rather than to local differences. That is why Honda created one universal car with minor technical modifications for specific markets.

The globalization of markets increases a company's profits because it is much more cost effective to market one single global brand than a variety of local brands. Marketing a single brand across countries creates significant *economies of scale*, that is, decreases in per unit production costs as the amount produced increases. Moreover, by reinforcing the same theme in their advertising, companies can build up a world image and a competitive advantage in a product category. Coca-Cola summarizes this advantage as "one look, one sight, one sound," meaning that its advertising message is being constantly reinforced, whether a consumer sees it at home or abroad.

THREATS IN INTERNATIONAL MARKETING

Every opportunity has its risks. This is especially true for international marketing, where every reason cited for entering foreign markets—higher growth rates abroad, the elimination of trade barriers, and the globalization of the marketplace—has its inherent threats.

First, looking abroad for growth may leave a company open to competitive inroads at home. This has occurred to General Motors and Ford, both of whom, while placing more emphasis on their European operations, have lost market share to Japanese competitors at home. Japanese manufacturers are producing quality cars at lower costs because of their higher productivity and consistently captured market share from American producers in the 1980s. Losses are continuing in the 1990s. In 1991, GM announced the closing of 21 plants and elimination of 74,000 jobs. Unless American car manufacturers stem these losses at home, they may be in no condition to compete effectively abroad.

Second, although decreasing trade barriers may create opportunities, they also create more-intense competition. Eliminating trade barriers in EC countries may make Europe more accessible to American companies in the short run. But in the long run, European companies may be strengthened by the elimination of trade barriers, because they will find it easier to market their products beyond their national boundaries. Facing larger and stronger European firms may make entry less desirable for American firms. Further, larger European companies could begin to compete with American firms at home. For example, Barilla, the leading pasta maker in Italy, has already extended its reach beyond its home borders to other EC countries. Once economic integration takes place, the company may grow faster and start competing in the United States as well.

Third, although the globalization of markets may create an opportunity for world brands, it may also encourage companies to standardize marketing strategies and to ignore local variations in tastes and customs. This may lead to problems, as was the case with Procter & Gamble's desire to standardize its strategies based on an American mold and its subsequent failures in Japan.

Overall, opportunities in the international marketplace are likely to outweigh threats. The threat of more-intense competition at home and abroad and the need to modify global strategies to account for local tastes are unlikely to deter companies from seeking opportunity abroad. The reasons for entering foreign markets are likely to shape marketing strategies into the next century.

ADAPTATION VERSUS STANDARDIZATION IN INTERNATIONAL MARKETING

The major concerns of international marketers are no different from those of domestic marketers: Develop a strategic plan for growth; ensure new product development; position products to targeted segments; manage, price, advertise, and distribute these products; and control marketing operations. The major difference is that a new dimension is added—a *country*. International marketers must adapt their strategies to differences among countries, yet they must also be aware of the opportunity to sell their products worldwide using more standardized approaches.

As a result, international marketers face a basic conflict that underlies any international marketing strategy—the desirability of selling on a standardized basis to reduce cost and to create a world image versus the necessity of adapting to local needs and customs. The key issue in developing international marketing strategies is where the company should position itself on the continuum from extreme standardization to extreme adaptation.

ADAPTATIVE STRATEGIES

Adaptive strategies *are strategies geared to differing customer needs, cultural norms, trade regulations, economic and political conditions, and competitors on a country-by-country basis.* Some companies follow an adaptive strategy for most of their offerings.[18] Nestlé's marketing managers stay in a particular country for years so as to understand local tastes and customs. The company then develops new products geared to the particular needs of local consumers. For example, Nestlé outsmarted Kellogg in Japan. Kellogg tried to overcome the Japanese tradition of eating fish and rice for breakfast by trying to sell the same kind of cereals sold in the United States, but their only market was kids who ate them as snacks. Nestlé developed cereals that taste like traditional Japanese dishes—seaweed, carrots, coconuts, and papaya. The company spent months testing various formulations until it developed cereals geared to Japanese tastes.[19] As a result, Nestlé outsells Kellogg in Japan.

STANDARDIZED STRATEGIES

Despite the importance of adjusting marketing strategies to local conditions, the trend in international marketing strategies in the last 20 years has been to greater globalization of products and advertising claims. **Standardized strategies** *are global strategies that cut across foreign markets.* This approach assumes that some products have universal appeal.

The advantages of a standardized approach are compelling. As we noted, a world brand avoids the significant costs of developing different brands and advertising campaigns for different countries. By having a worldwide advertising campaign, a company can achieve a dominant position across many countries, giving it a competitive advantage.

There are not many world brands. Colgate toothpaste, Marlboro cigarettes, and Coca-Cola all qualify because they market a leading product or service on a worldwide basis with little variation from country to country, and consumers in these countries have similar needs for the product. Coke "is it," whether you live in Buenos Aires, Seoul, or Montreal (see Exhibit 5.4).

THE KEY STRATEGIC DECISION: LOCAL VERSUS GLOBAL

Ultimately, the international marketer's selection of a standardized (global) or an adaptive (local) approach hinges on whether a product category is subject to regional variations in taste and usage. Products like airline travel, cameras, and automobiles reflect universal tastes. Most food and beverage products, clothing, and cosmetics do not. Coca-Cola is the exception as a world beverage. As we will see, the international marketer's decision on where the brand lies on a global-to-local continuum will affect every aspect of the marketing mix—product, promotion, distribution, and price.

EXHIBIT 5.4

Coca-Cola: A World Brand

Many international companies consistently pursue either standardized or adaptive strategies. Procter & Gamble follows an adaptive strategy. The smell of Camay, the flavor of Crest, and the formula for Head & Shoulders differ from region to region because its toiletries and household products are generally subject to regional variations. Black & Decker follows a global approach. When lower-priced Japanese imports undermined the company's leading position in power tools in the mid 1970s, it mounted a successfully coordinated worldwide response by looking for similarities among the 50 countries it markets to so as to introduce more standardized products, with relatively minor adjustments to account for different electrical systems and safety and industry regulations.[20]

Most international companies fall somewhere between the extremes of a totally standardized or adaptive approach. Figure 5.1 places several of the companies discussed so far on a global-to-local continuum. Coca-Cola and Black & Decker take a more global approach in standardizing their brands and, to a lesser extent, their advertising strategies. Procter & Gamble and Nestlé are closer to the local end of the continuum because their brands and subsidiaries operate independently.

FIGURE 5.1

International Marketers Graphed on a Global to Local Continuum

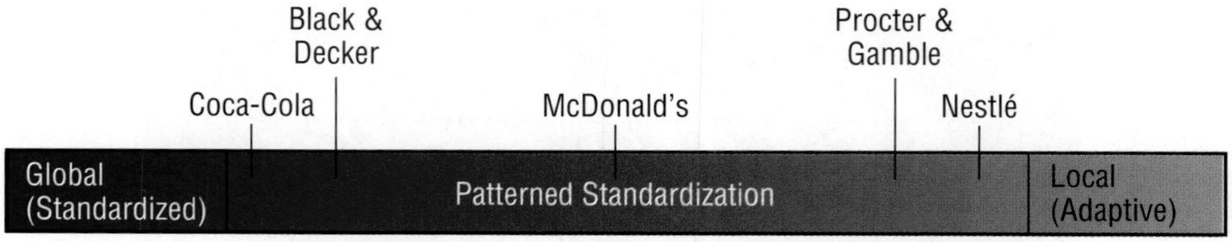

A compromise between a standardized and an adaptive strategy is patterned standardization. In a **patterned standardization strategy,** *a company establishes global marketing strategies while allowing executives in local markets, who are aware of national traits and customs, to vary the implementation of marketing strategies.* The concept behind patterned standardization is captured in a slogan that is becoming increasingly popular among American companies: "Be global, act local."[21]

McDonald's is an example of patterned standardization. Even though it provides the same services worldwide under the same name, it varies its offerings by region. The company offers beer in Germany, wine in France, mutton pie in Australia, and McSpaghetti in the Philippines to compete with local noodle houses.[22]

DEVELOPING INTERNATIONAL MARKETING PLANS AND STRATEGIES

Brands introduced into a foreign market require a marketing plan and a set of strategies. To ensure a brand's success, a number of steps are employed (see Figure 5.2) which are similar to the marketing planning process described in Chapter 3.

The first step is to *evaluate the international marketing environment.* This is the most important step, because it directly influences subsequent decisions on whether to enter an international market and how. Procter & Gamble acquired Rakona, the largest Czech detergent maker, for $45 million in 1991 as a base for expansion in Eastern Europe. Before making this decision, P&G had to assess the level of demand for detergents, the future purchasing power of consumers in the former Eastern-Bloc countries, the advertising and distribution facilities of the product, the trade regulations that might hinder sales, and the political climate.

After analyzing the international environment, management proceeds to the second step, which is to *develop objectives for market share, sales, and profits in foreign markets.* Based on an environmental analysis and a statement of related objectives, management proceeds to step three, which is to *determine whether to enter the market.* Despite environmental limitations, P&G decided to enter Eastern Europe because it saw future opportunity. Although the company anticipates difficulties in marketing products in the short term, it feels that Hungary, Poland, and Czechoslovakia will eventually establish free-market economies leading to increased consumer purchasing power, more major appliances, and an increased demand for detergents.

FIGURE 5.2

The International Marketing Planning Process

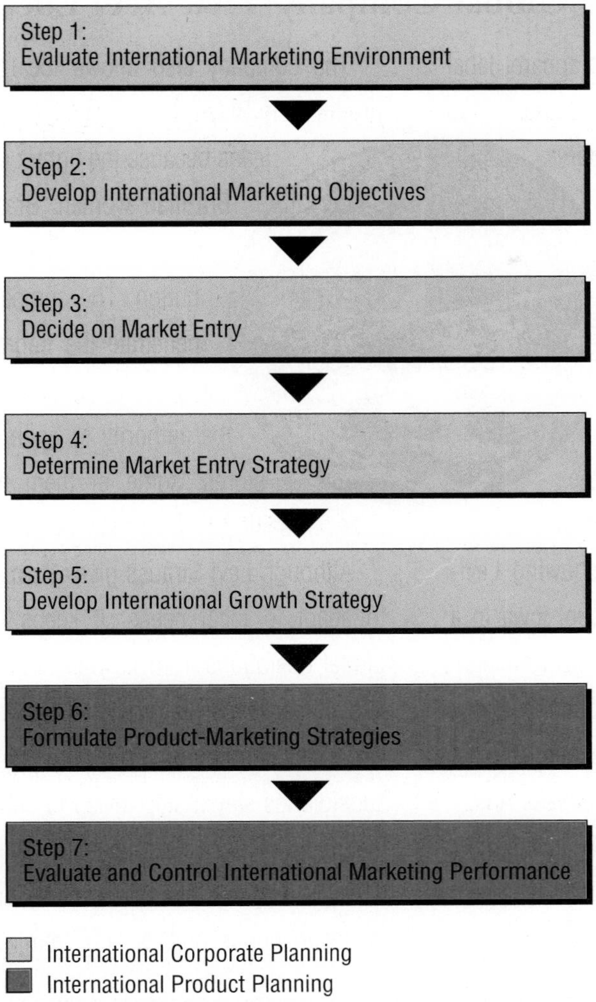

The fourth step is to *determine a market entry strategy*. A market entry strategy might involve building a plant abroad, acquiring a company, entering a joint venture with a domestic company, licensing out the technology, or exporting the product through domestic channels of distribution.

The fifth step is to *develop an overall international growth strategy that determines whether the company will follow a standardized or an adaptive strategy in the markets it is entering*. As we have seen, P&G generally follows an adaptive approach to account for local differences in needs and preferences for household products. At present, Rakona's detergent products are marketed only in Czechoslovakia. P&G will determine whether differences in needs and usage in Poland and Hungary warrant adjusting product formulations.

GLOBAL MARKETING STRATEGIES

Levi Strauss: A Global Company That Acts Local

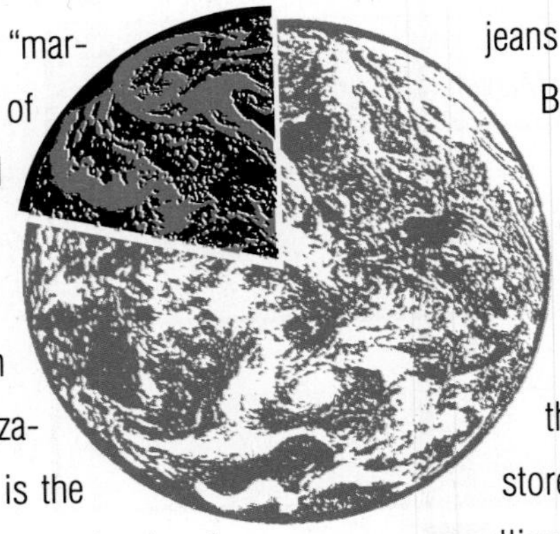

Levi's jeans is the only U.S. apparel label that can be called a world brand. It has capitalized on the Levi's name by "marketing it as an enshrined piece of Americana." Levi's success is based on its ability to present a unified world image while also encouraging local differences (an approach referred to as patterned standardization). The underlying world theme is the company's American roots. In Indonesia, local managers selected a TV commercial showing Levi-clad teenagers cruising around Dubuque, Iowa in a 1960 convertible as the basis for their campaign. Levi Strauss allows this variation because it recognizes that different advertising approaches work in different markets. In Japan, Levi Strauss uses American movie icons such as James Dean as the centerpiece of advertising because of the Japanese obsession with American cultural heroes.

The company also allows local variation in its products. In Brazil, it developed the Feminina line of jeans because the tighter cut is favored by Brazilian women. Brazilian managers can also call the shots on distribution. The company was able to penetrate the fragmented Brazilian market by giving local managers the authority to open a chain of 400 stores, some of them in remote rural areas, selling Levi's products exclusively.

Although Levi Strauss gives its managers latitude to adapt to local needs, it keeps tight control of global operations from its San Francisco headquarters. It approves all product introductions and advertising campaigns. And, to help its foreign subsidiaries stay a step ahead of competition, it has instituted a Quick Response System that links retailers to textile mills via computer and allows them to obtain goods quickly, thus minimizing inventory

The sixth step is to *formulate product marketing strategies*. The company's growth strategy establishes the framework for developing marketing strategies for individual products. If separate detergent brands are established for Poland and Hungary, product managers will be assigned to determine the price, advertising, and distribution strategies for these brands. The seventh and final step is to *evaluate the product's performance and control it by adjusting marketing strategies and expenditures*.

The remainder of this chapter will discuss in depth each of the steps in the international marketing planning process, with a particular emphasis on the first step, evaluating the international marketing environment.

GLOBAL MARKETING STRATEGIES

costs. Levi Strauss could have remained an American rather than a global firm by licensing its famous name to foreign companies. It rejected that approach because it would not have had control of its foreign operations, so it chose to establish company-owned subsidiaries abroad.

TIRAILLÉE, ÉCARTELÉE,
LA LIBERTÉ N'A TOUJOURS PAS CÉDÉ.
LEVI'S

Levi Strauss was not always an effective international marketer. In the mid 1980s, its international operations were losing money because the company lost its focus. It began selling specialty apparel and found that the Levi's name simply did not transfer to such lines. It then went back to its core business, jeans.

Levi's basic approach of maintaining a unified global image while giving local subsidiaries latitude to develop marketing strategies has worked well. In 1990, foreign sales accounted for 60 percent of the company's profits. International operations has the highest profit rate of any of Levi's seven divisions. The company's next step is to enter Eastern Europe and the countries of the former Soviet Union. When it does, chances are its marketing will be global, while managers are thinking locally.

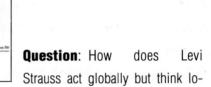

Question: How does Levi Strauss act globally but think locally? What type of patterned standardization approach should Levi Strauss use when it enters Eastern Europe and the new market economies of the former Soviet Union?

Source: "For Levi's, A Flattering Fit Overseas," *Business Week*, November 5, 1990, pp. 76–77.

EVALUATE THE INTERNATIONAL MARKETING ENVIRONMENT

The main difference between international and domestic marketing is that international marketing strategies must take into account differences between countries. Complete standardization of both product and advertising is almost impossible to attain. Even Coca-Cola, the hallmark of product standardization, introduces some variations in its product, making it less sweet in Thailand, for example, to accommodate local tastes. Thus, before entry, international marketers must thoroughly evaluate a country's environment—its cultural norms, business relations, economic conditions, trade regulations, competitive environment, and political environment.

CULTURAL NORMS

Culture *is a society's widely shared norms, values, and customs that lead to common patterns of behavior.* Culture affects how customers react to products and what they buy. In the past, American companies have frequently failed to take cultural norms in foreign markets into account. In 1981 Campbell was forced to call it quits in Brazil despite a $2 million award-winning advertising campaign, because it had failed to recognize that many Brazilian women felt inadequate if they did not make soup from scratch for their families.[23] The company also failed to account for consumer norms when it introduced its condensed soups in Britain, because it was not sensitive to the fact that English consumers were used to ready-to-eat soups in larger cans. As a result, Campbell's cans were at a disadvantage in stores because they appeared small to English consumers.

Companies have also committed gaffes as a result of a lack of knowledge of local languages and dialects. When Coca-Cola was introduced in China, shopkeepers made their own signs in calligraphy with the words *ke kou ke la*, which meant "bite the wax tadpole," hardly an association that encouraged sales. When the company discovered this, it came out with a different set of characters, *ko kou ko le* which not only sounded more like the real thing, but also meant "may the mouth rejoice."[24] Similarly, Pepsi-Cola had to change its slogan "Come alive with Pepsi" in certain Asian countries because the theme translated into "Bring your ancestors back from the dead."[25] And, General Motors discovered it could not use the name Nova on its models worldwide because in Spanish-speaking markets, the name translated to "won't go."[26]

When American companies have accounted for the norms and values of foreign consumers, they have been effective. SmithKline realized that it would have a problem launching its Contac cold medicine in China because of a cultural bent toward herbal medicines in that country and the fact that drugs were dispensed free of charge by a socialist health-care system. The company's research showed, however, that many Chinese consumers wanted to live more modern lives. The company associated the drug with modern living, and as a result, Contac is selling well in China.[27] Similarly, Ford recognized a growing independence among Japanese women in a traditionally male-dominated society, because many more were working full time. In 1990, Ford began targeting its Festiva car to single, young Japanese working women. In the past, carmakers have assumed that Japanese women would have deferred to fathers, husbands, or brothers in the purchase decision for a car.[28]

These examples show the importance of studying the norms, tastes, preferences, and language of consumers before entering a foreign market. McDonald's undertakes an intensive study of a market, first examining demographic trends, then conducting an analysis of political risk, and finally, determining a local population's receptiveness to its products. Further, as we have seen, it adapts its product offerings to local tastes.

BUSINESS RELATIONS

Differences in cultural norms and values not only affect consumer choice, they also affect the way business is conducted abroad. One of the frequent failings of

EXHIBIT 5.5

Getting Beyond an American View of the World

international marketers is to assume that business can be conducted abroad in much the same manner as it is conducted at home (see Exhibit 5.5). For example, Americans are very time-oriented and believe in getting right to the point in their business dealings. But business people from Asia and many Third World countries spend anywhere from 50 to 80 percent of the time talking about everything but business. Their purpose is to try to establish a personal relationship with the other party—a much less important priority to an American.[29]

Another characteristic of American businesspeople that sometimes gets them into trouble in Asian countries is that they are brought up to value individuality and independence of mind. In Japan, the culture dictates that decisions be made mutually. Negotiating sessions among Asians are frequently formalities meant to ratify decisions previously made by consensus. But to Americans, they are seen as a forum for individual give and take for which Asians are not prepared. As a result, misunderstandings develop and business is lost.

American companies are beginning to realize the need to educate their managers in the ways of foreign business relations. Compared to Japanese companies, however, they have a long way to go. Japanese companies generally send young executives abroad to learn the culture and business methods of other countries. For example, when China began opening its markets to the outside world in the 1970s, Mitsubishi, the giant trading concern, sent Chinese-speaking employees to backwater provinces as well as to major cities to establish relations with Chinese officials.[30] Few American companies send their executives abroad for the same purpose.

ECONOMIC CONDITIONS

Marketers must consider the economic environment of the host country before deciding on market entry. Economic considerations must include the country's economic infrastructure, its stage of economic development, and currency exchanges in the host country.

ECONOMIC INFRASTRUCTURE

A country's **economic infrastructure** *is its transportation, communication, power, distribution, and other facilities necessary to sustain economic activity.* A key consideration for international marketers is whether a country has the facilities to market a company's product. China may be encouraging foreign investment, but it lacks facilities to distribute goods outside the major cities. Advertising is restricted to occasional newspaper ads, making it difficult to communicate to potential consumers. Given these uncertainties, it is essential for marketers to evaluate basic facilities—a country's road system for transportation, warehouses for storage, mass media for advertising, and telephone ownership for marketing surveys—before deciding to enter a market.

One of the roadblocks to doing business in the former Soviet Union and Eastern Europe is the lack of modern communication and transportation facilities. The lack of an efficient phone system has frustrated many Western and Japanese businesspeople used to modern facilities. A standing joke in Hungary, where one usually has to wait up to a minute for a dial tone, is that you can identify Americans because they start dialing right away. Poor roads also inhibit distribution. One study estimated that it would require building 274,000 miles of new roads in Eastern Europe to support a Western-style distribution network.[31]

Reliance on a centralized economy has also stifled the ability to transfer goods efficiently to supply various sectors of the economy. For example, when McDonald's opened its first store in Moscow in 1990, it could not rely on local suppliers. It had to build its own plant to make beef patties. It also pasteurizes its own milk and bakes its own buns. Pizza Hut, on the other hand, chose to rely on local farmers and existing channels of supply. But its insistence on predictable deliveries and consistent quality mystified Soviet officials. One Soviet official summarized the reliability of local supplies by telling a Pizza Hut executive "If it's a good winter, you'll have more. If it's a bad winter, you'll have less."[32]

STAGE OF ECONOMIC DEVELOPMENT

A country can be classified by its stage of economic development as less developed, developing, or industrialized, depending on its gross national product, per-capita income, literacy rates, and the range and quality of products available. As a general rule, opportunities may seem to be greater in industrialized countries because of their greater purchasing power. But competition is also more likely to be intense, and a company may have to look elsewhere for future growth. Companies like McDonald's and Kellogg are already in most of the industrialized nations of the world.

International marketers are therefore likely to look to developing as well as industrialized countries for opportunity. Despite a poor infrastructure, Eastern Europe is likely to see increasing economic development. Since communism crumbled in 1989, Poland, Hungary, and Czechoslovakia have entered into 9,700 joint ventures with foreign companies to develop industries and resources.[33] All three countries are trying to make their economies as inviting as possible for foreign investment by offering incentives such as reduced taxes. As a result, companies like P&G, General Electric, Hewlett Packard, and AT&T have made substantial investments in Eastern Europe.

The rapid industrialization of some Pacific rim countries (South Korea and Taiwan in particular) is also drawing the attention of international marketers. A shift from a rural to an urban society, rising educational levels, and a greater proportion of working women have resulted in greater affluence in both countries. Dairy Farm, a Hong Kong chain, opened 25 supermarkets in Taiwan to accommodate working women who have less time to shop and are willing to pay higher prices for convenience.[34]

CURRENCY EXCHANGE RATES

Marketers also must consider the exchange rates of their country's currency relative to that in foreign markets. As the value of a country's currency increases, its goods become more expensive abroad. Many U.S. companies found themselves at a competitive disadvantage in the early 1980s as the dollar rose against foreign currencies. Japanese goods were finding it easier to make inroads into the American market, because they were cheaper based on the currency exchange. When the dollar dropped sharply after 1985, American exporters gained a competitive advantage, since their goods were less expensive abroad.

In most countries, companies can sell products, be paid in the local currency, and exchange it for dollars. This is not the case in China, the former Soviet Union, and Eastern Europe because their currencies are not exchangeable on foreign markets. As a result, companies doing business with these countries have had to resort to **countertrade**, *which is the acceptence, in lieu of currency, of local products that can be resold in the West.* PepsiCo, for example, signed a $3 billion deal with the Soviet government in 1990 to exchange its soda for Stolichnya vodka and for tankers.[35] It has countertrade agreements with Eastern European countries as well. In China, Pepsi exchanges soda for mushrooms used on pizzas by its Pizza Hut subsidiary.[36]

TRADE REGULATIONS

Countries establish trade regulations to protect their domestic industries from foreign competition. The most common regulation is the **tariff,** *a tax on imported goods.* Some countries also set import **quotas,** *which limit the amount of a product that can be imported.* Until the mid 1980s, the United States set import quotas on Japanese motorcycles to protect domestic manufacturers, primarily Harley-Davidson. Another set of trade barriers are *product standards,* which are product components or features required to permit a product to be imported. Japan has a variety of such standards to discourage American car manufacturers from exporting their cars. To sell an American car in Japan, one must go through volumes of documents on standards plus local testing, which adds at least $500 to the price of a car.[37].

Governments are motivated by two schools of thought in their attitude toward trade regulations. Some encourage market entry to further the development of domestic industries, increase the standard of living, provide sorely needed jobs, and supply foreign currency. For example, Italy has encouraged Texas Instruments to invest in the country's poorer south and has put up half of Texas Instrument's $1.2 billion investment in the region.[38] Other governments discourage foreign investment because they want to maintain government control over private enterprise, or they fear foreign domination of their economy. For example, Avon decided against entering the Nigerian market because the government required ownership of 60 percent of Avon's local operations.[39] Coca-Cola does not market in India, because in 1977 the government ordered it to divulge its closely guarded formula or cease operations. The company chose to leave.

Since World War II, there have been attempts to ease trade barriers to encourage international trade. In 1947, the United States and 22 other countries signed the General Agreement on Tariffs and Trade (GATT) to reduce tariffs in stages. Since 1947 the GATT agreement has reduced tariffs seven times. The average tariff today is less than one-fifth what it was after World War II. Despite these reductions, some countries make it difficult for foreigners to invest in their economies. So international marketers must determine whether market entry is worth the cost of tariffs, quotas, and rigid product standards.

Agreements between individual countries have also reduced trade barriers. The most significant has been the North American Free Trade Agreement of 1992 between the United States, Canda, and Mexico, eliminating tariffs and other trade barriers between the three countries so tariffs will reach zero by 1995.

1992 AND THE EUROPEAN COMMUNITY

One of the most significant events encouraging free trade occurred in 1992 when the European Community began to eliminate all barriers to the movement of people, products, services, and capital between its 12 member countries. The European Community had established 285 directives to remove all trade barriers by December 31, 1992, and to standardize everything from product labeling to the content of TV commercials. Brand names will be the same across countries, and prices for goods will be nearly identical. One result of these policies will be an expected 50 percent decrease in distribution costs as a result of the economies of scale in standardizing products and producing larger quantities for a larger market.

The European Community also plans to introduce a single currency by 1997. As a result, marketers will not have to worry about differences in exchange rates between countries. The introduction of a single currency will require establishing one central banking system for all EC countries.

American companies that have operations across Europe, such as IBM, Coca-Cola, and 3M, are well-positioned to take advantage of a single market. These companies dominate their respective industries on the continent. Other American companies with a less dominant European presence strengthened it in anticipation of 1992. For example, Ford purchased Jaguar, the British luxury carmaker. Sara Lee, owners of L'Eggs hosiery, bought Dim, the best-known hosiery company in France. Motorola and Intel are building large plants to increase production capacity in Europe.[40] Companies with minimal operations in Europe are also establishing a presence. General Mills entered into an agreement with Nestlé, the largest food marketer in the world, to distribute its cereals in Europe under the General Mills/Nestlé label.

This activity has given birth to the term **Eurobranding**, *which is the incorporation of several languages on a single package with the same brand name so that it can be introduced to all EC countries.* Sara Lee, for example, has selected Dim as its Eurobrand for socks, underwear, and lingerie (see Exhibit 5.6).

The changes that occurred in 1992 are also spawning increased competition. Japanese as well as American firms are positioning themselves as competitors as the barriers come down. Sony is a leader in electronics in Europe and sells more on the continent than it does in the United States. Kao, known as the Procter &

EXHIBIT 5.6

An Example of a Eurobrand

Gamble of Japan, has strengthened its hand in Europe by buying a leading German toiletry company. Sharp and Hitachi have expanded research and production facilities in Europe.[41] As the trade barriers come down, competition promises to shape up as a three-way battle between American, Japanese, and European firms. Despite greater competitive intensity , the net effect of the elimination of trade barriers is likely to be an increase in American exports to the European Community.

COMPETITIVE ENVIRONMENT

The degree of competitive intensity in a country must be considered by international marketers when evaluating market entry. If there are many competitors, or if certain companies have a competitive advantage in product quality, price, or distribution, market entry will be more risky. American companies without a firm presence in Europe will find entry risky in the face of competition from well-established European companies such as Unilever in household products and Nestlé in foods.

The most dramatic effects of foreign competition have occurred in the United States as foreign competitors, particularly Japanese companies, have eroded American leadership in electronics, personal computers, and, especially, in cars. In the 1970s, Japanese competitors found easy entry into U.S. markets. Five factors gave Japanese companies a competitive advantage in the United States in the 1970s and early 1980s. First, a weak yen and a strong dollar made Japanese products less expensive in the United States. Second, Japanese manufacturers established a competitive advantage by producing higher-quality products at lower costs. Higher productivity was made possible by giving Japanese workers greater responsibility on the production line, thus motivating them to high standards of efficiency. As a result, the price of GM cars averages $1,500 higher than that of Japanese imports.[42] Third, the Japanese could gain a competitive advantage by simply meeting customer needs. Japanese carmakers took the lead in meeting consumer needs for smaller and more-fuel-efficient cars in the 1970s.

A fourth factor giving Japanese companies an edge is that the Japanese government provides long-term support for research and development. Japan's Ministry of International Trade and Industry funds research to support private businesses, permitting Japanese companies to pursue promising technologies that American companies might give up because of the expense of development. Fifth, Japanese businesses have developed interlocking relationships known as *keiretsu. Keiretsu* are enormous conglomerates composed of companies that buy each other's products and protect each other's markets. Because their competitive position is protected at home, Japanese companies can devote more resources and attention to foreign markets.

These factors combined to produce a devastating toll on American industry. From 1975 to 1990, U.S. car manufacturer's share of the domestic market slipped from 81 percent to 62 percent, while the share of Japanese imports sales increased from about 10 percent to 30 percent (see Figure 5.3). In 1991, the best-selling car in America was the Japanese-made Honda Accord. Japanese competition caused General Electric to sell its TV and electronics business to a leading European competitor, because it simply could not meet Japanese quality and prices. Today, there is only one domestic manufacturer of televisions left, Zenith. It can survive only because it is concentrating on a niche that has not attracted Japanese competitors: televisions priced at over $1,000. Domestic carmakers also saw their market erode with Japanese competitors capturing close to 30 percent of the market.

Japanese competitors have also strengthened their hand by pouring money into research and development and stealing the lead from American companies in technology. In 1980, for example, seven of the ten most profitable patents in the United States were held by American companies and one was held by a Japanese company. In 1990 the tables were almost reversed: Five of the ten most profitable patents were held by Japanese companies and only three were held by American companies.[43] Japanese companies are taking the lead in developing higher-speed microchips for computers and high definition television (HDTV).

The competitive position of American firms has eroded in world markets as well

FIGURE 5.3

Share of the American Car Market Held by Domestic and Japanese Companies

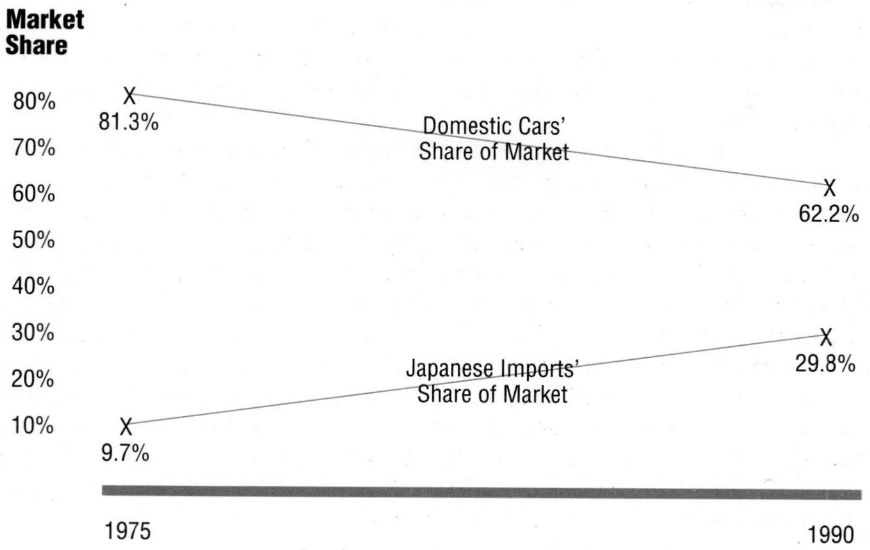

Source: *The U.S. Car Market: Prospects Through the 1990s* (London: The Economic Intelligence Unit, 1991), pp. 3-4.

as in the domestic market. From 1967 to 1989, America's share of computer exports went from 30 percent to 20 percent; its share of the world car market went from 20 percent to 10 percent; its share of electronics went from about 32 percent to less than 20 percent; and its share of telecommunications equipment went from 25 percent to 10 percent.[44] In each case, Japan gained world market share at the expense of the United States (see Figure 5.4). The eroding position of America's manufacturing base relative to foreign competition is one reason why the service sector of the American economy accounts for more dollars than the manufacturing sector.

Although the competitive picture for corporate America seems fairly dismal, there are bright spots. The productivity of American firms is improving. A weak dollar is also making Japanese goods more expensive in the United States. Further, as described in Chapter 1, American industry has learned the importance of being consumer oriented. As a result, foreign firms are finding it increasingly difficult to gain a competitive advantage based on productivity and greater sensitivity to consumer needs. In addition, the U.S. government is beginning to help domestic companies in research and development. For example, $260 million is being provided for a research project to help American car manufacturers develop an electric car to compete with future Japanese models.

POLITICAL ENVIRONMENT

The international marketer must also consider the political stability of the host country. The uncertainties of investing abroad are reflected in the upheavals created by the Yugoslav civil war which began in 1991, the Persian Gulf War the

FIGURE 5.4

Decline in America's Share of the World Market for Computers, Electronics, Autos, and Telecommunications: 1970 to 1990

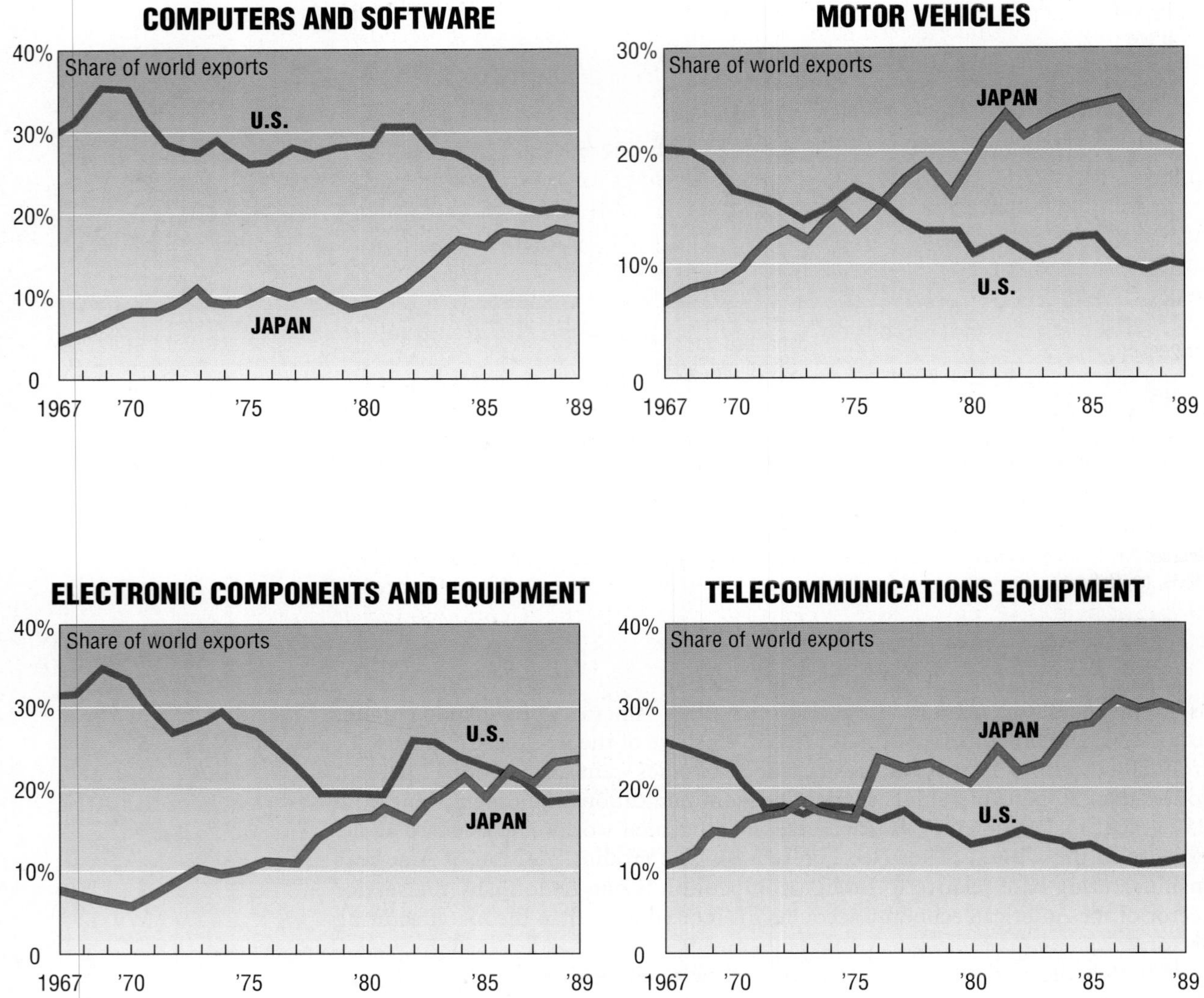

Source: Joseph R. D'Cruz, Faculty of Management, University of Toronto: "The New American Century: Where We Stand." Spring/Summer 1991 special issue, FORTUNE, p. 18. Used with permission.

same year, the crackdown on students in China in 1989, and the Iranian revolution in 1979. The destruction of Aramco's oil fields in Kuwait as a result of Iraq's invasion shows the uncertainties of operating abroad, even for long-established companies.

A country's political environment frequently has a direct impact on its economic policies. Events in the former Soviet Union are good examples: Mikhail Gorbachev's *glasnost*, the introduction of political reforms to open Soviet society, led to *perestroika*, that is, economic reforms designed to restructure the rigidly controlled Soviet system. *Glasnost* reached Eastern Europe in 1989 and led to the independence of the individual Soviet states in 1991. In both cases, the results were the elimination of centralized economic systems and the attempt to establish free-market economies.

Companies may not be able to predict political events such as the rapid demise of communism or the onset of the Persian Gulf War. But they can try to assess the overall political stability of a country. Spurred by unforseen political events like the Gulf War, many companies have set up staffs to track economic conditions and political events to better estimate financial exposure to risk on a country-by-country basis.[45]

FUTURE TRENDS IN THE INTERNATIONAL MARKETING ENVIRONMENT

A review of the international marketing environment provides us with an indication of future trends. First, key areas of the world will continue to draw the attention of international marketers. Increasing investments are likely in Eastern Europe, the former Soviet Union, and the Pacific rim countries. Further, despite the crackdown on student dissidents, China is continuing to try to attract foreign investments and to open its markets to foreign goods.

Second, trade barriers are likely to decrease in the next century. Free-trade agreements with Canada and Mexico and the economic integration of Western Europe are harbingers of more free trade in the future. Japan will probably further loosen trade barriers to avoid risking restraints on Japanese exports into the United States. Also, many Third World countries that now have rigid barriers to protect domestic industries are likely to loosen them to promote foreign trade as their country becomes more developed.

Third, the economic integration of the EC countries in 1992 will change the competitive map of the world. New and more-powerful alliances such as that between Nestlé and General Mills are going to be formed. Further, European companies now operating in one country will grow and become more-powerful competitors after economic integration occurs.

Fourth, the 25-year slide of corporate America in the face of onslaughts from Japanese companies and other foreign competitors is likely to come to an end. Increased productivity, a weaker dollar, greater sensitivity to consumer needs, and greater government support have all strengthened the position of American companies in the face of foreign competition. One report has found that America's competitive position is likely to continue to erode in certain areas such as electronics but that American industry is finding renewed strength in other areas such as biotechnology, pollution reduction systems, computer software, and database systems.[46] International marketers must anticipate such trends in assessing their potential in foreign markets.

DEVELOP INTERNATIONAL MARKETING OBJECTIVES

Once marketers have evaluated the international marketing environment, the next step is to establish objectives for possible entry into foreign markets. A company should be able to establish performance objectives for market share, sales, and profits based on its analysis of the potential in a particular country. For example, Procter & Gamble might have established market share objectives of 30 percent, sales of $200 million, and a 25 percent return on investment by the fifth year in its Eastern European detergent market.

Future objectives might be to have P&G's detergent brands available to 50 percent of Polish and Hungarian consumers within three years of entry as well as to establish cost limits for raw materials, production, distribution, and advertising.

These objectives must be based on estimates of the development of Eastern Europe's infrastructure—for example, the development of roads that would allow distribution to 50 percent of Eastern European consumers. Objectives must also take into account the degree to which the purchasing power of consumers in Eastern Europe will increase in the next five years, as well as the likelihood of competition from powerful European companies such as Dutch-based Unilever.

DECIDE ON MARKET ENTRY

Management's decision on whether to enter a particular market hinges on two key factors: first, whether the environment of the country in question offers opportunities for growth; second, whether the company has the facilities and know-how to exploit these opportunities. These two dimensions define the marketing planning matrix described in Chapter 2 (see Figure 2.2). Figure 5.5 translates the planning matrix to the international environment. Now, opportunity is defined based on an evaluation of the international marketing environment, and the firm's ability to exploit opportunity is defined by its resources and know-how in entering foreign markets. A high level of opportunity and a high ability to exploit opportunity define an *international window of opportunity.*

To assess an opportunity based on the international planning matrix, a firm must evaluate the marketing opportunity (environmental analysis) in a particular coun-

FIGURE 5.5

The International Marketing Planning Matrix

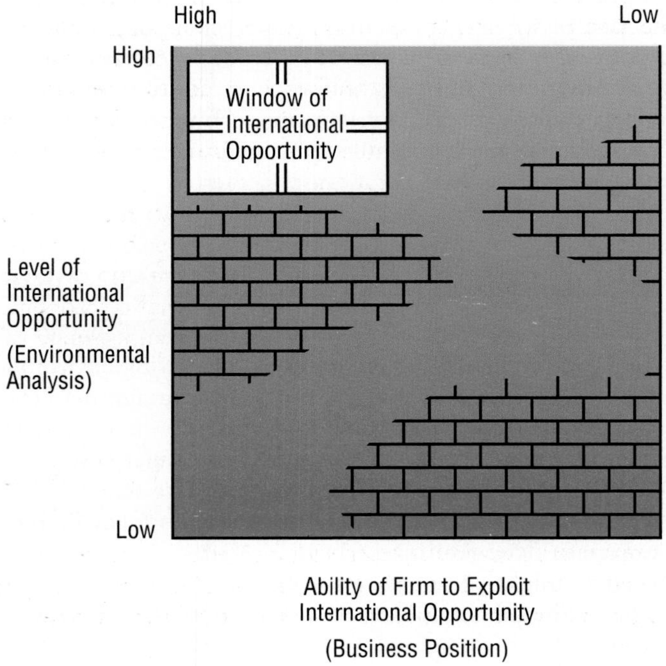

TABLE 5.1

Factors Defining International Marketing Opportunity and Business Position

FAVORABLE — NOT FAVORABLE	FAVORABLE — NOT FAVORABLE
+3 +2 +1 0 −1 −2 −3	+3 +2 +1 0 −1 −1 −3
A. INTERNATIONAL MARKETING OPPORTUNITY (Environmental Analysis)	**B. BUSINESS POSITION (Resource Analysis)**
Cultural norms	Local distribution facilities
Business relations	Local sales support
Economic infrastructure	Managerial know-how
Product regulations	Capital requirements
Tariffs	Plant capacity
Investment barriers	Marketing facilities
Competitive intensity	
Political stability	
Market size	
Market growth rate	

try or region and the firm's business position (resources). Table 5.1 cites the factors a business must evaluate if it is to be successful. An environmental analysis requires considering the factors described above—cultural norms, business relations, a country's economic infrastructure (distribution, transportation, and communications facilities), trade regulations (product regulations, tariffs, investment barriers), competitive intensity, and political stability. In addition, the firm must assess the size of the market and its potential growth rate. Managers will evaluate each factor and rate it as favorable or unfavorable. On this basis they will develop an overall assessment of the level of opportunity in a market.

Table 5.1 also lists some of the factors managers can use in evaluating a firm's business position, such as the company's local distribution facilities or sales support, managerial know-how to market abroad, and resources to invest in plant capacity and marketing facilities. Once the international market environment and the firm's business position are evaluated, managers can estimate sales and profit potential and decide on market entry.

DETERMINE A MARKET ENTRY STRATEGY

Once the international marketer has decided to enter a market, the next question is how. The continuum in Figure 5.6 shows five alternatives ranging from maximum to minimum investment in, and control of, marketing activities in the foreign country.

FIGURE 5.6

Market Entry Strategies Continuum

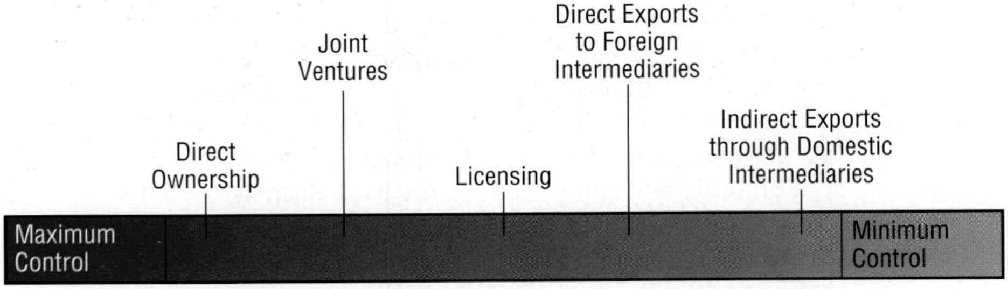

DIRECT OWNERSHIP

Direct ownership occurs when a company invests directly in a foreign company's manufacturing facilities. This represents the greatest commitment to, and risk in, a foreign market. Such direct investment is most likely when management determines that a country is politically stable and that the company therefore does not face the risk of expropriation or similarly drastic, unforeseen events.

Involvement abroad by American firms has been increasing greatly in recent years, spurred in part by the economic integration of Western Europe. In 1989, direct U.S. investment in Europe was $176 billion.[47] Companies that have an established base abroad, such as Ford or 3M, avoid trade barriers against foreign goods since they are considered domestic producers. Furthermore, firms can establish stronger relations with local wholesalers, retailers, and suppliers, making it easier to adapt to local needs.

An alternative to developing a foreign base over time is to achieve direct ownership quickly through acquisition. Many companies did not have the time to develop businesses in anticipation of 1992 and bought companies as a quick means of establishing themselves. Nestlé staked out a position in pasta by buying Buitoni. It also bought Carnation Co. to strengthen its hand in the dairy business.[48]

JOINT VENTURES

A *joint venture* is a business partnership with another company. Joint ventures are formed if a firm lacks the expertise or financial resources to enter a foreign market. Many Japanese companies use joint ventures to enter the American market. Toshiba, the electronics firm, has a joint venture with Westinghouse to produce color televisions and with AT&T to produce telephone-switching equipment.[49] U.S. companies have also used joint ventures to enter Japan. Apple sells its Macintosh through Canon, and Ford sells its Taurus through Mazda. U.S. companies have also used joint ventures to manufacture as well as to market their products abroad. Alcoa and Kobe steel of Japan entered a joint venture (KSC Alcoa Aluminum Co.) to produce and market aluminum sheet for the growing beverage container markets in Japan and other Asian countries (see Exhibit 5.7).

Joint ventures can also create synergies that might not exist when a single firm enters the market. Coca-Cola and Nestlé have agreed on a joint venture to market ready-to-drink coffees on a worldwide basis. The arrangement combines Nestlé's well-known brands such as Nescafé and Taster's Choice with Coca-Cola's massive beverage distribution system.[50]

EXHIBIT 5.7

An Example of a Joint Venture: Alcoa and Kobe

Rolls of Alcoa aluminum sheet await shipment in one of their joint plants. Alcoa and Kobe Steel of Japan formed a joint venture, KSL Alcoa Aluminum Company, to produce and market aluminum sheet for the growing beverage container markets in Japan and other Asian countries.

LICENSING

Licensing is when one company allows another to produce or market its product if the producer can guarantee the same quality. Granting licenses to foreign companies involves less investment in, and control of, foreign markets than does direct ownership or joint venture. It is a good way to shift the risks of production and marketing to the licensee, yet gain the benefits of entry into foreign markets. For example, Weight Watchers International has licensed its health products to 13 companies abroad.

Licensing creates a risk of lack of control over manufacturing operations, and thus over the quality of the product. PepsiCo licenses production of its flagship brand to government-owned companies in Egypt, and some consumers have complained that the Egyptian version of the drink lacks the flavor of the domestic product.[51]

EXPORTING *Exporting* is the selling of a product abroad from the company's home base. A firm exporting its products does not necessarily make any substantial investments abroad. Exporting is therefore the most frequently used method for market entry. Hershey exports directly to foreign intermediaries rather than making substantial investments in overseas production or joint ventures. A company can also export indirectly by using home-based organizations such as trading companies. This type of entry represents the least involvement in foreign markets, because the company is giving another organization responsibility for marketing its products. It is also the least expensive of the market-entry strategies shown in Figure 5.6.

A logical strategy for a company entering international markets is to begin with the least-expensive method, exporting through domestic intermediaries. If its products are successful abroad, the company can consider more-direct involvement through licensing, joint venture, or direct ownership.

DEVELOP AN INTERNATIONAL GROWTH STRATEGY

Once the international firm has determined a strategy for market entry, the next step is to decide on a **country–product mix,** *which defines the company's total product offerings on a global basis.* Such decisions should be made within the context of an **international growth strategy,** *an overall game plan for future growth in international markets based on the opportunities in each country and the company's ability to exploit them.* For example, General Foods sells chewing gum in France, ice cream in Brazil, and pasta in Italy. If selling chewing gum in France would put General Foods at a competitive disadvantage compared to domestic companies, those resources could be better used in another country. In other words, the global game plan requires deciding what products to sell in what countries, with an eye on the company's global offerings.

In developing an international growth strategy, a company must make two basic decisions: First, should it follow a standardized (global) or an adaptive (local) strategy in introducing its products abroad? Second, should it try to be in as many countries as possible or focus on a few key countries? The answers to these two questions result in the four strategic alternatives presented in Figure 5.7.

In **worldwide standardization**, *the international firm follows a fairly consistent marketing strategy across as many countries as possible.* This is essentially a world-brand strategy such as the one Coca-Cola follows—not only with its flagship brand but with its other soft-drink offerings. For example, Diet Coke is marketed in almost as many countries as Coca-Cola.

Because standardization provides economies of scale in advertising and production, a standardized strategy usually involves as many markets as possible (that is, a worldwide strategy). But standardization can also be used effectively on a more limited scale. Companies can use **standardization in key markets** *by applying standardization strategies only to markets where opportunity is greatest, particularly if customer needs in these markets are similar.* For example, Playtex markets its underwire bras in the United States and a few European countries using a standardized approach. The company could try to expand into other countries, but it feels that a product like an underwire bra does not have universal appeal because of different cultural norms outside the United States and Europe. Yet, a standardized approach is still desirable, because the size of the American and European markets makes economies of scale possible, and because of similar norms in these markets.

FIGURE 5.7

International Growth Strategies

Strategic Approach to International Marketing	Breadth of International Effort: As Many Countries as Possible	Breadth of International Effort: A Few Key Countries
Standardized (Global)	Worldwide Standardization (World Brands)	Standardization in Key Markets
Adaptive (Local)	Worldwide Adaptation	Adaptation in Key Markets

The most costly strategy is **worldwide adaptation**, *which requires selling different variations of a product in each country on a worldwide basis.* Such adaptation is necessary when differences in needs require it. Most of Procter & Gamble's brands are geared to specific countries or regions because of local differences. For example, the American version of Ariel, P&G's top-selling powder detergent in Europe and Latin America, is designed for lower water temperatures, greater sudsing, and faster performance. In Germany, washloads are soaked longer and at higher temperatures, so Ariel matches those conditions. In Japan, the product is formulated for shorter washing cycles and smaller machines.[52]

Adaptation in key markets *is a growth strategy in which a firm channels resources to a select group of countries.* Most companies simply do not have the resources of a P&G, allowing a worldwide adaptive strategy. Domino's Pizza follows a strategy of adaptation in key markets in ten countries where it varies its pizzas with what it calls "cultural toppings." For example, pizzas are topped with sweet corn in the United Kingdom, tuna in Japan, salami in Germany, and prawns in Australia.[53]

FORMULATE PRODUCT MARKETING STRATEGIES

Having developed an overall game plan for its operations in foreign markets, the international firm is in a position to formulate marketing strategies for each of its product lines. These strategies identify market segments and develop a mix of product, promotion, distribution, and pricing strategies for each market. The major strategic question is one we have addressed earlier: Where should these strategies fall on the continuum from standardization across markets to adaptation to each local market?

Most firms do not follow a strictly standardized or adaptive approach in developing product strategies. Marketers of world brands usually adjust their advertising to local conditions. For example, the Marlboro cowboy is generally regarded as a universal symbol. But there are significant local differences in implementation, such as showing the cowboy in a lighter colored hat in Hong Kong and China because of the positive cultural significance of the color white in the Far East (see Exhibit 5.8).[54] On the other side of the coin, brands designed for local conditions,

EXHIBIT 5.8

Adapting the Marlboro Cowboy to Local Customs

such as P&G's Ariel, have a standardized element across regions, for example, a common product characteristic (powdered detergent) or a common brand name.

When firms do follow a strictly standardized or adaptive approach, they tend to run into trouble. For example, Parker Pen tried to standardize every component of its marketing mix in 154 countries and failed in its international strategy because of inadequate attention to local differences. Its global advertising approach totally overlooked local variations such as the fact that Scandinavia is a ballpoint-pen market, whereas consumers in France and Italy want fancier pens.[55]

Because of the limits of a strictly standardized or adaptive product strategy, most firms follow an approach we identified in Figure 5.1 as patterned standardization; that is, developing a common product base that allows for substantial local variations. Patterned standardization allows companies to take advantage of economies of scale while meeting local needs. U.S. car companies have followed a policy of patterned standardization in selling abroad, because they need economies of scale to defray their high fixed costs. General Motors' X-cars were designed with a standardized body and interchangeable parts to allow for adaptation to local conditions. American Motors' Jeep (now owned by Chrysler) has a common design but with variations for 14 different countries.[56]

Generally, the product component of the international marketing mix is the most standardized, and the advertising component is the least standardized. Product and packaging characteristics can be standardized if product needs are similar across regions, but advertising almost always requires variations in language, symbols, and images to conform to local conditions.

EVALUATE AND CONTROL INTERNATIONAL MARKETING PERFORMANCE

The last step in the process of international marketing planning—evaluating and controlling the marketing effort—is more difficult than in domestic marketing for several reasons. One is that international marketers have less control over price because of tariffs and trade regulations. Frequently, the international firm must price its products higher than anticipated to absorb such export costs. Also, data on international markets are often incomplete, unreliable, and not comparable across countries. Such data are much harder to use for planning purposes. Finally, firms with foreign subsidiaries often find it difficult to control them from the home office because of differences in business customs and environment.

International firms must overcome these difficulties by establishing a system to control their foreign operations. A key requirement is establishing an information system for international markets. Such a system would provide data on differences in customer needs, trade regulations, and economic and competitive conditions between countries. With such information, managers could better evaluate opportunity within individual foreign markets based on the criteria listed in Table 5.1. In particular, data used to develop estimates of market potential and opportunity must be comparable across countries and regions. Coca-Cola's rating of the opportunities in China could then be compared to its assessment of the opportunities in India, for example. On this basis, the company could then determine where it could best allocate its resources in foreign markets.

ETHICAL AND ENVIRONMENTAL ISSUES IN INTERNATIONAL MARKETING

International marketers face serious ethical and environmental issues that must be considered when developing marketing strategies abroad.

ETHICAL ISSUES

The nature of international operations has created several ethical issues that have prompted debate in the business community. One of the most divisive ethical issues is the charge that some companies from industrialized nations sell products to developing and Third World countries that have harmful effects on consumers

ETHICAL AND ENVIRONMENTAL ISSUES IN MARKETING

Nestlé and the Infant Formula Controversy

In the late 1970s, a worldwide boycott of Nestlé products was initiated by consumer groups because of evidence of serious health problems among babies in underdeveloped countries who were fed Nestlé's infant formula products. Studies found that babies who were fed the formula frequently became ill, because contaminated water from local supplies was mixed with the formula. Once a mother opted to feed her baby infant formula, however, her natural milk dried up, and there was no alternative; the mother had to continue using infant formula. As stated by a doctor with the World Health Organization (WHO), "In the hands of the poor, bottle feeding often becomes a passport to death for the young child."

Infant formula is a $5 to $6 billion yearly business with Nestlé representing 40 percent of sales. The company has an obvious stake in supporting its use. Nestlé contended that infant formula was safe to use and promoted health by supplying babies around the world an alternative source of milk in cases where the mother could not or chose not to breast feed. The company's initial reaction to the controversy was to fight the allegations and to withhold cooperation from investigating agencies.

In 1981, the World Health Organization and UNICEF issued guidelines for the marketing of infant formula that proposed prohibiting the promotion of infant formula directly to mothers and suggested dispensing it through doctors and hospitals. It was the first time in the history of the United Nations that members voted an ethical code of conduct to control the activities of international marketers.

Nestlé subsequently accepted the WHO/UNICEF

or that take unfair economic advantage of them. The best-known case in this regard resulted in a worldwide boycott of Nestlé products in the late 1970s because of evidence that use of Nestlé's infant formula products resulted in the deaths of infants in Third World countries. The issue arose again in 1989 as Nestlé was charged with furthering distribution of infant formula in less-developed countries and faced another worldwide boycott. (see Ethical and Environmental Issues in Marketing box for a description of the controversy.)

Another issue that is drawing increasing attention is the charge that American cigarette companies are using less-developed countries as dumping grounds for their cigarettes because of greater health consciousness in the industrialized world. Many advocates of consumer rights feel that it is unconscionable to encourage smoking in countries where famine and disease are prevalent. A World Health Organization study found that marketing campaigns by U.S. cigarette companies have "caused immediate jumps in consumption among women and teens, traditionally non-smoking groups in less-developed economies."[57]

ETHICAL AND ENVIRONMENTAL ISSUES IN MARKETING

guidelines and assisted in resolving most of the problems that these organizations identified. To its credit, the company established a commission to audit compliance with the WHO/UNICEF code, chaired by Edmund Muskie, former senator and presidential candidate. Critics argued that the company's action was motivated by the fact that the boycott was beginning to hurt. Nestlé claimed it was trying to promote the health and welfare of infants. As a result of the company's actions, the boycott was suspended in 1984.

But the controversy surfaced again in 1989 when consumer groups claimed that Nestlé was renewing its marketing efforts in Third World countries. The issue was Nestlé's practice of distributing infant formula free to hospitals in less-developed countries. Critics contended that the practice induced mothers to depend on the use of the product for their newborn baby. The advice Nestlé received from its advertising agency—to infiltrate consumer groups so as to anticipate their future actions—only fueled the controversy. Fortunately, Nestlé did not take the advice of its advertising agency. But the company also continued to offer free infant formula to hospitals. As a result, there are now cries for a renewed boycott of Nestlé products.

Questions: Under what circumstances do you feel it is ethical for Nestlé to sell infant formula to mothers in Third World countries? Should it provide free infant formula to hospitals in Third World countries? Why or why not?

Sources: "Baby Alarms Ring for Nestlé," *Marketing*, June 1, 1989, p. 18; Carol-Linnea Salmon, "Milking Deadly Dollars From the Third World," *Business & Society Review* (Winter 1989), p. 43–48.

Consumer activists are emerging in Asian countries and are attacking cigarette marketing methods. They charge that American companies are manipulating Asian children by linking cigarettes to American themes such as the Marlboro cowboy. American companies play to children's dreams of becoming Americanized, prompting one activist to state that children are "smoking the American dream."[58] One consumer group was successful in stopping a rock concert in Taiwan sponsored by R.J. Reynolds in which admission was five empty packs of Winston.

American tobacco companies are motivated to sell abroad because of declining cigarette consumption in the United States. Their motives are profit driven, which are no different from those of other companies selling abroad. The key issue is the promotion of a harmful product among nonsmokers, particularly in economies where consumers can ill-afford the cost, let alone the effects of the product.

Another ethical issue is whether an international marketer should offer payoffs to buyers abroad if such payoffs are an accepted mode of doing business. Exporters of American products, particularly high-priced industrial goods, often protest that "if we don't, our competitors will, and we will lose the sale." However, such payoffs are little more than bribes for doing business. The fact that competitors offer them does not make the practice ethical. A firm could very well take a position that it sells its products based on quality and that payoffs will not be considered. Such a policy would be most effective if the largest sellers were to publicize it and discourage others from offering payoffs.

A third issue in international marketing is doing business in countries regarded as having reprehensible political policies, such as the apartheid policy in South Africa. Most American companies withdrew from South Africa in the 1980s at the urging of the U.S. government. Some, such as Mobil, remained, arguing that it is better to continue to do business in South Africa and try to support blacks economically through higher wages. Mobil finally quit South Africa in April, 1989, on economic rather than ethical grounds, citing restrictive tax laws passed in the United States making it difficult to continue doing business.[59] In July, 1991, the Bush Administration lifted many sanctions against South Africa as that country moved to end apartheid. But the issue applies to other countries as well, for example, ensuring that no business is done with Iraq in the aftermath of the Persian Gulf War.

ENVIRONMENTAL ISSUES

Environmental concerns will play an important part in the development of international marketing strategies in the 1990s. Consumers in Western Europe were environmentally conscious before their counterparts in the United States. "Green" political parties, which espouse a platform of environmental protection, emerged in the early 1980s in most Western European countries. Concern for the environment is increasing worldwide. In Germany, 75 percent of consumers consider environmental factors when making a purchase. In Holland, 91 percent of consumers feel that products that damage the environment should carry obligatory warnings.[60]

Germany is the most environmentally conscious country in the world because of its acid-rain problem, which was decimating the country's forests in the early 1980s. The country's federal environmental protection agency confers a "Blue Angel" label on products it considers environmentally sound. The German model will be adopted by the European Community in 1992 with the formation of a European Environmental Agency that will confer a similar environmental stamp of approval.[61]

Companies have responded to these concerns, and P&G has led the field. In 1987 it introduced refill packs for Lenor fabric softener to reduce the need for packaging. It introduced Ariel Ultra in 1989, a concentrated detergent that requires half the normal dose. The smaller package helps minimize waste. In 1990 it introduced Pump & Spray, a compressed-air pump replacing aerosol propellants which deplete the ozone layer of the upper atmosphere.[62] It also introduced a refill for Downy that can be poured into the original container to reduce packaging waste (see Exhibit 5.9).

Western Europe is not the only region with increasing environmental concerns. The opening of Eastern Europe and the former Soviet Union to Western trade also revealed rampant pollution and the sorry state of the environment in those countries due to uncontrolled industrialization. As other governments become more sensitive to the need for environmental controls, it is likely that marketers such as P&G will begin offering environmentally friendly products to consumers in these countries as well.

EXHIBIT 5.9

New Packaging Targets Environmentally Conscious Consumers

SUMMARY

1. **What are the reasons for entering foreign markets?**
   The primary reason for entering foreign markets is that domestic markets are stagnant. Government regulations at home may also drive companies to look abroad for growth. Decreasing trade barriers, particularly the elimination of trade barriers within Western Europe in 1992, are causing firms to look abroad. The globalization of markets is also creating opportunities abroad by facilitating the development of world brands and providing economies of scale in global distribution and advertising.
2. **What are the pros and cons of global versus local international marketing strategies?**
   A global (standardized) approach offers one product worldwide and uses a single advertising theme, usually with some local variations. The rationale for such an approach is that the world's consumers are developing similar needs and that a global approach permits companies to achieve economies of scale in production and advertising. But such an approach risks ignoring local differences in needs and customs.

A local (adaptive) approach adjusts marketing strategies to differing customer needs, cultural norms, and other environmental factors on a country-by-country basis. The advantage of this approach is that it directs strategies to the specific needs of individual markets. But it is costly to develop separate products and advertising campaigns for individual countries.

3. **What steps are involved in developing an international marketing plan?** The first step in international planning is to evaluate the cultural, political, and economic environment to determine the feasibility of entering the foreign market. If the company decides on entry, it establishes performance objectives and develops a market-entry strategy. Such a strategy might involve building a plant abroad, entering a joint venture with a domestic company, or exporting the product from the company's home base. In the next step, the company develops an overall strategic plan for operations abroad that determines whether it will take a global or local approach and that defines its country–product mix.

   The company also develops a marketing plan for each product sold abroad. This requires formulating strategies for product, promotion, distribution, and pricing. In the final step, the company evaluates and controls the international marketing effort.
4. **What environmental factors are likely to influence a firm's decision to enter foreign markets?** The international firm must determine cultural norms that might affect consumer needs and their reactions to the company's offerings. It must assess the nature of business relations in each country so that company executives will not blunder in dealing with foreign businesspeople. It must evaluate the economic infrastructure of a market to determine adequacy of distribution and communication facilities. It must assess trade regulations that might result in taxes, quotas, or restrictions on operations that will directly affect profit potential abroad. Also, it must evaluate competition to determine the profit potential of operations abroad. And finally, it must assess the political environment for signs of instability that might increase the risks of doing business in foreign markets.
5. **What strategies do firms use to enter foreign markets?** Firms can enter foreign markets by establishing or acquiring foreign subsidiaries. This affords greatest control over foreign operations. Firms can also enter into joint ventures with others if it lacks the expertise or financial resources to enter foreign markets. Licensing is also an option and permits a company to shift the risks of entering foreign markets to others. Finally, a firm can export its products from its home base. Licensing and direct exporting from the domestic market provide the marketer with the least amount of control over foreign operations.

KEY TERMS

International marketing (p. 138)
Adaptive strategies (p. 144)
Standardized strategies (p. 144)
Patterned standardization (p. 146)
Culture (p. 150)
Economic infrastructure (p. 152)
Countertrade (p. 153)
Tariffs (p. 153)
Quotas (p. 153)
Eurobranding (p. 154)
International growth strategy (p. 164)
Worldwide standardization (p. 164)
Standardization in key markets (p. 164)
Worldwide adaptation (p. 165)
Adaptation in key markets (p. 165)

QUESTIONS

1. For what reasons do companies enter foreign markets? Cite examples for each reason.
2. Cite examples of decreasing trade barriers in the 1980s and 1990s. What are likely to be the effects of looser trade regulations on international marketing strategies?
3. What are the opportunities and threats for American companies when economic integration takes place in the 12 European Community countries in 1992?
4. What are some opportunities and threats for American companies operating abroad in the 1990s?
5. What are the characteristics of a world brand? Cite examples. Can the strategy for a world brand account for differences in local needs and customs? If so, in what ways?
6. Why does McDonald's adapt its offerings to local markets, whereas Coca-Cola generally does not?
7. What environmental factors would P&G have to consider in marketing in Eastern Europe? Be sure to cite culture, business relations, the economic environment, trade regulations, competition, and the political climate.
8. What is meant by a country's economic infrastructure? How does the economic infrastructure of Eastern Europe, the former Soviet Union, and China affect market entry into these countries?
9. What factors gave Japanese companies competitive advantages in the United States? What factors are likely to help U.S. companies recoup their competitive position in the 1990s?
10. What market-entry strategies would you suggest for each of the following companies, and why?
    a. An American firm wants to introduce its line of high-quality biscuits in Western Europe and wants to maintain close control over the manufacture and marketing of the line.
    b. A manufacturer of household cleaners is just starting to sell abroad. It has limited resources for foreign operations but hopes to expand international sales in the future.
    c. A company wants to introduce its line of hydraulic lifts into an Asian country with strict export controls. It would like to establish manufacturing and marketing facilities in that country but does not have the resources to do so. Further, the company is not familiar with local regulations and customs.
11. What alternative strategies for international growth can a company follow? What is the rationale for pursuing each strategy? What are the risks?
12. Why is it more difficult to evaluate and control international marketing operations than domestic operations?
13. What are some key ethical issues in international marketing? Cite examples of how these issues affect marketing strategies.

QUESTIONS: YOU ARE THE DECISION MAKER

1. One advertising executive, citing the rationale for a global marketing approach, said:

   > *Different peoples are basically the same . . . An international advertising campaign with a truly universal appeal can be effective . . . The desire to be beautiful is universal. Such appeals as "mother and child," "freedom from pain," "glow of health," know no boundaries.*[63]

   Another marketing expert, citing the need for local adaptation simply said, "What makes sense in one country may not make sense in another."[64] What are the advantages and disadvantages of a global and a local approach to international marketing?
2. Are the two statements cited in Question 1 contradictory? Why or why not? How do marketers combine global and local strategies? Cite examples.

CHAPTER 6

Marketing Opportunity Through Competitive Advantage

YOUR FOCUS IN CHAPTER 6

To learn:

- *How a firm establishes advantages over its competitors.*
- *How marketing opportunities can be identified for establishing competitive advantage.*
- *How principles of military science can be applied in developing strategies to win competitive advantage.*
- *What strategies can be implemented to establish competitive advantage.*

The Cola Wars: Coke and Pepsi Fight for Competitive Advantage

Having been at each other's throats for close to 100 years, it is unlikely that Coke or Pepsi will declare a truce in the cola wars. In fact, competition is likely to heat up on every front in the 1990s—in diet colas, regular colas, fountain sales, and international sales.

With a substantial lead in sales both in the United States and abroad (Coke outsells Pepsi four-to-three domestically and four-to-one abroad), it is easier for Coke to take the initiative in the cola wars.[1] Coca-Cola did just that when it decided to change the formula of its flagship brand in 1985. The sweeter taste of the new Coke was meant to be more like Pepsi in order to appeal to teenagers, but all it did was alienate the real Coke loyalists—the adult cola drinkers. Pepsi was exultant. Roger Enrico, then president of Pepsi-Cola USA, issued his now-famous statement, "After 87 years of going at it eyeball to eyeball, the other guy just blinked."[2] When Coca-Cola brought back its original formula as Coca-Cola Classic, Pepsi saw it as an admission of a failed strategy.

Pepsi's advantage was short-lived. The national attention Coke gained with its new formula and quick about-face actually served to increase sales of Coca-Cola Classic. And although New Coke never made it off the ground, the combined Coca-Cola brands wound up with a higher market share than before the change.

But Coke did not rest on its market leadership. In 1990 it opened a broad offensive on various fronts. It decided to revitalize a dormant New Coke under a new name, Coke II, a new blue can that makes it look more like Pepsi, and an advertising campaign that clearly targets teenage Pepsi drinkers with the theme "Real cola taste, plus the sweetness of Pepsi."[3] It also decided to attack Pepsi on another front, by trying to draw Pepsi drinkers to Diet Coke. Coca-Cola saw a natural opening as teenagers loyal to Pepsi become weight conscious young adults. Its strategy was straight out of military textbooks—discourage a direct onslaught at the enemy; undermine his strength by flanking maneuvers. Coca-Cola's flanking maneuvers were to attack Pepsi on the regular cola flank with Coke II and on the diet cola flank with Diet Coke while leaving its flagship brand unscathed in the center of the field.

Coca-Cola attacked Pepsi on yet another front—fountain sales to restaurants. Coca-Cola has a commanding lead in this area, with 63 percent of fountain sales, based on key accounts such as Mc Donald's and Domino's Pizza, compared to Pepsi's 25 percent. It cemented this lead in 1990 when it won both Burger King and Wendy's from Pepsi.[4]

Coca-Cola is also unrelenting in pressing the cola wars in the international arena, and for good reason: In 1989, 80 percent of its earnings came from abroad.[5] It is expanding its base in China with ten bottling facilities. In 1987 it started selling Coke in Russia, and it is preparing to re-enter India.

What has been Pepsi's reaction to this onslaught? To hit back at every juncture. Shortly after Coke attempted to catch Pepsi's teenage following with New Coke, Pepsi returned the favor by trying to capture Coke's adult following with Slice. The juice-based soft drink was designed to appeal to the adult cola drinker's desire for a more nutritious and flavorful soft drink. Slice quickly reached $1 billion in sales before sliding back to about half that figure as competitors, including Coca-Cola, entered with their own juice-based drinks.

Pepsi also met Coke II head-on. When the brand was first introduced in Spokane in 1990, Pepsi fought it at every juncture. In the words of one Pepsi executive, "Coke II has vending machines; we've added . . . vending machines. They have advertising; we've beefed up our overall . . . advertising. They have 16-ounce cans; we're also going with 16-ounce cans."[6]

Pepsi did not take the loss of Burger King and Wendy's lightly. To maintain its share of fountain sales, it managed to contract with Howard Johnson restaurants and Marriott hotels to switch from Coke to Pepsi. On the international front, Pepsi countered Coke's moves by announcing a $1 billion plan to bolster sales in key areas not dominated by Coke, such as diet colas, fountain sales, and vending machines.[7]

Both Coke and Pepsi have followed sound principles in trying to gain competitive advantage: by trying to take the initiative away from the enemy (as Coke did when it won Burger King and Wendy's from Pepsi), by concentrating resources in key areas that are likely to lead to a strategic advantage (as Pepsi is doing in diet soft drinks and fountain sales abroad), and by anticipating the enemy's actions (as Pepsi did by expanding the flavors for Slice in anticipation of Coke's entry into the juice-based market). The cola wars may be almost a hundred years old, but they are still heating up.

DEVELOPING COMPETITIVE ADVANTAGE

As described in Chapter 4, competition is one of the main sources of marketing opportunity. To capitalize on that opportunity is to gain a **competitive advantage**, *that is, an advantage gained over a competitor by offering consumers greater value.* Greater value is provided when a company offers more benefits to consumers through its products or services, or the same benefits at a lower price than competitors.

Both Coke and Pepsi required a systematic approach to determine opportunities for competitive advantage and to decide on a strategy for attaining it. Figure 6.1 presents such a framework. The objective of this approach is to develop marketing strategies based on an analysis of competitive strengths and weaknesses.

The first step in the figure is to determine the bases for competitive advantage. Coca-Cola's competitive advantage is based on its dominance in the international market. Coca-Cola began establishing an international presence in the 1920s, but cemented its dominance abroad during World War II, when it followed the troops to Europe and the Pacific. Not only did it gain many loyalists among the GIs, it retained its bottling plants abroad and established a permanent presence. Pepsi-Cola's advantage is in having a lock on a key segment of the market that Coca-Cola will probably never break—teenagers. The basis for this advantage is the sweeter taste of Pepsi, and Pepsi has reinforced this advantage with advertising campaigns that are designed to appeal to teenagers.

The second step is to identify existing or emerging opportunities for competitive advantage. This is done through a **competitive analysis**, *which involves assessing the market's attractiveness, competitors' strengths and weaknesses, and the company's strengths and weaknesses.* Based on this analysis, a company proceeds to step three and develops competitive strategies to exploit the advantages that it identified in the previous steps. Such strategies will depend on whether the firm is a *market*

FIGURE 6.1

A Framework for Gaining Competitive Advantage

leader (as is Coca-Cola); a *challenger* (as was Pepsi when it advertised The Pepsi Challenge, showing consumers preferring Pepsi over Coke in taste tests); or a so-called *nicher*, as Pepsi is in looking for specific small, but profitable, segments of the market that are unlikely to be dominated by Coke, such as vending machine sales abroad.

Having determined its strategy, the firm proceeds to step four and tries to anticipate what the competitive responses will be. Pepsi correctly anticipated that Coke would follow its entry into fruit-based soft drinks by coming out with a fruit-based version of Minute Maid soft drinks. Pepsi tried to counter this move by offering Slice in a variety of flavors, making it more difficult for Coke to overcome Slice's lead. As is generally the case, pursuit of an opportunity such as fruit-based soft drinks carries with it the threat of competitive entry.

The remainder of this chapter presents the steps outlined in Figure 6.1 in greater detail. After discussing the bases for competitive advantage, we will consider how to identify opportunities for competitive advantage. We will then see how marketers develop strategies based on competitive analyses and, finally, how competitive responses can be anticipated.

DETERMINE THE BASES FOR COMPETITIVE ADVANTAGE

Michael Porter, a professor of business, has developed a theory of competitive advantage in which he cites two broad bases for establishing competitive advantage: a marketing advantage or a cost advantage.[8] **Marketing advantage** *is competitive advantage gained by superior products or services which do a better job than competitors in meeting customer needs.* **Cost advantage** *is competitive advantage gained by reducing production or marketing costs below those of competitors, enabling the company to reduce prices or to channel savings into advertising and distribution.*

Generally, a firm seeking a marketing advantage tends to be more consumer-oriented than one seeking a cost advantage, because product or service superiority requires doing a better job than the competition in meeting customer needs. But a firm seeking a cost advantage cannot ignore customer needs. If a firm is wholly production-oriented and focuses only on cost efficiencies at the expense of customer needs, any competitive advantage gained from lower costs will be short-lived.

Porter introduced a second dimension in his theory of competitive advantage; whether it is pursued on a market-wide basis or for a particular market niche. When Coca-Cola or Pepsi market their flagship brand, they follow a market-wide strategy, which is a strategy that appeals to as many consumers as possible. Even though Coke might target adults more heavily and Pepsi teenagers, the two giants cast a wide net in trying to attract cola drinkers to their flagship brands.

In contrast, a small company like A&W Brands tries to avoid competition with the two cola giants by marketing to small niches. *A* **market niche** *is a small segment of a market not actively pursued by other firms.* A&W's root beer and cream soda brands and regional brands such as its Squirt grapefruit drink are targeted to small segments unlikely to attract significant attention from Coke or Pepsi. As a result, A&W is able to be one of the market leaders in a category like root beer.

ETHICAL AND ENVIRONMENTAL ISSUES IN MARKETING

Have the Fountain Wars Between Pepsi and Coke Led to Unethical Actions?

The attempts by Pepsi and Coke to win restaurants to its brands have been relentless. One of the reasons that Coke was able to convince Burger King and Wendy to switch from Pepsi was the argument that Pepsi-Cola was a restaurant competitor. PepsiCo owns Pizza Hut, Taco Bell, and Kentucky Fried Chicken (KFC) making it the largest restauranteur in the country. These chains compete directly with Burger King and Wendy's, and Coca-Cola hammered that point home with ads in the restaurant trade press that said "If a PepsiCo restaurant is your competition, every time you serve Pepsi you're pouring money into your competitor's pockets." Coca-Cola also conducted marketing research to convince convenience stores such as 7-Eleven that PepsiCo's restaurants competed with them as well.

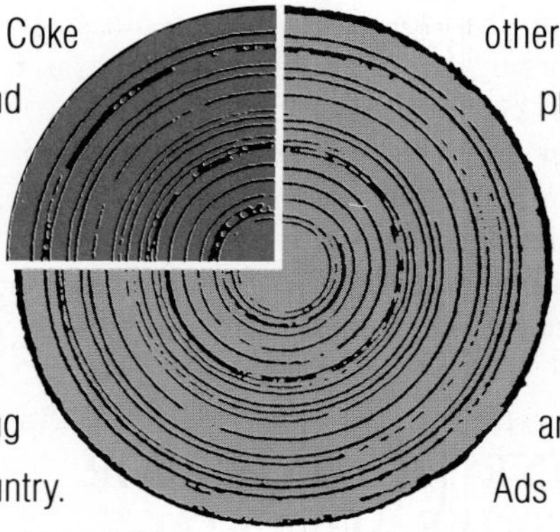

Not to be outdone, Pepsi convinced Howard Johnson and Marriott to switch from Coke with another argument, that Coke was giving preferential treatment to its largest account, McDonald's. Pepsi argued that Coke was charging McDonald's less than its other clients such as Hardee's, Baskin Robbins, and now Burger King and Wendy's. Ads in the trade press said that "Coke's pricing policy is requiring you to subsidize the operations of your largest competitor."

Now it was Coke's turn. It said the reason that Marriott switched to Pepsi was that it had asked Coke for a $50 to $100 million loan and that Coke had refused. Pepsi denied the accusation, with one Pepsi manager saying that "Coke's letter is grossly inaccurate and bad form."

Pepsi fired the final salvo in the fountain wars. It

The combination of marketing or cost advantages on a market-wide or market-segment basis produce the three pathways to competitive advantage shown in Figure 6.2: market-wide marketing advantage, market-wide cost advantage, and a market-niche advantage based on either marketing or cost leadership.

MARKET-WIDE MARKETING ADVANTAGE

A market-wide marketing advantage means that some aspect of a company's product or service has an edge over the competition. The most common basis for such a marketing advantage is to offer a *unique product or service.* Federal Express gained a competitive advantage by offering a unique service. It entered the package delivery market by trying to compete with Emery and Airborne as an air-freight forwarder. It then concentrated on the benefit of overnight delivery based on its hub-

ETHICAL AND ENVIRONMENTAL ISSUES IN MARKETING

attempted to further gain restaurant customers by offering the "Pepsi promise," a promotion guaranteeing a restaurant at least a 4 percent volume increase in the year following a switch to Pepsi. If the restaurant did not achieve the 4 percent increase, Pepsi would make it up.

This give and take between Pepsi and Coke reflects a practice that is fairly commonplace in advertising—the practice of ***comparative advertising,*** *which is directly naming a competitive product in an advertisement.* When Pepsi ran a campaign issuing the "Pepsi Challenge" to Coke and citing test after test that showed consumers preferred the taste of Pepsi, it was using comparative advertising to win consumers over.

But Pepsi's and Coke's attempts to win over business customers seem to be different from winning over consumers through comparative advertising. Pepsi and Coke went beyond that and accused each other of business practices that some observers might regard as unethical—for example, accusing one another of charging higher prices to larger customers without any cost justification or attracting a customer by an implicit loan guarantee. Whether either company substantiated their charges is not clear. A more basic question is whether either company should be using resources for negative competitive advertising that it could better spend elsewhere.

Question: Do you regard any of the actions taken by Pepsi or Coke in the fountain wars as unethical? Why or why not?

Sources: "Sorry, No Pepsi. How 'Bout a Coke?" *Business Week*, May 27, 1991. pp. 71–72; "Cola Feeding Frenzy," *Advertising Age*, April 1, 1991, p. 12; and "Pepsi Promises Sales," *Advertising Age*, November 5, 1990, p. 12.

spoke concept, directing all packages to its Memphis hub and branching out from there. Its focus on overnight delivery established a long-lasting marketing advantage based on superior service. United Airlines is likewise seeking competitive advantage with their new connoisseur class. (See Exhibit 6.1 for this and other examples cited below.)

There are several other ways to obtain competitive advantage through product/service superiority:[9] One is to build a *strong brand name* that will win shelf space in retail stores and gain customer trial for new products. If Kellogg comes out with a new cereal, Campbell Soup with a new soup line, or Black and Decker with a new line of power tools, both retailers and customers are likely to pay attention, because they recognize and respect these companies' names.

Providing *superior service* through speed of delivery and responsiveness to customer orders is another way to obtain competitive advantage. Thus, in the con-

FIGURE 6.2

Three Pathways to Competitive Advantage

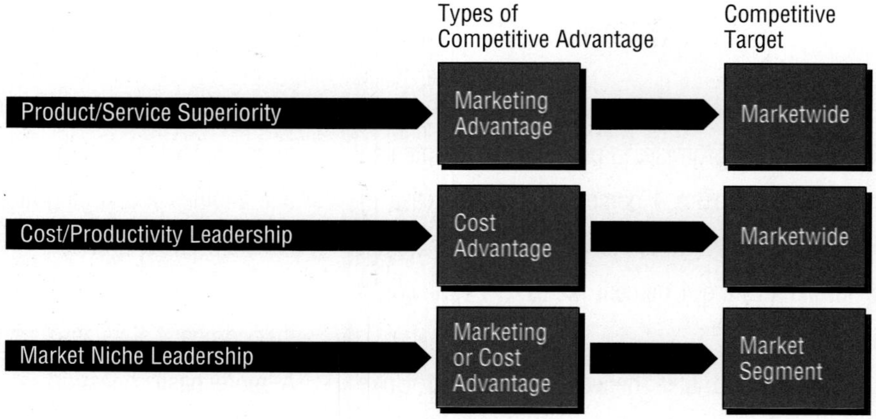

Source: Michael E. Porter, *Competitive Strategy,* (New York: The Free Press, 1980).

struction equipment market Caterpillar Tractor is known for its excellent dealer network that provides reliable service and spare parts for equipment used in situations where downtime is very expensive.

Technological leadership—being consistently among the first to provide innovative product features—can also provide a competitive advantage. One of Apple's advantages over IBM in the personal computer market has been its technological leadership in developing computer graphics. However, technological leadership does not always translate into a competitive advantage. RCA's leadership in electronics technology did not ensure its success in marketing videodiscs in the early 1980s because it failed to tie technology to the customer's need for recording capabilities, a need adequately met by VCRs.

A company that offers a *full line of products* stands a better chance of winning customer loyalty than a company that offers a limited line. Gerber has a competitive advantage in baby foods over Beechnut and Heinz because "it commands a baby food line so large it creates a billboard effect in supermarkets" by capturing so much shelf space.[10] Carrying a full line is particularly important to industrial buyers because they often need a variety of products to fill technical specifications. For example, corporate computer buyers like to deal with IBM because they can buy mainframe computers, microprocessors, PCs, printers, and software from the same source.

Still another way of gaining a competitive advantage is to develop *unique distribution facilities.* L'Eggs hosiery achieved competitive advantage by distributing its products in a unique way, through supermarkets. One of the reasons Gallo is the leading wine company in the United States is that it handpicked its distributors and demanded their loyalty in return for a strong product line.[11] The result was widespread distribution in liquor outlets.

The strategies just described have a common goal: to create greater customer loyalty that can insulate a company against its competition. These types of competitive advantages allow a company to keep prices at a profitable level. Cuisinart,

EXHIBIT 6.1

Pathways to Gaining Market-Wide Competitive Advantage

Product/Service Uniqueness (Left)
Service Support (Right)

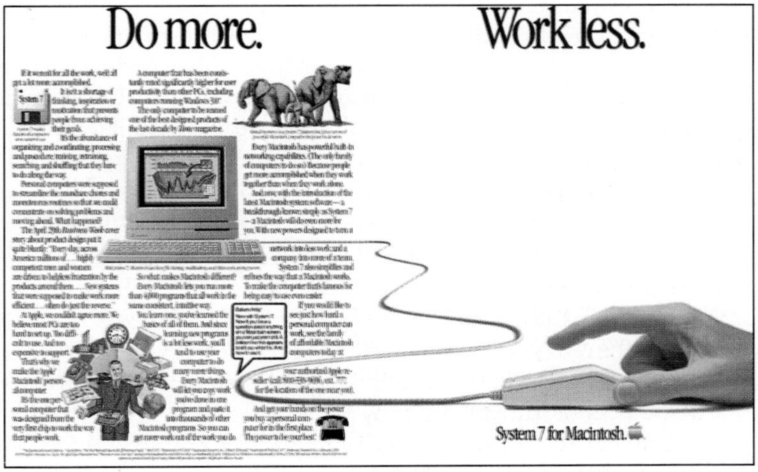

Technological Leadership in PC Market

Full Product Line

for example, can sell its food processors for four times as much as competitors because of unique product features. For a long time, Clorox was able to maintain a price differential for its bleach, even though it is a standardized product, because of superior name recognition among consumers.

MARKET-WIDE COST ADVANTAGE

A market-wide cost advantage is the ability to produce and/or market a product at a cost lower than competitors. Such an advantage allows a company to either pass the savings on to the consumer through lower prices or to maintain prices and plow increased earnings into greater marketing effort. In either case, the company's competitive position is strengthened.

How can a company reduce costs? One method is to develop *economies of scale* in production and/or marketing; that is, developing reductions in the per-unit cost of manufacturing or marketing a product as the amount produced increases. Such economies are achieved because certain fixed costs, such as the cost of machinery or the cost of trucks to distribute products, are spread out over more units. Economies of scale are developed in marketing by distributing and advertising a product on a mass-market basis or by distributing and advertising several products jointly. For example, when Folgers expanded its distribution nationwide from its western base, the increased quantity produced not only reduced per-unit manufacturing costs, it also reduced per-unit costs of distribution.

Experience can also help a company to achieve cost reductions. When a company manufactures or markets a product over time, the experience gained in production and marketing permits it to learn how to develop cost efficiencies that may not be available to a newcomer. Such efficiency can be gained more quickly if a company sells large volumes of a product, because it has a larger base for gaining experience. For example, Texas Instruments was able to establish cost leadership in electronic calculators by achieving lower costs based on its long-standing production experience. By lowering prices substantially, Texas Instruments pressured competitors to do the same, driving many of them out of business.

Still another way to reduce costs is by *greater productivity*. **Productivity** *is the ratio of output (production output, sales results) to input (manufacturing and marketing costs).* Improved productivity results from reduced labor costs, from adopting new technologies that increase production output at reduced costs, or from more-efficient procedures that reduce distribution and advertising costs. As described in Chapter 2, one of Toyota's biggest competitive advantages in producing cars in this country has been its greater productivity per worker.

One company that has actively sought a market-wide cost advantage is Heinz. In 1982, the company's CEO initiated a "low cost operator" program specifying cost-cutting goals for each of Heinz's subsidiaries. Managers had to either achieve these goals or start looking for another job. In one case, the ketchup group discovered that they could save $4 million a year by getting rid of the back label on ketchup bottles.[12] Based on its low cost program, Heinz wound up closing 16 plants, eliminating one-third of its managerial jobs, and generating an average of $55 million in profits per year.

Heinz's emphasis was on cost-cutting because of industry and economic conditions including slow growth, intense competitive pressures, and low profits. Also, Heinz is in an industry with few product differences among competitors. Product uniqueness or superiority is an unlikely reason for consumers to choose one brand of canned vegetables over another. Thus, cost reduction is the surest way to beat out competitors.

Lower costs produced higher operating margins for Heinz, with profits increasing an average of 17 percent a year in the mid 1980s. The company chose to plow these earnings into heavy advertising and sales promotions that in turn helped maintain a loyal customer base.

But a program of cost reductions must ensure product quality, otherwise a company cannot maintain a competitive advantage. By 1989, Heinz was losing its competitive advantage because cost cuts began taking their toll on quality. For example, cost reduction pressures at the company's Tater Tots frozen potato plants caused plant managers to step up line speeds and change cooking methods.[13] The result was that the once chunky insides turned to mashed potatoes. Although Heinz is still trying to achieve competitive advantage through lower cost, it is now also instituting a quality control program to ensure that cost reductions are not achieved at the expense of product quality.

MARKET NICHE

A third pathway to competitive advantage is to operate in a protected market niche. The question is how long a market nicher will be able to maintain its niche before the giants come in. Ironically, the better a company does in appealing to a particular market niche, and the more profitable the business, the greater is the likelihood that a large company will step in. As a result, market nichers tread a very fine line between maintaining a protected niche and attracting competition.

For example, a small company called Minnetonka established a niche by being the first to introduce liquid hand soap in 1981. The niche quickly attracted the industry giants, including Procter & Gamble. Minnetonka's sales plummeted, and the price of the company's share on the stock market fell from $18 to less than $2. To make matters worse, the company had been advertising its product, Softsoap, based on the slogan "soap without the soapy mess." Because the theme focused on the advantages of liquid soap in general rather than on the particular benefits of Softsoap, it helped pave the way for competition.[14]

A company can try to dominate a niche based on either product superiority or cost advantage. Most companies, like Minnetonka, rely on product superiority. Martin-Brower relies on cost to achieve a niche strategy. The company, the third largest food distributor in the United States, reduced its customers to eight leading fast-food chains. It met the specialized needs of these customers by stocking only their lines and positioning warehouses based on their locations.[15] As a result, the company was able to reduce the costs of its operations and provide its narrower customer base better service at lower prices.

CONDITIONS FOR SEEKING A PATHWAY TO COMPETITIVE ADVANTAGE

When should a firm seek a marketing advantage, a cost advantage, or a niche? A marketing advantage should be sought if the firm can answer an unmet need in the marketplace, such as the need met by Federal Express for more-reliable overnight delivery, or the need met by Apple for improved graphics in personal computers. Such a marketing advantage is most likely when a product is first introduced and competition has yet to enter. A cost advantage should be sought in mature markets where sales are stable or declining. In such conditions, few new products have been introduced, so the most effective pathway to market-wide advantage is to lower costs and use the additional margins to either lower the price to the consumer or increase advertising expenditures. Heinz chose the latter course.

A market-niche strategy is well suited to smaller businesses who are trying to coexist with the giants. Without this strategy, A&W could not exist in the soft drink industry, and Minnetonka could not have competed for a time as a small company in an industry dominated by giants. A niche strategy can also be used by larger companies who want to stake out a toehold in an industry as a basis for future growth. For example, Procter & Gamble followed a niche strategy in the soft drink market by acquiring Orange Crush and marketing it to a small, loyal segment. It viewed the acquisition as a testing ground to determine whether it should develop additional soft drink brands for a more forceful entry into the industry. It never established the strong bottler network necessary to be a success as a soft-drink marketer and sold Orange Crush to Cadbury Schweppes in 1989.[16]

Whether a firm gains a competitive edge through a marketing or a cost advantage, on a market-wide basis or in a particular market niche, the result tends to be greater profitability. However, a company cannot achieve advantage by one route while ignoring the other. Heinz's chief lesson in the 1980s was that a cost advantage is ineffective if product quality is ignored. Conversely, a marketing advantage is worthless if it makes the product prohibitively expensive.

COMPETITIVE ADVANTAGE IN INTERNATIONAL MARKETS

International markets provide a rich environment in which to gain a competitive advantage. The three dimensions of competitive advantage—cost, marketing, and market niches—can be applied to international companies operating abroad. The best example is found in Japanese companies looking for cost, marketing, and market niche advantages in the United States.

COST ADVANTAGE

As described in Chapter 5, Japanese companies have established a market-wide cost advantage in automobiles, electronics, and personal computers. The Japanese have been able to gain efficiencies in production by adopting a concept known as **statistical process control,** *which is an approach to production that seeks to control defects at the time they occur rather than after the product is completed.* Japanese workers on the assembly line are given the greatest autonomy possible and are responsible for identifying defects in their own work. Japanese workers are also inculcated from birth with a shared sense of responsibility to their co-workers and view the elimination of defects as a group responsibility.

In contrast, most American production lines focus on quality control after the fact. One estimate is that one-fourth of American workers are employed to fix the mistakes of the other three-fourths.[17] As a result, Japanese companies can maintain high quality at lower cost compared to their American counterparts. This is the primary reason that Japan drove American companies such as General Electric out of the television manufacturing industry.

Japan's ability to produce cars at lower cost based on statistical process control has put GM, Ford, and Chrysler at a severe competitive disadvantage. GM's average cost of producing a car is $1,500 higher than the comparable import.[18] In an attempt to learn Japanese production methods, GM entered a joint venture with Toyota to produce cars in a California plant. GM executives who "graduated" from the plant were highly enthused by what they learned and sought to pass it on to other divisions within GM.

MARKETING ADVANTAGE

Japanese companies producing packaged goods began mounting a concerted effort to seek a competitive advantage in the United States in the late 1980s. Whereas electronic and auto companies could establish a competitive advantage based on cost, Japanese producers of cosmetics, food products, and household goods had to pursue other avenues. A strong yen after 1985 made Japanese products expensive in the United States and eliminated most of their cost advantages. As a result, Japanese packaged-goods firms have pursued a marketing advantage. Kao, known as the Procter & Gamble of Japan, plans to pursue marketing advantages by introducing a raft of new products related to consumer needs. In the words of Edwin Artzt, Procter & Gamble's CEO, "their focus is on satisfying people up and down the line, in service, cost, and everything."[19] Kao has challenged the domestic market leaders in household products by introducing Attack, a superconcentrated detergent, and in skin care by introducing Actibath bath additive tablets and Ever Soft hand and body lotion. In 1988, it bought Andrew Jergens, a U.S. manufacturer of beauty lotion to establish a stronger domestic base for its new product efforts.

MARKET NICHE

Japanese packaged-goods firms also have targeted market niches. Kirin and Suntory, leading Japanese beverage companies, are following a market-niche approach. They are introducing iced tea and coffee to small segments of the market to avoid competition with the beverage giants. They are also introducing Japanese-style vending machines that offer up to fifty lines of food and drink as part of their niche strategy. These companies are powerful enough to expand beyond niches and can operate on a market-wide basis. Kirin, the world's number two beverage company, after Coca-Cola, began buying bottling companies in the United States to establish a possible base for introducing a line of beverages to challenge Pepsi and Coke.[20]

IDENTIFY OPPORTUNITIES FOR COMPETITIVE ADVANTAGE

Although firms may take various pathways to gain a competitive edge, these pathways are not always available, nor are they always suitable to a firm's resources. It is necessary for a company to assess a market and identify the opportunities for competitive advantage.

There are three requirements in identifying opportunities for competitive advantage: (1) determine the level of attractiveness of a market that might make it a good target for gaining competitive advantage; (2) identify competitors' strengths and weaknesses in the market; and (3) identify the company's capabilities to gain competitive advantage.

These three factors are shown as three dimensions in Figure 6.3. You may recognize Figure 6.3 as an offshoot of the marketing planning matrix described in Chapter 2 (see Figure 2.2). In that figure, a strategic window of opportunity is

FIGURE 6.3

Identifying the Opportunity for Competitive Advantage

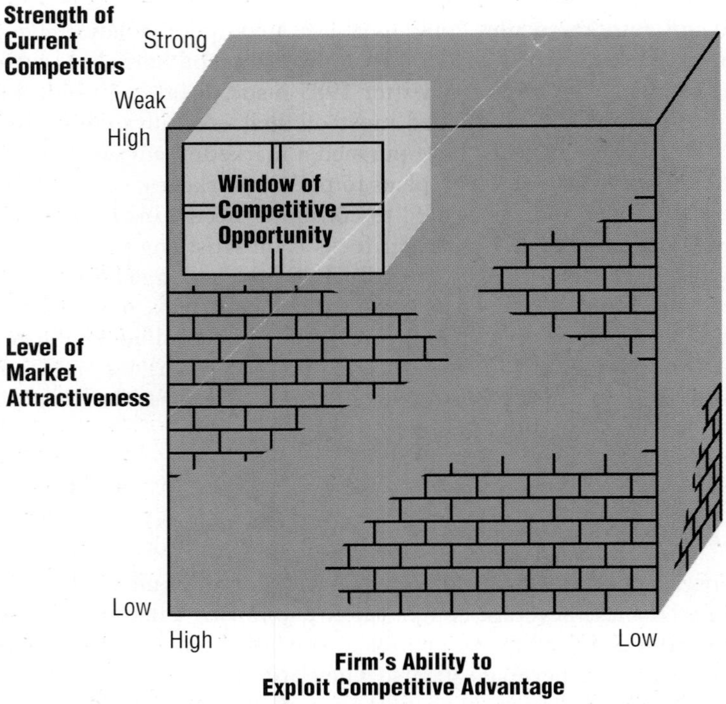

identified by a marketing opportunity that the firm has the resources to exploit. In Figure 6.3 a **window of competitive opportunity** *is now defined by a market's attractiveness as a source of competitive advantage, by competitive weakness, and by the firm's ability to exploit such a competitive advantage.* Opportunity is thus defined in a competitive context.

MARKET ATTRACTIVENESS

Michael Porter cites five factors that determine a market's attractiveness as a source of competitive advantage:[21]

1. Barriers to entry into the market
2. Competitive intensity
3. Availability of substitute products from other industries
4. Bargaining power of customers
5. Bargaining power of suppliers

The first two, barriers to entry and competitive intensity, are particularly important in defining the attractiveness of a market for a company considering entry. Procter & Gamble decided not to compete in the soft-drink industry primarily because of high competitive intensity and barriers to further expansion such as high costs of production and the expense of establishing a bottler network.

BARRIERS TO ENTRY

Barriers to entry *are factors that restrict a company's entry into a market.* They can be a plus if a company is already established, because such barriers serve to protect the company from further competition, or a minus if the company is considering entry into a market. The greatest barrier to entry is the existence of a competitor with a *significant marketing or cost advantage.* Federal Express created barriers to entry by being the first company to provide a unique service, guaranteed overnight delivery. Pepsi and Coke create barriers to entry with their constant advertising and promotional efforts. IBM creates barriers to entry because of a strong sales force, a full product line backed by service guarantees, and its historic reputation as the leader in the field.

At times, *entrenched competitors* will consciously develop barriers to prevent the entry of other companies into a market. When John Sculley left Pepsi-Cola to head Apple Computer, one of his stated intentions was to spend so much money advertising Apple products that the price of entry into the personal computer business would scare off newcomers.[22] Obviously, the threat could not scare off IBM, but Apple did raise the stakes by spending heavily in advertising and promotions.

Entrenched competitors are not the only barriers to entry. In fields such as telecommunications or mineral extraction, *capital requirements* may be so high that they virtually preclude new companies from entering the market. A related barrier is the need to attain *economies of scale* in production in order to reduce costs. If such economies cannot be achieved by a newcomer, the company will be at a cost disadvantage. *Patent protection* may also deter new entrants. Polaroid was able to block Kodak's entry into instant photography because of the patents it holds on the process.

The need for *adequate distribution facilities* is another barrier. Bottlers are a key link in the distribution of soft drinks, because they obtain the syrup from the manufacturer, bottle the products, and distribute them to supermarkets and other retailers. Pepsi and Coke have built a strong network of independent bottlers over the years. The expense of establishing such a bottler network has deterred newcomers. As we have seen, one reason P&G divested themselves of Orange Crush was that they could not establish a strong bottler network for the brand.

COMPETITIVE INTENSITY

When competition in a market is intense, the opportunities for gaining an edge over other companies tend to decrease. Competition tends to be most intense when sales in an industry are stable or decreasing. As competitors fight over a shrinking pie, revenues decrease. Companies cannot afford to develop superior products based on technological breakthroughs. Most product advances have been duplicated by competition, and the product is regarded as a virtual commodity.

For example, competition became more intense in the home-appliance industry as growth slowed because of a lower birth rate and major recessions in the early 1980s and 1990s. Sales leveled off in 1987 after four decades of steady growth and began to fall in 1990. The result was shrinking earnings and intense competition between the three major domestic manufacturers—General Electric, Whirlpool, and Maytag. The fight for market share in a declining industry has been described as brutal. As one GE executive said regarding the 1990s, "This war will be fought in the trenches."[23]

The reaction of all three manufacturers has been to look to international markets for future growth. The European Community, with a 4 percent annual growth rate for home appliances (compared to −2 percent in the United States) and a market 25 percent larger than that in the United States looks promising. In 1990, GE, Whirlpool, and Maytag announced expanded operations in Europe within weeks of each other through joint ventures with European companies or through outright acquisitions. As the European market for home appliances matures, competition is likely to be as intense as that in the United States. One factor that may deter more-intense competition is if consumers in the Eastern European countries begin to acquire increased purchasing power in a free-market economy. If so, the growth rate for home appliances is likely to increase beyond 4 percent, creating enough opportunity for everyone.

Competition also becomes more intense when there are fewer opportunities to reduce cost. In mature markets such as home appliances, there is limited potential to reduce marketing or manufacturing costs because cost reductions have already been "wrung out" by leading companies. As a result, profit margins are narrower. For example, profit margins at Whirlpool went from 19.5 percent in 1984 to 11.5 percent in 1989.[24] The result is more-intense rivalry for the limited profits available in the industry.

OTHER FACTORS DEFINING MARKET ATTRACTIVENESS

Three other factors were cited by Porter in influencing a firm's potential for gaining competitive advantage. One is the threat of substitute products from other industries. For instance, Pepsi and Coke are trying to increase the consumption of colas as a substitute for coffee, posing a threat to coffee producers.

The bargaining power of large customers can also inhibit a firm's ability to gain a competitive advantage. At times, companies sell to powerful customers who can force prices down, demand higher quality, or require more service. A large food chain like A&P or a merchandiser like Sears can force their smaller suppliers to reduce prices. Such actions by larger buyers increase competitive rivalry among their suppliers and reduce profits, making the market less attractive to enter.

Similarly, the bargaining power of a large supplier might decrease a market's attractiveness for a firm. A large supplier can exert bargaining power by raising prices or dictating the terms on which the product will be sold, making it more difficult for buyers to make a profit. In the past, auto companies have exercised bargaining power over their dealers by forcing them to take additional cars and to offer higher trade-in allowances. When suppliers can exert such power, it lessens the attractiveness of a market for a firm.

COMPETITORS' STRENGTHS AND WEAKNESSES

Analyzing market attractiveness tells a company which markets are the best to enter to win a competitive advantage. But managers must go beyond an overall view of the market to determine the strengths and weaknesses of individual competitors. There is no formula for analyzing competitors, other than to ensure that information is obtained from as wide a spectrum as possible. Certainly a company will want to evaluate a competitor's marketing objectives. For example, Pepsi-Cola is beginning to market a sports drink targeting Gatorade drinkers. In considering entry into the sports-drink market, Pepsi had to assess Gatorade's sales and market-share objectives. A firm will also try to predict a competitor's future strategies.

Will Gatorade introduce a diet version to try to outflank Pepsi? Will it introduce additional flavors? The assumptions a competitor makes regarding future market conditions must also be judged. Does Gatorade expect the demand for sports drinks to rise? Finally, a firm must assess the competitor's resources. Gatorade is owned by Quaker Oats, so the question is whether Quaker intends to expand the market for Gatorade based on its managerial, financial, production, and distribution capabilities.

Answering these questions is difficult at best. As described in Chapter 4, many firms have environmental scanning departments that gather competitive information from the business press, salespeople, trade sources, and marketing research. Marketing research includes surveys that evaluate consumer perceptions of competitive products, identify the strengths of those products, and uncover their potential weaknesses. The most difficult areas to assess are competitors' assumptions and intentions. These can frequently be gleaned from annual reports, articles in the business press, stock reports, and speeches.

Rich as all these sources may be, an assessment of competitors' strengths and weaknesses must ultimately depend on a manager's knowledge of the market, insight into the competition, and intuition.

COMPANY CAPABILITIES

The third component identifying competitive advantage is the company's capabilities. A company's strengths and weaknesses define its ability to exploit marketing opportunities and competitive weaknesses. When John Sculley came to Apple, the first thing he did was to assess the company's strengths and weaknesses relative to IBM. His assessment was that Apple was superior to IBM in technology and product superiority, but that its distribution network and promotional mix were inferior. Thus, one of his first moves was to strengthen Apple's distribution network and boost its advertising campaign.

This type of evaluation cannot be done "off the top of the head." Before making any major moves, Sculley spent a full year studying the company and the industry, developing an intimate knowledge of computer technology, fully understanding his management, and getting to know IBM almost as well as he knew Apple. What Sculley performed was a **marketing audit,** *a comprehensive review of the company's marketing operations and resources.* In studying Apple's capabilities, he analyzed the company's production, R&D, sales, distribution, product development, and promotion resources, and assessed the adequacy of these resources to exploit existing and future opportunities.

DEVELOP STRATEGIES FOR COMPETITIVE ADVANTAGE

The next step in a firm's pursuit of competitive advantage is to develop strategies to achieve it. The need to develop strategies with an eye on competition has led marketers to draw analogies from military science. Let us first consider how these rules of warfare might apply to gaining competitive advantage, and then consider alternative strategies.

RULES OF WARFARE APPLIED TO MARKETING

One of the foremost military strategists, B. Liddell Hart, said that "the object of war is a better state of peace."[25] Translated into business terms, this means that the object of gaining a competitive advantage is to achieve "peaceful coexistence" with your competitors—but *on your terms.* As a market leader, *peace* means acceptance of the company's leadership position. As a market challenger, it means establishing a secure position in the face of another firm's dominance or even displacing the firm as the market leader. As a market nicher, "peace" means being left alone to pursue profits in particular market segments.

If peace is not attainable on your terms, then the object of pursuing competitive advantage is *survival.* When Lever Brothers and P&G entered the liquid-soap market, Minnetonka was no longer thinking of a niche strategy as a means of peaceful coexistence with the giants. Its goal became survival in the face of market dominance, and its eventual solution was to hook up with a larger firm that had the resources to compete with the market leaders.

A study of the greatest military minds—Clausewitz, Napoleon, von Moltke—has led marketers to borrow four principles for achieving competitive advantage: (1) concentrate resources, (2) take the initiative, (3) maneuver resources, and (4) plan with flexibility.[26]

The first principle is to *concentrate resources* where they will have the greatest effect, because a firm's resources are limited. The best way to concentrate resources is not always clear. Should the firm go head to head with the market leader? Should it try to probe for weaknesses in the leader's position? Should it try to find select market niches? Pepsi's strategy for the 1990s appears to be to compete with Coke head to head in the United States while trying to find profitable niches abroad. The strategy makes sense, since Pepsi is on a near-equal footing with Coke in the United States and head-to-head competition is feasible. But it is far behind abroad, and attempting to compete with Coke on an equal basis in the 155 countries where Coke is sold would dissipate Pepsi's resources. Therefore, Pepsi will try to establish market dominance in certain countries like Russia (where it was marketed well before Coke) and India (where it moved in when Coke had a falling out with the Indian government) while finding profits in select niches like vending-machine sales abroad.

The second principle is to *take the initiative* by acting rather than reacting to environmental changes. Pepsi took the initiative in establishing the juice-based soda market, because it saw more of a need for nutritional drinks among adults and felt that the addition of juice was a means of meeting this need. Similarly, Coke took the initiative in appealing to both men's and women's desire for a diet cola with its introduction of Diet Coke.

The third principle is to *maneuver resources* so that overall objectives are accomplished in a coordinated fashion. In other words, "keep your eye on the ball" to ensure that all resources are directed toward corporate goals rather than being deflected to secondary areas of competition. Coca-Cola maneuvered its resources effectively in 1990 when it mounted its coordinated attack on Pepsi's two flanks—introducing Coke II to appeal to those who want a sugared cola and positioning Diet Coke to appeal to those who want to switch from sugared to diet colas.

The fourth principle is to *plan with enough flexibility* to anticipate both environmental change and competitive actions. Pursuing competitive advantage in a flexible way requires an ability to foresee changes in the environment and to anticipate what competitors might do. Pepsi faces an important strategic issue into the next century. As nutritional concerns mount, are people likely to turn away from sugared colas in greater numbers? If so, Pepsi's strength among teenagers may not be enough to sustain its flagship brand. Does Pepsi have enough strength in the non-sugared categories to sustain its soft-drink business? If not, it will either have to establish more strength in diet, noncaffeinated, and flavored drinks or devote less resources to soft drinks and more to its two other businesses, fast foods and snacks, thereby ceding dominance of soft drinks to Coca-Cola.

STRATEGIES FOR ATTAINING COMPETITIVE ADVANTAGE

Firms can develop strategies to attain competitive advantage on a marketing, cost, or niche basis. The application of principles of military strategy suggests two broad approaches to competition: **proactive strategies** *in which a company anticipates future competitive actions and environmental trends and attempts to make the first move,* and **reactive strategies** *in which a company responds after the competition make major moves.* In military terms, a proactive approach would be identified as an offensive strategy, a reactive approach as a defensive strategy.

Competitive strategies are categorized into proactive versus reactive strategies in Figure 6.4. These strategies are further divided by the firm's market position, because strategies are largely determined by whether a company is a market leader, a challenger, a follower, or a company that is trying to avoid competition with the larger firms altogether.

MARKET LEADER STRATEGIES

In a few industries, there is an undisputed leader such as Campbell Soup with an 80 percent share of the condensed soup market and AT&T with over 90 percent of the long-distance telephone market. A more common situation in consumer-goods industries is what economists call an **oligopoly**, *that is, an industry in which*

FIGURE 6.4

Strategies for Competitive Advantage

	Proactive Strategies	**Reactive Strategies**
Market Leaders	Market Expansion Market-Share Protection Preemptive Actions	Reaction to Competitive Challenge
Market Challengers or Followers	Head-to-Head Competition Flanking Strategies Encirclement	Follow the Leader
Companies Avoiding Competition	Market Niche Bypass the Competition	Status Quo

two or three firms dominate, and the actions of one firm directly affect those of another. For example, the constant give and take between Coke and Pepsi in the soft-drink industry is typical of an oligopoly.

Even though an oligopoly is dominated by more than one company, one firm typically has the highest market share and is acknowledged as the market leader. Thus, Coca-Cola is the market leader in soft drinks, Procter & Gamble in toothpaste, and IBM in computers.

Figure 6.4 illustrates three strategies identified with a market leader: market expansion, market-share protection, and preemptive actions.

MARKET EXPANSION

A **market expansion strategy** *is used by the market leader to expand demand for the product category.* The company attempts to increase demand by citing the benefits of the product category rather than focusing on the advantages of its brands. The objective is to either attract new users to the category or to get existing users to use more.

With a dominant share of the market for overseas calls, AT&T would clearly benefit from any increase in the demand for such calls. For example, it is trying to encourage customer segments more likely to have relatives abroad, such as Hispanic-Americans, to call them more frequently (see Exhibit 6.2). Coca-Cola's "Coke for Breakfast" campaign is also designed to increase demand for a product category—colas. In this case, Coke is trying to get existing cola users to drink more cola. But since Pepsi's U.S. share of the cola market is almost as large as Coke's, Coke's campaign could benefit Pepsi.

Another way to expand demand is to develop new uses for a product. S.C. Johnson found a new use for its furniture wax years back when it discovered consumers using it on their cars. It repositioned the product and created the market for car wax.

In each of these cases, the market leader's brands tended to be the beneficiaries, because they were the brands adopted by existing users, by new users, or for new uses.

MARKET-SHARE PROTECTION

A market leader not only tries to expand the market, it also employs a **market-share protection strategy**, *which is a strategy designed to protect its current share of the market.* Compared with other firms in the industry, a market leader has more to protect. Market leaders protect their share by outspending competition on advertising and by ensuring widespread distribution of their products. Such a strategy is more feasible for a market leader, because it operates with higher profit margins and thus has more resources to devote to capturing customers from competitors.

Pizza Hut, a division of PepsiCo, followed a market-share protection strategy when McDonald's started selling pizza. As the market leader in pizza, Pizza Hut had more at stake than McDonald's, the challenger. Pizza Hut mounted an advertising campaign ridiculing McDonald's pizza offerings. In one TV commercial, an 11-year-old girl asks "Does it come on a bun?" Another spot has a child saying "I don't like their pizza; I like their playgrounds." In a third spot, an adult is asked how he liked the pizza and says, "I'd just rather not talk about it now."[27] The

EXHIBIT 6.2

Market Expansion: AT&T Attempts to Increase the Demand for Out-of-Country Calls

question is, do the ads succeed in undermining McDonald's pizza offerings or do they just bring attention to them?

"HOLA MAMA. ¡FELIZ
Crisp clear connections to
DIA DE LAS MADRES!
Mexico bring AT&T customer Conchita Weaver
ES CONCHITA, ¿COMO
closer to her family.
ESTA LA FAMILIA?"
—Conchita Weaver
AT&T

PREEMPTIVE ACTION

A market leader may take **preemptive action**, *a strategy which anticipates or discourages competitive entry*. Quaker Oats is trying to discourage both Pepsi and Coke from establishing themselves in the sports-drink market. Pepsi is entering the market with Mountain Dew Sport, a low-calorie extension of its Mountain Dew brand. Coca-Cola is entering the market with PowerAde, a carbonated sports drink designed for fountain service only.

Quaker Oats is attempting to preempt Pepsi and Coke by introducing a better tasting extension of the Gatorade brand, called Freestyle, in citrus, lemon-lime, and tangerine flavors. It is also trying to head off Mountain Dew Sport by introducing Gatorade Light. The company is trying to preempt Coke and Pepsi by making sure it has all the market segments covered: Gatorade for the hard-core athlete, Gatorade Light for the calorie-conscious athlete, and Freestyle for the fitness-oriented consumer more interested in the taste of a sports drink than in performance.[28]

GLOBAL MARKETING STRATEGIES

Market Expansion Abroad: Kellogg versus General Mills

A cereal war is shaping up in Europe involving the two largest cereal makers—Kellogg and General Mills. The reasons for the companies' strategy of looking to Europe for growth are not hard to find: Cereal sales in the United States are leveling off after the spurt in cereal consumption due to greater nutritional awareness among adults. Helping to put a damper on cereal sales has been the Food and Drug Administration's actions in clamping down on claims that oat bran reduces cholesterol and that high-fiber cereals help prevent cancer.

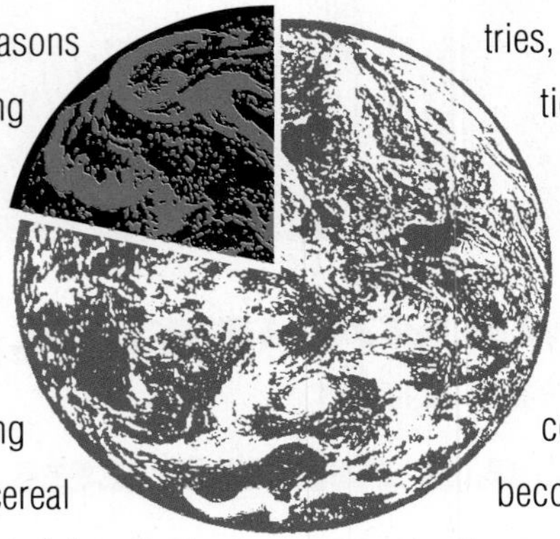

Cereal companies in Europe face no such restrictions. Further, cereal consumption is beginning to grow as more European consumers are becoming concerned about health and nutrition. In some countries, annual growth of cereal consumption is 30 percent.

Three other changes in Europe are boosting cereal sales. First, supermarkets are beginning to spring up across the continent. Second, commercial television channels are becoming more numerous, making it easier to reach large numbers of consumers. A third change is the development of satellite cable channels that cut across borders. These changes make mass marketing of cereals on a transnational basis possible. Further, they encourage more global marketing strategies since the same message can

REACTING TO A COMPETITIVE CHALLENGE

As Figure 6.4 shows, market leaders might follow reactive as well as proactive strategies by responding to competitive actions. The problem with reactive strategies is that they leave the initiative to the competitor. Flexibility of action calls for contingency plans to anticipate competitive moves so the company will not get caught in a reactive situation. A good example of a reactive strategy was General Foods' response to Procter & Gamble's challenge when it introduced its Folgers coffee into the eastern market. The competitive battle between General Foods' leading Maxwell House brand and Folgers was described by *Fortune* as follows:

> As the aggressor, P&G's coffee division is making most of the moves. But [General Foods'] troops countered quickly. When Folgers mailed millions of coupons offering consumers 45 cents off on a one-pound can of coffee, General Foods countered with newspaper coupons of its own. When Folgers gave retailers 15 percent discounts from the list price, General Foods met them head on. [General Foods] let Folgers lead off with a TV blitz

GLOBAL MARKETING STRATEGIES

reach consumers across Western Europe.

Kellogg has actually been on the European continent since the 1950s and has about 50 percent of the market but is now expanding its operations in anticipation of a rise in cereal consumption. General Mills is the new kid on the block. It would have faced formidable barriers to entry by trying to break into Europe in the face of Kellogg's dominance, so it selected a logical strategy: It hooked up with Nestlé, the largest food company in the world, but one that did not sell cereals. The synergies did not stop there. If General Mills could bring cereals to Nestlé, Nestlé could provide a network of plants—the distribution network that General Mills was lacking—and a renowned name in Europe.

Both companies see Europe, rather than the United States, as the basis for future market expansion. If they are right, the cereal wars may take a trip abroad.

Question: What are the reasons for Kellogg and General Mills stepping up operations in Europe? What are the risks?

Source: "Europe Cooks Up a Cereal Brawl," *Fortune*, June 3, 1991, pp. 175–179.

that introduced tidy Mrs. Olson to all those Eastern housewives . . . Then it saturated the airwaves [with its own TV advertising].[29]

MARKET CHALLENGER/ FOLLOWER STRATEGIES

Three major proactive strategies challenge a market leader: head-to-head competition (that is, a direct frontal attack on the leader), a flanking strategy in which the challenger looks for weak spots or gaps in the leader's offerings, and an encirclement strategy in which several challenges are mounted simultaneously, both directly and on the flanks. These strategies are described as proactive in Figure 6.4, because they take the initiative in challenging the market leader. They are presented visually in Figure 6.5, with examples of each strategy. In the next few paragraphs, we will look more closely at each of these strategies, as well as a reactive follow-the-leader strategy.

HEAD-TO-HEAD COMPETITION

Head-to-head competition *is a strategy in which a competitor directly challenges the market leader.* It is characteristic of oligopolies, because the second or third leading

FIGURE 6.5

Strategies to Challenge or Avoid the Market Leader

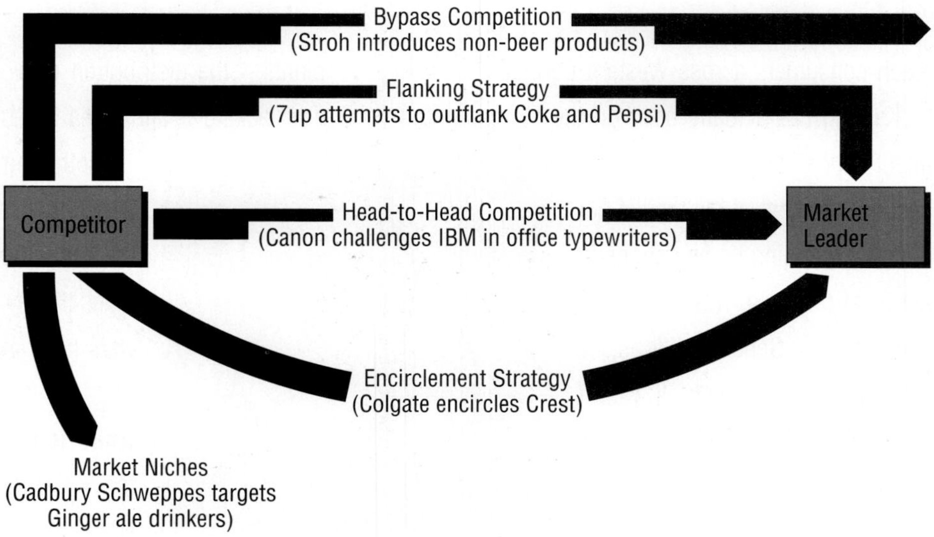

Source: Adapted from Philip Kotter and Ravi Singh, "Marketing Warfare in the 1980s." *The Journal of Business Strategy* (Winter 1982), 34.

company is likely to challenge the leader. General Foods' Maxwell House was the leading coffee brand in the United States until Procter & Gamble began moving Folgers from its strong West-Coast base. As we have seen, General Foods' reaction was to follow Folgers' lead. But even worse, in an attempt to reduce costs, General Foods began using cheaper beans and reducing advertising expenditures. By 1988, it was in second place, behind Folgers.[30]

When Philip Morris bought General Foods and Kraft and merged the two companies, they developed a more proactive strategy for Maxwell House. They improved the quality of their beans and changed the container from a can that one executive said made Maxwell House "look like it could have been motor oil," to a more streamlined look. In a direct challenge to Folgers, Kraft General Foods began an advertising campaign in 1990 that said consumers prefer the taste of Maxwell House to Folgers. Procter & Gamble retorted by saying the ads were misleading.[31]

A head-to-head challenge is not viable unless a challenger has some competitive advantage based on product superiority or cost. Canon has challenged IBM's dominance in office typewriters by claiming that it can go one better than IBM on features such as memory capacity, type of display, and ease of use. Although the ad in Exhibit 6.3 does not name IBM, Canon's target is clear, based on a claim of product superiority. Maxwell House is also claiming product superiority. The question is whether the consumer will accept Maxwell House's taste claim or simply regard it as advertising puffery.

The risk of head-to-head competition with the market leader is that it invites retaliation. Both Colgate and Procter & Gamble began expanding their presence in Europe in the 1980s as a result of stagnant detergent and toothpaste sales in the United States. The problem is that they had to compete head to head with

EXHIBIT 6.3

Canon Goes Head to Head Against IBM

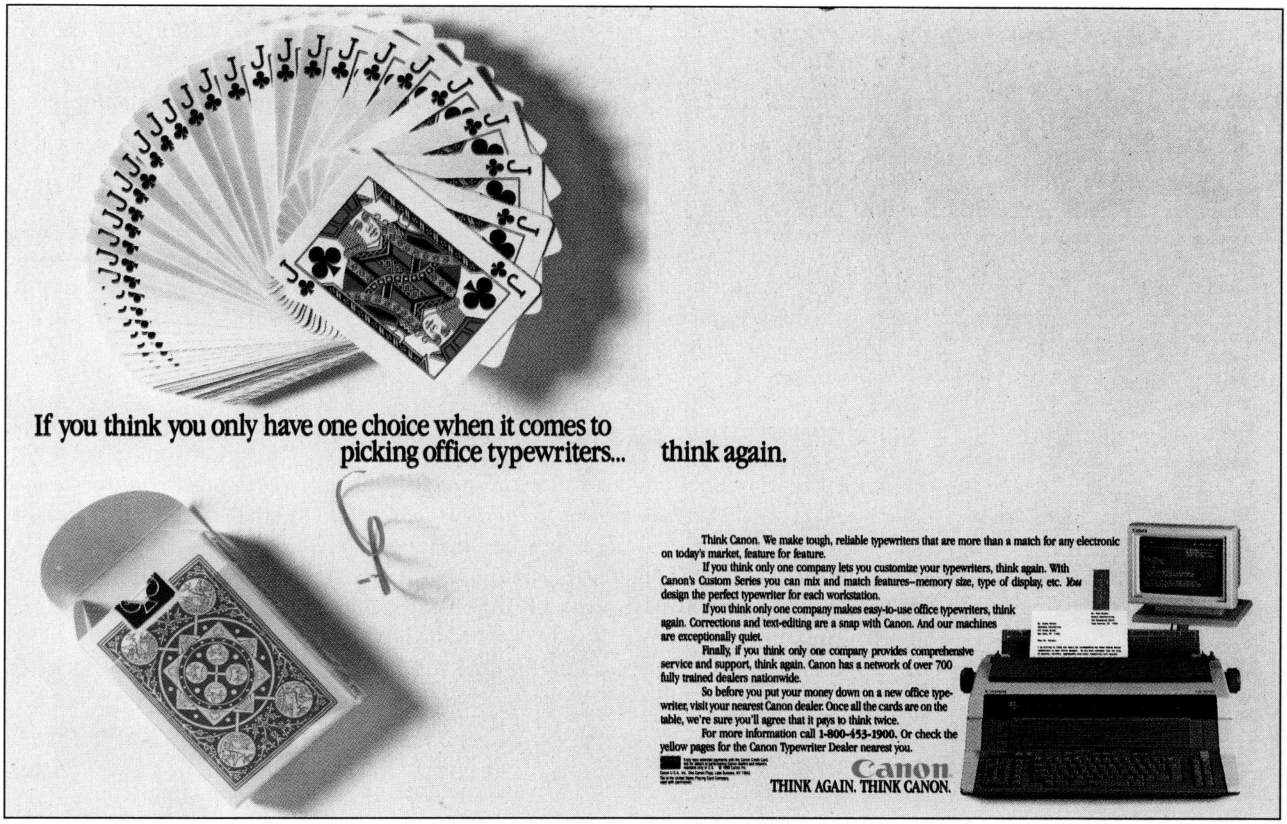

the European leader, Unilever. Unilever retaliated by bringing the battle to P&G's and Colgate's home turf.[32] It successfully introduced Snuggle, a new fabric softener, and increased promotional expenditures for existing brands such as Wisk detergent and Aim toothpaste.

Unilever's reaction demonstrates a further risk of head-to-head competition—that retaliation may occur in other markets. A logical reaction for a market leader under attack is to look at the challenger's home base as a source for retaliation.

FLANKING STRATEGY

A **flanking strategy** *challenges the market leader in areas not currently contested.* Many firms use this alternative of probing for weaknesses on the leader's flanks, because direct challenges are so risky. Such flanking strategies involve identifying consumer needs the leader may have overlooked and offering product improvements to meet those needs.

Seven-Up Co. sought a competitive advantage against Pepsi and Coke by advertising its flagship 7-Up brand as caffeine-free in the early 1980s. The strategy seemed a natural for the company because 7-Up never did have caffeine. In introducing the slogan "Never had it, never will," 7-Up tried to outflank Pepsi and Coke by appealing to a more health-conscious public, addressing a benefit the soft drink giants were ignoring. Flanking strategies have also been used for services. United Jersey, a group of banks in central and northern New Jersey, outflanked the larger banks such as Chase and Chemical by offering a new benefit, speedy loans. Their theme "the fast-moving bank," hit a responsive chord among customers.[33]

There are risks in a flanking strategy. If the leader retaliates quickly, it does not give the challenger time to establish an entrenched position. The challenger must have sufficient resources to sustain an attack. As we have seen in Chapter 3, when 7-Up began advertising its flagship brand as caffeine-free, Pepsi and Coke introduced their own noncaffeinated brands, undermining 7-Up's position. Eventually, the company went back to advertising the brand as "The Uncola," a theme it was using in the late 1970s to position 7-Up as a cola alternative.

ENCIRCLEMENT STRATEGIES

The third type of challenge, an **encirclement strategy,** *challenges the market leader on several fronts at the same time or in quick succession.* Such challenges are aggressive and require sufficient resources by the challenger.

In the early 1980s, Colgate began an encirclement strategy meant to wrest market leadership in toothpaste from Procter & Gamble's Crest. Colgate beat Crest in introducing gels, pump dispensers and toothpaste positioned for children. It then opened up a new set of benefits by switching the focus from tooth decay to gum disease and introducing tartar- and plaque-fighting toothpastes in paste and baking soda versions (see Exhibit 6.4). Colgate's market share climbed from 18 percent in 1980 to 28 percent in 1985, almost on par with Crest's.[34]

But Crest counterattacked and went one better than Colgate. It introduced an improved tartar-control formula, and Colgate's share began slipping. Crest went back to being the undisputed market leader with a 39 percent market share.[35] Although Colgate's encirclement strategy was successful for a time, it could not maintain a sustainable advantage in the face of Crest's product improvements.

FOLLOW THE LEADER

A **follow-the-leader strategy** *copies the market leader's moves.* Following the leader is a way to minimize the risks of retaliation due to a direct or indirect challenge. Such a "me too" strategy is unlikely to succeed if it only involves introducing carbon copies of leading brands. A market follower must provide some advantage to consumers, whether in service, location, convenience, or price.

Anheuser-Busch is using a follow-the-leader strategy in the draft-beer market. Miller's Genuine Draft, introduced in 1985, is the leader. In 1990 Anheuser-Bush announced plans to introduce Busch Cold Filtered Draft in a clear bottle with a shiny gold and red label, the same packaging as Miller Genuine Draft. One analyst said "It's Miller Genuine Draft in sheep's clothing." Another said that Anheuser-Busch risks selling a "me-too" product to which consumers will not respond.[36] The question is whether Anheuser-Bush can sufficiently differentiate its new entrant. It is saying that Busch Cold Filtered Draft is made from whole hops rather than the hops extracts used in making Miller Genuine Draft. But many marketers are skeptical whether this will be a sufficient point of differentiation.

EXHIBIT 6.4

Colgate Attempts to Encircle Crest

A follower strategy is often used in pricing by firms that produce standardized items such as steel, aluminum, paper, or fertilizers. Price competition tends to be unprofitable since a price cut will generally be copied, leaving everyone with lower profits. Therefore, the typical strategy is to follow the leader in pricing and attempt to obtain a competitive advantage in service and delivery.

But there are risks in a follower strategy. What if the market leader is pricing at an unprofitable level or offering the wrong services? To quote the vice-president of marketing at Compaq Computer, "To focus too much on the competition means you're relying on them to do their marketing job right. We'd rather make our own decisions."[37]

STRATEGIES FOR AVOIDING COMPETITION

Many companies seek profits by avoiding competition. They look for targets of opportunity that are unlikely to attract other companies, or that will give them enough time in a protected niche to ensure profits before a competitor enters the niche. Two proactive approaches for avoiding competition are a market-niche strategy and a strategy that seeks to bypass competitors. A reactive approach that avoids competition utilizes a strategy that maintains the status quo.

MARKET NICHE

One of the primary pathways to competitive advantage is to develop a market-niche strategy. A niche strategy entails pursuing markets that are too specialized or too small to attract the leaders. There are several alternative means of implementing such strategies. One is to focus on a particular *market segment.* Although Cadbury Schweppes is the third largest beverage maker in the world, it is a small player in the U.S. market and avoids competition with Pepsi and Coke through a niche strategy. For example, it targets its two ginger ale brands to specific niches: Canada Dry to "all-American types" and Schweppes to a more sophisticated and upscale segment. The company's strategy has been described as one designed to "plug niches and win [market] share without entering the cola wars."[38]

Coca-Cola is also following a niche strategy in the sports-drink market by aiming at a particular segment of the retail market, establishments that sell fountain drinks. Whereas Pepsi is going head to head with Gatorade by introducing Mountain Dew Sports, Coke is positioning PowerAde as strictly a fountain drink, thereby hoping to capture a niche that Gatorade has ignored.

Another market-niche strategy is to focus on a particular *price segment.* Hewlett-Packard, for instance, specializes in high-quality, high-priced hand calculators, thus avoiding direct competition with leaders such as Texas Instruments. A third strategy is to focus on a *geographic area.* Coors beer established a strong regional base in the Midwest, building a loyal following. Only when it went national did it lose its niche advantage, opening itself up to direct attack by Anheuser-Bush.

On the surface, market-niche strategies may seem similar to flanking strategies. There is a difference in emphasis, however. While a flanking strategy tries to take advantage of a competitor's weakness on an industry-wide basis, a niche strategy avoids competition by focusing on a market segment. The risk of a niche strategy is that the segment might become profitable enough to attract the industry leaders.

BYPASSING THE COMPETITION

A second proactive strategy for avoiding competition is a **bypass-the-competition strategy** *in which a company introduces unrelated product lines or enters noncompetitive areas.* For instance, Stroh Brewery is finding it increasingly difficult to compete with Anheuser-Busch and Miller and has had to shut down its biggest plant. Stroh's strategy has been to develop drinks other than beer in small market segments—including a malt-based cooler, a soft drink with 70 percent juice and 30 percent sparkling water, and a nonalcoholic malt beverage—while maintaining its current beer line.[39]

STATUS QUO

A more reactive way to avoid competition is to follow a **status quo strategy** *which is a "don't rock the boat" approach that avoids confrontation.* When Perrier was withdrawn from store shelves because benzene was found in the product, other competitors could have reacted by taking up the slack. But competitors like Evian Waters and San Pellegrino did not. Why? Because they feared that weakening the leader, Perrier, would weaken the bottled-water market. Since bottled water is a growth market in the United States, why rock the boat?

Marketing analysts were surprised by this status quo strategy. One former PepsiCo executive said: "This is the most gentlemanly market I've seen. Where I come from, when the competition does something wrong, you kill them. I would've gone to war." Another marketer said: "The best time to jump is when the competition is down . . . It's the only time to kick a leader."[40]

A status quo strategy is also appealing to these companies because it reduces the costs of competing with each other. If a status quo strategy proves to be the result of a direct understanding between companies, it is illegal under the antitrust laws because it involves collusion. Had Perrier's competitors come together and agreed on a "hands-off" strategy, the agreement would have been illegal.

ANTICIPATE COMPETITIVE RESPONSES

The last step in the process of gaining competitive advantage is to anticipate competitive responses. A company must always second-guess a competitor's responses to its strategies. Anticipating what competitors will do defines a proactive approach, because projected competitive responses influence the company's strategy.

An example is Unilever's introduction of Snuggle fabric softener to compete with P&G's Downy in 1985. Snuggle was a parity product offered at a lower price.[41] Lever's strategy had to be conditioned on the response it expected from P&G. If Lever had expected P&G to meet its price immediately, it would not have introduced the brand. If P&G either reduced the price of Downy or introduced a lower-priced fabric softener to outflank Snuggle within the first three years after introduction, Lever might have looked at operating margins more closely to see if there was room for a subsequent price cut. If it predicted no specific response from P&G in the first three years, however, Lever would have interpreted this as a clear signal to introduce Snuggle. Lever's prediction that P&G would not immediately respond to Snuggle's introduction was correct.

A marketer can select an appropriate strategy based on their estimate of competitive responses by using *expected value analysis*. This requires listing (1) the company's alternative strategies, (2) possible competitive responses, (3) the chance these responses will occur, and (4) the profit impact of the company's strategy. Assume Unilever has three options: as listed in Table 6.1—introducing Snuggle at a very low price ($1.59 for a 33-ounce container), a moderately low price ($1.89) or not introducing Snuggle at all. Since Downy sells for an average price of $2.19, both market entry strategies would undercut Downy's price.

Further assume that Unilever's management estimates there is a 20-percent chance P&G would meet Snuggle's price within one year, a 20-percent chance it would meet Snuggle's price within three years, and a 60-percent chance it would not respond in the first three years. Management then estimates the impact of its two pricing strategies on the return on investment (ROI). For example, if P&G meets the lowest price within one year, it would have a negative effect of 8 percent on ROI. If P&G does not respond within three years, there would be a positive effect of 5 percent.

To determine the best price level based on P&G's likely actions, management multiplies the likelihood of each contingency by the profit impact of the particular strategy. This determines the expected value of the pricing strategy. The expected value charging $1.59 is:

$$(.20 \times -8.0) + (.20 \times +2.0) + (60 \times +5.0) = +1.8\%$$

The profit impact of charging $1.89 is higher, +3.0 percent. By definition, the profit impact of not introducing Snuggle would be zero, so both pricing strategies

TABLE 6.1

Estimating the Best Marketing Strategy Based on Competitive Response

		PROFIT IMPACT OF COMPANY STRATEGIES (% IMPACT ON ROI)		
COMPETITIVE STRATEGIES	PROBABILITY OF COMPETITIVE STRATEGY	INTRODUCE SNUGGLE AT $1.59	INTRODUCE SNUGGLE AT $1.89	DO NOT INTRODUCE SNUGGLE
P&G reduces price for Downy within one year	.20	−8.0%	−4.0%	—
P&G reduces price for Downy within three years	.20	+2.0%	+1.0%	—
P&G does not respond in first three years	.60	+5.0%	+6.0%	—
EXPECTED VALUE OF EACH STRATEGY		+1.8%	+3.0%	0

would be preferable to doing nothing. The maximum pricing strategy based on P&G's expected response would be to charge $1.89.

SUMMARY

1. **How can a firm establish advantages over its competitors?**
   There are three broad pathways to competitive advantage: market-wide product or service superiority, market-wide cost leadership, and a market-niche strategy. A company seeking product superiority tries to do a better job than competitors in meeting customer needs in the total market. Product superiority can be obtained by providing a better product and/or doing a better job in positioning, promoting, and distributing the product.

   Cost leadership can be gained by reducing production or marketing costs below those of competitors. This gives a company the option of reducing prices or plowing higher operating margins back into advertising and promotions. A firm following a market-niche strategy tries to establish a product or cost advantage in a particular niche as a means of avoiding direct competition with larger companies in the industry.
2. **How can marketing opportunities be identified for establishing competitive advantage?**

Companies identify opportunities for competitive advantage by analyzing a market's attractiveness, their competitors' strengths and weaknesses, and their own strengths and weaknesses. A market is attractive to a potential entrant if competitive intensity is low, and there are few barriers to entry. A marketer analyzes competitors' strengths and weaknesses by evaluating their objectives, strategies, marketing assumptions, and resources. A company analyzes its own strengths and weaknesses in the same way.

3. **How can principles of military science be applied in developing strategies to win competitive advantage?**
A study of military science has led marketers to borrow four key principles to achieve competitive advantage: (1) concentrate resources where they will have the greatest effect; (2) take the initiative by acting rather than reacting to environmental changes; (3) maneuver resources so that overall objectives are accomplished in a coordinated fashion; and (4) plan with flexibility (contingency plans) to anticipate environmental change and competitive actions.

4. **What strategies can be implemented to establish competitive advantage?**
Strategies for competitive advantage can be categorized into proactive (offensive) strategies and reactive (defensive) strategies. The type of strategy to be selected will depend on the position of the firm in the marketplace—leader, challenger, follower, or nicher.

Market leaders tend to pursue strategies of market expansion, market-share protection, or preemptive actions to prevent competitors from entering new markets. Market leaders may also follow a reactive policy of waiting for a competitive challenge before taking action.

Market challengers pursue offensive strategies involving head-to-head competition with the market leader or flanking attacks that probe for gaps in the leader's offerings. They also pursue strategies of encirclement when they attack simultaneously (or in quick succession) on several fronts. A market follower pursues a reactive strategy by following the leader's initiative.

Companies can also gain competitive advantage by avoiding competition. Companies following a market-niche strategy avoid competition by targeting resources to profitable segments that leaders are unlikely to pursue. Companies can also try to bypass competition by seeking markets that are not closely related to those the leader is in. A company taking a more reactive stance avoids competition by trying to maintain the status quo—a "don't rock the boat" approach.

KEY TERMS

Competitive advantage (p. 176)
Competitive analysis (p. 176)
Marketing advantage (p. 177)
Cost advantage (p. 177)
Market niche (p. 177)
Productivity (p. 182)
Statistical process control (p. 184)
Window of competitive opportunity (p. 186)
Barriers to entry (p. 187)
Marketing audit (p. 189)
Proactive strategy (p. 191)
Reactive strategy (p. 191)
Oligopoly (p. 191)
Market-expansion strategy (p. 192)
Market-share protection strategy (p. 192)
Preemptive action (p. 193)
Head-to-head competition (p. 195)
Flanking strategy (p. 197)
Encirclement strategy (p. 198)
Follow-the-leader strategy (p. 198)
Bypass-the-competition strategy (p. 200)
Status quo strategy (p. 200)

QUESTIONS

1. What do we mean by competitive advantage? What are the alternative means of achieving competitive advantage?
2. What are the means by which companies can gain a marketing advantage? A cost advantage? Provide examples.
3. Under what circumstances is a company more likely to pursue a strategy of (1) product superiority, (2) cost leadership, or (3) market niche to achieve competitive advantage? What are the relative benefits of pursuing each of these pathways to competitive advantage?
4. What are the risks of pursuing competitive advantage based on cost? Based on a market-niche approach?
5. A company following a low-cost strategy to gain competitive advantage has two options: One is to undercut competition on price (as Texas Instruments did in the hand-calculator market). The other is to maintain price at competitive levels and put higher margins into advertising (as Heinz did in packaged foods).
   a. When is each strategy more likely to be used?
   b. What are the risks?
6. What market characteristics would give a new entrant a competitive advantage? How might these factors have influenced PepsiCo's decision to enter the sports-drink market? Do you agree with Pepsi's decision?
7. P&G's divestiture of Orange Crush probably required an assessment of (1) market attractiveness, (2) competitors' strengths and weaknesses, and (3) its own strengths and weaknesses in the soft-drink arena. What key questions did P&G probably ask in these three areas in deciding to divest Orange Crush?
8. Why did General Electric, Whirlpool, and Maytag look to Europe for growth? What means did these companies use to enter the European market?
9. Did Pepsi effectively apply the four principles of warfare cited in the text to gain competitive advantage over Coke? If so, how?
10. Why is the soft-drink industry considered an oligopoly? Has the automobile industry become more or less oligopolistic in the last ten years? Explain.
11. What are the differences between a (1) preemptive strategy, (2) flanking strategy, and (3) market-niche strategy? What types of companies are most likely to pursue each strategy? Why?
12. Why did Perrier's competitors follow a "Don't rock the boat" strategy when Perrier was taken off the shelves because of benzene in the product? What are the pros and cons of this strategy? What strategy would you have used? Explain.

QUESTIONS: YOU ARE THE DECISION MAKER

1. A marketing manager for a line of household cleaners commented on the steps described in Figure 6.1 to evaluate the potential for gaining competitive advantage. He said

   It looks good on paper. But in practice, competition won't give us the time to go through a formal competitive analysis to decide where and how to get competitive advantage. If a competitor comes out with a new ad campaign, increases its couponing, or introduces a special price promotion, you have to look at it and decide how you're going to react. If you go through all the steps suggested in your figure, it may be too late to do anything about a competitor's actions.

   Do you agree? Why or why not?
2. Scripto challenged Bic's leadership in disposable lighters by introducing a line of lighters priced from 69 cents to 99 cents. One marketing analyst felt that Scripto was likely to fail because "Bic makes a quality product and its distribution system is far superior to anyone else's."[42]
   a. What must Scripto do to be successful in its attempt at head-to-head competition with Bic?
   b. What are the risks?

PART III

Defining the Target Market

In order to direct the firm's resources to meet customer needs, market segments must be identified and targeted for marketing effort. Defining target markets requires collecting information on customers, which in turn, requires understanding customer behavior.

In Chapter 7, we discuss the development of marketing information systems to collect a broad range of information necessary to develop marketing strategies, and more specifically, marketing research to collect information on customer needs, characteristics, and behavior. Then, in Chapters 8 and 9 we describe final consumers and organizational buyers to gain a better understanding of how they arrive at purchase decisions. This information provides us with a basis for understanding how markets can be segmented, and what strategies to direct to these segments to meet their needs. Chapter 10 discusses alternative ways to define and target market segments, and the strategies companies use to segment their markets.

CHAPTER 7

Information and Research for Marketing Decisions

YOUR FOCUS IN CHAPTER 7

To learn:

- *The role of a marketing information system in developing marketing plans.*
- *The role of marketing research in marketing planning.*
- *How marketing research is conducted.*
- *The sources of marketing data.*
- *The nature of the "information revolution" that has occurred in marketing in the 1980s and 1990s.*

Frito-Lay: Using Marketing Research to Meet Customer Needs

Frito-Lay is relying more on marketing research to define consumer needs these days. Why? Because the snack food market has become highly fragmented. Consumers are developing more refined and specific tastes for snack foods, often on regional lines. Whereas potato chips once used to be just plain potato chips, today Frito-Lay sells its Lay's and Ruffle brand chips in a vinegar-flavored version in the Northeast, in mesquite flavors in the Southwest, and in a sour-cream flavor in the Midwest.[1]

Because of the increased fragmentation in the snack food market, segments can no longer be defined based on simple classifications such as older or younger and single or married. Consider the definition of the segment for Frito-Lay's new "Light" snack food line—35- to 54-year-old, college-educated , white-collar workers with annual incomes of more than $35,000.[2]

Developing new products and defining market segments with such precision requires a sophisticated database gathered through marketing research. Adding to its informational needs, Frito-Lay tests between 100 and 200 new product ideas during an average year, 15 of which are eventually marketed. To obtain the information needed to test new products and track existing ones, Frito-Lay interviews nearly 500,000 consumers each year.[3] It conducts taste tests of its products in shopping malls and in consumers' homes. It introduces new products into test markets to determine whether they should be marketed nationally. It periodically surveys consumers on a nationwide basis to determine which snack foods they prefer and what they plan to buy. It also collects information from retail stores on who is buying what brands, where they buy, in what quantities, and at what price.

All this information does not come cheaply. Marketing research costs the company about $30 million a year. But this is peanuts compared to what is at stake: Frito-Lay's 50 percent share of the salty snack chip market accounting for over $3.5 billion in sales each year.[4]

A good example of the importance of marketing research at Frito-Lay is its role in the introduction of the Light snack food line. American consumers have a love–hate relationship with snack foods. As ads frequently point out, once you start eating your favorite potato or corn chip, you can't stop. But consumers also put snack foods in the "junk food" category because of their low nutritional value.

Frito-Lay's solution was to cater to health concerns, not fight them. Its surveys showed that reducing oil in foods was one of the most common health concerns among the American public. So why not develop snack foods with less oil? There was one problem: In initial tests, consumers found that low-oil snack foods tasted terrible. But subsequent tests found that the company could reduce the oil by one-third without sacrificing taste. The new "one-third less oil" product was developed for the company's popular Cheetos, Ruffles, and Doritos brands. Test scores of each of these low-oil products were equal to the normal-oil counterpart—meaning that Frito-Lay could introduce the Light line without compromising taste and flavor.

Marketing research's role did not stop there. Product and taste tests are not enough to convince a company the risks of national introduction are worth taking. To minimize these risks, Frito-Lay first introduced the Light line into several test markets. Results from the test markets were designed to answer key questions such as whether a low-oil offering was required in each category, what sizes and packaging worked best, and what the target market for the line was.

To answer these questions, Frito-Lay employed the latest in market technology, scanner data. **Scanner data** *is collected when checkout clerks record sales by scanning product bar codes with a laser.* Sales data is stored in a central computer and is immediately available to product managers. Test markets were selected that had a good network of scanner supermarkets. Based on scanner data, Frito-Lay could determine sales results at various price and promotional levels for each brand in the Light line. This information helped Frito-Lay establish two key components of the marketing mix for the new product—price levels and in-store promotional strategies.

Scanner data alone did not tell Frito-Lay who its customers were. In the 1980s, research companies such as A. C. Nielsen and Information Resources Inc., developed the capability to identify who was buying what by establishing consumer panels. Consumers who agreed to be part of a panel were required to present a card when they shopped in scanner stores. The card identified their demographic characteristics and could link consumers to purchases. This was a major advance, because in the past, researchers had to rely on surveys to determine what consumers bought. These surveys were often unreliable because of faulty consumer recall or bias in citing prestige or higher-priced brands as being the ones purchased. With scanner data, marketers could directly tie purchases to consumer demographic characteristics by electronic means.

Based on test-market results, Frito-Lay introduced the Light line nationally in 1990. It did so because the product met its criterion for success in test markets: getting 15 to 20 percent of consumers to try the product and to buy it four or more times.[5] Whether a low-oil snack will make it nationally remains to be seen. One thing is for sure. Frito-Lay will continue to rely on marketing research to test new products and find new market segments in the 1990s.

THE MARKETING INFORMATION SYSTEM

In previous chapters, we have seen how marketers use knowledge of customers, competition, and the environment to identify opportunities as a basis for developing marketing strategies. The foundation of opportunity identification is *information* on consumer needs, competitive activities, changes in the marketing environment, and consumer reactions to the company's marketing strategies.

Marketers must also collect information on product and company performance in the form of sales and cost data. Environmental and company information must be integrated into a marketing information system so it can be used effectively by managers in developing marketing plans and strategies. *A* **marketing information system (MIS)** *is a company facility that integrates information from diverse sources, then disseminates it to managers in usable form to enable them to make decisions.*

ROLE OF THE MARKETING INFORMATION SYSTEM

The above definition cites three roles an MIS must fulfill, data collection, analysis, and dissemination. These roles are illustrated in Figure 7.1. An MIS must be able to *collect* information from diverse sources—customers, competition, salespeople, distributors, and published information from government and industry sources. Such data collection requires that an MIS have the capability to conduct surveys, test products, obtain information on competitive actions, and track changes in the environment such as new technologies.

An MIS must also have the capability to *analyze* the information once it is collected. This requires tying information from diverse sources together to try to assess its impact on company sales and profits. For example, data analysis in Frito-Lay's MIS would require tying together information on consumer life styles, attitudes, and brand preferences. Frito-Lay saw that changes in life styles were creating more negative attitudes toward snack food. Further, these changes led to a decrease in preferences for its traditional snack food lines, leading Frito-Lay to conclude that a light snack food line was necessary to maintain sales. The data analysis capability of Frito-Lay's MIS was thus able to relate changes in life styles and product attitudes to changes in brand preferences.

Dissemination of information requires sending data that has been analyzed to the right managers at the right time for marketing decisions. As a result, an MIS must be able to identify the type of information needed by various decision centers in

FIGURE 7.1

Role of the Marketing Information System

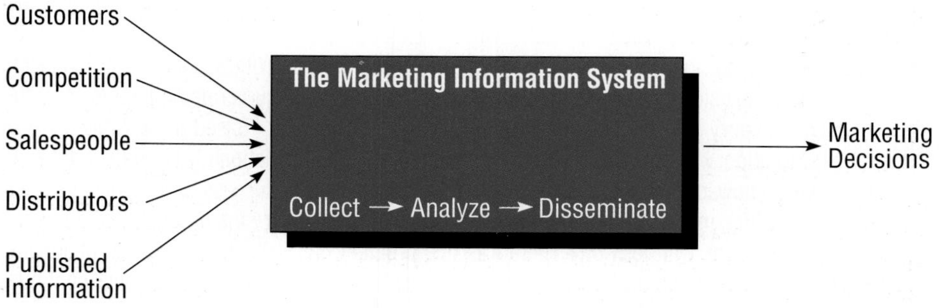

the organization. At Frito-Lay, information on changing life styles and attitudes toward snack foods was most important to the business manager heading the SBU responsible for chip-type snacks. This manager was responsible for identifying the need to develop a light snack line to accommodate nutritional concerns. Information on preferences for individual brands was disseminated to brand managers because they were responsible for developing strategy for individual brands. Once these brand managers recognized the likely erosion in sales of their brands because of nutritional concerns, they more readily accepted a recommendation from the business manager for line extensions such as Doritos Light and Cheetos Light.

The example we have cited focuses on the information needed to introduce *new products*. An MIS is also responsible for obtaining information that allows managers to develop marketing strategies for *existing products*. The sources of information are the same, but the type of information collected will differ. Now, the MIS is concerned with tracking product performance and determining what factors in the environment—customers, competition, technology—are responsible for changes in product performance. Once the Light line was introduced, Frito-Lay's MIS provided sales data by brand and cost data on marketing components such as advertising, couponing, distribution, and instore promotional efforts. Data on consumer attitudes toward the line, advertising recall, brand preferences, and future buying intentions were also provided to enable brand managers to try to assess the effectiveness of their marketing efforts.

COMPONENTS OF AN MIS

Data that is collected by an MIS is organized into three subsystems as shown in Figure 7.2, an internal reporting system, an environmental scanning system, and a marketing research system. The *internal reporting system* obtains data on company sales and marketing expenditures. An *environmental scanning system* obtains data on competition, technology, the economy, and legal and regulatory changes in the environment. A *marketing research system* obtains data on customer attitudes and behavior, and their reactions to the company's marketing strategies. The areas collected by each of these subsystems are summarized in Table 7.1.

Frito-Lay has an MIS composed of these three subsystems. Its internal reporting system provides information on company sales by price, store, promotional effort, and region, based primarily on scanner data. Its environmental scanning system tracks competitive sales, changes in technology, and changes in demographics and life-styles. Frito-Lay's environmental scanning system identified greater nutritional concerns as a potential threat to buying snack foods. Environmental scanning also identified improvements in technology permitting the development of low-oil snacks without a loss in taste based on the addition of enzymes to the product.[6] The marketing research system provides information on taste tests, consumer surveys, and test markets. This type of information led the company to introduce the Light snack line nationally.

Figure 7.2 shows that the three MIS subsystems feed into a decision support system. A **decision support system (DSS)** *is a computerized facility designed to store and analyze data from diverse sources.* Computers provide the basis for storing large amounts of information and organizing it. For example, a DSS would be required to allow Frito-Lay to organize sales data by brand, size, price paid, and store in which the brand was purchased. A DSS also provides the facility for analyzing data. Such analysis requires that a DSS have software allowing researchers to link one set of data to another. For example, price level can be related to store to determine

FIGURE 7.2

Components of the Marketing Information System

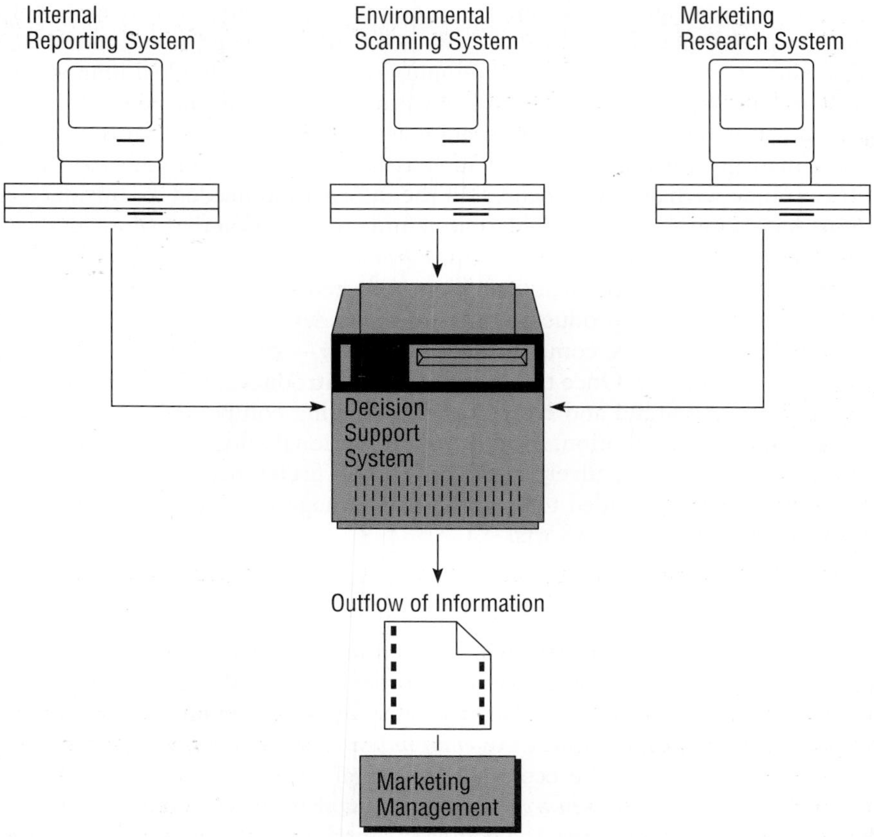

if certain stores are discounting Frito-Lay's brands more than others. Or data on attitudes toward health and nutrition could be linked to brand preferences to determine if health-oriented consumers are less likely to buy certain Frito-Lay brands.

In this section, we will describe the three subsystems in Figure 7.2, recognizing that they feed into a decision support system. We will then focus on the marketing research system for the rest of the chapter, because marketing research is the primary source of information related to customer needs—and customer needs must be central to the development of all marketing plans and strategies.

INTERNAL REPORTING SYSTEM

The internal reporting system provides management with data on factory shipments, retail sales, and marketing expenditures. **Factory shipments** *are the amount of goods the firm sells to retailers and wholesalers.* Data on retail sales to consumers are provided to companies by independent firms that specialize in such measurements. As Table 7.1 shows, retail sales data are broken out by brand, size of package, store in which purchased, price paid, and whether the brand was bought by

TABLE 7.1

Areas of Information Collected by MIS Subsystems

INTERNAL REPORTING SYSTEM	ENVIRONMENTAL SCANNING SYSTEM	MARKETING RESEARCH SYSTEM
Factory shipments	Competition Marketing expenditures Retail sales New products	Consumer needs attitudes brand preferences buying intentions advertising recall demographics life-styles
Retail sales by Brand Size Store purchased Price paid Coupon redemption In-store promotions	Social trends Demographics Life-styles	Advertising tests
Inventory levels	Economic trends	Product tests
Marketing expenditures Product development Distribution Advertising Sales promotions Sales force	Technology	Tests of price and in-store promotions
	Legal and regulatory	Test marketing

coupon or on promotion. Without such data, firms do not know how much of their products are sold by retailers at any given time, and cannot evaluate their marketing effort.

Scanner data has substantially improved the reliability of retail sales data by using electronic means to report sales. Prior to scanner data, retail sales were measured by **store audits** *in which auditors determined store inventories and identified sales of a brand* based on the following formula:

$$\text{Brand sales} = \begin{matrix}\text{beginning}\\\text{inventory}\end{matrix} + \begin{matrix}\text{product}\\\text{shipments}\end{matrix} - \begin{matrix}\text{ending}\\\text{inventory}\end{matrix}$$

Such audits were subject to human error and could not relate sales to in-store conditions such as price or coupon promotions, because these promotions often changed during the audit period. Of more importance, it took an average of three months to get store audit data to management.

Scanner data changed all that. Firms such as Frito-Lay, Procter & Gamble, and Kraft General Foods have internal reporting systems that provide managers scanner data within 24 hours. Quick data permits quick response. Frito-Lay did not have to wait three months to see a downturn in sales of its Tostitos tortilla chips in south Texas. Scanner data indicated that the downturn in sales occurred in markets where a regional competitor introduced El Galindo, a white-corn tortilla chip. Frito-Lay quickly responded by coming out with a white-corn version of Tostitos and recapturing lost sales.[7] Scanner data was able to link the decrease in sales to the introduction of El Galindo and was able to provide this information to Frito-Lay management in a matter of days.

EXHIBIT 7.1

A Frito-Lay Route Salesperson Recording Inventory with a Hand-Held Computer

Frito-Lay also supplements scanner data with information from its sales force. Each of Frito-Lay's 10-thousand salespeople who stock 400-thousand stores (known as route salespeople) are given hand-held computers to record brand inventory on store shelves and the amount stocked on the shelves on a day-to-day basis[8] (see Exhibit 7.1). This information accomplishes two things. First, it provides store audit data for those stores that do not have scanners, thus giving Frito-Lay a complete accounting of sales in all stores. Second, it gives management data that scanners do not provide, for example, inventory levels in various stores and shelf conditions such as stale products. The combination of scanner data and data from Frito-Lay's route salespeople provide Frito-Lay with a complete internal reporting system.

The internal reporting system also tracks and analyzes marketing expenditures. Key expenditures in the marketing mix for a brand are reported such as product development, advertising, sales promotional, distribution, and sales force expenditures. This information enables marketing managers to determine whether their costs are within the budget they originally establish for a brand. This information also permits managers to relate expenditures to sales to try to determine the effectiveness of their marketing effort. But as we shall see in a later chapter, the key difficulty in assessing marketing expenditures is that is is hard to separate product development, advertising, sales promotional, and distribution costs so as to identify a particular component of the marketing mix as being a determining factor in producing sales results.

ENVIRONMENTAL SCANNING SYSTEM

As we have seen in Chapter 4, the environmental scanning system tracks changes in the marketing environment that could create future opportunities or threats. Information compiled from diverse sources reveals potential changes in consumer demand, competition, technology, the economy, or government laws and regulations.

Compared to internal reporting and marketing research systems, environmental scanning is relatively unstructured. It does not rely on existing databases or formal studies but rather on a loose network of information that is channeled to a manager or department to review for insights and trends.

At Levi Strauss, a small environmental scanning group watches closely for environmental changes that could affect the demand for clothing, particularly demographic and life-style trends, as well as changes in family roles and government regulations. The group also tracks economic factors such as clothing imports, and technological trends such as improvements in synthetic fibers and in stretch fabrics.[9]

A firm that makes a business of environmental scanning, Inferential Focus, reviews more than 200 publications to find early warnings of political, economic, or social change that could affect the businesses of its subscribers. More than 50 clients pay $25,000 a year for this service. It was one of the first to detect a shift by baby boomers to a more sedentary, at-home life-style. It projected an increase in the sale of microwave ovens and frozen foods and decreased restaurant sales as a result.[10]

THE MARKETING RESEARCH SYSTEM

The marketing research system obtains data on consumer needs, attitudes, brand preferences, buying intentions, and characteristics. It also obtains information on consumer reactions to a company's marketing strategies through product tests, responses to advertisements, and tests of in-store promotional strategies. In cases where a new product is introduced, the marketing research system conducts market tests to determine consumer reactions to the product before it is introduced nationally.

These responsibilities are frequently divided for new and existing products in an MIS. This is the case for Kao's marketing research system, a company known as the Procter & Gamble of Japan. The company is the largest producer of household packaged goods in Japan. Kao's marketing research system has two subsystems providing information on new and existing products (see Figure 7.3 on page 218). If, for example, Kao is developing a new detergent product, it will conduct use tests in which households are asked to use the product and to compare it with their current detergent. It will also obtain consumer reactions to alternative packages, brand names, and advertising executions in developing an overall marketing mix for the product. This marketing mix is then introduced into test markets, where sales are tracked to determine both new and repeat buyers. A decision is then made whether projected revenues are sufficient to introduce the product to the national market.

Once the product has been introduced, Kao continues to obtain consumer feedback. It conducts in-store surveys of consumers to determine purchase motives and reactions to Kao's and competitive brands. It supplements this information with surveys conducted by telephone or personal interview to determine attitudes toward and usage of Kao and competitive products. It also conducts purchaser tracking studies in which information is obtained from the same customers over time to determine changes in attitudes, in usage patterns, and in intentions to buy. Such tracking studies serve as early warning systems to indicate if consumers are developing negative attitudes or are having problems with any of the company's products.

Of the three information systems described above, the marketing information system is the most important and complex because it obtains information directly from customers. As a result, the rest of this chapter will focus on the process and issues involved in collecting and using marketing research information.

GLOBAL MARKETING STRATEGIES

Marketing Information Systems in Western Europe

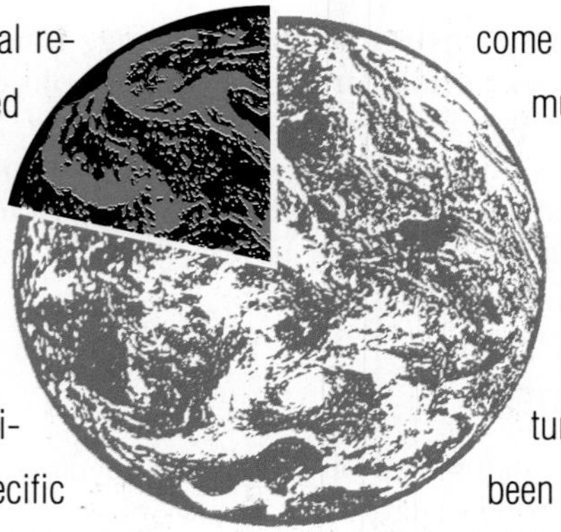

Information capabilities in the United States are the most advanced in the world in all three MIS subsystems. In the internal reporting system, scanner data is used more widely to track sales and to identify consumers buying the marketer's brands. In the environmental scanning system, census data is more detailed and sophisticated in its ability to identify specific demographic groups and to break out these groups by regions as detailed as individual zip codes. In the marketing research system, the United States has the most developed capabilities for conducting product tests, market tests, and surveys because of a wide network of firms specializing in various areas of marketing research.

Other regions of the world cannot match this informational capability, because the infrastructure does not always exist to provide the necessary information. A firm conducting a telephone survey of the buying habits of Eastern European consumers must realize that many households do not have phones and that its results might be biased as a result. A firm seeking information on demographic trends in, say, Malaysia must realize that census-taking has not been consistent and that demographic categories are not always defined in the same way over time. A firm trying to track retail sales in Brazil must realize that scanner technology has not yet become widespread and that store audits must be relied on for this purpose.

One region of the world that is catching up to the United States in informational capabilities is Western Europe. The research infrastructure in Western Europe has always been closer to that of the United States because of the more-developed economies of the countries in the region. But the economic integration of the European Community countries in 1992 provided a further impetus to improve informational capabilities. In the past, marketers had tended to focus on their informational needs one country at a time. Now, as marketers in Western Europe begin focusing on one large market, they are trying to develop integrated information systems across countries.

The need for a Pan-European information system has resulted in improvements in each of the three MIS areas. First, internal reporting systems that rely on the use of scanner data across countries are being developed. For instance, one research firm is offering a service called Euroscan that now provides scanner data to marketers in Germany, France, and England, and will soon be extending the capability to the rest of the EC countries as scanner technology

GLOBAL MARKETING STRATEGIES

becomes widespread.

Second, firms can begin to improve their environmental scanning capabilities because of promised standardization in census-taking across countries. As of now, census data from government agencies varies dramatically in its quality. Data in France, Germany, and the Scandinavian countries are excellent, whereas census data in Italy, Spain, and Portugal are poor. These differences will narrow as countries begin to adopt standardized codes for data collection across Western Europe. It is even possible that a Pan-European census might occur as early as the year 2000.

Improvements are also occurring in the third MIS area, marketing research. Standardized surveys are now asking the same questions of consumers in different countries to determine how they feel about various brands and product categories commonly available in Western Europe. In the past, surveys would be country-specific, making it difficult to reach conclusions for the region as a whole.

The greatest difficulty in standardizing the marketing research component of a marketing information system is language. Research companies are now providing central telephone facilities with a group of interviewers conducting the same survey in different languages to permit standardized data collection across countries. But the same questions in different languages may have different nuances and meanings. As a result, many companies first develop a questionnaire in French or English, then have local researchers translate it into their language, and then translate the questions back to French or English to determine if there are any differences in meaning.

Development of a standardized MIS capability in the European Community countries will be difficult. But it is happening, and it is improving the informational capabilities of European marketers.

Questions: What is the impetus for developing standardized marketing information systems in Western Europe? What improvements have occurred in this regard?

Sources: "Reaching the Real Europe," *American Demographics*, October, 1990, pp. 38–43 and 54; "Powerhouses Tear Down Europe Borders," *Advertising Age*, June 11, 1990, pp. S14–S16.

FIGURE 7.3

KAO's Marketing Research Information System

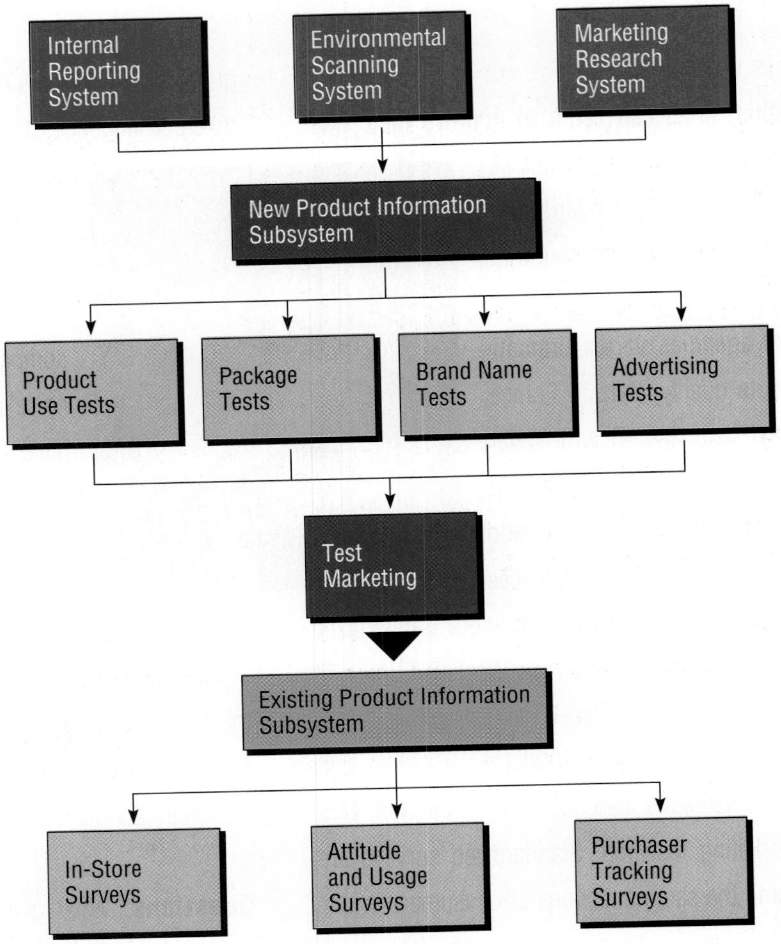

Source: Adapted from Masashi Kuga, "Kao's Marketing Strategy and Marketing Intelligence System," *Journal of Advertising Research 30* (April–May 1990), p. 24.

THE NATURE OF MARKETING RESEARCH

We will discuss the nature of marketing research by considering its importance, its role in the planning process, and the risks in its applications.

IMPORTANCE OF MARKETING RESEARCH

Marketing research is essential in providing marketing managers information to identify marketing opportunities and to develop strategies to benefit from these opportunities.

Marketing research serves an informational role in several key areas. First, it is essential in providing the informational base to introduce new products, as we have seen with the introduction of Frito-Lay's Light snack line. Second, marketing research can uncover opportunities for existing products. It was marketing research that led Colgate to make a global brand out of its Axion dishwashing paste that sold well in its Columbian subsidiary. Research indicated that the new formulation fit well with the dishwashing habits of consumers in the Far East and in other countries in Latin America.[11] Third, marketing research is important in identifying opportunities to revitalize brands when demand is lagging. When American Express saw card usage leveling off in the mid 1980s, marketing research identified an important consumer concern that spelled opportunity—paying hard-earned dollars for appliances that might break down, furniture that might crack, or electronics that might fail. As a result, American Express introduced the Buyer Assurance Plan, giving purchasers warranty protection on certain items bought with their American Express card. The plan was successful in expanding consumer use of the card beyond travel and entertainment. The novel concept of extending the manufacturer's warranties increased use of the American Express card on warranty items by 40 percent, and card applications soared.[12]

Another dimension reflecting the importance of marketing research is its scope. It is estimated that 72 million Americans were interviewed in surveys in 1990.[13] Procter & Gamble interviews well over one million people each year on literally thousands of projects to evaluate current brands and identify new opportunities. More money is also being invested in refining the accuracy of information on which decisions are made. For example, for the first time, marketers can determine which commercials specific households have watched and what their purchases were before and after seeing those commercials.

INTERACTION BETWEEN MARKETING RESEARCH AND MARKETING MANAGEMENT

To fulfill its role, marketing research must provide information to marketing management for decision making. This interaction is shown in a series of steps in Figure 7.4.

In the first step, a marketing opportunity or problem is identified. For instance, Stouffer's management felt that an opportunity to introduce a tastier line of diet

FIGURE 7.4

The Relationship of Marketing Research and Marketing Management

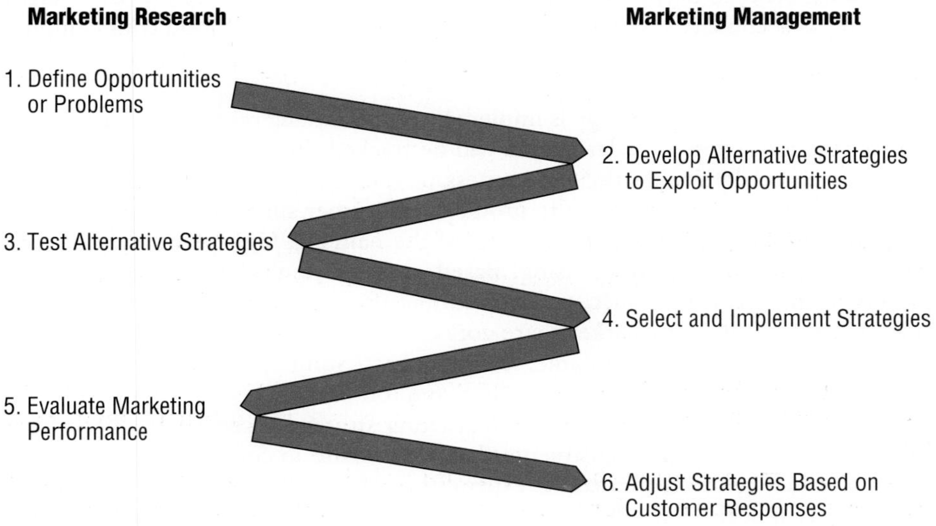

Source: Adapted from Henry Assael, *Marketing Management* (Boston, Mass: Kent Publishing, 1985), p. 191.

foods might exist, based on the increasing number of weight- and health-conscious Americans and the lack of enthusiasm for diet foods. Marketing research confirmed this opportunity. A survey of dieters identified four objections to existing diet foods: They were bland, lacked variety, were not filling, and did not look particularly appetizing. This dissatisfaction gave Stouffer's management the opening to introduce Lean Cuisine, which became the leading brand of frozen diet foods.

In the second step, management develops alternative strategies to exploit opportunity. Stouffer's strategy was to try to develop a tasty line of low-calorie entrees, a task that had eluded other marketers. The company spent five years in this effort.[14] Its development kitchens ground their own meat to control fat content and made heavy use of vegetables and herbs to develop tastier diet dishes. Simultaneously, management was considering how to position the prospective line. Three positionings were considered—a good-tasting food with a low-calorie appeal as secondary, a low-calorie food with good taste as secondary, or an emphasis on the line as a light food.

In the third step in Figure 7.4, marketing research tests alternative strategies formulated by management. Stouffer's tested various entrees on a panel of consumers to determine their reactions so it could make two key decisions; whether to introduce the product, and whether to introduce a broad or a narrow product line. In addition, mock-ups of sample ads were developed representing alternative positionings for the product line. One ad focused on the low-calorie appeal of the product based on the fact it had only 300 calories. Another emphasized good taste with the calorie appeal as secondary. These ads were tested on consumers to determine which had the greatest appeal for dieters.

In the fourth step, management selects a set of marketing strategies based on this research and implements them. Stouffer's found consumer reactions to many of the entrees positive. As a result, it decided to introduce a broad product line. Ten entrees were selected for market introduction based on consumer evaluations. Stouffer's also decided that the product should not be identified as a diet food, because dieters dislike being reminded they are on a diet. As a result, the name Lean Cuisine was selected. Consumer responses to alternative positionings also led management to decide to emphasize good taste, with low calories and weight watching as secondary themes. The rationale was that any diet food could emphasize low calories. Lean Cuisine's distinctive advantage was its good taste and appetizing appearance.

When the marketing strategy is implemented, marketing research evaluates consumer reactions (step 5). Sales results will be tracked. In addition, consumers will be surveyed to determine their awareness of the brand and the advertising and whether they are likely to buy the product. Consumer surveys after introduction of Lean Cuisine showed high awareness of the name. A high percentage of consumers also recalled the advertising. Based on sales results, it was apparent that Lean Cuisine was a huge success. Two months after introduction, it was the leading frozen diet food. Its market share continued to climb, and it became the second-largest-selling frozen food line, second only to Stouffer's regular frozen entree line. In two short years, it became a $500 million brand.[15]

In step 6, management adjusts the marketing strategy based on feedback from marketing research. Any adjustments that were made in Stouffer's strategies for Lean Cuisine involved increasing expenditures for the brand. The number of entrees was quickly expanded from 10 to 13 based on consumer responses, the

EXHIBIT 7.2

Shift in Lean Cuisine's Advertising Based on Marketing Research

From an Informational Appeal To An Image-Oriented Appeal

advertising budget was increased, and production capacity was expanded by 47 percent.[16] In addition, advertising emphasis began to shift. The initial ads were informationally oriented, explaining that Lean Cuisine was tastier and more appetizing because it had beef with less than 10 percent fat content and used naturally flavored foods. Marketing research showed that the target market was aware of these features, but consumers still had to be sold on what the product would do for them. So advertising shifted to a more image-oriented appeal[17] that currently uses the theme "Taste you can love for life," (see Exhibit 7.2).

RISKS OF MARKETING RESEARCH

In each of the cases discussed so far, marketing research identified an unmet need, and management successfully developed a product or service to meet it. But marketing research does not guarantee success. Companies face three types of risk in conducting marketing research: first, making the wrong assumptions about the research needed; second, conducting the wrong kind of research to fulfill the informational needs; and third, misinterpreting the data once the research is completed.

Although Colgate was successful in introducing Axion as a global dishwasher detergent, it fell prey to the first risk when it introduced Fab 1 Shot, a combined laundry detergent and fabric softener: It made the wrong assumptions. The company conducted its marketing research for the product on the assumption that purchases in the United States would be mostly for family use. But because Fab 1 Shot came in individual packets, it appealed more to convenience-minded singles. Because Colgate wound up interviewing the wrong consumers, advertising missed its target market and the brand is now languishing on store shelves.[18]

Coca-Cola's decision to change the formula of its flagship brand is an example of the second risk, the wrong kind of research. The company's rationale for changing the formula was logical—the brand was losing market share to Pepsi primarily among teenagers. So why not change the formula to make it sweeter and more appealing to that major segment. In extensive taste tests, the new formula for Coke was a consistent winner over the old Coke formula and it beat Pepsi more than 50 percent of the time.[19] Yet the uproar was heard around the world when Coca-Cola withdrew the old formula from the market and replaced it with the new formula. Disaffected Coke drinkers wanted their brand back. In two short months, Coca-Cola's management was forced to reintroduce the old formula as "Coca-Cola Classic."

What happened? The tests Coca-Cola conducted were "blind" taste tests; that is, there was no label on the can. As a result, consumers were reacting solely to taste, not to image. What would have happened if tests had been conducted with labels intact? Old Coke might very well have been a winner, because it represented more than just a soft drink to many people. The company assumed that Coca-Cola's competitive position could be determined based on taste alone. How consumers *felt* about the product was the key element Coca-Cola overlooked.

Ocean Spray Cranberries avoided the third risk—misinterpreting research data—by using scanner data in interpreting sales results of the company's new Mauna Lai guava juice. Data showed that the number of repeat purchasers was lower than company objectives to achieve the required market share. In years past, that information would have killed the brand. But scanner data was capable of showing that the fewer number of repeat purchasers were buying more of the brand, information that would not have been available from store audits. As a result of this greater frequency of purchase among repeat buyers, the company projected that it would eventually meet its sales objectives if it stuck with the brand. Mauna Lai turned out to be a highly successful brand.[20]

INSURING RIGOROUS MARKETING RESEARCH

If marketing research is to avoid the risks cited above and fulfill its managerial role, it must be conducted rigorously. Research is conducted rigorously when the data collected are valid, reliable, and representative.

Validity *is the collection of the* right *information to meet the purposes of the research.* One might question the validity of Coca-Cola's blind taste tests to measure preference for what is now Coca-Cola Classic versus New Coke and Pepsi. The assumption was that taste is the primary component of preferences for soft drinks. As we have seen, brand image also has a lot to do with preferences. A labeled test might have been more valid.

Reliability *measures the accuracy with which the data was collected.* Researchers should attempt to collect data without any inherent measurement biases. A reliable study should yield similar results if repeated. A case in which reliability was missing occurred some years ago when Pepsi tested its flagship brand against Coke. It conducted blind taste tests, giving consumers two identical bottles, one labeled with the letter M that always contained Pepsi and the other with the letter Q that always contained Coke. Pepsi was the clear favorite, and the company advertised this fact. Coca-Cola then did some research and found that consumers preferred an item labeled M rather than Q, regardless of its contents. In other words, many respondents preferred Pepsi not because of its taste, but because it was labeled M, and Coke was labeled Q. Coca-Cola concluded that on this basis, Pepsi's test was clearly unreliable. It advertised this fact, showing that when consumers were given two identical glasses of Coke marked M and Q, M was the clear favorite.

Representativeness *is the degree to which a sample of consumers represents the characteristics of a population.* Researchers can rarely interview every consumer in the market, so a *sample* is usually selected to represent the **population**, *that is, the total market under study*. For example, in testing New Coke, the population was defined as all cola drinkers. A sample can never be a perfect representation of the population, but researchers can try to make it as representative as possible. Generally, the larger the sample size, the greater its representativeness of a given population.

In testing New Coke, assume that 60 percent of the sample was teenagers but that data shows that only 40 percent of all cola consumption is accounted for by teenagers. Teenagers would thus be overrepresented in the sample. Since teenagers prefer a sweeter cola, overrepresenting them in the sample would create an unfair advantage for New Coke, given its sweeter taste. (Actually, though, it appears that Coca-Cola *did* select a representative sample of cola drinkers.)

Representativeness is becoming more of a problem for marketing researchers because of the increasing reluctance of many American consumers to participate in surveys. According to Walker Research, a company that tracks trends in marketing research, 36 percent of consumers declined to answer a phone survey in 1990 compared to a 24 percent refusal rate in 1986.[21] This would not be a problem except for the fact that people who do not respond are usually different from those that do. As a result, such high refusal rates increase the likelihood that a sample will not represent the population.

THE MARKETING RESEARCH PROCESS

Besides being rigorous, marketing research should be *systematic*, meaning it should follow a logical series of steps to achieve research objectives. These steps are outlined in Figure 7.5.

DEFINE RESEARCH OBJECTIVES

The first and most important step in the research process is defining the research objectives. This step is most important because it determines all subsequent steps. Defining research objectives can be difficult, because the research problem is not always obvious. Coca-Cola defined its research problem as determining whether reformulating its flagship brand would capture more of the teenage market from Pepsi. But the problem was not the Coca-Cola brand, it was the need to develop an effective strategy to appeal to teenagers. Had the company identified the research problem in this way, it might have directed its resources toward coming out with a new soft drink to appeal to teenagers rather than reformulating its flagship brand.

There are three types of research objectives. One is **exploratory**; *that is, an objective designed to define a problem so as to guide future research.* Had Coca-Cola defined

FIGURE 7.5

The Marketing Research Process

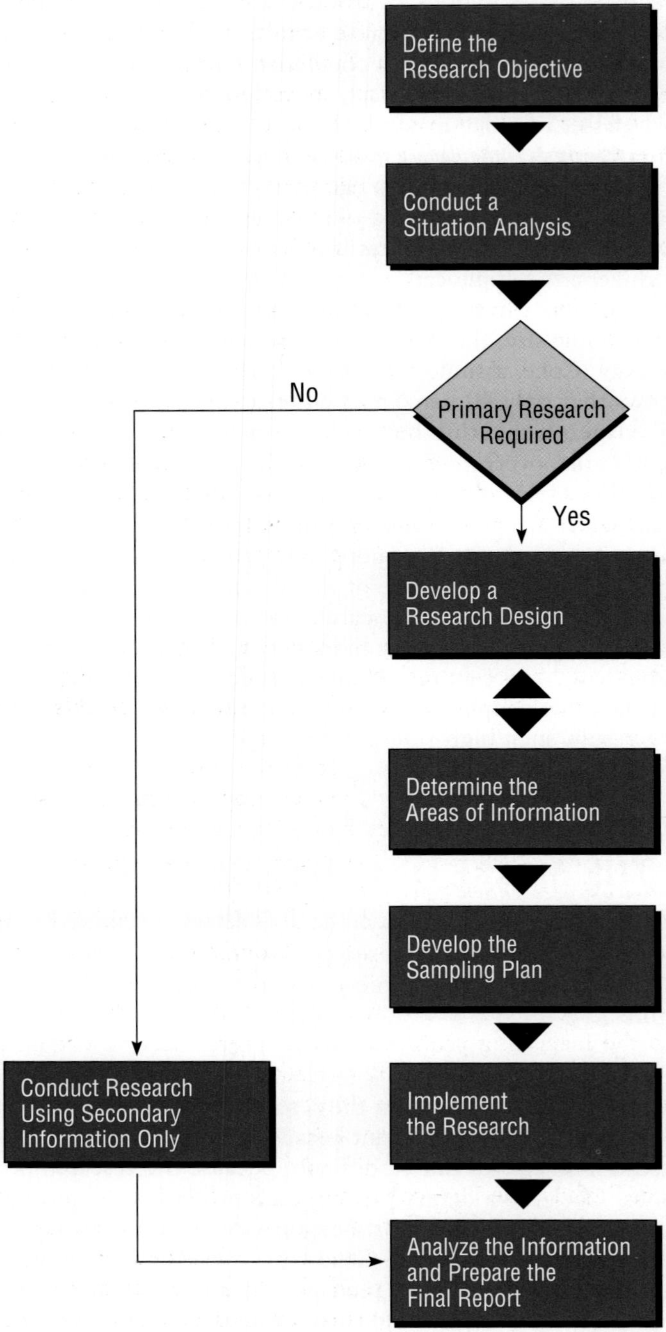

its objective as investigating how it could best appeal to teenagers, this would have been an exploratory objective. A second type of objective is **descriptive**; *that is, describing and explaining events in the marketplace*, such as sales trends for a product or changes in consumer attitudes toward a brand. Ocean Spray Cranberry's research objective in investigating sales trends of Mauna Lai in test market was descriptive. A third objective is **causal**; *that is, trying to determine cause and effect relationships.* An example is when Frito-Lay conducted taste tests to determine the effects of a one-third reduction in oil on taste. The objective was causal because Frito-Lay was trying to establish a cause and effect relationship between oil content and consumer taste responses. When marketing managers try to evaluate marketing performance, they have a causal objective in mind. For example, what is the *effect* on sales when coupons, price levels, or advertising expenditures change (the *causes*).

In considering the marketing research process in Figure 7.5, we will cite a research study conducted by AT&T. In the early 1980s, the company determined that it had little information on the telephone needs of its small-business customers. Its research objective was to obtain information on how to adapt its services and equipment to small businesses. This objective was exploratory in nature, because it required AT&T to gauge the telecommunications needs of small businesses and decide how it could best respond to them. The objective dictated all subsequent steps in the research process—the type of research to be conducted, the questions asked, the sample, and the data analysis.

SITUATION ANALYSIS

A **situation analysis** *is a preliminary investigation of information already available in the problem area.* Such information might be available from salespeople, from past research, or from published sources such as business periodicals, annual reports, or government data.

There are two key purposes to conducting the situation analysis. The first is to determine whether it is necessary for the company to incur the costs of marketing research. If the required information is available, additional research may not be necessary. *Existing data from published sources or from company records are* **secondary data**. *Data collected by a company for the specific purpose of answering its research questions are* **primary data**. Frequently, a company's research objectives can be met by secondary data. (We will discuss sources of secondary data available to researchers later in this chapter.)

A second purpose of the situation analysis is to help the researcher become familiar with the marketing problem. Marketing research is a staff function, and researchers called on to investigate managerial problems may not be fully familiar with the market or the customer. The situation analysis gives them the opportunity to talk to company managers, salespeople, and middlemen as well as acquaint themselves with existing data.

In the AT&T study, the research group responsible for the project first talked with product managers assigned to develop telecommunications products frequently purchased by small businesses and with salespeople in contact with buyers from small businesses. One of the reasons for the study was that AT&T could not allocate much personal sales efforts to small businesses because of their large numbers. Therefore, much of the selling to these businesses was done by phone. The lack of first-hand information related to the needs of this market indicated that primary data would be required.

Before collecting primary data, the research group investigated the availability of secondary data. They conducted a computerized search for secondary information, turning up 40 articles on the communication needs of small businesses. However, these articles did not refer directly to attitudes of small businesses toward AT&T or its equipment.

Figure 7.5 shows that the information from the situation analysis may be sufficient to fulfill the research objectives. If not, a research plan must be developed to collect primary data. In AT&T's case, it was apparent to management that it would have to conduct primary research to determine the telecommunication needs of small businesses and their attitudes toward AT&T equipment and service.

DEVELOP A RESEARCH DESIGN

If the researcher decides that primary information must be collected, the next step is to determine how. Figure 7.6 shows that when researchers conduct primary research, they use qualitative research, survey research, experimentation, observation, and case studies to implement a research plan.

QUALITATIVE RESEARCH

Qualitative research *is research that asks consumers to respond to questions in an unstructured manner*. As a result, analysis of the results rely totally on the interpretation of the researcher. Qualitative research is often used to collect primary data when the required information is too complex, vague, or potentially embarrassing to ask the respondent directly. It is also used to better identify a research area so that researchers will know what kinds of questions to ask in more-structured surveys or experiments.

Marketing researchers use two types of qualitative approaches: focus-group or depth interviews, and projective techniques. **Focus-group interviews** *are informal open-ended discussions guided by a trained moderator*. A group of eight to twelve respondents is asked to focus on a particular topic. Focus groups are a good vehicle for obtaining information, because respondents can talk freely and often encourage each other to talk more openly. *When such interviews are conducted on an individual rather than a group basis*, they are called **depth interviews**.

One study, conducted before flying was so commonplace, used focus groups to try to determine why men resisted flying for business purposes. The discussions found it was not so much fear of flying as guilt that if they died they would leave behind their loved ones. As a result, the airline sponsoring the study developed a campaign that focused on the joy of coming back to the family from a business trip rather than the more rational appeals of on-time arrival and direct flights. It is unlikely that this information could have been obtained by directly asking these businessmen why they chose not to fly.

Focus groups can be used as the main vehicle for data collection, but they are more often used as a means of determining areas of information to be collected in subsequent survey research. AT&T conducted focus-group interviews with owners of small businesses and found that those who were unwilling to consider competitive equipment gave AT&T's service reliability as their reason. As a result, a primary objective of a subsequent survey was to determine perceptions of AT&T's telecommunications services and the interaction between these perceptions and the willingness to consider competitive equipment.

Another approach to collecting qualitative data is through projective techniques. **Projective techniques** *are methods that present ambiguous materials to consumers designed to induce them to project subconscious feelings or attitudes*. If information is very

FIGURE 7.6

Types of Research Plans

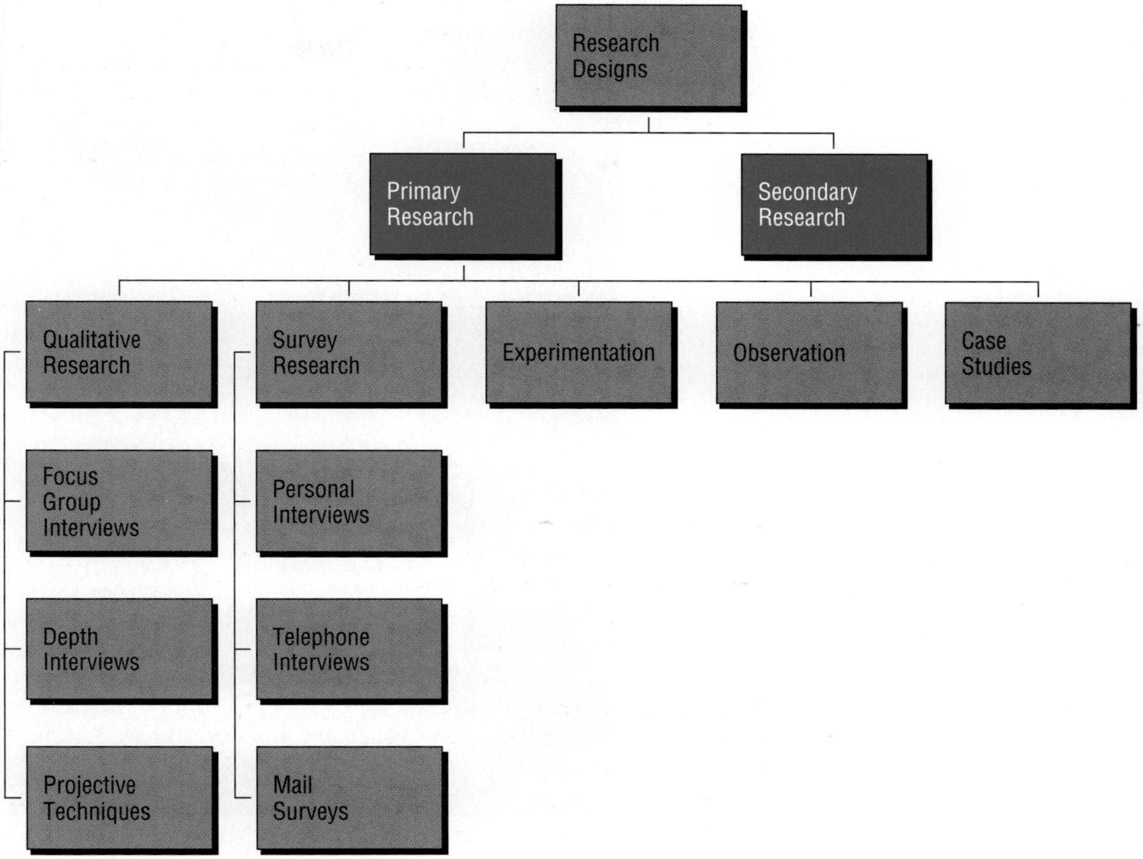

personal or potentially embarrassing, respondents can be given a situation, a cartoon, or an unfinished sentence and asked to react. They are more likely to project their true feelings, because the questions are not asked directly.

Panasonic used projective techniques to determine whether its positive image in consumer electronics could carry over to office automation. Researchers asked consumers to select photos of people they associated with IBM, Xerox, Canon, Epson, and Panasonic products. Respondents associated photos of older, distinguished and affluent people with IBM and Xerox. They selected photos of younger, upstart professionals with Panasonic.[22] The company used these findings in its campaign for office automation products. The campaign theme "Panasonic boom, the next generation" tries to capture the independent baby boomers of the 1960s and 1970s now moving into management positions (see Exhibit 7.3). The theme and image reflects consumers' perceptions of Panasonic "types."

SURVEY RESEARCH

The most important and commonly used method of collecting primary data is through consumer surveys. Surveys involve selecting a representative sample of

EXHIBIT 7.3

An Ad Campaign Based on Qualitative Research

respondents from a population, developing a questionnaire, asking the respondents questions, and analyzing the results.

A researcher must determine whether the survey will be conducted in person, by telephone, or by mail. Each method has its advantages and disadvantages, as summarized in Table 7.2.

PERSONAL INTERVIEWS A *personal interview* is usually necessary when a large amount of data are required, more-complicated questions must be asked, or when visual stimuli such as an advertisement or a new-product concept must be shown to consumers. The interviewer can help explain complicated questions, probe for additional information, and guide the respondent through the questionnaire.

But the potential for *response bias* due to the interaction between interviewer and respondent is high (many respondents like to give the answers they think the interviewer wants). Personal interviews are also the most expensive, costing three to four times as much as telephone interviews.

To reduce the costs of seeking out consumers in their homes, an increasingly popular method of personal interviewing is *mall intercept surveys*. These are surveys

TABLE 7.2

Characteristics of Three Methods of Survey Research

	PERSONAL INTERVIEWS	TELEPHONE INTERVIEWS	MAIL SURVEYS
Amount of data that can be collected	Large	Moderate	Moderate
Feasibility of complicated questions	Yes	Sometimes	No
Ability to present visual stimuli	Yes	No	Sometimes
Likelihood of cooperation (response rates)	Moderate	Moderate	Low
Time required to get data	Moderate	Quick	Slow
Potential response bias	High	Moderate	Low
Cost	Very high	Moderate	Low

done in shopping malls where interviewers approach respondents and conduct an interview, clipboard in hand. If visual stimuli such as ads or packages must be shown, researchers often set up a trailer or a booth and invite respondents to be interviewed. Mall intercept interviews are generally of short duration and obtain smaller amounts of data than regular personal interviews because most shoppers are "on-the-go."

TELEPHONE INTERVIEWS *Telephone interviews* are best used for shorter interviews that require no visual stimuli and when data is needed quickly. They allow the interviewer to probe for information and explain questions that are not understood. They also allow the interviewer to ask to speak to the individual with the desired characteristics, for example the female head of house or a teenager in the household.

Telephone interviews are not effective if the survey is designed to obtain confidential or complicated information. Although potential bias in responding to an interviewer is not as high as for personal interviews, it is still likely. Also, as we have seen, given the greater frequency of telephone interviews, more consumers are reluctant to cooperate. As a result, response rates are going down.

Telephone interviews have been used more frequently, because they are much more economical than personal interviews for national surveys. Companies can use networks of WATS (Wide Area Telephone Service) lines to call respondents from one central location. Such central interviewing facilities provide the added advantage of enabling a supervisor to monitor how interviewers are asking questions. Such interviewer control increases the reliability of the survey. A recent improvement in WATS line facilities is computer-assisted telephone interviewing, where the interviewer reads the questions from a video screen and types consumer responses directly into a computer (see Exhibit 7.4).

MAIL SURVEYS *Mail surveys* have several advantages. They are an inexpensive means of collecting data. They can be completed at the convenience of the respondent. They can be used to obtain a large amount of information if the survey is of interest to the respondent. And, there is less chance of response bias on the

EXHIBIT 7.4

An Example of Computer-Assisted Telephone Interviewing

respondent's part, because there is no interaction with an interviewer.

The main problem with mail surveys is that returns are low, leading to the likelihood that a representative sample may not be obtained. Also, a longer period of time is required to get data. Another problem is that the researcher cannot intervene to explain questions or to provide directions. So questions must be clear and simple.

In the AT&T survey, the company could have used any of the three methods in Table 7.2. It decided to test all three to see which was best. It found that mail surveys were the best approach, because owners of small businesses did not have the time to give to a phone call or personal interview. They could take a mail questionnaire home and send it back. Although response rates to mail questionnaires are generally much lower than for personal or telephone interviews, in this case response rates were high because of the respondents' interest in the survey.

EXPERIMENTATION

Experimentation *is research that attempts to test for cause and effect under controlled conditions.* In a marketing context, researchers try to determine the effects of marketing stimuli such as alternative product characteristics, advertising themes, or price levels (the cause) on consumer responses (the effect). In trying to establish such cause and effect relationships, the researcher must try to *control* all factors except the marketing stimulus being tested, so that consumer responses can be attributed to that particular stimulus. For example, if Frito-Lay wants to determine the effect of a coupon promotion on sales of Doritos in the southwest region of the country, it would want to make sure that advertising expenditures and prices stay the same. Why? Because if there was an increase in advertising expenditures, the brand manager would not know if a sales increase was due to the promotion or to advertising. If advertising stayed the same (that is, controlled by being held constant), then it is more likely that any change in sales is due to the coupon promotion.

Consider another example. Say Frito-Lay wanted to determine the effect of various levels of oil (the cause) on consumer taste preferences (the effect) for its light chip line. It is trying to determine the minimum level of oil it can introduce without adversely affecting consumer taste sensations. Frito-Lay introduces two formulations, one with one-third less oil and one with one-half less oil. The purpose is to determine the maximum reduction in oil without a serious deterioration in taste ratings. An experiment is necessary because the company is seeking the cause-and-effect relationship between oil level and consumer taste ratings.

To run the experiment, two groups of consumers are established to try each formulation. These groups have to be matched for brand preferences, frequency of snacking, and age. Why? Because each of these factors could influence taste ratings independent of oil level. For example, frequent snackers are likely to be more discriminating in their taste sensations for snacks. Assume the group trying the chip with one-half less oil had less-frequent snackers, and the group trying the chip with one-third less oil had more-frequent snackers. The company finds that both groups rated the chip as equally tasty. The chip with one-half less oil had an unfair advantage because it had a less-discriminating test group. If the groups were matched, the product with one-third less oil would probably have won.

In fact, Frito-Lay did run experiments under controlled conditions and found that it could reduce oil by up to one-third without loss of taste. Beyond that, taste ratings started plummeting. When it ran these tests, the company made sure to match groups trying various formulations to make sure that the results were due to the oil level in the chip rather than to some extraneous factor like frequency of snacking.

OBSERVATION

Through observation, researchers try to determine what consumers do in the process of buying a product, using it, or being influenced by some marketing communication. In observing the consumer, it is important that the process of observation does not influence the consumer's reactions, otherwise data from observations will be flawed.

It was through observation that Corning Glass found out why sales of its Pyrex measuring cup were slumping. Researchers watching consumers use the cup found that they were uncomfortable with the handle. They also had difficulty stacking the cup. As a result, Corning changed the handle and shape of the cup and sales soared.[23] Similarly, Q-tips were created when their inventor observed midwives wrapping cotton around wooden sticks, and Curad Battle Ribbon adhesive bandages were developed as a result of direct observation of children decorating bandages with crayons and felt-tip pens.[24]

The problem with these observational studies is that they are *obtrusive*; that is, respondents are aware of the presence of researchers, and this awareness can influence their behavior. *Unobtrusive* observation occurs when the consumer is not aware of the researcher. An example is when researchers, having determined that they could not get reliable estimates of alcohol consumption through direct questioning, then measured the number of empty bottles in the garbage.[25]

CASE STUDIES

Case studies are comprehensive analyses of a particular situation. They are used mainly by industrial marketers to study the purchasing process of their customers. For example, if an industrial firm wants to determine how buying groups operate in its industry, it might select four or five companies for intensive study to determine the composition of their buying groups, the criteria used by members for selecting vendors, and potential conflicts within the groups.

DETERMINE THE AREAS OF INFORMATION

Concurrent with establishing a research approach, the marketing researcher determines the areas of information to be collected (thus the double arrow between these two steps in Figure 7.5). In most cases, information is collected using a questionnaire administered by an interviewer. In the AT&T study, the questionnaire asked owners of small businesses for information on their telephone usage and equipment, their view of the importance of telephone service, the role of the telephone in conducting their business, and the likelihood of their buying competitive equipment (see Table 7.3).

Questions are of two types, open ended and structured. *Open-ended (unstructured) questions* ask consumers for a response without indicating the available choices. *Structured questions* list the available choices or ask consumers to rate a brand or company on specific criteria. For example, a question might ask the consumer for his or her income (open ended) or might provide income categories and ask consumers in which one they belong. The problem with open-ended questions is that they must be categorized, and such categories reflect the judgment of the interviewer. For example, question 4 in Table 7.3 asks, "In what ways are telephone communications important in your business." Such an open-ended question requires developing categories depending on the nature of the responses, so similar responses can be totaled and reported as one category. The next item, "Please rate the importance of telephone communications in each of the following areas" then structures the question.

Unstructured questions are used when it is difficult to develop pre-defined categories. They are useful in finding out what is in the consumer's mind rather than prejudging a response. That is why an unstructured question was asked in the AT&T study. But if a structured question can be asked in its place, the unstructured question should be avoided.

The questions in a questionnaire should be carefully crafted, because the same question asked two different ways can produce very different results. For example, when one researcher showed a picture of Ronald Reagan to respondents and asked, "You know who this man is, don't you?", most people correctly identified the picture. But when the researcher asked, "Do you have any idea at all who this man is?", only one out of fifteen people identified Reagan.[26] Similarly, consumers are more likely to answer that they purchased a particular brand when asked, "Did you buy brand X in your last purchase?" than if they are asked, "Which of the following brands did you buy the last time you purchased this product?"

Researchers should be aware of the following principles of questionnaire construction:

- Avoid leading questions such as, "Do you think that Brand X is better than all other brands?"
- Avoid putting the respondent on the defensive by asking questions such as, "Why didn't you buy brand X the last time you purchased?"
- Avoid identifying the sponsor of the survey. For example, questions on attitudes or perceptions of a company's brand should be asked along with those for competitive brands. If the company is to be identified, do so at the end of the questionnaire.
- Ask more-sensitive questions, such as those pertaining to income, at the end of the questionnaire, after a willingness to answer questions has already been established.
- Avoid ambiguous questions such as, "Why didn't you select your preferred brand instead of the brand you prefer less on your last purchase?"

TABLE 7.3

Selected Questions From the AT&T Study

1. How many telephone lines (i.e. separate telephone numbers) do you have in your place of business? ____________
2. What was the approximate dollar amount of your telephone bill last month? ____________
3. Please check if you have any of the following in your place of business.
   Beeper ________
   Pager ________
   Intercom ________
   Answering machine ________
   Call forwarding ________
   [*Additional items asked*].
4. In what ways are telephone communications important in your business?
5. Please rate the importance of telephone communications in the following areas:

	VERY IMPORTANT	SOMEWHAT IMPORTANT	NOT TOO IMPORTANT	NOT USED FOR THIS PURPOSE
Contacting prospects	________	________	________	________
Placing orders	________	________	________	________
Receiving orders	________	________	________	________
Communicating with employees	________	________	________	________

6–10. *[Series of quesions on ownership of AT&T equipment and subscription to AT&T service]*

11. Have you considered buying telephone equipment in the last six months? Yes ________ No ________
    If yes, from what company or companies?
12. Please evaluate the quality of AT&T service. *[Ratings from excellent to poor shown on the questionnaire.]*
13. Please evaluate the quality of the following AT&T equipment. *[Various categories of equipment listed and ratings from excellent to poor shown on the questionnaire.]*

DEVELOP THE SAMPLING PLAN

As we have seen, a sample of consumers is selected to represent a population, which is the market of interest to the researcher. In the AT&T study, the population was small businesses, defined in telecommunications terms as a business establishment with three lines (telephone numbers) or less. The sample size in the study was about 1,600 small businesses selected to be representative of all small businesses in the United States.

There are two approaches to selecting a sample: probability and nonprobability sampling. In **probability (or random) sampling**, *researchers use scientific rules to try to select a sample that is representative of the population.* Each individual in the population has an equal or known chance of selection. The AT&T study used this method by choosing respondents randomly from its list of small-business customers. But suppose there is no such list. Consider a survey of all individuals in the United States 18 years and older to determine their reactions to a brand of deodorant. In this case, a telephone survey can be used and household telephone numbers selected randomly by picking seven digits from a table of random numbers (area codes would be preselected). Using such a procedure, each household in the United States with a telephone would have an equal chance of selection.

Probability sampling is more accurate in assuring that the sample will tend to be representative of the population, but it is also much more costly than nonprobability sampling.

In **nonprobability sampling**, *selection is based primarily on the researcher's judgment.* This method is often used when the sample's representativeness is less important. For example, if a researcher is testing ten alternative package designs for a product, the purpose might be to weed out the clear losers so that two or three potential winners can be further investigated. Nonprobability sampling is adequate for such screening purposes.

Frito-Lay used nonprobability sampling in selecting respondents to test oil levels for its Light snack line. It did not need a representative sample of U.S. households. It only needed a matched set of consumers to determine the relationship between oil level and taste. Had the objective been to determine buying intentions for Light snacks in order to develop sales projections once it was introduced, a representative sample of U.S. households would have been required.

IMPLEMENT THE RESEARCH

When the areas of information and sampling plan are defined, the research is implemented. Most companies do not conduct their own surveys; they select marketing research companies to do them. In the small-business study, AT&T commissioned an outside research company to perform the research. Research companies may have their own interviewers or may contract out for them. They try to ensure reliability by training interviewers to ask questions without bias and to carry out the instructions for collecting information.

When interviews are completed, research companies are generally required by clients to validate a certain percentage of the interviews. Respondents listed on a questionnaire are called back to determine if they were in fact interviewed. This is necessary because in some cases, interviewers have been known to submit false questionnaires that they themselves fill out. Although this is not common, any such occurrence can result in the whole survey being invalid.

ANALYZE THE DATA

When interviews are complete, marketing research companies collect and analyze the data to be presented to management. *Data analysis* summarizes the data and shows the relationship between key variables.

The simplest analysis is a straight tabulation of the data. For example, the AT&T study found that only 13.5 percent of small-business owners were considering buying competitive equipment in the previous six months (see Table 7.4). The next level of analysis is a cross-tabulation. **Cross-tabulations** *categorize one variable by another.* For example, what variables are likely to increase or decrease the chances of owners of small businesses considering competitive equipment. Table 7.4 shows that among those who felt present AT&T telephone service was inadequate, 44 percent considered competitive equipment. Thus, a negative attitude toward AT&T telephone service meant that there was more than three times

TABLE 7.4

Straight and Cross-Tabulations: AT&T Study of Small Businesses

STRAIGHT TABULATION		
Percentage of small businesses who considered buying competitive equipment		13.5
CROSS-TABULATIONS		
Percentage of small businesses who considered buying competitive equipment by:		
	YES	**NO**
1. Whether they felt present telephone service is inadequate	44.2	10.7
2. Whether they considered cost of service very expensive	25.9	11.0
3. Whether they rated quality of service poor	24.9	22.1
4. Whether they rated cost of service most important factor in telecommunications	20.8	10.8

as much chance that a small-business owner would consider buying equipment from an AT&T competitor.

To go beyond two-way classifications, the researcher must use **multivariate statistical techniques**, *that is, techniques designed to examine more than two variables simultaneously and relate them to another variable* such as consideration of competitive equipment.

One such technique used by AT&T was designed to develop a complete profile of consumers most likely to consider competitive equipment. The program found that small businesses with (1) three or more lines, (2) who felt their present telephone service is inadequate, and (3) considered the cost of service expensive were five times as likely to consider competitive equipment as the average small business. Whereas 13.5 percent of the total sample of small business considered competitive equipment, among the group identified by these three variables, over 65 percent considered competitive equipment.

PREPARE THE FINAL REPORT

When the data is analyzed, researchers must submit a final report. Researchers must ensure that the final report is written in terms understandable to management to allow them to develop action recommendations. Although action recommendations can be made in the report, they are not necessarily required. In fact, some companies discourage such recommendations, because they feel strategy should be the purview of the manager, and the researcher's role should be to objectively report results. Other companies feel that because researchers are aware of the managerial objectives of the research, they should be given latitude in making action recommendations.

The AT&T report did make action recommendations. The report suggested targeting small businesses dissatisfied with service with ads for better service delivery, because these were the customers most likely to buy competitive equipment. Based on the findings, the report also suggested offering small businesses new products such as pagers and automatic dialers to better meet their telecommunication needs.

SOURCES OF MARKETING INFORMATION

In our discussion of the marketing research process, we focused primarily on collecting primary data; that is, data collected by a marketing organization for a specific research purpose. But, as we have seen, an important source of marketing information is secondary data—that is, past data that has been collected by the company or by other organizations such as trade associations, the government, or syndicated research firms that run continuous studies for subscribing organizations. Often, such data is sufficient to meet research objectives.

Figure 7.7 shows the sources of secondary and primary marketing data. Secondary data are shown first because researchers consider secondary data before committing to primary data collection. Data sources are further divided into data collected by the marketing organization (*internal data*) and data collected by outside agencies such as marketing research firms, advertising agencies, government organizations, and other environmental sources (*external data*). All data are directed toward marketing managers to allow them to identify opportunities and to plan for product and corporate strategies.

SOURCES OF SECONDARY DATA

Figure 7.7 shows that secondary data are available from external sources or from internal company records. Most firms will evaluate such data before incurring the costs of collecting primary data, since secondary data alone may satisfy the firm's research needs.

EXTERNAL SECONDARY DATA: ENVIRONMENTAL SOURCES

There are two major sources of external secondary data: (1) environmental sources such as government agencies, competition, trade publications, or consumer databases, and (2) syndicated research services.

The U.S. government is the largest environmental source, providing a rich storehouse of data useful to marketers in every field. The most important government source is the demographic information provided by the Bureau of the Census. As it begins to be disseminated, the 1990 census will provide companies with a rich source of data. We have seen in Chapter 3 that key demographic trends such as the increasing proportion of working women, more singles, and the decrease in the birth rate have affected the longer-term strategies of companies like Avon, Kellogg, and Gerber. Information from the 1990 census will be essential if these companies are to project future purchasing trends for their products. Marketers also use census data for planning. *Time* magazine uses census data to identify zip-code areas that have the highest income so that it can concentrate subscription mailings in these areas.[27]

Competition is another environmental source for secondary data. Firms can obtain valuable information from a competitor's annual report and financial reports required by the Securities and Exchange Commission, in addition to competitors' salespeople and distributors.

Trade and industry publications are a valuable source of information on demand trends, competitive activities, and government regulations. *Sales & Marketing Management* magazine provides a yearly survey of buying power that contains data on population, retail sales, and household income by county and city. The magazine develops an index of buying power based on this information for each area. An automobile manufacturer could use this buying-power index to determine purchase potential for its cars by region and thus identify areas warranting new deal-

FIGURE 7.7

Sources of Marketing Data

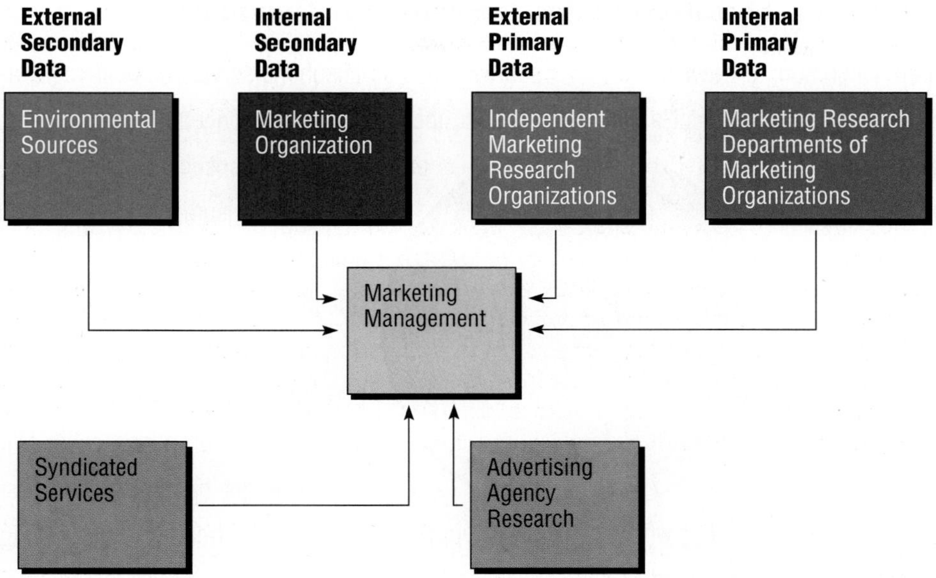

erships. *Fortune* publishes a directory of the 1,000 largest U.S. companies, with information on sales, assets, profits, and number of employees.

A controversial source of information that can provide more detail than any of the sources listed above is **consumer data bases**; *that is, demographic and financial information on individual consumers derived from applications for credit, drivers' licenses, or telephone service.* The agencies that collect this information make it available to data processing companies for future reference—for example, a bank sending loan application information on a consumer to a credit bureau.

Since the early 1980s, credit bureaus such as TRW Credit Data have amassed individual records on almost every adult in the United States. This data is sold to marketers who want to reach specific consumer groups—for example, sending loan applications to households who owe significant amounts on their credit cards.

Why are these databases controversial? Because the information collected for one purpose (credit) is being used for another (direct mail solicitations). Many feel this use of information represents an invasion of privacy. (See Ethics box).

EXTERNAL SECONDARY DATA: SYNDICATED RESEARCH

Marketing organizations often rely on **syndicated research,** *which is data collected periodically by firms that sell this research to subscribing companies.* The most important use of syndicated research services is to obtain retail sales data and data on advertising and media exposure.

SALES DATA We noted that before the advent of scanner data, retail sales were measured by store audits. Store audits are still used as the primary means to determine retail sales when scanner data is not available. The A. C. Nielsen Company, the largest marketing research company in the world, periodically audits the sales of a representative sample of food and drug stores nationwide. When bar codes

ETHICAL AND ENVIRONMENTAL ISSUES IN MARKETING

Consumer Databases: An Invasion of Privacy?

When Karen Hochman, a New York–based marketing consultant, got a call from an ITT representative to sell her long-distance service, she responded that she does not make many out-of-town calls. The sales rep then said he was surprised because her phone record showed that she called New Jersey, Delaware, and Connecticut frequently. Ms. Hochman was shocked. "If people are able to find out who I called," she said, "what else could they find out about me?"

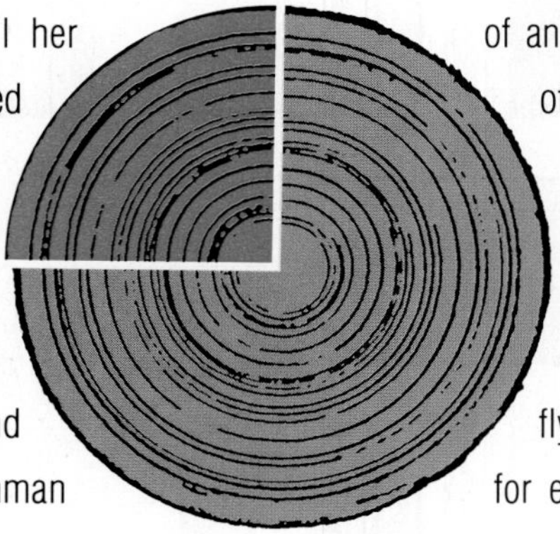

Karen Hochman is not alone in being concerned about her privacy. A recent Gallup poll found that 78 percent of consumers surveyed expressed concern about the amount of information marketers may have gathered about them without their knowledge. This concern is primarily focused on violations of privacy in consumer databases.

Banks send loan, mortgage, and credit card applications to credit bureaus for future reference. As a result, these credit bureaus have demographic and financial information on almost every adult in the United States. TRW alone has information on 140 million consumers. These credit bureaus can supplement loan information with data from other sources such as telephone service and car registrations, so they now know not only the financial status of an individual consumer, but the make of car the consumer owns and the amount spent on calls to various locations. Marketers could then buy lists of consumers from credit bureaus to target with direct-mail flyers, catalogs, or phone calls. ITT, for example, might have obtained a list showing customers who frequently call long distance.

Some credit agencies may be coming close to violating the law by making information obtained for one purpose available to marketers for another purpose. The Fair Credit Information Act of 1970 bars credit agencies from sharing this information with anyone except those who have a "legitimate business need." The question is whether these companies have the right to sell this information to marketers and whether marketers who buy information on individual consumers have a "legitimate business need."

The issue has not been tested, primarily because the Federal Trade Commission (the enforcing agency) has given privacy of information a low priority, and because the issue was further de-

ETHICAL AND ENVIRONMENTAL ISSUES IN MARKETING

emphasized during the Reagan administration. But the rising tide of consumer concerns is giving marketers pause in using databases from credit agencies. The Direct Marketing Association, representing the marketers most likely to use such databases, has promoted the right of consumers to confidentiality by encouraging consumers who are concerned to register with the Association to have their names removed from credit agency lists. To date, almost one million consumers have registered, but this is nowhere close to the number of consumers expressing concern about privacy, so this option is obviously not well known.

Companies providing information have also begun to tread lightly. Lotus, the software company, and Equifax, a large credit agency, had jointly developed a software package called Marketplace: Household, to be introduced in 1991 containing demographic and life-style information for 80 million U.S. households. Marketers could buy the software package and immediately establish the means of reaching individual households. But protests from the American Civil Liberties Union and consumer protection groups regarding invasion of privacy led Lotus to withdraw the package.

Despite these concerns, the three largest credit agencies, TRW Credit Data, Equifax, and Trans Union Credit Information continue to sell their databases. TRW Credit Data, for example, sells a list called Consumer Financial Database, which provides direct marketers with the identity of bankcards held by individuals and their outstanding balances and credit availability. Ironically, TRW Credit Data has a code of ethics which says, in part, that "Lists of names shall not be compiled from TRW Credit Data's files of credit information for sale." When asked about the disparity between its actions and its code of ethics, a TRW representative said that technological advances made the code no longer valid. The key question is whether consumer concerns will force these credit agencies to change their policies regarding the privacy of their information.

Questions: Is it unethical for credit agencies to sell the information they have on individual consumers? Why or why not? Under what circumstances, if any, would you approve of the sale of such information?

Sources: "Is Nothing Private?" *Business Week*, September 4, 1989, pp. 74–77; "Consumers Target Ire At Data Bases," *Advertising Age*, May 6, 1991, p. 3; "Lotus Forced to Cancel New Software Program," *Marketing News*, February 18, 1991, p. 11; "TRW Sells Its Conscience for Cash," *Business and Society Review* (Fall 1989),4–7.

began appearing on products in the early 1970s, in-store checkout scanners began to be used on a small scale. Sales were recorded both at the cash register and in a central computer file.

By 1991, over 77 percent of all supermarkets had scanner facilities.[28] By this time, services were established that supplied manufacturers with scanner data. Two companies dominate the field, Information Resources Inc. (IRI) and A.C. Nielsen. Both maintain large panels of consumers that buy groceries in scanner stores so that companies can relate brand sales to the characteristics of consumers who bought the brand. IRI's InfoScan service was the first to establish such a data source. The InfoScan panel is composed of 70-thousand households who buy from 2,700 stores located in 66 markets. Nielsen's SCANTRACK service is composed of 40-thousand households who shop in 3,500 scanner stores.

These services can provide companies with retail sales data for their brands as well as competitive brands broken down by the price paid for the item, whether it was bought with coupons or a price promotion, package size, region, and a demographic profile of new purchasers and repeat buyers of the brand.

As we have seen, scanner services are also available in Europe. Both IRI and Nielsen provide scanner data to marketers in Western Europe. GfK, the second largest research firm in Europe after Nielsen, also provides scanner data through its Euroscan service.[29]

ADVERTISING AND MEDIA EXPOSURE Several research firms offer services designed to determine exposure to print and TV advertising. For example, the Starch service conducts 240,000 interviews yearly, evaluating 30,000 ads, to measure awareness and readership of advertisements in magazines and newspapers.[30] It asks respondents whether they have seen the ad, remembered reading about a particular product or company, and whether they read the copy. Firms also offer services to measure exposure to TV advertising. Burke Marketing Research uses a day-after recall method in which a sample of consumers is asked whether they recall seeing a TV commercial the day after it appears.

Simmons Market Research Bureau provides the most-comprehensive data on exposure to print media. The company interviews 15,000 respondents yearly and obtains data on readership of 136 magazines and purchases of 500 product categories.[31] It can then determine whether purchasers of a particular product category are more likely to read certain magazines or newspapers. For example, if Simmons finds that purchasers of camping equipment are twice as likely to read *Popular Mechanics* as the average respondent, then a company knows that advertisements in that magazine would be very effective in reaching the camping market.

The A. C. Nielsen company is the largest service that measures TV exposure. It attaches an *audimeter* to a sample of 1,700 television sets nationwide that records what each household is viewing. Households in the sample also keep a diary of what each individual member watches. In this way, Nielsen can estimate not only if the set was on at a given time, but who was watching it. On the basis of this sample, the company projects TV exposure to the country as a whole and supplies the number of viewers watching a program, as well as a demographic profile of viewers by time of exposure. This information enables companies to determine the programs on which they should advertise in order to best reach a particular demographic target. For example, assume that purchasers of camping equipment tend to be nonurban, middle-income, blue-collar individuals between 25 and 40 and that this group is more likely to watch late-night movies. Then TV commercials for camping equipment should be shown on late-night movies.

Nielsen's data on TV exposure are also important to companies because TV networks use the program ratings to sell advertising time. The higher the rating, the more costly it is to advertise on a show. One of the costliest time slots on TV is the Super Bowl because of the millions of consumers watching the broadcast.

Nielsen also provides TV exposure data to marketers in seven foreign countries based on a sample of households with audimeters in these countries. An English-based company, AGB, provides similar services in thirteen countries based on a sample of households with audimeters.[32]

INTERNAL SECONDARY DATA

Internal secondary data includes data on factory shipments—showing the amount of revenue generated by each of the company's products—and cost data such as expenditures for research, advertising, personal selling, and distribution. The combination of revenue and cost data permits a company to evaluate a product's profit performance.

An industrial firm that analyzed its profits by product category based on internal company data found that 10 percent of its products accounted for 80 percent of its profits. Further, the most-profitable products were generally targeted to a small, well-defined group of customers. By eliminating many of its products and concentrating sales effort on the remaining product line and a smaller number of customers, the firm substantially increased its profits.

SOURCES OF PRIMARY DATA

Figure 7.7 shows that primary data can be collected externally or internally.

EXTERNAL PRIMARY DATA

Most companies use outside marketing research firms to conduct consumer surveys and product tests and to test alternative advertisements. When Coca-Cola ran its taste tests for New Coke, it first used Schrader Research, a New Jersey–based company specializing in taste tests, which had specially equipped trailers located in major markets nationwide to conduct the tests. It then turned to Cambridge Survey Research, a Washington D.C. company owned by political pollster Patrick Caddell, to conduct surveys to determine public reaction to a formula change.[33]

Another important source of external primary data is a firm's advertising agency, which conducts research to determine the best advertising approaches and to select the most effective media to reach the target group. Buick used its advertising agency, McCann-Erickson, to help it develop both the concept and the advertising for its Regal coupe. The effort began five years before its introduction with 20 focus groups across the country being asked what they wanted in a new car. Results showed they wanted a stylish but conservative car, one with lots of room, good acceleration, and gas mileage of over 20 miles per gallon. The agency then developed 20 ad concepts that were screened by consumers and narrowed down to 4, which were developed into TV commercials and print ads. These four alternative advertising approaches were again shown to consumers to help the agency select the best approach.[34]

INTERNAL PRIMARY DATA

Marketing organizations sometimes conduct their own studies. Procter & Gamble has a staff of 250 people in its marketing research department, with specific groups responsible for qualitative research, advertising tests, product and package testing, and data analysis.[35] It also has a bank of WATS lines it uses to conduct consumer surveys. At one time, the company ran 80 percent of its studies internally, but now it uses outside services more frequently.

Most marketing firms cannot afford the in-house marketing research facilities of a Procter & Gamble, but often conduct their own taste or package tests or other small-scale studies. This was the case with Frito-Lay when it conducted taste tests for the Light snack line.

THE INFORMATION REVOLUTION

A description of marketing research does not capture the remarkable changes that have taken place in the late 1980s and early 1990s in information technology. The quantity, quality, and accessibility of information have increased significantly. Today, marketers are capable of obtaining more-reliable sales information through scanner data, of accessing this information quickly through microcomputers, and of relating sales information to marketing expenditures—allowing managers to better measure the effectiveness of their advertising and sales promotions.

COMPONENTS OF THE INFORMATION REVOLUTION

Three developments have made this information revolution possible: electronic measures of TV exposure, scanner data, and the microcomputer. These three components are depicted in Figure 7.8 in a series of steps that illustrate the information revolution.

ELECTRONIC MEASURES OF TV EXPOSURE

The first component of the information revolution in Figure 7.8 is the electronic measurement of TV exposure (step 1). As we have seen, Nielsen attaches an audimeter to television sets to record the channel to which they are tuned. Consumers used to record who was watching the set through a diary questionnaire. But diaries were sometimes unreliable, because they required consumers to recall what they were viewing. In 1987, Nielsen replaced audimeters and consumer diaries with *People Meters*, hand-held devices that are supposed to be pressed when a member of the household starts and stops watching TV.

Whereas audimeters could only determine whether the set was on or not, People Meters record who is watching and what commercials are seen. Exposure to commercials now can be measured without asking consumers direct questions and having to rely on the accuracy of their recall. People Meters still lack perfect reliability, because there is no assurance that viewers will in fact "punch in" and "punch out" when viewing TV programs.

SCANNER DATA

We have described the second component in the information revolution, scanner data. Scanner information collected in retail stores is stored in a central computer and can be accessed by company managers from microcomputers in their locations. A manager can thereby determine sales of a particular product within a day or two of purchase.

The scanner panels established by IRI and Nielsen are shown in Figure 7.8 in steps 2 and 3. Members of these panels give the checkout clerk a computer-coded

FIGURE 7.8

Components of the Information Revolution

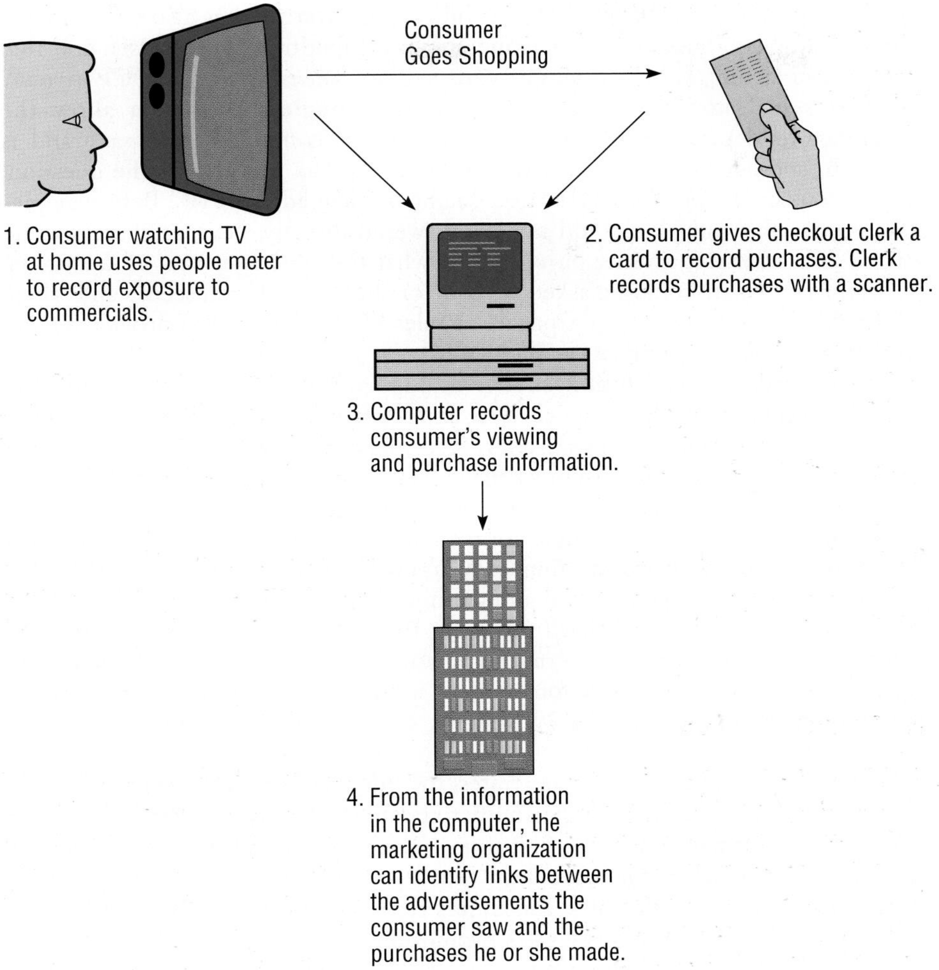

Consumer
Goes Shopping
1. Consumer watching TV at home uses people meter to record exposure to commercials.
2. Consumer gives checkout clerk a card to record puchases. Clerk records purchases with a scanner.
3. Computer records consumer's viewing and purchase information.
4. From the information in the computer, the marketing organization can identify links between the advertisements the consumer saw and the purchases he or she made.

card when they make a purchase. The researcher knows the demographic characteristics and past purchases of each consumer in the panel. When a consumer buys merchandise, the checkout clerk records the purchases, using a laser scanner, and punches in the consumer's card. This way, purchases can be associated with the demographic and past purchase characteristics of a particular consumer based on the card identification.

THE MICROCOMPUTER

As Figure 7.8 shows, through microcomputers, marketers have immediate access to purchase data from scanner stores and to TV exposure data from People Meters. Microcomputers at company locations provide on-line information at the manager's request. Further, managers can break out sales by price, region, or other factors to better assess a brand's performance.

SINGLE-SOURCE DATA Both IRI and Nielsen have equipped a subset of their consumer panels with meters to measure TV exposure. (IRI uses audimeters, Nielsen uses People Meters.) This way, they know what a particular consumer or household watches on TV *and* purchases (steps 1 and 2 in Figure 7.8). A third firm, Arbitron, has also established a scanner panel equipped with people meters, in competition with Nielsen and IRI.

This data facility, known as **single-source data**, *collects purchase and TV exposure from the same source—the individual consumer.* Single-source data allow the researcher to determine whether exposure to TV commercials for a brand is related to subsequent purchase of the brand. Such data can answer the question, "Did a consumer buy Coca-Cola after seeing a Coke ad on TV?" Before single-source data, this question could not be answered directly, because there was no way to link what a consumer purchased to what the consumer saw on television. At best, a consumer could be asked what he or she remembered seeing and when. By directly linking advertising exposure to sales, single-source data provide a more reliable measure of advertising effectiveness.

The information revolution shown in Figure 7.8 was an improvement in research quality in another respect. Consumers are never directly asked any questions. Rather, questions are answered by electronic measurement of their behavior and media exposure. This eliminates inaccuracies due to the potential bias in asking questions and relying on imperfect consumer recall.

Campbell effectively used single-source data in a test of two TV commercials for its line of Swanson frozen dinners. Campbell ran the test through IRI. One commercial showed a young man impressing his girlfriend with a fine meal she thought he had cooked but that turned out to be a Swanson frozen dinner. The other showed Swanson as an alternative to hot dogs or hamburgers. By determining purchases and TV exposure for the same individual, Campbell could determine that Swanson purchases were 20 percent higher among viewers of the first commercial.[36]

As the Campbell example demonstrates, the information revolution is providing managers with a powerful tool: the ability to relate marketing mix variables directly to product performance. For the first time, managers can evaluate how consumers respond in a store after they have been exposed to TV commercials. Scanner systems can also tell managers how consumers respond after having been exposed to various price levels and in-store sales promotions. Never before has it been possible to evaluate so accurately the impact of alternative marketing strategies on a product's sales performance.

SUMMARY

1. **What is the role of a marketing information system in developing marketing plans?**
   A marketing information system provides the capability to collect and analyze information from diverse sources and then disseminate it to decision makers. It should provide management with three capabilities: (1) to gauge a product's profit performance from information on sales revenues and costs, (2) to evaluate changes in the environment that might affect product performance, and (3) to evaluate customer perceptions, attitudes, and behavior that might affect product sales. These three requirements are filled by three subsystems of a marketing information system: an internal reporting system to provide company data, an environmental tracking system to identify environmental changes, and a marketing research system to provide customer data.

2. **What is the role of marketing research in marketing planning?**
The role of marketing research is to provide management with information to (1) identify marketing opportunities or problems, (2) develop alternative strategies to exploit these opportunities, and (3) evaluate consumer reactions to these strategies.
3. **How is marketing research conducted?**
Marketing research involves systematic steps to achieve a set of research objectives. Investigators first define the research objectives. They then conduct a situation analysis to review existing (secondary) data to determine if it might be sufficient to fulfill the research objectives. If not, they develop a plan to collect primary data, whether through qualitative research, a survey, or experimentation. If a survey is required, the researchers must determine if it is to be conducted in person, by telephone, or through the mail. Once the research approach is established, the researcher develops a questionnaire to collect the information and selects a sample of respondents for the study. Data is then collected and analyzed, and a final report is submitted to management.
4. **What are the sources of marketing data?**
Marketing data can be categorized as primary (data collected for the specific area being investigated) and secondary (data collected previously). Primary and secondary data can also be categorized as external (collected by outside agencies) or internal (collected by the firm). Most companies use outside marketing research firms to collect primary data. Some large firms such as Procter & Gamble have internal facilities for conducting surveys, product tests, and other types of research. Outside sources for secondary data include government agencies, competitors, publications, trade associations, and syndicated services.
5. **What is the nature of the "information revolution" that has occurred in marketing in the 1980s and 1990s?**
Three developments have created an information revolution in marketing: scanner data, electronic measures of TV exposure, and the microcomputer. Scanner data allows an instant record to be made of a consumer's purchases from the universal product code. Electronic measures of TV exposure determine the channel to which the set is tuned, and who is watching. Microcomputers make both sets of data quickly available to managers. Using these developments, researchers can collect single-source data, which link TV exposure to purchases and allow more-accurate measurement of the effectiveness of advertising.

KEY TERMS

Scanner data (p. 209)
Marketing information system (MIS) (p. 210)
Decision support system (DSS) (p. 211)
Factory shipments (p. 212)
Store audits (p. 213)
Validity (p. 222)
Reliability (p. 222)
Representativeness (p. 223)
Population (p. 223)
Exploratory research objectives (p. 223)
Descriptive research objectives (p. 225)
Causal research objectives (p. 225)
Situation analysis (p. 225)
Secondary data (p. 225)
Primary data (p. 225)
Qualitative research (p. 226)
Focus-group interviews (p. 226)
Depth interviews (p. 226)
Projective techniques (p. 226)
Experimentation (p. 230)
Probability (or random) sampling (p. 233)
Nonprobability sampling (p. 234)
Cross-tabulations (p. 234)
Multivariate statistical techniques (p. 235)
Consumer data bases (p. 237)
Syndicated research (p. 237)
Single-source data (p. 244)

QUESTIONS

1. What is the role of a marketing information system in making marketing decisions?
2. What were the roles of the internal reporting system, environmental scanning system, and marketing research system in Frito-Lay's introduction of its Light snack line?
3. What are the advantages of scanner data compared to store audits? in measuring retail sales? Specifically, why does such data give managers a better capability to evaluate sales results?
4. What are some potential problems in establishing marketing information systems abroad?
5. Assume that Pepsi-Cola conducted a study before it introduced Slice, its fruit-based soft-drink line, to determine the potential for the line. Its research objectives were to (a) determine if a fruit-based soft drink might better meet the nutritional needs of adults than existing colas and (b) identify the market for such a product. Describe the research process the company might have implemented based on the steps in Figure 7.4.
6. What are valid, reliable, and representative marketing data? In testing new Coke versus old Coke and Pepsi, how well did Coca-Cola meet the requirements of validity, reliability, and representativeness?
7. What is the purpose of a situation analysis? What kinds of information sources are used to conduct a situation analysis?
8. What type of research approach—qualitative, survey, or experimental—would a company be most likely to use in the following cases, and why?
   a. Identifying the demographic and life-style characteristics of potential buyers of a new fruit-and-nut snack.
   b. Testing two or three formulations of the product on consumers to determine which is most effective.
   c. Determining if consumers might have any deep-seated resistance to accepting fruit as a snack.
9. Because sales of men's hats have been slowly decreasing, a hat manufacturer is considering whether to get out of the business. Before it does, it would like to determine why sales have been decreasing to see if it can do something to reverse the trend.
   a. How can the company use focus-group interviews and projective techniques to evaluate why sales of men's hats are decreasing?
   b. What are the purposes of each of these techniques?
10. What are the advantages and disadvantages of personal interviews, telephone interviews, and mail surveys?
11. What is an example of an experiment in a marketing research study? Why would you classify the study you cited as an experiment?
12. What is the distinction between obtrusive and unobtrusive observational research? Provide an example of each. Why might obtrusive observation create biases in research results?
13. The investigation of the small-business market by AT&T warranted the collection of primary data through survey research. Why was it necessary to collect primary data? Under what circumstances might secondary data be sufficient to investigate a marketing research area? What are the dangers of relying only on secondary data?
14. An industrial producer of auto parts finds its sales slipping. Management feels the cause could be inefficient allocation of sales effort. How can the company use internal secondary data to investigate the cause of this decline?
15. What are single-source data? What is the significance of single-source data in evaluating advertising effectiveness?

QUESTIONS: YOU ARE THE DECISION MAKER

1. A manufacturer of hydraulic compressors says:

   Of the three components of an MIS, we rely primarily on the internal reporting and environmental scanning systems; internal reporting to track sales and costs, and environmental scanning to keep up to date on technology and our competitors. We do no marketing research to speak of. We find it sufficient to talk to our salespeople and to rely on business magazines and trade literature to assess the needs of our customers.

   What are the risks of doing no marketing research in evaluating customer needs?

2. A marketing executive for a leading producer of packaged foods commented on the steps in the marketing research process in Figure 7.5 as follows:

   These research steps certainly seem logical. But in our business, they are not always as structured as you make them out to be. Take the research we did for our new line of microwaveable snacks. We did not feel a situation analysis was necessary, because this was a brand new product with no past research. Further, we limited the amount of consumer testing and test marketing for the product because we wanted to get the product marketed quickly to beat out competition. So the systematic marketing research process you describe is not always necessary.

   Do you agree that a situation analysis is not necessary in introducing new products? What are the pros and cons of limiting product tests to ensure the product will beat competition to the market?

3. One marketing executive, commenting on the qualitative approach to marketing research, said:

   I always take these findings with a grain of salt. It's fine to say, for example, that men did not like to fly because of guilt in leaving their families behind, or that bathing is a ritual. But these findings are based on the comments of just a few consumers and rely on the researcher's insights. Some qualitative researchers admit that they might develop a hypothesis based on the comment of one respondent, "What happens if they are just plain wrong?"

   a. Is this marketing executive's concern with qualitative research justified?
   b. What might be a possible solution to the concern about (1) small samples and (2) relying on the interpretations of the researcher?

CHAPTER 8

Consumer Behavior

YOUR FOCUS IN CHAPTER 8

To learn:

- *How consumers go about making purchasing decisions.*
- *What factors influence a consumer's purchase decisions.*
- *How a consumer's needs, perceptions, and attitudes influence purchase decisions.*
- *How the consumer's characteristics and environment influence purchases.*
- *How marketers use knowledge about consumers and their environment to develop marketing strategies.*

Gerber Goes Back to the Consumers it Knows Best—Babies

In the mid 1980s, Gerber's earnings started looking like its baby foods—soft and strained. The company was buffeted by a series of missteps and mishaps so that by 1987, it was a prime takeover target. What happened? Quite simply, Gerber forgot who it was—the country's leading producer of baby foods, with a whopping market share of 72 percent of the baby food market.[1] In the process, it forgot about its primary consumers—babies—and its primary purchasers—their mothers.

What happened? By 1980 the company recognized that a long-term decrease in the birth rate meant a mature baby-foods market and started looking elsewhere for growth. But it began looking for growth in businesses it knew little about—trucking, furniture, and toy manufacturing.[2] These nonfood acquisitions proved disastrous; they started draining the company's profits from its steady performer, baby foods. Further, the new ventures deflected Gerber from developing new baby-food products. The company was ignoring its main business.

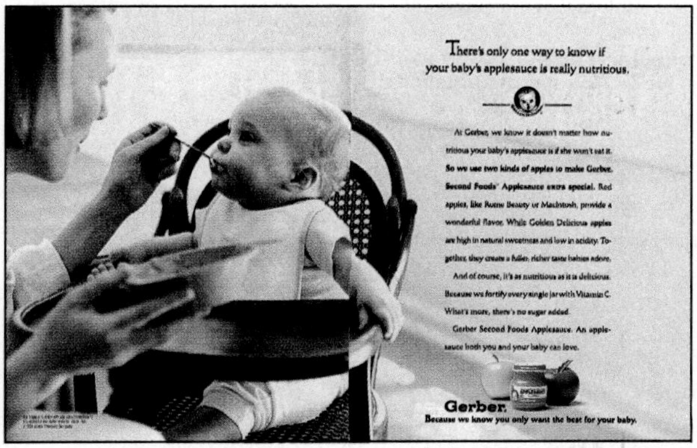

To add to its woes, in 1986 bits of glass were found in Gerber's peach jars in numerous states. The company refused to recall the peaches involved and reacted by not even responding to the publicity. Eventually, the Food and Drug Administration cleared Gerber of any wrongdoing in the matter, but the event caused a drop in Gerber's share, from 72 percent to 52 percent of the baby-food market.

By 1987, the company realized it had to do something. It boosted ad spending by 50 percent to counteract the negative publicity from the glass scare. Most important, the board of directors recognized the company had to reverse course and brought in a new management team headed by David Johnson, the executive that successfully took a regional baker, Entenmann's, national and made it one of the leading lines of baked goods in the country.

Johnson saw, in the words of one analyst, that the company could not afford to continue to "dilute top management's time and focus with cockeyed, nonfood, low-return businesses, and had to get [Gerber] back on the baby food business."[3] His first step was to divest Gerber of its truck, furniture, and toy companies. His next step was to refocus the company on baby foods. Johnson realized that Gerber had a natural advantage over its two main competitors, Heinz and Beech-Nut (owned by Nestlé). Both firms are food companies that have a baby-food line. Gerber's name, on the other hand, is synonymous with baby food.

But how could Gerber get extra growth from a market that was constrained by a long-term decline in the birth rate? The answer was fairly simple: introduce new products to extend the market down to younger babies and up to older ones. Gerber's traditional market was babies from six months to two years old. The company's first venture was First Foods, a new line of all-natural, extra-smooth fruits and vegetables in single servings designed for infants four months and older. The new line was successful in getting mothers to start babies on natural processed foods earlier. By 1989, it was capturing $30 million in sales.

Gerber also went in the other direction, introducing a new line for toddlers two to four years old called Gerber Graduates. The line is positioned as a more nutritional alternative to current feeding habits for toddlers, which involve canned foods, salt-laden adult foods, and fast foods.[4]

Despite these successes, management realized it was still in a low-growth market. The Census Bureau predicted an 8.2 percent drop in the number of children aged 4 and under in the next 20 years.[5] By 1990, Johnson's successors developed a strategy for growth beyond baby foods. Gerber would not make the mistake of looking for growth in nonfood areas. It would stick to foods under the umbrella of developing a family of products for various ages. Gerber's first step was to roll out Fruit Classics, a line of applesauce snacks positioned for school kids. But it carefully disassociated the Gerber name from the line, recognizing that grade-school children did not want to be caught eating anything that smacked of baby food. The company is also introducing Juice & More, a line of juice drinks with fiber for adults.

There is a second important element to Gerber's growth strategy: establishing a position for its baby foods in the international market. In 1991, Gerber announced it would start exporting its baby foods to Europe.[6] The prospects of low growth at home make the international market particularly appealing, especially since international sales currently account for only 5 percent of Gerber's total.

How has Gerber fared? Earnings more than doubled from 1988 to 1990.[7] And the company has not yet tapped into the potential for non-baby foods and for leveraging its name in the international market. Further, Gerber is showing a new-found sensitivity to consumer needs by introducing new baby food lines that mothers have accepted and by appealing to nutritional needs in these product introductions. Little did most people realize that going back to baby foods was just the first step in David Johnson's longer term strategy for growth.

IMPORTANCE OF CONSUMER BEHAVIOR

In Chapter 1, we defined marketing as all activities directed toward identifying and satisfying customer needs. According to this definition, understanding the customer is central to identifying marketing opportunities and to developing strategies for pursuing these opportunities.

UNDERSTANDING CONSUMER NEEDS

Successful marketing strategies hinge on identifying consumer needs. Kodak met the need among sophisticated amateur photographers for a finer grained film with better resolution by introducing Ektar. Apple was able to maintain its competitive advantage in the educational market by filling a need for user-friendly personal computers that had superior graphics. And Kellogg established the adult cereal market by recognizing the need among baby boomers for more nutritious breakfast foods.

In contrast, insufficient understanding of the consumer will put a company at a competitive disadvantage, sometimes severe enough to spell disaster. Avon began a long decline in the 1970s because it did not recognize the negative impact of more working women on door-to-door selling. Similarly, Polaroid and RCA could be cited for a certain corporate arrogance in being driven by their existing technology rather than by consumer needs when they introduced instant movies and videodiscs, products that consumers simply did not need.

CONSUMER BEHAVIOR AND MARKETING STRATEGY

If marketers are to understand their customers, they require marketing research to identify consumers' needs, perceptions of existing brand offerings, and brand attitudes. As we will see in this chapter, terms like *needs*, *perceptions*, and *attitudes* have specific meaning that largely determine what the consumer will purchase. Marketers must know these variables if they are to identify opportunities to better meet customer needs.

Gerber could successfully develop First Foods and Gerber Graduates by interviewing 75 thousand mothers to determine their needs in baby foods.[8] On this basis, the company developed an effective strategy for segmenting the baby-food market by age (see Exhibit 8.1). Its strategy was designed to meet the needs of each segment—for example, introducing First Foods in single-portion servings because mothers preferred smaller packaging to assist in feeding, while introducing Gerber Graduates in larger servings with more varieties such as vegetable stew with beef and spaghetti with meatballs for older infants.

Gerber also emphasizes the nutritional content of its new lines to meet the increasing health consciousness of baby-boom parents. In support of this emphasis, the company ensures that new parents leaving a hospital receive a Gerber care package providing information on baby nutrition and free samples. A subsequent direct mail program reaches two-thirds of new parents with child-care pamphlets, additional product samples, and coupons. In this way, Gerber is hoping that parents will go from First Foods to the regular Gerber line to Gerber Graduates.

Each segment of Gerber's strategy—segmentation, product positioning, promotion, and packaging—was developed with the purpose of appealing to the parent's feeding and nutritional concerns across the age spectrum from four months to four years. Each component of strategy was also tested—product tests to deter-

EXHIBIT 8.1

Gerber's Segmentation of the Baby-Food Market

mine babies' reactions to alternative foods, tests of advertising and direct mail to determine effectiveness in communicating nutritional information to parents, and package tests to determine parents' reaction to information on the label.

CONSUMERS AND ORGANIZATIONAL BUYERS

In Chapter 1, we cited two types of customers: final consumers and organizational buyers. Final consumers buy for themselves or their family. They are the last link in the chain of creating and distributing a product. Organizational buyers purchase for a company.

Because there are important differences in the purchasing behavior of these two types of buyers, a chapter will be devoted to each. This chapter deals with consumer behavior and the next with organizational buyer behavior.

A MODEL OF CONSUMER BEHAVIOR

Figure 8.1 presents a simple model of consumer behavior. Consumers are exposed to various **marketing stimuli**, *that is, purchase-related communications designed to influence consumers.* These stimuli can be the product itself or communications from marketers to consumers in the form of advertising, in-store stimuli, sales messages, or price. Marketing stimuli can also be word-of-mouth communications from friends, relatives, and acquaintances about products. Such communications generally exert more influence on consumers than marketing strategies because they are regarded as more trustworthy.

The consumer will react to these stimuli based on three sets of variables. First is the consumer's **psychological set,** *or general state of mind toward an object.* The consumer's psychological set will determine positive or negative reactions toward a brand. For example, Gerber had difficulty establishing itself in Brazil because

FIGURE 8.1

A Model of Consumer Behavior

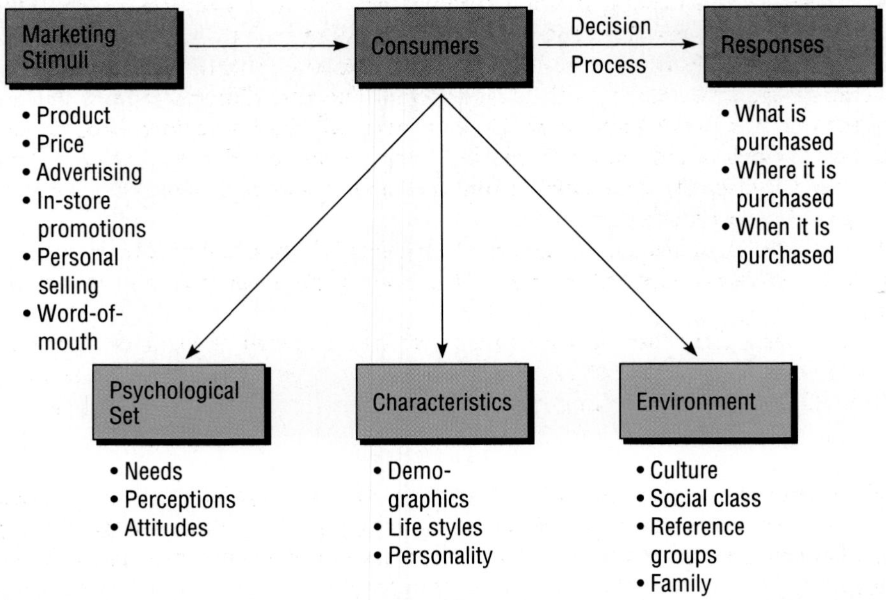

Source: Adapted from Jane F. Engel, Roger D. Blackwell, and Paul W. Miniard, *Consumer Behavior, Seventh Edition* (Fort Worth, Texas: The Dryden Press, 1993), S3.

mothers there traditionally prepared foods for their babies and were reluctant to buy processed foods. As a result, the Brazilian mother's psychological set toward Gerber was negative. The importance of the consumer's psychological set in influencing purchasing behavior will become clear when we define its determinants—consumer needs, perceptions, and attitudes.

The second set of factors that affect purchasing decisions are the consumer's *personal characteristics:* demographics, life-style, and personality. For instance, a baby's age (a demographic factor) and the parent's emphasis on nutrition (a life-style factor) are likely to influence the parent's decision to buy Gerber's First Foods.

Third are *environmental factors*, which include broad influences such as our *culture* (processed baby foods are acceptable in American culture but not in many other countries) and the consumer's *social class.* They also include more specific face-to-face influences such as the *family* (a mother prefers Beech-Nut to Gerber because her mother preferred it) and *reference groups* (that is, groups to which consumers refer for advice, opinions, and behavioral norms).

Figure 8.1 shows that the consumer's psychological set, characteristics, and environment are the inputs into a decision process that determines what the consumer buys, where the consumer buys it, and when it is purchased.

In the remainder of this chapter, we will examine these three components of consumer behavior. Before we do, we will first consider the consumer's decision process, because it defines how these factors work together to arrive at a consumer decision regarding what, where and when to buy.

THE CONSUMER'S DECISION PROCESS

Consumer decision making is not a singular process. The decision to buy baby foods or cereals is very different from the decision to buy a car. Figure 8.2 categorizes consumer decisions on two dimensions, the extent of decision making and the consumer's involvement with the purchase. The first dimension distinguishes between decision making and habit. In the process of decision making, a consumer evaluates various brands and searches for information about them. Habit, on the other hand, causes the consumer to buy the same brand repeatedly with little or no brand evaluation and information search.

The second dimension distinguishes between high and low involvement purchases. By **involvement,** *we mean the importance of the product decision to the consumer.*

Categorizing consumer decisions on these two dimensions produces the four types of decision processes shown in Figure 8.2: complex decision making, brand loyalty, limited decision making, and inertia.

HIGH-INVOLVEMENT PURCHASES

High involvement purchases *are purchases that are important to the consumer because they are more socially significant* (clothing) *or involve greater risk* (medicine). High-involvement purchases may require complex decision making or brand loyalty.

COMPLEX DECISION MAKING

Complex decision making *is a high-involvement purchase that requires a great deal of thought and deliberation.* A consumer is usually highly involved in a decision to buy a home, a car, or a computer because of the financial outlay and the importance of the product. In making a decision for these types of products, the consumer will search for information and carefully compare a number of alternatives

FIGURE 8.2

Types of Consumer Decision Processes

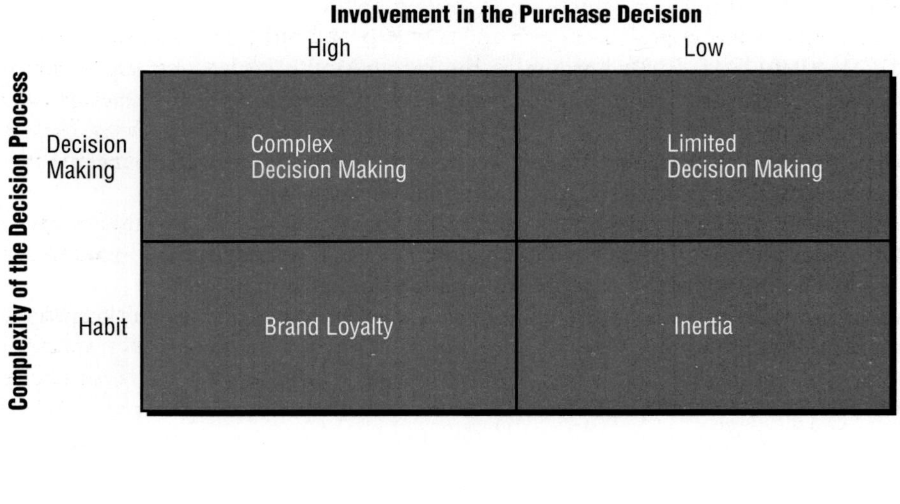

FIGURE 8.3

*Complex Decison Making**

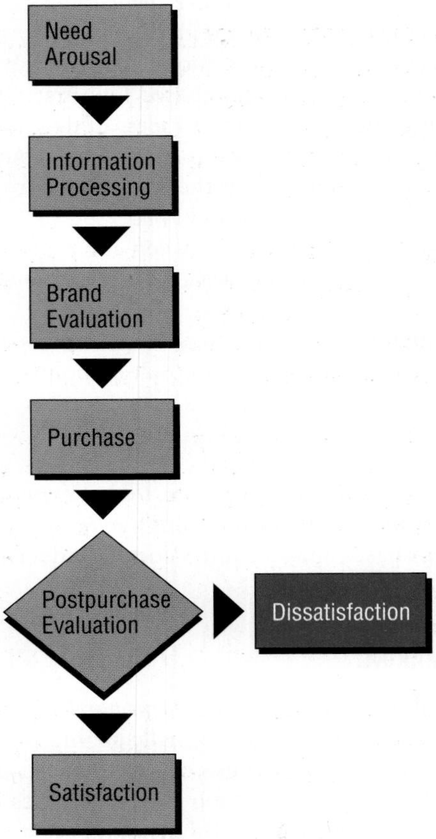

*Limited decision making involves the same steps as complex decision making, except that information processing and brand evaluation are much less extensive.

to determine which can best fill his or her needs. Figure 8.3 shows the steps in complex decision making, which are described below.

NEED AROUSAL Need arousal is the recognition of a need for a product or a brand. Such arousal can occur for many reasons, for example:

- past experiences (a college student realizes she needs an answering machine because she is constantly missing telephone messages)
- an immediate cue (a consumer's car breaks down)
- consumer characteristics (a middle-aged couple decide they need a smaller house because their children are no longer living at home)
- environmental influences (a couple decide they need a luxury car to keep up with their neighbors).

INFORMATION PROCESSING **Information processing** *is the process of noticing a marketing stimulus, understanding and interpreting it, and then retaining it* *in memory*. A mother of a newborn baby sees advertising for Gerber's First Foods, interprets the information as meaning she can feed processed food to her child earlier than she had expected, and retains this information in memory.

BRAND EVALUATION AND PURCHASE As consumers process information, they begin to evaluate brands that can satisfy their need. They will associate the characteristics of brands to desired benefits. If a mother wants her baby to begin to eat processed foods earlier and if she values nutritional foods, she is more likely to buy First Foods. The mother that does not value these characteristics is less likely to buy the brand.

POSTPURCHASE EVALUATION Once the product is purchased, the consumer will evaluate its performance. Continued satisfaction is likely to result in repurchase and eventually in brand loyalty. Postpurchase evaluation is critical to marketers since most brands depend on repurchases for success. If the consumer's expectations are not met, dissatisfaction will occur, and the consumer is unlikely to purchase again.

A consumer may also experience **post-purchase dissonance**; *that is, doubts as to whether the right decision was made.* Such dissonance is most likely if the decision between two alternatives was close, and the decision is an important one. Any negative information about the chosen brand is likely to heighten such dissonance. Consumers find postpurchase dissonance uncomfortable and try to reduce it. They can do so by ignoring the negative information, by seeking out positive information about the brand, or by rationalizing their experiences with the product (for example, the new car might have a lot of squeaks and rattles, but that is to be expected).

An important objective for marketers is to try to reduce a buyer's dissonance after the purchase. Themes like "Aren't you really glad you bought a Buick" are a direct attempt to assure the buyer that the right decision was made.

BRAND LOYALTY

Brand loyalty *is a commitment to a brand because of past satisfaction as a result of continued usage.* It causes repeat purchases made with little thought or deliberation but with high involvement. For example, the consumer might be loyal to a particular make of automobile because of consistent satisfaction with it over the years. Involvement with this type of purchase is high because an auto is an important symbol of achievement, but the complexity of the decision is low. The only decision is when to buy, not what to buy.

Consumer packaged goods may also generate involvement and brand loyalty. The outcry over Coca-Cola's plans to eliminate the original formula for its flagship brand clearly shows that soft drinks are high-involvement purchases for many consumers. Brand loyalty occurs in a high-involvement situation, because it requires a positive commitment toward the favored brand. If a store is out of a consumer's usual brand, a measure of involvement and commitment is whether the consumer would buy an alternative or go to another store. Camel cigarettes' old slogan, "I'd walk a mile for a Camel," advertised the involvement of loyal smokers with the brand. To many consumers, Coca-Cola was not just another soft drink. It was a symbol of the culture and environment in which they grew up, and a brand they would walk a mile for.

LOW-INVOLVEMENT PURCHASES

A **low-involvement purchase** *is one which the consumer does not consider important or risky enough to give it a great deal of thought and consideration.* Most products we buy are not particularly involving—toothpaste, batteries, gasoline, frozen vegetables.

When consumers are not involved with a product, they do not actively search for information about it. They use various strategies to minimize the time and effort in making a decision. One strategy is to buy the most familiar product on the store shelf. Another is to buy the lowest-priced brand or a leading brand that is being sold on a price deal or with coupons. Figure 8.2 shows two types of low-involvement purchases: limited decision making and inertia.

LIMITED DECISION MAKING

Limited decision making *is a low involvement purchase in which decision making takes place, but with minimal information processing and brand evaluation.* Whereas in complex decision making the consumer attempts to find the best choice (a process of optimizing), in limited decision making, the consumer is willing to find an acceptable choice (a process of satisficing.) Assume that a consumer notices a new brand of paper towel in the store. The consumer is not involved with the purchase, but noticing a new brand is enough to arouse mild curiosity. Information seeking is limited to examining the package and noticing that it says the brand is thicker and stronger than other paper towels. Brand evaluation is limited to comparing the new brand to the consumer's current brand and determining whether to try the new brand.

An important form of limited decision making is variety seeking. In **variety seeking,** *the consumer tries diverse brands to create some interest in the purchase and avoid boredom.* A decision process is involved in choosing the brand to buy, but involvement with the product is low. One study found that consumers who buy products such as salad dressing, potato chips, or cookies switch from one brand to another to try something new and different. These consumers see enough difference between brands of salad dressing or cookies to warrant seeking information about alternatives and to evaluate them but do not consider them important enough to give them a great deal of thought.[9]

INERTIA

Consumers seeking variety examine alternative brands and make a decision based on a minimal amount of information. In contrast, consumers buying by **inertia** *regard the purchase as unimportant and choose the same brand time and again with no information processing and brand evaluation.* Since items purchased by inertia are purchased frequently, it simply is not worth the time and trouble to make a decision every time the consumer has to buy. A consumer buying table salt might choose to buy Morton's because it is simpler to buy a recognizable name than to go to the time and trouble to examine alternative brands and make a decision. There would be no novelty in looking for another brand.

HABIT AND LEARNING

The level of involvement is one dimension in classifying consumer decisions. Another is the complexity of the decision process. Figure 8.2 makes the distinction between decision making and habit. The basic difference is a process of brand evaluation and information search in decision making and the absence of such a process in habit. Since we have already discussed decision making in the high-involvement decision section, we will focus on habit here.

HABIT

Habit *is repetitive behavior resulting in a limitation or absence of information seeking and evaluation of alternatives.* Habit leads to an almost automatic response when a need arises resulting in the repetitive purchase of the same brand. For example, a consumer who is out of antacid tablets buys the same brand with little thought or information search. As Figure 8.4 shows, the only elements in buying by habit are need arousal, purchase, and postpurchase evaluation. Thus, habit is the simplest purchasing process.

Both inertia and brand loyalty are classified as habit in Figure 8.2. With brand loyalty, the consumer is committed to a favored brand and is willing to go elsewhere if a store does not have it. With inertia, there is no commitment or strongly favorable attitude toward a brand. If a store is out of stock, the consumer will just buy an alternative brand. With brand loyalty, the consumer tries to optimize his or her satisfaction; with inertia, the consumer is quick to accept second best.

LEARNING

Both brand loyalty and inertia are a result of consumer learning. **Learning** *is a change in behavior occurring as a result of past experience.* As consumers gain experience in purchasing and consuming products, they learn what brands they like

FIGURE 8.4

The Process of Buying by Habit

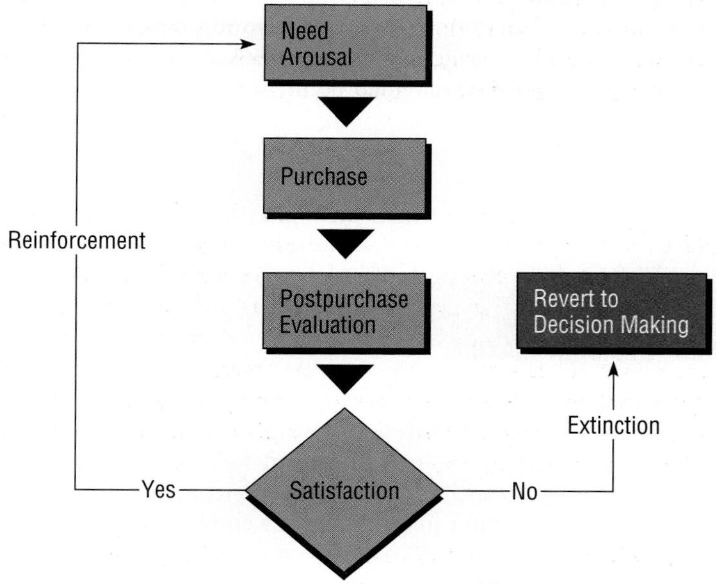

Source: Henry Assael, *Marketing Management, Strategy, and Action* (Boston, MA: Kent Publishing Co., 1986), p. 133.

and do not like and the features they like most in brands. They then adjust future behavior based on past experience. Learning may result in **reinforcement;** *which is continued satisfaction with a brand as a result of repeated usage leading to an increased likelihood the brand will be purchased again.* But learning can also result in **extinction,** *which is the elimination of expected satisfaction with the brand.* Extinction can occur fairly quickly if consumers are no longer satisfied with their usual brand. Figure 8.4 shows that extinction leads to a process of decision making in which the consumer begins to evaluate other brands. Thus, not only can decision making lead to habit when the consumer is satisfied, habit can lead back to decision making when the consumer is dissatisfied.

Consider a consumer who has bought Coca-Cola since he was a teenager. Every purchase of Coke *reinforced* his satisfaction with the brand, so today, when he wants a soft drink, he automatically thinks of Coke. Now assume our consumer buys Coke after the company decided to change the formula. He decides he does not like the new taste. It is too sweet. *Extinction* has taken place because the expected satisfaction has not occurred. The consumer is now faced with a decision as to which soft drink brand to buy next.

Marketers often use learning theory by linking their brand to a particular stimulus repetitively in advertising. If they are successful, *conditioning* has taken place. **Conditioning** *is the linkage between the brand and a stimulus in the consumer's mind so that just seeing the stimulus will evoke an awareness of the brand.* A good example is the longest running advertising campaign to date, the Marlboro cowboy campaign. Whether one believes that cigarette advertising is or is not ethical, it is generally recognized that the campaign has been the most successful in advertising history.

In the mid 1950s, Marlboro was languishing as a prestige-oriented brand targeted to light smokers. Philip Morris needed to revitalize the brand and decided to use the image of a cowboy to target the cigarette to heavy-smoking males. The repetitive use of the cowboy was so successful that consumers have become conditioned to associate Marlboro with cowboys. Since the cowboy is associated with a positive image of masculinity and assertiveness among many male smokers, the positive association was also transferred to the brand. As a result, Marlboro's net worth today is conservatively estimated to be in the billions of dollars for Philip Morris.

STRATEGIC IMPLICATIONS OF DECISION PROCESSES

Marketers develop very different strategies based on the type of decision process they think consumers are likely to use in selecting a brand.

HABIT VERSUS DECISION MAKING

Different advertising, distribution, and pricing strategies are appropriate for products typically purchased by habit than for those purchased as a result of decision making. In the latter case, advertising is likely to focus on brand attributes and features. Auto ads center around gas mileage, four-wheel drive, roominess, and comfort. Ads for over-the-counter pharmaceuticals emphasize quick relief, no side effects, and recommendations by doctors. In contrast, advertising for products purchased by habit aims primarily at reminding the consumer to buy and to reinforce postpurchase satisfaction. Philip Morris only has to show the Marlboro cowboy. No message or picture of the product are needed to remind loyal smokers to buy.

A market leader has a decided advantage if it is in a category purchased by habit, because many of its consumers are likely to be brand loyal. The market leader's objective will therefore be to remind consumers of the brand and reassure them. For example, Coke's former advertising slogan, "Coke is it," served as a reminder to drink Coke and reassured Coke drinkers by implying that there is no real alternative to Coke. Seven-Up tried to break Coke's and Pepsi's hammerlock on the market by advertising a new feature—no caffeine. The strategy was to get loyal Pepsi and Coke users to stop buying those brands by habit and to consider a noncola alternative.

The purchase process also helps determine distribution strategies. Brands purchased by habit should be readily available, because they are frequently purchased. Therefore, widespread distribution is necessary. Hershey is a classic example of a product relying on extensive distribution. Until the 1970s, it did no advertising, relying solely on its availability in almost every food store in the country to maintain its market leadership. Products purchased by complex decision making are bought less frequently. Often, these are technically complex items requiring the help of a salesperson and subsequent service. Consumers are more likely to shop around for such items. As a result, they are more likely to be distributed on a selective basis.

Pricing strategies also differ according to the purchase process. If a brand is purchased by habit, the best way a competitor can get a brand-loyal consumer to try something else is to offer a price deal, special sale, or a free sample. Such promotions are less effective with complex decision making. Consumers are less likely to switch because of a temporary price deal.

HIGH- VERSUS LOW-INVOLVEMENT DECISIONS

Marketing strategies will also differ depending on the degree to which the consumer is involved with the product. If there is little involvement, consumers are less likely to pay attention to advertising. As a result, ads should focus on a simple message and should try to increase the level of involvement. Crest linked an uninvolving product (toothpaste) to an involving issue (cavity prevention) by introducing fluoride. The Crest ad in Exhibit 8.2 illustrates a recent attempt to create involvement by linking the brand to the involving issue of keeping a youthful look.

Ads for high-involvement products should convey more information about product benefits, using an informational or emotional approach. Product benefits can be communicated based on emotions by showing good feelings and sympathetic scenes or by attempting to enhance the consumer's self-image. Benefits can also be communicated using an informational approach by directly describing product attributes. The ad for the Coustic car stereo in Exhibit 8.3 takes an informational approach. It details the characteristics and performance results of the product. The ad for the Clarion car stereo is clearly emotional.

Product-positioning strategies are also likely to differ based on the consumer's involvement with the product. Uninvolved consumers will not search for the best product; they will look for an acceptable product. Products that minimize problems rather than maximize benefits will catch their attention. Crest achieved its position as the leading toothpaste by advertising that it solves a problem—cavities—rather than maximizes a benefit (like whiter teeth).

EXHIBIT 8.2

Increasing Involvement for a Low-Involvement Product

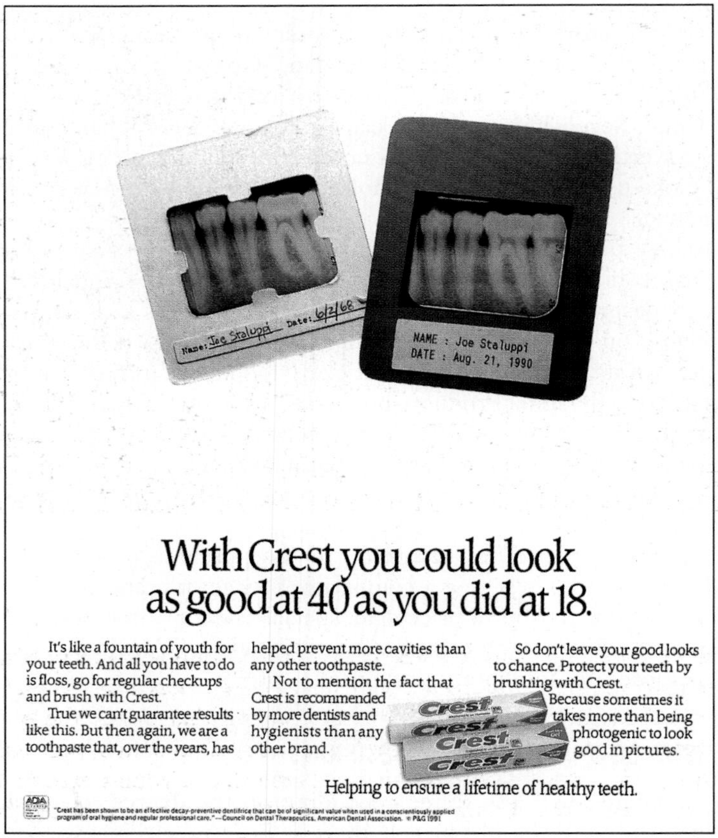
Name: Joe Staluppi Date: 6/2/68
NAME : Joe Staluppi
DATE : Aug. 21, 1990
With Crest you could look as good at 40 as you did at 18.
It's like a fountain of youth for your teeth. And all you have to do is floss, go for regular checkups and brush with Crest.
True we can't guarantee results like this. But then again, we are a toothpaste that, over the years, has helped prevent more cavities than any other toothpaste.
Not to mention the fact that Crest is recommended by more dentists and hygienists than any other brand.
So don't leave your good looks to chance. Protect your teeth by brushing with Crest.
Because sometimes it takes more than being photogenic to look good in pictures.
Crest
Helping to ensure a lifetime of healthy teeth.
ADA
"Crest has been shown to be an effective decay-preventive dentifrice that can be of significant value when used in a conscientiously applied program of oral hygiene and regular professional care." —Council on Dental Therapeutics, American Dental Association. © P&G 1991

Involved consumers will take the time and trouble to look for the best product available to meet their needs. In such cases, a product should be positioned as maximizing a benefit. Kellogg realized that adults would be more involved with cereals if they were positioned as meeting health and nutritional needs. It effectively changed cereals from an uninvolving children's product to an involving adult breakfast food by advertising nutritional benefits.

THE CONSUMER'S PSYCHOLOGICAL SET

In the remainder of this chapter, we will consider the three basic forces that influence consumer behavior in Figure 8.1, the consumer's psychological set, personal characteristics, and the social environment. Earlier, we defined the consumer's psychological set as his or her general state of mind toward an object. The psychological set is formed by a consumer's needs, perceptions of a brand or company, and attitudes toward that brand or company. These three variables are shown in Figure 8.5.

EXHIBIT 8.3

Ads for High-Involvement Products Using an Informational and an Emotional Approach

NEEDS

Needs *are goals that the consumer desires to attain.* To understand needs, we must also understand motives. **Motives** *are the underlying drives that channel and direct behavior toward attaining needs.* They are the engine that drives the consumer to fulfilling needs. Common motives include factors such as status, possession, economy, curiosity, pleasure, and dominance. Assume that a young executive is motivated by status and upward mobility. These motives may be translated into a need for a car that is stylish and will be seen as a status symbol among friends and neighbors. Therefore, needs and motives directly affect the specific criteria consumers use to evaluate brands.

Abraham Maslow developed a theory based on a *hierarchy of needs.*[10] According to Maslow, needs can be ordered from a lower to a higher level. An individual will satisfy the lowest need level first before the next higher set of needs becomes activated. Once these needs become satisfied, the next higher level is activated, and so forth. Maslow defined levels of needs from low to high:

1. physiological (food, shelter, sex)
2. safety (protection, security)
3. social (acceptance, friendship)
4. ego (prestige, success)
5. self-actualization (self-fulfillment).

Marketers use all five of Maslow's need levels in advertising; for example:

- physiological needs through sexual appeals, as in ads for personal grooming or clothing
- safety needs, as in messages advertising safer cars or promoting a safer environment

FIGURE 8.5

The Consumer's Psychological Set

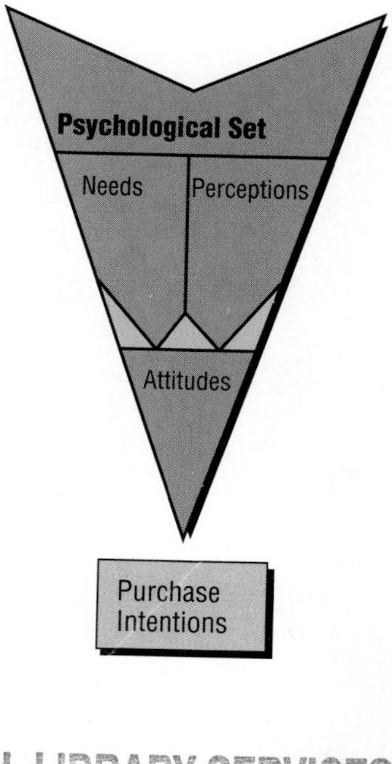

- social needs by showing group acceptance as a result of using a brand of soap or deodorant or wearing certain clothes
- ego needs by linking a product to success, such as driving a luxury car or drinking a certain brand of scotch
- self-actualization by showing self-fulfillment through personal pursuits such as fitness or travel

PERCEPTIONS

Perceptions *are the way consumers organize and interpret information about objects such as brands and companies.* Whereas needs and motives direct the consumer to certain actions, perceptions allow consumers to organize information to permit such action to take place.

Consumers perceive marketing information *selectively.* **Selective perception** *means that consumers can perceive the same information differently, because they have different needs, motives, and past experiences.* For example, one consumer views ads for a BMW, test drives the car, and decides that it provides luxury, good performance, and is worth the cost. Another views the identical ads, test drives the same car, and decides that it is overpriced and is just selling a luxury image.

There are three components to selective perception, exposure, comprehension, and retention. In order to perceive information, consumers must first be exposed to it, must comprehend it, and must retain it. Each of these processes is selective.

- *Selective exposure* means that people choose to see or to read what is most relevant to their needs. They also choose information that supports their views, reinforces their egos, and parallels their life-styles. For example, new-car buyers are more likely to perceive information that supports their brand choice and to ignore negative information about the selected brand.
- *Selective comprehension* means that consumers will interpret information so it is consistent with their psychological set. For example, a cigarette smoker may avoid antismoking ads or play down their importance. Accepting the message may mean recognizing that the smoker's actions are detrimental to his or her health.
- *Selective retention* means that consumers will remember information that is most relevant to their needs and that conforms to their psychological set. The recent purchaser of a BMW may retain information from ads that reinforce his purchase decision. Similarly, the heavy smoker is likely to quickly forget an antismoking commercial that shows the health risks.

In the process of perceiving marketing information, consumers form images of brands, stores, and companies. *An* **image** *is an overall perception of an object formed from information and from the consumer's past experiences.* The importance of brand image is demonstrated by Coca-Cola's experience when it changed the formula of its flagship brand. Coca-Cola conducted "blind" taste tests in which the brands were not identified, and consumers were asked their taste preferences for the new formula, the old formula, and Pepsi. Tests on 190,000 consumers found the new formula Coke to be the consistent winner.[11] The subsequent uproar when the old formula was withdrawn demonstrates the strength of Coca-Cola's image. Most consumers were not loyal to the brand based on taste; they were loyal because of brand image.

ATTITUDES

Attitudes *are the consumer's tendency to evaluate an object in a favorable or unfavorable way.* Attitudes have a thinking component (*beliefs*) and a feeling component (*brand evaluations*). **Brand beliefs** *are the characteristics we ascribe to a brand.* **Brand evaluations** *are our positive or negative evaluations of a brand.*

Consumer needs, perceptions, and the two components of attitudes interact to influence consumer purchase behavior as shown in Figure 8.6. The young executive we described has a *need* for a stylish, status-oriented car. He forms a *belief* that the BMW has a stylish design, a luxurious interior, and is highly regarded by friends and business associates from information that he *perceives* in ads and from word-of-mouth communication. Based on his beliefs, he decides that the BMW can meet his need for a status-oriented car, forms a positive *evaluation* of the car, and decides to buy it. The key link in Figure 8.6 is between needs and brand beliefs; that is, the belief that the BMW could meet the consumer's needs. This belief led to a positive brand evaluation and to an intention to buy.

STRATEGIC APPLICATIONS OF THE CONSUMER'S PSYCHOLOGICAL SET

Marketers will try to influence the consumer's psychological set by identifying needs and influencing brand images and attitudes.

NEED IDENTIFICATION

A company can gain a competitive advantage by defining unmet consumer needs. Coca-Cola defined the need for a diet cola among male cola drinkers, paving the way for the success of Diet Coke. Pepsi identified a need for a more nutritious noncola alternative among adults and established the juice-based soft-drink market with Slice.

FIGURE 8.6

How the Psychological Set Influences Consumer Behavior

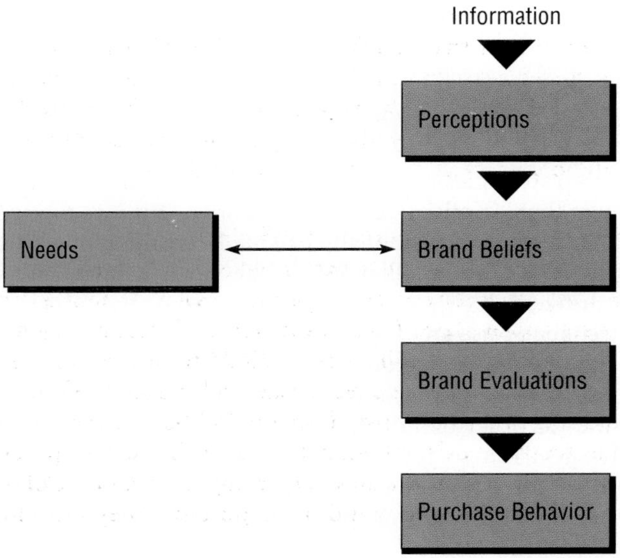

Consumer needs are the most important basis for identifying target segments. In determining the need for nutritious cereals, Kellogg identified a broad segment of health-conscious adults. But such a definition of the market was too broad to target specific brands and advertisements. As we have seen in Chapter 1, Kellogg defined more specific market segments such as a low-cholesterol segment, a fitness segment, and a low-calorie segment. Once Kellogg identified the market by needs, it addressed product development, advertising, and packaging strategies to these need segments.

BRAND-IMAGE FORMATION

Advertisers try to influence a consumer's brand image by positioning a brand so that it communicates desired benefits. Kellogg positioned All-Bran by communicating the benefits of high-fiber content; it positioned another cereal, Just Right, by touting the benefits of natural ingredients. Kellogg was successful in establishing a nutritional and health-oriented image for its complete line of adult cereals.

A major issue for a company is when a brand's image should be changed; that is, when the brand should be repositioned. Philip Morris repositioned Miller High Life after acquiring Miller Brewing in the early 1970s. High Life was positioned as "the champagne of bottled beer," conveying a high-quality image to a small segment of occasional beer drinkers willing to pay a premium price. Philip Morris changed the image to a heftier brew for the mass market with a campaign portraying blue-collar workers in positive situations associated with beer drinking. The campaign propelled High Life to the second-best-selling brand in the market.

Trying to change a brand's image can sometimes spell trouble for a company. Cadillac began making its cars smaller in the 1970s, after the energy crisis, to improve fuel efficiency. But a smaller Cadillac contradicted the brand image of Cadillac's core market. As Cadillac's director of marketing said, "You develop an image over an 83-year period, and it's hard to change."[12] Many loyal Cadillac customers wanted larger, more luxurious cars, even if they were gas guzzlers. As a result, sales began to slide, and Cadillac lost about one-fourth of its share of the luxury-car market. In an effort to recoup, the company brought back its king-size cars.

BRAND ATTITUDE FORMATION

Marketers develop strategies to either reinforce brand attitudes (an adaptive strategy) or to change them. Kellogg reinforced positive attitudes toward its cereal line as it introduced additional nutritionally oriented cereals. Philip Morris succeeded in changing attitudes toward Miller High Life when it linked the brand's image to heavy beer drinkers.

Marketers frequently use an adaptive strategy by introducing a line extension of a successful brand. The introduction of Diet Coke was built on the positive associations consumers have with Coca-Cola. The company had avoided using the Coca-Cola name for other brands, fearing it would dilute the position of its flagship brand. Its decision to introduce Diet Coke—and later Cherry Coke—reflected a change in management's thinking. The success of Diet Coke proved that positive attitudes toward one product can be effectively leveraged toward others.

EXHIBIT 8.4

Attempting to Create Positive Brand Attitude

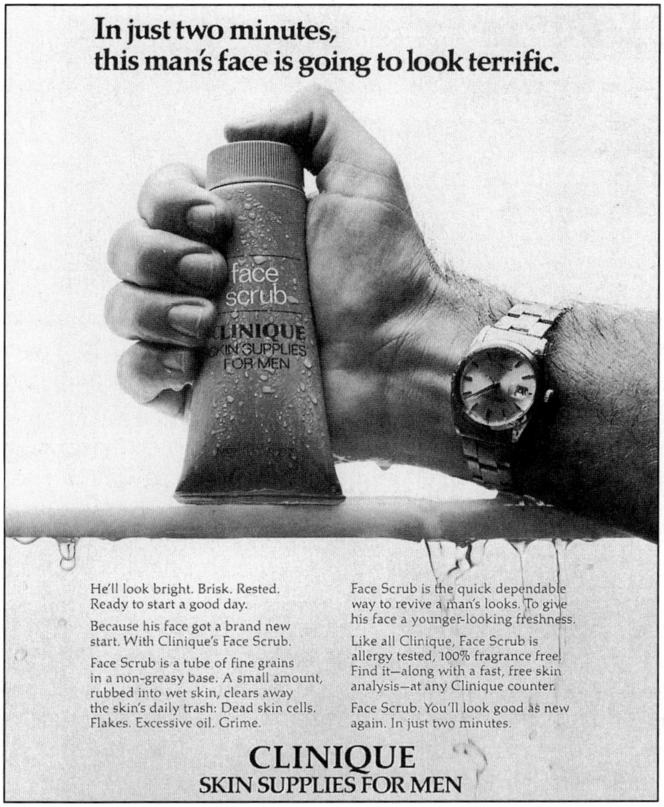

Cosmetics companies such as Brut, Ralph Lauren, Lancôme, and Clinique have had to use a change strategy to overcome men's reluctance to use skin-care products (see Exhibit 8.4). Their task, in the words of one executive, is to convince men "that there is nothing wrong with taking care of your skin. Your face is your calling card."[13]

CONSUMER CHARACTERISTICS

The second set of factors that influence purchasing behavior in Figure 8.1 are the consumer's personal characteristics. While the consumer's psychological set describes needs, perceptions, and attitudes toward specific brands, consumers' personal characteristics such as age or occupation are not brand-specific. Yet the age or occupation of a consumer could be just as important as perceptions and attitudes in influencing brand-purchasing decisions.

Marketers study three types of characteristics to better understand consumers: demographics, life-styles, and, to a lesser extent, personality.

DEMOGRAPHICS

In Chapter 4, we identified demographics as the objective characteristics of the consumer and cited broad demographic trends such as the greater proportion of working women, the increasing proportion of singles, and the greater number of older consumers. Marketers also study more-specific data on the demographic characteristics of current and prospective purchasers of their brands. In such cases, demographics are used to segment markets, to identify targets for new products, and to buy media to reach these target segments.

MARKET SEGMENTATION

Companies use demographics to define segments in the market. Kellogg is targeting most of its cereals by age segment—sugared cereals for children, fitness-oriented cereals such as Nutri Grain for young adults, and health-oriented cereals such as All Bran for older consumers. Avon is segmenting the market by income class and occupation, targeting more-expensive perfumes to affluent career women without the Avon label and its traditional Avon line of cosmetics to middle- to lower-income women.

IDENTIFYING TARGETS FOR NEW PRODUCTS

Demographics are also used to describe targets for new, as well as existing, products. In the 1970s, General Foods tested a new-product concept, a low-calorie breakfast strip designed as a more nutritious substitute for bacon. Research showed that two demographic segments were most likely to buy the product: older, downscale consumers and younger, more-affluent consumers. The older consumers were more likely to emphasize cholesterol content and health; the younger consumers, calories and nutrition. Such a split could suggest two ad campaigns for the same product or two separate products to appeal to each segment.

MEDIA SELECTION

Demographic characteristics also provide guidelines for media selection. When the demographic characteristics of a segment are identified, marketers try to select media that are more likely to be read or viewed by that segment. For example, when Lee introduced its Shawnee line of denim and corduroy jeans aimed at trend-conscious 14- to 19-year olds, the company's mix of media was based on this demographic definition of the target. Lee introduced the line with commercials on MTV, the music video station, ads in magazines such as *Glamour*, *Seventeen*, and *Young Miss* for the female line and *Sport* and *Rolling Stone* for the male line.[14]

LIFE-STYLES

In Chapter 4, we defined life-style characteristics as represented by a consumer's activities, interests, and opinions. Activities may be related to work, social events, entertainment, and the community. Interests may focus on the home, recreation, fashion, and food, to name a few areas. Opinions might concern the individual's job and personal achievements.

There is no standard definition of life-style variables as there is for demographics. Life-style categories are defined based on the nature and potential positioning of a product. A company positioning a detergent might identify segments such as compulsive housekeepers, homebodies, and achievement-oriented consumers, because these life-styles are likely to be related to attitudes toward detergents. A company segmenting a line of perfumes might develop different positionings—to self-indulgent, socially active, or inner-directed segments.

As with demographics, life-styles can identify broad trends such as the change in male–female roles and increasing emphasis on fitness and nutrition noted in Chapter 4. Life-style information has also been used more specifically to develop strategies for brands, particularly in defining market segments, positioning products, and selecting media.

MARKETING SEGMENTATION

The most widely used basis for segmenting consumers by life-style is through the VALS (Value and Life Style) program. Chapter 4 cited VALS as identifying eight life-style groupings based on the values and interests of American consumers. The first dimension distinguishes between outer-directed consumers driven primarily by their relationship to others versus those who are driven more by inner-directed needs. The second dimension distinguishes between consumers with more and with less economic resources.

One advertising agency that was trying to win Avon's business pointed out that Avon's highbrow ads featuring the theme, "The art and science of beauty," were geared more to an inner-directed group called *actualizers* (high-scale consumers who emphasize self-actualization and self-expression). The ad agency felt that Avon's target segment should be a group called the *strivers*, a more outer-directed and downscale group. For example, an Avon ad showing a high-fashion model gazing at beauty products inside geometric shapes just would not fly with the strivers.[15]

When Avon shifted its advertising business to the agency that gave it this insight, its new commercials, aimed at more-outer-directed consumers, featured young women—each looking like the girl next door—eating ice cream bars, sunbathing, or jogging, with the theme, "Look how good you look now." Currently, Avon is targeting the same group with the theme "They're dying to make you over. But who are they trying to make you into" (see Exhibit 8.5). The ad moves Avon more strongly away from its previous "art and science of beauty" campaign and appeals to "typical" women with more realistic views of themselves.

PRODUCT POSITIONING

The VALS groupings have been used to position products as well as to segment markets. MasterCard International took a look at American Express's "Don't leave home without it" campaign and realized that it was aimed at a VALS group called *achievers*, a high-income, status-oriented group, based on the idea of what other people would think about someone who does not have an American Express card. The company decided to distinguish itself from American Express by appealing to the more inner-directed and independent actualizer group. Celebrities such as Robert Duvall and Angela Lansbury pitched individualism based on the theme, "Master the possibilities" (see Exhibit 8.6). "Life's too short to worry about impressing other people," says Angela Lansbury in one commercial, "Don't talk to me about impressions. Give me possibilities."[16]

The fact that more consumers were becoming inner-directed reinforced MasterCard's positioning strategy. The MasterCard executive who conceived of the campaign described its rationale: "The consumer wants to be perceived as being his or her own person, capable of making choices. Substance and freedom have replaced style and status."[17]

EXHIBIT 8.5

Repositioning Avon Based on Life-Style Factors

They're dying to make you over.
But who are they trying to make you into?
Gee, they must have had you confused with Cleopatra, that's all.
And you're not alone.
Recently, a famous newspaper sent one of their reporters to have her makeup done at a bunch of fancy department stores.
The results?
One "aging glamourpuss" and two "kewpie dolls."
That's not how Avon looks at makeup.
We know you want to look pretty, but approachable. Real, only better.
With the new Avon personalized beauty computer, you've finally met your match.
With it, your Avon Representative will help you figure out just which colors will look the best on you.
It's absolutely goof-proof.
Because you can return or exchange anything you buy.
So call your Avon Representative. Or 1-800-858-8000 for service.
You don't have to drop a bundle.
A whole Avon makeup, soup to nuts, lipstick, lipliner, foundation, blush, eyeshadow, eyeliner, mascara, and nail polish costs an amazing $25.
AVON
THE SMARTEST SHOP IN TOWN

MEDIA SELECTION

Life-style characteristics can also be used to select media. For example, the National Turkey Federation tried to increase the consumption of turkey by appealing to specific VALS groups, using different media. It appealed to a downscale, need-driven group called *strugglers* by advertising bargain cuts in *True Confessions,* because readers of that magazine are downscale and older. Traditional cuts of turkey associated with holiday dinners were advertised to status-oriented VALS groups in *Better Homes and Gardens,* because these segments were more likely to read it. Finally, the most expensive, gourmet, cuts were aimed at the more-affluent, inner-directed, consumers—namely, actualizers, in magazines such as *Food and Wine* and *Gourmet.*

PERSONALITY

Personality *variables are those characteristics that reflect consistent, enduring patterns of behavior.* Compulsive, aggressive, or compliant behavior, for example, reflects deep-seated predispositions formed in childhood.

When researchers first began studying consumer behavior, they turned to existing personality theories to better explain consumer motives. First among these theories, Freud's **psychoanalytic theory,** *stresses the unconscious nature of personality as a result of childhood conflicts.* Freud's theories have been applied to marketing by stressing the unconscious motives for buying certain products. These motives would be extremely hard to determine by directly questioning a consumer, so behavioral researchers developed two techniques derived from psychoanalytic theory to uncover unconscious motives: depth interviews and projective techniques. Both techniques were described in the last chapter under the heading of Qualitative Research. Because of the focus on developing means to uncover unconscious motives, *applications of psychoanalytic theory to marketing are known as* **motivational research.**

EXHIBIT 8.6

Ads Targeted to Outer-Directed and Inner-Directed Consumers

Wilt Chamberlain. Cardmember since 1976.
Willie Shoemaker. Cardmember since 1966.
Membership has its privileges.
Don't leave home without it.

Another personality theory applied to marketing, **self-concept (or self-image) theory,** *holds that individuals have a concept of themselves based on who they think they are (the actual self) and who they would like to be (the ideal self).* Self-concept theory has been applied to marketing in two ways. First, consumers tend to buy products that reinforce their self-concept and are similar to it. Research has confirmed that consumers buy brands of beer, bar soap, toothpaste, and cars that they rate as more similar to themselves.[18] Self-concept theory might also be an explanation why McDonald's is more popular than Burger King. An advertising agency found that people described McDonald's as friendly and nurturing. Gimmicks such as Ronald McDonald and kiddie playgrounds further this nurturing feeling. In contrast, Burger King was described as aggressive, masculine, and distant.[19]

The second way in which self-concept theory has been used in marketing is to determine the differences between a consumer's actual and ideal self-image. The greater the difference, the greater the dissatisfaction with oneself. Such dissatisfaction could influence the purchase of products that enhance self-esteem. Marketers try to portray an idealized self in ads for perfumes or clothing in order to enhance one's self-image. In so doing, they convey the idea that "the better you look, the better you feel about yourself."

Both psychoanalytic and self-concept theory are nonempirical. In an attempt to introduce more empirical measures of personality, researchers have also applied trait theory to marketing. **Trait theory** *states that personality is composed of a set of measurable traits that describe general response predispositions* such as compulsiveness, aggressiveness, sociability, dominance, and stability. Such traits have occasionally been used to define market segments. A study by a large life-insurance company identified a target segment of purchasers as "dominant people who like to have control over situations with which they are involved. They tend to be self-reliant and will follow the counsel of experts only if it meets demands for accuracy and reliability."[20]

This personality profile suggests that life-insurance advertising to this segment should use an informational approach. An emotional approach such as fear of leaving a family destitute would be unlikely to work, because this group prides itself on control over its future and has probably planned ahead for financial security. Consumers in this segment are seeking information on how to better provide for future security; they do not need to be convinced that life insurance is a good idea.

Personality characteristics have not been used as widely as demographics and life-styles in developing marketing strategies, primarily because these variables are complex and harder to apply to marketing strategy. But the applications described suggest that they can be useful in better understanding consumer behavior.

ENVIRONMENTAL INFLUENCES

The final set of factors influencing consumer behavior in Figure 8.1 is the consumer's social and cultural environment. Influences range from broad cultural forces issuing from the society in which the consumer lives to more-specific group and family influences. These influences are shown as an inverted pyramid in Figure 8.7, with the broadest environmental influences at the top—culture (including crosscultural and subcultural influences), and social class—and narrower, face-to-face influences at the bottom (reference groups and the family).

CULTURE

Culture *represents the widely shared norms and values learned from a society and leading to common patterns of behavior.* The common patterns of behavior in American society are often reflected in what products consumers buy and the importance they

FIGURE 8.7

The Consumer's Environment

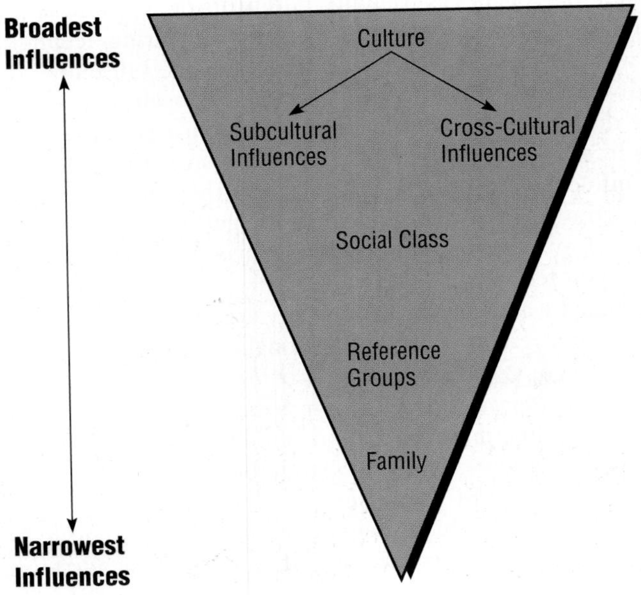

place on those products. The fact that cereal is the traditional breakfast food for children is specific to American culture, possibly the product of an emphasis on a hearty breakfast dating back to pioneer times.

Three American cultural values that have seen particular emphasis in marketing strategies are individualism, materialism, and youth. The emphasis on *individualism* has manifested itself in the search for distinctive clothing or furniture that reflects one's personality. As mentioned earlier, we often buy important products as extensions of our self-image, and such an extension often demands an expression of the individualism that is emphasized in American society.

Another dominant value in American culture is *materialism*. The traditional emphasis on materialism waned in the 1960s and 1970s as many Americans became increasingly skeptical of business and government because of the Vietnam War and Watergate. But a series of yearly surveys of first-year college students sponsored by the American Council on Education found a rising trend of materialism since the early 1970s. The 1987 survey found that more than three-fourths of the students surveyed felt that being financially well off was an essential goal, the highest proportion ever recorded by the study. Those who gave priority to developing a meaningful philosophy of life were the lowest proportion ever recorded.[21]

Another value emphasized in American society is *youth*. Ads for deodorants and cosmetics typically show young models even though the products are also directed to middle-aged adults. Ads directed to the mature market also reflect the value placed on youth. These ads are now using models over 50 but are emphasizing the youth and vitality of older people (see Exhibit 8.7).

CROSS-CULTURAL INFLUENCES

Cross-cultural influences *represent the differences in cultural values between countries.* As we have seen in Chapter 5, marketing abroad has become an increasingly important part of American business. American executives operating abroad cannot assume that the values of American consumers are universal. The traditional American values placed on achievement and materialism are not nearly as strong in many Asian countries, where an acceptance of one's place in society may dominate day-to-day behavior. Similarly, the strong individual bent of most Americans is not understood by the Japanese, who are raised to value the group and to submerge their individuality. Further, the emphasis on youth in Western culture is not likely to be reflected in other parts of the world, where age is more revered.

As a result of such differences, it is important for American executives marketing abroad to recognize and adapt to local cultural norms. We have seen that when Gerber tried to introduce processed baby foods into Brazil, it failed, because mothers there feel that only they can prepare food for their babies. Similarly, Singer Company found that its predominant form of promotion, demonstration classes for women, were ineffective in many Moslem countries, because women were not allowed to leave home to attend sewing lessons at Singer centers. It was only when men began attending the classes that they were convinced the lessons would be of value to their wives and allowed them to attend.[22]

American companies sensitive to crosscultural differences generally succeed. When General Foods tried to make Tang—its powdered soft drink—into a worldwide substitute for orange juice, it failed at first, because it did not account for variations in tastes and customs across countries. The Germans did not like the name, the British did not like the taste, and the French did not drink orange juice at breakfast. As a result, the company renamed the drink *Seefrisch* in Germany, sold a more tart version of Tang in Britain, and repositioned Tang as a refreshment for any time of day in France.[23]

EXHIBIT 8.7

Portraying a Youthful Mature Consumer

SUBCULTURAL INFLUENCES

In Chapter 4, we defined subcultures as groups of people having certain values in common that distinguish them from society as a whole. We also cited the increasing attention marketers are giving to the three largest subcultural groups in the United States: African Americans, Hispanic Americans, and Asian Americans.

AFRICAN AMERICANS

African Americans differ from other consumers in spending proportionately more for cosmetics, toiletries, and clothing. Because African Americans generally have lower income levels, they are likely to spend proportionately more on these categories. A greater proportion of money spent on necessities might make it appear that African Americans spend substantially less on luxuries. This assumption ignores the growing middle class in this group. One study found that a larger proportion of African Americans own CDs and answering machines than whites and are more likely to purchase cars, furniture, and VCRs.[24]

Companies have used two approaches in advertising to African Americans: One, using African American models to foster identification; and two, using the same advertising as to whites but placing the ads in African-American media. The ads for Delta Airlines in Exhibit 8.8 demonstrate the different campaign strategies.

EXHIBIT 8.8

Ads Appearing in African-American Media With and Without African-American Identity

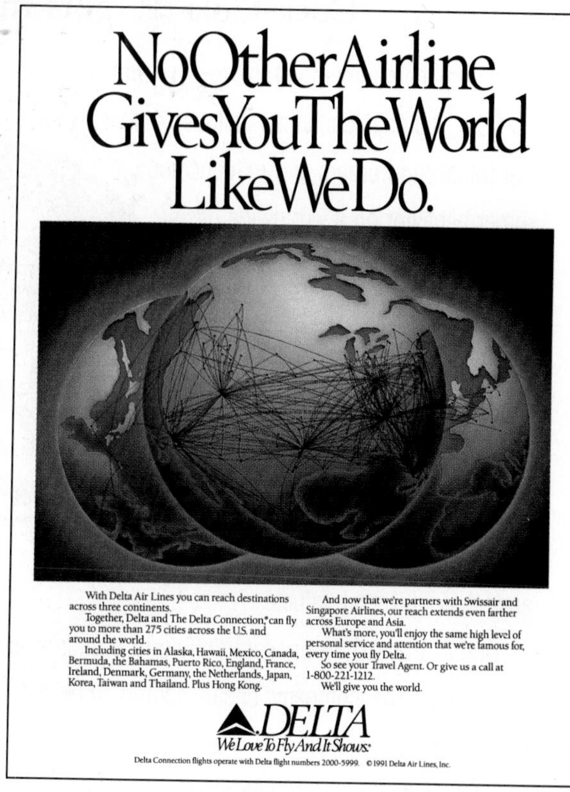

HISPANIC AMERICANS

As we noted in Chapter 4, Hispanic Americans are a distinct subculture, because they have largely resisted assimilation of their language and customs into American society. They prefer to speak Spanish at home and are more likely to cling to their culture, because many of them are recent immigrants.

Marketers generally have avoided segmenting the Hispanic market because of small budgets allocated to Hispanics and because of differences in customs and language between various Hispanic groups. Cubans primarily in Florida, Puerto Ricans primarily in New York, and Mexicans primarily in the Southwest have substantial differences in customs and language.

Companies targeting the Hispanic market have used the same two approaches to advertising as for African Americans: One, use the same ads as those in English, but with Spanish copy; and two, adapt the campaign to the specific values of the Hispanic market. As an example of the first approach, Pepsi-Cola used the same Pepsi Generation campaign for Hispanics as for the general market. In contrast, Polaroid geared advertising for its Spectra camera specifically to Hispanics by showing a father taking a picture of his wife and newborn baby to focus on an emotional moment. When it advertises to the general market, Polaroid focuses more on the camera and its features.

GLOBAL MARKETING STRATEGIES

Coca-Cola Targets the Global Youth Market

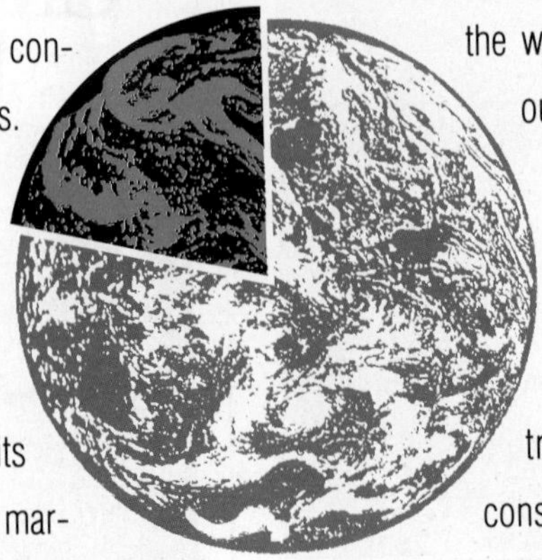

The counterpoint to crosscultural values is global consumer values; that is, values that transcend borders and influence consumer behavior on a worldwide basis. Such global influences would be a boon to marketers, because they could then use standardized product and advertising strategies across countries and reap the benefits of economies of scale. As a result, marketers seek *world brands;* that is, brands that can appeal to universal values.

One of the early proponents of world brands was Coca-Cola. The company began selling abroad in the 1920s, but it was only after World War II that international sales really took off. Coca-Cola's policy was to follow GI Joe in Europe and across the Pacific to ensure that every soldier had access to a Coke. In the process, civilians got to know the brand and wanted it. Coca-Cola decided to leave the infrastructure it had established for U.S. soldiers in place after the war—overseas bottling plants, sales outlets, and distribution facilities.

Coca-Cola's international infrastructure was well-suited for developments in the 1980s. Common communications and more-frequent travel encouraged more-common consumer values across countries and heightened Coca-Cola's international opportunities. This is most apparent for the youth market. Youth are less likely to be saddled by local customs and past traditions. They are more likely to wear jeans, listens to rock video channels, and go to fast-food establishments than their older brothers and sisters.

As a result, the marketing of world brands to the global youth market offered Coca-Cola special op-

ASIAN AMERICANS

Asian Americans are the most highly educated and affluent minority group. Asian Americans are even more varied than Hispanics and African Americans. The largest groups are Chinese, Filipino, Japanese, Vietnamese, and Korean. Most live in three states: California, New York, and Hawaii.

Few marketers direct advertising strategies to the Asian-American market because of its small size and fragmentation. But some companies are beginning to target Asian Americans because of their youth and greater affluence. Metropolitan Life has targeted this group in its advertising by influencing the role of insurance in planning for the future to guarantee a child's education. The firm is appealing to the Asian-American market's emphasis on education as a means of upward mobility.

GLOBAL MARKETING STRATEGIES

portunities. It could now use one universal advertising theme targeting youth globally. For example, its General Assembly campaign showing the youth of the world singing the Coke jingle in one big assembly ran worldwide in the late 1980s.

But Coca-Cola also recognizes that advertising cannot be completely standardized. Variations are required to reflect differences in language, cultural interests, and activities. For example, in the General Assembly campaign, ads running in various countries focused on a closeup of a local youngster. Similarly, another campaign portrayed a young boy offering sports stars a Coke. In the United States, the youngster offered "Mean" Joe Greene, the football star, a Coke at halftime. Since soccer was the universal sport in most other countries, Coca-Cola adapted the ad using children offering a Coke to local soccer stars.

The youth market is likely to become more similar on a worldwide basis, and Coca-Cola will be there with a universal appeal.

Questions: Why are the values of the youth market becoming more similar worldwide? Is Coca-Cola well positioned to take advantage of a global youth market? Why or why not?

Source: "The First Global Generation," *Adweek's Marketing Week*, February 6, 1989, p. 18; and "Coke's Intensified Attack Abroad," *New York Times*, March 14, 1988, p. D1.

SOCIAL CLASS

Social classes *define broad consumer groupings according to their degree of prestige and power in society.* In our society, prestige and power are defined by income, occupation, and education. In general terms, these criteria define the "haves" and "have nots." The most common way to categorize social classes are as upper, upper-middle, lower-middle, and lower.

The social class to which we belong influences what we buy. The upper class—composed of the social elite and top managers—tend to buy conservative clothing and avoid showy purchases. The upper-middle class—composed of professionals, managers, and some small-business owners—are career oriented and emphasize educational attainment. They stress quality and value in their purchases and are more likely to be comparison shoppers. Lower-middle class consumers—composed of white-collar employees and well-paid blue-collar workers—are more home and family oriented and buy with an eye to conformity and respectability. The lower class is composed of lower-paid blue-collar and unskilled workers.

EXHIBIT 8.9

Power Themes in Advertising Directed toward Different Social Classes

(Left) Power Theme Directed to Professional and Managerial Class Consumers
(Right) Power Theme Directed to Working-Class Consumers

Marketers have used social-class differences to define their advertising campaigns. Power and dominance have been used in advertising across different social classes. For example, working-class consumers (lower-middle and lower class) seek an escape from everyday drudgery. They express a need for power by buying more-powerful cars.[25] The "power and passion" of the Cherokee Jeep ad in Exhibit 8.9 is an expression of freedom and independence targeting this group.

In contrast, members of the professional and managerial group (upper and upper-middle class) express the need for power in terms of getting ahead in their occupations. The ad for the Macintosh in Exhibit 8.9 also advertises power. But in this case, it is "the power to be your best" in terms of getting ahead. Whereas the power appeal for the Cherokee is the independence of getting away from work, the power appeal for the Macintosh is one of getting ahead in work.

REFERENCE GROUPS

Consumers are also influenced by **reference groups,** *that is, groups that serve as a reference point for individuals in defining their needs and developing opinions.* In deciding what to buy, a consumer usually relies more on the opinions of reference groups than on information from ads or salespeople. Advertisers have a vested interest in providing only positive information about a brand; reference groups do not.

The most important reference groups are an individual's peer group (friends, neighbors, business associates) and family. Marketers frequently portray these groups in advertising. Ads for beverages as diverse as Hawaiian Punch, Lowenbrau beer, and Dry Sack sherry all show friends drinking the brand in a congenial setting. Fast-food chains such as McDonald's and Burger King usually advertise in a family-related context.

Reference groups exert three types of influence on consumers: informational, comparative, and normative. **Informational influence** *means the group is the source* *of believable information about brands and companies.* **Comparative influence** *means the group gives consumers something to compare their beliefs, attitudes, and behavior against.* The greater the similarity between a consumer's opinions and those of his or her reference group, the greater the comparative influence of the group. **Normative influence** *means the group persuades members to conform to its norms.* Sometimes groups use rewards and punishments to gain compliance. The family can reward children with praise and punish them with a scolding; social groups can reward members with compliments on their clothing or behavior and punish them by ignoring their words and actions.

To take advantage of the importance of reference groups, marketers try to duplicate these three forms of influence in advertising (see Exhibit 8.10). Marketers attempt to exert informational influence by using expert spokespersons who tell consumers about product features and performance. Such testimonials are accepted only to the degree that consumers view the spokesperson as being an expert on the product. Thus, information from Julius "Dr. J" Erving, the basketball star, about Dr. Scholl's foot powder is likely to be viewed as credible.

Marketers attempt to exert comparative influence by using a "typical consumer" approach to persuade consumers that people similar to themselves have chosen the advertised product to fill their needs. The ad for Subaru cars, American Express's corporate card in Exhibit 8.11 is an example. It shows a typical owner of a small business providing testimonials for the card.

Normative influence is wielded by depicting social approval from reference-group members. Praise from friends for good sherry or a comfortable auto ride are examples. The Johnny Walker ad in Exhibit 8.12 targets Hispanic Americans and shows reward power by associating the product with symbols of status and achievement such as a Mont Blanc pen. The tag line translates as "signature of excellence."

Normative influence can also be used more as a threat than as a reward. For example, the Hart Schaffner & Marx ad for men's suits in Exhibit 8.13 says that even though the right suit might not ensure success in the job, the wrong suit could lead to failure.

EXHIBIT 8.10

An Example of Informational Influence

EXHIBIT 8.11

An Example of Comparative Influence

CORPORATE
"I WANT IT TO TASTE LIKE HOME
AND SOUND LIKE HEAVEN."
"My first restaurant is famous for Bar-B-Q. My second one will have the finest Blues. And I'll track expenses for both places with the Corporate Card."
As your company grows, the benefits multiply. We'll itemize and categorize your employees' expenses, and when you travel you'll save at least 10% at participating hotels. Call 1-800-SUCCESS.
Keep on doing what you do best and let the Corporate Card do the rest.
TO YOUR SUCCESS

EXHIBIT 8.12

An Example of Normative Influence Using Implied Reward

Reference groups influence consumers through **word-of-mouth communication,** *that is, face-to-face communications between group members.* Such personal communication is the single most powerful influence on consumer behavior. One researcher summarized 6,000 consumer case studies and found that nearly 80 percent of purchases can be traced to word-of-mouth influence.[26]

The importance of such communication is illustrated by the quick success of Corona beer in the United States. The brand, a little-known Mexican import until the mid 1980s, did no advertising. It was sold on a limited basis and became the "in" beer among the young, affluent, urban set based on word-of-mouth communication. The beer's popularity spread like wildfire and caught the company by surprise. It had to quickly increase capacity and its distribution network to allow for expanded distribution into other areas. By 1987, Corona was the second largest imported beer in the United States, next to Heineken.[27]

A central element in word-of-mouth influences is the role of **opinion leaders,** *that is, individuals regarded by the reference group as having expertise and knowledge on a particular subject.* Marketers are interested in identifying opinion leaders, because if they can be convinced to buy a product, it will most likely be accepted by others in their reference group.

EXHIBIT 8.13

An Example of Normative Influence Using Implied Threat

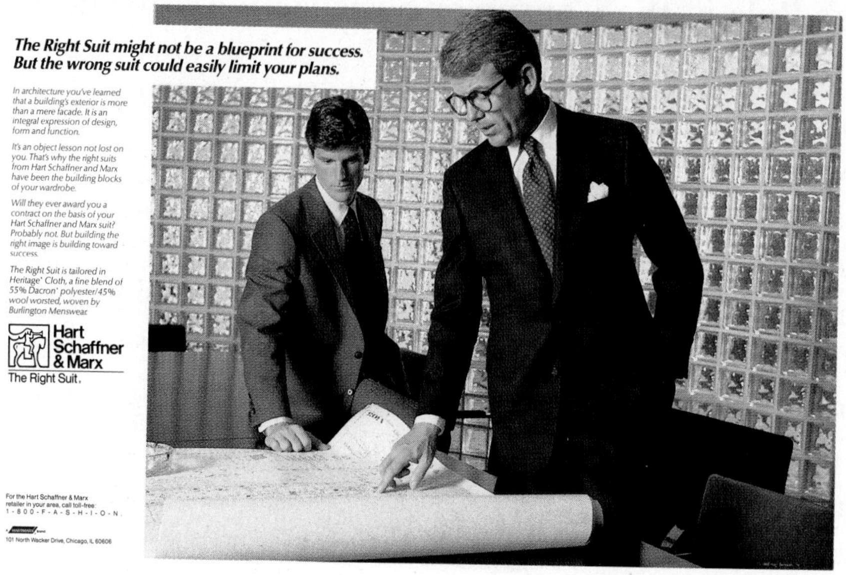

The Right Suit might not be a blueprint for success.
But the wrong suit could easily limit your plans.
In architecture you've learned that a building's exterior is more than a mere facade. It is an integral expression of design, form and function.
It's an object lesson not lost on you. That's why the right suits from Hart Schaffner and Marx have been the building blocks of your wardrobe.
Will they ever award you a contract on the basis of your Hart Schaffner and Marx suit? Probably not. But building the right image is building toward success.
The Right Suit is tailored in Heritage' Cloth, a fine blend of 55% Dacron' polyester/45% wool worsted, woven by Burlington Menswear.
Hart Schaffner & Marx
The Right Suit.
For the Hart Schaffner & Marx retailer in your area, call toll-free: 1-800-F-A-S-H-I-O-N.
101 North Wacker Drive, Chicago, IL 60606

THE FAMILY

The most important reference group is the family. Spouses influence each other's choice in clothing. Family influences occur between husbands and wives and between parents and children. Marketers are interested in who is likely to have the most influence on purchasing decisions so they can develop advertising and select media targeting that person.

HUSBAND–WIFE INFLUENCES

Traditionally, wives have had the most influence in buying foods, toiletries, and small appliances, while husbands have dominated decisions for automobiles, insurance, and financial services. But as we have seen in Chapter 4, these traditional patterns have changed. The increasing power of working wives has given them a greater say in decisions for financial services, insurance, and automobiles.

Carmakers are beginning to recognize these changing family roles by directing more of their effort toward women. In the mid 1980s, Chevrolet began allocating 30 percent of its ad budget for messages that appeal to women. But even then, much of this advertising was geared to fashion and style rather than to performance. One study found that 65 percent of women felt misrepresented in auto advertising that implied they were more interested in appearance than in technical data.[28]

On the other side of the coin, greater involvement by husbands in home and child care have given them more influence over purchases of foods and household items.

PARENT–CHILD INFLUENCES

Consumer socialization *is the process by which children learn how to be consumers.* This process is perhaps the most important legacy of the family in marketing

ETHICAL AND ENVIRONMENTAL ISSUES IN MARKETING

Advertising's Role in the Consumer Socialization of Children: Is It Ethical?

There is widening concern about the influence of advertising on children—and for good reason. Concern centers primarily on a young child's lack of ability to evaluate advertising and to distinguish between an ad and regular programming. Concern is heightened by the fact that children from 6 to 13 years of age spend more time in front of the television than at school.

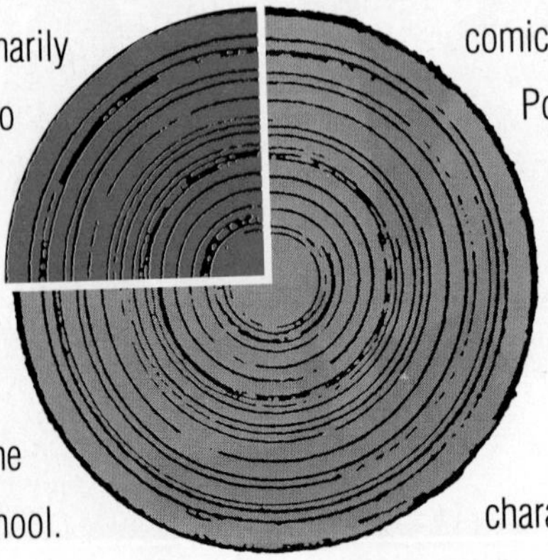

Research supports these concerns. One study found that younger children do not understand the purpose of a commercial as well as older children. Another found that children between the ages of three and five had difficulty distinguishing between TV programming and commercials.

Some advertisers have stimulated these concerns by seeming to take advantage of children's lack of ability to evaluate advertising. One example, cited by a consumer advocacy group, is an Instant Quaker Oatmeal ad that appears to be a full-page Popeye comic strip. To resolve the cartoon crisis, Popeye proclaims "Can the spinach! I want me Instant Quaker Oatmeal." Children are thus encouraged to believe that the ad is actually a cartoon.

Advertisers are also using cartoon characters such as the Teenage Mutant Ninja Turtles to promote cereals and other food products of questionable nutritional value. One study found that of 222 products advertised to kids on Saturday-morning programming, only 20 were within the guidelines for avoiding high-fat, high-sugar, and high-sodium.

Some marketers have gone out of their way to avoid unduly influencing children. The founder of Little Tikes toys refused to advertise to children be-

terms. Parents can try to teach children to be more-effective consumers by helping them to distinguish fact from fantasy in advertising, by trying to show them the relationship between price and product quality, and by teaching them how to be effective comparison shoppers.

In recent years, children have acquired more purchasing influence than ever before. Since many children come from dual-income and one-parent families, they often have to do the shopping and take care of the house when they come home from school. As a result, the process of consumer socialization is occurring much faster than it used to. Children must learn to be consumers, because they are often the purchasing agents for the family. This recognition led Kraft General Foods to tailor more of its food advertising to girls age 12 to 19. It places ads for convenience dinners in magazines such as *Seventeen.*

Many marketers try to influence the consumer socialization of children by getting them to recognize company and brand names early—even if these companies

ETHICAL AND ENVIRONMENTAL ISSUES IN MARKETING

cause he believed that parents should make toy purchase decisions for their kids. He even refused to advertise on television to avoid "the faddish lures kids are susceptible to."

Little Tikes is the exception, however. Expenditures for advertising targeting children has been growing, primarily because children between the ages of 6 and 17 pack $53 billion in purchasing power.

Growing concern over the influence of advertising on younger children led Congress to approve a bill in 1990 which reduced the amount of commercial time allowed on children's television programming. In addition, since children have difficulty distinguishing between the show and the commercial, legislation requires advertisers to announce when they are going to a commercial or to a show with statements like "and now, back to our show."

The majority of advertisers recognize that they have a responsibility to avoid unduly influencing impressionable children. Yet some advertisers continue to encourage confusion between ads and programming. Until such practices stop, government regulation of children's advertising is likely to increase.

Questions: What are the ethical issues in advertising to younger children? What can advertisers do to ensure that advertising to children is responsible?

Sources: Ronald S. Rubin, "The Effects of Cognitive Development on Children's Responses to Television Advertising," *Journal of Business Research 4* (1974), 409–419; Nancy Stephens and Mary Ann Stutts, "Preschoolers' Ability to Distinguish Between Television Programming and Commercials," *Journal of Advertising 11* (April–May 1982),16–25; "The Backlash Over Clutter in Kidland," *Adweek's Marketing Week*, October 8, 1990, p. 4; and "Little Tikes With a Grown-Up Dilemma," *Adweek's Marketing Week*, September 10, 1990, p. 18.

do not sell children's products. Black & Decker has licensed its name to a line of toys that are miniature versions of its small appliances. One company executive reasoned, "Youngsters don't buy Black & Decker drills. But they might someday, if they start out on toy Dustbusters."[29]

Such strategies might be effective in capturing a child's loyalties at an early age, but they must be closely monitored by parents to avoid exploiting children, especially because children are more easily influenced by a marketer's appeal than adults.

THE FAMILY LIFE CYCLE

Another dimension of family influence is the **family's life cycle**, *which is the progression of a family from formation to child-rearing, to middle age, and finally to retire-*

ment. The stage of the life cycle influences purchasing behavior. For example, newly married couples are more affluent because both frequently work and do not have the expenses of child care. They are good markets for travel, entertainment, autos, and durable goods. As children arrive, discretionary income decreases as expenditures on appliances, furniture, and infant products increase.

As children grow, financial pressures continue, especially if they enter college. Discretionary income then increases sharply as children leave home. At this point, husband and wife are probably at the peak of their earning potential, yet expenses have decreased. Such middle-aged "empty nesters" are excellent markets for travel, sporting goods, apparel, and home-improvement items.

In the later stages of the life cycle—older married couples and widows and widowers—discretionary income starts decreasing, as these individuals begin to live off fixed-income pensions and annuities. Expenditures increase for drugs, medical services, hobby-related items, and leisure products.

As an example of marketing products by stage of the life cycle, banks and brokerage houses have positioned financial services according to the desire for growth in equity in the early phases of the life cycle, for short-term appreciation and willingness to take risks in the middle years when discretionary income is greatest, and for protection of equity in the later years when husband and wife may be living on a fixed income.

SUMMARY

1. **How do consumers go about making purchasing decisions?**
Consumers first determine their needs, then search for information on brands that might fill their needs, evaluate alternative brand choices, and finally choose the brand that they feel will most likely fill their needs.

   Decisions will vary depending on the extent to which such information search and brand evaluation takes place. They will also vary depending on the degree of involvement of the consumer with the brand. Complex decision making involves extensive information search and brand evaluation. Where brand loyalty exists, information search is minimal. In low-involvement decision making, the consumer wants to minimize the time and effort spent in selecting a brand.
2. **What factors influence a consumer's purchase decisions?**
Three sets of factors influence a consumer's purchase decisions: the consumer's psychological set, characteristics, and environment. The psychological set is composed of the consumer's needs, perceptions, and brand attitudes. Consumer characteristics are the consumer's demographic, life-style, and personality variables that are likely to influence brand choice. The consumer's environment is the society in which brand choice takes place and the groups with which the consumer associates, particularly the peer group and the family.
3. **How do a consumer's needs, perceptions, and attitudes influence his or her purchase decisions?**
Needs are forces that direct consumers toward the achievement of certain goals. Perceptions are the way consumers organize and interpret information about brands and companies. Consumers develop brand images that represent their overall perceptions of a brand. Attitudes are the tendency to evaluate a brand or company in a favorable or unfavorable way. Needs, perceptions, and

attitudes determine the purchase decision. When a brand is perceived as filling a consumer's needs, a positive attitude is likely to result, leading to a greater likelihood the brand will be purchased.

4. **How do the consumer's characteristics and environment influence purchases?**
Whereas a consumer's perceptions and attitudes are specific to a brand, consumer characteristics are more general. Three types of characteristics affect brand choice: demographics, life-styles, and personality. Demographics are the objective characteristics of the consumer, such as age, income, and education. Life-styles represent the consumer's activities, interests, and social attitudes. Personality variables are characteristics that reflect consistent and enduring patterns of behavior, such as compulsiveness, compliance, and dominance.
Environmental factors also influence consumer behavior. These factors range from broad cultural influences to more-specific group and family influences. Cultural values such as the emphasis in American society on youth and materialism influence our choice of brands. Social class—that is, the status grouping in which a consumer belongs based on income, education, and occupation—influences preferences for a range of products from beer to cars.
Groups have the most direct influence on brand choice through face-to-face influence. Family influences occur between husbands and wives and parents and children. A key element in family influence is the consumer socialization of children; that is, the process by which children learn how to evaluate marketing information and select brands.

5. **How do marketers use knowledge about consumers and their environment to develop marketing strategies?**
Marketers use the three basic influences on consumer behavior—the consumer's psychological set, characteristics, and environment—to develop a range of marketing strategies. These variables are most commonly used to define market segments. Once the target segments are defined, brands are positioned to the needs of these segments. Definition of the target segments also helps identify the proper media to reach these groups. In particular, demographic and life-style characteristics are used to identify magazines or newspapers most likely to be read and TV or radio shows most likely to be seen or heard by the target group.

KEY TERMS

Marketing stimuli (p. 251)
Psychological set (p. 251)
Involvement (p. 253)
High-involvement purchases (p. 253)
Complex decision making (p. 253)
Information processing (p. 254)
Post-purchase dissonance (p. 255)
Brand loyalty (p. 255)
Low-involvement purchase (p. 256)
Limited decision making (p. 256)
Variety seeking (p. 256)
Inertia (p. 256)
Habit (p. 257)
Learning (p. 257)
Reinforcement (p. 258)
Extinction (p. 258)
Conditioning (p. 258)
Needs (p. 261)
Motives (p. 261)
Perceptions (p. 262)
Selective perception (p. 262)
Image (p. 262)
Attitudes (p. 263)
Brand beliefs (p. 263)
Brand evaluations (p. 263)
Personality (p. 268)
Psychoanalytic theory (p. 268)
Motivational research (p. 268)
Self-concept (self-image) theory (p. 269)
Trait theory (p. 269)
Culture (p. 270)
Cross-cultural influences (p. 271)

Social class (p. 275)
Reference groups (p. 276)
Informational influence (p. 276)
Comparative influence (p. 277)
Normative influence (p. 277)
Word-of-mouth communication (p. 278)
Opinion leaders (p. 278)
Consumer socialization (p. 279)
Family life cycle (p. 281)

QUESTIONS

1. Consider the four types of decisions in Figure 8.2. Which decision process is most likely to apply to each of the following product categories?
   a. cigarettes
   b. adult cereals
   c. canned vegetables
   d. cookies
   e. automobiles

   Describe your rationale for associating a particular decision process with each product category.
2. Use the model of complex decision making in Figure 8.3 to describe the decision-making process you went through in selecting a business school. What are the implications of the decision process you described for the school's
   a. positioning strategy (features to meet student needs)?
   b. product strategy (course offerings)?
   c. pricing strategy (tuition level and financial assistance programs)?
3. What is the distinction between brand loyalty and inertia? What are the strategic implications of this distinction?
4. a. Under what circumstances might a consumer switch from complex decision making to habit in buying a car? What might cause the consumer to stop buying by habit and to revert to complex decision making?
   b. What might cause a consumer to switch from being uninvolved to being highly involved with a product like cereals?
5. What is meant by reinforcement of consumer behavior? What is the role of the product in achieving reinforcement? Of advertising?
6. When Kellogg introduced adult cereals, it changed cereals from an uninvolving to an involving product for many consumers. What are the different strategic implications in advertising cereals as an uninvolving product versus advertising them as involving?
7. How does the conflict between the positive taste tests for "new" Coke and the subsequent outcry among consumers to bring back "old" Coke demonstrate the importance of brand image?
8. How have marketers used demographic and life-style characteristics to (a) segment their markets and (b) select media? Cite specific examples.
9. How can psychoanalytic theory contribute to better understanding consumer behavior? Self-concept theory? Describe specific applications of each to marketing.
10. How do the ads in Exhibit 8.10 to 8.13 demonstrate the three types of reference group influences?
11. Why have children gained more purchasing influence in the family? How have some marketers directed more of their effort toward children?

QUESTIONS: YOU ARE THE DECISION MAKER

1. A product manager for a well-known brand of bar soap commented on the distinction between low- and high-involvement purchasing decisions as follows:

   Your emphasis on low-involvement decisions is overblown. I just don't agree that consumers aren't involved with most decisions. Consumers get their egos tied up with a lot of packaged goods—soaps, toothpaste, deodorants, hair spray. Anything that has to do with how we come across socially has to be involving. Even items like detergents and floor cleaners are going to be involving for many consumers that take pride in the way they and their homes look. So I just don't buy your focus on low involvement.

   Do you agree with the product manager's statement? Why or why not? Are marketing executives likely to think consumers are more involved with their products than they actually are?

2. An electronics company decides to diversify and buys a company that produces canned vegetables. Company executives have been accustomed to marketing electronics as items purchased based on information search and brand evaluation. They must now market products likely to be purchased by habit. What are the different strategic implications the company's executives are likely to face in marketing a product purchased by habit rather than complex decision making?
3. An auto manufacturer is marketing a new, high-priced model to professionals and managers. Its main line of cars is positioned primarily to blue-collar workers, based on themes of escaping from everyday drudgery. What differences in positioning strategies might be developed in appealing to professionals/managers versus blue-collar workers.
4. An executive of one of the leading liquor companies that targets both whites and African Americans says:

   Our marketing strategy is to use the same advertising campaign for both African Americans and whites. We feel the focus should be on the product, not on the ethnic character of the market. We will advertise in media targeting African Americans, but we do not develop specific ads or promotions for this group.

   What are the pros and cons of the company's strategy regarding the African-American market.

CHAPTER 9

Organizational Buyer Behavior

YOUR FOCUS IN CHAPTER 9

To learn:

- *The similarities and differences between organizational buying behavior and consumer behavior.*
- *The types of decisions organizational buyers make.*
- *The role of group decision making in organizational buyer behavior.*
- *The individual and environmental influences on organizational buyers.*
- *The strategies business-to-business marketers use to influence organizational buyers.*

IBM—Struggling to Satisfy its Organizational Customers

Once-mighty IBM is in trouble. Instead of "Big Blue," the company's nickname, industry analysts are now calling IBM "black and blue." After forty years of sustained growth and the preeminent role in establishing computer industry standards, 1985 saw a sharp reversal in IBM's fortunes with its first drop in earnings. By 1991, earnings decreases were commonplace. The company's world share of the computer market had dropped to 23 percent from a 1980s high of 36 percent.[1]

What happened? IBM's dominance went to its head and it started ignoring its organizational customers. In years past, selling computers to companies was easy. The IBM salesperson would walk in, tell the information manager what his or her company needed, and the advice was accepted. The FUD factor was pervasive—fear, uncertainty, and doubt of buying anything but IBM machines.

Open systems.
Everyone agrees they're good, but not everyone agrees how to get there.
IBM

With the advent of new technologies—personal computers, workstations, and powerful microcomputers—organizations began to realize that they no longer had to rely on the large mainframe computers on which IBM relied to maintain its dominance. Companies became more systems oriented; that is, they wanted to tie together computers from different companies to create the best information system to meet their particular needs. But IBM continued to push its mainframes and proprietary software to ensure that only IBM machines would be used.

Not surprisingly, IBM began losing sales to smaller and more-efficient companies such as Compaq, NEC, and Microsoft. By 1986 John Akers, the company's new CEO, realized that IBM would have to become more customer oriented. The first step was to reeducate IBM's sales force to think in terms of systems rather than individual products and to begin focusing on customer needs. To encourage a customer orientation, the sales force was organized on industry lines so that separate sales groups could specialize on meeting the information and data-processing needs of such diverse businesses as banks, life-insurance companies, airlines, or auto manufacturers. Further, IBM developed a software package called Office Vision Systems to link together all the computers in one organization so they could communicate with each other. Most revolutionary of all, IBM allowed its salespeople to work with other computer companies in establishing custom-made systems for customers and even allowed them to suggest competitors' machines.

By 1987, these changes appeared to help, as profits began inching up. But they were not the answer. IBM was just too big to change with any quick fixes. One organizational buyer said, "The people I deal with still have the Big Blue attitude: Do it our way or not at all."[2] Although top management was committed to a customer orientation, the message did not always filter down through the ranks. Further, IBM was still wedded to its proprietary software when companies were calling for "open systems"; that is, a universal standard for software to ensure compatibility between computers made by different companies.

IBM's ponderous bureaucracy was also interfering with its ability to respond to customer needs. It was late in coming out with workstations (multi-function personal computers), laptops, and notebook computers; when it did, its products were often inferior to the competition's. In an industry where the lifespan of a notebook computer is as short as three months, IBM's models were often obsolete by the time they reached the market.[3]

By 1991, John Akers was getting increasingly frustrated as he saw IBM's stock sink to almost half of what it was in 1987. It was apparent to Akers that IBM would have to become a leaner organization, one that could respond to the quickly changing needs of its business customers and one that could compete effectively with smaller and more efficient computer makers.[4] But how?

In November 1991, Akers came up with what might be the answer. A few months before, he had established a precedent-setting alliance with IBM's archrival in personal computers, Apple Computer, to better integrate Apple's Macintosh computers into IBM networks. In the past, the two systems were incompatible, but now this new capability would allow companies to integrate Apple and IBM computers in one system.[5]

Then, in December, Akers made a startling announcement: IBM would break up into a number of smaller, autonomous companies, one responsible for personal computers, another for printers, another for software, and so forth. The purpose was to eliminate one big IBM and create more-flexible operating units that could better develop computer products geared to the needs of IBM's business customers. The move was also designed to get the company away from its emphasis on mainframes and focus it more on the small, powerful workstations and personal, laptop, and notebook computers that were becoming the core of many companies' processing systems. As part of the move, IBM was giving up its emphasis on proprietary systems and embracing the open systems concept to allow linkages with other computer makes.

These moves were designed to permit IBM to develop custom-made systems for business organizations, without being fettered with a mainframe mentality and the necessity to stick to only IBM hardware and software. The move may mean that IBM will no longer be "black and blue," but it will never be Big Blue again either.

THE NATURE OF ORGANIZATIONAL BUYING BEHAVIOR

Most of the buying and selling in the American economy is not from an organization to a final consumer but from one organization to another. In fact, organizational buying represents more than $2 trillion in sales, an amount that is greater than purchases of goods by final consumers. Further, companies that sell to organizational buyers spend more money marketing their goods than those that sell to final consumers. This is because organizational buyers usually require face-to-face contact with sellers whereas final consumers usually do not.

Organizational buyers *are those individuals responsible for purchasing goods for companies that either use these goods in the process of production and distribution or that resell them.* Organizational buyers purchase for manufacturing firms, for institutions such as hospitals and schools, for government agencies, and for intermediaries such as wholesalers and retailers. *Companies that market to these business organizations are known as* **business-to-business marketers.** For example, when Westinghouse sells a factory automation system to a team of General Motors buyers, Westinghouse is the business-to-business marketer and the GM team is the organizational buyer. Just as marketers of consumer goods must base marketing strategies on an understanding of the needs of final consumers, business-to-business marketers must base their strategies on an understanding of the needs of organizational buyers. Westinghouse must develop a factory automation system based on their understanding of GM's production and scheduling needs.

IMPORTANCE OF A CUSTOMER ORIENTATION

A business-to-business marketer can become product oriented more easily than a consumer-goods marketer for one reason: Business-to-business marketers are more likely to sell high-technology, finely engineered products. As a result, they are more likely to become wed to their technologies rather than to the customer. This was true for IBM. It had become more focused on its product lines than on customer needs.

In some cases, business-to-business marketers that become technology-oriented are too late in recognizing the need for a customer orientation and go out of business as a result. On occasion, these are the same companies that were the technological innovators in the industry. For example, an English company called Electric and Musical Industries (EMI) developed the CT scanner, the device that takes hundreds of X-ray slices from different angles, then uses a computer to reconstruct the total picture. EMI rested on its laurels as the innovator, without ever developing a marketing capability to keep a tab on customer needs. EMI's first device was a head scanner, but customers (hospitals) wanted a body scanner capable of faster resolution time in taking the X-rays.[6]

EMI was slow to respond, and its take-it-or-leave-it attitude turned off many customers. By the time it produced the desired machines, General Electric had developed a third generation of CT scanners, a superior sales force, and an ability to adapt to market needs. Six years after EMI introduced the device, it was out of the CT-scanner market, and losses incurred as the result of declining sales made it an acquisition target.[7]

TYPES OF ORGANIZATIONAL BUYERS

If business-to-business marketers are to develop strategies based on the needs of their customers, they must be aware of the different types of organizational buyers—industrial buyers, institutional buyers, government agencies, or resellers. Table 9.1 lists some examples of products and services purchased by these buyers.

Industrial buyers *buy products and services that they use to further process other products.* They buy products used in manufacturing, mining, or construction. For example, General Electric buys generators to create power, General Motors buys factory automation equipment to produce cars, and Black & Decker buys conveyor belts to transport parts from one part of its plant to another. A manufacturer might also buy services such as a contract to service generators or trucks, an inventory control system to ensure adequate inventory levels, or a marketing research study to identify prospective buyers.

TABLE 9.1

Examples of Purchases by Organizational Buyers

TYPE OF BUYER	PRODUCTS	SERVICES
INDUSTRIAL BUYERS	Pollution control company buys industrial generator	Auto producer buys maintenance and repair contract for machinery
	Metal processor buys forklift trucks to transport fabricated parts	Industrial cable company buys inventory control system
		Computer manufacturer buys marketing research study
INSTITUTIONAL BUYERS	Hospital buys drugs	Hotel buys janitorial and cleaning services
	Hotel buys food	Airline buys consulting services
GOVERNMENT AGENCY	Census Bureau buys computers	State Department of Tourism hires an advertising agency
	Department of Defense buys military equipment	City drug-rehabilitation program hires professional counseling services
	School system buys educational supplies	
RESELLERS	Distributor buys electrical cable for resale to utility company	Retailer buys store-location study
	Wholesaler buys drugs for resale to drug stores	Distributor buys accounting services
	Retail druggist buys pharmaceuticals for resale to final consumer	

Whereas industrial buyers buy for organizations that process goods, **institutional buyers** *buy for organizations that provide services,* such as hospitals and schools, hotels and restaurants, airlines and railroads. Buyers for Humana, an organization that runs a chain of 80 hospitals in 50 cities, purchase drugs, medical equipment, and hospital supplies. Buyers for Marriott Hotels purchase food, linens, and professional services from lawyers and accountants. These goods and services are purchased to provide other services rather than to process products (see Table 9.1).

Government agencies *represent federal, state, and local governmental units* both in the United States and abroad. They are a significant proportion of organizational buying with over 80,000 federal, state, and local government units in the United States that account for over $1 trillion in purchases. Federal agencies such as the Census Bureau or the Department of Defense will buy products ranging from computers to military equipment. A local school system might buy educational materials. Government agencies also buy services. For example, a state agency might hire an advertising firm to promote tourism. Or a city drug-rehabilitation program might hire psychologists for professional counseling services.

Resellers *are wholesalers and retailers that buy products to resell.* They do not process goods. Rather, they act as purchasing agents for other organizational buyers or for the final consumer. A distributor such as W. W. Grainger buys electrical cable from a manufacturer and sells it to a public utility. A drug wholesaler such as McKesson buys from pharmaceutical companies to resell to drugstores. A retailer such as Sears buys a wide range of products to resell to the final consumer. Here also, resellers buy services to support their activities, such as studies to determine the best location for new store outlets or accounting services for bookkeeping and tax returns.

We will consider reseller activities in a later chapter. For now, we will focus on industrial and institutional buying behavior.

COMPARISON WITH CONSUMER BEHAVIOR

Organizational buyer behavior is similar to consumer behavior in many respects. Each of the steps in complex decision making cited in the previous chapter—need arousal, information search, brand evaluation—apply to organizational buying. Further, the types of factors influencing organizational buyers are similar to those influencing consumers—the buyer's psychological set, characteristics, and group influences through word-of-mouth communications.

Traditionally, organizational buyers have been thought of as more rational and scientific in their purchase decisions. Since they often rely on a set of technical product specifications, their purchasing is more likely to be based on measurable product attributes and seller capabilities. Yet, studies have shown that organizational buyers are also governed by emotion, inertia, and interpersonal relations in making purchasing decisions. For example, one study of purchasers of computer terminals found that word-of-mouth influence was as important in making the decision as objective sources such as technical specifications.[8]

The differences between organizational and consumer behavior tend to outweigh the similarities primarily because of the greater complexity of products purchased by organizational buyers. Greater complexity means that a lot more can go wrong with the product, so more risk is involved in the purchase. Organizational buyers have more at stake—sometimes including their jobs—if they make the wrong decision. Because of this risk, organizational buying decisions are more likely than consumer buying decisions to be made on a group basis. As a result, organizations frequently form buying centers. *A* **buying center** *is a group of executives that provide the different skills necessary to make a buying decision.* Most often, the group is composed of a purchasing agent, an engineer, and a production manager.

Technical complexity also means that buyers are likely to base their purchases on a set of formal product specifications. **Product specifications** *are performance requirements set by prospective users of the product* (such as lifting capacity for forklift trucks). As a result, a purchase decision is based on the degree to which product or service attributes meet these specifications. The purchase decision will also be based on vendor (that is, supplier) attributes such as reliability, on-time delivery, and service. In consumer buying, the consumer usually decides on a product first, then on the store to buy it from. In organizational buying, the product and vendor decision are closely intertwined.

Business-to-business marketing and consumer-goods marketing also differ from the seller's standpoint, primarily in the greater role of personal selling in business-to-business marketing. The salesperson's technical knowledge of the product is essential, and postpurchase follow-up and service are necessary. In business-to-business marketing, buyers negotiate with sellers on price, delivery dates, and product specifications. In consumer buying, such negotiations are rare. Advertising is likely to play only a supportive role to personal selling in organizational buying and serves to provide information to lay the groundwork for a subsequent sales call.

A MODEL OF ORGANIZATIONAL BUYER BEHAVIOR

Figure 9.1 presents a basic model of organizational buyer behavior representing key influences on either individual buyers or the buying center, the types of decisions made by these buyers, and the decision outcomes.

INFLUENCES ON ORGANIZATIONAL BUYERS

Five influences on organizational buyers are shown in Figure 9.1. As with the consumer, the organizational buyer is exposed to *marketing stimuli* (that is, the marketing strategies developed by business-to-business marketers to influence organizational buyers). Assume that Citicorp wants to buy a customized computer system for its retail banking divisions so that managers can have instant access to information for each branch. The bank establishes a buying center made up of the information systems manager, the purchasing manager, and the data-processing manager, and directs this group to solicit information from several computer firms. These companies provide information on a customized system, including specifications on software and hardware. They also provide information on price, prospective installation dates, training schedules for users of the system, and maintenance service. This information represents marketing stimuli that will be evaluated by the buying center, which will influence their decision.

The organizational buyer will also be influenced by his or her *psychological set and characteristics*. For example, assume that the purchasing manager has purchased mostly IBM equipment in the past and has a favorable attitude toward that company (the buyer's psychological set). He is older and more risk averse than the

FIGURE 9.1

A Model of Organizational Buyer Behavior

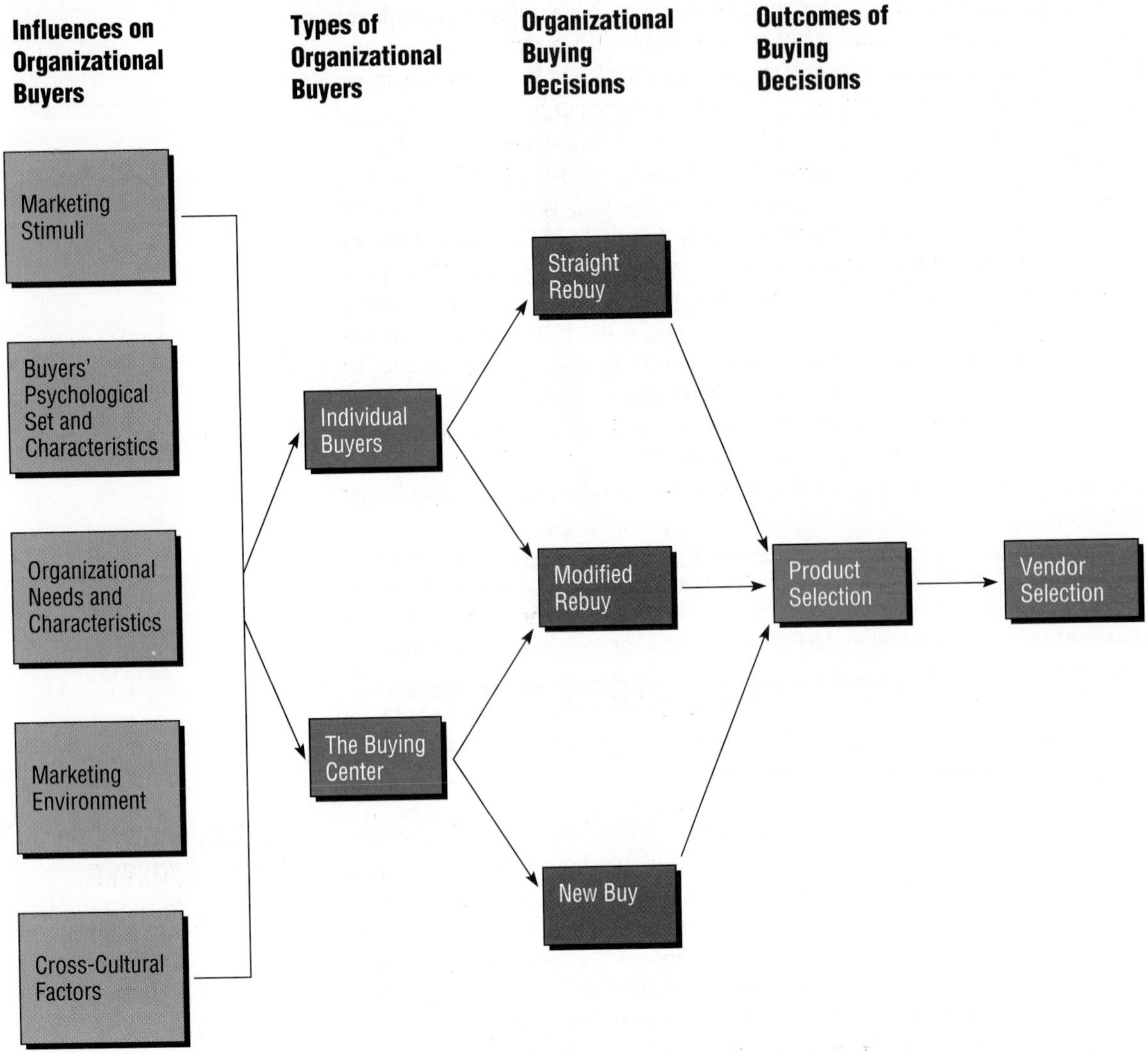

other members of the group (the buyer's characteristics) and does not want to make any waves by trying a totally new supplier. Based on these individual buyer influences, the purchasing manager is initially in favor of the IBM system, whereas the information systems and data-processing managers have no strong preferences.

The third major influence on the organizational buyer is the organization itself. Organizational buyers must be guided by the *needs of the organization.* The Citicorp buying group defined the nature of the informational linkages required to better supply branch information to managers, and then developed specifications for an information system to best meet their needs. The buyer is also influenced by the *characteristics of the buying organization,* including factors such as purchasing roles, the nature of personal influence, and the degree to which decision making is centralized. In the Citicorp example, the information systems manager has the most influence over software specifications, because she is familiar with the data and analytical needs of managers in a branch office information system (purchasing role). As a result, she wants to consider a wider range of software alternatives and tries to prevail on the purchasing manager not to be so committed to past vendor relationships (personal influences). Since Citicorp is relatively decentralized, the lines of authority between the data processing, information systems, and purchasing managers are not clear-cut (degree of centralization). This means the information systems manager has to rely on persuasion rather than on direct power and authority in trying to get the purchasing manager to consider other vendors.

Influences of the *marketing environment* such as the level of competition, technology, and regulatory constraints are the fourth set of factors that will affect the decision of the buying group. For example, several of Citicorp's competitors are considering establishing similar systems to provide their managers with quick information on the status of branch deposits and transactions. Advances in information-processing technology make it essential that Citicorp maintain a state-of-the-art system. The economic uncertainty as a result of the 1990–92 recession has also made banks more cost conscious, and an effective system to track deposit and transaction activity might help reduce costs. Finally, the trend toward deregulation means that new competitors are coming in to challenge the traditional banking system, putting more pressure on the banks to improve efficiency through better information.

Organizational buyers operating in international markets are also influenced by *cross-cultural factors*. For example, Europeans tend to be much more formal in buyer-seller interchanges than Americans. Status and titles are more important. In Japan, establishing a personal relationship based on mutual trust is a necessary prerequisite to productive buyer-seller interactions. American buyers doing business abroad must be aware of these cross-cultural differences.

ORGANIZATIONAL BUYING DECISIONS

An organizational buying decision can be made by an individual or a buying center. When product purchasers are relatively simple, individual buyers are responsible for the decision. When products are complex or involve large expenditures, a buying center will be responsible. Figure 9.1 shows that individuals and buying centers make very different types of decisions. Individual buyers are more likely to make decisions known as *straight rebuys*, buying centers decide on *new buys*, and either individual buyers or buying centers make decisions for *modified rebuys*.

The **straight rebuy** *is a recurring purchase that can be handled on a routine basis*, such as when an institution buys office supplies or a manufacturer buys metal fasteners. These purchases involve standardized products with routine usages. Little information search is required. Usually, a straight rebuy will be triggered by a low inventory level. It is similar to habitual purchasing in consumer behavior. Vendors are often selected from an approved list. *An* **approved vendor list** *is a list of sellers that have been approved by the company* based on factors such as product quality, delivery and service reliability, and past performance. 1991, Sonoco was an approved vendor for Monsanto, providing products to help make synthetic textiles (see Exhibit 9.1).

A **modified rebuy** *is a recurring purchase that requires some information on product specifications and vendor capabilities*. A modified rebuy might involve reevaluating a straight rebuy because of a new product or a change in technology—for example, the introduction of a bonded adhesive in place of a metal screw. More complex modified rebuy decisions are made by buying centers.

EXHIBIT 9.1

Sonoco and Monsanto Have an Approved Vendor Relationship

Sonoco Products Company workers perform quality tests on fibre drums at the Pittsburg, California plant. Sonoco's comprehensive quality program earned the Sonoco Fibre Drum Division a "preferred" supplier designation from its customer Monsanto Chemical Company. Products like fibre drums may be purchased as a straight rebuy from a supplier on an approved vendor list.

A **new buy** *is a decision that has not occurred before and requires extensive information search on product specifications and vendor capabilities* since there is little experience to go on. In the Citicorp example cited above, the microcomputer network for a branch-banking information system was a new buy.

OUTCOME OF THE BUYING DECISION

Organizational decisions also require selection of a product and a vendor. Selection of the product should determine selection of the vendor. In the Citicorp example, each of the companies being considered provided different sets of specifications for the microcomputer network. Therefore, selection of the system determines selection of the vendor.

But frequently, it is the other way around—the vendor is selected based on past loyalties or just plain inertia on the part of the manager, and the product is selected as a result of vendor selection. One study found that many organizational buyers are reluctant to change to new sources because of an inability to cope with any complications resulting from such a change.[10] The purchasing manager in the Citicorp example would have selected the IBM system regardless of systems specifications. He felt comfortable with IBM based on past associations and was trying to minimize risk by avoiding selection of a new vendor.

THE ORGANIZATIONAL BUYING DECISION PROCESS

In the rest of this chapter, we consider the basic components of organizational buyer behavior in Figure 9.1. We will start by considering the organizational buying decision process, because it gives us a perspective on different types of organizational buying. We will then discuss the influences on organizational buyers shown in Figure 9.1. We reserve for last the marketing strategies business-to-business marketers direct to organizational buyers.

TYPES OF BUYING DECISIONS

The three types of organizational buying decisions—new buys, modified rebuys, and straight rebuys—parallel the processes of complex decision making, limited decision making, and habit cited in the last chapter (see Table 9.2).

COMPLEX DECISION MAKING

Complex buying decisions (new buys) are usually made by a group because of the financial and performance risks involved in buying a new product. The characteristics of complex decision making in Table 9.2 are high risk, extensive information search, and a detailed evaluation of alternative vendors. An approved vendor list is rarely used, because it would be too risky to limit choice only to firms from which the company already buys. Once the decision is made, postpurchase evaluation is also extensive, because product performance is monitored carefully. In a new-buy situation, the people with the most influence are usually engineers, because they have the best capability to set and evaluate specifications for complex products.

TABLE 9.2

Types of Organizational Buying Decisions

DECISION-MAKING PROCESS	COMPLEX DECISION MAKING → (NEW BUY)	LIMITED DECISION MAKING → (MODIFIED REBUY)	HABIT (STRAIGHT REBUY)
TYPES OF DECISON MAKING	Group →	Group or Individual →	Individual
FINANCIAL AND PERFORMANCE RISK	High →	Moderate →	Low
INFORMATION SEARCH	Extensive →	Limited →	None
EVALUATION OF ALTERNATIVE VENDORS	Extensive →	Moderate →	Minimal
USE OF APPROVED VENDOR LIST	Rarely →	Sometimes →	Usually
POSTPURCHASE EVALUATION	Extensive →	Moderate →	Minimal
POSITION WITH GREATEST PURCHASE INFLUENCE	Engineering →	Production or Purchasing →	Purchasing

FIGURE 9.2

Complex Decision Making in Organizational Buying

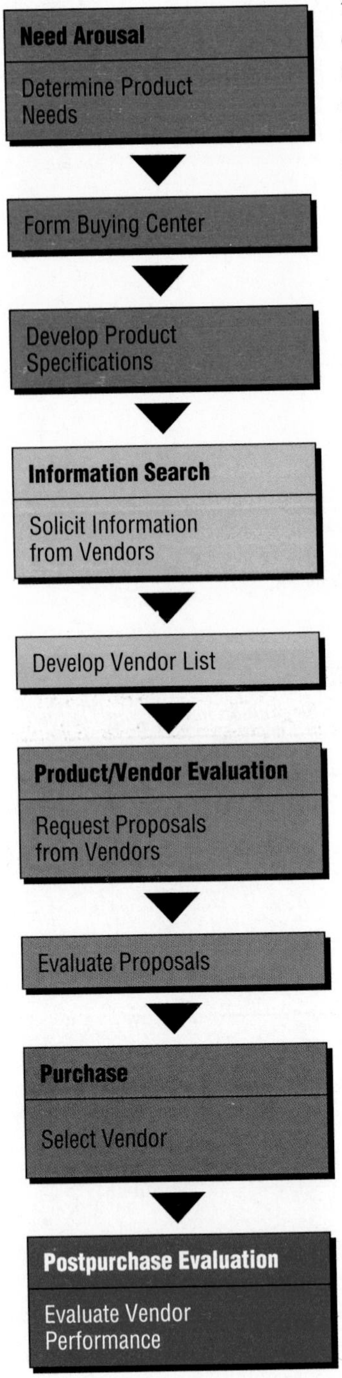

Complex decision-making processes in organizational buying have the same five steps as in the consumer behavior model—need arousal, information search, product and vendor evaluation, purchase, and postpurchase evaluation (see Figure 9.2). Initially, an organization determines a product need, then forms a buying center that develops the specifications for a product to meet this need. In the Citicorp example, the company first determined it needed an on-line branch information system to provide deposit and transaction information to its managers. A buying center was then formed, and it developed specifications for the type of information required, linkages between mainframe and microcomputers, and core capacity requirements.

Information search involves soliciting information from vendors regarding their capabilities. Based on this information, the buying center develops a list of vendors from which it will solicit proposals. These may be totally new vendors or vendors with which the company has dealt in the past.

Product and vendor evaluation involves submitting the product specifications to the approved vendors and requesting a proposal detailing how each vendor plans to fill the specifications. Proposals are then evaluated by the buying center, based on its original specifications.

In the final stages, the buying center selects a vendor and evaluates the vendor's performance on delivery, product installation, product performance, and service to determine if the company should buy from that vendor again. Assume that based on its overall assessment, the buying group at Citicorp concluded that Digital Equipment would do the best job in developing, installing, and maintaining an on-line branch information system. The other members prevailed on the purchasing manager (who favored IBM) to go along with their decision for Digital Equipment. All were satisfied with Digital's installation, personnel training, and service performance, and decided to consider the company in future systems purchases.

LIMITED DECISION MAKING

Limited decision making is analogous to a modified rebuy. If a company decides to buy an existing product with some modifications, a buying group may not be required. The decision might instead be made by one or two individuals, with a more limited search for information and fewer vendors under consideration.

The characteristics of limited decision making in Table 9.2 are limited information search and vendor evaluation, occasional use of an approved vendor list, and limited postpurchase evaluation. Production and purchasing executives are the most influential parties—production initiating a request, and the purchasing department filling it. The expertise of an engineer is less important since the product or service is not new.

An example of a modified-rebuy process is the purchase of steel plate by James Hampden Ltd. The Glasgow-based company is a producer of customized and standardized units of air- and gas-handling equipment such as large fans and blowers, circulators for gas-cooled nuclear reactors, and rotary heat exchangers.[11] When producing customized units, it buys steel plate on a special-order basis. This is not a new buy, but a modified rebuy, since these steel products have been purchased before.

An order for steel plate is usually initiated by a production manager or engineer. The order states the product specification, quantity required, and delivery date.

The purchasing agent then initiates a request for quotes from an approved vendor list. (Companies get on the approved vendor list if they meet Hampden's requirements for product quality, financial soundness, and condition of plant and equipment.)

The purchasing agent selects a supplier to fill the order from the approved list. Sometimes, the purchasing agent negotiates price and delivery with the vendor, but usually the vendor with the lowest price and best delivery date is selected. Postpurchase evaluation of product quality and on-time delivery determines whether the vendor stays on the approved list.

HABIT

Straight rebuys are similar to habitual purchasing behavior. As Figure 9.3 shows, straight rebuys are usually initiated when a product's inventory level reaches a reorder point. Purchasing is then automatic. A purchase order is issued to an approved vendor, who fills it based on prearranged terms for price and delivery. A vendor is on the approved list because past performance has been satisfactory. If its prices become higher than those of competitors, or product quality deteriorates, or delivery slows down, the vendor will probably be taken off the approved list. The process in Figure 9.3 can be better described as ordering rather than purchasing. The vendor is only filling an order rather than meeting a set of specifications. As Table 9.2 shows, ordering is the responsibility of the purchasing department. There is no information search or vendor evaluation, and postpurchase evaluation is minimal. Hampden buys steel for standardized products based

FIGURE 9.3

Habit in Organizational Buyer Behavior

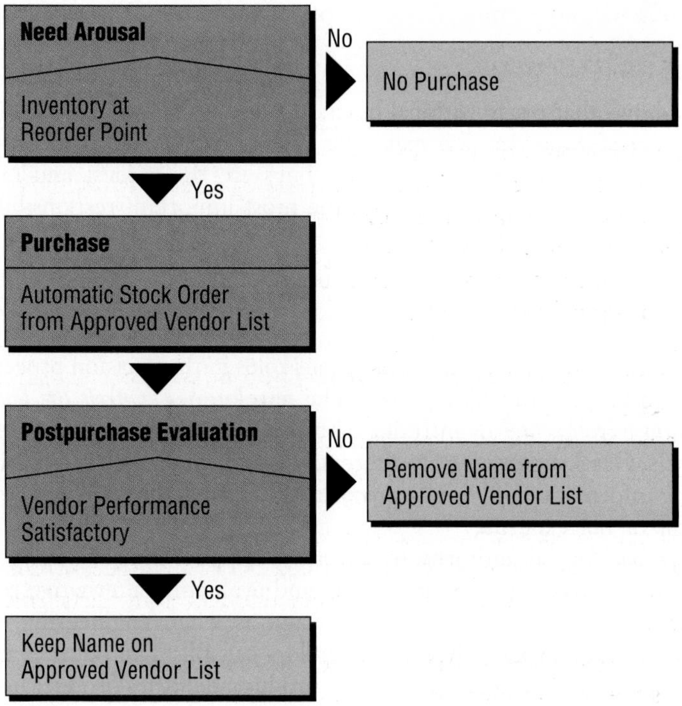

on a straight rebuy process. Steel plate for standardized products is maintained at specified stock levels. When inventory falls below these levels, the stock control department issues a purchase order that is sent to an approved vendor and quickly filled.

VENDOR LOYALTY Straight rebuys can reflect vendor loyalty or inertia. **Vendor loyalty** *is the consistent use of the same vendor as a result of past satisfaction.* Frequently, the same vendor is used when an automatic reorder point is reached. One study found that vendor loyalty is most likely for small orders and when significant cost savings can be had by dealing with the same vendor.[12]

Dealing with the same vendor has the advantage of providing a constant and assured source of supply. Xerox has cut its approved vendor list from 2,000 to less than 350 highly reliable suppliers. As a result, it has been able to substantially reduce the need to inspect incoming parts.[13]

But when the price of a product is high, and the product is technologically complex, vendor loyalty can be risky. As technology advances, other vendors may offer superior products or the same product at lower costs. A company that buys complex products should be wary of consistently buying from the same vendor.

INERTIA **Inertia** *in organizational buying occurs when buyers rely on the same vendors in the belief that it is better to avoid the risk of trying someone new* even if another supplier might offer better prices, quality, or delivery dates. Also, the organizational buyer may wish to avoid starting a new process of information search and vendor evaluation. In addition to the advantage of a long-term relationship, dealing with the same vendor offers the benefits of reciprocity. **Reciprocity** *is when two business organizations agree to buy each other's products.* For example, an auto manufacturer might buy materials from a steel company, which then buys its fleet of cars from the auto manufacturer. Such reciprocity encourages inbreeding and a failure to look for more efficient sources of supply.

GROUP DECISION MAKING: THE BUYING CENTER

Figure 9.1 shows that organizational buying decisions can be made on a group or individual basis. Group decision making is most likely for new buys and is organized around a buying center. Since new buys are the riskiest and most costly buying decisions, the buying center has the most important responsibility in the organizational buying process.

ROLES IN THE BUYING CENTER

Members of the buying center assume various roles in the decision process, termed gatekeeper, influencer, buyer, and user. The **gatekeeper** *controls the flow of information into the buying center* by introducing materials from salespeople, ads, or technical journals. Gatekeepers identify alternative products and vendors in the process of gathering information. The *influencer* sways other members of the buying group based on his or her expertise.

The *buyer* has formal authority to select the supplier and to arrange terms of purchase and also has a role in identifying and evaluating alternative vendors. At times, the buyer's authority may be restricted as when engineering establishes product specifications that only certain vendors can fill. The buyer is usually the purchasing agent. The ultimate *user* of the product identifies product needs, helps establish product specifications, and evaluates the product once it is used.

These roles are not always firmly defined by the buying group and may vary depending on whether a product or a vendor is being selected. For example, the engineer is likely to be the gatekeeper for product information, whereas the purchasing agent usually serves as gatekeeper for vendor information. Engineers exert influence regarding technical specifications, purchasing agents regarding cost and delivery criteria.

CONFLICT IN THE BUYING CENTER

In the process of group decision making, conflicts are likely to arise between members of a buying center. For example, engineers are interested in product specifications and are more likely to sacrifice quick delivery or a cheaper price to get the materials they want. Production managers are most interested in keeping the factory running smoothly and avoiding delays. Like engineers, they will emphasize quality products, but they also emphasize on-time delivery. Purchasing agents are most interested in getting good products at the lowest cost, with adequate delivery and service. They are more focused on good vendor relations, whereas engineers and production managers are more concerned with product specifications. Frequently, engineers and production managers view the purchasing department as a service function operating to fill their needs, while purchasing agents see themselves as having independent authority to select vendors and negotiate terms of sale.

Usually, these differences in opinion are resolved when the buying center collects information about a product or vendor and reaches a joint decision. In the example cited above, the information systems manager at Citicorp felt that Digital Equipment had the capability to provide the services necessary to install and maintain an on-line branch information system, but the purchasing manager felt that IBM was better able to perform these functions. As additional information was collected, members of the buying center decided on Digital Equipment, and the purchasing manager was persuaded to go along.

At times, however, conflict among members of a buying center can be intense, particularly if there is mistrust among groups in the organization. Consider the following statements by a purchasing agent and a production manager:[14]

> Purchasing Agent: The company doesn't realize that we are an important contributor to profits and not merely a service-providing mechanism for other departments.
>
> Production Manager: Those people in purchasing are trying to build their own little empire without regard for our needs. It's about time they were put in their place.

In such cases, the only option might be to ask top management to step in and resolve the conflict.

PRODUCT AND VENDOR SELECTION

A new-buy or modified-rebuy situation involves two interrelated decisions: which product to purchase and which vendor to supply the product. Figure 9.1 suggests that the product decision should be made first and then vendors selected to fill predetermined product specifications. The decision process for product and vendor selection will differ in several respects: First, buyers will use different criteria in selecting products and vendors; second, they will use different sources of information in evaluating each; third, the influence of members of a buying center will differ when product and vendor decisions are made.

SELECTION CRITERIA

Quality and performance are likely to be the most important criteria in choosing a product, with technical specifications dominating. Suppliers are most likely to be chosen based on price, service, delivery, and dependability (see Table 9.3).[15]

An important factor in vendor selection is potential risk. Selecting the wrong vendor could mean product failure, missed delivery dates, or poor service. Organizational buyers use several strategies to reduce these risks. One is to buy from proven vendors on an approved vendor list. A second strategy to reduce risk is multiple sourcing. **Multiple sourcing** *is buying from several vendors so that the risk is spread among them.*[16] A third strategy is simply to select the vendor that offers the lowest price so as to minimize the potential for financial loss.

None of these strategies completely eliminates the risk of poor vendor selection. Using the same vendor from an approved list can mean missed opportunities to get better prices or performance elsewhere. A few bad performers in the selected group will cause multiple sourcing to fail, and buying based on price leaves one open to possible product or service failure.

SOURCES OF INFORMATION

Buyers turn to different sources of information depending on whether they are selecting a product or a vendor. As mentioned, technical information is likely to be most important in product selection. Such information is obtained from technical journals, trade magazines, customer catalogs, trade shows, and government publications.

For information on vendor capabilities, the most important sources are the vendor's salespeople and past performance. The salesperson can describe the vendor's product offerings, pricing structure, and service and delivery capabilities. If the vendor has been used over time, the buyer's purchasing agent can track vendor performance on product reliability, delivery, and service.

The vendor's advertising and sales literature can provide additional information. So can more-objective sources such as trade and government publications. A key source of information that is sometimes overlooked in both product and vendor selection is word-of-mouth communication from colleagues both inside and outside the company. Studies of both product and vendor choice have found that such sources are particularly important in the later stages of complex decision making, when the buyer is close to making a decision,[17] and also when the purchase involves a high degree of risk.[18]

Figure 9.4 categorizes information on products and vendors on two dimensions. The first is personal sources (salespeople, colleagues, friends) versus impersonal sources (advertising, literature, and data). The second dimension is commercial (marketing) sources versus noncommercial sources (trade associations and government agencies). As with consumer behavior, personal sources are a more important influence on buyers than impersonal sources. In organizational buying, however, personal commercial sources (the salesperson) are much more important, whereas in consumer buying, personal noncommercial sources (friends and relatives) are likely to dominate.

TABLE 9.3

Criteria Used for Product and Vendor Selection

PRODUCT CRITERIA	VENDOR CRITERIA
Overall quality	Overall reputation
Quality of parts	Financing terms
Features conform to buyer's specifications	Flexibility in adjusting to buyer's needs
Durability	Technical services
Compatibility with present equipment	Confidence in salespeople
Speed of obsolescence	Convenience in placing order
Economy	Price
Value	Training offered by vendor
Flexibility to accommodate future growth	Reliability of delivery
Product reliability	Ease of maintenance
Ease of use	Post-purchase service
Training time required	

Sources: Donald R. Lehmann and John O'Shaughessy, "Difference in Attribute Importance for Different Industrial Products," *Journal of Marketing 38* (April 1974), 38; and John I. Coppett and William A. Staples, "Product Profile Analysis: A Tool for Industrial Selling," *Industrial Marketing Management 9* (1980), 208.

FIGURE 9.4

Sources of Information for Organizational Buyers

	Commercial	Noncommercial
Personal	Salespeople	Colleagues Friends Consultants
Impersonal	Advertising Sales Promotions Trade Shows Catalogs	Trade Association Literature Government Data Technical Journals

RELATIVE INFLUENCE IN THE ORGANIZATION

Some areas in the organization exert more influence on product selection, others on vendor selection. Generally, engineers have more influence on product selection, particularly for new buys and modified rebuys. They have the technical expertise and are more likely to influence setting product specifications.

ETHICAL AND ENVIRONMENTAL ISSUES IN MARKETING

Influencing the Organizational Buyer: When Does It Become Bribery?

Organizational buyers wield a significant amount of influence in vendor selection, especially in new-buy situations. Vendors will naturally try to influence buyers to choose the vendor's firm. It is clearly acceptable to try to influence the buyer based on the characteristics of the seller's product, price, reliable service, or prompt delivery. Occasionally, vendors will try to "grease the wheels" in doing business by taking the buyer out for lunch, giving small promotional souvenirs, or sending a holiday gift. But the vendor could also offer a buyer a free trip to Acapulco if the vendor's firm is awarded a contract. When such actions influence the buyer to select the vendor, even if the vendor's offer is not the best deal for the buyer's firm, then the vendor's actions could be considered bribery.

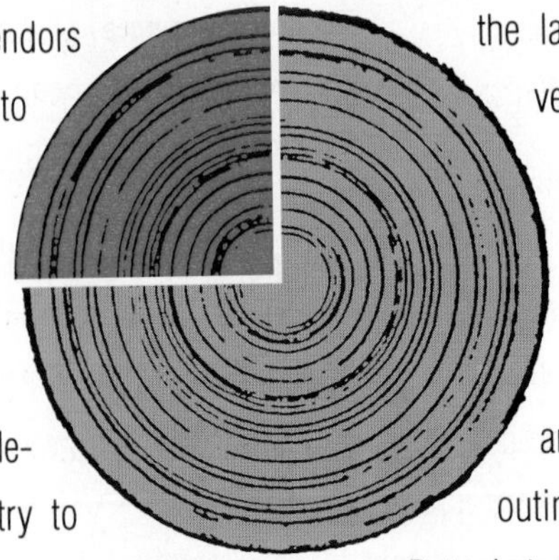

What constitutes ethical behavior on the part of buyers and sellers in the negotiating process is relative and depends largely on the perceptions of the parties. A recent survey of the ethics of purchasing agents in the United States found that most considered it acceptable to be taken out to lunch or dinner and to be offered small advertising souvenirs. But the large majority found that gifts from vendors, such as clothing or appliances, offers of vacation trips, and loans of money constituted unacceptable behavior that is unethical. Grey areas included gifts of food and liquor, holiday gifts, and golf outings.

But what about the other side of the coin, the organizational buyer using his or her power to encourage a bribe? Such actions are rare in the United States, but bribing buyers to obtain lucrative contracts is often an accepted mode of behavior for doing business abroad. The most famous example occurred in the late 1800s when Charles M. Schwab, head of Bethlehem Steel, presented a $200,000 diamond and pearl necklace to the mistress of Czar Alexander's nephew. Not coincidentally, Bethlehem Steel won the contract to supply the rails for the Trans-Siberian railroad soon after.

The issue of bribing foreign buyers as an accepted form of business came to a head in the mid-

There is a danger, however, that engineers may set product specifications that are too technologically oriented. They tend to want better designs and more features than their organization may need. For example, if the engineering group at Hampden Ltd. develops specifications for a large fan blower for an automobile assembly line, it may decide to buy finely tempered steel for quieter operation,

ETHICAL AND ENVIRONMENTAL ISSUES IN MARKETING

1970s when it was discovered that Lockheed Aircraft paid millions of dollars to Japanese government officials to get lucrative airline contracts. One study found that from 1970 to 1977, almost $412 million in questionable payments were made by U.S. companies to foreign buyers. As a result, in 1977 Congress passed the Foreign Corrupt Practices Act making it illegal for American companies to bribe foreign buyers. One Minnesota-based company was fined close to $1 million in 1989 under the act for paying bribes to officials in the Republic of Niger to retain aircraft service contracts.

Many international marketers argue that restrictions against paying bribes hinder their ability to compete abroad, because similar restrictions do not apply to sellers from most other countries. They say the United States should not apply its moral principles to other cultures where bribery is prevalent and accepted. But other executives argue that bribery ultimately corrupts the buyer–seller relationship and undermines legitimate negotiations. If bribes are accepted, these executives say, they may encourage loose moral standards among both buyers and sellers and lead to low employee morale. If a company loses a contract because it did not offer a bribe, so be it; the relationship was not worth fostering.

Ethical standards in the United States generally condemn bribes. But behavior abroad is more variable. Most large companies have official standards of business conduct that are adhered to in various degrees. Ultimately, the behavior of the organizational buyer and seller will be governed by two factors: their own personal standards and those of their firm.

Question: Should U.S. companies be allowed to pay bribes to foreign buyers if that is a prevalent practice in the country? Support your position.

Sources: Laura B. Forker and Robert L. Janson, "Ethical Practices in Purchasing," *Journal of Purchasing and Materials Management* (Winter 1990),19–26; Deon Nel, Leyland Pitt, and Richard Watson, "Business Ethics: Defining the Twilight Zone," *Journal of Business Ethics 8* (October 1989), 781 –791; Michael R. Czinkota and Ilka A. Ronkainen, *International Marketing* (Chicago: The Dryden Press, 1990), 111–113; and Philip R. Cateora, *International Marketing* (Homewood, IL, Richard D. Irwin, Inc., 1983), 179.

whereas the plant manager may be willing to pay less for a noisier fan system, because noise is not a critical factor on the assembly line.

When it comes to vendor selection, the purchasing agent generally has the most say. Purchasing agents are responsible for maintaining relations with vendors on an ongoing basis and know more about delivery and service capabilities. In a straight-rebuy situation, where product choice is predetermined, the purchasing agent usually acts alone. In a new-buy situation, the product specifications set by engineering may narrow the choice to a few vendors, at which point purchasing steps in for the final decision.

INFLUENCES ON ORGANIZATIONAL BUYERS

Throughout the decision-making process, organizational buyers respond to the influences shown in Figure 9.1. We consider marketing stimuli (that is, the strategies business-to-business marketers use to influence organizational buyers) in the next section. Here, we describe the individual buyer's psychological set, the characteristics of the buyer's organization, the marketing environment, and cross-cultural influences.

INDIVIDUAL BUYER INFLUENCES

Like consumers, organizational buyers are influenced by their psychological set and characteristics in deciding on vendors and products. The only major difference is that consumers purchase according to individual needs and preferences, whereas organizational buyers attempt to purchase to maximize organizational profits.

Organizational buyers go into purchasing situations with prior notions and predispositions about products and suppliers. The importance of this psychological set was apparent in the Citicorp example where the purchasing agent preferred IBM. Because he placed the most emphasis on service, delivery, and installation, and because he had a positive perception of IBM's capabilities in that regard, he naturally had a positive attitude toward the company.

The characteristics of organizational buyers also affect their approaches to decision making and their choice of products and suppliers. One early study of the decision-making process for buying computers found that less-educated buyers who were more closed minded were less likely to purchase computers for their company.[19] Another study found that younger and better-educated buyers were more likely to use a variety of information sources in evaluating products and suppliers.[20]

The purchasing agent in the Citicorp example was older and more risk averse than the other members of the buying center. As a result, he did not seek new vendors. His past relationship with IBM led him to favor IBM products.

ORGANIZATIONAL CHARACTERISTICS

The organizational characteristics of the buyer's firm will influence his or her actions. Studies have shown that the firms most likely to adopt new products are larger and are in industries with rapid technological change.[21] Organizational buyers in such firms are more likely to experience new-buy situations and to make group decisions in a buying center.

The structure of the organization is important, too. Highly centralized, bureaucratic organizations are more likely to adopt routine purchasing procedures and are less likely to consider new products or vendors. Firms with a freer and more open decision-making style are more likely to encourage risk taking. One study found that such firms are more open to information and facilitate the flow of information into the firm.[22] Such a flow is likely to encourage consideration of new products and vendors.

ENVIRONMENTAL INFLUENCES

The environmental factors that most influence organizational buyers are (1) competitive intensity, (2) technological advances in the buyer's industry, (3) the state of the economy, and (4) legal and regulatory factors. Another important component of the environment is the availability of the materials being purchased. In the 1970s, companies became increasingly aware of their vulnerability to shortages in fuel, precious metals, and other raw materials. As a result, many began signing longer-term contracts with their suppliers.

Another characteristic of the environment facing the organizational buyer is that the demand for industrial products is derived. **Derived demand** *is demand for a product that depends on the demand of another product.* Hampden Ltd. buys steel plate according to the demand for blowers and other air- and gas-handling systems. These systems are used in factories that make autos, appliances, and other consumer products. Therefore, the demand for steel plate, blowers, and air- or gas-handling systems is derived from the demand for consumer goods such as autos and appliances.

When demand for a product is derived, it fluctuates more. Any cutback on purchases of the final product has a ripple effect throughout related industries. As a result, organizational buyers must be careful not to overbuy, or they may find themselves with excess inventory when a decrease in demand for consumer goods decreases the demand for industrial goods.

CROSS-CULTURAL INFLUENCES

Organizational buyers are likely to react differently to the buyer–seller relationship based on the norms and customs of their country. Nowhere is this more apparent than in differences between Japanese and American bargaining styles in buyer–seller negotiations. The Japanese value harmony, consensus, and loyalty to the group. Americans value individuality and directness.

In the Japanese framework, negotiating decisions are frequently formalities meant to ratify decisions previously made by the group so as to preserve harmony. Further, the Japanese tradition is to avoid a direct "no" at all costs in negotiations. For Americans, negotiations are seen as a forum for give and take for which Japanese business people may not be prepared.

Consider the following outcome that resulted because American negotiators were not sufficiently aware of Japanese business customs and traditions:

> The Japanese executive sucks in air through his teeth and exclaims "That will be very difficult." What he really means is just plain "no." But the Japanese consider an absolute "no" to be offensive and usually seek a euphemistic term. That's why in Japan the "difficult" really may be impossible. The American on the other side of the negotiating table knows none of this and presses ahead to resolve the "difficulty." The Japanese finds this inexplicable persistence to be abnormally pushy. The atmosphere deteriorates and, sure enough, the big deal falls through."[23]

Differing norms and customs may affect the outcome of negotiations in other countries as well. Consider the following episode that occurred between an American and an Arab negotiating team:

> American executives negotiating a contract in the Middle East found that there wasn't time to have their revised negotiating proposal typed, submitted a hand-written version, and thought nothing of it. But the Arabs

GLOBAL MARKETING STRATEGIES

IBM's Disadvantage in Japan: Coming Up Against the "Keiretsu" System

IBM started selling computers in Japan when they were first commercially developed in the mid 1950s. The company started with a virtual monopoly of the computer industry. It is now a poor third behind NEC and Fujitsu.

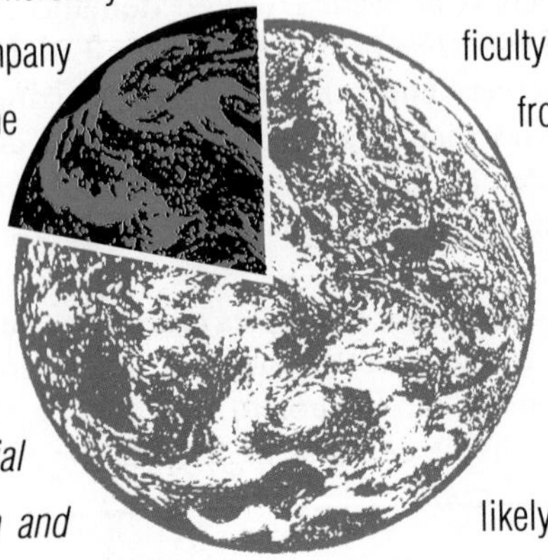

Why? Because of the *Keiretsu* system. ***Keiretsu*** *is a network of Japanese companies that have partial ownership in each other, buy from and sell to each other, share technology, and cooperate to fend off foreign competition.* There are six *Keiretsu* in Japan that represent 30 percent of that country's total corporate assets. A *Keiretsu* is made up primarily of companies in different industries, although there are some competitors in the same *Keiretsu.* At the center of each *Keiretsu* is a large bank that provides capital to its members for R&D expenditures and other activities. NEC, the largest Japanese computer maker, belongs to the Sumitomo *Keiretsu,* named after the Sumitomo bank. The ten largest banks in the world are part of Japan's *Keiretsu* system.

The *Keiretsu* system has established a protective barrier around Japanese companies to exclude foreign competition. The fact that they practice reciprocity, that is, buy from and sell to each other, means that a foreign company like IBM will have difficulty approaching organizational buyers from a *Keiretsu* company. Any company in the Sumitomo *Keiretsu* will buy only NEC computers. Thus, IBM is shut out from a significant portion of Japanese industry.

Unlike the United States, which is likely to view a *Keiretsu* as a potential violation of antitrust laws, the Japanese government fosters the *Keiretsu* system. In the 1950s, the Japanese Ministry of International Trade and Industry (MITI) pressured IBM to give Japanese companies access to basic patents in exchange for granting the company permission to produce in Japan. In a further effort to get Japanese computer makers off the ground, MITI sunk $6 billion of government money into the Japanese computer industry for research and development and new equipment. As a result, market share of foreign-made computers (primarily IBM) went from 93 percent in 1958 to about 35 percent today.

The *Keiretsu* system is well-suited to the Japanese preference for harmony and consensus, because it relies heavily on cooperation between

GLOBAL MARKETING STRATEGIES

participants. Further, it allows Japanese companies to commit to long-term research and development, because funding from *Keiretsu* partners is generally assured. This is one of the basic reasons for Japan's growing technological dominance over the United States.

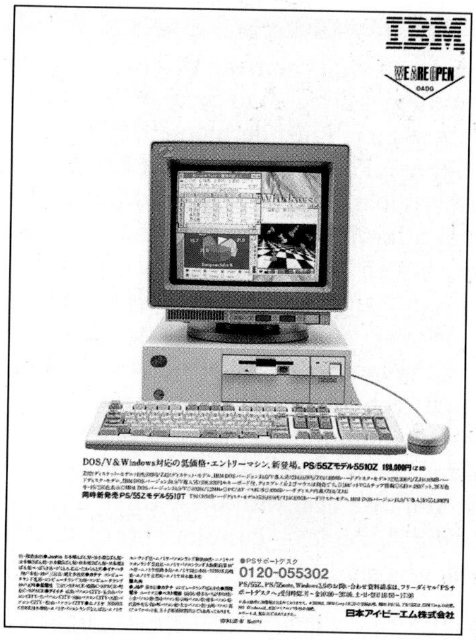

IBM has decided not to battle the *Keiretsu* system but to emulate it. It is cooperating with Japanese companies to sell its machines. For example, it entered into an agreement with Ricoh, Japan's largest manufacturer of copy machines, to sell IBM computers. It is also entering into joint ventures with Japanese companies—for example, an agreement with Matsushita Electric to develop personal computers and manufacture workstations. It is also involved with Mitsubishi Bank to develop and market on-line banking systems. If this sounds like IBM is trying to establish its own *Keiretsu,* it is. The company has come to the realization that the best way to do business in Japan is to establish long-term cooperative ventures that will permit it entry into Japanese companies.

IBM's ultimate motive in these joint ventures is not just to develop and manufacture computers in Japan, but to gain access to the Japanese organizational buyer to help it sell computers by establishing itself as a cooperative company in the *Keiretsu* mold. Who knows? IBM may become the first foreign *Keiretsu* in Japanese history.

Questions: Why is IBM at a competitive disadvantage in selling its computers in Japan? How has the company reacted?

Sources: Charles H. Ferguson, "Computers and the Coming of the U.S. Keiretsu," *Harvard Business Review 68* (July–August 1990), 55–57 and 60–68; Marie Anchordoguy, "A Brief History of Japan's Keiretsu," *Harvard Business Review 68* (July–August 1990), 58–59; "Losing the High-Tech Lead," *InfoWorld*, September 23, 1991, 40–44; and "IBM Fights Back," *Datamation*, January 1, 1988, 68–2 to 68–5.

across the bargaining table considered the gesture so bizarre that they began to analyze it intensely, seeking messages. Some concluded the Americans were trying to imply that they considered the whole contract unimportant.[24]

STRATEGIC APPLICATIONS OF ORGANIZATIONAL BUYER BEHAVIOR

Perhaps the most important set of influences on organizational buyers are the marketing strategies directed to them by business-to-business marketers. Business-to-business marketers must develop effective strategies to meet the needs of organizational buyers. The most important component of the marketing mix in business-to-business marketing is personal selling. The salesperson is the main channel for communicating information about product offerings and vendor capabilities. Advertising, though important, plays a supportive role by paving the way for the salesperson rather than a dominant role by influencing purchases.

Before marketing strategies can be developed, prospects for sales must be identified. Today, the average cost of a sales call on a prospective customer is over $300. In some high-technology industries requiring careful preparation and a more detailed presentation, the cost rises to more than $1,000. With costs like these, it is essential to screen companies and carefully identify prospective customers.

In this section, we deal with these three major components of business-to-business marketing strategies—customer prospect identification, personal selling, and supportive advertising strategies.

PROSPECT IDENTIFICATION

Traditionally, business marketers have pinpointed customers for sales calls by relying on industry classifications. The government has established a detailed system of identifying organizations called the *Standard Industrial Classification (SIC)*. Each class of business in the United States is given an SIC code. For example, the code for companies producing blowers and exhaust fans, like Hampden, is 3564. A company specializing in selling steel plate to manufacturers of air blowers can consult the SIC codes and find that there are 337 such plants in the United States. This information may be sufficient for the seller to identify its prospects.

But the steel plate company may also want to sell to other industry groups such as companies making machine tools and accessories. Now its prospect list grows to over two thousand prospects. To concentrate its sales effort, it therefore decides to sell its products only in one region of the country, the Western states. Further, it might decide it is uneconomical to call on firms with net sales of less than $20 million. So it now wants to identify prospects by size and location.

The government does not have data on the organizational characteristics of individual businesses. Dun & Bradstreet (D&B), the information conglomerate, has such data on most companies in the United States, based on its file of companies' credit ratings. The steel plate company decides to use the D&B database to identify air blower and machine tool companies in the West with sales of over $20 million. As a result, it pares its prospect list from 2,000 companies to 280. The company's 20-person sales force can directly contact this prospect group.

EXHIBIT 9.2

Targeting Prospects

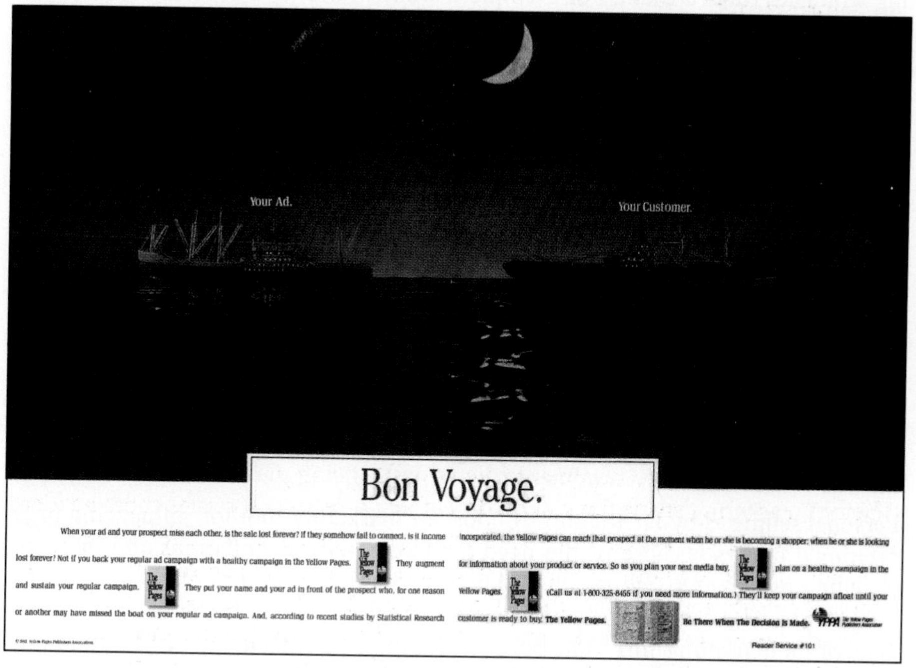

IDENTIFYING PURCHASE INFLUENCERS

The procedure for prospecting just described identifies an organization. But it does not identify those with purchasing influence within the organization. Usually, the first person to contact is the purchasing agent, who then directs the seller to those with purchase influence, such as a design engineer or production manager.

But some organizations are a labyrinth of divisions, customer groups, and business units. If a certain individual is more likely to have purchase influence for particular types of products, the job of prospecting is much easier. Advertising can be used to introduce a company's product line, and salespeople can follow up by contacting a specified individual within a company. The right of Exhibit 9.2 shows an ad for *PC World*, a magazine for managers who buy PC hardware. The ad is directed toward sellers of such equipment and points out that the magazine reaches key prospective buyers.

The ad on the left of Exhibit 9.2 provides an alternative to prospecting: using advertising to encourage prospects to call the company. *The Yellow Pages* is a good vehicle for such advertising by business-to-business marketers since, as the ad implies, any prospect who calls can be turned into a buyer. Such advertising reduces the need to use salespeople to seek out individuals with purchase influence in the buying organization.

SEGMENTING PROSPECTS

Business marketers identify customers with unmet needs and then direct marketing strategies toward them. For example, a study of over 300 organizational buyers responsible for buying computers identified four segments based on the computer needs of each company.[25] Segment 1 emphasized price and delivery in buying computers, segment 2 favored the supplier's visibility among the company's top management, segment 3 preferred performance factors such as ease of operation and amount of training required, and segment 4—which was more systems oriented—emphasized the software support and broad line of products that would facilitate establishing systems networks.

This information allowed computer marketers to pinpoint prospects. For example, before IBM's slide, segment 2 would have been its strongest prospect because of the company's leadership in the industry and visibility among top management. But the increasing emphasis on systems solutions makes segment 4 more important.

SALES STRATEGIES

Personal selling is by far the most important marketing tool for influencing organizational buyers because of the need for face-to-face negotiations and influence in selling most industrial products. The overriding importance of personal selling means that a business-to-business marketer's sales strategy is the central component of its marketing mix. The single most important factor in IBM's attempted turnaround in 1987 was its shift in strategy from selling individual products to selling systems solutions. Salespeople had to become intimately familiar with their customers' needs and organization to sell systems solutions.

This shift in emphasis from a product to a systems orientation in selling is reflected in Exhibit 9.3, an ad for Brock Control Systems. Brock helps business-to-business marketers design systems to better analyze and evaluate their sales efforts, for example, to determine how to best allocate a salesperson's time to prospects. Such scientific analysis of sales effort is just one more indication of the greater sophistication of business-to-business marketers in selling to organizational buyers.

A central part of a more effective sales strategy is the **National Account Marketing (NAM)** *concept in which a team of salespeople is responsible for satisfying the needs of a single organization.* The NAM concept is becoming more widely accepted among business-to-business marketers selling to large accounts. A NAM team coordinating a seller's marketing effort is better able to determine customers' needs and also to overcome any obstacles or misunderstandings between buyer and seller. One study confirmed that organizational buyers prefer to deal with a team from a supplier rather than separate salespeople offering different lines from the same company.[26]

Measurex, a California-based seller of computerized manufacturing control systems, has implemented the NAM concept very successfully, making the transition from being product to systems oriented in the interest of meeting the needs of its organizational buyers. The heart of Measurex's strategy was to make salespeople more aware of customer needs and operations. Its focus on personal selling is reflected in an average field cost for each of its salespeople of over $250,000 a year. The average cost of a sales call is $1,000.[27]

EXHIBIT 9.3

Developing More-Effective Sales Approaches for Business-to-Business Marketers

Business marketers are also beginning to use **telemarketing**, *that is, contacting prospects by phone*, on a widespread basis to supplement the efforts of their salespeople. Telephone selling is becoming a cost-efficient means of reaching smaller accounts or those hard to reach by salespeople. Trained company representatives can provide smaller customers with product information, answer questions, and send them more-detailed information by mail.

ADVERTISING STRATEGIES

Advertising plays a supportive role in business-to-business marketing by paving the way for the salesperson to call on the organizational buyer. Advertising has two main roles: first, to communicate product features; second, to communicate vendor capabilities. These two roles reflect the two main decision areas of the organizational buyer—making product and vendor decisions.

The ad for NEC in Exhibit 9.4 demonstrates the first of these roles—to communicate product features. The ad cites key features of NEC's cellular phone for business customers such as lighter weight, more talk time, and digital clock features.

EXHIBIT 9.4

Advertising Product Features to Organizational Buyers

Introducing a somewhat lighter portable phone.
At 15.3 ounces light, 2.3 inches narrow, 7.2 inches short and a mere inch thin, the NEC Portable Phone promises to be a success story of incredible proportions. It can go from a car to a boat to a pocket in seconds. Its high-performance slim-packaged battery (with low battery indicator) provides 80 minutes of talk time or 18 hours of standby time. Plus escalating call alert, digital clock and automatic wake-up features. Interested in picking up your profits? Pick up the phone. For more information, call 1-800-643-8820.
NEC
C&C

The second role of advertising in business-to-business marketing is to communicate the vendor's capabilities. This is illustrated in the ad for INCO, formerly International Nickel, in Exhibit 9.5. The ad cites INCO's capabilities in stainless steel applications, its metallurgic ingenuity, and its reliability. The ad is designed to increase awareness of the company's capabilities and its name change.

SUMMARY

1. **What are the similarities and differences between organizational buyer behavior and consumer behavior?**
   The same types of factors that influence consumers influence organizational buyers, namely, the buyer's mind set, characteristics, and environment. Like consumers, organizational buyers are governed by their needs, attitudes, and perceptions of product offerings. The main differences between organizational buyers and consumers are a function of the technical complexity of business

EXHIBIT 9.5

Advertising the Capabilities of Business-to-Business Marketers

WE'VE BEEN ON THE TIP OF YOUR TONGUE
FOR OVER 75 YEARS. Not to put words in your mouth, but you probably already know us as the International Nickel Company. Today, it's simply Inco. And while our name isn't on all that we make, it's surprising how much we're in.
Over 60 per cent of total nickel production goes to make stainless steel stainless. And from its initial use in cutlery, our metallurgic ingenuity has put it to work.
For instance, stainless steel's endless applications in food processing equipment—up to and including the kitchen sink. Not to mention its widespread use in architecture, aerospace and under-sea technology.
This same kind of innovative thinking has kept us on the leading edge, to the point where we now hold one-third of the world nickel market. And with fixed-volume arrangements accounting for a large portion of our sales, we can effectively plan for the years ahead. You have our word on it.
INCO
STRONGER FOR OUR EXPERIENCE
For more information, write N.K. Barnes, Director, Investor Relations, Inco Limited, One New York Plaza, N.Y., 10004.

products, which leads to more decisions being made on a group basis through buying centers. Organizational buyers are also more likely to develop product specifications to fill their needs and to negotiate the fulfillment of these specifications at particular prices with sellers.

2. **What types of decisions do organizational buyers make?**
   Organizational buyers make new-buy, modified-rebuy, and straight-rebuy decisions. A new buy can be characterized as complex decision making. It requires extensive information search on product specifications and vendor capabilities,

careful consideration of a number of alternative vendors, and a process of group decision making. Generally, new-buy decisions are made by a buying center.

A modified rebuy is a recurring decision that is not routine. It can be characterized as limited decision making. It might involve reevaluating a straight rebuy or repurchasing a new product. Some information search is required, but it is not extensive, and brand evaluation is limited to a few vendors.

A straight rebuy is a recurring decision that can be handled on a routine basis. It parallels habit in consumer decision making. Little or no information search is required, and a vendor is chosen from an approved list.

3. **What is the role of group decision making in organizational buyer behavior?**
Group decisions are likely in organizational buying because products are complex and decisions risky, requiring the collective expertise of several individuals organized into a buying center. Members of a buying center serve a number of roles. The gatekeeper controls the flow of information into the group, the influencer sways other members, the user evaluates product needs and assesses the product's performance, and the buyer has formal authority to select a supplier and arrange terms of purchase.
4. **What are the individual and environmental influences on organizational buyers?**
Organizational buyers are influenced by their psychological set—their needs, perceptions of vendors, and attitudes toward these vendors—and their demographic characteristics. The nature of the buyer's organization also influences organizational buyers. For example, highly centralized, bureaucratic organizations are likely to encourage routine purchasing procedures and to discourage the flow of new information or consideration of product alternatives. The broader business environment also influences buyers through factors such as technological change, the degree of competitive intensity in the buyer's industry, the state of the economy, and government laws and regulations.
5. **What strategies do business-to-business marketers use to influence organizational buyers?**
Business-to-business marketers must first identify prospects based on factors such as industry grouping, size, and location. Then they must develop sales and advertising strategies to meet the needs of these prospects. Personal selling is the most important component of the business-to-business marketing plan. Advertising strategy is used to pave the way for the salesperson and has three objectives: to advertise product features, to advertise solutions to buyers' problems, and to advertise vendor capabilities.

KEY TERMS

Organizational buyers (p. 288)
Business-to-business marketers (p. 288)
Industrial buyers (p. 289)
Institutional buyers (p. 290)
Government agencies (p. 290)
Resellers (p. 290)
Buying center (p. 291)
Product specifications (p. 291)
Straight rebuy (p. 293)
Approved vendor list (p. 293)
Modified rebuy (p. 293)
New buy (p. 294)
Vendor loyalty (p. 298)
Inertia (p. 298)
Reciprocity (p. 298)
Gatekeeper (p. 298)
Multiple sourcing (p. 300)
Derived demand (p. 305)
***Keiretsu* (p. 306)**
National account marketing (NAM) (p. 310)
Telemarketing (p. 311)

QUESTIONS

1. What actions did IBM take in 1986 and in 1991 to reverse its slide in sales? What do these actions have to do with organizational buyer behavior?
2. What are the differences among industrial buyers, institutional buyers, and resellers?
3. What are the differences between organizational buying behavior and consumer behavior? What are the strategic implications of these differences for business-to-business marketers?
4. What are the similarities between the model of organizational buyer behavior in Figure 9.1 and the model of consumer behavior in Figure 8.1? What are the differences? What are the strategic implications of these differences in marketing to consumers versus organizational buyers?
5. Consider the three types of decisions in Table 9.2—new buy, modified rebuy, and straight rebuy. Which decision process is most likely to apply to each of the following categories and why?
   a. Purchase of a pollution control system for a chemical company's processing plants
   b. Purchase of office supplies for a bank's branch offices
   c. Purchase of various grades of aluminum by a manufacturer of kitchen utensils
   d. Purchase by an airline company of a computerized scheduling and booking system
6. Under what circumstances might a company switch from a new buy to a modified rebuy in making a decision to purchase industrial generators? Under what circumstances might the company switch from a straight rebuy to a modified rebuy in making a decision to buy metal fasteners?
7. A purchasing agent for a large industrial company tends to buy products from the same vendors because of long-established relationships with the salespeople from these companies. The purchasing agent is confident about the vendor's products and service reliability.
   a. How is this vendor loyalty an advantage to the buyer?
   b. What are the potential risks?
8. What strategies do organizational buyers use to reduce the risk of vendor selection? What are the problems with each of these strategies?
9. What are the similarities and differences in the roles of the family purchasing agent and the organizational purchasing agent?
10. A pharmaceutical company is considering converting its plants to reduce industrial emissions and limit pollution. What are likely to be the differences in criteria used to evaluate alternative vendors' proposals by the (a) purchasing, (b) engineering, and (c) production departments?
11. How do the characteristics of the buyer's organization and the buyer's environment influence product and vendor choice?
12. In what ways do American and Japanese negotiating styles differ? How can this affect buyer–seller negotiations?
13. What is the *Keiretsu* system? What is its purpose?
14. Why is personal selling the most important component of the business-to-business marketing mix?
15. What roles does advertising play in the business-to-business marketing mix? Cite examples.

QUESTIONS: YOU ARE THE DECISION MAKER

1. A product manager for Procter & Gamble is about to take a position as product manager for Westinghouse's factory automation systems division. When asked whether there might be a problem in this job transition, the product manager said:

   Marketing is marketing. The basic principles of trying to influence the buyer are pretty much the same. You advertise to try to influence and inform the buyer, and you price to create value for the buyer.

   In what ways is the product manager right and in what ways is the product manager wrong?

2. An organizational buyer responsible for purchasing petrochemicals used to manufacture plastics considered the difference between vendor loyalty and inertia and made the following comments:

   Any organizational buyer that buys from the same vendor based on inertia should be fired. When we buy petrochemicals, even on a straight rebuy to replenish stocks, we are always evaluating a supplier's performance. We would take a supplier off the approved list in a minute if we saw a decrease in quality or a failure to meet delivery dates. Just because a buyer feels comfortable with the same vendor is no reason to continue to deal with the company. We are supposed to maximize our company's profits, not to lie low and avoid making waves.

   An organizational buyer working for a producer of electrical cable takes a completely different view and said the following:

   There is a lot to be said for inertia. Why should I spend a lot of my time and effort comparing vendors for a standardized item like cable when I have two or three reliable suppliers who give me good prices and reasonable delivery dates? I can better spend my time for the company in other ways.

a. What are the reasons for these very different views of accepting inertia as a basis for vendor selection?
b. Do you agree with each buyer's views on the subject? Why or why not?
c. Would you fire an organizational buyer who is motivated to buy based on inertia?

3. One American executive, in commenting on Japan's *Keiretsu* system, says quite simply:

   Americans should establish their own Keiretsus. *This is the only way to compete effectively with Japanese companies. We have to beat the Japanese at their own game.*

   Do you agree with this statement? What are the difficulties of establishing the equivalent of *Keiretsus* in the United States?

4. A marketer of air-pollution control systems, when asked about the company's market segmentation strategies, said:

   We don't have any. Market segmentation is simply not relevant when you develop a specific system for one customer. Each customer is its own segment.

   Do you agree? Can a producer of air-pollution control systems segment the market, even though each system is customized? In what ways?

CHAPTER 10

Identifying and Targeting Market Segments

YOUR FOCUS IN CHAPTER 10

To learn:

- *The advantages of a strategy of market segmentation.*
- *Why there has been a recent trend toward market segmentation.*
- *How companies can identify market segments.*
- *What criteria marketers can use to decide which segments to target for marketing effort.*
- *The alternative strategies companies can use to segment markets.*

Levi Strauss—From Mass Marketing to Marketing Segmentation

Until recently, Levi Strauss successfully sold its jeans on a mass market basis. The leading jeans maker used one ad campaign with a basic message that Levis are for everyone.[1]

Then in the 1980s, it began to be apparent that jeans were no longer for everyone. Total sales of jeans took a slide, going from 516 million in 1981 to 400 million in 1988.[2] What happened? Baby boomers were no longer teenagers and were getting out of jeans. Worse, the company could not rely on teenagers to replace lost sales, because teens were a shrinking proportion of the population. In addition, older consumers had already switched from jeans to conservative slacks.

"Woman In Straw Hat"
Levi's
JEANS FOR WOMEN
Levi's® 512™ Slim Fit Jeans. Tight hip, slim thigh, narrow ankle.

What was the answer to Levi's problems? A strategy of *market segmentation,* designed to develop different lines for different age segments: one line to teenagers, another to baby boomers, and another to the mature market. It made sense, but baby boomers and mature adults were less likely to wear jeans. One solution to this problem was based on research that showed that the strength of the Levi name could be extended to slacks. Why not develop a line of slacks under the Levi name targeted to baby boomers and the mature market?

Levi's age-based segmentation strategy was initiated in 1987 when a group of Levi executives noticed a pair of baggy cotton slacks marketed by their Japanese subsidiary. With aging male baby boomers in mind, they brought the pants back to the United States and, with an $11 million advertising campaign, introduced them under the Dockers label. The brand was an immediate success because of Levi's positive image among male baby boomers and their desire for a dressier and more-comfortable alternative to jeans. By 1991, Dockers represented close to half a billion dollars in sales.[3]

But the company did not stop there. It realized that if it was really going to hedge against a decline in the sales of jeans, it would have to go after the mature market as well. Levi already had a line called Action slacks for males over 50, but the company never gave the line much attention because of its mass-market focus on jeans. By 1987, that focus began to change. Levi developed a national advertising campaign for Action slacks and made sure to differentiate them from Dockers by making them more conservative, with a looser cut.

In the process of targeting baby boomers and mature males, Levi did not forget that its core area of business was still the $1.5 billion jean market, and its core target segment was still teenagers. As a result, it developed the 501 line of "button-fly" jeans specifically targeted to males 14 to 24 years old and introduced the line with documentary-style advertising showing youths in various parts of the country doing things characteristic of that region, such as boating in a Louisiana bayou. Continuing with the creative tone, the company introduced a campaign in 1991 with Spike Lee as a voice-over for a button-fly jeans report featuring strange things that happened to teens when wearing 501 jeans. Teens responded enthusiastically to Spike Lee because they were able to identify who was behind the voice.[4]

To make sure that it was not limiting jeans just to teenagers: Levi introduced the 505 jeans line, with a fuller cut positioned to baby boomers; another line positioned to the 8-14 set, with a "Wild Creatures" ad campaign showing kids doing wild things in jeans like flipping on a skate board; and a third line of jeans targeted to female baby boomers.[5]

The female line—introduced in 1988 with a $12 million advertising campaign—was a departure for Levi, because its mass-market approach always relied on a general male-oriented positioning for jeans, with purchases by females regarded as an extra bonus. A segmentation strategy dictated a specific positioning so as to better design jeans for the female figure. As a result, Levi advertises the jeans, called its 900 line, as "cut, styled, and sized for women."

Levi's segmentation strategy is not without risk. By targeting demographic groups across the age spectrum, Levi is substantially increasing its marketing costs. It must now develop separate advertising campaigns to each segment as opposed to one national campaign across all segments. Its product development and distribution costs are also substantially higher. Further, Levi risks alienating one demographic group in advertising to another. For instance, when Levi spent $2 million to advertise Dockers in the 1991 Super Bowl game, a sizeable part of the market were teenagers.[6] As Levi's marketing manager says, "We have to make sure our ads for men don't turn off our teenage audience, and vice versa."[7]

But the benefits of Levi's segmentation strategy far outweigh the risks. Levi can now retain customers from 8 to 80 years old as they move from the kids line to 501 jeans, to the 505 line, to Dockers, and to Action slacks. Further, the company is now better meeting the needs of half the population—women. As a result, segmentation is creating more revenues than costs. By 1991, Levi had reversed its sales slide and increased sales by 40 percent over 1988. In the international market (representing 39 percent of Levi's revenue), sales went up by 30 percent.[8]

Levi is now a more profitable company because it is targeting key demographic segments.

PURPOSE OF MARKET SEGMENTATION

Market segmentation *is a strategy of dividing a market into groups of customers with similar needs and meeting those needs with marketing efforts.* It is the opposite of mass marketing, in which a company offers one basic product without catering to different customer needs and characteristics. Today, almost all companies follow a strategy of market segmentation to some degree.

Directing marketing efforts to meet the needs of market segments usually involves developing a new product or targeting an existing product. Dockers was a new product positioned to meet the baby boomer's need for a dressier and more-comfortable substitute for jeans. Levi also positioned its existing jeans to various demographic segments by providing variations such as a fuller cut for baby boomers and a better fit for women. In each case, a segment of consumers had similar needs, and the company's marketing effort was directed toward that segment.

Most of the examples of market segmentation in this chapter cite consumer goods companies. As we will see, industrial firms have lagged behind in segmenting their markets. But business-to-business marketers are beginning to recognize the benefits of a segmented approach, and applications in the industrial sector are increasing.

WHY SEGMENT MARKETS?

A strategy of market segmentation is a reasonable, marketing-oriented approach to identifying and satisfying consumer needs. But does it lead to greater profitability? Someone could reasonably argue that mass marketing is more profitable since a company can enjoy economies of scale in both production and marketing. One advertising campaign is bound to be cheaper than fragmented campaigns geared to various market segments, and one production run for a homogeneous product is much less expensive than separate runs for different products.

Despite its higher costs, the profits generated from targeting a number of segments are likely to be higher than the profits from selling one product to a mass market. Why? First, segmentation allows marketers to better focus on customer needs. If markets are segmented, the marketer can develop specific products, promotional strategies, distribution efforts, and prices for each segment. A mass-market approach does not allow for such variations. As Henry Ford once said when asked whether he was going to offer consumers different colors for the Model T car, "They can have any color they want as long as it's black." Ford was following a classic mass-marketing strategy to achieve economies of scale and keep costs down so the Model T could be affordable. Such an approach is unlikely to succeed in today's marketplace. Consumers are unlikely to accept a lack of variation in most product offerings. Their needs have grown to be too varied.

A second advantage of segmentation is that it promotes new product ideas. The introduction of Dockers, Action Slacks, and the 505 and 900 lines of jeans was the result of Levi's attempt to target separate demographic segments.

Third, segmentation helps marketers develop an effective marketing mix. Understanding a segment's needs helps in developing an advertising strategy. The ads for Dockers show a group of men between the ages of 25 and 45 reminiscing about memorable times together. The ads play on the greater importance of family and friends to baby boomers and the positive associations with the Levi name. The company also developed its retail strategy based on an understanding of baby boomers' needs. Management knew that Dockers could not be presented in a traditional setting—hung on rack after rack in a wood-panelled showroom—because Dockers' customers grew up shopping for jeans in "hip" boutiques with blaring rock music.[9] So Levi helped retailers establish Dockers boutiques to mirror baby boomers' tastes.

A fourth benefit of a segmentation strategy is that it helps guide the allocation of marketing resources to various products. A large baby-boom segment and a shrinking teenage segment prompted Levi to switch resources from jeans to slacks.

The profitability of a segmentation strategy was illustrated in a study by J. Walter Thompson, a large advertising agency, for one of its clients.[10] Sales of one of the company's leading food products was stagnant. The product was advertised based on its distinctive taste. The ad agency suggested introducing a separate campaign targeting a health-oriented segment with a "natural ingredients" appeal. When a $2 million ad campaign was directed to the taste segment only, it resulted in $3.8 million in revenues. When separate $1 million campaigns were directed to taste and health-oriented segments, $6.3 million in revenue was generated. By following a segmentation strategy, the company generated an additional $2.5 million in revenue with the same advertising expenditures.

All segmentation strategies will not necessarily be as profitable, but the study suggests that by dividing the marketing effort and targeting it to well-defined segments, profitability will improve.

MICRO, SEGMENTED, AND MASS MARKETING

Figure 10.1 shows various levels of marketing effort on a continuum from the individual consumer to the total market. At the most individual level is **micromarketing**, *which involves directing marketing strategies toward individual consumers.* Companies have appealed to individual consumers by mail or through telephone solicitations. Consumers have traditionally been identified for direct marketing efforts through mailing lists. The advantage of micromarketing is that companies can gear their messages to the characteristics of individual consumers—for example, using car registration data to target new-car buyers with direct mail ads for low-interest car loans. As we have seen in Chapter 7, marketers must be careful not to infringe on the consumer's right to privacy when using data on individual consumer characteristics.

Where mailing lists do not exist, marketers have begun to use **geo-demographic analysis** *which identifies individual households as targets by analyzing data at the zip code level and linking zip codes to demographic characteristics.* For example, geo-demographic analysis can identify all zip codes in the United States with a high proportion of retirees. If a marketer wants to reach retired individuals in the sun belt, it can identify zip codes in sun-belt states with a heavy proportion of retirees and use direct mail to reach households in these zip-code areas. Not all households in the zip-code areas will be retirees, but the high proportion of retirees in the area would make direct mail cost efficient.

A form of micromarketing is **customized marketing**, *which is the development of tailor-made products to meet the needs of individual buyers.* Firms producing pollution-control systems, for instance, must design them to the specifications of individual companies. Clothing can be made to the specifications of individual consumers. Even "mass-produced" cars have come close to being produced on a customized basis. The number of options on a Ford Thunderbird resulted in

FIGURE 10.1

Levels of Market Segmentation

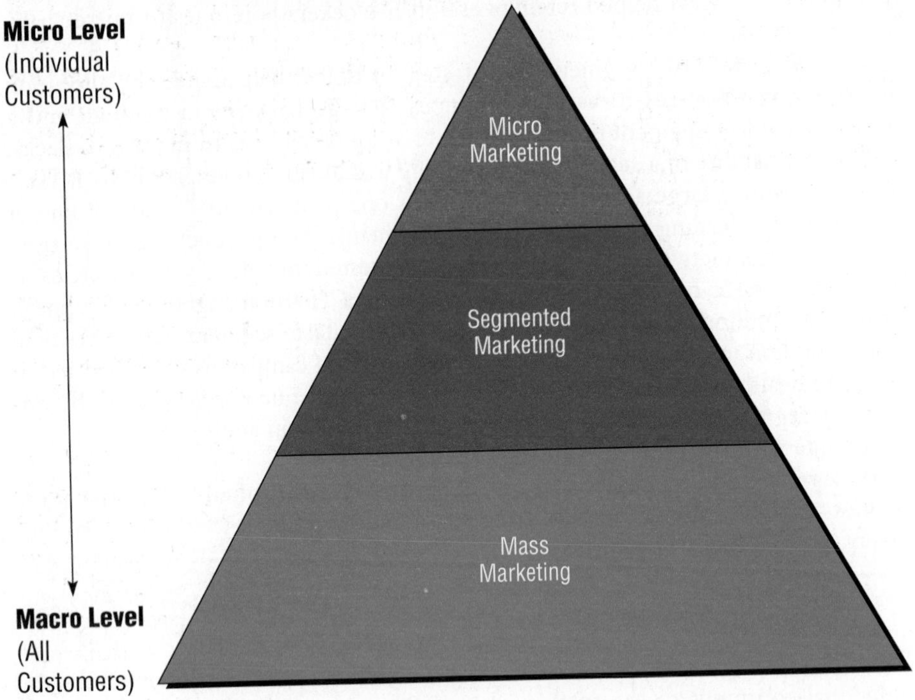

69,120 combinations, meaning that consumers came close to designing their own cars if they specified all the available features.

At the other extreme in Figure 10.1 is **mass marketing**, *which is a uniform marketing strategy directed toward as wide a market as possible.*

Although micromarketing and mass marketing are relevant, they have limitations. Micromarketing is limited by the ability to identify and reach individual consumers and by the cost involved in developing tailor-made products to individuals. As we will see, micromarketing is most relevant for industrial products, where it is often necessary to develop products for individual customers and to direct marketing effort toward these customers. Mass marketing is limited by its ability to meet customer needs. With the increasing fragmentation of the American marketplace and the development of more-specific customer needs, mass marketing has become a less-viable marketing strategy.

As a result, our focus in this chapter is a strategy that lies between micromarketing and mass marketing: segmented marketing. As we have seen, segmented marketing requires developing products to meet the specific needs of well-defined customer groups.

Figure 10.1 suggests that market segmentation is on a continuum, meaning that a marketer can target a very small segment, and approach micromarketing, or target a larger segment and approach mass marketing. For example, Liggett & Myers is targeting smaller segments because, according to its CEO, it "couldn't compete head to head with Philip Morris or R. J. Reynolds in advertising spending."[11] The company introduced Eve 120mm to appeal to female smokers who buy 120mm cigarettes, even though this segment accounts for only 2 percent of smokers. Eve sales totaled over $50 million, a small but profitable sales level for the brand.

In contrast, Philip Morris targets larger segments that generate more sales revenues. Its Benson & Hedges brand is positioned to an upscale segment of both male and female smokers. Marlboro is positioned to a more downscale, male macho segment; Virginia Slims is positioned to independent, modern women; and Merit is positioned to concerned smokers who want a low-tar, low-nicotine cigarette. Each of these segments is larger than the niche targeted by Liggett & Myers' Eve, and pursuing them all allows Philip Morris to cover most of the cigarette market.

THE TREND TOWARD MARKET SEGMENTATION

Like Levi, many venerable names in corporate America have shifted from a mass-marketing to a segmented-marketing strategy. In the past, companies such as Ford, Chevrolet, Coca-Cola, Pepsi-Cola, Hershey, and Kodak sold one or two product lines to a national market. By the 1960s, these companies began to recognize the benefits of a more segmented approach.

Why the changeover from mass to segmented marketing? There were two major reasons: economic change and demographic or life-style change. Economic change came first. As we have seen in Chapter 1, until the 1960s marketers did not need to pay that much attention to customers. During the Depression, customers could not afford to buy; during World War II and the Korean War, customers could afford to buy, but the goods were frequently unavailable. Only by the 1960s were customers becoming more selective, because they finally had the buying power at the same time that the goods were available.

Many marketers reacted by trying to offer customers what they wanted. The best way to do that was to recognize the diversity of customer needs. In the automobile industry, for instance, carmakers began to divide the market into middle-aged and younger segments; luxury and economy segments; performance and style segments; and rural, suburban, and urban segments. A similar pattern emerged in the soft-drink industry, where manufacturers divided the market first into cola and noncola segments, then into taste, diet, and health-oriented segments. In each case, new products or extensions of existing products were directed toward these segments.

A second change that contributed to the emergence of market-segmentation strategies was the shift in demographics and life-styles that became apparent in the 1970s. As we have seen in Chapter 4, the increase in working women (a demographic change) led to a shift away from the traditional assumption that car purchases were a male preserve. Car features and advertising began to be directed more specifically toward women. The greater focus on health and nutrition (a life-style change) prompted the introduction of adult cereals, caffeine-free versions of soft drinks, and a host of low-calorie foods. In each case, companies began to identify different demographic and life-style segments because of changing needs, directing their marketing effort toward these segments.

PROCTER & GAMBLE—A PAINFUL TRANSITION

The shift to segmented marketing is sometimes painful for companies that have traditionally relied on mass marketing. At Procter & Gamble, this change has been particularly difficult. The giant consumer packaged-goods company traditionally used a mass marketing approach.[12] Mass marketing was a successful strategy for P&G, because its products—toothpaste, soap, and detergents—had a relatively homogeneous market; they could be sold to consumers across age, income, and regional lines. Also, brands such as Crest, Ivory soap, and Tide detergent were the market leaders. Consumers were convinced they were among the best offerings in the market. If a brand has established itself as a leader over the years through mass marketing, it can continue to be marketed uniformly until it faces a competitive challenge. And, as we have seen in Chapter 4, challenging a market leader is difficult.

But P&G's environment was changing, because the assumption of homogeneous demand no longer held true. As one marketer put it,

> [P&G] soon discovered that demographic and lifestyle changes had delivered a death blow to mass marketing and brand loyalty. A nation that once shared homogeneous buying tastes had splintered into many different consumer groups—each with special needs and interests.[13]

As competitors recognized this diversity in demand, they began to chip away at P&G's dominance—Kimberly Clark in disposable diapers, Colgate in toothpaste, Lever in detergents. P&G's response was to offer more product options to try to accommodate the diversity in demand. Where Tide had once been a single product sold uniformly across the country, today consumers can choose from regular Tide, liquid Tide, Tide in 10-box Redi-Paks, and Tide in multi-action sheets (see Exhibit 10.1). The largest mass marketer finally had to adopt market segmentation in order to survive.

COCA-COLA—A FULLY SEGMENTED PRODUCT LINE

Coca-Cola's product line illustrates the extent of the shift from mass marketing to segmented marketing. Figure 10.2 is a product-market matrix of Coca-Cola's products. It is produced by the intersection of six market segments defined by common needs and five product types directed to these needs. Coca-Cola was one of the first to recognize the importance of diet products when it introduced Tab in 1963 as a diet cola positioned to women. Twenty years later, it used the magic name Coke on a product other than its flagship brand for the first time, introducing Diet Coke positioned to men. The year 1983 also saw Coke introduce caffeine-free versions of Coca-Cola, Diet Coke, and Tab, positioned to health-oriented consumers.

In 1985, Coca-Cola introduced Cherry Coke to meet the needs of teenagers who wanted a sweet cola drink and to break Pepsi's lock on the teenage market. The most famous move of all, the introduction of New Coke, was made for the same reason—to better appeal to teenagers who favored Pepsi.

When Coca-Cola brought back the original brand because of the consumer outcry, it inadvertently followed a sound segmentation strategy: positioning one brand (New Coke) to the segment that wants a sweeter drink and another brand (its flagship brand) to the segment that does not.

Coca-Cola also introduced Minute Maid soda as a fruit-based drink in reaction to Pepsi's introduction of Slice. The brand is positioned to appeal to a segment that likes the taste of fruit juice, as well as to health- and nutrition-conscious consumers. Filling out the product line is Sprite, the company's lemon–lime entry positioned to consumers who like a lemon–lime flavor.

EXHIBIT 10.1

P&G Goes From Mass to Segmented Marketing

FIGURE 10.2

Market Segmentation of Coca-Cola's Product Line

Market Segments	Products: Cola	Diet Cola	Caffeine-Free	Fruit Based	Lemon-Lime
Taste Oriented: Like Sweet-Tasting Colas	New Coke Cherry Coke				
Taste Oriented: Like Unsweetened Colas	Coca Cola Classic				
Taste Oriented: Like Fruit Juice				Minute Maid	
Taste Oriented: Like Lemon-Lime					Sprite
Health/Nutrition Conscious			Caffeine-Free Tab, Coke, and Diet Coke	Minute Maid	Caffeine-Free Sprite
Weight Watchers		Diet Coke, Tab, and Diet Cherry Coke			

Coca-Cola's shift to segmented marketing is reflected in the share of revenue represented by its flagship brand. In 1979, Coke represented 70 percent of sales. By 1988, it represented only 50 percent of the company's soft-drink sales, as more brands were marketed to specific segments.[14]

COUNTERSEGMENTATION

So far, we have emphasized the shift to market segmentation. A reverse trend, known as countersegmentation, emerged in the 1980s. **Countersegmentation** *is the grouping together of several segments, and directing a single marketing effort to these segments to reduce costs.* For example, rather than producing a paper towel for a segment desiring heavy-duty use, another for a segment that desires absorbency, and a third for a segment that desires a decorative towel, a company might produce one lower-price towel to appeal to economy-oriented consumers cutting across all three segments. It may still produce a two-ply towel for the heavy-duty segment, but now the distinction is between an economy and a quality segment. As a result, the company is appealing to two rather than three segments. Countersegmentation does not mean eliminating a strategy of market segmentation, it means appealing to fewer segments on a more economical basis.

There are two reasons for this trend. First, segmentation is a costly strategy. A company may move too far in the direction of market segmentation by defining more segments than are necessary to meet customer needs. Such *oversegmentation* means that the costs of appealing to these segments are greater than the revenues derived. Soft-drink companies like Coca-Cola or Pepsi have occasionally been criticized for oversegmenting the market. For example, is it necessary to produce a caffeine-free version of Tab, given its low market share, when a caffeine-free version of Diet Coke is available? A tongue-in-cheek representation of the dangers of such oversegmentation is shown in Figure 10.3.

A second reason for countersegmentation is the greater price sensitivity of consumers as a result of recessions in the early 1980s and 1990s. Consumers are willing to accept lower-priced products as long as they meet basic quality requirements. As a result, consumers are more likely to buy generic cigarettes, no-frills furniture, and modular housing. In each case, consumers are sacrificing product features tailored to their needs for lower-cost alternatives. A slow recovery from the 1990-92 recession is likely to result in continued price sensitivity on the part of consumers. As a result, companies are likely to expand their offerings of lower priced goods.

Countersegmentation does not reduce the importance of market segmentation. It shows that there are limits to a segmentation strategy based on the costs of meeting the needs of particular segments.

THE MARKET-SEGMENTATION PROCESS

Although Procter & Gamble's shift to a segmentation strategy was prompted by the strategies of its competitors, the process of identifying segments is far more complicated than simply looking over one's shoulder to see what the competition is doing. Figure 10.4 illustrates this process. It shows market segmentation as part of the marketing planning process discussed in Chapter 3. Before selecting segments for a marketing effort, the company conducts a situation analysis of the market and identifies marketing opportunities.

FIGURE 10.3

A Hypothetical Example of Oversegmentation

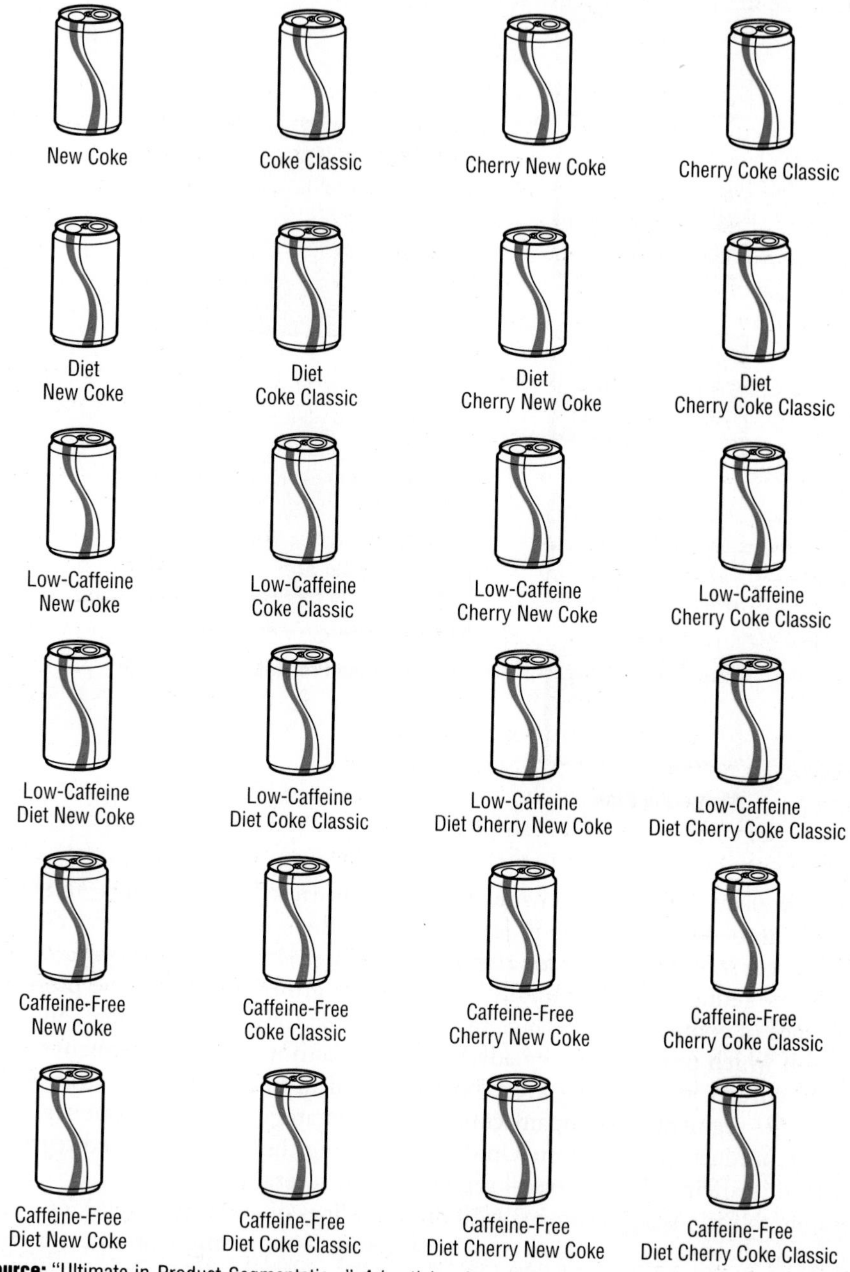

Source: "Ultimate in Product Segmentation," *Advertising Age,* September 23, 1985, p. 18. © Terry Sharbach.

After taking these steps, the company can segment its markets. Market segmentation requires two steps, identifying and targeting market segments. *Identifying segments* requires dividing the market based on a given criterion associated to consumer needs. Segments can be identified by similarity in the benefits customers seek, by their behavior, or by their characteristics. Levi divided the jeans

FIGURE 10.4

The Process of Identifying and Targeting Market Segments

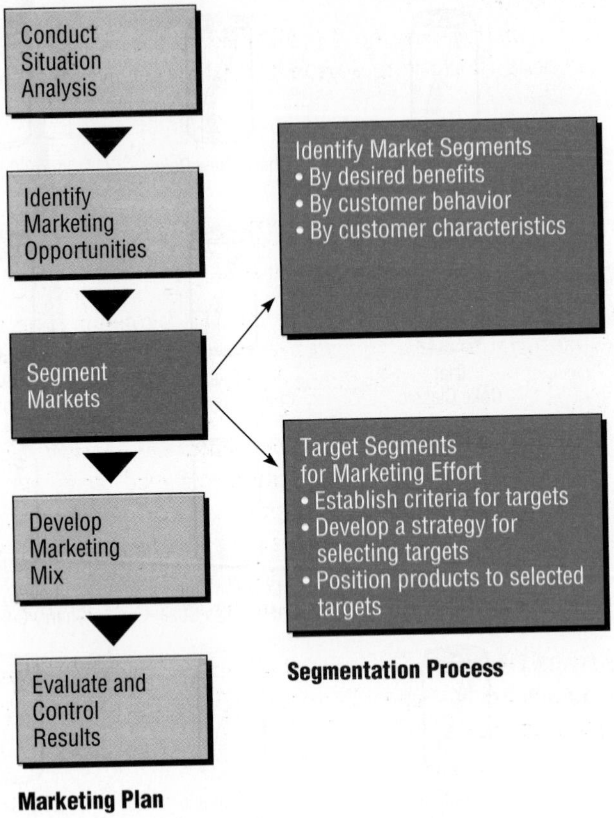

market by a key demographic characteristic, age, because kids, teenagers, and baby boomers needed different cuts in jeans and wore them on different occasions.

Targeting *segments requires selecting one or more segments for marketing effort.* Criteria for targeting a segment might be its size, its growth potential, the presence or absence of competitive offerings that are directed toward the segment, and the ease with which products can be advertised and distributed to the segment.

Once criteria for targeting are established, a firm must develop a strategy to select target segments. A company could follow a strategy of pursuing one segment with one product (just as Seven-Up did in targeting the health-oriented segment with its no-caffeine claim), several segments with several products (as Levi did in appealing to various age segments with different lines of jeans and slacks), or some strategy in between. The third step in targeting is to position products to the selected segments.

Once segments have been selected for targeting, the remaining steps in the marketing planning process are implemented: developing a marketing mix, and evaluating and controlling the marketing effort. Marketing-mix strategies follow segmentation since these strategies are determined by the needs of the target segment. For example, Iveco, a manufacturer of medium-sized trucks, found that truck owners who deliver food are particularly concerned with maneuverability in food distribution centers.[15] Having defined this segment, Iveco developed an integrated strategy to meet the target segment's needs. The company improved the maneuverability of its trucks and positioned them to food-delivery companies on this basis. Its advertising and personal-selling programs were coordinated to emphasize maneuverability.

In the remainder of this chapter, we will discuss the two steps in the market segmentation process: identifying segments and targeting them for marketing effort.

IDENTIFY MARKET SEGMENTS

There are three approaches to identifying market segments. The first, **benefit segmentation,** *identifies segments by what consumers want.* An example would be Nestlé identifying a decaffeinated segment that wants a better tasting decaffeinated coffee and positioning Taster's Choice freeze-dried decaffeinated to this benefit segment. A second approach, **behavioral segmentation,** *segments by what consumers do.* An example would be Nestlé identifying heavy iced-tea drinkers and directing its Nestea brand to this behavioral segment. A third approach, **segmenting by consumer characteristics,** *identifies segments by demographic, regional life-style, or personality characteristics.* An example would be Levi's identifying baby boomers as needing jeans with a fuller cut and positioning its 505 jeans line to this demographic segment.

Table 10.1 summarizes the types of variables marketers use to identify segments by these three approaches. As we will see, the approach marketers use will depend on their strategic purpose.

BENEFIT SEGMENTATION

Marketers use benefit segmentation to determine the need for a new product. Segments are identified by the benefits they seek. Segments whose needs are not being met represent targets for new product offerings. For example, a soft-drink company might determine that women over age 50 find few beverages that satisfy their need for health and nutrition. The company then develops a new soft drink with a high fiber content and markets it to this segment. The new product opportunity resulted because few beverage products provided the health and nutritional benefits sought by older women.

Table 10.2 shows how the snack-food market is segmented by benefits. The table is based on data compiled by a large food manufacturer that was investigating new product opportunities for nut and chip-type snacks. The company interviewed 1,500 snack-food users and identified six segments according to the similar benefits perceived by consumers in each group. The second row of the table shows the benefits sought by each segment. For example, nutritional snackers want a nutritious, natural snack with no artificial ingredients, whereas weight watchers want a low-calorie snack that provides quick energy. The study also identified the demographic, life-style, and personality characteristics of each benefit segment and the types of snacks they usually eat.

The company already was doing well in the "party" and "indiscriminate snacker" segments with its existing chip and nut snacks, but it also wanted to appeal to the growing nutritional segment. It developed a nut-and-dried-fruit

TABLE 10.1

Variables Used to Identify Consumer Market Segments

BENEFIT SEGMENTATION	Nutrition Health Economy Good taste		Prestige/luxury Performance Style Service
BEHAVIORAL SEGMENTATION	Brands purchased (e.g., users of Tide) Product category purchased (e.g. users of liquid detergents) Frequency of purchase (e.g., heavy, medium, or light purchasers of liquid detergents)		
SEGMENTING BY CONSUMER CHARACTERISTICS			
DEMOGRAPHICS	Income Age Sex	Race Occupation Region	Family size Stage in family life cycle
REGIONAL	International regions National regions Zip codes		
LIFE-STYLES	Achievement oriented Societally conscious Health conscious Sociable Family oriented	Isolate Venturesome Innovative Outdoor type	
PERSONALITY	Aggressive Compliant Dominant	Compulsive Authoritarian Ambitious	

snack positioned to nutritional snackers. Preliminary product tests showed that consumers in this group liked the product, and it was then introduced into test markets.

Data on the demographic, life-style, and personality characteristics of nutritional snackers showed that these consumers are a young, well-educated, self-confident group. As a result, the company developed an advertising campaign featuring young, upwardly mobile consumers on the go, having a tasty and nutritional snack. Demographics also helped the company select magazines for its print advertising and time slots for its TV advertising aimed at young, upscale consumers.

BEHAVIORAL SEGMENTATION

While benefit segmentation is most effective in guiding new-product development, marketers who want to develop strategies for existing brands and product categories are guided by what people do. In behavioral segmentation, consumers are grouped by their purchases. For example, the adult cereal market might be segmented by those consumers who buy bran cereals, vitamin-fortified cereals, low-calorie cereals, and sugared cereals. Marketers then would determine the

TABLE 10.2

Benefit Segmentation of the Snack Food Market

	NUTRITIONAL SNACKERS	WEIGHT WATCHERS	GUILTY SNACKERS	PARTY SNACKERS	INDISCRIMINATE SNACKERS	ECONOMICAL SNACKERS
PERCENTAGE OF SNACKERS	22	14	9	15	15	18
BENEFITS SOUGHT	Nutritious No artificial ingredients Natural snack	Low calorie Quick energy	Low calorie Good tasting	Good to serve guests Proud to serve Goes well with beverage	Good tasting Satisfies hunger	Low price Best value
DEMOGRAPHICS	Better educated Have younger children	Younger Single	Younger or older Females Lower socio-economic group	Middle aged Nonurban	Teens	Larger families Better educated
LIFE-STYLE AND PERSONALITY CHARACTERISTICS	Self-assured Controlled	Outdoor types Influential Venturesome	High anxiety Isolate	Sociable	Hedonistic	Self-assured Price oriented
CONSUMPTION LEVEL OF SNACKS	Light	Light	Heavy	Average	Heavy	Average
TYPE OF SNACKS USUALLY EATEN	Fruits Vegetables Cheese	Yogurt Vegetables	Yogurt Cookies Crackers Candy	Nuts Potato chips Crackers Pretzels	Candy Ice cream Cookies Potato chips Pretzels Popcorn	No specific products

demographic and life-style characteristics of each behavioral segment. If, for example, the group buying bran cereals has more consumers who are over 50, in a higher-income group, and express health concerns, this information would be used to position the product (use health-oriented claims in the advertising) and to select media (buy TV time on programs most likely to be watched by upscale consumers over 50, or select magazines most likely to be read by this group).

SEGMENTING CONSUMERS BY BRANDS PURCHASED

The most frequent form of behavioral segmentation is to segment by what brands people buy. There are two main reasons for segmenting by brands: to target actual purchasers and to identify prospective purchasers.

When VF—the producer of Lee jeans—bought Wrangler dungarees in 1986, it had to target two very different groups of jeans purchasers. Lee purchasers tended to be stylish, suburbanite women who bought their jeans in specialty stores; Wrangler purchasers were rural consumers who bought dungarees at mass-merchandise outlets such as K Mart. VF made sure to market differently to each segment so as to maintain the loyalty of both. In the words of its president, "These are separate companies that will operate separate businesses, and what one does will have no bearing on the other."[16] Segmenting by brand-purchasing behavior led VF to a strategy of ensuring brand distinctiveness and separation. The brands continued to be sold in separate stores, with separate advertising campaigns, rather than being linked under a single corporate umbrella.

Another reason to segment by brands purchased is to identify prospective rather than actual brand users. When Yamaha chooses the cities in which to open new motorcycle dealerships, it identifies the demographic characteristics of owners of its motorcycles and assumes that prospective purchasers will have similar characteristics to existing Yamaha owners. It then uses census data to locate new Yamaha dealerships in those areas whose demographic profile most closely matches the demographic profile of Yamaha owners.[17]

SEGMENTING CONSUMERS BY PRODUCT CATEGORIES PURCHASED

Another basis for segmenting markets behaviorally is by identifying users of a product category rather than a brand. Defining users as product category rather than brand users casts a broader net and includes users of the company's and competitive brands. For example, it might make more sense for Dannon to appeal to yogurt users in general than to users of Dannon yogurt in particular. As a result, Dannon would identify the characteristics of yogurt users and develop strategies to appeal to this broader group.

Another reason to segment by product category is to target heavy product users. This requires segmenting markets by frequency of product usage. Dannon may wish to target heavy yogurt purchasers rather than yogurt purchasers in general. In so doing, the company is more effectively directing its marketing dollars toward those who are most likely to buy. Nestlé segmented the iced-tea market by level of usage to determine how to better position its iced-tea brand to heavy users. It found that the heaviest-user segment (17 percent of iced-tea users) drank twice as much (47.5 glasses a month) as the average drinker (about 24 glasses a month). By questioning the heavy users, it learned that this group emphasized two things in drinking iced tea: It restores energy, and it is a good year-round drink. Nestlé then developed its advertising around these two benefits to appeal to the heavy-user segment.

SEGMENTING BY CONSUMER CHARACTERISTICS

The third approach to market segmentation involves grouping consumers by their characteristics. On this basis, markets have been segmented by consumers' demographic, regional, life-style, and personality characteristics. The purpose of such segmentation is to help the marketer develop a marketing mix for a brand. Demographics can guide the selection of media to target consumers, regional segmentation can guide the development of products to satisfy different regional preferences, life-style and personality variables can guide the nature of the advertising appeal and the positioning of the brand.

DEMOGRAPHIC SEGMENTATION

In demographic segmentation, consumers are grouped according to variables such as income, education, occupation, age, sex, or race (see Table 10.1). This type of segmentation is used for two reasons: First, demographics are often linked to consumer needs and behavior. Age largely determines brand preferences in the soft-drink market, with teenagers preferring sweeter drinks and adults noncola, fruit-based drinks. Second, demographics are easier to determine than benefits or behavior and thus are more easily applied in segmenting markets.

The usual categories for demographic segmentation are income, age, sex, and ethnic origin. Each will be discussed.

SEGMENTING BY INCOME Holiday Inn uses income as the basis for demographic segmentation of its markets, dividing hotel users into three categories: affluent, middle-income, and budget-conscious. Its Holiday Inn chain has an established position in the middle-income group. To appeal to the upper and lower end of the market, it developed two other chains: Crowne Plaza hotels for the affluent segment and Holiday Inn Express for the budget conscious. Holiday's strategy for each of its chains is a function of the income segment, the chain targets. Holiday Inn Express, for example, has low rates and minimal service and is advertised as a no-frills chain, using media that reach a downscale segment. Segmenting by income thus provides Holiday Inn with a basis for differentiating marketing strategies for its three chains.

SEGMENTING BY AGE Companies often position their products to different age groups. Age is the basis for Levi's segmentation strategy. Similarly, Richardson Vicks uses age segmentation to position its Life Stage vitamin line, with Children's Formula in chewable form designed for 4- to 12-year-olds, Teens Formula for teenagers, and Men's and Women's formula for adults. Both Levi and Richardson Vicks reflect a trend toward extending products beyond their original niches—jeans from teens to baby boomers and vitamins from adults to children. Other companies have also followed this trend. Johnson & Johnson successfully positioned its baby shampoo to adults and positioned adult-oriented sunscreens to children.[18]

This strategy makes sense only if the product meets the needs of the age segment. Baby shampoo was successfully marketed to adults, because it met the needs of a segment who wanted a milder shampoo. However, companies may be going too far in looking for new age segments. Quaker is positioning its Gatorade sports drink to children (see Exhibit 10.2). Some nutritional experts question whether kids need the minerals in Gatorade and consider fruit juice to be more nutritional.[19]

SEGMENTING BY SEX American Express segments its market on the basis of another demographic characteristic, sex. In attempting to increase the number of women who are American Express cardholders, it waged an "interesting lives" campaign that provided a realistic portrayal of women's roles in a series of short vignettes. Toiletry companies that have long segmented their cosmetic and hair-care lines for women are now beginning to segment male consumers. Lancôme, for example, advertises its line of skin-care products for men with, "Take what you have and make it better."

EXHIBIT 10.2

Segmenting by Age

SEGMENTING BY ETHNIC ORIGIN As we have seen in Chapter 4, the vast purchasing power of African Americans and Hispanic Americans has led marketers to segment these groups. For example, Ford worked with an African-American advertising agency to develop ads for its LTD Crown Victoria positioned to African Americans interested in luxury. The appeals are the same as to white consumers—luxury, comfort, roominess, and a more-powerful engine. Nissan, on the other hand, has begun to target an African-American segment interested in economy and practicality. The segmentation of African Americans by luxury versus economy parallels the same strategy used by carmakers for whites.

Marketers are also beginning to segment the Hispanic-American market. Anheuser-Busch, the leading beer among Hispanics, segments the market by using different advertising for Mexican, Cuban, and Puerto Rican consumers. The Puerto Rican commercial is set in a disco and features salsa rhythms; the Mexican commercial is set in a rodeo to mariachi music; and the Cuban commercial takes place on a private boat, because Cubans are the most affluent Hispanic group. This segmentation strategy ensures that "each campaign should pick up on the regional nuances of [these] groups."[20]

REGIONAL SEGMENTATION

Marketers have given more emphasis to regional segmentation in recent years because of differences in consumer needs and purchasing behavior by region for many product categories. Campbell soup has led in the trend to regional segmentation. Until the mid 1980s, the company had relied on a mass-marketing approach by utilizing nationwide campaigns to sell its soups. Themes such as "Mmm, Mmm good," "Soup for lunch," and "Soup for one," were designed to sell canned soups in general rather than specific types of Campbell's soups. The top of Exhibit 10.3 on page 338 is an example of Campbell's former mass-marketing approach. Campbell's strategy of stimulating demand for canned soup made sense since the company had over 80 percent of the canned soup market.

By 1986, Campbell recognized the demographic and life-style fragmentation of the American market place. The increasing proportion of singles, working women, weight watchers, and the nutritionally oriented meant that a mass-marketing approach would no longer work. Campbell would have to target specific types of soups to demographic segments rather than sell canned soup as such. Campbell chose regional segmentation because of significant differences in soup preferences by region (see bottom of Exhibit 10.3). The company has established twenty-one regional marketing centers in the United States, each responsible for developing and promoting products suited for that area. For example, a spicier version of Campbell's nacho-cheese soup was introduced in Texas and California, creole soups to southern markets, and a red-bean soup to Hispanic markets. Campbell also designed a line of low-fat, low-salt prepared foods for health-conscious northeastern urbanites.[21]

General Motors is also adjusting its effort on a regional basis, with a special eye on the California market. It sold its Cavalier line nationally as a family utility vehicle, but in California introduced a special version with a bigger engine, subtler styling, and a campaign that emphasized the sportiness and excitement of the car.[22]

GEO-DEMOGRAPHIC SEGMENTATION An important form of regional segmentation is *geo-demographic segmentation*, which identifies demographic segments by zip code. On this basis, marketers can target similar types of neighborhoods across regions through a zip-code analysis. Claritas, a market research firm, used the 1990 census to group the thousands of zip codes in the United States into similar neighborhoods by their demographic characteristics. It came up with 40 neighborhood groupings. One such group, identified as "Blue Blood Estates," includes Chappaqua, New York, and Winnetka, Illinois. This group is described as "America's wealthiest neighborhoods, populated by established managers, professionals, and heirs to old money." Another category, labeled "Shotguns and Pickups" includes Weatherford, Texas, and Waverly, Ohio. It is described as the "hundreds of small, outlying townships and crossroad villages that serve the nation's breadbasket and other rural areas."[23]

Companies can determine whether product consumption varies by these zip code categories. For example, Dannon yogurt could determine average yogurt consumption in each of the 40 clusters and then distribute products to clusters such as "Blue Blood Estates" or "Shotguns and Pickups" based on the average amount of yogurt purchased. The company also could distribute coupons or mailers to those clusters that represent the heaviest consumption groups.

REGIONAL SEGMENTATION AND THE EUROPEAN COMMUNITY Regional segmentation has particular relevance for the European Community as

ETHICAL AND ENVIRONMENTAL ISSUES IN MARKETING

RJR Tobacco's Attempt to Segment By Race Backfires

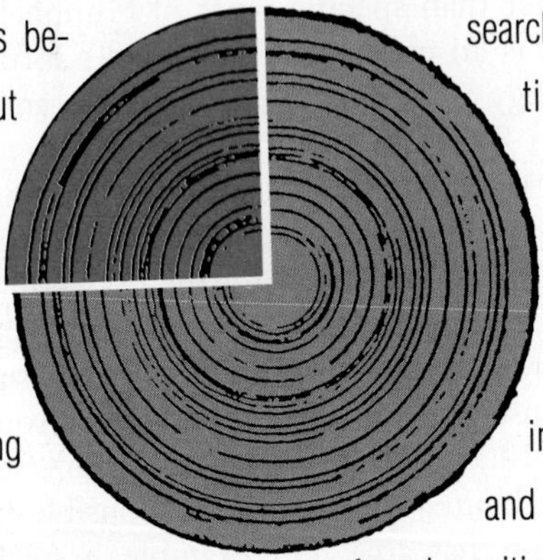

In January 1990, Dr. Louis Sullivan, a cabinet-level official heading the Department of Health and Human Services, was becoming increasingly uneasy about RJR Tobacco's plans to market a new cigarette. The cigarette, called Uptown, was positioned to African Americans and was slated to be test marketed in Philadelphia the following month.

Cigarette, alcohol, and beer companies had targeted minorities before by directing advertising to African-American and Hispanic consumers. For example, a substantial portion of the marketing budget for Salem and Newport cigarettes goes to targeting African Americans. Miller and Anheuser-Busch target minorities by advertising in African-American and Hispanic media and by promoting rock concerts and special events. However, these companies do not position their brands exclusively to minorities. RJR's strategy was a first—announcing that a cigarette would be targeted to a minority group.

The company's motives were clear. Domestic cigarette sales were sliding. The incidence of smoking among African Americans was about 20 percent higher than among whites. Further, RJR's Salem brand was losing share to Newport, meaning that the company's market position among African Americans was deteriorating. What better way to increase sales than to market a cigarette to African Americans? Research showed that a significant proportion of African-American smokers wanted a lighter menthol flavor than Salem and that many Newport smokers open their packages upside down. So Uptown was to be introduced with a light menthol flavor and with cigarettes packed in the preferred position. The name *Uptown* was meant to convey a sophisticated life-style, reflected in magazine ads and billboards for the brand. The tagline in the advertising was to be "Uptown. The Place. The Taste."

The apparent risk and insensitivity of RJR's approach escaped company management. The cigarette's content should, in itself, have sent warning signals. Uptown would have been the company's second most potent cigarette—next to Camels—based on tar and nicotine content. As one critic said, "They [RJR] probably assumed that since many African Americans normally are able to spend less on smoking, a high-potency product was the best way to get them addicted quickly."

RJR immediately came under attack by a coalition of antismoking and African-American consumer groups. These groups coalesced their actions in

ETHICAL AND ENVIRONMENTAL ISSUES IN MARKETING

Philadelphia in anticipation of Uptown's February 5, 1990, launch. Members of the coalition mounted public protests and a boycott of all RJR-owned products such as Nabisco cookies. They charged that RJR was targeting an underprivileged and vulnerable minority with a deadly product. Further, many African Americans could ill-afford the expense of smoking, and they could ill-afford the medical expenses that smoking might incur. RJR reacted by blasting its critics, countercharging that they were eroding free enterprise and that African-American smokers had the right to choose the cigarette they want.

It took Dr. Sullivan to put a halt to RJR's plans. On January 19, he was slated to give a speech in Philadelphia. His staff urged him to come out publicly against Uptown. Sullivan rewrote his speech and launched a broadside against RJR, calling its plans "slick and sinister." He asked Americans to "resist the efforts of tobacco merchants to earn profits at the expense of the health and well-being of poor and minority citizens." Within the week, RJR announced it was canceling its Uptown launch.

RJR's Uptown experience has deterred it from launching another cigarette aimed at minorities. Whether it has increased the company's sensitivity in targeting vulnerable groups is doubtful: Two weeks after RJR canceled Uptown, an RJR document surfaced in the press citing plans to introduce a cigarette called Dakota targeted to blue-collar women under 21. The document suggested not identifying the cigarette with the RJR name, a first for the company. RJR's plans immediately came under attack by antismoking groups which claimed the move would violate the tobacco industry's informal code against targeting consumers under age 21.

Although there was no evidence RJR planned to introduce Dakota, the company's tentative plans raised further questions about its segmentation approach. Both the Uptown and Dakota experience suggest that marketers of cigarettes, alcohol, and beer will be increasingly wary of targeting minorities and younger age groups.

Questions: What was the distinction in RJR's approach in marketing Salem and Uptown to African Americans? Is it unethical to design and market a cigarette exclusively for a particular minority group? Why or why not?

Source: "Why Big Tobacco Woos Minorities," *Adweek's Marketing Week*, January 29, 1990, pp. 20–30; "In Philadelphia, R.J. Reynolds Made All the Wrong Moves," *Adweek's Marketing Week*, January 29, 1990, pp. 20–22; and "New RJR Brand Under Fire," *Advertising Age*, February 19, 1990, pp. 1 and 74.

EXHIBIT 10.3

From Universal Appeal to Regional Favorites

A 1932 CAMPBELL AD: THE DAYS WHEN MARKETERS USED NATIONAL CAMPAIGNS TO SELL PRODUCTS 'SHORE TO SHORE' MAY SOON BE OVER

(Above) Campbell's Former Mass-Market Approach
(Right) Chowders Are a Favorite in New England

economic and political integration begins to be implemented in 1992. Many marketers are citing the EC countries as one mass market because of economic integration. In reality, regional customs are likely to continue to affect purchase behavior for many categories. Regional differences are likely to persist in purchases of foods, beverages, and clothing. Citing each European country as a separate segment is probably too local, just as citing Europe as one mass market is probably too global.

As a result, marketers have looked to some rational basis for regional segmentation of the EC countries. One such scheme is shown in Table 10.3. It divides Europe into six regions that cross national lines. France, Italy, and Germany, for example, fall into more than one segment.

There are significant differences between regional segments. Segments 5 and 6, the two most southerly European regions, are significantly younger and poorer

TABLE 10.3

A Regional Segmentation of the European Economic Community

SEGMENT 1: UNITED KINGDOM AND IRELAND

Average Income: $11,450
Age Profile: Average of EC countries
Language: English

SEGMENT 2: CENTRAL AND NORTHERN FRANCE, SOUTHERN BELGIUM, CENTRAL GERMANY, AND LUXEMBOURG

Average Income: $15,470
Age Profile: Middle aged and older
Language: French and German

SEGMENT 3: SOUTHERN GERMANY, NORTHERN ITALY, SOUTHEASTERN FRANCE, AND AUSTRIA (IF IT JOINS)

Average Income: $16,740
Age Profile: Middle aged
Language: French, German, and Italian

SEGMENT 4: DENMARK, NORTHERN GERMANY, THE NETHERLANDS, NORTHERN BELGIUM, AND SWITZERLAND AND THE SCANDINAVIAN COUNTRIES (IF THEY JOIN)

Average Income: $19,420
Age Profile: Middle aged
Language: Scandinavian, French, Italian, and German

SEGMENT 5: SPAIN AND PORTUGAL

Average Income: $6,530
Age Profile: Young
Language: Spanish and Portuguese

SEGMENT 6: GREECE AND SOUTHERN ITALY

Average Income: $7,610
Age Profile: Young
Language: Greek and Italian

Source: Sandra Vandermerwe and Marc-Andre L'Huillier, "Euro-Consumers in 1992," in John K. Ryans, Jr., and Pradeep A. Rau, eds., *Marketing Strategies for the New Europe* (Chicago: American Marketing Association, 1990), pp. 151–164.

GLOBAL MARKETING STRATEGIES

Goodyear Tire Segments International Markets Across Regions

A key issue in segmenting international markets is whether segments should be defined by region (as in Table 10.3) or across regions. Regional segmentation makes sense if particular needs, tastes, and purchasing behavior are conditioned by regional identity and custom. For example, it would make sense to segment an outerwear clothing line on a regional basis simply because of differences in climate.

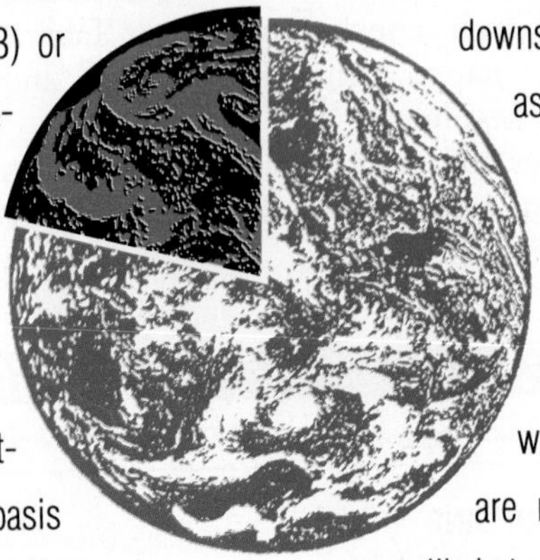

Goodyear Tires uses a more global approach to segmentation, because tires are a universal product, but it also does some regional fine-tuning. The company decided to identify segments in international markets by what consumers emphasize in purchasing tires—brand, price, or the retail outlet. It identified four segments that cut across regional lines. Those who emphasize the brand, Goodyear called *quality buyers*. They tend to be upscale, brand loyal, and buy major brands. Since consumers in Belgium and Italy tend to be more brand loyal, they are more likely to be in the quality segment.

The second segment, labeled *trusting patrons*, is very loyal to a particular retail outlet. This group is downscale and regards the brand of tires as unimportant. As a result, it relies on the retail outlet to recommend a brand. These outlet-oriented shoppers are likely to be found in less-developed countries around the world, because attitudes toward tires are not well formed. Retail outlets are more likely to be regarded as specialists. As countries become more economically developed and these consumers become more familiar with a product category like tires, the consumers are more likely to become quality oriented.

There are two price-oriented groups. *Value-oriented shoppers* consider the brand first and price second. This group tends to buy major brands, has low retailer loyalty, and does a detailed comparison of brands. A high proportion of consumers in France and Greece are value oriented. The second price-oriented group, *bargain hunters,* rely exclusively on price. They tend to be younger and are the least

than the rest of Europe. Marketers of appliances, electronics, and cars are likely to find greater price sensitivity in these regions and should be prepared to offer lower-priced lines. Interestingly, the richest regions (Segments 2, 3, and 4) all have significant French- and German-speaking populations, meaning marketers can more easily use one homogeneous advertising strategy in these areas.

The regional segmentation in Table 10.3 is helpful in developing guidelines for marketing in the EC countries as economic integration takes hold.

GLOBAL MARKETING STRATEGIES

brand loyal. They regard buying tires as a necessary nuisance and delay the purchase as long as possible. The greatest proportion of bargain hunters are found in the United States.

Goodyear varies its marketing strategy in each country, depending on which segment is predominant. For quality buyers, the company uses image advertising through TV and radio to emphasize the latest in technology. Distribution is through specialty tire stores and department stores. There is little discounting. Brand-image advertising is also used to appeal to value buyers, but Goodyear also uses periodic price promotions to appeal to the price orientation of this group.

Goodyear uses a retail-oriented approach in appealing to the "trusting patron" group. Ads emphasize the store, with frequent attempts to link Goodyear tires to local store advertising. As for bargain hunters, price is the only motivating factor in Goodyear's marketing mix. Distribution is primarily through discount stores. The approach to the fourth group, bargain hunters, is strictly price-oriented with frequent price promotions directed to this group.

Goodyear's international segmentation scheme shows an attempt to transcend regional boundaries and use a more global approach in segmenting markets. Given that it obtains a higher margin and profit from the quality segment, its motto might well be "Quality buyers of the world, unite."

Questions: What is the rationale for Goodyear's segmentation of its international markets? How does the company vary its strategy by segment?

Source: Adapted from "Attitude Research Assesses Global Market Potential," *Marketing News*, August 1, 1988, pp. 10 and 13.

LIFE-STYLE SEGMENTATION

Life-style segmentation groups consumers according to their attitudes, interests, and opinions. Achievement orientation, societal consciousness, health consciousness, and family orientation would be examples of the characteristics associated with consumer needs and brand preferences.

Merrill Lynch used life-style segmentation to change its corporate image. In the early 1980s, the company found that its advertisements portraying a herd of bulls

EXHIBIT 10.4

Change in Merrill Lynch's Image Due to Life-Style Segmentation

Example of "We're Bullish on America" Campaign.

Example of "A Breed Apart" Campaign.

with the theme, "We're Bullish on America," appealed to conventional and risk-averse consumers. To attract those people who were more upscale and willing to experiment, the company identified a more achievement-oriented group as its target. It then changed its advertising theme to "A Breed Apart" (see Exhibit 10.4).

Life-style segmentation has also been used to segment international markets. One large advertising agency identified a global life-style group known as *strivers*—young adults who lead active lives, are frequently under stress, and prefer products that are sources of instant gratification. Given their time constraints, strivers would be a good target for a global fast-food chain such as McDonald's. Instant gratification and fast foods would also go hand in hand. A second group, *achievers*, are affluent, assertive, and their country's opinion leaders. They value status and quality in brands. They would be a good target for luxury products such as designer clothes and high-priced cars. A third group, *traditionalists*, embody the traditional values of their country, are resistant to change, and buy familiar products. Traditionalists would be a good target for local, home-spun products.[24]

SEGMENTING BY PERSONALITY CHARACTERISTICS

Personality characteristics are another important basis for segmenting markets. Traits such as aggressiveness, compliance, and compulsiveness are more deep seated than life-styles, because they reflect more enduring patterns of behavior. As a result, they are particularly relevant to consumer purchase behavior.

Anheuser-Busch developed personality profiles of beer drinkers in an effort to determine which market segments the company's major brands were reaching. It linked four drinking types to personality factors. Reparative drinkers are light drinkers who are attuned to the needs of others; social drinkers tend to be ambitious and manipulative; indulgent drinkers drink heavily when alone and blame others for their shortcomings; and oceanic drinkers drink heavily with others to escape awareness of their shortcomings.

The study found that Michelob and Budweiser appealed to different personality segments and allowed the company to specify target segments to be reached by each brand based on personality types. For instance, advertising aimed at reparative drinkers might show men and women drinking beer together in a relaxed, congenial setting. Michelob would be positioned well to this group. An appeal to oceanic drinkers might use a male-oriented setting geared to the heavier drinker by linking beer-drinking to some occupational or social success to overcome a sense of failure. Budweiser would be positioned well to this group.

The study was also helpful in pinpointing the best advertising media for each beer. For example, reparative drinkers were more likely to watch TV, while oceanic drinkers were more likely to read *Playboy*. Personality segmentation thus enabled more-effective advertising directed to particular market segments.[25]

TARGET THE MARKETING EFFORT

Once a firm has identified market segments, it must target marketing effort to selected segments. Figure 10.4 shows that there are three steps in selecting segments for targeting: first, establish criteria for selecting segments; second, develop a strategy for selecting segments; and third, once target segments are selected, position products to meet the needs of these segments.

ESTABLISH CRITERIA FOR SELECTING TARGET SEGMENTS

There are five generally accepted criteria for selecting segments for targeting:

1. Similarity of customer needs within the segment
2. Unmet needs
3. The size of the segment
4. The segment's growth potential
5. The accessibility of the segment

Nestlé used these five criteria in a study that segmented the instant coffee market and eventually led to the introduction of Taster's Choice decaffeinated.

SIMILARITY OF CUSTOMER NEEDS

Consumers in a segment must have similar needs if they are to be targeted for marketing effort. If a group's needs are not similar, there is little basis for directing marketing strategies to a segment, because no single product will offer the benefits the segment wants.

In the early 1970s, Nestlé did a study of instant coffee drinkers and identified four benefit segments: convenience, taste, lift and pickup, and no interference with sleep (that is, the decaffeinated segment). Each of the segments could be identified by consumers who emphasize one of these four primary needs.

The similarity in needs within a segment permitted Nestlé to direct specific instant-coffee brands to specific targets. Thus, Nescafé is positioned to two segments, the convenience and lift/pickup segments, Nescafé Decaffeinated is positioned to the "Lets Me Sleep" segment, and Taster's Choice freeze-dried coffee is directed to the taste segment.

Even when firms use an approach other than benefit segmentation, the assumption is that needs within the segment are similar. Hence, when Holiday Inn segments its market by consumer characteristics (income), it is assuming that low-, middle-, and higher-income consumers will have different traveling needs in terms of the service and amenities for which they are willing to pay.

UNMET NEEDS

A second basic criterion in targeting a particular segment is whether its needs are being met by competitors. If they are, a firm entering the segment runs the risk of being a "me-too" brand with little competitive advantage. If the segment's needs are not being met, then a strategic window exists, assuming the firm has the competency to target the segment.

Nestlé defined a strategic window when it identified a significant group of decaffeinated users who were dissatisfied with the taste of existing brands. As a result, it introduced a decaffeinated version of Taster's Choice. The breakthrough was not so much in identifying this group, for it was long known that many decaffeinated users thought existing brands such as Sanka tasted medicinal. Rather, the breakthrough came with the technology that developed the freeze-drying process, allowing a decaffeinated coffee to be developed that retained more of the flavor of the original beans. Having already developed Taster's Choice, Nestlé obviously had the know-how to introduce a freeze-dried decaffeinated version.

SIZE OF THE SEGMENT

Another important criterion in selecting segments for targeting is the size of a segment, because size is linked to profitability. A firm would prefer to go after a segment with more consumers—therefore, higher revenue potential—as long as the segment is identified by similar needs, and the company can establish some competitive advantage. The segment of coffee drinkers who wanted a better-tasting decaffeinated coffee was large enough to pursue, so Nestlé targeted this segment for its Taster's Choice decaffeinated brand.

The size of a segment is not always related to profitability, however. Relatively small segments may be highly profitable as long as the company can establish a unique and sustainable competitive advantage. For example, Le Peep International is a breakfast-only restaurant chain that provides a unique offering—"power" breakfasts in a quiet setting with tablecloths, flower vases, and skylights—to a small, but profitable, segment; young professionals.[26]

GROWTH POTENTIAL

Still another criterion in targeting segments for marketing efforts is the potential for growth. A segment that is likely to attract more consumers in the future is preferable to one that is in a stagnant position in a mature market.

Although coffee consumption is decreasing because of greater health awareness, the decaffeinated market segment is increasing for the same reason. Thus, Taster's Choice decaffeinated is well positioned to address these concerns in a growing segment of the coffee market. Similarly, Le Peep is likely to find a growing segment of young professionals attracted to the idea of breakfast in a nice environment. The danger of a growth segment is that growth is likely to attract competitors. Le Peep may soon find it will not be the only elegant breakfast chain in town.

ACCESSIBILITY OF SEGMENTS

The last opportunity-related factor in evaluating a segment is its accessibility. To reach a segment, a firm must have access to media to deliver its advertising messages and to store outlets to deliver its products.

Demographics provide the basis for selecting media and for establishing distribution efforts to reach the segment. Le Peep, for instance, can select media to reach young urban professionals by advertising in magazines such as *Time* or *Fortune.* The chain can also locate its restaurants in downtown office areas where young professionals are most likely to work. Similarly, Nestlé can use the fact that decaffeinated drinkers tend to be over age 50 to help establish a target for its advertising for Taster's Choice decaffeinated coffee.

Accessibility is also related to region. To implement its regional segmentation strategy, Campbell must select local TV shows and magazines capable of reaching consumers in specific regions. Similarly, since Le Peep is a regional chain, it must select media directed to its regions. National magazines such as *Time* now have the capability to produce copies by region so that an advertiser like Le Peep can buy space in the regional edition where it is located. Without this facility, Le Peep would have to buy space in a national edition and most of its advertising dollars would be wasted.

If a segment does not have certain distinctive demographic characteristics, accessibility may be difficult. The only way to appeal to such a segment is to advertise to everyone through the mass media. This is inefficient, however, for the vast proportion of advertising dollars will be wasted on consumers outside the target group. Demographics that identify a segment permit the marketer to pinpoint advertising to the specific target.

DEVELOP A STRATEGY FOR SELECTING TARGET SEGMENTS

Having established criteria for targeting segments, a firm must decide what type of strategy will be most effective in selecting segments for marketing effort. As Figure 10.5 shows, firms can market one or several products to one or more segments, producing four alternative strategies: concentrated segmentation, market-segment expansion, product-line segmentation, and differentiated segmentation.

CONCENTRATED SEGMENTATION: ONE PRODUCT TO ONE SEGMENT

Concentrated segmentation *involves targeting one segment with one product.* Concentrated segmentation tends to be used by smaller firms with limited resources. These firms become profitable by gaining a strong market position in one segment. Le Peep markets one product, power breakfasts, to a single segment, young professionals.

"Putting all your eggs in one basket" can be risky, however. A large firm can enter a segment and undercut a smaller firm. Minnetonka followed a concentrated

FIGURE 10.5

Alternative Strategies for Targeting Market Segments

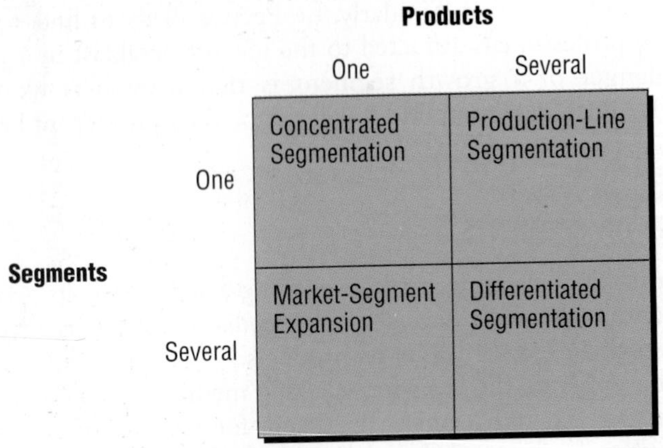

segmentation strategy when it developed liquid hand soap in a pump dispenser and appealed to a small segment with the product. As we have seen in Chapter 6, the product's success prompted larger companies such as Lever and P&G to enter the market. Minnetonka was quickly outgunned and forced to merge with a larger, foreign-owned packaged-goods company to survive.

MARKET-SEGMENT EXPANSION: ONE PRODUCT TO SEVERAL SEGMENTS

A firm that uses **market-segment expansion** *markets one product to several segments.* Thus, the market base for one product is expanded, increasing profitability. Typically, a company starts with a concentrated segmentation strategy, then embarks on a segment-expansion strategy to increase the product's base. Kellogg expanded its base from children to adults when cereal sales stagnated because of a declining birth rate. Johnson & Johnson expanded its shampoo market from babies to adults for the same reason.

DuPont, on the other hand, started with a strategy of market-segment expansion when it introduced Kevlar, a synthetic material that is both lighter and stronger than steel. The product was targeted to three very different market segments: commercial fishermen, aircraft designers, and plant engineers. Commercial fishermen found that a boat hull made from Kevlar saves fuel, increases speed, and permits more fish to be carried in the boat because of its light weight. Aircraft designers like Kevlar because of its high strength-to-weight ratio and the additional lift it provides, and plant engineers like Kevlar because it eliminates the need for asbestos in pumps and other devices.[27] DuPont developed three different advertising campaigns to communicate these benefits to each target group (see Exhibit 10.5).

Market-segment expansion is viable only if specific segments have well-defined needs for the same product and if appeals directed toward one segment will not alienate another segment. Coors is the first beer company to direct its advertising specifically toward women, even though women buy only 17 percent of the beer

EXHIBIT 10.5

One Product Directed to Several Segments: DuPont's Kevlar

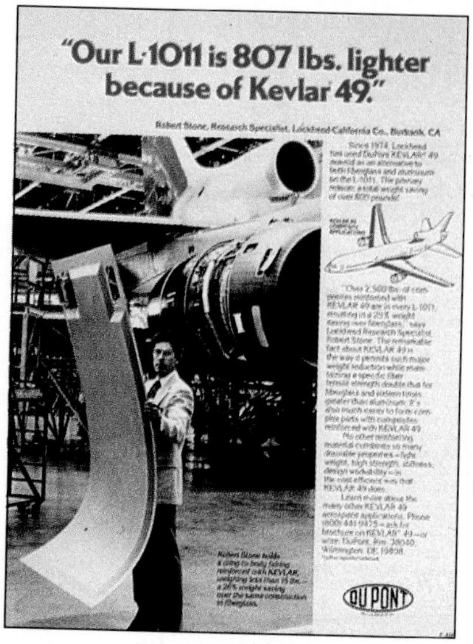

sold in the United States. Other companies have not targeted women for fear that their ads may alienate male users. As one industry analyst said, "If you gear ads to men, women will buy the product. But if you gear ads to women, men won't buy the product. You're dealing with the fragile male ego here."[28] Coors is willing to take the risk since women's 17 percent share of the beer market still amounts to $6.5 billion a year. That means almost $400 million to Coors for each additional share point it can gain by appealing to women.

PRODUCT-LINE SEGMENTATION: SEVERAL PRODUCTS TO ONE SEGMENT

Product-line segmentation *directs several products to one segment.* This is called product-line segmentation because the several products being directed to the one segment are usually part of a single product line.

Toddler University is a small company created to target one segment, babies, with one line of products, shoes. But the company approaches the baby-shoe market with a distinctive positioning. It operates like an athletic shoe company by dividing its line by performance category. For example, there is a shoe for babies in the crib, another for toddlers, and another for babies who are just starting to walk.[29] Toddler University's walking shoes are designed to look like their adult counterparts (see Exhibit 10.6).

The risk in a product-line segmentation strategy is the same as that for concentrated segmentation—putting all your eggs in one basket by appealing to one segment. If larger companies like Reebok or Nike begin to appeal to the baby market, Toddler University might face the same fate as Minnetonka—being outgunned by larger companies.

EXHIBIT 10.6

An Example of Product-Line Segmentation: Toddler University

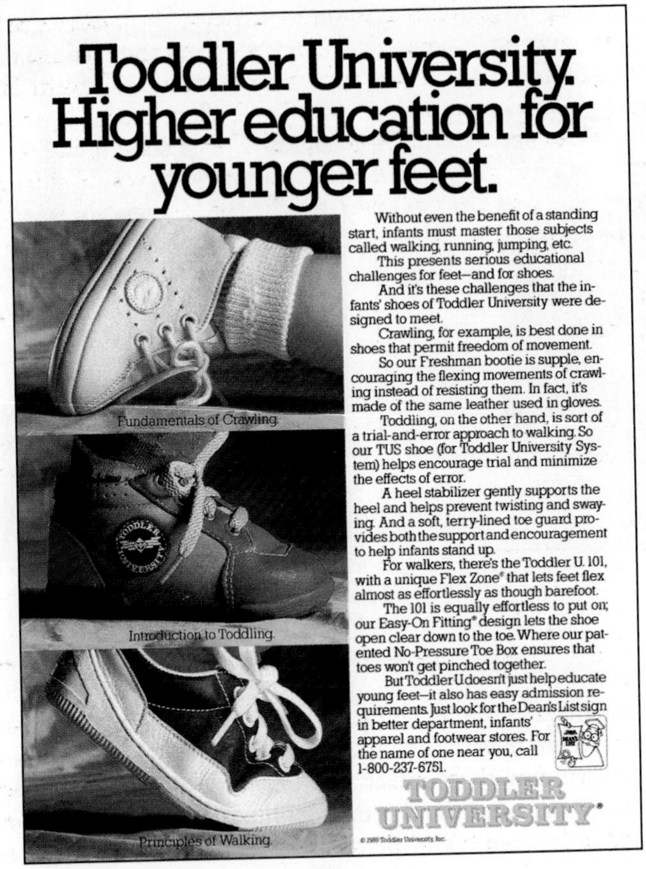

DIFFERENTIATED SEGMENTATION: SEVERAL PRODUCTS TO SEVERAL SEGMENTS

Many firms, particularly larger ones, operate in several segments by marketing several specific products to each segment. This fourth strategy is referred to as **differentiated segmentation,** *because the firm is differentiating its product offerings to meet the needs of particular segments.* Companies, such as Levi, that used a mass marketing approach in the past, can use differentiated segmentation to cover the total market with separate offerings to specific segments.

In marketing its charge-card line, American Express changed its strategy from concentrated segmentation, to segment expansion, to differentiated segmentation. Until 1980, the American Express card represented one product targeting one segment, male executives. As card membership leveled off, the company followed a segment expansion strategy by marketing the green card to working women, senior citizens, owners of small businesses, and students.

To ensure continued growth, the company's next step was to expand its product line through a differentiated-segmentation strategy. It first introduced the gold card, which provided additional services to business people. It then offered the platinum card as a symbol of prestige. American Express's next step was to introduce the Optima card designed to extend credit to cardholders. The Optima, green, gold, and platinum cards segmented the market from lower to higher socioeconomic class. As a result of this strategy, American Express has been cited as one of the few service companies that has mastered the art of market segmentation.

Differentiated segmentation is a powerful strategy, but it carries risks. As a firm appeals to more segments, it must fragment its efforts and increase its costs. Production costs go up as production runs become smaller. Advertising costs also increase, since different campaigns must be used to reach different segments. Finally, product-development costs go up as products are modified to meet the needs of each segment. As we have seen, the higher costs of differentiated segmentation have led some firms to follow a policy of countersegmentation, reducing the number of segments to which they appeal. Countersegmentation does not mean that these firms are abandoning a differentiated-segmentation approach, they are still following it by attempting to cover the total market. However, they are dividing the market into fewer segments so as to reduce costs.

POSITION PRODUCTS TO TARGET SEGMENTS

Once a company has decided which market segments to target, it must position products to meet the needs of those segments. Chapter 3 defined positioning as communicating product benefits to customers. DuPont positions Kevlar as the synthetic material as strong as steel. Toddler University positions its shoes as the performance shoes for babies, in a conscious attempt to create parallels to the adult athletic-shoe market. In each case, specific segments are targeted for these appeals. Because other competitors might threaten to go after these same segments, an effective positioning strategy is a means of gaining a competitive advantage.

We also have seen in Chapter 3 that there are various ways to position products to communicate benefits—by focusing on product features, solutions to problems, symbols, or comparisons with competition. All these approaches to positioning have one common element: the need to first define a target segment before developing the positioning strategy. Therefore, market segmentation and product positioning go hand in hand in the marketing plan: Market segments are defined, and products are positioned to meet the needs of these segments.

INDUSTRIAL MARKET SEGMENTATION

The same reason applies for segmenting markets in the industrial sector as in the consumer sector—developing products to meet the needs of customer groups. However, industrial firms have lagged behind in applying segmentation strategies. One reason is that industrial firms tend to be more engineering oriented, focusing on product specifications. As a result, they frequently let product design (rather than consumer needs) drive marketing strategy.

Another reason is that industrial marketers are more likely to be in one of the two extremes on the marketing continuum in Figure 10.1, micromarketing or mass marketing. Buyers often require unique products, for example, customized telecommunications or information systems. As a result, many industrial marketers are not required to segment markets into groups of buyers. They are producing for individual customers.

When customized marketing is not required, a mass-market mentality seems to prevail. As one industrial marketing expert said:

TABLE 10.4

Variables Used to Identify Industrial Market Segments

BENEFIT SEGMENTATION	
Product Criteria	Product performance Durability Economy Ease of use
Vendor Criteria	Delivery Reputation Economy Convenience
BEHAVIORAL SEGMENTATION	Products purchased Frequency of purchase Type of purchase (new buy, modified rebuy, straight rebuy)
SEGMENTING BY ORGANIZATION CHARACTERISTICS	Location Number of employees Annual sales volume Net worth Number of years in business Number of establishments Industry grouping

> Industrial firms frequently have a product emphasis and little or no real market segmentation identification. . . . Many industrial companies tend to think of a market as one large unit that buys and uses similar products.[30]

Despite these limitations, we have seen the application of effective industrial segmentation strategies by DuPont for Kevlar. Similarly, Deere, a large farm-equipment manufacturer, effectively applies a product-line segmentation strategy in marketing high-horsepower machinery to larger farms. Deere focuses on one major segment—larger farms that require large-horsepower equipment—and positions its full line of farm machinery to this segment.

Industrial firms that implement segmentation strategies use the same three bases for segmentation as those used by consumer firms: segmenting by benefits, by behavior, or by customer characteristics. As Table 10.4 shows, however, the variables used to segment the market differ from those in consumer marketing. For example, industrial marketers are more likely to identify benefit segments by the need for performance, durability, economy, or ease of use, because organizational buyers tend to emphasize these factors in selecting products. Industrial marketers also identify benefit segments by the buyer's emphasis on delivery, reputation, or convenience, because organizational buyers emphasize these factors in selecting vendors.

Organizational buyers can be segmented behaviorally by the products they buy or the frequency with which they buy them. We have seen in Chapter 9 that organizational buyers can be classified by the type of purchase (new buy, modified rebuy, straight rebuy), and buyer segments can be defined on this basis.

As for the third approach to segmentation—by customer characteristics—consumer-goods firms use demographic characteristics to segment consumers, whereas industrial firms use organizational characteristics. Industrial marketers might segment buyers by size of the firm, total number of employees, industry grouping, and number of years in business.

A good example of benefit segmentation in the industrial sector is DuPont's segmentation of potential Kevlar users into three segments: customers who need a stronger synthetic material, a lighter material, and a material that can be an asbestos substitute. An AT&T study is an example of behavioral segmentation in industrial marketing. AT&T separated the telecommunications market into large, medium, and small businesses based on the number of telephone lines owned. It then determined the telephone needs and characteristics of each segment. The AT&T study cited in Chapter 7 described the steps taken to further research the needs of the small business segment. Both Hewlett-Packard and IBM provide an example of segmenting by organizational characteristics. They group computer buyers by industry type and then develop systems for these industry groupings—for example, systems for aircraft designers, branch bank managers, or retail inventory managers.

SUMMARY

1. **What are the advantages of a strategy of market segmentation?**
   Market segmentation generally leads to greater profitability, because it better satisfies the diverse demands of the marketplace. In general, firms can generate more revenue by appealing to the needs of specific consumer segments. Market segmentation also helps a firm identify opportunities, develop new products, and allocate marketing resources to areas of opportunity.
2. **Why has there been a recent trend toward market segmentation?**
   Many companies have recently shifted from a mass-marketing approach to a market-segmentation approach for two reasons. First, economic conditions since the 1950s have prompted firms to focus on consumer needs in order to remain competitive. The best way to focus on consumer needs is by developing products to meet the needs of particular consumer segments. Second, demographic and life-style changes in the 1970s and 1980s have fragmented the market into more-discrete groupings, furthering the need for a market-segmentation approach.
3. **How can companies identify market segments?**
   Companies can identify segments by the benefits they seek, by their behavior, and by their characteristics. Benefit segmentation identifies segments by their needs; it is an effective tool for developing new products, because it pinpoints segments with unmet needs. Behavioral segmentation focuses on the brands consumers buy or the extent to which a product category is used. This approach assists marketers in developing strategies for brands or product categories. Segmenting by consumer characteristics—such as age, income, race,

life-style, and personality traits—is useful in providing guidelines for positioning products in advertisements and also for selecting media to reach target segments.

4. **What criteria can marketers use to decide which segments to target for marketing effort?**
   Marketers use two sets of criteria in selecting segments for targeting: (1) opportunities for revenue in marketing to the segment and (2) a firm's competency to pursue these opportunities. Factors related to revenue potential are the extent of similarity in the needs of customers within a segment; the existence of unmet needs within the segment; the size and growth potential of the segment; and the segment's accessibility through marketing efforts such as advertising or distribution. The firm's competence is a function of its marketing and manufacturing know-how, as well as its resources, in targeting a particular segment.
5. **What alternative strategies can companies use to segment markets?**
   A company can follow a strategy of pursuing one or several segments with one or several products. Directing one product toward one segment, concentrated segmentation, is most often chosen by smaller firms seeking to gain competitive advantage. Market-segment expansion, which directs one product toward several segments, allows a firm to expand the market base for a product. Directing several products toward one segment, product-line segmentation, usually involves the products of a single product line being directed toward one segment. Differentiated segmentation involves directing several specific products toward several segments.

KEY TERMS

Market segmentation (p. 320)
Micromarketing (p. 321)
Geo-demographic analysis (p. 321)
Customized marketing (p. 321)
Mass marketing (p. 322)
Countersegmentation (p. 326)
Targeting (p. 328)
Benefit segmentation (p. 329)
Behavioral segmentation (p. 329)
Segmenting by consumer characteristics (p. 329)
Concentrated segmentation (p. 345)
Market-segment expansion (p. 346)
Product-line segmentation (p. 347)
Differentiated segmentation (p. 348)

QUESTIONS

1. What environmental trends prompted Levi to adopt a market segmentation strategy?
2. What are the advantages and disadvantages of:
   a. micromarketing
   b. market segmentation
   c. mass marketing
3. Why was Procter & Gamble successful in following a mass-marketing approach in the face of the trend toward segmented marketing? Why did the company shift from a mass-marketing approach to a segmented-marketing approach?
4. Why did a trend toward countersegmentation develop in the 1980s? Did this trend conflict with the trend toward market segmentation described in the chapter? Why or why not?
5. Consider the following situations:
   a. A company wants to direct its marketing efforts toward heavy snackers.
   b. A company wants to determine the potential for a new nut-and-dried-fruit snack.
   c. A company wants to determine the life-style characteristics of its customers to obtain insights for developing its advertising strategy.

   What kind of segmentation approach should be used to identify segments in each of these cases? What is the strategic purpose of each approach?

6. What are the implications of the benefit-segmentation study of the snack market (Table 10.2) for:
   a. new-product development
   b. developing advertising themes
   c. media selection
7. Why is it important to identify a segment whose consumers have similar needs? What problems arise if a company targets a segment whose consumers have different needs.
8. What are the implications for marketing the following products to European countries, based on the regional segmentation categories in Table 10.3:
   a. jeans
   b. financial-planning services
   c. day-care centers
9. How could a company developing retirement communities use the Claritas service (see p. 335) to locate potential sites.
10. Why is it difficult to market to a segment whose consumers have no distinctive demographic characteristics?
11. What are the risks of a:
    a. concentrated-segmentation strategy
    b. market-segment-expansion strategy
    c. differentiated-segmentation strategy
12. Why do product-positioning decisions necessarily follow selection of target markets? Cite examples from the chapter of the link between selecting target segments and positioning products to them.
13. Why have industrial firms lagged behind consumer-goods firms in applying market-segmentation approaches?
14. What is the main difference in segmenting markets for industrial firms versus consumer-goods firms?

QUESTIONS: YOU ARE THE DECISION MAKER

1. A marketing executive for a producer of household cleaning products takes a cautious view when it comes to market segmentation. He says:

   Market segmentation works for companies who can offer consumers something different, something they need that competitors are not giving them. But many of our products are standardized items in mature, low-growth industries. We can't segment markets and offer something different to each segment. We advertise across the board and try to attract consumers with couponing and low prices. On this basis, we pretty much fall on the right-hand side of your continuum [Figure 10.1]. We are likely to remain mass marketers for the foreseeable future.

   a. Do you agree that market segmentation is not applicable for relatively standardized products such as detergents and bleach?
   b. What is the danger of this company following a mass-marketing approach for the foreseeable future?
2. An executive for one of the "Big Three" car manufacturers commented on the trend toward countersegmentation as follows:

   We are considering a countersegmentation policy by reducing the number of options we offer. In so doing, we will not be appealing to as many segments as we used to. We continue to find ourselves at a cost disadvantage compared to Japanese manufacturers, and reducing options is one way to reduce our costs and make our cars more price-competitive with Japanese makes.

   a. What are the pros and cons of this strategy?
   b. Do you agree with it? Why or why not?
3. When Stroh Brewery introduced Sundance, a sparkling beverage with 70 percent juice, it took the position that it was a beverage company, not just a brewery. Stroh saw an increasingly health-conscious population and realized it could not appeal to it by being a brewery, so it created a product that taps into the age of moderation and health.[31] Sundance's target audience is upscale adults, age 25 to 45, in urban areas, who are health and fitness conscious. What type of segmentation strategy is Stroh following in introducing Sundance—concentrated, product-line, or differentiated segmentation? Explain.

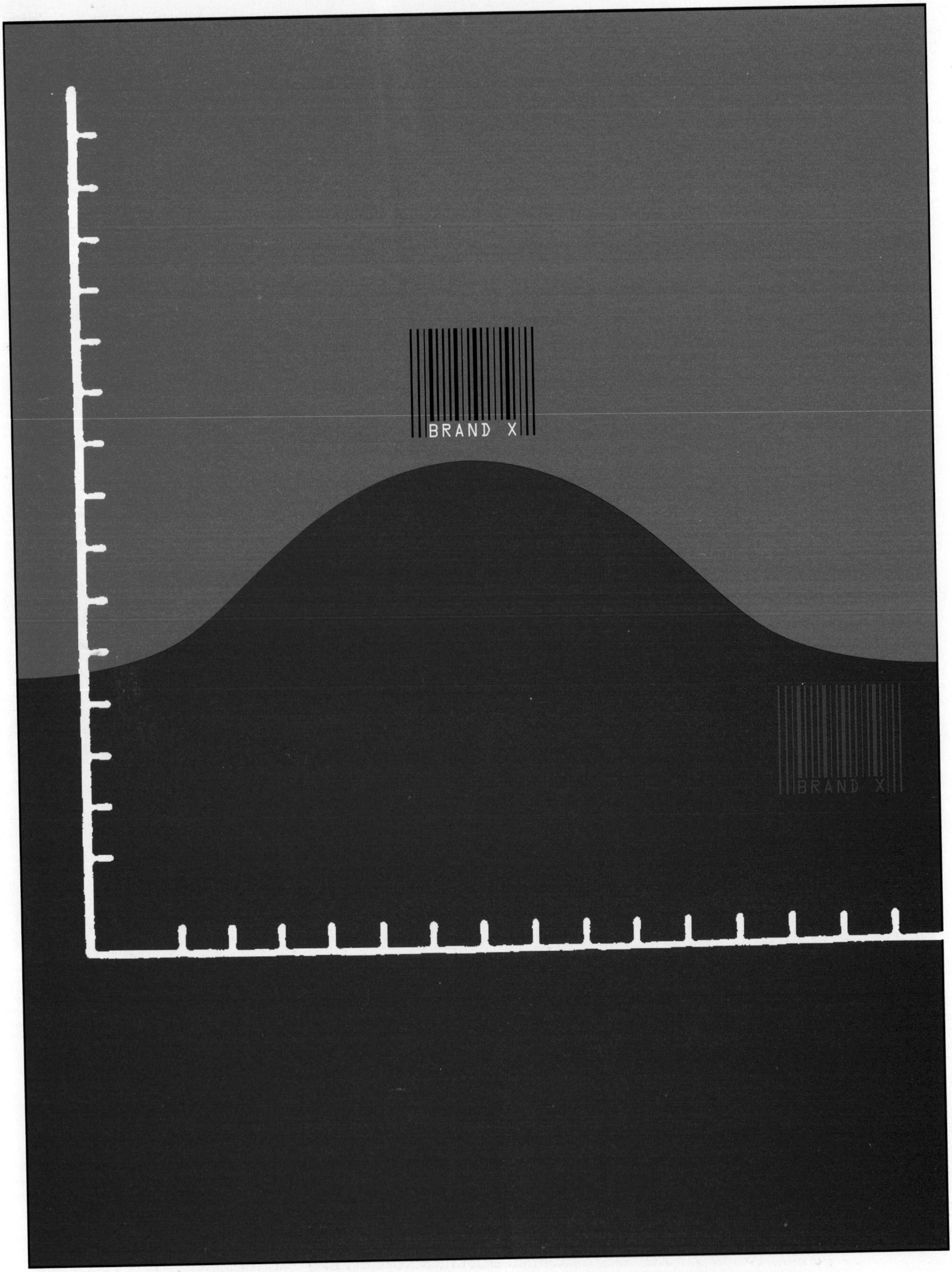

BRAND X
BRAND X

PART IV

Developing the Marketing Mix

The central component of the marketing plan is a marketing mix of product, distribution, promotional, and pricing strategies necessary to ensure that the product will meet the needs of targeted customers. This section considers each of these four components of the marketing mix.

The section on *product* (Chapters 11–13) describes developing new products, managing existing brands and products, and marketing services by profit and nonprofit firms. The area of *distribution* (Chapters 14–16) includes a description of alternative methods of distribution, and the nature of retailing, wholesaling, and physical distribution. *Promotion* (Chapters 17–19) describes the components of the promotional mix, namely advertising, sales promotions, publicity, and personal selling. The final section on *pricing* (Chapters 20–21) describes pricing strategies and methods of price determination.

CHAPTER 11

Developing New Products

YOUR FOCUS IN CHAPTER 11

To learn:

- *The definition of a product and a new product.*
- *Why new products are essential to a firm's profitability.*
- *The reasons for new-product successes and failures.*
- *What steps are involved in new-product development.*
- *Some of the ethical issues in new-product development.*

3M'S New Product Development Process Produces Another Winner

3M researchers knew they were onto something. It was 1987, and the company's marketing researchers had been fanning out across the country. The objective? Find out why sales were increasing beyond expectations for 3M's line of sandpaper designed for in-home use. The answer would lead to one of 3M's greatest success stories.

What the marketers found was that 3M consumers were mainly using 3M's sandpaper for refinishing wood furniture, a cottage industry that has boomed, because 75 percent of all U.S. households engage in some home-improvement.[1] Within six months, a 3M development manager named JoAnn Fernandez had been given the green light to translate that desire into a new product.

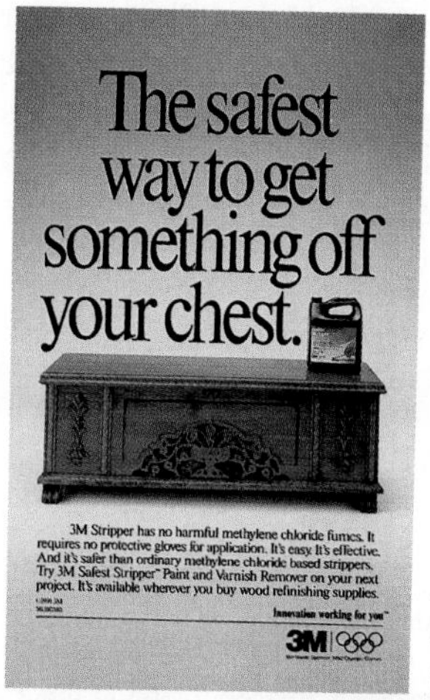

The safest way to get something off your chest.
3M Stripper has no harmful methylene chloride fumes. It requires no protective gloves for application. It's easy. It's effective. And it's safer than ordinary methylene chloride based strippers. Try 3M Safest Stripper™ Paint and Varnish Remover on your next project. It's available wherever you buy wood refinishing supplies.
Innovation working for you™
3M

In focus group interviews, Fernandez kept hearing that home improvers liked the sense of accomplishment that came with stripping away corroded paint and watching the pristine wood emerge. But they worried about the active ingredient in most refinishers: methylene chloride. It bubbled the paint away like acid but, if spilled, could easily burn through rubber gloves and singe skin. Such worries had already reached the ears of regulators at the U.S. Consumer Product Safety Commission (CPSC), who were investigating the chemical's potential as a carcinogen.[2]

The early focus group returns and CPSC debate convinced Fernandez that 3M had stumbled onto a major new product opportunity. By this time, more than a dozen 3Mers from the company's 42 divisions had been pulled onto a task force, dubbed XX, that came up with several novel ideas, among them creating a chemically-lined bag that furniture could be placed in overnight so that by morning it would be stripped. A second wave of marketing researchers fanned out across the country, stopping mall shoppers to ask them what they thought about the innovation. None liked the bag idea much, but the notion of a non-toxic gel brought the kind of approval rating that led Fernandez to move into high gear.[3]

To get a feel for which of the half-dozen formulations developed by 3M scientists worked best, Fernandez started close to home. She shipped samples to 3M's in-house woodworking club and dozens of employees. Based on the positive responses, she took the two most popular versions and gave it to 400 outside consumers whom 3M had previously used in tests. Within three months, she was sitting on a finished product. But what would she call it?

In the product tests, consumers kept raving about the fact they could use it indoors without gloves, and it really did strip. "But we had a positioning challenge," Fernandez says. "How were we going to communicate safety and effectiveness?" The answer became the brand name "Safest Stripper."

By early 1988, there was no question Safest Stripper would launch an entirely new category, and dozens of new products that could be used with it were either on the boards or in test phases. Ordinarily, a product is first introduced into a few markets (known as *test markets*) to determine consumer reactions before it is introduced nationally. But with so much at stake, Fernandez decided she could not risk tipping off her competitors by introducing Safest Stripper in test markets. Instead, while 3M's ad agency was busily designing a campaign, Fernandez took her creation to the 1988 National Hardware Show in Chicago. Chains such as Wal-Mart and Home Depot lined up to place their orders.

Volume shipping began in January 1988, and by the time Safest Stripper appeared on store shelves, 3M was advertising the slogan "You don't have to dress up to strip anymore."[4] The ad read, "Now there's a paint and varnish remover that doesn't require protective clothing."

In another company, Safest Stripper might never have been developed, because most other companies do not have the systematic and rigorous new-product development process of a 3M—and other companies do not mandate that a quarter of their $13 billion in revenues come from new products. To foster an atmosphere of innovation, 3M researchers are told to spend 15 percent of their time developing pet projects. When one looks promising, an "action team" is formed. The team decides how to develop and market the product. As the product clears each hurdle, everyone involved profits. For instance, if sales reach $5 million, the product's originator becomes a project manager, at $20 million a department manager, and at $75 million a division manager.[5] Fernandez, for example, has become marketing operations manager for 3M's Do-It-Yourself division.

It all happened because 3M wanted to know why its customers were using more sandpaper than the company expected.

WHAT IS A PRODUCT?

When we think of a product, we visualize a tangible object with physical properties. But often, we also ascribe intangible attributes to a product. When you think of your car as "powerful," a soft drink as "refreshing," or a computer as "user friendly," you are citing performance characteristics that describe the product's ability to satisfy consumer needs.

The success of many products is due more to such intangible attributes than to tangible characteristics. The new breed of mountain bicycles are a prime example. When Cycle Composites of California introduced its state-of-the-art Kestrel line—designed with a rugged, carbon, one-piece frame, wide tires, and upright seating—it focused on the bike's tangible features (see Exhibit 11.1). But the rugged design and light weight was more than a functional advancement, it was a fashion statement for Europeans who quickly traded their stylishly designed Italian bikes for these new symbols of the American pioneering life-style. Mountain bicycles quickly became an international hit, appearing in Paris boutiques with pricetags of more than $3,000 and quickly grew to account for more than half the 15 million bicycles sold in Europe.[6]

EXHIBIT 11.1

Mountain Bikes Have Both Tangible and Intangible Product Attributes

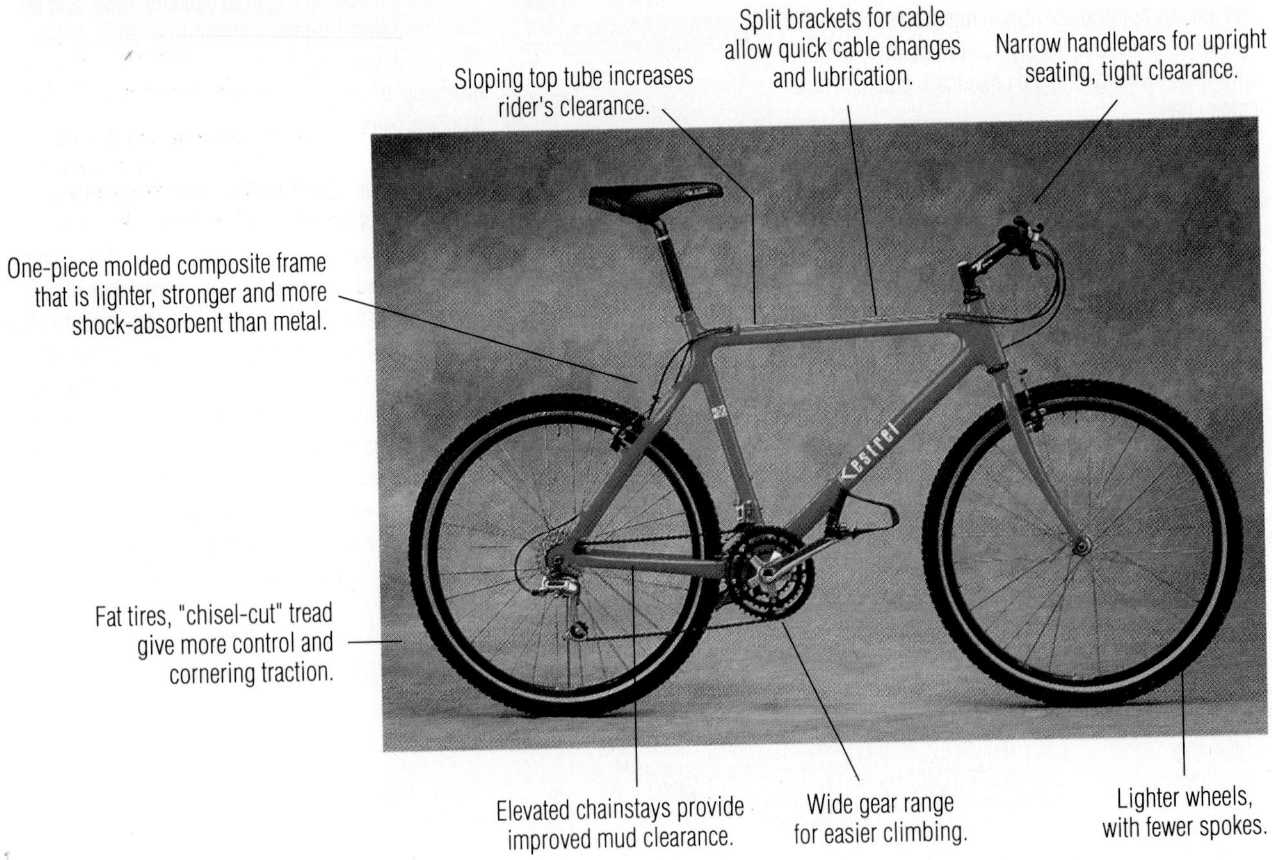
Split brackets for cable allow quick cable changes and lubrication.
Narrow handlebars for upright seating, tight clearance.
Sloping top tube increases rider's clearance.
One-piece molded composite frame that is lighter, stronger and more shock-absorbent than metal.
Kestrel
Fat tires, "chisel-cut" tread give more control and cornering traction.
Elevated chainstays provide improved mud clearance.
Wide gear range for easier climbing.
Lighter wheels, with fewer spokes.

PRODUCT COMPONENTS

The mountain bicycle example implies that a product is defined as much by how the consumer sees it as by its physical characteristics.

A product is therefore composed of intangible benefits as well as tangible characteristics. As a result, a **product** *is defined as a bundle of attributes and benefits designed to satisfy customer needs.* The fact that consumers seek different benefits means that they will see products differently. Therefore, a product is not a uniform, well-defined entity. When PepsiCo introduced its juice-based Slice brand in 1985, it appealed to a segment of soda drinkers who also wanted the benefit of nutrition; but others merely saw adding fruit as a gimmick to increase prices. One consumer may see Lexus's LS 400 sedans as a purveyor of luxury and prestige; another may see it as crass and tasteless. These consumers will define each product very differently.

The definition of a product cites two of its components: the benefits it conveys and its attributes. A third component is support services. These components are shown in Figure 11.1. The benefits of the product are those characteristics consumers see as potentially meeting their needs. Figure 11.1 shows that *product benefits identify the* **core product**, because benefits determine whether the consumer buys it. For many Kestrel buyers, the benefit was status and image. For purchasers of 3M's Safest Stripper, the key benefit was being able to refinish their home furniture safely and easily.

Marketers must turn desired benefits into product attributes. *Product attributes identify the* **tangible product** in Figure 11.1. Cycle Composites and other moun-

FIGURE 11.1

The Components of a Product

Source: Philip Kotler and Gail Armstrong, *Principles of Marketing.* (Englewood Cliffs, N.J.: Prentice-Hall, 4 ed., 1989), p. 244.

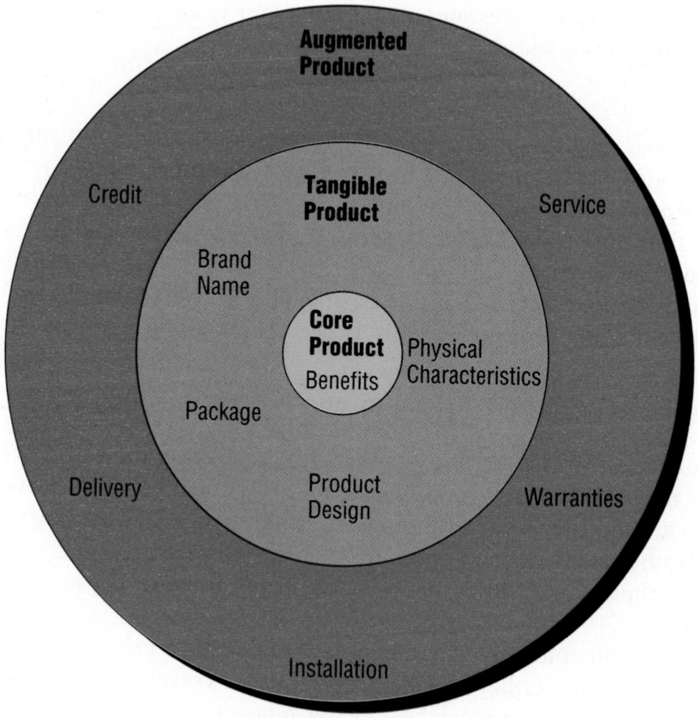

tain bike makers may not have created Europe's fascination with the outdoorsy American life-style, but they were able to tap into it with their improvisational and daring designs. 3M turned its customers' desire for an odorless furniture refinisher into a tangible product with Safest Stripper.

Figure 11.1 shows that product attributes not only include physical characteristics such as the gear range of a bicycle, they are also represented by the package and the brand name. How a package is wrapped can sometimes be more important than its content. For example, the ingredients in a product like baby shampoo are fairly standardized across brands. But many parents prefer Johnson & Johnson because they regard it as a known and dependable brand, and they do not want to risk using anything else on their baby. In this case, brand name is more important than content. The packaging can also be critical. One of the reasons Campbell's Juice Works failed was because competitive brands were in aseptic packages, and Juice Works was not.

Product design is another important attribute. Products such as automobiles, electronic items, and many industrial goods require good design of the visible components of the product. These may be as important to purchasers as their mechanical characteristics. Luxury was a key element in Toyota's design of its Lexus LS 400 sedans; as a result, the $43,000 model became a dominant player in the prestige market.[7]

The third element of a product is post-sale support. Many products are purchased on credit. Purchases also sometimes include delivery, installation, warranties, and service. *A product that includes post-sales support features is referred to as an* **augmented product** because terms of sale include elements other than the tangible product. The augmented product is particularly important in industrial marketing, because many industrial products require post-sale support. In recent years, Digital Equipment Corporation established a competitive advantage over IBM by providing stronger post-sales support for computer systems in the way of instruction, servicing, and software.

PRODUCT CATEGORIES

So far, we have used the term *product* as a single classification. Actually, a product can represent a brand or a product category. A **brand** *is a name or symbol that represents a product.* A **product category** *is the generic class to which the brand belongs.* Brands within the product category provide the same functional benefits to consumers and can serve as substitutes for one another. Safest Stripper is a brand within the product category—furniture-stripping products. Similarly, Macintosh is a brand name; the product category is personal computers.

DIFFERENCES BETWEEN COUNTRIES IN PRODUCT DEFINITIONS

Some product categories are likely to be defined the same the world over, because they have the same role and provide the same functional benefits across countries. Teenagers around the world tend to view jeans the same way, and carbonated soft drinks is a universally defined product category. However, the definition of many product categories will differ between countries because consumers see them differently.

For example, in countries where bicycles are seen as a primary means of transportation or recreation, they may be broken out into several categories depending on their function—mountain bikes, racing bikes, tandems, and three- and ten-speed bikes. Each of these types of bicycles would be represented as a separate category because they serve a different functional purpose. Yet, in countries such as the United States, where bicycles are not an important part of day-to-day living, different types of bicycles are likely to be lumped together into one product category. Similarly, whereas U.S. consumers might define jeeps, station wagons, sedans, and sports cars as different product categories, in China automobiles might be regarded as one product category because of their scarcity. Chinese consumers are unlikely to draw fine lines between automobile types.

Even in the same country, different segments of consumers might define product categories differently. An American bicycle maven might make the same distinctions between bicycles as a typical French consumer and view the definition of bicycles as a single product category as oversimplified.

DISTINCTION BETWEEN BRANDS AND PRODUCT CATEGORIES

The distinction between brand and product category is important for several reasons. First, the product category defines the brand's competition. Defining the product category broadly or narrowly will therefore affect a brand's strategy. Avia sneakers are a good example. While Reebok spends more than $70 million on promotion to define its categories—and Nike $100 million—Avia has only $10 million to spend. If it defined its sneakers so that they appealed to the broadest audience, Avia would be up against all of Reebok's and Nike's products. Given its limited promotional budget, Avia would be at a great disadvantage. Instead, it markets its sneakers narrowly to health-club enthusiasts. In playful ads, people in airports are asked by an announcer to identify Avia and give answers ranging from "an Arab head covering" to "bathroom tissue." The announcer then asks people in health clubs to do the same. They, of course, answer correctly. The narrowly-defined message is that while most people may not know the Avia brand, health club enthusiasts swear by it.[8]

A second reason why the distinction between brand and product category is important is that a company may wish to develop a **product line**; *that is, a line of offerings within a certain product category.* ConAgra is hitching its fortunes to its best-selling Healthy Choice frozen meal label by expanding it into an umbrella category that will include everything from microwavable meals that need no refrigeration to frozen breakfasts.[9] In the deodorant category, Ban has a complete product line composed of roll-ons, dry sprays, and sticks. The definition of the product category determines what is in the product line.

A third reason for distinguishing between brand and product category is that, at times, a company may be as interested in stimulating demand for the product category as for its brand. 3M positioned Safest Stripper in the context of its entire line of Do-It-Yourself refinishing products by creating an ad picturing children and featuring the slogan, "Before creating our furniture stripper, we considered people who don't even own furniture." The objective was to stimulate demand for the category—furniture-stripping products—as well as the brand.

PRODUCT CLASSIFICATIONS

The large number of different products in the marketplace makes classifying them difficult. Yet, marketers need to classify products so that similar strategies can be developed for those in the same class. Two important types of product classifications bear on marketing strategies: degree of product tangibility and type of product user.

DEGREE OF PRODUCT TANGIBILITY

Products can be classified by the degree to which they represent tangible physical characteristics. Figure 11.2 shows three categories on this dimension: durable goods, nondurable goods, and services.

The most tangible product offerings, **durable goods,** *are products that are used over time.* Cars, appliances, and electronics are durable goods. **Nondurable goods** *are items consumed in one or a few uses.* These products are divided in Figure 11.2 into packaged goods, such as toothpaste, detergents, or candy bars, and nonpackaged goods, such as gasoline.

Services *are intangible benefits* that are purchased by consumers but do not involve ownership. When we buy an airline ticket, we are buying the services offered by riding in someone else's plane. Since services represent more than half the Gross National Product of the United States, we will consider how they are classified and marketed in Chapter 13.

As we will see, there are major differences in marketing strategies for durables, nondurables, and services. For example, customers are likely to deliberate more in buying durables and consult a wider range of information sources. As a result, personal selling is a more important part of the marketing mix. Advertising is more likely to provide consumers with information. Durables are also distributed selectively rather than on a widespread basis. Nondurables involve less consumer deliberation. Advertising is more likely to be used to convey images and symbols than to provide information. Distribution is fairly extensive, and sales promotions such as couponing and price deals are used frequently to encourage consumers to switch to a company's brand.

Because services are intangible, advertising is used to try to make their benefits more tangible. Most services are delivered on a person-to-person basis and are often variable, so an important element in the marketing mix is to ensure that services are offered at a standard level of quality.

TYPE OF BUYER

The other important product classification is by type of buyer. The most important distinction is between products directed toward consumers versus organizational buyers. As we have seen in Chapter 1, consumer goods are sold directly to individuals for final consumption. Industrial goods are designed to be used in producing other goods (raw materials such as steel or lumber) or in support of such production (generators to produce electricity, typewriters to prepare reports, post-sale services to maintain products). The distinction between a consumer good and industrial good is not based on the characteristics of the product, but on the purpose for which it is used. A typewriter or computer used at home is a consumer good; the identical product used in a business organization is an industrial good.

FIGURE 11.2

Classifying Products by Degree of Tangibility

CONSUMER GOODS

Consumer goods can be classified as convenience, shopping, and specialty goods (see Table 11.1). **Convenience goods** *are goods that consumers purchase frequently with little deliberation or effort.* They are generally packaged goods such as toothpaste, detergents, cereals, and coffee. We have seen in Chapter 8 that such low-involvement products are characterized by little information search and by repeat buying based on inertia rather than on brand loyalty.

The product classifications in Table 11.1 are of interest, because they suggest different marketing strategies. Because consumers purchase convenience goods frequently, they must be distributed widely. Since product involvement and brand loyalty are low, coupons and price promotions are frequently used to induce consumers to switch brands. High advertising expenditures are necessary because of intense competition in many convenience goods categories. Low involvement also means that advertising strategies are more likely to use symbols and imagery rather than information to increase brand awareness and to influence purchases. For example, ads for colas might show teens on the beach to capture the spirit of youth and vigor the marketer is trying to associate with the brand. Rarely will a cola ad focus on product attributes such as sweetness or carbonation.

Shopping goods *are those products for which consumers are likely to spend more time shopping and comparing on specific characteristics, because they are involved with the product.* As a result, a process of complex decision making is likely, requiring greater information search. Examples of shopping goods are clothing, furniture, major appliances, cosmetics, and medical services.

TABLE 11.1

Classification of Consumer Goods

	CONVENIENCE GOODS	SHOPPING GOODS	SPECIALTY GOODS
CONSUMER PURCHASING CHARACTERISTICS	Frequent purchases Low involvement Purchase by inertia or limited decision making	Less-frequent purchases Higher involvement Purchases by extensive decision making	Infrequent purchases Highest involvement Purchases by brand loyalty
TYPES OF PRODUCTS	Toothpaste Detergents Cereals Coffee	Appliances Clothing Cars Medical services: general practitioner	Rolex watch Nikon camera Gucci handbags Medical services: specialist
STRATEGIC CHARACTERISTICS	Low price Widespread distribution Fewer product differences Frequent use of sales promotions High level of advertising expenditures Frequent use of symbols and imagery in advertising	High price Selective distribution Many product differences Emphasis on product features in advertising Importance of personal selling	Highest price Exclusive distribution Unique brand Emphasis on status in advertising Importance of personal selling

The marketing mix for a shopping good is very different from that for a convenience good. Prices are higher. Coupons and other price incentives are unlikely to be used, because it is difficult to get buyers in a high-involvement category to switch brands based on price. Distribution is likely to be selective, because products are not purchased as frequently. Product characteristics are likely to be more distinct. Whereas the ingredients in toothpaste or detergents brands are similar, the characteristics of clothing, cars, or medical services can differ markedly. As a result, advertising is likely to focus on these differences. Personal selling is likely to be important, because consumers seek information about alternative brands.

Specialty goods *are products with unique characteristics for which consumers make a special effort to search and buy.* These products have the highest level of consumer involvement. Their purchase is often the result of brand loyalty. These are products of high status such as luxury cars or yachts, prestige items such as Rolex watches, Gucci handbags, or Mercedes Benz cars, and brands having a reputation for high performance such as Nikon cameras. Medical services could also be a specialty good if a consumer seeks treatment from a specialist rather than a general practitioner.

Strategies for specialty goods are characterized by high prices, because consumers in this case are insensitive to low-price appeals. Distribution is on an exclusive basis to ensure a status image. Products must have an element of uniqueness for consumers to view them as specialty items, and this uniqueness will be advertised. Personal selling is particularly important in guaranteeing continued loyalty and good service.

It is important to recognize that the same item could be a convenience, shopping, or specialty good. This is because products are classified based on how consumers view them rather than on any inherent physical characteristics. Thus, a skin moisturizer is a convenience good for the consumer who thinks all moisturizers are alike and buys the cheapest one. It is a shopping good for the consumer who sees distinct differences between brands and goes through a process of extensive decision making in comparing them. It is a specialty good for the consumer who seeks out one particular moisturizer that can only be purchased from exclusive cosmetics retailers. Consequently, marketers might position their brand either as (1) a convenience good, as the lowest-priced moisturizer on the market; (2) a shopping good, as the product that has the best and safest ingredients to moisturize the skin; or (3) a specialty good, as the most distinctive and highest-quality product on the market, available only from certain exclusive sources.

Another point is that many consumers view certain product categories differently as they lose their distinctiveness. When compact disc players were first introduced, they were a specialty item, a new way to play music with little distortion. As they are becoming more widespread, they are viewed as shopping goods with consumers comparing many alternative brands more closely.

The definitions of consumer, shopping, and specialty goods are also likely to differ across countries because of different stages in economic development. Packaged goods are classified as conveniences in advanced capitalistic economies, because they are generally available and frequently purchased. But when consumers in Eastern Europe and the former Soviet Union must go from store to store and wait in long lines for milk, vegetable oil, or chocolate syrup, these items can no longer be regarded as convenience goods. Similarly, whereas VCRs or compact disc players are no longer unique in most advanced economies and are regarded as shopping goods, in less-developed economies their ownership would connote status, and they would be considered specialty goods.

INDUSTRIAL GOODS

As we have seen in Chapter 9, sales to organizations account for more dollars than sales to final consumers. This means that industrial goods represent more sales in our economy than consumer goods. Industrial goods can be classified in three ways: production goods, installations and accessories, and supplies and services (see Table 11.2).

Production goods are products used to manufacture a final product. Examples are steel, aluminum, and lumber products. Component parts required by manufacturers are also included in this category—for example, a producer of computer chips selling this component to a manufacturer of computers. Since production goods are fairly standardized, they are usually bought on a straight-buy or modified-rebuy basis. A purchasing agent or materials-ordering manager is responsible for buying; often, purchases are made from the same vendor. In some cases, however, production goods are specialized and purchased on a new-buy basis. An example would be highly tempered steel plate used in the construction of submarines. Since most production goods are standardized, companies selling them are likely to gain a competitive advantage by offering superior service and delivery. Buyers tend to be price-sensitive, so lower prices can create a competitive advantage.

Industrial goods categorized as **installations and accessories** are used in support of the manufacturing process. Examples are generators, truck fleets, factory-automation systems, or pollution-control systems. These are differentiated goods often produced to specification. Purchases are made on a new-buy basis by a buying center, with little loyalty to any single vendor. Sold primarily based on their features rather than on price or delivery, these products are likely to be developed to meet buyers' specification. Consequently, salespeople must have the technical

TABLE 11.2

Classification of Industrial Goods

	PRODUCTION GOODS	INSTALLATIONS AND ACCESSORIES	SUPPLIES AND SERVICES
CUSTOMER PURCHASING CHARACTERISTICS	Straight rebuy or modified rebuy Vendor loyalty Purchased by purchasing agent or materials-ordering manager	New buy Purchased by buying center	Straight rebuy or modified rebuy Vendor loyalty Purchased by purchasing agent
TYPES OF PRODUCTS	Steel Aluminum Lumber Component parts	Generators Trucks Factory automation systems Pollution-control systems	Typewriters Maintenance and repair services Business stationery
STRATEGIC CHARACTERISTICS	Marketed based on delivery and vendor reliability Price conpetition Sales-force acts as order takers	Marketed based on product performance Sales force requires technical expertise Price not a determining factor	Marketed based on vendor reliability Price competition Sales force acts as order takers

expertise necessary to describe product performance. Buyers tend to be price insensitive and buy based on product performance.

Supplies and services are products that support the manufacturing process but are not part of it. Examples are personal computers, maintenance and repair services, or business stationery. As with production goods, these products are likely to be purchased on a straight-rebuy or modified-rebuy basis by a purchasing agent, often from the same vendor. Reputation and reliability of the vendor and price are particularly important selection criteria.

WHAT IS A NEW PRODUCT?

An understanding of the nature of a product and types of consumer and industrial products allows us to consider the specifics of product strategy. Perhaps the most important strategic concern of marketers is developing and introducing new products to the marketplace. As we will see, the ability to effectively develop and market new products largely determines a company's profitability and competitive position.

Before we consider the nature of new-product development, we should address the question, "What is a new product?" This question has some strategic relevance, because a product viewed as new is likely to go through a more rigorous development and testing process than one viewed as a simple extension of an existing product.

In 1991, IBM began test-marketing a revolutionary new computer that it dubbed the "notepad." Shaped like a legal pad, the new-generation computer translates handwritten letters into type via an electronic stylus used to write on the computer's screen (see Exhibit 11.2). IBM had a choice. Did it view the notepad as an extension of its entrenched personal-computer line, which had become an industry standard, or did it view it as a totally new product? Because IBM identified the target market as professionals who had no need for personal computers but would view the flexibility of notepads favorably, it decided to treat the notepad as a new-product innovation.[10]

NEW TO THE CONSUMER OR NEW TO THE COMPANY?

Booz Allen & Hamilton, a leading consulting firm, studied 13,000 new products introduced by 700 companies in the early 1980s.[11] It classified them based on whether they were new to a company, new to consumers, or new to both. A product is new to a company when the company goes through a process of development, testing, and market introduction. (IBM's notepad is an example.) A product is new to consumers when they have no prior awareness of the product category when it is introduced (for instance, cellular phones when they were first introduced).

This classification produces three types of new products, as shown in Figure 11.3. An **innovation** *is a product that is new to both consumers and to a company.* About 10 percent of the products in the Booz Allen & Hamilton (BAH) study were classified as innovations. Sony's Digital Audio Tape players or NutraSweet's Simplesse-brand fat substitute are two examples of this kind of product. Innovations usually result in some change in consumer behavior and consumption patterns. Compact discs are a clear example. The LP, which was the standard for five decades, has virtually died, as has sales of turntables. Consumers have grown accustomed to the

EXHIBIT 11.2

IBM Develops a New Product Innovation: The Notepad

starkly clear sound of CDs and the ease of play they offer. CD technology has also spurred a boom in subsidiary industries such as CD-ROM, a system for storing and retrieving printed information.

A **new-product duplication** *is a product that is known to the market but is new to the company.* About 20 percent of the products in the BAH study were in this category. When Kodak followed Polaroid by introducing instant cameras, they were new to the company but known to consumers. Clorox engaged in new-product duplication with disastrous results during the late 1980s and early 90s when it invested $225 million in detergent products that were new to the company, but did not offer any advantages to consumers when compared to more established brands from Procter & Gamble and Unilever.[12]

Product extensions *are products known to the company but that are new to consumers.* The purpose is to allow the firm to present the consumer with a seemingly new product offering or improvement without requiring a costly new-product development process. There are three types of product extensions: revisions, additions, and repositionings. A **product revision** *is an improvement in an existing product*—for example, adding fruit to yogurt or vitamins to cereals. The BAH study classified 26 percent of new products as revisions. A **product addition** *represents*

FIGURE 11.3

New-Product Classifications

New to the Company	New to the Consumer: Yes	New to the Consumer: No
Yes	Product Innovations (10% of New Products)[a] • Compact disks • Cellular telephones	New-Product Duplications (20% of New Products) • Clorox detergents • Kodak instant cameras
No	Product Extensions – Revisions (26% of New Products) • Vitamin-enriched cereals – Additions (26%) • Ritz bits crackers – Repositionings (7%)[b] • Tums with calcium	Not a New Product

[a]Percentages cited are new products classified in the Booz Allen & Hamilton study. See *New Product Management for the 1980s.* (New York: Booz Allen & Hamilton, 1982), pp. 8–10.

[b]Percentage of new products adds up to 89% of those studied in the Booz Allen & Hamilton study. The remaining 11% were classified in ambiguous categories.

EXHIBIT 11.3

A Nabisco Product Line Extension: Bite Sized Ritz Crackers

an extension of an existing product line. Nabisco lifted its fortunes with product additions in the late 80s, introducing dozens of extensions such as Ritz bits and a line of Mini Oreo Cookies, both bite-sized versions of the original brands (see Exhibit 11.3).[13] The BAH study classified another 26 percent of new products as additions. A **product repositioning** *is communicating a new feature of a brand without necessarily changing its physical characteristics.* When Tums was repositioned as a product that would fight calcium deficiencies in women, no product change was required. Tums always had calcium but women were unaware of it. Several food makers ran afoul of the Food and Drug Administration in 1991 when they repositioned their unchanged corn oils by advertising that the products lack cholesterol. (The FDA's objection was that because all corn oils were 100-percent cholesterol free, the manufacturers were falsely implying differences existed.)

INNOVATIONS OR NEW-PRODUCT REFORMULATIONS?

This classification of new products shows that the vast majority are either reformulations of existing products or additions to existing product lines. Only one out of ten new products in the Booz Allen & Hamilton study are classified as *innovations*—that is, new to the world.

Companies that emphasize innovations, such as 3M, put more of their resources into research and development and technical expertise. Such firms are willing to take the risk of introducing new and untried products and to spend advertising dollars on educating consumers on their use. In contrast, firms that introduce non-innovative products put more focus on existing markets, spending marketing dollars to attract customers from competitors rather than to create new customers. Their rationale for being a follower is that new-product development is expensive, and it is less risky to let others develop and introduce new products.

Further, in high-technology areas, frequent changes in technology increase the risk of new-product development. Polaroid was the innovator in instant photography, establishing the category and educating customers in product use. Kodak, which introduced its own model in the late 70s, was the follower, attempting to convince customers its cameras were as good as Polaroid's. But entry into the market with a "me too" product is highly risky, especially if the product is too similar and offers no new advantages. In 1988, Kodak suffered the risks of a "me too" approach by losing a $500 million suit for violating Polaroid's patent on instant cameras.

NEW PRODUCTS AND PROFITABILITY

Even though some firms do not emphasize new-product development, most leading companies try to ensure a continuous flow of new products, because new-product development is closely tied to profitability. These firms expect to see a substantial part of their sales represented by new products. As we have seen, at 3M about one-fourth of company sales come from products introduced during the previous five years.

New products have an especially strong profit potential because they are designed to satisfy unmet customer needs. The link between new-product development and profitability is illustrated in Figure 11.4. The first curve (curve A) is the sales volume for a typical product over time.

When the product is first introduced, brand awareness and distribution must be established. As a result, expenditures usually exceed revenues, and the brand shows a loss. As the brand begins to be accepted, sales accelerate, and the brand shows a profit (curve B). (The horizontal line in Figure 11.4 is the dividing line between profits and losses.)

FIGURE 11.4

Profits and New-Product Introductions

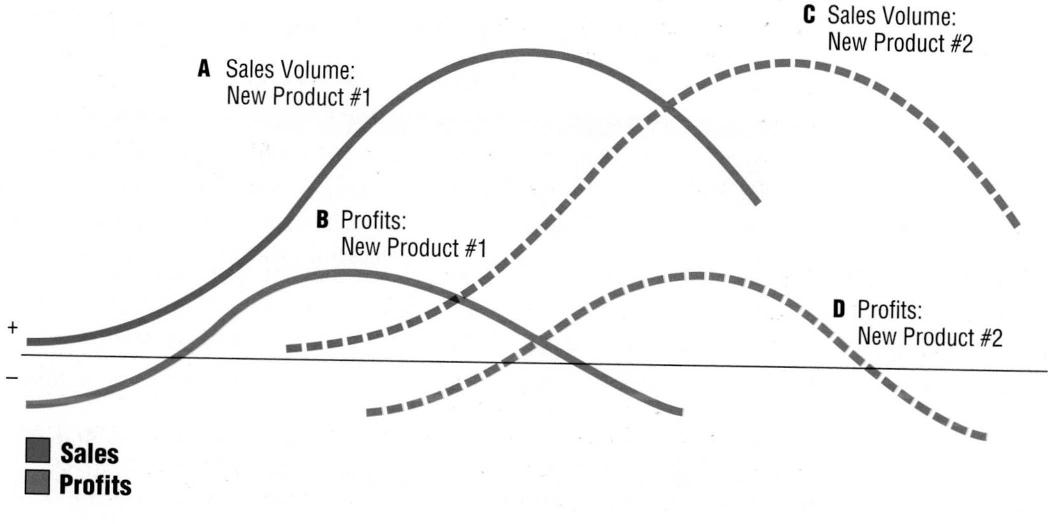

Higher profits tend to attract competition. As this happens, sales continue to increase, but not as rapidly, and profits begin to level off. As competition intensifies, the firm loses its competitive advantage, since many brands have the same basic features and advertise the same benefits. As sales begin decreasing, the brand starts showing a loss.

The sales history of the new product in Figure 11.4 is known as the product's life cycle. The **product life cycle** *represents the sales curve for a product or brand that over time goes through stages of introduction, growth, maturity, and decline.* Changes are required in marketing strategies to meet changing consumer demand and competitive conditions at each phase.

We will be discussing the concept of the product life cycle in Chapter 12. Here, the life cycle shows that a firm cannot rely on any one new product for profitability. Profits can be maintained only by a constant flow of new products. This is demonstrated by the introduction of a second new product just as the profits of the first begin to decline. Sales from the second product (curve C) begin to increase, and profits (curve D) take up the slack just as losses begin to appear for the first product. As a result, overall profitability is maintained. Over time, a third and a fourth new product will be introduced to maintain profits. This scenario assumes that many of the firm's new products will be successful. Any firm recognizes that some of its new products must fail. But if the firm has an effective new-product development process, its overall success rate should assure profitability over the long term.

The introduction of the Apple computer is an illustration of the link between new-product introductions and profitability in Figure 11.4. When the Apple was first introduced, it showed a loss because of the need to spend for advertising and distribution before the product was established. As consumers accepted the Apple, sales increased, and it became profitable. IBM's entry into the personal computer market slowed Apple's growth. Profits began to decrease. To survive, Apple began revitalizing its product line with a series of variations on the original model and the introduction of the new Macintosh, which was positioned to the business market. After that failed to pay the dividends Apple had hoped, the company entered into a joint venture with IBM to create new software both could use in future products, thereby increasing Apple's share of the business market. This move is designed to ensure a steady stream of new products to maintain Apple's profitability over time.[15]

FACTORS IN THE SUCCESS AND FAILURE OF NEW PRODUCTS

The failure rate for new products is high. In 1990, 12,000 new products entered the marketplace—few the result of new technology—and approximately 80 percent of them failed.[16] Since new product failures are expensive, marketers must be aware of the factors associated with successful product introductions to avoid the risks of such failures.

WHY NEW PRODUCTS SUCCEED

Factors generally recognized as keys to new-product success are as follows:

1. *The degree to which the product matches customer needs.* In 1990, Pert Plus became the world's best-selling shampoo. Why? Because it met the busy con-

sumer's need to save time by providing a combination shampoo and conditioner. Ironically, Procter & Gamble did not know what it had on its hands. At first, it did not anticipate a positioning based on time-saving convenience and marketed Pert Plus as an improved shampoo. Only after P&G spent a modest sum test-marketing it in Seattle did executives realize they had a sure-fire winner based on the benefit of time-saving convenience.[17]

2. *Use of existing company know-how.* A new product is most likely to succeed if it is developed within the company's core markets, so that the company can use its expertise in selling it. When an experimental drug went awry at Merck, company managers saw the potential for a totally unexpected application. The result was Mevacor, a drug that prevents cholesterol formation and has turned into a $430 million a year blockbuster. Merck, which grew 22 percent annually during the latter half of the 1980s, might have missed out on Mevacor if not for the company's internal know-how.[18]
3. *A superior product.* A new product is more likely to succeed if it is superior to those already on the market. An upstart Silicon Valley computer software company called Go has become a $30 million powerhouse in three years by offering a new computer operating system called PenPoint that radically simplifies personal computing commands. Although Microsoft's DOS system is the established leader, PenPoint's design eliminates the cumbersome commands that DOS users must trudge through. As a result, IBM has invested heavily in PenPoint and is using it in its prototype notepad computers (see Exhibit 11.2).[19]
4. *An organizational environment that fosters entrepreneurship.* Successful new products are often developed within an entrepreneurial business environment. This environment is found when top management encourages its middle managers to take risks in the process of new-product development. At 3M, this risk-oriented philosophy is called "*intra*preneuring," because it is fostered in-house. It takes the form of new-product "venture groups" that operate like small companies within the parent corporation. The ethic is summed up by a 3M saying, "The captain bites his tongue until it bleeds," meaning that top executives must keep their hands off a project once it has begun.[20]
5. *An established new-product development process.* Finally, successful new products are often the result of a well-defined new-product development process. The disastrous performance of Frito-Lay in the late 1980s underscores this. When the company was pressured by its parent, PepsiCo, to introduce more new products, it went on a new-product binge, ignoring all its own new product development rules. It introduced cheese-topped crackers, cheese-filled snacks, and granola nuggets, with little research or testing. As a former Frito-Lay executive said, "They tried too much. There were too many new types of products and the pace was just too quick."[21] The misguided frenzy caused a 13 percent loss in operating profits and the resignation of the PepsiCo division's president.[22]

WHY NEW PRODUCTS FAIL

There is no easy formula to predict product failures. But marketing managers can use past failures to develop the following general prescriptions as to why new products fail:

1. *Misreading customer needs.* One of the main reasons new products fail is that management misreads customer needs. In some cases, companies misread the market because of inadequate market analysis. The first low-calorie beer,

GLOBAL MARKETING STRATEGIES

From Tokyo to Taiwan: Introducing Foreign-Born Products in the United States

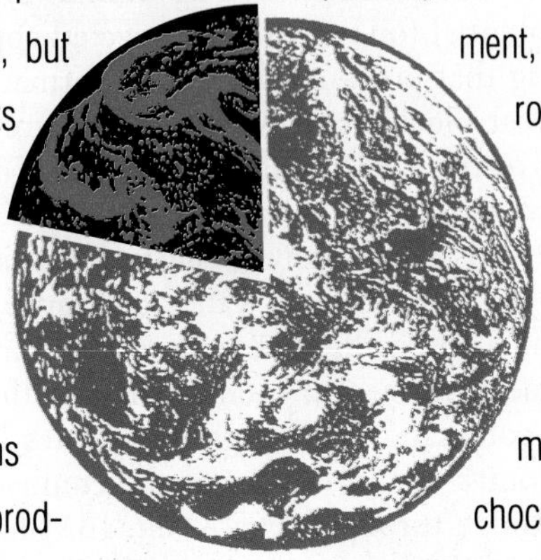

The recession of the early 1990s caused dozens of expensive new-product development projects to be put on hold, but that did not mean new products stopped appearing on supermarket shelves.

The early 1990s saw a wave of new introductions born in Europe, where such multinational corporations as Procter & Gamble find the new-product development process less expensive. In late 1989, P&G began testing Cheer With Color Guard in Arizona, a new version of its Cheer brand that had already been unveiled in Japan. The residents of Tucson did not know they were using a product pre-tested in Tokyo—after all, what can be more American than Cheer? But the move allowed P&G to save millions of dollars in development work.

The trend may have begun with the recession, but by 1992 it seemed to have taken on a life of its own. "Most big companies are systematically scanning the world for new product ideas," one analyst told the *Wall Street Journal*. "[They're] saying, 'Instead of spending all this money on research and development, lets go to the treasure trove of Europe and Asia.'"

Hershey Foods, for example, mined other continents for its next big product before settling on Symphony, a creamier candy bar modeled after the smoother-tasting chocolate of Europe. Dry beers, one of the fastest-growing categories in the domestic alcohol market, were pioneered by Japanese brewing plants such as Sapporo Breweries Ltd. Even cat food has felt the foreign touch. Mars Inc. changed the recipes in its Kal Can cat food to mirror its overseas products which bring in $1 billion in annual sales and even changed the venerable brand name to Whiskas—its overseas trademark.

Marketers who look beyond their shores for new products are also looking for ways to appeal to ethnic groups that they have had little success reaching. After Colgate-Palmolive failed to dent the Hispanic-

Rheingold's Gablinger, was a failure because it was positioned as a diet beer. Adequate market analysis would have shown that beer drinkers do not want to link the enjoyment of beer to the pain of dieting. Miller succeeded in meeting consumer needs by introducing a "light" beer; Gablinger's failed by introducing a "diet" beer.

2. *Poor product positioning*. The annals of marketing are full of cases of poor product positioning resulting in new-product failures. One of the most dramatic involved Fab 1 Shot, a pre-measured single-packet detergent and soft-

GLOBAL MARKETING STRATEGIES

American market, it increased sales by using a Central American television commercial to sell its soap to American Hispanics. It also began importing its Fabuloso cleaner from Central America and positioning it to Hispanic Americans.

However, assuming winners abroad will be successful at home can spell disaster. European-style hair mousse crested briefly in the United States during the mid 1980s, then all but disappeared because the products' stickiness and inconvenience quickly turned off consumers. Similarly, Kellogg was forced to pull its LeShake drinkable yogurt off supermarket shelves in the mid-1980s because, even though it had been popular in Europe, American consumers were not ready for a yogurt beverage.

Kellogg learned its lesson, however. One of its most successful introductions of recent years has been Mueslix, a cereal loaded with fruit, grains, and nuts, pioneered by its Swiss division. The product dovetailed neatly with the domestic trend toward high-vitamin diets.

The rash of foreign-born products introduced into the United States is likely to continue as new-product development costs escalate. But companies must research these products in the home market to ensure they are acceptable to domestic consumers. Such product introductions involve competitive risks as well. Shortly after P&G moved Cheer With Color Guard into Arizona, Japan-based Kao Corp. began researching consumers to determine whether it too should move in with its own product, Attack.

Question: What are the opportunities and risks of introducing foreign-born products into the United States?

Sources: "More Companies Shop Abroad for New-Product Ideas," *The Wall Street Journal*, March 14, 1990; and "P&G products immigrate to U.S.," *Advertising Age*, October 30, 1989.

ener. Colgate-Palmolive went all out to sell Fab 1 Shot to its biggest customers, households with large families, by virtually giving it away through coupons and rebates. Within a year, it had captured 4 percent of the $2.5 billion market. But two years later it was being withdrawn. What went wrong? Once the rebates ended, large families could not be induced to keep buying the packets, which proved insufficient for big loads. The correct niche for the product, college students and singles who ranked convenience high, had been ignored by Colgate-Palmolive's marketing strategy.[23]

FIGURE 11.5

The New-Product Development Process

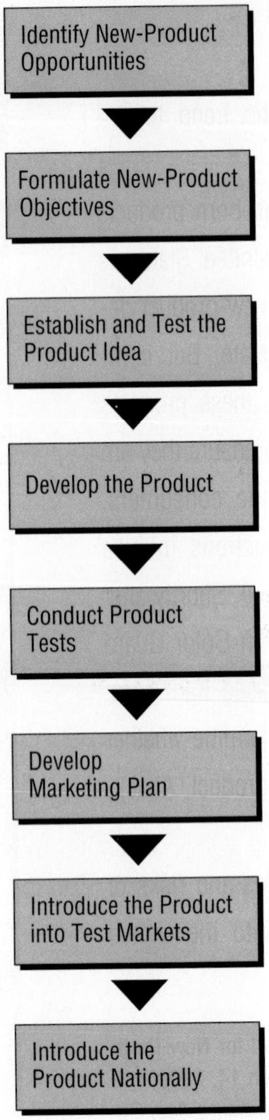

3. *Poor product performance.* A product can always be repositioned if it provides consumer benefits, but an inferior product is doomed to failure, regardless of its positioning, unless the company goes back to the drawing boards and reformulates it. General Electric staked its whole $2 billion refrigerator business on what it thought was a pioneering compressor designed in its Kentucky headquarters. It turned out, in the words of a GE executive "to be our worst nightmare come true." Blunders committed at every stage of the design process made the compressors unworkable, and the company replaced them in 1.1 million models. Ultimately, GE was forced to buy its compressors from overseas, the very thing it sought to avoid. The result was GE taking a $450 million pre-tax loss in 1988.[24]
4. *Inadequate marketing research.* Companies sometimes fail to adequately project product desirability before they incur the costs of market entry. AT&T convinced itself in the mid 1980s—through product tests and market research—that there would be a $5 billion market awaiting its picture-phone. By 1991, it was a dead proposition. What happened? Consumer responses to the picture-phone were positive, but they were reacting to the technology. AT&T never researched the value of the picture-phone to the consumer. Consumers were not willing to pay $1,500 for the phone, and an extra $100 a month for service, while getting a video image of dubious quality.[25]
5. *Inadequate competitive analysis.* Another reason new products fail is that companies often seem to have blinders on when it comes to estimating competitive reactions. A case in point is Simple Pleasure, NutraSweet's ice cream made with the Simpless fat-substitute. NutraSweet thought it would capture the segment of health-conscious ice-cream buyers who were worried about high-fat diets. The company failed to foresee that its competitors would flood the market with fat-free entries, making the fledgling fat-substitute category redundant. Simple Pleasures is languishing because NutraSweet failed to anticipate competitive reactions.[26]

THE PROCESS OF NEW-PRODUCT DEVELOPMENT

Whatever the explanation for new-product failure, its high costs have caused marketing management to put more emphasis on an effective process of new-product development. Figure 11.5 presents an outline of this process.

The first step in the new-product development process is to identify new-product opportunities. When Weyerhaeuser looked at the disposable diaper market, it saw an opportunity to establish a new brand—a lower-priced product with more features—despite the fact that P&G and Kimberly Clark had 85 percent of the market. Once the opportunity was identified, new-product objectives were established. The main objective was to capture at least the 15 percent of the market not occupied by the two leaders and hopefully penetrate the leader's share as well. As the third step of Figure 11.5 shows, new-product ideas are then established and tested. On this basis, Weyerhaeuser developed the product by deciding what features to introduce into its diaper (step 4 in Figure 11.5). It decided on cushy waistbands, superabsorbent pulp woven into the pad to keep babies dryer, and a cloth-like cover.

The fifth step in the new-product development process involves testing the actual product. Weyerhaeuser tested the diapers by providing samples to mothers and getting their reactions. These tests showed some problems with the diapers, so Weyerhaeuser went back to steps 4 and 5 in Figure 11.5 by reformulating the diaper (adding such things as cuffs to block leakage) and tested it again. This time, the new version stimulated enough consumer interest to convince Weyerhaeuser to introduce the brand in a test market.

At this point, a marketing plan was developed (step 6) to set the strategy to be used in test marketing and possibly a national introduction. (A **test market** *is a market in which the product is placed to gather sales and marketing information so as to make a decision whether and how to introduce the brand nationally.*) Weyerhaeuser decided it wanted to make its product the hybrid of a national brand and a private brand (that is, a brand sponsored by a retail store). The box would bear the brand name UltraSofts, but it would also feature the name of the store where it was sold. The Wegmans Food Markets chain of New York was chosen for the test-run (step 7). The chain created awareness of the new brand with $1 off coupons mailed to shoppers' homes. Based on the fact that Wegmans shoppers preferred UltraSofts to other brands two to one, a launch was begun.[27] In the following pages, we will review each of these steps.

IDENTIFY NEW-PRODUCT OPPORTUNITIES

As we have seen in Chapter 4, unmet customer needs are one of the main sources of marketing opportunity. There are other bases for new product opportunities, including competitive weakness, new technologies, and changes in laws and regulations. But the most systematic approach to identifying opportunities has been in the analysis of customer needs. Gaps in the marketplace—determined by identifying customer segments dissatisfied with current offerings—represent potential new-product opportunities. Consider the following examples:

- When a Nabisco executive saw her baby-boom friends moving into their child-rearing years, she got the idea of creating a bite-sized version of the company's Honey Graham crackers, since graham crackers are often the first treat parents give toddlers. The success of the product led Nabisco to turn miniature snacks, a previously non-existent market, into a growth vehicle for the 1990s.[28]
- Several companies are introducing iced cappucino products to appeal to the growing segment of adult drinkers who have turned away from coffee because of heath concerns over caffeine and younger drinkers who dislike its bitter taste. Because tests show the richer, chilled concoctions appeal to both groups, analysts project that iced cappucino products may command $1 billion in sales by the year 2000.[29]
- Companies sometimes stumble into finding gaps in the market. When a 3M executive could not get scraps of paper to stick in his church-choir hymnal book, he remembered a 3M scientist's idea to create an adhesive strong enough to hold but easy enough to remove. This fortuitous accident created Post-it-Notes, which has grown into a 340-item line for 3M.[30]

FORMULATE NEW-PRODUCT OBJECTIVES

Each new product should have specific profit and sales goals as a basis for evaluating performance. We have seen in Chapter 3 that the three performance goals most frequently cited are sales volume, market share, and return on investment. *Dollar sales volume* is the most frequently stated new-product objective. Sales goals are also stated in units, because *unit sales* objectives can be more easily translated into production requirements.

Market-share goals indicate expected product performance relative to the competition. Usually, market-share goals for products entering established markets are relatively modest. For example, when PepsiCo introduced Slice, its goal was to attain a 2 percent share in the first year. In newer markets, goals might be much higher. Procter & Gamble anticipated obtaining a substantial share of the relatively new liquid soap market when it introduced Ivory Liquid. A company can also aim at capturing market share from specific competitors. When General Motors launched Saturn, its goal was to wrest a share of the small-car market from the Japanese. GM wanted Saturn to reduce Japanese auto makers' 26-percent share of the compact market and to increase its own 33-percent share. Toward that end, its objective was that 80 percent of Saturn sales would come from buyers who did not own a GM car.[31]

Return on investment provides a key performance measure in terms of a product's profitability and contribution to company resources. The basic assumption in most strategic plans is that existing products provide the resource base to support new products until they are profitable and that successful new products will provide the resource base for the next generation of new products.

Another frequently used performance measure for new products, its **payback period**, *is the period of time it takes for the cash flow generated by the product to become positive* (that is, to be on the plus side after accounting for all past expenditures and investments). The payback period is important in showing how long it takes the product to be a cash generator with the ability to support other new-product ventures.

ESTABLISH AND TEST THE PRODUCT IDEA

The third phase of new-product development is establishing the product idea and testing it. This is a three-step process. First, many new ideas are *generated.* Next, these ideas are *screened* to narrow the field to a few alternatives. These alternatives are then formulated as a *product concept statement*, and consumers are asked to react to them. (A **product concept** *is a detailed description of the product idea and is designed to communicate product benefits to consumers.*)

The Booz Allen & Hamilton study found that organizations are putting more emphasis on these steps and increasing their efficiency. As a result, companies have had to test fewer ideas per successful new product. In a 1968 study, Booz Allen & Hamilton found that companies screened an average of 58 new-product ideas to get one new-product success. By 1981, it took an average of only seven new ideas to get a success (see Figure 11.6).

IDEA GENERATION

If new products are expected to be an ongoing source of profits to the firm, product ideas must be generated. The most important sources are:

- *Research and development:* Basic breakthroughs often come from an R&D group. As we have seen, R&D work done by the Go company of Silicon Valley enabled IBM to create its revolutionary computer notepad. Ford's R&D department recently upstaged other carmakers by inventing a front seat that adjusts between six and ten different ways and can be narrowed or widened to suit the occupant.[32]
- *Focus groups:* We have seen in Chapter 7 that focus groups are often used to identify unmet customer needs. The ones used by 3M revealed the need for a

FIGURE 11.6

Mortality of New-Product Ideas During Product Development: 1969 versus 1981

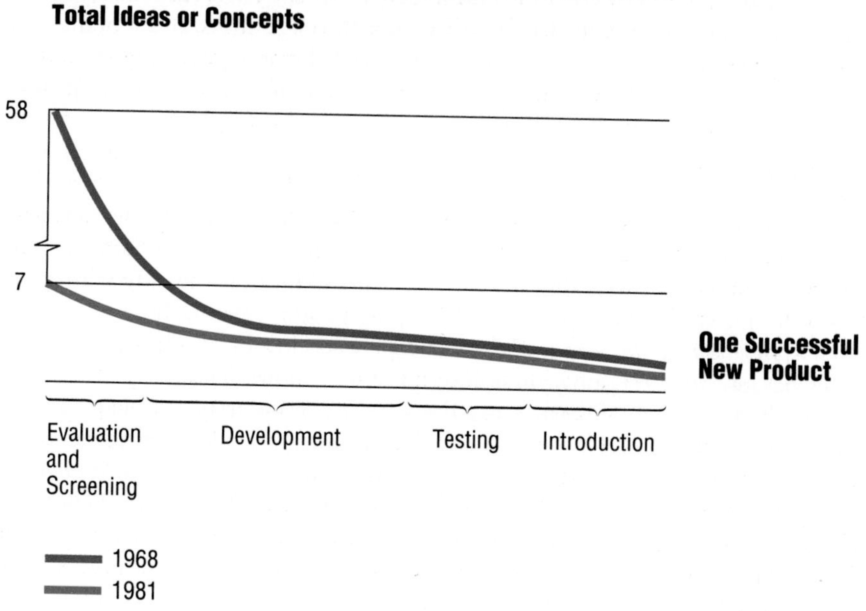

Source: Adapted from "New Product Strategy: How the Pros Do It," *Industrial Marketing,* May 1982, p. 50.

product that later became Safest Stripper. There is some dispute regarding how many focus groups are needed to generate product ideas. Major companies may use eight or more groups in research that often costs in excess of $200,000. Some analysts, however, maintain that two groups in two markets is adequate.[33]

- *Customer suggestions:* Some companies encourage customers to suggest new products. For instance, IBM has developed an Installed User Program in which software packages are developed by users.[34]
- *Competitors:* Products introduced by competitors are often acquired and tested in company labs. Companies might develop a competitive edge in their labs and introduce an improved version of the product.
- *Salespeople and distributors:* Suggestions often come from the company's own sales force and its distributors, both of whom have direct contact with customers. Industrial firms are much more likely to rely on the sales force for new-product ideas and opportunities. A good sales force has the technical proficiency to identify and interpret customer needs.

IDEA SCREENING

As Figure 11.6 shows, a firm cannot afford to develop and market all the ideas it generates. Thus, screening is an essential part of establishing the product idea. Companies use two general approaches to weed out ideas that do not warrant further consideration: managerial judgment and customer evaluations.

Managerial judgment refers to a process in which managers rate new-product ideas on key criteria related to a product's profit potential, such as market size, projected growth rate, and required resources. Since managerial judgment is usually not sufficient, *customer evaluations* are also used to screen new-product ideas. Mobil Chemical asked consumers to rate 20 new product improvement ideas against competitive offerings for products such as storage bags, trash bags, and bug killers. Consumers were asked to rate the new product ideas and whether they would buy the new product if it was introduced. Ideas that scored highest on "intention to buy" were then subjected to the next step, a product concept test.

CONCEPT TESTING

In a concept test, a company develops a description of a product's characteristics and benefits as well as an illustration of the product and presents it to the consumer. Consumers evaluate the product idea, providing the company with a final check before it incurs the expense of developing **product prototypes,** *that is, preliminary production of the new product.* Concept tests do not require product prototypes because they rely only on a description of the product.

At one time, General Foods tested the concept of an artificial bacon product with less fat than regular bacon. It asked consumers to evaluate the degree to which they expected the product to be less fatty than bacon and more nutritious. It also asked their intentions to buy the product on a scale from very likely to not likely at all. Responses to the concept test would determine if General Foods incurred the costs of developing product prototypes and asking consumers to try them in a product test.

DEVELOP THE PRODUCT

If the concept test is positive, the company has a green light to go on to the next step, developing the new product. We tend to think of a product in terms of its physical attributes and what it can do, but another product quality is also important to a company: its design. We will examine how companies formulate both physical attributes and design as they develop new products.

FORMULATING THE PRODUCT'S PHYSICAL ATTRIBUTES

Formulating the product requires translating consumer preferences into physical product attributes. For example, the idea of an artificial bacon product had to be translated into a product that looked and tasted like bacon but was less fatty and more nutritious.

This process of developing physical product attributes to satisfy intangible consumer benefits is one of the most difficult tasks in marketing. Bic tried to play on its reputation as the leader in disposable products when it introduced a line of $5 perfumes and colognes. It failed because it concentrated on the novelty of its "disposable" perfume rather than the product's chief attribute: its smell. As a result, consumers had little reason to be interested.[35]

Part of the problem in developing products to meet consumer needs is that research and development (R&D) and marketing have very different objectives and perspectives in the new-product development process. R&D personnel tend to emphasize high-quality, well-engineered products, and such products require sufficient time for development. Although marketing personnel also appreciate quality, they argue that perfectly engineered products may not be what consumers want and that the long period necessary to develop such products may give competitors an edge. Kodak's rush to be the first to market a lithium battery resulted in insufficient testing of its claim to a longer shelf life. Many batteries failed to perform adequately within the guaranteed time. As a result, Kodak had to delay introducing the product.

Coordination between R&D and marketing is particularly important for industrial firms because of the high development costs of many industrial products. Frequent advances in technology result in more product changes, and these changes have to be attuned to customer needs. Industrial marketers must work closely with their R&D counterparts to ensure that products meet customer specifications. Organizational buyers will often work directly with marketers and R&D personnel in setting specifications, making coordination with R&D even more important and potentially more difficult.

Production as well as R&D must be coordinated with marketing in formulating new-product attributes. New production facilities may have to be established, and the nature of these facilities will determine the quantity that can be produced as well as the speed with which products can be delivered to the marketplace. These are critical factors for the marketing manager. Marketers are more likely to emphasize speed and product quality in the production process, whereas production managers are more likely to emphasize cost-effectiveness.

DEVELOPING AN EFFECTIVE PRODUCT DESIGN

For many products, exterior design is almost as important as development of the product itself. Consumers buying cars, typewriters, or kitchen appliances are often first drawn to the product by its design. For example, Philips Industries, the giant Dutch electronics firm, designed its roller radio with huge circular speakers to convey a sense of sound and an outside handle "that blares 'pick me up and carry me.' " The company had forecast sales of 70,000 units for 1986; the product sold 500,000 in that year, largely due to the new design.[36] But, as General Electric's refrigerator compressor fiasco proved, design cannot save a product that fails to deliver consumer benefits. Philips also introduced a microwave oven that could be used on the dining-room table and was supposed to remind people of an old-fashioned cooking vessel. Instead, the product reminded consumers of a nuclear power plant, something few people wanted on their tables while they ate (see Exhibit 11.4).

The Philips example shows that the same company can be the source of both effective design and bloopers. In another illustration, the Lexus LS 400 sedan became a dominant player in the prestige market because of its cachet-driven design, but its lower-priced partner, the ES 250, languished because it was modeled on Toyota's Camry. Its older styling was not exciting or luxurious enough for the status-conscious buyers who wandered through Lexus showrooms.[37]

CONDUCT PRODUCT TESTS

The next step in the new product development process, the *product test*, is the first actual exposure consumers have to the product. At this point, the company must invest in production of prototypes to be used in the concept tests. Consumers might be given the product to use over a period of time at home and compare it to their regular brand, or they might be invited to company facilities to try the product and rate it. Based on the response, the company decides whether to introduce the product into test markets.

Product testing for industrial firms is sometimes limited by the expense of prototype production. For example, a firm developing nuclear imaging machines that

EXHIBIT 11.4

Product Designs from Philips that Succeeded and Failed

Philips' Roller Radio: A Success

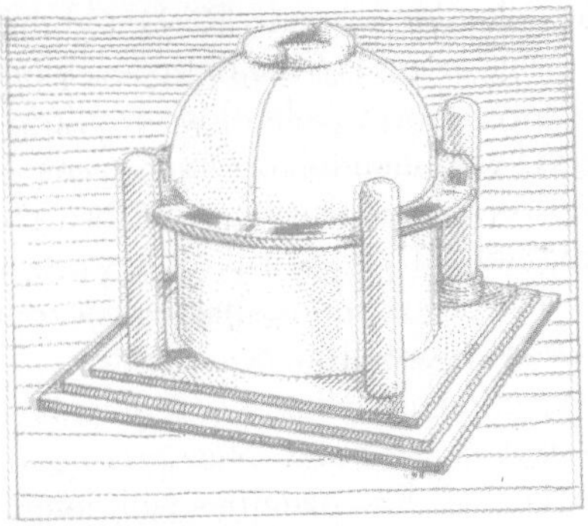
Philips' Microwave Oven: A Failure

cost close to $1 million might be able to develop, at most, one or two prototypes to test their effectiveness. Some industrial firms use their sales force to conduct informal concept tests on customers before committing to expensive prototype production.

Whether testing is for consumer or industrial goods, an important indication that the product-development process is on track is a good "fit" between results in the concept and product tests. The benefits that appeal to consumers in the concept must be actually delivered when the product is used. General Foods faced a problem with its artificial bacon product. In the concept test, consumers expected the product to be lean and moderately appetizing. When the consumers used the product, they found it to be too fatty, but actually more appetizing than expected. Because the major benefit of the product was supposed to be its low fat content, General Foods had to reformulate and retest the product. This required conducting steps 4 and 5 in Figure 11.5 a second time.

DEVELOP THE MARKETING PLAN

Once the product is developed and tested, management must formulate a marketing plan that will be effective for introducing and sustaining it in the market. Because the marketing planning process was already described in Chapter 3, we will not repeat the points made there.

It is important to note, however, that there are generally two marketing plans: a plan for introducing the product into the test market and a plan for a subsequent regional or national introduction. The test-market plan sets out the product's positioning, defines target segments, establishes a marketing mix, and identifies media schedules and distribution requirements for the markets in which the product will be tested. The test market plan is then modified on the basis of the product's performance to produce the marketing plan used in a national launch. The target market might be redefined, advertising themes changed, budgets for specific marketing-mix components increased or decreased, and price levels adjusted based on results in test markets. The revised marketing plan provides the blueprint for introducing the product.

INTRODUCE THE PRODUCT INTO TEST MARKETS

The last step in new-product development before national introduction is **test marketing,** *which requires introducing the product in several markets with a complete marketing plan to simulate a national introduction.* Results of the test market are then projected nationally to determine if the product is likely to be successful. This stage differs from earlier concept and product tests, which ask the consumer, "If this product was in the market, would you buy?" Test marketing gives consumers an actual opportunity to buy and is the "dress rehearsal" for introduction. If results do not meet sales and profit goals, there is still time for management to withdraw the product to avoid market failure. In addition to determining consumer reactions in a realistic environment, test marketing also allows management to evaluate marketing strategy before introducing the brand nationally and to project sales and revenues from test areas to the national market.

In selecting test markets, management tries to ensure that they are representative of the product's target segment and reflect competitive conditions nationally. Introducing a product into test markets where competition is weak would bias sales results upward. Management must also ensure that the product is in test markets long enough to determine the repurchase rate—an important factor in national projections of sales.

RESULTS OF TEST MARKETING

In addition to providing data on purchase and repurchase rates, test markets provide information that the company can use to fine-tune the marketing mix. For example, in 1984 Campbell test marketed its Home Cookin' Soups, a thicker soup that looked more homemade with chunks of meat and vegetables. These tests provided the company with a clear idea of what worked and what did not. What worked was that consumers thought the soup tasted good; what did not work was everything else, from the packaging to the variety of flavors available.

As a result of these findings, Campbell reformulated the marketing plan for the product. It broadened the line of flavors, introduced a larger 19-ounce can that would appeal to family users and, at the same time, captured more shelf space. The original "Tastes like I made it myself" advertising message changed to focus more on the nutritional benefits of the food. Management attributes the success of the brand to the lessons learned in the test market.[38]

ALTERNATIVES TO TEST MARKETING

Despite successes such as Campbell's, test marketing is both costly and time-consuming. Also, having a product in test market for months allows competitors to duplicate the product. As a result, many firms are using alternatives to test marketing that are of shorter duration and are less expensive. One type of test, known as a **simulated store test,** *asks consumers to shop in experimental supermarket facilities in which new products are introduced and tracks their purchases.* Another, known as a **sales wave experiment,** *places new products in consumer homes, determines reactions to the product, and gives consumers a chance to purchase the product over time in order to track repurchase rates.* Companies are increasing their use of these techniques to avoid the risks of competitive duplication and the high costs associated with test marketing.

Most test marketing and less-costly alternatives are conducted by consumer rather than industrial firms. It would be prohibitively expensive to test market complex, high-technology products—and such tests would invite competitors to acquire and possibly duplicate the new technology. Further, many business-to-business marketers have a limited number of customers, often located in a few regions. Test marketing prior to introduction is not necessary since these firms can go directly to individual customers to do a concept test or to test product prototypes.

NATIONAL INTRODUCTION

A company's most crucial decision is whether to introduce the product nationally. The substantial investment in production and marketing makes this a risky decision. If a company decides to introduce the product, it must choose between a region-by-region *rollout* or an immediate national introduction. To minimize risk, most companies choose a rollout, releasing the product first in regions where competition is weakest. Procter & Gamble rolled out Folgers coffee from a strong regional base on the West Coast, across the center of the country, and finally introducing the brand on the East Coast, where General Foods' Maxwell House brand was strongest.

In contrast to its Folgers strategy, Procter & Gamble frantically scurried to go international with Pert Plus, a combination shampoo and conditioner that met the busy consumer's need to save time. When the Seattle test-market results showed it was a sure-fire winner, the company went national and then began testing it abroad.[39] The two-in-one benefit was universally appealing, but the company could not use the Pert name in many countries. So today, it is sold as Rejoice in Hong Kong and Singapore, Rejoy in Japan, and under the Vidal Sasoon label in Europe. It is now the world's best-selling shampoo.

The decision to use a regional rollout or a national introduction depends on the company's competitive position and risk orientation. General Motors used a regional rollout for its Saturn car in 1990 because of a slumping car market. It could not afford a high-stakes national introduction. P&G, on the other hand, was in a strong competitive position with Pert Plus, since it was the first combination shampoo/conditioner, and consumers could not seem to get enough of it. The company was willing to take the risk of going national immediately, because it did not want to risk competitive duplication by taking a more cautious region-by-region approach.

RISKS OF NEW-PRODUCT DEVELOPMENT

Companies sometimes forego some of the eight steps in new-product development in Figure 11.5 in the interest of saving time and money or gaining a quick competitive advantage. Even if a company follows each step to the letter, it still faces serious risks.

The greatest risk in the new-product development process is its cost. In the initial phases of idea generation and screening, costs are relatively low. If a company decides to test a product, prototypes must be made, and the company incurs its first substantial costs. Research and development must be brought into the process to work on the development and design of the product. In many cases, new production facilities must be built. When the company begins test marketing, it incurs costs of advertising, sales promotions, and distribution. Finally, when the product is introduced, costs escalate because of the expenses of national advertising and distribution. These costs have increased in recent years, so that by 1988 it cost an average of $20 million to introduce a new brand.[40] Costs of market entry have increased correspondingly. Transportation costs and the costs of TV advertising have outpaced inflation. As a result, the risks of new-product introductions have escalated.

A second risk of new product development is the threat of quick competitive duplication. PepsiCo's advantage in introducing Slice, the first nationally marketed juice-based soft drink, was quickly dissipated as Coca-Cola's Minute Maid and P&G's Orange Crush introduced competing versions. Another risk is unforseen technical problems that cause delays in new-product development, as when Kodak experienced technical problems in trying to ensure the shelf life of its new lithium batteries.

A third risk is changes in technology that can quickly make a new product obsolete. RCA's videodisc was no sooner on the market than it began facing competition from video-cassette recorders. The superior technology of VCRs, providing recording capabilities, soon made videodiscs for home use obsolete.

A fourth risk is a failure to ensure distribution prior to introduction. A number of years ago, Heinz introduced Great American Soups based on positive consumer reactions but could not get retailers to give it the shelf space required to effectively compete with Campbell's.

STRATEGIES TO REDUCE THE RISK OF NEW-PRODUCT DEVELOPMENT

The high costs of new-product development and the associated risks have caused marketers to try to seek ways to reduce these risks. One risk reduction strategy cited in the Global Marketing Strategies box is to introduce successful foreign products into the United States to avoid high development costs. Such products were developed for a different market and culture, however, and reactions by domestic consumers must be researched carefully to ensure they are acceptable.

A second approach is to follow a "me too" strategy by offering minor improvements of existing entries. But a "me too" product may not provide sufficient improvements to warrant consumer acceptance. A third strategy to avoid risk is to reposition existing brands, as when Seven-Up began advertising its flagship brand as having no caffeine. No development was required since the product never had caffeine.

By far the most common strategy to avoid the risks of new-product development is **brand leveraging;** *that is, introducing a new product with the name of an existing brand.* Diet Coke and Ivory Liquid are examples. Although brand leveraging does not eliminate product development, it does reduce the risks of introduction by giving the new brand the protection of an established and successful name.

ETHICAL AND REGULATORY ISSUES IN NEW-PRODUCT DEVELOPMENT

Consumers have a right to safe products, to products that perform well, and to full information regarding product ingredients. These three rights constitute the major ethical responsibilities of marketers in developing new products.

ETHICAL AND ENVIRONMENTAL ISSUES IN MARKETING

Hell on Wheels: How ATVs Drew the Government's Ire

Few products have been swept up in the regulatory firestorm that has surrounded All-Terrain Vehicles (ATVs), the rugged motorcycle hybrids that exploded onto the American landscape in the early 1980s. From the desert ranges of Baja, California to the dirt roads of Maine, outdoor enthusiasts rushed to catch the ATV craze, and none were more passionate about it than children.

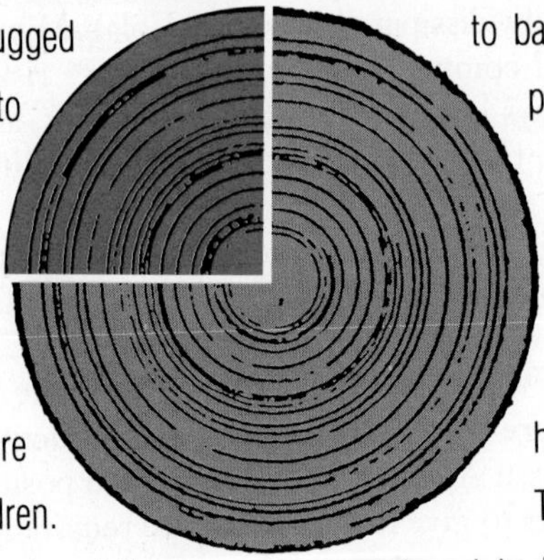

Then the accidents started. Kids found themselves losing their balance, tipping in ruts, and literally being run over by the machines. Children with ATV-related injuries flooded emergency rooms. Parents began wondering about the machines. And so did the federal Consumer Product Safety Commission (CPSC).

In 1984, with the injury toll mounting, the CPSC began pressuring the five major ATV makers—Suzuki, Yamaha, Honda, Kawasaki, and Polaris—to voluntarily enforce safety measures, but the manufacturers dragged their feet. This blasé attitude would come back to haunt the manufacturers. As ATV horror stories found their way onto nightly news shows, Congress opened hearings on suggested legislation to ban the three-wheel models. The proposed legislation was not binding, but by 1985—when 85,900 injuries and 295 deaths had been blamed on ATVs—the CPSC had come under so much public fire that it had to act.

The agency called on the Justice Department to bring suit under an emergency provision in the Consumer Product Safety Act that allowed the CPSC to recall dangerous products. By December 1987, the manufacturers found themselves under such pressure that they agreed to a consent decree which required them to stop selling three-wheel models and restrict sales of the four-wheel models to children. The decree made no mention of a recall, however, leading the most passionate consumer activists to criticize it as unduly lax.

If anyone thought that would end the controversy, they were wrong. Despite the consent decree, more than half the nation's ATV dealers continued recom-

PRODUCT SAFETY Most companies try to ensure product safety and reliability in the course of new-product development. But abuses exist, and the consumer's welfare requires government to have a role in ensuring product safety. The primary government agency responsible for product safety is the Consumer Product Safety Commission (CPSC), established in 1972.

The CPSC can ban the sale of products, require manufacturers to perform safety tests, and require repair or recall of unsafe products. It operates a "hot line,"

ETHICAL AND ENVIRONMENTAL ISSUES IN MARKETING

mending adult-sized models to kids. As a result, more than 40 percent of the deaths and injuries on ATV's were still suffered by riders under the age of 16.

Embarrassed, the CPSC again cracked down on the ATV makers, leading to a 1990 agreement in which the manufacturers promised to conduct undercover investigations of dealers, terminate those found to be ignoring the provision banning sales to children, and ensure that safety information was prominently displayed.

By 1991, with the ATV-related death rate among all age groups down 40 percent and the injury rate down 50 percent, the CPSC voted against suggesting further design recommendations to reduce injuries.

Like the 1988 consent decree, the 1990 decision—passed by a 2–1 vote among the agency's commissioners—was controversial. Said Anne Graham, the dissenting commissioner, "The commission cannot afford to use the achievements of the past as justification for future inaction."

Commissioner Jacqueline Jones-Smith defended the decision by insisting that the very nature of the sport—rough riding on rugged terrain—lent itself to injury. Moreover, she said, redesigning the vehicles could cause more problems than it solves. While total injuries were halved since 1986, deaths on the four-wheel models had doubled, and ATVs were still responsible for 60,000 injuries.

The CPSC's inaction has left the final onus on ATV manufacturers, who must now prove they can effectively regulate an inherently risk-oriented sport.

Questions: What additional actions might manufacturers of ATVs have taken to avoid injuries? What additional action might the CPSC have taken? Are ATV manufacturers and dealers equally guilty of unethical behavior?

Sources: "Study Assails Dealers in All-Terrain Vehicles," *The New York Times,* December 5, 1989, p. A33; "For Want of a Wheel," *AEI Journal on Government and Society,* Regulation 1988 Number 1, pp. 7–10; "ATV Makers Agree to Discipline Dealers," News from CPSC press releases, July 2, 1990; "Two More ATV Makers Agree To Discipline Dealers Found Selling Adult-Sized Vehicles To Children," News from CPSC press release, October 5, 1990; "Safety Commission Votes Continued Enforcement of ATV Consent Decrees," News from CPSC press release, May 15, 1991 and attached statements by Commissioners Jacqueline Jones-Smith and Anne Graham.

allowing consumers to report hazardous products and runs a National Electronic Injury Surveillance System, a computer-based system that monitors 119 hospital emergency rooms across the country. On the basis of this system, the commission computes a *Product Hazard Index*. Among products with the highest hazard index are cleaning agents, swings and slides, liquid fuels, snowmobiles, and all-terrain vehicles (ATVs). The CPSC is also active in recalling products, recalling an average of 200 a year.[41] Another agency with recall powers is the National Highway

Traffic Safety Administration, which sued General Motors to force a recall of 1.1 million X-body cars because of faulty brakes.

The Food and Drug Administration (FDA) also has an important role in ensuring product safety. It has the authority to ban or seize food and drug products it regards as a menace to public health and to require companies to test products before they are marketed. The agency required NutraSweet Co. to test a new, low-calorie fat substitute. It had also challenged R.J. Reynolds' new smokeless cigarette, claiming that it should be treated as a drug (see Exhibit 11.5).

In addition to government regulation, consumers have recourse to sue manufacturers for damages. Unfortunately, such product-liability claims come into play only after consumers have incurred some harm as a result of product use. Over 10,000 former users of Dalkon Shield, an intrauterine device, brought suit against A.H. Robbins, its manufacturer, only after experiencing illness and infertility.

Although there is a need for government to regulate product safety, some companies recognize their responsibilities in this area. In 1991, General Motors did the unheard of when a bad batch of engine coolant ruined water pumps in almost all of its 2,000 Saturn cars—30 percent of the total sold up to that time. Instead of simply correcting the glitch, GM gave brand-new cars to all affected Saturn owners and went out of its way to identify the company responsible. The strategy was designed to build confidence in the car and accountability in the suppliers.[42] It is a good example of self-regulation to ensure product safety.

PRODUCT PERFORMANCE

Manufacturers should be concerned with more than product safety. They also have a responsibility to ensure that products perform in an acceptable manner. If a fabric shreds, a kitchen appliance fails, or a battery goes dead soon after it is purchased, performance, not safety, is the issue.

Most companies try to ensure that a product will meet consumer expectations for the simple reason that, if they don't, consumers will not buy again. Also, negative word-of-mouth communications about the product will discourage new buyers.

Since good product performance is generally in their interest, most manufacturers use quality controls to achieve it. They also reduce the financial risk to consumers of purchasing expensive products such as cars or appliances by offering warranties that assure repairs or replacement in a certain period of time. Industry associations have also established performance standards such as energy usage for major appliances.

The government can do little to legislate adequate product performance if consumer safety or environmental concerns such as pollution are not at issue. Consumers can bring a manufacturer to court when it has not adequately remedied a product failure; but few do unless product safety is involved. Fortunately, the link between good performance and profitability is a compelling motivator for most companies to regulate themselves.

PRODUCT INFORMATION

Another consumer right that bears on new-product development is the information on product ingredients provided on the package. Consumers have a right to know these ingredients so as to make a safe and informed choice.

The FDA is responsible for regulating label and package information. As we have seen in Chapter 4, a new FDA chief reinvigorated the agency in 1991, prom-

EXHIBIT 11.5

Premier Smokeless Cigarette: An Issue of Product Safety

ulgating new labeling rules and actively seizing products such as Citrus Hill because of misleading packaging claims. The most dramatic labeling proposal will require all food makers to compare their products' fat, cholesterol, fiber, and sodium content with the maximum recommended daily allowance. Additional laws seeking to protect consumers through full information have resulted in health-warning labels on cigarettes and sugar substitutes.

SUMMARY

1. **What is the definition of a product? A new product?**
A product is an offering by an organization represented by a bundle of product attributes and benefits designed to satisfy customer needs. Products are classified as consumer goods (products sold directly to individuals for final consumption) and industrial goods (products to be used in producing other goods or in support of the production process). New products are products new to consumers, to a company, or to both. A product is new to consumers when they have no prior awareness of the brand or product category. A product is new to a company when it has to go through a process of development, testing, and market introduction. Many products that are new to both companies and consumers are classified as innovations—that is, products that result in changes in consumer behavior and consumption patterns.
2. **Why are new products essential to a firm's profitability?**
Because existing products eventually mature and begin to decline, firms need a series of successful new-product entries to maintain profits over time.
3. **What are the reasons behind new-product successes and failures?**
New products tend to be successful when the company has matched product characteristics to customer needs well, when it has been able to use its know-how in marketing the new product, when the product has a distinct competitive advantage, and when the company's environment fosters taking risks.
New-product failure results from misreading customer needs, poor positioning of the product, a product that does not perform well, and inadequate marketing research and competitive analysis.
4. **What steps are involved in new-product development?**
   - Identifying new-product opportunities based primarily on unmet customer needs
   - Developing new-product objectives
   - Generating and screening new-product ideas to fill customer needs
   - Testing the product concept, then the product itself
   - Developing the product
   - Developing a marketing plan for product introduction
   - Testing the product in several market areas
   - Introducing the product.
5. **What are some of the ethical issues in new-product development?**
The major ethical issue in new-product development is the marketer's responsibility to ensure safety. Most marketers try to do so during the development

process. But abuses have occurred, making action by government agencies necessary. The most important of these agencies is the Consumer Product Safety Commission (CPSC). Another key issue is full disclosure of information about product ingredients on packages. Again, most marketers do so, but laws had to be passed to guarantee full information on packages of all appropriate products.

KEY TERMS

Product (p. 359)
Core product (p. 359)
Tangible product (p. 359)
Augmented product (p. 360)
Brand (p. 360)
Product category (p. 360)
Product line (p. 361)
Durable goods (p. 362)
Nondurable goods (p. 362)
Services (p. 362)
Convenience goods (p. 363)
Shopping goods (p. 363)
Specialty goods (p. 364)
Production goods (p. 365)
Installations and accessories (p. 365)
Supplies and services (p. 366)
Innovations (p. 366)
New-product duplication (p. 367)
Product extensions (p. 367)
Product revision (p. 367)
Product addition (p. 367)
Product repositioning (p. 368)
Product life cycle (p. 370)
Test market (p. 375)
Payback period (p. 376)
Product concept (p. 376)
Product prototypes (p. 378)
Test marketing (p. 381)
Simulated store tests (p. 381)
Sales wave experiments (p. 381)
Brand leveraging (p. 383)

QUESTIONS

1. An industrial engineer commented on the definition of a product as follows:

   As far as I'm concerned, the product is the various parts that make it work. It's fine to say that the brand name and package may influence sales when we are dealing with consumers goods. But for industrial goods, it is the physical product entity that counts. Everything else is window dressing.

   a. Do you agree with this statement?
   b. Could product components other than the physical product be decisive in influencing sales for industrial goods? Why?
2. Why is the distinction between a brand and a product category important?
3. What is the distinction between a personal computer classified as a consumer good and a personal computer classified as an industrial good. What are the strategic implications?
4. A company that has tended to rely on product reformulations and extensions of its existing line is considering putting more emphasis on innovations. What risks might the company face as a result?
5. Why does the identification of products as convenience, shopping, and specialty goods vary from one country to another? Provide examples.
6. What are the implications for new-product development of the relationship between profits and sales in Figure 11.4?
7. The chapter cited five reasons why new products succeed. Were each of these factors important in 3M's successful introduction of Safest Stripper? Explain.
8. What are some differences in the new-product development process between consumer goods and industrial goods?
9. Many companies are avoiding test marketing. Why? What are the risks of *not* test marketing a product? What are the alternatives to test marketing?
10. What are the risks of new-product development? What strategies do companies use to reduce these risks? What are the pros and cons of this position?
11. How have federal agencies operated to ensure product safety? What can companies do to ensure that they market safe products?

QUESTIONS: YOU ARE THE DECISION MAKER

1. A manufacturer of major appliances is considering acquiring a company that produces cleaning products, such as oven and floor cleaners, to offer a broader range of products for the kitchen and home. It staffs some product management positions with managers from its appliance business. Based on Table 11.1, what changes in the marketing mix will these managers most likely have to consider in shifting from appliances to cleaning products? Would you consider the transition from one type of business to the other an easy one?
2. A company introduced a new hand-cream preparation marketed to older women and positioned to "get the wrinkles out of aging hands." Consumers liked the product in concept and product tests. Trial rate for the product in test markets was so high that the company decided to shorten the test-marketing period and introduce the product nationally. It flopped badly. What hypothesis could you develop as to why the product was successful in tests but failed after national introduction? Based on your hypothesis, explain a course of action better suited to the product and market.
3. Consider the following statement made by a marketing manager at a large electronics firm:

   We have some of the best engineers and scientists in our R&D labs. But those people waste most of their time on esoteric ideas with no market applications. And when they do hit on an idea that is marketable, they're interested in making the perfect product. Well, consumers aren't usually willing to pay for the perfect product. If it was up to me, I would have R&D report to marketing to ensure product development is geared to what the market wants.

   a. Do you agree with this statement?
   b. What problems might arise if R&D were under the control of marketing?
   c. What problems might arise if R&D were divorced from marketing?
4. The president of a firm that manufactures small appliances says:

   New products are one road to profitability, but not the only road. The problems with investing heavily in new-product development are that (a) it is expensive, (b) it is risky, because competition can follow you in very easily, and (c) it opens you up to losses due to changes in technology. I would prefer to let the other fellow take the lead and then follow when I think the market is ripe.

   What are the pros and cons of this position?

CHAPTER 12

Managing Brands Over the Product Life Cycle

YOUR FOCUS IN CHAPTER 12

To learn:

- *The role of the product manager in marketing a brand.*
- *The responsibilities of product managers for brands, product lines, and the company's overall product mix.*
- *What important decisions product managers must make for brands and product lines.*
- *What is meant by a product life cycle, and how this concept helps managers develop brand and product-line strategies.*

The Changing Orthodoxy at Procter & Gamble

Neil McElroy was miserable. The soap Procter & Gamble had hired him to advertise, Camay, was being ignored in favor of a P&G old-timer called Ivory. Sensing that his young career was in jeopardy, McElroy dashed off a three-page memo to his bosses, challenging them to give him control of Camay and the resources to let it go head-to-head with Ivory. The year was 1931. Procter & Gamble would never be the same.

Previously, companies milked their brands until newer ones came along to knock them off the shelf. McElroy was asking P&G to do the unthinkable: let two viable brands co-exist. He won, and his innovation ushered in P&G's golden age.[1]

Joy, Crest, Zest, Tide, and dozens of today's other superbrands became profit centers unto themselves, managed by brash, swaggering *brand managers,* in the McElroy mold, who were bent on thrashing their competition—even if it came from within P&G. They acted as overlords with all the company's resources at their disposal. True, there was a chain of command above them, but these brand managers formed the nucleus of P&G's profit wheel, and if any doubted their power they had only to remember that McElroy eventually became chairman of P&G.[2]

The *brand management system* was so successful, it was copied by nearly every packaged-goods company in the world. By the 1980s, however, the successes at P&G were fewer, and cracks in the brand-management system began to show. There were three problems. First, brand managers took a mass-market approach. They were naturally motivated to get as many consumers to buy their brand as possible, but the increasing proportions of singles, working women, divorced parents, and affluent baby boomers reflected a fracturing of the mass market. Brand management did not lend itself to developing new products more finely tuned to the needs of specific market segments.

Second, brand managers tended to focus on a single brand. They lost sight of the total marketplace. As a result, several brands in a product category would go after the same customers with the same marketing strategies. For example, P&G's Tide and Cheer detergents often issued price-off coupons at the same time. The resulting *cannibalization* (competition between a company's brands for the same buyers) was beginning to hurt P&G.

Third, a rigid command structure was beginning to inhibit the quick responses necessary to market new products to smaller segments. The 92 brand managers at P&G had to go through three or four layers of management to get a decision approved.[3] One brand manager recalled having to wait one year to get approval for a simple change in package design. This rigidity let Kimberly-Clark capture a swath of Pampers' market by introducing refastenable tabs on its disposable diapers. P&G's research people had a similar invention, but it languished in development. Suddenly, the one-man one-product marketing approach began to look rusty and dated.[4]

By the mid 1980s, P&G decided it had to revitalize the brand management system. Rather than having a single brand manager run the show, it began forming teams of managers from advertising, research and development, distribution, and marketing to develop marketing strategies for a total product category. For example, a team would be responsible for all offerings in P&G's line of detergents—Tide, Cheer, Duz, Dash, Bold, and Ivory Flakes. Brand managers were now one cog in a larger wheel. The purpose was to coordinate strategies so as to better target new and existing products to defined segments and thus avoid cannibalization.

But who would head the brand management teams? A new level was created known as a *category manager.*[5] The category manager would have responsibility for coordinating the various brands in a category and would have profit responsibility for all these brands. Brand managers would now report to P&G's category managers. By 1990, P&G had 26 category managers responsible for 39 separate product categories.[6]

The category management system was designed to correct the weaknesses in brand management and make P&G more attuned to a changing marketplace. First, response time was quickened. If a brand manager wanted a package change or a change in positioning strategy for a particular brand, the category manager could immediately approve it.

Second, the category management system moved P&G from an individual brand to a total product line approach. Under category managers, team after team began building on the strength of existing brands by introducing new offerings under existing brand names. This concept came to be known as *brand leveraging* and resulted in products such as Crest Tartar Control toothpaste and Pampers Superabsorbent diapers. The rationale was simple: It is cheaper and more effective to target specific segments with extensions of existing brands than to introduce them as totally new brands.

Third, the category management system shifted P&G from a mass marketer to a market segmenter. Teams could better market individual brands in a product category to individual segments. And fourth, category managers could better coordinate all brands in a category to avoid cannibalization.

Category management may be the death knell for McElroy's brand management orthodoxy, but McElroy was an innovator. Chances are, he would have been the first one to revise his memo if he were living today.

THE PRODUCT MANAGEMENT SYSTEM

All managers who deal with brands or product categories work within what is called the *product management system.* The **product management system** *is designed to develop and implement marketing strategies at three levels: the brand, the product line (or product category), and the product mix.* As we have seen in Chapter 11, a **brand** *is a name or symbol that represents a product.* Crisco and Puritan are brands of corn oil made by Procter & Gamble; Pepsi-Cola is a brand of cola made by PepsiCo.

A **product line** *is a group of products in the same product category, frequently with the same brand name.* Kleenex tissues (including Ultra, Boutique, and so on) and Minute Maid juices (which range from apple juice to lemonade) are product lines under one brand name. A product line can also be a collection of brands with different names. As we have seen, P&G's line of detergents include five or six different brands.

A **product mix** *is the array of product categories that a company or strategic business unit (SBU) offers to the public.* (We defined SBUs in Chapter 2.) When Greyhound Dial Corp. needed revamping, CEO John Teets created separate SBUs responsible for personal care, food, household, and laundry products. Each were given their own sales, advertising, marketing, and research staffs. As a result, the personal care unit rolled out Dial liquid soap, while the food unit introduced microwave-ready lunch meals.[7]

Table 12.1 shows the three types of managers associated with these three levels—brand managers, category managers, and business managers—and the strategic decisions for which they are responsible. We will refer to all three managers generically as *product managers,* because they are part of the product management system. **Brand managers** *have profit responsibility for particular brands and are responsible for positioning the brand, identifying its target segments, and establishing price, promotional, and distribution strategies.* Companies that rely on brand managers emphasize the brand as the focal point for marketing strategy. Until the mid 1980s, Procter & Gamble focused on individual brand names rather than on product lines.

After the mid 1980s, the product management focus at P&G shifted from brands to product lines and from brand to category managers. **Category managers** *have profit responsibility for all brands in a product category.* As we have seen, teams at P&G under the direction of a category manager began managing product lines. One result was the extension of most P&G lines into new offerings under existing brand names. Another result was a better coordination of brands within product lines.

Product-mix decisions involve evaluating all of a firm's or business unit's product offerings and allocating resources to the firm's product categories. As we have seen in Chapter 2, such decisions are made by business unit or corporate managers, responsible for developing a strategic plan. Product-mix decisions shape a company's future growth and affect its profitability. Arm & Hammer was a one-product company in the early 1970s, until it extended its trusted name in baking soda to toothpastes, carpet deodorizers, and laundry detergents.[8]

In the remainder of this chapter, we focus on the three levels of product management just described.

TABLE 12.1

Three Levels of Product Management

	BRAND →	PRODUCT LINE →	PRODUCT MIX
MANAGEMENT	Brand manager	Category manager	Business or corporate manager
STRATEGIC FOCUS	Brand positioning	Coordinate brands within product line	Allocate resources to product lines
	Identify target for brand	Product-line positioning	Evaluate product portfolio
	Develop marketing mix for brand	Identify target for product line	Add new lines; delete existing lines
		Develop marketing mix for product line	
		Develop product-line extensions and determine deletions from line	
PLANNING	Marketing plan	Marketing plan	Strategic marketing plan
EXAMPLES	Tide detergent	P&G's detergent offering: Tide, Cheer, Dash, Bold, Duz, Ivory Flakes	P&G's total product offering: detergents, toothpaste, coffee, disposable diapers

THE BRAND

A brand name associated with a quality product is one of the most valuable assets a company can have. The name Campbell is worth more than all of the company's soup-making facilities. The name Reebok, although unknown before 1981, has become synonymous with stylish athletic footwear.

COMPONENTS OF A BRAND

Most products in the marketplace are **branded**, *that is, they have a name and/or symbol that is identified with the product.* If we accept the broad definition of a product in the last chapter, then a brand means more than a name, such as Pillsbury, or a symbol, such as the Doughboy. It is also represented by the benefits it conveys (the *core product*), the package it is in (the *tangible product*), and any warranties and services associated with it (the *augmented product*). We will consider each of these.

BRAND NAMES

Companies spend millions of dollars establishing brand names and keeping them before the public eye. For Walt Disney, General Electric, Johnson & Johnson, and Xerox, the brand name means competitive advantage.

Although brand names are generally associated with consumer goods, they can be equally important for industrial products. As we have seen in Chapter 9, the name IBM carried such weight in computers that many information managers feared to buy anything else. As many said, "You can't get fired for buying an IBM product." Similarly, the name Deere in farm equipment or Boeing in aircraft has value for customers that substantially contributes to the net worth of the company.

The term **brand equity** *refers to the value that a brand name develops over time* for its owner. When Grand Met purchased Pillsbury for $57 billion in 1989, Pillsbury's Green Giant and Totino's brands were worth $4.3 billion alone to the new owners. Philip Morris estimates that the Marlboro cowboy is worth over $10 billion, representing one-third of the company's total market value. Some British companies have even begun quantifying the value of their brand names on their balance sheets.[9]

The value of a brand name is illustrated by the Hong Kong–based Semi-Tech group's purchase of Singer Sewing Machine for $300 million in 1989. Even though Singer was languishing, Semi-Tech founder James Ting saw that consumers who shopped in Singer's 30,000 shops worldwide had a very positive association with its products—so he took advantage of this brand equity by slapping the Singer name on everything from video recorders to phones to boom boxes, hoping to turn the 139 year-old sewing icon into a global consumer electronics powerhouse. The returns on Ting's experiment are not in yet, but he believes the cornerstone to its success will be Singer's well-known name.[10]

One of the more blatant manifestations of brand equity is one company using another's established brand to sell their product. In a 1991 ad campaign, Weber barbecue grills pictured its product in front of a Chevrolet Corvette and used the tag line, "One of these babies really cooks." The little-known Weber hoped to bask in Corvette's brand equity.[11]

ATTRIBUTES OF A GOOD BRAND NAME If possible, a brand name should suggest product benefits. Sunkist oranges, Easy Off oven cleaner, Beautyrest mattresses, and Pampers disposable diapers are other examples of names that suggest product benefits.

Also, a brand name should fit the brand image. Tiffany is a good name for jewelry because it gives the impression of being exclusive, fine, and status-oriented. Nissan's Pathfinder is a good name for a four-wheel drive vehicle because it brings to mind adventure and exploration.

The name should be easy to pronounce and recognize as well. When IBM reviewed its branding policies, it found that its product developers were coming up with computer software names such as "Expert Systems Reasoning Method." The developers were sent back to the drawing boards, and the result was more-user-friendly names like "Knowledge Tool."[12]

For international marketers, the name should be able to be translated into other languages without altering its meaning. A 1990 survey of Soviet shoppers found that the brands with the highest name recognition were Sony, Adidas, Ford, Toyota, Mercedes-Benz, Fanta, Pepsi-Cola, Volvo, Fiat, and Panasonic, all names that translate well into Russian.[13]

Finally, as we have seen in Chapter 4, the Lanham Act forbids use of a brand name previously registered by another company.

HOW ARE BRAND NAMES SELECTED? Given these objectives, companies use both managerial judgment and consumer tests to select a brand name.

A management team at Sony selected the name Walkman. Names such as "Hot Line" and "Sound-About" were considered and rejected as not reflecting product benefits. Managers liked another name, "Stereo-Walky," but Toshiba had already registered the name. The team liked Walky, and Sony's ad agency even developed a logo with two legs sticking out from the bottom of the A in "walk." That gave someone the idea of combining walk and man, and the name was born.[14]

Instead of relying entirely on managerial judgment, most companies use some kind of consumer testing as well. Typically, the company generates a large number of names which are then weeded down by management to 10 or 20 finalists. These are then tested on consumers.

BRAND SYMBOLS

Brand symbols can be as important as brand names in establishing product associations and a brand image. Immediately after Grand Met took over Pillsbury, they resuscitated the languishing Doughboy, trimming him down and pasting him on everything from cake mixes to kitchenware (see Exhibit 12.1). As a symbol, the Doughboy was worth as much, if not more, than the Pillsbury name, and Grand Met doubled his ad budget to make the most of it.[15]

EXHIBIT 12.1

A Symbol that Plays a Key Role in Brand Identification: Pillsbury's Doughboy

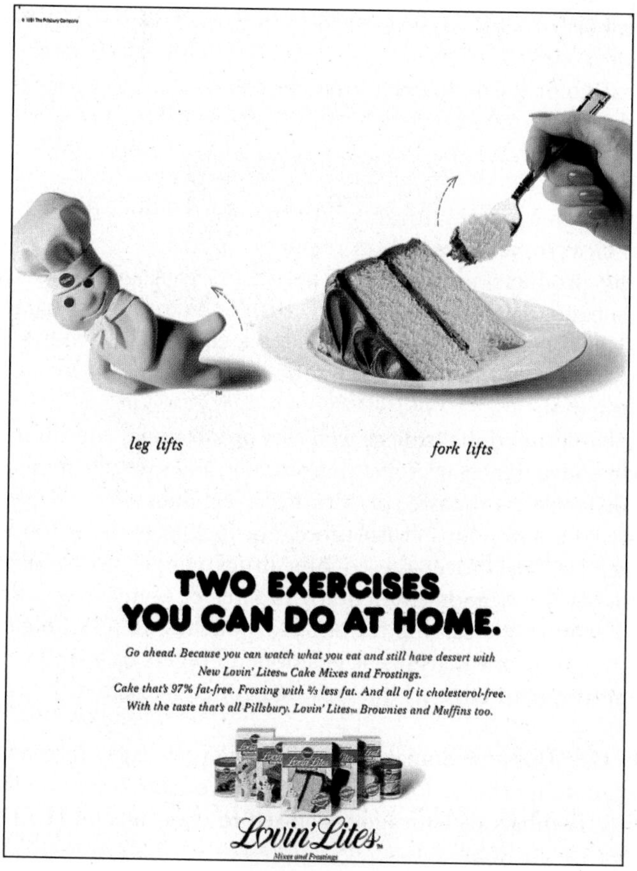

leg lifts
fork lifts
TWO EXERCISES
YOU CAN DO AT HOME.
Go ahead. Because you can watch what you eat and still have dessert with
New Lovin' Lites™ Cake Mixes and Frostings.
Cake that's 97% fat-free. Frosting with ⅔ less fat. And all of it cholesterol-free.
With the taste that's all Pillsbury. Lovin' Lites™ Brownies and Muffins too.
Lovin' Lites™
Mixes and Frostings

When brand identification is weak, symbols may be even more important than names. Because consumers regard all glass-fiber products similarly, Owens-Corning decided to exploit the one visual factor that distinguished it from competitors—its pink coloring. It adopted the Pink Panther as its symbol. This cartoon character became the centerpiece for the advertising campaign with the theme "Put Your House in the Pink." For the first time, buyers began to specify Owens-Corning Fiberglass insulation.[16]

THE PACKAGE

A third important component of a brand is packaging. Its importance is reflected in the fact that 10 cents of every dollar spent by consumers goes to package development. One survey by a design firm found that many executives considered packaging the most important element in the consumer's decision to buy.[17]

ROLE OF THE PACKAGE The package plays a number of important roles. First, it identifies and promotes the brand. Hershey's distinctive brown package was so successful in this regard that the company found advertising unnecessary until the early 1970s.

Second, distinctive package design can attract consumers' attention and increase sales. This was clearly the case with Pasta LaBella macaroni, which was introduced by American Italian Pasta, with a label that created a sophisticated European feel. One supermarket owner said the brand tripled his pasta sales.[18]

Third, a package can identify a line of products. When Murrie White Drummond & Lienhart of Chicago was asked to create a look for H_2O skin products, it came up with a jet-black plastic label shaped like a wave. Each H_2O product had a different color bordering the wave. For example, Tahiti Twist moisturizing gel was bordered in orange, while Primrose moisturizing cream was set around lavender. The sleek, futuristic design makes H_2O's products immediately identifiable (see Exhibit 12.2).[19]

Fourth, packaging communicates information on ingredients, quantity, and product use. Government regulation requires disclosure of ingredients for many food and drug products and dating of perishable packaged products. Packaging also communicates product benefits or changes in product characteristics that might appeal to consumers. Procter & Gamble changes Crisco oil's labels once a year, and the labels of cake mixes more often, to make room for new recipes and product information.[20]

Packaging has a functional role as well as a promotional and informational role. It can provide convenience, preservation, storage, and safety benefits. Pumps make it easier to dispense toothpaste, plastics make ketchup more squeezeable, cylindrical cans make potato chips crush-proof, zip-lock bags make foods fresher, and seal-tight openings make over-the-counter drugs tamper-proof. All are examples of improvements in packaging functions. Procter & Gamble was first out of the gate with coffee in single-serving tea bag-like pouches. P&G's Folgers Singles not only carried higher profit margins, it positioned Folgers to a convenience-minded niche, helping it get an edge in the crowded coffee market.[21]

PACKAGE DESIGN Companies either design packages internally or employ special package design firms for this purpose. (We have seen how Murrie White Drummond & Lienhart of Chicago was hired to dress up the H_2O skin products line.)

EXHIBIT 12.2

Packaging that Promotes Product Identification: H_2O

Package design was central in Coca-Cola's decision to bring back the original brand after introducing the new formula. A new can had to be developed that would distinguish what is now Coca-Cola Classic from New Coke. The challenge for the package designers was to fit the product into the Coke family while giving it a distinctive identity that would appeal to traditionalists.[22] The name Coca-Cola would be used instead of Coke, and Classic would be attached to appeal to the brand's loyal followers. The name appeared in a script style reminiscent of old ads, and the words "original formula" encased in a circle resembling an official seal were added to the can.

THE WARRANTY

Another component of brands is the *warranty* that is sometimes provided by manufacturers and retailers. **Warranties** *are written statements that describe a company's commitment to replace or repair products that are defective or perform poorly.* There are *limited warranties,* which stipulate areas that are not covered, and *full warranties,* which have no restrictions. Sears made headlines with a first-of-a-kind full warranty on children's clothing that offered to replace any piece that became damaged or torn.[23] The catch, as Sears made clear, was that the item had to be returned while the child was still able to wear that size.

Sears was not walking out of step. Many companies desperate for market share are using warranties as enticements. The offers vary widely. Hampton Inn Hotel chain offers a 100-percent satisfaction guarantee, while Domino Pizza has promised to give its pizzas away for free if delivery isn't made in 30 minutes. The dual benefit for companies is that warranties give them something they rarely get: feedback. Studies suggest that most customers who have complaints do not air them.[24]

The Magnuson-Moss Warranty Improvement Act of 1975 requires manufacturers to state the limits of any warranty including its length, specific areas of performance, and whether it includes labor and routine maintenance. The act also requires full warranties to meet certain minimum standards, including reasonable repairs and replacement.

GLOBAL MARKETING STRATEGIES

Barbie: Extending Brand Equity to International Markets

Can a Valley Girl make it in Japan? John Amerman thinks so, especially if her name is Barbie.

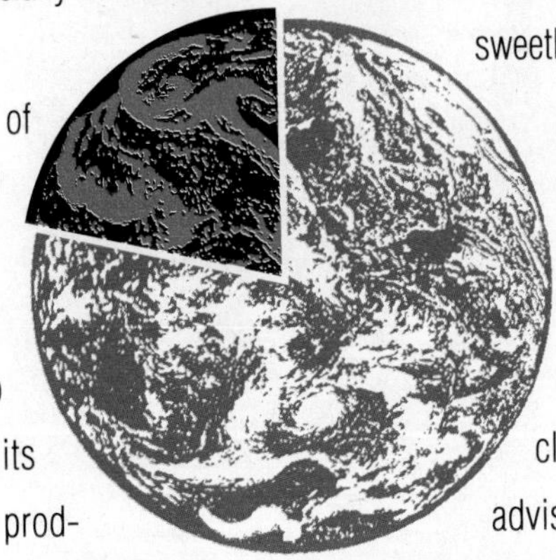

When Amerman took the reigns of Mattel in 1987, most analysts had given the toy company up for dead. Years of unchecked expansion and a disastrous plunge into electronic toys had wiped out its choke-hold on cutting-edge kids products. Profits were down—so were spirits—and Mattel's management was letting one of its chief assets, the Barbie doll, languish. To Amerman, that made as much sense as locking a fortune in a vault and forgetting the key. Barbie was a gold mine in brand equity because almost every girl in America had one. Amerman decided it was about time Mattel started to capitalize on her name. By 1990, he was spending $220 million to promote her. Little girls were buying everything from Barbie '57 Chevys to $500 Barbie mansions, and Mattel's growth rate was soaring past the 30-percent barrier.

Barbie had become America's darling again. And Amerman was ready to make her the world's sweetheart.

Barbie had been in Japan since 1958, but Mattel's old management could not seem to find the right way to market her. In her first formulation, she was a bosomy clothes-horse. Then, when Japanese advisors suggested she would do better with an Oriental look, Mattel gave her doe-eyed features and a decidedly flatter chest. That did not help either, especially since Japanese girls—unlike their American counterparts who cram shoe boxes full of Barbie paraphernalia—considered her a traditional decorative doll who only needed one dress.

The problem was not with the doll, Amerman decided. It was with Mattel's decision to market her differently in Japan. If she represented the universal aspiration of all young girls to act adult and dress stylishly, then she should be marketed universally as well. That meant pitching her not to Japanese par-

BRAND IMAGE

A **brand image** *is the overall impression created in the consumer's mind by a brand's physical characteristics, name, symbols, package, and reputation for service.* That image may be the most important factor in a purchase decision.

It is unlikely Dole would have succeeded branding fresh produce if consumers did not already strongly associate it with fresh pineapples. Dole relied on that asso-

GLOBAL MARKETING STRATEGIES

ents—as the company had done—but to the kids, just as it did in the United States.

When Amerman put his thoughts into practice, he discovered two things: Japanese mothers would buy whatever their daughters asked for, and the daughters were asking for Barbie. Bypassing the wholesalers who traditionally have had a lock on distribution, Mattel International began selling to retail outlets and laying plans to tap into a network of 1,400 mass-merchandise superstores. Barbie began disappearing off store shelves, leading Mattel to predict it would sell $150 million worth of branded Barbie goods by the mid 1990s, doubling the present volume of all fashion-doll sales in the country.

Barbie is not stopping there, either. As soon as the Berlin Wall came crashing down, Amerman was faced with the problem of introducing Western-quality and goods to Eastern Europe. His solution: Freedom Barbie. "Children's wants and desires, their play patterns, are the same all around the world," he says, predicting Barbie will become a billion-dollar phenomenon by 1995.

She has already demonstrated that an established brand name can make a company a global powerhouse, as long as it is marketed with savvy, style, and a '57 Chevy.

Question: What strategy did Mattel use to capitalize on Barbie's name on a global basis? What risks did it face in implementing its strategy?

Sources: "Barbie Does Budapest," *Forbes,* January 7, 1991; "Now a Glamorous Barbie Heads to Japan," *The Wall Street Journal,* June 5, 1991; and "Mattel Inc. Resumes Its Leadership of the Toys Parade," *The Wall Street Journal,* June 5, 1990.

ciation when it began tilling thousands of acres of California farmland to grow lettuce, broccoli, celery, peppers, grapes, and 50 types of fruits.[25]

In another context, Izod Lacoste polo shirts were the standard-bearer of chic during the early 1980s, but became bargain-basement fare after owner Crystal Brands agreed to sell them to discount chains. While they accounted for $450 million in sales in 1982, the figure in 1990 was estimated to be only $125 million.[26]

The essence of image marketing may best be summed up by a 1991 report in the magazine *Consumer Reports.* The publication discovered that in blind taste tests, only 7 of 19 self-proclaimed Coke and Pepsi fans could pick their brands. Diet-soda tasters did worse. Why then does Coke and Pepsi stand head and shoulders above its competition? Maybe it has something to do with the $300 million both companies spend reinforcing their brands' image.[27]

THE VALUE OF BRANDING

If the marketing strategy for a brand is successful, all of its components—name, symbol, packaging, and service reputation—act to form a strong positive association in consumers' minds. As a result, branding can be valuable to both the company and the consumer.

ADVANTAGES OF BRANDING FOR MANUFACTURERS

A brand name has at least four advantages for manufacturers. First, when a brand name is associated with a successful product, it will attract *loyal customers.* At the Robinson Brick Company, a study told executives that loyal customers thought Robinson had higher-quality bricks than competitors, a greater choice of colors, and faster delivery. Robinson's management team did not need to think twice about what to do next. Playing on this consumer confidence, they began elevating their name in ads to strengthen brand association. Soon after, hardware store customers began asking for Robinson bricks in the same way they specified Anderson windows or Levolor blinds.[28]

Second, a brand that has built a loyal consumer base has *staying power.* One study found that of 30 leading brands in 1930, 27 are still leaders in their category today, including Ivory soap, Campbell soup, Gold Medal flour, and Crisco shortening.[29]

A third reason branding is important to manufacturers is that a brand with strong consumer loyalties also tends to *win distribution support* more easily. Reebok had to scrounge for support from shoe distributors in its early years. Now that it is an established brand, it has no problem getting shelf space.

Finally, a strong brand can be *leveraged* by applying it to spin-offs within a product line. In the space of 20 months, Procter & Gamble leveraged its brand names onto 90 products.

ADVANTAGES OF BRANDING FOR CONSUMERS

Branding gives consumers some important advantages. A brand name *identifies a product* so that consumers know what they are getting. Consumers do not need to worry about variations in content and quality from one purchase to the next. As a result, branding *facilitates shopping.* Recognizable brand names allow consumers to buy with little need for comparisons and information search.

Brand names also give consumers *information.* Consumers remember the taste, ingredients, price, and performance of brands; they remember which brands satisfied them and which did not. This is why branding creates the opportunity for consumers to become brand loyal. Crest toothpaste has many loyal users because the brand has become equated in consumers' minds with cavity protection: It was the first fluoridated toothpaste and received the endorsement of the American Dental Association. That association is still invaluable years later.

There are signs, however, that consumers are no longer as committed to buying brands as they once were. One 1990 survey showed that 62 percent of consumers polled bought only well-known brand names, down from 77 percent in 1975.

Another showed that the number of consumers who regarded brand names as an assurance of quality dropped from 68 percent in 1989 to 61 percent in 1990.

PROTECTING BRANDS

Because brand recognition is so important in guiding consumer purchases, a brand is valuable property to the company that has established it. The power of brand names is evident when people refer to copying papers as Xeroxing, caulk used to patch cracks as Spackle, or a tissue as Kleenex. These are all specific product names, and their owners protect them by registering them as trademarks with the U.S. patent office. As we have seen in Chapter 4, the Lanham Act (1946) protects such trademarks from duplication.

Why does generic use of a brand name pose a threat to the brand's manufacturer? Because if a brand is too successful, its name may pass into the vocabulary and, as a result, companies may lose the right to use them. Thermos, cellophane, and shredded wheat were once brand names until the companies that produced them lost the right to their names in court cases because they were so commonly associated with the product category.

Some current brand names are also in danger of losing their identity. One survey found that 56 percent of the respondents called all tissues Kleenex. Similarly, 61 percent referred to Band-Aids instead of bandages, 52 percent to Scotch Tape instead of cellophane tape, 49 percent to Xeroxing instead of copying, 48 percent to Q-tips instead of cotton swabs, and 42 percent to Jell-O instead of gelatin.[30] Rollerblades is using an advertising campaign to protect its name because the public is beginning to identify the name with the sport rather than with the company's products (see Exhibit 12.3).

Conversely, companies seeking to use new product names sometimes find themselves thwarted by little-known brands that already hold the trademark. This happened to Cosmair's L'Oréal division when it wanted to call a green and purple hair dye Zazu. A Hinsdale, Illinois hair-styling salon with the same name sued Cosmair and won damages of $2.1 million. Some marketers believe that suing over trademark names has become a cottage industry, with obscure companies filing multimillion dollar suits any time they catch wind of a larger firm using a name that sounds even remotely similar. "It's a real challenge to find a clean name without any conflicts," said one trademark attorney.[31]

MARKETING DECISIONS CONCERNING BRANDS

We have been looking at the advantages of branding and the stake that companies have in the brands they own. Because brands are so important, the way in which they are marketed is of great strategic relevance. Let us look at two important marketing decisions concerning brands: first, the extent to which the manufacturer controls the marketing of its brand; and second, the way in which a company identifies its brands.

BRAND CONTROL

Although we have seen that many companies go to great lengths to develop and protect their brands, not all manufacturers choose to control the marketing of their products. Some even permit their products to be sold without brand names. Companies must make two decisions regarding brand control. First, will they control the marketing of their brand, or will they produce for retailers and wholesalers and let these intermediaries control the product? Second, regardless of who controls the brand, will it be supported by advertising and promotional efforts?

EXHIBIT 12.3

Protecting Valuable Brand Names

Yes-or-no decisions on these two issues produce the four alternatives to brand control shown in Figure 12.1—manufacturer's brands, private brands, generic products, and price brands.

MANUFACTURER'S BRANDS *Brands that are both produced and marketed by the manufacturer are called* **manufacturer's brands.** These are also known as **national** or **regional brands**, depending on the geographic area in which they are marketed. Most of the brands cited in this chapter, including Crest toothpaste, Kleenex tissues, and Tide detergent are manufacturer's brands sold nationally. Coors beer was a regional brand centered in the Midwest until it began to expand nationally to challenge Budweiser.

FIGURE 12.1

Types of Brands Based on Who Controls Them

Control over Brands

Marketing Support	Manufacturer	Retailer/Wholesaler
Yes	Manufacturer's Brands • Crest Toothpaste • Kleenex Tissues	Private Brands • A&P Ann Page Coffee • Safeway's Truly Fine deodorant soap
No	Price Brands • P&G's Summit Paper towels • Ralston Purina Mainstay dog food	Generic Products • L&M produces generic cigarettes

PRIVATE BRANDS **Private brands** *are manufactured for retailers or wholesalers and marketed under their label rather than the manufacturer's label.* Large retailers such as Sears and A&P often buy products from leading manufacturers such as Michelin, Heinz, or Ralston Purina, then sell the products under the retailer's own brand name to consumers. According to SAMI Information Services, store-brand dollar volume in grocery stores was $16.3 billion in 1988, or 12.6 percent of every dollar spent. They were the first, second, or third brand in more than 40 percent of the 476 categories that SAMI monitors.[32] Often, advertising expenditures on private brands such as Sears' DieHard battery or A&P's Ann Page coffee are equal to expenditures on leading manufacturer's brands.

Why do retailers and wholesalers market private brands when they have to support them with advertising and promotional expenditures? Because they can buy these products at lower cost from manufacturers who want to use up excess capacity. As a result, prices for private brands average 15 percent to 30 percent below those of national brands.[33] Even after spending money on advertising, retailers and wholesalers can offer goods that are often comparable in quality to manufacturer's brands at substantially lower prices. Thus, Safeway can claim that its Truly Fine deodorant soap is comparable to Dial, and its Nu-Made mayonnaise is comparable to Hellmann's.

The next question is why manufacturers sell products for private branding when they know that private brands may undercut the price of their own brands? There are several reasons. First, excess capacity may cost a manufacturer heavily if production facilities go unused. Second, manufacturers can reduce marketing costs by selling products for private branding. This is one reason companies such as Ralston Purina, Scott Paper, and Heinz regularly sell products for private branding, in some cases using up to 40 percent of their production capacity for this purpose. However, other manufacturers, such as Procter & Gamble and Kellogg, refuse to produce for private brands, citing their product superiority and market leadership as evidence that their efforts are best directed to their own brands.

The competition between retailer's brands and manufacturer's brands has been called the **battle of the brands**. The battle is over shelf space and the consumer's dollar, and in this battle, retailers have the advantage. Consumers have become more educated regarding brand alternatives and recognize the value of private brands. Also, retailers control shelf space and can give their own brands preferred positions. This was the case when the Kroger supermarket chain introduced under its own label the first low-calorie yogurt with NutraSweet.[34] All these factors were reflected in an A.C. Nielsen study that found consumers spend 14.2 percent of their total grocery dollars on private-label brands.[35]

GENERIC PRODUCTS A third brand category, **generics**, *are unbranded products sold with no promotional support.* They are produced by manufacturers and controlled by resellers, generally supermarkets. They often appear in plain white boxes with black letters identifying the product category—detergent, paper towel, and so forth. Generic products sell at an average of 40 percent below national brands and 15 to 20 percent below private brands.[36]

Generics first appeared in the United States in 1978; by 1982, they were selling in 80 percent of American supermarkets. Consumers accepted generics in the early 1980s because of greater price sensitivity during a steep recession. The popularity of generics peaked in 1982, with a 12 percent share of unit sales in supermarkets; since then, this share has been declining. However, sales of generics continue to be strong in certain categories that consumers view as undifferentiated, such as granulated sugar, apple juice, baking soda, and canned vegetables.[37]

Manufacturers are even less willing to produce generic items than private brands. Yet, some manufacturers who are losing market share and looking to utilize capacity will probably opt to produce generics. Liggett & Myers' sharp decline in cigarettes, for instance, prompted it to begin producing generics in 1981. By 1984, L&M's generics had captured a substantial 4 percent of the cigarette market. Its success prompted other cigarette companies to introduce generics and lower-priced brands.

PRICE BRANDS **Price brands** *are low-priced brands under the manufacturer's control that are sold with minimal advertising and promotional expenditures.* A manufacturer introduces price brands to compete with private brands and generics. This strategic purpose has also led price brands to be called **fighting brands.**

Procter & Gamble has adopted this strategy because it avoids producing private brands and generics. It introduced a line of low-priced paper towels, called Summit, without advertising support in an attempt to counteract the inroads being made by generics and private brands. Similarly, Ralston Purina eliminated advertising and reduced the price of its Mainstay brand of dog food to compete with generics, and L&M introduced Pyramid, a cigarette priced 25 percent below regular brands to further support its dominant position in lower-priced cigarettes.

As the number of low-priced brands in the market increases, however, greater pressure is placed on higher-priced manufacturer's brands to maintain both advertising and product quality in order to ensure the loyalty of current users. Many of these brands are experiencing a decline in their market shares as consumers switch to price brands, private brands, and generics. As a result, there may be fewer manufacturer's brands in the future.

BRAND-IDENTIFICATION DECISIONS

Companies have several options in trying to establish brand identity, depending first on whether the brand is an individual brand or part of a product line, and second on whether its name is specific to the brand or part of a corporate umbrella. These decisions produce the four alternatives for brand identification shown in Figure 12.2.

INDIVIDUAL BRAND NAMES Procter & Gamble follows a strategy of **individual brand names** *in which each brand a company offers is sold individually and will stand or fall on its own.* New brands are identified with the P&G name only for the first few months after introduction; from that time on, all reference to P&G is discontinued. Even when P&G offers several brands in a product line, there is no strong corporate identification.

An individual-brand strategy such as that used by P&G offers some advantages but also some risks. The company can market separate brands in a category to separate market segments and thus capture more consumers. But there is a possibility of **cannibalization** *in which a new brand that the company introduces draws consumers from the company's existing brands.* For example, when P&G introduced Cheer, some of its users had previously been Tide purchasers. Cannibalization should not deter a company from introducing a new brand, especially if it is an improvement over the existing brand that is being cannibalized. An improved brand will probably draw more customers from the competition than from the company's own brands. But if most of the new brand's business represents consumers switching from one of the company's existing brands, cannibalization could lead to a net loss.

Increasing cannibalization between its brands is one reason P&G introduced the category management system. A category manager can coordinate strategies so that the different brands a company offers within a product category are marketed to different segments. For example, a category manager might decide to position Tide to a convenience segment and Cheer to a segment that puts more emphasis on a powerful cleaner. Further, if P&G decided to introduce a superconcentrated

FIGURE 12.2

Brand-Identification Alternatives

		Type of Name Identification Brand Name	 Corporate Name
Single Brand or Product Line	Single Brand	Individual Brand Name • Crest • Pampers	Corporate Brand Name • Kellogg's Raisin Bran • GE refrigerators
	Product Line	Product-Line Brand Name • Kenmore appliances • Homart home installations	Corporate Family Name • Heinz's 57 Varieties

ETHICAL AND ENVIRONMENTAL ISSUES IN MARKETING

Using Doctors to Promote Brand Names: Is It Ethical?

Carnation has followed a corporate-brand-name strategy for many of its brands including Carnation Slender, a breakfast diet drink, and Carnation Good Start, its entry in the infant formula market. But as just another packaged goods company, Carnation felt it needed to add legitimacy to its infant formula claims, especially since Good Start was positioned to milk-sensitive children. It therefore enlisted doctors to be spokespersons in order to add legitimacy to its infant formula claims.

For example, one doctor, a member of the American Academy of Pediatrics, appeared on the syndicated talk show Hour Magazine in 1988 and raved about Good Start's anti-allergenic benefits for milk-sensitive children. What the viewing audience never learned was that this was not an unsolicited view. The doctor was a paid consultant to Carnation.

Within three months, the Food and Drug Administration began receiving complaints that Good Start caused severe allergic reactions in some babies, prompting nine state Attorneys General to open independent probes into Carnation's health claims. As evidence mounted that Good Start wasn't all it was advertised to be, the company scrapped its marketing strategy, withdrawing claims that the formula was a pediatric breakthrough.

The uproar opened a rare window onto the ethically dubious ways some companies use doctors to launch products. It also shows why the relationship is beginning to fray.

During the mid-to-late 1980s, hundreds of new products were carrying health claims. It seemed natural, therefore, for brand managers to use doctors in marketing the new products. Among the firms that did so were Evian mineral water, which hired a famed cardiologist to support the claim that babies had a greater risk of dehydration than adults; and Kellogg, which used a well-known nutritionist in ads that claimed its fiber-filled Heartwise (now known as Fiberwise) breakfast cereal reduced the risks of heart disease.

The trend toward using doctors as spokespersons was allowed to flourish under Ronald Reagan, but in

version of Tide, the category manager would try to position it to minimize cannibalization with other detergents in the line.

CORPORATE BRAND NAME Instead of identifying products by individual brand names, many companies choose a strategy of using **corporate brand names** *that link the brand name to the company's name.* Kellogg follows such a strategy for its cereal brands—for example, Kellogg's Rice Krispies and Kellogg's Raisin Bran—because the diversity of these products might otherwise lead to confusion

ETHICAL AND ENVIRONMENTAL ISSUES IN MARKETING

the early 1990s, new Food and Drug Administration chief David Kessler began an aggressive crackdown. Among his promises: Medical experts involved in any "illegal promotion effort" would be thoroughly investigated by the FDA. In short order, consumer advocates began calling for bans on food advertising during children's television programming, and the doctor–marketer union devolved into a nasty round of finger-pointing.

To see how the union was forged in the first place, one need look no further than Good Start. The formula was introduced as a medical breakthrough at a New York press conference by Carnation's president, who stood under a picture of Belgian twins reportedly cured of sleeplessness by Good Start. Coverage of the press conference was aired on CNN, and among those interviewed was a University of California doctor who said the innovation was promising. It was not disclosed that this doctor was another Carnation paid consultant.

Carnation followed up with ads in magazines such as *Parenting, American Baby,* and *Essence.* The ads did not mention Good Start, but advised parents that commonplace symptoms such as vomiting and sleeplessness could mean their babies were allergic to their present formula. Meanwhile, doctors were reading Carnation ads in pediatric journals that billed Good Start as a breakthrough formula that had been safely fed to more than 25 thousand European infants. A toll-free number for samples was listed—the hope being that when parents saw the Carnation ad and called their doctors, these doctors would be ready to recommend Good Start.

Was this ethical marketing? By not disclosing that doctors acting as spokespersons were paid consultants, was Carnation withholding pertinent information from consumers? Ultimately this is an issue of public safety, and marketers who play doctor tread on very thin ice.

Questions: Consider the two questions in the last paragraph.

Sources: "Marcus Welby, Brand Manager," *Adweek's Marketing Week,* July 29, 1991; and "Marketers Pay A High Price for A Doctor's Advice," *Adweek's Marketing Week,* April 2, 1990.

and a lack of consumer loyalty. As we have seen, P&G does not feel the need for corporate brand name identification because it establishes such strong individual brand names, such as Pampers, Crest, and Folgers, with intensive advertising.

PRODUCT-LINE NAME A **product-line name** *is applied to several offerings within a product line*, as in Sears' Kenmore appliance line, its Kerrybrook women's clothing line, and its Homart home-installations line. Sears' product lines require separate identification because of their diversity. The alternative—naming all products under the Sears corporate umbrella—would create too much confusion in consumers' minds.

P&G is following both an individual brand and a product line strategy. It has put more emphasis on product lines to better coordinate brands in the same category and to encourage extension of existing brands into new offerings.

CORPORATE FAMILY NAME Some companies *identify their products under a corporate umbrella—that is, a* **corporate family name** strategy. This strategy requires all of a company's products to be advertised under the company's name as a family of brands. It is feasible under three conditions: (1) if the company's product mix is not too diverse and can be easily identified by consumers with the company name, (2) if the company has a strong corporate identity, and (3) if individual brand identification is difficult. Heinz follows a corporate-family-name strategy because it has a relatively homogeneous mix of food products, it has a strong corporate identity, and it would be difficult to establish separate brand identities for each of its 57 varieties of food products. An important advantage of this strategy to Heinz is the economies of scale available in promoting many products in the same advertisement.

THE PRODUCT LINE

Whereas branding decisions are concerned with the marketing strategy for a particular brand, product-line decisions are concerned with the makeup of the brands offered in a given product line. There are no hard-and-fast rules in defining a product line. Some firms may define it very broadly; for example, a line of kitchen appliances under one category manager. Others define it more narrowly; for example, separate lines of refrigerators, washing machines, dryers, stoves, and dishwashers. Sometimes, a line is identified with a particular brand name, as with the line of Slice soft drinks in different flavors. At other times, a line can include different brands within a product category, as with Kellogg's line of adult cereals that includes Mueslix, Product 19, Fiberwise, and All Bran.

Regardless of definition, the category manager must determine how many offerings will be included in the line, whether individual items should be added to or deleted from the line, and the overall positioning of the line.

PRODUCT-LINE DECISIONS

The key questions determining the makeup of the product line concern its depth and its breadth.

DEPTH OF THE LINE

The **depth of the line** *refers to the number of different sizes, models, or flavors within a particular product line,* such as the number of adult cereals offered by Kellogg or the number of flavors offered by Slice.

When Sony wanted to deepen its Walkman line, for instance, it spun off 41 separate versions of the Walkman, including the sporty Outback, a waterproof beach version, and a children's version called "My First Sony" (see Exhibit 12.4).

EXHIBIT 12.4

Sony Increases the Depth of its Product Line

A full line is particularly important for industrial sellers, because buyers often want a full range of products. A company may carry hundreds of variations of industrial valves or fasteners, even if some of them are losing money. It is worth losing money on a few items to avoid losing customers because the particular product they need is not produced by the company.

There is such a thing as too much depth, however. Brand additions that offer nothing new are likely to cannibalize sales from existing products in the line. As a result, the company has incurred the costs of introducing a line extension without increasing sales.

BREADTH OF THE LINE

The **breadth of a line** *refers to the diversity of products in a line.* Whereas deepening a product line means adding items within its current range, broadening a line means extending it beyond its current range, usually into related product categories, thus increasing the diversity of the line. For example, if Häagen-Dazs ice cream adds new flavors such as butternut crunch, it is deepening its line, but when it adds yogurt, sherbet, and ice-cream pops, it is broadening the line into categories related to ice cream. In so doing, it is providing a broader set of alternatives to consumers.

Although broadening a product line can be strategically important, it is not without risk. As with increasing the depth of a line, the primary danger is cannibalization. Gillette had a strong, premium shaving-cream brand with Right

FIGURE 12.3

Product-Line Strategies

		Type of Change: Additions to Line	Type of Change: Deletions from Line
Dimension of Change	Depth of Line	Line Extensions	Line Pruning
	Breadth of Line	Brand Leveraging	Line Retrenchment

Guard but decided it wanted to attack the low-price end of the market occupied by competing Barbasol. Since Gillette's Good News! razors were successful on the low end, Gillette launched Good News! Shaving Cream. Instead of drawing consumers away from Barbasol, it cannibalized Right Guard. The problem was that consumers felt they could save money by buying Good News! and get the benefits of Right Guard.[38]

PRODUCT-LINE STRATEGIES

Category managers may try to modify existing lines by adding or deleting offerings to change the depth or the breadth of a line. These possibilities create the matrix of four strategies shown in Figure 12.3: line extensions, brand leveraging, line pruning, and line retrenchment. We will examine each of these.

LINE EXTENSIONS

Line extensions *are additions to the line in the same product category and serve to deepen the line.* Extensions give customers a fuller range of alternatives in the product line and help a company avoid being flanked by a competitor's introduction of a similar modification. Arrow Shirt's strategy of extending its line beyond the traditional, conservative, white shirt for which it was known is shown in Exhibit 12.5.

BRAND LEVERAGING

Category managers may use another strategy besides line extensions for adding to a line. Instead of deepening a product line, a company may broaden it by leveraging a successful brand through the introduction of products in related categories under the same brand name. **Brand leveraging** *is the introduction of a new product under an existing brand name.* The introduction by Häagen-Dazs of frozen yogurt leveraged the Häagen-Dazs name from ice cream to yogurt. The introduction of butternut crunch ice cream merely extended the ice-cream line.

Brand leveraging has become a popular strategy because companies find it is about 40 to 80 percent less expensive to introduce a new product under an existing brand name than to launch it under a new name.[39] It should be no surprise that two thirds of the 5,779 new packaged goods introduced in 1989 were marketed under existing brand names.[40]

Brand leveraging works best when the brand name has value, is well-known, and can be associated with the new product. For example, Reynolds successfully leveraged its name from aluminum foil to plastic wrap and food storage bags because

EXHIBIT 12.5

A Line Extension Strategy for Arrow Shirts

What do you get after spending 75 years making America's favorite dress shirt?
Bored.
Arrow

the Reynolds' name is well-known to consumers in the context of wrapping products[41] (see Exhibit 12.6).

A risk in brand leveraging is that it can dilute the value of the original brand. Critics say that while leveraging provides quick cash, in the long run it exhausts the loaned brand's equity, which in many cases took decades to create. The fear of diluting its brand name is one reason Coca-Cola insisted that the name be used only on its flagship brand. Before 1982, there were frequent proposals to use the Coca-Cola name on other products. The company finally relented in 1983 with the introduction of Diet Coke because of the growth of the diet-cola market and research that showed that a diet brand of Coke would be a leader in the category.

The introduction of Diet Coke did not dilute the strength of the flagship brand, but the company may have gone too far in a brand leveraging strategy when it

EXHIBIT 12.6

Reynolds Leverages Its Name to Plastic Wrap

licensed its name to clothing manufacturers. The failure of the clothing line shows that the most venerable brand name can not be leveraged unless it is logically associated with a product category. It also demonstrated the risk of diluting the equity in the flagship brand.

LINE PRUNING

Both line extensions and brand leveraging strategies add to the number of products in a line, but these strategies may lead to overextending a line. When this happens, products must be deleted either through line pruning or line retrenchment.

Line pruning *is reducing the depth of a product line by cutting back on the number of alternative sizes, models, or flavors in the line.* Pressure often comes from salespeople to offer additional variations in the line to satisfy buyers, and many product managers have a tendency to favor such line extensions. As items are added, however, the costs of design, inventory, order processing, and transportation all rise, and the line may become unprofitable.

The effective category manager realizes that line pruning can be just as important as line extension. But when should a line be pruned? Three conditions serve as a signal: (1) a number of items in the line are not making an adequate contribution to profits, either because of low sales, or because they are cannibalizing

EXHIBIT 12.7

A Failure in Leveraging: Bic Perfume

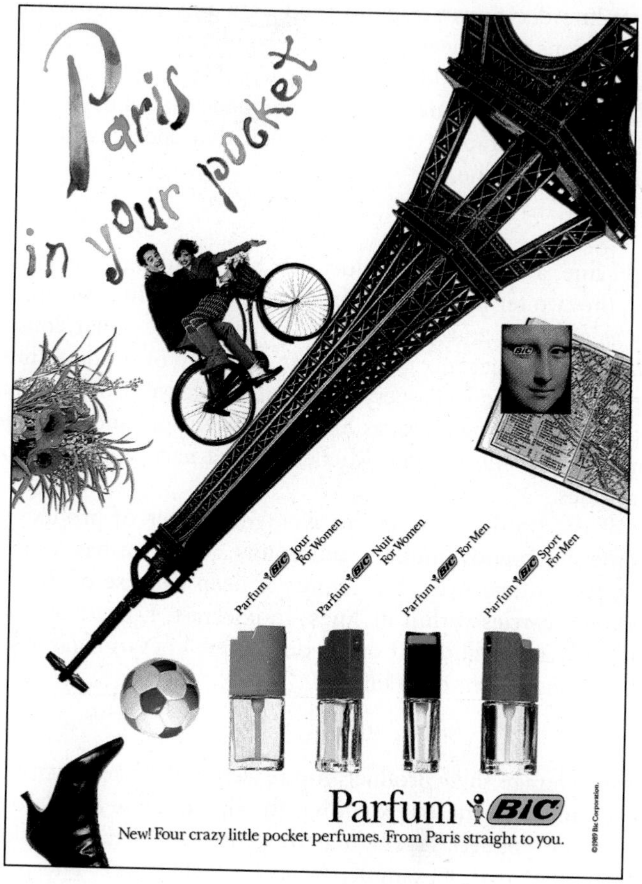

other items in the line; (2) manufacturing and distribution resources are being disproportionately allocated to slow-moving items; and (3) many items in the line may be outdated because of product improvements.

LINE RETRENCHMENT

Whereas line pruning reduces the depth of the line by cutting back on offerings in a given product category, **line retrenchment** *reduces the breadth of the line by cutting back on the diversity of items offered in related product categories.* Such retrenchment is usually caused by a failure to leverage the brand into a related category.

Successful leveraging requires the right conditions: a strong brand name; a logical association of the new product with the brand umbrella; and successful introduction of the leveraged product without alienating users of other products in the line. When these conditions are not met, companies are likely to fail in leveraging their brand. The Disney name has always had a certain amount of magic. But when the company tried to get into movies for adults, the Disney name failed, because that magic applied only to child-oriented products. As a result, Disney developed adult films under a different name, Touchstone. Similarly, Bic attempted to leverage its name from pens and disposable lighters to perfumes, but consumers simply did not see the association (see Exhibit 12.7).

THE PRODUCT MIX

While product-line decisions are concerned with the individual items in a line, product-mix decisions are concerned with the combination of product lines offered by the firm and the possible addition of new lines or deletion of existing lines. As shown in Table 12.1, product-mix decisions are made by business-unit or corporate managers, usually in a strategic marketing plan that specifies how much money will be allocated to each line.

BREADTH, DEPTH, AND CONSISTENCY OF THE PRODUCT MIX

Like a product line, a company's product mix has breadth and depth. In this context, however, the two terms take on a broader meaning, since we are talking about the company as a whole, and not the pieces (that is, lines) that comprise it.

The *breadth* of a product mix refers to the diversity of product lines offered by the firm. General Electric has a very broad mix because it offers a large number of lines in business units as diverse as lighting, major appliances, medical imaging, aerospace, and factory automation. Michelin has a narrow product mix, offering just a few tire lines.

The *depth* of the product mix is the average number of product variations in each line—different brands, models, and colors. Michelin has a narrow product mix because it only offers tires. But its mix is deep because of the large number of different tires it carries within its lines. In contrast, Liggett & Myers' product mix is both narrow and shallow: It offers only a few lines of cigarettes and a small number of variations within each line.

LEVERAGING TO BROADEN THE PRODUCT MIX

Companies can leverage their product mix as well as their product lines. Whereas leveraging a product line means extending the brand name in related areas (from ice cream to frozen yogurt), leveraging the product mix means using the brand name in unrelated areas (for example, Coca-Cola clothing). The principle is the same: The company is mining a known brand's equity to launch something new. Leveraging the product mix is riskier, because it goes far afield from the original brand's customer base. For example, Playboy met with disaster when it used its name to get into family resorts and air fresheners. On the other hand, Arm & Hammer was successful in leveraging its name—first into detergents and household products and then into toothpaste.[42]

An offshoot of leveraging is **licensing**, *where companies sell to other companies the rights to use their brand names.* Everlast, the maker of boxing gloves, gets $14 million from licensing its name to clothing manufacturers. Fisher-Price, the toymaker, licenses its name to S.C. Johnson for a line of children's soap products (see Exhibit 12.8). Such licensing by manufacturers allows them to reap the benefits of leveraging without assuming any new-product development costs.

THE PRODUCT LIFE CYCLE

The marketing strategy for a brand or product line cannot stay constant over a **product's life cycle**, *that is, the phases through which a product goes from introduction to growth to maturity and decline.* Variations in positioning, advertising, pricing, and distribution strategies occur in each of these stages.

EXHIBIT 12.8

Fisher-Price Licensed Its Name to S.C. Johnson & Sons for this Children's Soap Product

Figure 12.4 shows the product life cycle for record albums, cassettes, and compact discs. Records are in the declining phase of the life cycle because of new technologies. By 1989, less than 40 million records were sold compared to ten times that number in 1977. Cassettes are entering the mature phase of their life cycle, with sales leveling off for the first time in 1988. Compact discs are in the growth stage of their life cycle, with sales growing at an increasing rate. Sales for CDs will continue to rise and may level off as new technologies with even finer audio clarity, such as digital audio tapes, enter the market.

STAGES OF THE PRODUCT LIFE CYCLE

Figure 12.5 shows the traditional, bell-shaped sales curve for a product or a brand as it passes through the life-cycle stages of introduction, growth, maturity, and decline. These stages tend to be associated with the types of brand strategies shown at the top of the figure: brand development, reinforcement, revitalization, harvesting, and, possibly, revival. The figure also shows the strategic objectives as well as the four Ps—product, place (distribution), promotion, and price strategies—associated with each stage. In the following paragraphs, we will look more closely at each stage in the life cycle.

FIGURE 12.4

The Life Cycle for Three Product Categories

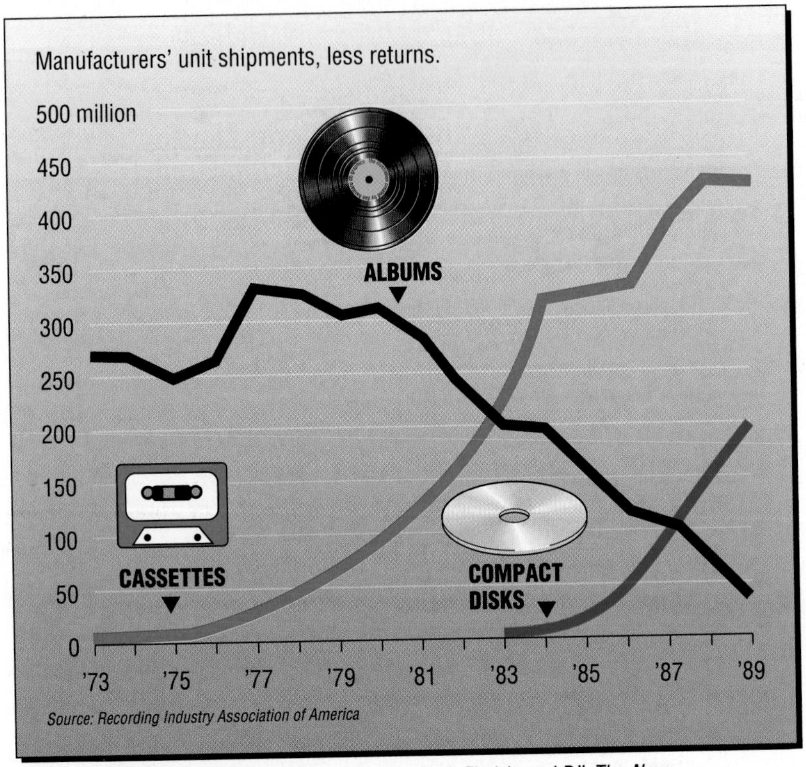

Source: "Recording Enters a New Era, and You Can't Find It on LP," *The New York Times,* April 1, 1990, pp. 1 and 24. Copyright © 1990 by the New York Times Company. Reprinted by permission.

THE INTRODUCTORY STAGE

When a brand is introduced, the main purpose of marketing strategy is to establish it, not only with consumers, but with wholesalers and retailers as well. **Brand establishment** *entails building a distribution network to make the product available to consumers and convincing consumers to try the product in its introductory phase.*

The product must have some competitive advantage in terms of quality or cost in order to attract consumers. The goal of advertising is to inform consumers of these benefits. To influence wholesalers and retailers to stock a brand, firms may offer favorable trade discounts and allowances for advertising and in-store promotions.

Brand managers can follow two types of pricing strategies in the introductory stage. With a **penetration strategy,** *the brand is introduced at a low price to induce as many consumers as possible to try it.* A penetration strategy is usually coupled with the use of price deals and coupons, particularly for food products and toiletries. With a **skimming strategy,** *the brand is introduced at a high price so as to maintain a select image and to appeal to a smaller target segment.* As competition intensifies, prices are slowly lowered.

Paris-based L'Oréal's successful introduction of Plénitude skin-care products in 1989 illustrates the basic principles of brand establishment. Known primarily for its hair-care products, L'Oréal introduced color cosmetics to the United States in 1983, but found itself unable to translate the booming sales it generated in Europe.

FIGURE 12.5

Marketing Strategies Over a Brand's Life Cycle

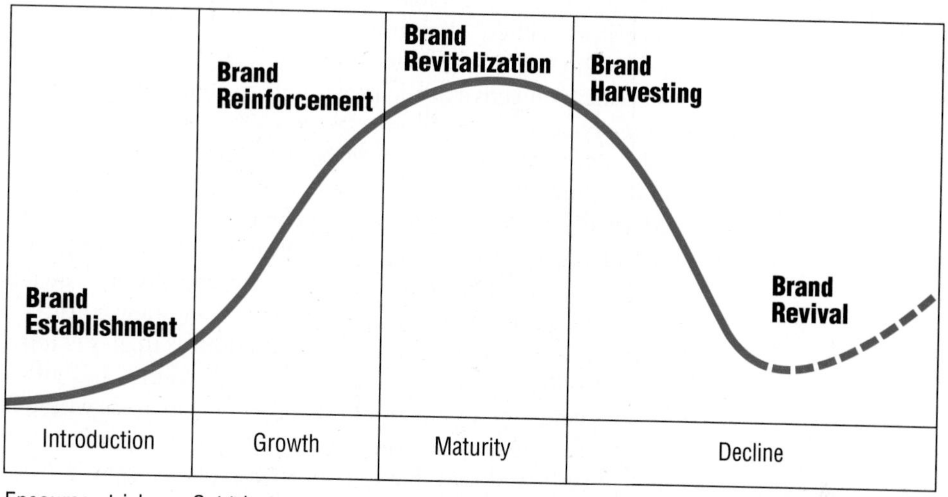

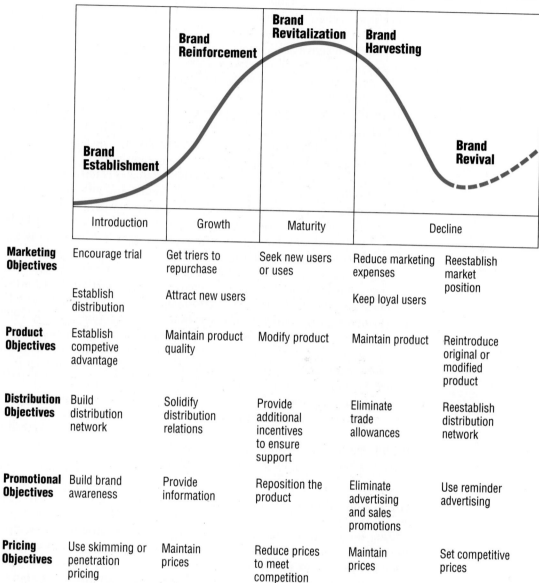

	Introduction	Growth	Maturity	Decline	
Marketing Objectives	Encourage trial Establish distribution	Get triers to repurchase Attract new users	Seek new users or uses	Reduce marketing expenses Keep loyal users	Reestablish market position
Product Objectives	Establish competive advantage	Maintain product quality	Modify product	Maintain product	Reintroduce original or modified product
Distribution Objectives	Build distribution network	Solidify distribution relations	Provide additional incentives to ensure support	Eliminate trade allowances	Reestablish distribution network
Promotional Objectives	Build brand awareness	Provide information	Reposition the product	Eliminate advertising and sales promotions	Use reminder advertising
Pricing Objectives	Use skimming or penetration pricing	Maintain prices	Reduce prices to meet competition	Maintain prices	Set competitive prices

Gimmicky promotions, which never gave consumers a clear idea about the products' benefits, siphoned profits and led to widespread returns. By the time L'Oréal launched its Plénitude line in 1989, it had learned from its mistakes.

Seeking to communicate a clear message, L'Oréal lobbied drugstores and department stores to create a separate skin-care section. Winning that fight, it then shipped more than 20 million samples, positioned Plénitude as high-quality but affordable, and supported the line with $18 million in advertising. Following its long-held strategy of building a line around a "star product," L'Oréal spent most of its ad budget promoting Plénitude's Eye Defense Gel-Cream. Within two years, Plénitude's 14-product line captured 9 percent of the market, second only to Oil of Olay.[43]

THE GROWTH STAGE

A brand enters the growth stage when sales increases are sustained, and the brand begins to become profitable. If it is an innovation, by this time it will have attracted competitors. When Minnetonka introduced the first liquid soap, 42 competitors appeared on the market after only one year.[44]

The main objective of the growth phase is **brand reinforcement**, *that is, to reinforce the brand's position by getting consumers who have tried the brand to repurchase it and by continuing to attract new users.* If a substantial number of first-time purchasers do not rebuy, the brand will fail.

Marketing-mix strategies during the growth stage are all aimed at maintaining and building upon the competitive advantages won during the introductory stage. The primary product objective is to maintain product quality, although if competition is intense, a company may have to add new features, improve packaging, or add services. The objective of distribution strategies is to solidify relations with distributors by continuing to offer trade discounts and allowances. At the same time, the company will seek additional outlets in areas where brand sales are weak. During this stage, an attempt is made to maintain prices; occasionally, however, prices must be reduced due to competitive pressure, as in Minnetonka's case when it lowered its price as competitors entered the liquid soap market.

Whereas the promotional goal of the introductory stage was to create brand awareness and encourage users to try the product, the goal of the growth stage is to inform consumers about brand performance. In 1982, Reebok was a fledgling sneaker outfit trying to gain consumer awareness of its offerings. By 1989, however, with a claim on 40 percent of the $4.3 billion athletic shoe industry, Reebok was intent on continuing to fuel its growth. The company invested $60 million in a "power marketing" blitz, almost half of which went to promoting its Energy Return System shoe introduced the year before and engineered with windows on the soles to show iridescent tubing that was supposed to return energy to the wearer. Televised spots interspersed tight close-ups of the shoe with action shots of grunting weight-lifters, breathless runners, and fast-moving basketball players. With Nike hot on its heels, Reebok considered the hefty ad budget a key component in reinforcing its leading position in the market.[45]

THE MATURITY STAGE

During the maturity stage, sales begin to level off because of increasing competition. The brand attracts few new buyers; instead, it relies on repeat purchases to maintain its market position. Greater competitive intensity leads to more price competition, lower prices, and reduced operating margins. As a result, profits begin to decrease.

A strategy of **brand revitalization** *is followed by brands in the mature phase of the life cycle to counter decreasing profits.* This strategy can be approached three ways: (1) market expansion, (2) product modification, and (3) brand repositioning. A firm may follow one or all of these strategies.

Market expansion can mean finding new users for the brand or new uses. Polaroid was looking for *new users* when, in a unique move, it agreed to let Japan's Minolta begin selling its top-of-the-line Spectra Pro model. It marked the first time since a federal court decision forced Eastman Kodak out of the market that anyone other than Polaroid sold instant cameras. With its fortunes flagging, Polaroid needed to expand beyond its domestic base. The move let Polaroid avail itself of Minolta's extensive distribution network and created a new source of business for Polaroid's high-margin film division.[46]

Industrial products go through the same life-cycle stages as do consumer products, and marketers may apply similar strategies. One such company, Alcan, is trying to expand the market for aluminum by finding *new uses* such as aluminum-powered batteries, aluminum rail coal cars, aluminum containers for microwave cooking, and aluminum-coated hard disk drives for computers.[47]

Companies following a strategy of *product modification* attempt to revitalize a product by changing it in some substantial way to increase demand. After a decade of economic drought and fierce competition for the equipment needs of American farmers, John Deere was stuck in a rut. With sales of its most important farm machines down 70 percent, Deere overhauled its existing tractor lines in 1990 with modifications like quieter cabs and a new spot for the exhaust pipe so farmers could see more clearly through their rear-view mirrors.[48]

Brand repositioning requires changing the brand's appeal to attract new market segments. Repositioning a brand may or may not require modifying it. Because Corn Flakes has been stagnant for years, Kellogg is trying to revitalize it by appealing to a new segment, adult baby boomers, with a nostalgic theme beckoning them to try the cereal they grew up with.[49]

PRODUCT DECLINE

The fourth product life-cycle stage, decline, is characterized by decreasing sales and profits and eventually by losses. Decline may be due to a variety of causes: technology making the brand obsolete, lower-cost competitors undercutting the brand, changes in consumer preferences, or ineffective attempts at revitalization. A company cannot sustain a brand in a declining phase for long. It must choose either of the two strategies outlined in Figure 12.5: brand harvesting, with a likelihood of eventual elimination, or brand revival.

BRAND HARVESTING As we have seen, one of the product-line manager's most important responsibilities is to prune the line to eliminate unprofitable brands. Most companies do not give enough attention to brand-elimination decisions, and few brand managers get rewarded for eliminating brands. Companies prefer to add new products than eliminate unprofitable ones. Unprofitable brands are often carried too long, creating a drag on profits and decreasing the cash available for pursuing new market opportunities.

Although some products are dropped abruptly, a company will often *harvest* a brand before eliminating it. A **harvesting strategy** *requires decreasing marketing expenditures to almost zero and allowing the brand to continue on its own steam by relying on the purchases of loyal customers.* This strategy might make the brand profitable on a much smaller sales base, and some brands have been harvested for years.

Lever Brothers has been harvesting its Lux Beauty Bar since it stopped advertising the brand in 1970, yet Lux is generally available because it is distributed with other Lever toiletry products. Without advertising, Lux's profit margin is 5 percent greater than most other soaps. This situation will not continue indefinitely, however, for Lux's loyal consumer base is literally dying out. Once the brand begins to lose money, it will be eliminated.

A risk of a harvesting strategy is that a firm might begin cutting marketing costs too soon and force the brand into further decline. It might have been possible, for example, to revitalize Lux by repositioning it as a deodorant soap. Additional advertising expenditures to increase brand awareness might also have revitalized the brand. Managers must be sure that a brand has no long-term earnings potential before harvesting it.

BRAND REVIVAL A strategy of **brand revival** *requires bringing brands that are being harvested or have been eliminated back to life on the strength of their names.* Managers realize it is much cheaper to resurrect a brand name than to create a new one. Although a resurrected brand usually has no competitive advantage other than its name, that one advantage may be significant in a mature market where few brands are in a unique position.

For instance, Beecham is reviving Geritol, the iron and vitamin supplement for older consumers, by advertising it as "the brand for amorous middle-aged people, not the Lawrence Welk generation."[50]

Old names can also be leveraged and used on new products. We have seen how one of the oldest toy brands in America, Barbie, was the key to Mattel's turnaround. By promoting the doll's thirtieth anniversary with a slew of new extensions (among them cereal, trading cards, and clothes), Barbie amassed $600 million in domestic sales in 1989.[51]

THE PRODUCT LIFE CYCLE AND INTERNATIONAL MARKETS

The stage of a product in its life cycle is likely to vary by country. Products in the mature or declining stage in one country may be in the introductory or growth stage in another. Such differences have to do with the stage of economic development in different countries. Products such as answering machines and VCRs are in the mature phase of their life cycle in the United States but are in the introductory or growth phase in less-developed countries. Similarly, the life cycle for CDs is more advanced in the United States than in most other countries.

Differences in the stage of the product life cycle also have to do with different patterns of usage and customs between countries. Cigarettes are in the declining portion of their life cycle in the United States because of increasing health consciousness. But in Japan and most European countries, smoking continues unabated, and cigarettes are in a growth or mature phase. Conversely, skin-care products are in the mature phase of their life cycle in countries such as Hungary and France, where women have been more concerned with their skin because of cultural tradition. These products are in the growth phase in the United States because of a more recent awareness among women of the importance of skin care.

A brand's as well as a product's life cycle may vary by country. Ajax cleanser is in a declining position in the United States because the brand came out with fewer packaging innovations and product formulations compared to Comet. Yet in Europe, it is in its growth phase because of a more active marketing program involving more product-line extensions.[52]

LIMITATIONS OF THE PRODUCT LIFE CYCLE

The product life cycle is a useful tool in suggesting strategies over the life of a brand and in indicating when changes in strategies should take place, but brand sales do not necessarily follow the symmetrical curve in Figure 12.5. As a result, it is not always easy for a brand manager to determine a brand's position in the life cycle. Sales may rise during the introductory stage, for instance, then suddenly drop off. In this case, reliance on the life-cycle concept would have led the brand manager to mistakenly predict a growth phase, perhaps allocating more money to advertising and distribution in the coming period.

Another complication is that the length of the life cycle may vary. It is very hard to predict how long it may take a brand to move from introduction to growth to

FIGURE 12.6

Variations from the Normal Product Life-Cycle Curve

A. Product with Slow Adoption (Home Computers)

B. Product with Fast Adoption (Compact Discs)

C. A Fad Product (Teenage Mutant Ninja Turtle Dolls)

D. Product with Frequent Revitalization (Semiconductors)

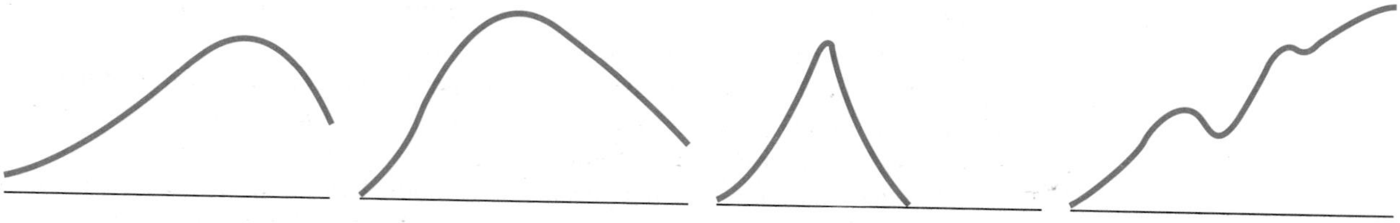

maturity. New technologies may shorten a product's life cycle, much as the advent of the compact disc shortened the life cycle of records. A successful strategy of revitalization may lengthen the maturity phase beyond what might have been predicted and may even cause a product to go from growth to maturity and back to growth.

Figure 12.6 illustrates some of the more common variations from the normal life cycle curve. The first curve shows a product that has a long introduction stage, because it is adopted slowly by consumers. Home computers are an example of this type of product. The second curve illustrates products such as compact discs, which are rapidly adopted and have a shorter than expected introductory stage. The third curve is yet another deviation, a fad product with a rapid rise and a rapid decline. Movie spin-off products, such as Teenage Mutant Ninja Turtle dolls, follow such a curve. Finally, the fourth curve shows a product that has been frequently revitalized, going through periods of decline and subsequent growth. High-technology products such as semiconductors might follow such a life cycle.

In each of these cases, it is difficult for a brand manager to determine what stage the product is in and the appropriate strategic course based on its position in the life cycle. Thus, while principles derived from the life cycle provide useful guides for strategy, their application must be tempered by the particular nature and history of each brand.

SUMMARY

1. **What is the role of the product manager in marketing a brand?**
   The product (or brand) manager is responsible for developing marketing strategies for a brand and for the brand's profit performance. Product managers collect all information that might affect brand performance, set goals for the brand, and plot marketing strategies to achieve these goals.
2. **What are the responsibilities of product managers for brands, product lines, and the company's overall product mix?**
   Product managers develop strategies at three levels: for brands, product lines, and the firm's product mix. Brand managers are responsible for positioning the brand, identifying its target segments, and establishing it in the marketplace. Category (also known as product-line) managers are responsible for a group of

brands in the same category. They coordinate the marketing strategies for the brands in the line and decide on additions to and deletions from the line.

SBU or corporate managers are responsible for product-mix decisions that involve evaluating a firm's or business unit's overall product offerings. These managers evaluate the portfolio of product offerings and allocate resources to the firm's product lines.

In recent years, category managers have assumed more responsibility for brand management because of the need to coordinate marketing strategies for brands in a product category. Such coordination attempts to avoid cannibalization between brands in a firm's product line.

3. **What important decisions must product managers make for brands and product lines?**
A brand represents the name and symbols associated with the product as well as the package in which it is purchased. In some cases, a warranty is given with the brand.
A firm must decide whether it will control its brands or produce for private branding to allow retailers to put their own name on the company's products and to market them. Managers must also decide on whether a brand will stand alone or will be part of a family of brands and if it will bear a corporate name.
Managers also make product-line decisions. They must decide on the depth and breadth of the product line. In addition, they must determine brands to add to the line to provide more depth or breadth. They must be wary of cannibalization when making additions to the line, that is, taking sales away from existing products when adding a new brand with little net addition in sales. It is as important to delete unprofitable products as to add potentially profitable ones.

4. **What do we mean by a product's life cycle? How does this concept help managers develop brand and product-line strategies?**
Most products pass through stages of introduction, growth, maturity, and decline. The product life-cycle concept proposes that a manager can develop marketing strategies depending on where a brand or product is in its life cycle. Taking advertising strategy as an example, the introductory phase is marked by an objective of creating brand awareness, the growth phase by informing consumers of product benefits to gain a competitive advantage, the maturity phase by trying to differentiate the brand from competitors, and the decline phase by a cutback in advertising. Integrated strategies can be associated with each phase in the life cycle—brand establishment in the introductory phase, reinforcement in the growth phase, revitalization in the maturity phase, and either harvesting or revival in the decline phase. Brands and products are likely to be in different stages in the life cycle in different countries. This is because of variations in economic development, custom, and usage by product category.

KEY TERMS

Product management system (p. 392)
Product line (p. 392)
Product mix (p. 392)
Brand manager (p. 392)
Category manager (p. 392)
Branded (p. 393)
Brand equity (p. 394)
Warranty (p. 397)
Brand image (p. 398)
Manufacturer's brand (p. 402)
National/regional brands (p. 402)
Private brands (p. 403)
Battle of the brands (p. 404)
Generics (p. 404)
Price brands (p. 404)
Fighting brands (p. 404)
Individual brand name strategy (p. 405)
Cannibalization (p. 405)
Corporate brand name strategy (p. 406)
Product-line brand name strategy (p. 407)

Corporate family name strategy (p. 408)
Product-line depth (p. 408)
Product-line breadth (p. 409)
Line extensions (p. 410)
Brand leveraging (p. 410)
Line pruning (p. 412)
Line retrenchment (p. 413)
Licensing (p. 414)
Product life cycle (p. 414)
Brand-establishment strategy (p. 416)
Penetration pricing strategy (p. 416)
Skimming pricing strategy (p. 416)
Brand reinforcement strategy (p. 418)
Brand revitalization strategy (p. 418)
Harvesting strategy (p. 419)
Brand revival strategy (p. 420)

QUESTIONS

1. What is the product management system? Why was it developed?
2. How has the product management system changed since it was first adopted by Procter & Gamble in 1931? Why have these changes taken place?
3. What is meant by brand equity? What is the role of the package in establishing brand equity? Cite examples.
4. Why is creating a strong brand name such an essential ingredient of marketing strategy? Cite an example of a company that created a strong brand name. What were the key strategic elements in doing so?
5. When Coca-Cola brought back the original formula as Coca-Cola Classic, it was essentially admitting that brand image can be more important than taste in influencing consumer purchases of soft drinks. Explain why.
6. Is there a danger that a company can be too successful in establishing a strong brand name? Explain.
7. What is meant by "the Battle of the Brands?" What is the role of price brands and private brands in this battle?
8. Why is a family brand strategy relevant for Heinz but not for Procter & Gamble? What are the advantages and disadvantages of such a strategy?
9. What do we mean by cannibalizing a product? Why did General Foods introduce Maxim freeze-dried coffee when it knew the brand was likely to cannibalize its Maxwell House brand? When should a company forego introducing a new product because of projected cannibalization?
10. What do we mean by brand leveraging? Cite examples of successful and unsuccessful leveraging strategies. Why were these companies successful or unsuccessful in leveraging their brands?
11. What is the distinction between the breadth and depth of a product line and the breadth and depth of a product mix? Cite examples.
12. What are the alternatives in revitalizing a brand in the mature stage of its life cycle? Are these alternatives mutually exclusive, or could a firm use all of them for the same brand?
13. Why does the stage of a product's or brand's life cycle differ across countries? Cite examples.
14. What are the limitations of using the product life-cycle concept to develop strategies for a brand? How should the product life-cycle concept be used by a brand manager?

QUESTIONS: YOU ARE THE DECISION MAKER

1. The president of a large financial services company offering insurance, brokerage, and financial-planning services does not believe in the product management system. He says:

   Brand managers are fine for firms producing packaged goods that spend millions advertising their brand name. But we do not build brand identification for our services; we build corporate identification. Without brands, what is the point of having brand managers?

   a. Is the brand or product management system irrelevant if a firm advertises its corporate name rather than advertising individual brand names?
   b. Should a financial-service firm use a product management system, even though it is selling services rather than products?
2. Most consumer-goods manufacturers produce national brands and frequently spend millions of dollars to establish a positive brand image. In view of this, why would a firm manufacture products to be sold by retailers or wholesalers as private brands or generic products?

CHAPTER 13

Marketing Services by Profit and Nonprofit Firms

YOUR FOCUS IN CHAPTER 13

To learn:

- *Why services have become a major part of our economy.*
- *The differences between services and products and the strategic implications of these differences.*
- *How service firms develop marketing strategies for their offerings.*
- *The distinctions between marketing nonprofit services and marketing services at a profit.*
- *Why it is more difficult to market nonprofit services than services in the profit sector.*

Federal Express—How Fred Smith Marketed His Way to Creating a $1 Billion Business

Fred Smith sat in a Memphis office early in 1973 and watched the idea that earned him a C in his college economics course bomb.[1] It was the first day of business for his overnight package delivery service, and just eight shipments had been ordered. To make matters worse, seven of them were from his own staff.[2] It was an inauspicious start for a company with such a grandiose name—*Federal Express*.

By the end of Federal's first year, it had brokered less than a million deliveries and was losing a million dollars a month. What went wrong? Smith was not marketing his service correctly. He was targeting shipping executives, reasoning they were his natural clients, but they were not producing enough business. After huddling with his staff, Smith decided to go after the general business market, from secretaries to CEOs.

At first, Federal's TV ads focused on its unique hub-and-spoke system (all packages are routed to Memphis, then sent to their destinations). While intriguing to shipping professionals, the novelty was lost on results-oriented line managers. So Smith's advertising team tried again—and more successfully. A single, catchy slogan summed up Federal's *raison d'être:* "When it absolutely, positively has to be there overnight."[3] The message got through to line managers: Federal Express could provide an important benefit—guaranteed overnight package delivery. This time, the broader business market took notice. By 1983, the company's revenues were topping $1 billion and a new industry had been born.[4]

Inevitably, copycat operations began to arise, threatening to make Smith a victim of his own success. He reacted by broadening Federal's base even further, creating something that would make the company stand out from the crowd and keep generating new business. It was the Federal Express shop.

The one-stop service boutiques not only advertised Federal Express's growing line of services and reinforced its trademark red and purple logo, but they also provided far more flexibility than the original door-to-door delivery system. For instance, customers who did not want to wait until 10:30 A.M. for their package to arrive could pick it up at a Federal Express shop at 9 A.M. and pay less for the option. To get the first wave of 60 stores up and running, Smith threw gala grand-opening parties, which reinforced the concept of immediacy and convenience. To promote the 9 A.M. pick-up service, he launched a direct marketing campaign featuring a teddy bear, conveying the feeling it was simple and easy. The teddy bear promotion paid an unexpected dividend: package recipients who had grown used to picking up their overnight parcels also got used to dropping off outgoing ones, creating new business and saving Federal Express money on couriers.[5]

To keep Federal growing, Smith created such innovations as contracting with retail catalog houses. By selling the fact that these retailers could win several extra weeks worth of orders during the crucial Christmas season by guaranteeing overnight delivery, Federal Express was able to lure more than 200 new clients.[6]

By 1991, Federal Express was handling more than a million packages a day with 380 planes, 31,000 vans, and 95,000 employees.[7] To make sure it all works like clockwork, Smith implemented a quality control system that is based on what he calls his "Hierarchy of Horrors"—an index that measures late deliveries, incorrect billings, and damaged packages. About 2,100 customers are randomly polled every three months, and the results are used to guide Quality Action Teams in the company's 11 divisions. In 1990, the innovative system won Federal Express the prestigious Malcolm Baldrige National Quality Award.[8]

Like all combat veterans, however, Smith has his battle scars. A foray into the fax business known as ZapMail was an unmitigated disaster, leading to $350 million in losses before Smith pulled the plug in 1986.[9] Even that failure pales when compared to his riskiest gambit—express delivery abroad.

Despite committing $1.5 billion to overseas operations since 1985 (including the $895 million purchase of Tiger International—the world's largest carrier of heavy cargo), Federal Express still has only a miserly share of the market in Europe and Japan.[10] Moreover, its overseas presence is draining money from its domestic operations just when rivals UPS and Airborne are becoming competitive in pricing and on-time delivery.

The challenge for Smith must be to stem his overseas losses and reposition Federal Express for its third decade.

THE IMPORTANCE OF SERVICES

The United States economy is vastly different today than it was in the two decades following World War II, when the manufacturing sector was responsible for turning the United States into an economic powerhouse. Since Korea, Taiwan, and other developing countries now offer cheaper labor and competitive technology, America's manufacturing base has receded and has been replaced with a service-oriented economy. The service sector encompasses everything from the brokerage houses of Wall Street to fast-food restaurants, diaper delivery services, and health clubs. Whereas in 1945 the service sector accounted for one-third of our Gross National Product (GNP), today it accounts for over one-half (see Figure 13.1). Three-fourths of all Americans are employed, directly or indirectly, in delivering services.

THE DEVELOPMENT OF A SERVICE ECONOMY

Why have we become a service economy? As we have seen in Chapter 4, demographic changes can bring about economic changes. The increasing number of working women, single parents, and senior citizens has resulted in a more service-dependent economy. The time crunch suffered by dual-income families, the economic pressures on modern parents, and the needs of the elderly are fueling the growth of new service companies while leading old ones to provide more variety.

FIGURE 13.1

Growth in the Service Sector of the U.S. Economy

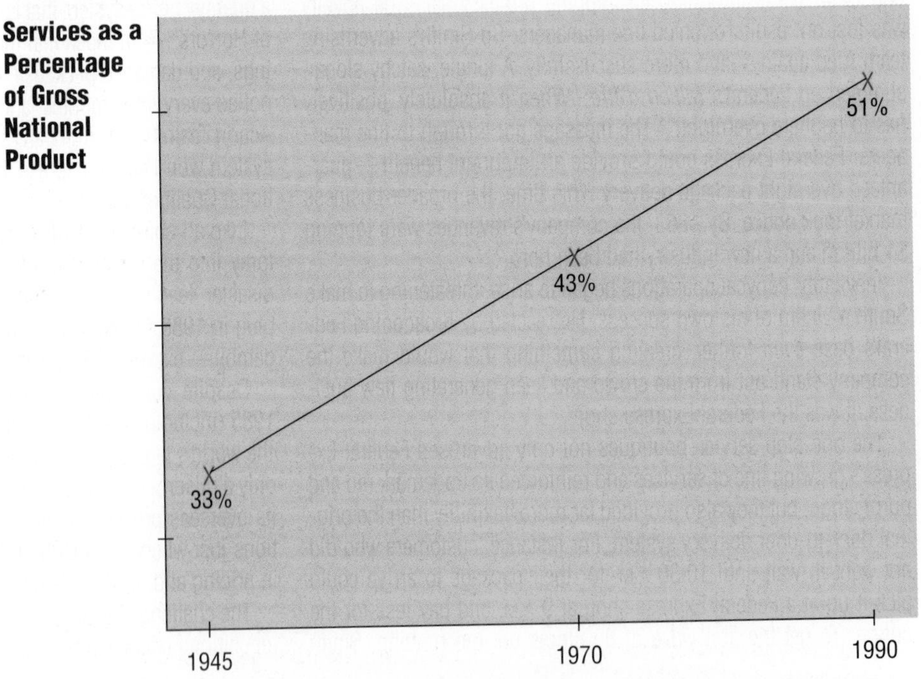

Source: U.S. Bureau of Economics Analysis, *The National Income and Products Account of the United States 1929-82* (Washington, D.C. Government Printing Office, 1983) and U.S. Bureau of the Census, *Statistical Abstract of the United States* (Washington, D.C. Government Printing Office, 1990), p. 433.

These new demographics have also created the affluence that allows consumers to purchase more services. Just as the demand for personal services from lawn care to beauty care to car care to child care has increased, so too have expenditures for services such as travel and entertainment.[11] More Americans are in hotels, in restaurants, on the road, and in the air than ever before.

The most successful companies are those that were able to predict these trends and respond swiftly. We have seen how Fred Smith turned Federal Express into a $1 billion business by anticipating the public's desire for a quicker, more-dependable way to send packages. There has been an explosion in health-care and fitness services fueled by the increasing longevity and greater health consciousness of Americans. Exercise and fitness centers are now part of the American landscape. Health Maintenance Organizations (HMOs) have flourished, because they fill the need for a wide variety of affordable health-care services under one roof.

Legal and regulatory changes have also expanded the service economy. For instance, when the Securities and Exchange Commission removed the gentlemanly restraints on competition among financial service firms in 1975, well-heeled Wall Street stock traders found themselves under siege by discount brokers. To stay profitable, they had to offer new services. Merrill Lynch, for one, created the Cash Management Account—a fund that let the public have access to an array of financial instruments and receive checking, loan, and credit-card privileges. The CMA has gone on to become one of the most successful financial service plans in history, representing $210 billion in investment in 1990.[12]

The deregulation of the airline and telephone industries has also thrown open those once-closed fields. This was true of AT&T. With its long-distance business under attack from MCI and Sprint, and its phone equipment division suffering from foreign competition, AT&T needed to find a new high-growth vehicle. As a result, it moved head-long into financial services. Reasoning that its 70 million customers were a resource that could not be ignored, the company set to work on developing Universal—a credit card that AT&T customers could use to charge meals, make phone calls, and get money from bank automatic teller machines (ATMs). Universal was unveiled in ads during the telecast of the 1990 Academy Awards and garnered 70,000 calls in that one night (see Exhibit 13.1). Eleven weeks later, AT&T passed the million-person account mark.[13]

Foreign competition is another factor in America's transition to a service economy. Intense Japanese competition has driven General Electric out of manufacturing televisions and small appliances and into service and technology businesses such as insurance and factory automation. Our trade deficits are a stark reminder of how effective foreign competitors have been in reducing America's manufacturing base. They are also a big reason companies such as GE are finding it more profitable to sell services than products.

A MARKETING ORIENTATION FOR SERVICES

With the emergence of a service economy, it has become increasingly important for service firms to develop a marketing orientation. Hotel chains such as Holiday Inn, Hyatt, and Marriott are targeting specific income segments by expanding their offerings to include luxury, medium-priced, and budget-oriented facilities. Hospitals are beginning to advertise to consumers, and they are also redesigning drab facilities to counter competition and meet consumer needs. Professionals such as lawyers, accountants, dentists, and doctors are also beginning to advertise their services, and nonprofit organizations such as universities, charitable organizations, and museums are now recognizing that they must gear their services to customer needs in order to survive.

EXHIBIT 13.1

AT&T Expands into Financial Services with the Universal Card

In the boom years of the mid 1980s, demand for financial, travel, and entertainment services was often greater than supply. Service companies could offer their services to customers on a take-it-or-leave-it basis. This was demonstrated in 1983, when Citicorp (one of the more astute marketers in the banking industry) forced customers with average balances of less than $5,000 to use automatic teller machines (ATMs) exclusively. The hue and cry from disgruntled customers who disliked being prevented from dealing in person with bank employees forced Citicorp to rescind the requirement.

As the earning power of the average consumer ebbed during the recession of the early 1990s, shoppers began demanding more from services. Service companies could no longer ignore customers. They reacted by stressing quality and reliability in their marketing campaigns. Delta sold itself with the slogan, "We love to fly and it shows." The ITT Hartford Life Insurance Company marketed itself in commercials that proclaimed "When you need us most we're at our best," and Citibank replaced its gaudy catchphrase "For those who want to succeed, not just survive" with "Not just banking. Citibanking."

The trend toward customer-driven service marketing was reflected in a report by one quality control consultant who found that although only 10 percent of service companies had quality enforcement programs in 1991, more than 70 percent were expected to have them in place by the year 2000.[14]

THE NATURE OF SERVICES

Service firms cannot advertise a physical product; hence, their marketing strategies differ from those of a consumer-goods firm. In order to understand these differences, we must first understand the characteristics that distinguish services from products and the different types of services that are offered.

CHARACTERISTICS OF SERVICES

In Chapter 11, we defined *services* as intangible benefits purchased by consumers that do not involve ownership. Besides being more intangible, three other characteristics distinguish services from products: Services are more variable, more perishable, and their production is often simultaneous with their consumption. As we will see, each of these characteristics creates more risks for the marketer, but also creates more opportunities.

INTANGIBILITY

A consumer can squeeze Charmin paper towels, pour a Diet Coke, and smell Aramis cologne. Products can be examined before purchase and compared to competitive offerings; after purchase, consumers have something to show for the money they spent. However, consumers cannot feel, see, or smell services before they are purchased, and although some services produce tangible results, such as a haircut or clean laundry, most do not.

This intangibility does not mean that consumers get less for their money when they buy a service compared to a product. A Merrill Lynch CMA account that earns its bearer thousands of dollars, or a Federal Express delivery that produces a business gain, yields more important benefits than toothpaste, detergent, or packaged foods. However, intangibility makes it more difficult to communicate the benefits of what is being sold. Service marketers can turn this disadvantage into a competitive advantage by making their service more tangible to consumers than that of their competitors. One way to do this is to link the service to a symbol such as the Merrill Lynch bull, or Prudential's rock (see Exhibit 13.2). The bull is associated with financial success, the rock with stability.

Another way to make a service more tangible is to focus on the people who provide it, because the service provider is more tangible than the service. Car service ads show competent mechanics (Mr. Goodwrench, see Exhibit 13.2), health maintenance organizations promote their caring doctors, and bank advertising emphasizes the personal attention of its executives with themes like "Your Anchor Banker," or "You've Got a Friend at Chase."

VARIABILITY

Services rely primarily on people to provide them, and people are much more variable than products. A shopper may find salespeople helpful and courteous on one trip and rude on another; a traveler may have a flawless flight on one occasion, but have her baggage lost the next time she flies the same airline. Such variability makes it a risky business to market services, because customers experiencing poor service delivery may not come back, and they may tell others of their experiences.

Like intangibility, variability provides an opportunity to gain a competitive edge. Consumers will try to minimize the risk of service variability by choosing the most

EXHIBIT 13.2

Creating Tangibility for Services Through Symbols and People

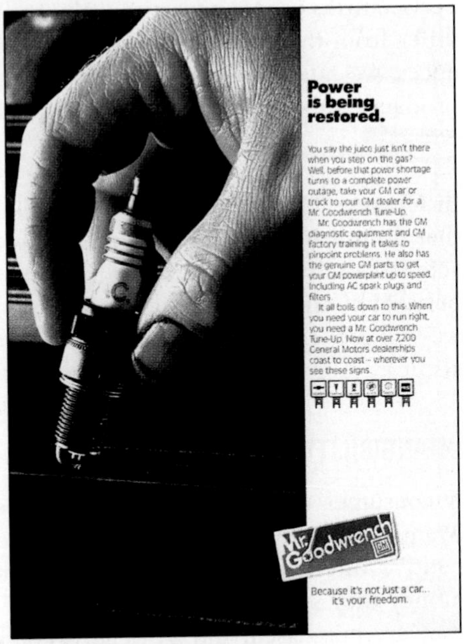

reliable service providers. More effective company standardization procedures help create reliability. For example, Federal Express became the leader in air package delivery by ensuring on-time delivery through its own airplane fleet, novel hub–spoke concept, and rigid adherence to routine.

Another way to reduce variability is by relying on technology to switch service delivery from people to machines. Fidelity Investments employs high-tech workstations to improve customer service. In the mid 1980s, Fidelity discovered its customers were irritated by long delays that accompanied their calls for stock information. Fidelty then invested hundreds of millions of dollars in computer workstations that could provide answers with lightning speed. One station can monitor 20 securities, retrieve news articles from the previous three months on a given stock, zero in on a company's product profile, and enter brokerage transactions simultaneously.[15]

Banks have both expanded their services and reduced the variability of teller services by giving customers the option of using 24-hour ATMs. Seattle-based Seafirst bank dispenses postage stamps from its ATMs and accepts the most cash cards (Visa, MasterCard, Sears' Discover, CIRRUS and so on) in the Northwest.[16]

PERISHABILITY

A third distinction between services and products is perishability. If services are not consumed when offered, they immediately go to waste. An airline seat cannot be stored in inventory: If it is not filled, its value is lost. The lawyer whose services are not being used cannot store them for use at some future time. Whereas shifts in demand for products can be accommodated through inventory control, services do not have the same flexibility to regulate supply to meet demand.

Perishability provides service marketers with a basis for competitive advantage if they can regulate supply or demand. On the supply side, marketers can try to cut back on facilities during slack periods. Thus, a restaurant might close off one of its rooms and hire fewer waiters when demand is low. In peak periods, marketers can try to increase capacity by using part-time employees or by letting customers perform certain services at a discount, such as pumping their own gas.

Service marketers can also use several strategies to regulate demand to avoid unsold capacity. Airlines, telephone companies, and utilities provide lower rates in off-peak periods to encourage greater use by consumers and higher rates during peak periods when demand might exceed available supply. Service companies also like to pre-sell services so they can more easily determine the facilities that will be used at a given time. That is why airlines stipulate that customers taking advantage of lower fares must buy their tickets in advance.

A failure to adequately manage supply and demand can cause a service firm to go out of business. This is what happened to People Express. The airline overestimated demand and bought fifty Boeing 727 jets in 1985, then was unable to book enough passengers during the winter months, when only 50 percent of its seats were filled.[17] Because of People Express's low-fare policy, it had to fill a higher percentage of seats than its competitors to break even. As a result, the company reported a net loss of $27.5 million in 1985 and eventually went out of business.[18]

SIMULTANEOUS PRODUCTION AND CONSUMPTION

Unlike products, which are produced, sold, and then consumed, services are often sold first, then produced and consumed at the same time. A consumer paying school tuition, buying an airline or theater ticket, or giving a lawyer a retainer for services to be delivered will consume these services at some future time as they are being produced.

Like the other characteristics of services, simultaneous production and consumption creates both risk and opportunity. The risk is that the service being consumed might be provided by a rude, rushed, or ill-informed employee. Who would blame the customer for not coming back?

Every time a service employee meets a customer, it is called a *moment of truth, that is, a moment that requires a service delivery*. One moderately-sized freight company found its drivers, dispatchers, and office workers encountered 152,800 such moments a day.[19] For larger service firms, the number might be multiplied fivefold. That is why when Marriott was preparing to open its first hotel in Poland, it worried about the local workforce's unfamiliarity with American-style hotel etiquette. To ensure local Poles would be as solicitous as Mariott's U.S.-trained employees, it flew 20 managers from Warsaw to Boston and made them go through extensive training that included customer role-playing. Said one of the trainers: "It helped more than [having] three hours of lectures, because it made trainees think like customers."[20]

IMPACT OF SERVICE CHARACTERISTICS ON INTERNATIONAL MARKETING

Certain service characteristics create greater risks for marketing services in the international compared to the domestic arena. International marketers find it harder to overcome the problems of intangibility, variability, and simultaneous production and consumption in marketing their services.

Intangibility is a greater problem for international marketers because of the necessity to use symbols that have a common meaning across countries. As we have seen, symbols are used to convey tangibility for intangible services, but when Merrill-Lynch uses the bull as a symbol of investor initiative and independence (with an association to a "bull" or strong stock market), it cannot assume that the symbol will have the same meaning in other countries. The use of the bull as such a symbol would be resented in Spain and Mexico, where bullfighting is a national sport, and the bull is regarded as a symbol of aggression.

If a company can establish a global service symbol, it can reap the benefits. Thus, the golden arches have been successfully associated with McDonald's on a worldwide basis.

Variability in service delivery is another problem that is more severe in international markets. Although most of us have encountered rude hotel or restaurant employees, the standards for service in the United States are generally much higher than in the rest of the world. Service amenities are few, for example, in Eastern European countries. If these countries are to move to a market economy, and increase the level of tourism in the process, service delivery will have to improve. That is one reason why Marriott decided to train its Polish employees in the United States rather than in Poland. Variability of service in Poland is a generally accepted norm, and Marriott felt this mindset could be better changed in the United States.

Simultaneous production and consumption of services becomes riskier given the variability of services abroad. The "moment of truth" in service delivery is more likely to fall short. As a result, international service providers in transportation, hotels, and financial services must institute quality control programs to ensure more standardized service delivery.

CLASSIFYING SERVICES

Risks and opportunities vary according to the type of service being offered. Therefore, it is important to categorize services to understand strategy development. Figure 13.2 presents a three-part classification of services into product-related, equipment-based and people-based services.

Although we have discussed services as primary offerings, **product-related services** *play a supporting role to products.* For instance, warranties provide post-sale service support to purchasers of automobiles, electronics or appliances. Repairs independent of warranties also require service delivery. Normal maintenance may also require product-related service delivery, for example, an oil change for a car or maintenance of factory automation systems in a plant. In a crowded field, service support can be the determining factor in a product's success. Weyerhauser has been able to charge higher prices for its wood products, because it provides stores with a computer system that enables customers to design their own home-improvement projects.[21] In contrast, Olivetti failed to crack the U.S. office equipment market, despite a superior product, because of poor service.[22]

When service is the primary offering, *products play a supportive role if they are needed to deliver a service. These are called* **equipment-based services**, and they rely on the consumer's belief that a provider has the best type of equipment to execute the service. This is why airlines such as Delta promote the care they take in maintaining their aircraft, and phone companies such as MCI advertise their fiber-optic networks. In cases where the equipment is not automated, service companies often

FIGURE 13.2

A Classification of Services

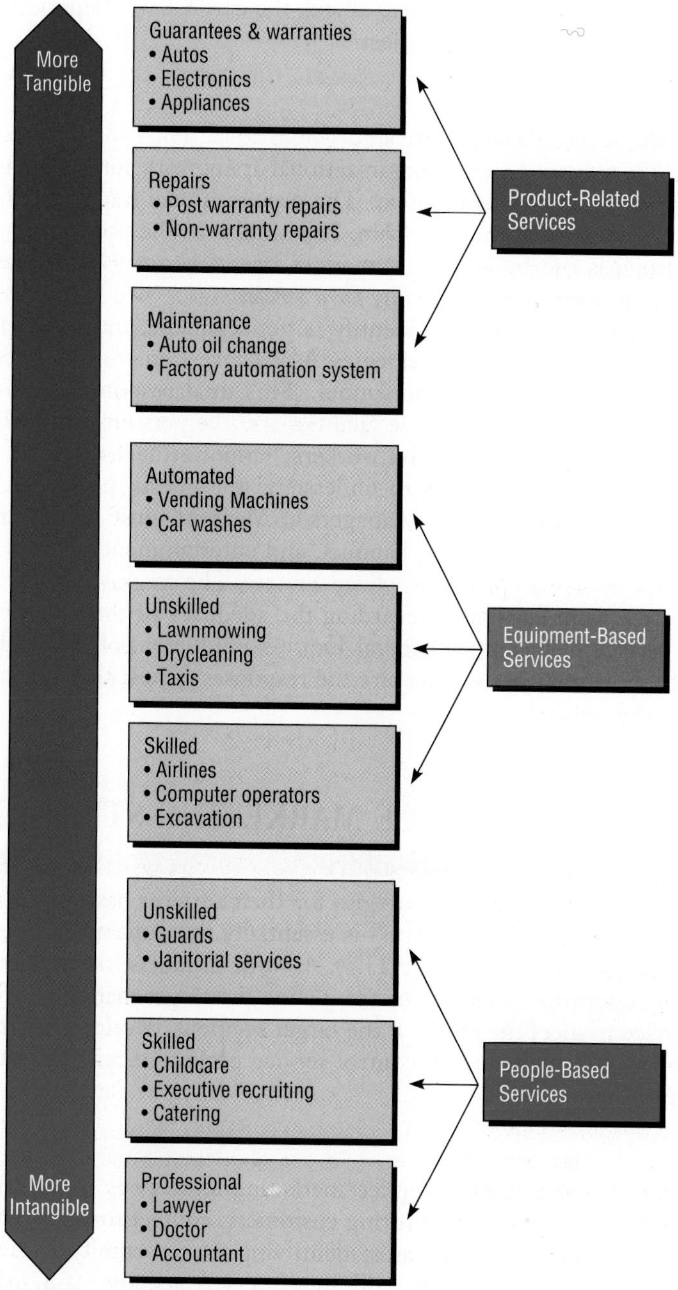

advertise the people behind the equipment—that is, friendly phone operators or flight attendants and experienced pilots.

People-based services *are primary service offerings that rely on people rather than equipment for delivery.* These include unskilled services (lawn care), skilled services (child care), or professional services (legal counseling or medical care).

Product-related services are the most tangible types of services; people-based services are the least tangible. The services provided by an auto mechanic are more tangible than those provided by a lawyer because consumers can associate the effectiveness of repairs with a physical object, the car. A lawyer's performance can not be associated with a physical object.

THE SERVICE MANAGEMENT SYSTEM

Services, as well as products, require an organizational framework to market them. In Chapter 12, we saw that the organizational framework for products was the product or brand management system. The organizational framework for service firms is a **service management system.** It is similar to the product management system in that it is run by **service managers** *who develop marketing strategies and have profit and performance responsibility for a service.*

The service manager's job is to identify target segments, and develop advertising, personal selling, and pricing strategies. As we have seen, many services require both physical installations and personnel. This dual responsibility is critical, because consumers evaluate both the facilities and the personnel in selecting services. Marriott gives its 70,000 hotel workers "empowerment training" to enable them to "step outside" their jobs to understand the guests' point of view when solving guest problems.[23] Service managers at Marriott must also ensure proper maintenance of room, reservation, banquet, and entertainment facilities to ensure that its hotel workers also properly deliver services. The service manager must also obtain feedback from customers regarding the adequacy of these services. As we have seen, service managers at Federal Express randomly poll more than 2,000 clients every three months and measure the responses against the company's quality index.

DEVELOPING SERVICE MARKETING STRATEGIES

Service managers must develop strategies for their services based on a marketing plan. The marketing planning process is essentially the same as that described in Chapter 3 for products (see Figure 13.3). As with products, the service manager must identify opportunities for a service, define the target market segment, position the service to meet the needs of the target segment, develop a marketing mix for the service, and evaluate and control service performance. This section considers each of these steps.

IDENTIFY SERVICE OPPORTUNITIES

The first step in developing a service marketing strategy is to identify service opportunities. This requires monitoring customers, competitors, and the broader marketing environment. In some cases, identifying an opportunity leads to the creation of a new service. When Merrill Lynch developed the cash management account (CMA), it identified an important need for one-stop servicing of financial accounts. Seeing that no one else was offering consolidated financial management, Merrill Lynch successfully stepped into the strategic "window of opportunity." It saw that baby boomers wanted more financial options, and that dual-earning households meant greater affluence as well as less time to devote to juggling several financial accounts. These demographic trends spelled the need for more flexibility and simplicity in financial management, and the CMA was the answer.

FIGURE 13.3

Marketing Planning for Services

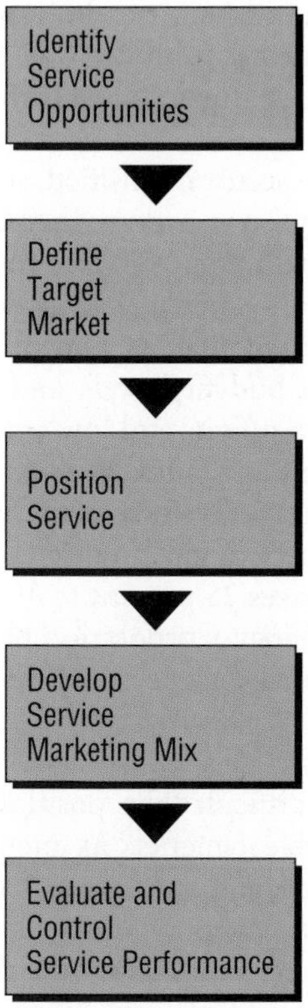

Service firms also look to new high-growth areas for opportunity when existing services mature. When McDonald's average per-store sales went into a two-year free-fall in the early 1990s, the company quietly decided to expand into day care by opening a test center near Chicago called Leaps & Bounds. The idea was to turn the threat of intense competition in the fast-food industry into opportunity by leveraging McDonald's popularity with children. It is too early to tell if McDonald's will be successful, but it shows that the company is looking to branch beyond its traditional fast-food service domain.[24]

In others cases, identifying a service opportunity leads to revitalizing an existing service. When the Paris-based hotelier Accor found itself unable to expand in Europe, it purchased the American Motel 6 chain for $1.3 billion. Although skeptics doubted Accor's chances for success in the oversaturated low-priced motel niche, the deal gave Accor 157,000 rooms—the most of any hotel in the world—an enviable customer base and a powerful competitive advantage in transatlantic marketing. It could lure its European customers to Motel 6 and its American clients to Formula 1, the $23-a-night chain it is cloning across Europe.[25]

DEFINE TARGET MARKETS

A plan to develop new services or revitalize existing ones must define the target segments for these services. Service firms have lagged behind product firms in segmenting markets. When demand for services was greater than supply, service firms did not feel the need to target specific segments. When they did, they tended to define their markets on narrow grounds by following a *concentrated segmentation strategy* (one set of services to one segment). For example, hotels and motels tended to identify their target segment on the low, middle, or high end of the socioeconomic spectrum. Howard Johnson was targeted to budget travelers, Holiday Inn to the mid-priced segment, and Hyatt to the higher income luxury segment.

As competition in the service sector intensified, service firms began to recognize that they could no longer rely on a narrow segmentation strategy. They could make more profits by offering different services to different segments, that is by moving from a concentrated to a *differentiated segmentation strategy*. For instance, when Holiday Corporation found that its mid-priced Holiday Inn hotels were caught in a squeeze between budget hotels and luxury chains, the company responded by expanding into the high- and low-price ends of the market. On the high end, it developed Crowne Plaza, a luxury hotel chain of multiple-room suites targeting mainly upscale business travelers; at the low end, it developed Holiday Inn Express hotels, a limited-service chain targeting the value-conscious business or pleasure traveler, offering prices 25 percent to 30 percent below typical Holiday Inns.[26] For good measure, Holiday Corporation has also introduced Homewood Suites, a chain of hotels designed for guests usually staying five nights or more.

POSITION SERVICES

Positioning a service is more difficult than positioning a product because of the need to communicate intangible benefits. As mentioned earlier, Merrill Lynch adopted the symbol of the bull and the slogan "We're Bullish on America" to convey its optimism about the economy and to encourage investments through Merrill Lynch. However, research showed that the theme was attracting the wrong kind of customer. It appealed to people who "flow with the crowd and prefer the conventional" instead of the innovative customer who Merrill Lynch felt would experiment with its new investment services.[27] As a result, the company kept the symbol of the bull but changed its slogan to "A breed apart." This repositioning effectively attracted the more-entrepreneurial investor that the company wanted.

DEVELOP THE SERVICE MARKETING MIX

The service manager must develop a marketing mix designed to deliver a service to the target segment based on the same mix of elements as a product marketing mix—namely, establish brand identity, advertise the service to the target segment, distribute it through the personal selling process, and set a price.

BRAND IDENTITY

Services have brand names just as products do. Frequently, services are identified by the corporate name—for example, Federal Express and AT&T. But separate brand names are often developed for individual services, as when McDonald's created Leaps & Bounds, and Holiday Corp. established Crowne Plaza.[28]

Unlike products, brand identity for services cannot be associated with a physical entity such as Pepsi-Cola's red, white, and blue cans. Consequently, it is all the more important for a company to establish brand names and symbols for its services, since such identification makes the intangible service more tangible in the consumer's mind.

ADVERTISING

The intangibility of services makes it more difficult to communicate their benefits through advertising. One approach to solving this problem is to try to spell out the service as clearly as possible through informative advertising. American Express has used such an informational approach in advertising to baby boomers. Its direct-mail campaign helps educate prospective investors about financial facts, even sending consumers a wallet-sized card with practical information such as tips on how to purchase insurance.

Another approach is to use symbols and imagery to convey the benefits of the service. Metropolitan Life initially took an informational approach in advertising its health-care plans. This informational approach was beginning to encourage a negative image of Metropolitan as a faceless entity, however, and company management decided it had carried the educational campaign far enough.[29] It decided instead to use symbols as tangible manifestations of the service, selecting Snoopy and the Peanuts comic-strip gang as its official representatives (see Exhibit 13.3). The Peanuts characters gave Metropolitan a friendly face. The campaign was effective in conveying an image of personal and reliable medical care.

EXHIBIT 13.3

Symbol Oriented Service Advertising

PERSONAL SELLING AND DISTRIBUTION

Since most services are produced and consumed simultaneously, the service provider both manufactures and distributes the service through a process of personal selling. As a result, the salesperson plays a more important role in service firms than in those producing products.

The point of contact between the service provider and the customer (referred to above as the "moment of truth") is, potentially, the weakest element in the service marketing mix. We have seen the variability in service quality caused by a lack of motivation on the part of service providers and the many moments of truth an employee encounters in an average day. One of the service manager's most difficult tasks is to try to motivate salespeople to deliver better and more consistent service, to be sensitive to customers, to gain their trust, to determine how satisfied they were with service delivery, and, in so doing, to convey an impression of professional competence.

The Averitt Express freight company of Tennessee motivates its drivers by expanding their job descriptions to include personal selling. They go out on the road armed with business cards and the power to solicit orders wherever they drop off packages. Averitt's drivers earn additional income for their efforts.[30]

Although the channel of distribution for services is generally limited to a buyer and a seller, occasionally intermediaries such as travel agents are needed. Carnival Cruise Lines has boosted revenues 30 percent since 1980 by aggressively targeting these agents. It sends employees masquerading as customers to their offices, and if an agent suggests a Carnival cruise first, he or she can win up to $1,000. Many passengers polled by the company report that Carnival was the first cruise mentioned by their travel agent.[31]

Service firms can establish a competitive advantage by providing more convenient access to services. Kentucky Fried Chicken is one of the growing number of fast-food chains using roving restaurants to increase their distribution reach. A KFC trailer, known as a mobile restaurant (see Exhibit 13.4), may show up on a busy street corner one afternoon and at a horse show the next. The advantage is that if one location does not provide sufficient sales, KFC does not have long-term liability; it can just pick up the mobile coach and move it to another site. They are also less expensive—The KFC trailers cost $200,000 compared to $1 million for a brick-and-mortar restaurant.[32]

Another strategy for increasing service access is to provide more outlets. Thus, banks may increase their number of branches, and further extend the distribution of services, by means of ATMs. Providing many outlets to consumers is costly, however. To make this strategy more cost-effective, many service firms have developed one-stop service shopping. By concentrating several services in one location, firms can decrease the cost and give the customer greater convenience. The trade-off is that often customers must travel a longer distance to reach the facility. HMOs have followed this strategy. They provide a broad range of health services in one facility, thereby decreasing medical costs and providing the customer with more medical services, but at remote locations.

PRICING

The cost of a product to a consumer is its price. Consider, however, the diversity of terms used in referring to the price of services—college tuition, finance charges, insurance premiums, lawyer's fees.

EXHIBIT 13.4

Increasing an Access to a Service: KFC's Mobile Restaurants

Services can be priced on a *cost-plus* basis by determining service costs and adding a fixed margin, or they can be priced by a *target return* method that determines the price that will yield a targeted return on investment. Both methods may be difficult to apply for people-based services, since it is harder to establish the cost of a service delivered by a person than by a machine. As a result, many service firms use **value-based pricing** *by setting prices based on what the consumer is willing to pay.* For example, an accountant may set the fees for preparing tax returns based on what individual customers are willing to pay for the service, rather than on actual costs of preparation. (We consider price determination for services in Chapter 21.)

EVALUATE AND CONTROL SERVICE PERFORMANCE

Services are much more difficult to evaluate and control than products because of the variability in service performance. Although no simple solutions exist for improving a service manager's ability to evaluate and control services, two essential requirements are: (1) to minimize performance variability by motivating service providers and (2) to obtain feedback regarding customer satisfaction with the services provided.

A few strategies are useful in motivating service providers. One approach is to "sell" them on the importance to the firm of the services they provide. Management is essentially marketing the firm to its employees. Federal Express uses a "quality communicator" whose sole job is to instruct Federal's workforce how to deliver the company's services more effectively. The communicator acts as a clearinghouse for suggestions that one division might have for improving productivity at another.[33]

GLOBAL MARKETING STRATEGIES

Citibank in Japan: Service Marketing in a Global Environment

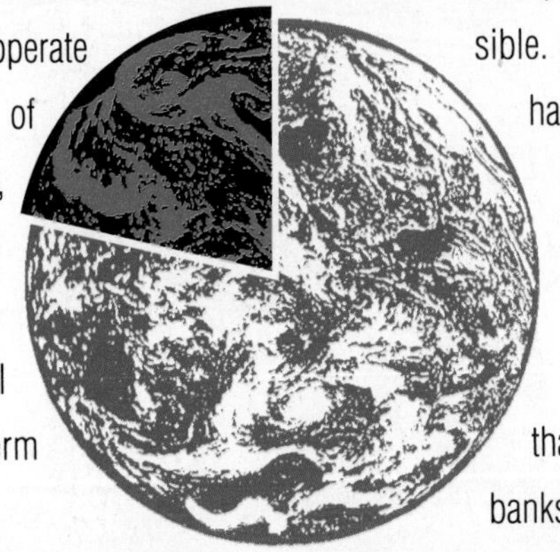

Although more than 80 foreign banks operate in Japan, they are nowhere near as successful as Japanese banks that operate abroad. Japan controls 14 percent of all bank assets in the United States, while American institutions in Japan barely control 1 percent. Citibank is aiming to change all that. How? By redefining the term customer service in Japan.

From the beginning, Citibank faced some formidable hurdles in making its presence felt in Japan. First, Japan's 13 major banks had long enjoyed favorable treatment from the country's finance ministry compared to foreign banks. The finance ministry tried to mute foreign competition by stressing how safe Japanese banks were and trumpeting the collapse of American banks. It even blocked Citibank from taking over a troubled 100-branch Tokyo bank.

Second, local tradition also played a role in inhibiting Citibank. The Japanese pay for almost everything with cash, shun checking accounts, and have their paychecks deposited directly by employers. As a result, local banks with extensive networks of automatic teller machines and long-term relationships with employers were able to discourage foreign banks from making inroads. Third, the high cost of land made opening new branches nearly impossible. Little surprise then that Citibank had only two branches in Tokyo and one in Yokohama during the mid-1980s.

What Citibank had going for it, however, was a vision. It reasoned that the choke-hold of Japan's local banks could be broken if someone could make Japanese customers realize what they were missing. After the United States began exerting pressure on Japan's finance ministry to stop favoring domestic banks, Citibank saw the wedge it needed. It quickly unveiled one flashy new service after another—all aimed at the well-to-do cosmopolitan Tokyo residents whom Citibank identified as being investment oriented toward their savings and liquid assets.

Its first offering was an account that paid a starkly higher interest rate than rival banks if deposits were made in U.S. dollars. The success of that program led Citibank to launch Multi-Money, a multiple currency account that offered customers a choice of depositing their money in six currencies, banking by mail or phone, a fully integrated statement in the

Another strategy is to establish customer-service divisions in which managers try to establish clear standards for performance, define goals for service personnel, and specify the means to attain these goals.

Equally important is the need for systematic feedback from customers. Hotels, airlines, and other service establishments encourage customers to fill out questionnaires rating facilities and personnel. Larger firms also rely on national surveys

GLOBAL MARKETING STRATEGIES

customer's choice of languages, and an automatic credit line. In its first 12 days, Multi-Money lured an amazing 12,000 customers.

But Citibank did not stop there. It began offering retail customers who had been shut out of the luxurious waiting rooms of Japan's private banks such things as checkbooks, gold credit cards and ATMs that accepted deposits and transferred cash between accounts.

All of this did not overshadow the fact that Citibank still was hobbled by its lack of branches. A deal giving it access to the 20,000-strong Japanese ATM network called BANCS certainly helped, but not enough. So Citibank began using direct mail to invite customers to open accounts by phone. The novelty of being able to open an account by phone intrigued the Japanese enough that before long, Citibank was receiving 10,000 inquiries a month. Today, one-fifth of all new accounts are opened without a customer setting foot in a Citibank branch. The Japanese have been so taken with phone banking that by 1990, almost a third of Citibank's Japanese transactions were being done by call-in, a figure that translates to 60,000 calls each month.

Citibank hopes to open 50 branches in Japan by the mid 1990s, and has its horizons set on becoming a dominant player in Japan's financial world. Timing has been on its side, since the finance ministry is intent on making Citibank a shining example of its liberalization policy. It also does not hurt to have friends in high places. When Japan's prime minister had an impromptu meeting with President George Bush in 1990, Bush made it clear he wanted no more obstacles put in Citibank's path the next time it wanted to buy an ailing institution. The message was swiftly relayed to Japan's bankers.

Questions: What hurdles did Citibank have to overcome to become an effective service provider in Japan? How did it overcome these hurdles?

Sources: "Citibank Builds Full-Service Strategy in Japan," *The Bankers Magazine*, July/August 1990; "A Tale of Tellers in Distant Places," *The Economist*, July 7, 1990; "Citicorp Branches Out in Japan," *Tokyo Business Today*, January 1989; and "How Citibank Created a Retail Niche for Itself in Japan," *Planning Review*, September/October 1989.

to obtain more reliable and systematic information on the customer's image of the firm and reactions to its services.

As with products, the evaluation-and-control process also involves phasing out services that prove ill-conceived or unmanageable. We have seen how Smith abandoned ZapMail at Federal Express after the fax-based service drowned in a tide of red ink.

MARKETING NONPROFIT SERVICES

Although this chapter has focused primarily on marketing services for a profit, services provided by nonprofit institutions also represent big business in our economy. Institutions such as colleges, museums, charitable organizations, cultural centers, and religious institutions are not necessarily motivated by profit-maximizing goals in providing services to the public. Few people realize that the nation's nonprofit sector—which one study numbers at six million organizations—accounts for over 20 percent of economic activity in the United States. This activity translates into more than $250 billion spent disbursing nonprofit services annually.[34] Charitable organizations alone receive more than $30 billion in yearly contributions.[35]

THE NATURE OF NONPROFIT SERVICES

Nonprofit services are similar to services in the profit sector in that they are intangible, variable, immediately perishable, and are produced as they are consumed. As most students know, a class taught by an instructor (a service in the nonprofit sector) is difficult to evaluate objectively; it can be highly variable from one week to the next; it is perishable (that is, it is lost to students who do not show up); and it is "consumed" by students as it is "produced" by the instructor.

Marketing nonprofit services is more difficult than marketing services in the profit sector. Before considering these difficulties, let us briefly consider some types of nonprofit services and how they develop a marketing orientation.

TYPES OF NONPROFIT ORGANIZATIONS

Different types of nonprofit organizations can be classified as follows:

- Cultural (for instance, museums, operas, and symphonies)
- Knowledge oriented (colleges, schools, research organizations)
- Philanthropic (foundations, charities, welfare organizations)
- Social causes (environmental, consumer, feminist groups)
- Religious (churches and religious associations)
- Public (city, state, federal services; quasi-governmental services such as the U.S. Postal Service and Amtrak)

THE EMERGENCE OF A MARKETING ORIENTATION

Nonprofit services at one time had an almost total lack of awareness of the benefits of marketing. Many were relatively unresponsive to client needs, because their revenues were derived from contributions, endowments, and subsidies and were therefore not dependent on satisfying customers. This seeming independence from the consumer led many nonprofit organizations to place considerations such as adequacy of facilities or service delivery lower on their scale of priorities than they should have. Museum managers, for example, would typically ignore lack of parking and long lines, assuming that art should be able to sell itself despite all obstacles.

This view has had to change in recent years. The deep recession of the early 1990s and cutbacks in grants by the Reagan and Bush administrations have intensified competition and forced nonprofits to scramble for funds while attempting to adopt higher public profiles. This has led to a new era of marketing among nonprofits. Social cause agencies are fast becoming full-service marketers and advertisers in their own right, developing sophisticated promotional and awareness-raising activities to keep their philanthropic missions intact.[36] Colleges now use marketing to influence alumni to give donations, as well as to recruit students. Charitable organizations such as the Heart Fund and the American Cancer Society use national advertising campaigns to influence people to stop smoking. Government institutions such as the Department of Agriculture use marketing techniques to sell ideas such as improving children's eating habits.

DIFFICULTIES IN MARKETING NONPROFIT SERVICES

Developing marketing strategies for nonprofit services is particularly difficult because of several characteristics of such services. First, nonprofits market to **multiple publics** *since they must attract resources from donors as well as allocate resources to clients.* Marketing to donors is likely to be very different from marketing to clients. For example, the American Cancer Society uses direct mail to solicit contributions from donors, then uses these funds to prepare antismoking commercials for the general public.

A second characteristic of nonprofits is that they require **multiple exchanges** *of resources in dealing with donors and clients.* While an average of 83 percent of all philanthropic gifts are given by individuals,[37] a charitable organization such as Save the Children Foundation must also deal with corporate contributors and government agencies in trying to attract funds. It then allocates funds to projects ranging from basketball courts on Indian reservations to nutrition-training centers in the Dominican Republic. Similarly, a nonprofit hospital must be concerned with exchanges among financial contributors, physicians, nurses, drug and equipment suppliers, and patients. In contrast, exchanges for services tend to be simpler in the profit sector, usually occurring directly between consumer and service provider, occasionally with the help of an intermediary.

A third characteristic of nonprofit companies is that they are *more likely to be influenced by government agencies*, lobbyists, and other public agencies than are organizations with a profit goal. Such nonmarket pressures require many nonprofit firms to offer services to uneconomical segments: for example, the postal service maintains rural services, and Amtrak provides services to thinly populated areas. Many rates charged by nonprofits are also subject to review by government agencies. Examples of this are postal rates and fees for health services under Medicaid and Medicare.

Another reason it is more difficult to market services in the nonprofit sector is that many nonprofit firms are trying to change people's behavior by *selling an idea*, whether it be influencing them to drive more slowly, to use mass transit, or to buy nonpolluting products. Such goals are beneficial to society, but represent either inconvenience or added cost to individual consumers. Trying to convince people of the dangers of smoking, drinking, or drug abuse is also difficult because these actions are often habitual, and, as we have seen in Chapter 8, a marketing strategy is more likely to be effective when it reinforces current behavior than when it attempts to change it.

Still another difficulty in marketing nonprofit services is that what they have to offer is often *more vague and less tangible* than for-profit services. The benefits of air travel, telecommunications, or bank services are easier to convey than the benefits of religion, culture, or knowledge. Further, level of awareness of the activities of nonprofit organizations is often low. This was revealed when the United Way conducted a survey of Horry County, South Carolina, to see how widely known the group's efforts were there. The results showed that only half of those surveyed could cite any specific United Way program, even though the vast majority said it knew of the organization's presence in Horry County.[38]

Finally, marketers of nonprofit services find it *harder to control their resources* than do marketers of services for profit. In many cases, nonprofit organizations must use the commercial air time that is contributed by media and thus have no say as to when their ads will be shown or heard.

DEVELOPING MARKETING STRATEGIES FOR NONPROFIT SERVICES

Despite these difficulties, managers in nonprofit institutions have become increasingly adept at developing and implementing marketing strategies. The process of developing strategies in the nonprofit sector are the same as those for services in the profit sector: identifying opportunities, defining target segments, positioning the service, developing a marketing mix, and evaluating and controlling service delivery. We will briefly explore each of these.

IDENTIFYING OPPORTUNITIES FOR NONPROFIT SERVICES

Nonprofit agencies must identify opportunities both for attracting clients and for attracting donors. A study conducted for the Kennedy Center, a cultural facility for music and drama in Washington, D.C., serves as a good example of identifying new opportunities to attract clients. In trying to attract people who did not ordinarily attend its performances, the center interviewed a sample of residents of the greater Washington D.C. area. The survey found that non-attenders placed a higher priority on parking facilities and convenience than those who attended Kennedy Center events and rated the center low on both criteria. The clear implication was that the Kennedy Center should advertise the adequacy of its parking facilities and the convenience of its location to public transportation.

The survey also found that those who did not attend the Kennedy Center enjoy dinner theater, country-and-western music, and pop music more than attenders. If the Kennedy Center changes its mix of entertainment to provide more of these types of shows, it might attract more customers.

DEFINE TARGET MARKETS FOR NONPROFIT SERVICES

Nonprofit firms must identify targets for their efforts, from the standpoint of identifying both clients and donors. The Department of the Army identifies its "clients" as potential recruits, specifically young people who want independence, the chance to mature, and the opportunity to travel.[39] Demographically, these individuals are most likely to be lower-middle-class males age 17 to 21 who live at home. The army directed a $30 million-plus advertising drive toward this segment.

Nonprofit firms must also identify a target for donations. Colleges identify donor targets from their alumni list based on income, age, and past history of donations. In a bid to expand their donor base, some nonprofits are matching computer-generated models of their current donors with zip code lists so as to identify nondonors living in the same zip code areas as donors.[40] The assumption is that nondoners who live near donors are better prospects than the average consumer.

EXHIBIT 13.5

Positioning a Nonprofit Service: The Shanti Project

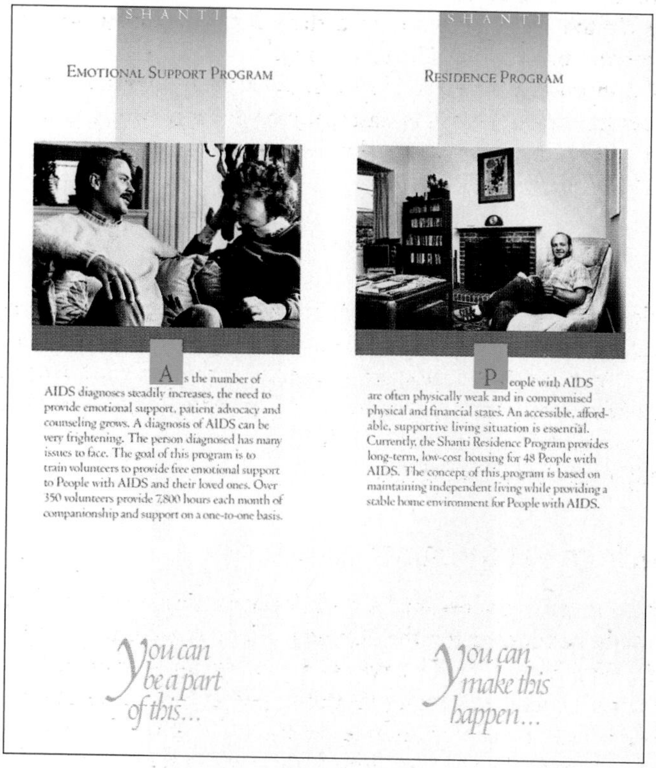

POSITIONING NONPROFIT SERVICES

The importance of positioning services in the nonprofit sector can be seen in the case of the Kennedy Center, which discovered through research that nonattenders were more likely to view it as too formal and stuffy. To dispel these notions, the center was repositioned as friendly and unimposing.

In another area of the nonprofit sector, a San Francisco AIDS center had difficulty attracting volunteers to seminars designed to help them cope with the strains of their work (known as the Shanti Project). With the help of a volunteer marketer from Levi Strauss, the Shanti Project conducted a survey that found that volunteers would attend if the program's topics were expanded to include how they could avoid awkward feelings toward AIDS patients who were gay, poor, or drug addicts. As a result, it adopted a catchy name for the seminar—"The Courage to Care: Healing Yourself to Help You Care Better"—and sent out brochures to 15,000 Bay Area health-care professionals (see Exhibit 13.5). As a result, the seminars quickly sold out.[41]

MARKETING MIX FOR NONPROFIT SERVICES

Like other service firms, marketers of nonprofit services must develop a mix of brand, advertising, distribution, personal selling, and pricing strategies to attract funds and deliver services to clients.

EXHIBIT 13.6

Establishing Brand Identity

BRAND IDENTITY The U.S. Postal Service established Express Mail services after research showed that customers would be willing to pay a significant amount to guarantee overnight delivery. It established a brand identity for Express Mail through advertising to compete with air express services such as Federal Express and Purolator Courier in the profit sector. It succeeded in establishing an association between Express Mail and next-day service (see Exhibit 13.6).

ADVERTISING Advertising is used by nonprofit firms to influence both donors and clients. Organizations such as the Salvation Army and the Heart Fund use advertising to solicit contributions (see Exhibit 13.7). Direct-mail advertising is most frequently used to solicit contributions.

Advertising is also an effective means of encouraging people to use nonprofit services. Colleges, museums, opera companies, charities, and public institutions frequently advertise their services in newspapers and on radio and TV. The creative use of advertising by nonprofit firms with limited budgets sometimes rivals that of larger profit-making firms. Consider the relatively low-budget campaign for the San Diego Zoo on its seventieth birthday in 1986. The campaign helped increase attendance to over 3 million people a year.[42]

Even religious institutions are beginning to advertise. One ad shows Bubba Smith sitting under a tree, reading as Dick Butkus approaches. TV viewers might

EXHIBIT 13.7

The Salvation Army Uses Advertising to Solicit Contributions

Nobody's as hip as we are.
THE SALVATION ARMY
Photograph courtesy: Bodi
What do you want to know about the drug scene? The counter culture? Street people? And street talk?
Your friends like to wear old clothes from our thrift shops? Our friends have to. Your friends into alcohol *and* drugs? Ours are dying from it. You have pals who are always broke, bummed out and up-to-here with society? Ours are destitute, schizophrenic and suicidal. Pregnant teenagers? Tell us about it.
And all too often we're the only thing standing between our friends and real tragedy. Us in our dowdy uniforms and old-fashioned attitudes.
Yet somehow we do it.
Author Peter Drucker says, "The Salvation Army probably does a better job with the poor than anyone else."
"And frugally," adds *Fortune* (11/9/87). "Of each dollar it receives, 86 cents goes to the needy." In a business where 50 or 60 cents is good enough.
Yes, we're religious. But we're no fanatics. You can't do what we do and be a pollyanna, a goody-goody or holier-than-thou.
But hipper-than-thou? Probably.
Places you wouldn't venture into, we live and work. People you wouldn't touch, we embrace. Scenes you couldn't look at, we live with. And deal with. Every day.
So go ahead and kid us all you want to about "saving souls." But for God's sake help us save lives.
We're fighting for you.
The Salvation Army of Greater New York, 132 West 14th Street, New York, NY 10011-7388. (212) 807-4200

expect a Miller Lite ad coming up when they see these two burly former football players. But Butkus snatches the book from Bubba Smith and begins pouring through it with interest. It is the Bible.[43]

DISTRIBUTION Unlike services for profit, distribution strategies for nonprofit services are usually directed to both donors and clients. Increasing the number of locations where donations can be made can stimulate contributions. That is why Salvation Army collectors solicit funds at so many locations between Thanksgiving and Christmas.

Increasing the number of service locations can also expand the use of nonprofit facilities. Thus, many health maintenance organizations are allowing people to use an expanded network of doctors. Similarly, colleges in cities have added branches in suburban areas to increase enrollment. Adelphi College in New York conducted courses on a commuter train at one time to try to gain a competitive advantage.

PERSONAL SELLING Since direct mail is effective in soliciting funds primarily from smaller contributors, nonprofit agencies use personal selling to attract funds from larger donors. The United Fund found that 1 percent of its contributors donated 10 percent of its funds.[44] When giving is so concentrated, direct

ETHICAL AND ENVIRONMENTAL ISSUES IN MARKETING

Halo Marketing: Are Nonprofits Trading Saintliness for Sawbucks?

What does the American Association of Retired Persons, a nonprofit agency, have in common with your local pharmacy? Maybe not much at first thought. But consider this: The AARP sells its membership list to pharmaceutical companies, who in turn market their goods to AARP members under the organization's name. Since proceeds from the sales are tax exempt, the AARP and drug makers can undercut prices offered by the local pharmacy, sometimes by 50 percent.

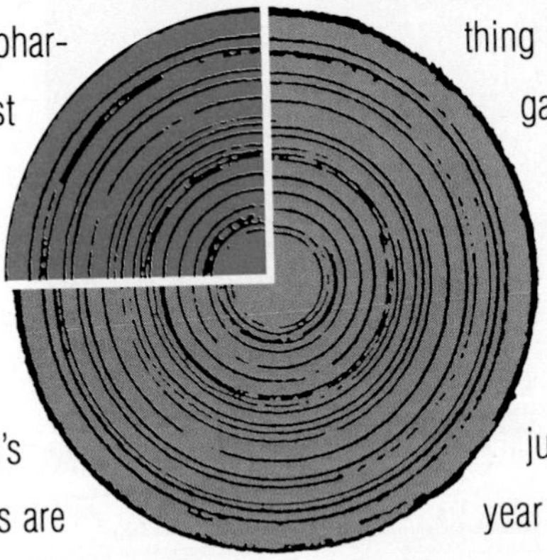

The practice of using a nonprofit's tax-exempt status to market goods which are "related" to its social aim is called *halo marketing*, and it has small-business owners in an uproar. Their claim is that nonprofit firms are abusing their status and reputations to gain an unfair advantage over for-profit firms. Moreover, they say nonprofits have become so adept at using their tax-exempt status to sell related services that these services now encompass anything even tangentially related to the organization's social aims. Few question the legitimacy of charitable institutions and their efforts on behalf of the nation's poor for example, but it takes some creative imagining to justify their tax-free sale of $680-a-year health club memberships, liquor, and foreign cars—all under the guise of the "related religious, charitable or educational" exemption.

Congress designed tax-exempt status for nonprofits to achieve a two-fold aim. When applied to charities, it is supposed to create a fiscal climate that allows them to survive. When applied to companies such as Farmland Industries, an agricultural cooperative, it is supposed to give the service time to incubate. In theory, when the service is mature enough to compete, the designation should be taken away.

contact is an effective means of fundraising. Stanford University, like many other educational institutions, uses personal solicitations to appeal to donors who have the potential to contribute large amounts.

Nonprofit organizations may also use personal selling to deliver their services. Outreach workers in social programs, family planners, and community organizers try to get individuals in need of social services to use them. In some cases, salespeople are required to sell the goods of nonprofit agencies in much the same way as for-profit companies. For example, UNICEF relies on an army of field volunteers to sell their greeting cards to retailers.

PRICING A major difference between profit and nonprofit services is that the former are priced to maximize profits, whereas the latter are priced at a "fair" level based on clients' needs and ability to pay. Most nonprofit firms do not expect to

ETHICAL AND ENVIRONMENTAL ISSUES IN MARKETING

Small-business owners say that is not happening, and nonprofit firms are becoming bolder than ever, in some cases leveraging their names just like for-profit companies do with successful products. Consider the Mayo Clinic lending its name to health foods or a hospital peddling hearing-aids that are backed by its reputation.

Is it unfair price competition? Look at the case of one New Jersey travel agent who said she has to compete against Harvard and Yale alumni associations which sponsor "continuing education" cruises to France. "They can mail a brochure for 8 cents that would cost me 39 cents and we lose commissions," she said.

Where does all the money go? Ideally, it gets poured back into the charity's social outlets—into, say, the American Red Cross's disaster relief unit or the Ford Foundation's art grants program. But with few restrictions on how such revenues may be spent, it is not uncommon to see some of the money funneled into employee perks and lavish headquarters such as the Red Cross' Beaux Arts building in Washington or Ford's crystal palace in New York.

"I'm not opposed to the Girl Scouts having an annual cookie sale," the New Jersey travel agent concluded, "But if the Girl Scouts want to open a cookie store next to Mrs. Fields cookies, they should have to pay the same taxes."

Questions: Is tax-exempt status creating an unfair price advantage for nonprofit firms when they compete with for-profit companies? What are the pros and cons of such a price advantage for nonprofit organizations?

Sources: "Businessmen with Halos," *Forbes*, November 26, 1990; and "Profits? Who, Me?" *Forbes*, March 23, 1987.

recoup costs. College tuition payments rarely cover costs, and social agencies often provide their services for free.

Nonprofit firms must also take account of the nonmonetary costs incurred by their clients. Health-care facilities should be aware of the costs of waiting time, inconvenience, discomfort, and insecurity involved in medical care. Minimizing such costs helps to attract more customers. Alcoholics Anonymous charges a very high nonmonetary cost for membership—public admission of being an alcoholic and commitment to refrain from drinking.

EVALUATING AND CONTROLLING NONPROFIT SERVICES

Evaluating the performance of nonprofit institutions is both simpler and more complex than for profit-making organizations. It is simpler, because it is relatively easy to track the effectiveness of a nonprofit organization's fundraising efforts. Institutions such as the United Way can easily measure the number of new donors attracted yearly and the average amount of giving per donor, but the amount of resources a nonprofit organization attracts is only one dimension of performance.

The difficult part is evaluating how these resources are used. Consider a college. Administrators might attempt to obtain feedback from students concerning many aspects of college service, from the quality of teachers to the adequacy of library, dorm, and computer facilities. Ultimately, such feedback provides only short-term answers. The real criterion of effectiveness for a college is how well it has performed in equipping its students to be successful in society, whatever path they choose. This kind of measure is very difficult to obtain, given the diverse factors that affect individual success.

Nonprofit organizations also face the same problems as the profit sector in controlling performance: Management must motivate personnel to provide services in a customer-oriented fashion. Presumably, employees in nonprofit firms are motivated by the altruism of working for worthy causes such as fighting cancer, protecting the environment, or improving minority education, not by the pay, which is much lower than in the profit sector. But judging by the low level of performance in many public and private agencies, such altruism does not always result in effective service delivery. Nonprofit firms need to institute the same types of educational programs as in the profit sector to motivate employees to provide services effectively.

SUMMARY

1. **Why have services become a major part of our economy?**
   Basic demographic changes have propelled services to the forefront of our economy. First, the increase in the proportion of working women made time more valuable, then the greater affluence of dual-earning households made it possible to buy more personal services to alleviate the time crunch. More health-conscious and fitness-oriented life-styles have also resulted in increased expenditures on services.

   Foreign competitors have added to the emergence of a service economy by winning out over domestic manufacturers with superior goods at lower prices. As a result, many manufacturers have been forced to shift to service businesses to ensure growth.
2. **What are the differences between services and products? What are the strategic implications of these differences?**
   Services are less tangible and more variable in quality than products. They are also more perishable because they cannot be stored. If they are not used when offered, they go to waste. Another difference between services and products is that services are usually consumed as they are produced.

   These differences make the marketing of services more difficult than products. Managers try to overcome these difficulties by employing various strategies. They try to make their services: (1) more tangible by associating them in the consumer's mind with physical objects or people; (2) less variable by using machines, where they can, to create standardization and by training their salespeople to provide better and more-reliable service; and (3) less perishable by varying price to encourage use during off-peak periods.

3. **How do service firms develop marketing strategies for their offerings?**
Service firms develop marketing strategies in the same way firms producing products do. Service managers first identify an opportunity in the marketplace leading to the development of a new service or the revitalization of an existing service. Services are then marketed to defined segments and positioned to meet their needs. Service managers must then establish a marketing mix to deliver services to the target segment.
A service marketing mix will involve a plan to: (1) establish brand identity for the service, (2) distribute the service by ensuring that it can be obtained conveniently, (3) communicate the service benefits through advertising, and (4) price the service to provide an adequate return on investment. The final step in strategy development is to provide for evaluation and control. Such evaluation is more difficult for services than products, given their variability and intangibility.
4. **What are the distinctions between marketing nonprofit services and marketing services at a profit?**
Nonprofit services are distinct from services in the profit sector in that they must attract resources from donors as well as allocate these resources to clients. The service manager must develop marketing strategies for these multiple publics. As a result, nonprofit agencies must establish multiple exchanges when they market to donors and clients. Resources must be donated to service organizations, then passed on to their clients, often through an intermediary. A third difference is that nonprofit firms are more likely to be influenced by nonmarket forces such as government agencies, lobbyists, and other public agencies.
5. **Why is it more difficult to market nonprofit services than services in the profit sector?**
There are a number of reasons why nonprofit service marketing is more difficult. First, many nonprofit agencies are trying to sell ideas and to change behavior. Second, nonprofit services are more vague and less tangible than services in the profit sector. Third, nonprofit firms have less control over their resources and marketing strategies.

KEY TERMS

Product-related services (p. 432)
Equipment-based services (p. 432)
People-based services (p. 433)
Service management system (p. 434)
Service manager (p. 434)
Value-based pricing (p. 439)
Multiple publics (p. 443)
Multiple exchanges (p. 443)

QUESTIONS

1. If service marketing is different from product marketing, why have financial-service firms such as Citicorp hired product managers from consumer packaged-goods firms such as Procter & Gamble and General Foods to manage their services?
2. What factors have led service firms to become more marketing oriented in the 1980s and 1990s?
3. Do Federal Express's overnight delivery services have the four characteristics of a service: intangibility, variability, perishability, and simultaneous production and consumption? If so, in what ways? How did the company try to deal with the problem of variability in its services?
4. A fast-food chain finds significant variability in service, particularly in several

locations where customer complaints are frequent. The company fears if it does not decrease the variability of its service, it will begin to lose customers to competition. What strategies can it develop to reduce service variability?

5. What are the marketing responsibilities of the service manager in the service management system?
6. In what way did Merrill Lynch's introduction of the cash management account fill an important gap in customer needs for financial services? What demographic trends identified an opportunity for introducing this service?
7. Some marketers feel that establishing brand identity for services is more important than for products.
   a. Do you agree? Why or why not?
   b. What are some examples of services that have established brand identity? Has the brand name or symbol helped market the service?
8. How did Citibank use service distribution strategies to overcome its lack of branches in Japan?
9. Why are problems of service delivery greater in international markets than in domestic markets?
10. The director of marketing at a large cultural institution has felt frustrated in trying to influence top management to use more-constructive pricing and promotional strategies to market musical and theatrical events. She says, "I am beginning to think that top management feels there is no reason to be marketing oriented, because they are used to being in a sellers' market. But that may change, forcing them to take a closer look at marketing techniques."
    a. What factors are likely to cause nonprofit organizations to be more marketing oriented?
    b. What factors have caused management in nonprofit firms to resist the use of marketing techniques?
11. A marketing manager who moved from a large financial institution to head the marketing effort for a large philanthropic agency said, "My former job was a piece of cake compared to this one. Not only is marketing more complicated here, it's less controllable."
    a. Explain why the marketing of nonprofit services is more difficult than the marketing of for-profit services.
    b. Specify what characteristics of nonprofit services make it more difficult to formulate marketing strategies and make these strategies less controllable.
12. How do distribution and advertising strategies differ in attracting donors versus attracting clients for nonprofit services?
13. What is the role of personal selling in the marketing of nonprofit services?

QUESTIONS: YOU ARE THE DECISION MAKER

1. Assume that a life-insurance company has developed a new life-insurance plan targeting working women to make benefits more comparable to those for men. It is concerned about the difficulties of communicating intangible benefits such as security, protection, and peace of mind. What strategies can the company develop to communicate these benefits?
2. One airline executive in business for over 40 years reflected on the variability in airline services as follows:

   I'm tired of hearing how variable services are compared to products. Yes, we have had delays, bumped passengers, lost baggage, and even had discourteous flight attendants at times. But these things are the exception, not the rule. Airline service is a lot better than when I got started in this business. And, I think it is less variable than some products. Personally, I think there is more variability in the cars I buy than in the service we provide. Overall, I think our customers understand some degree of variability in service is inevitable—and are willing to accept it.

   a. Do you agree with this executive's position? Why or why not?
   b. Are there any risks in a service company assuming that "customers understand some degree of variability in service is inevitable and are willing to accept it?"

3. A regional airline finds it is overbooked during peak periods and has significant excess capacity during slack periods. It is trying to compete with larger airlines on its routes by offering better service and price. It recognizes the inherent problems of service perishability in transportation.
   a. What strategies can it develop to try to manage supply and demand?
   b. How would these strategies put the company in a better competitive position?
4. Evaluate your college as a provider of a nonprofit service.
   a. Is it effective in communicating its programs and facilities to prospective students?
   b. What steps would you take to improve your college's marketing program?

CHAPTER 14

Distributing Products and Services

YOUR FOCUS IN CHAPTER 14

To learn:

- *Why intermediaries are used to distribute products and services.*
- *What channel systems are, and what types of channel systems are most effective for distributing consumer goods, industrial goods, and services.*
- *The key steps in establishing a system of distribution and in developing distribution strategies.*
- *Why conflicts occur within a channel system.*

Avon—Reinventing Door-to-Door Selling for the Nineties

In 1972, Avon stock traded at a galloping $140 per share. A year later, it was down to $18.[1] How does an empire crumble that fast? By squandering a golden distribution network. Avon pioneered door-to-door selling, then let it's network disintegrate. Now, two decades later, the Avon lady has come back with a vengeance, and Avon is clawing its way back to the top.

In its heyday, Avon had what many thought to be a foolproof distribution system. Its representatives would get a 40 percent commission on each sale but no base salary, and with no need for wholesalers or retailers, Avon walked away with profit margins that were the envy of the industry. The formula, however, worked only as long as someone was home to answer the doorbell. But as the proportion of working women increased, Avon experienced the ultimate "double whammy"; few women at home to buy and few women available to take on part-time jobs to sell. By the mid 1970s, Avon's door-to-door distribution system began falling apart as legions of women moved from home to the workplace.[2]

At first, Avon executives were too insular to pay much notice. But by 1980, Avon was suffering 12 percent average annual profit losses,[3] and it appeared too late to reverse the damage. Since the company did not pay much attention to marketing (it never polled its representatives to build a customer profile, for instance), it had no idea where its losses were coming from, or why.[4] By 1983, a new management team concluded that Avon would have to place less reliance on door-to-door selling.

To stem the tide of red ink, the new Avon team jumped into a diversification frenzy. It acquired health-care concerns, Tiffany & Co., perfume makers, and even a specialty-chemical producer. As it turned out, Avon either bought the wrong companies or paid too much for good ones, leaving itself drowning in $1.1 billion of debt.[5]

As the rest of Avon was sinking, James Preston, then president of its direct-selling unit, began rethinking the conventional wisdom that his 500,000 Avon ladies were has-beens. Maybe their numbers were dwindling (by 1982, for the first time in its history, Avon's sales force was shrinking). Maybe they were demoralized. Maybe there was too much middle management getting in their way. But, Preston came to realize, they were not dinosaurs. So he set out to reinvent the wheel by marrying marketing and distribution in a way Avon's old guard never fathomed.

After studies found that the primary reason women stopped buying Avon products was that they lost contact with the Avon saleslady, Preston revamped Avon's territorial structure. Instead of giving representatives a two-block stretch of apartment buildings, he assigned them to floors of huge office buildings. He also set out on a 32-city tour to find out what his representatives were thinking and found that the modern woman wanted to be an Avon sales representative as a career, not a hobby.

To satisfy them, he let them set up mini-selling groups that could recruit other representatives and keep a cut of the profits. He also revised the commission structure so the top producers were earning more and sent out a 500,000-piece direct-mail campaign to representatives who had stopped selling. Finally, Preston targeted younger women likely to spend more on their appearance instead of relying on Avon's traditional core market of women older than age 50.[6]

Preston's moves turned the ostracized direct-selling group into Avon's star once again, boosting sales from $95 million in 1985 to $157 million in 1987.[7] By 1988, Preston had been named CEO.[8]

Now, Preston is taking Avon ladies into the 1990s by linking them to catalog and phone sales. For instance, under a program called Avon Select, the company pays its representatives for each customer name they submit. Avon then sends these customers catalogs with the representative's name printed on it. The customer can either call the representative or call Avon. Either way, the representative gets a commission which continues to be paid so long as the customer keeps ordering.[9]

The next leap will be direct-response advertising, whereby Avon customers will be invited to call Avon directly. While this may be viewed as undercutting the Avon lady, Preston believes it will attract customers in areas where Avon does not have a presence, furthering growth. Preston's strategy has succeeded in not only revitalizing door-to-door selling, but also in broadening Avon's distribution base to telephone sales. As a result, he expects sales, which grew 2 percent in 1990, to leapfrog to 7 percent by 1995.

Says Preston, "We're back to a business we know."[10]

THE IMPORTANCE OF DISTRIBUTION

The Avon story shows that distribution is a key ingredient in a company's marketing strategy. Although Avon had a $22 million ad budget in 1988, it was sliced down to $4.6 million in 1990, proving that distribution, not advertising, was the key part of the company's turnaround.[11]

The importance of distribution is also reflected in its cost (averaging about 25 percent of the product's price).[12] Manufacturers could sell directly to their customers, but most use intermediaries such as retailers, wholesalers, or manufacturers' agents for two reasons: (1) Intermediaries do a better job in getting the right product to the consumer at the right time and at the right place; (2) and they do so more cheaply than manufacturers. As a result, the nature of the distribution system established by a manufacturer—whether direct to consumers or through intermediaries—can be the single most important element in determining the success or failure of a product.

This chapter, and the next two, explore the implementation of distribution systems. Our perspective in this chapter is primarily that of the manufacturer, whose goal is to distribute products to consumers in the most effective manner. Throughout these three chapters, it is important to remember that these distribution strategies must be integrated with other elements of the marketing mix: product, promotion, and price strategies.

NATURE OF THE CHANNEL SYSTEM

The distribution process has been compared to a pipeline or channel because it represents a series of flows. As Figure 14.1 illustrates, information regarding consumer needs flows to manufacturers, passing through intermediaries on the way. It then flows from manufacturers back to consumers in the form of information on prices, product characteristics, and availability. There is also a flow of orders from intermediaries to manufacturers that reflects consumer needs. The flow of products goes from manufacturers through intermediaries to consumers, and a flow of payment goes from consumers through the channel back to manufacturers.

The distribution of information, orders, products, and payments requires cooperation between manufacturers, wholesalers, and retailers in order to work smoothly. These three parties work as a **channel** (or **distribution**) **system**, that is, *a group of independent businesses composed of manufacturers, wholesalers, and retailers designed to deliver the right set of products to consumers at the right place and time.* In the following paragraphs, we will look at the role played both by intermediaries and manufacturers within the channel system. First, however, it is important to understand exactly what intermediaries are.

TYPES OF INTERMEDIARIES

There are three general types of intermediaries in the channel system: retailers, wholesalers, and agents and brokers. **Retailers** *are distinct from other intermediaries in that they sell to final consumers.* As such, they are used primarily by producers of consumer goods, not industrial goods. The importance of retailing is measured by the existence of over 2 million retail establishments in the United States, accounting for over $1 trillion in sales. These establishments range from large department stores such as Dayton Hudson, to supermarket chains such as Kroger, to general

FIGURE 14.1

Flows through the Distribution Channel System

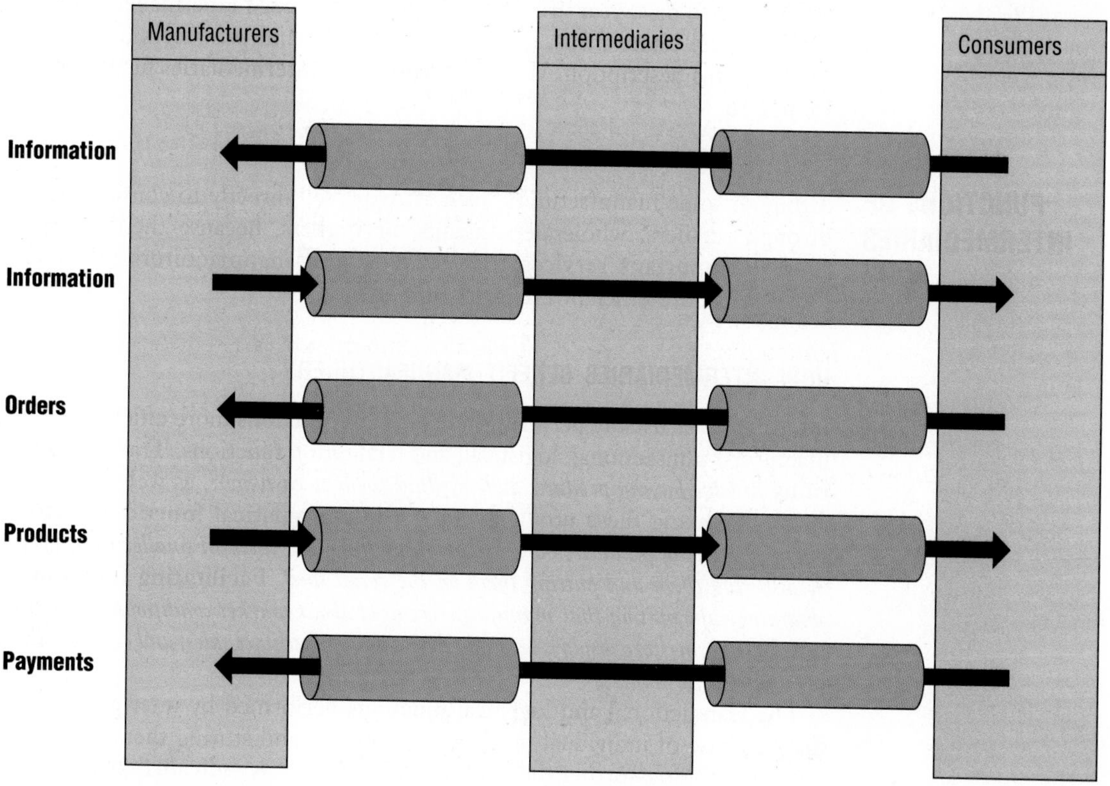

merchandisers such as Sears, to small specialty retailers and "mom and pop" food stores.

Wholesalers (also referred to as **distributors** *when selling industrial goods) buy and resell merchandise to other wholesalers or to retailers.* Unlike wholesalers of consumer goods, distributors sometimes sell directly to a final user. They often specialize in a certain line of industrial goods and have the sales staff and technical expertise to sell direct.

The third category of intermediaries, agents and brokers, differ from other intermediaries in that they do not take title to products. They provide an important facilitating function by bringing buyers and sellers together, charging a commission for this service.

Agents differ from brokers by serving as an extension of the manufacturer's marketing organization. There are two types: **Manufacturers' agents** *sell a company's products in a specific geographic area, usually on an exclusive basis.* They specialize in particular product lines and can also carry the products of noncompeting companies. They are used by industrial machinery and equipment producers, auto-supply companies, computer firms, and, occasionally, consumer-goods producers. Sales agents go beyond manufacturers' agents in representing the company. **Sales agents** *have authority to set prices and terms of sale and sometimes even assume the manufacturer's total marketing effort by setting promotional and distribution policy for the products.* Sales agents are used by small firms that cannot afford a marketing or sales staff.

In contrast to agents, **brokers** *serve solely to bring buyers and sellers together and have no continuous relation with the seller.* They inform sellers of possible buyers and negotiate transactions for a commission. Sellers who are not trying to sell a product or service on a year-around basis and do not need a permanent sales staff use brokers. Real estate firms, insurance companies, and producers of seasonal items would fit this description. We will discuss these intermediaries further in Chapters 15 and 16.

FUNCTIONS OF INTERMEDIARIES

Although some manufacturers, such as Avon, sell directly to consumers, most sell through retailers, wholesalers, agents, or brokers, because these intermediaries provide important services that benefit both manufacturers and consumers through a more efficient exchange of goods.

HOW INTERMEDIARIES BENEFIT MANUFACTURERS

Intermediaries usually perform three types of functions more efficiently than manufacturers: transactional, logistical, and facilitating functions. **Transactional functions** *involve buying products and reselling them to customers,* as well as incurring the risks of stocking these products in inventory. **Logistical functions** *require assembling a variety of products, storing them, and providing them in smaller units to customers by assorting them and putting them on the retail shelf.* **Facilitating functions** *involve obtaining information that manufacturers need about market conditions, promoting products through in-store displays or local advertising to facilitate sales, and occasionally extending credit to customers.*

The transactional and logistical functions performed by intermediaries require the purchase of individual products, assembling and storing them in greater varieties, and then assorting them so they can be sold as individual products. Assume that J.C. Penney *buys* athletic shoes and sportswear from four manufacturers: Nike, Reebok, Adidas, and Converse. In so doing, it *assembles* a variety of different types of products—athletic shoes, jogging outfits, and other sportswear—and *stores* them in its warehouses. It then distributes them to its retail outlets, which *assort* the various shoes by unpacking cartons and showing shoes and clothing samples on the retail floor. As a result of buying, assembling, storing, and assorting, Penney has made a variety of athletic shoes and sportswear available to individual customers, so it can *sell* one pair of shoes or one jogging outfit. In the process, it has also reduced the number of transactions required to buy and sell the manufacturers' products: With four manufacturers and four customers, eight buy–sell transactions are required (see top of Figure 14.2).

The bottom of Figure 14.2 shows what would happen without an intermediary. Each manufacturer would have to store its own products, then assort them. Taking on the storing functions would substantially increase inventory costs, and the sorting functions would substantially increase transportation costs, because items would have to be shipped as individual units to customers. Further, with four customers, each manufacturer would have four sales transactions instead of the one required if an intermediary was used. The total number of transactions for the four manufacturers would be sixteen instead of the eight required with an intermediary. If, as is more likely, there are 1,000 customers instead of four, each company would have to complete 1,000 transactions to sell to each customer instead of one shipment to Penney. The total number of transactions for the four manufacturers would be 4,000 instead of the four required with Penney as an intermediary.

FIGURE 14.2

How Intermediaries Make Exchange More Efficient

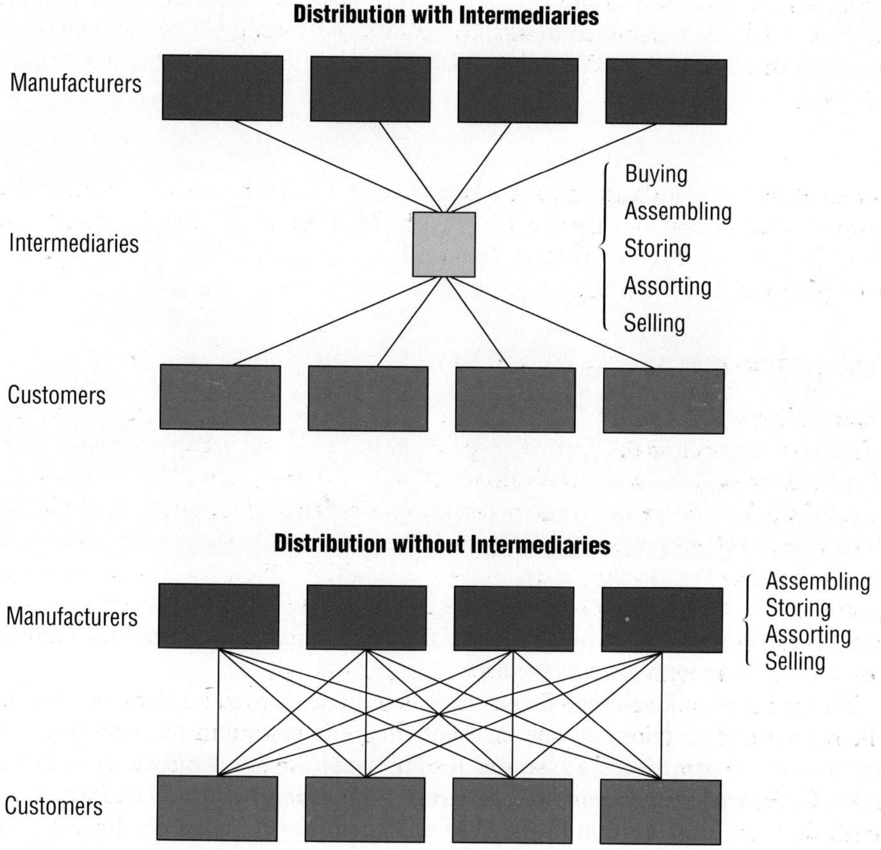

HOW INTERMEDIARIES BENEFIT CONSUMERS

Consumers also benefit from intermediaries. Distribution channels create possession, time, and place utility for consumers. **Possession utility** *means providing consumers with the right assortment of products.* Benetton, the Italian clothing manufactuere, relies on its retailers to determine consumer preferences, allowing the company to make the right products. **Time utility** *means having the product when you want it.* A key ingredient in Benetton's success is the speed with which information on color preferences reaches the factories, and the speed with which quick-dyed sweaters are shipped to retail stores. **Place utility** *means having the product available in convenient locations.* Benetton provides place utility with more than 750 stores in all 50 states.

FUNCTIONS OF MANUFACTURERS

If intermediaries play an essential role in the channel system, so does the manufacturer. In some cases, this means selling directly to consumers and taking on the transactional, logistical, and facilitating functions necessary for distributing products and services. Such direct marketing is more prevalent for industrial than consumer goods since industrial markets are likely to have fewer buyers. As a result, there is less need for intermediaries to reduce the number of transactions. Further,

EXHIBIT 14.1

Benetton's Performance Has Been Driven by Distribution Rather Than by Advertising

the high cost and bulk of many industrial products makes it cheaper to sell them directly than through an intermediary.

Even when manufacturers do not distribute their own goods directly, they are likely to play an important role in channel coordination and management. Any distribution system needs a **channel leader** *responsible for coordinating the flow of information, product shipments, and payments in the channel system.* The largest and most powerful organization in the channel system usually takes on this role, and that is generally the manufacturer (although at times, a large retailer like Sears or wholesaler like McKesson is channel leader). The manufacturer also frequently provides managerial and financial assistance to its intermediaries. For instance, automobile companies often help finance dealers opening new outlets and extend credit to help them maintain an inventory of cars. Manufacturers may also provide dealers with managerial assistance in running their businesses and may even extend cooperative advertising allowances to pay part of their local advertising costs.

Benetton is a channel leader. The company gained worldwide recognition for its sweaters by building a distribution empire of 5,000 franchised retailers in 70 countries. Benetton established its global clout by borrowing a deceptively simple business principle from the Japanese. The principle, called **Kanban** (also known as **just-in-time** or **JIT**) *says that a company should produce and distribute only what consumers need when they need it.*[13] *Kanban* meant that Benetton could ship products directly to the retail stores that ordered them. The company did not have to keep large product inventories, since the products were presold. Retailers did not have to stock large inventory either. Once the colored sweaters were received, they went right on the shelf and moved briskly off.

To control its distribution outlets, Benetton used independent agents to recruit retailers willing to stock only Benetton goods, adhere to 80 percent markups, and pay for orders within 90 days. So many joined up that Benetton was able to create a highly profitable global distribution network that minimized inventory and warehousing costs.

The number of Benetton stores worldwide, plus its JIT system, ensures that the right product will be at the right place at the right time, thus giving consumers time, place, and possession utility. This competitive advantage has produced profits 30 percent higher than the U.S. apparel industry average.[14] As with Avon, Benetton's performance has been driven by distribution supported with advertising (see Exhibit 14.1).

SELECTING DISTRIBUTION SYSTEMS AND STRATEGIES

A key marketing decision, generally made by the manufacturer, is that of selecting a channel system to distribute the company's goods. Figure 14.3 presents the steps required in this decision process and serves as a model for the rest of this chapter.

The first steps require the market organization to consider alternative forms of distribution and simultaneously evaluate the nature of the distribution environment. The marketer can then identify distribution objectives, determine the channels of distribution to be used, ensure the cooperation of the channel members, and develop distribution strategies to gain adequate coverage. The final step in the process is to evaluate the channel system and consider ways to improve it.

IDENTIFY ALTERNATIVE DISTRIBUTION SYSTEMS

Distribution systems will vary depending on whether a consumer good, industrial good, or service is being distributed.

DISTRIBUTION SYSTEMS FOR CONSUMER GOODS

Figure 14.4 shows the five most-common types of distribution channels for consumer goods.

DIRECT MARKETING TO CONSUMERS Some consumer-goods firms use a **direct marketing channel system** *to sell products directly to consumers, thereby avoiding the use of intermediaries.* Four methods are employed: door-to-door sales, company-owned retail stores, telephone orders, and catalogs.

Amway, with 750,000 sales representatives selling soap and related products, and Avon, with over 500,000 representatives selling everything from cosmetics to lingerie, are by far the largest *door-to-door sellers.* Other companies that rely on door-to-door sales are Mary Kay Cosmetics, Fuller Brush, Electrolux vacuum cleaners, and Shaklee nutritional products. Tupperware sells its housewares directly by having its sales representatives arrange Tupperware parties.

Some manufacturers have set up *company-owned retail outlets* to sell their goods directly to consumers. In this way, they bypass the cost of both wholesalers and independent retailers and keep the majority of profits on every sale. This strategy is feasible, however, only if manufacturers can perform the wholesaler's and retailer's functions more economically. Bill Hayden, a former Texas Instruments engineer, started CompuAdd by hawking his low-priced computers from the back of a Chevette. When business took off, he branched into catalogs; when that blossomed he built more than 150 retail stores. Hayden, who envisions his bargain-priced chain as the computer world's version of Wal-Mart, concluded that his strength lies in selling direct to the consumer and not using intermediaries.[15]

FIGURE 14.3

The Process of Selecting Distribution Systems and Strategies

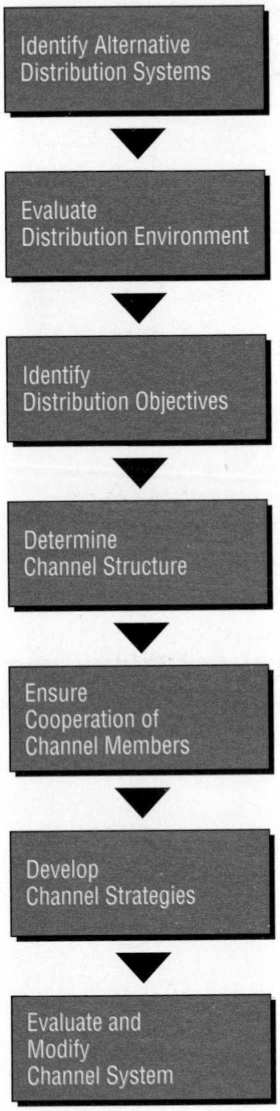

A third approach to direct marketing is *telephone sales.* In contrast to CompuAdd, Dell Computer sells its low-priced computers directly to consumers, without relying on retail outlets. Buyers can order Dell computers only directly from the company by phone on one of their 800 lines or by mail (see Exhibit 14.2). Buyers must know the exact options they want, from type of display to disk drives, because the computer is going to be built within three to four days based on these specifications. Dell's low-price strategy is made possible by eliminating the usual retailer's markup of 22 percent.[16] Dell's target is "computer mavens" who are aware of the company's direct sales policy and know the exact configuration they want in a personal computer.

A fourth means of direct marketing to consumers is through *mail-order catalogs.* While CompuAdd uses them to augment direct retail sales, and Avon employs them to bolster its door-to-door network, others use catalogs as the primary distribution channel. This group includes L.L. Bean, Fingerhut, Horchow, and Fraenkel's Shop America. Fraenkel's, which does a robust American business, expects to add 500,000 customers to its rolls through its placement of catalogs in 4,000 7-Eleven stores in Japan. By paying a $7.70 membership fee, consumers are able to place orders for everything from compact discs to Chanel No. 5 perfume at discounts of up to 50 percent.[17] Japanese travelers abroad are encountering cheaper prices because of the high value of their currency, the yen. 7-Eleven's catalog operation is a means of offering Japanese consumers lower prices at home as well.

MANUFACTURER TO RETAILER Most manufacturers do not market their own products directly to consumers but rely instead on intermediaries. One method, illustrated in the second channel system in Figure 14.4, is to bypass wholesalers and sell directly to retailers. Large manufacturers with their own sales staff sell directly to large chains such as Kroger, Sears, K Mart and Dayton Hudson. Manufacturers can sell economically to these retailers because they purchase large amounts and, as we noted, can sometimes perform the wholesaler's functions more economically.

Compaq's use of the manufacturer-to-retailer channel system has helped it establish a competitive advantage in the personal computer market by offering retailers a margin of 36 percent of sales, about 10 percent higher than the average. It is also responsive to retailers, adding product features and adjusting inventory levels based on their feedback. As a result, Compaq has won the loyalty of computer retailers and is the only company other than IBM and Apple to win substantial shelf space in computer stores.[18]

When a large retailer like Sears is the channel leader, it will sometimes bypass wholesalers and buy directly from manufacturers, as it did when it began carrying IBM's PS/1 personal computer, thus forming a manufacturer-to-retailer channel. There are several reasons for retailers to bypass wholesalers. Like manufacturers, they may be able to perform the facilitating, transactional, and logistical functions more cheaply than wholesalers. In addition, direct contact with manufacturers gives large retailers a better capability to control the variety of goods they buy. It also may speed delivery, a particularly important factor when goods are perishable.

FIGURE 14.4

Primary Distribution Channels for Consumer Goods

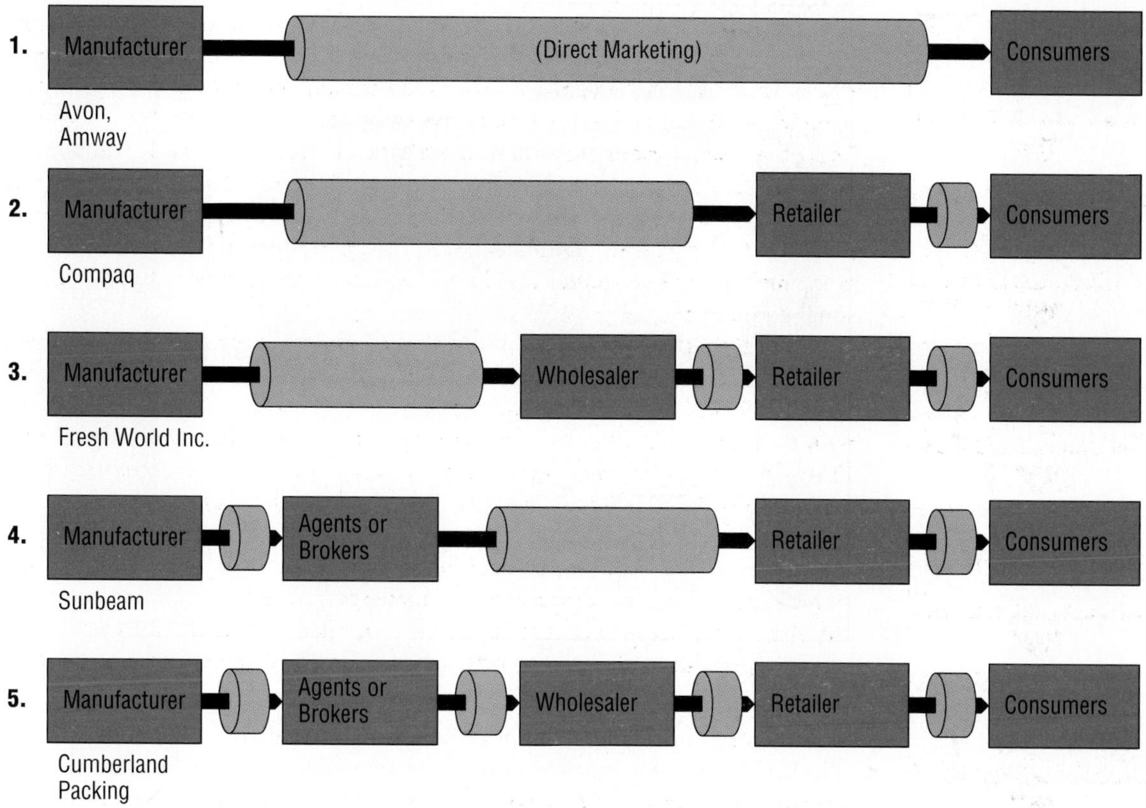

MANUFACTURER TO WHOLESALER TO RETAILER As shown in the third channel system in Figure 14.4, some manufacturers use wholesalers as intermediaries, either because they are too small to sell directly to retailers, or because the retailers are too small to make direct sales economical. Most large consumer-goods manufacturers such as Kraft General Foods or Procter & Gamble use wholesalers to sell to smaller retailers, even though they may sell directly to larger retailers.

Wholesalers tend to spring up in new business areas, where they are uniquely suited to assemble a variety of products from many manufacturers and do so more economically than retailers. For example, they began to be used by retailers in selling computer software because wholesalers could better screen the many offerings from software manufacturers. Few computer retailers had the time or expertise to do so.[19] Wholesalers are also valuable to new product makers as was the case when FreshWorld Inc. wanted to push its specially bred carrot and celery sticks into supermarkets under the name VegiSnax. It signed on with Sunkist Growers of Florida, the nation's largest citrus fruit wholesaler, to ensure its products would reach supermarket shelves.[20]

USE OF AGENTS AND BROKERS The last two channel systems in Figure 14.5 use agents or brokers to either sell directly to retailers or to sell to wholesalers

EXHIBIT 14.2

Advertising Toll-Free Numbers to Prompt Telephone Sales

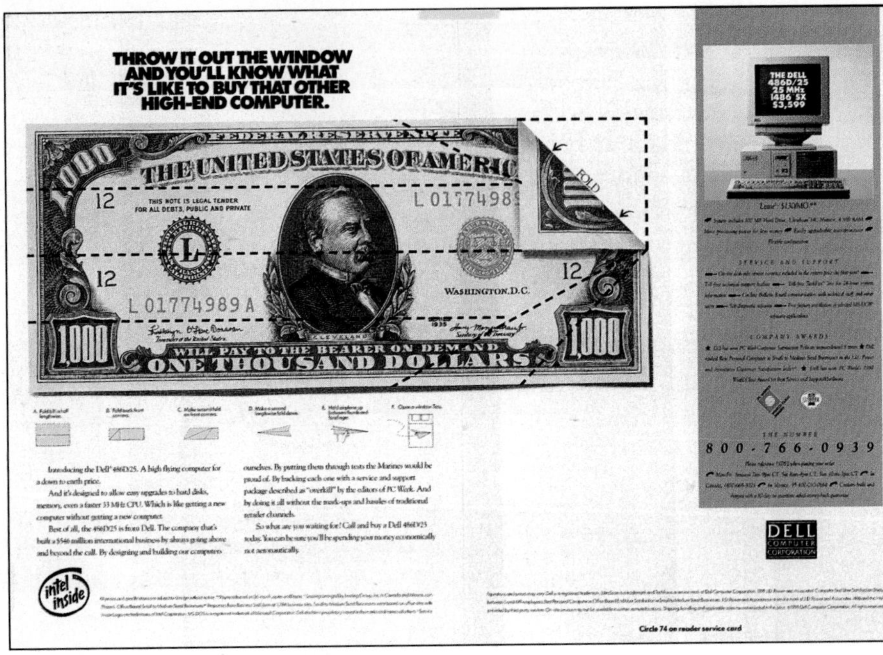

who then sell to retailers. Sunbeam's personal-care division illustrates the former. The division was too small to develop its own sales staff to sell its line of grooming appliances, so it hired 21 manufacturer's agents to call on retailers, coordinate in-store demonstrations, and present the line in a professional manner (system 4 in Figure 14.4). Cumberland Packing, producers of Sweet'n Low artificial sweetener, uses a network of sales agents nationwide to sell to wholesalers (system 5). In 1965, Sweet 'n Low was a lackluster sugar substitute with sales of under $3 million. Now its sales have increased tenfold as a result of the use of sales agents to convince wholesalers to stock and push the item.[21]

Manufacturers also use brokers to distribute items. Fuji had always used agents to sell its floppy computer discs to office supply dealers. As personal computers became fixtures in people's homes, Fuji decided to treat the floppies like a packaged good and sell them in supermarkets. It did not have the sales force to sell to supermarkets, so it contracted with 10 broker groups to sell the newly repackaged discs on a commission basis to such chains as Kroger and Shopko. An unexpected bonus in the deal was that the brokers also began handling Fuji's film and audiotape business, thus assuring broad merchandising support.[22]

International marketers often use brokers and agents to support their marketing efforts abroad. These intermediaries are important when a company does not have the know-how and facilities to enter foreign markets. Agents and brokers can provide much needed expertise to effectively enter these markets.

DISTRIBUTION SYSTEM FOR INDUSTRIAL PRODUCTS

Industrial goods require different types of distribution systems than consumer goods. Figure 14.5 shows the four most-common distribution channels for indus-

FIGURE 14.5

Distribution Channels for Industrial Goods

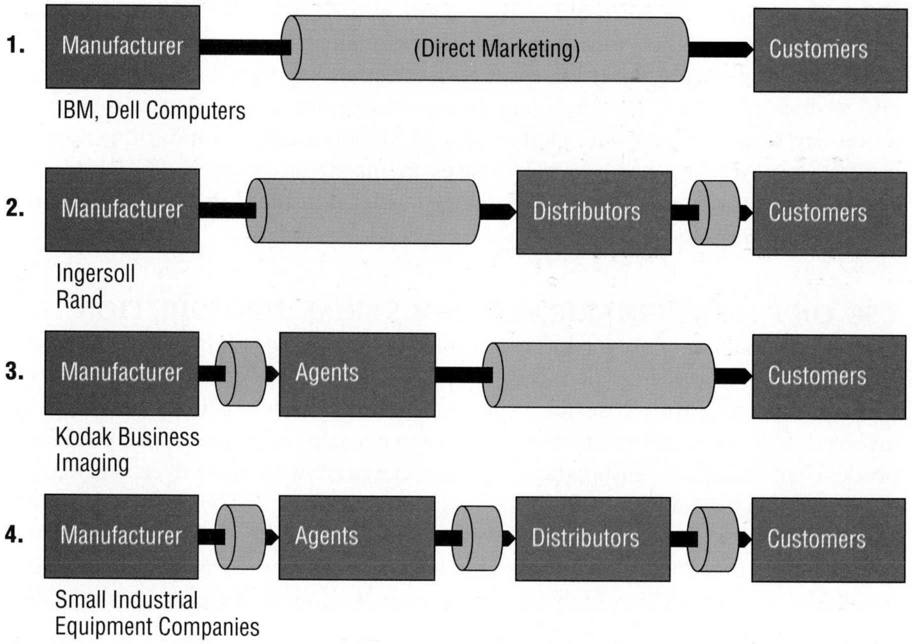

trial products—direct marketing and three different systems that involve agents and/or distributors as intermediaries.

DIRECT MARKETING TO INDUSTRIAL BUYERS Direct marketing is much more common for industrial than consumer products for a number of reasons. First, many industrial marketers have just a few buyers, making direct sales more economical. Second, industrial buyers prefer to deal directly with manufacturers because of the high price and technological complexity of many products. This way they can rely on the technical expertise of the company's sales staff rather than that of an intermediary. One producer of factory-automation equipment summarizes the problems of distributing through intermediaries: "You have lots of very fine equipment, lots of industries that can use the equipment, and just about no middlemen who understand how to implement the equipment to the particular needs [of customers]."[23]

Industrial manufacturers use three methods for selling directly to buyers: their own sales force, telemarketing, and catalog sales. IBM sells most of its mainframe computers and about 20 percent of its PCs to large accounts through its own sales force. Other large industrial companies such as Hewlett-Packard, GTE, and National Cash Register also sell directly to large accounts.

The high cost of a sales visit makes it impractical for small industrial manufacturers to make in-person calls, so some are beginning to use **telemarketing**, *that is, contacting customers and prospects by phone.* Telemarketing generally utilizes Wide Area Telephone Services (WATS) lines to reach customers nationwide. Michael Dell turned Dell Computer from a college sideline to a $400 million business in six years by using a 175-person telemarketing staff to educate potential corporate clients about his low-priced, custom-configured IBM PC clones. Dell played up the fact that it could ship customized computers anywhere within seven days and ensure clients round-the-clock service.[24] Large companies also find it too expensive to make in-person calls to smaller customers and use telemarketing to reach them. Companies like IBM, Hewlett-Packard, and AT&T cite 800 numbers in ads directed to industrial customers to encourage smaller customers to call.

Although telemarketing is the most cost-effective way to sell to smaller customers, it does not work in a vacuum. Many companies augment it with catalogs describing their product line. Dell sends out 30,000 catalogs a month, generating requests by inserting business reply cards in magazines such as *PC World.* The combination of telemarketing and catalogs has let him build the country's leading mail-order computer house.[25]

USE OF INTERMEDIARIES IN INDUSTRIAL DISTRIBUTION The three additional channels for industrial goods—involving selling through distributors (that is, wholesalers of industrial goods) and/or agents—pose some risks, because manufacturers lose direct control over sales when intermediaries are involved. It is often more effective for a company sales representative to negotiate product specifications, installation, and maintenance with the buyer. Agents and distributors are usually more effective when a company is trying to reach many smaller buyers and when it is not well-established in the market. These intermediaries are more likely to be used for lower-priced items and goods purchased in smaller quantities, in which case, they can develop economies by assembling small orders for many different buyers.

Ingersoll-Rand began using distributors (system 2 in Figure 14.5) to sell its pneumatic tools because of expanded use of its lines. Until the mid 1970s, the company sold directly to large users in the construction industry. In the late 1970s, pneumatic tools began to be demanded by smaller buyers, and distributors were able to give better local service to this broader market.

Kodak's Business Imaging Systems (BIS) division, which engineers sophisticated film-processing equipment, uses manufacturer's agents to reach its customers (system 3 in Figure 14.5) because it believes professional sellers are more creative and attentive to its products. Kodak's BIS arm has ceded vast parts of the country to its agents, making them an extension of its marketing arm and allowing it to save on the fixed expense of maintaining an internal sales force.[26]

Still another industrial channel that involves intermediaries is the use of agents to sell to distributors (system 4 in Figure 14.5). This channel is most effective if a company is selling a new line and is having trouble establishing itself with distributors. Agents have the expertise in industrial products to facilitate product acceptance among distributors. This channel is typically used by small industrial equipment manufacturers who wish to delegate responsibility for marketing their line to sales agents while gaining the broader distribution base afforded by distributors.

DISTRIBUTION SYSTEMS FOR SERVICES

As we have seen in Chapter 13, distribution for services differs from that for products because most services are delivered directly to consumers at the time they are consumed. Figure 14.6 shows three channel systems for services. The first, direct delivery, is the most common. Professional and personal services, health-maintenance organizations, airlines, hotels, and cultural organizations generally provide their services directly (see Exhibit 14.3).

FIGURE 14.6

Distribution Channels for Services

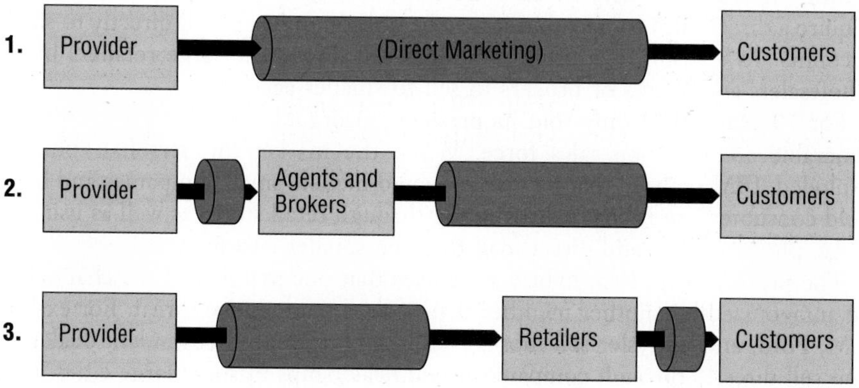

EXHIBIT 14.3

Humana Delivers Its Services Directly to Consumers

In some cases, these services are sold through agents and brokers (system 2 in Figure 14.6). Airline and hotel reservations can be obtained through travel agents, and home buyers often use the services of real estate brokers. Consumers are likely to use agents and brokers when they cannot locate the desired service or product on their own. A travel agent might facilitate finding the right vacation package, a real estate broker the right home.

When services are product related, a retailer is often required to deliver the service (system 3 in Figure 14.6). For example, automobile and appliance manufacturers require retailers to provide repair and maintenance services for their products.

HYBRID DISTRIBUTION SYSTEMS

Many companies use more than one distribution system. This is known as a **hybrid distribution system**. Such systems are necessary because larger accounts often require a direct sales contact, but it may be uneconomical to sell directly to smaller accounts. As a result, manufacturers often sell directly to large retailers but use wholesalers and agents or brokers to sell to smaller accounts.

For 70 years, IBM only sold its products to organizational buyers through its venerable 5,000-person sales force. When the market for personal computers exploded, IBM realized that its market would include small companies and household consumers, so it began distributing through retail stores as well as using catalogs, phone orders, and direct mail to reach smaller customers.

The problem with such hybrid systems is that one member of the channel may be antagonized by another member that poses a competitive threat. For example, GM, Ford, and Chrysler sell most of their cars through independent dealers but also sell directly through company-owned dealerships in some large cities. Company-owned stores are established because it is too expensive for independents to operate them in these markets. The problem is that such stores antagonize nearby dealers who own their own stores, since the company is competing with them. While a danger, it does not appear to be deterring many executives from employing hybrid distribution. In a recent survey of senior managers, 53 percent said they would have hybrid systems in place by 1992; the figure was 33 percent in 1987.[27] The increasing use of hybrid systems is due to the manufacturer's need to reach small as well as large buyers to assure adequate sales.

Retailers, as well as manufacturers, have turned to hybrid methods. When the Staples office supply company found their retail stores were not doing well with large firms, it began accepting phone orders and later branched into direct mail and catalogs to snare big clients. It is also considering adding a direct-sales force to handle the most valuable accounts.[28]

VERTICALLY INTEGRATED DISTRIBUTION SYSTEMS

Regardless what alternative is selected, the distribution system must be coordinated by a single organization (the channel leader) if the channel is to be effective and profitable. This need for coordination requires development of a **vertically integrated channel system**; that is, *a system where companies at different levels—manufacturers, wholesalers, retailers—work together to distribute goods.*

Figure 14.7 illustrates three ways to vertically integrate the distribution system: company ownership, contracting with intermediaries, or a channel leader administering the distribution system. In identifying alternative distribution systems (step 1 in Figure 14.3), the manufacturer must determine which of these three systems is best to achieve vertical integration.

COMPANY-OWNED SYSTEMS The most direct way to integrate the channel system is to own it outright. When a manufacturer owns the distribution system, it usually owns the retail stores in the system. For example, Matsushita, the company that makes Panasonic products, runs 27,000 stores in Japan that account for 60 percent of its sales.[29] Tandy became the United States' largest consumer electronics maker by owning its exclusive distributor, Radio Shack.[30] Such ownership allows the manufacturer to control the way its products are sold and to coordinate the activities of its retail outlets for maximum efficiency. Manufacturer

FIGURE 14.7

Vertically Integrated Distribution Systems

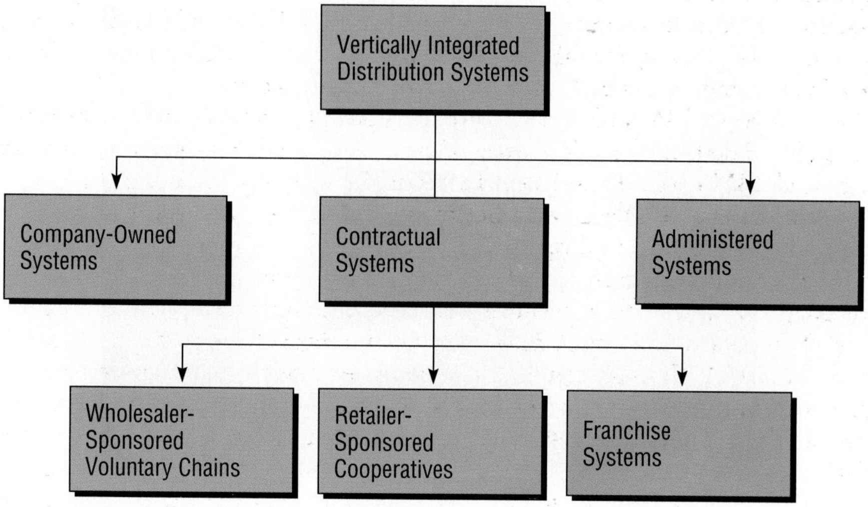

ownership of retail outlets is known as **forward integration** *because the company is acquiring outlets closer to the consumer in the distribution chain.*

Intermediaries can also serve as channel leaders for purposes of integrating and controlling their channel activities. When a retailer or wholesaler owns the distribution system, it often owns manufacturing facilities. For example, the wholesaler McKesson manufactures some of the food and drug items it distributes. The retailer Sears Roebuck obtains 50 percent of its products from manufacturers in which it has part or full ownership. Such ownership gives retailers and wholesalers the means of controlling their sources of supply and is known as **backward integration** *because the intermediaries are acquiring facilities that are further removed from the consumer in the distribution chain.*

CONTRACTUAL SYSTEMS Another method of integrating distributive functions is through **contractual systems**. *Here, independent manufacturers or intermediaries enter into a contract with other intermediaries to coordinate distributive functions that can be performed more efficiently in tandem than separately.* Three types of contractual systems account for about 40 percent of retail sales: wholesaler-sponsored voluntary chains, retailer-sponsored cooperatives, and franchises.

Wholesaler-sponsored voluntary chains *are groups of retailers organized into a chain operation by a wholesaler to help them obtain the same economies in purchasing as larger retail chains.* The wholesaler can provide goods and services more economically than if it had to sell to each retailer separately. For example, McKesson created the Valu Rite voluntary chain to help independent druggists gain the buying economies available to drug chains. Valu Rite makes independent druggists more competitive with the chains by helping them buy, market, and advertise their products. Members get the benefits of being part of a large network while keeping their neighborhood orientation.[31]

Retailer-sponsored cooperatives *are groups of independent retailers who band together to set up a wholesale buying office.* Retailers purchase through this cooperative

EXHIBIT 14.4

Ace Hardware: An Example of a Retailer-Sponsored Cooperative

and collaborate on promoting products and setting prices. These coops are also effective in combatting large chains, as evidenced by Ace Hardware which serves as a distribution center for 5,200 independently owned hardware stores (see Exhibit 14.4). Ace's 14 retail-support centers from Washington to Florida set pricing, inventory, and store layout strategies and provide advertising support for its members. Members pay up to 10 percent above Ace's cost for most items in order to support the cooperative.[32]

Franchise systems *require a parent company (usually a manufacturer) to grant a channel member (usually a retailer, sometimes called a* **dealer***) the right to sell the company's products under the company name and usually specifies that the franchisee will be the exclusive representative of the company in a certain area.* The franchisor may assist the retailer in establishing the store, promoting it, and training personnel and usually establishes strict guidelines as to how the store is to be laid out and operated. Franchise systems are the most important type of contractual agreement. Almost one-fourth of retail establishments in the United States are franchised, accounting for about one-third of retail sales.[33]

Most manufacturers award franchises to retailers under specific conditions. For example, gas stations are required to stay open a certain number of hours and to stock the company's line of products. Soft-drink companies such as PepsiCo and Coca-Cola franchise bottlers who are required to buy the concentrate from the manufacturer, then bottle and promote their soft drinks, and distribute them to retailers.

Manufacturers are utilizing franchising as a means of expanding overseas operations. Adidas is establishing a network of franchised stores to sell its athletic shoes and sportswear in Eastern Europe. In 1990, it offered franchises to 35 sporting-goods retailers in Hungary and is likely to use franchising to expand operations in other Eastern European countries.[34] One difficulty is the different rules that govern franchise contracts in foreign countries. As a result, companies franchising abroad cannot operate with the same standardized procedures that might apply to operations in the United States.

Service firms also franchise retailers. This is the case with PepsiCo's Pizza Hut, which had about 6,000 franchised retail locations in 1991 and plans to triple that

EXHIBIT 14.5

Franchised Outlets Sell a Diversity of Goods and Services

number by reaching exclusive distribution pacts with football stadiums, grade-school cafeterias, airport kiosks, and even airlines. All of this led Pizza Hut's Steven Reinemund to say he considers the chain "a pizza distribution company."[35] Motel chains such as Howard Johnson, and car rental companies such as Avis, also franchise their service operations. In so doing, they organize a channel system for bringing their services to consumers (see Exhibit 14.5).

ADMINISTERED SYSTEMS The third type of vertically integrated distribution system is an **administered channel system.** *Here, integration of distributive activities is accomplished through the power of a channel leader rather than through ownership or contractual arrangements.* The most powerful member of the distribution system assumes the role of channel leader and, as such, influences channel members to cooperate in performing distributive functions. Without such cooperation, inefficiencies may occur in delivery, inventory controls, or administration of warranty claims.

Large manufacturers such as Procter & Gamble, General Electric, and IBM have been able to obtain cooperation from retailers regarding displays, preferable shelf space, and pricing policies. In other cases, it is the retailer or wholesaler who assumes the role of channel leader. As we have seen, McKesson is the channel leader for drug retailers; Sears is the channel leader in dealing with its suppliers.

DISTRIBUTION IN THE INTERNATIONAL ENVIRONMENT

The channel systems we have described typify the U.S. marketplace. Any marketer that assumes the domestic distribution structure is typical of foreign markets is likely to run into trouble. International markets must adapt to the distribution structure of the host country.

In selecting distribution channels, international marketers generally choose one of the approaches shown in Figure 14.8. A company can distribute indirectly by selling to domestic intermediaries, which then sell to foreign intermediaries, or it can sell directly to foreign intermediaries through its headquarters organization.

FIGURE 14.8

International Distribution Channels

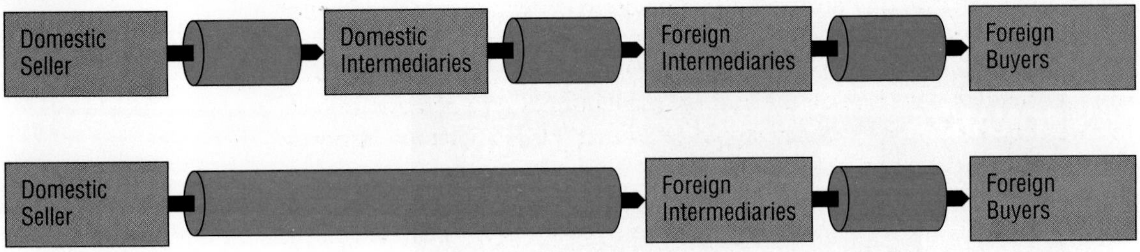

Because smaller companies do not have the resources to sell abroad, they use domestic intermediaries. One is an **export trading company**, *which is a company that will buy the firm's products and assume all distribution and marketing abroad.* If the firm does not want to give up title to its goods, it can use an **export management company**, *which serves as an export agent by marketing a firm's products overseas on a commission basis.*

Larger firms tend to export directly through foreign intermediaries. They may do so through wholesalers, through foreign agents and brokers, or directly to retailers. When larger companies can develop more-direct control over foreign distribution, they will do so. Deere has set up sales branches in Latin America so that it can deal directly with the independent dealers who distribute its agricultural equipment. These branches give the company direct control over the way foreign intermediaries handle sales and service.[36]

Figure 14.8 does not capture the unique nature of the distribution structure in certain countries. In Japan, for example, small "mom-and-pop" retailers predominate over larger stores. Wholesalers are essential to reach the large number of small retailers. Further, these wholesalers will do business with a manufacturer only if a highly personal and stable relationship is established in contrast to the more impersonal relationship typical of manufacturer–wholesaler relations in the United States.

When Schick began doing business in Japan in 1960, it quickly realized the importance of establishing a strong relationship with Japanese wholesalers. Partly as a result, it gained 70 percent of the razor-blade market in Japan.[37] Procter & Gamble was slow to learn this lesson and alienated local wholesalers by discounting Cheer detergent and undercutting their margins. As a result, P&G found itself at a competitive disadvantage to domestic competitors, such as Kao, with stronger distribution relationships.[38]

An added complication of doing business in Japan is that distribution is not a simple two-stage process from manufacturer to wholesaler to retailer. The wholesale structure is a labyrinth of different types of wholesalers requiring manufacturers to distribute through three or four different types of wholesalers before their goods even get to the retailer. P&G adjusted its distribution to account for this complex structure. It sells soaps and detergents first to general wholesalers, who sell to specialty wholesalers, who sell to regional and local wholesalers, who finally sell to retailers. P&G is not always happy with this mode of distribution, because the longer the channel, the less control it has over the way its products are sold. However, the company has little choice if it wants to do business in Japan.

Another example of the unique nature of Japanese distribution is that 75 percent of new cars are sold door-to-door by auto salesmen.[39] Apparently dealer showrooms are considered too impersonal.

One important characteristic of foreign distribution not shown in Figure 14.8 is the high cost of distributing products abroad. Foreign intermediaries are smaller, and the channels of distribution tend to be longer, so prices are higher as a result of the margins required to compensate each channel member. Poor warehousing and storage facilities also increase the cost of distribution. Prices sometimes escalate to three or four times what they would be in the domestic market, largely as a result of these higher distribution costs.

Another complication is that some countries do not have the necessary economic infrastructure to distribute goods from abroad. In Eastern Europe and the former Soviet Union, the road systems, storage facilities, and wholesale and retail institutions are inadequate to support the emerging market economies. Franchises have taken hold because they offer ready-made distribution systems. Thus, we see Payless Rent-a-Car, Adidas, and Mister Donut stores appearing in Hungary, McDonald's in Russia, and Raddison looking to ring the entire Eastern Bloc with its hotels. The combined effect has been to infuse the region with marketing prowess that would otherwise take decades to obtain.[40]

Developing economies are also fertile grounds for direct selling, as Avon proved when it exported the Avon lady to China. Since it arrived in 1985, Avon has become the country's leading cosmetics supplier, selling about $1.5 billion in 1991. One reason for the success is that Avon's 6,000 representatives earn about $1.75 an hour, twice the average wage, thereby ensuring a healthy sales pool. The target customers are Chinese women between 25 and 30 years of age who are likely to spend more for foreign products. Avon believes the formula could be easily transported elsewhere, since it is already at work in Brazil and Mexico.[41]

EVALUATE THE DISTRIBUTION ENVIRONMENT

As the manufacturer identifies alternative distribution systems, it must engage in the second step in Figure 14.3—evaluating the distribution environment. These two steps occur simultaneously, because environmental factors such as customer needs, competitive practices, legal regulations, and the nature of the company's products largely determine the best channel system for the manufacturer.

CUSTOMER AND COMPETITIVE FACTORS

Customer characteristics clearly influence channel selection. A company that sells its products to a few large customers in geographically concentrated areas may find that direct marketing is economically feasible. If it sells to many small, geographically dispersed customers, however, that company will need intermediaries.

Competitive factors are also important in selecting a channel system. If competition is intense, companies may look to distribution to seek a competitive advantage. For example, competition in the luxury import auto market was so fierce that when Mitsubishi unveiled a new line of cars in 1991, it decided to buy Valu Rent-A-Car to give American consumers exposure to the product. Valu turned out to be a crucial cog in Mitsubishi's distribution wheel, not only because it offered free advertising and exposure, but because it was an outlet for the cars Mitsubishi's dealers could not sell.[42]

Companies may also choose new and innovative channel systems to help them gain competitive advantage. Although L'Eggs hosiery had no unique product features, they gained an edge on the market by being the first hosiery product to be distributed through supermarkets.

GLOBAL MARKETING STRATEGIES

Japan's Distribution Revolution Changes Prices on Everything from Tape Decks to Tomatoes

Where does an apple cost $2 and a dinner for four run $600? In Japan, where government-protected mom-and-pop stores have held the country's retail sector in a choke-hold for almost a century. Today, however, Japan's ancient system is in the throes of a revolution. Desperate to shed its claim to the highest prices in the world, the Japanese government is blessing discount retailers, direct sellers, and superstores. The result: a new age of distribution.

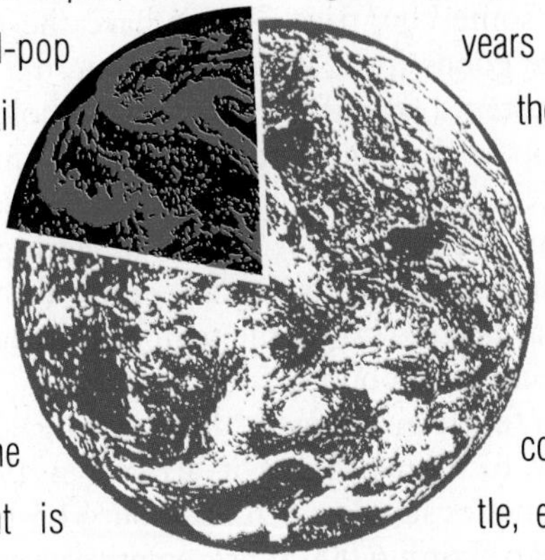

Since the turn of the century, the engine of Japan's distribution system has been small retailers usually employing one or two people. The government had favored them by giving local chambers of commerce sweeping powers to bottle-up applications by larger stores that posed competitive threats. A cultural predisposition against competing with a neighbor also led to situations where a shopkeeper might be the only seller of food for blocks and could mark-up prices at will.

It proved to be an enduring formula until a new generation of Westernized Japanese youth decided against going into the family business. In the six years prior to 1988, a total of 100,000 of these stores closed, paving the way for a new breed of entrepreneurs schooled in Western distribution methods. They understood that after years of hard work, Japanese consumers wanted to slow down a little, enjoy the fruits of their labors, and stop paying outlandish prices for goods priced much more cheaply abroad.

Social trends also played a role. As more Japanese women entered the workforce, they had less time to visit neighborhood grocers or druggists. This led to the rise of supermarkets such as the Summit chain, which could offer lower prices by circumventing wholesalers and negotiating directly with manufacturers. Cut-price mass merchandisers also sustained phenomenal growth, selling in excess of $4 billion a year. Chains like I World, Mr. Max, and The Price Club began anchoring shopping malls that sprouted up across the landscape. The effect on Ja-

LEGAL REGULATIONS

Legal regulations are another important factor in the distribution environment, for they may restrict the choice of intermediaries or otherwise affect distribution strategies. The legality or illegality of several distribution practices often depends on whether they restrict competition. This means that a number of distribution practices may be judged legal in one context but illegal in another.

GLOBAL MARKETING STRATEGIES

pan's mom-and-pop stores was shown in a 1985 study that found 94 percent of small shopkeepers said they felt threatened by large stores.

We're an Honored Guest in the Japanese Home
Amway
Amway (Japan) Limited

The Japanese Ministry of Trade and Industry (MITI) is using the momentum toward larger stores to exact more-sweeping change. To begin the phase-out of mom-and-pop stores, MITI has ordered that chambers of commerce take no more than 18 months to decide large store applications, and their powers in this area may soon be stripped entirely. As a result, 2,500 stores with more than 500 square feet of space will open in Japan by 1993—more than double the rate of the late 80s—allowing consumers access to broad lines of goods at competitive prices. MITI's elimination of curbs on where stores may be placed is also giving a boost to the emerging convenience-store sector, where more than 50 chains have emerged.

All of this is forcing the hand of manufacturers, which previously felt no need to price competitively. For instance, in the clothing sector, the fastest-growing chains have begun designing their own clothes. Whereas local stores once tamely went along with whatever manufacturers said, the power of Japan's new retailers is forcing manufacturers to begin putting the consumer first.

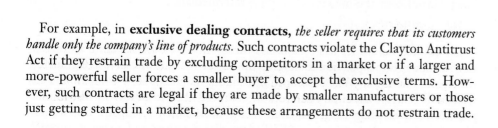

From tomatoes to tape decks, Japan's distribution revolution is lowering prices across the board and proving that a thriving distribution network is a consumer's surest ally.

Questions: What forces in Japan are decreasing the importance of mom-and-pop retail stores? Who is most likely to benefit from these changes and how?

Sources: "Reforms in Store," *Far Eastern Economic Review,* January 17, 1991; "Japan Bends Grudgingly on Retailing," *The New York Times,* November 12, 1990; "Ready, Set, Sell—Japan is Buying," *Fortune,* September 11, 1989; "Convenience Stores in Japan Set Sights on Catalog Business," *The Wall Street Journal,* November 30, 1990, A9C.

For example, in **exclusive dealing contracts,** *the seller requires that its customers handle only the company's line of products.* Such contracts violate the Clayton Antitrust Act if they restrain trade by excluding competitors in a market or if a larger and more-powerful seller forces a smaller buyer to accept the exclusive terms. However, such contracts are legal if they are made by smaller manufacturers or those just getting started in a market, because these arrangements do not restrain trade.

A second type of distribution practice that is sometimes judged illegal involves **tying contracts** *that require a buyer to take less-popular products in a manufacturer's line in order to get the desired merchandise.* For example, an automobile manufacturer may insist that a dealer take a quota of less-popular models along with the most-popular ones. Such arrangements are illegal when the seller is large enough to restrain trade or when a substantial volume of business is tied to the contract.

Finally, the granting of **exclusive sales territories** *by manufacturers to a wholesaler or retailer, giving it the sole right to sell the manufacturer's products in a certain area,* is sometimes judged illegal. Such arrangements seek to avoid retailers or wholesalers competing with each other for the same customers when selling the company's products. Their legality is judged on a case-by-case basis. For example, the Supreme Court found territorial restrictions imposed by Schwinn Bicycle on its intermediaries to be illegal because it restrained trade, yet it found soft-drink manufacturers to be within their rights in granting bottlers exclusive territories, because such contracts do not restrain trade at the retail level.

PRODUCT CHARACTERISTICS

The characteristics of the product are also important in selecting a channel system. One of the most elementary decisions—whether to use intermediaries or to use direct marketing—is in large part dictated by the product. If a product is technologically complex, expensive, or bulky, it is usually more effective to market it directly. Mainframe computers fit all three criteria, so most manufacturers sell them directly to industrial buyers. The complexity of mainframe computers makes it necessary to provide the technical expertise of a company's sales staff to explain the product and to service it once it is sold; their high price prompts industrial buyers to insist on dealing directly with the company; and their bulk makes it more economical to avoid the transportation and handling costs of shipping through intermediaries.

COMPANY CHARACTERISTICS

The characteristics of the company are another consideration in determining what type of distribution system will be most effective for a product. A company that is just starting out may not have the leverage to get its products accepted by wholesalers or retailers; thus, it is more likely to rely upon agents. Once established, it may be able to dispense with the agents' services and perhaps even with wholesalers. At its start, Häagen-Dazs marketed itself in California by using wholesalers to reach large numbers of ice-cream vendors. As the company became established, it was able to sell directly to supermarket chains.

Size is another important factor in selecting a distribution system. Large companies have more resources to sell directly to customers; they can establish sales staffs and the required warehouse facilities more easily than can small companies. Large companies are also more likely to administer the channel system and to exert control over the operations of their intermediaries.

DEVELOP DISTRIBUTION OBJECTIVES

Once the channel leader has established the groundwork for selecting a distribution system, it is in a position to develop the objectives that will serve as a guideline for channel selection. When Compaq introduced its line of IBM-compatible PCs, it knew it did not have the resources to compete head to head with IBM's sales staff. This overriding environmental factor determined Compaq's distribution objective: to avoid competing with IBM in direct selling and to work through intermediaries. This initial objective guided Compaq's selection of a retailer-only system of distribution.

IBM faced a different distribution environment than Compaq; therefore, its distribution objectives differed. Its client base was composed of both large and small accounts, so it developed an objective of selling differently to each group. As a result, it established a dual system of direct sales to large accounts and the use of intermediaries to sell to smaller accounts.

DETERMINE THE STRUCTURE OF THE DISTRIBUTION SYSTEM

The fourth step in selecting a distribution system is to determine its structure. A marketing organization must make four decisions in this regard. The first decision is whether to use intermediaries or to market directly. If intermediaries are to be used, the next two decisions involve the length of the channel system, and the intensity of distribution. **Length of distribution** *refers to the number of different intermediaries that will be used.* Direct marketing is, by definition, the shortest channel, because no intermediaries are used. A channel that requires agents, wholesalers and retailers is the longest. **Intensity of distribution** *refers to the degree of coverage provided by the distribution system.* This can range from the intensive distribution of a product like Hershey bars or Coke, (both of which can be found at virtually any food or candy store) to the exclusive distribution of products such as autos, Rolex watches, or Pucci sportswear.

The final decision in determining the structure of a distribution system is the selection of specific intermediaries to be included in the channel system. Wholesalers and retailers must be selected according to specific criteria such as their size, location, and expertise in distributing the company's products.

WHETHER TO USE INTERMEDIARIES

As we have seen, the decision whether to use intermediaries depends on whether the company feels it is more economical to market directly. How can managers estimate these costs? Suppose an industrial manufacturer is faced with the decision to use manufacturers' agents or to establish its own sales force, and has the following facts:

- Manufacturers' agents receive a 5 percent commission on sales.
- If the company sells direct, its sales representatives receive a 3 percent commission.
- The cost of supporting and administering a company sales force adds $500,000 a year to the cost of direct selling.

To determine which alternative is more economical, company management must estimate the sales level at which the cost of using either method is equal. This level can be computed by setting the costs of manufacturers' agents and direct selling equal to each other as follows (with x representing the sales level where costs of the two methods are equal).[43]

$$.03x + \$500{,}000 \text{ (the cost of selling direct)} = .05x \text{ (the cost of selling through manufacturers' agents)}$$

Solving for x, the point of indifference is $25 million. This means that if sales are less than $25 million, it will be cheaper to use manufacturers' agents; if sales are higher than $25 million, it will be more economical to use company sales representatives. This is logical, because as sales increase, the fixed costs of the company's sales force will be defrayed. Thus, the decision to use intermediaries depends in large part on the amount of sales a company forecasts.

Even if economics dictate using intermediaries, some companies may still bypass them to control the marketing of their products. IBM continued to sell its PCs through company-owned stores, even when it was uneconomical to do so, in the interest of control.

LENGTH OF THE CHANNEL

If management determines that intermediaries should be used, the length and intensity of coverage of the channel must be decided upon. Shorter channels offer more control, because there are fewer intermediaries. Franchising is popular because emerging companies such as the Gloria Jean's chain of exotic coffee shops can deal directly with their franchisees, stipulating conditions for store operations and sales under contract. Gloria Jean went from a single shop in 1979 to a 77-store chain in 29 states by keeping its business close to the vest, controlling everything from lease negotiations to electrical fixtures at its franchised shops.[44] Large retailers such as Home Depot or Wal-Mart also prefer shorter channels that permit them to deal directly with their suppliers.

Most smaller consumer packaged-goods companies do not have the luxury of shortening their channels and require wholesalers to sell to retailers. Even here, though, some have tried to bypass wholesalers. Goya Foods uses 120 salespeople to sell its Hispanic food line to the *bodegas* (grocery stores) in Spanish-speaking neighborhoods. Goya is able to sell directly to *bodegas* because they are well-targeted geographically and demographically.

INTENSITY OF DISTRIBUTION

Distribution coverage can be viewed as a continuum from intensive to exclusive, with selective distribution between the two extremes. The nature of the product will determine the type of coverage (see Figure 14.9). **Intensive distribution** *involves selling in many outlets* and is required for inexpensive, frequently purchased products. Most consumer packaged goods require intensive distribution through food and drug stores. Intensive distribution provides consumers with the convenience necessary to purchase items frequently. A disadvantage of intensive distribution is that it increases the manufacturer's difficulty in controlling the way products are priced and displayed, particularly since retailers can control shelf space.

In **selective distribution,** *a limited number of intermediaries who can provide the desired sales support and service are used.* These intermediaries give the company's products special attention, although they also carry the goods of competitive manufacturers. Selective distribution is common for durable goods such as small appliances, stereo equipment, and furniture and for industrial goods that are sold on a nonexclusive basis. Buyers often go out of their way to shop for these items, permitting manufacturers to limit distribution to a smaller number of intermediaries and thereby better control how their products are sold.

In **exclusive distribution,** *manufacturers grant intermediaries exclusive territorial rights to sell their products in a certain area.* Franchises are an example. Exclusive distribution is most common for consumer goods requiring service (autos, appliances) or projecting quality images (jewelry, high-styled clothing) and for industrial goods where the products' complexities require sophisticated sales techniques. Exclusive distribution offers the manufacturer the advantage of having stores sell only its brands and obtaining maximum control over how they are sold (see

FIGURE 14.9

Intensity of Distribution Varies by the Nature of Products

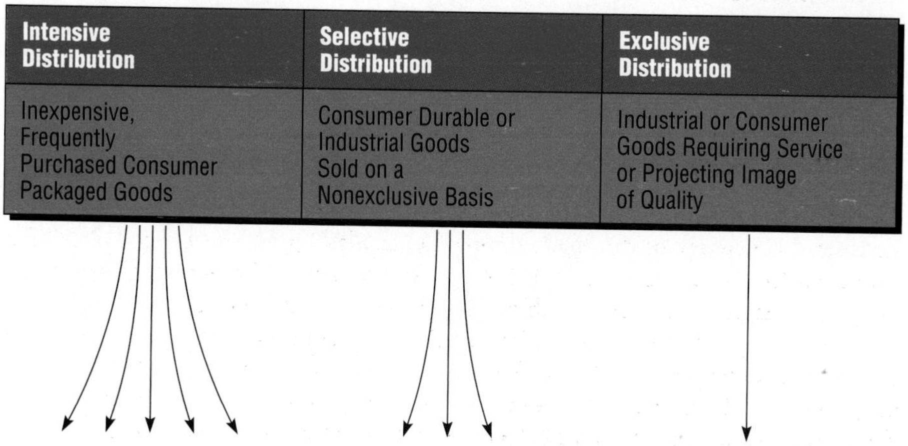

Exhibit 14.6). Exclusive distribution also has disadvantages: There is greater potential for channel conflict as the more-powerful manufacturers try to exert control over independent dealers, and the manufacturer may lose some sales in limiting distribution to one intermediary in an area.

SELECT SPECIFIC INTERMEDIARIES

The most important criterion in selecting intermediaries is their ability to reach the target market and perform the distribution functions at a reasonable cost. Other considerations in selecting wholesalers and retailers are size and financial resources, experience, geographic areas covered, service and delivery record, growth record, product expertise, and reputation in the field.

Industrial firms seek distributors or agents that have the technical expertise to market their goods. Consumer-goods firms, on the other hand, must find wholesalers who can distribute economically to smaller retailers. Producers of a variety of products in a particular line must find wholesalers who have the warehousing facilities and inventory control systems to handle many items in small quantities.

ENSURE THE COOPERATION OF CHANNEL MEMBERS

Once the manufacturer has selected a distribution system, it is necessary to ensure the cooperation of channel members (the fifth step in the channel selection process in Figure 14.3). We might assume that such cooperation should be taken for granted since members of a distribution system depend on each other to do business. For example, General Motors needs its network of close to 20,000 dealers to distribute its cars: It would be economically infeasible for even the largest manufacturing entity in the United States to set up 20,000 company-owned dealerships and distribute its cars directly. At the same time, GM dealers cannot do business without the company's cooperation in providing cars and extending financing.

The common desire to make a profit over the long term enforces some degree of cooperation, but conflict sometimes goes hand in hand with cooperation, as a natural outgrowth of differing economic objectives among channel members and differing views of the way the business should be run. Let us first review the nature of these distributive conflicts and then discuss how they can be resolved.

EXHIBIT 14.6

An Example of Exclusive Distribution

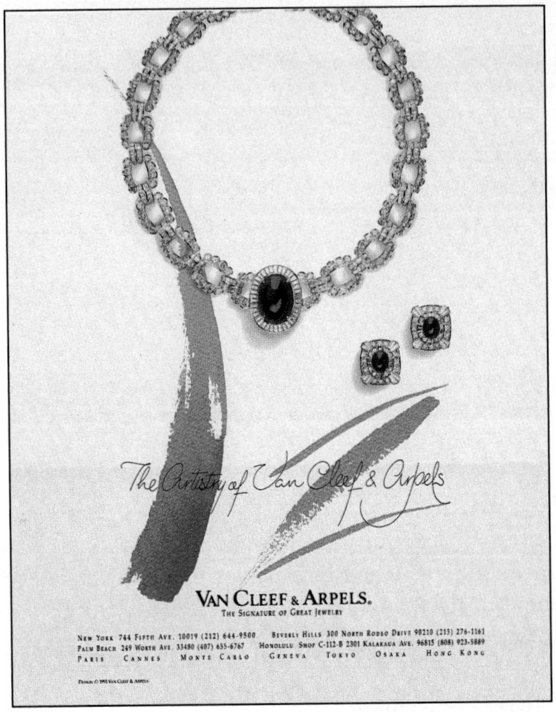

CONFLICT

There are at least four sources of conflict between channel members in a distribution system. One is *differing economic objectives*. The drive to maximize short-run profits sometimes prompts channel leaders to view relations with other channel members as a zero-sum game—that is, my gains are your losses, and vice versa.

TCBY (which stands for The Country's Best Yogurt) franchises retail stores to sell its frozen yogurt. In the late 1980s, it kept scoring record increases in sales by adding new outlets. However, existing franchisees saw their sales decrease as more TCBY stores were opening, often in their neighborhoods. Whereas the manufacturer saw more outlets as a means of generating more sales, existing franchisees viewed TCBY's store-expansion policy as an economic threat.[45] TCBY's gains were its dealers' losses. A decrease in sales of frozen yogurt resolved the conflict by convincing TCBY that a store expansion policy was no longer sound.[46]

A second source of conflict in the distribution system is that *a channel leader sometimes competes with its intermediaries for sales*, thus performing the distribution functions of the intermediary. This is illustrated by the case of Quaker State motor oil. To boost short-term profits in the late 1980s, Quaker State ordered its dealers to stock its products exclusively or lose the account. Many capitulated, only to find themselves losing money to competitors who stocked broader lines. Already disgruntled, these dealers broke ranks when they saw Quaker State bypassing them by dealing directly with mass merchandisers such as Kmart and Wal-Mart and giving them huge discounts. Because Quaker State lost the support of its dealers, gross profit margins on oil operations nosedived from 11 percent in 1986 to 2.4 percent in 1989.[47]

A third source of conflict is that *manufacturers have a national perspective, whereas most intermediaries have a local perspective.* Having spent millions in product development and advertising, manufacturers want to make sure that intermediaries will sell the product effectively and give it adequate shelf space, so the manufacturer will often try to exert control over store operations to make sure their product receives the right support. Retailers and wholesalers, on the other hand, often sell many other items beside the manufacturer's line. They are more concerned with local competitive conditions that will affect store sales than the potential of the manufacturer's product for nationwide sales.

A fourth source of conflict is that intermediaries are independent business people that often *resent being controlled by the channel leader.* Tom Carvel, founder of Carvel ice-cream stores, was called an "iron-fisted tyrant" because he insisted that his franchisees do business his way. Dealers particularly resented being pressured to buy everything from cones to napkins from Carvel at inflated prices. Franchisees finally brought suit against Carvel for these practices.[48] This situation reflects conflict between a franchisor who wants to control and standardize retail operations and independent franchisees who resent this control and want to maintain their independence.

In general, channel conflicts are less intense for industrial products compared to consumer products, primarily because industrial firms do not use retailers, and many of the conflicts just cited are between manufacturers and retailers. A study of the historic pattern of distribution conflicts in several industries found that the most intense conflicts have occurred in the drug, automobile, petroleum, and food industries, all of which use retailers.[49]

COOPERATION

Although conflict is virtually inevitable in a distribution system, it impedes the transactional, logistical, and facilitating functions that are necessary for a profitable operation. As the most-powerful organization, and the one that has the most at stake, the channel leader usually takes the initiative in providing assistance to other members of the channel.

Manufacturers have tried to ensure the cooperation of intermediaries by helping them make their business operations more profitable. For example, after a period of ignoring the needs of its retailers, Reebok began sending managers to client stores at least three days a week to deal with orders, delivery schedules, and customer service.[50] Similarly, Xerox makes distinctly different models of its personal copiers for its different channel members (appliance stores, department stores, telemarketers, and so on) so they do not cannibalize one another.[51]

Industrial firms also recognize the importance of gaining the cooperation of their distributors and agents. As we have seen, Caterpillar gained a competitive edge by providing its dealers with detailed marketing plans that helped them address industry trends, future demand, and inventory management. Inventory management is especially important since Caterpillar's machines require high transportation and storage costs. In addition to localized training, the company often flies its dealers to its Peoria, Illinois, headquarters for four-day sessions that are split between class and lab work. Caterpillar also has training centers in Brazil, Japan, Australia, and Spain for its global operators.[52]

Channel leaders who are intermediaries also offer support to other channel members. McKesson extends finance terms to its 20,000 drug retailers and also provides managerial assistance. Sears provides financing to many of its suppliers.

ETHICAL AND ENVIRONMENTAL ISSUES IN MARKETING

Ethics and Channel Conflict: Revenge of the Retailers

When Hormel came out with a line of microwave-ready entrees that did not need refrigeration in the mid 1980s, the company's marketing staff knew they would face an uphill climb getting the items onto supermarket shelves. What they did not count on was that the hill would have to be lined with money. Stop & Shop, a major Boston retailer, refused to carry the line unless Hormel paid a fee for shelf space. Hormel balked, and Stop & Shop waved goodbye.

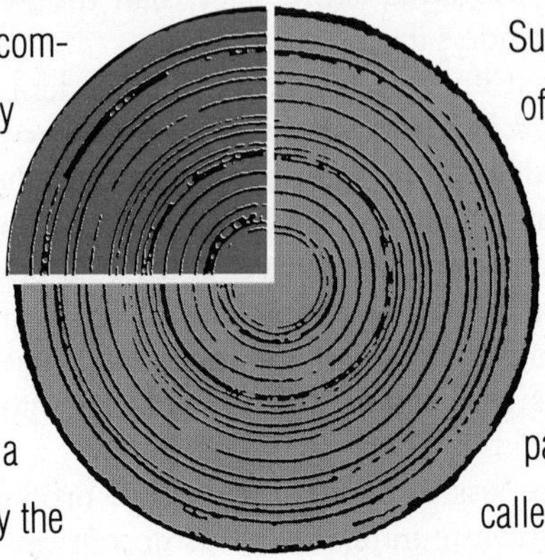

A retailer's demand that a manufacturer pay to have a new product stocked is called a **slotting fee**. Slotting fees are meant to help cover the costs of entering new products into store computers, finding warehouse space, and redesigning shelves. Fees for a six-item line introduced to a 50-store chain might average $70,000. Some manufacturers view these fees as extortion, because they cannot be justified by the retailer's costs. They complain that slotting fees are increasing and, on average, eat up 44 percent of their marketing budget.

Such complaints have reached the ears of officials at the Federal Trade Commission, which has begun eyeing the practice. The central issue is whether giant food manufacturers can secure preferential treatment by paying huge slotting fees, commonly called "street money," while smaller companies get frozen out. Fees tend to be highest for products that compete for shelf space, such as frozen dinners and cake mixes, and lowest or nonexistent for highly popular products.

Slotting came into play after retailers gained access to powerful checkout scanners that allowed them to track sales. Through the 1980s, major consumer-goods firms bullied retailers into jamming thousands of new products into their already crammed warehouses, thereby depressing profits. Since these products often cannibalized existing

DEVELOP CHANNEL STRATEGIES

So far in this book, we have emphasized marketing's role in influencing the consumer to buy. But unless intermediaries see the advantage of stocking the company's products, consumers will never have the opportunity to buy. Two types of strategies, *push* and *pull*, are effective in influencing intermediaries.

PUSH AND PULL DISTRIBUTION STRATEGIES

Companies use **push strategies** *to influence wholesalers and retailers to stock and promote their products,* thus "pushing" the product through the channel to the final consumer. They may offer intermediaries higher margins for carrying a particular

ETHICAL AND ENVIRONMENTAL ISSUES IN MARKETING

ones, they rarely generated new profits for the stores and, to make matters worse, robbed them of much needed space for real growth brands. Since most stores operated on margins of barely 1 percent, manufacturers forced supermarkets to absorb often-devastating losses. The scanners allowed retailers to calculate—sometimes to the dollar—the costs of carrying these products, and they began demanding compensation from the manufacturers.

The practice has grown to include **failure fees,** *or charges assessed when products don't live up to sales projections.* This particularly galls food manufacturers that insist stores can make more money by killing products than stocking them. There has also been talk of some supermarket chains charging hundreds of dollars just to listen to a sales pitch.

Slotting fees are not cast in stone, however. One gourmet popcorn maker who could not afford them bypassed supermarkets altogether and started selling to mom-and-pop stores. The popcorn proved to be such a hit, supermarkets began clamoring for it and waived or reduced their charges.

Whether the FTC acts or not, some see the mere fact that it is studying the issue as a plus. "It's a rampant disease, but it has been too secretive to be resolved," said one food-marketing executive who believes the FTC's involvement could lead to negotiated settlements between the warring camps. But not all are so optimistic. Said another, "Frankly, retailers are so powerful now that if slotting allowances were outlawed, they would find another way to get bonus money" from marketers.

Questions: Is there any cost justification for retailers to charge slotting fees? Do you regard the practice as unethical? Why or why not?

Sources: "Slotting Fees May Get FTC OK," *Advertising Age,* June 18, 1990; and "Shelf Control," *New York Magazine,* January 22, 1990. "Want Shelf Space at the Supermarket? Ante Up," *Business Week,* August 7, 1989.

product, allowances for retail advertising, quantity discounts, contests and bonuses to reward retailers and wholesalers for higher sales, and in-store promotions and displays to make it easier for the retailer to sell the product.

Pull strategies *influence the consumer to go to the store and "pull" a product out of the channel system.* Advertising, coupons, and cents-off promotions are used to create brand awareness and encourage consumers to try the product. (We will be discussing push and pull strategies more fully when we consider sales promotional strategies in Chapter 17.)

Manufacturers do not rely solely on either push or pull strategies, because these strategies serve different purposes. The important question is which type of strategy should the company allocate more of its resources to—influencing the trade (push) or influencing consumers (pull). In general, companies that are small or are not yet established in a market must put more emphasis on push than on pull, because getting the product on the shelf is a prerequisite to selling it. This strategy proved effective for Snapple when it contracted with bottlers to get the product onto supermarket shelves within 48 hours of orders.[53]

Industrial companies are also more likely to use push than pull strategies by influencing buyers through their own sales force or indirectly through intermediaries. Established consumer-goods companies, on the other hand, do not have to rely on push strategies, because wholesalers and retailers will readily stock well-known brands. One wholesaler, commenting on P&G's leverage over its retailers, said "When they [P&G] enter a market with an item, you've got to carry it."[54]

Sometimes, however, established companies may make a mistake in putting too much emphasis on the pull and not enough on the push. When Philip Morris bought Seven-Up, it ignored the need for a push strategy. Assuming that its distributor relations were rock-solid, the company cut back on promotional support and trade discounts to bottlers and retail stores. When bottlers responded by reducing distribution support, Philip Morris reinstituted a more-balanced approach between push and pull.[55]

INTEGRATING CHANNEL STRATEGY INTO THE MARKETING MIX

While this chapter has shown that distribution may often be the most important aspect of a company's marketing mix, we must remember that it does not operate exclusive of sales, advertising, and promotion strategies. If P&G launches a coupon drive to induce consumers to buy a new product, that product must be on the shelves, otherwise the effort is futile.

The U.S. strategy of Great Waters of France (GWF) for Perrier is a good example of integrating channel strategy into the marketing mix. The product was first sold through gourmet food outlets in large cities. GWF realized that to expand sales, it would have to sell through supermarkets. To ensure the support of retailers and get the product on the shelf, GWF offered retailers margins that averaged 10 to 30 percent above those of most other soft-drink producers.

Pricing was critical to achieving mass distribution. GWF reduced the retail price from 99 cents to 69 cents a bottle, just 10 cents more than large sizes of club soda. To increase sales to a point permitting such a substantial reduction in price, GWF inaugurated a national advertising campaign of $800,000, a significant budget considering its previous years' sales were only $1 million. The campaign emphasized Perrier as an alternative to regular sugared soft drinks with the slogan "naturally sparkling."[56]

The marketing program resulted in a sixteenfold increase in sales in two years. Most importantly, this increase was achieved by an integration of distribution, price, and advertising strategies. Expanded distribution permitted a lower price which allowed further expansion of distribution. Advertising fueled this expansion by providing the pull to the initial push given retailers through favorable margins.

EVALUATE AND MODIFY THE CHANNEL SYSTEM

Manufacturers must evaluate the performance of the channel system to determine whether changes are needed (the last step in the channel selection process in Figure 14.3). We have seen how such an evaluation led the Staples office supply chain to conclude that it needed to broaden its network from retail outlets to telemarketing and direct sales.

Manufacturers must also evaluate how well individual channel members perform by comparing actual sales to projections, as well as evaluating each intermediary's record of inventory levels, on-time deliveries, service fulfillment, and use of in-store displays and promotional programs. After a decade of being on the cutting edge of the personal computer industry, Apple grew lax and allowed its distribution network to rust. Evaluation has led it to phase out its "major accounts" direct-sales force and turn those duties over to local dealers, revive sales to schools and colleges, and use service-integration firms such as Arthur Anderson & Co. to better coordinate all its channels.[57]

When a review of channel performance shows a need for change management must develop a strategy to modify its channels, either changing their length or their intensity of coverage. For instance, we have seen that IBM increased the length of its channels by relying more on retailers and distributors to sell its PCs when it saw that direct sales were not economical. Warner Lambert, on the other hand, changed the intensity of distribution for Entenmann's Bakery products after it bought the company. The bakery had previously distributed its products in the Northeast and Florida by selling directly to retailers from its own trucks. Within months of acquiring the company, Warner Lambert decided to add trucks, warehouses, and production facilities to make nationwide distribution possible. Entenmann's distribution system did not change; its intensity of coverage did.

SUMMARY

1. **Why are intermediaries used to distribute products and services?** Intermediaries such as retailers and wholesalers minimize the number of transactions required to sell products to consumers. They also perform key transactional, logistical, and facilitating functions in getting products to consumers. Manufacturers bypass wholesalers and sell directly to retailers when they determine they can perform these distribution functions more economically.
2. **What are channel systems, and what types of channel systems are most effective for distributing consumer goods, industrial goods, and services?** A channel system is a system of interdependent businesses composed of manufacturers and intermediaries designed to deliver the right set of products to consumers at the right place and time. Manufacturers of consumer goods utilize retailers, wholesalers, and agents and brokers to distribute their goods. Industrial firms use distributors (wholesalers distributing industrial goods) and agents. Manufacturers of both consumer and industrial goods also have the option of selling directly to consumers, although this alternative is more likely to be used by industrial marketers. Most services are distributed directly to customers, because services are consumed as they are delivered. Sometimes agents are used to bring buyers and sellers together.

   Vertically integrated distribution systems are those that establish the means to coordinate and manage the channel members. These can be company-owned systems, systems using intermediaries that are administered by a channel leader, or contractual systems. The most frequently used contractual systems are franchise systems, in which a parent company grants an intermediary the right to sell its products on an exclusive basis.

3. **What are the key steps in establishing a system of distribution and developing distribution strategies?**

When introducing new products, manufacturers must establish a channel system and make key decisions regarding distribution strategies. In so doing, they must first identify the alternative distribution systems available, then evaluate the distribution environment—namely, the nature of customer demand, competitive influences, legal regulations, and product and company characteristics. On this basis, they can identify distribution objectives and determine the channel structure.

Once the channel is selected, manufacturers are in a position to develop distribution strategies to influence intermediaries to stock their goods. The final step in channel development is to evaluate performance of the channel system and to modify the channel if necessary.

4. **Why do conflicts occur within a channel system?**

Conflicts are a natural outgrowth of the differing economic interests of channel members. Actions to maximize profits by one channel member often hurt another. Another reason for conflict is that the channel leader will sometimes bypass its intermediaries and take on their functions, thus competing with them. Conflict also results from the national, product-oriented perspective of the manufacturer versus the local, store-oriented perspective of the retailer.

KEY TERMS

Channel (distribution) system (p. 456)
Retailers (p. 456)
Wholesalers (p. 457)
Distributors (p. 457)
Manufacturers' agents (p. 457)
Sales agents (p. 457)
Brokers (p. 458)
Transactional functions (p. 458)
Logistical functions (p. 458)
Facilitating functions (p. 458)
Possession utility (p. 459)
Time utility (p. 459)
Place utility (p. 459)
Channel leader (p. 460)
Kanban or Just-in-Time (JIT) (p. 460)
Direct marketing channel system (p. 461)
Telemarketing (p. 465)
Hybrid distribution system (p. 468)
Vertically integrated distribution systems (p. 468)
Forward integration (p. 469)
Backward integration (p. 469)
Contractual systems (p. 469)
Wholesaler-sponsored voluntary chains (p. 469)
Retailer-sponsored cooperatives (p. 469)
Franchise systems (p. 470)
Dealers (p. 470)
Administered channel systems (p. 471)
Export trading company (p. 472)
Export management company (p. 472)
Exclusive dealing contracts (p. 475)
Tying contracts (p. 476)
Exclusive sales territories (p. 476)
Length of distribution (p. 477)
Intensity of distribution (p. 477)
Intensive distribution (p. 478)
Selective distribution (p. 478)
Exclusive distribution (p. 478)
Slotting Fees (p. 482)
Push strategies (p. 482)
Failure fees (p. 483)
Pull strategies (p. 483)

QUESTIONS

1. What were the causes for a decrease in Avon's door-to-door sales? How did Avon counter the threat?
2. How did Benetton's distribution strategy create possession, time, and place utility for its consumers? What role did the *Kanban* process adopted by Benetton have in creating time, place, and possession utility?
3. What are the functions of a channel leader in a distribution system?
4. Cite examples of manufacturers that have developed a competitive advantage based on the distribution system they

developed. Is their competitive advantage sustainable?

5. What are the differences between industrial and consumer-goods firms in (a) the distribution systems they use and (b) the types of distribution strategies they are most likely to employ?
6. Consider the case of a manufacturer of industrial pipe insulation that sells to many small buyers. Order sizes tend to be small, and sales are fairly routine.
   a. What type of distribution system is this manufacturer likely to develop?
   b. What factors might cause this manufacturer to change the distribution system it is currently employing?
7. Provide examples of a manufacturer-controlled hybrid distribution system and a retailer-controlled hybrid distribution system. Why was a hybrid distribution system used in each case?
8. What are some of the differences between distribution systems in Japan and in the United States? How is the distribution structure in Japan changing? Will these changes make distribution in Japan more or less similar to that in the United States? Explain.
9. Is intensive, selective, or exclusive distribution most likely to be used for the following products? Why?
   a. A new soft drink fortified with calcium.
   b. Low-salt foods.
   c. An electronic-mail terminal.
   d. A new low-calorie dog food.
10. What are the bases for the conflicts between manufacturers and their intermediaries? For each conflict cited, who do you think has the stronger argument, the manufacturer or the intermediary?
11. Why are companies that first enter the market more likely to use push strategies? What types of push strategies might they use?
12. When Philip Morris began distributing Seven-Up, one bottler said, "Philip Morris hasn't recognized that this industry requires as much 'push' at the local level as 'pull' through national ads."[58] What are the dangers of too much push and not enough pull? Of too much pull and not enough push?

QUESTIONS: YOU ARE THE DECISION MAKER

1. Consider the case of a manufacturer of personal computers that is starting to sell to corporate accounts. It is considering two alternative forms of distribution to sell to corporate buyers: through distributors or by direct selling. The company has traditionally used distributors because it never developed a strong sales staff. It now feels that the economics of selling direct warrant considering developing its own sales capability.
   a. What specific criteria could management use in evaluating the benefits of direct selling?
   b. Do the pros and cons of selling direct differ for industrial and consumer goods?
2. An automobile executive cites the changing nature of company–dealer relations as follows:

   Twenty years ago we would go in and tell the dealer, "Take so many cars or parts and accessories; handle warranty claims in this or that way," and so forth. The company's attitude was that if the dealers didn't like it, let them find someone else to supply them with cars. Today it is totally different. We recognize the dealer as an independent businessperson who might have legitimate grievances, and we try to accommodate our policies to the economic interests of our dealers.

   a. Why do you suppose this automobile manufacturer shifted to a more dealer-oriented view?
   b. What are some recent policies that reflect a greater dealer orientation?

CHAPTER 15

Retailing

YOUR FOCUS IN CHAPTER 15

To learn:

- *What are the most significant trends in retailing today.*
- *The most important types of retailers.*
- *How retail marketing strategies are developed at the corporate and store levels.*

Sears: Has it Lost its Retail Identity?

Through the 1980s, Sears took one big slide. The 103-year-old company started the decade as the nation's number one retailer, but by the dawn of the 1990s, it had slid to third-place behind Wal-Mart and Kmart. Sears was caught between deep discount stores with bargains and upscale specialty shops with cachet.[1] It was also grappling with high overhead, aging stores, and garish displays that made upwardly mobile consumers feel that Sears was a dinosaur.[2] Put simply, the store that grew up with America had become stagnant, unable to pounce on trends, because it had lost its focus.[3]

Then, suddenly, Sears began lurching to extremes. Hoping to lure back value-conscious customers, CEO Edward Brennan shut down all 824 of Sears' stores in 1989 and reopened them 42 hours later behind a media blitz trumpeting a new low-pricing policy. By slashing prices on 50,000 items and introducing brand names, Sears seemed to be turning into a discount merchandiser[4] (see photo).

At the same time, executives were worrying about Sears' image with women. Sears, long considered the "bag lady" of apparel retailing, was being ignored by women in shopping malls, a vast market considering more than two-thirds of its stores are mall-based. After hiring a women's fashion director—a position that had been vacant for nine years—the chain started stocking trendier fashions and employing a new "power format" with dramatic displays routinely found in trendy department stores. It even launched a new ad campaign behind the redesign, promoting expensive new collections in upscale magazines such as *Vogue* and *Mademoiselle*.[5] Not to let any market go untouched, Sears also tried catering to baby boomer families through a series of free-standing McKids clothing stores in shopping malls.[6]

So what was Sears trying to become? A discounter, a department store, or a specialty retailer? If Sears did not know, how could its customers? The confusion has kept the Chicago-based company on the ropes. Its price policy has failed, the apparel changes have not significantly improved its standing with women, and the McKids stores have been closed.

If there is a symbol for all that has gone wrong at Sears, it is the company's catalog division, a mainstay of Americana. Founded in 1897, it once had the largest revenues of any mail-order concern. But the lack of focus that permeated the stores infected the catalogs, making them highly vulnerable to slicker specialty products put out by mail-order concerns such as Land's End and Victoria's Secret. By 1991, Sears' venerable division began losing ground and money. Retail analysts began speculating Sears might have to sell its catalog division or shut it down completely.[7]

The only bright spot for Sears seems to be its powerhouse financial-services division. Insurance, stock brokerage, and real-estate services are offered in many Sears outlets. A recent addition to Sears' financial services was the Discover credit card. Introduced in 1986, it is now held by 33 million Americans and accepted in 1.1 million stores, making it a rival to MasterCard and Visa.[8] Ironically, analysts have valued Sears financial services division at $17.8 billion, while only valuing the company as a whole at $8.2 billion.[9] Analysts have little confidence in the ossified retailer and see its merchandising group as a drain on the healthier units, hence, the negative value on Sears' retail operation.

Now, Brennan is trying to waken the sleeping giant by stepping on its toes. Answering Wall Street's complaints about its high cost of operations (30 cents on every dollar of sales goes to overhead), Brennan cut 21,000 jobs—or ten percent of the national store workforce in late 1990. He is also instituting a Store Simplification Program designed to make the stores more efficient, attractive, and convenient. Talk abounds that a merger is planned with Montgomery Ward.[10]

These moves may satisfy Wall Street, but will they prompt customers to rediscover Sears? Driven by a deep recession, Sears' core store and catalog earnings nosedived from $656 million in 1984 to $37 million in 1991.[11] One does not have to be a CEO to know this means Sears has a long way to go to re-establish a retail identity in the 1990s.

IMPORTANCE OF RETAILING

We defined retailing in Chapter 14 as the sale of products and services to a final consumer. Many people associate retailing with small stores and independent merchants. This might have been true a hundred years ago, but retailers such as Sears represent large, powerful organizations that serve as the channel leaders in their distribution system.

Compared to manufacturers, retailers are becoming larger and more powerful in the channel system. The growth of private brands has led retailers to rely less on manufacturers for products and to have more control over what goes on the store shelf. Even when large retailers such as Wal-Mart, Kmart, and Sears buy name brands, they generally have the upper hand in price and quantity negotiations. As we have seen in Chapter 14, some large retailers even demand payments from manufacturers for putting new products on their shelves. For example, Shop-rite Stores asked for $86,000 to stock a new brand—Old Capitol microwave popcorn—then withdrew the brand from its shelves six weeks later because it was not selling.[12]

The importance of retailing can also be measured by its role in the economy. Total U.S. retail sales are over $1.5 trillion a year. Retailing is the third largest employer in this country, representing about 14 percent of jobs. Sales are made by close to two million retail establishments.

The importance of retailing goes beyond economic concentration and sales. Retailing is essential in providing *time*, *place*, and *possession utility* to consumers. For example, mass merchandisers such as Wal-Mart give consumers more possession utility by offering a greater variety of name brands, thus increasing the range of goods available at various prices. They also provide place utility by locating in shopping malls that give users the benefits of one-stop shopping. One-stop shopping also provides time utility by decreasing shopping time.

TRENDS IN RETAILING: PAST AND PRESENT

Retailing is a field of dynamic change, as illustrated by the following review of past and present trends. This dynamism affects the role of retailing in marketing strategies.

THE WHEEL OF RETAILING

Some observers have described a **wheel of retailing** *that produces new institutions in retailing as a result of cyclical change.*[13] New types of institutions enter into retailing with the same competitive advantage: lower prices as a result of fewer services and lower operating costs. Over time, these outlets begin to add services, increase their prices, and become less efficient, thus opening up the field for other innovative retailers to come in with the same low-service, low-price advantage. As a result, the wheel of retailing turns again (see Figure 15.1).

We can begin the cycle before the turn of the century with the introduction of department stores. Department stores undercut the then prevalent general stores in price by eliminating personal service and by purchasing products in larger quantities. They then became higher priced and added "bargain basements" for economy-minded shoppers. Following World War II, higher prices in department stores created an opportunity for the entrance of discount stores, which offered lower prices in exchange for reduced services. The 1970s saw another turn of the

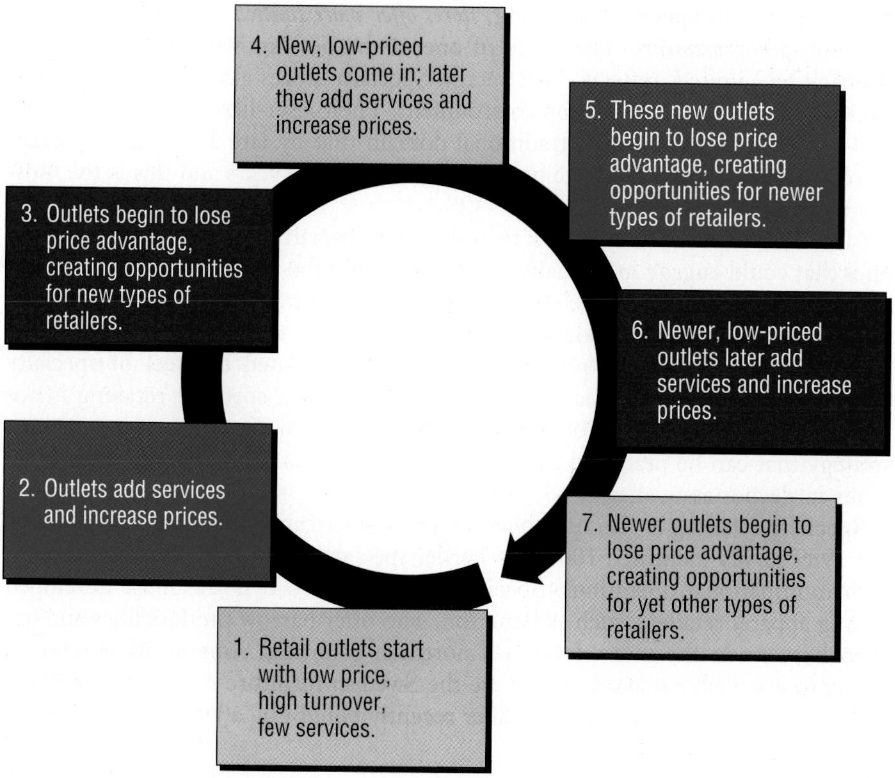

FIGURE 15.1

The Wheel of Retailing

wheel with the advent of warehouse clubs. These were the largest retail outlets yet. They sold products in a warehouse setting with almost no services and at prices well below discount stores. Warehouse clubs found an opening because discount stores could not hold down both operating costs and prices to maintain their competitive advantage.

CURRENT TRENDS

The wheel of retailing continued to turn in the 1980s, with new forms of retailing—specialty retailing, off-price retailing, nonstore retailing, and consolidated retailing. The wave of takeovers and acquisitions among department stores also introduced a new element to retailing: leveraged debt. As more and more department stores borrowed heavily to grow, their debt-to-earnings ratio skyrocketed. Smaller and more-profitable retailers are also emerging to compete with department stores. These changes may result in yet another turn of the wheel in the 1990s: the demise of department stores.

SPECIALTY RETAILING

After World War II, retailers such as Sears and Montgomery Ward came to be known as *mass merchandisers* because they offered a wider variety of goods at lower prices. Discount houses such as Korvettes and Goldblatt reinforced the trend toward mass merchandising.

The trend toward mass merchandising ended in the 1970s, as demographic changes resulted in fragmentation of the market. Consumers wanted name brands and a greater selection of specialty merchandise. Speciality retailing emerged as an alternative. In **specialty retailing,** *stores offer more limited lines of specialty items but in deeper assortments.* The name of one of the best known specialty clothing stores, The Limited, reflects this strategy. Specialty stores also offered more personalized service in a small-shop environment. Their laser-like focus cut so deeply into the mass merchandiser's traditional domain that by late 1990 one key executive was forced to admit, "I've been in this business 40 years and this is the most disquieting time I've ever seen."[14]

Mass merchandisers were quick to realize that specialty stores were not the only ones that could engage in specialty retailing. During the 1980s, every leading mass merchandiser climbed on the specialty retailing bandwagon. For example, Sears CEO Brennan unveiled a boutique strategy to reverse sagging sales in 1988. He divided stores into eight "power formats" that simulated the feel of specialty stores.[15] These moves by mass merchandisers show that specialty retailing is not practiced just by specialty stores such as The Limited or The Gap, it is actually a strategy that can be practiced by any retailer that wants to offer more-specialized items in deeper assortments.

Specialty retailing is also no longer a purely American phenomenon. A December 1989 survey identified 100 cross-border specialty retailers in Western Europe with multinational operations. Specialty retailing abroad is the most developed among apparel retailers, such as Benetton, who offer narrow product lines and has been heaviest in the more-developed northern countries. Among other retailers trying to establish a market abroad are the Swedish furniture manufacturer IKEA and Aquascutum, the menswear retailer recently bought by a Japanese company.[16]

OFF-PRICE RETAILING

A greater emphasis on quality also has led to a trend toward **off-price retailing,** *which involves offering brand name merchandise at deep discounts.* Many middle-class shoppers, looking for brand names and designer labels as a guarantee of quality, were nevertheless unwilling to pay the high prices charged for such items by department stores. This gave some knowledgeable retailers exactly the type of opening predicted by the wheel of retailing—offering the same quality merchandise for lower prices. Stores like Plum's, Loehmann's, and T. J. Maxx buy manufacturers' overruns, or orders canceled by department stores, and sell this merchandise at significant discounts for cash with no exchanges. In one of the largest segments, apparel, off-price retailers saw their market share grow from 6.8 percent in 1987 to 7.5 percent in 1989.[17]

Off-price retailing is not restricted to discount retailers such as Plum's or Loehmann's. Like specialty retailing, it is a strategy that can be used by any retailer. In fact, off-price retailing goes hand in hand with specialty retailing, because both are based on the popularity of high-quality, brand-name merchandise. Thus, when Wal-Mart, the newly minted number one American retailer, offers brand name merchandise at reduced prices, it is engaging in both specialty retailing and off-price retailing at the same time. Sears' abrupt 1989 price rollback was an attempt to battle Wal-Mart and ascendant discounters like Home Depot by engaging in round-the-clock off-price retailing instead of using periodic sales as a weapon.

Japan is fast becoming another fertile ground for off-price retailing. The first large American retailer to try to establish a presence in Japan is Toys "Я" Us. The company's Pacific Rim expansion called for the opening of five huge discount stores in the early 1990s, but an outcry from Japanese merchants, who claimed the stores would strangle local retailers, cast doubt as to how fast Toys "Я" Us would be allowed to advance by the Japanese government. It is being viewed by other major American retailers as a test case of the viability of exporting retail operations to Japan.[18]

NONSTORE RETAILING

Another trend that marked the 80s and is gaining strength in the 1990s is **nonstore retailing**, *which is any method of selling to a final consumer other than in a store.* It includes catalog sales, door-to-door selling, selling by vending machines, and in-home buying by telephone or by newer means such as computer-assisted videotex systems (see Chapter 4). By 1985, nonstore retailing represented about 14 percent of retail sales and is projected to account for about one-third of retail sales by 1995.[19]

Retail sales through door-to-door, catalogs, and vending machines have been around for a long time; however, two new trends in nonstore retailing emerged in the 1980s. First was the growing importance of catalog sales (about half of American adults buy products by mail at least once a year)[20] and their transformation from mass merchandise to specialty vehicles. Second was the increasing importance of shopping at home, particularly through electronic retailing shop at home shows (see Exhibit 15.1).

CONSOLIDATED RETAILING

In the decade between 1974 and 1984, the U.S. population grew by 12 percent while space in shopping centers went up by 80 percent.[21] Then retailers began to realize that limited population growth meant fewer shoppers in the long term, so more and bigger stores were obviously not the answer to long-term growth.

EXHIBIT 15.1

Nonstore Retailing

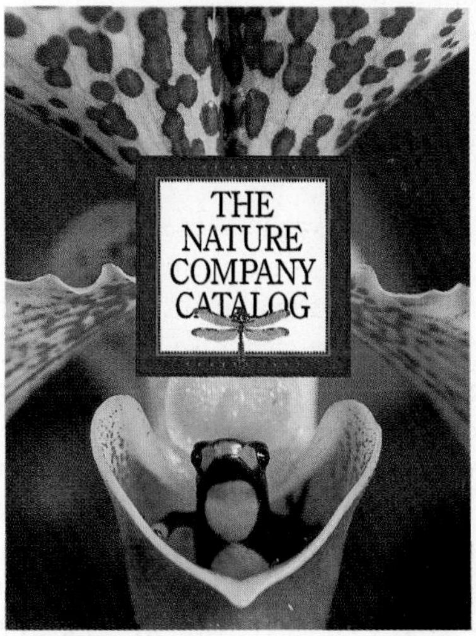

Rather, smaller and more specialized stores were needed to cater to the needs of more-particular and more-affluent consumers.

Through **consolidated retailing,** *retailers began to slow growth by cutting back on product lines and the addition of new stores.* For instance, Kmart announced plans to reduce its nonapparel inventories by $1.8 billion in early 1991.[22] Larger retailers in more-mature businesses believed the best way to grow was to acquire smaller, faster-growing specialty retailers rather than add new stores. For example, J.C. Penney acquired Units, and The Limited acquired another specialty retailer, Henri Bendel.[23]

TYPES OF RETAILERS

The major types of retailers are divided in Figure 15.2 into merchandisers (sellers of finished, nonfood items), and food stores. These outlets are classified by level of service, price, variety of product lines, depth of assortment in given lines, and size of establishment. In addition to merchandisers and food stores, we will also discuss non-store retailers.

MERCHANDISERS

Four types of merchandisers are shown in Figure 15.2 on a continuum, with specialty stores on the full-service, high-price, limited-product-line end of the continuum and warehouse centers on the limited-service, low-price, and broad-variety end.

FIGURE 15.2

Types of Merchandisers and Food Stores

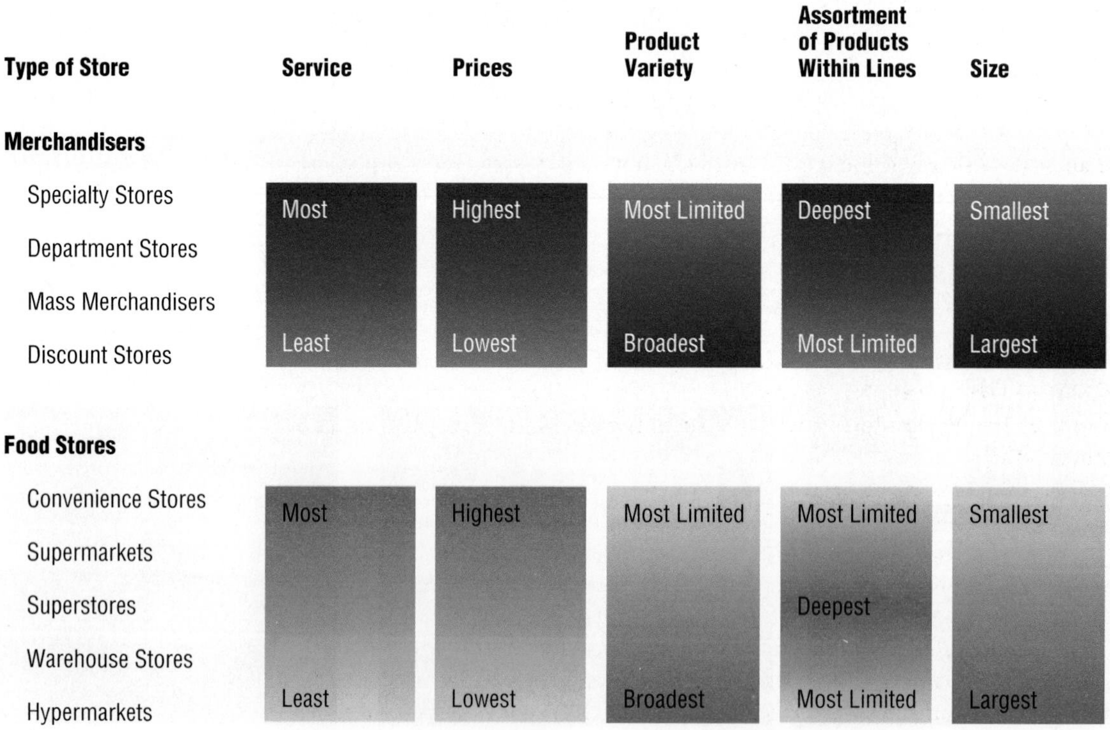

Type of Store
Service
Prices
Product Variety
Assortment of Products Within Lines
Size
Merchandisers
Specialty Stores
Department Stores
Mass Merchandisers
Discount Stores
Most
Least
Highest
Lowest
Most Limited
Broadest
Deepest
Most Limited
Smallest
Largest
Food Stores
Convenience Stores
Supermarkets
Superstores
Warehouse Stores
Hypermarkets
Most
Least
Highest
Lowest
Most Limited
Broadest
Most Limited
Deepest
Most Limited
Smallest
Largest

SPECIALTY STORES

Specialty stores *are small, carry few product lines, and provide a deep assortment of items in these individual lines.* Examples include clothing stores; furniture outlets; electronics outlets; and stores that sell specialized services, such as beauty salons. With the exception of off-price specialty stores such as Home Depot, they provide full service at higher prices.

Most specialty stores are managed by independent retailers, as opposed to department stores or mass merchandisers, which are usually part of a **retail chain** *(retailers with more than four outlets).* As we have seen, specialty stores caught the demographic wave in the 1980s and were the fastest-growth sector in retailing.[24] The most successful are those that can target their line to a particular niche willing to pay for a wider choice and better service. For example, The Body Shop, a London-based retailer, provides all-natural body lotions and cosmetics to an ecologically minded clientele through a chain of outlets worldwide.

DEPARTMENT STORES

In contrast to specialty stores, **department stores** *offer a broader choice of merchandise (usually clothing, furniture, and household goods) in some depth.* Department stores ran into trouble in the 1980s as they began to lose customers for two reasons: (1) Specialty stores such as The Limited's Express stores (see Exhibit 15.2) offered a higher level of service, greater depth of merchandise, and greater responsiveness to fashion trends; and (2) mass merchandisers such as Wal-Mart, Kmart, and Sears offered lower prices on profitable items such as toys, sporting goods, and appliances.

Many department stores reacted by trying to emulate the competition. For example, J.C. Penney spent the 1980s trying to transform its stores into specialty divisions and attempting to lure brand-name designers such as Halston. Dayton Hudson, meanwhile, acquired specialty retailers while expanding its sphere through the purchase of Chicago-based department store Marshall Field's. Others, such as Macy's and Bloomingdale's, moved closer to specialty retailing by establishing departments with higher-quality, specialized merchandise.

Some department stores were too late in seeing the need to upgrade their merchandise and establish a new identity. B. Altman shut its doors in 1989 after a long slide. Garfinckel's, Burdine's, Rich's, Stix Baer & Fuller in St. Louis, and the Wieboldt stores in Chicago all ran into trouble in the 1980s for the same reasons.

MASS MERCHANDISERS

Another type of outlet, **mass merchandisers,** *offer a broad assortment of goods at lower prices than department stores or specialty retailers but do not offer the same depth of assortment or service.* Examples are stores such as Wal-Mart, Sears, Kmart, and Montgomery Ward.

Because of their traditional focus on lower-priced, often lower-quality merchandise, mass merchandisers found themselves at a competitive disadvantage to specialty retailers in the 1980s. They tended to concentrate on their own private brands rather than on name brands and, as a result, were bucking the demographic trends that dictated more emphasis on quality and product image.

Now, mass merchandisers are reacting by moving heavily into specialty retailing without totally giving up their mass-merchandise orientation. Kmart is giving its 2,204 stores facelifts and is offering leading brands as it searches for a trendier

EXHIBIT 15.2

A Specialty Store

image.[25] Montgomery Ward has taken the most-drastic steps to change its merchandise and its image. For years, it was regarded as the doormat of mass merchandisers because it lacked direction and focus on any particular market segment. A new CEO, Bernard Brennan (brother of Sears' CEO Edward Brennan), moved quickly to transform the company from a mass merchandiser into a collection of value-driven specialty stores. The first prototype specialty store—called Focus Montgomery Ward—was opened in 1986 and carried apparel, home furnishings, appliances, and electronics.[26] Montgomery Ward also established stand-alone Auto Express stores for automotive accessories and Electric Ave. stores for electronic goods (see Exhibit 15.3).

We have seen how Sears is dividing its operations to make its stores more like a collection of value-driven boutiques.

DISCOUNT STORES

Consumers seeking low prices prefer **discount stores,** *which offer a wide variety of goods at the lowest prices on a self-service basis.* These stores offer a variety of product lines but very limited selections within each line. They first made their appearance in the 1950s, when innovative retailers realized they could sell the same merchan-

EXHIBIT 15.3

A Mass Merchandiser Who Utilizes a Specialty Store Within a Store

dise as department stores for substantially less by cutting back on facilities and service. Stores such as Korvette's, Goldblatt's, and Target established themselves as the low-priced alternatives to department stores. Eventually the wheel of retailing turned, and as these stores began to offer more services, their operating costs increased, and they began to lose their price advantage. Many then went out of business. A few, such as Target and Toys "Я" Us, survived by discounting brand-name items and becoming off-price retailers. Now, Toys "Я" Us is testing the formula in Japan, Britain, France, and Germany. The toy retailer's product selection—which ranges from candy to computers—will lure consumers in Western Europe and the Pacific Rim who are presently making do with "mom-and-pop" outlets. Toys "Я" Us plans to invest $1.5 billion in its global expansion by the year 2000.[27]

In the mid 1970s, a new type of discounter emerged, the warehouse club. **Warehouse clubs** *are discount stores that offer the widest variety of goods on a self-service basis in warehouse-like facilities.* Just as the discount stores of the 1950s undercut the department stores, the warehouse clubs of the 1970s undercut the mass merchandisers. Warehouse clubs' no-frills setting and low operating costs give them a competitive advantage over mass merchandisers. The first of these outlets was The Price Club, opened in San Diego in 1976. In unheated, unadorned warehouses covering more than two acres, the clubs stocked a wide variety of products—but with limited choices in each product line. Customers had to carry heavy items to the cash registers, pay cash, bag their own merchandise, and pay a membership fee (hence the term warehouse "club"). The Price Club soon grew to 40 stores, with sales of over $5.6 billion in 1990.[28] Warehouse clubs are billed as the hottest concept in the 1990s retailing with Wal-Mart and Kmart investing heavily in them.

Another type of discounter that has emerged in the 1980s is the **factory outlet store** *which is a company-owned store that sells excess inventory and defective merchandise at deep discounts.* Manufacturers such as Liz Claiborne clothes, Coach leather goods, and Hathaway shirts have opened outlet stores. Factory outlets have begun to cluster together in suburban areas to offer economy-minded shoppers a variety of products.

FOOD STORES

Figure 15.2 compares five types of food outlets. Note that convenience stores and hypermarkets are on the opposite ends of the price, service, and product-variety continuum.

CONVENIENCE STORES

Consumers who are willing to pay more in order to buy food quickly often shop at **convenience stores,** *neighborhood outlets that stay open longer than most supermarkets, carry a limited number of high-turnover convenience items, and charge higher prices because of their higher costs of operation.*

Convenience stores have been profitable in recent years because of the greater number of working women requiring off-hour and speedy shopping and the growing number of singles who buy in smaller quantities. Demographic studies indicate this trend will continue. The increasing popularity of fast-food establishments has further fueled convenience store growth, since consumers are less likely to eat at home and tend to purchase smaller amounts of food and necessities. These stores have grown almost twentyfold in the last 30 years.[29]

Most convenience stores are managed by independent retailers. The largest chain is 7-Eleven, which has over 7,000 stores in the United States and has spawned the powerful Seven-Eleven Japan Company. Once little more than a fledgling subsidiary, Seven-Eleven Japan generated $1 billion in revenues at the end of fiscal 1990. Ironically, when 7-Eleven's Dallas-based parent, the Southland Corporation, ran into money troubles, Seven-Eleven Japan bailed it out with $430 million.[30]

SUPERMARKETS

Most food purchases are made at **supermarkets**—*low-price, high-volume food outlets that carry a wide variety of products (an average of 12,000 different products) and offer few services.* Supermarkets give the most prominent display to high-turnover convenience items. Most supermarkets are chain-store operations. The largest are Kroger, American Foods, and A&P. Many carry their own private brands in competition with national brands.

Demographic trends such as the increasing proportion of singles and working women hurt supermarkets in the 1980s. The greater time crunch led more consumers to use convenience stores, and greater affluence resulted in more consumers eating out, further cutting into supermarket sales.

Supermarkets can ill afford decreased sales. They generally operate on slim profits, averaging 1 percent of sales. Some have tried to increase profits by eliminating low-turnover food items and by allocating shelf space to more-profitable nonfood items such as toiletries and hardware. *Carrying a combination of food and nonfood items, known as* **scrambled merchandising,** has improved profits.

Most chains now realize that scrambled merchandising is not sufficient to adjust to the environment of the 1990s. They have learned the same lesson as the mass merchandisers—that a highly segmented population means they can no longer take a standardized approach to selling. They have to apply the same concepts of specialty retailing that merchandisers such as Sears and Kmart are adopting. Specialty retailing applied to food stores means more services, such as home delivery and later hours, as well as more specialty food items in the stores, such as bakery products, imported goods, and gourmet foods.

Supermarkets have also had to use a more targeted approach to maintain profits. A&P, for example, targets suburban shoppers with its Super Fresh stores, ethnic New York shoppers with its Waldbaum's units, and upscale suburbanites with its Future Store outlets (see Exhibit 15.4). Set up like a holding company, A&P uses its logo on only about half its stores, thereby allowing it to format each store to a particular market segment.[31]

EXHIBIT 15.4

A&P's Future Store Targets Suburbia

SUPERSTORES

Supermarkets in the 1980s introduced a wider variety of food and nonfood lines and greatly expanded store size into what became known as superstores. **Superstores** *are almost twice as big as the average supermarket*—over 40,000 square feet compared to an average of 25,000 square feet for supermarkets— *carry about twice as many items, and engage in extensive scrambled merchandising.* Kroger, Stop & Shop, and A&P all began building superstores at a fast pace. By 1985, one out of five supermarkets was a superstore and they accounted for over 20 percent of total food sales.[32] Kroger's superstores include service departments for meats, cheeses, seafood, deli items, gourmet foods, and baked foods. They also have nonfood sections for drugs, photo finishing, health foods, and flowers. The objective is to compete with convenience stores by staying open just as many hours, yet also provide the advantage of warehouse clubs by offering one-stop shopping through greater variety.

WAREHOUSE STORES

Warehouse stores *are deep-discount, no-frills outlets that offer food products in cartons straight from the manufacturer and require customers to bag their purchases.* They are the food-outlet equivalent of warehouse clubs. Like the warehouse clubs, they offer significantly lower prices by buying on a high-volume basis, by selling in a warehouse setting, and by avoiding service costs. Their operating costs are about one-half those of conventional food stores. Warehouse stores are four times the size of supermarkets and carry more items than superstores. Most carry a wide range of nonfood items. These stores accounted for only 1 percent of food sales in 1976, but by the mid-1980s they accounted for more than 10 percent.

The largest chain of warehouse stores is owned by Super Valu, the largest food wholesaler in the country, which runs 16 Cub warehouse stores in the Midwest. Originally, Super Valu viewed the chain as a way to expand its wholesale business, but Cub is now viewed as a profit center in its own right. Supermarket chains began to open warehouse stores in the 1980s. These include Safeway's prototype, Food Barn Warehouse; in Kansas City, A&P's Sav-A-Center warehouse stores; and Ralph's Giant stores in Southern California.

HYPERMARKETS

Another segment of the trend toward larger food stores offering lower prices is the establishment of **hypermarkets,** *mega-stores that combine the characteristics of food stores and mass merchandisers.* They offer all the products of a supermarket, as well as a larger variety of nonfood items than superstores or warehouse stores. In addition, most hypermarkets have departments typical of mass merchandisers, such as automotive supplies, hardware, clothing, and electronics. Some even have beauty salons, fast-food restaurants, and playrooms for children while their parents shop.

To offer the ultimate in one-stop shopping, hypermarkets require huge facilities. Some are over 300,000 square feet, eight times the size of the average superstore and three times the size of the average warehouse store.[33]

EXHIBIT 15.5

Wal-Mart's Hypermart Offers One-Stop Shopping

Hypermarkets were first introduced in Europe, with the philosophy of providing supermarket facilities and then drawing shoppers to nonfood items to increase profits. They were introduced into the United States in the early 1970s, but most failed because American shoppers were not accustomed to buying merchandise and food in the same outlet. As a result, the first hypermarkets could not cover their operating costs. They reappeared on the American scene in earnest in 1987 with the establishment of two outlets by Carrefour—a large European-based hypermarket operator—the opening by Wal-Mart of four hypermarkets (see Exhibit 15.5), and the planned introduction of additional ones by Kmart.[34] These retailers are reintroducing hypermarkets, because improvements in physical distribution make it possible to operate these outlets more efficiently than was the case in the early 1970s.[35]

NONSTORE RETAILERS

Another category of retailers is nonstore retailers, including those selling by catalog, home shopping networks, vending machines, door-to-door, and direct mail. Nonstore retailing is expected to gain an increasing proportion of retail sales in the 1990s because of the increasing numbers of singles and working women for whom time constraints are most severe and for whom home shopping by catalog and TV home-shopping networks is therefore more desirable.

Catalogs grew explosively in the 1980s. Most of the growth was the result of specialty mail order catalogs such as Victoria's Secret and The Sharper Image, which were respectively geared to fashion-conscious working women and gadget-obsessed yuppies. Such venerable catalog houses as L. L. Bean and Spiegel

EXHIBIT 15.6

Vending Machines in Japan

expanded their business as well. The importance of catalogs is shown by the number mailed out yearly—close to 9 billion. In all, the catalog segment accounts for $35 billion in sales.[36] However, in the early 1990s, there was evidence that the boom years for catalogs had peaked. For instance, Penney's experienced the first losses in five years from its catalog division in 1990, and it was not alone: Spiegel and Lands' End both suffered losses. With catalog mailings up almost 75 percent since 1983, some analysts conclude that the industry is approaching maturity.[37]

Home shopping networks use a combination of television (to view the merchandise) and telephone (to place orders). Such shows increased with the spread of cable TV. By 1987, more than half of all homes with TV sets were able to tune into home shopping networks; 3 million consumers are regular watchers of these shows; and 2 million consumers buy regularly. Many of these people regard home shopping as a social event as much as a shopping event, calling in regularly to chat with the host and other viewers.

Vending machines are yet another means of nonstore retailing. They are used to sell to consumers in off-store locations and they have the advantage of 24-hour service. The price of vended items is 25 to 30 percent higher than store-bought items in the United States because of machine breakdowns, pilferage, and the need to frequently restock widely scattered machines. But in Japan's scrupulously lawful society, glitzy high-tech vending machines are rarely pilfered and are such a rage that Coca-Cola is installing them at the rate of 120,000 a year (see Exhibit 15.6).[38] In addition to convenience items such as candy, soft drinks, and snack foods, some retailers have also begun selling clothing and cosmetics through vending machines. In Paris, businesses sell Levi's jeans for $47 each in vending machines.[39]

Some manufacturers serve as retailers by selling *door to door*. Companies such as Avon and Mary Kay Cosmetics are essentially nonstore retailers. In Japan, for instance, door to door marketing has become such a staple that Mutow—the country's largest mail-order house—which sells things such as vacations door to door, has been increasing the ranks of its sales representatives at the rate of 20 percent a year.[40]

Consumers can also buy items solicited by *direct-mail* flyers, letters, and brochures. Certain companies specialize in compiling mailing lists, which are then sold to marketers employing direct mail to sell books, magazines, insurance, and novelty items, to name a few categories.

DEVELOPING RETAIL STRATEGIES

Retailers must develop marketing strategies, just as manufacturers do, but for a different purpose. Retailers' strategies are more focused on getting consumers into their stores and ensuring that they have an assortment of goods from which to choose. A marketing planning framework similar to that described in Chapter 3 for manufacturers is also used for developing retailing strategies (see Figure 15.3). Retailers must evaluate their environment, develop objectives, assess alternative strategies, and then evaluate and control them, just as manufacturers do.

Figure 15.3 includes the development of strategies for the entire retail corporation and of the individual store. At the corporate level, retail chains must develop strategic plans that will determine to what extent they will be specialty or general merchandisers, full or off-price merchants, and store or nonstore retailers. Also, corporate planning is necessary to determine whether the company should acquire other retail units or even other businesses outside of retailing. At the store level, retailers must identify target segments and appeal to these segments by developing a marketing mix appropriate for each store.

EVALUATE OPPORTUNITIES IN THE RETAIL ENVIRONMENT

The first step in developing retail strategies is to evaluate the opportunities and risks in the retail environment. Consumer, competitive, technological, legal, ecological, and economic influences are involved.

THE CONSUMER

Retailers must assess the environmental trends that affect consumer needs. Two of the most important influences on retail strategies—greater affluence and less time for shopping—have resulted from environmental trends such as the increasing proportion of singles and working women, the greater number of dual-earning households, and the greater affluence of baby boomers approaching middle age. These trends have had a major effect on the strategies of the three key retailing sectors—merchandisers, food stores, and nonstore retailers.

It was a key demographic trend—the increasing proportion of working women—that led Sears to reorient its apparel line. CEO Brennan feared that Sears was ignoring this powerful demographic category by stocking its stores with tired old merchandise, such as a $6.99 pair of pull-on pants made of spongy polyester, so he hired Lee Hogan Cass away from the Southern California-based Broadway department-store chain to become his fashion director. Her job was to fill Sears' aisles with dress-for-success clothing that women would feel comfortable wearing to work. But it was hard going. Shortly after her arrival, Ms. Cass told one of the store's scarf buyers that he had just handed her "the ugliest merchandise I've ever seen." In order to appeal to working women, said Cass: "There's only one way to go, which is up, meaning higher priced, higher quality merchandise."[41]

Retailers also study the way individual consumers evaluate and select stores. The process of selecting a store is not that different from the process of brand selection described in Chapter 5. Consumers process information about a store from various sources—friends, salespeople, advertising, and their own experiences. They develop an image of the store and this influences their selection. They will then assess their shopping experience and decide whether they would like to return to the store. If they begin to shop at the same store, they may develop store loyalty in the same way they develop brand loyalty.

FIGURE 15.3

Developing Retail Strategies

Retailers attempt to influence consumer images of their stores to foster store loyalty. For example, when Tandy began to worry about static growth in its consumer electronics segment in 1990, it opened a fleet of stores specifically targeting women, under its new The Edge division. Tandy executives were convinced that women offered a whole new market but were turned off by the hardware-heavy orientation of most of their Radio Shack outlets. The Edge stores were boutique like, with products encased in glass, extra sales help, and soft features that mirrored fine jewelry stores—a complete change in image from the typical Radio Shack store.[42]

COMPETITION

In order to develop a competitive advantage based on price, quality of merchandise, or service, retailers must evaluate the actions of their competitors. Most retailers were competing on two fronts in the 1980s. First, they were competing with retailers that sold the same types of goods. For example, Kmart was competing with Sears, A&P with Kroger, The Limited with The Gap. Second, they were competing with different types of retailers. When Montgomery Ward started selling electronics in stand-alone stores, it found itself competing with electronics specialty stores such as Newmark and Lewis.

Competition became more intense on both fronts in the last decade. Store expansions in the 1960s and 1970s meant that the same types of stores were competing for consumers. Many of these retailers concluded that the best way to gain a competitive advantage was to go beyond their traditional retail domains and compete in specialty and off-price retailing. As a result, competition between different types of retailers heated up, and the lines between mass merchandisers, department stores, and specialty retailers became more blurred.

This blurring has put some of the largest retailers on a collision course. Analysts estimate that within five years, Wal-Mart, Kmart, and Target—which together account for 70 percent of the discount retail business—will have 75 percent of their turf in common and overlap in about 40 percent of their territories.[43]

Greater competitive intensity and decreasing retail profits are forcing retailers to reduce their costs in order to maintain profits. More retailers began to use scanners to electronically check out products, and automated merchandise-handling systems in their distribution centers as a way to reduce costs. Toys "Я" Us and Wal-Mart developed a competitive advantage by selling at lower prices made possible by the lower costs of their more-efficient physical distribution systems. Home Depot's near fanatical focus on technology has caused them to install point-of-sale registers that tie in with headquarter's main computer system, thereby allowing them to instantly analyze consumer preference. Little wonder that Home Depot is being called the next Wal-Mart.[44]

INTERNATIONAL COMPETITION

The European community's creation of a Common Market—a single market of 320 million people in 1992—heralded a new era of competition abroad. This Pan-Europeanism is leading local retailers to look at untapped markets beyond their borders.

GLOBAL MARKETING STRATEGIES

Japan: Door-to-Door Salmon?

Japan may be a global cutting-edge producer of high-technology products, but when it comes to demographic trends, it is at least a decade behind the United States. Hence, Japanese retailers are just now beginning to deal with the rise of working women and the advent of baby boomers as their society demands more convenient forms of shopping. As Japanese merchants are forced to become more consumer oriented, they have embraced nonstore retailing with a passion.

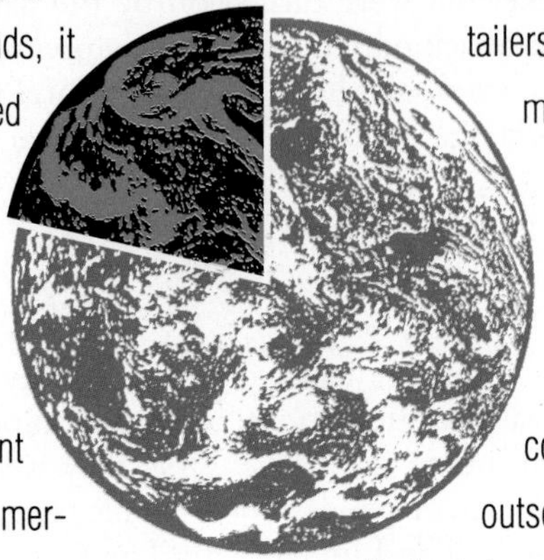

While the Avon lady may be an American anachronism, door-to-door selling is sweeping Japan, and many companies are undertaking recruitment drives to expand their operations. Gakken, a retailer of school supplies, boasts the largest direct-sales force in the country, with 80,000 employees. It uses its field representatives not only to sell but to cull data on its youth market so that it can develop better products and later sell the information to other retailers seeking opportunities in the youth market. The rise in door-to-door selling, however, has bred competition in some strange quarters. For instance, when trucking firms began shipping salted salmon direct to consumers in the mid 1980s, they outsold department stores that traditionally had done well with the fish during gift-giving seasons.

The Japanese are also perfecting another form of nonstore retailing: Kiosks are beginning to appear in offices, railway stations, and other public locations, allowing commuters to buy such products as shirts while they wait for trains or take coffee breaks. In 1987, the leading Japanese retailer, Matsuzakaya, went so far as to develop a satellite link with a West German department store so that its customers could

Some companies are simply expanding their chains. For instance, UK-based Laura Ashley went into Belgium, Switzerland, France, Norway, and eight other countries. Others are seeking to expand via acquisition or joint partnerships. Delhaize "le Lion," one of Belgium's largest retailers, has taken a 40-percent stake in a joint venture with Pingo Doce, a Portugal food retailer, to develop a Portuguese foodstore chain. A third group of retailers, outside the twelve-nation European Community, are adding to the competitive mix by gaining a foothold in the new market. U.S.-based Toys "Я" Us is already operating in France and Germany, while Switzerland's Bally footwear outlets have branches throughout Europe.

International competition may also take the form of foreign retailers using American techniques to change the way business is conducted on their own soil. In Japan, for instance, the Daiei chain has prospered into a 204-store giant by mirroring American-style discounting. In early 1991, its CEO, Isao Nakauchi,

GLOBAL MARKETING STRATEGIES

choose from a wide array of European goods in its kiosks—and get them in half the time it takes to receive traditional mail-order merchandise.

Catalogs have also become a retailing mainstay—accounting for roughly a third of nonstore sales—and the Japanese are innovatively adapting them to their customs. For example, wedding couples are expected to present gift-giving guests with tokens of their appreciation that have roughly half the value of the original wedding gift. Respecting the custom can be torture for couples who get hundreds of presents. Enter Seibu. The company offers catalogs that list items by price and provide a gift-giving service that takes care of choosing appropriate selections. For their troubles, Seibu and others in the field get to expand their mailing lists while sending wedding guests their catalogs.

If the rise of nonstore retailing in Japan carries risks, it is for small merchants who will find themselves victims of convenience and the new internationalization of Japanese consumers. The larger chains view nonstore retailing as an opportunity to establish alternative channels of distribution and they expect revenues from nonstore retailing to far outweigh any declines in store sales. Nonstore retailing promises to be a growth industry in Japan in the 1990s.

Questions: Why is nonstore retailing becoming increasingly popular in Japan? What are the opportunities and risks of nonstore retailing for Japanese retailers?

Source: "The Japanese Yen for Non-Store Retailing," *Direct Marketing*, April 1989, p. 24.

announced his intent to buy-out two Tokyo rivals and to become the Wal-Mart of Japan. Such a move is expected to usher in an unprecedented era of local competition.[45]

TECHNOLOGY

In addition to electronic check-out systems and automated distribution centers, 1990s technology is producing another innovation on the retail landscape—electronic retailing; that is, out-of-store kiosks with computer terminals that permit shoppers to obtain product information and to order by using their credit cards. An offshoot of this is in-store video retailing. Wal-Mart has invested heavily in several prototype "stores of the future," which feature shopping carts equipped with video screens that flash product and price data for each department. The store also features the Wal-Mart Arts Report and Wal-Mart Sound Associates, twin stations that let consumers preview movies and music.[46]

Advances in technology have also improved the physical distribution of goods. As we have seen in Chapter 4, automated check-out counters using electronic scanners have become more widespread. Electronic scanning systems, such as that used by Toys "Я" Us, allows the company to obtain instant sales information from its retail stores and to maintain inventory levels based on sales. Retailers have also developed automated merchandise-handling systems. Many of Toys "Я" Us warehouses have automated facilities that process, store, and assemble merchandise for shipment. These advances in physical distribution are considered in Chapter 16.

LEGAL INFLUENCES

Retailers are prohibited from engaging in **horizontal price fixing,** *which is an agreement among retailers to set a common price in a given area,* and **vertical price fixing,** *an agreement between retailers and manufacturers to fix prices.* In addition, if a larger retailer puts pressure on smaller manufacturers to give it preferential prices, it is guilty of violating the Robinson-Patman Act (see Chapter 4). A&P was involved in a five-year battle with the FTC over charges that it tried to force its suppliers to grant it lower prices than those charged to other buyers.[47]

Retailers are also prohibited from using deceptive practices such as **bait-and-switch pricing,** *in which they systematically advertise products at unusually low prices to get consumers into the store, then claim they are out of the advertised item and attempt to persuade consumers to buy a higher-priced product.*

ECOLOGICAL ISSUES

As we have seen in Chapter 1, the 1980s brought a new groundswell of concern about ecological issues, and the 1990s promise to see this concern widen. The trend finds retailers in a win–win situation as many discover they can make a tidy profit while performing a public service.

Bloomingdale's was among the first to jump on the environmental bandwagon, opening 100% Natural Shops in 14 of its 16 locations during the Christmas 1990 season. At the same time, Woodward & Lothrop set up Planet Earth shops in its 30 outlets, featuring T-shirts that carried wildlife messages, toys crafted from plantation-grown trees, and calendars made on recycled paper. Wal-Mart has also encouraged environmental consciousness by identifying with green tags products that improve the environment.[48]

THE ECONOMY

Retailers are particularly sensitive to changes in economic conditions, because a good proportion of retail sales are tied to disposable income. The only retail segment that is truly resistant to economic downturns is food stores. In an economic downturn, consumers are more likely to cut down on purchases of apparel, furniture, jewelry, or automobiles than on basics such as food and toiletries. Hence, the 1990–92 recession claimed a record number of bankruptcies—50 major retailers representing $23.7 billion in sales.[49] Many surviving retailers revised their sales estimates downward and put more pressure on store managers to control inventories because of the poor economic outlook.

Perhaps the only winners in the 1990–92 recession were warehouse clubs, which grew so fast that experts began using words such as "mind-boggling" to describe their future promise. Among the specialty stores that emerged in surprisingly strong shape were The Gap, which had an audience highly focused on its moderately priced apparel, and The Limited, which had a diverse portfolio.

DEVELOP RETAIL OBJECTIVES

The second step in developing retail strategies is to set objectives based on the opportunities identified in the organization's environmental analysis. These objectives should be broad enough to guide corporate strategies in the form of an overall mission statement and also be specific enough to measure performance at the store level.

CORPORATE MISSION

Retailers must develop a *mission statement* to guide strategies at the corporate level. For example, Leslie Wexner, founder of The Limited, saw the need for specialty apparel stores across socioeconomic groups. As a result, he developed a mission for The Limited to "blanket every segment of the women's apparel business" with a separate chain of stores and "become a $10 billion company with 10 percent after-tax profits by the mid 1990s."[50] This mission statement determined the company's acquisition strategy. For example, the company bought Lerner Stores to appeal to price-conscious shoppers, Sizes Unlimited to sell budget-priced large sizes, and Lane Bryant to target women who wanted more expensive large-sized apparel.

PERFORMANCE GOALS

Performance goals must be established to evaluate the success of the company and the individual stores' retail strategies. Goals at the corporate level involve total company sales, return on investment, and net profits. Goals at the store level involve more specific criteria such as sales by department and by individual item. A good measure of effective space utilization is dollar sales per square foot. Wal-Mart's expenses are nearly six percentage points lower than Kmart's, because Wal-Mart has higher sales per square foot.[51] Another criterion of performance is the **stock turnover rate,** *that is, the rate at which a store's inventory moves over a specific period of time.* One study found that retailers with the highest profits also have the highest stock turnover.[52] Supermarkets require stock turns averaging 25 to 30 times a year or about once every other week to be profitable. Mass merchandisers require an average of 15 to 17 stock turns a year.[53]

Another effective measure of performance is **return on assets,** *which is the product of the stock turnover and the profit margin.* (**Profit margin** *is net profits as a percent of sales.*) Thus, a supermarket with a stock turnover of 25 and a 1 percent profit margin is achieving a 25 percent return on assets.

DEVELOP CORPORATE RETAIL STRATEGIES

Larger retailers must develop strategies at the corporate level before considering more-specific store strategies. These corporate strategies generally involve decisions regarding whether to promote growth by external acquisitions or by internal development through store expansion.

ETHICAL AND ENVIRONMENTAL ISSUES IN MARKETING

The Day Dave Nichol Saw Green

At first, Dave Nichol thought it was the dullest, dumbest book he'd ever seen; then it made him a fortune.

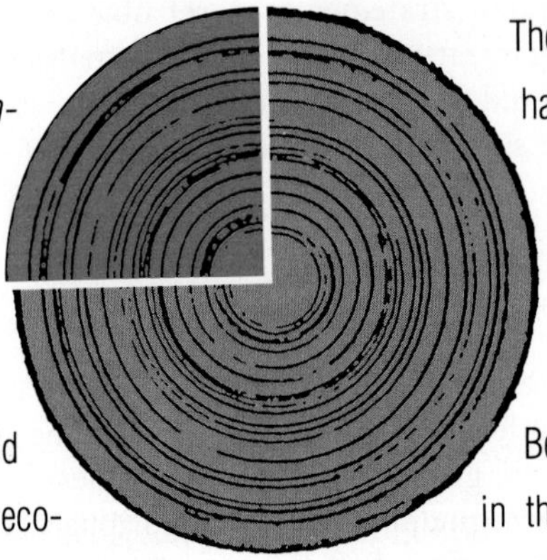

The book was *The Green Consumer Guide,* and Nichol, the product-development president of the 350-store Canadian supermarket chain Loblaw Co., picked it up on a swing through London. "Why would people want to know where to buy ecologically correct diapers," he chuckled dismissively. But when Nichol returned to Canada and discovered the *Guide* was a UK best seller, his smile disappeared.

Today, Nichol is on the cutting edge of eco-marketing and father to the world's first supermarket line of "environment friendly" products. His 100-item line of GREEN products ended its first year in June 1990 by generating $52 million in sales, with profit margins roughly equal to non-GREEN competitors.

The GREEN line fused concepts that had been brewing in Europe for some time: Chlorine-free coffee filters were sold in Sweden, nonchlorine-pulp diapers in Britain, and vegetable oil-based cleaning products in Belgium. Even Loblaw had its fingers in the pie, with a few brands under a now-defunct Nature's Choice logo. But it took Nichol to sew the threads together.

During development of the $8.7 million line, Nichol set about polling environmental groups to see what they wanted on supermarket shelves. This served a dual purpose. Not only did he gain insights, but he gained their trust, and a business relationship ensued. For instance, in exchange for backing seven

EXTERNAL ACQUISITION

Many retail chains have reacted to slow growth in their areas by acquiring higher-growth retailers. For example, Kmart, in the face of competition from Wal-Mart's fast-growing Sam's stores, bought 51 percent of the Dutch warehouse company Makro. Kmart also acquired Builders Square, to confront Home Depot, and the Sports Authority chain to compete in the growing athletic apparel market.

Some retailers reacted to slow growth by trying to find profit opportunities outside retailing. The leader in this acquisition strategy has been Sears. The company sought growth in financial services by first establishing Allstate Insurance and then acquiring financial-service firms such as Dean Witter, the country's fifth largest stock broker; Coldwell Banker, the largest real-estate firm; savings-and-loan operations in California; and a mortgage life-insurance company. Sears introduced many of these financial services in its retail stores. Some analysts believe that these acquisitions have further confused Sears' image in shoppers' minds (see Exhibit 15.7).

ETHICAL AND ENVIRONMENTAL ISSUES IN MARKETING

GREEN products, the group Pollution Probe got $65,000 a year in royalties. It's director even appeared in commercials with Nichol, who had replaced Star Trek star William Shatner as the chain's spokesman.

Then, controversy hit. The Pollution Probe spots made its director face charges of "selling-out" and forced his resignation. Greenpeace attacked GREEN's fertilizer as being potentially toxic, unaware the Canadian government possessed Loblaw tests showing it was toxin-free. In four weeks, the GREEN line was the talk of Canada, with Loblaw research showing more than 80 percent of the country was familiar with its GREEN name.

Despite bad feelings among some environmental groups that feel they were used, GREEN has turned into a powerhouse. Witness its $20 high-efficiency light bulb, which sold 75,000 units in two months. "It's the most amazing product that I have seen in 18 years in the supermarket business," says Nichol. "Twenty-dollar light bulbs and people are lining up to buy them. I guess that's what you call a win–win situation."

Nichol has shown the world that eco-marketing is a powerful new force.

Questions: Do you regard Loblaw's GREEN line as a promotional ploy or a legitimate endeavor to promote environmental protection? Explain your position.

Source: "Loblaws," *Advertising Age*, January 29, 1991.

Yet as we have seen, the financial services division is one of the few bright spots on Sears' otherwise bleak landscape—accounting for close to 40 percent of Sears' revenue. Three years after Sears launched Discover Card, the card accounted for $80 million in revenues. By not charging annual fees, and by offering rebates for its use, Sears convinced 33 million Americans to carry the card.[54]

INTERNAL DEVELOPMENT

Another way to promote corporate growth is through internal development—primarily by expanding the number of stores in a chain. Wal-Mart has followed a strategy of store expansion—and with good reason: Its phenomenal success in the South and Southwest is being repeated in rural and suburban areas in the rest of the United States.

Retailers can also seek growth through internal development by repositioning themselves in the marketplace, as when the nation's number four retailer, J.C. Pen-

EXHIBIT 15.7

Do Sears' Acquisitions Confuse Its Image?

ney, changed its image to go after the high-end department-store market occupied by R.H. Macy and Dillard's. Exhibit 15.8 shows an example of J.C. Penney's attempt to create a more upscale image with its Jacqueline Ferrar line of clothing. Such a strategy carries significant risks. First, the J.C. Penney name may continue to be associated with mass merchandise like lawn mowers and paint, not boutique-style offerings. The company redesigned its catalogs and advertising to counteract this perception. Second, the company may alienate its core customers—middle-to-lower-income, price-conscious consumers—in attempting to attract a more upscale clientele. Third, management is not as familiar with specialty retail operations as it is with mass merchandising.

Needless to say, a strategy of corporate repositioning should be reviewed carefully and pursued only when sales are stagnating and survival is at stake, as was the case at J.C. Penney.

IDENTIFY TARGET SEGMENTS AND POSITION STORES

Analyzing the environment and establishing objectives permits a retailer to identify appropriate target segments for its stores and to position stores to meet the needs of these segments. For example, the increasing proportion of working women led Sears and J.C. Penney to target more upscale females. Similarly, The Limited's objective of developing specialty stores to appeal to segments across the socioeconomic spectrum required targeting separate stores to separate socioeconomic segments. In each case, management must target customers by demographic and life style criteria. It must then position the store by developing an appropriate assortment of merchandise to appeal to these groups and develop advertising appeals to reflect the desired store image.

EXHIBIT 15.8

J.C. Penney Attempts to Upscale Its Image

Jacket, $64. City short, $42.
Jewelry and straw hat available
in Women's Accessories.
It's a whole new kind of spirit.
Jacqueline Ferrar™
JCPenney Fashion comes to life
Available at most large stores. Select Jacqueline Ferrar fashions are available in the JCPenney Catalog. Call toll-free anytime 1-800-222-6161.
Prices higher in Alaska, Hawaii and Puerto Rico. ©1991, JCPenney Co., Inc.

DEVELOP THE RETAIL STORE'S MARKETING MIX

Once the target segment is identified and a positioning strategy established, retailers can focus on individual stores by developing a marketing mix to give each store a consistent image and to ensure its appeal to the appropriate target segment. A store's marketing mix requires decisions on product mix, service, in-store decor, advertising, price, and location.

PRODUCT MIX

Retailers must make decisions about the variety of products they offer and the depth of offerings in individual product lines.

As we have seen, J. C. Penney and Sears have followed vastly different strategies regarding product assortment. Penney has deleted major appliances, paint, hardware, fabric, lawn and garden supplies, and automotive products from its stores, and is increasing the depth of offerings in a more limited line of soft goods. In 1988, clothing accounted for 69 percent of Penney's sales, compared with 49 percent in 1981.[55]

Sears shows no sign of giving up its mass-merchandise orientation, despite its move to include more specialty items in its product mix. The company continues to sell appliances, hardware, automotive supplies, and apparel. The risk in this example, is that the combination of general and specialty merchandise may confuse the consumer about the retailer's image.

SERVICE

The level of service offered by a retail store can be the most important component in the marketing mix. One study found that seven of the eleven most important reasons shoppers cited for switching stores were service-related factors such as poor sales help, wrapping, credit, and delivery.[56] Many retail experts identify the quality of sales help as the biggest problem in retailing today. Reduced sales staffs, inadequate employee training, and indifference on the part of sales personnel all contribute to this problem.

Perhaps no retailer is as service minded as Ikea, the Swedish furniture retailer whose American invasion was heralded by a New Jersey store that offered an infant changing room, staff to play with toddlers, a restaurant selling low-cost Swedish specialties, and endless aisles marked by eye-catching information displays.[57] Small merchants also find service a key. In Dacorah, Iowa, local retailers banded together to confront a new Wal-Mart by offering home-spun service, such as sending Christmas cards to customers, that the retail giant can't match.[58]

IN-STORE DECOR

Atmospherics, *that is, the in-store decor,* is an important influence on store image and consumer behavior. Barney's, the New York clothing store, sparked its turnaround from a modest men's discount shop to a beacon of high-fashion by redesigning its flagship mid-Manhattan store. Out went the jammed aisles and drab colors. In came an art-deco spiral staircase, gleaming lacquered counters, and antique Viennese furniture. As one writer noted, "The place is so gorgeous you can almost peel your eyes from the price tags."[59]

Kmart decision-makers believe that one of the main ways it can keep pace with archrival Wal-Mart is by upgrading the appearance of its aging chain. By 1995, executives promise all 2,204 stores will get a $2.3 billion face lift that will erase its reputation for clutter. By then, they hope Wal-Mart's new fleet will have aged enough to give Kmart an advantage.[60]

PROMOTIONS

Retailers use the same key promotional tools to influence consumers as manufacturers—personal selling, sales promotions, and advertising. Personal selling is most important when the consumer is uncertain of the purchase and seeks additional information. A consumer buying carpeting, appliances, or electronics may seek the advice of a retail salesperson. Retail stores can develop a more positive image if salespeople are trained to assist consumers in meeting their needs rather than pressure them to buy the store's products.

EXHIBIT 15.9

An Example of Institutional Retail Advertising

©1991 Barneys New York
The suitable spectrum. In New York the best place to buy a $600 suit is the store that sells more $1500 suits than most any store in the world, because of expertise, selection, and value. And now you don't have to go to New York.
BARNEYS NEWYORK
Chestnut Hill Cleveland Dallas Houston Manhasset Manhattan Seattle Short Hills South Coast Plaza Westport

Sales promotions are most important when price is a factor and it is important to try to get consumers into the store. Sales promotions include price-off promotions, two-for-one deals, in-store displays, and contests. Such promotions are most likely to be used for frequently purchased consumer packaged goods.

Advertising is used by most retail stores to either sell the store (*institutional advertising*) or to sell the merchandise in the store (*promotional advertising*). Institutional advertising is most likely to be used by retail chains to create an image, as when Barney's in-house advertising staff used classic black-and-white photographs in a high-concept magazine campaign that tried to convey the store's distinctiveness (see Exhibit 15.9).[61] Advertising also allows chains to respond to the retail environment with mid-course corrections. When The Gap decided the recessionary 1990s were souring consumers to its stylized, celebrity-oriented campaign, it switched to a campaign emphasizing the practical aspects of its products.[62]

Promotional advertising is used by individual retail shops to advertise prices and special sales. It has a shorter-term impact and usually appears in newspapers. The 1990–92 recession caused some retailers to shun promotional advertising to reduce their costs. By giving up weekly price promotions, Home Depot reduced ad expenses as a percentage of sales from 3.2 percent in 1985 to 1.5 percent in 1989 and has passed the savings on to the consumer.[63] It seems to be following the lead of Wal-Mart, which has the lowest ratio of ad spending to sales of any mass merchandiser.[64]

PRICE

Consumers could be alienated or confused when a store's advertising decor does not match the price of the merchandise. For example, frequent price promotions by a store trying to convey a prestige image would be counterproductive. Therefore, retailers must follow a general pricing policy that reflects their store image.

In setting price levels, most retailers use a *markup* approach, adding a certain margin to the cost of the item to cover their expenses and to try to meet profit goals. A typical markup might be 50 percent of the selling price, but the percentage varies greatly among product lines. Lower-priced items can carry lower markups because they are likely to turn over faster.

Other pricing decisions concern the level and timing of *markdowns*. Discounters and off-price retailers are likely to mark-down merchandise early to promote higher stock turnover. Stores that do not mark down on a daily basis run holiday sales or semiannual clearances to sell slow-moving merchandise. Retailers sometimes mark down their merchandise in stages, offering a greater markdown as the item remains in stock longer.

LOCATION

The starting point for a store's location decisions must be the definition of its target segment. A retailer must first identify the most-attractive communities in which to locate by the degree to which they represent the target segment. For example, when Toys "Я" Us decided to target upscale urbanites in 1990, it opened its first multilevel store as the glitzy anchor of a mid-Manhattan shopping center across from Macy's. Said the company's chairman: "If this store succeeds, the avenues of growth for similar downtown stores in large cities are enormous."[65] On the other hand, the location of convenience stores such as 7-Eleven cannot be positioned as precisely based on consumer characteristics, because these stores must be in diverse neighborhoods to provide easy accessibility.

After determining the area, the retailer must choose a specific site, based on pedestrian and vehicular traffic, distance of prospective shoppers from the site, and number of competitive retailers in the area. Additional considerations are local market characteristics such as population size, population density, income level, and household composition.

EVALUATION AND CONTROL

The last step in the process of developing retail strategies is evaluation and control of retail operations. Performance at the company-wide level is compared with projected performance on sales and returns on investment. Performance at the store level is compared with projected sales by department and by product line. Stock turnover and return on assets are also evaluated.

The areas that create the most control problems in retailing are shrinkage, space utilization, inadequate stock turnover, and product proliferation. **Shrinkage** *is the theft of merchandise by customers or employees.* The cost of shrinkage represents 7 percent of retail sales.[66] Retailers try to control it by store cameras, security guards, and automatic alarms that sound when unchecked merchandise is taken out of the store.

Poor use of space is an even more serious problem, and it is one of the reasons that Sears' selling costs are higher than Wal-Mart's. Only about 55 percent of Sears' floor space in its large shopping-mall stores is devoted to sales compared with nearly 80 percent for Kmart stores. Most of the rest of Sears' floor space is used for storage.

Stock turnover is tied to space utilization, because greater turnover means more sales per square foot. When Sears reduced its prices in 1989, it achieved a higher turnover rate on its merchandise, thus reducing its inventories and converting some of its storage space to more profitable sales usage.[67] Reduced inventory as a result of higher turnover could be counter-productive, however, if it leads to out-of-stock situations.

Another control requirement is tracking the profitability of specific products and deleting them if they fail to meet profitability or turnover objectives. The Seven-Eleven Japan Company is revolutionizing this area. The average store is less than half the size of its American counterpart, but sells roughly twice as much. With personal computers and advanced software, store owners can instantly call up full-color graphs showing the pattern of sales by category and by age and sex of customers. A hand-held version allows employees to scan their aisles and to track sales by product.[68]

SUMMARY

1. **What are the most significant trends in retailing today?**
   The 1980s saw important changes in the retail environment, the most important being the increasing importance of specialty retailing. Greater affluence meant that shoppers wanted name brands and a greater variety of merchandise. Another important trend was off-price retailing, that is, offering high-quality name-brand items at deep discounts. A third trend saw an increase in sales through nonstore retail facilities, particularly catalogs and TV shopping networks. This trend was spurred by the time-saving convenience of buying at home. A fourth trend was the shift from expansion to consolidation in retailing. Retailers began concentrating on becoming more productive in existing facilities rather than expanding by building new facilities.
2. **What are the most important types of retailers?**
   Retailers can be classified as merchandisers, food stores, and nonstore retailers. The most important types of merchandisers are specialty stores (small stores carrying a few specialty lines), department stores (full-service outlets that carry a greater number of lines), discount stores and mass merchandisers (limited-service stores that offer a broad variety of product lines at low prices). Food stores including convenience stores (neighborhood food stores that offer the convenience of longer operating hours), supermarkets (low-cost, high-volume outlets that carry many different products), superstores (large stores carrying twice as many items as supermarkets), warehouse stores (deep-discount, no-frill outlets that offer merchandise in warehouse facilities), and hypermarkets (giant-sized outlets that offer both food and a variety of nonfood items at low

prices). Nonstore retailers include companies that sell by mail order catalog, home shopping networks, through vending machines, door-to-door, and by direct mail.

3. **How are retail marketing strategies developed at the corporate and store levels?**
Retailers must evaluate their environment, develop objectives, assess alternative strategies, and then evaluate and control them. At the corporate level, they may follow acquisition strategies for growth or grow through internal development by opening new stores or by repositioning themselves to enter new lines.
Retailers must develop a mix of strategies to give their stores a consistent image and to ensure they appeal to the appropriate target group. Store managers must make decisions regarding the product mix, service, in-store advertising, price, and location.

KEY TERMS

Wheel of retailing (p. 490)
Specialty retailing (p.492)
Off-price retailing (p. 492)
Nonstore retailing (p. 493)
Consolidated retailing (p. 494)
Specialty stores (p. 495)
Retail chains (p. 495)
Department stores (p. 495)
Mass merchandisers (p. 495)
Discount stores (p. 496)
Warehouse clubs (p. 497)
Factory outlet stores (p. 497)
Convenience stores (p. 498)
Supermarkets (p. 498)
Scrambled merchandising (p. 498)
Superstores (p. 499)
Warehouse stores (p. 499)
Hypermarkets (p. 499)
Horizontal price fixing (p. 506)
Vertical price fixing (p. 506)
Bait-and-switch pricing (p. 506)
Stock turnover rate (p. 507)
Return on assets (p. 507)
Profit margin (p. 507)
Atmospherics (p. 512)
Shrinkage (p. 515)

QUESTIONS

1. How does retailing provide time, place, and possession utility to consumers?
2. According to the "wheel of retailing" concept, on what basis do institutions first enter into retailing, and how might they lose their competitive advantage?
3. What were some of the most significant trends in retailing in the 1980s? Cite examples of each.
4. Specialty retailing was described both as a trend and as a type of store. Explain.
5. How does J.C. Penney's strategy to reposition itself as a specialty retailer differ from Sears'. What are the risks of J.C. Penney's strategy?
6. What was the impact of the following environmental trends on retail strategies in the 1980s?
   a. More singles and working women
   b. Technological advances in retailing
   c. The recession of 1990–92
7. What are the advantages of hypermarkets? What problems have they faced in the United States? Why?
8. Why did nonstore retailing experience rapid growth in the 1980s?
9. How have multinational retailers reacted to the integration of the twelve-nation European Community in 1992?
10. What corporate strategies have large retailers followed to promote growth? Cite examples.
11. What are some key areas of performance that retailers try to control? Why are these areas of concern to retailers?

QUESTIONS: YOU ARE THE DECISION MAKER

1. One department-store executive commented on in-home shopping as follows:

   I just don't think sales through home-shopping networks are going to continue to increase. This is a passing fad. Most people want to see merchandise, compare items, and ask a salesperson's advice. And despite their name, home-shopping networks don't let people shop. We were considering buying into a cable home-shopping show, but I strongly recommended against it.

   a. Why did in-home shopping increase in the 1980s?
   b. Do you agree with the reasons cited by the executive as to why people are unlikely to buy from home-shopping networks?

2. An executive of a large department-store chain, reflecting on the company's strategy of acquiring nonretail businesses in the 1970s, said:

   Buying into businesses that had growth potential looked good on paper. But we quickly discovered we are retailers, not drug manufacturers, electrical distributors, or appliance producers. We had to go back into the retailing business.

   a. Do you agree with the statement? Why or why not?
   b. Why did retailers such as Sears follow a policy of acquiring businesses outside of retailing?

CHAPTER 16

Wholesaling and Physical Distribution

YOUR FOCUS IN CHAPTER 16

To learn:

- *The most significant trends in wholesaling today.*
- *The various forms of wholesaling.*
- *The nature of the physical distribution process.*
- *Why physical distribution is a system.*
- *The nature of physical distribution activities, namely: order processing, merchandise handling and storage, inventory control, and transportation.*
- *What a just-in-time distribution process is.*
- *The relationship of physical distribution to other components of the marketing mix.*

McKesson Corp.—Making Physical Distribution A Fine Art

At McKesson Corp, the potential for mayhem is always lurking in the shadows. With 20,000 customers, 2,000 suppliers, and an inventory that spans from soap to prescriptive drugs, the mega-wholesaler must route millions of items to all corners of the United States every day. How does McKesson do it? Through a state-of-the-art system of *physical distribution.*

In the 1960s, McKesson was a staid San Francisco drug distributor with a plodding, if steady clientele. After merging with a California dairy in 1967, it went on an acquisitions frenzy, buying up dozens of smaller wholesalers and expanding the diversity of products it distributed. Ultimately, however, the diversity was too great, and the strain frayed its all-important distribution arm. McKesson's core customers—pharmacists—were getting hair spray when they wanted aspirin, billing errors were manifest, and at times it seemed the whole operation was on the verge of collapse.

To bring order from the chaos, McKesson began experimenting in the late 1970s with a computer that would later revolutionize physical distribution. It was called the Economost. Until its unveiling, druggists would make mental notes about what they needed and phone orders into McKesson when they ran low on inventory. The pharmacist might go a month without calling, and then place 20 orders in two weeks.

The Economost program was designed to streamline the unwieldy and time-consuming ordering process. In its original design, the Economost was a crude adding machine-type instrument mounted on a shopping cart and powered by a car battery. A pharmacist would walk through the pharmacy aisles, calculate what needed to be restocked, print out the tally, and send it to McKesson in regular weekly intervals. It was a breakthrough, not the least because it ended the helter-skelter ordering system of old.

Based on early trials in California, McKesson decided to roll out Economost nationally, and today it lies at the heart of the drug wholesaler's national distribution network. The 1990s Economost is a hand-held, laser-guided computer with a wand that reads bar-code information on a product's label (also known as the Universal Product Code or UPC). When a druggist finds an item low in stock, he or she waves the wand over its label, presses the computer keypad to indicate quantity, and then downloads the data via modem to McKesson's national data center in Rancho Cordova, California.

From there, McKesson's system kicks into high gear. The Rancho Cordova center sorts the orders by geographic location and forwards them to one of McKesson's 45 distribution centers, where warehouse workers (called *pickers*) take the printed order sheets and fill them using boxes pre-labeled for the druggist. The centers—which generally contain 25,000 different items—are laid out to maximize efficiency. For instance, the most frequently ordered goods are stacked waist high, giving easy access to the scores of pickers who roam the aisles.

Once the box is filled, it then travels along a conveyer belt to a computerized sorting center which prepares the shipments for dozens of trucks that wait by loading bays. The computers figure out not only which box goes on what truck, but also which boxes need to be placed closest to the front of the truck to accommodate the driver's route. The boxes are then fed along the conveyer belts and loaded into the trucks. The system is so precise that when a druggist opens the box (waiting at the store by opening time) the items are already sorted according to the store's layout.

The Economost program allowed McKesson to institute the *Just-In-Time distribution system* (JIT) followed by many Japanese companies. The system requires a company to produce and distribute only the quantity consumers need just at the time they need it. As a result, this state-of-the-art process let McKesson claim an 18 percent increase in profits in 1990. It also allowed the wholesaler to perform a variety of *value added* functions for its clients. For instance, the company furnishes monthly reports for druggists, telling them which segments of their business are rising, stagnating, or in decline, and suggesting alternative orders. It also provides professionals who help new clients stock and manage new stores.

McKesson's pioneering physical distribution network gives its clients a competitive edge and keeps them returning to McKesson for more. It is a sure prescription for success.[1]

THE LINK BETWEEN WHOLESALING AND PHYSICAL DISTRIBUTION

Wholesaling is a main link in the chain that routes goods from the manufacturer to the consumer. As we have seen in Chapter 14, wholesalers are defined as organizations that buy and resell merchandise to other businesses. They sell to other wholesalers, retailers, and industrial buyers, but not to the final consumer.

As we described in the McKesson example, wholesalers must often devise intricate systems to move their goods along the distribution chain. These systems include order processing, merchandise handling, storage, and transportation functions. Combined, they form the physical distribution network that will also be a focus of this chapter.

Physical distribution is not just the province of wholesalers. Manufacturers and retailers have their own systems, but it is particularly important for wholesalers, given their place in the middle of the retail channel and their understandable concern over logistics. As we have just seen, McKesson moves millions of products across the country each day.

In this chapter, we first examine the importance of wholesaling; then the types of wholesalers responsible for distributing goods and services; and finally, the physical distribution network that is required to ensure an efficient flow of goods from manufacturers to consumers.

IMPORTANCE OF WHOLESALING

The importance of wholesaling can be measured by its economic magnitude. Wholesale sales are actually greater than retail sales, making it a $1.8 trillion-a-year industry.[2] The reason is that the wholesale sector sells both industrial and consumer goods, whereas by definition, retail sales represent only consumer goods.

Wholesaling plays a critical role in providing *time*, *place* and *possession utility* to industrial customers and final consumers. Without wholesalers, manufacturers would have to deal directly with retailers or with their customers, and retailers would have to buy directly from manufacturers. Most retailers and manufacturers are too small to buy and sell direct; they need wholesalers.

Wholesalers also provide essential services to larger retailers and manufacturers. Many of these firms have found that it is cheaper to use storage and transportation facilities owned by wholesalers rather than to set up their own physical distribution facilities. In fact, the trend in the last decade has been for manufacturers and retailers to increasingly rely on independent wholesalers rather than to sell direct.

Another measure of the importance of wholesaling is its increasing power in the channel system. As wholesalers have provided more services to manufacturers and retailers, they have become a more indispensable part of the distribution link to the customer. Larger wholesalers have served the role of channel leader by managing the flow of goods from manufacturers to retailers and industrial users. McKesson helps some of the manufacturers it buys from manage their inventories, collect and analyze market data, plan sales campaigns, and even develop new products based on market feedback. We have seen how it helps its druggist clients by setting up computerized ordering systems. It also provides in-store promotional programs to its druggists and organizes them into voluntary chains so they can achieve economies of scale in buying.

An indication of the increasing power of wholesalers is that some of them have acquired their own retail units. Food wholesaling giant Super Valu earns 30 percent of its income from its Shopko retail chains and spent a third of its 1990 capital budget expanding the chain. Super Valu is even venturing into hypermarkets.[3]

TRENDS IN WHOLESALING: PAST AND PRESENT

Wholesaling was not as important 50 years ago as it is today. The Great Depression in the 1930s caused many manufacturers to become more cost conscious and to reassess the role of the wholesaler. Viewing wholesalers as mere order takers, they decided to "bypass the wholesaler" and perform the wholesale function themselves—usually more cheaply and efficiently.

The trend of bypassing the wholesaler persisted into the 1970s. Then, a remarkable shift began taking place in the wholesaler's role: from routine order taker to an intermediary providing greater distribution efficiency. Many wholesalers had realized that the only way they could grow was to offer more services and to do so more efficiently.

This transformation, known as **value-added wholesaling,** *improved wholesaling productivity by providing more services and lowering the cost of these services through automation.* McKesson was one of the first to implement it—with the automated physical distribution facilities described earlier. As a result, by 1991, drug companies were selling 75 percent of their products through McKesson, compared to only 45 percent in 1970.[4]

Other wholesalers followed McKesson's lead. The largest food wholesalers—Super Valu, Fleming, Wetterau—have automated distribution centers and computerized systems that equal McKesson's. As a result of their move to value-added wholesaling, the number of retail food chains distributing through wholesalers doubled in the 1980s.[5] Today, most wholesalers are following the value-added trend, with three out of four having computerized order-processing systems.

But even value-added wholesaling was not enough to rescue wholesalers from the 1990–92 recession. In 1987, the industry reported an 11.3 percent annual gain, however, 1990 gross profits for wholesalers totaled $358 billion—a mere 4.8 percent rise over the year before.[6]

TYPES OF WHOLESALERS

The various types of wholesalers in the distribution system are as diverse as the different types of retailers described in Chapter 15. So far, we have assumed that wholesalers are independent businesses such as McKesson or Super Valu. Figure 16.1 shows that the wholesaling function can also be performed by manufacturers and retailers. In this section, we talk about both company-owned and independent wholesalers.

FIGURE 16.1

Types of Wholesalers

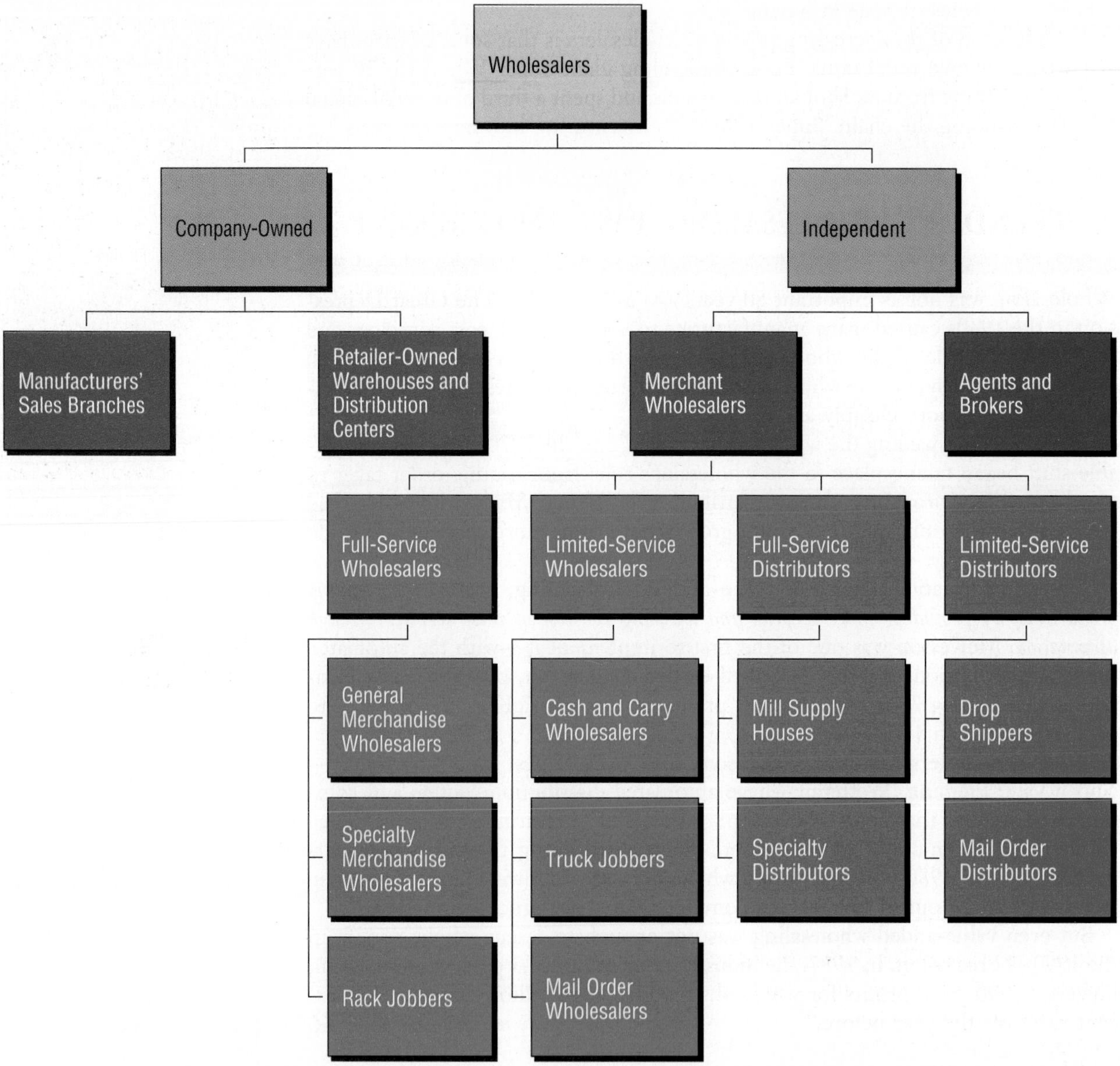

COMPANY-OWNED WHOLESALERS

We have seen in Chapter 14 that some manufacturers market directly to their customers, primarily to industrial firms, by integrating forward and assuming the wholesaling function. In Japan, the largest manufacturers maintain an iron grip on prices and service by tightly controlling their wholesaling operations. American companies such as IBM, 3M, and General Electric use dual-distribution systems in which they market both directly and also through independent wholesalers.

Manufacturer-owned warehouses designed to handle merchandise and store inventory are known as **sales branches.** Manufacturers use branches to sell to the largest

EXHIBIT 16.1

Wal-Mart's Distribution Nerve Center

retailers and industrial buyers and distribute to smaller customers through independent wholesalers. Manufacturers' branches represent about 10 percent of wholesale facilities, yet account for over one-third of wholesale volume, reflecting the fact that they sell to the largest accounts.

Large retailers integrate backward by owning their own warehouses and distribution facilities, enabling them to buy directly from manufacturers. Mass merchandisers such as Kmart and Sears, and food chains such as Safeway and Kroger all use their own storage and shipment facilities when they buy from larger firms. These facilities provide retailers with less spoilage, better inventory control, and quicker delivery. Wal-Mart has 17 distribution centers (that is, large computerized warehouse facilities) that are linked to its 1,800 stores by an automated system widely regarded as the most sophisticated in retailing. When a consumer makes a purchase, the information goes from the checkout counter into a main computer bank at Wal-Mart's nerve center in Bentonville Arkansas (see Exhibit 16.1). This information allows Wal-Mart's distribution centers to determine up-to-the-minute inventory levels. In this way, Wal-Mart knows what products to direct to its stores. About three-fourths of Wal-Mart's products are distributed in this way. It uses independent wholesalers to distribute the other one-fourth.[7] Such facilities provide retailers with better inventory control, quicker delivery, and a price edge.

INDEPENDENT WHOLESALERS

Independent wholesalers may be merchant wholesalers or agents and brokers. Figure 16.1 shows the various categories of each. **Merchant wholesalers** *purchase and take ownership of goods;* agents and brokers (discussed in Chapter 14) serve as intermediaries between buyers and sellers without taking ownership of the merchandise. Merchant wholesalers may sell consumer or industrial goods on a full-service or limited-service basis. When they sell industrial goods, they are known as distributors.

FULL-SERVICE WHOLESALERS

Full-service wholesalers perform a range of services such as storing goods, controlling inventory, processing orders, and transporting merchandise. Larger, full-service wholesalers extend credit to retailers and help them set up order-processing and inventory-control systems. Examples are McKesson and Super Valu.

Full-service wholesalers are classified by the assortment of merchandise they carry and services they perform. **General merchandise wholesalers** *provide full service and carry a broad assortment of merchandise (many different product lines), but in so doing, sacrifice depth in each line.* For example, McKesson carries both drug and nondrug items. It stocks almost every product line that can be found in a drugstore but may not carry every brand of analgesic or stomach remedy. The larger, full-service wholesalers provide more than 100 services to clients, from site location and financing to insurance and advertising.

Specialty merchandise wholesalers *also provide full service, but specialize in certain product lines such as health foods, automotive parts, or luxury items and carry a deep assortment of alternatives in each line.* Bista has carved out a niche among Asia's wholesalers by carrying deep assortments of Cross pens, Van Cleff watches, and Elizabeth Arden products.[8]

A particular type of full-service wholesaler is a **rack jobber,** *which displays merchandise in the store by stocking the racks, thus relieving retailers of inventory control and ordering.* Rack jobbers sell these items on consignment—that is, they bill the retailer only when the item is sold, in effect extending the retailer credit. They appeared on the scene when food retailers began to stock nonfood items and found the ordering and merchandise-handling costs for these products too high. As a result, independent wholesalers began to take over these functions.

The McLane Company of Texas, for instance, has followed convenience stores into the nonfood sector with great success by providing merchandising help and customizing rack displays for independent owners. Its clients are offered both food and nonfood merchandise.[9]

McKesson sometimes acts as a rack jobber for jewelry and cosmetic items in drugstores since many owners lack the time or know-how to properly order and display these items. Close to 1,000 McKesson employees service stores from all 58 of the company's distribution centers. Once McKesson took over as a rack jobber, sales in these categories shot up 80 percent.[10]

LIMITED-SERVICE WHOLESALERS

Limited-service wholesalers eliminate certain distributive functions such as transportation, merchandise handling, and credit and can offer buyers lower prices as a result.

Cash-and-carry wholesalers *sell from warehouse facilities, and require buyers to pay cash and transport their merchandise.* These facilities are the same as retail warehouse clubs, except that cash-and-carry wholesalers will sell only to business firms, whereas retail clubs also sell to consumers. Makro Self-Service Wholesale is one of the largest cash-and-carry wholesalers in the country. It owns four 200,000-square-foot distribution centers and sells exclusively to business people. Stores carry an average of 35,000 items in a variety of categories from food to typewriters. Makro's Washington store has sales of over $200 million a year.[11]

Truck jobbers *are small wholesalers that specialize in storing and quickly delivering perishable items such as dairy products, baked goods, fruits, and vegetables.* They sell directly from their trucks to small retailers for cash.

Mail-order wholesalers *sell out of a catalog to small retailers, usually in outlying areas that full-service wholesalers would find too costly to serve.* They sell items such as hardware, specialty foods, and jewelry.

INDUSTRIAL WHOLESALERS

Industrial wholesalers (often called distributors), can provide full or limited services. They also may carry general or specialty merchandise. *A full-service distributor that sells a variety of lines is sometimes referred to as a* **mill supply house**. These distributors, like their wholesaling counterparts, are increasing in scope. Premier Industrial, for example, has 14 separate divisions, ranging from J.L. Holcomb Manufacturing (cleaning agents and brushes) to Certanium Alloys (welding electrodes and brazing alloys).[12] **Specialty distributors** *also provide full service, but concentrate on specific lines such as generators, power tools, or industrial fasteners.*

Two types of limited-service distributors are drop shippers and mail-order distributors. **Drop shippers** *(sometimes called desk jobbers) take title to the goods they sell* *but never possess them.* They obtain orders from industrial buyers or other distributors and forward these orders to producers for shipment. They do not store, handle, or transport the items ordered. They sell primarily bulky items having high transportation costs, such as coal, lumber, chemicals, or industrial machinery. **Mail-order distributors** *sell specialized items out of a catalog that can be easily shipped by mail or truck.* They are the same as mail-order wholesalers except that they sell to industrial buyers.

DEVELOPING WHOLESALE STRATEGIES

Like retailers, wholesalers must establish marketing strategies, but they have been less systematic in doing so. With the move to value-added wholesaling, many began to develop strategies based on the steps described in Chapter 15 (see Figure 15.3). As with retailers, wholesalers must formulate corporate marketing strategies and a marketing mix.

CORPORATE MARKETING STRATEGIES

Many wholesalers have followed a policy of acquiring other wholesalers as a means of expanding their facilities and offering more and better services, thereby leading to consolidation. Fleming, the largest U.S. wholesaler, has been the most rabid acquisitor, spending $1 billion over the past decade to buy 12 wholesalers representing $7.5 billion worth of sales.[13] The corporate mission guiding these acquisitions was to establish Fleming as a value-added wholesaler and to apply its network of automated services to all its customers.

Other wholesalers have used acquisitions to get into retailing. As we have seen, Super Valu acquired food chains, reasoning that owning retail establishments would (1) give them assured outlets for their products and (2) improve efficiency by using an integrated ordering and inventory-control system. Retailing also allows wholesalers to sell inventory that would otherwise have to be returned to the manufacturer. Wisconsin Toy Company decided that instead of merely returning overstocks, it could profit by selling them itself. As a result, it opened a 75-store chain called Toy Liquidators that rings up sales of roughly $40 million a year.[14]

Some wholesalers have tried to grow by internal development rather than by acquisition, building warehouses and distribution centers in new markets. Wallace, a $79 million Houston distributor of pipes, decided to invest heavily in worker training, spending $2 million to develop teamwork among its 280 employees. As a result, it boosted on-time deliveries to 98 percent. Super Food Services, another food wholesaler, followed a market-expansion route through a $45-million capital improvement program to build new distribution centers and modernize existing facilities.[15] Its president believes that owning retail stores would result in Super Food Services competing with its own customers—retailers. So the company is expanding its wholesaling facilities.

THE WHOLESALER'S MARKETING MIX

Like retailers, wholesalers must make product-assortment, price, promotional, and location decisions. Regarding *product assortment,* wholesalers must decide whether to carry a full line of products or to specialize in a few lines. Just as there is a trend toward specialty retailing, there is a strong trend toward specialty wholesaling—

GLOBAL MARKETING STRATEGIES

Wholesaling in Japan: Nothing Is Too Small, Is It?

In Chapter 14 we saw how strict government controls over Japan's retail sector has led to some of the highest prices in the world. (Remember the $600 dinner for four?) What we did not see is how Japan's wholesaling system evolved in step with those controls, and how it poses unique challenges to American manufacturers.

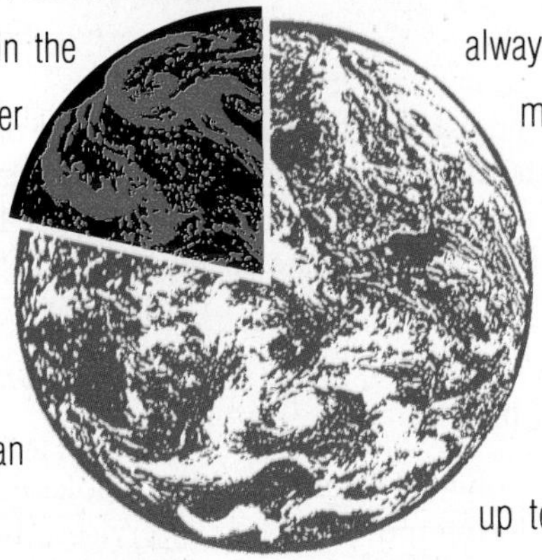

The small-sized shelves of Japan's government-subsidized mom-and-pop stores pose a foreboding barrier to American marketers, not the least because the wholesalers who stock those shelves feel no need to carry large inventories. When Americans come knocking on the door of Japanese wholesalers, they are often told there is just not enough room for their products.

The system evolved for some very Japanese reasons. First, there is precious little flat land, meaning that stores are small, clustered together, and have no storage room. Second, Japanese people eat more fresh foods than Americans and since they do not always have room for refrigerators, they must shop daily. These factors account for the fact that Japan has 1.6 million retail outlets, or one for every 74 citizens—twice the American proportion.

Food wholesalers cope by making up to three deliveries a day, sometimes in minuscule quantity. Campbell's Japanese wholesaling subsidiary delivers as few as six cans to a single store. The added work has forced Campbell to push the price of tomato soup to $1.45 a can.

Japan's massive supply needs have given rise to more than 400,000 wholesalers, some employing fewer than five people. The process has grown so unwieldy that a single item may pass through four wholesalers before reaching the retail shelf. To sell tabasco sauce, Toyota Tsusho (the car-maker's trading division) must import the product, truck it to its

concentrating on fewer, but more profitable items and providing a higher level of service for those items. For instance, Fleming is deepening its mix by increasing the amount of meat, deli, and dairy items it carries.[16]

Wholesalers usually set *prices* on a markup basis, often 20 percent to cover expenses and to produce profits that average anywhere from 1 to 3 percent of sales.

Wholesalers generally do little advertising, although some advertise in trade publications. They *promote* their goods primarily through personal selling. An important aspect of value-added wholesaling is to ensure that the salesperson is more than an order taker and to assist retailers in making the right decisions regarding product assortment and inventory control. In the industrial sector, sales-

GLOBAL MARKETING STRATEGIES

warehouse, and sell it to a primary wholesaler, such as Nikko Shokai. Then, Nikko Shokai sells the sauce to yet another wholesaler like CGC Japan, a cooperative that services 268 small grocery chains.

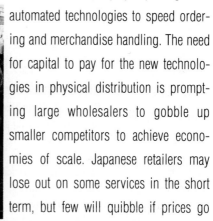

Just as Japanese citizens are accustomed to getting premium service from local merchants, so too have Japan's wholesalers come to expect pampering by exporters. To become Japan's leading supplier of pacemakers, an American exporter had to invent customized computer programs to allow wholesalers to identify research surgeons as the target. An exporter of filofaxes had to specially wrap them in expensive boxes and absorb the cost to satisfy Japanese wholesalers.

High prices and government pressure to bring them into line with those in the rest of the world are causing a shakeout in Japanese wholesaling, however large wholesalers realize they need the same automated physical distribution facilities as their American counterparts if prices are to come down. American companies are helping by exporting these automated technologies to speed ordering and merchandise handling. The need for capital to pay for the new technologies in physical distribution is prompting large wholesalers to gobble up smaller competitors to achieve economies of scale. Japanese retailers may lose out on some services in the short term, but few will quibble if prices go down as Japanese wholesalers become larger and more efficient.

Questions: Why are there so many Japanese wholesalers? What pressures are causing them to decrease in number?

Sources: "Distribution System Faces Changed Environment," *Business Japan,* August 1990, pp. 89–93; "Selling In Japan Gets Less Befuddling," *Business Week,* February 20, 1989, pp. 122B, 122D, & 122F; "How McIlhenny Drenched Japan with Tabasco Sauce," *Business Week,* February 20, 1989, p. 122D.

people must act almost as consultants. One tool distributor has gone so far as to begin keeping inventories of what its customers *might* need, giving them broad leeway to adapt to market conditions.[17] Another says that his company does not employ salespeople but rather, "specialists who are qualified to assist our customers with a wide range of questions concerning applications."[18]

Wholesalers must also make decisions about where to *locate* warehouses and distribution centers. These facilities should be located in areas that will minimize transportation costs to customers. Wal-Mart clusters its stores within 200 miles of its distribution points, ensuring deliveries can be made daily.[19] Another factor in the locational decision is the cost of establishing a distribution center that may run several hundred thousand square feet. Low-rent areas and industrial parks are favored.

Overall, wholesalers have become more sophisticated in developing marketing strategies to meet customer needs. They have shown a remarkable resilience in the past decade by increasing their efficiency and by demonstrating to manufacturers and retailers that it is generally more economical to use the wholesalers' services rather than bypass them in the distribution channel.

NATURE OF PHYSICAL DISTRIBUTION

Physical distribution *encompasses all activities involved in moving goods from where they are produced to where they are purchased or consumed.* When McKesson orders beauty supplies from Procter & Gamble to sell to drugstores, it takes responsibility for merchandise-handling, storage, transportation to the retailer, and, in some cases, shelf-stocking in the store itself. *This combination of order processing, merchandise-handling, inventory, storage, and transportation functions represents the* **physical distribution system.**

The goals of such a system are to provide on-time shipments; to ensure dependability of deliveries so that products arrive regularly, safely, and in the correct form and quantity; and to secure accurate information on customer needs. Toys "Я" Us is able to gain a competitive edge by consistently providing the right mix of products to its stores on time, dependably, and based on accurate customer information.

Physical distribution is particularly important for industrial marketers, which supply materials that buyers use in the production process. Products that arrive late, in the wrong quantities, or in defective condition can delay production runs and result in substantial losses to industrial buyers. For example, in the mid 1980s, Zytec, a Minnesota manufacturer of power supplies, suffered when its assembly line lapsed into disarray because suppliers routinely ran late delivering parts or furnished them in the wrong quantity. The result was defective products that led Zytec's customers to defect en masse. By 1985, it was teetering on bankruptcy. The company's management responded by firing suppliers who could not meet stringent delivery and quality demands. Assurance of on-time delivery improved assembly line operations so that by 1990, Zytec had a 99.5 percent customer acceptance rate.[20]

PHYSICAL DISTRIBUTION AS PART OF THE CHANNEL SYSTEM

Physical distribution is part of the channel system described in Chapter 14. It is responsible for the product flows from the manufacturer to the customer. It is necessary for manufacturers, wholesalers, and retailers to have physical distribution capabilities to ensure that products are delivered on time and in good condition.

Manufacturers such as Procter & Gamble, Lever Brothers, Colgate-Palmolive, and Compaq computers have their own merchandise handling and storage facilities to sell directly to retailers (see Exhibit 16.2).

Wholesalers require sophisticated physical distribution systems, because they are in the middle of the channel network, managing a steady stream of goods from manufacturers and sorting them for delivery to retailers. W.W. Grainger, one of the largest wholesale distributors of industrial products, services 921,000 customers through 300 branches throughout the United States, using computers to

EXHIBIT 16.2

Compaq Computer Corporation Can Ship Orders from Retailers in Less Than Four Hours

Interior of Company's Houston Warehouse

process customer orders and transmit them to automated warehouses, where merchandise is retrieved and delivered to loading platforms for shipment. The company stocks 22,000 items in its warehouses, ranging from one-ton industrial generators to featherweight semiconductors.[21]

Large *retailers* also have their own physical distribution systems. Toys "Я" Us, the first retailer to sell toys as a mass merchandiser at discount prices, has a computerized information system that hooks up every cash register in every company store to a central computer at company headquarters.[22] The capability to obtain immediate sales information from its stores permits the company to implement a just-in-time (JIT) distribution system. Merchandise is kept in warehouses for only a short time. Rapid inventory turnover means higher profits. On-time shipments are made to its 20 warehouses strategically located throughout the country within easy trucking distance of each of the stores it services. A fleet of Toys "Я" Us trucks ship the merchandise from the warehouses to the retail stores.[23]

The channel leader, whether a manufacturer, a wholesaler, or a retailer, has responsibility for integrating the varying elements of physical distribution. As channel leader, McKesson will coordinate shipments from manufacturers to fill druggists' orders. It will provide information to its suppliers to help them establish production schedules based on demand and to its retailers to help them order goods, anticipate trends, and set their inventory levels accordingly.

IMPORTANCE OF PHYSICAL DISTRIBUTION

The importance of physical distribution is reflected in its cost, estimated by one study to average 20 percent of sales.[24] (The average amount spent on advertising or sales promotions is significantly less.) Physical distribution costs for intermediaries are even higher due to their role in assembling and sorting products. Order processing, merchandise handling, storing, inventory management, and transportation all account for a portion of the cost.

Managers view physical distribution as a key component of the marketing mix because of its central role in creating time, place, and possession utility and in achieving distribution efficiencies. One study of industrial buyers found that they rate physical distribution second to product quality in evaluating alternative suppliers.[25] For many industrial buyers, the starting point in selecting a vendor is not identifying the company offering the lowest price but the company offering the best delivery and service reliability.

Physical distribution is also rated important by marketers of consumer goods, who cannot afford to risk running out of stock due to poor inventory control or delivery. Consumers are becoming less brand loyal, and when they find their preferred brand out of stock, they are increasingly likely to buy an alternative product.

Further, physical distribution is an important means of gaining a competitive advantage. For example, Hillenbrand Industries has buried its competition by offering made-to-order caskets in just two days. Instead of maintaining a large (and costly) inventory, Hillenbrand runs a mail-order system through which funeral directors call orders into one of 59 distribution centers and receive delivery within 48 hours. With its savings, Hillenbrand offers funeral directors such value-added services as videotaped management training programs and advice on multicultural burial customs.[26]

Eastman Kodak's experience with instant cameras in the late 1970s serves as an example of poor physical distribution leading to competitive disadvantage. Its promotional campaign aroused consumer interest, but when consumers went to retail stores to look at the camera, retailers were often out of stock.[27] As a result, many consumers lost interest, and sales fizzled. Even the best advertising campaign or the most aggressive pricing strategy is useless if the company does not have an effective physical distribution system to ensure the product is on the right shelves at the right time.

PHYSICAL DISTRIBUTION IN THE INTERNATIONAL MARKETPLACE

Physical distribution represents the infrastructure necessary for the flow of goods from manufacturer to consumer. The United States has one of the most sophisticated and advanced physical distribution systems in the world. Physical distribution in other parts of the world is much more primitive. Poor road systems cause delays in transporting goods. Poor telecommunications systems inhibit data transmission by computers through phone lines and even make telephone ordering difficult. Poor refrigeration means that many products spoil by the time they reach their destination. Lack of warehouse facilities means that products must often be discarded if they cannot be used right away.

As a result, when we talk of automated physical distribution systems such as those used by McKesson or Toys "Я" Us, we are assuming an infrastructure that exists in an advanced market system. We cannot assume such facilities in most Third-World countries.

Physical distribution capabilities in a country are likely to be influenced by many of the trends in the international marketplace cited in Chapter 5. For example, the move to a market economy by Russia and the Eastern European countries will require better road systems and improved telecommunications to allow more advanced order-processing and merchandise-handling systems and more efficient transportation. Without these facilities, it is unlikely these countries can establish a strong, market-based economy.

The economic integration of the 12 European Community nations also has direct implications for physical distribution. The elimination of trade regulations will facilitate standardizing distribution systems between countries. A necessary expedient like creating uniform transport regulations will be made easier. As a result, large automated order handling and storage facilities (known as distribution centers) will be able to serve all of Western Europe. In 1992, Donna Karan, the fashion house, established a distribution center in Europe in anticipation of economic integration. The center will have a computer network to handle orders and distribution throughout Western Europe.[28] Before 1992, such a unified distribution system would not have been possible.

When we discuss establishing physical distribution systems in the next section, it is important to remember that we are assuming an infrastructure, such as that in the United States or in Western Europe, that permits the establishment of automated physical distribution systems.

THE PHYSICAL DISTRIBUTION PROCESS

Figure 16.2 shows the steps required to effectively perform physical distribution activities. The first step is to establish objectives. Next, managers develop facilities to perform the key physical distribution functions—order-processing, merchandise handling and storage, inventory management, and transportation. Finally, the process also must be evaluated and controlled to produce maximum consumer satisfaction at a reasonable cost. In the remainder of this chapter, we will consider each of these steps.

DEVELOP PHYSICAL DISTRIBUTION OBJECTIVES

Physical distribution objectives can be stated in terms of improving customer satisfaction and/or reducing costs. A customer-oriented objective might be to minimize delivery of damaged goods by use of effective merchandise handling. Another objective might be to minimize out-of-stock conditions through more-efficient inventory management procedures. A third might be to ensure on-time delivery of customer orders through an efficient transportation system.

L.L. Bean has defined key areas in its physical distribution system, among them ease of order placement, in-stock levels, shipping costs, and delivery time. However, L.L. Bean's management recognizes that objectives must be specific to provide operational control over physical distribution.[29] A reasonable set of physical distribution objectives for its lines of clothing might be:

- Enough turnover so that no product stays in inventory more than one month
- A turnaround period of no more than one day between when an order is received and when it is shipped
- 100 percent on-time delivery

Cost objectives could also be specified (for example, physical distribution costs not to exceed 15 percent of sales). The cost of particular physical distribution activities might also be spelled out. If a company uses a just-in-time system, it might want to specify that transportation costs do not exceed 50 percent of total physical distribution costs.

DEVELOP ORDER-PROCESSING CAPABILITIES

Once physical distribution objectives are defined, managers must establish the components of the physical distribution system. The first step is to develop **order-processing** *capabilities; that is, to receive and process customer orders, transmit them to warehouses, fill the order from inventory, prepare a bill, and issue shipping instructions.*

FIGURE 16.2

Establishing the Physical Distribution System

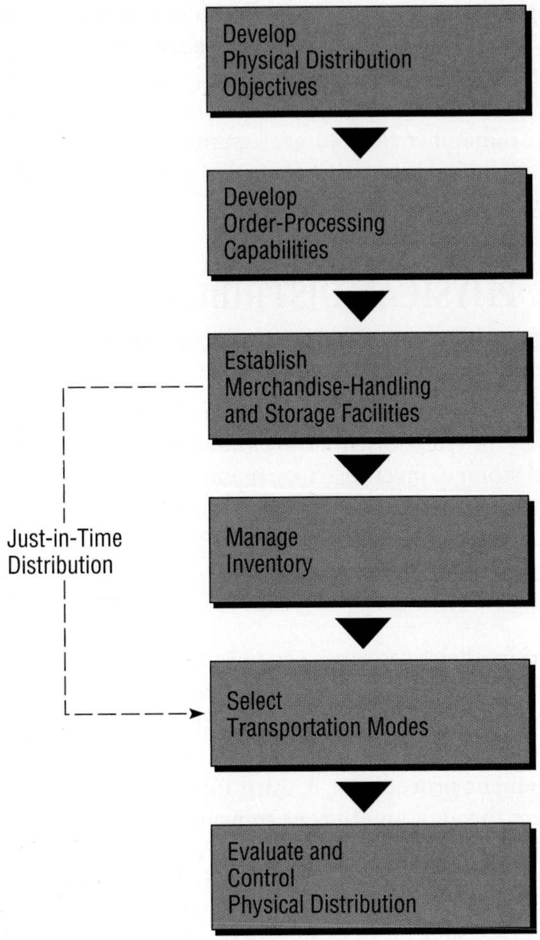

Order processing systems of most large companies are entirely automated. We have seen how McKesson's system is automated, right down to the conveyer belts that load packages on trucks according to each package's destination. Channel-leading retailers have also developed pinpoint order-processing systems. In 1990, Kmart unveiled a state-of-the-art order-processing network whereby a clerk records purchases with a scanner at the checkout counter, and this sales data is fed to a computer at Kmart headquarters in Troy, Michigan (see Figure 16.3). The computer automatically reorders goods for the stores based on sales rather than waiting for requests from the field—which used to arrive only after a store's shelves were bare.[30] Orders are transmitted to one of Kmart's warehouses, where the goods are located and prepared for shipment to the store.

ESTABLISH MERCHANDISE-HANDLING AND STORAGE FACILITIES

The next set of components required for a physical distribution system, merchandise handling and storage facilities, provide the link between order processing and shipment.

FIGURE 16.3

Kmart's Automated Order-Processing System

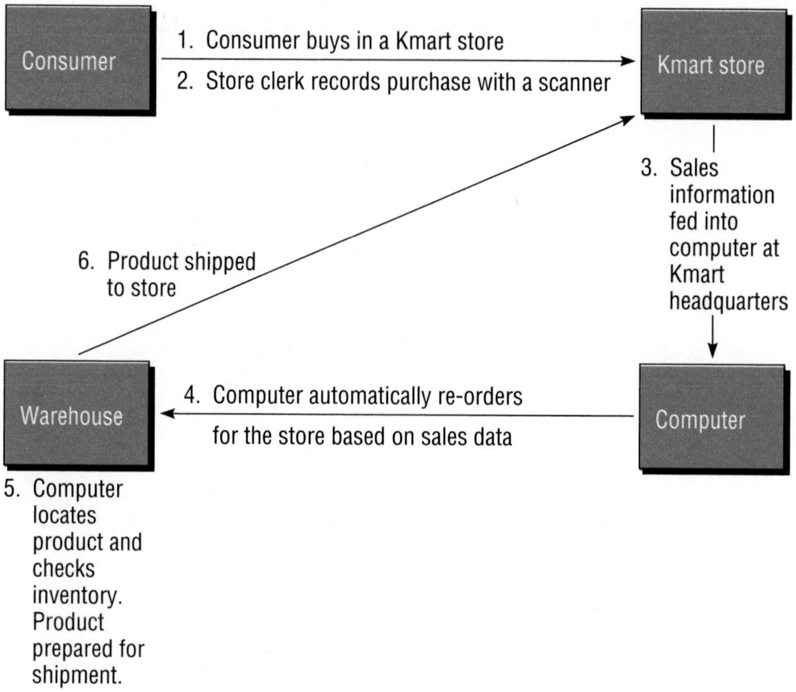

MERCHANDISE HANDLING

The activities of **merchandise handling** *are locating an item in inventory, conveying it to an assembly area where it is sorted and packed for shipping, moving it to a shipping platform, and loading the item on a transportation vehicle for shipment to the customer* (see left-hand side of Figure 16.4). For the Giant supermarket chain of Virginia, these activities are handled by a computer-controlled warehouse system dubbed the Ordermatic—a 10-story-tall behemoth with 5,400 separate "gravity flow" lanes and conveyer belts. (The right hand column in Figure 16.4 illustrates the merchandise handling steps controlled by the Ordermatic computer.)

When a product order comes from a Giant supermarket, the Ordermatic locates the desired item in the warehouse by zeroing in on its bar code. Once located, the item is picked up by either robot or human arms, placed in crates, and dropped onto one of the Ordermatic's moving conveyers. All the conveyers flow into the Ordermatic's computer "brain," a glass-enclosed sorting center that separates the crates according to their destination.

After being sorted, the crates travel down metal rollers and into several shipping lanes that feed Giant's delivery trucks. Workers stationed at those lanes use a laser scanner to check the bar codes and confirm that the item has been correctly slotted. The Ordermatic can send 7,200 cases an hour to bay doors for delivery.[31]

STORAGE FACILITIES

Warehouses permit a firm to consolidate a variety of items in one location close to the buyer. Retailers and wholesalers can buy a variety of items in larger quantities and take advantage of quantity discounts because of warehouse facilities.

FIGURE 16.4

A Merchandise Handling System

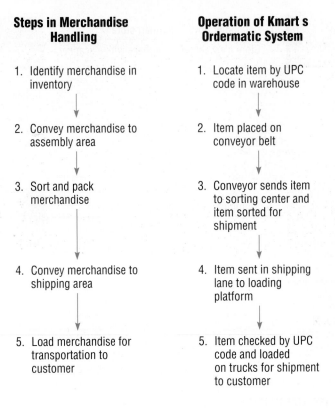

Steps in Merchandise Handling	Operation of Kmart s Ordermatic System
1. Identify merchandise in inventory	1. Locate item by UPC code in warehouse
2. Convey merchandise to assembly area	2. Item placed on conveyor belt
3. Sort and pack merchandise	3. Conveyor sends item to sorting center and item sorted for shipment
4. Convey merchandise to shipping area	4. Item sent in shipping lane to loading platform
5. Load merchandise for transportation to customer	5. Item checked by UPC code and loaded on trucks for shipment to customer

Manufacturers can ship larger quantities of items from a warehouse location and save in transportation costs.

Warehouse facilities may be either public or private. **Public warehouses** *provide storage facilities to a firm on a rental basis.* There are over 10,000 such facilities in the United States. For companies that produce seasonal products or products with cyclical demand, public warehouses are more economical than the fixed costs of building warehouse facilities that would not be needed on a consistent basis. Some public warehouses offer specialized facilities such as refrigeration for frozen foods or climate control for wines and tobacco.

Private warehouses *are facilities owned by firms that need storage on a consistent basis, that is, manufacturers with a large variety of goods requiring storage between production and delivery.* Retail chains and distributors shipping to a large number of retail outlets are also likely to own their own facilities.

One trend among retailers, however, is to cut down on their warehousing costs by forging deals whereby manufacturers ship to stores directly. Montgomery Ward asks vendors of "high-ticket" items, such as General Electric, to ship directly to its stores.[32]

Another recent development is the establishment of **distribution centers** *which are large, automated warehouses with computerized order-processing and merchandise-handling facilities.* They are usually one-story facilities (avoiding the need for elevators) and are located near highways or railroads to facilitate transportation (see W.W. Grainger's 1.4 million square-foot distribution center in Exhibit 16.3).

EXHIBIT 16.3

W. W. Grainger's Distribution Center

The Lazarus department store chain was able to custom design its merchandise-handling system through its $14 million purchase of a 1.2 million square-foot distribution center in Sharonville, Ohio. The suburban center offers access to multilane highways that feed right into Lazarus's major markets. Its size also facilitated the creation of separate loading bays for each of the chain's 41 stores, cutting down on mix-ups and delay.[33]

Some firms use smaller warehouse facilities to first gather items and then ship them to distribution centers, where they are consolidated for shipment to various points around the country.

MANAGING INVENTORY

Warehouses and distribution centers require a system to manage inventory. An inventory management system must answer two questions: how much to reorder to maintain optimal inventory (the *optimal reorder quantity*) and how often (the *optimal reorder frequency*). The optimal reorder quantity and optimal reorder frequency are easiest to determine for products that have a consistent demand pattern throughout the year. Consumer repurchase rates for items such as toothpaste, cereals, or deodorants are predictable, and inventory levels and reorder frequency can be keyed to known demand. Inventory management is more difficult for seasonal products such as iced tea or suntan lotion. Companies prefer to manufacture these items year-round to spread out the fixed costs of production facilities and ensure steady work for employees. As a result, inventory builds up in off-season periods. Thus, to operate on a year-round basis, management trades lower per-unit production costs for significantly higher inventory carrying costs.

Determining optimal inventory levels and reorder points is most difficult for products with erratic demand such as fashion items or toys. Many manufacturers and retailers have found a solution to erratic demand by maintaining minimum inventory levels through a just-in-time system and ordering by closely tracking consumer demand.

ETHICAL AND ENVIRONMENTAL ISSUES IN MARKETING

Trade Loading: How RJR Manipulated Its Order Processing System to Inflate Profits

A good order-processing system ensures that customer purchases determine orders by wholesalers or retailers and that orders determine a manufacturer's production schedule.

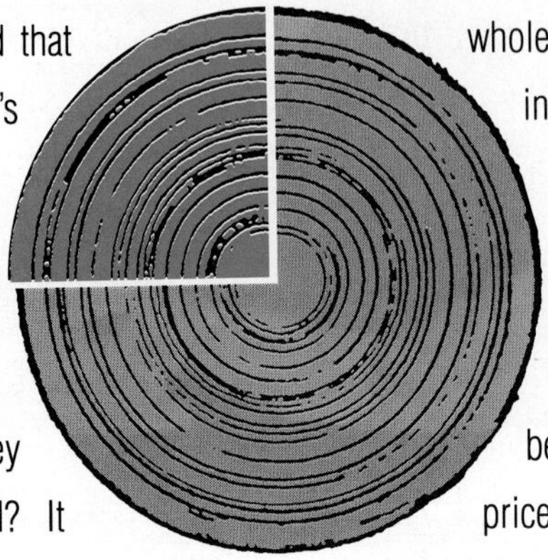

So what would happen if the system was thrown out of whack by a manufacturer who sent its wholesalers far more than they needed or the customer wanted? It should mean bad business. But when RJ Reynolds did it in the late 1980s, it meant $250 million in new revenues. How? A misguided but not illegal bookkeeping gimmick called *trade loading* was used by RJR to inflate its profits and market share.

The genesis of trade loading came in 1982, when RJR's wholesalers went on a buying spree to stock up on cigarettes before a 16 percent federal excise tax went into effect. After they made huge profits by reselling the cigarettes when the tax went into effect, wholesalers realized they could keep making money by buying large volumes before a price increase and they clamored to institutionalize the practice. RJR was only too happy to oblige. Every June and December through the 1980s, it hiked its prices so that wholesalers who "loaded up" beforehand could charge higher prices and increase their profits. The benefit for RJR was clear: It could show sales surges on its quarterly reports during June and December, just before it increased its prices.

If the system seemed innocuous at its beginning, it became dangerous when RJR grew addicted. By 1987, the company was using trade loading to inflate

OPTIMAL REORDER QUANTITY

The optimal amount to reorder to maintain appropriate inventory levels depends on inventory costs. As shown in Figure 16.5, there are three types of inventory costs: carrying costs, out-of-stock costs, and procurement costs. **Carrying costs** *are the costs of tying up capital in inventory and some additional costs such as taxes and insurance on inventory.* These costs can be substantial, often as much as 25 percent of the value of the inventory itself. The longer an item stays in inventory, the higher the carrying costs. **Out-of-stock costs** *are the costs of sales lost because the item is not available.* The greater the demand for a product, the greater is the out-of-stock cost. **Procurement costs** *are the costs of reordering an item and include the costs of processing and transmitting the order and the cost of the item itself.*

The optimal reorder quantity depends on these costs. As inventory levels go up, out-of-stock costs go down because it is more likely the product will be available.

ETHICAL AND ENVIRONMENTAL ISSUES IN MARKETING

claims that it held a 32 percent share of the domestic market—a benchmark RJR officials were obsessed with, because retailers always gave better exposure to Philip Morris, the market leader.

Also by the late 1980s, many Americans had already quit smoking, and the "loaded" cigarettes were piling up in warehouses across the country. RJR's wholesalers ideally should have had about 4½ days of stock. By 1988, they were holding six weeks worth. With so many cigarette cartons piled up, wholesalers were having trouble telling which were fresh and which were stale. In the confusion, stale cigarettes were being trucked to market, creating widespread customer irritation.

The trade-loading scam began unraveling in 1989, after Kohlberg Kravis Roberts (KKR) bought the consumer-products giant for $25 billion. The new team was horrified to discover RJRs doctored balance sheets and inflated warehouse stocks. No one could even seem to agree how many billions of stale boxes were out there. Some said 13 billion, others 15 billion.

KKR decided to kill the practice, announcing in late 1989 it was discontinuing trade loading and foregoing $340 million in operating profits. RJR could afford the write-off, but the withdrawal pains were acute for the wholesalers who had grown fat from the quarterly surges. Said one: "Take away those profits without giving us something in their place and you've got blood in the streets."

Questions: What is trade loading? How did it create inefficiencies in the physical distribution system?

Source: "The $600 Million Cigarette Scam," *Fortune,* December 4, 1989.

Procurement costs also go down, since orders will be less frequent; but carrying costs will go up. The reorder quantity to maintain an optimal inventory level is the point where all three of these costs are minimized. This is at point Q in Figure 16.5.

FREQUENCY OF REORDERS

The frequency of reorders will depend on the optimal reorder quantity and the level of demand. A firm estimating the number of times it will have to reorder an item might determine that the optimal reorder quantity is at 2,000 units and that estimated annual demand is 50,000 units. The product would then have to be reordered 25 times a year. If demand is consistent, this would mean reordering about every other week. If demand is seasonal or erratic, reorders are likely to cluster at points of peak demand.

FIGURE 16.5

Inventory Costs

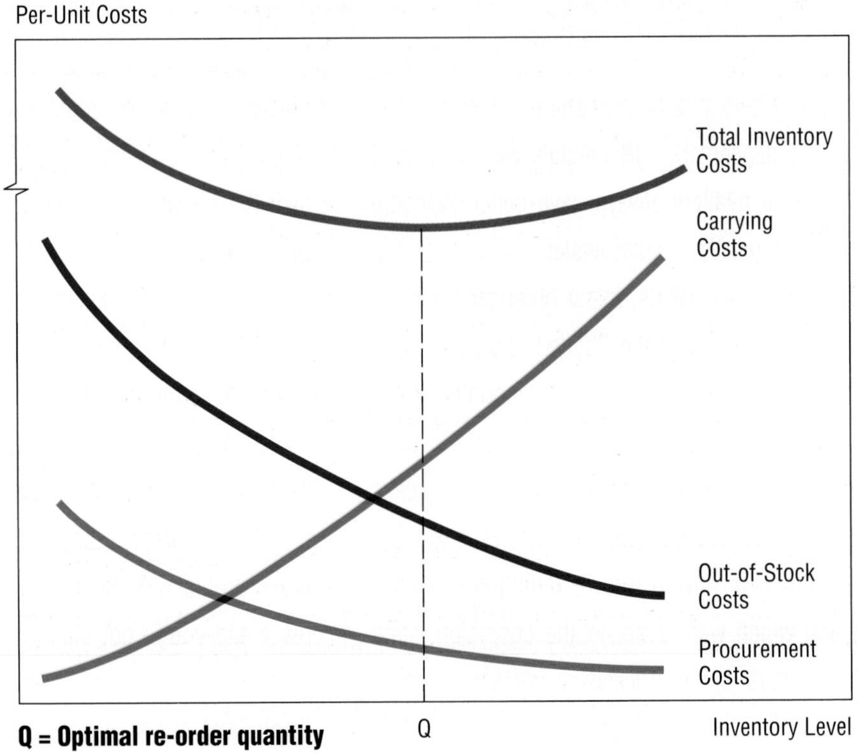

Frequent reorders minimize inventory levels and keep inventory carrying costs down. But they increase procurement costs and the chances of being out of stock. Conversely, ordering less frequently requires higher inventory levels, resulting in higher carrying costs but lower procurement costs and less chance of being out of stock.

JUST-IN-TIME (JIT) DISTRIBUTION

An alternative to maintaining substantial inventory levels is the just-in-time distribution process that minimizes inventory levels to reduce physical distribution costs. **Just-in-time (JIT) distribution** *means producing exactly what is required by the market just in time to be delivered to customers.* Figure 16.2 shows a JIT capability by the dotted line from merchandise handling to transportation. The objective is to minimize inventory and storage costs. JIT systems are most feasible when demand is consistent and predictable. As we have seen, McKesson instituted a JIT capability as part of its Economost system, allowing the company to ship only what was immediately required by its pharmacists, thus keeping its inventory low.

JIT systems were developed by the Japanese as a production-control method rather than a distribution system. The idea was to get materials to the production line exactly when they were needed so as to reduce inventory costs involved in production. In its first applications, it was therefore most relevant to industrial marketers trying to ship materials to their buyers (other manufacturers) for use on the production line.

The concept was extended to distribution primarily in the early 1980s, when high interest rates substantially increased inventory carrying costs. The best means to reduce carrying costs was by eliminating inventory, and JIT was the way to do it. Not only did it get materials to the production line when needed, but it produced the finished product when it was needed by customers.

There are four requirements for a JIT system. First, rapid feedback from customers regarding their needs so manufacturers can produce on an as-ordered basis. Toys "Я" Us is able to operate with a JIT system because it can obtain immediate information on customer purchase trends and transmit orders to toy manufacturers on this basis. The result is lower inventory costs, which permits the company to sell its products at lower prices. The company also avoids the risk of holding unsold inventories in the highly volatile toy market, simply by placing more frequent orders with manufacturers.

A second requirement for JIT to work is an effective computer system. If products are to pass quickly from manufacturer to customer on an as-ordered basis, then they must be identified on the assembly line to fill customer orders. This must be done by computers, most frequently by laser scanners identifying bar codes with the information fed into the manufacturer's computer at both the plant and at the consolidation point. As one druggist who was new to the JIT system remarked, "It does just about everything but tie my shoelaces."[34]

A third requirement is quick and efficient transportation. The greater frequency of deliveries under this system means that smaller quantities are shipped, thus transportation costs increase and inventory costs decrease. A fourth essential component is **consolidation centers,** which *are ship-through facilities that look like distribution centers—large one-floor buildings—where products are brought for delivery rather than storage, permitting them to be sent quickly to customers.*

SELECT TRANSPORTATION FACILITIES

The last physical distribution activity, transportation, accounts for an average of 45 percent of physical distribution costs. This proportion is even higher in JIT systems, because inventory and storage costs are minimized. Because of its cost, selection of transportation facilities is one of the most important decisions in the management of the physical distribution system. The key modes of transport are by truck, rail, air, water, and pipeline. The advantages and disadvantages of each are summarized in Table 16.1.

Large wholesalers and retailers usually employ a combination of transportation modes. Chicago-based Spiegel ships 15 million packages a year to customers who buy from its catalogs. The company relies on Viking Freight Systems to provide shipment by truck, rail, and air depending on the customer's location.[35]

TRUCKS

More money is spent on truck transportation than on any other mode, even though it comes in second to railroads in terms of total ton-miles of goods delivered. There are over 25,000 independent trucking companies in the United States, shipping a variety of products. Most of the products shipped are packaged goods or lighter industrial goods.

The most important advantages of trucks are speed, on-time dependability, and availability of routes. In addition, trucks have the flexibility of picking products up at a plant and delivering them directly to customers, an important advantage in a JIT system. However, motor transportation is expensive and cannot carry large loads. Hackney Trucking tries to overcome this disadvantage by advertising double

TABLE 16.1

Characteristics of Alternative Modes of Transportation

	ADVANTAGES	DISADVANTAGES
TRUCK	Fast On-time dependability Extensive routes Flexibility in pickup and delivery Frequent shipments	High cost Small size of loads Weather sensitive
RAIL	Extensive routes Handles large loads Handles a variety of products	Slow Limited flexibility in pickup and delivery Limited frequency of shipments
AIR FREIGHT	Fast Frequent shipments Less risk of damage	High cost Limited variety of products Weather sensitive Limited on-time dependability
WATER	Low cost Handles large loads Handles a variety of products	Slow Limited routes Infrequent shipments Limited on-time dependability
PIPELINE	Low cost On-time dependability Frequent shipments	Limited variety of products Slow Limited routes

trailers that carry large loads directly to end users, thus reducing warehouse costs (see Exhibit 16.4).

Some of the larger trucking companies provide important services to their customers. John Cheeseman Trucking performed some of Torrington's merchandise-handling and storage functions through its own consolidation centers. The Danzas Corporation, which was founded in 1815 by an officer in Napoleon's defeated army, runs 650 international distribution centers. Customers who seek out its express fleet of 4,500 trucks are also offered access to its air and ocean shipping divisions. Danzas' reputation for value-added service led McDonald's to choose the Swiss-based transportation company for its move into Moscow (see Exhibit 16.5).[36]

RAIL

Railroads are the most widely used means of transportation, representing about one-third of delivered tonnage. In 1950, they represented 57 percent of delivered tonnage. The decrease was due to the increasing use of trucks and the advent of air transportation. With 200,000 miles of lines, railroads provide a wide availability of routes. Companies producing bulky items such as coal, lumber, and paper products usually ship by rail. But railroads are slow, do not ship as frequently as truck and air transport, and have limited flexibility in picking up and delivering products.

Obsolete tracks and equipment, poor service, and damaged merchandise helped reduce the use of rail transport in the 1950s and 1960s. A series of bankruptcies

EXHIBIT 16.4

Advertising Economical Truck Transportation

EXHIBIT 16.5

Danzas Trucks in Moscow

resulted in the mergers of many railroad lines, leading to modernized equipment and more streamlined companies that offer improved services. As a result, railroad companies are in better shape today than they were 20 years ago.

AIR FREIGHT

Air is about three times as expensive as trucks and fifteen times as expensive as rail. As a result, its use is limited to specialized products. But it is very fast and decreases the risk of damaged merchandise. Some combination of truck and air is usually required to get products to airports and then to customers.

Speed is sometimes worth the greater cost of air transport, particularly for perishable goods or high-cost items that must reach customers quickly. Beauty For All Seasons, a cosmetic company, switched from truck to air transport because the latter cut down on damaged merchandise. The company found that its lipsticks were melting when shipped in the south, and its face creams froze when shipped in the northeast. Quick delivery in temperature-controlled planes solved the problem.[37]

Air express companies such as Federal Express and Purolator Courier provide overnight delivery for smaller packages (under seventy pounds) by routing them through central hubs. Emery Air Freight established a niche in the market by concentrating on overnight delivery of heavier packages, making it appealing to companies that need quick delivery as part of a JIT system. Like Federal Express, Emery routes all packages through a hub—Dayton, Ohio—which operates like one giant consolidation center for rerouting to customers nationwide.

WATER TRANSPORT

Water transport can be by ship on the Great Lakes or the St. Lawrence Seaway, by barges on inland waterways, or transoceanic to foreign markets. Water transport is a major means of hauling low-cost, bulky items such as coal and iron. Delivery is slow, the routes are limited to navigable waterways, and shipments are infrequent compared to other modes. But costs are one-fifth that of rail.

PIPELINES

Pipelines are used to move liquids such as oil or chemical products and natural gas products over long distances. The more than 200,000 miles of pipelines in the United States make them a more flexible means of transportation than many people realize. They are inexpensive and reliable, but slow and limited to certain routes and products.

INTERMODAL TRANSPORTATION SYSTEMS

One of the important advances in physical distribution is the development of intermodal transportation systems. **Intermodal transportation systems** *combine modes of transport such as links between rail, truck, and ship.* **Piggybacking** *describes a transfer of containers from truck to rail;* **trainship** *involves a combination of rail and ship transportation.* A necessary facility in such intermodal transport is **containerization**; *that is, putting goods in containers that can be transferred between trucks, ships, and railroad cars.*

CSX, one of the largest railroads, is an intermodal company that offers services in rail, ocean shipping, trucking, and warehousing (see Exhibit 16.6). The company uses container ships capable of conveying railroad-car loads to 76 ports in 64 countries. In addition, it runs an in-coastal barge fleet, a trucking company, and pipeline facilities. These are not stand-alone facilities. They are interconnected in that CSX's rail lines can connect with its trucks, and its rail and truck fleet can load onto its ships and barges. One service is its Orange Blossom Special for citrus growers, combining rail service through its Seaboard System with CSX-owned trucks that pick up from the growers and deliver directly to customers.[38] CSX provides the advantage of multiple transportation services within one company.

EXHIBIT 16.6

Example of an Intermodal Facility

Another One Of Our Trains Arrives At The Station.
If you think we're just a railroad, take another look.
We're a lot more. We're Sea-Land, one of the largest container ship lines on earth, serving 76 ports in 64 countries.
We're also trucks. Barges. Pipelines. Energy resources. Fiber optics. Resorts and property development. And, of course, the railroad. And we're developing new technology to make it all work together.
We're CSX, the first true global transporter. If you've never heard of one before, it's because there's never been one before. This is a company on the move.
CSX
The Company That Puts Things In Motion.
Transportation/Energy/Properties/Technology
©1987, CSX Corporation

EVALUATION AND CONTROL

Once decisions have been made regarding order processing, merchandise handling, storage, inventory management, and transportation, a company must evaluate its performance of these activities (the last step in establishing the physical distribution system). Control requires comparing performance with physical distribution objectives. Looking back to the objectives stated earlier, some key indicators of performance would be:

- The amount of time it takes to process an order
- The amount of time it takes to deliver an order
- The proportion of items that arrive undamaged
- The amount of time products are in inventory
- The proportion of times items arrive on time
- Physical distribution costs as a percentage of sales

Failure to meet objectives based on these criteria could spell problems with the physical distribution system, warranting examination of each of the activities in the system.

Companies are likely to put more emphasis on controlling particular physical distribution activities, depending on the nature of the system and the strategy they select. For example, a JIT approach requires more emphasis on control of transportation and less on inventory. As a result, managers will keep a closer watch on the proportion of on-time deliveries and a less-careful watch on inventory turnover. Conversely, a company that maintains a large number of warehouses because of seasonal or erratic demand will keep a closer watch on storage and inventory carrying costs.

As an example of control over physical distribution, the Oldsmobile Division of General Motors has established a special Reduction of Auto Damage (ROAD) team responsible for ensuring damage-free transit and delivery of cars from the assembly line to dealer showrooms. The team analyzes travel conditions along the routes taken by trains transporting Oldsmobile cars and has authority to alter schedules and routes in response to potential hazards.[39] As a result of ROAD teams, Oldsmobile has cut transit time from an average of 50 hours to 36 hours and substantially reduced delivery of damaged vehicles.

PHYSICAL DISTRIBUTION TRADEOFFS

The physical distribution activities cited in Figure 16.2 are closely interrelated because they involve cost tradeoffs. Figure 16.6 shows the per-unit costs of physical distribution activities by order quantity (that is, the size of a single order). As order quantity increases, per unit transportation costs decrease because of economies of scale in transporting a larger number of items. The cost of processing orders also decreases, because larger order quantities result in fewer orders. Storage costs (that is, the costs of building and maintaining warehouses) increase because of the need to maintain more units in stock. Inventory costs (the costs of keeping products in stock) also increase, because more inventory capacity is required to handle larger volume.

If a company finds that costs of a certain physical distribution component are too high, it can try to reduce costs of that component; but total costs may not be reduced. For example, if transportation costs are too high, they can be decreased by using slower means of transport such as rail; but this would increase inventory and storage costs and might also aggravate customers by delaying deliveries.

In summary, Figure 16.6 shows a tradeoff between inventory, transportation, order-processing, and storage costs. A just-in-time system increases the frequency of orders and reduces order size. Transportation and order costs are high, but storage and inventory costs are minimal (left-hand side of Figure 16.6). Conversely, accumulating units into one large order minimizes transportation and ordering costs, although it increases storage and inventory costs (right-hand side of Figure 16.6). Total physical distribution costs are minimized somewhere between these two extremes at point X in Figure 16.6.

Ultimately, there must be a tradeoff between total distribution costs and customer satisfaction. Maximizing customer satisfaction is likely to increase distribution costs because it may require larger inventories to avoid stockouts, speedier transportation to ensure on-time reliability, and more warehouses, all of which increase distribution costs. For instance, Wilson Plastics won its battle for supremacy with Formica by building a costly network of 15 regional warehouses that provide one-day delivery and by designing its products with simplified, albeit more

FIGURE 16.6

Physical Distribution Costs

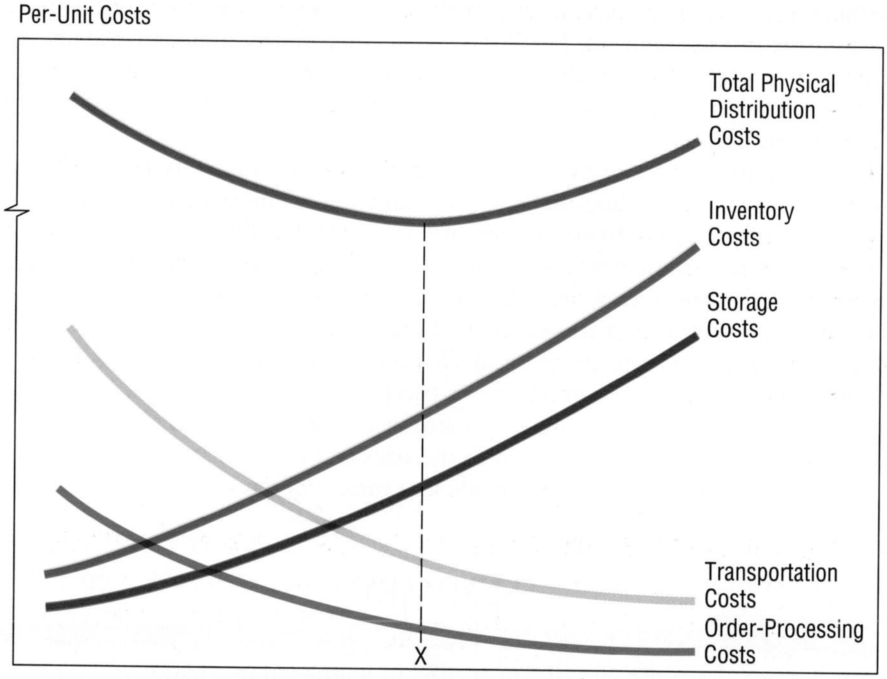

X = Order quantity that minimizes total physical distribution costs.

expensive, resin that allows Wilson to quickly make items that distributors do not have in stock.[40]

After weighing these alternatives, distribution managers must decide on the costs deemed necessary for customer satisfaction. One reason newer, automated inventory-control and order-handling systems are a source of competitive advantage is that they are cost-efficient in improving customer service. If physical distribution is to be used as a means of gaining competitive advantage, enough must be spent on it to ensure customer satisfaction and distribution efficiency.

INTEGRATING PHYSICAL DISTRIBUTION INTO THE MARKETING MIX

Physical distribution activities must be integrated with other components of the marketing mix—product, promotion, price, and distribution strategies.

Products can develop a competitive advantage based on the services provided through physical distribution activities. Campbell Soup instituted a JIT system in distributing its Le Menu frozen food line. Products were produced only when needed, improving on-time delivery to supermarkets and reducing damage due to perishability.[41]

Promotional factors also interact with physical distribution. The product must be on the shelf before it is advertised. Perrier, for instance, blundered with a $25 million ad campaign that was launched after the discovery of benzine in some of its bottles forced a full-scale recall. The subsequent campaign, designed to keep customers aware of Perrier, featured the slogan: "Perrier. Worth waiting for." But without any Perrier on supermarket shelves, customers shrugged it off as irrelevant. Critics of the campaign felt that Perrier should have waited until the product was on the shelf before it resumed advertising. Said one marketing consultant, "The strategy of keeping Perrier in consumers' minds isn't as effective when the brand is out of sight, and people have to wait months for it."[42]

Pricing must also be integrated with physical distribution; its costs must be accounted for in the selling price. For example, one company gave quantity discounts to its customers based on freight costs, ignoring the warehouse handling costs. As a result, some items were underpriced and others overpriced depending on their merchandise-handling requirements.

Because physical distribution is part of the overall distribution system, a company must also integrate its physical distribution activities with those of other channel members. Thus, Wal-Mart uses computers to tie its physical distribution system to those of manufacturers by spewing out sales data that alerts manufacturers to coming orders, right down to the sizes and colors that are needed. Shipments from manufacturers can be made in a matter of days.[43]

SUMMARY

1. **What are the most significant trends in wholesaling today?**
   The most significant trends in wholesaling have been a shift from an old-fashioned order-taker mentality to a focus on higher productivity through computerized order-processing systems, automated merchandise-handling methods, and modern distribution centers. This recent focus on efficiency and productivity has come to be known as value-added wholesaling.
2. **What are the most important types of wholesalers?**
   Wholesaling can be performed through company-owned or independent wholesalers. Company-owned outlets may be manufacturers using sales branches or retailers using company-owned warehouses. Most wholesalers are independents, divided into those that take ownership of goods (merchant wholesalers) and those that do not (agents and brokers). Some merchant wholesalers provide full services. These include general-merchandise and specialty wholesalers and rack jobbers. Merchant wholesalers that provide limited services include cash-and-carry wholesalers and truck jobbers. Merchant wholesalers that sell to industrial buyers are called distributors. These may also be full- or limited-service wholesalers.
3. **What is the nature of the physical distribution process?**
   Physical distribution is responsible for the flow of products from the manufacturer to the customer. Intermediaries and manufacturers engage in physical distribution activities to get the right products to customers at the right time and place. These activities are order processing, merchandise handling, development of storage facilities, inventory management, and delivery of products by utilizing various modes of transportation.
4. **Why is physical distribution a system?**
   Physical distribution is a system for two reasons. First, physical distribution activities are interrelated because of cost tradeoffs. For example, decreasing

transportation costs may increase storage and order-processing costs because of an increase in average order size. Reducing inventory levels by speeding up delivery reduces inventory carrying costs but increases transportation costs. Second, physical distribution activities are designed for a common goal—distribution efficiency in the form of trying to minimize distribution costs and maximize customer satisfaction.

5. **What is the nature of physical distribution activities such as order processing, merchandise handling and storage, inventory control, and transportation?**
Order processing requires receiving and processing customer orders, transmitting them to warehouses or distribution centers, filling orders from inventory, and providing billing and shipping instructions.
Merchandise handling requires locating an item in inventory; conveying it to an assembly area where it is sorted and packed for shipping; and sending it to a shipping platform, where it is loaded for shipment. Warehouse facilities permit a firm to consolidate a variety of items in one location, store them, and then select them for shipment. A recent development is the establishment of distribution centers—large, automated warehouses with computerized order-processing and merchandise facilities.
Inventory management requires determining how much to reorder to maintain optimal inventory levels and how often to reorder. The optimal reorder level balances inventory carrying costs, out-of-stock costs, and procurement costs. Finally, transportation modes are selected based on criteria such as cost, speed, on-time reliability, and route availability.

6. **What is a just-in-time distribution process?**
Just-in-time (JIT) distribution means producing exactly what is required by the market just in time to be delivered to customers. The objective is to minimize inventory levels. A JIT system allows manufacturers to produce on an as-ordered basis. Transportation is a key component, because such a system requires more frequent delivery of smaller quantities. Another essential component of a JIT system is computers and bar codes to allow products to pass quickly from manufacturer to customer.

7. **What is the relationship of physical distribution to other components of the marketing mix?**
Physical distribution is related to every component of the marketing mix. A product can gain a competitive advantage through on-time, damage-free delivery. Advertising cannot succeed unless physical distribution is effective in putting the product on the shelf in time to meet demand. The price of a product must take account of physical distribution costs, and a company's physical distribution activities must tie in to the distribution activities of other channel members to ensure smooth delivery from manufacturer to consumer.

KEY TERMS

Value-added wholesaling (p. 521)
Sales branches (p. 522)
Merchant wholesalers (p. 523)
General merchandise wholesalers (p. 523)
Specialty merchandise wholesalers (p. 523)
Rack jobbers (p. 524)
Cash-and-carry wholesalers (p. 524)
Truck jobbers (p. 524)
Mail-order wholesalers (p. 524)
Mill supply house (p. 524)
Specialty distributors (p. 524)
Drop shippers (desk jobbers) (p. 524)
Mail-order distributors (p. 525)
Physical distribution (p. 528)
Physical distribution system (p. 528)
Order processing (p. 531)

Merchandise handling (p. 533)
Public warehouses (p. 534)
Private warehouses (p. 534)
Distribution centers (p. 534)
Carrying costs (p. 536)
Out-of-stock costs (p. 536)
Procurement costs (p. 536)
Just-in-time (JIT) distribution (p. 538)
Consolidation centers (p. 539)
Intermodal transportation (p. 542)
Piggybacking (p. 542)
Trainship (p. 542)
Containerization (p. 542)

QUESTIONS

1. What is value-added wholesaling? What steps did McKesson take to become a value-added wholesaler?
2. Why do many large manufacturers and retailers distribute through wholesalers when they have the resources to sell directly to retailers or to industrial buyers?
3. What is the distinction between full-service and limited-service wholesalers? Cite examples of each, specifying why they are full- or limited-service wholesalers.
4. Why is physical distribution one of the most important marketing activities?
5. How can physical distribution give a company a competitive advantage? Provide examples.
6. What are the cost tradeoffs in establishing a physical distribution system? What are the risks involved?
7. What events in the international marketplace are likely to affect the development of physical distribution systems abroad? In what ways will physical distribution be affected by these events?
8. A manufacturer of regular and instant coffees is considering producing a new line of canned iced coffee. What problems might occur in managing inventory for the new product that the manufacturer did not experience with its regular and instant coffee lines? What can the manufacturer do about these problems?
9. Toy products such as hula hoops and Cabbage Patch dolls experienced a rapid rise in sales, several years of popularity, and then a rapid fall-off. What problems did toy manufacturers have in determining production and inventory levels for these fad items? What solutions might there be for reducing the risk of manufacturing and inventorying such items?
10. Why is transportation the most important physical distribution activity in a just-in-time system? What facilities must transportation companies maintain to ensure just-in-time distribution?
11. The manufacturer of the new iced coffee line cited in question 9 maintains a just-in-time system of distribution for its regular and instant coffees. It is considering using the same system for its iced coffees.
    a. What problems might there be in using a JIT system for iced coffees?
    b. What types of companies are most likely to use a JIT system? Why?
12. What type or types of transportation would be the best for the following products and why?
    a. Fresh lobsters transported to fish markets
    b. Coal transported to manufacturers
    c. Natural gas transported to storage facilities
    d. Soft drinks transported to retail outlets
13. How do physical distribution requirements affect the following components of the marketing mix?
    a. Promotional strategies
    b. Packaging
    c. Pricing strategies

    How does a product's characteristics affect physical distribution activities?

QUESTIONS: YOU ARE THE DECISION MAKER

1. One well-known marketing writer commented on management's attitude toward physical distribution: "American management's philosophy has been: 'If you're smart enough to make it, aggressive enough to sell it—then any dummy can get it there!' "[44] What is wrong with this philosophy?
2. A producer of over-the-counter pharmaceutical items recently introduced a just-in-time system for most of its products. The distribution manager said:

   Our JIT system is the greatest thing since sliced bread. It has substantially reduced our inventory costs, improved on-time deliveries, and gotten our products to customers in better condition. If I had my way, I would try to totally eliminate inventory by using even quicker modes of transportation and moving our products more rapidly through our distribution centers.

   What are the risks of relying totally on a JIT system?

CHAPTER 17

The Promotional Mix, Sales Promotions, and Publicity

YOUR FOCUS IN CHAPTER 17

To learn:

- *The components of a promotional mix, and the purposes of each component.*
- *The marketing communications process required to transmit the promotional mix.*
- *How managers select a promotional mix for a brand or product category.*
- *The types of sales promotional tools that can be used to promote a brand.*
- *The types of publicity tools that can be used to promote a brand or company.*

The Promotional Mix: How a Lousy Ad Showed Burger King the Value of a Good Promotion

When the wife of Burger King CEO Barry Gibbons had trouble cashing a check in a Miami grocery store without identification, she complained so loudly that it gave her husband a brainstorm. Service companies have too many rules, he thought, and if you want to keep customers happy sometimes you have to break the rules.[1]

By 1990, "Sometimes you've gotta break the rules" had become Burger King's nationwide advertising slogan, with a majority of the company's $215 million marketing budget devoted to it. The company had been burned by the 1986 "Search for Herb" fiasco, an irrelevant advertising campaign based on a search for a figure called Herb, because he never went to a Burger King. Now, the fast-food chain finally thought it had hit upon a slogan that would position it as being more individualistic and flexible than archrival McDonald's.[2] It would soon discover otherwise.

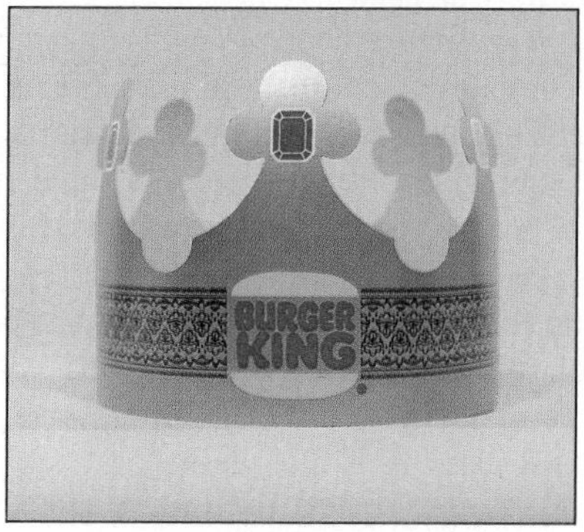

Customers could not understand what the slogan meant, and franchisee's complained that it seemed to encourage lawlessness. "Are we telling kids to go out and buy drugs?" one wondered.[3] Having gone through eight campaigns since 1976, Burger King was determined not to flip-flop again, and it tried clarifying the theme with a second wave of ads. One depicted a Burger King manager letting members of his staff use the restaurant after closing for their rock band's practice. "Helping someone realize a dream can be as important as the dream itself," an announcer intoned at the commercial's close.

Unfortunately, as much as Gibbons wanted to stand by the campaign, the new ads did not help, and complaints were growing too loud to ignore. Franchisees were in near revolt, demanding the company do something to increase foot traffic in their restaurants. Reluctantly, Gibbons agreed to divert most of the money earmarked for the ad campaign to Burger King's sales-promotion department.[4]

One of Burger King's favorite promotional tools had been using popular cartoon characters to appeal to children, and with the "break the rules" campaign floundering, the strategy became even more critical. In a tie-in promotion for its minimuffins breakfast, for instance, Burger King sold 11 million dolls modeled after characters from "The Simpsons" television show.[5] It also scored a coup by stealing from McDonald's the rights to use Walt Disney characters and themes in joint promotions and premiering the alliance with a massive blitz surrounding Disney's popular movie *Beauty and the Beast*. Even more ambitious was the *Keys to the Castle* campaign, which coincided with Disney World's twentieth anniversary; customers received a pop-up replica of the park that contained one of five keys, and those who collected all five won a trip to Disney World.[6]

The most successful promotion, however, was Burger King's Kids Club. A multimedia program unveiled early in 1990, Kids Club enabled children who signed up at local restaurants to receive a newsletter, stickers, posters, and other gifts. Almost all of Burger King's 5,400 restaurants participated, and many reported kids lining up to join. Within a year, the company had lured 2.7 million customers under the age of 12, and the club was credited with helping to boost sales to $6.2 billion—$500 million more than the year before.[7]

Yet by 1991, Burger King realized it could not sustain growth with expensive tie-in and club promotions alone. So it embarked on another course, this time jettisoning the "rules" campaign in favor of a new slogan: "Your way. Right away," a campaign that employed the value of Burger King's food products. Analysts saw the shift as a way for Burger King to get back to the basics of reinforcing its brand-name products, namely the Whopper.[8]

Not surprisingly, Burger King reinforced the slogan by changing its promotional strategies to match the advertising campaign. It replaced glitzy Disney-type cartoon promotions with price and value-oriented programs—the "your way" campaign. For instance, to promote its double cheeseburger, the chain unveiled a two-for-one deal. It also trumpeted a budget breakfast menu to coincide with its introduction of the Breakfast Buddy, an egg and bacon sandwich that premiered at 59 cents. The move mirrored a trend in the fast-food industry toward price promotions.[9]

What lies ahead for Burger King? Less-conventional promotions for sure. Currently, drivers wheeling up to get gas in some Amoco stations are seeing Burger King menus positioned above the pumps. By picking up the phone, they can order while they pump, then pick up their food at the nearby restaurant.[10]

Burger King may have finally found the answer in its search for an identity. The answer lies in a balanced promotional mix requiring value-oriented advertising supported by value-oriented promotions. Thankfully, Burger King no longer has to look for Herb. It seems to have found "Its way . . . right away."

THE PROMOTIONAL MIX

Burger King's advertising, sales promotions, and publicity constitute its promotional mix. *A* **promotional mix** *is the combination of communications strategies that a company uses to convey brand benefits to customers and to influence them to buy.* Four elements are involved: advertising, sales promotions, personal selling, and publicity. The promotional mix is such an important part of the overall marketing mix that each of its components will be examined in detail—sales promotions and publicity in this chapter, advertising in Chapter 18, and personal selling and the management of the sales effort in Chapter 19. A brief introduction to each of these components follows.

ADVERTISING

Advertising *is a paid, ongoing, nonpersonal communication from a commercial source such as a manufacturer or retailer.* It communicates messages about a product, service, or company that appear in mass media such as television, magazines, or radio.

Advertising has several communications objectives. One is to make consumers *aware* of a product. For example, in the early 1980s, Polaroid saw sales in its core market of instant cameras almost halved in the face of increasing sales of 35mm cameras. Polaroid's solution was to develop the Spectra, an instant camera with automatic focusing and a self-timer, that produces pictures close to 35mm quality.[11] Polaroid introduced Spectra with a $45 million advertising campaign. As a result, the majority of potential purchasers became aware of the availability of the camera. Advertising is also designed to *inform.* Polaroid's objective was not only to create awareness, but to inform consumers of Spectra's picture quality and features.

Advertising is also meant to *influence* consumers to buy. Influencing consumers often requires ads with emotional as well as informational content. United Airline's "Fly the friendly skies" or Burger King's "Your way. Right away." are themes that are meant to stir up good feelings about the product or service and thus encourage purchase.

Finally, the most important purpose of advertising is to keep the product or service *visible* to consumers over the long term. The idea is to keep existing customers loyal while ensuring that noncustomers continue to remember the product's existence. In this respect, advertising is insurance against the possibility that the product might fade out of existence. In a sense, it is more of a capital investment, like building a factory to ensure production over the next 20 years, than a short-term expedient to gain sales.

A classic example of the disastrous results of misunderstanding the role of advertising occurred at the turn of the century. The leading bar soap at the time was a brand called Sapolio, with Ivory second. The managers of Sapolio felt their brand was so firmly entrenched that they could cut back on advertising. Soon their market share began slipping, and eventually Sapolio slipped into the history books. Ivory, on the other hand, continued to advertise and thereby has maintained brand awareness to this day.

SALES PROMOTIONS

There are two types of sales promotions, consumer promotions and trade promotions. **Consumer promotions** *are short-term inducements of value to consumers to encourage them to buy a product or service.* Sales promotional tools directed to consumers include *coupons* that can be redeemed for cash, *sweepstakes* and *contests* that involve prizes, and *rebates* on a purchase. Most of these techniques are used to promote consumer packaged goods.

Trade promotions *are inducements to retailers and wholesalers to get them to stock the brand.* They include *cash allowances* and *discounts.* Occasionally, contests and sweepstakes are also directed to intermediaries to generate interest in the company's product.

Consumer promotions are more closely integrated with advertising strategies and are often meant to encourage nonusers to try a brand in the hope that they will continue to use it. This was Häagen-Dazs's objective when it ran a special promotion to pitch its ice cream as an alternative to roses on Mother's Day.[12] In most cases, consumers who switch to the promoted brand will switch back to their regular brand once the deal is off, but some might switch loyalty to the new brand. A study by the Promotion Marketing Association of America found that those most likely to change their purchasing behavior because of price promotions are not the lower-income consumers, but upscale middle-aged college graduates. It also found that the categories most likely to induce a switch in loyalty are batteries, coffee, personal appliances, shampoo, and toothpaste.[13] But even attracting temporary users over the short term can be profitable.

As we have seen with Burger King's "Keys to the Castle" promotion, sales promotions are also designed to motivate existing customers to buy more frequently. Attracting new customers is secondary in these cases.

Most sales promotions must be combined with advertising in order to be effective. The price incentive of the sales promotion needs to be complemented by the communication of product or service benefits that advertising provides. When the sales promotion is no longer running, and the price incentive is not available, advertising maintains the product's message.

PERSONAL SELLING

Personal selling *is face-to-face communication between a company sales representative and a customer and is designed to influence the customer to buy the company's products or services.* It is a powerful element of the promotional mix, because the marketer does not have to establish a message beforehand. The salesperson can assess the customer's needs, develop a sales message accordingly, evaluate the customer's reaction, and adjust the approach. Even when it does not result in a sale, personal selling is likely to at least get the attention of the customer and elicit some sort of response that may lead to a later sale.

Personal selling has a broad-based role in the promotional mix. Direct buyer-seller contacts are essential in marketing industrial goods, services, and many consumer goods such as clothing, appliances, automobiles, and electronics. In these cases, personal selling is often the most important component of the promotional mix. Advertising and sales promotions play a supportive role by setting the stage for buyer-seller interaction. For example, an organizational buyer who sees an ad for an industrial product might become more aware of the product's benefits and therefore more receptive to a salesperson's influence.

Personal selling is a powerful and effective means of communication, but it is expensive. Average costs of a call on an industrial buyer are estimated at over $300, whereas reaching an industrial buyer through a business publication costs an average of about 25 cents.[14] Of course, personal selling is a much more important influence on industrial buyers than magazine advertising, so higher costs are usually justified.

ETHICAL AND ENVIRONMENTAL ISSUES IN MARKETING

Cause-Related Marketing: Riding the Coattails of Crisis?

An interesting extension of joint promotions is cause-related marketing campaigns. **Cause-related marketing** *involves the firm agreeing to give a fixed amount of money to a chosen charity in return for being able to use the charity's name in promotional ads and events.* Since American Express launched the first cause-related ad in 1983 by associating itself with the Statue of Liberty restoration campaign, companies have tried to link themselves with causes that reflect their ideals. Buy Birds Eye and fund a food bank; wear Reebok sneakers and help Amnesty International; eat Ben & Jerry's ice cream and save the rain forests. Are marketers suddenly coming down with an acute case of good intentions, or is there something more cynical at play?

With federal funds in short supply, cause-related marketing has given some charities a much-needed boost. For instance, Johnson & Johnson embarked on a drive to help battered-women's shelters in the late 1980s with a campaign called Shelter-AID. By using coupons, point-of-purchase displays, and national ads for its feminine-protection products, Johnson & Johnson was able to raise tens of millions of dollars for women's shelters across the country.

What is troubling about such pairings is that they raise questions concerning whether it is ethical for a company to sell products on the coattails of the abused, poor, hungry, or sick. Besides profiting, Johnson & Johnson received reams of free publicity. Its director of promotions was even called upon to act as a spokesperson for domestic violence! She said to one interviewer: "We weren't trying to come up with a good cause. We were trying to come up with a good promotion that would move product, and this was it."

Supporters of cause-related marketing reply that

PUBLICITY

Publicity *is unpaid communication about the company or its product or service in the mass media.* Most companies try to supplement their paid promotional efforts with publicity by providing press releases for radio, newspapers, and magazines; films for television news shows; public appearances by corporate executives; and subsidies for notable figures on the national scene. An example of the latter was when Cadillac agreed to sponsor yachtsman Dennis Conner's defense of the 1992 America's Cup. The car company hoped it would become associated with the national fervor surrounding Conner's defense of the prized sporting trophy.[15]

Publicity is a subset of a company's broader public relations effort. **Public relations** *are organized efforts to present a company and its products in a positive light by influencing relevant groups such as stockholders, consumers, government officials, and other*

ETHICAL AND ENVIRONMENTAL ISSUES IN MARKETING

it creates a win–win situation—more revenue for the company, new funding for the charity. Clearly this has been the case with the American Red Cross, which benefits mightily through tie-in promotions with R.J. Reynolds, Maxwell House, Pepsi, and Burger King. In fact, a six-week Burger King promotion to aid survivors of Hurricane Hugo and the California earthquake in 1989 netted $5.7 million for the Red Cross—the largest cash gift ever given to a charity. Lesser-known charities, however, are hard pressed to find such lavish help, leading critics to complain that most companies seek out only those organizations that are popular and recognizable. An often-heard refrain is that groups working to help victims of AIDS receive little of that type of largesse.

At times, companies have chosen their alliances poorly and suffered backlashes. Witness the case of Philip Morris, which sponsored the National Archives celebration of the Bill of Rights bicentennial. Antismoking advocates accused the maker of Marlboro of using the cause to circumvent rules that prohibited it from advertising on television. It finally pulled out of the sponsorship.

Ultimately, marketers must ask themselves if they are promoting a worthy cause or merely using it as window dressing for ads that would not otherwise get noticed. Said one veteran public service advertiser, "Consumers are pretty shrewd, and if the sponsor is overtly trying to profit in a real, bottom-line sense, there will be a backlash not unlike the kind that follows negative political advertising."

Question: Is cause-related marketing a legitimate activity, or is it a questionable activity designed only to gain support for a company and its brands? Fully explain your position.

Sources: "Cause-Related Marketing: Doing Well While Doing Good," *Sales & Marketing Management*, March 1991; "Line between Public Service, Paid Ads Blurs," *Advertising Age*, October 8, 1990; "Doing Well by Doing Good," *Industry Week*, November 5, 1990; "Doing Well by Doing Good," *Business Week*, December 5, 1988.

business executives. For example, a company might lobby for legislation beneficial to it or initiate contact with consumer activists such as Ralph Nader in order to convince them that the company is operating in the consumer's interest. Some publicize earnings reports and actions of benefit to the company's stockholders. McDonald's public relations effort involves supporting children's hospitals with its free Ronald McDonald Houses for visitors. Its attempt to communicate these efforts through news releases and reports in the media is the publicity element of its public relations campaign.

Publicity can be both positive and negative. A company tries to encourage positive news and contain or counteract negative news. Procter & Gamble's image was heavily damaged by the 1991 disclosure that it used the Cincinnati district attorney's office to subpoena phone records of a *Wall Street Journal* reporter who had written stories critical about the company's food division.[16] Even though P&G's top management tried to contain the bad publicity, the outcry from civil libertarians was so fierce that P&G was ultimately forced to publicly renounce its investigation.

MARKETING COMMUNICATIONS AND THE PROMOTIONAL MIX

The key process underlying each of the four components of the promotional mix is *communications.* Therefore, to understand how the promotional mix influences customers, we should understand the nature of the communications process, particularly in the field of marketing. Any communication, whether it is an advertisement, a word-of-mouth message such as a salesperson's opinion about a product, or a news message such as a newspaper report or a TV commentary, has certain elements in common. Figure 17.1 shows the steps in the communications process. The marketing organizations responsible for each step in the process are shown at the bottom of the figure.

THE SOURCE

The first step in the communications process shows that a communication must have a source. The source of the marketing message is the company offering products or services. In its role as the source, the company develops communications objectives and identifies a target for its communications.

As the source of the message for its Spectra camera, Polaroid's promotional objective was to convince consumers that Spectra was the equal of 35mm cameras with the added advantage of instant pictures. With a price tag of $225, Spectra had to target a younger and more upscale segment than Polaroid's traditional consumers. As a result, message development and media selection were aimed primarily at baby boomers.[17]

FIGURE 17.1

The Communications Process

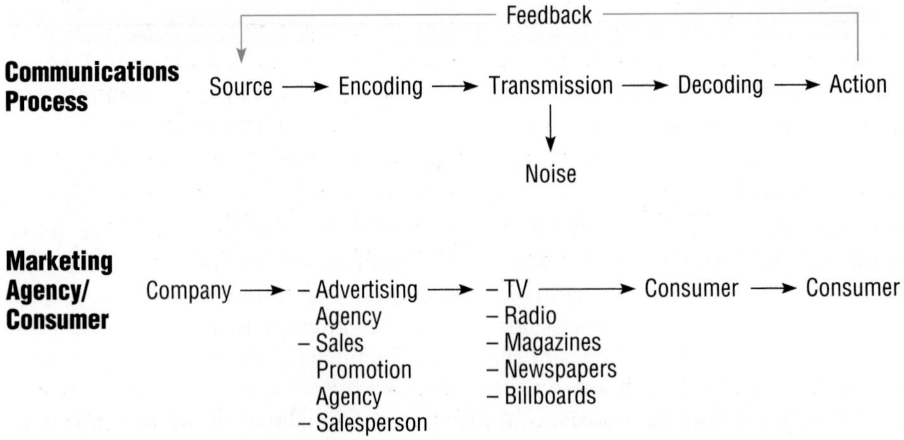

ENCODING

Encoding *is the process by which the source translates its objectives into an advertising or sales promotional strategy that will communicate the appropriate message.* An advertising agency, sales promotional agency, salesperson, or public relations department of a company may be responsible for encoding the message depending on the component of the promotional mix.

To get across its message of Spectra's parity with 35mm camera quality, Polaroid's advertising agency decided to use Ben Cross, star of the movie *Chariots of Fire*, as a spokesperson. The agency felt that Ben Cross had an upscale image and that baby boomers would identify with him. Polaroid also developed a direct-mail catalog that emphasized the same message about Spectra as its advertising—parity of Spectra to 35mm pictures.

TRANSMISSION

Transmission *is the process of communicating the message to the target audience.* Advertising agencies develop a media plan that outlines how to reach the target with a selected mix of vehicles—television, radio, magazines, newspapers, billboards.

Figure 17.1 shows that a byproduct of transmission can be noise. **Noise** *is interference that may occur during transmission* because of the clutter of messages competing for the consumer's attention. For example, if in the course of a day's viewing, a consumer sees 20 TV commercials, the message communicated in any one commercial may become confused with the others and may be lost in a jumble of competing claims. Such competition for the consumer's attention diminishes a message's effectiveness.

The primary media vehicle to communicate the Spectra message was TV commercials on the major networks. The Ben Cross commercials and other ads comparing Spectra with 35mm pictures appeared on network TV. In addition, print ads were scheduled to appear in all major upscale magazines, and Spectra was advertised on billboards in 25 markets.[18]

DECODING AND ACTION

Decoding *is the way consumers interpret marketing messages* and determines how consumers will react to them. This process involves (1) noticing the message *(awareness)*, (2) interpreting and evaluating it *(comprehension)*, and (3) retaining it in memory *(recall)*.

In our Spectra example, the company hoped that a consumer looking for a simpler alternative to a 35mm camera would (1) notice Spectra ads, (2) interpret and evaluate them as meaning that the Spectra produced comparable pictures to a 35mm camera, and (3) remember the message long enough to *act* on it by buying. Judging by the successful introduction of Spectra, the company knew that the basic message had indeed been decoded by the targeted consumers as hoped.

Action—that is, a purchase by the consumer, expressed in sales figures—is the primary criterion for evaluating the effectiveness of a marketing communication. If most consumers had remained unpersuaded that any instant camera could be as good as a 35mm, the sales figures would have shown that the promotional campaign was a failure.

FEEDBACK

Feedback *is evaluating the impact of the communications on the consumer.* Feedback is necessary to judge the success of a communication. Determining this impact is difficult, because the marketer does not know whether a consumer purchases primarily because of the advertising, the recommendations of a friend, a price reduction, poor strategies on the part of competitors, or a host of other environmental factors that might affect consumer actions.

It is almost certain that marketing communications will have some impact on sales, but the key question is how much of an impact. A statement made by John Wanamaker, the famous Philadelphia retailer, over 100 years ago is still largely true today: "I know that half of my advertising expenditures are wasted, but I don't know which half."

One solution to this problem is to look at other criteria in addition to sales—that is, to measure the degree to which consumers are aware of the advertising messages, how they comprehend them, and whether they recall them over time (the three parts of the decoding process). The simple assumption is that a consumer who is aware of the advertising is more likely to buy than one who is not, a consumer who evaluates the ad positively is even more likely to buy, and a consumer who evaluates the ad positively *and* retains the message over time is the most likely to buy. Given the difficulty of linking advertising to sales, advertisers are forced to depend mostly on these measures of effectiveness (awareness, comprehension, and recall).

When the Spectra campaign was evaluated in this way, it proved effective on all counts. Awareness of the campaign was high among the target group of affluent baby boomers. They generally evaluated the campaign positively, and a significant proportion recalled the advertising. Sales confirmed these findings, exceeding expectations and reaching close to 800,000 units the first year.[19] Of equal importance, some experts concluded that the advertising campaign was so successful that it created a more positive image for Polaroid's older instant camera models.

SELECTING THE PROMOTIONAL MIX

Marketing managers must select a mix of each of the promotional elements—advertising, sales promotion, personal selling, and publicity—and allocate resources to each. Firms vary widely in the degree to which they rely on these various elements. Frito Lay relies heavily on TV advertising for its potato chips. Borden Company, its chief competitor, does not have the resources to compete directly with the larger advertising budget of Frito Lay, so it relies almost exclusively on trade discounts and consumer sales promotions in marketing its Cottage Fries potato chips.[20]

Figure 17.2 shows the steps involved in selecting a promotional mix. First come promotional objectives such as establishing brand awareness, influencing product trial, and encouraging repeat purchasing. Next, managers must evaluate the factors that are likely to influence the promotional mix in order to determine the relative importance of each component. On this basis, a promotional strategy can be developed—that is, the combination of promotional tools required to meet marketing objectives. Now a budget can be formulated in which resources are allocated according to the importance of each element of the promotional mix. The final step is to evaluate the results of the mix and make adjustments where appropriate. Each of these steps will be examined in detail.

FIGURE 17.2

Developing the Promotional Mix

ESTABLISH PROMOTIONAL OBJECTIVES

Promotional objectives are formed in terms of what will influence the consumer to buy. If the brand is being introduced, the first objective is to establish brand awareness. The next is to create a positive attitude toward the brand. A third objective is to encourage product trial, and a fourth objective is to influence existing users to buy again. These objectives—awareness, positive brand attitudes, trial, and repeat purchasing—attempt to create a base of loyal consumers over time.

As an example, when Nabisco premiered its Teddy Graham cookies in 1988, its promotional objective was to influence trial by appealing to baby boomers' nostalgic memories of eating graham crackers when they were young. Animated advertisements picturing singing bears imitating Elvis Presley were designed to cement that nostalgic association while also stimulating the interest of baby boomers' children. Nabisco's specific promotional goals might reasonably have been to establish brand awareness among 50 percent of cookie buyers in the first six months after introduction into the U.S. market, to achieve trial use among 20 percent of them, and to attain a 5-percent share of the cookie market within two years after introduction. As it happened, Teddy Graham's were a hit and achieved the objective, a percent share of the market representing over $150 million in sales.[21]

EVALUATE FACTORS THAT INFLUENCE THE PROMOTIONAL MIX

Once objectives are set, managers must evaluate the factors that determine the relative importance of advertising, sales promotion, personal selling, and publicity. Three factors are particularly important in this regard: the type of customer, type of product, and stage of the product in its life cycle.

TYPE OF CUSTOMER

The type of customer to whom the product is targeted affects the relative emphasis on the various components of the promotional mix. For example, personal selling is more important and cost effective for industrial buyers because of their smaller numbers, specialized needs, and geographic concentration. Advertising would be concentrated in specialized magazines such as *American Machinist*, *Electrical Construction & Maintenance*, or *Coal Age* since they reach prospective industrial buyers.

Confining advertising to specialized publications is also effective for nonindustrial manufacturers if they are on limited budgets. When the Leading Edge personal computer tried coming back from a disastrous bout with bankruptcy, it concentrated its anemic $5 million media budget in business and computer magazines in the hopes they would reach corporate decision makers.[22]

Another set of customers that companies must reach with their promotional mix are retailers and wholesalers. The main vehicles for influencing these intermediaries to stock the company's products are trade promotions and personal selling. Discounts and payments to support a retailer's or wholesaler's promotional efforts are called *push money*, because they are designed to push the product through the channel of distribution. Personal selling is part of the push, too.

Companies directing appeals to the final consumer rather than to the trade put more emphasis on advertising and consumer promotions. They rely more on a strategy of *pulling* products through the channels by influencing final consumers to seek them rather than *pushing* products by influencing the trade to offer them. When Polaroid introduced the Spectra, it relied heavily on the pull of advertising to get prospective buyers to camera stores.

TYPE OF PRODUCT

A product's characteristics will help determine the emphasis placed on each component of the promotional mix. Figure 17.3 shows the relative importance of the four promotional tools for different categories of products—consumer packaged goods, durables, services, and industrial products. Sales promotions are most important for consumer packaged goods because they are frequently purchased, lower-priced items, and consumers are price sensitive about such items. A consumer intending to buy one roll of Bounty paper towels may buy three rolls during a price promotion. As a result, coupons, premiums, and price deals are effective tools in promoting packaged goods. Sales promotions aimed at the retailer (such as trade discounts) are important in gaining marketers of packaged goods valuable shelf space.

Advertising is most important for consumer durable goods, because advertisers must communicate product features and benefits over time. Since consumers pay a higher price for durables such as cars, furniture, or personal computers, advertising must convince prospective purchasers that the product will deliver the expected benefits. Moreover, once a car or a personal computer is purchased, advertising must reassure consumers that they made the right choice.

FIGURE 17.3

Importance of Components of the Promotional Mix by Type of Product

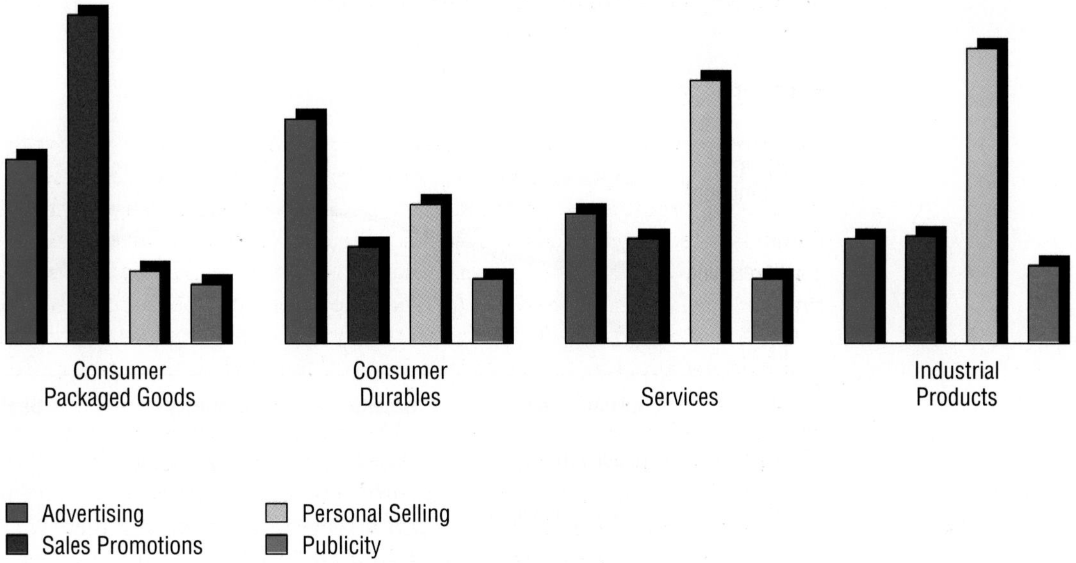

Personal selling is the dominant element in the promotional mix for service firms, because services are often delivered by a salesperson, whether it is a stockbroker offering investment advice or a clothing salesperson arranging for alterations and delivery. Also, complex products—products bought on specification—and higher-priced products warrant an emphasis on personal selling. These characteristics tend to describe industrial goods.

Publicity is likely to be more important for larger firms that must convey a message of corporate good will to stockholders, customers, and other factions of the public than for smaller firms. Such companies cut across all classes of products. Even for larger firms, however, publicity is rarely a dominant element; rather, it serves an important supporting role.

STAGE IN THE PRODUCT'S LIFE CYCLE

The composition of the promotional mix will change over a product's life cycle. In Chapter 12, we cited variations in overall marketing strategies across the life cycle. Figure 17.4 shows the impact of these variations on the two most important components of the promotional mix—advertising and sales promotions.

In the *introductory phase* of the life cycle, advertising's role is to create brand awareness. The role of sales promotions is twofold: First, trade promotions provide the *push* to ensure shelf space; second, consumer promotions provide the *pull* to generate product trial. Both advertising and sales promotional expenditures will be high during the introductory period. In general, more money will be spent on trade than on consumer promotions. Without trade support, companies run the risk of spending millions on advertising or consumer promotions only to have consumers unable to find the product on the shelf.

When Schering Plough introduced its highly successful Fibre Trim diet product in 1987, it used a combination of advertising, consumer promotions, and trade

FIGURE 17.4

The Advertising and Sales Promotional Mix over the Product Life Cycle

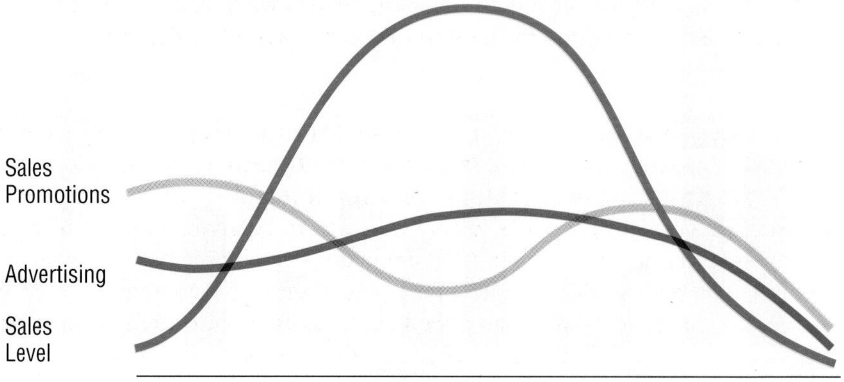

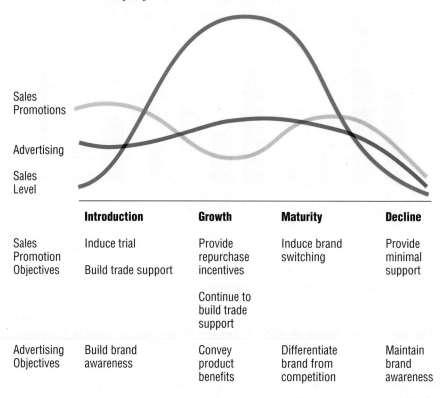

	Introduction	Growth	Maturity	Decline
Sales Promotion Objectives	Induce trial Build trade support	Provide repurchase incentives Continue to build trade support	Induce brand switching	Provide minimal support
Advertising Objectives	Build brand awareness	Convey product benefits	Differentiate brand from competition	Maintain brand awareness

promotions. Trade promotions to drugstores involved merchandise discounts, premiums, and window decals. Consumer promotions offered first-time purchasers \$1 off the purchase price of the second box. Sales promotions were backed by a \$25 million advertising campaign promoting the dietary benefits of fiber. As a result of this strategy, four out of five purchasers said they would rebuy the product, and the introduction was described as the most successful of any diet product.[23]

In the *growth phase* of the life cycle, the product is generating increased sales, and advertising expenditures are likely to be maintained or increased. Having established brand awareness, the advertising strategy shifts to communicating product benefits. The purpose is to attract new buyers and convince existing buyers to repurchase. Sales promotional expenditures are likely to take a sharp drop, because many customers have tried the product. Moreover, continued use of consumer promotions might cause buyers to view the brand as a low-priced, low-quality entry.

Sales promotional expenditures are likely to increase in the *mature phase* of the life cycle, the point where sales growth stabilizes or begins to decline. Since competition is more intense, the company is likely to provide price inducements to coax its users to remain loyal and competitive brand users to switch to the company's brand. As price competition intensifies, the use of coupons, premiums, and price deals increases.

The *decline phase* of the life cycle is marked by cutbacks in all promotional expenditures. Sales promotions may support the brand with occasional coupons and price deals, and advertising will attempt to maintain brand awareness among brand loyalists, but it is also possible that the company may choose to *harvest* a brand in the decline phase. *A* **harvest** *strategy involves cutting off most or all promotional support for a brand and relying on sales from loyal buyers for continued profits.* This was the strategy employed by Standard Brands when it withdrew its support for Chase & Sanborn coffee in the face of a continued sales decline.

DEVELOP A PROMOTIONAL STRATEGY

The third step in selecting a promotional mix is to develop a strategy that will best meet promotional objectives. If the primary objective is to gain brand awareness and develop a positive brand image, then advertising will receive the most emphasis. If the main objective is to communicate and demonstrate complex product features, then personal selling will dominate. If the objective is to gain maximum trial for a new product or encourage switching from a competitor, then sales promotional components such as coupons, free samples and special events might be employed, combined with incentives to influence the trade to stock it.

A good example of the sales promotional component is the strategy that Diet Pepsi launched in Tulsa, Oklahoma, to overcome the half-point advantage which Diet Coke held in market share. The promotion began with 200,000 Tulsa homes receiving cans of Diet Pepsi and a sweepstakes entry form (see Exhibit 17.1) touting a grand-prize vacation at Club Med. To enter, consumers had only to answer six questions about soft-drink consumption. From the 20,000 responses, Pepsi managers were able to build a database of consumers loyal to Diet Coke, loyal to Diet Pepsi, and prone to switching. The Diet Coke drinkers were then sent coupons for a free six-pack of Diet Pepsi, the Diet Pepsi customers were sent 75-

EXHIBIT 17.1

Example of a Sales Promotion to Encourage Brand Switching

cents-off coupons for cases, and the switchers were given enough coupons to keep them drinking Diet Pepsi for a month.

Realizing that the coupons would have to be redeemed somewhere, Pepsi executives identified the stores where diet-soda drinkers were most likely to shop. Once identified, the stores were lavished with incentives to set up elaborate point-of-purchase displays that encouraged switching by Diet Coke loyalists. Among the incentives were cash prizes for the stores that sold the most Diet Pepsi. Finally, Pepsi salespeople were ordered to fan out across Tulsa and create events to further promote the soda. One such event, the Diet Pepsi Cheerleader Challenge, used neighborhood cheerleaders to spur on sales. By the promotion's end, Diet Pepsi sales had skyrocketed 27 percent in the Tulsa market, leaving it one full point ahead of its rival in market share.[24]

SET THE PROMOTIONAL BUDGET

The total amount of money that will be spent on the promotional mix will depend on the promotional strategies the firm intends to follow. The amount allotted to each element in the mix will depend on its relative importance.

TOP-DOWN VERSUS BOTTOM-UP BUDGETING

Chapter 3 cited two approaches to budgeting, a top-down and a bottom-up approach. Both approaches apply to budgeting for promotion. Figure 17.5 shows that in a top-down approach, managers establish one overall expenditure level for the promotional mix and then allocate these funds to the components of the mix. In contrast, a bottom-up approach first requires developing separate budgets for advertising, sales promotions, personal selling, and publicity. The sum of these four components is the total promotional budget.

A top-down approach has the advantage of treating the promotional mix as an integrated part of marketing strategy and determining how much effort is required overall to inform and influence the consumer. The danger in using a top-down approach is that the manager might lose sight of the specific objectives and roles of the individual components of the promotional mix.

A bottom-up approach has the advantage of focusing on the tasks required to achieve specific advertising, promotional, personal selling, or publicity objectives—but possibly at the expense of exceeding necessary limits on the total promotional budget. In building up a budget, the manager might allocate too much money to the promotional mix, because each promotional component independently establishes a spending level based on its objectives.

Burger King tends to take a top-down approach to promotional budgeting. It establishes an overall spending level for the year and then allocates expenditures primarily to advertising and sales promotions. Once advertising expenditures are established, the company further allocates resources to network TV, local TV, magazines, radio, and billboard advertising. As we have seen, Burger King has shifted more resources to sales promotions in recent years and has allocated the bulk of its advertising budget to network TV.

TECHNIQUES FOR SETTING THE PROMOTIONAL BUDGET

Three techniques have been widely used for setting the promotional budget—an objective-task approach, a percent of sales approach, and a competitive parity approach. More arbitrary approaches have also been used. All these approaches can be used on a top-down or bottom-up basis.

FIGURE 17.5

Top-Down versus Bottom-Up Promotional Budgeting

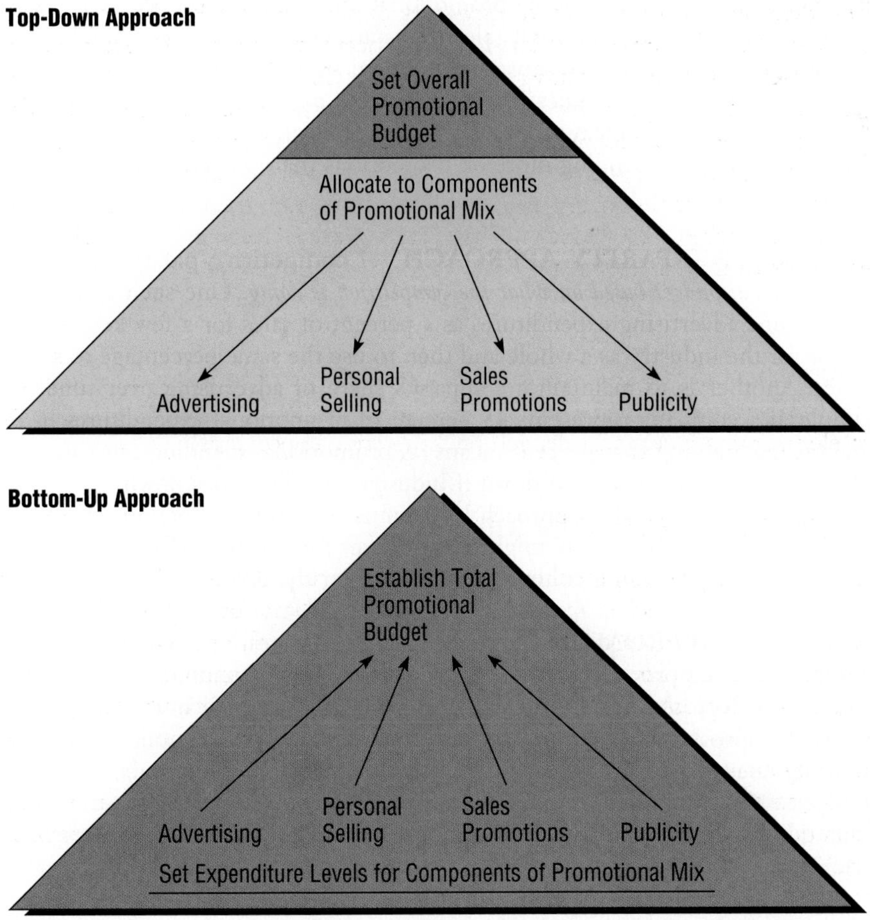

OBJECTIVE-TASK APPROACH An **objective-task approach** *requires defining promotional objectives, determining what strategies (tasks) are required to attain them, and computing how much those strategies will cost.* Once the budget is established to fulfill the tasks, the company can determine whether it can afford the expenditures. If not, objectives must be scaled down.

Pillsbury used an objective-task method in setting the advertising budget for its Totino's frozen pizza line. The overall objectives were to increase sales by 30 percent and profits by 100 percent by increasing product quality and distribution. The promotional objectives called for a 70-percent increase in brand awareness, a 20-percent increase in trial, and a 40-percent increase in the repurchase rate.[25] These ambitious goals required Pillsbury to put substantially more money into television advertising while maintaining its level of consumer and trade promotions. Since management felt these goals were attainable, it approved a substantial increase in the advertising budget.

PERCENT-OF-SALES APPROACH *The* **percent-of-sales** *approach sets the promotional budget as a certain percentage of the company's sales.* For example, in the late 1970s, Sears set its advertising budget at 3 percent of forecast retail sales and advertising expenditures for its catalog were set at 5.75 percent of forecast catalog sales.[26] This frequently used approach has the advantages of being simple and varying promotional expenditures with a brand's performance. It has serious flaws, however. First, the level of sales is determining the promotional mix, when actually the opposite should be true—the promotional mix should influence sales results. Second, some products with high sales levels are not particularly profitable. Yet, these products would receive more promotional support than would more profitable products with lower sales levels. Third, the percent-of-sales approach may inhibit a manager from trying to transform a promising brand into a star. Such an effort would require spending more on promotions than warranted by the brand's sales level.

COMPETITIVE-PARITY APPROACH *A* **competitive-parity** *approach sets the promotional budget based on what the competition is doing.* One such approach is to determine advertising expenditures as a percent of sales for a few key competitors or for the industry as a whole and then to use the same percentage to set the budget. Another is to maintain a company's share of advertising over time. For example, if a company represents 15 percent of promotional expenditures in the industry, maintaining that percent means its promotional spending must go up if industry spending goes up and down if industry spending goes down.

The problem is that this approach lets competition set the spending pace, and what is right for one company might not be right for another. Moreover, such an approach might just lead a company into following the errors of its competitors.

ARBITRARY APPROACHES Companies that do not have a systematic promotional planning process often use simple and arbitrary methods. Smaller firms that have no formal planning methods are most likely to fall into this category. One such approach is to set budgets for raw materials, production, distribution, and other needs and then allocate what is left to the promotional mix. Another is to increase the promotional budget by a fixed percent each year. These methods suffer the disadvantage of not being tied to promotional objectives or product performance.

ALLOCATE THE PROMOTIONAL BUDGET

In a bottom-up approach, the firm has already determined how much it will spend on each component of the promotional mix as part of the budgeting process. In a top-down approach, the firm has established a total promotional budget that must be allocated among the components of the promotional mix. The amount allocated to advertising, sales promotion, personal selling, and publicity will depend on the importance of each component as determined by the factors discussed above—the type of customer, type of product, and stage in the product's life cycle. As we have seen, more money will be allocated to advertising for consumer durables, to sales promotions for consumer packaged goods, and to personal selling for industrial products and services.

Once a firm has implemented its promotional plan, it will try to assess the effectiveness of each component of the promotional mix and reallocate funds to those components that are most effective. Burger King, for example, shifted money from advertising to sales promotions when it determined that promotions such as giveaways, sweepstakes and two for one deals were more effective than advertising in attracting customers. The amount of money that will be shifted from one component to another depends on the effect additional expenditures have on revenues. Burger King will stop shifting money to sales promotions when it finds that sales promotions no longer outperform advertising in increasing revenues.

The same allocation principle applies to other components of the promotional mix. A retailer might shift money from personal selling to advertising if it finds that it must create store awareness before personal selling can be effective. In such a case, additional expenditures on advertising create more revenue than additional expenditures on personal selling.

EVALUATE THE PROMOTIONAL MIX

The last step in selecting the promotional mix in Figure 17.2 is evaluation. Several key questions are involved here. First, have the promotional objectives been translated into an effective marketing message? Returning to the Teddy Graham example, the animated singing bears were very effective in communicating nostalgia, fun, and good taste. Second, has the target group been defined? Nabisco narrowly tailored the campaign to reach baby-boom mothers and their young children.

Third, is the right promotional mix being used to influence the target group? It is hard to imagine Nabisco doing any better. It successfully influenced baby-boom mothers through network television ads in which the singing bears evoked the musical sounds of the 1950s. The ads aired during "A Current Affair" and "Lifestyles of the Rich and Famous," shows heavily watched by the target group. Simultaneously, Nabisco tried influencing children with ads broadcast on such perennially watched syndicated shows as "Gilligan's Island" and "The Flintstones." To augment the advertising campaign, Nabisco employed sales-promotion tools such as the Teddy Graham's fan club, a membership organization that, like Burger King's Kids Club, returned premium gifts to children who joined. The fan club had the dual benefit of helping Nabisco develop a database for later use in direct marketing.[27]

Fourth, to what extent does exposure to each component of the promotional mix result in sales? The ideal approach in evaluating the effectiveness of each component of the promotional mix is to determine how much an additional dollar spent on advertising, sales promotion, personal selling, and publicity produces in sales. Given the difficulty in determining the sales produced by each component of the promotional mix, managers try to assess the effectiveness of these components by other means—effectiveness in creating brand awareness, conveying product benefits, inducing product trial, or encouraging repurchase of the brand.

Generally, sales promotional strategies are easier to evaluate than advertising, because they can often be tied directly to sales. For example, a company can determine the number of products purchased with coupons. Similarly, sales can be related directly to a premium or sweepstakes promotion, because these are short-term inducements. Sales increases that occur during the promotional period can generally be attributed to the promotion.

SALES PROMOTIONS

In the remainder of this chapter, we will consider in more detail two components of the promotional mix, sales promotions and publicity. In the next two chapters, we consider the other two components, advertising and personal selling.

INCREASING IMPORTANCE OF SALES PROMOTIONS

The amount of money spent on sales promotions has increased markedly since the mid 1970s. Figure 17.6 shows that in 1976 marketers spent about $30 billion on sales promotions. Ten years later, they were spending over $100 billion. Expenditures on advertising also rose during this period, but not as fast. By 1988, more

FIGURE 17.6

Growth in Sales Promotion and Advertising Expenditures: 1976–90

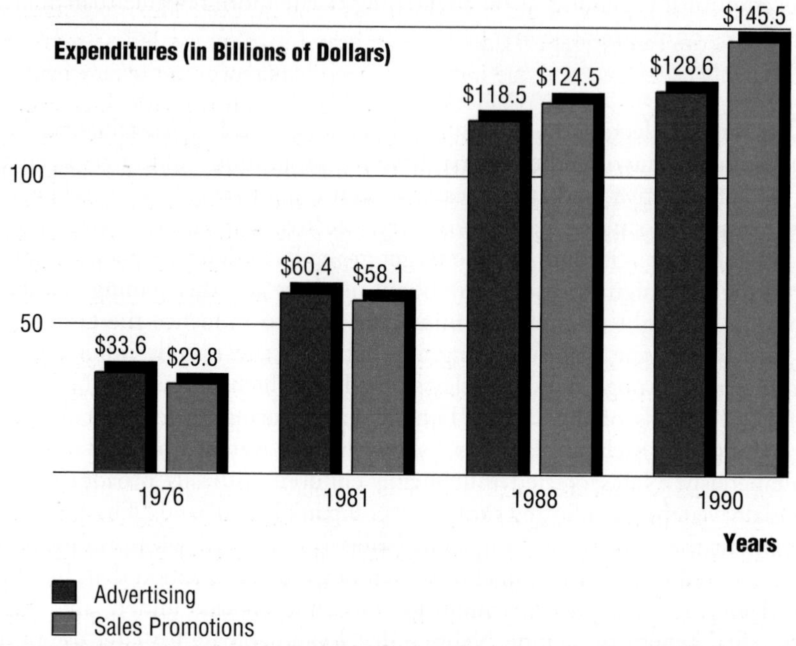

Source: Sales promotion expenditures from "Sales Promotion: The Year in Review," *Marketing & Media Decisions,* July 1987, July 1988, and July 1989, pp. 124–126. Advertising expenditures for 1976 and 1981 from *Statistical Abstract,* 1980 and 1987, figures for 1988 from "Ad Spending Outlook Brightens," *Advertising Age,* May 15, 1989. 1990 figures for sales promotion from *Donnelley Marketing Surveys of Promotional Practices,* 1991. 1990 figures for advertising from McCann Erickson.

money was being spent on sales promotions than on advertising. The gap widened further by 1990, with $146 billion spent on sales promotions compared to $129 billion on advertising.[28] Sales promotions were growing at an annual rate of 9 percent compared to only a 5-percent growth rate for advertising.

Burger King's promotional strategy reflects this change. In the early 1990s, the company shifted most of its promotional budget to sales promotions, partly as a result of its ineffective advertising, partly because of the effectiveness of promotional incentives in attracting customers to Burger King outlets. But the company realized it could not rely on sales promotions alone. An effective promotional mix requires advertising to reinforce Burger King's name and to maintain loyalty among its customers.

There are several reasons for the relative shift of promotional dollars from advertising to sales promotions. First, the cost effectiveness of advertising through the mass media has been decreasing. As markets have become more segmented, it has become increasingly expensive to reach targets through national advertising campaigns. One study estimated that from 1983 to 1987, maintaining the same level of advertising expenditures would have produced almost 20 percent less revenue.[29] This decrease in advertising productivity is projected to continue.

Second, the popularity of VCRs and cable television has resulted in fewer consumers watching nationally televised commercials. In addition, with more women in the workforce, viewing of daytime television commercials has decreased. Most of the dollars formerly spent on network TV went to sales promotions.

Third, with the U.S. population growing at only 0.8 percent annually, growth in per-capita consumption of most products has been modest. This, combined with excess production and a general decrease in brand loyalty, has led to more competition for market share and the increased use of price promotions to secure it.[30] Consumers are more willing to buy many products on a price basis, increasing the effectiveness of sales promotional tools such as coupons and price deals. One result of the decrease in brand loyalty is that more consumers are making their purchase decisions in the store rather than deciding on a brand beforehand. A study by the Point-of-Purchase Advertising Institute found that over 80 percent of supermarket purchases are decided in the store.[31] When consumers make decisions in the store, they are more likely to be influenced by in-store displays, store coupons, and price deals.

Fourth, greater similarity among brands in many product categories also encourages this trend toward sales promotions. When brands are similar, consumers are more likely to make choices based on price. As a result, sales promotions are more effective than advertising.

For some companies, the increased reliance on promotion was indispensable. Consider the well-known case of Johnson & Johnson, which used coupons rather than advertising to get Tylenol back on its feet after a series of cyanide deaths due to tampering. Its mass distribution to American households of 40 million coupons worth $2.50 each (the price of a small bottle of Tylenol) brought former Tylenol users back to the brand, enabling the company to recapture lost market share.[32]

While price promotions helped Tylenol, they are often blamed for undercutting the brand equity of other products or services. McDonald's employed price-based promotions when it found customers complaining that its prices had risen too high. But the subsequent spate of ads which focused on those promotions led analysts to worry that the chain was squandering its carefully managed image merely to build short-term profits. Said one, "McDonald's whole brand character is beginning to erode. With all these promotions, you begin to lose the sense of who they are, what they stand for, and what their values are."[33] Ironically, Burger King did not have the same problem when it shifted much of its budget to sales promotions, because past advertising never established a strong brand identity.

RISKS OF INCREASING USE OF SALES PROMOTIONS

The McDonald's example typifies the risks of promotional activities. Indeed, something of a backlash began to emerge in the early 1990s as more and more marketers gave voice to worries that excessive promotion was destroying the brand equity that many manufacturers have spent decades developing. In one survey of 600 media buyers, 40 percent said the future had to hold more image-based advertising.[34]

Part of the problem is that emphasis on sales promotions may condition consumers to expect constant price cuts. Since many consumers see little difference among brands, when a promotion on a given brand ends, they will simply switch to another brand being promoted. As a result, many marketers will be forced to continually use sales promotions to keep their market share from eroding. Yet, the constant use of sales promotions decrease profits.

These risks have caused some companies to reverse the trend shown in Figure 17.6 and to start putting more money into advertising. For example, Volkswagen bucked the trend of the automotive industry by eliminating all rebates and committing itself to long-term brand building through advertising. With many customers trained to expect such rebates, Volkswagen's sales tumbled eight percent

EXHIBIT 17.2

Volkswagen Shifts Resources from Rebates to Advertising

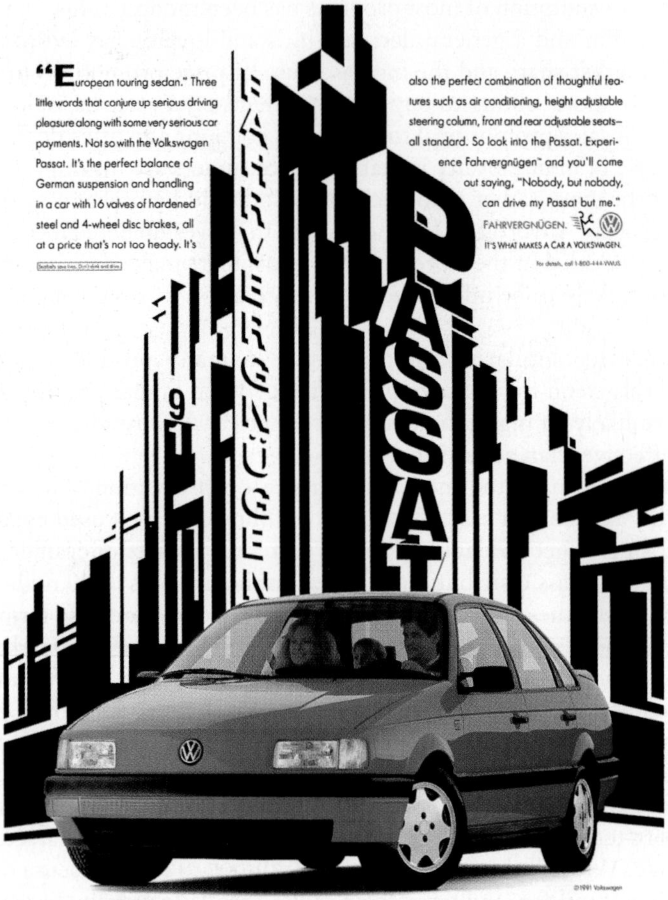

in the first four months of the experiment, but they began nudging up again after the company devoted more money to its *Fahrvergnugen* (translated as "the pleasure of driving") ad campaign designed to draw attention to the company's European heritage (see Exhibit 17.2).[35]

Many other companies are following Volkswagen's lead. One such company is Kraft General Foods. In an effort to maintain the value of its brand names, the company is changing its promotional mix to allocate less to sales promotions and more to advertising. Nevertheless, the relative shift from advertising to sales promotions is likely to continue into the 1990s for most companies.

TYPES OF SALES PROMOTIONS

As noted, sales promotions may be directed toward consumers or toward the trade. The division of expenditures between advertising, trade promotions, and consumer promotions is shown in Figure 17.7. Somewhat more money is spent on trade than on consumer promotions. Of the $146 billion spent on sales promotions in 1990, about $66 billion was spent on consumer promotions and about $80 billion on trade promotions.

FIGURE 17.7

Distribution of Expenditures by Types of Sales Promotions

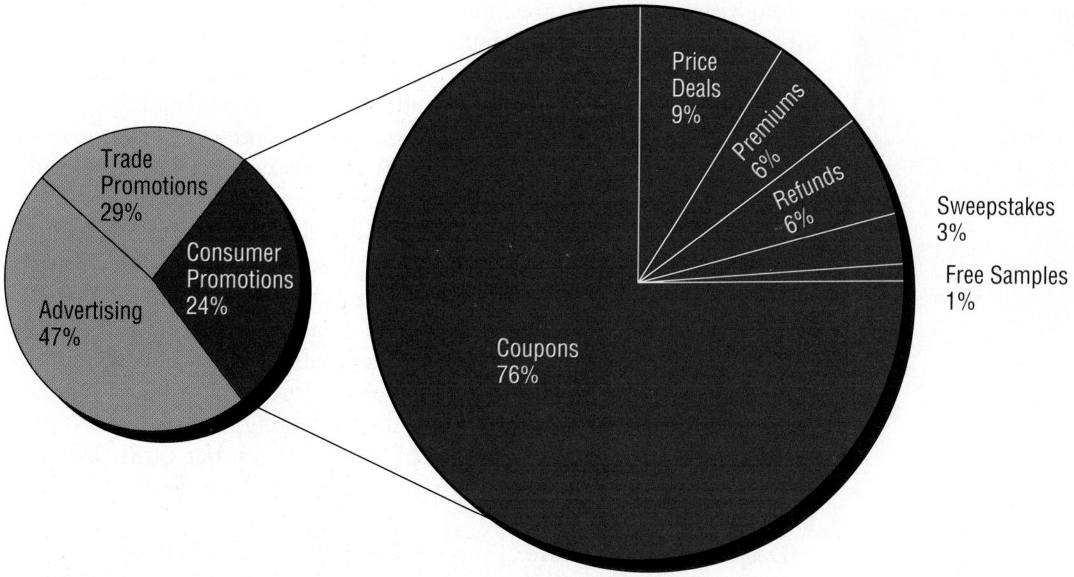

Source: "Sales Promotion: The Year in Review," *Marketing & Media Decisions,* July 1989, pp. 124–126. *Donnelley Marketing Annual Surveys of Promotional Practices,* 1990, 1991.

CONSUMER PROMOTIONS

As shown in Figure 17.7, consumer promotions include coupons, price deals, premiums, rebates, sweepstakes, and free samples. A recent survey by the Promotion Marketing Association of America found that coupons were the most popular with consumers (98 percent of the respondents said they had used them), refunds were second (54 percent), sweepstakes were third (26 percent), and premiums were last (17 percent).[36] We will now examine the various forms of consumer promotions in detail.

COUPONS The vast majority of promotions—76 percent—are coupons. **Coupons** *are certificates that offer a discount off the regular price of a brand when they are redeemed.* They are used to encourage nonusers to try a product or existing users to buy more frequently. Like other sales promotions, coupons are more effective in inducing short-term switches to a brand than in retaining consumers over the long term. Most consumers that have switched to another brand because of coupons will revert to their regular brand when coupons are no longer offered. Companies such as Procter & Gamble, Coca-Cola, Quaker, and Gillette rely heavily on them to sell health-and-beauty aids, frozen foods, cereals, prepared foods, and household products.

Coupons are the most effective means of getting consumers to try a product or to switch a brand. A study by the Promotion Marketing Association of America found that more than 10 percent of respondents bought a brand they never tried before or purchased a different brand because of a coupon.[37] Other promotional devices such as rebates, premiums, and sweepstakes were only half as effective in attracting consumers.

EXHIBIT 17.3

Example of a Free-Standing Insert

One reason coupons are more popular is that they are the best money-savers for consumers. In 1990, 279 billion coupons were distributed, and about 9 billion of these were redeemed, a redemption rate of 3.2 percent.[38] These redemptions saved consumers a total of over $3 billion. About 80 percent of coupons are **free-standing inserts,** *meaning they are distributed as inserts in newspapers* (see Exhibit 17.3 for an example). The remaining 20 percent are distributed by mail, in newspaper or magazine ads, or directly in stores.

The latest wave in direct store coupons are **electronic coupons** *that are delivered from dispensers at the time the customer receives his or her receipt.* Usually, the coupons are for products that rival the ones a shopper has just bought. For example, jam manufacturer JM Smucker recently ran a promotion in which electronic coupons that were good for a free jar of Smucker's jam were automatically dispensed to anyone who bought rival Sorrell Ridge's all-fruit jam.[39] The potential for such couponing is enormous. CitiCorp is already testing a frequent-shopper program in which members are given personal bar-coded scanner cards. When presented in certain supermarkets, the register automatically awards discounts and rebates for specific products.[40]

Despite their wide use, coupons have several disadvantages. First, they are expensive. A single-page, four-color coupon appearing as a free-standing insert in Sunday newspapers across the country costs well over $500,000. In addition, more than 95 percent are not redeemed. Finally, the market is becoming saturated with coupons, diminishing their effectiveness. Yet coupons continue to be by far the most influential sales promotional method because of their effectiveness in inducing consumers to try a brand.

PRICE DEALS **Price deals** *are short-term discounts offered by manufacturers to encourage nonusers to try the brand and existing users to buy more.* Most price deals are printed directly on the package, indicating so many cents off. These deals are an effective way for a company to meet a competitor's coupon offer or to compete with a price reduction. Some marketers use price deals so frequently that consumers assume they are part of the established price. When the product goes "off deal," consumers may regard it as a price increase and be reluctant to buy it. Constant use of price deals can in this way dilute brand loyalty and discourage repeat purchases.

PREMIUMS **Premiums** *are gifts offered for free or at reduced prices as an incentive to buy the promoted brand.* To be most effective, the premium should be related to the product. Kodak successfully employed this tool with its 1991 campaign (shown in Exhibit 17.4) featuring Kolorkins, three fuzzy stuffed animals that Kodak film buyers could get for their children by mailing proofs of purchase to the company. More than a simple incentive to buy Kodak, the dolls reminded film buyers of Kodak's high color quality while their names—Rewind, Shutter, and Focus—reinforced the association between Kodak and picture taking.[41]

Another type of premium is *frequent-shopper programs,* designed to give customers bonuses for repeated use of the company's products or services. These programs were started by airlines, but are now being used widely by hotels and credit

EXHIBIT 17.4

Employing a Premium as an Incentive to Buy a Brand

card companies. Marriott hotels offer bonus points providing discounts and free stays to repeat customers. American Express offers gold card members frequent-flyer miles on six airlines for use of its card. A variety of other companies are using the frequent-shopper concept. Waldenbooks recently unveiled a frequent-shopper club that automatically entitles repeat shoppers to 10-percent discounts, a $5 certificate with every $100 in purchases, and benefits such as automatic check acceptance.[42] Supermarkets are also becoming involved in frequent-shopper bonuses. Sperry & Hutchinson updated its venerable S&H Green Stamp program by issuing supermarket shoppers magnetic cards that automatically issue points toward merchandise awards every time they are presented at checkout lanes.[43]

REBATES **Rebates** *are short-term price inducements which allow the consumer to recover a portion of the original cost of an item.* They began to be used widely by auto companies in the mid 1970s as a result of rising gas prices. After almost going into bankruptcy, Chrysler used the technique to help it gain a 12 percent share of the auto market. The use of rebates for autos spurred other industries to try them, sometimes in imaginative ways. Toro realized that consumers were reluctant to buy an expensive snow blower because it did not always snow. As a result, the company started a promotion called "Snow Insurance," involving a rebate of 50 percent to 100 percent off the purchase price if snowfalls were significantly less than average in the buyer's community. Sales exceeded projections by 20 percent during the promotion.[44]

The problem with rebates is that they are disguised price cuts that might undermine the quality image a company is trying to establish. Consumers may also come to expect rebates as a standard part of the price offer. By 1990, the major car companies began to realize that rebates were eroding the equity they had built up in their brand names. As a reaction to that, Ford announced in 1991 that it was dropping most of its rebate programs and funneling the money to support its dealers.[45] As we have seen, Volkswagen had already done the same.

SWEEPSTAKES **Sweepstakes** *are contests in which the consumer has a chance to win prizes or sums of money simply by submitting his or her name and address.* Sweepstakes lend excitement to sales promotions and appeal to the American consumer's sense of gamesmanship. In the months after the Persian Gulf War, when air travel was light, British Airways tried to stimulate business with what it called "The World's Greatest Offer." The airline received more than 1.5 million entries by promising to give away thousands of tickets for free travel to London and other European capitals.[46]

One of the most elaborate sweepstakes ever, found NBC teaming up with McDonald's for the McMillions contest that promised $35 million in cash prizes. McDonald's customers were encouraged through ads that appeared on NBC to pick up a different game piece from the chain's restaurants every day. Each card bore a number and time to watch NBC. The network would air the winning number at the appointed time. The campaign benefitted NBC because McDonald's shifted the bulk of its massive advertising budget to the network during the promotion.[47]

FREE SAMPLES **Free samples** *are new products offered free as a way to get consumers to try them.* Free samples are feasible only for low-cost, frequently purchased items; otherwise they become prohibitively expensive. When Gillette introduced its Trac II razor, it distributed over 12 million free samples backed up by a one-dollar refund offer for new purchasers. Thus, a rebate was combined with the free sample.

Many free samples are wasted because they are given to nonusers or to people who already use the product. Some companies avoid such waste by offering free samples to consumers who are sufficiently interested to write in for them.

POINT-OF-PURCHASE PROMOTIONS **Point-of-purchase (POP) promotions** *are store displays and decorations* such as advertising signs, window displays, and end-of-aisle display racks for products. Such in-store displays provide more impact at the point of purchase. Since most customers make their purchasing decisions in the store, point-of-purchase displays are considered one of the most cost-effective tools available to marketers. This is why more than $13 billion is spent on *POP* materials each year.[48] In the early 1990s, Anheuser Busch responded to competition from Coors and Miller by shifting its emphasis from expensive national advertising to grass-roots point-of-purchase promotions. Said one industry executive, "They think they're getting beat at the store level, so now the 'buy Bud' message will come at you not [just] from the TV but from the store."[49]

JOINT PROMOTIONS Companies have often joined forces when using the sales promotional techniques described above. For example, Procter & Gamble and General Motors' Chevrolet Division launched a joint promotion, the $9 million Great American Key Hunt, to introduce Chevy's 1988 cars. Hidden inside containers of seven of P&G's top brands were Mylar card keys. Any buyer who found a key was invited to visit a Chevrolet dealer to find out if it was one of the designated keys for 750 cars being given away.[50] Chevrolet was interested in teaming up with P&G because 97 percent of U.S. households use one or more of the seven P&G products in the promotion. The contest not only sold P&G products, it produced a great deal of traffic in Chevrolet dealerships. It was the biggest promotion run by either P&G or Chevrolet.

Such joint promotions reduce the costs of running expensive efforts such as sweepstakes or premiums, making them affordable even for smaller companies. Given the high cost of sales promotional activities, the use of joint promotions is likely to increase.

TRADE PROMOTIONS

Trade promotions *are promotions directed toward retailers and wholesalers in order to get them to stock the company's products.* They represent the *push* in the promotional effort as opposed to the *pull* provided by consumer promotions and advertising.

Three types of promotions specifically geared to the trade are merchandise allowances, case allowances, and direct payments for stocking goods known as slotting allowances. **Merchandise allowances** *are payments by manufacturers to reimburse retailers for in-store support of the product,* such as window displays or in-store shelf displays.

Case allowances *are discounts on products sold to retailers.* Bowater Computer Forms offers its office-supply dealers direct discounts depending on how much paper they agree to buy, as well as coupons that are good for discounts on its other products. The company also absorbs freight costs on shipments of ten cases or more.[51] **Slotting allowances** *are direct payments to retailers, generally food chains, for stocking an item.* As we have seen in Chapter 14, some food chains are requiring direct payments of $70,000 or more for each new product introduced. Food companies are increasingly willing to pay these allowances because of the intense competition for shelf space.[52]

Price deals, coupons, and sweepstakes can be directed to intermediaries as well as to consumers. For example, Amtrak tried to boost sagging ridership to ski areas through trade promotions directed toward ski resorts, ski retailers, and travel agents. Amtrak established booths at ski shows, promotional posters for distribution to the trade (see Exhibit 17.5), and incentives for ski retailers and travel agents that sell Amtrak ski tour packages. The company combined these trade promotions with sweepstakes and point-of-purchase displays aimed at the consumer. As a result, sales of Amtrak packaged tours through travel agents and ski retailers increased 15 percent.[53]

SALES PROMOTIONS FOR INDUSTRIAL PRODUCTS

Sales promotional tools for industrial products are essentially the same as those for consumer products. These tools are rarely used for higher-priced industrial products, since buyers are unlikely to select a vendor based on a promotional offer when a substantial purchase is involved. Instead, they are used primarily for lower-priced products and services.

For example, Airborne Express used a Lotto Sweepstakes to try to influence high-volume corporate customers to use its air freight service. The purpose of the promotion was to build awareness of Airborne and to attract first-time shippers.

EXHIBIT 17.5

A Promotional Poster Directed to the Trade

The total investment was $8 million in network TV advertising and in direct-mail announcements and a $1 million prize to the winner. Out of 1.3 million mailings, Airborne received only about 20 thousand responses.[54] The winner was determined by an airbill number drawn from these responses. Although the promotion did not pay for itself, the company felt it was worth it in building awareness among prospective customers.

Promotions directed toward intermediaries are especially important to industrial manufacturers. Nissan Industrial Equipment found that although its distributors were knowledgeable about the company's standard forklifts, they had very little information about its higher-end machines and therefore could not offer customers a compelling reason to buy them. To change that, Nissan launched a contest where salesmen were given multiple-choice tests about its Marathoner line of electronic lifts. For coming in the top 30th percentile, the salesperson got a silver emblem; those in the top 10th percentile received a gold emblem. The grand-prize winner won a trip to Hawaii. Nissan's Marathoner sales increased by 40 percent after the promotion.[55]

One promotional device specific to industrial products is the trade show, in which booths are set up by various vendors in one large meeting place to dispense information about their products to prospective customers. Trade shows are instrumental in attracting about one-fourth of industrial sales.[56] They are particularly important as a means of reaching customers who are not contacted by a company's direct-sales force. The trade show provides an efficient means of identifying prospects, introducing new products, and delivering a sales message to many buyers.

EXHIBIT 17.6

A Sales Promotion for Financial Services

SALES PROMOTIONS FOR SERVICES

Sales promotions have become an increasingly important part of the promotional mix for services. Because services cannot be stored, unused service capacity is wasted. Consequently, airlines and hotels use price deals and coupons to encourage customers to use their facilities during off-peak periods. For example, the Milford Plaza tried to combat sharply reduced hotel occupancies in New York by attracting nonbusiness travelers. Their Broadway Sleeper package offers guests a $10 credit toward a room on presentation of a theater ticket stub.[57]

Financial-service firms have also begun to use sales promotions more often. Consumer banking services have become more standardized and competitive, so offering promotions is a way of distinguishing a bank's services. For example, Citibank gave away 500 "Citibikes" in connection with its "Cititour" pro bicycle race (see Exhibit 17.6). The promotion included a free T-shirt for those who showed a Citibank ATM card and a free cycling cap for those who had a coupon from the Cititour Sweepstakes brochure.[58]

PUBLICITY

Publicity has become a more important part of the promotional mix. More companies are recognizing its value—not only as an effective means to get favorable news stories and announcements about a product or company in the mass media but also to counteract negative news.

ADVANTAGES AND DISADVANTAGES OF PUBLICITY

One advantage of publicity is its credibility. When information appears in a neutral source such as a newspaper or television news broadcast, it is more likely to be believed than when it comes directly from an advertiser. Most consumers accepted the fact that Johnson & Johnson was not at fault for the cyanide tampering of Tylenol, because this view was reported in news stories rather than in company advertising. A second advantage of publicity is that it is inexpensive. There are few costs other than maintaining a public relations department or printing company communications. Third, publicity can support the other components of the promotional mix. Burger King's donations to the American Red Cross create goodwill for the chain and reinforce the image of its prime corporate character in advertising and sales promotions.

A major drawback in the use of publicity is that it has received stepchild treatment as a component of the promotional mix. It is not usually well coordinated with the other components of the promotional mix. This is because the responsibility for publicity usually lies with a corporate public relations department rather than a marketing group. As a result, strategies to develop favorable publicity for

GLOBAL MARKETING STRATEGIES

How Sales Promotions Helped Chiquita Sell Bananas in Belgium

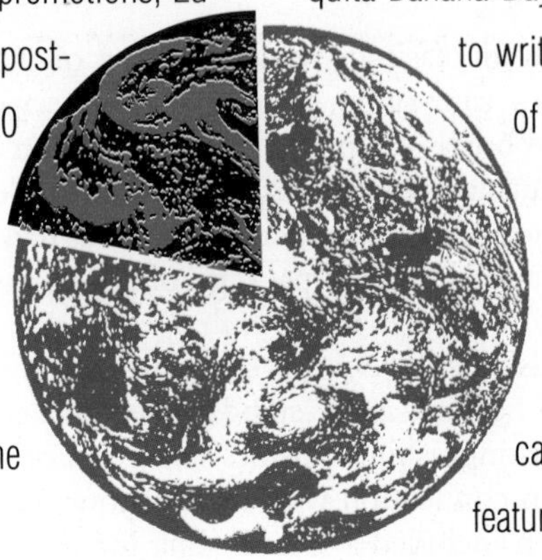

Although the United States leads the world in expenditures on sales promotions, Europe and Japan are fast catching up, posting growth rates that exceed 20 percent a year. What accounts for this rapid change? As more companies try to make their products truly global, they realize that promotional campaigns must become global as well.

Consider the case of Chiquita's race to boost its banana sales in Belgium. During Belgium's dark and dank winter, Chiquita's sales are robust, but when summer arrives, they trail off badly due to competition from the country's locally-grown fruits. How, Chiquita wondered, could it change that?

The answer was to build a promotional campaign around a sweepstakes promotion that offered families an all-expense day at Walibi Park, Belgium's top amusement park. The event was aptly named Chiquita Banana Day, and to enter, children were asked to write a sentence about a Walibi (a type of bear) and send it to Chiquita along with proofs of purchase of a month's worth of bananas.

To make sure word got out, the agency built a print and television campaign around the sweepstakes, featuring a cute brown Walibi eating, of course, a Chiquita Banana (see ad). Luckily, Chiquita was the first to take advantage of the newly deregulated Flemish airwaves, meaning that the Walibi spot was the first commercial to appear on Flemish TV. That fact alone guaranteed Chiquita tons of free publicity. But to ensure nothing was left to chance, Chiquita's ad agency sent out dozens of press releases informing reporters about the sweepstakes. By July, a groundswell had begun.

a product or company tend to be divorced from advertising, sales promotion, and personal selling.

Another drawback is that publicity is not within the company's control. When a company sends a press release to the media, it has no influence as to how it will be treated. McDonald's publicity claims of nutritional value for its foods have sometimes backfired when nutritional groups and state agencies challenged these claims. Of more serious consequence, events such as the Exxon Valdez oil spill or the gas leak at a Union Carbide plant in Bhopal, India, often result in little more than damage control by a company. When companies are forthright in the face of negative publicity, such as Johnson & Johnson's immediate recall of Tylenol after the cyanide poisonings and its introduction of tamper-proof packaging, negative publicity leaves no long-lasting damage.

GLOBAL MARKETING STRATEGIES

Chiquita ensured the excitement continued throughout the summer by organizing beach volleyball and other games on the Belgian coast. Winners received coupons for 2 pounds of bananas, and when they redeemed them, they were automatically entered in the Walibi drawing.

Chiquita's well-established campaign included trade promotions, because retailers had to be counted on to make sure there were plenty of Chiquita bananas on hand to meet demand. A second competition was held for them. For every box of bananas ordered, retailers were told they would receive a game card making them eligible to be chosen as one of 50 VIP grocers at Walibi Park, where a drawing would be held awarding winning card holders such prizes as video cameras and stereo equipment. More than 6,000 retailers responded.

With this massive buildup, Chiquita Banana Day attracted 25,000 people and created a mile-and-a-half traffic jam. More importantly, Chiquita's market share in Belgium went from 60 percent to 80 percent, and summertime sales rose 60,000 boxes over the previous year!

Questions: What components of the promotional mix did Chiquita use in its campaign in Belgium? How did it coordinate these elements into one promotional campaign?

Sources: "What Makes a Winner in Europe?" *Adweek's Marketing Week*, August 20, 1990, p. 35; and "Needed: A New U.S. Perspective on Global Public Relations," *Public Relations Journal*, November 1990, p. 18.

TYPES OF PUBLICITY

Most publicity efforts involve press releases, company communications, and, more recently, special events.

PRESS RELEASES

Press releases might be used to announce a new product or technology, to communicate news about the company, or to counteract some negative event or rumor. The British conglomerate Grand Metropolitan sent out a press release to announce its acquisition of Burger King. Johnson & Johnson used press releases to announce that it was reintroducing Tylenol in a tamper-proof package rather than pulling the brand off the market after the cyanide poisonings. Perrier used press releases extensively when announcing that it was ending the recall forced upon it when traces of benzine were found in some of its bottles. One trend in this area is *video releases*; that is, videotaped press releases sent to television stations. A 1990 study of 900 local stations found that 52 percent had aired company video releases as news stories over a two-year period.[59]

COMPANY COMMUNICATIONS

Companies will also try to get stories into newspapers, magazines, or on television news shows in a more comprehensive publicity campaign involving various company communications.

McDonald's mounted an issue-oriented publicity campaign to counter negative publicity generated by nutritional groups' criticisms about the fat and salt content of its foods and the disadvantages of fried foods. The company reduced the sodium level of many of its foods, fried them in vegetable shortening instead of animal fat, and introduced fresh salads on the menu.[60] It publicized these changes through press releases and by offering a booklet in each of its outlets on the nutritional content of its products. The company also introduced a number of ads in medical trade magazines touting the nutritional content of its foods and explaining how they contribute to a balanced diet. (These ads were challenged by several groups, however, as exaggerations.)

SPECIAL EVENTS

Increasingly, many companies sponsor special events such as musical or sports events as a means of promoting good will among consumers, stockholders, and other relevant portions of the public. These events are then publicized by the company through the mass media.

McDonald's sponsors an All-American high-school basketball team each year composed of the top senior basketball players in the country. It then holds an annual McDonald's All-American game between these players, with the proceeds of the game going to Children's Charities. Millions of viewers watch the game on ABC. As a result, McDonald's gets nationwide publicity and good will for its sponsorship of the event.

EVALUATING PUBLICITY

The effectiveness of a company's publicity efforts can be measured by the amount of space or air time that a company or its product receives and by the number of people reached by the message. For example, Absolut Vodka launched a $1 million print ad campaign during the 1987 holiday season that featured a microchip which played the tune "Jingle Bells." The innovative ad was featured on several national television shows, including the "NBC Nightly News," which prominently mentioned Absolut while explaining how the ad was engineered. According to a public relations agency that tracked the amount of air time Absolut received, the ad generated about $8 million of free publicity. In fact, since distilled spirits cannot be advertised on television, Absolut literally received more exposure than money could buy. Sales of the vodka wound up wildly exceeding projections.[61]

Effectiveness can also be measured by the degree to which a campaign changes consumers' opinions. The marketer can measure this by conducting a survey. The Potato Board instituted a publicity campaign to convince consumers that potatoes are not fattening and are actually nutritious. Then it conducted a survey and found that the number of people who believed that potatoes are rich in vitamins and minerals had risen from 36 percent before its publicity campaign to 67 percent after.

SUMMARY

1. **What are the components of a promotional mix and the purpose of each component?**
   A promotional mix combines advertising, sales promotions, personal selling, and publicity. Advertising is a paid, ongoing, nonpersonal communication from a commercial source such as a manufacturer or a retailer. Advertising is designed to inform consumers about a brand and to influence them to buy. Its primary value is its long-term effect of keeping consumers aware of the brand and maintaining consumer loyalties.
   Sales promotions are shorter-term inducements of value to consumers that encourage them to buy a product or service. They are aimed at attracting new users and encouraging existing users to buy more frequently.
   Personal selling is face-to-face communication by a company representative to influence the customer to buy a product or service. It is more flexible than other components, because the salesperson can assess the customer's needs and design a message accordingly.
   Publicity is unpaid communications in the mass media about a company, product, or service. Consumers often see it as more believable than advertising, but the message is difficult to control.
2. **What is the nature of the marketing communications process?**
   Marketing communications require a source (the advertiser) that develops a message (encoding) that is transmitted to an intended receiver who then interprets (decodes) it. The advertiser then evaluates the response to the message (feedback). Evaluating the effectiveness of the marketing communication process is difficult, because a host of other environmental factors influence sales as well.
3. **How do managers select a promotional mix for a brand or product category?**
   Managers first establish promotional objectives. They then evaluate the factors that determine the importance of each component of the promotional mix, such as the type of customer, type of product, and stage in the product's life cycle. On this basis, they develop a strategy that determines the mix of advertising, sales promotion, personal selling, and publicity to effectively promote the product. Next, a promotional budget is determined and allocated to each component of the promotional mix. The final step is to evaluate the promotional mix by assessing its impact on the target audience.
4. **What types of sales promotional tools can be used to promote a brand?**
   Sales promotions have become a growing part of the promotional mix, recently exceeding advertising in terms of total expenditures. Consumer promotions are designed to influence consumers to try a brand and to get existing consumers to buy again. Trade promotions are designed to get retailers and wholesalers to stock the brand. Trade promotions push the product through the channels; consumer promotions pull it through. Coupons are the most frequently used type of consumer promotions. Other types of consumer promotions are price deals, premiums, refunds, sweepstakes, free samples, and point-of-purchase displays. Trade promotions include merchandise allowances, case allowances, and direct payments to get intermediaries to stock a brand.
5. **What types of publicity tools can be used to promote a brand or company?**

Companies use press releases and communications to try to get favorable news disseminated. An increasingly frequent component of publicity efforts is sponsorship of sports or musical events. News of such sponsorship is then publicized to generate goodwill for the sponsor.

KEY TERMS

Promotional mix (p. 552)
Advertising (p. 552)
Consumer promotions (p. 552)
Trade promotions (p. 553)
Personal selling (p. 553)
Publicity (p. 554)
Public relations (p. 554)
Encoding (p. 557)
Transmission (p. 557)
Noise in communications (p. 557)
Decoding (p. 557)
Feedback (p. 557)
Harvest strategy (p. 563)
Objective-task budgeting (p. 565)
Percent-of-sales budgeting (p. 565)
Competitive-parity budgeting (p. 566)
Coupons (p. 571)
Free-standing inserts (p. 572)
Electronic coupons (p. 572)
Price deals (p. 572)
Premiums (p. 572)
Rebates (p. 573)
Sweepstakes (p. 574)
Free samples (p. 574)
Point-of-purchase displays (p. 574)
Trade promotions (p. 575)
Merchandise allowances (p. 575)
Case allowances (p. 575)
Slotting allowances (p. 575)

QUESTIONS

1. Did Burger King have a well-integrated promotional mix? Why or why not?
2. What different roles do advertising, personal selling, sales promotion, and publicity fill in the promotional mix?
3. To evaluate the effectiveness of marketing communications, what basic questions should a promotional manager ask at each stage of the process? Apply these questions to the promotional campaign for Polaroid's Spectra camera.
4. Why is it easier to evaluate the effectiveness of sales promotions than of advertising? How have advertisers dealt with the difficulty of directly relating advertising to sales?
5. Which component of the promotional mix is likely to be most important for each of the following, and why?
   a. A company marketing pollution control systems to chemical firms
   b. A leading cereal manufacturer trying to combat competition from lower-priced brands
   c. A brand of coffee that wants to expand from its western base and is finding it difficult to gain shelf space in supermarkets in the east
   d. A manufacturer of household products trying to create awareness for a new detergent
   e. A company trying to create an image for a perfume which targets the achievement-oriented working woman
   f. A financial services firm trying to ensure that its customers receive proper attention and advice from its sales representatives
6. Figure 17.3 indicates that sales promotions are most important for consumer packaged goods, advertising for consumer durables, and personal selling for services and industrial goods. Why?
7. How do (a) sales promotional objectives and (b) advertising objectives change over a brand's life cycle?
8. What is the distinction between a top-down and a bottom-up approach to promotional budgeting? What are the advantages and disadvantages of each approach?
9. What are the problems with a percent-of-sales approach and a competitive-parity approach as a basis for establishing the advertising budget? Why are these approaches widely used in setting promotional budgets despite these problems?
10. Why has the relative importance of sales promotions increased while that of advertising has declined?

11. What are the risks in using sales promotions?
12. What sales promotional tools would you use in each of the following situations, and why?
    a. A company introducing a new brand of toothpaste is trying to encourage trial
    b. A company with a coffee brand in the mature phase of the life cycle would like to regenerate interest in the brand
    c. A fast-food chain would like to encourage customers to eat at its outlets more often
    d. A small company introduces flavored sparkling waters and is trying to influence wholesalers and retailers to stock the line
    e. A manufacturer of major kitchen appliances is trying to check a decline in its market share
13. What are the advantages and disadvantages of using publicity in the promotional mix?

QUESTIONS: YOU ARE THE DECISION MAKER

1. A marketing executive for a producer of kitchen appliances commented on the use of nonsales criteria to evaluate advertising as follows:

    I have a real problem using consumer awareness of my advertising as a measure of its effectiveness. Advertising awareness does not tell me anything about what the consumer did. I have to justify my advertising expenditures by their effect on profits, and the only way I can do that is to try to determine how they influence sales.

    Do you agree with the executive's statement? Why or why not?
2. One product manager for a premium-priced coffee brand made the following comments about sales promotions:

    All I hear these days is the increasing amount spent on sales promotions relative to advertising. I just don't understand it. For my money, advertising will produce higher returns over the long run. It keeps brand awareness high, maintains our loyal customer base, and communicates our product's benefits so as to attract new customers. What do coupons and price deals do? Such promotions may attract some customers based on price incentives. But most of these customers just go right back to their original brand when the promotion is off. So how much have we gained? Even worse, the promotion means our regular customers are buying what they would ordinarily purchase, but at a lower price. Overall, I would put more money into advertising than sales promotions.

    a. Do you agree with the product manager's assessment of the value of sales promotions? Why or why not?
    b. How is the fact that this executive manages a premium-priced brand likely to color her evaluations of sales promotions?
3. A marketing manager for a line of personal computers made the following comments about slotting allowances:

    I think paying retailers to stock our items is outrageous. We spend millions to develop what the consumer wants, so why should we pay retailers to stock our products? I would prefer to use advertising and occasional consumer promotions to pull the products through the store than have to pay retailers to push them through.

    a. Do you agree with this executive's position on slotting allowances? What are the risks of his position?
    b. Would a manager for a packaged good like cereals take a different position regarding slotting allowances than a manager for a line of personal computers?

CHAPTER 18

Advertising

YOUR FOCUS IN CHAPTER 18

To learn:

- *The types of advertising marketers use most widely.*
- *How firms develop advertising strategies.*
- *The different types of messages advertisers develop to communicate product benefits.*
- *How advertisers select the proper media to transmit their messages.*
- *How marketers evaluate advertising effectiveness.*
- *What is socially responsible advertising.*

Eveready: Using a Bunny to Advertise Batteries?

When Ralston Purina bought Eveready in 1986, its executives didn't have the faintest notion how to sell batteries. After all, this was not cat food. They could not parade a cute, fuzzy pet across the screen, could they? But it did not take a battery expert to see that rival Duracell was closing in on Eveready's 52-percent share of the $2.5 billion U.S. battery market[1] and that Eveready spokesman Robert Conrad wasn't getting the job done.[2]

Just as things began to look hopeless, Eveready CEO Patrick Mulcahy noticed that an eccentric square-jawed soccer star named Jacko Jackson was setting Eveready's sales on fire in Australia. After viewing Jacko's spots, Mulcahy decided that with a little grooming, Jacko could become a U.S. phenomenon too. With barely any testing, he sank $30 million into a TV and print campaign that featured the sports star growling "Oy" and demanding that viewers "Get Energizer."

ENERGIZER
STONEHENGE, WILTSHIRE, ENGLAND.
STILL GOING.
NOTHING OUTLASTS THE ENERGIZER.

The campaign violated a basic principle of advertising, "Communicate product benefits." Not only didn't Americans get Energizer, they didn't get Jacko either. Many grew to loath him as a loud-mouthed irritant.[3] "The sales force looked at us and said 'How could you do that? We expected more from our new parent,' Mulcahy later recalled. To make matters worse, the Jacko fiasco enabled Duracell to pull even with Eveready, leaving each with 45 percent of the battery market. Desperate, Mulcahy went back to Eveready's ad agency, DDB Needham Worldwide, looking for something new.[4]

DDB Needham came up with an approach that poked fun at Duracell's earlier commercials, where toys with Duracell batteries were shown winning endurance contests against toys with "ordinary" batteries. DDB Needham's answer was a commercial showing an Eveready bunny marching into a crowd of Duracell bunnies as a voice-over complained that no one ever invited Eveready to Duracell's "party." The spot so encouraged Mulcahy that he asked it to be turned into a larger campaign. But DDB did not see turning the bunny into a campaign. They saw it only as a one-time commercial. Given Mulcahy's pet-food roots, it is not surprising that he really liked the bunny campaign and decided to pursue it with another agency, Chiat/Day.

Chiat/Day's creative team came up with the idea for a series that would begin with a parody of typical TV commercials. Each parody would last a few seconds before being interrupted by the drumming Eveready bunny. "Still going," a voice-over would intone. One of Chiat/Day's parodies advertised the fictitious foreign film *Dance with Your Feet*, another advertised the make-believe Soviet drink "Sputnik" ("Made with 10 percent real beet juice!").

The ads delighted Mulcahy, who gave the green light for them to be unveiled during the 1989 World Series and supported them with $22 million for TV advertising in that year's fourth quarter.[5] In short order, viewers began taking notice of the new Duracell campaign. Wait a minute. *Duracell*?

Yes; because the bunny was a spin-off of the earlier work from Duracell, consumers associated the "Still going" appeal with Duracell's earlier endurance theme. As a result, Eveready's name did not stand out. In one survey, a full 40 percent recalled the spot being a Duracell commercial. Even more galling was evidence that the campaign was boosting Duracell's sales.[6]

Mulcahy stood his ground, renewing the campaign for a second year and tripling its media budget. The new phase found the bunny doing such things as wearing a gas mask while mocking a spot for the fictional "Airedale" air freshener. The campaign was also moved into print, where an ad that featured the bunny breaking through a full page of type was published in *Newsweek*, *People* and *Sports Illustrated* magazines. In a further extension, the bunny appeared in a pseudo-movie trailer that was shown in theaters.[7] By late 1990, Eveready claimed that brand awareness rose 33 percent from the year before, while recall of the advertising message was up 50 percent.[8]

But critics were pointing to another advertising principle that the campaign might be violating: "Do not let humor overwhelm the message." The danger was that consumers might remember the bunny, but might not connect it to the message—that Eveready batteries are longer lasting.

It is too early to tell whether the Eveready bunny can stem Duracell's gains. One 1991 survey found that Duracell had a 44 percent share of the highly competitive alkaline segment to Eveready Energizer's 36 percent.[9] Somehow Ralston Purina managed to sneak in a pet to sell batteries. The question is whether the bunny is communicating the message.

IMPORTANCE OF ADVERTISING

Marketers may be spending more money on sales promotion than advertising, but advertising is still the mainstay of a company's communication strategy, informing the consumer about product benefits and keeping the product visible over time.

ADVERTISING EXPENDITURES

In 1982, total advertising expenditures were about $62 billion. By 1991, they had more than doubled to $132.6 billion.[10] Projections are that advertising expenditures will be nearly $500 billion by the turn of the century.

Table 18.1 lists the ten top advertisers in 1990. Most are firms that sell consumer goods. Procter & Gamble became the leading advertiser when its acquisition of new cosmetics companies and its decision to shore up its diaper, detergent, and cleansers divisions spurred a 50-percent hike in spending. P&G was bucking the tide that saw the top 100 companies tighten their belts during the economic downturn of 1990. Philip Morris had been the leading advertiser with the acquisition of General Foods and Kraft in the mid-to-late 1980s, but slipped into second place in 1990.[11]

Fast-food outlets and producers of consumer packaged goods such as drugs, toiletries, and food typically spend over 5 percent of sales revenues on advertising. For example, McDonald's spends close to 20 percent of sales on advertising, P&G spends 15 percent, Grand Metropolitan (owners of Pillsbury and Burger King) spends 11 percent, and Philip Morris and PepsiCo spend 6 percent. Large retailers (Sears and Kmart) spend less. The leading auto companies spend no more than 2 percent of revenues on advertising.

TABLE 18.1

Leading Advertisers in the United States for 1990

	ADVERTISING EXPENDITURES (IN MILLIONS)	AD EXPENDITURES AS A PERCENT OF SALES
1. Procter & Gamble	$2,284	15.0
2. Philip Morris	2,210	6.1
3. Sears, Roebuck	1,507	2.9
4. General Motors	1,502	1.7
5. Grand Metropolitan	882	11.0
6. PepsiCo	849	6.0
7. AT&T	796	2.1
8. McDonald's	764	19.7
9. Kmart	693	2.3
10. Time Warner	676	7.9

Source: "100 Leading National Advertisers," *Advertising Age*, September 25, 1991, p. 1; and company annual reports.

EXHIBIT 18.1

Purposes of Advertising

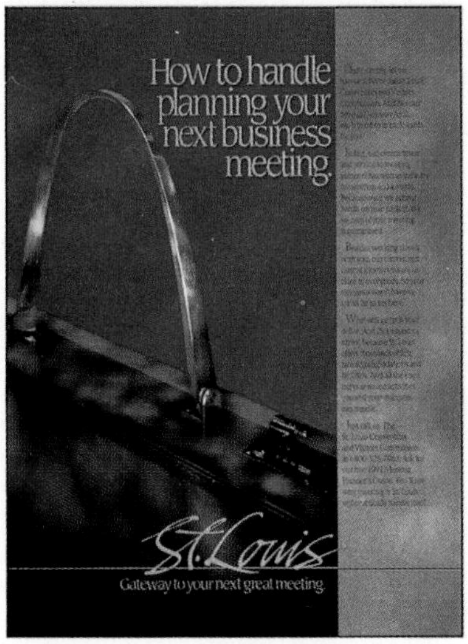

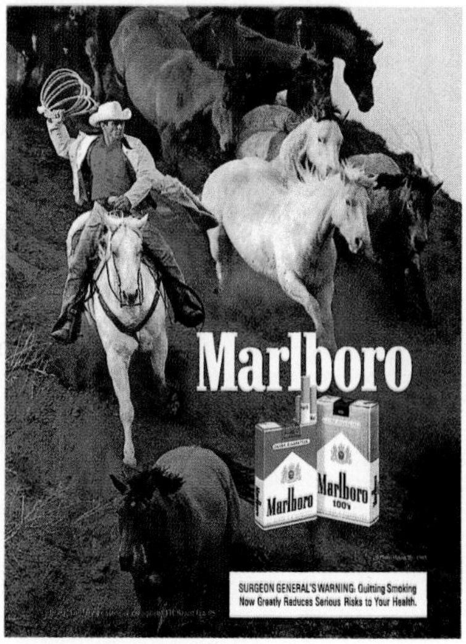

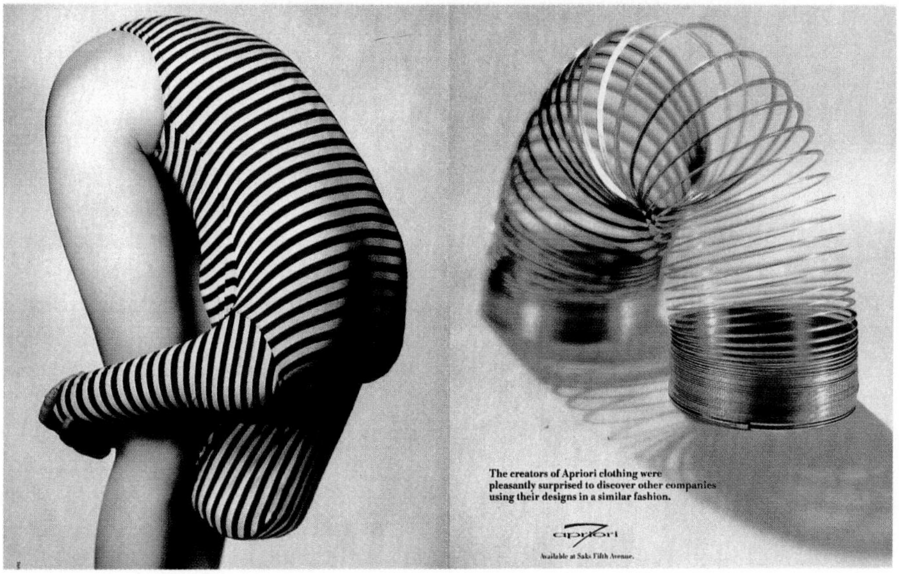

(Top Left) Advertising to Create Awareness

(Top Middle) Advertising to Inform

(Top Right) Advertising to Maintain Product Visibility

(Lower Left) Advertising to Influence Consumers

PURPOSES OF ADVERTISING

As we have seen in Chapter 17, advertising has four basic functions. Exhibit 18.1 provides an example of each. The ad for the St. Louis Convention Center was designed to *create awareness* of the center by using the image of a briefcase handle from an attaché case to associate managers' conference needs with the city's famous arch.

Advertising is also meant to *inform* customers about product or service benefits. The "keep your body at its peak" ad campaign used by Evian in the late 1980s was designed to inform amateur athletes that Evian helps prevent dehydration and helped the bottled water company double its sales to $65 million. Exhibit 18.1 shows how Evian continued the theme into the 1990s.[12]

Another purpose of advertising, to *influence* consumers to buy, is demonstrated by the Apriori ad in Exhibit 18.1. When Apriori wanted to convey the message that its stylish clothes were perfect for exercising, the ad agency of Weiss Whitten Carroll Stagliano juxtaposed a model in an Apriori leotard with a Slinky. While the visually captivating ad provided little actual information about Apriori clothing, it left the viewer with the strong impression that Apriori's clothes are stylish and comfortable.

Finally, one of the most successful advertising campaigns in history, the Marlboro Man, fulfills a fourth function of advertising, to *maintain product visibility*. The campaign was launched in the mid 1950s and has been used to maintain product visibility for over 30 years. The image of the strong, quietly confident, masculine cowboy transformed the brand into a market leader.

TYPES OF ADVERTISING

Most advertising campaigns are designed to influence consumers to buy a particular brand. The ads in Exhibit 18.1 for Apriori, Evian, and Marlboro represent brands in a product category. Three other types of advertising can be as important as brand advertising in the promotional mix—product advertising, corporate advertising, and cooperative retail advertising.

BRAND ADVERTISING

Brand advertising *is designed to maintain awareness of a brand among consumers and to increase its market share.* Marketers try to increase the share of their brands primarily by attracting users of competitive brands. Such brand advertising tries to stimulate **selective demand,** *that is, the demand for a particular brand.* One Pepsi ad showed rap star Hammer interrupting a raucous concert after accidentally sipping Coke and then begin singing a campy rendition of the lounge song "Feelings." It was a clear attempt to stimulate selective demand for Pepsi by attracting Coke drinkers. Brand advertising also attempts to keep current customers "sold" on the brand. Pepsi's ad was designed to reinforce its place among youthful soda drinkers.

PRODUCT ADVERTISING

Product advertising *is designed to attract new users by stimulating* **primary demand,** *that is, demand for a general product category.* As such, product advertising is trying to make the industry pie bigger, whereas brand advertising is trying to redistribute the pie so the advertiser gets a larger share.

Companies band together at times to advertise a product category on an industry-wide basis. Such advertising is usually meant to counter an industry-wide decrease in demand by stimulating primary demand. Rather than spending their money to compete with each other in the face of a shrinking pie, these companies contribute a percentage of their revenues to a cooperative advertising effort to prevent the pie from shrinking further.

Exhibit 18.2 shows how the California Milk Advisory Board sponsored a campaign to compete with soft-drink makers in an attempt to lure youthful drinkers.

EXHIBIT 18.2

Advertising a Product Category

The ad was designed to convince teens not only that drinking milk was hip but also that it created a good physique. It was executed by picturing a trendy blond-haired teen holding a carton of milk in an exuberant action shot.

Companies sometimes try to stimulate demand for both the brand and the product. Bayer is promoting the product category, aspirin, by advertising its benefits in reducing the chances of a heart attack. It is also promoting its brand by saying that athletes such as former tennis star Arthur Ashe takes Bayer for this purpose.

CORPORATE ADVERTISING

More companies than ever are advertising their corporate name as well as their brands. There are three types of corporate advertising: patronage, image, and issue advertising (see Exhibit 18.3).

Corporate-patronage advertising *is designed to encourage customers to patronize the firm.* The ad for Mitsubishi shows the range of products the company produces. It is designed to communicate the company's diversity and technological leadership worldwide, and in so doing, encourage customers to buy the products shown in the ad. Interestingly, Mitsubishi heads one of the six Japanese *Keiretsu* (see Chapter 9).

Corporate-image advertising *attempts to establish a corporate identity.* Bell & Howell conducted research that found that most consumers associated the company with cameras, even though it had sold its camera division in 1979. The company launched a campaign to convey the fact that it was a conglomerate. The ad had little copy and did not detail specific products. Rather, it conveyed an image that the company was in a wide range of product areas.

Corporate-issue advertising *states a company's position on an issue of public importance.* Shortly after the Exxon Valdez—a single-hull tanker—ran aground in Alaska, DuPont sponsored an ad that supported double-hulled tankers, thereby positioning itself as an environmentally friendly company.[13] Mobil Oil regularly runs an ad in the opinion section of *The New York Times* for policy statements on a host of public issues that affect it. Clothing maker Benetton combines issue and public image elements in print ads that promote racial harmony.

EXHIBIT 18.3

Types of Corporate Advertising

Corporate Patronage Advertising

Corporate Issue Advertising

Corporate Image Advertising

COOPERATIVE ADVERTISING

Cooperative advertising *is brand-related advertising in which manufacturers offer retailers allowances to advertise their brands* and permit retailers to insert the store's name in the ad. Cooperative advertising—which accounts for $11 billion in advertising a year—helps manufacturers because it is a means to get retailers to stock and to more aggressively sell their products. In this respect, it represents a "push" effort in contrast to the "pull" of brand or product advertising. Companies as diverse as IBM, Levi Strauss, General Electric, Bristol-Myers, and Ford provide extensive co-op support. To boost car sales in the summer of 1990, Ford gave its dealer groups $31 million in co-op funds—an increase of nearly a third over the same period the year before.[14] Cooperative advertising is also important to manufacturers as a source for local advertising to balance their national advertising campaigns.

Cooperative advertising helps retailers as well. Most manufacturers pay from 50 to 75 percent of advertising costs to push certain products. In this way, retailers can afford to advertise in newspapers, on radio, and even on TV. The economic downturn of the early 1990s left retailers in even greater need of this support. One study found that most manufacturers were raising co-op budgets from 12 to 20 percent to spur sales during this period.[15] Marshall Field's is a good example of how retailers use co-op budgets. At the department store chain, apparel buyers will plan a campaign months in advance and then decide on the number of manufacturers needed to support it. For instance, clothing manufacturers were asked to contribute $5,000 each to support a campaign for "juniors" apparel.[16]

DEVELOPING ADVERTISING PLANS AND STRATEGIES

FIGURE 18.1

The Advertising Planning Process

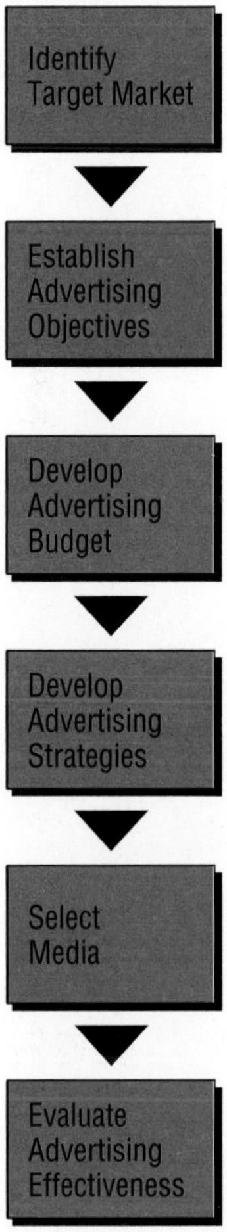

Companies develop advertising plans to communicate product benefits to consumers and to influence them to buy. The process of advertising planning is shown in Figure 18.1. This process parallels the steps in the communications process described in Chapter 17. The advertiser (the source of the message) identifies the target market for the advertising campaign, establishes advertising objectives to influence the target to buy, and develops an advertising budget. The advertising agency then develops an advertising strategy—that is, encoding a set of messages that communicate product benefits—and selects media to transmit the message to target consumers. The advertiser will then evaluate the effectiveness of the campaign based on how consumers interpret (decode) the message and act on it.

We will focus for the remainder of this chapter on the six steps in the advertising planning process in Figure 18.1.

IDENTIFY THE TARGET MARKET

The first step in advertising planning is identifying the target for the advertising campaign. In Chapter 10, we saw that many companies have shifted from a mass-market approach to a segmented-market approach requiring a more precise definition of the target market. For example, before 1980 most car advertising targeted male audiences. With the recognition among marketers that an increasing proportion of women influence and make car-buying decisions, the auto companies began directing ads toward specific segments of women buyers, such as budget-minded, performance, and luxury-oriented segments.

The definition of the target market will influence the positioning of a product and the advertising themes used. An example of this link between target market definition and advertising strategy is Nike's print ads targeting women. They were widely heralded for their honesty and integrity. One, featuring a photo of Marilyn Monroe, begins with the statement, "A woman is often measured by the things she cannot control." It continues by describing how society measures women by their physical attributes and ends with the phrase, "Statistics lie." The only suggestion of Nike is an understated logo in the upper right corner, yet the ad creates the strong impression that Nike is far more sensitive to women's needs than its competition.[17]

Similarly, AT&T turned its pursuit of college-age customers into a campaign in which students were pictured offering down-to-earth, personal testimonials to the company.[18] Like Nike, AT&T scored by not talking down to its target audience. College students rated the campaign their third favorite of 1989.

ESTABLISH ADVERTISING OBJECTIVES

Once marketers identify a target, they must formulate advertising objectives to determine the level of marketing effort needed to influence the target group. These objectives should help advertisers determine the advertising budget and advertising strategies. Objectives also provide the basis for evaluating results of the advertising campaign.

Advertising objectives might be to reach a certain percentage of the target group or to increase the number of times an average consumer in the target group has seen the advertising. When Admiral introduced its "A La Mode" refrigerator with a stir freezer that makes ice cream and frozen desserts, its objective was to reach at least 80 percent of the target group, upscale consumers between the ages of 24 and 54. Additional objectives for Admiral might have been to achieve awareness of the A La Mode refrigerator within one year among at least two-thirds of the target group and to create a preference for the product among at least 20 percent of the target.

Ultimately, the key objective must be to influence customer behavior. As a result, advertising objectives are often stated in terms of sales goals; for example, achieving first-year sales of $20 million for the A La Mode refrigerator. Behavioral objectives can also be stated more specifically in terms of goals for increasing new users, increasing usage levels among existing users, or increasing the level of brand loyalty.[19]

DEVELOP THE ADVERTISING BUDGET

The advertising budget is a component of the overall promotional budget. We described approaches for establishing the promotional budget in Chapter 17. Advertisers can use the same approaches to set advertising expenditure levels—an objective-task method, a percent-of-sales approach, a competitive-parity approach, or some arbitrary method.

The most widely used approach is the objective-task method. Sara Lee used it to establish the advertising budget for its line of Le Sandwiche croissants. The company set a market-share goal for the product line and then determined the proportion of the target group it would have to reach and the frequency of exposures required to attain the market-share goal. It then estimated the advertising budget required to meet these "reach" and "frequency" objectives.[20] Sara Lee's approach can be summarized as:

1. *Objective* → Market-share goal
2. *Task* → Reach and frequency required to meet market-share goal
3. *Budget* Advertising budget to achieve reach and frequency objectives

ESTABLISH ADVERTISING STRATEGIES

The central component of the advertising planning process in Figure 18.1 is developing advertising strategies. Once the target is identified, objectives are established, and an advertising budget is set, management is ready to consider how to go about influencing the consumer to buy. Advertisers first determine an overall campaign strategy. They then consider what specific messages should be used to inform and influence consumers.

DETERMINING THE CAMPAIGN STRATEGY

Advertising strategies can be designed to *maintain* a brand's position by continuing an advertising campaign over time, or strategies can be designed to *change* a brand's image and expand its base of users. A market leader such as Marlboro tries to maintain its market position and uses advertising as a reminder effect to reinforce current users. However, most brands cannot rely on the same campaign for 30 years. They must adapt to changing market conditions by revitalizing their image, which requires a change in advertising strategies over time.

Maintenance or change strategies can be implemented by (1) informing consumers of product benefits and characteristics or (2) using symbols and images to influence consumers to buy. Informational campaigns are often used to tell consumers about new products or to suggest new uses for existing products. The Wrigley company suggested a new use for gum when it positioned its Spearmint gum as an alternative to cigarettes in cities that had banned smoking in the workplace.[21] Informational campaigns are particularly important in industrial advertising, because buyers often make decisions based on product specifications.

Informational campaigns are also prevalent for consumer electronics, appliances, and other durables, because companies can get an edge on their competitors based on product features. The ad for the Sony videocamera in Exhibit 18.4 is meant to inform consumers of product features. The photo is designed to draw consumers into the ad so that they read the copy.

Advertising campaigns can also be based primarily on symbolism and imagery rather than on information. The Halston perfume ad in Exhibit 18.4 is based strictly on imagery. The apple is meant to suggest Eve tempting Adam to eat the forbidden fruit, with the tag line "irresistible."

Figure 18.2 categorizes advertising strategies based on the two factors just cited—maintenance versus change and information versus imagery. These dimensions do not represent sharp distinctions. Most informational ads have components of imagery. The ad for Halston shows the product and is therefore partly informational, but the intent is clearly to convey symbolism.

There are four basic types of strategies shown in Figure 18.2. *An* **information-oriented maintenance strategy** *is designed to reinforce the positioning of a brand or a company by conveying information about it.* Mercedes Benz uses such a strategy. The company's advertising has been conveying the same message for 20 years on an informational basis. Mercedes' advertising agency realized early on that it could

EXHIBIT 18.4

Ads Based on Symbolism and Information

Advertising Based on Symbolism

Advertising Based on Information

FIGURE 18.2

Advertising Campaign Strategies

Content

Objective	Information	Imagery/ Symbolism
Maintenance	Information-Oriented Maintenance Strategy	Image-Oriented Maintenance Strategy
Change	Information-Oriented Change Strategy	Image-Oriented Change Strategy

not describe Mercedes' quality without using long copy. This approach required print advertising packed with technical facts.

An **image-oriented maintenance strategy** *reinforces the brand's or company's positioning through imagery*. Merrill Lynch uses such a strategy by consistently relying on the Merrill Lynch bull as a unifying company symbol that is meant to represent confidence in both the company and the American economy.

Information-oriented change strategies *are designed to revitalize brands by advertising new product features*. For example, Seven-Up shifted from a campaign

EXHIBIT 18.5

An Image-Oriented Change Strategy: Changing the Image of Jeans to Target Adult Women

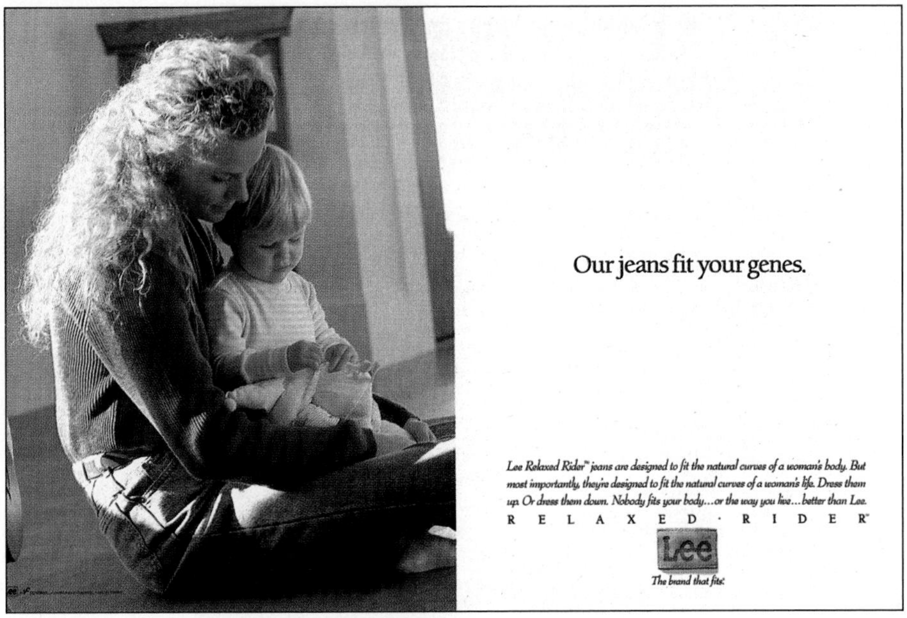

advertising its flagship brand as "The Uncola" to one touting the caffeine-free benefits of the brand by using an information approach with the slogan, "Never had it, never will."

An **image-oriented change strategy** *is meant to revitalize a brand through imagery and symbolism.* The three leading jeans companies, Levi Strauss, Lee, and Wrangler all target adult women by trying to change the perceptions of jeans as a male-oriented product. The image that Lee jeans is trying to project in implementing this strategy is shown in Exhibit 18.5.[22]

DEVELOPING THE ADVERTISING MESSAGE

Once the direction of the overall campaign is established, advertisers must develop specific messages to communicate product benefits and to influence the consumer to buy. Whether a campaign is based on information or imagery directly affects the development of the advertising message. Advertisers must address certain key issues in developing messages, specifically:

- Should the message be based on emotional or rational appeals?
- Should the advertiser consider using fear appeals to encourage purchase of the brand?
- Should humor be employed?
- Should spokespersons be used to communicate product benefits?
- Should comparative advertising be used to attack competitors?

Another issue in message development that we will address is the use of *subliminal advertising*; that is, messages that are shown so quickly that consumers are not aware of them, but they do register in the consumer's mind.

EXHIBIT 18.6

Using Emotional Appeals

A LOT OF TIRES COST LESS THAN A MICHELIN. THAT'S BECAUSE THEY SHOULD.
To everyone out there looking to save a few dollars on a set of tires, let's not mince words. You buy cheap, you get cheap.
There may be a lot of tires out there that cost less than a Michelin. The only question is, what do you have to give up if you buy one?
Do they handle like a Michelin?
Do they last like a Michelin?
Are they as reliable as a Michelin?
Then ask yourself this: Do you really want to find out?
At Michelin, we make only one kind of tire.
The very best we know how.
Because the way we see it, the last place a compromise belongs is on your car.
As a matter of fact, we're so obsessed with quality we make the steel cables that go into our steel-belted radials. We even make many of the machines that make and test Michelin tires.
And our quality control checks are so exhaustive that they even include x-rays.
These and hundreds of other details, big and small (details that may seem inconsequential to others), make sure that when you put a set of Michelin tires on your car, you get all the mileage Michelin is famous for.
True, there may be cheaper tires. But if they don't last like a Michelin, are they really less expensive?
So the next time someone tries to save you a few dollars on a tire, tell him this: It's not how much you pay that counts. It's what you get for your money.
And then *he'll* know that *you* know that there's only one reason a tire costs less than a Michelin.
It deserves to.
MICHELIN
BECAUSE SO MUCH IS RIDING ON YOUR TIRES.

EMOTIONAL VERSUS RATIONAL APPEALS

An important issue for advertisers is whether the message should "pull at the heartstrings of the consumer" or should be directed to transmitting information. One advertising agency executive voices the consensus among advertisers that the 1980s saw "emotion playing a greater role in advertising [by becoming] less product-feature oriented and much more nonverbal."[23]

Why this recent trend to emotion? There are several reasons. First, many products have become more standardized. When a car advertiser has no unique product claim, what better approach than to develop an emotionally based position? Second, advertisers have begun to recognize that many of the products they advertise are not particularly involving. Emotional advertising is a way to increase that involvement. When Chevrolet draped the American flag across its "Heartbeat of America" ads at the height of the Persian Gulf War, it barely even showed its cars. Yet, Chevrolet was very successful in involving viewers who were proud of American soldiers fighting in the Gulf.[24] Third, the intensity of competition has increased in many categories. More product alternatives make it harder for any one product to be noticed. What better way to stand out from the crowd than to take an emotional approach?

As Exhibit 18.6 shows, Michelin effectively stood out from its competition by taking an emotional approach. The ad makes the point that anyone worried about their child's safety should buy a Michelin tire, despite its higher price.

EXHIBIT 18.7

An Appeal to Fear

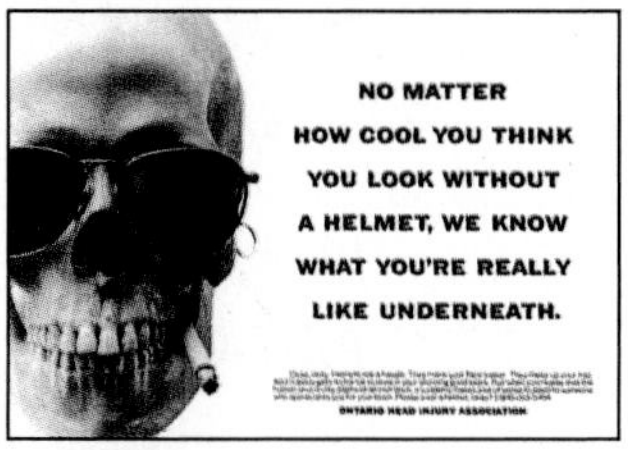

USING FEAR APPEALS

Most advertising informs consumers of the advantages of using a product. *Fear appeals* focus on the potential problems of using a product (cigarettes) or not using a product (seat belts). They are largely used for public service advertisements, such as the one shown in Exhibit 18.7 that warns of the dangers of riding motorcycles without a helmet. The effectiveness of the ad is questionable, however, because those who ride motorcycles without a helmet probably think they are invincible and are likely to ignore the message.

Fear ads also run the risk of alienating their targets by being overbearing. Early antismoking ads showing terminal cancer patients were ineffective, because they produced such a high level of anxiety that many smokers simply chose to ignore them.

Appeals to fear are likely to work when they show the consumer what to do to avoid a problem. Kellogg employed a successful appeal to fear when it introduced All-Bran as a high-fiber cereal that could help ward off colon cancer.

EMPLOYING HUMOR

Humor can be a memorable and persuasive way to sell a product. It is a good attention-getting device and may create a positive mood toward the advertiser, because people like to laugh. The British, who use humor liberally in their ads, think that it also aids recall and comprehension.[25] Combos pretzels used humor in its advertising to show things that go together (pretzels and nacho cheese), as opposed to things that do not go together (grandmas and motorcycles).

But humor can be an absolute dud if it is not used in good taste or if it is not closely tied to product benefits.[26] Perrier was roundly criticized for TV ads that had pseudo-newscasters reporting how Americans were clamoring for the bottled water after a contamination scare forced its recall. The spot was in bad taste since it trivialized a very real public-health concern.[27]

USING SPOKESPERSONS

Celebrity spokespersons have been used with increasing frequency. Table 18.2 lists the most popular entertainers and celebrities used in 1991 ads.

Well-known spokespersons can be effective in getting an ad message across if they are *likeable.* One survey found 39 percent of those polled said likable celebrities are more memorable than most other types of commercials.[28] "Murder She Wrote" television star Angela Lansbury was a successful spokesperson for Bufferin aspirin because of her image as a kindly mother figure. Similarly, Bill Cosby worked well in promoting Jell-O pudding pops because the ads were directed toward fans of his television show.

Spokespersons are also more effective in conveying a message when they are viewed as *credible.* Basketball star Michael Jordan has been an enormously successful spokesperson for General Mills' Wheaties cereal because it is marketed to sports fans, and Jordan is one of the reigning kings of the sports world. Conversely, Ringo Starr humiliated Sun Country when he sought treatment for alcohol abuse in the midst of a campaign for its wine coolers.[29] Similarly, Diet Pepsi quickly disassociated itself from Mike Tyson when he was charged with rape.

TABLE 18.2

Most-Popular Celebrity Spokespersons as of 1991

ENTERTAINERS	ENDORSEMENTS	ATHLETES	ENDORSEMENTS
Bill Cosby	Jell-O, Kodak Colorwatch	Michael Jordan	Nike, McDonald's, Hanes, Wheaties, Gatorade
Ray Charles	Diet Pepsi	Bo Jackson	Nike
Paula Abdul	Diet Coke	Tommy Lasorda	Ultra SlimFast
Candice Bergen	Sprint	Earvin "Magic" Johnson	Converse, Pepsi, Kentucky Fried Chicken
Linda Evans	Clairol, LensCrafters	Joe Namath	Flex-All, The Wiz
Ed McMahon	American Family Publishers, Colonial Penn Insurance	Bob Uecker	Miller Lite
Angela Lansbury	Bufferin	Joe Montana	Diet Pepsi
Kathie Lee Gifford	Carnival Cruise Lines, Ultra SlimFast	Nolan Ryan	Advil
Hammer	Pepsi, British Knights	Hulk Hogan	Right Guard
Lynn Redgrave	Weight Watchers	Arnold Palmer	Jiffy Lube, Hertz, Sears

Source: Video Storyboard Tests Inc., as reported in "Celebrity Pitchman Are Popular Again," *The Wall Street Journal.*

A spokesperson can also fall flat if cast in the wrong role. Bill Cosby was used as a spokesperson for the brokerage house, E. F. Hutton, intoning the company's tag line, "When E. F. Hutton talks, everybody listens." The hope was that his good-guy image would help repair the firm's reputation after it was rocked by a management scandal. But as one wag said, "When Cosby talked, nobody listened." Why? Because his lovable TV character was not perceived as having any special financial know-how. Cosby lacked credibility, which was the main requirement for a spokesperson for a financial-services firm.

A celebrity need not be a sports or entertainment star. Dave Thomas, owner of Wendy's fast-food chain, has become the engine behind its growth because of his everyman persona. It is unlikely that even Madonna could do more for the chain. Given the proliferation of ads that use media celebrities, a backlash may be developing against their use. Some marketers have predicted that the 1990s will be the "non-celeb decade."[30]

COMPARATIVE ADVERTISING

Comparative advertising *names competitors and cites their disadvantages relative to the advantages of the advertised brand.* Many American carmakers are attacking the Japanese in ads that show sedans side by side.[31] Exhibit 18.8 shows an ad from Pontiac that boasts its Grand Am GT outperforms the Nissan 240SX and the Toyota Celica GT at a lower price. In another case, the Hardee's restaurant chain tried to undercut McDonald's introduction of the McLean Delux hamburger in ads for its own Real Lean Delux. The ads ridiculed the fact that McDonald's used a sea-

EXHIBIT 18.8

An Example of Comparative Advertising

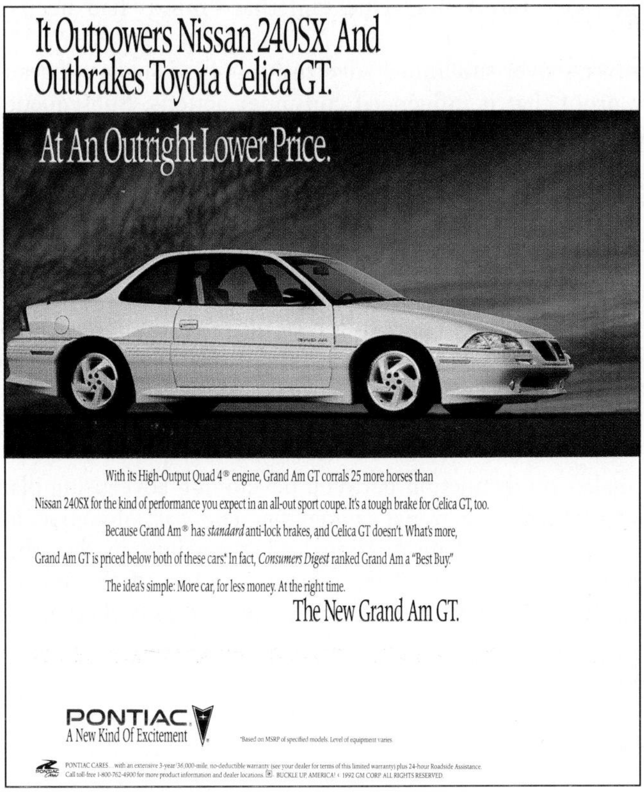
It Outpowers Nissan 240SX And Outbrakes Toyota Celica GT.
At An Outright Lower Price.
With its High-Output Quad 4® engine, Grand Am GT corrals 25 more horses than Nissan 240SX for the kind of performance you expect in an all-out sport coupe. It's a tough brake for Celica GT, too.
Because Grand Am® has *standard* anti-lock brakes, and Celica GT doesn't. What's more, Grand Am GT is priced below both of these cars.* In fact, *Consumers Digest* ranked Grand Am a "Best Buy."
The idea's simple: More car, for less money. At the right time.
The New Grand Am GT.
PONTIAC
A New Kind Of Excitement
*Based on MSRP of specified models. Level of equipment varies.
PONTIAC CARES ... with an extensive 3-year/36,000-mile, no-deductible warranty (see your dealer for terms of this limited warranty) plus 24-hour Roadside Assistance.
Call toll-free 1-800-762-4900 for more product information and dealer locations. BUCKLE UP, AMERICA! © 1992 GM CORP. ALL RIGHTS RESERVED.

weed derivative to hold its burgers together in the place of fat. "We would never consider using fillers, flavor enhancers—seaweed," says a Hardee's actor.[32]

Comparative advertising has been increasing since a 1976 Supreme Court decision held that an advertiser has the right to name a competitor under freedom of speech. In fact, the rise has been so dramatic that Coca-Cola felt compelled recently to petition the three television networks for committees that would judge all comparative claims for truthfulness. The idea is under study.[33]

Coke's request points up the risks in using comparative advertising, namely that a challenger should steer clear of it unless there is a legitimate claim to superiority. Otherwise, the brand could lose credibility in the consumer's eyes and even risk a court challenge. Also, comparative ads risk leading the consumer to mistake the challenger for the competitor. And despite the popularity of comparative advertising among manufacturers, studies have found that it yields no more benefit in sales than noncomparative advertising.[34]

SUBLIMINAL ADVERTISING

Subliminal advertising *is advertising that is shown so quickly that consumers can perceive it only at a subconscious level.* In 1957, two messages, "Eat popcorn" and "Drink Coca-Cola," were shown in a New Jersey movie theater for 1/3000th of a second at intervals of every five seconds.[35] Popcorn sales in the theater increased by 58 percent and Coca-Cola sales by 18 percent compared to periods in which there was no subliminal advertising. These results immediately raised serious ethical questions, since consumers could be influenced by messages without their approval or knowledge. *New Yorker* magazine said that "minds had been 'broken and entered'." [36]

The controversy over subliminal advertising proved shallow, because there was little further proof that it influenced consumer actions. Subsequent attempts to replicate the 1957 movie experiment did not succeed.[37]

Today, advertisers shun subliminal advertising, but some advertising critics claim that advertisers use techniques that approach the subliminal. These critics cite rapid changes in scenes or sound levels and the use of quick, repetitive phrases as a means of getting the advertising message in the consumer's subconscious. Such strategies are said to be most effective for low-involvement products. Since consumers are unlikely to pay close attention to the ads, communications devices not directly related to the product such as variations in sound or color might be used to register the message when the consumer's level of attention is low.

DEVELOPING INTERNATIONAL ADVERTISING STRATEGIES

Figure 18.1 makes no distinction between developing advertising plans and strategies for domestic or international campaigns. There is, of course, a basic difference between domestic and international ad campaigns in that the latter must consider differences between entire countries. One of the most contentious debates among international marketers revolves around whether a single *global strategy* can be used for advertising or whether *local strategies* should be developed to reflect differences between countries.

GLOBAL STRATEGIES

Global advertising is highly desirable because it achieves economies of scale in advertising through one universal campaign. Yet, it runs the risk of failing to adapt to local needs. Global advertising is feasible if products appeal to universal needs and can therefore use universal symbols and imagery. McDonald's golden arches, the Marlboro cowboy, and the Coca-Cola can are universal symbols reflecting common needs for fast foods, cigarettes, and soft drinks. Such common needs allow the marketing of world brands.

Recently, globalized strategies have become more feasible as a result of reduced trade barriers and the creation of pan-European television networks that make it easier than ever to reach large audiences with a single message. Another reason global advertising campaigns are becoming more feasible is the convergence of tastes and preferences across countries. As we have seen in Chapter 5, consumers are being exposed to the same products and ads worldwide because of global communications and consumers' increased travel. This trend has made it easier to appeal to consumers globally. For example, Visa has run identical ads in various countries for its card, with only a change in language (see Exhibit 18.9).

Although the standardized approach taken by Visa is becoming more feasible, it is still the exception. Most firms that try to follow a standardized approach use a strategy referred to in Chapter 5 as *patterned standardization*; that is, a global theme that is adapted in some way to the local environment. Coca-Cola's Assembly TV campaign shows children singing the Coke jingle, but the camera focuses on youngsters of the particular country in which the ad is shown.

Regardless of whether the extent of advertising standardization is truly global or is patterned, American companies must make sure the image they are selling

EXHIBIT 18.9

An Example of a Global Advertising Strategy

abroad is understood. When Philip Morris unveiled Marlboro in Hong Kong, for instance, the company's local advertising staff wanted to picture the Marlboro cowboy jumping on a bullet train. American executives had to tactfully explain that the scene didn't quite fit the company's carefully crafted image of the Marlboro cowboy on horseback.[38]

LOCAL STRATEGIES

Some products lend themselves to global advertising more than others. While a razor ad might work well on the world stage because everyone has similar shaving needs, food ads are more problematic due to cultural differences. This is why most firms use global campaigns for certain products and geographically specific campaigns for others. One study found that two-thirds of firms advertising internationally utilize both global and local strategies, depending on the brand.

Colgate-Palmolive, one of the first consumer goods firms to embrace global advertising, is now in the odd position of bucking the trend by tailoring all its international marketing to a country-by-country strategy. Company officials believe that concentrated marketing effort at the local level is the only means by which they can make products such as Fab and Ajax international brand leaders.[39] Similarly, Renault advertises its Clio differently to various European countries because of differences in the features consumers consider important. The company emphasizes performance and safety in Switzerland, quality and value in Germany, style in Spain, and luxury in France (see Exhibit 18.10).

EXHIBIT 18.10

An Example of a Local Advertising Strategy

Germany: Quality and Value

Spain: Style

Switzerland: Performance and Safety

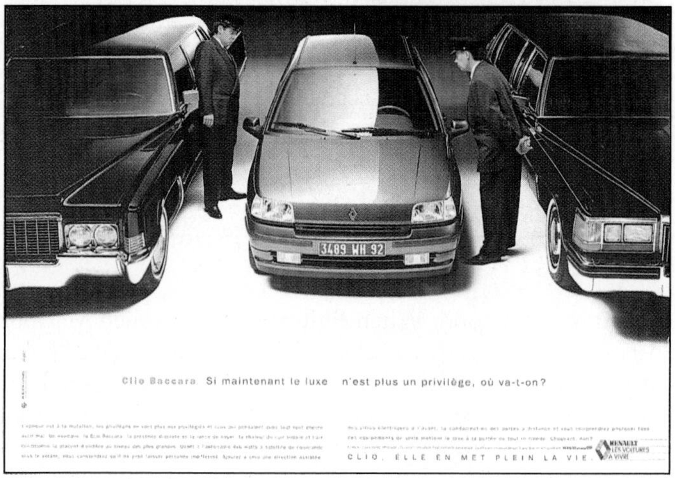

France: Luxury

SELECT MEDIA

Once advertisers have established a strategy for their brand, they must select the media to transmit the message. Selecting media is a difficult task because of the diversity of options. Advertisers can use TV, radio, magazines, newspapers, billboards, or direct mail; within each of these categories, the number of options is almost limitless.

TYPES OF MEDIA

The media vehicles available to advertisers can be broadly divided into broadcast media (TV and radio) and print media (newspapers, magazines, billboards, direct mail). These six types are shown in Figure 18.3. Advertising expenditures in 1990 are shown in dollars and as a percentage of all spending.

FIGURE 18.3

Distribution of Advertising Expenditures by Type of Media, 1990 (Dollars in Billions)

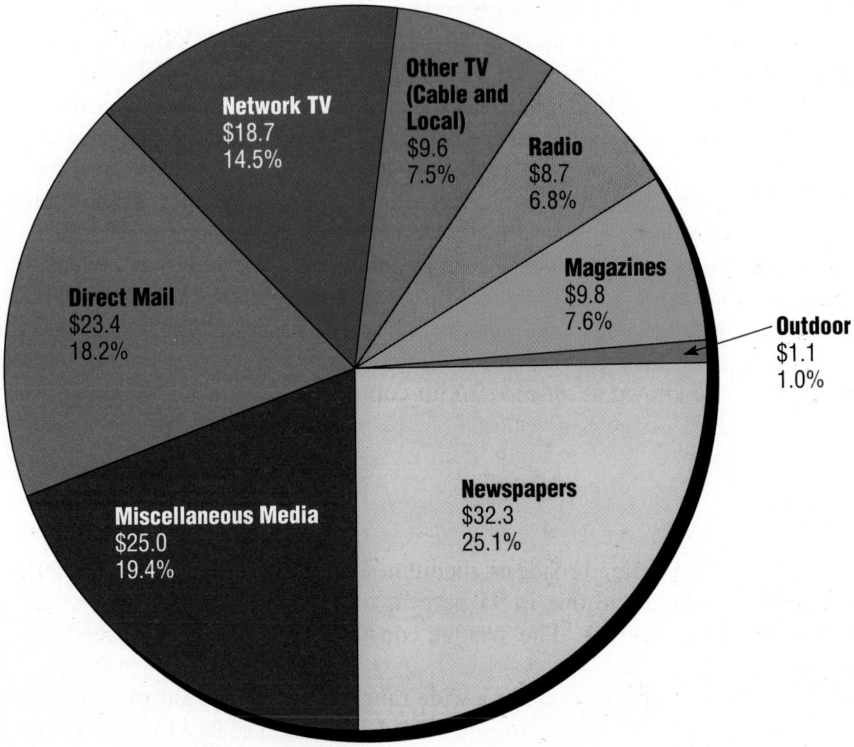

Source: *Mediaweek's Guide to Media,* 3rd Quarter, 1991.

TELEVISION

The mainstay of most national advertising campaigns is television—a medium in sound, color, and motion that can visually associate symbols with products, demonstrate product usage, and show consumer reactions. Figure 18.3 shows that television (network, local, and cable) accounted for over 20 percent of advertising expenditures in 1990. Over 97 percent of U.S. households have a TV set. These households watch an average of six hours of TV a day, most of the time on one of the three major networks. Although the networks' stronghold is declining, network TV is still viewed as the most effective medium for advertising products on a mass market basis.

Network TV's national scope is also a potential weakness. The medium is not selective in pinpointing target markets. As a result, advertisers turn to local TV stations to reach specific geographic markets more effectively and to cable TV and magazines to reach specific demographic groups. Also troubling to advertisers is that the network audience is declining. Fewer than 65 percent of the country routinely tunes into the Big Three (ABC, NBC, and CBS) in the evening, turning instead to a wide choice of cable channels. Daytime viewership is also down.

As audiences have shrunk, costs have risen. While it cost an average of $2.30 for a television advertiser to reach 1,000 people in 1967, costs rose to $6.81 per thousand in 1986 and to $9.74 in 1990, over four times the 1967 rate. Such fees have led advertisers to allocate less of their budgets to the networks, although they still accounted for a staggering $9.4 billion in ad revenue in 1989.[40] Despite the high cost of TV advertising fees, network TV remains the single most important part of the media mix for national brands.

Cable TV, subscribed to by over 50 percent of the nation's homes, is a cross between network TV and magazines. It provides the same visual advantages as network TV, but it also offers the selectivity of magazines. Since most cable channels are oriented to specialized interests such as news, sports, weather, and movies, commercials on these channels can be targeted to more specific groups than the network TV audience. For example, Lifetime, a cable station built around female-oriented programming, targets upscale women between the ages of 18 and 49. As a result of stations like these, cable TV has come to be referred to as *narrowcasting*, compared to network TV's *broadcasting*.[41]

Another advantage of cable TV is that commercials can be longer because they cost less. Because they communicate more information, cable TV commercials have come to be known as *infomercials*, in contrast to network TV's *commercials*.[42]

RADIO

Radio is the other major broadcast medium. With an average of more than five radios per household and one in 95 percent of cars and 61 percent of offices, it provides constant coverage. The average consumer listens to over three hours of radio a day.[43]

Radio is also flexible in reaching a wide range of audiences. Burger King is one of the largest users of the medium, spending $25 million of its $150 million media budget on targeted radio advertising. Companies such as Volkswagen and Pepsi have also discovered that radio provides an ideal way to fill local or regional gaps in a national campaign. While Pepsi was using Michael Jackson in its 1989 television campaign, it was also using the Texas band Asleep at the Wheel for radio ads in Austin.[44]

Radio is also more economical. The cost of radio advertising has increased at a rate less than that of all the other major media. From 1967 to 1987, its rate of increase was half that of network TV.[45] As a result, advertisers have increased radio expenditures from $1.8 billion in 1974 to $8.7 billion in 1990.[46]

NEWSPAPERS

Newspapers are the biggest advertising medium, accounting for more than 25 percent of advertising spending. Most of this is for retail advertising. Sales, price specials, coupon offers, and all types of merchandise are advertised on a day-to-day basis. Much of this expenditure might be better categorized as sales promotions rather than advertising, given its short-term nature.

Most national brand advertisers use newspapers on a limited basis, usually in conjunction with retailers by offering allowances for cooperative local advertising. However, national advertisers are paying closer attention to newspapers for several reasons. First, heavy newspaper readers tend to be upscale and have more discretionary purchasing power. Second, the cost of newspaper advertising has been increasing at a much lower rate than that of television. And third, newspapers are an excellent medium for targeting specific geographic segments.

MAGAZINES

Magazines have several major advantages over other types of media: First, since they are saved, picked up more than once, and often passed along to others, a consumer may be exposed to a magazine ad more than once, and a single ad is likely to be seen by more than one reader.

Magazines also provide a means of drawing the consumer's attention to the printed word through colorful illustrations or clever headlines. This effectiveness of magazines in communicating information makes them the most important component of the media mix for industrial advertisers. This is why ads in business publications such as *Iron Age* or *Aviation Week* are essential in providing key information on product attributes and performance and paving the way for subsequent sales calls.

A third advantage of magazines is selectivity. Magazines have become the most selective means of reaching target groups based on special interests and demographic characteristics. Since 1970, there has been a flood of specialty magazines geared to such interests as health, fashion, foods, electronics, sports, and so forth. Ten years ago, when Grape Nuts wanted to advertise to women aged 24 to 54, it turned to *Readers Digest*. Today, it splits its budget among 30 magazines, including *Backpacker*, *Prevention*, and *Shape*.[47]

A fourth advantage of magazines, flexibility, makes them an effective means of positioning consumer as well as industrial goods. Absolut became the number one vodka in the country through a high-gloss magazine campaign that grew more elaborate each year. The, first ad, which appeared in 1980, featured a halo over a bottle of Absolut and simply read, "Absolut Perfection." More recent ads present this playful theme to regional markets. (see Exhibit 18.11). By 1990, electronic chips that played music, snowflakes, even a workable jigsaw puzzle had all been employed in Absolut magazine ads. "We could not have had this success without the magazine medium," one Absolut manager said.[48]

In the not-too-distant future, a process called selective binding will give magazines the added flexibility of direct mail operations, allowing advertisers to target by zip code and, ultimately, even street address.[49]

DIRECT MAIL

Direct mail is the fastest-growing medium for advertisers and the most flexible. Figure 18.3 shows that direct mail (advertising or promotions mailed to specific customers) was the third most prominent medium after newspapers and TV, representing over 18 percent of all advertising expenditures in 1990.

Direct mail's advantage is the ability to target specific segments at relatively low cost compared to the mass media. It is a particularly important vehicle in industrial advertising for delivering catalogs to buyers and providing flyers detailing product specifications and prices. It can target industrial advertising directly to the individuals who have buying influence, without the waste of reaching nonbuyers through mass-media advertising.

Direct mail is also used for consumer goods and services. Mailing lists have been developed to target specific markets. For example, R. L. Polk, a Detroit-based research group, has data on all households with cars. R. L. Polk developed a mailing list for Subaru of 500,000 professional car-owning women with incomes over $35,000. Subaru was interested in this group, because more than 60 percent of its

EXHIBIT 18.11

Basing a Campaign on Magazine Advertising

cars are bought by women. The mailing included a brochure on Subaru's models and a 13-page kit that provides vehicle purchasing tips, a list of Subaru ownership advantages, and a discussion of leasing versus purchasing.[50]

OUTDOOR

Outdoor advertising is represented primarily by billboard advertising, but other forms include advertising on buses and even on parking meters. Colgate-Palmolive used bus billboards to promote its toothpaste in Russia.[51] The cost per advertising exposure is much lower for outdoor than that for TV, radio, or magazine advertising. To be effective, outdoor must convey the message within two or three seconds, so it must capture attention with creative illustrations and few words.

Outdoor advertising represents only 1 percent of advertising spending. But billboards are enjoying something of a renaissance as people spend fewer hours at home and more time traveling in their cars to and from work. The top users of billboards for national advertising are health care, banking, and resort companies. Outdoor advertising is also an effective medium for local advertisers, since it can be placed near retail establishments.

NON-TRADITIONAL MEDIA

The relentless drive for advertising efficiency has led marketers to explore some new options. One is the inclusion of commercials at the beginning of video rentals. A Schweppes soft-drink commercial, placed before the video version of *A Fish Called Wanda* was seen by 95 percent of the households that rented the movie.

The rate, which was better than some prime-time TV ads, astounded experts who assumed viewers would just skip right to the movie.[52]

Another medium is shopping cart advertising. In some supermarkets, an infrared sensor triggers advertisements to appear on small video display monitors attached to a product's shelf. Every time the cart passes certain products, the monitor flashes a message. Whether videocarts succeed or not, they indicate that advertisers are trying new and less-costly media to reach their target markets.[53]

CRITERIA FOR MEDIA SELECTION

An advertiser must select media based on their effectiveness in reaching the target group. Effectiveness is determined by the degree of exposure advertising produces and its cost.

ADVERTISING EXPOSURE

Advertising exposure *is the extent to which a particular ad is seen, read, or heard by a target group.* The potential advertising exposure that a medium can deliver is determined by its reach and frequency. **Reach** *is the percent of the target group exposed to the medium.* **Frequency** *is the number of times an individual in the target group is exposed to the message.* Assume Subaru supports its direct-mail campaign to professional women with magazine advertising. It finds that *Working Woman* magazine reaches 30 percent of Subaru's target of upscale working women. Subaru plans eight full-page ads a year and estimates readers will be exposed to half of them.

Advertising exposure is measured by reach multiplied by frequency, a measure known as **Gross Rating Points (GRPs)**. Subaru's estimated GRPs for *Working Woman* would be

$$30 \text{ (reach)} \times 4 \text{ (frequency)} = 120$$

The company would then investigate other magazines and select those that gave it the highest GRP to the target group at the lowest cost.

There is a tradeoff between reach and frequency. For a given advertising budget, greater emphasis on reach means less on frequency, and vice versa. The balance between the two depends on the advertising objectives. Reach is important for nationally advertised products that cut across many segments—for example, products such as toothpaste, detergents, and soft drinks. Frequency is important to establish brand awareness when a new product is introduced. Generally, several exposures are necessary for such awareness. Frequency is also more important when trying to influence a particular target group. The objective is to reach fewer people a greater number of times; whereas in advertising on a mass-media basis, the reverse would be true.

In the Subaru example, the advertiser could try to use a greater number of magazines to increase reach to working women, but much of this advertising would be wasted on consumers outside the target. A more likely course would be to use fewer and more-specialized magazines and more insertions in each magazine to increase frequency to a more-select group of upscale working women.

ADVERTISING IMPACT

One problem with using advertising exposure to select media is that exposure does not reflect the impact of advertising. Two magazines might deliver the same GRPs, but an advertisement in one might have more of an impact than an ad in the other.

GLOBAL MARKETING STRATEGIES

Selecting Media Strategies in Emerging Economies: Advertisers Find None of the Comforts of Home

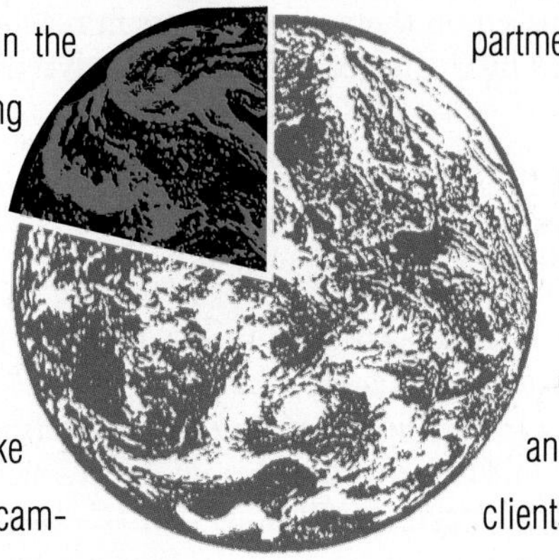

When Hugh Salmon visited Vietnam's Ho Chi Minh City in 1989, the only foreign ad he saw was a Sanyo billboard in the center of town. It made the managing director for Ogilvy & Mather's Thailand office realize just how far the agency would have to go if it wanted to advertise in Vietnam.

One assumption advertisers make when they design international campaigns is that a media infrastructure exists to convey the message to the consumer. A typical U.S. campaign involves a mix of television, radio, print, and outdoor media. In some developing countries, a marketer is lucky to be able to utilize just one of those vehicles.

In Vietnam, for instance, print ads were not allowed until recently, ads for soft drinks are still banned, and the country's one television network allows only 15 minutes of commercials a day—all of which must be prescreened by the government's Department of Culture and Information.

Vietnam is not alone in lacking many of the tools that Americans depend upon to advertise. In Eastern Europe, ad agencies are encountering one setback after another as they try to keep pace with clients who are flooding the region with exports. Procter & Gamble, Colgate-Palmolive, General Motors, and R. J. Reynolds are all looking to become major players in Eastern Europe and are expecting their ad agencies to give them support.

One example of how difficult this can be is the problem agencies have booking commercial time on Czech television. "In dealing with Czech TV, we feel like beggars," said one U.S. agency executive referring to the fact that there are no fixed slots for com-

An ad for a tennis racket in *Sports Illustrated* is likely to have more of an impact on the reader than the same ad in *Time* because of the differing editorial content of these magazines, even though both might have produced the same GRPs. Media planners must, therefore, account for the nature of the medium and its fit with the product.

COST

Advertisers select media based on advertising exposure relative to the cost of obtaining such exposure. GRPs alone cannot be the basis for media selection. The more appropriate criterion would be the *cost per gross rating point.*

Consider the following example: At one time, McDonald's media plan called for achieving 150 GRPs among children for each weekend of TV, split between 15- and 30-second commercials. The company was willing to allocate up to $650,000

GLOBAL MARKETING STRATEGIES

mercials. Requests for air time often go unanswered, leaving agencies guessing until the last minute about whether the spots will be broadcast. A more basic dilemma is trying to phone in the request. Few East Europeans have phone service, and the system is routinely overloaded.

Then there is the paucity of local print media. The Communist party's past stranglehold over print outlets has left much of Eastern Europe without the variety of newspapers and magazines that foreign advertisers consider necessary for successful mass-market campaigns. There are signs this will improve, but not soon.

The collapse of communism has played into advertisers hands in at least one respect: billboards. All of the billboards that used to carry propaganda have to be used for something, so foreign marketers are plastering them with ads for cigarettes in East Berlin and elsewhere.

As international marketers expand into Eastern Europe, Russia, and Asia, they will have to continue to use their ingenuity to overcome the lack of a media infrastructure for advertising campaigns.

Questions: What are some of the difficulties in executing a national advertising campaign in Eastern European countries? In Vietnam?

Sources: "Foreign Products Flooding Vietnam," *Advertising Age*, October 15, 1990, p.4a; "Marketing Is a New Game in the Old East Germany," *Adweek*, October 29, 1990, p.24; and "E. Europe: Opportunity in Chaos, *Advertising Age*, September 3, 1990, p.5a.

each weekend to achieve this purpose. Suppose the company allocated its advertising as in Table 18.3. Given these results, it would benefit the company to put more money into 15-second commercials, since they cost less per GRP. It would also be more effective to buy more 15-second commercials on Sunday rather than Saturday morning, since the cost per GRP is lower then.

On this basis, the media planner would try to determine the schedule that would achieve the most cost-effective delivery of advertising exposure given the advertising objectives and budgetary constraints.

SELECTING THE MEDIA MIX

Media planners use criteria such as cost per GRP to select a mix of vehicles to advertise their brands. Few rely on only one type of medium. Since there are so many alternatives, computer programs have been developed to help determine the

TABLE 18.3

Selecting Media by Cost per Gross Rating Point

	SAT. MORN. (30 secs.)	SAT. MORN. (15 secs.)	SUN MORN. (30 secs.)	SUN MORN. (15 secs.)
1. Frequency (Number of commercials)	2 ads	1 ad	2 ads	1 ad
2. Reach (Percent of children reached)	30%	30%	20%	20%
3. GRPs (1 × 2)	60	30	40	20
4. Total Cost	$300,000	$90,000	$180,000	$55,000
5. Cost per GRP (4 ÷ 3)	$5,000	$3,000	$4,500	$2,750

optimal combination of media based on the advertiser's objectives and cost constraints. Such programs might suggest, for example, that Subaru use radio advertising and cable TV as well as direct mail and magazines to reach upscale working women and would indicate the most effective combination of these media.

One such program, known as MEDIAC, estimates the GRPs a particular ad might produce in a given medium—for example, the estimated GRPs if Subaru were to run a commercial on a financial news channel on cable TV. It then computes the schedule that will maximize GRPs within budget constraints. These programs cannot take over as a substitute for the advertiser's judgment. In fact, they are based on the objectives and constraints dictated by the advertiser.

Another approach to media selection would be to use marginal analysis. For example, the optimal selection of the media alternatives in Table 18.3 would be at the point where gaining each additional GRP costs the same amount of money. Using marginal analysis, the media planner would shift expenditures from 30- to 15-second commercials and from Saturday to Sunday, until the added cost of achieving an additional GRP is equal across all media vehicles.

ESTABLISHING THE MEDIA SCHEDULE

Once a media mix is selected, a time schedule must be established to specify when the ads will be run. An important consideration in timing is *seasonality* in a product's sales. Many products have some seasonality based either on variations in consumption (iced tea in the summer) or on special events (watches or cameras for graduation and Christmas). Advertisers must decide whether to increase spending during these periods.

Another issue in timing is whether advertisers should use pulsing or continuity. **Pulsing** *is spending most of the advertising budget in a few large bursts at various times.* **Continuity** *is spending the advertising budget steadily over time.* Some advertisers feel that advertising has a greater effect when it is presented in concentrated bursts; others feel it is more effective to advertise consistently over time to constantly keep the brand visible. Research conducted by Anheuser Busch concluded that advertising for Budweiser could stop for at least a year without any serious effect on sales. The company could then provide a six-month burst of advertising to maintain previous growth. This finding led Anheuser to adopt a pulsing strategy.

Pulsing is most relevant for new products to provide an initial burst and establish brand awareness. It is also used for seasonal products to advertise more heavily during peak periods. It is sometimes used in conjunction with sales promotions to provide support for price or coupon incentives.

Continuity is used to sustain an ad campaign and establish awareness over time. It is particularly important to maintain a continuous level of advertising expenditures in the face of intense competition. However, if the same campaign is run for a long period of time, there is a danger of consumer wearout. **Wearout** *is a decrease in the effectiveness of advertising over time because of boredom and familiarity.* As a result, advertisers will try to vary the message when they maintain continuous advertising.

EVALUATE ADVERTISING EFFECTIVENESS

The last step in developing advertising strategies is evaluating the effectiveness of advertising. Overall, advertising has a positive effect on a firm's profits. One study examined advertising expenditures of 700 consumer-goods firms from 1970 to 1986 (see Figure 18.4). The study found that firms who advertise much more than their competitors had a significantly higher return on investment (an ROI of 32 percent). Firms that spent much less than average had an ROI of only 17 percent.

The study in Figure 18.4 shows that advertising is positively related to profits. But it does not indicate what types of advertising are most effective and for what brands. Advertisers deal with these questions by evaluating their advertising strategies in three ways. First, they evaluate the *effects of individual ads* on consumers. Does the ad create brand recognition? Does it create a positive attitude toward the brand? Is it likely to influence the consumer to buy? Second, they assess the *effectiveness of various media* in delivering the message. Third, they evaluate the *effect of the overall campaign* on sales results.

FIGURE 18.4

Advertising's Effect on Profitability

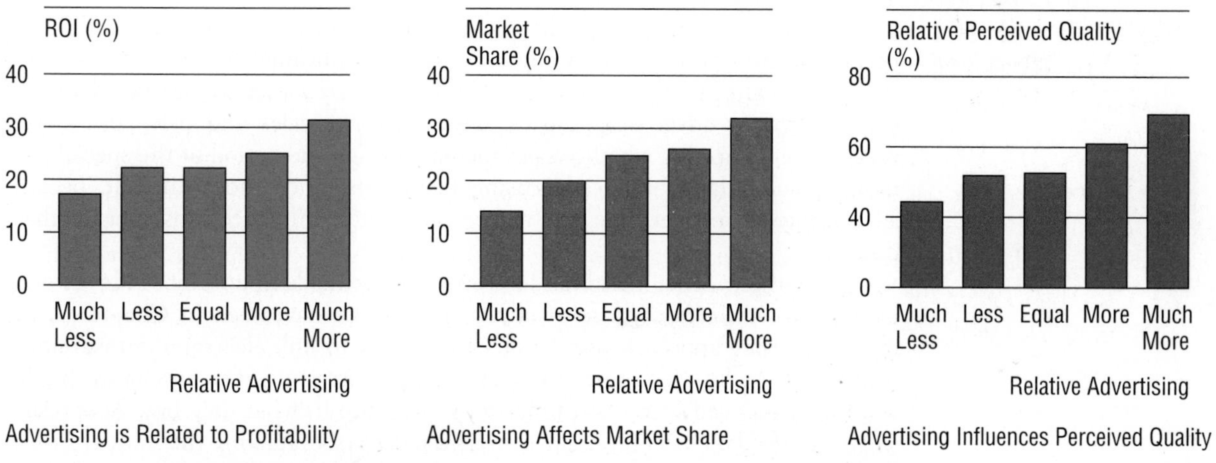

Source: *The Impact of Advertising Expenditures on Profits for Consumer Businesses* (New York: The Ogilvy Center for Research & Development, 1988), pp. 6, 15.

EVALUATING INDIVIDUAL ADS

Chapter 7 described different techniques to test print and broadcast ads. In each case, ads are tested before they are introduced (pretesting) and after (post-testing). The most common form of pretesting print ads is to give respondents a portfolio of dummy ads in a magazine format and ask them to recall copy points. Pretests of TV commercials are conducted in theaters and special trailers. In both cases, consumers are asked to record their reactions to the commercials through a hand-held electronic device or by a questionnaire. Testing the ad before it is introduced allows the advertiser to determine the effectiveness of individual ads based on criteria such as awareness of the ad, recall, and reaction to the contents.

The most common method of post-testing print ads is to ask consumers to look through an actual magazine and report which ads they remember seeing (the *in-magazine recognition test*). The most common method of post-testing TV ads is to interview consumers the day after a TV ad appears to determine what they remember about it (the *day-after recall test*).

EVALUATING MEDIA EFFECTIVENESS

Advertisers must gauge the potential effectiveness of various media in delivering their message. As we have seen, the most commonly used measure is cost per gross rating point (GRP). To compute GRP for magazines or newspapers, the advertiser must know the number of readers a publication reaches and the frequency of exposure to the ad. Some research firms specialize in running syndicated studies to measure readership, the most important being W. R. Simmons for magazines and Scarborough research for newspapers.

Cost per GRP can also be computed for TV. Chapter 7 noted that A. C. Nielsen provides a syndicated service to measure TV exposure by attaching an electronic device, known as an audimeter, to TV sets in a representative sample of U.S. households. On this basis, the percentage of households tuned in to various shows can be determined, as well as the frequency of exposure, thus providing a basis for determining GRPs.

EVALUATING ADVERTISING'S EFFECT ON SALES

The most important criterion in measuring advertising effectiveness is its effect on sales. As we have seen in Chapter 17, relating advertising to sales is difficult, because so many other factors might influence a consumer to buy.

The sales effects of certain kinds of advertising are easier to measure than others. Newspaper advertising usually describes store sales and price deals. The retailer can determine whether sales increase during the period of the special promotion, but linking brand advertising to sales is much more difficult, because advertising occurs over time, and many other factors influence consumer purchase decisions.

Despite these difficulties, brand advertisers have made important strides in evaluating the sales effectiveness of advertising. As we have seen in Chapter 7, the most promising approach uses single-source data to link electronic measurement of TV viewing to electronic scanners that measure consumer purchases. In this way, marketers can link a consumer's TV exposure to what they buy. As a result, single-source data have given advertisers a means of evaluating the sales effectiveness of their ad campaigns. These new technologies are only now beginning to be widespread.

ENSURING SOCIALLY RESPONSIBLE ADVERTISING

Most advertising is socially responsible, but, unfortunately, some advertising willfully deceives or misinforms the public. Other advertising, while not deceptive, is irresponsible. Ads that are in bad taste, promote socially unacceptable conduct, or stereotype minority groups can all be counted as irresponsible.

DECEPTIVE ADVERTISING

Deceptive advertising *is advertising that gives false information or that willfully misleads consumers about the benefits of the brand.* It is unethical and is controlled both through the self-regulation of responsible advertisers and through government action. On the national level, the Federal Trade Commission monitors advertising and takes action against ads regarded as deceptive by using a cease-and-desist order. For instance, the FTC ordered liquid-diet marketers to stop touting their products' miracle benefits when medical evidence suggested they caused significant health problems in some users.[54]

The federal Food and Drug Administration (FDA) can also flex its muscles over advertising when it believes false claims are being made on labels. When a slew of food companies advertised that fiber cereals could help reduce the risk of heart disease, the FDA ordered them to prove it or drop the campaign. Kellogg reacted by changing the name of its Heartwise cereal to Fiberwise and toning down heart-related claims. Deceptive advertising can also be attacked on the state level by elected Attorneys General. Kellogg's Heartwise decision was also influenced by a suit from the Texas Attorney General's office.[55]

Cease-and-desist orders cannot correct a false impression created by past advertising, so the FTC can use a second remedy, corrective advertising. **Corrective advertising** *requires a company to publicly correct past claims through new advertising.* Without corrective advertising, companies might benefit from false claims made in the past, even after they have stopped making them. The FTC required Warner Lambert to correct the claim that Listerine mouthwash prevents colds. It also required Hawaiian Punch to correct its claim that its drink was composed of natural fruit juices. The impact of corrective advertising was illustrated by a study that found that the proportion of consumers who believed that Hawaiian Punch had little fruit juice went from 20 percent to 70 percent when the company started correcting the claim.[56]

In the end, however, claims that a product is the highest in this or the most effective in that have dubious value. One poll showed a high degree of skepticism among consumers when it comes to such claims. Only 15 percent said they believed statements such as "nothing works better" and "better than ever." Even the claim that ranked highest in believability, "low in cholesterol," managed to convince only 47 percent of those polled.[57]

IRRESPONSIBLE ADVERTISING

An advertisement need not be deceptive to be unethical. Sometimes ad agencies take humor, comparative advertising, and emotional advertising too far, ending up with ads that are irresponsible. **Irresponsible advertising** *depicts or encourages irresponsible behavior* (for example, encouraging children to smoke) *or portrays groups in an irresponsible manner* (for example, portraying women as stupid).

Witness the case of the television ad created by the Chiat/Day/Mojo agency for Reebok sneakers in which two bungee-cord jumpers are shown diving from a

ETHICAL AND ENVIRONMENTAL ISSUES IN MARKETING

Volvo: A Case Study in Deceptive Advertising

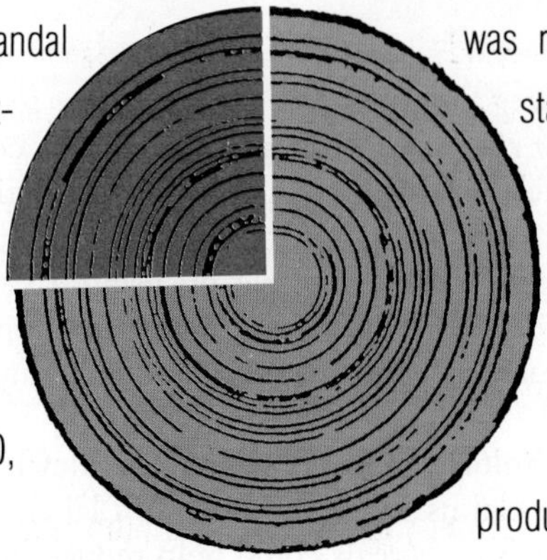

No one bats an eyelash when an ad agency airbrushes a model's features to enhance her beauty. Nor is it a scandal when a fast-food company tries dozens of different camera angles to make its hamburgers look large and juicy. But there are limits: When Volvo premiered its Monster Truck Pull advertisement in 1990, those limits were shattered.

The genesis of the ad came in early 1989, when copywriters at Volvo's ad agency, Scali, McCabe, Sloves of New York, saw a video of an exhibition in Vermont where a Volvo was the only one of a dozen cars to survive being mauled by a monster truck. Since Scali had previously trumpeted Volvo's structural soundness—notably in an ad that pictured a cargo trailer propped atop a Volvo's roof—the Vermont exhibition seemed tailor made for the campaign. Scali decided to recreate it.

Unluckily for Volvo, history did not repeat itself. The Texas Exposition and Heritage Center in Austin was rented for the re-creation, a Volvo station wagon was placed between several other cars, and a 13,000-pound truck called "Bear Foot" rolled over all of them. The Volvo was totaled as was every other car. At that point, an employee of the production company hired by Scali to film the commercial called a local welder. The welder later recalled being told to "do whatever it took to make the Volvo hold up." Not only did this mean reinforcing the Volvo's roof with steel, it meant weakening the roof supports of the other cars. So little was left to chance that when it came time for a close-up of Bear Foot rolling over the Volvo, only a single tire was used.

Extras who were hired to cheer in the background were so shocked at the rigging that they went right

bridge. The final shot shows only the Reebok jumper connected to his bungee cord; the other cord has a pair of empty Nike's attached to it. This Chiat/Day/Mojo spot was supposed to combine comparative and humorous advertising, but by giving viewers the impression that the Nike wearer plunged to his death, Chiat/Day/Mojo insulted the consumer's sense of decency. As *Adweek* magazine later editorialized, "This is the sort of thing that gives bad taste a bad name." [58]

Some of the most irresponsible types of advertising have occurred in campaigns that target children, women, and minorities.

ADVERTISING TO CHILDREN

Advertisers have a responsibility to avoid manipulating young children, who tend to be more gullible than the rest of the population. As we have seen in Chapter 8, children cannot adequately process information to evaluate advertising claims.

ETHICAL AND ENVIRONMENTAL ISSUES IN MARKETING

to Texas Attorney General Jim Maddox. After reviewing what they brought him, Maddox decided he had a major consumer fraud suit on his hands.

When raw footage was delivered to New York, Scali's copywriters came up with the tag line: "Volvo, a car you can believe in." They also depicted the Texas stunt as a real event, quoting Bear Foot's driver as saying, "I tried everything, the darn thing wouldn't give." According to the suit Maddox filed after the ad aired, the driver was really told, "Do all you can to the others but take it easy on the Volvo."

Volvo's internal investigation concluded that Scali's usually vigilant manager was not on hand for the filming, and most of the fault lay with the production company. But few consumers were listening by the time that finding was released. As part of a settlement with Attorney General Maddox, Volvo printed letters of apology in *The Wall Street Journal* and *USA Today.* Its reputation for trustworthiness was in tatters.

The ad did more than harm Volvo, however. It cast a pall over the entire industry. As *Adweek's Marketing Week* later editorialized, "The Volvo mess called into question the credibility of all ads."

Questions: Who was at fault in creating Volvo's deceptive ads—the ad agency, the production company, Volvo itself? Should Volvo have been required to do any more than stop the deceptive advertising and print letters of apology in newspapers?

Sources: "Four More Volvo Ads Scrutinized," *Advertising Age*, November 26, 1990; "Candid Camera: Volvo and the Art of Deception," *Adweek's Marketing Week*, November 12, 1990; and "A Year of Controversy And Self-Inflicted Wounds," *Adweek's Marketing Week*, December 17, 1990.

The potential for taking advantage of children led the Federal Communications Commission to limit the amount of advertising in children's shows to 10 minutes per hour on weekends and 12 minutes on weekdays. Under the rules, such popular shows as *Teenage Mutant Ninja Turtles* would be deemed commercials if replicas of the characters were advertised during its airing.[59]

Considerably more troubling than using cartoons to sell toys is the use of cartoons to sell alcohol and tobacco. Witness the introduction by R. J. Reynolds of Old Joe, a cartoon camel character. The campaign rescued the flagging Camel brand from obscurity to make it the sixth most popular in the nation (see Exhibit 18.12). While R. J. Reynolds' stated intent is to appeal to smokers over the age of 21, antismoking activists insist that the cigarette maker's real desire is to attract teens with a likeable cartoon character. There has been a 32 percent rise in Camel's market share among teens since Old Joe was introduced. Because of Joe Camel's

EXHIBIT 18.12

Cigarette Advertising that Appeals to Children

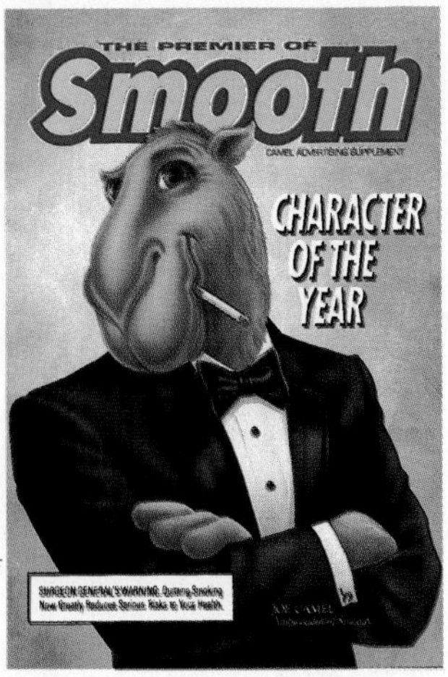

success, a coalition of major health associations, including the American Cancer Society, lobbied the Federal Trade Commission in early 1992 to ban all cartoon characters used to sell cigarettes because of their appeal to minors.[60]

PORTRAYAL OF WOMEN

Historically, the advertising profession has not been particularly sensitive in its portrayal of women. The National Advertising Review Board found that until the late 1970s, women were typically shown as "stupid—too dumb to cope with familiar everyday chores unless instructed by children or a man." [61] In the early 1980s, some advertisers went to the other extreme and portrayed "superwoman"—a working woman who could serve the family breakfast, run off to the office, glide in to make dinner looking perfectly breathtaking, and carry on a stimulating conversation with her husband while taking care of the kids.

Advertisers are now more sophisticated in dealing with the female audience and are portraying women in more-realistic roles. For example, Subaru's campaign to women, cited earlier, changed the traditional image of women as being interested only in the styling and interior of a car. Its campaign focused on specific performance characteristics to attract upscale working women.

PORTRAYAL OF AFRICAN AMERICANS

Advertising's portrayal of African Americans has also improved over time, although troubling questions still exist about how frequently African Americans appear in mainstream ads. A survey of major national magazines by the New York City Department of Consumer Affairs found that although African Americans make up 12 percent of the U.S. population and 11 percent of magazine readers, they appear in only 4.5 percent of general-circulation magazine ads.[62] Moreover, in some publications (for example, *Time, Esquire, Vogue*), the survey found the proportion of advertisements featuring African Americans had actually declined in the past 20 years.

Another reason for concern is that the survey found most African Americans were depicted as athletes, musicians, or objects of charity. While such depictions may signal an improvement over the days when African Americans were depicted as 'can't-do-anything-but-have-a-good-time' types, they still offer too narrow a view of African Americans in advertising.

SUMMARY

1. **What types of advertising do marketers use most widely?**
   The most common types of advertising are brand, product, corporate, and cooperative advertising. Brand advertising is designed to increase the market share of a brand by getting users of competitive brands to use the company's

brand. It is also designed to reinforce the decision of current users to continue to buy the brand.

Product advertising is designed to increase the demand for a product category. Corporate advertising encourages customers to buy the firm's products, tries to establish or change the image of the company, or takes a position on an issue that is important to the company. In cooperative advertising, manufacturers offer retailers an allowance to advertise in their stores at the local level. Advertising includes the manufacturer's name and provides a local presence for the manufacturer's products.

2. **How do firms develop advertising strategies?**
Advertising strategies are developed by an advertising planning process. Advertisers identify a target for their communications, define advertising objectives to influence the target to buy, and establish an advertising budget. The advertising agency is then responsible for developing an advertising strategy. Such strategies may try to maintain a brand's position over time or may be designed to change a brand's image to expand its base of users. Strategies can be based on transmitting information, developing positive brand associations through images and symbols, or some combination of both. Once strategies are established, the advertising agency selects the media with which to transmit the message to the target. The final step is to evaluate the effectiveness of advertising strategies based on how consumers interpret the message and whether they act on it.

3. **What different types of messages do advertisers develop to communicate product benefits?**
Advertisers have various alternatives in developing messages. They must decide whether the message should be based on emotional or rational appeals. The trend in recent years has been toward using more emotional appeals, because they are likely to stand out and involve the consumer in the message.

The ad may use fear appeals or humor. A fear appeal can be effective if it provides the consumer a way to remedy the problem the ad is illustrating. Humor can be effective if it creates a positive mood toward the brand and if it is linked to product benefits.

Another issue in message development is the use of spokespersons. They are effective if they are either seen as experts or are likeable and are matched to an appropriate product. Finally, advertisers must decide whether to attack competitors in their messages. Such comparative advertising is occurring more frequently, but it is risky unless the advertised brand is clearly superior to the named competitor.

4. **How do advertisers select the proper media to transmit their messages?**
Media are selected primarily based on the degree to which they reach the target group and the frequency of exposure within the group. The combination of reach and frequency is known as gross rating points (GRPs). Cost per gross rating point is the cost of achieving a given level of reach and frequency in the target group when using a particular medium. Another criterion is advertising impact, that is, the effectiveness of the ad in a particular medium based on its editorial content or the nature of its programming. The difficulty in examining the thousands of combinations of media in the process of developing a mix of vehicles has led many ad agencies to use computer programs to help in selecting an effective combination of media vehicles to reach a target group.

5. **How do marketers evaluate advertising effectiveness?**
Advertisers evaluate individual messages, the media in which they appear, and the overall campaign. Print ads are frequently evaluated by in-magazine rec-

ognition tests, whereas broadcast commercials are often evaluated based on day-after recall tests. Media are evaluated based on effectiveness in reaching the target group. Evaluating the overall campaign requires relating advertising expenditures to sales. Recently, this has been done by using single-source data, which measure ad exposure and purchases for the same household through electronic means.

6. **What is socially responsible advertising?**
Advertising is socially responsible if it is truthful and informative. Deceptive advertising willfully misinforms the public. It is combatted by self-regulation through industry standards and by government regulation through the actions of the FTC. Advertisers also have a responsibility to avoid taking advantage of children. Another area in which advertising must demonstrate social responsibility is in portraying women and minority groups realistically.

KEY TERMS

Brand advertising (p. 588)
Selective demand (p. 588)
Product advertising (p. 588)
Primary demand (p. 588)
Corporate-patronage advertising (p. 589)
Corporate-image advertising (p. 589)
Corporate-issue advertising (p. 589)
Cooperative advertising (p. 590)
Information-oriented maintenance strategy (p. 593)
Image-oriented maintenance strategy (p. 594)
Information-oriented change strategy (p. 594)
Image-oriented change strategy (p. 595)
Comparative advertising (p. 598)
Subliminal advertising (p. 599)
Advertising exposure (p. 607)
Reach (p. 607)
Frequency (p. 607)
Gross rating points (GRPs) (p. 607)
Pulsing (p. 610)
Continuity (p. 610)
Wearout (p. 611)
Deceptive advertising (p. 613)
Corrective advertising (p. 613)
Irresponsible advertising (p. 613)

QUESTIONS

1. What was the purpose of using a bunny to advertise Eveready batteries? What advertising principle might the campaign violate?
2. How do the ads in Exhibit 18.1 illustrate the four basic functions of advertising?
3. What is the distinction between brand and product advertising? What are the purposes of each? Under what circumstances would a manufacturer want to stimulate demand for a product category (such as analgesics) as well as demand for the company's brand (such as Bayer)?
4. What are the purposes of the three corporate ads shown in Exhibit 18.3?
5. When would advertisers be most likely to use an information-oriented advertising campaign? An image-oriented advertising campaign?
6. Why are advertisers using emotional themes in their messages more frequently?
7. Do you agree with the statement, "Michelin tires should not have used an emotional approach in its advertising (see Exhibit 18.6) because tires are selected based on objective criteria"? Support your opinion. Can emotional themes be effective in advertising products that are selected based primarily on objective criteria?
8. A number of years ago, the Men's and Boy's Clothing Institute tried to encourage men to be more clothes conscious by using a fear appeal. Ads showed a daughter concerned with the appearance of her father. She asks her mother, "Couldn't Daddy stay upstairs when Jim comes?" The ad concludes, "Dress Right—you can't afford not to." Based on the requirements for the effective use of fear appeals, do you think this ad was effective in promoting greater clothes consciousness? Why or why not?
9. Why was Bill Cosby a successful

spokesperson for a food product targeted primarily to families but not for a stock brokerage firm?

10. What is subliminal advertising? Why did it create such a furor when it was first used? Is subliminal advertising used today?
11. What are the advantages and potential risks of using global advertising strategies? Why are global advertising strategies becoming more feasible?
12. What are the advantages and disadvantages of using network TV as the primary vehicle in a brand's media mix? Why are fewer viewers watching network TV?
13. What might be the primary medium selected by advertisers for each of the following products? Why?
    - An industrial robot used on assembly lines
    - A new line of Kodak 35mm color film
    - A special sale of children's clothing at a local department store
    - A more comprehensive health-insurance policy for the elderly
    - A line of food products targeting Hispanic families.
14. When should advertising be scheduled based on pulsing? On continuity?
15. What criteria could an advertiser use in evaluating the social responsibility of the firm's advertising?
16. A manufacturer of toy cars and trucks advertises them on Saturday morning and uses cartoons to blend the commercial in with program content. At the end of the commercial, a voiceover says "Make sure to ask your mom to buy you a [brand name] so you won't be the only kid without one." Is this advertising unethical? Why or why not? Would you regard the ad as deceptive? As irresponsible? In what ways?

QUESTIONS: YOU ARE THE DECISION MAKER

1. One manufacturing executive who considered offering retailers advertising allowances stated why he chose not to do so:

   Why should I offer retailers advertising allowances? When I do, half of them don't use it, and the other half use it in the wrong way. We spend millions of dollars trying to establish a national message. I want to control my advertising to maintain this image. Retailer cooperative advertising does not permit me that control.

   What are the risks of not having a cooperative advertising program?
2. One advertiser, commenting on the distinction between information- and image-oriented advertising, said:

   That distinction is overdrawn. Sure, there are ads that are primarily informational, and there are ads that are primarily image-oriented. But all advertising really represents a mix between information and image.

   Do you agree? Do the ads in Exhibit 18.4 represent a mix between information and image? In what way?
3. One advertising executive, commenting on the issue of global versus local advertising, says flatly:

   I just don't believe in a global advertising strategy. If you standardize your theme worldwide, you'd be shooting yourself in the foot. A consumer orientation requires adjusting advertising strategies to the particular needs and customs of each country. Standardizing an ad theme is like Henry Ford saying "You can have any color Model T as long as it's black."

   What did the ad executive mean by quoting Henry Ford? Do you agree with the statement? Why or why not?

CHAPTER 19

Personal Selling and Sales Management

YOUR FOCUS IN CHAPTER 19

To learn:

- *How consultative-selling, order-getting, and order-taking approaches to personal selling differ.*
- *Important trends in personal selling that are taking place in the 1990s.*
- *The nature of the selling process.*
- *The key steps in managing the sales effort.*
- *How the sales effort is implemented and evaluated.*

For Xerox, Being Customer Oriented Meant Upgrading Its Sales Force

When Xerox customers call Chuck Horton, they sometimes hear a recorded message on his answering machine that says, "Hello caller. Right now I'm probably out trying to understand my customer's needs."[1] The message is an ironic reminder that not long ago, Horton's colleagues in the sales department might well have said, "I'm not here, and that's your tough luck." Xerox, the wonder company of the 1960s, had grown so top heavy and arrogant that it lost sight of its customers' needs, leading to steadily worsening sales and a crisis in confidence. How did Xerox claw its way back? By reinvesting in what made it succeed to begin with: its sales force.

The story begins in 1982, when David T. Kearns became CEO of Xerox. After joining the company from IBM ten years earlier, the ex-navy sailor was aware that companies that once only bought copiers were beginning to invest in integrated office systems. As a result, they wanted to hear from salespeople who could offer everything in one package—copiers, electronic typewriters, personal computers, and printers. Xerox could not compete in this fast-changing market, because its copying and information-systems divisions were warring fiefdoms that operated independently of each other.[2]

The sales structure in each division seemed logical enough. At the top, 300 sales representatives known as national accounts managers worked on the largest national accounts. Next came 1,000 major account managers, operating out of Xerox's 80 sales districts, who dealt with clients that represented at least $10,000 in sales. Customers good for sales of $5,000 to $10,000 were taken care of by account representatives, with the smallest accounts being serviced by marketing representatives. While the system looked good on paper, the reality was that sales representatives in the copying and information-services divisions were poaching on each other's clients. To an outsider seeking a cohesive sales pitch, Xerox looked like a company in disarray. Xerox had the capability to sell individual product lines, but not integrated office systems.

To develop the capability to sell systems, Kearns realized he would have to create a single force responsible for selling all of Xerox's copying, electronic publishing, printing, and computing systems. Sales teams, composed of representatives of every Xerox division, were formed to sell systems solutions to larger accounts.[3] Gone were the days where a copier salesperson could not talk computers and a computer salesperson could not talk copiers. In was the new umbrella mantra of "systems selling."[4]

Of course, all these salespeople could not absorb all there was to know about every Xerox product overnight. A $20-million-a-year, three-tier training program had to be installed to bring them up to speed. The first stage involved classroom seminars; the next stage offered videos to be studied in local offices; and in the third stage, Xerox computers were given to salespeople to learn in their homes, and workstations were installed to be learned in their offices.[5]

With this internal work done, Kearns could begin erasing Xerox's outward image as an arrogant company that didn't give a hoot about its clients. What better way, he reasoned, than to tie its sales representatives' salaries to customer satisfaction. Using Xerox's Customer Satisfaction Measurement System (CSMS)—a questionnaire that regularly asked 40,000 customers worldwide how the company was doing—Kearns created an incentive program whereby salespeople could increase their salaries by 20 percent if they met customer satisfaction goals that were measured by CSMS scores.[6] By 1990, old-line sales representatives raised in the "you'll have to buy what I'm selling" school had been replaced by a new generation of representatives who were being evaluated by the satisfaction they generated among their customers.

Kearns might have been aiming at the larger customers with his systems-oriented sales force, but he was not ignoring smaller customers that might want an individual product. To sell these customers, Kearns turned to one of the fastest growing trends in personal selling—*telemarketing*. Telemarketing provides customers with a toll-free number staffed by sales reps that can process orders, take requests for service, and handle complaints. The company initiated this facility through an ad campaign for copiers featuring a three-year full-replacement guarantee policy and the tag line, "Small businesses run risks. A copier shouldn't be one of them." Each ad contained a toll-free number. Within seven months, customer-initiated leads rose a whopping 41 percent.[7]

Xerox still isn't totally out of the woods. It's glitzy $150,000 image processing machines—which combine the functions of image scanners, laser printers, copiers, and fax machines—have gotten off to a slow start, and the company as a whole has not posted two years of steady growth since the 1970s. Still, the ability of Xerox's sales force to focus on office systems rather than individual products helped the company post a 20 percent revenue increase in its office systems business in 1990 and may yet put the $18 billion company back on track.[8]

THE IMPORTANCE OF PERSONAL SELLING

Many marketers would cite personal selling as the most important component of the promotional mix. Certainly it is the most important component in business-to-business marketing, where face-to-face interaction between buyer and seller is essential, because marketers often develop goods to the specification of the buyer. This is true of Xerox because it develops systems solutions to meet customer needs. Even when industrial products are not customized, though, many are complex enough to require personal interaction to explain product features and performance.

By the early 1990s, companies were spending more than $200 billion annually on personal selling (more than twice as much as on advertising). Most of this spending occurred in the industrial sector, where the average cost of a sales call was $240.[9] More specifically, selling expenses averaged 12 percent of total revenues for office supplies companies, 7 percent for computer companies, and 4 percent for producers of light machinery. In contrast, selling expenses averaged less than 2 percent of revenues for consumer packaged foods and household items.

The importance of personal selling is increasing in the 1990s as industrial America is becoming more systems and productivity oriented. Companies which once dealt with their problems in piecemeal fashion are now looking for far-ranging solutions to take them through this decade and beyond. Marketers such as Xerox have responded by developing selling teams to offer a range of integrated products. These salespeople often need an engineering or design background and frequently act more as consultants than as traditional salespeople. The character of Willy Loman, the tragic fast-buck salesman in Arthur Miller's play *Death of a Salesman*, is out of touch with the professionalism that characterizes the new breed of salesperson. Paying for today's breed, however, is also more expensive than ever. The cost of a business-to-business sales call has been rising at an annual rate of 11 percent, while most companies have not been able to raise prices more than five percent.[10]

Although personal selling dominates the promotional mix for industrial products, it is also important in marketing services. Stockbrokers, real-estate agents, and travel agents, for example, sell their services at the same time that they perform them, so personal selling becomes their prime means of satisfying customers. Personal selling can also be the primary means of communication and customer satisfaction for some consumer goods, as in Avon's reliance on door-to-door selling and General Motors' reliance on its dealer network to sell cars.

Personal selling is also important as one of the most common entry positions for those going into marketing. Sales has been both a stepping stone to a higher management position and a career path in its own right. Individuals choosing a sales career do so because they like the personal interaction with buyers, they enjoy solving buyers' problems, and they like the freedom afforded by a sales position. Salespeople also like the link between effort and reward, since sales results are usually linked to commissions.

THE NATURE OF PERSONAL SELLING

The role of the salesperson varies greatly depending on the selling situation. At one end of the spectrum are the sophisticated sales teams developed by companies such as Xerox, IBM, and Hewlett-Packard. At the other end are simple order takers.

TYPES OF SALESPEOPLE

Table 19.1 classifies salespeople on a continuum from consultants to simple order-takers. In between is a category of salespeople we will refer to as order-getters.

CONSULTATIVE SALESPEOPLE

Consultative salespeople *are those who take the initiative in defining customer needs and recommending a set of solutions to meet these needs.* They do the most creative selling. A consultative salesperson might be an engineer who develops a set of specifications for a custom-designed computer network or air pollution–control system, or a travel agent who develops a vacation package to meet a family's needs.

A consultative salesperson must develop an intimate knowledge of the customer and the factors underlying customer needs, and must initiate a series of meetings that involve a two-way dialogue to define these needs. For instance, when the West Company—the world's biggest marketer of specialized packing materials—decided to become more market driven, it retrained its salespeople to become "packaging consultants" instead of just product pitchmen.[11]

Consultative salespeople require in-depth technical knowledge and often have an engineering or programming background. Such training is extensive and expensive, but since it costs five times more for a company to attract a new client than

TABLE 19.1

Types of Salespeople

	CONSULTATIVE SALESPEOPLE	ORDER GETTERS	ORDER TAKERS
TYPICAL EXAMPLES	Computer systems salesperson Pollution control systems salesperson Industrial generator salesperson Architect (sells home design) Travel agent (sells vacation package)	Door-to-door salesperson Clothing store salesperson Petrochemicals salesperson Steel plate salesperson Office supplies salesperson (offers new line of products)	Food product salesperson (stocks supermarket shelves) Pharmaceutical salesperson (stocks drugstore shelves) Department store salesperson Office supplies salesperson (takes orders based on inventory levels)
SALES APPROACH	Unstructured, interactive	Structured, one-way	Simple inquiry
SALES PRESENTATION	Need satisfaction	Standardized	Stimulus–response
COMPLEX PRODUCT	Usually	Sometimes	No
LEVEL OF TECHNICAL EXPERTISE	High	Low to medium	Low
TRAINING	Extensive	Moderate	Moderate
PROSPECTING	Usually	Usually	No
TEAM SELLING	Usually	Rarely	No

keep an old one, many CEOs find that costly up-front investments in consultative selling help the bottom line over the long haul.[12] Because of their training, these salespeople—sometimes called "knowledge workers"—usually have the authority to specify prices, define product specifications, and set delivery dates in negotiations with the buyer.

All this does not mean they work alone, since defining customer needs and developing solutions usually requires a combination of expertise that a single salesperson rarely has. As a result, team selling is the norm. Xerox's strategy to stay competitive was to switch from an order-getting approach to a consultative-selling approach. As we have seen, this required selling systems solutions rather than individual products. To sell systems solutions, Xerox established National Accounts teams to work only with the company's biggest clients (for example, the federal government or multinational corporations) to ensure that their interrelated computer systems run without any hitches. The teams are staffed by the most experienced salespeople in Xerox's worldwide R&D, marketing, and sales departments.[13]

ORDER GETTERS

Both order getters and consultative salespeople must focus on customer needs. But an **order getter** *is more product oriented in trying to steer the customer to the company's products and demonstrate product benefits.* The consultative salesperson is more interested in developing a custom-made solution to the customer's problems. Salespeople in clothing stores, door-to-door salespeople, and sellers of standardized industrial products such as petrochemicals or steel plate are examples of order getters.

The job of the order getter is to sell a line of standardized products, whereas the consultative salesperson sells custom-made products. The order getter is more likely to initiate a one-way transmittal of information from seller to buyer, whereas the consultative salesperson must initiate a two-way flow of information. The types of products sold by order getters are of low to moderate complexity since they are part of a standard line. As a result, the salesperson does not require a high level of technical expertise. Training is required, however, to inform the salesperson of the company's product line and to teach an effective sales approach. Order getters are also expected to prospect for new accounts.

Order getters also differ from order takers. The ad for Willamette Industries in Exhibit 19.1 makes this distinction. The ad says that Willamette's salespeople don't just take orders for the company's line of products, they *fill* them by making sure buyers get exactly what they want.

A good example of effective order getting is the sales approach used by Ball Corporation's commercial glass division, which sells a standardized line of glass containers to food packers.[14] Salespeople first inform prospective buyers of Ball's capabilities, including capabilities in its high-tech divisions, such as building guidance systems for space vehicles and launching solar observatories. The salesperson then elicits a reaction to better identify customer needs. Prospects are invited to visit the company's plant and R&D labs.[15] The primary focus of the sales approach is to inform the customer of company capabilities. The sales approach is fairly standardized compared to a consultative-selling approach.

ORDER TAKERS

Table 19.1 shows that *an* **order taker's** *sales approach is a simple inquiry as to customer needs* which are then met by taking an order. This approach is characterized as

EXHIBIT 19.1

Making the Distinction between Order Taking and Order Getting

Anyone can take orders over the phone.
But when it comes to *filling* orders for wood products, that's where Willamette breaks rank.
Our salespeople know their way around the mill because they go there often. They check the quality of the
Mike Huycke, Western Lumber Sales
lumber and plywood first-hand, to make sure you're getting exactly what you've ordered.
Besides knowing their products, they also know your market. And when it's time to fill orders for your customers, the products you need are at your command.
So if you're looking for a few good men and women to do business with, call Willamette.
After all, if we only took orders, we might as well sell fast food.
Instead of wood.
Willamette Industries, Inc.
Lumber & Plywood Divisions
Western Lumber and Plywood
Albany, OR (503) 926-7771
Southern Lumber and Plywood
Ruston, LA (318) 255-6258
Atlantic Plywood
Rock Hill, SC (803) 328-3844
We don't just take orders.

stimulus-response. For example, a stimulus such as running low on steel plate in the production line elicits an order to restock the item. The salesperson merely fills the order. Little technical expertise is required to sell such products.

Most food and drug companies have what is known as a *route sales force* composed of order takers responsible for contacting store managers and stocking food and drugstore shelves with the company's products. Stocking shelves does not involve selling in the traditional sense. Route salespeople simply enter a store, inspect the shelves, and restock them with the company's product when required. Periodically, they will contact store managers to determine required changes in inventory levels, requests for new products, or requirements for in-store displays. In so doing, the effective route salesperson is meeting the needs of the store manager.

Frito-Lay uses a 10,000-plus route sales force to service 325,000 food stores. The company spent $45 million to equip these salespeople with hand-held computers to track movement of product off the shelf and thus justify a request for more shelf space for its products. The hand-held computers are also used to automate orders and help speed deliveries.[16]

Many people regard order takers as low-status positions. But a position as a route salesperson is often an entry-level pathway to a higher-paying managerial job. At Frito-Lay, a route sales position is considered one of the most important tasks in the company and is a necessary stepping-stone to a sales management position.

TRENDS IN PERSONAL SELLING

The development of national account marketing teams, the increase in information accessible to salespeople, and the greater use of telemarketing to avoid the higher costs of personal selling are the most important selling trends of the 1990s.

NATIONAL ACCOUNT MARKETING

National account marketing (NAM) teams *are groups composed of salespeople and other managers who are required to define the needs of their larger customers and develop solutions to meet these needs.* These teams specialize in certain industries and develop an intimate knowledge of their customers' businesses. NAM teams were developed in response to the needs of larger customers to buy complex systems such as those involving computers, factory automation, or medical diagnostics, rather than individual components and equipment. Selling these systems required developing new levels of expertise that went beyond the capabilities of a single salesperson. As such, NAM teams engage in consultative selling rather than order getting or order taking.

Since NAM teams sell to larger customers, they usually represent well over 50 percent of a company's sales. Such teams are effective. One study found that sales increased in over 90 percent of companies once they established NAM teams.[17] The concept certainly worked for Reynolds Metals. When Reynolds' president decided he wanted to win Campbell's Soup as a customer, he rolled up his sleeves and put a NAM team made up of sales, marketing, graphic design, and engineering employees on the assignment. It took them five years, but the team finally persuaded their counterparts at Campbell that Reynolds' aluminum packaging was more cost effective and a public relations plus since it is recyclable. The deal helped Reynolds sales soar past $6 billion in 1989, even as the price of aluminum was dropping.[18]

A NAM team is headed by a *national account manager*, a sort of "super-salesperson" responsible for creating a close working relationship with the customer, coordinating the activities of other members of the NAM team to meet customer needs, providing follow-up service, and maintaining relationships for future sales. To facilitate an open dialogue, NAM teams usually deal with buying centers (see Chapter 9) in the customer's organization. As a result, an engineer on the NAM team can deal with an engineer in the buying group, an information specialist in the NAM team can deal with the information specialist in the buying group, and so forth.

INFORMATION ACCESSIBILITY

One of the important developments of the 1980s which is continuing explosive growth in the 1990s is technology that gives salespeople greater access to information while they are on the road. Personal computers, portable fax machines, photocopiers, cellular phones, electronic diaries, and the like are turning salespeople's cars into movable headquarters, freeing the salesperson to resolve customer problems without being anchored to desks. Many salespeople now obtain inventory and product information by personal computers through interactive hookups with the home office, and send in sales information to headquarters at the end of the day. The ad from GRiD Systems for the GRiDPAD in Exhibit 19.2 illustrates this technology. The importance of such information accessibility was reflected in a recent *Sales & Marketing Management* survey which found that two-thirds of the country's top sales managers felt such new technologies would be a critically important productivity lever in the 1990s.[19]

Ryder, for example, has supplied its salespeople with computers to enable them to instantly analyze a customer's transportation needs through a program known as Rydernomics. The program includes a computer model that the salesperson uses to help a customer consider the projected costs of owning versus leasing a fleet of trucks over several years. If leasing is determined to be the most economical solution, another model compares the cost of leasing Ryder trucks to that of competitors' trucks. The cards are not always stacked in Ryder's favor, since the model sometimes shows that going with the competitor will be cheaper.[20]

TELEMARKETING

The escalating cost of personal selling in the value-conscious 1990s is spawning another trend—the increasing use of telemarketing. It costs less than one-sixth as much to sell by phone compared to a personal contact.[21] Many industrial firms use telemarketing to sell to smaller accounts, freeing the sales force to concentrate on more-profitable accounts. Dow Chemical, for example, determined that it would be uneconomical for its sales force to visit accounts representing less than $50,000 in revenue. These accounts are sold by phone.[22]

EXHIBIT 19.2

Making Information Accessible

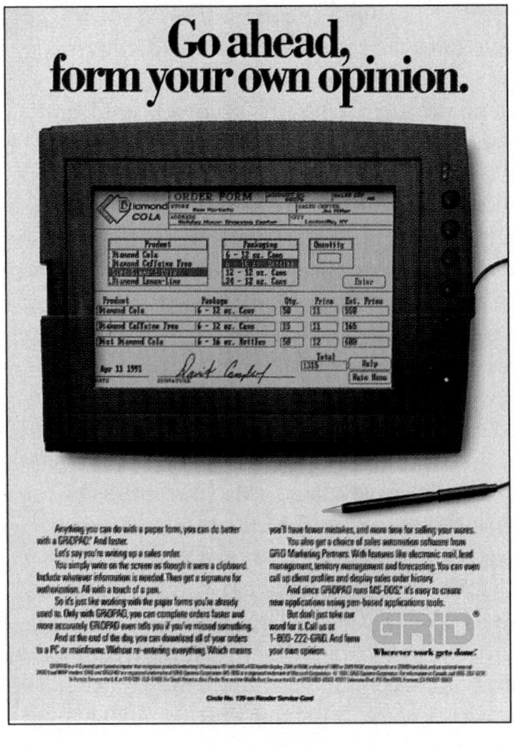

Products like the GRIDPAD® computer help sales representatives improve productivity. Sales people fill in order forms on screen with a pen and download information into a personal or mainframe computer at the end of a day. Reps can also store and access customer profiles, display sales order histories, and other sales and marketing information.

EXHIBIT 19.3

Data General Uses Inbound Telemarketing to Sell Its Services

Smaller firms also use telemarketing because they may not be able to afford the costs of personal selling. The Codex Corporation, a small computer manufacturer, tries to finalize all its sales calls over the phone because it wants to avoid the estimated $400 cost of an in-person sales visit.[23]

Firms using telemarketing generally have inbound and outbound facilities. **Inbound telemarketing** *involves taking calls from customers.* The ad touting Data General's AViiON System in Exhibit 19.3 is an example. Callers are likely to be screened to determine whether they are prospects. Requests for service from small businesses are taken by phone. If the customer is large enough, information on the inquiry will be given to a sales representative for a possible personal sales call. Hewlett-Packard has established a telemarketing center to identify prospective purchasers and supply its sales force with this information. Operators at the center handle customer phone inquiries on 800 numbers and determine which customers might be good prospects for a follow-up by the appropriate salesperson.[24] The company has found that when salespeople work in tandem with its telemarketers in this way, they reduce the costs of making a sale by 12 percent.[25]

If the prospect is a smaller company, it may not be economical for a salesperson to make a call. As a result, an **outbound telemarketing** facility *is used, which involves a trained salesperson contacting a prospect to try to make the sale by phone.*

Companies will usually integrate either inbound or outbound telemarketing into advertising campaigns. For instance, when AT&T's New Jersey General Business Systems subsidiary wanted to telemarket its Merlin cordless phone to small business owners, it timed its outbound calls to arrive just after the prospect received a piece of AT&T direct mail. The one–two punch helped AT&T double its response rate for the mailer.[26]

THE PERSONAL-SELLING PROCESS

A model of the personal-selling process is shown in Figure 19.1. It reflects a problem-solving approach most likely to be used in consultative selling. The steps in Figure 19.1 can also apply to order getters and order takers, as when an order taker interacts with a store manager to determine the manager's needs regarding product inventory, displays, and in-store promotions.

A salesperson first identifies prospects and determines which ones to visit. In making a sales call, the salesperson's first priority is to determine customer needs. He or she then formulates a sales approach and communicates information to help meet the buyer's needs. In the process of communicating, the salesperson may alter the approach in response to buyer comments. There should be a two-way flow of communication between seller and buyer. In the final step, the salesperson evaluates the effectiveness of the sales approach and modifies it accordingly.

IDENTIFY AND QUALIFY PROSPECTS

One of the most important roles of a salesperson is **prospecting**, *that is, identifying and qualifying potential customers. Salespeople* **qualify** *potential customers by identifying the best prospects and screening out poor ones.* Prospects can be qualified by determining their need for a product, financial resources, net assets, and potential for

FIGURE 19.1

A Model of the Personal Selling Process

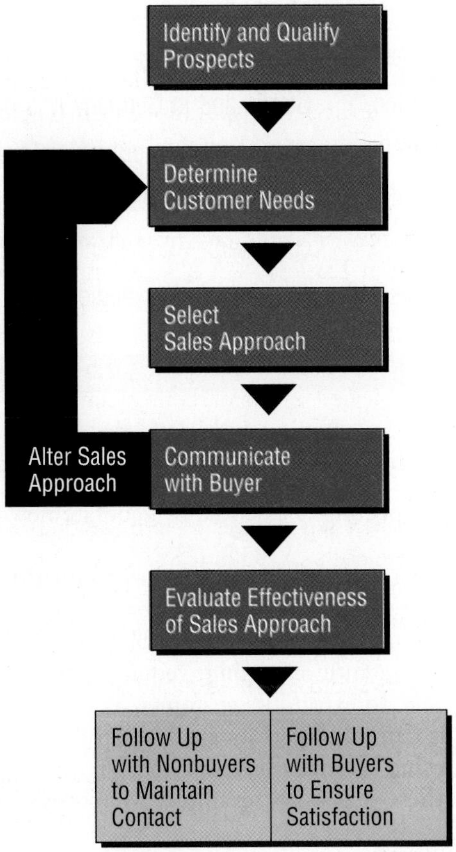

GLOBAL MARKETING STRATEGIES

Telemarketing Booms in Europe But Challenges Americans

Jim Mishek knew his Wilson Tools produced sheet-metal fabrication products that were twice as good as anything produced in Europe. The problem was, his prospective clients in Europe didn't. How, Mishek wondered, could he change that from behind his desk in Minnesota?

The answer lay in telemarketing and a campaign that would increase his European sales by ten percent in six months. Mishek began by sending prospective clients a glossy brochure that described his offerings in detail. If the client was interested, he was instructed to call a toll-free number that reached Wilson's headquarters. When Mishek found that many Europeans were afraid to make the first call for fear of appearing too pushy, he began having his salespeople call them to build relationships. Before long, his phones were ringing off the hook.

What Mishek tapped into was one of the fastest-growing selling methods in Europe. In 1990, U.K. telemarketing sales jumped six percent, Germany's sales rose 10 percent and France's total was up by 16 percent. These figures are expected to grow even more when Europe's trade barriers come down in 1992, and marketers who have been stymied from expanding suddenly find all of Europe a giant market waiting to be tapped.

Even so, there are still unique challenges facing American manufacturers who try to telemarket in Europe. Consider marketers of consumer goods using telemarketing to encourage phone orders. The level of phone ownership in the United Kingdom and France is one-third less than that in the United States, and in Germany it is one-half less. Although this was not a problem for Mishek—his goods were so specialized he could easily identify prospective customers—it challenges marketers who depend on reaching a wider audience.

future growth. Such prospecting is essential to generate new business and ensure continued profitability.

The importance of prospecting has increased as competition, particularly from foreign producers, has intensified. Sellers must generate new accounts to maintain their market share. The rapid rate of technological change means that a company's customer base is also constantly changing, requiring prospecting in new areas. Hewlett-Packard was able to expand its customer base by prospecting small businesses that it viewed as natural targets for its desktop laser printers. Furthermore, many companies are going into new business areas, requiring their salespeople to identify prospects in these areas. For example, Memorex's expansion into audio

GLOBAL MARKETING STRATEGIES

Marketers must also take into account the different cultural attributes of European phone shoppers, notably the fact that they do not use credit cards the way their American counterparts do. (When the equivalent of the Home Shopping Network opened up in France, only 20 percent of its callers charged their purchases!) The effect is that phone sellers must wait for cash to arrive before they can ship their products, increasing inventory and storage costs.

Because Europe does not have the toll-free services that are available in the United States, another practical consideration must be where to base the telemarketing facility. The U.K. has 17 cities with populations in excess of 500,000 people, while Germany has 12, and France has six. Since most calls will be placed to these urban areas, it would hardly be practical to have the phone center placed in a faraway town. The most effective European telemarketers therefore create calling centers in each of the largest areas they wish to target.

Finally, regulations that vary from country to country have given international telemarketers numerous headaches. In Germany, for instance, it is against the law to make outgoing prospecting calls, while in France it is illegal for one company to sell potential customer lists to another.

Despite these pitfalls, telemarketing has flourished in Europe. After the 1992 unification, it is a good bet that the industry will grow by even greater leaps and bounds.

Questions: What problems do marketers face in using telemarketing facilities in Europe? Did Jim Mishek of Wilson Tools face these problems?

Sources: "International Telemarketing," *Direct Marketing*, April 1990; and "Internationally Speaking," *Direct Marketing*, December 1988.

components and AT&T's move into the credit-card market have required identifying new business prospects.

The most frequently used sources for prospecting are leads from other salespeople in the firm and referrals from satisfied customers.[27] However, most sales managers agree that their sales force does not spend enough time on prospecting, usually because its members prefer to visit existing customers rather than chance wasting time on new prospects. As a result, companies try to identify potential targets for its salespeople.

Most companies use two approaches to generate sales leads. One is to identify prospects based on inquiries from 800 numbers. Honeywell generates more than

50,000 sales leads a year from customer inquiries through its inbound telemarketing facility. The company sends these leads to its sales force by computer within 12 hours of receiving an inquiry.[28]

The second method of prospecting is for a company to generate a database of potential customers and call them directly. Xerox uses the 40,000 quality management questionnaires it sends out to clients to create an internal database that it sorts according to the client's business and needs. The database has been invaluable in helping Xerox prospect current clients when it introduces a new line.

Another good source for prospects is at trade shows. Salespeople often identify prospects at such shows for follow-up sales calls. One firm, Giltspur, specializes in training salespeople to meet and qualify prospects at these shows (see Exhibit 19.4).

DETERMINE CUSTOMER NEEDS

Whether the customer is a prospect or an existing account, the key step in the selling process is to identify needs. This step, often referred to as the *preapproach* phase, requires that the salesperson learn as much as possible about the customer so that he or she can better identify customer needs and solve customer problems.

Customer need identification has become much more important in the selling environment of the 1990s, because increased competition in many industries requires salespeople to be more attuned to customers. As we have seen in Chapter 5, foreign competition has made substantial inroads into many industries in the United States, particularly autos, electronics, and computers. As a result, domestic companies have had to sharpen their marketing skills to remain competitive. A

EXHIBIT 19.4

Advertising the Importance of Prospecting

sales force attuned to customer needs is essential in such a competitive environment. Another factor creating competitive intensity is the greater maturity and standardization of products in many industries. As products move along the life cycle and become more standardized, a greater burden falls on the sales force to determine how company offerings can better meet customer needs.

There is no easy formula for identifying customer needs. However, to be prepared to ask the right questions, the salesperson must have information on the customer before the sales call. During the sales call, he or she should encourage two-way communication. The most-effective salespeople are problem solvers who consistently probe to determine customer needs, devoting the greater percentage of the sales call to discussing these needs.

Salespeople for Gould Computer, a division of NEC, allow customers to identify their own circuit designs by a computer-aided library of design alternatives. Customers know best what they want in a circuit design, so permitting them to develop their own design allows Gould to meet customer needs effectively while controlling costs.[29]

In the service sector, where consumers do not have something tangible to hold onto, defining needs is even more important. GTE runs a yearly opinion survey of 20,000 business customers to determine their view of GTE quality and capabilities in key areas that drive customer satisfaction, such as reliability, quality of voice transmission, and repair responsiveness. GTE advertises its reliance on these surveys as an example of its ability to better meet customer needs.[30]

SELECT A SALES APPROACH

Once the salesperson has defined customer needs, he or she must select an approach to inform and influence the customer that the company's offerings can meet these needs. Two general strategies are used. The salesperson can emphasize his or her expertise, which requires a demonstration of specialized knowledge, or he or she can emphasize similarity to the customer, which requires building up rapport and showing the customer that the salesperson has had to make similar decisions.

Salespeople often use a combination of both expertise and similarity, but expertise is likely to be more dominant for complex products—particularly in the industrial sector—whereas similarity is more important for consumer services such as life insurance or travel, where personal rapport might be essential.

The sales approach will also vary depending on whether the salesperson is trying to reinforce the customer's preferences or change them. The first task is obviously easier. Inducing the customer to switch to the company's products means that the salesperson must change the customer's beliefs about the relative merits of the company's offerings and requires the presentation of new information on product capabilities, price, delivery, or services.

For example, assume that a salesperson for a manufacturer of exercise machines learns that a chain of neighborhood health spas is expanding to ten new locations and needs to fill them all with the latest in weight and aerobic machines. The spa's owner has had past dealings with the salesman's company and has lingering reservations about its selection and ability to deliver on time. The salesperson will try to convince the spa owner that the company has revamped its lines since their last dealing and has instituted a just-in-time delivery system. The strategy is to subtly change the buyer's beliefs about the company and its offerings. If the salesperson does not win the buyer over on this sales call, at least a basis has been established for possibly making a sale in future calls.

COMMUNICATE WITH THE BUYER

Having formulated a sales approach, the salesperson must communicate it during a sales presentation. Companies have used three approaches in the sales presentation, a canned, a formula, and a problem-solving approach. In a **canned approach,** *the salesperson follows a predefined script without regard to the customer's response.* As a result, every customer is treated the same, regardless of need. A canned approach is useful in telephone selling when time is short and the message must be conveyed quickly. It is also useful in door-to-door sales when little is known about customer needs. But when a customer's needs must be defined, a canned approach is ineffective because it does not encourage two-way communication.

A second approach, **formula selling,** *provides information to customers in a step-by-step manner to persuade the customer to buy.* It differs from a canned approach in requiring the salesperson to first identify customer needs, and then to develop a step-by-step sales presentation to meet these needs. As a result, most salespeople have a number of formulas depending on customer needs. An interesting variant of the formula approach used in telephone sales is *electronic scripting* in which the computer leads the salesperson through a series of sales messages depending on the customer's response.

The third approach, **problem solving,** *requires the salesperson to spend time obtaining an in-depth understanding of the customer and formulating a sales approach accordingly.* Whereas in a canned and formula approach, the salesperson does most of the talking, in a problem-solving approach the salesperson is a listener and continually probes the customer to gain a better understanding of his or her needs. Therefore, ongoing two-way communication is essential. A problem-solving approach is required in consultative selling since products and services are usually custom-made to meet customer needs. To a lesser extent, problem solving is also required in order getting and order taking. For example, two-way communication is often needed by a route salesperson to gain an understanding of the store manager's needs and to solve the store manager's problems.

Both formula selling and problem solving allow for an alteration in the sales approach based on communication with the buyer. Figure 19.1 shows that such an alteration is based on redefining customer needs to gain a better understanding of how to meet them.

Our spa example illustrates a problem-solving approach. The salesperson listened to the owner explain his needs and concerns, then described the changes that occurred in the company's offerings. Assume that the spa owner now expresses interest in a number of the latest high-tech cardiovascular exercise machines which no other health club in the area offers. He asks specifics on potential delivery dates and price for several dozen units but expresses concern about one thing—the machines are so big, they take up more room than he may be able to devote. The salesperson tells the owner that he may be able to get the manufacturer to alter the design. Moreover, he invites the buyer to try out two models for a week to see for himself whether they are proven customer pleasers. The buyer agrees. The problem-solving sales approach with two-way communication has paid off.

EVALUATE THE EFFECTIVENESS OF THE SALES APPROACH

After completing the sales call, the salesperson will evaluate the effectiveness of the sales approach to determine what action to take in the future—writing the company off as a prospect, waiting for a while before making the next contact, following up immediately, or possibly even following up with a sales team to provide technical information beyond the salesperson's expertise. The salesperson also evaluates the sales approach to improve his or her effectiveness in future sales contacts.

Evaluating the sales approach provides the information necessary for appropriate follow-up after the sales call. Figure 19.1 shows two types of follow-up. In the absence of a sale, a follow-up maintains contact and builds on the relationship that has been established. If a sale has been made, follow-up is necessary to ensure the customer is satisfied with delivery, service, and product performance.

In our spa example, the salesperson is satisfied that there is an excellent chance the prospect might buy three dozen of the cardiovascular exercise machines from his company. Thus the selling approach is judged to have been appropriate, and follow-up will be made after the buyer has tested the products.

FIGURE 19.2

The Sales Management Process

MANAGING THE SALES EFFORT

Besides the salesperson, key players in a firm's selling process include divisional sales managers and district sales managers. Both are involved in managing the sales effort. The *divisional sales manager* is responsible for sales of a total division and is often given the title of vice-president of sales. A *district sales manager* usually has responsibility for a particular geographic territory and reports to the divisional sales manager. Procter & Gamble recently appointed 22 divisional managers to coordinate the company-wide work of scores of district managers and thousands of salespeople. Previously, each division of P&G (for example, food and beverage, packaged soap) had their own sales force.[31]

A number of steps are involved in managing the sales effort, as shown in Figure 19.2. The divisional sales manager is responsible for planning the sales effort, the district sales manager for implementing it. In planning the sales effort, the divisional manager first establishes sales objectives for the division and for individual sales territories. The divisional manager then determines the sales budget and organizes the sales effort.

The district sales manager is responsible for managing the sales force in his or her territory and implementing the plans laid out by the divisional manager. Implementation requires recruiting salespeople, training them, and motivating them.

The final step in the sales-management process is evaluation. The divisional manager evaluates the overall sales performance of the division and the performance of each district sales manager. District managers evaluate the performance of individual salespeople.

ESTABLISH SALES OBJECTIVES

Companies establish sales objectives for a total division (such as the personal computer division of a company like Hewlett-Packard), for sales territories within the division, and for individual salespeople within each territory.

DIVISIONAL SALES GOALS

At most companies, the overall sales goal for a division is based on a *volume target* stated in dollars or units, usually based on a sales forecast for the coming year. Although volume targets are the most common sales objectives, they are not always the most relevant, because a sales manager could achieve volume goals at the expense of profits. Firms are therefore turning more to *profitability objectives,* which consider the expected contribution to profits of a particular product line or sales territory. Profitability objectives have the advantage of accounting for both volume and costs in establishing performance expectations.

The difference between the two measures is best illustrated by the case of a computer manufacturer that was one of the volume leaders in its market with $200 million in annual sales but was posting virtually no profit. It turned out that although its 100-person sales force had one of the leading products to sell, it consistently gave retailers deep discounts of 25 percent or more. Why? Because their quotas were based on volume, not profit. They earned a 3-percent commission by closing the sale regardless of how much profit was involved. Once the company recognized this, it changed its system to pay less than 1-percent commission for sales booked at 40 percent off list price, 2.5 percent for sales at 20 percent off list, and 6 percent for sales made at list. By year's end, 40 percent of the company's sales were being made at list price versus none the year before.[32]

SALES GOALS BY TERRITORY

Volume and profitability objectives are both allocated by territory. A territory's goal is stated as a **sales quota**—*that is, the expected sales performance for the area in a given period of time*. Territorial quotas can be determined by estimating the sales potential of each territory based on potential demand and economic conditions in the territory.

For example, the Equitable Life Insurance Company segments its customers in each of its sales districts by categories reflecting their potential such as business owner, emerging affluent, very affluent, retired, and dual-income families with no kids. Using these measures, the company creates a sales-potential index by sales district. The greater the number of potential purchasers of life insurance in each area, the higher the index. Based on this index, Equitable establishes sales goals by territory and by segment.[33]

Sales goals can also be established based on the characteristics of industries and organizations. A manufacturer of hydraulic lifts might find that sales are greatest among heavy-machinery manufacturers with 500 or more employees. A territory that has more companies with these characteristics will have proportionately higher sales goals compared to other territories.

OBJECTIVES FOR INDIVIDUAL SALESPEOPLE

Objectives must also be developed for individual salespeople. Many firms allocate a territory's sales quota to individual salespeople based on a combination of past performance, changes in competitive conditions, and changes in demand among the salesperson's customers. If a salesperson accounted for $5 million in sales last year, but competition promises to be more intense in the coming year, it would be unfair to hold the salesperson to the same sales quota. The salesperson's quota should be scaled down, or rewards should be increased for other activities such as prospecting.

Just such a problem convinced Monier Roof Tile of Orange, California, to revamp their compensation package in the mid 1980s. After the economic downturn of 1981, Monier realized that its sales goals assumed a booming industry. Whereas previously, it rewarded its sales representatives based on sales volume, it revised its commission structure to reward representatives who brought in new customers. In so doing, it recognized that the focus should be on building a long-term client base rather than increasing short-term sales volume.[34]

Total sales volume should be only one among several objectives for salespeople. Objectives might also be stated in terms of *contribution to profit.* Profitability rather than volume objectives might ercourage a salesperson to allocate effort to products with the highest profit margins. Other objectives might be to contact a certain number of prospects per week or to make a minimum number of sales calls each week.

DETERMINE THE SALES BUDGET

The sales budget is usually established by determining the number of salespeople required to meet a division's objectives, then calculating the cost to recruit, train, and pay them.

Several methods can be used to determine the optimal size of the sales force—a marginal-revenue, objective-task, percent-of-sales, or competitive-parity approach.

MARGINAL-REVENUE APPROACH

The marginal-revenue approach is ideal for determining the sales budget, because it identifies the number of salespeople required to optimize contribution to profits. The principle behind this approach is to continue to expand the sales force as long as the marginal revenue gained from adding a salesperson is greater than the marginal cost of that salesperson. The optimal size of the sales force is achieved when marginal revenue gained from adding another person equals marginal cost. The problem with this approach is the difficulty of estimating marginal revenues and costs for each additional salesperson.

OBJECTIVE-TASK APPROACH

The most widely used approach in determining a sales budget is the objective-task method. The size of the sales force is based on an objective of reaching a certain number of existing and prospective customers and the required sales effort to reach this group. Assume a company wants to reach the following number of large, medium, and small customers each month and estimates the required sales calls to each customer as follows:

	LARGE CUSTOMERS	MEDIUM CUSTOMERS	SMALL CUSTOMERS
Number of customers	200	400	1,000
Estimated sales calls per customer per month	10	5	1
Total number of calls per month	2,000	2,000	1,000

Total calls are estimated at 5,000 per month. If the average salesperson makes 50 calls a month, the size of the sales force should be 100 people. The weakness in this approach is that the number of sales calls may not be related to profitability, so this approach may not identify the sales-force size that maximizes profits.

PERCENT-OF-SALES APPROACH

A firm can also establish the sales budget as a percentage of sales. The advantage of this approach is that selling costs are controlled, because they are a constant percentage of revenues. The problem is that there is no rational basis for setting the sales budget based on a constant percentage. The percentage selected is arbitrary and does not take account of the specific environment the company is facing.

COMPETITIVE-PARITY APPROACH

A firm can also base the size of its sales force on how many salespeople are employed by close competitors. This is the least defensible basis for determining the sales budget, because it assumes that what is right for competitors is also right for the company.

ORGANIZE THE SALES EFFORT

Once a sales budget is established, the divisional sales manager can turn to organizing the sales force. Developing a sales organization requires several decisions: Should the company maintain one sales force to service all accounts, or should it develop a **sales force mix**; *that is, a combination of different sales organizations to service large, medium, and small customers?* Should it rely on its own employees to sell, or should it use outside facilities? Should it organize its sales force along product, customer, or geographic lines?

DEVELOPING A SALES FORCE MIX

Many firms have developed a mix of sales organizations to deal with customers, as shown in Figure 19.3. National account marketing teams deal with the largest clients representing a small percentage of a company's client base (usually 10 percent or less of total customers), but up to 50 percent of its sales. At Xerox, about 300 NAM teams service only 350 customers, but each of these customers represents millions of dollars in sales.[35] Individual salespeople deal with medium-sized clients in the sales-force mix. At Xerox, these customers are served by about 1,000 individual account managers. Smaller customers are serviced by either salespeople or by telemarketing facilities. About 2,000 salespeople known as account representatives take care of these small customers at Xerox, while the company's telemarketing facility takes up the slack in servicing the smallest orders.

More and more firms are following a sales-mix strategy, because they find it more cost effective to let sales teams concentrate on the largest accounts, individual salespeople on mid-sized accounts, and telemarketing facilities on the smallest accounts.

FIGURE 19.3

The Sales Force Mix

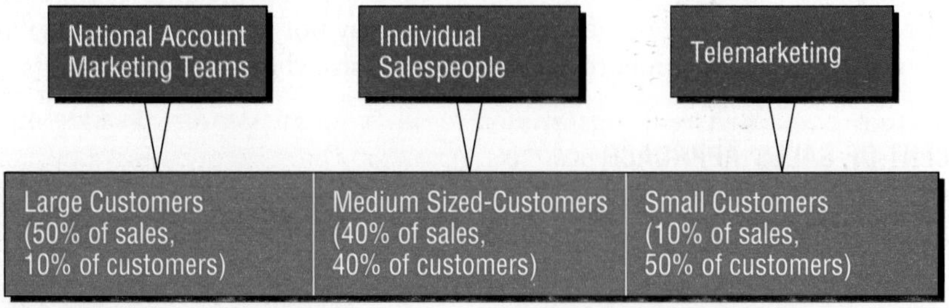

USE OF OUTSIDE SALES FACILITIES

Another important organizational decision is whether the firm should use outside facilities such as manufacturers' agents, sales agents, or distributors to supplement, or even to replace, the firm's sales staff. As was shown in Chapter 14, agents and distributors can reduce selling costs by contacting smaller and geographically dispersed accounts that may be sapping the efforts of the company's own sales force. If sales revenue is not high enough to support a company's own sales force, such outside facilities will be used.

For example, Airwick felt its own sales force was not producing sufficient revenue to justify its cost, so the company replaced its 10 sales offices with 93 independent distributors. The company is helping its distributors hire and train salespeople, control inventory, and install better accounting systems.[36]

Using agents and distributors carries some risks, particularly if they are the primary means of selling. Since they usually work for more than one company, they are less motivated to sell a company's line than the company's sales staff would be. They are also less knowledgeable about the company's products and technical specifications. Apple scrapped its network of manufacturers' representatives in favor of its own sales force in order to gain better control over its sales effort.[37]

ORGANIZING BY TERRITORY, PRODUCT, OR CUSTOMER

Another key decision in organizing the sales force is whether to structure it by territory, by product, or by customer type. In a *territorial* organization, each salesperson is responsible for selling the complete line of company products to customers in a territory. A territorial structure has several advantages. It clearly defines the salesperson's performance, since it is associated with the territory. It motivates the salesperson to develop prospects and build business in the territory, since the salesperson's compensation is tied to territorial performance. A territorial organization also has the advantage of reducing travel expenses and eliminating duplication of selling effort.

If special expertise is required to sell certain products or to sell to certain customers, a strictly territorial organization will probably not work. In this case, companies are likely to organize the sales force by *product line.* This type of organization is logical if the company is selling technical products requiring special sales expertise. However, many companies have tended to move away from a product organization because of the trend toward integrated selling. Buyers generally prefer to purchase from one salesperson who can sell many products rather than from several salespeople selling individual lines. If a firm's products are not interconnected, though, a product organization may be feasible.

A sales force can also be organized by *customer type.* For example, IBM might organize its sales force for integrated computer systems so that there are sales units for specific industries such as aerospace, automobile, chemical, and metal processing. The advantage of this type of organization is that salespeople can become more knowledgeable about specific types of buyers and develop a better capability to define their needs. Many companies have moved to a customer-based sales organization because of the greater importance of developing custom-made solutions to customer problems. Hewlett-Packard switched from a product-based organization to a customer-based organization to allow its sales force to sell computer systems rather than individual products. Another factor encouraging a customer-based sales organization is the trend toward developing a sales-force mix, since the type of organization shown in Figure 19.3 requires organizing the sales force by customer size.

IMPLEMENT THE SALES EFFORT

The next steps in the sales-management process involve implementing the selling effort. At this point, primary responsibility for the sales effort shifts from the divisional manager to the district sales manager and from planning the sales effort to managing the sales force. Implementing the selling effort requires recruiting salespeople, training them, and motivating them through compensation plans and other incentives.

RECRUITMENT

One of the most important responsibilities of the sales manager is recruiting salespeople. Effective recruiting means a better performing sales force and greater profitability from the sales effort. But what makes a good salesperson? Studies have shown that there is no apparent answer to this question; the evidence is contradictory. One study of life-insurance salespeople found that industry experience was related to performance; another found it was not.[38] Similarly, one study of oil company salespeople found that their intelligence was related to sales performance; another study found it was not.[39] These contradictory findings probably mean that salespeople need different traits depending on whether the job calls for order-taking, order-getting, or consultative-selling.

The recruiting process requires attracting applicants and selecting them. A company attracts applicants by obtaining names of potential recruits from its own salespeople, employment agencies, and college placement services. In attracting applicants, recruiters have had to counter misconceptions about selling, for example, that sales positions are low in status, are low paying, and require a "fast talking" approach. In fact, many sales positions are (1) a starting point for top marketing executive positions, (2) have attracted significantly higher pay in recent years, and (3) require an increasing amount of expertise as products in many industries become increasingly complex.

Once having attracted applicants, companies must establish objective selection procedures. Most rely on interviews to assess candidates. To avoid the subjective nature of such interviews, many firms like IBM, Gillette, and Procter & Gamble also test their applicants to assist interviewers in the selection process. These tests are generally developed by the company and are based on years of experience in observing what factors seem related to sales performance. Such tests are only one element in the selection process, however. Ultimately, the sales manager's judgment is the deciding factor.

TRAINING

Sales managers are closely involved in developing training programs for salespeople. Since the cost of training one salesperson averages over $20,000, the sales manager is concerned with developing the most effective program for the money.[40] The sales manager must also decide whether the company should hire experienced salespeople rather than train new ones. Most firms favor training a new staff, because hiring experienced personnel is much more costly. In some cases, however, experienced people are necessary to fill gaps in the sales force and meet the business' particular needs. This is especially true for service firms, because without tangible products to sell, their salespeople need to be more adept at explaining what they offer.

Any training program will vary depending on whether a firm is training an order taker, order getter, or consultative seller. The objectives of a training program for order takers are to communicate proper operating procedures and standards.

Burger King established a training program for the employees of its 4,200 fast-food outlets. The objective was to "achieve consistent adherence to strict operating standards" so as to maintain good service.[41]

Training objectives for order getters might be to acquaint them with the company's products and to teach them how to sell. Consultants are likely to go through a more intensive but less structured program. The program will not focus so much on how to sell, but rather on developing technical skills and an understanding of the customer's industry. The purpose of the program is to equip salespeople with the information necessary to develop custom-made solutions to solve customer problems. At Merck's pharmaceutical division, trainees spend six months to a year on selling the products under supervision to ensure that they understand medical applications and diseases (see Exhibit 19.5).[42]

EXHIBIT 19.5

Sales Training

A training coordinator at Merck shows a company sales representative how to use an interactive video program to learn about the physiological process of heart disease. Training provides new hires and experienced sales people with technical skills and information to help them work with customers to solve problems.

MOTIVATION

Salespeople must be motivated to achieve sales objectives; otherwise, recruitment and training procedures are meaningless. There are two key issues in motivation: Are sales quotas viewed as attainable? Are the rewards for performance satisfactory?

Quotas must be set in line with the potential in the salesperson's territory. If they are set at unreasonable levels the salesperson might become discouraged. Sales managers must discuss quota objectives with salespeople and try to help them achieve them. Some managers even go on the road with their salespeople to try to help them. Salespeople who see such a commitment on the part of their sales managers are more likely to give their maximum effort.

The second component of motivation—and perhaps the most important—is financial reward. Three types of compensation plans have been used to reward salespeople: straight salary, straight commission, and a combination of the two. A *straight salary* plan is simple to administer, but it is the least likely compensation plan to stimulate performance, because compensation is not tied to sales levels.

Straight-commission plans provide direct financial incentives tied to sales volume. They encourage salespeople to increase sales and to make more effective use of their time. But a straight-commission plan gives a salesperson no incentive to do anything but sell. Salespeople are also supposed to search for prospects, fill out call reports, supply information to their customers, and help in customer service and product installation. A straight-commission plan does not reward them for these nonsale activities. Moreover, a decrease in industry demand or increase in competition could demoralize a sales force on straight commission, since sales and compensation would go down for reasons beyond their control. Problems with straight salary and commission plans have led most companies to adopt a *combination* plan. One study found that 22 percent of the companies surveyed use straight salary, 21 percent straight commission, and the remaining 57 percent a combination of the two.[43] These combination plans attempt to balance the security of salary and the incentives of commissions.

Nonfinancial incentives such as a sense of accomplishment, respect from one's peers, and recognition are also very important in motivating high performance.[44] These nonfinancial incentives are likely to be influenced by an organization's attitude toward its sales force. Some organizations treat selling as a low-status position. It is difficult to motivate salespeople in such a climate. Other organizations make it a point to communicate the importance of personal selling.

Some firms use sales contests and recognition programs as nonfinancial incentives to enhance the sales force's motivation. Companies often have awards for best or most-improved performance. Some have special clubs for high performers that enhance their status in the firm. Contests that reward high performers through trips or gifts are also an effective way to increase motivation.

EVALUATE AND CONTROL THE SALES EFFORT

The last step in the sales management process is evaluating and controlling the sales effort. The divisional sales manager evaluates sales performance for the total division; the district sales manager evaluates the performance of individual salespeople in his or her territory. Table 19.2 summarizes the criteria for evaluating the total sales effort and the effort of individual salespeople, along with the problems associated with using each criterion.

TABLE 19.2

Criteria for Evaluating the Sales Effort

	CRITERIA	PROBLEMS AND LIMITATIONS
EVALUATING THE TOTAL SALES EFFORT	Profit return on sales expenditures	Difficult to isolate effects of sales effort on sales results
	Divisional contribution to profits	Difficult to isolate contribution of sales effort as distinct from other components of the marketing mix
	Sales volume and market share	Not necessarily related to profitability
	Contribution to profits	Difficult to determine if performance is result of sales manager's and sales force's actions or due to uncontrollable market conditions
EVALUATING A SALES-PERSON'S PERFORMANCE	Sales quota	Not necessarily related to profitability
	Contribution to profits of salesperson	Difficult to isolate influence of individual salesperson on results
	Sales volume for more-profitable product lines	Does not take account of nonsale activities
	Number of new accounts	Does not take account of nonsale activities
	Completion of sales reports	Does not take account of sales performance
	Expenses per sales call	Does not take account of sales performance
	Customer satisfaction	Not empirical and difficult to assess

EVALUATING THE TOTAL SALES EFFORT

The ultimate criterion of the effectiveness of the sales effort is profitability. Ideally, managers would like to establish a relationship between the amount spent on selling and the revenue generated from this effort (that is, a profit return on sales expenditures). However, too many other factors affect a customer's decision to buy to be able to isolate the specific impact of a sales contact.

These difficulties have led companies to rely on general measures of sales performance. Divisional managers compare their division's performance to sales volume and the market share of other companies in the industry. But, any volume and share increases could be unprofitable because of the high sales costs in obtaining them. The division's contribution to profits is a better criterion of evaluation, but it is difficult to isolate the contribution to profits from the sales effort alone as distinct from contributions from advertising, product development, or other components of the marketing mix. In short, there is no one perfect measure of sales performance.

If performance falls short, the divisional manager will want to know whether it was because of environmental factors beyond the firm's control, such as a general decrease in customer demand, or whether it was some shortcoming in the company's sales approach, such as a failure to adequately prospect new accounts.

The divisional manager also evaluates the performance for each sales territory. If a territory is below its quota, the divisional manager will determine if the problem is beyond the district manager's control or if it is correctable. Low performance could be the result of poor recruitment and training procedures, inadequate prospecting for new accounts, or poor leadership by the district sales manager in motivating the sales force. Any of these reasons would require corrective action.

EVALUATING THE SALESPERSON

In evaluating individual salespeople, the sales manager first looks at their sales volume relative to quota objectives set out at the beginning of the year. Sales volume should not be the only, or even the primary, criterion, however, because it may not reflect profitability. A salesperson might have achieved a high sales volume by pushing less-profitable lines that are easier to sell, by failing to prospect for new accounts, or by ignoring the record-keeping required to detail sales calls and results.

Information such as (1) sales volume for more-profitable lines, (2) number of new customers sold, and (3) expenses per sales call should be used to evaluate sales performance and determine how much each salesperson contributes to profits. Accordingly, salespeople are required to file *sales reports* that include such information.

CONTROLLING THE SALES FORCE

In controlling the sales effort, the sales manager's primary focus is on expenses. Expenses incurred by salespeople, especially travel and entertainment expenses, must be controlled to maximize profitability.

The sales manager will also try to control the way the salesperson spends his or her time. Since salespeople typically prefer to pursue existing customers, sales managers try to influence them to spend more time on prospecting for new accounts. Salespeople are also notorious in trying to avoid the paperwork associated with sales reports. They feel their time could be better spent in the field trying to close a sale. Sales managers will try to control the allocation of time to ensure that sales reports are submitted. Hewlett-Packard found that an important advantage of supplying its salespeople with personal computers was that less time was spent on paperwork, since salespeople could directly file their sales reports on the computer. This allowed them to spend more time with customers and lessened the need of management to control the completion of paperwork.

The importance placed by marketers on evaluating and controlling the sales effort reflects its role in the promotional mix. In many cases, sales expenditures far outweigh expenditures on advertising and sales promotions, particularly for industrial goods and services. As a result, managers must carefully track the profit results of their sales effort.

ETHICAL ISSUES IN PERSONAL SELLING

The preceding discussion assumes that salespeople will sell a company's products or services in an ethical manner—making a good-faith effort to determine what the customer wants, conveying truthful and accurate information about the company's products, trying to provide customers with full information, and addressing any subsequent customer complaints.

The vast majority of salespeople conduct themselves in such a responsible manner, especially with today's greater emphasis on a problem-solving approach. At times however, salespeople engage in undesirable high-pressure sales tactics. Movies like *Glengarry Glenn Ross*, about real-estate agents who would do anything to make a sale, or like *Tin Men*, about sellers of aluminum siding who trick innocent homeowners into signing contracts, give the impression that this type of unethical sales behavior is the norm rather than the exception.

The greatest problems in selling occur with door-to-door and telephone sales. Although companies such as Avon and Mary Kaye have established sound reputations based on a professional door-to-door sales staff, other companies have abused door-to-door selling. In one of the most disturbing examples of this, agents of the American National Insurance Company were found to have scanned Los Angeles newspapers for articles that chronicled bloody gang violence in low-income neighborhoods. They would then travel to the neighborhoods, knock on doors and wave the articles in front of residents as they tried to sell $10,000 policies as hedges against the possibility of deadly violence.[45]

Telephone sales practices are also prone to unethical behavior. In one approach, the customer is led to believe he or she has won a prize only to be told of various conditions involved requiring the purchase of a product. In another, the caller claims to be conducting a survey, but then attempts to induce the customer to buy products. Such practices undermine legitimate sales and marketing research efforts by phone.

Government has become more interested in regulating telemarketing practices. More than 30 states have passed laws restricting home solicitation and/or automatic-dialing recorded messages. Florida, for instance, has a law prohibiting telemarketers from dialing anyone who chooses to place an asterisk next to their name in the phone book. An even more cutting edge area for regulation is fax marketing. In 1989, Connecticut became the first state to enact a law where senders of unsolicited fax ads can be fined $200.[46]

By and large, however, government can do little to legislate fair sales practices. If outright fraud has occurred, consumers have recourse in the courts. Consumers have availed themselves of this option in complaints regarding pyramid selling schemes. In pyramid selling, members are asked to recruit other salespeople and get a commission on the recruit's sales. When the recruit in turn recruits people, the pyramid begins to form. Where such schemes run into trouble is when the goal is not to sell a product, but merely to get hundreds upon hundreds of members to pay a fee. After a while, an area can become so flooded with salespeople that the number of sellers far outstrips potential buyers.

In general, consumers must rely on the self-regulation imposed by companies. Fortunately, companies have become more sensitive to the need to maintain high standards in selling. The greater complexity of many products, the greater amount of information available to salespeople, and the trend to team selling have encouraged a problem-solving approach that creates higher standards in personal selling. Salespeople generally view their field as a responsible profession. An example of the professionalization of selling is a certificate program awarded to life-insurance salespeople by the American College of Life Underwriters based on a rigorous training course that emphasizes responsible selling.

ETHICAL AND ENVIRONMENTAL ISSUES IN MARKETING

The Hard Sell: How Oracle Got Carried Away by Success

Lawrence Ellison liked the grand theatrical gestures. There was the time, for instance, that he held a press conference aboard the Concord to tout the performance of his company's computer database software. As the CEO of Oracle Systems, Ellison wanted the salespeople he employed to be just as aggressive as he. He would later regret the extent to which his wish came true.

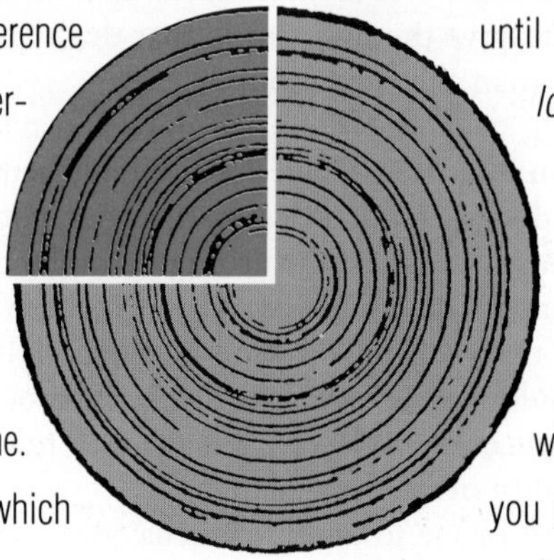

Oracle climbed to the top of the cutthroat database software market by combining innovation with Ellison's hyper-aggressive sales philosophy. By adapting its state-of-the-art programs to all types of computer brands and sizes, Oracle's R&D department was able to constantly stay one step ahead of its competition. The work of its sales force was even more phenomenal: 100 percent growth every year for 10 years. By 1988, sales of $280 million led Ellison to predict Oracle would be a $5 billion company by the mid 1990s. But the figures masked a bothersome reality whose full measure would not be revealed until 1991, when the company reported it *lost* $12 million on sales of $1 billion.

What happened? In their drive to realize Ellison's dreams, Oracle's managers set unrealistic goals for their salespeople. "It didn't matter what you thought you could do when you sat down at the end of the year to make your forecasts," said a former executive. "You were given a [quota] from your manager and you knew it would be double [the figure from the year before]." To make good on their quotas, salespeople started cutting corners. Since they received their commissions when the sale was made—not when the buyer actually paid for the product—salespeople would sell software that wouldn't be ready for months.

So blinded were they by their need to close sales that Oracle's salespeople would sign letters prom-

SUMMARY

1. **How do consultative-selling, order-getting, and order-taking approaches to personal selling differ?**
Consultative salespeople define the needs of their buyers and develop custom-made solutions to meet these needs. Most often, they sell complex product systems on a team basis. They must have a technical background and must develop an intimate knowledge of the customer's operations. Order getters influence the buyer to select the company's products by demonstrating its benefits. Products are usually part of a standard line and are not highly technical. An order taker fills a predefined need, most frequently replenishing a buyer's stocks when inventory is low. Little interaction is required with the buyer.

ETHICAL AND ENVIRONMENTAL ISSUES IN MARKETING

ising its products would fit certain specifications without ever asking Oracle's R&D people whether such promises could be guaranteed. Moreover, some would try to collect payments before the software arrived. Things got worse when Oracle redrew its sales territories and no one was quite sure where they should be selling.

Then the false promises began coming back to haunt the company. Facing mounting losses, it rushed out a financial database package that was riddled with errors. When customers began looking for salespeople to complain to, they could find no one. "When you'd call with problems, you got run-arounds," said a member of one user group. Given the fact that Ellison was running his billion dollar company the same way he did when it took in a fifth of the revenue, inadequate controls were in place to stem the tide of red ink. By 1990, the company had only collected $468 million on sales of $971 million.

To avoid bankruptcy, Ellison began reining in his sales force and insisting that Oracle's software be represented accurately. Today, Ellison is doing all he can to institute the controls needed to make Oracle a respected leader once again. Customers have begun reporting that Oracle's products have fewer bugs and customer service is vastly improved. In retrospect, Ellison now realizes that setting unrealistic goals for his sales force initiated the debacle. Given the company's high-quality product, he did not have to push his salespeople to the edge. "The arrogance was unnecessary," he says. Whether Oracle can regain its position as a respected leader in software remains to be seen.

Question: What could Ellison have done to ensure that the sales force did not misrepresent Oracle's offerings and capabilities?

Sources: " 'The Arrogance Was Unnecessary'," *Forbes*, September 2, 1991; and "The Selling Frenzy That Nearly Undid Oracle," *Business Week*, December 3, 1990.

2. **What important trends in personal selling are taking place in the 1990s?**
One of the most important developments was the establishment of national account marketing (NAM) teams to develop custom-made systems solutions to fill the needs of larger customers. In addition, technology has given salespeople greater access to information. Salespeople with personal computers have almost instant access to information. Finally, telemarketing facilities are increasingly used to handle customer inquiries and to try to sell to smaller customers by phone. Telemarketing is a way to reduce the high costs of personal contacts by limiting these contacts to larger customers.
3. **What is the nature of the selling process?**
The selling process requires a logical series of steps to influence the customer to buy. First, the salesperson must identify a prospective customer. Next, the

salesperson determines customer needs by probing for information in a two-way discussion. In so doing, he or she decides on the appropriate approach to inform and influence customers that the company's products and services can fill their needs. Having formulated a sales approach, the salesperson communicates it to try to influence the buyer. Finally, he or she evaluates the effectiveness of that sales approach and decides whether further sales calls are warranted.

4. **What are the key steps in planning the sales effort?**
   Planning the sales effort is the responsibility of a divisional sales manager. It requires setting sales objectives and establishing a sales budget for the division, then organizing the sales force based on (1) what combination of NAM selling teams, individual salespeople, and telemarketing will be used; (2) whether or not outside sales facilities such as manufacturers' agents and distributors will be used; and (3) whether a product, geographic, or customer organization is appropriate.
5. **How is the sales effort implemented and evaluated?**
   Implementing the sales effort requires recruiting salespeople, training them, and motivating them to perform. This is the responsibility of the district sales manager. Recruitment criteria and training programs differ for order takers, order getters, and problem solvers. Motivation is frequently based on a combination of straight salary and sales commissions. Implementation requires that the divisional manager evaluate the total performance of the division and that the district sales manager evaluate the performance of individual salespeople based on sales objectives.

KEY TERMS

Consultative salespeople (p. 623)
Order getters (p. 624)
Order takers (p. 624)
National account marketing (NAM) team (p. 626)
Inbound telemarketing (p. 628)
Outbound telemarketing (p. 628)
Prospecting (p. 629)
Qualify prospects (p. 629)
Canned sales approach (p. 634)
Formula selling approach (p. 634)
Problem solving approach (p. 634)
Sales quota (p. 636)
Sales force mix (p. 638)

QUESTIONS

1. How did Xerox increase the effectiveness of its sales force in the mid 1980s? What factors prompted the company to make these changes?
2. Why is personal selling the most important component of the promotional mix in business-to-business marketing?
3. What are the differences in the sales approaches of consultative salespeople, order getters, and order takers? What kinds of products are each type of salesperson most likely to sell?
4. What reasons are behind the growing use of national account marketing (NAM) teams and telemarketing facilities in the 1980s? What kinds of firms have been most likely to use NAM teams? Why?
5. Consider each of the following situations:
   - A seller of custom-made hydraulic lifts uses the specifications formulated by the customer's engineering department as a basis for submitting a proposal for the sale of the specified product. The salesperson's presentation to the buyer focuses primarily on price, delivery dates, and installation.
   - The sales staff for a leading snack food manufacturer uses its route salespeople to fill orders for supermarket chains. It provides little service or information, because chain store buyers know the products they want.
   - The sales force for a large telecommunications firm communicates the firm's new capabilities in information-processing and office systems.
   - A seller of pollution-control systems

works jointly with the buyer in developing specifications to the buyer's needs. Both the salesperson and buyer are trained engineers who work together with their design staffs in developing, installing, and servicing the system.

a. Which sales approach does each of these situations reflect: consultative selling, order getting, or order taking? Why?
b. Do any of these situations reflect the use of a NAM team?

6. When sales of Massey-Ferguson's farm machinery began declining in the early 1980s, the company substantially decreased its sales force and began using telemarketing facilities to maintain contact with most of its customers.
   a. Was this a proper use of telemarketing facilities?
   b. How do you think customers reacted to being contacted by phone rather than in person?
7. A sales manager for a producer of hydraulic lifts believes that prospecting has become more important in the last decade. The company is a leader in the field, but the sales manager is concerned that new entrants will have more innovative and technically oriented salespeople who are better able to identify prospects.
   a. Is the sales manager's concern well founded?
   b. Why has prospecting become more important in the last decade?
8. What are the responsibilities of a divisional sales manager in managing the selling effort? Of a district sales manager?
9. What are the pros and cons of using outside sales facilities like manufacturers' agents and distributors? Why did Apple Computer stop using manufacturers' agents and establish its own sales force to sell its personal computers?
10. When is a company likely to organize its sales force by territory, by product, or by customer type? Why have more companies organized their sales effort by customer type in recent years?
11. How will recruitment criteria and training programs differ for order takers, order getters, and consultative salespeople?
12. Why is a combination of salaries and commissions the most popular method for compensating salespeople?

QUESTIONS: YOU ARE THE DECISION MAKER

1. A salesperson of over-the-counter products for a pharmaceutical company says:

   Going in with a canned (standardized) approach usually doesn't work for me. The most difficult part of selling is when you are trying to overcome a customer's resistance to what is new and unfamiliar. For example, it is difficult to try to sell a new high-potency nonprescription pain reliever when the druggist is used to Bayer, Bufferin, and Tylenol. The creative part of selling is adjusting to the customer's frame of reference or trying to change it.

   a. Do you agree with this statement? Why or why not?
   b. What are the implications of the statement for an order-getting approach versus a consultative-selling approach?
2. A salesperson for a small computer company commented on the increasing use of NAM teams to sell as follows:

   I really mistrust selling on a team basis. I realize the team gives you something extra in the expertise of other individuals. But as you bring more people into the selling process, there is more chance of crossed signals between team members and miscommunication with the buyer. I have seen situations where one person on the NAM team says one thing while another says something else. As far as I'm concerned, the best sales approach is one-on-one selling where you can directly influence the buyer and can service the buyer's needs without having to work through a team.

   a. Do you agree with the salesperson's criticism of NAM teams? Why or why not?
   b. Have you found it difficult to work with teams on school projects? If so, do the salesperson's comments apply to your experiences?
   c. What are the advantages and disadvantages of selling on a team basis?

CHAPTER 20

Pricing Influences and Strategies

YOUR FOCUS IN CHAPTER 20

To learn:

- *Why price has increased in importance as a component of the marketing mix.*
- *How a company goes about determining prices for a product.*
- *How demand and other environmental factors influence price determination.*
- *What types of pricing strategies companies develop for existing and new products.*
- *What types of pricing practices are unethical, and how they can be regulated.*

Apple Computer: Rebuilding Market Share with a Low-Price Strategy

The 1980s were good to John Sculley, the CEO of Apple Computers. So good, they almost killed his company.

In 1984, Apple had taken the worlds of design and publishing by storm with its new line of Macintosh computers. The Mac's superb graphics and user-friendly features were unlike anything that had come before, as was its price. What was meant to be a $1,000 machine had turned into a $2,500 product because of cost overruns and a lavish marketing effort. Luckily for Sculley, since no one could figure out how to duplicate the technology, his customers had no where else to go.[1] Within a year, the Mac line was an international best seller, and Apple executives were proclaiming that they would "blow IBM away." [2]

In their optimism, however, Sculley & Co. were ignoring a central irony of their strategic plan. By keeping their technology a secret, they could not share in the economies of scale enjoyed by rivals who collaborated on "open systems"—ones which enabled many different vendors to share the costs of innovation and development. As a result, Apple had to keep pushing up its prices to pay for R&D.[3] By 1989, Apple computers were costing as much as 36 percent more than comparable models from IBM or Compaq.[4]

Macintosh Classic at $999

It was at this juncture that a debate began to rage in the company's executive suite. The competition still had not matched the Mac's technological edge (the OS/2 operating system created by Microsoft in 1987 to give IBM users Mac-type graphics was not selling).[5] Given Apple's competitive advantage, some executives felt that the time was ripe to drop prices and pursue market share. A high price would only encourage competitive entry. Sculley, however, would not listen. He kept ordering price hikes, some by as much as 29 percent.[6]

What he refused to see was that Apple's strategy of playing to the market's high-end was running out of steam. Its original corporate customers were finding it harder to justify spending $10,000 on workstations, and first-time PC buyers did not want to take a $3,000 plunge.[7] Even though foreign sales kept Apple from going into the red, by 1990 its U.S. market share had nosedived to 9 percent from 15 percent three years before. Sculley was forced to admit that his sales were "dead in the water."[8]

Making matters worse was that software houses—the life blood of a computer maker—had stopped writing many programs for the Mac, and Microsoft had returned from its OS/2 disaster with a program called Windows that was selling well. Many analysts began worrying that Apple was nearing the point of no return.[9]

Enter Mark Spindler, a fast-talking native of Germany whom Sculley had thrust into the chief operating officer spot. Realizing he did not have time to engineer a new generation of Macs, Spindler took the most straightforward remedy available: In 1991, he plunged Apple into the low-end market with the $999 Mac Classic, a stripped down version of the regular Mac that retained its graphic capabilities. At the same time, he dropped prices on its higher-end models.

Whether he realized it or not. Spindler switched from a cost-oriented to a demand-oriented method of pricing. Instead of determining R&D and other costs and tacking on a profit margin to determine price, Apple was now willing to ask itself "What value do consumers place on our offerings, what are they willing to pay, and can we make a profit at that price level?"

The results of Apple's value-based pricing approach were better than anyone could have expected. Two hundred thousand Macs were shipped in 1991—an 85 percent increase over the year before[10]—and 700,000 more were expected to be sold in 1992.[11] For a lean company, that should have meant a profit bonanza. But Apple was far from lean. It was a corporate spendthrift. As a result, the lower profit margins that resulted from lower prices left Apple unable to afford its old life-style, and a painful period of retrenchment followed. Workers were fired, the organization was reshuffled, and Sculley emerged preaching a new low-price religion. "We're going to catch up," he told one interviewer.[12]

Perhaps he will. But with the lower margins, Sculley can no longer afford to be the R&D loner he once was. This is why he has agreed to develop products with one-time archrival IBM. The pact may be viewed as an admission that Sculley's attempt to go it alone at the high-priced end of the computer market has failed.

THE IMPORTANCE OF PRICE

The price level of a product can spell its success or failure. Price must be consistent with the quality consumers perceive they are getting. If it is set too high, consumers will feel they are not getting enough value for their money. If it is set too low, consumers will question the quality of the product, because they have learned that in most cases, lower price means lower quality. An important component in Apple's comeback was that the budget-priced Mac Classic enticed buyers who knew of Apple's quality but had previously felt they could not afford it. With the new model, these consumers recognized they were getting value for their money.

PRICE AS A DETERMINANT OF PROFITS

Ultimately, the importance of price must be measured by its impact on a brand's profitability. Profit is total revenue minus total cost, and total revenue is determined by price times quantity. So, price is a direct determinant of profits.

These are basic facts known to all marketing managers. Therefore, it is surprising that until recently, price was not regarded as a particularly important decision area in developing marketing strategies. Until the mid 1970s, pricing was primarily a matter of determining costs and adding a target return on these costs. This prevailing cost-oriented method of pricing considered consumer demand after the fact. If consumers would not buy at the price that was set, the marketer would reduce the price and see if consumers were then willing to buy.

By the early 1980s this method began to give way to a more demand-oriented strategy, where marketers began setting prices to achieve certain goals, such as maximization of short-term profits. Such strategies required knowing how much consumers would buy at various price levels. As we have seen, Apple initially priced its Macs based on cost, and only began to consider what consumers were willing to pay when it realized its prices were too high.

INCREASING IMPORTANCE OF PRICE IN THE 1980s AND 1990s

Starting in the mid 1970s, marketing executives began to cite price as the most important component of the marketing mix.[13] This emphasis on price has become even stronger in the 1990s. There are at least four reasons for this increasing emphasis on price. First, *sharp recessions* in the early 1980s and 1990s decreased consumer purchasing power, making them more price sensitive. They began to shop around and to buy lower-priced generic brands and private labels, making price a prime weapon among manufacturers eager to gain competitive advantage. For example, failure of the economy to emerge from recession in 1991 prompted P&G to announce "everyday low prices." Rather than offer consumers frequent coupons and price promotions, the company announced lower prices across the board in response to consumers' restricted purchasing power.

A second reason for the greater strategic importance of price is *foreign competition.* The trickle of lower-priced foreign goods that began to flow into the U.S. market in the 1970s had turned into a flood by the late 1980s, creating downward price pressures in many industries such as autos, electronics, and steel. One of the reasons Apple was forced to abandon its high-end strategy was because of the enormous appeal of low-cost foreign-made IBM PC "clones." Japanese auto makers, by providing higher quality cars at lower prices, have given American consumers more value for the money. The American auto industry reacted by using rebates and discounts to compete. By the 1990s, companies like General Motors were desperate to stop using rebates but found that rebates had become an ingrained part of the company's competitive pricing policies.[14] Other firms have reacted by ceding the low-price end of the market to foreign competitors and carving a niche on the high end. As we have seen in Chapter 6, Zenith, the only remaining company in the United States making televisions, is focusing on the premium-price niche, offering sets retailing for more than $1,000 with features such as large screens and built-in cabinets.[15]

A third factor increasing the importance of price is the *fragmentation of many markets* into segments demanding different price levels. Companies that offer one brand to a mass market are losing out to firms that offer premium-priced and lower-priced brands to different segments. Philip Morris, the leading cigarette company, is beginning to segment the market based on price by coming out with lower-priced brands to compete with generics. Companies that have formerly targeted a mass market are able to survive by narrowly targeting the high-price or low-price ends. Liggett & Myers, once a leading cigarette company, reacted to a long slide in market share by specializing in producing generic and low-priced cigarettes. On the retail level, swanky stores such as Neiman Marcus and budget outlets like Wal-Mart are prospering while mid-priced department stores like Macy's are slowly dying.[16]

Finally, *deregulation* has increased the importance of price. Before 1975, pricing was regulated in basic industries such as airlines, trucking, railroads, financial services, and telecommunications. The deregulation of all of these industries resulted in intense price competition (see Exhibit 20.1 for price-oriented ads as a result of deregulation). For example, airlines began slashing prices once Congress removed the Civil Aeronautic Board's power to regulate them. In the first five years after deregulation, airline prices decreased 50 percent.[17] By 1991, the price wars had claimed such venerable but unprofitable carriers as Pan Am and Eastern.

EXHIBIT 20.1

Results of Deregulation: Increased Price Competition in Two Industries

FIGURE 20.1

A Model of Price Determination

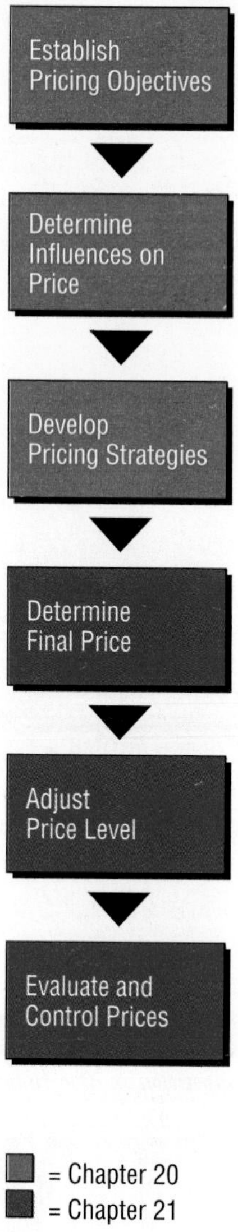

THE PROCESS OF PRICE DETERMINATION

Figure 20.1 presents a model of the process of price determination. This chapter examines the steps in the shaded boxes, and the remaining steps will be considered in Chapter 21.

The first step in the model is to establish pricing objectives. McDonald's, for example, had established a pricing objective of offering reasonable quality at the lowest prices, but in the mid-to-late 1980s, the company strayed from its pricing objectives and began increasing its menu prices to offset a decline in traffic in its U.S. restaurants. After it became clear that its reputation as a value leader was becoming endangered, McDonald's initiated a full-scale review of its pricing strategies.[18]

The next step in Figure 20.1 is to evaluate pricing influences such as costs, consumer demand, and competitors' prices. McDonald's evaluation led it to conclude that its short-sighted pricing policy had allowed competitors to gain market share. On the low end, Taco Bell was stealing away customers with 39-cent tacos. On the higher end, chains such as Dallas-based Chili's were skimming business by offering casual sit-in dining and more-elaborate menus for only marginally higher prices. McDonald's needed to decide on which end of the price ladder it wanted to compete.

The third step is to develop a pricing strategy that maps out how the company will meet its pricing objectives. While McDonald's policy of hiking prices faster than inflation during the mid-1980s reflected an aggressive approach, the company decided that to fend off the advances of its rivals it needed to revert to its original strategy. As a result, it went back to a value pricing strategy to reaffirm its place in the market's low-price end.

Once it has established a pricing strategy, the company should determine the price level at which the product will be sold. In McDonald's case, it decided to slash most menu items by 20 percent, leaving its cheeseburgers to sell for 69 cents. McDonald's also applied the same low-price strategy to new offerings such as corn-on-the-cob and salads, charging 20 percent less than it would have in previous years.

Pricing adjustments are likely to be part of a company's pricing strategy. For a manufacturer, such adjustments require offering retailers and wholesalers discounts for providing certain services or for paying on time. In McDonald's case, it frequently offered its customers discounts in the form of price promotions to try to increase store traffic. One such discount was a "value pack" of meal coupons.

The last step in Figure 20.1 involves evaluating and controlling prices. To evaluate customer responses to price, the company can measure sales results and determine whether additional customers bought because of a price change. On that score, McDonald's was quite pleased. After the 1991 price cuts, sales of its burgers jumped 30 percent. The responses of retailers and distributors must also be evaluated. While McDonald's franchisee's were pleased with the increased foot traffic, they were also worried that lower prices might cut into their profits. Eventually, most were satisfied that the additional sales volume from lower prices outweighed the lower profit margins on each item sold.

Prices must be controlled, as well as evaluated, if sales goals are to be met. Thus, McDonald's had to make sure that its franchisees followed its pricing strategies and that lower prices were offered uniformly to all customers. In the remainder of this chapter, we consider the first three steps in price determination shown in Figure 20.1; establishing pricing objectives, determining pricing influences, and developing pricing strategies.

PRICING OBJECTIVES

A manager determines price levels based on pricing objectives. Pricing objectives can be based on cost, competitive actions, sales, or customer demand. *Cost-oriented pricing objectives* are the most common. The most frequently used objective is a *target return on investment.* For example, a firm might cite an objective of a 15 percent return on investment for a product and set a price that it estimates will meet this goal. When Eli Lilly, a leading pharmaceutical company, introduced Treflan, an agricultural herbicide, its initial objective was to obtain an adequate return to recoup its investment in a reasonable period of time.[19] This objective dictated a high price, which was a feasible strategy because Treflan was under patent protection.

Competitive pricing objectives can also be set such as trying to deter competitive entry. When Treflan's patent was about to expire, Lilly changed its objective to one of trying to discourage competitive entry. This led to a sharp reduction in price.

Many firms establish *sales-based pricing objectives*; that is, they set prices to achieve dollar sales goals. Such goals provide a more direct measure of the firm's success in increasing its revenues through its pricing strategies.

A fourth category of objectives, *demand-oriented objectives*, are designed to set prices based on customer responses. The most frequently stated demand-oriented objective is short-term profit maximization, but determining customer demand for a brand in order to set a profit-maximizing price is difficult, because the firm must estimate how much customers will buy at various price levels.

PRICING INFLUENCES

The two most important influences that affect pricing decisions are demand and cost. Consumer *demand* defines the amount consumers are willing to buy at various prices and determines revenue. *Cost* factors are used to establish prices on a target return or markup basis. Whereas consumer demand defines a ceiling above which prices cannot go to remain profitable, costs define a floor below which prices cannot go. Besides cost and demand influences, a number of other environmental characteristics affect price, such as competition and the trade.

As we will be using various demand and revenue concepts in our discussion of pricing, we recommend that you review Appendix 20A, "Basic Demand and Revenue Concepts," at the end of this chapter before you read further.

DEMAND FACTORS

Marketers should have some idea of the quantity customers are willing to buy at various price levels in order to set prices. This information is estimated in the form of the consumers' *demand curve* and *price elasticity*, or sensitivity to price.

THE CONSUMER DEMAND CURVE

The consumer **demand curve** *is a curve that shows the quantity of a product that customers buy at various price levels.* Marketers attempt to estimate a demand curve for customers when they introduce new products or want to change prices of existing products.

FIGURE 20.2

Hypothetical Demand Curves for the Saturn Car

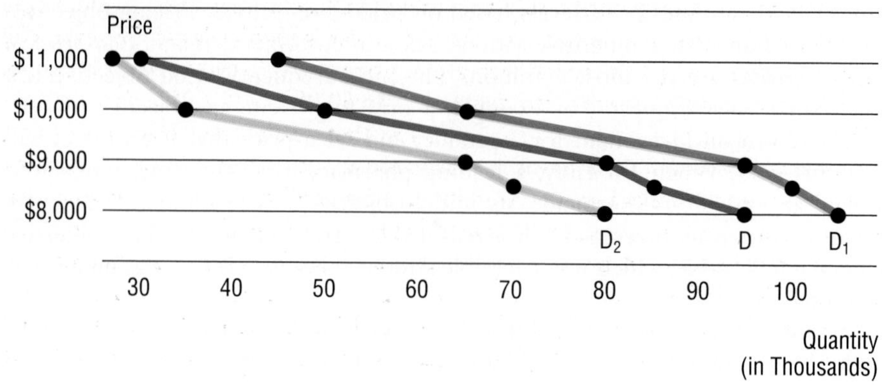

Suppose General Motors tested five prices ranging from \$8,000 to \$11,000 for its new subcompact Saturn car line before it was introduced in 1991. Based on these tests, GM estimates demand at 30,000 units at the \$11,000 price, 95,000 units at the \$8,000 price, and various units in between at the intermediate prices. On this basis, the demand curve for the Saturn is estimated (Curve D shown in Figure 20.2).

Any change in the level of consumer demand at a given price results in a new demand curve. For example, assume that GM introduces the Saturn line at a price of \$8,000, and finds that its estimates of demand are fairly accurate. In the first year after introduction, it sells close to the 95,000 cars it projected at a price of \$8,000 for total revenue of \$760 million (95,000 × \$8,000). But now, an unanticipated event occurs in GM's favor: Congress imposes a strict import quota on all Japanese cars, resulting in a decrease in competition in the sale of subcompacts. As a result, in the second year after introduction, GM sells 110,000 cars at a price of \$8,000. There is now a new demand curve for the Saturn, represented by Curve D_1 in Figure 20.2. The demand curve for the Saturn has shifted to the right, meaning that demand has expanded. Now total revenue, at a price of \$8,000, is \$880 million rather than \$760 million. GM has gained a windfall of \$120 million more in revenues based on Congress's actions.

On the other side of the coin, suppose Congress took no action, and Japanese manufacturers entered the United States with new lines of cars priced even lower than in previous years. Now, General Motors can only sell 80,000 Saturns at \$8,000 (curve D_2) for a total revenue of \$640 million, or \$120 million less than anticipated. In this case the demand curve for the Saturn shifted to the left. Thus, an increase in demand means the demand curve shifts to the right; a decrease means it shifts to the left.

PRICE ELASTICITY OF DEMAND

Price elasticity *is the percentage change in quantity that results from a percentage change in price*, as shown by the following index:

$$\text{Price Elasticity of Demand} = \frac{\text{Percent Change in Quantity}}{\text{Percent Change in Price}}$$

Price elasticity is a measure of a buyer's sensitivity to price. When the percent change in quantity is more than the percent change in price, consumers are *price sensitive* (that is, *price elastic*). A decrease in price will produce a more than proportionate increase in quantity, resulting in an increase in revenues. The example in Figure 20.2 shows that demand for the Saturn car is highly elastic. For example, Curve D shows that a 10 percent decrease in price from $10,000 to $9,000 results in a 60 percent jump in estimated demand from 50,000 to 80,000 units.

When the percent change in quantity is less than the percent change in price, consumers are *price insensitive* (that is, *price inelastic*). An increase in price will produce a less than proportionate decrease in quantity, resulting in an increase in total revenue. Consider the hypothetical demand curve for a Jaguar auto in Figure 20.3. A 33 percent increase in price from $45,000 to $60,000 results in a decrease in sales from 20,000 to 16,000 units, or only 20 percent. A price increase pays, because at a price of $45,000, total revenue is $900 million ($45,000 × 20,000 cars), whereas at a price of $60,000, total revenue is $960 million ($60,000 × 16,000 cars).

When consumers are price elastic, they will switch brands based on price. When they are inelastic, they tend to remain loyal to a brand. Price is fairly elastic for items ordinarily purchased in supermarkets or drugstores. It is inelastic for prestige products such as gourmet foods or luxury cars. However, demand can be inelastic even for everyday products. The consumer who insists on buying Michelob beer or Pepperidge Farm cookies is loyal to those brands and may continue to buy even if prices increase by 10 or 20 percent.

UPSIDE AND DOWNSIDE ELASTICITY

Upside elasticity *is the elasticity for a product when prices are increasing and* **downside elasticity** *is the elasticity when they are decreasing.* Upside and downside elasticity for a product may differ. For example, consumers may decrease consumption if prices increase but may not necessarily increase consumption if prices decrease. When coffee prices increased sharply in the mid 1970s, coffee consumption decreased, because many consumers switched to tea and other products. When prices began to decrease, some of these consumers continued to drink other prod-

FIGURE 20.3

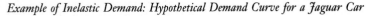

Example of Inelastic Demand: Hypothetical Demand Curve for a Jaguar Car

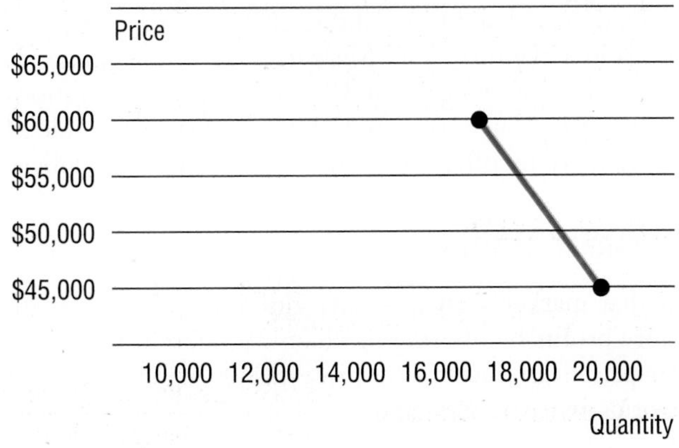

EXHIBIT 20.2

Creating Upside Price Inelasticity and Downside Price Elasticity

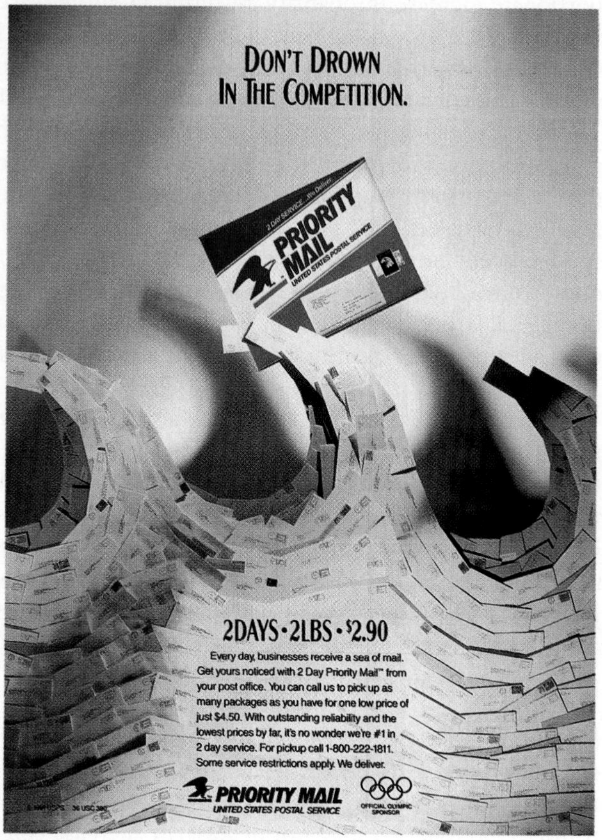

ucts, so consumption did not increase as much as expected. These consumers demonstrated upside price elasticity (sensitivity to increases in price) and downside inelasticity (insensitivity to decreases in price).

Ideally, a marketer would want things the other way around—upside price inelasticity (no substantial change in consumption as prices go up) and downside elasticity (increased purchases as prices go down). Marketers try to encourage upside price inelasticity by advertising products on a prestige basis. For example, the ad for Red Devil wood stain in Exhibit 20.2 tries to convince the consumer that the product is in a class by itself. Marketers try to encourage downside price elasticity by advertising lower prices and by using price promotions. The ad for the Post Office's Priority Mail Service in Exhibit 20.2 is an example of encouraging downside price elasticity by offering a low rate for overnight delivery.

ELASTICITY BY MARKET SEGMENT

By recognizing that market segments have different price elasticities, marketers can generate more profits by offering products at different prices to different segments—a lower-priced product to the price-elastic segment and a higher-priced product to the price-inelastic segment.

The airlines have long followed a pricing policy based on the fact that business travelers are more price inelastic than vacationers. They will pay a higher price if they can get to the right place at the right time. Vacation travelers want lower prices more than they want scheduling flexibility, so airlines offer them lower fares at restricted times.[20]

COST–REVENUE RELATIONSHIPS

Estimating the demand curve for a product enables the manager to compute revenues generated at various prices. This information, in turn, is part of the calculation of profits, which are revenues minus costs. Costs are more easily estimated than revenue, since the firm already knows its costs for labor, raw materials, marketing, and administration, but must predict revenue. At this point, it would be useful to review the basic cost concepts summarized in Appendix 20B before considering cost–revenue relationships.

DETERMINING PROFITS

As we noted, the quantity customers are willing to buy at a certain price determines total revenue. If the manager also knows the cost of producing these items, then profits can be determined. Managers will try to set prices at the point where they will maximize profits. The price–quantity relationships in Curve D of Figure 20.2 for the Saturn car are shown in Table 20.1, along with the total costs of production and distribution. The last column shows the profits (total revenue minus total cost).

On this basis, gross profits would be greatest when cars sell for $8,500. Assume GM sets its price for the new cars accordingly, but the company also realizes that if it reduces price to $8,000 because of competitive pressures, or if it decides to raise the price to $9,000, there would be little loss in profits. As a result, GM has price flexibility in the range of $8,000 to $9,000.

MARGINAL ANALYSIS

Marginal analysis *attempts to establish a profit-maximizing price based on the revenue gained by selling additional units of a product and the costs to produce and market the*

TABLE 20.1

Determining Profits at Various Price Levels

PRICE *(P)*	QUANTITY *(Q)*	TOTAL REVENUE *[P · Q]* (in Millions)	TOTAL COST (in Millions)	PROFITS (Total Revenue–Total Cost)
$11,000	30,000	$330	$410	–$ 80
$10,000	50,000	$500	$500	$ 0
$ 9,000	80,000	$720	$600	$120
$ 8,500	87,000	$740	$618	$122
$ 8,000	95,000	$760	$646	$114

additional units. The profit-maximizing price is at a point where marginal revenue equals marginal cost. This principle of marginal analysis in pricing means that as long as the additional revenue gained from the last unit produced (the marginal revenue) is greater than the cost of producing that last unit (the marginal cost), the company should produce the additional unit. If, for example, the 87,000th Saturn car produces $2,900 in revenue and costs $2,800 to produce, it is profitable to produce the additional car because it is contributing $100 to profits. Once the last unit is no longer contributing to profits, then it does not pay to produce more units. Since the sale of an additional unit of a product depends on consumer demand, marginal analysis is a demand-oriented approach to pricing.

The principle of marginal pricing says that if demand is elastic, when marginal revenue is greater than marginal cost, prices should decrease as long as the additional units demanded bring in more revenue than the cost of producing them. This is known as *pricing down the demand curve.* The marketer keeps decreasing prices (moving down the demand curve) as long as these decreases contribute to profit. If demand is inelastic, when marginal revenue is greater than marginal cost, prices should increase as long as the additional units demanded bring in more revenue than their cost. This is known as *pricing up the demand curve.* The marketer keeps increasing price as long as these increases contribute to profits.

In the Saturn example, demand was elastic. The following marginal revenue and marginal cost figures are shown in Appendixes 20A and 20B for prices of $9,000, $8,500, and $8,000:

PRICE	QUANTITY	MARGINAL REVENUE (*MR*)	MARGINAL COST (*MC*)	MARGINAL CONTRIBUTION TO PROFIT (*MR* − *MC*)
$9,000	80,000	$7,330	$3,300	$4,030
$8,500	87,000	$2,860	$2,570	$ 290
$8,000	95,000	$2,500	$3,500	−$1,000

In the preceding table, the **marginal contribution to profit** *is the contribution made by the last unit produced.* As long as the last unit is making a marginal contribution to profit, prices should keep decreasing. At a price of $9,000, each additional unit is making a contribution to profits of $4,030, so it would pay GM to reduce the price further so as to sell more cars. At a price of $8,500, marginal revenue is almost the same as marginal cost. By the time we reach a price of $8,000, marginal costs exceed marginal revenue, and there is no contribution to profit by producing any more cars. So the optimal price is a little below $8,500, because at that price each additional car produced is still making a small ($290) contribution to profit.

At a price much below $8,500, any additional car produced would not be making a contribution to profit. This is almost exactly the same result we obtained in Table 20.1 when we identified the price that maximizes profits as $8,500. (That is the price at the point of greatest difference between total revenue and total cost.)

This principle of marginal analysis is illustrated in Figure 20.4. The intersection of the marginal revenue and marginal cost curves is at the point that maximizes total profit (that is, the point that produces the greatest spread between total revenue and total cost).

The problem in using marginal analysis to determine the profit-maximizing price is that the method depends on the accuracy of the estimated demand curve.

If consumers buy 75,000 units at $8,500 instead of the projected 87,000, the profit-maximizing price would not be $8,500.

ENVIRONMENTAL PRICE INFLUENCES

In addition to consumer demand and cost factors, a number of environmental factors influence a manager's pricing decisions. These influences include the customer's pricing perceptions, competitive reactions, trade reactions, and economic conditions.

CONSUMER PRICE PERCEPTIONS

Based on their past experience, customers develop expectations regarding price levels. They judge prices as too high or too low based on those expectations. They also frequently regard price as an indicator of product quality. Managers must determine both consumers' pricing expectations and the associations they make between price and quality.

FIGURE 20.4

Defining the Point of Profit Maximization for the Saturn Car / Note: Hypothetical Example

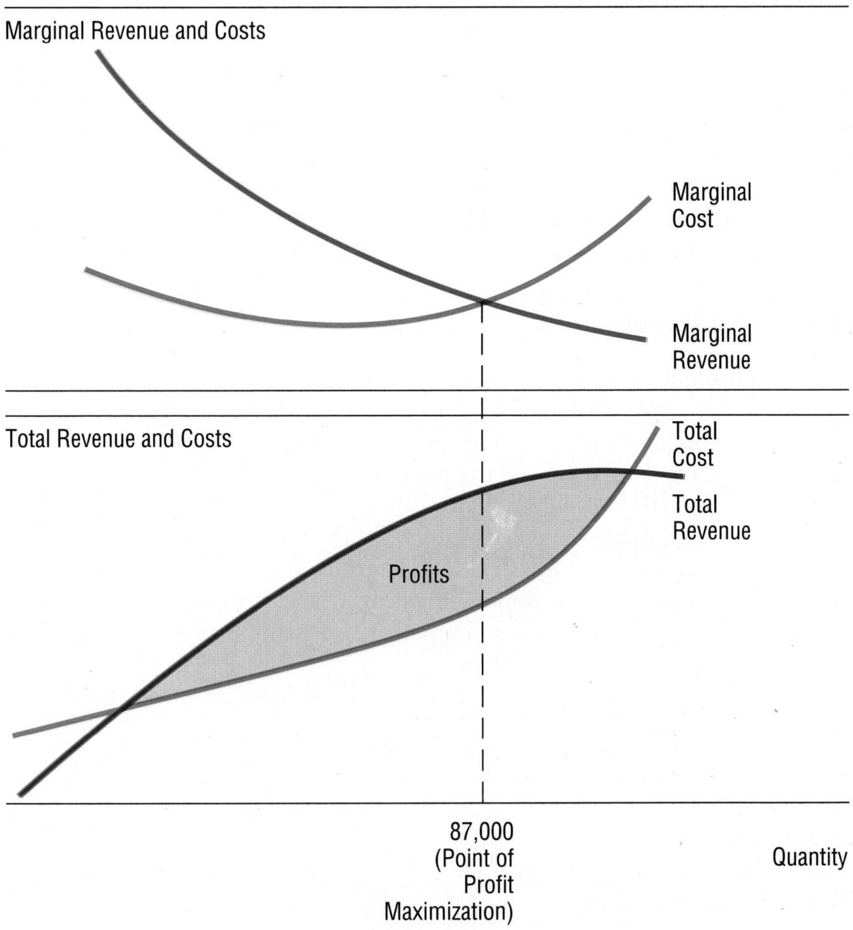

Most consumers develop an **acceptable price range** *for a product category, that is, a price range they view as being realistic.* They will not buy a brand priced above that range because the product is not worth it to them. That reality hit Mercedes-Benz squarely between the eyes in 1991, when its new model prices started at a whopping $90,000. Even die-hard Mercedes buyers found it difficult to justify the price-tag, and sales plunged 24 percent. Mercedes reacted by rolling out a mid-size sedan priced at $55,800.[21]

At the same time, consumers will also not buy below the range because they fear the product would be of inferior quality. Sears came to realize this after its disastrous foray into discount pricing. The retailer believed it could get consumers through its doors by touting everyday low prices, but many just wound up believing that if the items were selling so cheaply they must not be high quality. "I think we overemphasized price and we need to return to the value platform," the store's president reflected in 1990.[22]

As these examples show, different segments of the market will have different acceptable price ranges. Therefore, the product manager must determine the acceptable price range for a particular target segment and develop a price within it.

Consumers also develop perceptions about the character of a company based on the price of their offerings. The E&J Gallo Winery is a dominant player in the volume wine business, routinely selling upwards of 67 million cases a year, but its association with low-cost wines has prevented it from making a significant dent in the elite ranks of chardonnays and zinfandels. Part of the problem is that the company steadfastly refuses to use any name other than the one adorning its lower-end wines.[23]

Another issue in pricing is the associations consumers make between price and quality. Since many consumers regard price as an indicator of quality, marketers must make sure that price is in line with product quality. Consumers who feel the price was too high for the quality they received will not buy again and may pass the word on to other consumers. The higher the price, the greater the risk of disappointing the consumer with what is perceived as inferior quality.

COMPETITIVE INFLUENCES

Marketers must take competitive reactions into account when setting prices. Competitive reactions can be evaluated by determining the likelihood that a competitor will react to a company's price change, and the anticipated effects of such a reaction on sales. When Apple reduced the price of its Macs to $999, it had to evaluate the likelihood that IBM would retaliate with a series of price cuts on its personal computers. Further, Apple would have to assess the effects on its sales of a minor, moderate, or major price cut by IBM. If it determined that there was a high probability that IBM would exceed Apple's price cuts, the effect could be to cancel any sales gains made by Apple. Such a competitive evaluation might have dissuaded Apple from cutting prices on its Macs.

Some companies have used price to retaliate for competitive actions. When Miller and Coors, the country's second and fourth largest beer companies, decided to grab share away from their struggling third- and fifth- place competitors, Stroh Brewery and G. Heileman Brewing, they did so by launching a price war. What Miller and Coors did not foresee was that they were also taking a shot at the profits of Anheuser Busch, the industry leader. Anheuser retaliated by cutting prices even further. That petrified the other two leaders, because Anheuser Busch could better afford to absorb price cuts, since its operating profits were $14.31 on each barrel it sells compared to $4.67 for Miller and $4.27 for Coors. As one analyst said, "Miller and Coors went after the elk and deer, but they wound up shooting the elephant."[24]

TRADE INFLUENCES

Manufacturers must anticipate how retailers and wholesalers will react to their pricing strategies. If a manufacturer cuts prices, and many distributors decide to stop carrying the product because of reduced margins, such a price decrease could be counterproductive. If manufacturers are small or are new in the business, they may not have the leverage to convince wholesalers and retailers to stock their offerings. Their only option might be to offer the trade higher margins.

Another factor in pricing strategy is the manufacturer's desire to control prices at the retail level. When a manufacturer spends millions of dollars in advertising trying to establish a high-quality image for a brand, price discounts at the retail level can undermine the strategy. When Sony found many of its dealers selling its merchandise at lower prices to discounters to get rid of unwanted inventory, it was concerned, because lower prices would tarnish its image. As a result, it stopped selling to these dealers.[25]

A manufacturer can suggest prices, but is prohibited from forcing retailers to sell at the manufacturer's price under restraints against vertical price fixing. One legal way to control prices at the retail level is to franchise retailers so that their pricing actions can be controlled by the manufacturer. Sony switched from selling to independent retailers to franchising its stores so that it could control prices at the retail level. Another option would have been for Sony to sell directly to customers through its own outlets, but this is an expensive alternative since it would require Sony to incur the distribution costs of a large network of independent retailers.

ECONOMIC INFLUENCES

Periods of inflation, recession, and shortages have a direct effect on pricing actions. In inflation, prices to consumers rise to keep pace with the increasing costs of raw materials and labor. Shortages such as the oil crises in the 1970s will also drive up prices because of increased costs. In a recession, marketers face pressures to cut prices to remain competitive because of decreases in demand for many categories.

During the steep recession of the early 1990s, consumers' price sensitivity increased sales of generic and price brands, so that they now account for nearly one-fifth of supermarket sales.[26] As if that was not enough to cause shudders among managers of national brands, Sam Walton announced in late 1991 that his Wal-Mart stores, the nation's largest retailer, was introducing its own private label line under the name of Sam's American Choice.[27]

Hoping to stem the flight from their products, packaged-goods companies began introducing their own budget brands. Campbell's Soup introduced frozen foods under the Budget Swanson and Great Starts Budget Breakfast labels to attract value-conscious senior citizens. Wilkinson Sword launched an Economie line of razors to attack private labels head-on,[28] and Revlon's Charles of the Ritz, usually an upscale cosmetics maker, got into the act by introducing a collection of affordable products under the Express Bar nameplate.[29]

In addition to extending their product line to low-priced brands, manufacturers have also cut the price of their regular brands. Procter & Gamble's introduction of a low-price strategy for all its major brands is an example.

PRICING STRATEGIES

Based on its pricing objectives and the influences on price, a company develops an overall pricing strategy for its brand or product line (step 3 in Figure 20.1) that determines a range of prices for a product or service. Pricing strategies can be developed for existing products, for new products, and for product lines.

PRICING STRATEGIES FOR EXISTING PRODUCTS

Pricing strategies for existing products deal with two key areas: the appropriate price level and the changes in price from the current level.

PRICE LEVEL

Price-level strategies can position a brand from the lowest to the highest price. These extremes are shown in Exhibit 20.3, with the positioning of the Toyota Tercel at the low end of the car market (with a price of $6,998) and the Porsche at the higher end (with a price of $39,850). Price-level strategies are meant to delineate the pricing position of a brand—as an economy, mid-priced, or premium-priced brand.

The tendency in recent years has been to position products as either economy or premium brands. Low-price strategies target price-elastic consumer segments. A variety of forces described at the beginning of this chapter have caused marketers to put more emphasis on low-price strategies. The increasing popularity of private brands, generics, and off-price retailers is a reflection of the price-elastic consumer market. The low-price focus has enabled the Ikea furniture chain to flourish at a time when the $30 billion home-furnishings industry was otherwise

EXHIBIT 20.3

Positioning Brands at Two Extremes of the Price Range

EXHIBIT 20.4

Prism Competes in the High Priced End of the TV Market

flat. Ikea offers stylish but low-priced items in an environment totally devoid of service. In fact, it is not uncommon for consumers to wait hours in several lines to obtain their purchases. Yet, few seem to mind when an entire living room can be furnished for about $1,000.[30]

A high-price strategy is designed to appeal to a price-inelastic segment of the market. There are several reasons why many manufacturers are choosing this course. One is that the low end is either unprofitable or filled with too many competitors. Both reasons factored into Panasonic's decision to abandon the low end of the color television industry—despite the fact it accounted for 30 percent of the company's sales—and work only on the higher end in the late 1980s. Its new line, called Prism, features televisions ranging from a 20-inch set that sells for $700 to a $4,300 51-inch projection model.[31] As a result, Panasonic now competes directly with Zenith in the high end of the television market (see Exhibit 20.4). Similarly, when Honda saw Hyundai breathing down its neck in the super-economy car market, it abdicated its position there and moved up the price ladder with its new Acura division.[32]

The purchasing power resulting from the increasing proportion of working women and the greater number of single-member households is fueling this high-price niche. New entrants such as Frusen Gladje, a super-premium ice-cream brand, can sell for double the price of a premium brand like Breyers. In the words of one supermarket manager, "It's the quality and the name. People don't care what it costs."[33]

Another reason companies follow a high-price strategy is as part of an overall marketing strategy to establish a prestige image for a brand. A higher price is consistent with the quality image established in the advertising. In a groundbreaking series of ads run in 1992 by the high-fashion clothing designer Donna Karan, a

EXHIBIT 20.5

A Quality Image Associated with a High Price

woman is shown running for the office of president of the United States. As shown in Exhibit 20.5, the ads picture the woman on the campaign trail, in her office, and being sworn in. Nowhere is price alluded to. In fact, even the name Donna Karan is mentioned in only one panel of the series. It is all designed to highlight the exclusivity of her line and the powerful people who purchase it.

One peculiarity of pricing prestige products is that if the price is set too low, demand may actually decrease, because price falls below the consumer's acceptable price range. This is illustrated by the backward-bending demand curve in Figure

20.5. If, for example, the price of a Jaguar was set at $30,000 instead of its normal $45,000 to $75,000 range, buyers might feel it had lost its prestige value and might look for another car that had status and prestige at higher prices. Marketers of prestige products want to price above the point at which demand decreases if price goes down. (This would be at a point at $40,000 in Figure 20.5.) Backward-bending demand curves are common for prestige products such as designer clothes, yachts, or luxury cars.

PRICE STABILITY VERSUS CHANGE

Another major pricing decision for existing products is whether prices should be changed from current levels or remain stable.

STRATEGIES FOR PRICE STABILITY Some industries try to maintain *price stability* to avoid *price wars.* Price wars are likely to occur in industries with standardized products such as gasoline. Since there is little difference among brands, a decrease in price will attract a large number of customers and force other companies to match the decrease. Some companies may retaliate by decreasing prices even further, thus setting off a price war. In such a war, the smaller and weaker companies are forced out of the industry, leaving a few, large manufacturers to control prices.

Historically, this type of situation has produced a **price leader;** *that is, a company that tacitly sets a price that every other company follows.* Having a price leader avoids price wars, since companies in the industry accept the principle that only the leader will change prices. U.S. Steel (now USX), Alcoa, Owens-Illinois, and Dow Chemical assumed price leadership in the steel, aluminum, glass container, and chemical industries to achieve price stability. However, today, many industries can no longer maintain price stability because of foreign competitors coming in with lower prices. As a result, USX and Owens-Illinois are no longer price leaders in their industry.

FIGURE 20.5

Demand Curve for a Prestige Product

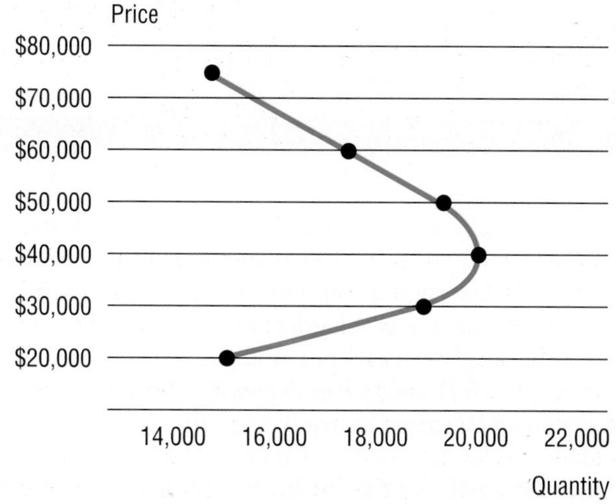

GLOBAL MARKETING STRATEGIES

Pricing Strategy: How Japan's Carmakers Are Going for the Hearts and Wallets of American Luxury-Car Buyers

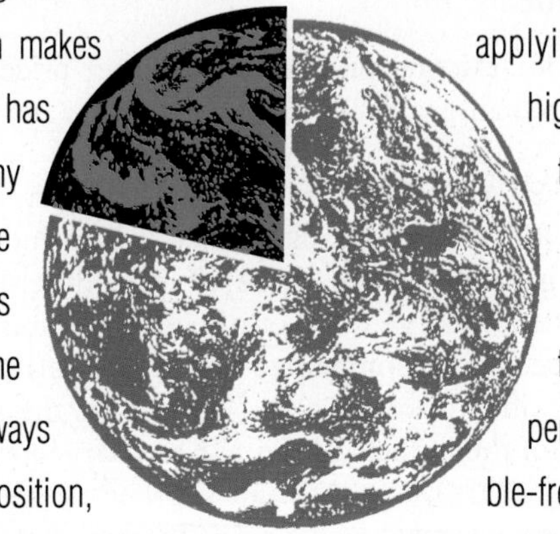

In the offices of Detroit's battered automakers, an idea is making the rounds that could transform the way Motown makes cars. It posits that since America has already lost the battle over economy cars to the Japanese, the Big Three should get out of that business and concentrate on producing the roomy luxury cars they have always made best. It is an alluring proposition, but it is no longer viable because by combining exceptional quality, service, and price, the Japanese automakers are waging a no-holds-barred war for the hearts and wallets of America's luxury car buyers—and they are winning.

In Detroit's heyday, companies like General Motors followed a simple formula: The young adults who bought Chevrolets would ultimately grow up to buy Pontiacs, Oldsmobiles, Buicks, and then Cadillacs. Today, the Japanese are following a similar strategy. Toyota, Nissan, and Honda spent the 1970s and 1980s learning how to build cheap and dependable economy cars that suited American tastes. Now that their customers are aging, the Japanese are applying the same principals to their high-end cars. "They have redefined the meaning of luxury," one Chrysler executive said recently. "Their cars are not ultracomfortable, ultrafast, or ultracostly, but they have perfect manners: They are totally trouble-free."

Because of that, Japanese nameplates adorned 14 percent of the upscale autos sold in the United States at the end of 1990, and the numbers are growing. Part of what allows the Japanese to price so aggressively is their edge in productivity. It takes significantly less time for them to assemble a car compared to American companies, and they spend $10 an hour less per worker doing it. Consider the $31,000 Mitsubishi 3000GT VR-4 made in Japan and marketed by Dodge as the Stealth. Even though it is loaded with features, it sells for $6,000 less than its prime U.S. rival—the Corvette. Similarly, after

Attempts at price stability are not limited to industries with standardized products. Some candy-bar manufacturers have maintained prices by changing the size of their bars. M&M/Mars engineered a disguised price cut by increasing the weight of its bars without changing the price. Its purpose was to gain a competitive advantage, which it held for two years before finally increasing its prices.[34] On the other side of the coin, McDonald's has decreased the size of its hamburgers to avoid price hikes due to increased costs.

STRATEGIES FOR PRICE CHANGE Companies may also try to increase or decrease prices for existing products as a part of their strategy. Companies have

GLOBAL MARKETING STRATEGIES

only 14 months on the market, Toyota's $44,000 Lexus LS400 managed to outsell competing models from Mercedes-Benz, BMW, and Ford-owned Jaguar.

Detroit has tried competing by dressing up the cars it already has in production. Chrysler, for instance, gave birth to the $26,000 Imperial in 1990 by stretching the wheelbase of its $15,000 Dodge Dynasty and embellishing its interior. Even though first-year sales were encouraging, demand for such models are not expected to grow significantly. Why? Because big V-8-powered cars do not appeal to drivers who have learned to drive on small Toyotas and Hondas.

The inevitable march of the Japanese through Detroit's last car stronghold has created some ill will between the nations. After President George Bush traveled to Tokyo in 1991 and failed to win voluntary quotas, a wave of protectionist feeling swept the United States. The fact remains, however, that consumers buy on the basis of price and quality, and the Japanese are masters of both. Considering that two million luxury cars will be available by 1995—about 400,000 more than the market can absorb—Detroit does not have much time to fight back.

Questions: What competitive advantages do Japanese car manufacturers have over American producers in the luxury-car market? What advantages do American car makers have over the Japanese?

Sources: "New Luxury Cars," *Fortune*, July 2, 1990, pp. 59–65; "Can American Cars Come Back?" *Fortune*, February 26, 1990, pp. 62–65; "The Final Battle," *Tokyo Business Today*, February 1990, pp. 27–31; "Why Toyota Keeps Getting Better and Better and Better," *Fortune*, November 19, 1990, pp. 66–79.

increased prices as a result of (1) increases in raw material and labor costs or (2) a change in the quality and features of their product. It was an increase in raw material costs that prompted coffee companies to increase their prices in the mid 1970s. In contrast, M&M/Mars increased its prices based on a change in product features. When the company increased the weight of its candy bars, it waited two years before increasing price by five cents a bar. Retailers welcomed the increase and reacted by increasing the price of all their candy bars by five cents. As a result, other manufacturers had no choice but to follow Mars' price increase.[35]

Price decreases can also be part of a pricing strategy. One reason to reduce prices is to cover overhead when plant capacity is not being fully utilized. The reduced price causes an increase in volume, which covers overhead (fixed costs). This principle of reducing price so as to use capacity and make a contribution to overhead is well illustrated in airline pricing. If airlines charge regular fares, many of their planes will have empty seats. An empty seat is a lost seat. As long as the airlines can cover the variable cost involved in filling an additional seat (personnel and handling costs for the customer's tickets and baggage), it pays to reduce the price to fill the seat. Any price above its variable costs will contribute to paying off the cost and maintenance of the plane. That is why airlines reduce their fares substantially for standby travelers.

Other firms reduce price because they have been able to reduce costs and hope to gain a competitive advantage by passing the savings to the consumer. A third reason companies reduce price is as a reactive strategy to a competitive move rather than as a proactive strategy to gain competitive advantage. Major airlines such as American and TWA followed Continental's lead by reducing prices on most of their routes. Similarly, Compaq reacted to a price assault by IBM on its feature-rich computers by slashing prices by up to 25 percent.[36]

A fourth reason to reduce prices is in reaction to a change in the marketing environment, such as an economic downturn. When Polaroid wanted to bolster sales of its OneStep Flash camera during the 1990–92 recession, it dropped the price to $30 from its $35 to $40 range. The result was a 46 percent rise in OneStep sales over the year before and—surprisingly—growth in Polaroid's other lines as well.[37]

STRATEGIES FOR PRICING NEW PRODUCTS

Developing a price for a new product is difficult, since managers have little basis for assessing consumer demand. The more innovative the product, the more difficult it is to assess consumer reactions to price prior to market introduction. As we have seen in Chapter 11, two types of strategies used in pricing new products are skimming strategies and penetration strategies.

In a **skimming strategy**, *the price is set high, with the idea of possibly reducing it as competitors begin to enter the market.* A skimming strategy works best if demand for the new product is inelastic and if the company has patent protection. When Polaroid first introduced its instant cameras and film, it could do so at a high price because of the uniqueness of the product. Interested consumers were insensitive to the price, and Polaroid had patent protection. Over time, as the product was adopted on a more widespread basis, Polaroid developed a fuller product line by introducing less-expensive cameras positioned to a broader segment of the market while maintaining the positioning of its more-expensive cameras to quality-oriented camera buffs.

In a **penetration strategy**, *a company prices a new product at a low price to deter competitive entry.* This makes sense if the company has no patent protection and the demand for the product is elastic. Bausch & Lomb followed a penetration strategy when it introduced soft contact lenses in the early 1970s. It priced aggressively with a price 50 percent below the industry norm. When its chief competitor, Cooper-Vision, retaliated by lowering the prices on its lenses, Bausch & Lomb lowered prices even further, to $10 to $15.[38]

STRATEGIES FOR PRICING PRODUCT LINES

Companies set prices for product lines by using a strategy of **price lining,** *that is, marketing products in the line to different segments at specific price points.* A firm can create more profits by offering products to different segments depending on their price sensitivity, compared to offering a product at a single price. In following such

EXHIBIT 20.6

Lorus Competes with Swatch's Chrono at the Low End of the Price Line

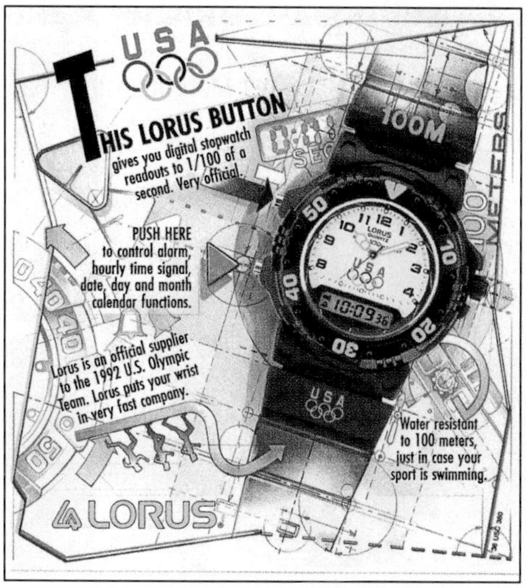

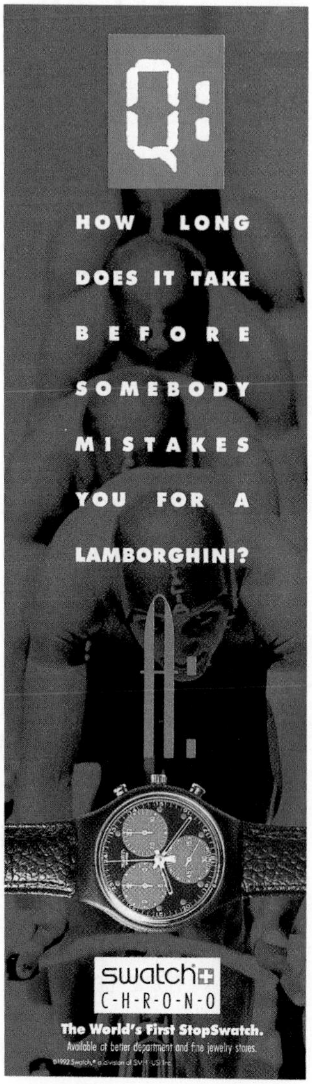

a strategy, the company is covering the demand curve by marketing products to appeal to economy-minded customers, customers at the mid-price level, and customers interested in prestige products. Each product is aimed at a segment with a different price elasticity. For example, Seiko offers a low-priced Lorus line of watches at about $50, a mid-priced line at $250, and a high-priced Lassale line at $1,000 or more. In targeting these prices to different segments of the market, Seiko is assuming that these are logical price points and that additional offerings at intermediate price ranges will not increase profits. Offering a watch at a price of $400 is unlikely to get the $250 consumers to trade up or the $1,000 consumers to trade down.

Price lining is an important strategic tool. Seiko's price lining strategy is meant to fend off advances from interlopers on both the high and low end. The company's line was designed to attack the status-oriented offerings of Rolex and Patek-Phillippe at the high end, while its Lorus line was designed to go head-to-head with Swatch's Chrono line at the low end (see Exhibit 20.6). Seiko's purpose is to give consumers more choices at different price levels in the hope that many of them will trade up to more expensive watches.[39]

ETHICS AND REGULATIONS IN PRICING

Pricing practices are regulated by the government more forcefully than other areas of the marketing mix (such as personal selling, distribution, or even advertising) because pricing illegalities are made explicit in acts such as the Sherman Act, the FTC Act, and the Robinson-Patman Act (see Chapter 4). Four areas of pricing are considered unethical and illegal: Deceptive pricing, unfair pricing, discriminatory pricing, and price fixing.

Deceptive prices *are those meant to deceive customers and to take unfair advantage of them.* They are illegal under the Federal Trade Commission (FTC) Act. One

ETHICAL AND ENVIRONMENTAL ISSUES IN MARKETING

At Craftmatic, One Man's Upselling Is Another's Bait-and-Switch

Stanley Kraftsow calls it "upselling," that is, encouraging consumers to consider a higher-priced product. His critics call it the bait-and-switch. What's all the fuss about? Beds. More precisely, the $400 Craftmatic adjustable bed that Kraftsow features in his ubiquitous late-night ads.

"If you wake up in the morning tired and aching, suffering from flat-bed-caused aches and pains, then you need a Craftmatic," they begin, going on to promise hospital-quality at a cost "hundreds less than . . . quality flat beds." Then the price of $400 flashes across the screen as does a toll-free number. It all seems simple and straightforward—until the viewer phones for a brochure. Within days of receiving the brochure, the prospective customer also receives an endless stream of calls from operators plugging for an in-home appointment with a salesperson. Those who agree get more than they bargained for. They get to see the Kraftsow "upsell" first hand, and very often, it is a costly show.

According to two former salespeople who spoke to *Forbes* magazine in 1990, sales representatives are taught to walk into a customer's house with a beeper that they activate, pretending it is a call from the office. Before answering it, they give the salespitch, showing a 15-minute videotape about the bed and quizzing the customer about his or her medical problems. "Then you hit 'em with the price," the ex-salesman told *Forbes*. It is not the $400 price they are expecting, however. It is $4,500.

The roller coaster thus begins.

The salesperson gradually drops the price to about $3,800, and if the customer still has not bitten, he begins packing his bags. But before he gets out the door, he asks to return the "page" he received

type of deceptive pricing, **bait-and-switch pricing,** *is a low-price offer intended to lure customers into a store, where a salesperson tries to influence them to buy a higher-priced item.* Another deceptive practice is to offer a discount off an inflated price. Since the price is inflated, the consumer is not actually getting a discount.

Unfair pricing *uses pricing practices to drive competitors out of business.* Predatory pricing is the most apparent of these practices. **Predatory pricing** *is decreasing prices below cost to drive competitors out of the market.* When competitors are driven out, the company then raises prices back to their former level. The Sherman Act prohibits such practices. The FTC brought action against General Foods for predatory pricing in 1976. It claimed that GF priced its Maxwell House coffee too low in an attempt to drive competitors like Folgers out of areas where it was the market leader. General Foods claimed that it was competing in good faith against

ETHICAL AND ENVIRONMENTAL ISSUES IN MARKETING

earlier. The call turns out to be from a phantom "Mr. Smith." "What is it?" the salesperson asks into the phone, loud enough to be heard. "You need another testimonial letter?" At that point, he turns to his hosts and asks if they would be willing to write a letter singing the praises of the bed he has been trying to sell them. The hook is that he claims his boss has authorized him to sell them the bed for $3,000 if they help.

By then, the customer is probably wondering what is going on. According to *Forbes*, the salesperson then dials his office again and puts his hosts on the phone with the so-called Mr. Smith, who begins knocking down the price for their "help" in providing a testimonial. How far will Mr. Smith drop his price? Down to $1,800.

Such tactics have led Craftmatic into seven separate consent agreements with state attorneys general, where it agreed to cease and desist its sales practices. In at least two cases, it was forced to set up a $300,000 restitution fund.

Kraftsow defends himself when talking about the latest order he has signed—one with the state of Pennsylvania. There, the company sent out 500,000 direct-mail pieces for its $400 bed, but only sold ten of them. Kraftsow insists it was not a bait-and-switch, because his salespeople never disparaged the $400 product or refused to deliver it—two key elements of the scam. "If the customer wants it, we'll deliver it. We have it in stock," Kraftsow said through his lawyer.

Perhaps he is right on a technical level, but few consumer activists would say it is the best example of an ethical pricing policy.

Questions: Was Kraftsow's sales approach "upselling" or bait-and-switch pricing? What is the distinction between the two?

Source: "Upselling," *Forbes*, January 8, 1990, pp. 70–72.

Procter & Gamble's introduction of Folgers into the eastern market.[40] Since GF did not subsequently raise prices to take unfair advantage of a strong market position, it is questionable whether the company's actions were unethical. In trying to protect General Foods' competitors, the FTC might have been encouraging higher coffee prices.

Price discrimination *is selling the same product to buyers at different prices without any cost justification.* Theoretically, price discrimination maximizes profits by enabling sellers to charge price-inelastic customers higher prices than elastic customers are charged. It can be unethical if it leads to charging similar buyers different prices for the same goods. The Robinson-Patman Act of 1936 states that price discrimination is illegal, but it makes a number of important exemptions. First, the restriction applies only to sales to organizational buyers, not to final consumers. General Motors cannot sell the same cars at different prices to its dealers, but the dealers can charge consumers different prices for the same car.

Also, the act says that price differences to similar buyers are legal if such differences have some cost justification. A manufacturer may charge a lower price to a buyer who orders a large quantity or is closer to the factory, since the seller is passing on legitimate savings to the buyer. And a seller may charge different prices for the same item to similar buyers if the seller is meeting lower prices from competitors in certain areas of the country. Finally, if sellers can show that charging different prices for the same product caused no injury to competition, they are unlikely to be prosecuted under the act.

Price fixing *is an agreement among firms in an industry to set prices at certain levels.* The Sherman Act prohibits it because such actions restrict price competition. **Horizontal price fixing** *is an agreement among competitors to fix prices at artificially high levels.* **Vertical price fixing** *is an agreement between different levels in the business chain to fix prices;* for example, an agreement between manufacturers and retailers or between manufacturers and distributors. Generally, vertical price fixing involves an agreement that the product will be sold at the manufacturer's suggested price and will not be discounted by the retailer or wholesaler.

Eight colleges and universities agreed in 1991 to stop collaborating on financial aid requests after the federal Justice Department accused them of meeting annually to discuss the applications of 10,000 students who had been accepted to more than one institution in the group. In a form of *horizontal price fixing*, the Justice Department said the gatherings violated the Sherman Act because their purpose was to illegally restrain price competition on financial aid to prospective students.[41]

Panasonic was accused of *vertical price fixing* by forcing its retailers to raise prices of its electronics products by 5 to 10 percent. Retailers who did not comply were threatened with being cut off from Panasonic products. The FTC forced Panasonic to cease the practice, to pay $16 million in rebates to consumers who were charged higher prices, and to advertise the settlement.[42]

As with other areas of the marketing mix, most firms have acted ethically in setting prices. They do not attempt to deceive customers or to use pricing actions to restrain competition. Perhaps the greatest spur to responsible pricing is competitive forces in the market place. Unless it is a monopoly, a firm charging artificially high prices will be undercut by a competitor. A firm willfully deceiving consumers through pricing actions will eventually lose out to more responsible competitors as consumers learn that they are being duped. Although government regulation is important in pricing, competitive forces are the best regulators in ensuring ethical pricing.

SUMMARY

1. **Why has price increased in importance as a component of the marketing mix?**
Several factors have led price to become a more important component of marketing strategy. First, recessions in the early 1980s and 1990s made consumers more price sensitive. Second, competition from lower-priced foreign imports has led American firms either to try to compete on a price basis, or to escape price competition by going after high-price segments. Third, companies have realized the benefits of segmenting markets by price and are offering high-, medium-, and low-priced brands in a product line. Finally, deregulation in

many industries has led to greater price competition, increasing the importance of price.

2. **How does a company go about determining prices for a product?**
A company must first establish price objectives. It must then evaluate pricing influences—in particular, cost and demand for the product. Based on this information, the company establishes pricing strategies that define the general range of prices that the company should consider. The company then determines the price level based on a demand-oriented or cost-oriented method of pricing. It then adjusts the final price to offer consumer and trade discounts. Once the price is set, it evaluates the impact on customers and competitors. In the final step of the price-setting process, the company controls prices by trying to ensure objectives are being met.

3. **How do demand and other environmental factors influence price determination?**
To set prices, marketers should know how customers react to alternative prices. Ideally, a firm will try to establish a demand curve; that is, the amount of a product consumers will purchase at various price levels. This allows marketers to determine total revenue, which information, along with costs, enables marketers to measure profits at various price levels and set the most profitable price. The demand curve also measures price sensitivity. To increase revenues, marketers can set higher prices when customers are less price sensitive and lower prices when they are more price sensitive. Marginal analysis identifies a profit-maximizing price as the point where marginal revenues of the last unit sold equal its marginal costs.
A number of environmental factors will influence these pricing decisions, such as customer price expectations, customer price–quality associations, competitive reactions to price, reactions of the trade, and economic conditions.

4. **What types of pricing strategies do companies develop for existing and new products?**
Pricing strategies for existing products focus on establishing the appropriate price level and on deciding whether to change prices from current levels or to maintain price stability. Pricing strategies for new products include skimming and penetration pricing. A skimming strategy, which sets a high initial price, is feasible if demand is inelastic or if the company has patent protection. A penetration strategy, which sets a low initial price, makes sense if demand is elastic. Pricing strategies are also developed for product lines. Various offerings in a product line target different price segments to appeal to economy-minded, mid-price, and prestige-oriented customers.

5. **What types of pricing practices are unethical, and how can they be regulated?**
Several types of pricing practices are unethical, because they either deceive the customer, are discriminatory, or restrain competition. Deceptive pricing attempts to deceive consumers as to product availability at a certain price or as to price level. Discriminatory pricing attempts to sell the same product to similar buyers based on what they are willing to pay, without any cost justification for the price difference. Pricing in restraint of trade involves agreements among competitors to set prices to discourage new entrants or to set prices below cost to drive existing competitors out.
These actions are illegal under the Sherman, FTC, and Robinson-Patman Acts. Ultimately, competitive forces act as regulators to ensure fair pricing practices, since companies that deceive customers or restrain trade are likely to lose out to companies that price according to customer benefits.

KEY TERMS

Demand curve (p. 655)
Price elasticity (p. 656)
Upside price elasticity (p. 657)
Downside price elasticity (p. 657)
Marginal analysis (p. 659)
Marginal contribution to profit (p. 660)
Acceptable price range (p. 662)
Price leader (p. 667)
Skimming strategy (p. 670)
Penetration strategy (p. 670)
Price lining (p. 670)
Deceptive pricing (p. 671)
Bait-and-switch pricing (p. 672)
Unfair pricing (p. 672)
Predatory pricing (p. 672)
Price discrimination (p. 673)
Price fixing (p. 674)
Horizontal price fixing (p. 674)
Vertical price fixing (p. 674)
Total revenue (p. 677)
Average revenue (p. 677)
Marginal revenue (p. 678)
Fixed costs (p. 678)
Variable costs (p. 678)
Total costs (p. 678)
Marginal costs (p. 678)

QUESTIONS

1. Why did price become a more important element of the marketing mix in the 1980s and 1990s? How did the increasing importance of price affect the methods used to determine price levels?
2. How can a company estimate the consumers' demand curve for a product? What are the risks of using estimates of consumer responses to various price levels as a basis for setting prices?
3. What was the rationale for the change in the pricing strategy for Apple's Macintosh computer.
4. The demand curve for the Saturn car in Figure 20.2 was cited as probably being elastic. The demand curve for the Jaguar in Figure 20.3 was cited as probably being inelastic.
   a. What does this mean? What are the implications for setting prices?
   b. What types of products are likely to have elastic demand? Inelastic demand?
5. What is the distinction between upside and downside price elasticity? Apply these concepts to the experience of coffee producers when coffee prices went way up and then came down again in the mid 1970s.
6. What principle defines the profit-maximizing price for a product? Has this principle been applied to other components of the marketing mix? How?
7. What factors have encouraged companies to follow a low-price strategy for certain products? What factors have encouraged them to follow a high-price strategy?
8. What types of industries are most likely to seek price stability? Why? Why do many of these industries have price leaders?
9. What do we mean by price lining? How can firms better maximize profits through this strategy? What are the risks in following such a strategy?
10. Cite examples of deceptive pricing practices, discriminatory pricing practices, and pricing practices in restraint of trade. How do natural market forces act to discourage these practices?

QUESTION: YOU ARE THE DECISION MAKER

A General Motors dealer, reading the section describing the demand-oriented pricing approach for the company's new Saturn line, said the following:

> *I know GM doesn't price like that. They develop a target on their investment and set a price that they think will give them enough revenue to reach the target return. Pricing based on trying to estimate the demand curve for a new car is a pretty chancy proposition. We are not dealing with a brand of cereal or toothpaste that can be test marketed to determine demand. We are dealing with a car. You might ask people whether they would buy it at a certain price; you might even ask them after they test-drive it. But what they say and do are two different things. I would take your marginal approach to pricing with a grain of salt.*

a. Do you agree with the GM dealer's assessment of using marginal analysis to determine price?
b. What might be the problem with using a cost-oriented approach like the one the dealer described?

APPENDIX

20A

BASIC DEMAND AND REVENUE CONCEPTS

TOTAL REVENUE

Total revenue (TR) *is the total amount of money received from the sale of a product.* It equals the price *(P)* times the quantity sold *(Q)*, or

$$TR = P \times Q$$

General Motors introduced its new Saturn line of low-priced subcompact cars in 1991. GM planned the introduction of the Saturn line for almost a decade. It has attempted to decrease costs of the car to a level that will enable it to compete with Japanese imports on a price basis. Assume that it introduced the car at a price of $8,500 and sold 50,000 cars. Total revenue would be $425 million ($8,500 × 50,000 cars). Sales of 80,000 cars at this price would produce a total revenue of $680 million.

AVERAGE REVENUE

Average revenue (AR) *is the average amount of money received for selling one unit of a product.* It is computed as total revenue divided by quantity, so

$$AR = TR/Q$$

The demand curve is also known as the average revenue curve since it shows the average revenue (that is, price) that is obtained at various levels of consumer demand (that is, quantity).

In the above example, the average revenue for the Saturn car at 50,000 units is $425 million/50,000 or $8,500. This is also the price of the car, so average revenue is the same as price.

Suppose GM asks consumers whether they would buy a Saturn at $8,000; $8,500; $9,000; $10,000; and $11,000. Consumer responses allow the company to estimate the quantity likely to be purchased at each price. It can then establish a demand curve for the Saturn. Let us assume that GM establishes the price–quantity relations in the first two columns of Table 20.2. The resulting demand curve is shown as Curve D in Figure 20.2 in the chapter.

TABLE 20.2

Revenue Information from Demand Curve for Saturn Car

PRICE	QUANTITY	TOTAL REVENUE (in Millions) *[P × Q]*	CHANGE IN QUANTITY	CHANGE IN TOTAL REVENUE (in Millions)	MARGINAL REVENUE [Change in *TR*/ Change in *Q*]
$11,000	30,000	$330	—	—	—
$10,000	50,000	$500	20,000	$170	$8,500
$ 9,000	80,000	$720	30,000	$220	$7,330
$ 8,500	87,000	$740	7,000	$ 20	$2,860
$ 8,000	95,000	$760	8,000	$ 20	$2,500

MARGINAL REVENUE

Marginal revenue (MR) *is the change in total revenue (ΔTR) obtained by selling an additional unit of a product (ΔQ).* Therefore, MR = $\Delta TR/\Delta Q$.

In the Saturn example, Table 20.2 shows that a cut in price from $10,000 to $9,000 would result in sales of an additional 30,000 units. The total revenue at $10,000 is $500 million, and at $9,000 it is $720 million. So ΔTR is $220 million, and ΔQ is 30,000. As a result, if 80,000 units are sold, then

$$MR = \$220 \text{ million}/30{,}000 \text{ units} = \$7{,}330$$

The $7,330 in marginal revenue is the revenue derived from selling car number 80,001.

APPENDIX 20B

BASIC COST CONCEPTS

FIXED COSTS

Fixed costs *are expenses that are constant regardless of the quantity produced.* For example, the cost of constructing a plant is fixed, regardless of the quantity produced in the plant.

VARIABLE COSTS

Variable costs *are costs that vary directly with the amount produced.* They include the cost of labor and raw materials used to make the product, plus the cost of distribution and personal selling. *Average variable costs (AVC)* are the variable costs in producing one unit of a product at a certain quantity. *Total variable costs* are average variable costs times the quantity produced; that is,

$$TVC = AVC \times Q$$

TOTAL COSTS

Total costs (TC) *are the total expenses incurred in producing and marketing a product.* Total costs are the sum of *total fixed costs (TFC)* and *total variable costs (TVC)*; therefore,

$$TC = TFC + TVC$$

MARGINAL COST

Marginal cost (MC) *is the changes in total costs (ΔTC) that result in producing and marketing an additional unit of a product (ΔQ).* Therefore,

$$MC = \Delta TC/\Delta Q$$

TABLE 20.3

Cost Factors in Producing the Saturn Car

AVERAGE COST PER UNIT *[AVC]*		QUANTITY *[Q]*		TOTAL VARIABLE COSTS *[TVC]*		TOTAL FIXED COSTS *[TFC]* (in Millions of Dollars)		TOTAL COSTS *[TC]*	CHANGE IN *Q*	CHANGE IN *TC* (in Millions)	MARGINAL COST [Change in *TC*/ Change in *Q*]
\$7,000	×	30,000	=	\$210	+	\$200	=	\$410	—	—	—
\$6,000	×	50,000	=	\$300	+	\$200	=	\$500	20,000	90	\$4,500
\$5,000	×	80,000	=	\$400	+	\$200	=	\$600	30,000	100	\$3,300
\$4,800	×	87,000	=	\$418	+	\$200	=	\$618	7,000	18	\$2,570
\$4,700	×	95,000	=	\$446	+	\$200	=	\$646	8,000	28	\$3,500

COST INTERRELATIONSHIPS

The interrelationships between these costs are demonstrated in Table 20.3. Assume that the fixed costs in establishing the production facilities for the Saturn are \$200 million. At 30,000 units of production, average variable costs (*AVC*, that is, the variable costs in producing one unit of a product) are \$7,000 per car. Total variable costs would be \$210 million (\$7,000 × 30,000 units). Total costs would be \$410 million (total variable costs plus total fixed costs).

Note that as more cars are produced, average variable costs per unit go down. This is because the company is achieving economies of scale in production. If GM can lower average variable costs sufficiently through better production methods, it can follow a low-price strategy to compete more effectively.

Table 20.3 also shows marginal costs decreasing until the company produces 87,000 cars. By the time 87,000 units are produced, it costs only an additional \$2,570 to produce the 87,001 unit. At this point, marginal costs begin to rise, possibly because the company is coming close to reaching its full production capacity.

CHAPTER 21

Pricing Methods

YOUR FOCUS IN CHAPTER 21

To learn:

- *How companies use cost-, demand-, and competition-oriented methods to set price.*
- *How companies adjust the final price.*
- *How they evaluate and control prices.*
- *What pricing methods are used for services and for industrial products.*

General Motors: The Pricing Pitfalls of Being the High-Cost Producer

General Motors, the world's largest industrial company, is in deep trouble. Its market share went from 45 percent in 1981 to 35 percent in 1991 in an industry where each share point represents about $2 billion in revenue.[1] In 1991, GM lost an average of $1,500 on each of the more than 3.5 million cars and trucks it made in North America, a total loss of over $5 billion. To try to stem the tide, the company announced it would close six assembly plants and fifteen factories and lay off 74,000 workers by 1995 to reduce capacity by one-sixth.[2] The cuts were a a stark admission that the company did not expect to quickly recapture market share.

What does GM's troubles have to do with pricing? A lot. GM is the highest-cost producer in the industry. Its cars each cost $200 to $300 more to build than the average Ford and $750 more than the average Japanese car.[3] The problem is that GM prices on a cost-oriented basis. It starts out by designing a car for a particular target segment, checking on competitive prices, and making a rough estimate of the volume that it can sell. The company then estimates its fixed and variable costs per unit at this volume level and adds a certain profit margin to determine the price. It then evaluates the market to determine whether consumers are likely to buy the projected volume at the proposed price. If it appears the price is too high to achieve the target return, the company can either try to cut costs or withdraw the model.[4]

Pontiac Firebird and Chevrolet Camaro Z28

As the high-cost producer, GM has two options, neither of which are particularly desirable: set prices above those of competitors or hold the line on price and see profit margins shrink. An additional problem with GM's cost-oriented pricing approach is that it does not take account of the consumer's response to price. When GM recently announced a 5-percent average price hike based on increased costs, one industry analyst summarized the problem succinctly:

> *Customers don't care a lot about a company's costs. If prices were set by the relative value of the product offered to the customer, then costs could follow price . . . rather than the other way around.*[5]

In other words, if price is based on consumer demand, then the next step is to determine whether costs permit the company to produce the product profitably at the proposed price. This is what the executive means by costs following price. But GM was letting price follow costs.

How did GM wind up being the high-cost producer in the industry? By maintaining an inefficient production base and failing to bolster the productivity of its workers. Rather than accept methods shown by Japanese manufacturers to increase productivity, such as giving workers on the assembly lines direct responsibility for quality control, the company continued to rely on a highly centralized style of management that discouraged worker initiative.

GM's attempt to become cost effective actually compounded its problems. The company realized it would have to start cutting costs to maintain its market leadership as far back as 1979. Its reaction was to try to achieve economies of scale by using common parts across divisions and centralizing car designs.[6] The attempt to avoid duplication of design and engineering across divisions blurred the historic distinctions between them. In the late 1920s, Alfred P. Sloan Jr., the founder of GM, established five divisions based on a concept of price segmentation. Moving from Chevrolet to Pontiac, Oldsmobile, Buick, and Cadillac the cars got bigger, fancier, and more expensive. In this way, a consumer could stay with GM cars for life at any socioeconomic level.

The use of common parts and designs blurred these historic distinctions. Consumers could not tell the difference between a Chevrolet and a Pontiac or an Olds and a Buick. Some Buicks even looked like Cadillacs. Consumers no longer saw the value associated with the price of a GM car just at the time when high-quality Japanese cars were being introduced at lower prices. The result? A steady and precipitous drop in market share and profits.

GM recognizes it must get its costs down to remain competitive. It is slowly changing from its centralized, autocratic approach in an attempt to improve worker productivity. One result is that the quality of GM cars has improved significantly as measured by defects per car. In addition, GM's new Saturn car was produced by relying on cost-saving quality-control techniques based on worker initiative.

There are even signs that GM may be switching to a more consumer-oriented basis for pricing. The company set the price for the Saturn by first considering at what price level consumers would consider the car to be competitive with lower priced imports such as the Toyota Tercel, Nissan Sentra, or Honda Civic.[7] Having decided the proper price would be approximately $8,000, the company then worked back and determined the production and design costs required to produce the car at that price. It designed its Saturn plant accordingly. In other words, Saturn's price level was set by letting costs follow price.

If this is a trend, there is hope for GM in the future.

DETERMINING THE FINAL PRICE

In Chapter 20, we saw how marketers set the groundwork for determining prices by defining objectives; estimating consumer demand, costs, and profits; and then developing pricing strategies. In this chapter, we continue to focus on the process of determining a particular price for a product. We will now consider the shaded areas shown in Figure 20.1, namely alternative approaches marketers use to determine the final price, the adjustments they make to this price, and how they evaluate and control pricing actions.

In this section, we will describe three methods of setting prices (see Figure 21.1). *Cost-oriented* methods determine a product's costs and then add a percentage markup or target return on profits to determine price. *Demand-oriented* methods first determine consumer demand at various price levels and set prices at the level that optimizes profits. *Competition-oriented* methods set prices based on what the competition does, often following competitors in their pricing strategies or setting prices a certain percentage above or below competitors' prices.

COST-ORIENTED PRICING METHODS

As Figure 21.1 suggests, cost-oriented pricing methods are the most widely used. There are several reasons. First, they are simple. Costs are determined and a certain margin or target return is added on. Second, cost-oriented pricing methods are less risky, because they are based on a known factor, costs. The alternative—to base prices on consumer demand—creates more uncertainties, because demand forecasts are often unreliable. Third, cost-oriented methods tend to lead to more-stable prices over time, because prices are set based on factors internal to the company, such as labor costs and availability of raw materials.

FIGURE 21.1

Methods of Price Determination

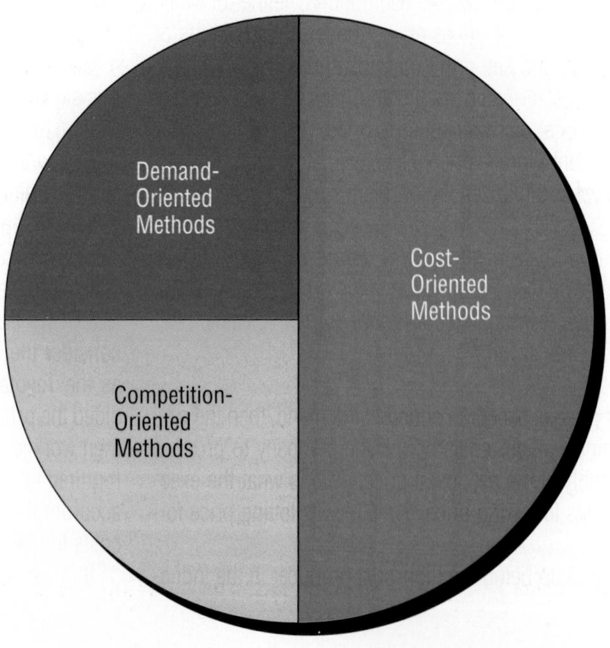

But these advantages also suggest the basic limitation of cost-oriented methods, namely that in ignoring consumer demand they may be setting prices at unrealistic levels. In setting prices based on costs alone, a high-cost manufacturer may be pricing its goods out of the market. Conversely, a low-cost manufacturer may be pricing at levels well below what consumers are willing to pay. As the high-cost producer in automobiles, General Motors' cost-based pricing has placed it at a competitive disadvantage.

Cost-based methods work reasonably well only in industries where consumer demand and competition are stable. In these cases, companies can price based on cost because consumer demand and competitive responses are determinate.

Two cost-oriented pricing methods are used most widely, cost-plus pricing and target-return pricing.

COST-PLUS PRICING

In **cost-plus pricing**, *the marketer determines the unit costs for producing an item (variable and fixed costs per unit) and adds a margin to meet a profit objective.* Assume that a firm decides to introduce a superpremium brand of ice cream and prices it on a cost-plus basis. It determines its variable costs for producing the superpremium brand (primarily raw materials and labor) at \$1.50 per pint. It assumes that variable costs will not change much as a function of quantity, because it anticipates few improvements in productivity or other labor efficiencies as volume increases.

The company determines that fixed costs (cost of plant and machinery and administrative costs) are approximately 30 percent of variable costs, or 45 cents per unit. Its profit objective is to achieve a 20 percent return on variable costs, or 30 cents per unit (\$1.50 × 20%). On this basis, it computes price as

Variable costs per unit	\$1.50
Fixed costs per unit (30% of variable costs)	.45
Profit margin (20% of variable costs)	.30
Price per pint of ice cream	\$2.25

The price of \$2.25 is what the company charges retailers for its ice cream. Now assume that a retailer also uses a cost-plus approach in determining the price it will sell to final consumers. In most cases, retailers will determine price based on a **markup**, *that is, a profit margin based on the final selling price rather than the total cost of the item.* Assume a retailer marks up the ice cream by 25 percent. The final selling price that will give the retailer a profit margin of 25 percent can be computed as follows:

$$\text{Retail Selling Price} = \frac{\text{Average Cost of the Unit}}{1 - \text{Desired Margin}}$$

In our example, this would be:

$$\text{Retail Selling Price} = \frac{\$2.25}{1 - .25} = \$3.00$$

The final selling price to the customer would thus be \$3.00 based on the retailer's margin of 75 cents.

As noted, the problem with a cost-plus or markup approach is that there is no guarantee it will produce a final price in line with what consumers are willing to pay. Consumer responses to price never enter into the decision. Further, a company following a cost-plus approach may price itself out of the market if its costs are higher than those of competitors.

TARGET-RETURN PRICING

Many firms set a target return on their investment or on costs and then price to achieve this target. **Target-return pricing** *determines the price that will achieve a profit target at a specified volume level.* In contrast, cost-plus pricing determines price by tacking a fixed profit margin onto costs regardless of volume.

There are two types of target-return pricing: *target return on investment* and *target return on costs.* **Target return on investment** *establishes a return on investment (ROI) objective and prices to meet it.* Suppose the ice cream producer's initial investment to establish the business and manufacturing plant was $500,000. The company sets an ROI objective of 10 percent, because this is the best return it could expect if it were to put its $500,000 in some other investment such as government bonds. The company's profit objective in the first year of operation is therefore $50,000.

Assume projected sales of the superpremium ice cream is 100,000 units. We noted previously that variable costs in producing the ice cream are $1.50 per unit, and fixed costs are 45 cents per unit. So total costs are $195,000:

$$[\$1.50 + .45] \times 100{,}000 \text{ units} = \$195{,}000$$

With a profit goal of $50,000, we can find the price that will achieve that goal as follows:

$$\text{Price} = \frac{\$50{,}000 \text{ (Profits)} + \$195{,}000 \text{ (Costs)}}{100{,}000 \text{ units}} = \$2.45$$

A price of $2.45 will achieve a profit goal of $50,000 if 100,000 units of ice cream are sold. However, this approach does not tell us whether consumers will actually buy 100,000 units of the ice cream at $2.45.

A firm can also determine price based on a **target return on cost** *that establishes an objective based on return on total costs at a specified volume level and the price required to meet it.* This is the method the American auto companies generally use. An example for pricing a compact is shown in Table 21.1. Variable costs, including raw materials and labor (vehicle assembly), total $3,974. Fixed costs are estimated at 40 percent of variable costs, or $1,590. The profit target is 10 percent of total costs, or $556 (10% of $3,974 + $1,590). Additional unallocated costs (research and development, tooling) are $2,472. The sales price to the auto dealer totals $8,592. The dealer's markup of 22 percent would result in a final price of $11,016, but the company might decide to list the car for $10,995 for promotional purposes.

COST-ORIENTED PRICING IN INTERNATIONAL MARKETS

Most international marketers first entering a foreign market use cost-oriented pricing methods, because they have insufficient information to estimate consumer

TABLE 21.1

Pricing by Target Return on Cost in the Auto Industry

ASSEMBLY PLANT		CORPORATE HEADQUARTERS		DEALER SHOWROOM	
Body	$1,104	Total variable cost (TVC)	$3,974	Cost to dealer	$ 8,592
Transmission	$ 180	Fixed costs (TFC): 40% of TVC	$1,590	Dealer markup (22%)	$ 2,424
Engine	$ 622				
Chassis	$1,002	Profit target: (10% of TFC + TVC)	$ 556		
Vehicle assembly	$1,066	R&D, special tooling	$2,472		
Total variable costs	$3,974	Total cost to dealer	$8,592	List price	$11,016

Source: Adapted from "Why Detroit Can't Cut Prices," *Business Week,* March 1, 1982. Costs adjusted to reflect 1992 prices.

demand or competitive responses.[8] These marketers tend to use two pricing strategies. The first is to set prices based on the marketer's total cost. However, exporters often run into problems using a cost-plus approach, because their distribution and transportation costs are higher than those of domestic companies, resulting in a higher price than that of domestic products.

As a result, many international marketers set prices lower than their costs so as to establish themselves in foreign markets. Such a practice is known as **price dumping,** *that is, selling a product below the cost of production to stimulate sales in foreign markets.* If the product is accepted at lower prices, the marketer can eventually raise the price and make a profit. The objective of the foreign entrant may be not only to gain entry, but to drive out weaker domestic producers and dominate the market. This occurred when Japanese electronics companies entered the U.S. market with lower-priced televisions in the 1970s and eventually drove most domestic manufacturers out of business. These actions prompted Zenith to bring suit against Matsushita and other Japanese television manufacturers for unfairly agreeing to sell in the U.S. market at lower prices to drive out domestic companies. The Supreme Court dismissed the suit in 1986 for lack of evidence.[9]

As this case illustrates, price dumping has become a sore spot in Japanese–American trade relations because of charges by American manufacturers that Japanese companies have entered the market with lower-priced goods to drive domestic companies out of business and dominate the market (see Global Marketing box).

Another, less common, reason for price dumping is to get rid of excess inventory at home. A foreign firm might find itself with an excess supply of goods that can not be sold in the domestic market and will look abroad to "dump" them at lower prices. Selling below cost is economical because the firm is still contributing to its overhead by reducing inventory, but such pricing actions have led to charges of a "beggar thy neighbor policy." That is, when a company sells at a lower price abroad because of weakness in its home markets, it is exporting that weakness by undermining the profitability of foreign firms.

GLOBAL MARKETING STRATEGIES

Price Dumping: A Japanese–American Issue in Trade Relations

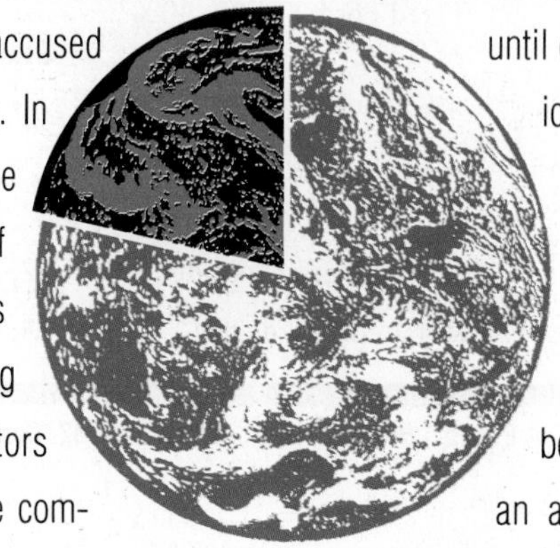

Price dumping has become a sore spot in Japanese–American trade relations. Several American industries have accused Japanese firms of price dumping. In the best known case, three of the largest American producers of semiconductors brought charges against Japanese firms for selling memory chips and semiconductors below the cost of production. The companies charged that the Japanese firms' intent was to drive American producers from the market. In an attempt to improve the trading climate with the United States, the Japanese government agreed to stop Japanese semiconductor firms from selling below costs and to open their markets to American producers of semiconductors.

Because the agreement was not carried out, President Reagan imposed $300 million in trade sanctions against Japanese semiconductor producers in 1987 and ordered tariffs on certain types of memory chips. The sanctions and tariffs will remain in effect until dumping stops and access for American manufacturers improves.

In a 1991 case, GM, Ford, and Chrysler charged Japanese carmakers with dumping minivans in the United States by selling them below production costs. As proof of an attempt to drive domestic minivan producers from the market, the companies cited a 20-percent decline in sales of domestically produced minivans from 1990 to 1991 while the sale of Japanese-produced minivans doubled. Toyota and Mazda were named as the worst offenders for selling their minivans for up to 30 percent less than what was regarded as fair value. The case is under review by the International Trade Commission.

In a third case, domestic auto parts makers accused Japanese companies in 1991 of dumping auto

DEMAND-ORIENTED PRICING METHODS

Demand-oriented methods base price on what consumers are willing to buy at various price levels: That is, price is based on the consumers' demand curve. Marketers are paying more attention to demand-oriented pricing because cost-oriented methods are too rigid for the competitive environment of the 1990s. If costs are stable, a company's prices are stable; if costs go up, its prices go up; but price changes are not in response to customer demand or competition.

The need for greater price flexibility has increased because of the greater price sensitivity of American consumers as a result of deep recessions in the early 1980s and 1990s. The availability of high-quality foreign goods at lower prices also made marketers aware that they would have to compete with foreign companies by providing the same value to consumers, dollar for dollar.

There are three demand-oriented pricing methods from which to choose: mar-

GLOBAL MARKETING STRATEGIES

supplies in the United States. This case is particularly important because car parts bought from Japan represented one-fourth of the $41 billion trade deficit with that country in 1991. Widespread dumping by Japanese suppliers would worsen the trade deficit and weaken the American economy. As proof of their dumping charge, American companies cite Japanese statistics showing that car parts in Japan are from four to eight times more expensive than Japanese parts sold in the United States.

Mazda MPV

The issue of price dumping has clearly aggravated trade relations between the United States and Japan. Some feel Japanese companies are being charged unfairly because they are promoting healthy price competition in the United States, and it is in the consumer's interest to encourage lower prices. Others feel that price dumping by Japanese firms could drive out domestic companies, leading to a weaker American economy.

Questions: Why do companies engage in price dumping? Can price dumping be justified as a legitimate pricing strategy? Why or why not?

Sources: Andrew R. Dick, "Learning by Doing and Dumping in the Semiconductor Industry," *Journal of Law and Economics* (April 1991), pp. 133–159; Jan Mares, "The Semiconductor Agreements: A Glance Back, a Look Ahead," *Business America*, August 15, 1988, pp. 8–11; "The Ambush Awaiting Japan," *Economist*, July 6, 1991, pp. 67–68; "Big 3's Complaint on Japan Minivans Is Upheld by ITC," *Wall Street Journal*, July 11, 1991, p. A3.

ginal pricing and flexible break-even pricing, which rely on an estimate of the demand curve, and demand-backward pricing, which does not.

MARGINAL PRICING

Marginal pricing *requires the marketer to change price up to the point where marginal revenue equals marginal cost.* If demand is inelastic, prices will increase to reach this point; if it is elastic, prices will decrease.

The principle is illustrated using the example of the Saturn in Figure 21.2. In our previous example, GM determined that the point at which marginal revenues equal marginal cost for the last unit produced is at about 87,000 units. This is the point where the marginal revenue and cost curves intersect (point x in the figure).

FIGURE 21.2

Marginal Pricing

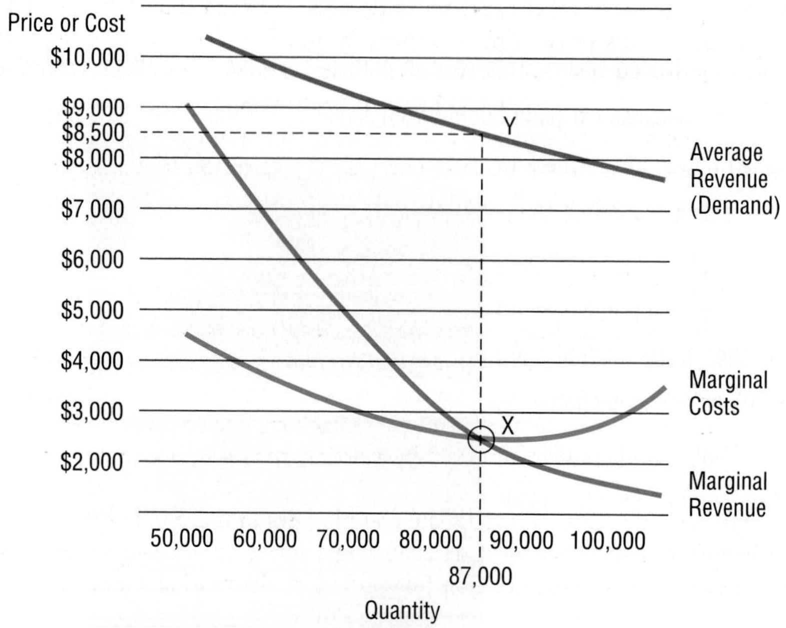

But how does GM know what price to charge at that point? By referring to the demand curve. The demand curve in Figure 21.2 (we have seen in the addendum to Chapter 20 that this is the same as the *average revenue curve*) shows that consumers are willing to buy 87,000 units at a price of $8,500. This is determined by identifying the intersection of the marginal revenue and cost curves, then extending a line up to the average revenue (that is, *demand*) curve (point *y* in the figure). At that point, the profit-maximizing price is $8,500.

Marginal pricing identifies the profit-maximizing price, but it requires estimating the demand curve. The difficulty in determining how much consumers are willing to buy at various price levels is the main reason that marginal pricing is not used more widely.

FLEXIBLE BREAK-EVEN PRICING

In **flexible break-even pricing** *price is determined by maximizing the difference between total revenue and total cost across various levels of demand.* (Since flexible break-even pricing is an offshoot of break-even analysis, it would be helpful to review the principles of *break-even analysis* described in the addendum to this chapter.) In this type of pricing, a number of alternative prices are considered, producing a different *total revenue curve* for each price. Assume that an ice cream manufacturer tests a superpremium ice cream at four prices, $1.75, $2.25, $3.00, and $3.50. Figure 21.3 shows the total revenue (price × quantity) for each price level. The area of profitability is the difference between total revenue and total cost; this is the shaded area in the figure. The marketer wants to maximize this shaded area.

Assume that the company tested each price in a test market in order to estimate demand. At a price of $3.50, demand is estimated at 100,000 units; at $1.75 it is estimated at 400,000 units. The difference between total revenues and costs at the level demanded at each price is shown by the dotted vertical line. At a price of $1.75, the company would be breaking even because total revenues equal total costs. At the other three prices, the company would be making a profit. Profits would be greatest at a price of $3.00 because the difference between total revenue and total cost is greatest at this price. This is shown by the fact that the solid vertical line is longest at a quantity of 300,000 units (the total demand at a $3.00 price level).

Because flexible break-even pricing requires estimates of consumer responses to prices, it is a demand-oriented method of pricing. It should produce results similar to those of marginal analysis, because both use the criterion of maximizing profits based on consumer demand.

DEMAND-BACKWARD PRICING

In **demand-backward pricing**, *prices are set by determining what consumers are willing to pay for an item, then deducting costs to determine if the profit margin is adequate.* This is considered estimating "backwards" because the marketer starts with a final price based on consumer demand and works backward to the profit estimate. It is more common to estimate "forward" by starting with a cost and adding a profit margin.

Demand-backward pricing avoids the complexities of marginal or flexible break-even pricing methods. Instead of determining a series of price–quantity relationships in the form of a demand curve for a product, the marketer only has to learn

FIGURE 21.3

Flexible Break-Even Pricing

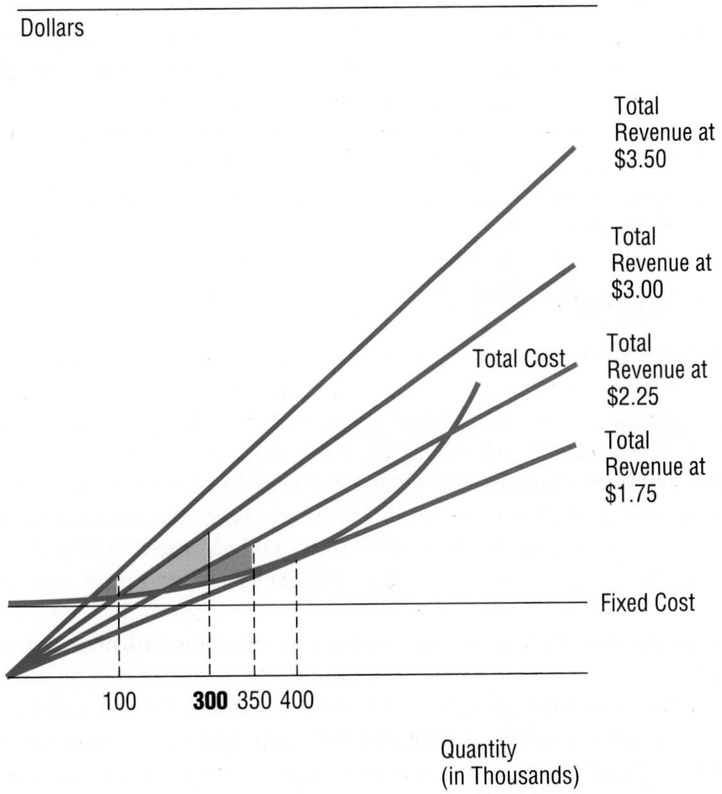

one price–quantity relationship, the price consumers are willing to pay and the estimated volume for the particular product at that price. The catch is knowing this single price.

Dell Computer, a manufacturer of IBM-compatible personal computers, used demand-backward pricing when it determined what price for its PCs would be competitive with IBM's Personal System/2 line. It knew it wanted to come in with a price under $1,000, then determined if it could do so profitably. It did, with a price of $995.

COMPETITION-ORIENTED PRICING METHODS

Some companies base their prices on what competitors do. In this case, they risk setting prices that do not take account of distinctions between their products and those of competitors. Three types of pricing methods are based on competitive actions: follow-the-leader pricing, pricing pegged to prevailing industry norms, and pricing based on projected competitive responses.

FOLLOW-THE-LEADER PRICING

A **follow-the-leader** *price strategy develops when competitors decide to follow the pricing strategy of a price leader in the industry.* As we have seen in Chapter 20, industries producing standardized products seek price stability, because price competition can lead to destructive price wars. A company emerges that is recognized by others as a price leader, and a tacit understanding develops that companies will use a follow-the-leader pricing strategy. Such pricing is most likely to occur in an **oligopoly,** *that is, an industry dominated by several large companies in which the pricing actions of one company directly affect the others.* Since products are standardized, a price reduction by one company would force others to follow, resulting in a price war. As a result, it is in the interest of companies in an oligopoly to create price stability by agreeing to follow a price leader.

Follow-the-leader pricing is less common than it once was, because the government has frowned on such methods as a form of price fixing, even when there is no overt agreement to fix prices. Also, as we have seen, greater foreign competition and consumer price sensitivity have led to a need to develop more-flexible methods of pricing.

Some industries still have price leaders, however. IBM is regarded as the undisputed price leader in computer software. One software competitor said, "IBM sets the trends we all follow." Another described a clear follow-the-leader policy: "The higher IBM's prices are, the more we can charge."[10] But IBM's prices are not followed as rigorously by competitors as Alcoa's and U.S. Steel's once were in the aluminum and steel industries.

PEGGED PRICING

A **pegged pricing** *policy establishes a company's price based on an industry norm.* Companies in an industry without a price leader might carry out such a strategy to gain price stability. Candy-bar manufacturers have tended to use such pegged pricing. They establish a price norm for an individual candy bar, and most companies stick to the norm.

Some companies use the industry norm as a baseline and price a certain percentage above or below it. This is a common practice for a company trying to establish a niche on the high or low side of the market. The marketer then works back from this premium or economy price to determine if a reasonable profit can be made.

TABLE 21.2

Determining Price Based on Estimated Competitive Responses

PRICE DECREASE FOR TREFLAN	ESTIMATED RETURN ON INVESTMENT (ROI)	PROBABILITY OF NO COMPETITIVE ENTRY AT STATED PRICE	EXPECTED ROI IF NO ENTRY (ESTIMATED ROI TIMES PROBABILITY OF NO COMPETITIVE ENTRY)
5%	15%	20%	3.0%
10%	12%	40%	4.8%
12%[a]	10%	50%	5.0%
15%	6%	80%	4.8%
20%	4%	90%	3.6%

[a]Optimal price change to maximize expected ROI

PRICING BASED ON PROJECTED RESPONSES BY COMPETITORS

Some firms set price levels based on their estimate of competitive responses to their actions. Consider the example of Eli Lilly's pricing strategy for its agricultural herbicide, Treflan. Lilly wanted to reduce prices for the product to discourage competitive entry since Treflan's patent was about to expire. The appropriate price reduction will largely depend on the likelihood of competitive entry at that price.

Assume that Lilly is considering the five price reductions for Treflan shown in Table 21.2. Return on investment falls with each price decrease: a 15 percent return on investment if the price of Treflan is reduced by 5 percent, a 12 percent ROI if price is reduced by 10 percent, and so forth. Lilly's managers estimate that there is only a 20-percent chance that competition will *not* enter the market if the price of Treflan is reduced by 5 percent, a 40-percent chance if the price is reduced by 10 percent, and so forth (column 3 in Table 21.2).

The last column weights ROI by the chance of no competitive entry. As we see, expected ROI is maximized when the price of Treflan is reduced by 12 percent. At that price reduction, *expected* ROI is 5 percent. If the price reduction is any less than 12 percent, the chance of competitive entry is too high. If the price reduction is any more than 12 percent, ROI decreases to unacceptable levels. So management decides to decrease the price by 12 percent, largely based on estimated competitive reactions to the company's price changes.

PRICE ADJUSTMENTS

The price that the marketer establishes in the previous step is the quoted or **list price,** *that is, the company's "official" price subject to discounts.* This is the price that might appear in a catalog or be quoted by a salesperson. The list price is sometimes the same as the final selling price, but in the majority of cases, the manufacturer makes some adjustment in the list price. This is the fifth step in the process of price determination.

These adjustments to list price are often made both to the trade and to the final customer. When IBM offers a discount to computer retailers buying a large number of personal computers, when Folgers offers a price promotion on its coffee,

EXHIBIT 21.1

An Example of Adjustments on the List Price

or when Ford authorizes its dealer to offer trade-in allowances on used cars, these companies are adjusting their list price downward. The Buick ad in Exhibit 21.1 shows a $19,556 list price for the Electra with options. Two discounts are shown: a discount for selecting the option package and a cash rebate of $1,000. The actual price after adjustments is $18,166.

Five types of adjustments off the list price are frequently used as shown in Figure 21.4: discounts, allowances, price promotions, geographic price adjustments, and odd–even prices.

DISCOUNTS

A **discount** *is a reduction off the list price offered by the seller if the buyer takes certain actions that reduce the seller's costs.* The discount could be based on an incentive to buy in quantity, perform certain marketing functions, buy at a certain time of year, or pay bills quickly.

QUANTITY DISCOUNTS

Quantity discounts *are given to buyers for buying in volume.* Volume purchases decrease the costs of order taking, processing, and delivery, and may also decrease the unit costs of production because of economies of scale in larger production runs.

Quantity discounts may be noncumulative or cumulative. *Noncumulative discounts* are limited to one order. For example, IBM offers up to 40 percent off list price to retailers buying large numbers of its Personal System/2 computers at one time.[11] *Cumulative discounts* allow a buyer to aggregate all purchases over a year. For example, a manufacturer of industrial generators might offer distributors a 10-percent discount if they buy more than 100 units in a year. Cumulative discounts are an important strategic tool, because they encourage the customer to continue to buy from the same company to qualify for a discount.

Some companies not only offer cumulative discounts for one of their products, but also allow buyers to accumulate discounts across their product lines. Assume that a company like Merrill Lynch buys 20 different computer systems from IBM over the course of a year, and IBM gives Merrill Lynch a 16 percent discount on these purchases. Such a discount encourages customers to buy a range of products from the same manufacturer to qualify for a savings. It is a means of encouraging vendor loyalty.

TRADE DISCOUNTS

Trade discounts *are granted by producers to retailers and wholesalers for performing the marketing functions required to sell to the final consumer.* The trade discount is the retailer's and wholesaler's *profit margin*, because it represents the difference between what retailers and wholesalers pay the manufacturer and what they can sell the product for. Trade discounts are also a way producers can get retailers and wholesalers to stock a new item. The traditional retail discount for personal computers is 22 percent. A new computer manufacturer might offer a 30 percent discount to get computer retailers to stock its products.

Table 21.3 shows an example of a trade discount structure for a superpremium ice cream that lists for $3.00 a pint. Assume that the manufacturer distributes the ice cream through food brokers, who then distribute to wholesalers and retailers. The trade discount is stated as $3.00 less 30/10/5. This means the discount is 30

FIGURE 21.4

Types of Price Adjustments

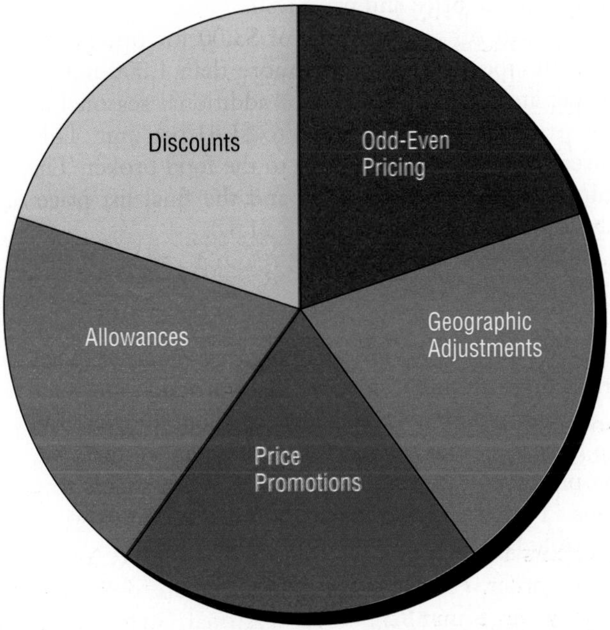

TABLE 21.3

Discount Structure from the List Price

List price	$3.00
Trade discount ($3.00 less 30/10/5)	
Retailer discount at 30%	– .90
Wholesaler's selling price to retailer	$2.10
Wholesaler discount at 10%	– .21
Broker's selling price to wholesaler	$1.89
Food broker discount at 5%	– .09
Manufacturer's selling price to broker	$1.80
Quantity discount	
10% off list price	– .30
Manufacturer's selling price to broker with trade and quantity discount	$1.50
Seasonal discount	
4% if purchased from December to March	– .06
Manufacturer's selling price to broker with trade, quantity, and seasonal discount	$1.44
Cash discount (2/10 net 30)	
2% if paid in 10 days; net due in 30 days	– .03
Manufacturer's selling price to broker with all discounts	$1.41

percent to retailers, 10 percent to wholesalers, and 5 percent to food brokers. (The intermediary closest to the consumer is listed first.) The reason that retailers get more of a discount than wholesalers or food brokers is that they usually perform more functions in selling to consumers.

Starting with the list price of $3.00, a 30 percent discount to retailers means they are buying the product at $2.10 per unit. Wholesalers get 10 percent off the suggested retail price of $2.10 and pay $1.89 for the product. Food brokers get 5 percent off the wholesale price and pay $1.80. The company also offers a quantity discount of 10 percent off the list price of $3.00 for orders of one thousand or more. Assuming the food broker orders more than 1,000 items, the price would then be $1.50 per item to the broker. An additional seasonal and cash discount could bring the price to the broker down to $1.41 per unit. This is the price that the manufacturer gets for selling the item to the food broker. The spread between the manufacturer's selling price of $1.41 and the final list price of $3.00 is represented by the various discounts in Table 21.3.

SEASONAL DISCOUNTS

Seasonal discounts *are price incentives to encourage customers to buy in the off-season.* Manufacturers facing seasonal demand for their product offer such discounts. Buyers obtain the products more cheaply and stock them for the busy season. Seasonal discounts help buyers, because savings are usually more than the additional costs of keeping the products in inventory. They also help sellers to smooth out their production runs. The alternative would be higher unit costs of production in-season, and possible layoffs in the off-season.

Products such as boats, ski equipment, or snow blowers are good candidates for seasonal discounts. Table 21.3 shows a seasonal discount being offered by an ice cream manufacturer in the winter months when demand is lowest. Because ice cream is perishable, the discount is not meant to encourage retailers to stock the item in the winter and sell in the summer. Rather, it is meant to get them to spur demand for the product during the winter months through in-store promotions and favorable shelf positions in freezer compartments.

CASH DISCOUNTS

Cash discounts *are incentives manufacturers offer buyers to encourage them to pay their bills quickly*. This permits manufacturers to maintain their liquidity and to avoid the costs of collecting bills that are past due. Buyers find it economical to pay quickly, because the savings usually outweigh any revenues they might obtain by holding onto their money longer.

In Table 21.3, the cash discount is stated as 2/10 net 30, which means that the food broker can take a 2 percent discount on the selling price of $1.44 by paying the amount within 10 days of the billing date, but the net amount is due in 30 days. If the food broker buys 2,000 units, this would represent a savings of 3 cents a unit, or $60.

Companies also offer consumers cash discounts. Examples include lower prices at cash-only gas pumps and discounts offered by some stores for cash sales rather than those paid with checks or credit cards.

ALLOWANCES

Allowances are payments to the buyer from the seller in exchange for goods or for taking certain actions. The most common type is a **trade-in allowance,** *which is a price reduction for trading in a used product as part payment for a new one*. Car dealers can lower the price of a car without changing the list price by simply offering more for a used car. Some retailers also allow electronics and appliances to be traded in.

Promotional allowances *are allowances that manufacturers give to retailers to advertise their products*. As we have seen in Chapter 17, such allowances form the basis for cooperative advertising between manufacturers and retailers. Retailers insert their name into the manufacturer's ad, allowing the retailer to advertise on the local level while making the manufacturer's products more visible.

PRICE PROMOTIONS

Price promotions *are short-term discounts offered by manufacturers to induce consumers to try a product*. They allow a manufacturer to temporarily reduce the price without changing the listed price. As we have seen in Chapter 17, promotions such as cents-off deals are effective in countering competitive price reductions or in getting users of competitive brands to try the product.

Manufacturers use price promotions primarily for lower-priced goods in their line. Kraft General Foods frequently runs price promotions for its regular Maxwell House coffee brands but does not run promotions for its top-of-the-line Maxwell House Private Collection coffees. Similarly, our ice-cream manufacturer would be wary of running a price promotion on its superpremium brand for fear of hurting its quality image.

If not overused, price promotions are an effective means of adjusting price to short-term changes in competitive conditions.

GEOGRAPHIC PRICE ADJUSTMENTS

In **geographic price adjustments**, *companies adjust their prices to reflect differences in transportation costs based on the seller's or buyer's location.* These adjustments are most important for bulky products with high transportation costs. The methods for pricing to reflect transportation costs are called *free-on-board (FOB) origin pricing* and *delivered pricing.*

FOB ORIGIN PRICING

In **free on board (FOB) origin pricing,** *the price is determined at the seller's location* and does not include transportation costs. The buyer gets the product delivered on board some vehicle such as a truck or a railroad car at the point of origin (usually the seller's plant) and pays for all transportation costs to the final destination.

Prices quoted FOB are the same to all buyers. Since buyers must absorb transportation costs, the buyer that is most distant from the seller is at a cost disadvantage. As a result, most buyers try to purchase at closer points of origin. Sellers using FOB pricing try to establish plants and warehouse locations across the country so that a point of origin is reasonably close to almost any buyer.

DELIVERED PRICING

In **delivered pricing,** *the price is adjusted to include transportation costs.* There are four widely used methods of delivered pricing: Single-zone pricing, multiple-zone pricing, basing-point pricing, and freight-absorption pricing.

Single-zone pricing *means that all buyers pay the same price for the product regardless of where they are located.* The seller includes average transportation charges per unit as part of the total cost of the item but does not vary price depending on the buyer's location. This means that buyers close to the seller are subsidizing the transportation costs of buyers further away. Kraft General Foods charges the same list price for a can of Maxwell House to retailers across the country. If the point of origin is the New York area, then a supermarket in New York is actually paying a higher price per mile for transportation than a supermarket in California.

A company is most likely to use single-zone pricing when transportation costs are a small part of the final price. In such cases, customers closer to the seller are unlikely to make an issue of the fact they are absorbing freight costs of more-distant customers.

In **multiple-zone pricing,** *a firm divides its selling territory into geographic zones, and the price depends upon transportation costs from the seller's location to the buyer's zone.* A zone system makes sense if transportation costs are high. Customers close to the seller would object to a uniform price. Zones provide a basis for accounting for different transportation costs in different parts of the country. Under such a system, an appliance manufacturer might charge a different price depending on whether a customer is in New England, in the Midwest, in the South, or in the West.

In **basing-point pricing,** *the company establishes a location called a* basing point *from which transportation charges are added to the list price.* The steel industry used basing-point pricing for years, charging for steel from Pittsburgh, the basing point, because the city was the historic center of the steel industry. Under this system, if a firm is located in Indianapolis and buys steel from nearby Fort Wayne, Indiana, it will still be charged for transportation from Pittsburgh. Such *charges for non-existent freight are known as* **phantom freight.**

EXHIBIT 21.2

An Example of Odd-Even Pricing

Multiple-zone and basing-point pricing could both be illegal if there is evidence that firms have conspired to establish the zones and fix prices. If, for example, several firms have exactly the same zones and the same price differences across zones, it could be construed as evidence of collusion in setting up geographic areas and freight charges and therefore be regarded as illegal.

As the name implies, *in* **freight-absorption pricing** *the seller absorbs the total cost of transportation.* The buyer is allowed to deduct the cost of freight from the list price. If freight is an important part of the total cost, absorbing these charges provides the seller with an important advantage over competitors. Companies trying to expand their sales territories absorb freight charges to try to attract buyers in more-distant regions. The problem is that such a practice can become very costly.

ODD–EVEN PRICING

In **odd–even pricing**, *a company adjusts the list price to end in an odd number that is just under a round number.* Using odd–even pricing, our ice-cream manufacturer might offer regular, premium, and superpremium brands at 99 cents, $1.99, and $2.99 respectively.

Odd–even pricing is a commonly used type of price adjustment, because consumers see a product as significantly less expensive if it is priced just under the round number. For example, the difference between 99 cents and $1.00 would be perceived as more than one cent. Several studies also have found that odd prices were seen as providing more value than even prices.[12] For this reason, odd–even pricing is sometimes referred to as *psychological pricing*.

The popularity of odd–even pricing is reflected in the fact that 61 percent of supermarket items have prices ending in a 9.[13] Odd–even pricing is also used for a variety of products outside the supermarket. The Chrysler Le Baron is priced at $13,495, not at $13,500. Similarly, Hilton hotels advertise their "bounce back vacation" special at $89, not $90 (see Exhibit 21.2).

EVALUATING AND CONTROLLING PRICES

The last step in the process of price determination in Figure 21.1 is to evaluate and control prices after they are introduced into the marketplace.

EVALUATING PRICES

Evaluating prices requires assessing customer and competitive responses to a product's price level.

EVALUATING CUSTOMER RESPONSES

Evaluating customers' responses to price requires tracking their purchases over time and determining whether estimates of demand are correct. If they are not, the marketer may have to change the price. For consumer packaged goods, the best means of tracking consumer responses to price is *scanner data.* As we noted in Chapter 7, marketers can track the quantity of a product purchased at various price levels by scanner data in order to provide a basis for estimating price–quantity relationships. Marketers can then determine whether an upward or downward change in the price level is warranted based on current demand.

Marketers must also evaluate consumers' responses to price for products not tracked by scanner data—cars and appliances, for example. GM could obtain sales data from its dealers regarding consumer response to a list price of $8,500 for the Saturn. It could also estimate consumer reactions to trade-in allowances, cash rebates, and price deals on options. This should give GM some indication of price elasticity of the Saturn at the $8,500 level and whether a decrease or increase in price is warranted.

EVALUATING COMPETITIVE RESPONSES

Marketers must account for competitive reactions in setting prices. Eli Lilly probably felt a price cut of 12 percent for Treflan was deep enough to deter competitive entry, but Lilly would have to track competitive responses after the price reduction to verify this. If enough competitors entered the market despite the price cut, Lilly might have to consider an even deeper price cut to deter further competitive entry. On the other hand, if competition was much less than Lilly anticipated, it might consider raising prices close to their former levels, despite the expiration of its patent.

In either case, Lilly would be adjusting prices in response to competitive reactions to its initial price move. Such action and counteraction in response to competition are typical in pricing. Adjusting prices requires carefully assessing competitive responses to the company's pricing strategy to determine if a change from the initial price is warranted.

CONTROLLING PRICE LEVELS AND STRATEGIES

Controlling prices requires determining whether prices should be changed after they have been introduced, and adjusting pricing strategies in response to customers, competitors, and the trade. Managers must be concerned with two key questions in controlling prices, as shown in Table 21.4. First, are profit and sales objectives being met? Second, are price levels and strategies in line with the other components of the marketing mix, namely product, promotional, and distribution strategies?

TABLE 21.4

Issues in Controlling Prices

KEY QUESTIONS	REQUIRED ACTION
ARE PROFIT AND SALES OBJECTIVES BEING MET? IF NOT, IS IT DUE TO	
– Consumer demand and/or	Assess consumer responses to price and adjust prices to reflect consumer demand
– Competitive responses	Assess competitive response to price and adjust prices to anticipate competitive responses
IS PRICE IN LINE WITH OTHER COMPONENTS OF THE MARKETING MIX?	
1. *Product Strategy*	
– Is price in line with product quality?	Adjust price so it is in line with consumer perceptions of product quality, *or* Adjust product quality so it is in line with price *or* Advertise to change perceptions of product value so it is in line with price.
– Are prices in the company's product line differentiated to reflect value of each product?	Adjust prices in product line to ensure proper range between premium and economy brands
2. *Promotional Strategy*	
– Is the advertising message consistent with consumers' price-quality perceptions?	Change the advertising message *or* Advertise to develop desired price-quality associations
– Are price promotions run too frequently?	Control frequency of price deals to ensure that discounted price will not become permanent price
3. *Distribution Strategy*	
– Are distribution outlets consistent with the product's price-quality association?	Change distribution outlets so image is in line with product's price level
– Are trade and other discounts adequate?	Improve discounts to trade if required to ensure adequate distribution

MEET PROFIT AND SALES OBJECTIVES

An important question in controlling prices is whether failure to meet profit or sales objectives is due to the firm's pricing actions. Poor performance could be due to advertising strategies, lack of adequate distribution, a weak sales force, misestimation of demand, or a host of factors other than price. Unless the impact of

ETHICAL AND ENVIRONMENTAL ISSUES IN MARKETING

How Baseball Controlled Prices Through Price Fixing: The Owners Throw a Spitball at Their Players

One aspect of controlling prices is the cost of the product being sold, an especially important concern if the company uses a cost-plus pricing method. In the case of baseball, the owners found one of their main costs, players' salaries, spiralling out of control in the late 1970s. Their solution? Agreeing to control their players' salaries—actions that verged on price fixing in violation of the Sherman Antitrust Act.

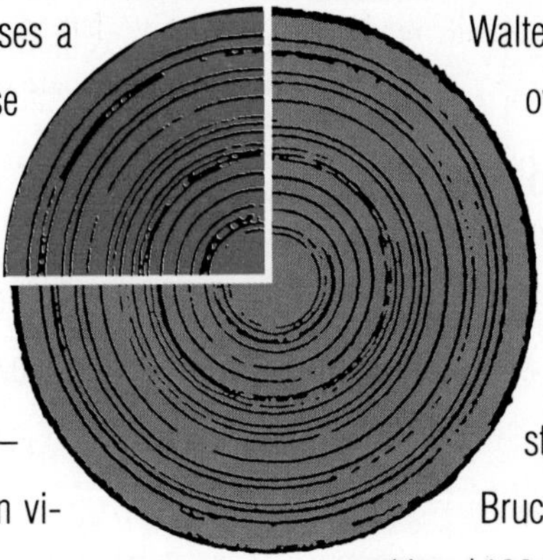

The story starts in 1975 when an arbitrator ruled that pitcher Andy Messersmith could become a free agent when his contract expired. Until then, baseball's *reserve clause* tied a player to his team for life. Free agency meant that owners had to bid for ballplayers in an open market. They had to establish a price for the players' services that was either accepted or rejected. Not surprisingly, the free-agency system escalated salaries. From 1976 to 1985, average salaries per player rose 700 percent to $369,000.

In 1985 a tough, hard-nosed executive became commissioner of baseball: Peter Ueberroth. One of the first things he did was to show owners such as Walter Haas, head of Levi Strauss and owner of the Oakland A's, and Ted Turner, founder of Turner Broadcasting and owner of the Atlanta Braves, that they were running their clubs like the corner grocery store. In one case, he pointed out that Bruce Sutter of the Atlanta Braves was making $100,000 an inning, in another that Omar Moreno of the New York Yankees was being paid $700,000 to sit on the bench.

The culprit, Ueberroth pointed out, was free agency, and the owners had to act together to stop it. How? By agreeing not to bid on each other's players. Once the owners agreed to a process that amounted to collusion, the effects were immediate and startling. Kirk Gibson, star of the Detroit Tigers, was the first to know something was wrong. He was ready to sign with the Kansas City Royals as a free agent when, suddenly, the Royals said they were no longer interested. Tim Raines, the 1986 National

price on sales and profits is determined independent of other elements in the marketing mix, the company might wind up changing prices when such a change is not warranted.

To determine the effects of price on sales and profits, the firm must evaluate consumer and competitive responses to its prices to determine if it misestimated

ETHICAL AND ENVIRONMENTAL ISSUES IN MARKETING

League batting champion, tried testing the free-agent market when the Montreal Expos offered almost the same salary as the previous year. The result? No takers. The final scorecard of the 1985–86 season was that, of 33 free agents (among the best players in baseball), 29 went back to their old teams with a 5-percent average increase in salary. The remaining four were players the home clubs were willing to let go.

The results on the teams' profitability were immediate. In the 1985–86 season, baseball saw its first profit in eight years. In the following year, revenues were up 15 percent while players' salaries took a dip for the first time in years. By 1988, baseball's revenues hit $1 billion and operating profits $121 million.

The Players' Association was quick to react, charging the owners with collusion and price fixing. Delaying tactics by the owners dragged out hearings for three years until, in 1989, a series of arbitration decisions went against them. Price fixing and collusion were out, free agency was back in. Salaries started climbing again. In 1991, the average Oakland A's player was making $1.35 million. Whereas every team was profitable in 1989, by 1991 ten were losing money. The owners moaned that they were back where they started in 1985.

Baseball's experience raises an important issue. Should businesses be allowed to collude and fix prices if that is the only way they can make a profit? Clearly, the answer in a free-market system is no, as it was in the case of baseball.

Question: Do you believe the owners had a right to agree among themselves as to how they would deal with free agents? Why or why not?

Source: "How Peter Ueberroth Led the Major Leagues in the 'Collusion Era,'" *The Wall Street Journal*, May 20, 1991, pp. A1 and A12.

customer demand or competitive responses. Such an evaluation frequently leads the firm to change its initial price.

Scanner data is particularly important in determining the effects of price on consumer and competitive responses. Since scanners immediately record consumer purchases, the marketer can track the amount of a company's and competitive brands purchased at various price levels. The marketer also needs to consider factors other than price that might influence sales such as changes in the company's advertising expenditures, whether a price deal was running for the product, and whether a competitive promotion was running at the time.

COORDINATE PRICE WITH OTHER ELEMENTS IN THE MARKETING MIX

Table 21.4 shows that the second key area in controlling prices is to ensure that price levels and price strategies are consistent with other elements of the marketing mix. The table shows areas of control to ensure that price is coordinated with product, promotional, and distribution strategies.

PRODUCT STRATEGY A key issue in coordinating price and product strategies is whether the price of a product is in line with consumer perceptions of its quality. Dell Computer's strength is that buyers see value in the product for its price. If consumers do not perceive sufficient value for the price, then the company should consider a price decrease, an upgrade in product quality, or an advertising campaign to educate the consumer about the product's features.

A second issue regarding product strategy is control over prices in a product line. One of GM's problems was that its price-lining strategy was out of control. Models were not sufficiently differentiated across divisions to reflect price differences. In such a case, the company must either realign prices or realign the products to be consistent with current price lines.

PROMOTIONAL STRATEGY The main requirement in coordinating price with promotional strategy is to make sure the advertising message is consistent with the product's price level. An ad for a high-priced product must reinforce a quality image. The advertisement for Porsche in Chapter 20 is an example. Conversely, advertising for a low-priced product should convey value for the money.

Another area of control required to coordinate price and promotional strategies is sales promotions. Marketers must control the frequency of sales promotions to avoid a situation where coupons or price discounts are being used more often than not. Product managers prefer to promote their products to increase sales and market share. But a longer-range perspective might show that such frequent promotions only encourage consumers to switch in the short term and win few loyal consumers for the brand.

DISTRIBUTION STRATEGY An important issue in coordinating price and distribution is whether the product's price level is consistent with the distribution outlets being used. A high-priced, prestige product should be distributed on a selective or exclusive basis; Rolex watches, for example, through exclusive jewelry stores. Lower-priced products should be distributed on an intensive basis to make them available to a broader price-sensitive market. When price level is not consistent with the distribution outlet, a product's image can suffer. J.C. Penney convinced Halston to sell its designer line of clothing through Penney outlets, but Halston's higher prices were inconsistent with Penney's image. The move was intended to enhance Penney's image, but it had the effect of reducing Halston's prestige.

Another issue in coordinating price and distribution is whether trade and other types of discounts are giving the product the distribution clout it needs. Such discounts are essential to ensure trade support, particularly for smaller companies trying to compete with market leaders for shelf space. Smaller computer companies producing IBM-compatibles have had to provide higher trade discounts to retailers to try to break IBM's hold on the distribution channel.

PRICING SERVICES AND INDUSTRIAL PRODUCTS

Generally, the same methods of determining prices are used for consumer goods, services, and industrial products. However, there are enough differences in price determination for services and industrial goods to warrant special attention.

PRICING SERVICES

Services are more difficult to price than products for several reasons. First, because services are intangible, it is hard to estimate demand. A company evaluating a new service would have to rely on a description of the service's features, then ask consumers their intentions to use it. Demand estimates for a product, on the other hand, can rely on actual in-home or market tests to assess customer demand.

It is also difficult to estimate the cost of a service, particularly a personal service. Costs of producing a product (raw materials and factory labor) are more easily identifiable because products tend to be more standardized. A lawyer's or accountant's fees are often based on hourly rates, but the time required to provide these services is highly variable.

The difficulty in estimating demand for and costs of services means it is harder to apply the most frequently used pricing methods such as cost-plus, target-return, or demand-oriented pricing. As a result, service marketers have relied on two approaches particular to services: value-based pricing and bundled pricing.

VALUE-BASED PRICING

Value-based pricing *sets a price that reflects the highest value a consumer might place on the product.* It is pricing by "what the market will bear." In the absence of any systematic demand-oriented or cost-oriented approach, value-based pricing sets the price at a level the marketer thinks the consumer will accept. The price is then gradually raised, almost by trial and error, to test buyers' price elasticities for the service. If a price rise results in a sharp decrease in demand, the price reverts to its previous level.

Value-based pricing is more complicated than it may sound. It requires establishing prices for different services, often at different rates during different times, depending on the value customers place on the service. Airlines use it in setting fares higher for vacationers during peak holiday periods, and utilities set higher rates during peak usage hours. These differential rates are meant to maintain a constant price–value relationship at different times. That is, if it costs one-half as much for a kilowatt hour of electricity at 4 A.M. compared to at noon, the assumption is that electricity is valued twice as much at noon.

BUNDLED PRICING

Bundled pricing *is the practice of offering two or more products or services as a single package for a special price.* For example, some banks offer credit cards at no annual fee and free travelers' checks to customers with large certificates of deposit. Airlines sometimes bundle vacation packages combining air travel with car rentals and lodging.

Bundling is more effective for services than for products for two reasons. First, services often are interdependent. Travelers who fly generally need lodging and rental cars. Banking customers who use checking services frequently need loans or want to take out certificates of deposit. It is more economical for a firm to offer such services as a bundle, because demand for one service stimulates demand for the other.

A second reason bundling is more common for services is that when one agency books airline, hotel, and car-rental arrangements, it spreads order-processing and administrative costs across several services. Similarly, when a customer opens a checking account, the marginal costs of servicing the customer on a certificate of deposit or a loan are fairly low. Teller processing, computer time, and sales costs are spread across several services.[14] Costs of bundled services are much lower than if each service were sold separately.

Bundled pricing has also been used as a means of segmenting markets based on price. For example, Interleaf, a software producer, offers its core Technical Publishing Software at a price of $2,500. Customers can add on modules to this core product such as the Advanced Graphics module for an additional $4,500 or the Book Catalog module for $2,500. In bundling its offerings in this way, Interleaf can offer its core software package to price-sensitive consumers and its combined (that is, bundled) packages to more-specialized and less-price-sensitive segments such as the graphic arts or technical document markets.[15]

PRICING INDUSTRIAL PRODUCTS

Pricing industrial products is also more difficult than pricing consumer goods, because it is harder to estimate customer demand. Demand for industrial goods is derived from demand for consumer goods. Therefore, business-to-business marketers have more than one industry and more than one demand curve to estimate in setting prices. Moreover, this *derived demand* is more volatile than final consumer demand. A change in demand for processed foods will accentuate a change in demand for food machinery.

The volatility of derived demand makes it difficult to use demand-oriented methods of price determination for industrial goods. As a result, the dominant method of setting prices in the industrial sector is based on costs. Although business-to-business marketers use the same type of cost-oriented methods of pricing as consumer marketers—cost-plus and target-return pricing—two pricing procedures are particular to industrial products: bid pricing and delayed-quotation pricing.

BID PRICING

In **bid pricing,** *organizational buyers send out requests for proposals that invite prospective sellers to bid on a set of specifications developed by the buyer.* Buyers solicit bids from an approved vendor list and compare proposals. Generally, the vendor that submits the lowest bid while meeting the buyer's specifications will get the contract.

Sellers must balance the desire to bid low to win the contract with the desire to maintain profit targets in setting the price. In so doing, they must try to estimate the level of competitive bids. Assume that Citicorp sends out specifications for the development of an integrated branch management information system to several vendors on an approved list. One vendor considers four prices for the sys-

TABLE 21.5
Example of Bid Pricing

COMPANY'S BID	ROI ESTIMATE	PROBABILITY OF GETTING CONTRACT WITH THIS BID	EXPECTED ROI (ESTIMATED ROI × PROBABILITY)
$2 Million	7%	80%	5.6%
$2.5 Million	8%	70%	5.6%
$3.0 Million[a]	12%	50%	6.0%
$3.5 Million	18%	20%	3.6%

[a]Optimal bid price to maximize expected ROI

tem and estimates return on investment for each price, as shown in Table 21.5. The vendor then estimates what competitive bids might be and develops a probability of getting the contract at each of the four prices. On this basis, the vendor estimates the highest chance (80 percent) of getting the contract is with a bid of $2 million, but ROI is only 7 percent at that price. The expected ROI weighted by the chance of getting the contract is 5.6 percent (actual ROI of 7 percent times the estimated chance of getting the contract of 80 percent).

Based on the expected ROI, the best price to bid is $3 million, even though there is only a 50 percent chance of getting the contract at that price. The company would prefer to accept a lower probability of getting the contract rather than raising the probability by lowering the price, because lower prices produce unacceptable returns on investment.

DELAYED-QUOTATION PRICING

In **delayed-quotation pricing**, *the seller delays quoting a price for a product until delivery.* Such pricing passes much of the risk of cost overruns and faulty production schedules to the buyer. Business-to-business marketers find delayed-quotation pricing desirable because the production process for industrial goods is usually longer than for consumer goods. For example, the development, sale, and installation of an air-pollution-control system for a large manufacturer may take years. Costs, specifications, and requirements from regulatory agencies may change significantly during this time. As a result, many business-to-business marketers are reluctant to commit themselves to a fixed price years in advance.

The potential risks of committing to a fixed price are illustrated by Westinghouse's agreement in the mid 1970s to sell 80 million pounds of uranium to nuclear power plants through the 1990s as part of its agreement to sell generating equipment. It committed itself to sell the uranium at $9 a pound. By 1977 uranium was selling at $41 a pound, and Westinghouse sold only one-fifth of the amount contracted.[16] The company lost $500 million because of these fixed-price contracts.

Some sellers try to balance their risks by quoting a wide price range in advance. This combines a fixed price (since there is a commitment to a price range) and a delayed quote (since the final price is specified within the agreed-to range at the time of delivery).

SUMMARY

1. **How do companies use cost-, demand-, and competition-oriented methods to set price?**
Cost-oriented pricing is usually cost-plus pricing or target-return pricing. In cost-plus pricing, the marketer determines the unit costs of producing an item and adds a margin to meet a profit objective. In target-return pricing, the marketer determines a profit objective based on return on investment or on costs, then determines the price that will achieve the profit target at a specified volume level.
Demand-oriented pricing methods require estimating consumers' demand curve for a product by asking consumers what they intend to buy or by using market tests to determine sales at different price levels. Based on this information, companies can set prices with marginal pricing or flexible break-even pricing.
In competition-oriented pricing, marketers base their prices on what competitors do. The company may follow a price leader in the industry, peg prices to a prevailing industry norm, or price based on how competitors might react to the firm's price.
2. **How do companies adjust the final price?**
The price established by a company through cost-, demand-, or competition-oriented methods is the base, or list, price for a product. Adjustments to the base price can be in the form of discounts, allowances, price promotions, geographic adjustments, or odd–even pricing.
Discounts are provided to customers as an incentive to buy in quantity, to perform certain marketing functions that enable customers to buy, to buy at a certain time of year, and to pay bills quickly. Allowances are payments to the buyer in exchange for some benefit to the seller. Price promotions are short-term discounts offered by manufacturers to induce consumers to try a product. Geographic adjustments are designed to take account of transportation costs in the final price. In odd–even pricing, the list price is adjusted to end in an odd number that is just under a round number and gives consumers the impression of being less expensive.
3. **How do companies evaluate and control prices?**
Companies evaluate prices by assessing the responses of customers and competitors to the price levels they set. This requires tracking consumer purchases to determine whether the demand estimates on which prices are based are accurate. It also requires evaluating competitive responses to prices in order to determine whether some countermove is warranted. Both cases might require a change in the list price.
Controlling prices requires a company to determine whether profit and sales objectives have been met and, if not, whether a price change is warranted.
4. **What pricing methods are used for services and for industrial products?**
Service companies tend to price based on their estimate of the value of the service to customers. They are more likely to bundle services into one package at a special price because of the cost efficiencies of bundling.
Sellers of industrial products must face more-volatile demand trends for their products. As a result, they are reluctant to commit to fixed prices and are more likely to delay price quotes until the time of delivery. Business-to-business marketers must also respond to requests for bids and must estimate prices in competitive bidding situations.

KEY TERMS

Cost-plus pricing (p. 683)
Markup (p. 683)
Target-return pricing (p. 684)
Target return on investment (p. 684)
Target return on cost (p. 684)
Price dumping (p. 685)
Marginal pricing (p. 687)
Flexible break-even pricing (p. 688)
Demand-backward pricing (p. 689)
Follow-the-leader pricing (p. 690)
Oligopoly (p. 690)
Pegged pricing (p. 690)
List price (p. 691)
Discount (p. 692)
Quantity discount (p. 692)
Trade discount (p. 693)
Seasonal discount (p. 694)
Cash discount (p. 695)
Trade-in allowances (p. 695)
Promotional allowances (p. 695)
Price promotions (p. 695)
Geographic price adjustments (p. 696)
Free on board (FOB) origin pricing (p. 696)
Delivered pricing (p. 696)
Single-zone pricing (p. 696)
Multiple-zone pricing (p. 696)
Basing-point pricing (p. 696)
Phantom freight (p. 696)
Freight-absorption pricing (p. 697)
Odd–even pricing (p. 697)
Value-based pricing (p. 703)
Bundled pricing (p. 703)
Bid pricing (p. 704)
Delayed-quotation pricing (p. 705)
Break-even analysis (p. 708)

QUESTIONS

1. What is the difference between cost-plus pricing and target-return pricing? What are the problems with each method?
2. Why are new entrants in international markets more likely to use cost-oriented pricing methods? Why might they use a price-dumping strategy?
3. Why are demand-oriented pricing methods more flexible than cost- or competition-oriented methods?
4. How can a company estimate a consumer demand curve for new and existing products? What are the problems with using these approaches to estimate demand?
5. Why did companies in the steel and aluminum industries prefer to follow a price leader rather than set prices independently? What was likely to happen if a competitor priced above or below the leader?
6. How does IBM use cumulative discounts to encourage customers to remain loyal to its products?
7. What is the rationale behind odd–even pricing? Should it be used only for low-priced brands? Why or why not?
8. What key areas must be considered in controlling prices? What actions might the marketer take in each of these areas?
9. Why are service firms more likely than other companies to use value-based pricing? Why are they more likely to bundle their services and price them as a single package?
10. Why do marketers of industrial products have more difficulty in estimating customer demand than marketers of consumer goods? What are the implications for determining prices?

QUESTIONS: YOU ARE THE DECISION MAKER

A General Motors dealer, after reading the introduction to this chapter, commented as follows:

I think you're giving GM a bum rap in implying that they are shortsighted using a cost-oriented pricing method. Their cost-oriented pricing reflects the realities of the auto industry, namely that we have high fixed costs that must be covered and that it is very difficult to estimate consumer demand for a new model car. Granted, GM's costs have gone up. But the company is now more conscious of the need to improve productivity and to get its costs down.

a. Do you agree with this justification of GM's cost-oriented approach to pricing? What are the pros and cons of cost-oriented pricing methods?
b. What difficulties might GM have if it switched to a demand-oriented basis for pricing?

APPENDIX

21A

BREAK-EVEN ANALYSIS

Break-even analysis *identifies the point where total revenue equals total cost, and profits are zero.* As volume increases beyond the break-even point, the company begins earning profits. To create a break-even chart, a total revenue curve is first determined for a given price level. The chart in Figure 21.5 is for the Saturn at a price of $11,000. At this price, if the company produces 30,000 units, total revenue will be $330 million. At 40,000 units, total revenue would be $440 million, and so forth. As a result, the total revenue curve at a given price is a straight line representing price multiplied by quantity.

The figure shows total fixed costs at $200 million. This remains constant. Total costs rise, because total variable costs (primarily raw material and labor) go up as more units are produced. The break-even point for the Saturn at a price of $11,000 would be at 50,000 units. At this price, total revenue and total cost are both $550 million. Beyond 50,000 units, GM would start making a profit.

How can we determine the break-even quantity? We know from the appendixes in Chapter 20 that

$$\text{Total Revenue} = \text{Price } (P) \times \text{Quantity } (Q)$$

and that

$$\text{Total Cost} = \text{Total Fixed Cost } (TFC) + (\text{Average Variable Cost } [AVC] \times \text{Quantity } [Q])$$

Therefore, because the break-even point is where total revenue equals total cost, then

$$P \times Q = TFC + (AVC \times Q)$$

FIGURE 21.5

Break-Even Chart for the Saturn at a Price of $11,000.

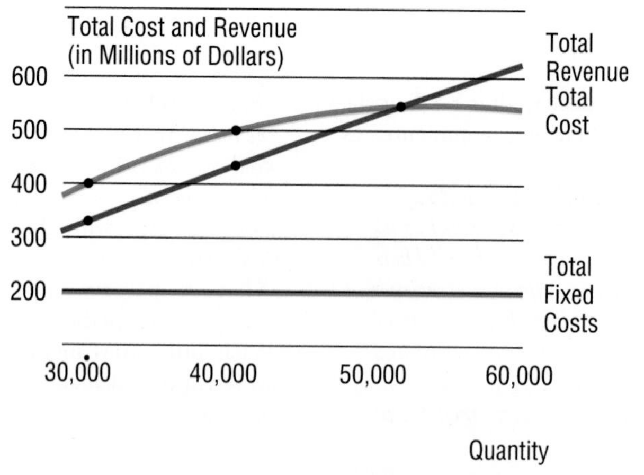

where Q is the amount of production required to break even. Solving for Q gives us

$$Q \text{ (to break even)} = \frac{TFC}{P - AVC}$$

Assuming an average cost per unit of \$7,000, the break-even point for the Saturn at \$11,000 would be

$$Q = \frac{\$200{,}000{,}000}{\$11{,}000 - \$7{,}000} = 50{,}000 \text{ units}$$

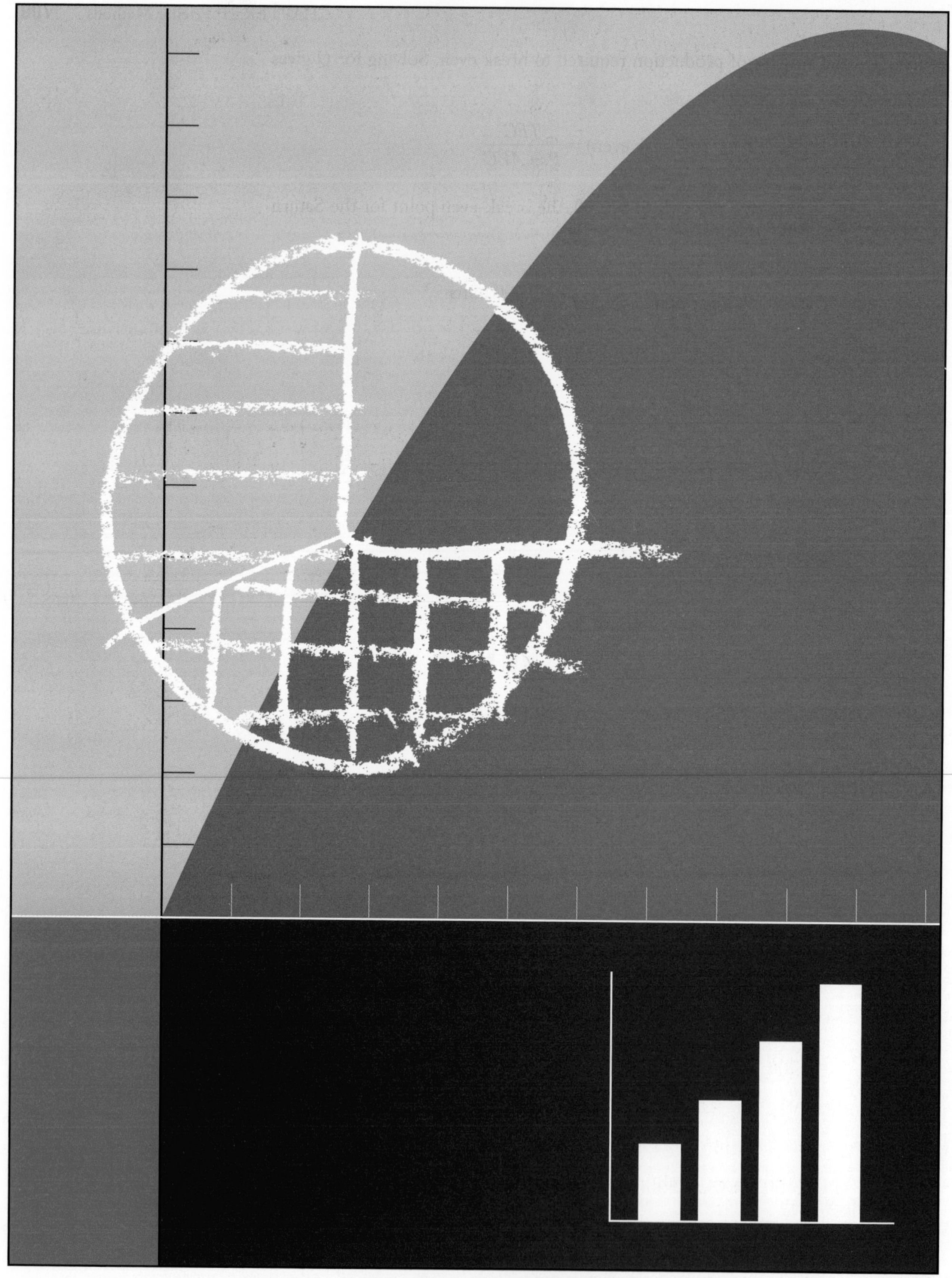

PART V

Strategic Planning, Evaluation, and Control

In this last section of the book, we consider marketing in a broader perspective. In Chapter 22, we reintroduce the need for a strategic marketing plan to tie together all the components of marketing strategy into an overall corporate game plan that guides the future direction of the firm. We describe how firms develop strategic plans and formulate marketing strategies at the corporate and business unit levels.

In Chapter 23, we then discuss the process of evaluating and controlling the entire marketing effort. This last chapter emphasizes the greater focus of American firms on increasing productivity to better control marketing operations and more effectively compete with foreign companies.

CHAPTER 22

Strategic Marketing Planning

YOUR FOCUS IN CHAPTER 22

To learn:

- *The nature of the strategic marketing planning process.*
- *The role of the strategic business unit (SBU) in the strategic marketing planning process.*
- *How a firm can best evaluate its business and product mix.*
- *The alternative routes to corporate growth.*

Philip Morris' Strategy for Survival: From Cigarettes to Food

Philip Morris has so radically transformed itself that in fifty years, students may have trouble believing it once made cigarettes. While Philip Morris has been synonymous with Marlboro since the 1920s, today it is also the second largest food company in the world, owning well-known brands such as Post cereal, JELL-O, and Oscar Mayer meats. How did the nation's premier cigarette manufacturer become a consumer-products colossus?

The story starts in 1970 when TV commercials for cigarettes were outlawed. Philip Morris' cigarette business was thriving despite mounting evidence that cigarette smoking is linked to cancer and heart disease. The company concluded that a long-term decline in cigarette sales was inevitable. It would have to look elsewhere for growth to ensure survival into the next century.

The first product it looked at was beer. Why? Because heavy beer drinkers have the same demographic and life-style profile as heavy cigarette smokers. Further, both categories relied heavily on supermarket sales. Philip Morris acquired Miller Brewing in 1970, a company that was going nowhere quickly. The first thing Philip Morris did was reposition Miller High Life, a brand that targeted the occasional beer drinker with the slogan "the champagne of bottled beer."

Philip Morris had a ready-made strategy at hand—Marlboro. In the mid 1950s, Marlboro was an elite brand positioned to light-smoking women and was ready for extinction when Philip Morris repositioned it to heavy-smoking males with the now famous Marlboro cowboy. The company applied the same strategy to Miller. With the theme "it's Miller time," Philip Morris repositioned the brand to heavy beer-drinking, blue-collar workers. As one analyst said, "Philip Morris successfully took Miller out of the champagne bucket and put it into the lunch pail."

Things went well for Philip Morris until the early 1980s. The acquisition of 7-Up was turning sour, because the company never established strong relationships with 7-Up bottlers, so essential to success in the soft-drink industry. As a result, bottlers did not provide the necessary support to aggressively distribute 7-Up's brands to supermarkets and food stores. A mass-marketing cigarette-style campaign for 7-Up's flagship brand also flopped. On top of that, sales for Miller started sliding in the face of an onslaught from Budweiser. The only two bright spots were Marlboro and Miller Lite, but the company could not rely on two brands for long-term growth, particularly in the face of the increasing emphasis on health.

Enter Hamish Maxwell, an urbane, chain-smoking visionary who took the company's reins in 1984. He was determined to move Philip Morris further away from cigarettes and to channel its wealth into foods. Within 16 months, Maxwell wrote a $5.7 billion check for General Foods, and the metamorphosis was underway. With General Foods, Philip Morris inherited some of the best-known names on supermarket shelves.[1] It also got a company that had been coasting through much of the 1980s.[2] By installing a hand-picked chairman, Maxwell hoped to make his new acquisition more nimble. He also paid an unusual amount of attention to its operations, pushing through such things as a new decaffeination process for the Sanka brand to give it more market share.[3] By 1988, however, it had become clear that troubled General Foods was not rebounding.

About that time, Kraft caught Maxwell's eye. Maxwell was particularly interested in how Mike Miles, Kraft's CEO, had managed to increase unit sales of Kraft's stodgy Cheez Whiz by 35 percent by promoting it as a microwaveable hot sauce.[4] Kraft was not cheap, but Philip Morris' tobacco division was a cash engine that generated $10 million a day and owned 11 percent of the 5.3 trillion-unit world market. Even if Maxwell was not looking for an acquisition target, the sheer build-up of cash would have forced him to swallow one. So, in the fall of 1988, Maxwell paid $13 billion for Kraft. It gave him the world's second-largest packaged-goods company, with such venerable brands as Kraft cheeses, Breyers ice cream, and Parkay margarine. Just as important, it gave him Miles.[5]

Merging two huge food companies was an unparalleled task, but Maxwell's faith in his new executive was strong enough that he divided the new Kraft General Foods (KGF) into seven strategic business units under a command chain that ended with Miles.[6] Miles moved quickly. He brought out a number of line extensions under the Maxwell House name that brought the brand to within a hair of catching industry-leading Folgers and also instituted a broad strategy of introducing fat-free formulations of many KGF products. Miles boldest step, however, was engineering the deal to buy the European operations of Swiss coffee and chocolate giant Jacobs Suchard for $4.1 billion.[7]

By 1991, Philip Morris' food units contributed more than half of its $58 billion in revenues. Not surprisingly, when it came time to choose a successor for Maxwell, several veterans of Philip Morris' tobacco division were passed over in favor of Miles.[8]

Critics warn that many brands at Kraft are mature, and the new CEO has a long way to go to learn about tobacco while keeping up Maxwell's enviable management record. But with cash flow expected to total $18 billion by 1995, Miles certainly has the resources to buy more.[9] And with a lifetime of studying consumer products companies, he seems well suited to lead Philip Morris as it continues to transform itself through the 1990s.

THE NATURE OF STRATEGIC MARKETING PLANNING

Until now, we have focused primarily on how to market a product. In this chapter, we take a broader view of marketing and consider the development of a **strategic marketing plan**, *that is, a corporate "game plan" that will map out where the company should be going over the next five years and how to get there.* As we have seen in Chapter 2, the strategic marketing plan differs from the plan for an individual product in that it deals with the marketing of all the company's product offerings.

THREE LEVELS OF MARKETING PLANNING

In Chapter 2, we saw that marketing activities take place at three levels in the organization: the corporate level, the strategic business unit (SBU) level, and the product level. Figure 22.1 shows that these three planning levels produce a corporate strategic plan, an SBU strategic plan, and a marketing plan for individual products.

Strategic marketing planning takes place at the two highest levels in the organization: the corporate level and the strategic business unit level (SBU). (As you may remember from Chapter 2, an SBU is a unit within a company that organizes its marketing effort around customers with similar demand, such as Kraft General Foods' coffee, breakfast foods, or frozen foods SBUs.) The Philip Morris example focused on Hamish Maxwell's corporate strategy in defining what businesses Philip

FIGURE 22.1

Characteristics of Three Marketing Planning Levels

	Management Level	Type of Mix	Strategies	Allocations	Time Horizon
Corporate	Top management	Business mix	Corporate growth strategy	To SBUs	5 years
Strategic Business Unit (SBU)	Business management	Product mix	SBU growth strategy	To products	5 years
Product Market Unit (PMU)	Product management	Marketing mix for products	Market segmentation and product positioning	To marketing mix components	1 year

Morris should be in, but business units must also develop strategies to determine the mix of products they should offer.

At the corporate level, strategic planning is the responsibility of the company's top management, including an executive vice president for marketing. The plan focuses on the firm's **business mix,** *that is, the combination of businesses the firm should be in.* The development of a business mix is central to the firm's long-term strategy for growth because the business mix defines the markets the firm will be in and the customers it will appeal to. Top managers must plan to develop a mix of mature and growing businesses. The mature businesses represent cash generators that fund growth areas. These growth areas will, in turn, become mature businesses that will fuel future growth areas, and so on as the firm's business mix evolves.

As we have seen, Philip Morris changed its business mix by adding Kraft and General Foods, divesting itself of 7-Up, and buying Jacobs Suchard. The cigarette business remains the primary cash engine to fuel growth areas in nutritional and convenience foods to be developed at KGF. These moves were developed in the corporate strategic plan. In the process of determining this mix, top management does two things: First, it formalizes its future plans for the company in the form of a corporate growth strategy that identifies the nature of the business mix. Second, it allocates resources to the SBUs based on the corporate growth strategy. These plans are generally developed with a five-year time horizon.

The SBU strategic plan parallels the corporate plan, except it is done at the business-unit level. The plan is the responsibility of the business managers who run the SBU and report to top management. The SBU strategic plan focuses on the unit's product offerings. At Philip Morris, that might mean that the business manager for KGF's coffee division would be concerned with issues such as introducing a new line of continental coffees or extending the decaffeinated line because of increasing health concerns. These considerations are incorporated into an SBU growth plan that requires allocations to individual product offerings. The SBU growth plan focuses on the unit's **product mix**, *that is, the combination of products the business unit should offer.* Because the SBU plan is submitted to top management to help with the development of corporate plans, the time horizon is also usually five years.

The third level of planning, the product marketing plan, is the responsibility of product managers. As we have seen in Chapter 12, the primary concern of product managers is developing a mix of product, distribution, promotional, and pricing strategies for their products. In the process, product managers must identify the market segments representing greatest opportunity and position the product to these segments. At Philip Morris' Miller beer division, that meant introducing a new Genuine Draft brand made with an innovative cold-filtering process in the hopes it would appeal to premium beer buyers. Product managers make allocations to the individual components of the marketing mix—expenditures for product development, advertising, and distribution. Product marketing plans have a much shorter time horizon, usually one year.

Although strategic plans usually have a five-year time horizon, this does not mean they are developed every five years. In a fast-moving marketplace, companies cannot wait five years to assess their environment. They develop strategic plans yearly, but with a longer-term perspective. As a result, *the strategic plan is a moving five-year plan,* with objectives and strategies changing yearly to account for changes in the marketing environment. It is a working document designed to account for environmental change on an ongoing basis.

TOP-DOWN VERSUS BOTTOM-UP STRATEGIC PLANNING

There are two approaches to strategic planning: a top-down approach and a bottom-up approach. In the *top-down approach*, allocation decisions are made by a centralized planning group at the corporate level and passed down to the SBUs, which then allocate resources to their individual product lines. Top-down planning is thus a *centralized* planning process in which corporate planners call the shots.

In contrast, the *bottom-up approach* is more *decentralized*, taking place primarily at the SBU level. The central part of the strategic plan is each individual SBU's evaluation of its product mix. The company's growth strategy is a composite of all the SBUs strategies. In the bottom-up approach, the SBU planners call the shots in the strategic planning process: They "drive" the corporate game plan.

The top-down and bottom-up approaches do not merely describe differences in the process of strategic marketing planning, they also describe substantial differences in philosophy and end results. Because it is centered at the corporate level, a top-down approach tends to focus more on corporate resources. Corporate planning managers tend to place more emphasis on the internal evaluation of company strengths and weaknesses than on the external evaluation of environmental opportunities and risks. Concern tends to be more toward maximizing shareholder's equity than customer satisfaction, with the primary focus on increasing the value of the company's stock.

By definition, a bottom-up approach is more marketing-oriented, focusing on the opportunities in the SBU's markets. SBU managers are more interested in evaluating opportunities and risks, leaving it to the corporate managers to place constraints on the money they can spend. The process is *market-driven* rather than *resource-driven*.

General Electric operated on a top-down basis until the mid 1980s, with corporate planners determining SBU strategies and direction. This caused some marketing blunders such as the conclusion among GE's corporate planners that since families were getting smaller, kitchen appliances should get smaller. Line managers at the SBU level realized that the kitchen was one room that was not shrinking and that working women wanted big refrigerators to reduce shopping trips.[10] The realization that business unit managers know their markets better than corporate planners caused GE's CEO, Jack Welch, to institute a bottom-up planning approach. He cut the corporate planning group from 58 to 33 people, established 15 SBUs, and gave the SBUs responsibility for determining their future course.

Top-down planning is still used in many companies, particularly where a company is in disarray because of rapid environmental changes or a lack of adequate controls on operations. In such cases, a new management team usually steps in and exerts control from the top. When Jack Welch first took over General Electric in 1981, he led a top-down transformation that divested low-growth manufacturing businesses such as televisions and electronics and built up high-growth areas such as medical imaging, factory automation, and aerospace. Only when he felt the company was in the right set of businesses did Welch institute a bottom-up approach.[11] GE's experience shows that if a company is customer-driven, eventually top management will assign strategic planning responsibilities to the SBUs.

THE STRATEGIC MARKETING PLANNING PROCESS

How can strategic marketing plans be developed at the corporate and SBU level to ensure future growth? Figure 22.2 illustrates the required steps. In the first step, management must define the **corporate** or **SBU mission,** *that is, what business or* *businesses the firm or business unit should be in.* Miles' corporate mission for Philip Morris is to continue weaning the company away from its dependence on cigarettes. Welch's mission for GE is to make it a worldwide leader in advanced technology and services.

At both these companies, the mission serves as the basis for defining a set of *corporate objectives.* These objectives might specify criteria for acquiring new businesses or divesting existing ones and for establishing earnings targets and return-on-investment goals. As a direct outgrowth of its corporate mission, GE's corporate objectives were:

- to be first or second in key technology and service businesses such as medical imaging and factory automation
- to change the firm's business mix through acquisitions and divestment, so that 80 percent of earnings would come from technology and services by 1995
- to maintain a minimum earnings growth rate of 10 percent in each business
- to achieve a return on investment of 15 percent in each business.

Objectives were also developed for each of GE's 15 SBUs. For example, GE's medical imaging unit might have established objectives such as developing nuclear imaging capabilities, maintaining an earnings growth rate of at least 15 percent (50 percent higher than the corporate guideline), and broadening its international marketing base.

With these general objectives in place, top management next evaluates the firm's *business mix* to identify which SBUs should be supported with more investment, which should be maintained at current levels, and which should be divested. Such an analysis evaluates each SBU's growth and profitability potential and results in an overall *corporate growth strategy* designed to allocate funds to each business unit. GE's business mix analysis led it to:

- sell its small appliance division to Black & Decker
- sell its television and electronics business to Thompson International, the leading electronics producer in France
- acquire Government Reinsurance Corporation and Kidder Peabody, a stock brokerage firm, to establish a base in financial services
- acquire RCA for $6.3 billion to give it a foothold in broadcasting (RCA owned NBC) and to gain its aerospace business
- sink $8 billion into development of technology for its factory automation and medical imaging businesses.

Each business unit must also evaluate its mix of products to meet SBU and corporate objectives. Based on an analysis of the product mix, business-unit managers will then develop an SBU growth strategy spelling out allocations for the unit's product offerings. For example, acceptance of GE's second-generation CT-scans led the medical imaging unit to allocate money to develop third-generation CT-scans and nuclear imaging capabilities.

The final stage in strategic marketing planning is *evaluation and control.* Top management must evaluate the plan to determine if corporate objectives have been met and must also institute controls to make sure the plan remains on course. The SBUs implement their plans, evaluate the results to determine if they are in line with corporate and SBU objectives, and institute controls.

We will be focusing primarily on large companies in this chapter because such companies are usually multi-divisional firms likely to be organized on an SBU

FIGURE 22.2

The Strategic Marketing Planning Process

basis, and it is important to recognize the role of the business unit in strategic planning. But the steps in Figure 22.2 are just as relevant for smaller companies. A small company like Bowater Computer Forms needs a strategic plan to adapt to an ever-changing computer environment. It must establish *sales and profit objectives* for its key businesses: computer paper, diskettes, and computer software. It must also constantly evaluate its *business mix* in light of anticipated changes in the computer environment. In so doing, Bowater must establish a *corporate growth strategy* to determine the relative emphasis it will place on each of its businesses and to allocate future resources accordingly. Finally, it must *evaluate and control* its strategic plan every year while focusing on a five-year planning horizon.

In the remainder of this chapter, we will review the major components of the strategic planning process shown in Figure 22.2.

DEFINE THE CORPORATE MISSION

A corporate mission should give a company's management a sense of purpose and direction. The question "What business are we in?" provides the focus for a corporate mission statement.

A company could take a product-oriented view in defining its mission or a customer-oriented focus. A product-oriented view is likely to frame the company's mission in terms of existing resources and technology, while a customer-oriented focus is likely to frame the mission in terms of satisfying customer needs.

A strict product focus tends to be far more limiting than a need-oriented focus, inhibiting the search for new opportunities. Imagine how history would have changed if railroad companies such as Penn Central or Baltimore & Ohio had conceived of their business as the transportation business rather than the railway business. What would have prevented such railroad companies from buying a small airline or bus company in the 1930s?[12]

As we have seen in Chapter 2, Kodak went from a product to a customer orientation by changing its mission from a "photography company" to an "imaging company." This shift prompted a change in the company's corporate advertising approach. Before the change in mission, most of its advertising was for individual products that focused on the company's photography business. After, the company embarked on an umbrella campaign that featured electronic publishing, printing, color imaging, and digital scanning systems. The basic ad theme, "The new vision of Kodak," (see the bottom of the ad in Exhibit 22.1) reflected the change in corporate mission to imaging.

DETERMINE CORPORATE OBJECTIVES

Although the corporate mission of companies like American Express and Kodak ultimately leads to strategies such as divesting an insurance company or developing imaging products, their mission statements are too broad to direct such strategies. Corporate mission statements need to be translated into a set of more-specific objectives. That is why Philip Morris' mission of growth in its food divisions was

EXHIBIT 22.1

Defining Kodak's Corporate Mission: Imaging

translated into the specific objective that these businesses would account for more than half of its $58 billion in revenues by 1991.

Westinghouse, one of America's most diverse conglomerates—with interests in broadcasting, financial services, truck refrigeration, and waste disposal—defines its mission as maximizing short-term profits. On this basis, objectives for each SBU are an 8.5-percent annual growth in sales, 10-percent annual increase in pre-tax earnings, and 18- to 20-percent return on equity. Some critics say short-term profit maximization is hardly a mission and that this short-term view has led the company to get rid of businesses that would have been profitable had they been given a chance. The company's focus on the short term has increased immediate earnings, making stockholders happy. At the close of the 1980s, Westinghouse trailed only Philip Morris, Merck, and McDonald's in growth.[13] But its short-term focus came back to haunt it in the early 1990s when Westinghouse found its stable of businesses were mature and short on growth potential.

In contrast, GE has taken a longer-term view of where it is headed. Its single-minded focus on making the company a leader in high technology areas such as medical imaging and factory automation has resulted in a willingness to forego short-term earnings objectives for longer-term growth. Its investment of $8 billion into R&D for these areas is an example.

EVALUATE THE BUSINESS AND PRODUCT MIX

One of the most important responsibilities of any company's top management is deciding what its business mix should be. This was certainly true of Philip Morris. Figure 22.3 shows the changes in Philip Morris' business mix from 1987 to 1991. Whereas in 1970, 100 percent of Philip Morris' sales were derived from cigarettes, by 1987 only 53 percent of sales were from cigarettes primarily as a result of the acquisition of Miller and General Foods. By 1991, the company had further reduced its dependence on cigarettes to 42 percent with the acquisition of Kraft. Foods now account for the major part of the company's sales. Figure 22.3 also shows the decreasing role of beer in the company's mix, going from 13 percent to 6 percent of company sales in four years. Philip Morris' corporate growth strategy is to increase its foods businesses while maintaining the cigarette business for its cash-generating potential. The acquisition of Suchard in 1990 supported this strategy.

BUSINESS PORTFOLIO ANALYSIS

Before a company can embark on transformations such as Philip Morris' switch from cigarettes to foods, management must have some systematic approach to determining its business mix. Such an approach, **business portfolio analysis,** *esti-*

FIGURE 22.3

Change in Philip Morris' Business Mix: 1987–91

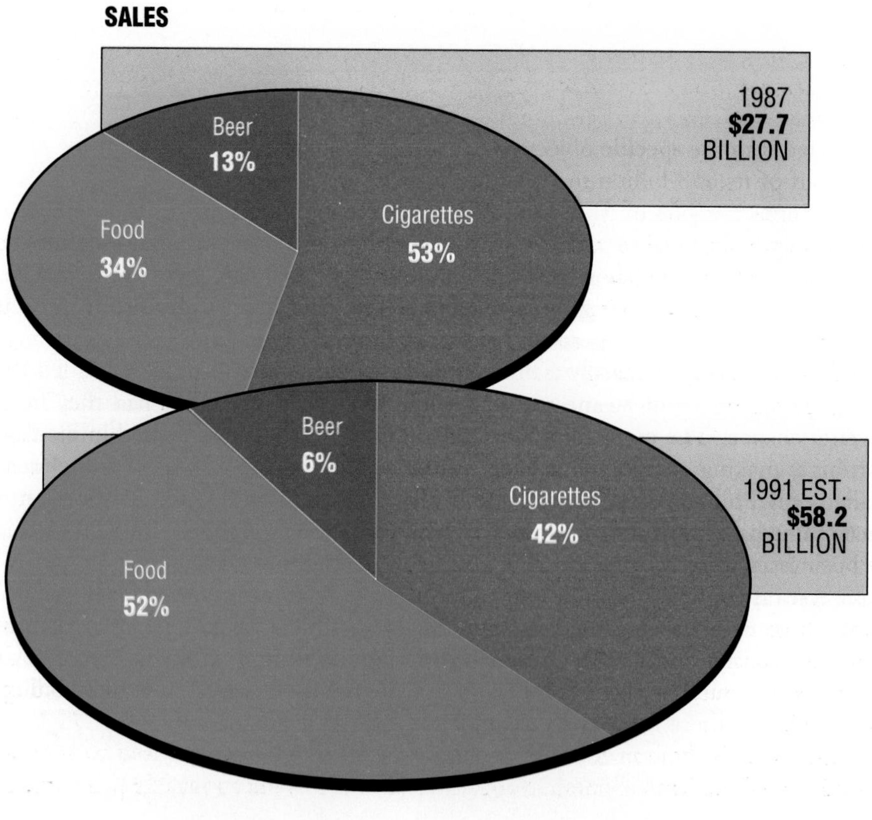

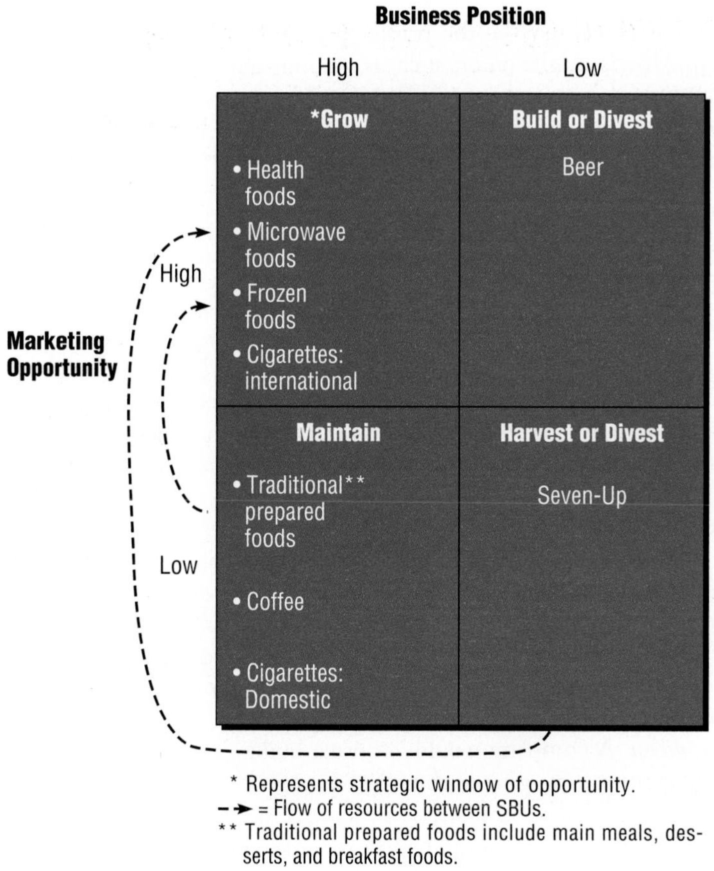

FIGURE 22.4

Philip Morris' Business Portfolio

mates the revenue potential of each business and allows management to allocate resources to these businesses accordingly. Revenue potential for each business is evaluated on two criteria: *marketing opportunity* and the company's *business position,* that is, its ability to exploit opportunity (see Figure 22.4).

As we have seen in Chapter 4, marketing opportunities are defined by environmental factors such as changing demographics, life styles, and cultural values. Marketing opportunities can also result from a low level of competition, favorable economic conditions, new technologies, or laws and regulations that favor certain industries. A company's business position is determined by its level of management expertise in key businesses and by its resources, primarily financial, production, R&D, and marketing resources.

Marketing opportunity and business position are the two dimensions that form a business portfolio matrix in Figure 22.4. In Chapter 2, we defined a *strategic window of opportunity* as businesses that are areas of opportunity and that the company has the resources to exploit (top left in Figure 22.4). But all of a company's businesses cannot be strategic windows since areas in the upper left of the matrix require resources. As a result, portfolio analysis is designed to develop a mix of businesses that generate and require cash. The revenue-generating businesses will supply cash to fuel future growth for the strategic windows of opportunity. On this basis, business portfolio analysis views the corporation as a portfolio or mix of businesses, each with a different mission, market, set of resources, and earnings potential.

Philip Morris' base in tobacco generates revenues that can be used to support future growth at Kraft General Foods in areas such as microwavable products. In ten years, microwavable products may be the prime source of cash for growth in newer areas that Philip Morris might enter, such as vitamin-enriched food additives. Based on this framework, there are several approaches to portfolio analysis. They all rely on the common matrix shown in Figure 22.4 in which opportunity-related criteria are listed on one dimension and company-related factors on the other.

BUSINESS PORTFOLIO STRATEGIES

The four alternatives shown in the matrix in Figure 22.4 are known as **business portfolio strategies**, *that is, strategies that specify resource allocations for each business.* As shown in Figure 22.4, the upper left hand portion of the matrix (the strategic window) represents areas of high opportunity that the firm is in a position to exploit. If an SBU is in this area, the decision should be for it to *grow*. This strategy requires investing in the SBU's future growth potential.

If opportunities are low, but the firm is in a strong position, as shown in the lower-left portion of the figure, then the company should invest in the business unit on a limited basis to *maintain* its present position. SBUs following a maintain strategy are cash generators that can support strategic windows of opportunity.

If opportunities are good, but the company is in a poor position to exploit them, as in the upper-right quadrant, two strategies are possible: (1) invest in the SBU by acquiring the resources to exploit opportunity, a *build* strategy, or (2) get out of the business, that is, *divest.* A company would choose a build strategy only if it felt it could develop the resources to pursue the opportunity.

If opportunities are poor, and the company is in a weak position (the lower-right portion of the matrix), its strategy should be to *harvest* the business by reducing costs faster than decreases in revenues. A profit in the short term can result through these cutbacks, but by eliminating support for the business, the company realizes its days are numbered. The alternative to harvesting is for the company to immediately *divest* itself of the business.

PHILIP MORRIS' BUSINESS PORTFOLIO

Figure 22.4 shows how Philip Morris might have applied portfolio analysis in making business-mix decisions concerning a number of its current and past SBUs. Health, frozen, and microwavable foods are seen as strategic windows of opportunity warranting further investment due to greater emphasis on health and more of a focus on convenience as a result of the increasing proportion of singles and working women. The portfolio strategy for these businesses is growth through additional investment.

Tobacco is split into two SBUs, domestic and international. The international SBU is thriving because, with the exception of Western Europe, health concerns and advertising restrictions have not taken hold in most other countries. This SBU is in a moderate growth position because Philip Morris predicts greater restrictions on the sale of cigarettes abroad and an eventual decrease in demand. The North American cigarette SBU is in the lower half of Figure 22.4, meaning low growth potential, because of rising health concerns and a general recognition of the risks of smoking. Philip Morris' business position is strong because it has the world's best-selling brand—Marlboro. As a result, the company will continue to invest in product development, advertising, and distribution to *maintain* its leadership position.

Coffee is in a maintain position for similar reasons. Kraft General Foods has leading brands such as Maxwell House and Yuban, but a long-term decrease in coffee consumption has limited growth, warranting a maintain position. KGF's traditional prepared foods—divided into main meals, desserts, and breakfast foods SBUs—are also in the maintain quadrant. Many of these brands such as Oscar Mayer meats have experienced declines because of concerns about cholesterol and calories. However, since these brands represent leaders in their category, the business units continue to be cash generators.

Philip Morris is in a difficult position with its beer business. Growth is moderate because of increasing acceptance of light, draft, and nonalcoholic beers, but long-term predictions are not encouraging. Further, the company is in an increasingly weak position due to a loss of market share for its flagship brand to Budweiser. As a result, Philip Morris must either build the business by continuing to strengthen Miller Lite and its new entry, Miller Genuine Draft, or it must consider harvesting and divesting the business.

Under Philip Morris' ownership, 7-Up was a no-growth company. Accustomed to national marketing, Philip Morris could not get the knack of dealing with powerful local bottlers who ran their own campaigns. It also failed to secure adequate distribution, leading to a disaster when it tried introducing a new soda called Like. Before divesting 7-Up, Philip Morris began harvesting it by cutting back on its investment in the company, watching as its market share slid from 6 percent to 4 percent. In 1986, 7-Up was sold and is now thriving under new owners.

The dotted line in Figure 22.4 shows the flow of resources between businesses. Businesses in low areas of opportunity supply a flow of cash for investment to businesses in higher areas of opportunity. Cigarettes, coffee, and traditional prepared foods supply cash as market leaders. 7-Up provided cash when it was sold. As a result of these moves, Philip Morris has a good balance of cash generators and cash users. It is conforming to an important goal of business portfolio analysis—to ensure a mix of cash-generating and cash-using businesses so that the former can support the latter's growth. Further, Philip Morris has few businesses on the right-hand part of the matrix. This is also positive, because businesses in the build and harvest/divest portions of the matrix generally represent problems.

APPROACHES TO BUSINESS PORTFOLIO ANALYSIS

Although the goal of business portfolio analysis is always to provide an optimal mix of businesses, the analysis can be approached in a number of ways. The most widely used approaches are the Boston Consulting Group's (BCG's) growth/share analysis and GE/McKinsey's market attractiveness/business position analysis. (The latter was developed by General Electric and the large consulting firm, McKinsey & Co., as an alternative to the BCG approach.) We will consider both approaches here, because they demonstrate different ways of systematizing the processes of selecting a business mix and allocating funds to businesses.

BCG'S GROWTH/SHARE ANALYSIS

The Boston Consulting Group, a leading management consulting company, developed an approach that uses two criteria to evaluate a firm's business units: the market growth rate and the relative market share of its products. Relative market share is calculated by dividing the SBU's market share by the market share of its leading competitors. Thus, if Budweiser has a 40-percent share of the beer market and Miller High Life has a 20-percent share, Budweiser's relative share is 2.0 (40/20) and Miller's is .5 (20/40).

FIGURE 22.5

BCG's Growth/Share Matrix

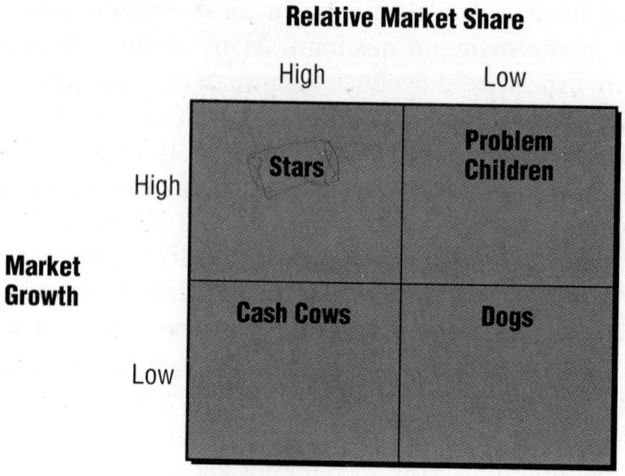

The growth rate for an SBU's market is regarded as a summary measure of marketing opportunity, while the firm's relative market share is regarded as a summary measure of its strength or weakness (that is, its business position) in that market. As a result, the BCG matrix parallels the basic portfolio matrix presented in Figure 22.4. The reason BCG uses market growth and relative market share as the two criteria for evaluating SBUs is because studies have shown that these two factors are related to profitability.[14]

BCG's matrix presents four alternative SBU positionings that are shown in Figure 22.5 and parallel those in Figure 22.4:

- *Stars* are products with a high growth rate and market share. These products warrant a growth strategy and need significant cash to finance rapid growth.
- *Cash cows* are SBUs in low-growth areas that have high market shares. They generate more cash than is required to maintain them. Excess cash is used to finance high-growth areas.
- *Problem children* are SBUs that have a low relative market share in high-growth situations. Their eventual direction is not clear, and the firm must determine whether to build them into stars or to get rid of them. Any course in between is dangerous, because it could just dissipate resources.
- *Dogs* are low-share SBUs in low-growth areas. They should be either harvested for short-term profits or divested.

The BCG approach provides a useful overview of a company's business mix, and its labels of businesses as stars, cash cows, dogs, and problem children are widely used. It has serious flaws, however. The most serious is its assumption that market share is linked to profitability and should be the criterion for a company's strength. Many other factors affect the firm's business position besides market share, including financial resources, marketing know-how, and distribution facilities. And although market share is generally related to profitability, there are many exceptions. As we have seen in Chapter 6, low-market-share firms can be very profitable when they operate in protected niches.

A second major flaw in the BCG analysis is that it relies on the single factor of market growth to measure opportunity. As we have seen in Chapter 4, a host of factors other than market growth affect marketing opportunity, including competitive intensity, legal and regulatory factors, and technology.

GE'S MARKET ATTRACTIVENESS/BUSINESS POSITION MATRIX

General Electric began using the BCG analysis in the early 1970s but soon recognized the limitations of relying on only one factor to measure opportunity and one factor to measure business position. As a result, GE asked McKinsey & Company, a large management consulting firm, to help it develop a better portfolio approach. The result was a matrix shown in Figure 22.6, which evaluates market attractiveness and business position. (Market attractiveness is closely analogous to marketing opportunity and relates opportunity to specific markets.) This matrix rates an SBU on *multiple criteria* related to market attractiveness and business position, such as:

Market Attractiveness	**Business Position**
Market size	Market share
Growth rate	Product quality
Cyclicality of demand	Price competitiveness
Seasonality of demand	Marketing capability
Competitive intensity	Production strength
Rate of technological change	Financial strength
Barriers to entry	Distribution capability
Economies of scale	Sales effectiveness
Required capitalization	Capacity utilization
Legal regulations	Technological skills

FIGURE 22.6

GE's Market Attractiveness/Business Position Analysis

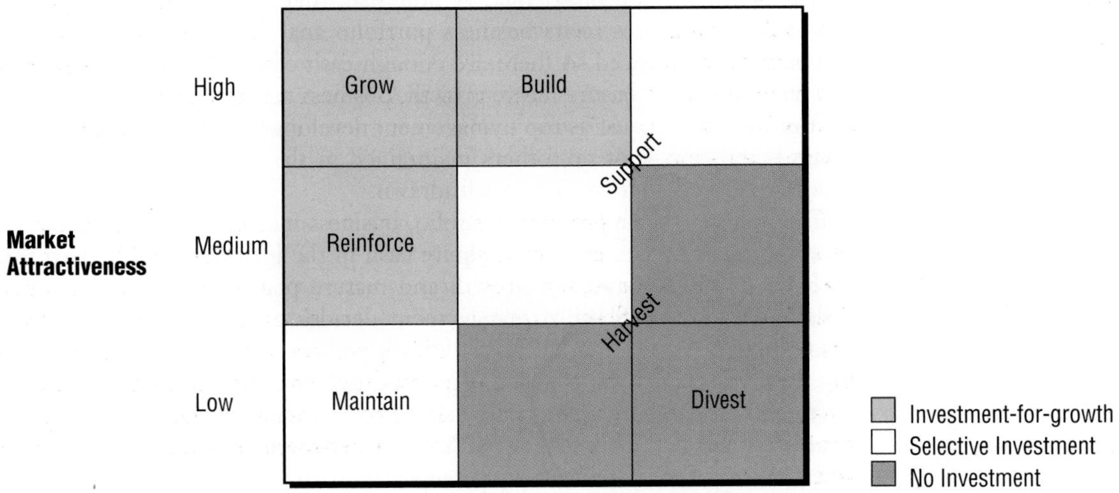

Once the SBU is rated, it is positioned on the two dimensions in the matrix shown in Figure 22.6. The matrix shows three general portfolio strategies. SBUs with high market attractiveness that are in a strong business position are candidates for investment for growth. SBUs in the middle range are candidates for selective investment to generate short-term earnings, and SBUs with low attractiveness and business position warrant no further investment.

Figure 22.6 also shows that a company can generate more specific portfolio strategies within each of these three alternatives. In the investment-for-growth area, three strategies are shown: grow, build, and reinforce. As shown in Figure 22.4, a grow strategy is warranted for a new SBU in a strategic window of opportunity and a build strategy if market attractiveness is high, but the firm does not have the resources to exploit it. A reinforce strategy is used for a more mature SBU that is in a strong business position but facing increasing competition. This strategy requires greater advertising and sales support.

Two different types of portfolio strategies would be appropriate in the selective investment category. A support strategy would apply to an SBU that has a unique competitive advantage in appealing to a particular market segment. The company would allocate resources to the SBU on a selective basis to protect its competitive advantage. For example, American Motors invested selectively in its Jeep line to support a protected niche that was not threatened by the Big-Three auto makers. In a maintain strategy, the company would allocate enough funds to ensure the SBU's leadership position but would not try to increase market share, since the unit is in a stagnant market.

As shown in Figure 22.6, a firm follows a strategy of harvesting or divesting the SBU when opportunity is low and the business position is poor. A harvesting strategy is best if a firm has a group of loyal customers that will continue to buy its brands despite little advertising and a lack of widespread distribution. In the absence of such a core of loyal users, the business is unlikely to maintain short-term earnings and should be divested. As we have seen, Philip Morris harvested 7-Up by cutting back on advertising and distribution support before fully divesting it in 1986.

PRODUCT PORTFOLIO ANALYSIS

Just as corporate management evaluates its mix of businesses, SBU managers must evaluate their unit's product mix. In doing so, they use the same principles that top management uses in its business portfolio analysis—namely, that a product mix should be balanced so there are enough cash cows to support potential stars and enough stars to ensure future growth. Business managers thus develop product portfolio strategies, just as top management develops business portfolio strategies: Some brands are built up, others maintained in their cash-generating positions, others harvested, and yet others withdrawn.

In developing their product portfolio, business managers must manage it over the product life cycle. Products require cash in the introductory phase of the life cycle, generate cash in their growth and mature phases, and may again require cash in the decline phase if management decides to try to revitalize them (for example, the decision to revitalize 7-Up with a "no-caffeine" claim). To develop a mix of brands in the introductory, growth, and mature phases of the life cycle, business managers must ensure a stream of new products over time. Successful new products that are initially cash users then become cash generators as they mature, and fuel more new products that serve as the basis for future growth.

Of the two approaches to business portfolio analysis discussed in the preceding section, GE's market attractiveness/business position approach is more suitable for a product portfolio analysis. The reason is because a range of factors reflecting market attractiveness and business position determine the movement of a product along its life cycle. Standard Brands, now a part of RJR Nabisco, used the GE-McKinsey approach to analyze its mix of grocery products.[15] Product managers received a data package with projections of inflation, economic growth, demographic, and other environmental changes that they used to evaluate their individual products on market attractiveness and business position.

The result was the product portfolio matrix illustrated in Figure 22.7. Piñata Foods and Planter's Nuts, specialty and snack food categories that the company acquired because of their growth potential, were in an investment-for-growth position. Fleishman's Corn Oil was also in the investment-for-growth category. Although an established brand, it had growth potential because corn oil is recognized as being healthier than other oils.

Several product lines were in the selective investment category. Souverain Wines was not a major factor in the domestic wine industry because of competition from more established companies such as Gallo. Therefore, Standard Brands had to decide whether to build up the line or to get out of the wine business. Fleishman's Yeast and Royal Gelatin Desserts appealed to well-established consumer segments. Standard Brand's candy-bar and confectionery products were in a strong position but in a mature, low-growth market. The company was willing to invest selectively to maintain these brands for their cash-generating potential.

Finally, several products were in the harvest/divest category. Pet foods was a candidate for divestment because of declining sales. Chase & Sanborne, once a leading coffee brand, was in the declining phase of its life cycle and had only a 4-percent share of the market in 1979. Because the brand had a small but loyal

FIGURE 22.7

Standard Brand's Past Product Mix

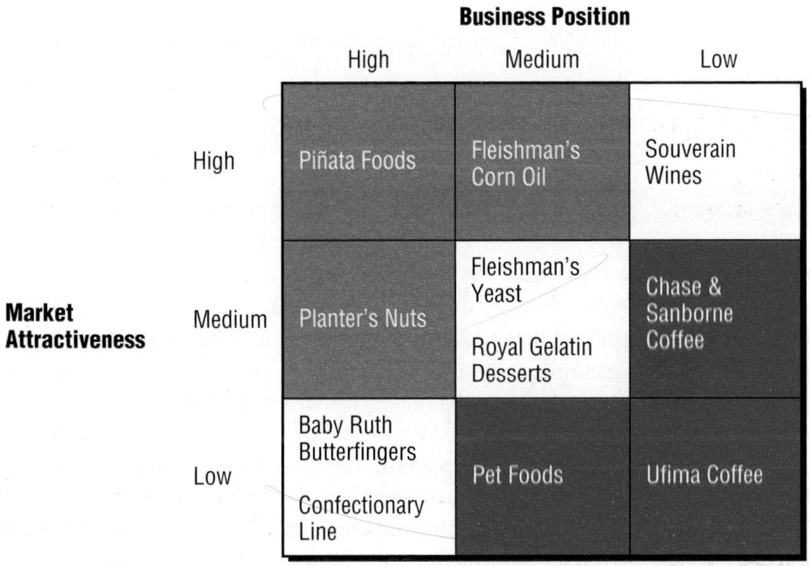

GLOBAL MARKETING STRATEGIES

How P&G's Portfolio Analysis Took Cover Girl Global

When Edwin Artzt was named chairman of Procter & Gamble in 1989, few thought the 60-year-old executive was anything more than a caretaker. After all, P&G's revenues were double that of a decade earlier thanks to outgoing CEO John Smale. But Artzt, nicknamed the Prince of Darkness because of his late-night work habits, was not the sit-back type. Within two years, he would leave his indelible stamp on the company by leading it into a global battle for the world cosmetics market.

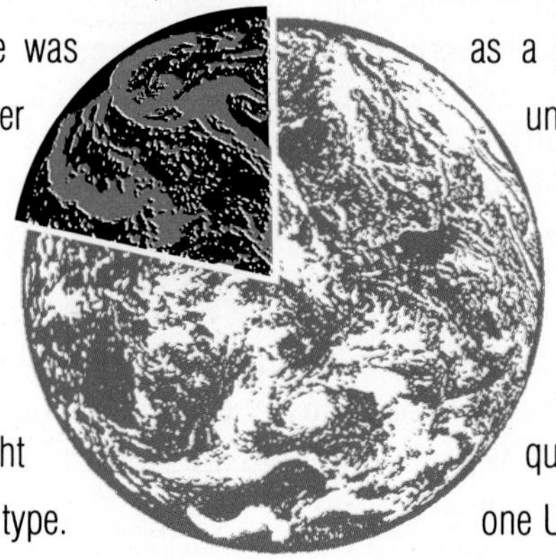

What Artzt saw upon assuming the helm of P&G was that many of its staple products were in mature markets where competitors were growing ever more aggressive. To have a healthy future, P&G needed to be able to act faster to seize opportunities in high-growth markets. And few were higher-growth than cosmetics. To prove the point, Artzt had only to look toward P&G's experience with Oil of Olay, the skin cream it inherited after buying Richardson Vicks in 1985. Having previously been marketed to older women as a conditioner, Oil of Olay was repositioned as a youth cream to a broader market under a P&G ad campaign that said "Why grow old gracefully?" By 1990, sales zoomed up 60 percent.

With the youth market in mind, one of Artzt's first acts was to acquire Cover Girl in 1990, the number-one U.S. cosmetics brand. After doubling its ad budget and stylizing its packaging, P&G's ad agency was able to shed the line's girl-next-door image and replace it with a higher fashion one. It was the first step toward taking the brand global; but, with barely a fifth of Cover Girl's revenues coming from abroad and a weak distribution network there, Artzt realized that it could take him several years to achieve his goal. Much more effective, he reasoned, would be an acquisition strategy where he could buy an already developed distribution network.

What was available? As it happened, Revlon's two

following, management felt it could still generate profits for several years by cutting back marketing expenditures and harvesting it. The same was not true of Ufima Coffee, a French coffee subsidiary. Its low returns prompted Standard Brands to divest it.

This product portfolio strategy produced sound results. Overall, about 50 percent of sales came from brands in the investment-for-growth category, 30 percent from brands in the selective investment category, and 20 percent from brands in the harvest/divest category. This 50/50 split between cash-generating and cash-using brands reflected a balanced product portfolio.

GLOBAL MARKETING STRATEGIES

cosmetics divisions, Max Factor and Beatrix, were going on the block at just that time. What Artzt liked about these two divisions was their international presence. Two thirds of Max Factor's $600 million in revenues came from abroad, and the German-based Beatrix—which did not even sell its products in the United States—had well-developed distribution networks throughout Austria, Italy, Spain, Sweden, and Switzerland. The fit was too good to pass up and in 1991 Artzt signed a $1.1 billion check for the two divisions.

Suddenly, P&G went from having no fragrance business in Europe to $130 million in sales and from $28 million in sales on its cosmetics lines to $210 million. The news was equally good in Japan, where Max Factor was well accepted. P&G cosmetics sales instantly went from zero to $225 million there. The numbers led one impressed analyst to project that Artzt had cut at least three years off the time it otherwise would have taken to make Cover Girl a world brand. His competitors were equally shell-shocked, since no other company had ever attempted to develop a Pan-European cosmetics line in such quick order.

However, Artzt believes that the only way to lead Procter & Gamble into the future is by redefining its mission so that it begins thinking of itself as a leader in the high-growth international cosmetics market. To him, the moves are far from audacious, they are just plain common sense.

Questions: What was the reasoning behind Artzt's acquisition of Max Factor and Beatrix? How did it tie in to his earlier acquisition of Cover Girl?

Sources: "Procter & Gamble Is Following Its Nose," *Business Week*, April 22, 1991; "A New World of Beauty for P&G," *Adweek's Marketing Week*, April 15, 1991; "At Procter & Gamble Change Under Artzt Isn't Just Cosmetic," *The Wall Street Journal*, March 5, 1991.

CORPORATE GROWTH STRATEGIES

At the corporate and the SBU level, the key element in the strategic marketing plan is the company's growth strategy—its overall *game plan* for the next five years. A corporate growth strategy can be specified, however, only when the company's mission, objectives, and business portfolio have been developed.

In contemplating growth, the major question to be addressed is whether to emphasize acquisitions or internal development. If a company relies on external

EXHIBIT 22.2

The Results of ConAgra's Acquisition Strategy

acquisitions, it means that the company is not satisfied with its current business position and is looking for new businesses to fuel growth. In so doing, it wishes to broaden its resources and capabilities. If it relies on internal development, management is satisfied with its resources and is looking for opportunities to better satisfy customer needs by introducing new products.

For instance, Abbott Laboratories, the pharmaceutical company, has rejected a strategy of acquisitions for growth; instead, it is maintaining a competitive advantage in the health-care industry by constantly developing new products in the medical diagnostic market such as a desktop blood analyzer and a blood test to detect the AIDS virus.[16] Abbott has yet to find an outside business with more profit potential than the businesses it has developed internally.

In contrast, ConAgra has pursued an aggressive acquisition strategy to become one of the nation's largest food companies. In 1981, ConAgra's sales were split equally between branded foods, food processing, and agricultural products. In a move to get away from the commodity-oriented agricultural and processing businesses, the company established a goal of seeking branded food companies with good earnings records that are leaders in their market. Purchases such as Banquet Foods, RJR Nabisco's frozen-food business, Beatrice, and Golden Valley Microwave Foods resulted in 77 percent of ConAgra's sales being in branded foods by 1991. The company now has such venerable brand names as Hunt's ketchup, La Choy Chinese foods, Peter Pan peanut butter, and Orville Redenbacher's popcorn (see Exhibit 22.2). ConAgra's sales skyrocketed from $1.4 billion in 1981 to $19.5 billion in 1991.[17]

Most companies, however, do not rely on only one strategy for growth. Sony pursued an acquisition strategy when it paid $3.4 billion for Columbia Pictures (giving it two film studios, a TV unit, and the Loews theater chain) and $2 billion more for CBS Records. Simultaneously, it was following an internal development strategy by developing such products as digital audio tape players and 8mm VCRs.

The synergy in the dual strategy is evident. The CBS deal gave Sony a roster of the world's best-selling artists whose music could be released on tapes and discs. The Columbia acquisition allowed it to begin releasing the studio's films on formats such as 8mm VHS and laser disc.[18]

INTERNAL DEVELOPMENT STRATEGIES

Figure 22.8 classifies corporate growth strategies by two criteria: whether they are directed toward new or existing markets, and whether they require new or existing products. These two dimensions produce three alternative strategies for internal development: market penetration, market expansion, and product development.

MARKET PENETRATION

A **market penetration strategy** *requires investing in existing brands directed toward existing markets.* Many companies have followed a strategy of acquisition outside of their core areas only to discover that they do not have the managerial or marketing know-how to run the businesses they have acquired. After a painful process of divestment, they go back to emphasizing existing brands.

General Mills followed this path. In 1985, it divested businesses in fashion (Izod) and toys (Parker Brothers, Kenner) and went back to emphasizing existing brands in its lower-growth core businesses, cereals and cake mixes. The company is now counting on product reformulations and changes in packaging to sustain older brands such as Cheerios, Wheaties, Total, and the Betty Crocker cake mix line.[19] But a company cannot rely solely on a strategy of market penetration. New products are required for future growth. General Mills recognizes this fact by combining market penetration with a strategy of new product development.

MARKET EXPANSION

A second internal development strategy, **market expansion**, *involves expanding existing products into new markets.* The seven regional U.S. phone companies, dubbed Baby Bells, are following this approach. Stymied by restrictions in the

FIGURE 22.8

Corporate Growth Strategies for Internal Development

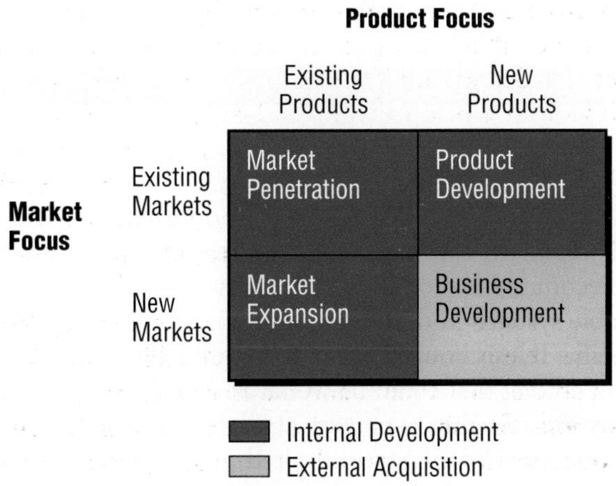

ETHICAL AND ENVIRONMENTAL ISSUES IN MARKETING

For Companies Expanding into Europe, the Message Is: "Welcome Aboard, But Leave Your Trash at Home"

The European Community's 12 member states have a simple message for the foreign marketers who want to set up shop on the continent: "Welcome aboard, but leave your trash at home."

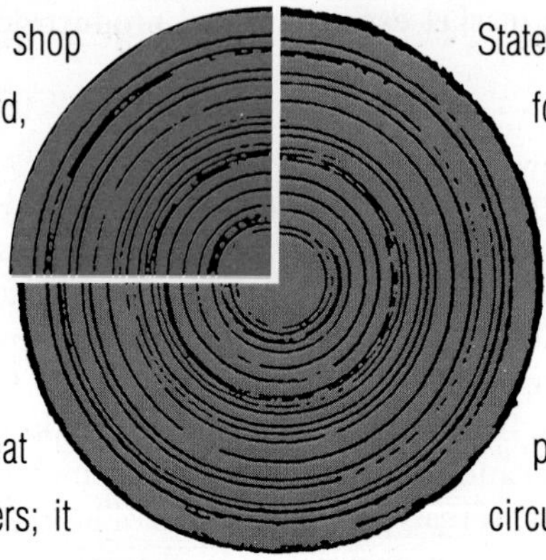

The European Community (EC) recognizes that by dismantling its trade barriers in 1992, it has created an economic powerhouse that will be attractive to foreign marketers; it also realizes that market growth cannot come at the expense of the environment. So the council has announced that firms wishing to do business with it must first document that their operations will cause minimal ecological damage. The edict is forcing corporate planners to weigh ecological concerns far more heavily than ever before as they draft strategic plans for Europe.

One of the best examples of the EC's seriousness is a rule that requires Detroit's Big-Three auto makers to submit to European pollution-control tests instead of merely certifying that they have passed U.S. tests. If there is a bright spot, it is that the European tests are virtually identical to those in the United States. The same cannot be said, however, for many of the other Euro-pollution rules.

Since a key EC guideline allows individual countries to pass laws that are more rigorous than existing pan-European ones when "ecological circumstances" warrant, a host of restrictive laws are hitting the books. Consider the German law that requires consumers to leave superfluous packaging materials such as cardboard containers for batteries at a retail outlet when they make their purchase. The law is so strict it even makes retailers responsible for collecting such things as yogurt containers for recycling. If 7-Eleven was creating a strategic plan for moving into Germany, provisions for recycling facilities would clearly have to be included.

Prospective European marketers must also consider how the new laws increase their environmental

United States that limit their rate of return on local service and their ability to sell telephone equipment, the Bells are scouring Europe's potential $20 billion hardware and telecommunication market. Southwestern Bell, for instance, is helping build new cable systems in the Liverpool region of Britain, while a consortium that includes Pacific Telesis bought a license to build West Germany's cellular telephone system—a project that could be worth $6 billion over 20 years. This global push grew out of the fact that managers at each of the Baby Bells believed that legal regulations in the United States limited growth potential enough to make Europe an attractive growth frontier.[20]

ETHICAL AND ENVIRONMENTAL ISSUES IN MARKETING

liability. The EC has ruled that parent corporations can be held accountable for the misdeeds of subsidiaries and third-party waste disposal firms. Such laws have led to a boom among waste management companies that can offer strategic planners peace of mind. In Spain, which projects annual economic growth at 40 percent but has been slow to comply with the EC's eco-guidelines, pollution-control equipment has been ranked as the second best prospect for exporters.

Concerns about environmental liability have also sparked a new cautiousness among underwriters who supply insurance to multinationals. Many are calling on their prospective clients to certify their good-faith with "ecological audits," that is, a thorough review of the environmental controls a company has in place to control pollution. These audits have also become popular with American companies that are interested in European acquisition targets but concerned about their environmental soundness.

Given the long-term benefits of operating in Europe, strategic planners must do their utmost to ensure they keep up with the latest regulations. Perhaps the most vigilant company in this regard has been Bayer, which is pouring 20 percent of its manufacturing budget into environmental planning and protection. Bayer's motto might best be described as: "If it's not clean, it's not profitable."

Question: What provisions will companies expanding into Europe have to make in their plans for environmental controls? Cite examples.

Sources: "EC Balances Trade with the Green Revolution," *Business America*, September 9, 1991; "Toughened Environmental Regulation Looms in EC," *National Underwriter*, October 14, 1991; and "The Dirty Dozen," *The Economist*, July 20, 1991.

PRODUCT DEVELOPMENT

In the third internal development strategy in Figure 22.8, **product development,** *a company emphasizes development of new products or extensions of existing product lines, in most cases for existing markets.* Syntex, the first company to make a birth-control pill in the 1960s, adopted this strategy when it switched from external acquisitions in the mid 1980s, selling its beauty and eye-care businesses so that it could stick strictly to pharmaceuticals. Committing to pharmaceuticals meant relying on its expertise in biotechnology to introduce new products. The company upped its

R&D budget and introduced new drugs to fight ulcers, hypertension, and arthritis. It has doubled its sales force to help sell these new drugs.[21]

In the case of drug maker Warner Lambert, an increasing focus on new products is the result of the expiration of patents on several of its leading drugs. The company is investing heavily in research to develop a new generation of drugs. One of the fruits of this strategy is Cognex, which if approved by the Food and Drug Administration, would be the first drug available for the treatment of Alzheimer's disease.[22]

EXTERNAL ACQUISITION STRATEGIES

When a company aims new products to totally new markets, it requires new resources such as technology, marketing know-how, distribution networks, a sales force, and manufacturing facilities. This strategy, shown in the lower right-hand box in Figure 22.8, is referred to as **business development,** *that is, establishing new businesses for new markets.* Although companies occasionally develop new businesses internally, such as GE's development of its factory automation business, business development usually requires following a strategy of external acquisition. Here, it is important to make a distinction: Until now, our discussion of external acquisitions has focused on companies diversifying into unrelated lines and getting into trouble as a result. There are other, less-risky, routes to external acquisition, however.

Figure 22.9 presents the alternatives for corporate growth through acquisition along two dimensions. First, a company can acquire businesses similar to those it is now in, or it can acquire new businesses in unrelated areas. Second, a strategy of business development can be followed through diversification of its businesses or through integration of its operations. A diversification strategy is meant to expand a company's business mix, as when Philip Morris expanded into consumer packaged foods. An integration strategy is meant to expand the company's resource base, as when A&P acquired food manufacturers to assure itself of a source of supply for its private brands.

On this basis, four strategies for external acquisition are shown in Figure 22.9. **Divergent acquisition** *is a strategy of diversifying into new businesses.* Companies

FIGURE 22.9

Corporate Growth Strategies for External Acquisition

Type of Business		Type of Strategy: Diversification	Type of Strategy: Integration
	New Businesses	Divergent Acquisitions	Vertical Integration
	Similar Businesses	Convergent Acquisitions	Horizontal Integration

EXHIBIT 22.3

A Convergent Acquisition: Black & Decker Acquires Price Pfister

such as Philip Morris, GE, and Sony have changed their corporate missions to better enter the business environment of the 21st century by acquiring new businesses outside their traditional areas of competency.

Convergent acquisition *is diversifying into related busineses within a company's core areas of competency.* Black & Decker has consistently followed a convergent acquisition policy by folding into its business mix companies that are in the home improvement business. The first example of that was when it acquired General Electric's small appliance division. Later, it bought a stable of brand names that included Price Pfister faucets (see Exhibit 22.3) and True Temper lawn tools.[23]

Horizontal integration *is acquiring companies in the same business* to improve the firm's managerial competence and resource base. For example, Philip Morris' acquisition of Kraft was designed to integrate Kraft's resources with General Foods. Kraft had the managerial talent in new product development lacking at General Foods, and its dairy and microwavable product lines represented areas that GF did not market.

In **vertical integration,** *a company acquires new facilities backward or forward in its chain of operations.* **Backward integration** *is when a company acquires facilities that precede its operations in manufacturing and/or distribution.* For example, Tandy, a manufacturer of electronic goods, has acquired companies that make plastic molding, epoxy boards that hold microprocessors, and extruded wire from ingot rods to make electronic cables.[24] These companies provide the materials for the huge variety of electronic parts that Tandy manufactures. **Forward integration** *is when a company acquires facilities that enable it to carry out tasks that are further along in its manufacturing and/or distribution processes.* Tandy has also established its own retail stores—Radio Shacks—because of a desire to control the marketing of its products and be closer to the final consumer.

EVALUATE AND CONTROL THE STRATEGIC PLAN

Once corporate growth and portfolio strategies have been implemented, management must evaluate the strategic plan to determine if objectives have been met. Control over the strategic plan occurs at both the corporate and the SBU level.

At the corporate level, planners must determine whether the necessary resources are being allocated to the business units to achieve objectives. General Electric's objective of being a leader in factory automation required an investment of billions of dollars in R&D to develop this field. Corporate planners must also ensure that business strategies are consistent with overall objectives. For instance, requests by the lighting or appliance units at GE for increased R&D expenditures that might reduce the funds available for key technology and service areas might be rejected because they are not consistent with GE's overall objectives.

The management of strategic business units must also exert controls, tracking allocations to individual products and ensuring that the product mix has the right balance of stars and cash cows, with any dogs being harvested or divested so they do not serve as a cash drain. One of the most difficult aspects of strategic marketing planning is achieving the delicate balance between too much corporate control, which might stifle the initiative of the business units, and too little control, which might lead units to drift from corporate objectives.

This latter situation occurred at Westinghouse and led to a series of disastrous ventures. Westinghouse formed a business unit to build low-cost housing on government contracts and gave the SBU's management a blank check to achieve growth. The business unit began to acquire contracts without regard for profitability, and substantial losses resulted.

In contrast to Westinghouse, General Mills exerted too much control over some of its business units. When sales started to decrease at Parker Brothers, the company responded by getting involved in a business it did not really know—games. It introduced its own managers into the company, thus undercutting Parker managers who knew the business best. Similarly, when the company's Izod line of clothes began to slip, and Izod's managers tried to rush new lines to market, General Mills' corporate staffers held them back, allowing competitors to take business away from Izod.[25] These examples show the importance of effective, not excessive, control by corporate management.

SUMMARY

1. **What is the nature of the strategic marketing planning process?**
   The purpose of strategic marketing planning is to provide a corporate game plan to chart where the company should be going for the next five years. Developing a corporate game plan requires management to:
   a. define the firm's corporate mission and objectives
   b. evaluate the company's mix of strategic business units
   c. develop a corporate growth strategy to allocate funds to the SBUs
   d. evaluate and control the plan
2. **What is the role of the strategic business unit in the strategic marketing planning process?**
   Business-unit managers must evaluate the SBU's product mix just as top management evaluates the company's mix of business units. Managers will then

develop strategies for each of their products and submit an overall request for funds to corporate management. Once corporate approves funds, business-unit management implements the plan, evaluates results, and institutes controls.

3. **How can a firm best evaluate its business and product mix?**
A company can best evaluate its business mix through portfolio analysis. This approach views a company's businesses as a portfolio of SBUs that should be balanced between established, cash-generating brands and newer, cash-using brands that have potential for growth. Each business unit is evaluated on two criteria—marketing opportunity and the company's business position in the market. Business units are positioned on these criteria. Portfolio strategies are then developed for each unit depending on its position. For example, a strategy of investment-for-growth would be appropriate for an SBU with high marketing opportunity and in a strong business position. A strategy to maintain a brand would be appropriate for an established SBU in a strong market position but with limited growth potential. An SBU's product mix can be evaluated on the same basis—analyze marketing opportunity and business position for each product, then develop allocation strategies to achieve a balance between stars (products with high growth potential where the firm is in a strong position to exploit opportunity) and cash cows (established brands that can generate cash to support stars).

4. **What are the alternative routes to corporate growth?**
The strategic marketing plan must specify the degree to which a company will rely on internal product development or external business acquisition for growth. Most companies rely on both, but generally either internal development or external acquisition is more dominant.
One strategy for internal development, market penetration, focuses on increasing the market share for existing products to existing customers through more advertising, more sales promotions, or price cuts. Market expansion looks for growth by identifying new target markets for existing products. In product development, a company introduces new products to existing customers.
Strategies of external acquisition focus on businesses rather than products. These strategies can involve diversification into new businesses or integration of operations. Diversification can be convergent if the company acquires businesses within the company's core market areas, or it can be divergent if businesses in unrelated areas are acquired. Integration is vertical when a company acquires businesses that are earlier or later in the manufacturing and distribution chain—for example, the manufacturer owning its own retail stores, or a retailer owning manufacturing facilities. Integration is horizontal when a company acquires a direct competitor—as when Stroh Brewing acquired Schlitz.

KEY TERMS

Strategic marketing plan (p. 714)
Business mix (p. 715)
Product mix (p. 715)
Corporate mission (p. 716)
Business portfolio analysis (p. 720)
Business portfolio strategy (p. 722)
Market penetration strategy (p. 731)
Market expansion strategy (p. 731)
Product development strategy (p. 733)
Business development strategy (p. 734)
Divergent acquisitions (p. 734)
Convergent acquisitions (p. 735)
Horizontal integration (p. 735)
Vertical integration (p. 735)
Backward integration (p. 735)
Forward integration (p. 735)

QUESTIONS

1. What was Philip Morris' corporate mission in the early 1970s? What were the implications of its mission for (a) the mix of business units it developed, and (b) the company's acquisitions and divestments.
2. What is the distinction between top-down and bottom-up strategic planning? What are the implications of each planning approach for (a) who does strategic planning and (b) what gets emphasized in the strategic plan?
3. What are some of the problems that result from a top-down strategic planning process? Did General Electric have a problem with top-down planning? In what way? How did the company react to these problems?
4. Consider the five basic business portfolio strategies—grow, build, maintain, harvest, divest. Which strategy would be most applicable for each of the following businesses and why?
   a. a business with declining sales in a low-growth market, but with a small group of loyal consumers who are likely to continue buying the SBU's products
   b. a business in a mature industry in which the company has the second largest market share
   c. a business that has a number of high-technology products developed by the company, with good prospects for growth
   d. a business outside the company's core area that was recently acquired because of a strong R&D capability in a growing industry
5. What are the limitations of BCG's growth/share approach to portfolio analysis? How does GE's market attractiveness/business position analysis overcome some of these limitations?
6. What is the distinction between a strategy of market penetration and market expansion? When would a company be likely to use one or the other as the primary vehicle for growth? Give examples.
7. What is the distinction between a strategy of product development and business development? When would a company be likely to use one or the other as the primary vehicle for growth? Give examples.
8. What risks have companies experienced in following (or attempting to follow) strategies of:
   a. divergent acquisitions
   b. vertical integration
   c. horizontal integration

   Give examples of these risks.
9. When Mobil Oil purchased Montgomery Ward, the large mass merchandiser, Mobil pushed it to take certain actions to improve its earnings record. One action was to expand a Montgomery Ward Florida-based discount chain to national status. On the other hand, when Nestlé acquired Beech Nut, it allowed the new SBU's management to develop a plan to challenge Gerber and Heinz. What are the pros and cons of Mobil's more-activist position and Nestlé's more hands-off attitude?

QUESTIONS: YOU ARE THE DECISION MAKER

1. A manager for a one-business company commented on strategic marketing planning as follows:

   Strategic marketing planning is fine for a company organized on a business-unit basis. But a company in one business does not really need strategic planning. What is the point of developing a corporate mission, doing a portfolio analysis, or formulating a corporate growth strategy if you are only in one business?

   Do you agree? Why or why not?
2. A large Hollywood movie studio establishes a new marketing division with responsibility for researching, advertising, and distributing its movies. The director of the marketing division feels the company's corporate mission should be defined as "developing movies to meet changing customer tastes in a dynamic cultural and social environment."
   a. Do you agree with the definition of corporate mission? Why or why not?
   b. Does the definition of mission exclude certain corporate growth alternatives?
3. A marketing executive for a producer of computer software commented on the various alternatives to growth outlined in

Figures 22.8 and 22.9 as follows:

> *That classification looks logical. But it is a little too simplistic when you look at the way we do things. We don't say we are going to achieve growth in our business through "market penetration," or "market expansion," or "product development." We evaluate each business' potential for increasing sales on a range of factors—competition, customer demand, technology—and then decide how we can apply our expertise to increase growth. We might have ten different growth strategies for ten different businesses. Classifying a business' growth strategy into one of your boxes tends to hide the different and unique conditions each of our businesses face.*

Do this executive's comments mean that a business unit should not formulate an integrated corporate growth strategy along the lines suggested in Figures 22.8 and 22.9?

CHAPTER 23

Controlling the Marketing Effort

YOUR FOCUS IN CHAPTER 23

To learn:

- *The distinction between strategic control and product-marketing control.*
- *How companies control marketing operations.*
- *The primary focus of strategic control.*
- *The primary focus of product-marketing control.*
- *The types of systems companies use to implement control processes.*

How Heinz's Cost Control Strategy Went Out of Control

The hundred executives listening to Tony O'Reilly could not believe their ears. Here was the CEO of Heinz, a man who had quadrupled profits and more than doubled sales over a decade, spelling out a doom-and-gloom scenario that seemed out of touch with reality. Instead of reveling in the fact that Heinz's sales were still growing, O'Reilly was obsessed with the corporate culture he had created. This was the day, he told his managers, to start destroying it.[1]

O'Reilly's philosophy through most of the 1980s had been to achieve growth by mercilessly slashing production costs. Since most Heinz products were in the mature phase of their life cycles—achieving little better than 2 percent annual growth—he had to spend heavily on advertising to defend their market share. By the same token, he insisted that all his products be the lowest-costing competitor in their category, so their profit margins could support Heinz's ad budget and earnings goals. When one group reported they could save $4 million a year through moves like taking the back label off catsup bottles, he demanded more.[2] For a while, the relentless strategy—dubbed the Low Cost Operator program (LCO)—seemed to be working.[3] Company-wide sales had increased by $1 billion annually and profits by $500 million since 1983.[4]

Tony O'Reilly, Heinz CEO

By the time O'Reilly took to the podium that day in 1988, cracks in the foundation had begun to show. Ore-Ida, its frozen-french-fried-potato unit, slipped four market share points in two years, while its 9 Lives cat food division nosedived six points in half that time. O'Reilly was not about to wait for the damage to get worse. "We cannot continue with past management practices," the Irish-born one-time star rugby player told his audience. Low costs had to be accompanied by higher quality if productivity was to improve. Heinz had allowed the balance to tilt and was paying the price.[5]

Ore-Ida, for instance, doubled its output by stepping up assembly line speeds, adding technology that let it reclaim oven heat, and changing cooking methods. But no one ever bothered asking whether its products still tasted good. As it turned out, customer favorites like Tater Tots were being ruined. The snack's once-chunky insides had been turned into mashed goo and its crispy coating made soggy. When sales started sliding, Ore-Ida's managers (whose salaries were based on the savings they produced) were too afraid of O'Reilly to look at the root cause and unconvincingly blamed changing eating habits.[6]

Then there were the problems at StarKist tuna. In the early 1980s, imports of canned tuna increased by 77 percent, driving down the average price of a can by 18 percent. To match rivals who were using low-paid Thailand labor, O'Reilly closed his Terminal Island, California plant and cut the work force in his remaining plants in Puerto Rico and Samoa by five percent.[7] It was another case of a move making sense on paper only. In practice, workers became so overwrought that they started leaving tons of white meat on fish bones and not separating out the dark meat that normally went into Heinz's pet food products.[8] The quality of StarKist nosedived.

About that time, O'Reilly began reading marketer Philip Crosby's book *Quality Is Free*. Its premise that one could save money by making things right the first time struck him like a ton of bricks. Although O'Reilly's low-cost operator program was effective initially, the Ore-Ida and StarKist experience showed that LCO was starting to cut into bone. O'Reilly began acknowledging that his relentless drive to cut costs may have done more harm than good.[9] Suddenly, a new term was being heard in Heinz's executive suites in downtown Pittsburgh—Total Quality Management or TQM.

Total Quality Management meant accepting the Japanese-based concept of quality circles. Teams of workers were given responsibility for quality control on the assembly line. Each team of workers was told that they would be responsible to the next team down the line for maintaining quality. TQM also meant that Heinz would now consider cost controls only in the context of maintaining quality. For example, TQM was responsible for introducing a notion that would have been heresy in the old culture: that adding workers can boost quality and lower costs. At troubled StarKist, by adding 400 hourly employees and retraining the entire work force at a cost of $5 million, O'Reilly was able to cut out $15 million in waste and bring the brand back to its previous level of quality.[10]

TQM also impacted on Ore-Ida. Quality teams brainstormed with assembly-line workers to repair the product damage. By slowing down the production lines, managers were able to churn out more uniform morsels and restore Tater Tots' flavor. Consumers reacted by driving sales up 18 percent. After being in operation for two years, TQM helped increase 1990 profits at Ore-Ida by 15 percent.

O'Reilly believes that TQM's controls will make Heinz stronger and more productive as it does battle in the 1990s, and for the first time he is talking about brand building. In 1992, the CEO authorized his managers to spend $650 million on marketing—double the average of previous years.[11] He also began planning to turn Heinz's Weight Watchers division into a global player by tripling its size through a range of new-product introductions.[12]

Still, some analysts wonder whether O'Reilly waited too long before he evaluated his weaknesses and moved to control them. As of 1991, StarKist's earnings were off 50 percent thanks to the price cuts of rivals, and 9 Lives was suffering from the entry of Alpo into the cat-food business. One Heinz watcher observed that "A company that had a hard time building volume should have been moving much earlier (on quality control)."[13] Whether Heinz moved early enough to control quality as well as costs remains to be seen.

THE NATURE OF MARKETING CONTROL

Control *refers to directing or redirecting a company's actions to ensure that they meet objectives.* **Evaluation** *refers to determining whether results are on target.* Evaluation is a necessary adjunct of control because any time company actions are controlled, they must first be evaluated.

The Heinz story illustrates the importance of control, particularly over marketing activities. By cutting production costs to the bone, Heinz gave up market share by allowing the quality of its goods to slide. Heinz also wasted money on the manufacturing end. One example: The company had to throw out untold cans of StarKist because faster assembly lines sent them bumping into the sharp edges of packaging machines, leaving the cans dented and unsightly.[14]

When applied to marketing, control has two dimensions: a corporate or SBU dimension and a product dimension. These two dimensions parallel the marketing planning levels cited in Chapter 22. Control at the corporate or SBU level is **strategic marketing control**—*that is, an attempt to keep the components of the strategic marketing plan on target and to redirect them if they are not.* Control at the product level is **product marketing control**—*an attempt to keep the components of a product's marketing plan on target.*

STRATEGIC MARKETING CONTROL

Strategic marketing control requires top management to evaluate the company's business mix and SBU management to evaluate the unit's product mix in order to determine whether they have effectively judged new business and product opportunities and the company's ability to pursue these opportunities. Unless the strategic plan is absolutely on target, which is unlikely, the process of strategic control will lead managers to make adjustments in resource allocation.

Westinghouse attempted to exert strategic control in the 1980s when it instituted controls over every aspect of its strategic plan—identification of marketing opportunity, growth strategies, acquisition strategies, and its business mix. A new management team began spinning off dozens of businesses with poor short-term earnings—cable television, the major appliance group, the company's lamp business, and its office furniture division. Strict market share and profitability criteria were used to determine these divestments: If a subsidiary was not first or a strong second in its industry, it was a candidate for divestment. Further, the company increased productivity by cutting costs and improving quality.[15]

But, Westinghouse's divestment of businesses that were failing to produce short-term earnings left it with a mix of mature businesses by 1990. Although the company's attempt at instituting strategic controls seemed sound in the 1980s, the 1990s showed that Westinghouse's focus was too short term.[16] Westinghouse had divested potential winners such as cable TV and electric motors because it did not have the patience to support them in their growth phase. Strategic control requires divesting businesses with a lack of long-term growth prospects, not short-term earnings potential. By 1991, Westinghouse was reeling under poor earnings reports.

PRODUCT MARKETING CONTROLS

Whereas strategic controls deal with the total business and product mix, product marketing controls deal with the marketing mix for an individual product. Product managers must evaluate the effectiveness of product, distribution, promotional, and pricing strategies and reallocate resources as appropriate.

When Roger Enrico stepped into the president's job at Frito Lay in 1991, he found the company's snack foods under assault from rivals such as Anheuser Busch's Eagle Snack Foods division who were heavily discounting their brands. Enrico reacted on the product level. He instituted tight cost controls to allow for deep price cuts on his entire line, further controlled production to cure such things as an inordinate number of broken chips in bags of Ruffles, and broadened distribution channels for new products such as the multigrain Sunchips. The underlying issue was controlling production and marketing costs to allow Frito Lay products to compete in the face of fierce price competition.[17]

IMPETUS FOR MARKETING CONTROL

The control of marketing operations has received more attention in the late 1980s and early 1990s for three reasons: the intensification of foreign competition, the debt incurred by many companies during the 1980s acquisition spree, and the deep recession in the early 1990s.

FOREIGN COMPETITION

As we have seen in Chapter 5, foreign competitors, particularly Japanese companies, have been able to capture market share in key industries by offering quality products at lower prices than U.S. companies. In 1991, for instance, *Consumer Reports* found 28 of the 31 top-rated cars were Japanese.[18] The basis for their competitive advantage is no secret—higher productivity because of more efficient production methods and lower labor costs. American companies have reacted by putting more emphasis on productivity. Such improvements in productivity can be achieved only by greater cost and quality controls in production and marketing.

Many American companies have adopted two widespread practices based on the productivity of Japanese competitors: just-in-time distribution systems and quality-circle programs. Combined, these practices are the central components of a Total Quality Management (TQM) program. We have seen in Chapter 16 that *just-in-time (JIT) distribution* has cut down on production and distribution costs by producing for existing demand rather than for anticipated demand and by delivering raw materials and finished products on an as-needed basis. **Quality circles** *are groups of autonomous workers who are responsible for their output* and are motivated to perform quality work based on the recognition that their mistakes will affect the autonomous work group next down the line (see Exhibit 23.1). Underlying the formation of quality circles is a deceptively simple notion: It is better to control quality at the point of production to try to avoid mistakes than to identify and correct mistakes through random inspection of products after they are produced. As noted, Heinz and Westinghouse have adopted quality-circle programs in an attempt to improve productivity. The traditional concept of a foreman controlling workers has been replaced by workers being given responsibility for quality control.

EXCESS DEBT

Another reason control has received more attention is the huge debt levels accumulated by companies in the 1980s and 1990s. Unisys is a good example. Its $350-million purchase of workstation maker United Technologies in 1990 drove its debt well above industry norms. This led James Unruh, Unisys's CEO, to comb the books looking for sell-offs to reduce its crushing interest payments on debt.[19]

EXHIBIT 23.1

Compaq Utilizes Just-in-Time Distribution

At Compaq Computer Corporation's Houston, Texas plant, the assembly line is U-shaped so that workers at the beginning and end of the line can easily confer. This arrangement facilitates group interaction processes such as the quality circle meeting pictured here.

Many other companies realized that gobbling up high-growth businesses outside their areas of core competence was antithetical to growth. Examples are Quaker Oats' entry into electronic toys, American Express' experiment with world banking, and Horn & Hardart's purchase of a southern fried chicken chain. Each purchase ultimately led to a painful control strategy: divestiture.

THE 1990–92 RECESSION

A third factor encouraging marketing controls was the deep recession during the early 1990s. Reduced consumer purchasing power meant that many manufacturers had to cut prices to maintain volume. Kraft, which normally sells premium brands, lopped 40 percent off the price of many products. Such price cuts required tighter control of costs to maintain profit margins. The emphasis was not on costs alone, it was also on productivity. **Productivity** *is the ratio of quality to cost.* Greater productivity means higher quality without increasing cost, or lower cost without decreasing quality. Cost controls in the early 1990s were introduced with quality in mind. For example, Heinz's Total Quality Management program meant ensuring higher quality to keep its products competitive but at reasonable costs.

A MODEL OF MARKETING EVALUATION AND CONTROL

A firm must have a systematic basis for evaluating and controlling marketing operations at both the corporate and the product level. A model of marketing evaluation and control is shown in Figure 23.1.

In the first step, the firm must define criteria by which it will evaluate performance. Assume that Westinghouse establishes sales and profitability criteria for its robotics (factory automation) division. The second step is to project performance of the division based on these criteria. Westinghouse might forecast sales of $65

FIGURE 23.1

A Model of Evaluation and Control

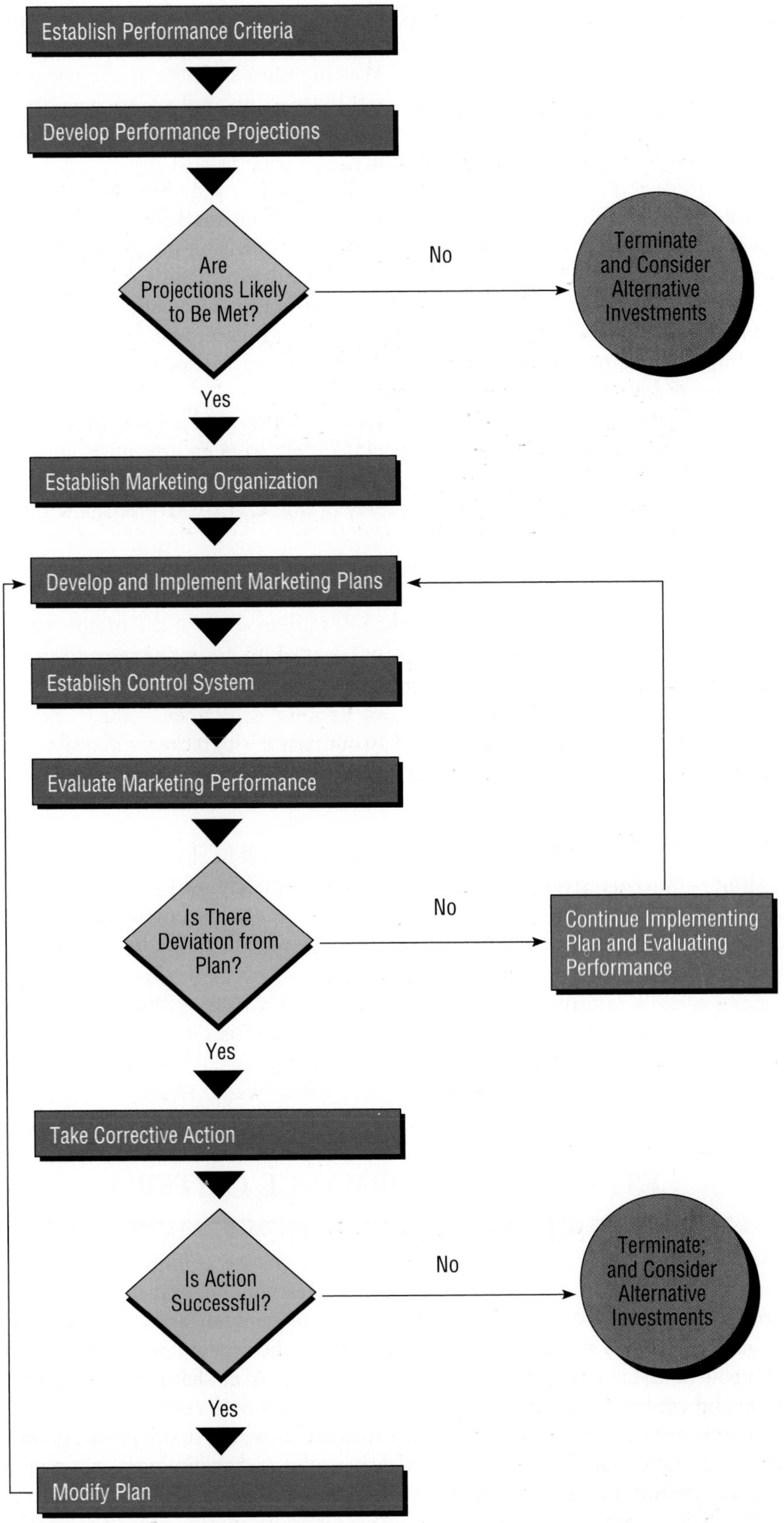

million in the first year, rising to $120 million by the fourth year, an average of 13 percent return on investment for the first five years and an expectation that the division will account for 10 percent of Westinghouse's profits at the end of five years. If management finds it unlikely that a business or product will meet its minimal performance goals, it will terminate the business or product and use the funds in some alternative investment opportunity.

The third step in the control process is to establish a marketing organization capable of developing, implementing, and controlling marketing plans. Part of Westinghouse's organizational plan for the robotics division might be to establish quality-circle groups to ensure quality control and to establish national account marketing (NAM) teams to sell to large users of factory automation systems, such as General Motors. Once such an organization is in place, managers can develop and implement a marketing plan to achieve the objectives spelled out in the performance projections.

In the fifth step, management must evaluate performance. Evaluation requires a control system that will allow a company to track costs and revenues and determine whether profit and ROI goals have been met. If performance is on target, implementation of the plan can continue. If it is not, corrective action should be considered.

Westinghouse's robotics division did not meet expectations when it was first acquired in 1983. Sales were expected to rise above $60 million the year after the business was purchased but reached only $40 million. Part of the reason was that General Motors, the unit's largest customer, went into a joint venture to produce automated systems for itself. Also, many companies preferred electric robots to Westinghouse's hydraulic robots.[20]

Westinghouse's corrective action was to put more emphasis on electric robots and to seek clients outside the auto industry. Westinghouse also established a productivity center to develop new techniques in robotics for cost reductions and quality control.[21]

If corrective action is not successful, the business will be divested or the product eliminated. If corrective action is successful, the company uses what it has learned so as to modify the plan and redirect its efforts to meet objectives. This final step in control is critical since it provides the company with feedback for the next planning cycle.

The remainder of this chapter considers each of the steps in evaluation and control shown in Figure 23.1.

ESTABLISH PERFORMANCE CRITERIA

The three primary criteria used to evaluate performance at both the product and the corporate/business-unit level are profits, sales volume, and market share. In some cases, these criteria do not always move in tandem, and a firm may consciously emphasize one at the expense of another. For example, a firm entering a market—or defending one—might try to "buy" market share at the expense of profits by advertising heavily, cutting prices, and providing retailers or wholesalers with higher margins. Since costs increase to achieve market share, profits go down. The firm might incur these additional expenses to establish itself, but the goal remains maximization of long-term profits.

This chapter is particularly concerned with profit criteria, because they ultimately dominate evaluation of a product's or business unit's performance. The profit criteria most commonly used in evaluating performance are *contribution to margin* and *return on investment (ROI)*. It would be helpful at this point to review the cost and profit concepts involved, by turning to the appendix to this chapter.

CONTRIBUTION TO MARGIN

Contribution to margin is a logical criterion for evaluating product performance, because it takes into account only those costs that are directly assignable to the product. As a result, it is also known as *direct* (that is, assignable) *costing*. In contrast, an approach based on net profit and return on investment is known as *full costing*, because it takes account of all costs, both assignable (direct) and nonassignable (indirect).

Using contribution to margin as a profit criterion makes it easier to evaluate product performance. Procter & Gamble evaluates its products using an approach it calls Direct Product Profitability (DPP), which relies solely on direct costs to evaluate product performance. The DPP approach has shown that some products with high sales volume have a low contribution to margin because they have high handling costs. P&G began focusing on reducing handling costs so as to increase margins. For example, it found that if it redesigned its Ivory shampoo bottle from a teardrop shape to a cylindrical container, it would save 29 cents a case in handling and storage costs[22] (see Exhibit 23.2). If P&G had evaluated Ivory shampoo based on net profits or return on investment, it would have had to allocate indirect (nonassignable) costs to the product. Handling costs would have been harder to isolate and might have been overlooked.

EXHIBIT 23.2

A Result of Direct Costing at Procter & Gamble: A Change in Packaging to Reduce Costs

NET PROFIT/RETURN ON INVESTMENT (ROI)

Return on investment (ROI) is based on net profits and therefore requires allocating all costs to a product or business unit. Given the problems cited with allocating nonassignable costs, why would a firm use net profits or return on investment as a performance criterion? One reason is that return on investment gives a firm some indication as to how effective it is in using its capital. Was Westinghouse's expenditure of $107 million to acquire the robotics business worthwhile?[23] The best way to answer that is to consider alternative uses of the capital. In 1992, it projected a 13.1 ROI. Had Westinghouse put the money in the bank, it might have received a 6 percent return, at best. So a projected 13.1 percent would be a good return.

A second reason for using a return-on-investment measure is that it is more valid when evaluating a business unit rather than a product. This is because most of the costs incurred by a business unit are assignable. For example, most of the costs of manufacturing automated equipment can be directly assigned to the robotics division, but if the division produces 20 different robotics systems, it would be difficult to allocate manufacturing costs to each of these products. So, in general, it is much easier to allocate costs to a business unit than to a product.

USE OF PERFORMANCE CRITERIA

What criteria are used most frequently in evaluating marketing performance? A study of 233 American firms found that most used more than one criterion, with sales volume the most frequently used (88 percent of the companies in the study used it). The next most frequently used criterion was contribution to margin, used by 44 percent of the companies, followed by net profit/ROI used by 30 percent.[24]

The finding that sales is a more popular performance measure than profitability should be of concern if it reflects current procedures in corporate America. As we know, sales are not always related to profitability. A firm that does not use some profitability criterion can quickly lose sight of rising costs.

DEVELOP PERFORMANCE PROJECTIONS

Once the firm has established the criteria it will use to evaluate marketing performance, it develops performance projections for products and business units, in the form of a profit and loss (P&L) statement.

Performance projections are in the form of expected performance, usually for a minimum of one and a maximum of five years. The best way to set out these projections is in a *profit-and-loss (P&L) statement* for a product or business unit.

Assume that Westinghouse's management developed a five-year P&L projection for the robotics division in 1987 for the period 1988 to 1992. The projected P&L is shown in Table 23.1. Sales are forecast at $65 million in 1988, and are expected to increase to $110 million in 1990, and then level off. Variable costs rise more sharply at the start of business, then level off as learning effects begin to reduce the average cost of production and marketing per unit. Assignable fixed costs are more constant, because they do not vary as much with sales volume. Contribution to margin is projected to rise steadily from $7 million in 1988 to $29.5 million in 1992. When nonassignable fixed costs are allocated, there is a net loss in 1988, but a more substantial net profit by 1990 that then levels out, producing an ROI of 12 to 13 percent.

Because the five-year P&L is a projection, it serves as a performance yardstick. The comparison of actual performance to projected performance gives manage-

TABLE 23.1

Hypothetical Five-Year Profit-and-Loss (P&L) Projections for Westinghouse's Robotics Division (in Millions) (1988–1992)

	1988	1989	1990	1991	1992
1. Sales	$65.0	$80.0	$110.0	$120.0	$114.0
2. Variable Costs	30.0	40.0	48.0	55.0	50.0
3. Assignable Fixed Costs	28.0	30.5	34.0	35.0	34.5
4. Contribution to Margin (1 − [2 + 3])	7.0	9.5	28.0	30.0	29.5
5. Nonassignable Fixed Costs	9.0	10.5	15.0	16.0	15.5
6. Net Profits (1 − [2 + 3 + 5])	−2.0	−1.0	13.0	14.0	14.0
Contribution to Margin as a Percent of Sales (row 4/row 1)	10.8%	11.9%	25.5%	25.0%	25.9%
Return on Investment (row 6/initial investment of $107 million)	0	0	12.1%	13.1%	13.1%

ment a basis for determining whether corrective action is necessary to get performance on target. As we know, sales of the robotics division did not meet expectations after the unit was purchased, and it probably took longer than the three years projected in the P&L statement to make the division profitable.

DEVELOP A MARKETING ORGANIZATION

The next step in the process of evaluation and control requires establishing a marketing organization capable of implementing and evaluating marketing strategies. The two most widely used approaches to organizing the marketing effort are a *product-based organization* and a *market-based organization.* These approaches are shown in Figure 23.2.

In each case, the marketing organization is headed by a vice president of marketing. Under the vice president are several marketing managers responsible for various functional tasks. There is a marketing manager for administration and planning who is responsible for developing marketing plans for each product and for supplying input into the business unit's strategic plan. A national sales manager is responsible for overseeing the efforts of regional and district managers to ensure that existing and prospective customers are contacted and sold. A marketing research manager is responsible for providing line managers with enough information on customer needs and the marketing environment to make marketing

FIGURE 23.2

Two Types of Marketing Organizations

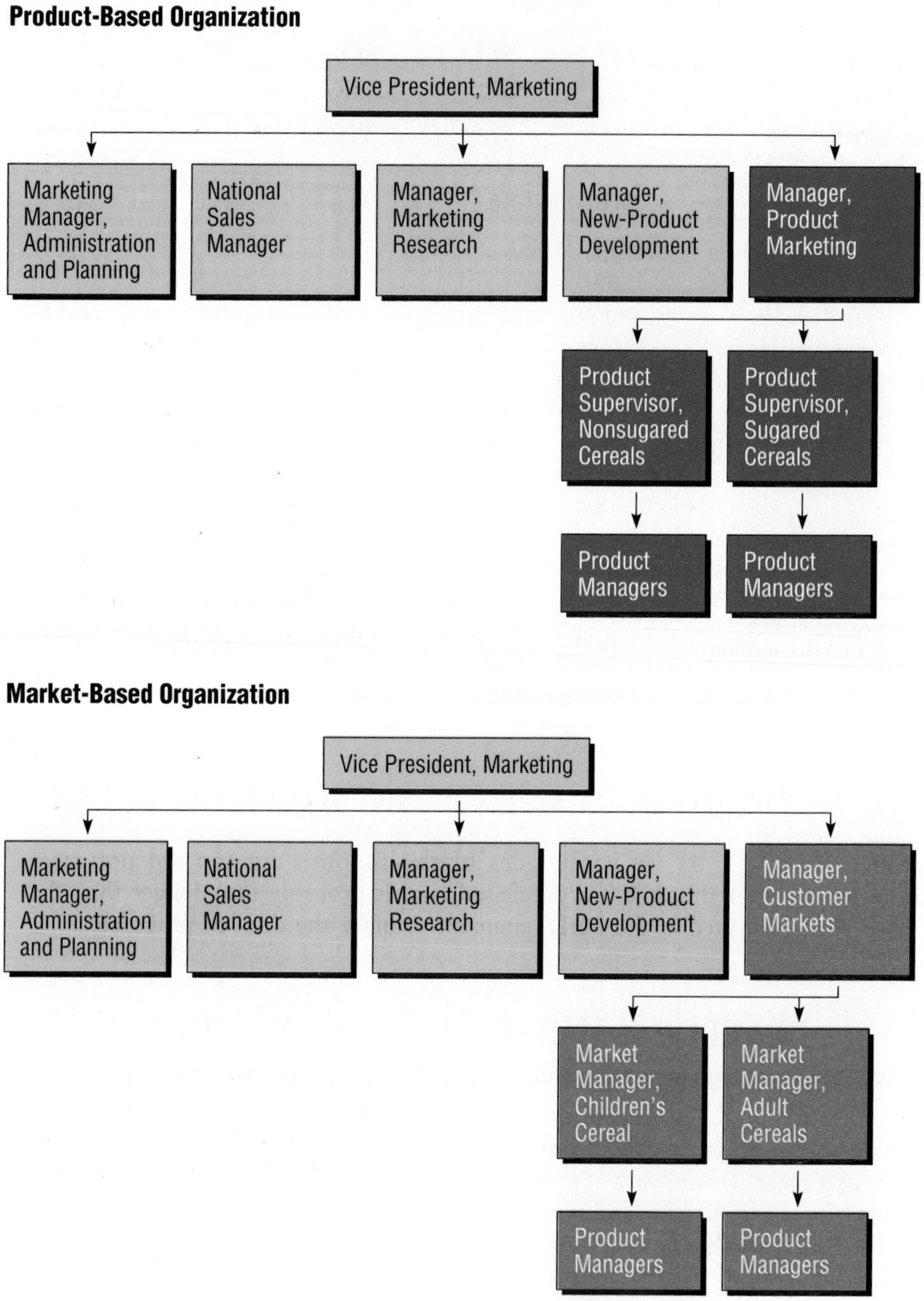

decisions. And a marketing manager for new-product development initiates new-product ideas and oversees the process of development, product testing, and test marketing.

The two organizational charts differ in the way marketing strategies are implemented. If Kellogg followed the product-based form of organization depicted at the top of Figure 23.2, the basic product division might be between sugared and unsugared cereals. A manager of product marketing (the extreme right-hand box) might be responsible for both units. Under this manager might be a supervisor of all sugared cereals and a supervisor of all unsugared cereals. Under each of these supervisors would be product managers for individual cereal brands.

The alternative to a product-based organization is organizing marketing activities by broad customer segments (see the bottom of Figure 23.2). The basic organization is the same except that under the vice president of marketing is a manager of customer markets. Kellogg is actually organized on this basis, across two broad markets, children's cereals and adult's cereals. A market manager is responsible for each of these groups across all product categories. For example, the market manager for children's cereals is responsible for marketing all brands to this segment. Product managers responsible for individual brands report to their respective market managers.

A product-based organization is most appropriate when customer needs are differentiated by product characteristics. For example, a basic distinction in soft drinks is between cola and noncola products. Cola drinks tend to appeal more to teens, because cola drinks are sweeter and more carbonated. Noncola drinks appeal more to adults, because noncola drinks are less sweet and more flavor oriented. In contrast, with cereals, the basic distinction is not between product characteristics but between markets. The appeal to children is based on taste and nutrition; the appeal to adults is based on diet, health, and fitness. Although sweetened cereals are primarily positioned to children, so are many nonsweetened products. Kellogg's Corn Flakes directs appeals toward both groups. Given that this basic distinction between the needs of children and adults frequently cuts across individual products, a market-based organization makes sense.

DEVELOP AND IMPLEMENT THE MARKETING PLAN

Much of this book has been devoted to the process of developing and implementing marketing plans. What we have not discussed is the human dimension of implementation—that is, the problems managers encounter in trying to implement marketing plans and the importance of adequately motivating subordinates to meet objectives. Evaluation and control involve not only costs and revenues, but also people.

One large consulting firm, McKinsey & Company, believes that one of the recent problems with implementation in American industry is that management has focused too much on analytical techniques and not enough on the human element. Japanese companies may have attained higher productivity precisely because they have done the exact opposite. The development of quality circles is an example of a focus on the human element in implementation.

PROBLEMS IN IMPLEMENTATION

One source of problems in implementing marketing plans is resistance to change. The more far-reaching the changes in the marketing plan, the greater the potential for such resistance. A common scenario is a company in trouble and a new management team coming in with a strategic plan calling for changes such as severe cost cutting, more emphasis on new-product development, divestment of certain business units, or entry into new lines of business. These changes contradict "the way we do things around here" and are resisted.

AT&T ran into serious problems in implementing a new set of strategies after divesting its subsidiaries in 1984. In that year, James Olsen, the company's chief financial officer, tried to launch a plan to strengthen the company's core business of long-distance services and phone equipment and bolster its fledgling computer business. The strategy involved cooperation and trade-offs between divisions—for example, combining the sales force for telephone and computer equipment and eliminating duplication in accounting and data-processing services across various divisions. Business managers refused to buy in, because in the old Bell System they ran their units like fiefdoms and were not accustomed to compromise.[25] Only when Olsen was promoted to chairman two years later would business managers agree to the plan, but when a new CEO, Robert Allen, took over the reins in 1988, he still found resistance to change in AT&T's top management ranks.

Managers also face problems in implementing plans because of conflicts between corporate staffers and line (operational) managers. Line managers see staffers as being divorced from day-to-day operations and being concerned primarily with analytical planning techniques that often produce unrealistic goals. Conversely, staffers feel that line managers do not see the "big corporate picture" and are too focused on their individual tasks.

As a result of this conflict, alienated line managers often ignore staffers, even when staffers are right. For example, General Electric's corporate staffers correctly predicted that Japanese manufacturers would make a dent in the U.S. small-appliance market as early as 1970, but the warning was ignored by the Appliance Group's line managers.[26] On the other hand, GE staffers recommended building smaller refrigerators because of smaller families. Line managers could have told them that kitchens were not getting smaller, despite smaller families, because working mothers were stocking more food.

REQUIREMENTS FOR EFFECTIVE IMPLEMENTATION

There are no clear-cut solutions to implementation problems, but there are a few prescriptions to take account of the human element. One is to ensure that performance goals are understood and that employees accept them. Olsen saw this requirement as his major task when he took over as head of AT&T.

Another prescription is to reward employees for good performance. At Heinz, an executive's bonuses are tied to his or her performance in reducing costs and increasing quality, the two basic components in Heinz's Total Quality Management program.

A third prescription is to foster open communications and participative management. A study of 43 successful U.S. companies found that most had a high level of informality and a decentralized structure that fostered open communications. Quality circles are highly motivated because of their autonomy and informality. Productivity of these groups tends to be much higher than that of traditional work groups supervised by foremen. As a result, more than a third of American companies are expected to involve three out of four of their workers in quality circles by the mid-1990s. The figure is more than double the rate of the mid-1980s.[27]

A fourth prescription for effective implementation is to make sure that people know their responsibilities. IBM's chief executive, John F. Akers, spent much of 1991 holding company seminars in which he tried to light a fire under lackluster managers he believed were to blame for the company's declining worldwide market share. "I'm sick and tired of visiting plants and hearing nothing but great things about quality, only to then visit customers who tell me of problems," Akers told one group. "If the people in the labs and plants miss deadlines, tell them their jobs are on the line."[28]

ESTABLISH A CONTROL SYSTEM

Once marketing plans are implemented, one step remains before these plans can be evaluated—establishing a control system to track performance and let managers know when corrections are necessary. Companies use three types of systems to control marketing performance: after-the-fact, steering, and adaptive control.

AFTER-THE-FACT CONTROL SYSTEM

An **after-the-fact control system** *controls marketing performance at the end of the planning period.* If performance does not meet objectives, managers take corrective action to bring performance back into line for the next planning cycle. Assume that Westinghouse finds its actual sales revenues in 1992 were close to the projected $114 million in Table 23.1. But, also assume distribution costs were projected at $10.5 million and actual costs were much higher than projected. Management breaks out distribution costs further to compare projected to actual performance and finds the following:

DISTRIBUTION COSTS	PROJECTED	ACTUAL	PERCENT DIFFERENCE
Transportation costs	$6.2 million	$8.2 million	+32%
Inventory costs	$2.7 million	$3.7 million	+37%
Order-handling and processing costs	$1.6 million	$1.7 million	+ 6%

Management further determines that (1) transportation costs are out of line because of increases in trucking costs and (2) inventory costs are above projections, because products are staying in inventory longer than expected. Management decides to institute a just-in-time (JIT) system so that production will be more closely tied to existing orders, thus reducing product inventory levels. It must continue to ship by truck because of the need for rapid delivery with a JIT system, but it institutes a more rigorous review of alternative shippers in an attempt to control transportation costs.

STEERING CONTROL SYSTEM

In a **steering control system,** *deviations in performance are detected during—rather than at the end of—the planning period, allowing for prompt corrective action.* Steering control avoids the key problem with an after-the-fact control system: that management must wait until the end of the planning period to make adjustments, and such delays could cost a company millions of dollars.

Steering control can be implemented through the use of control charts, such as the ones shown in Figure 23.3, that track hypothetical distribution costs for Westinghouse's Robotics Division. The control charts show the projected (dotted line) and actual (heavy solid line) distribution costs by quarter in 1992. The parallel lines above and below projected costs are an allowed 10-percent deviation above or below budget. If costs stray more than 10 percent beyond projections, the deviation is immediately brought to management's attention so it can attempt to "steer" costs back into line. The control charts show that by the second quarter of 1992, distribution costs were out of line and needed to be brought into control. Further, the two components of distribution that caused costs to exceed budgets were transportation and inventory costs.

Since taking corrective action more quickly makes the most sense, why would any company use an after-the-fact control system? Because after-the-fact control

FIGURE 23.3

*Control Charts for Steering Control System**

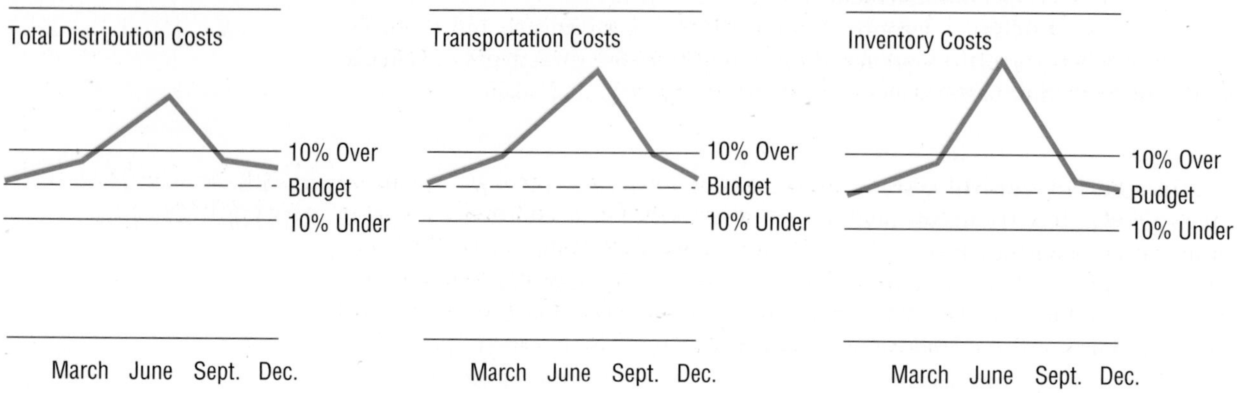

* Hypothetical Distribution Costs for Westinghouse's Robotics Division, 1991.

is simpler to implement. Many companies do not have the resources and managerial know-how to track performance and make immediate adjustments. In some cases, after-the-fact control may be justified in its own right because expenditures cannot be changed until the end of the planning period. For example, media schedules are fixed well in advance, and it might not be feasible to change advertising expenditures during the year.

ADAPTIVE CONTROL SYSTEM

Both after-the-fact and steering control systems are designed to bring performance into line with prior objectives. But what happens when the environment changes to such a degree that the objectives are no longer relevant or when the objectives were so wrong in the first place as to require revision? Such a situation calls for an **adaptive control system** *that allows for changes in objectives as well as in performance to meet objectives.* This system requires tracking environmental factors such as competitive intensity, level of customer demand, and technology to determine if objectives are still relevant. If not, objectives are changed to meet the new environmental contingencies, resulting in a new set of guidelines for performance.

For example, Westinghouse may have been overly optimistic in its expectations that factory automation might be the answer to increasing productivity. Rather than relying solely on automation to increase productivity, many companies have begun to rely more on quality circles to reduce labor costs (see Global Marketing Strategies box). As a result, sales of factory robots have begun to lag behind forecasts. If Westinghouse had established an adaptive control system, it might have scaled back its sales and cost forecasts rather than waiting until the end of the planning period to make adjustments.

Both adaptive and steering control allow for changes during the planning period. The difference is that with adaptive control, objectives can change, whereas with steering control, they remain fixed. In this way, adaptive control is a *proactive* system: Management anticipates changes in the environment and acts to develop a new set of ground rules for evaluating and controlling performance. After-the-fact and steering control are *reactive* systems: Management reacts to a situation that is out of control and tries to repair it.

EVALUATE MARKETING PERFORMANCE

Once plans are implemented and a control system is established, managers are able to evaluate performance. There are two dimensions in marketing evaluation: the strategic dimension, which evaluates corporate and business unit performance, and the product-marketing dimension, which evaluates product performance.

STRATEGIC MARKETING EVALUATION

The elements of marketing performance we will consider in strategic evaluation involve costs, product quality, and corporate growth. Costs and product quality determine a company's level of productivity. As we have seen, one of the major concerns of American firms is their level of productivity compared to that of foreign competitors. America's future economic well-being is likely to be determined by the degree to which American companies increase their productivity.

MARKETING PRODUCTIVITY

The productivity of a company's marketing operations is defined by its *efficiency*, which is the ratio of output to input: Increased efficiency means more output for less input. Given the importance of satisfying customer needs, marketing productivity should be measured by the quality level of a company's product offerings, but with the proviso that product quality be attained at reasonable cost. Therefore, **marketing productivity** *is measured by the ratio of product quality to the cost of producing and marketing the item.*

This is illustrated in Figure 23.4 as the marketing productivity triangle. One leg of the triangle is lower costs, the other is higher quality. The higher the quality and the lower the cost, the higher the company's marketing productivity and profitability. The cost/quality trade-off at the bottom of the triangle means that an emphasis on lower costs could result in lower quality, and higher quality could result in higher costs.

FIGURE 23.4
The Productivity Triangle

ETHICAL AND ENVIRONMENTAL ISSUES IN MARKETING

Environmental Control: How Monsanto Gave Adaptive Control a Green Hue

After taking office in 1981, Ronald Reagan put ecological issues on the back burner and sharply cut funding for the Environmental Protection Agency. Taking their cue from the president, most Fortune 500 executives felt little pressure to worry about the environment as they mapped out control strategies for the 1980s—and Richard Mahoney, CEO of Monsanto, was no different from his fellow CEOs.

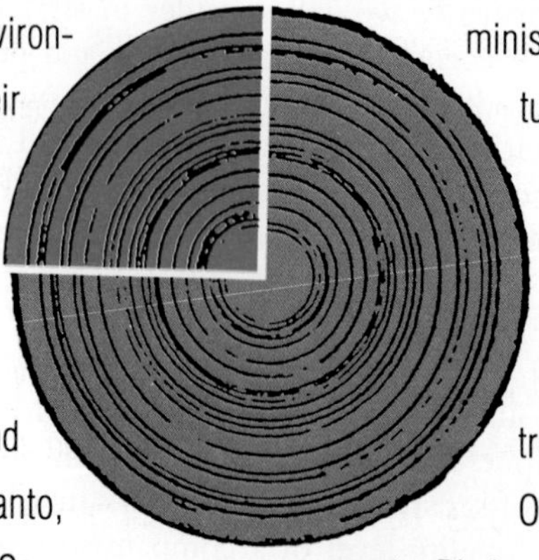

However, Mahoney saw the public's increasing concern with the environment and recognized that the end of the Reagan era would bring with it a need for greater environmental controls. The need for a new environmental policy at Monsanto became apparent. This policy began to take shape in the summer of 1988 when Mahoney was fretting over a report that showed his company had released 20 million pounds of toxic emissions into the air the year before. "I don't like these numbers," he said, staring at the executives gathered in his office. His first concern was his company's public image, but a bottom-line mentality was also at play. A new administration in Washington would eventually make Monsanto clean up its act, and who knew what the cost would be then. Better to act first, he reasoned, and get a jump on rivals while gaining the public's trust.

Out of that session came the Monsanto Pledge. It stated that the company would voluntarily reduce its emissions of 307 toxic chemicals to only 10 percent of 1987 levels by 1992 and eliminate 70 percent of waste by-products by 1995.

By rerouting pipes, resealing valves, and redesigning processes to eliminate solvents, Mahoney thinks his company can fulfill the pledge while staying within its normal budget. More important, however, Mahoney believes that he can actually make money from it. The idea of zero emissions fits snugly with Monsanto's goal of zero defects. By inspiring his ecologically minded employees, Mahoney hopes

This cost/quality tradeoff was apparent when Heinz's Low Cost Operator program began to affect quality. The company's introduction of its Total Quality Management program was an attempt to maintain the balance between quality and cost illustrated in Figure 23.4.

COST CUTTING During the recession of the early 1990s, a period described by many economists as the hangover left from the free-spending 1980s, cost cutting was one of the main means used to pare down debt and improve productivity. As we have seen in Chapter 21, General Motors had to downsize its operations by almost 20 percent to reflect a loss in market share, primarily to Japanese imports.

ETHICAL AND ENVIRONMENTAL ISSUES IN MARKETING

he can infuse the company with an atmosphere of *environmental control* as well as quality control. Traditional quality control must now include safeguards for environmental control, even if these controls increase production and marketing costs. As an outgrowth of this plan, Monsanto was the first to publicly release an environmental audit which details how the company spends its annual pollution-control budget of $350 million.

If the public begins clamoring for other companies to do the same, then Mahoney would not be disappointed. The others would then be forced to play catch-up, and federal regulators would hold Monsanto up as proof that the battle can be won. Even if that never comes to pass, Mahoney expects that his investment in environmental control will eventually show up in the bottom line.

Monsanto's 1988 pledge to reduce pollution reflects an *adaptive control system* at work. Mahoney correctly anticipated the need for tighter environmental controls and set the wheels in motion to institute these controls without waiting to be forced to do so by government agencies. He sees these actions as a competitive advantage for Monsanto. In his words, "I believe that people who outperform on the environment will have the same advantages as those who outperform on superior marketing or anything else."

Questions: Why could Monsanto's pledge be regarded as an example of adaptive control? Mahoney thought of environmental controls as a vehicle for profit maximization and competitive advantage. Was this ethical?

Sources: "The Greening Of Corporate America," *Business Week*, April 23, 1990, pp. 96–103; "Goody Two-Shoes," *The Economist*, November 2, 1991, p. 68; "Monsanto," *Chemicalweek*, July 17, 1991, pp. 66–76; "Monsanto Efforts Revitalized," *Chemicalweek*, July 17, 1991, pp. 104–105; and "A Matter of Perception," *Financial World*, January 23, 1990.

Cost cutting alone cannot be a solution to improving productivity. Like Heinz, General Motors tended to ignore the quality side of the productivity equation by continuing to build look-alike cars with similar frames and common parts. As a result, consumers had difficulty justifying the price differences between General Motors cars and imports based on perceived quality differences.

QUALITY CONTROL The second leg of the productivity triangle is quality. Many American companies have subscribed to the traditional notion that quality control is best attained by inspections after the fact. As a result, they have been at a competitive disadvantage to foreign competitors, particularly the Japanese. One estimate is that one-fourth of American workers are employed to fix the mistakes

EXHIBIT 23.3

Ford's Emphasis on Quality Control

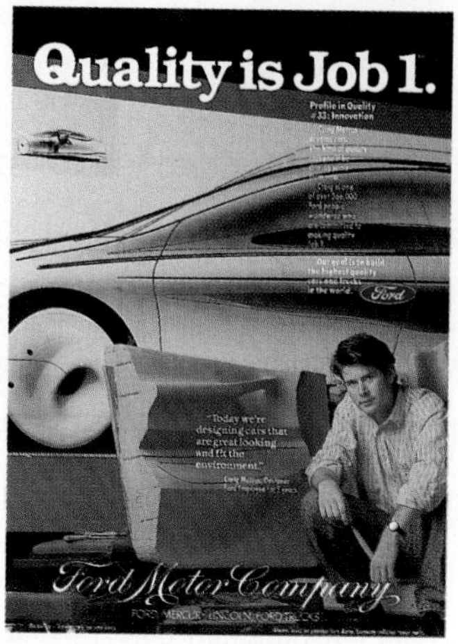

of the other three-fourths, and that quality control costs the average American firm 10 to 20 percent of sales.[29]

In contrast, the Japanese have adopted the concept of **statistical process control**, *which seeks to control defects at the time they occur rather than after the fact*. This is accomplished through quality circles that give workers responsibility for identifying defects in their own work and encouraging them to be as conscious of quality as possible. It requires that workers have the greatest amount of autonomy possible.

Effective quality control decreases the incompatibility between high quality and lower costs, because quality can be improved while costs are reduced. This has been Ford's approach to improving productivity: Let improvements in quality drive cost cuts, the idea being that product quality, not costs, is the key to marketing success. General Motors' approach has been the opposite: Let cost cuts drive any subsequent improvement in quality.

Ford's approach to quality control has been to establish quality circles, each trained to regard itself as a customer of the preceding group on the assembly line and as a supplier to the next group. If one group assembles circuit boards, it is a customer of whoever makes the chips for the board and is a supplier to the next group down the line who gets the board and puts it into the car. Being accountable to one's co-workers for quality makes each member of the quality circle more responsible for his or her work output.[30] The ad in Exhibit 23.3 illustrates Ford's approach: quality control through prevention rather than through correction.

The focus on product quality has produced results. Ford averages 10-percent fewer defects in producing its cars compared to General Motors and Chrysler, and since 1982 its sales have grown faster than those of GM or Chrysler (see Figure 23.5). Further, in 1986, Ford's profits surpassed GM's for the first time and have stayed above since. It is apparent that the evaluation of performance in the context of quality control is paying off.

CORPORATE GROWTH AND ACQUISITIONS

Corporate growth strategies are another component of the strategic marketing plan that must be evaluated and controlled. Smart executives realize the limitations of unbridled growth and pull back before their operations go out of control.

An important component in evaluating corporate growth strategies is company acquisitions. The 1970s and 1980s saw many of the largest companies in America acquiring firms far from their core areas of expertise. These companies wrongly assumed they could run these businesses. When they found that they did not have the managerial or marketing know-how to do so, most of the acquisitions were divested.

The key requirement in evaluation and control is for a company to establish marketing, managerial, and financial criteria for acquisitions. Sara Lee, a company with a mix that includes Hanes hosiery, Jimmy Dean sausage, Coach leather goods, Eyelab stores, and Isotoner gloves, defines itself as being a branded consumer products manufacturer. As a result, it specifies that any company it considers for acquisition should have a well-known branded product but not be in a category with intense competition (a marketing criterion). Further, the company must have an uncomplicated management and employment situation (a managerial criterion). Sara Lee also requires high profits and a low ratio of capital to sales (financial criteria).[31]

PRODUCT MARKETING EVALUATION

The second area that must be evaluated for purposes of control is the product marketing plan. Management will want to evaluate three product-specific areas: the adequacy of the new-product development process in adding profitable products to the company's offerings; the adequacy of the company's process of deleting unprofitable products; and the effectiveness of the product's marketing mix—that is, advertising, sales, distribution, and pricing strategies.

FIGURE 23.5

Results of Ford's Drive for Product Quality: Outperforming GM and Chrysler in Sales

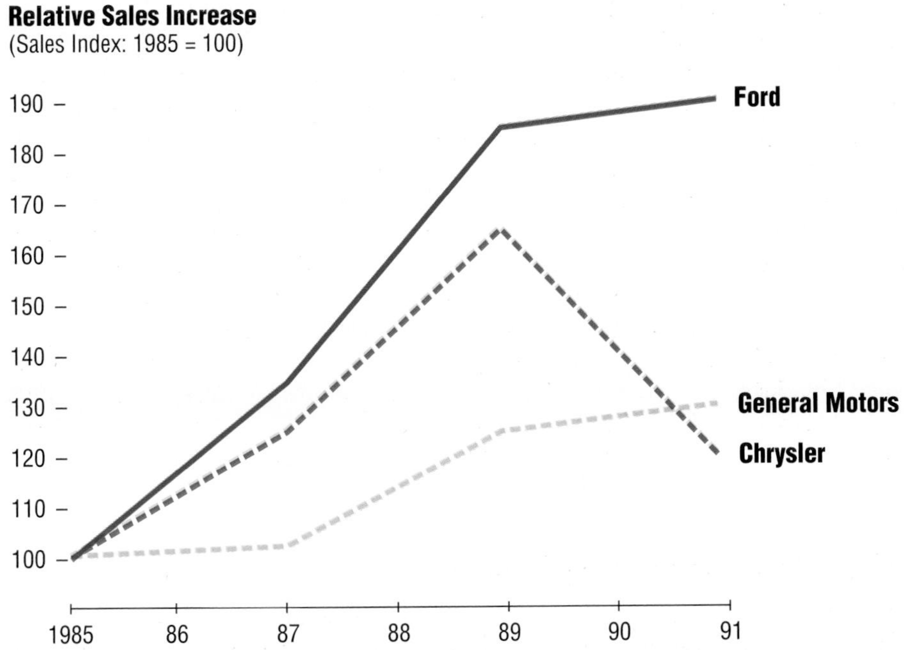

GLOBAL MARKETING STRATEGIES

How the Japanese Plan to Maintain Their Productivity Advantage into the Twenty-First Century

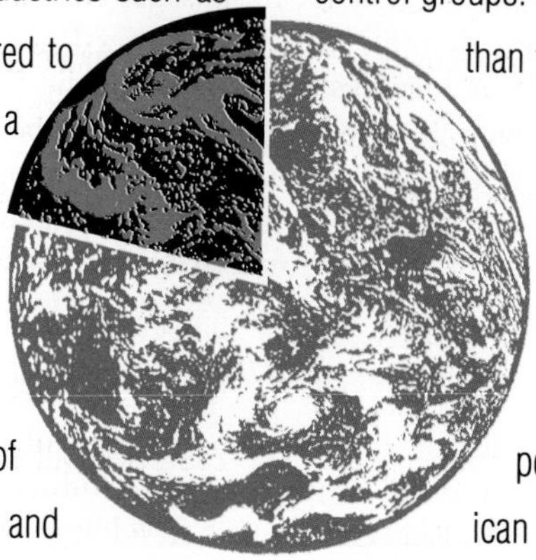

The Japanese have established a clear lead in productivity in key industries such as automobiles and electronics compared to American companies by following a simple philosophy: If you control quality during, rather than after, production, costs will take care of themselves. This focus on quality emerged as the basic philosophy of corporate Japan in the early 1950s and was implemented by what we now know as quality circles.

This quality control philosophy became known as *quality circles*, because teams of workers were assigned responsibility rather than individuals. This suited the Japanese culture's concept of shared responsibility in all societal actions. Another reason the Japanese were quick to accept the concept of quality circles was that they were starting from scratch—their economy was nowhere in early 1950. Such a concept was much harder to swallow in the United States because it would have meant changing work ethics and well-entrenched union procedures. Further, in the early 1950s, the Japanese just did not have the manpower to establish separate quality-control groups. What better way to solve the problem than to give responsibility to the workers?

The success of quality circles enabled Japanese car and electronics manufacturers to produce high-quality products at reasonable costs, giving them a distinct competitive advantage compared to American companies. The fact that American companies such as Heinz and Westinghouse are adopting the concept is a tribute to its effectiveness. Companies, such as General Motors, whose corporate culture has made it difficult to adopt the quality-circle concept, find themselves at a competitive disadvantage. Witness the GM plant closings and layoffs announced in 1992.

Given the fact that corporate America's increasing adoption of quality circles is helping it to catch up to Japan's rate of productivity, Japanese executives are asking themselves how they can maintain their productivity advantage into the next century. The answer appears to be a further advance in quality control known as Quality Function Deployment (QFD).

PRODUCT ADDITIONS

As we have seen in Chapter 11, firms emphasize new-product development to sustain profitability over time. A typical objective for firms such as DuPont, Westinghouse, and 3M is that one-fourth of their earnings come from products developed in the past five years. The effectiveness of the new-product development

GLOBAL MARKETING STRATEGIES

Although the Japanese excelled in quality control on the production line, they did not always develop products to meet customer needs. Establishing quality control for a product with the wrong characteristics to meet customer needs is not going to help a company gain a competitive advantage, so the Japanese are now promoting control of the product design process to ensure that the right specifications are introduced into the product in the first place.

QFD therefore extends the concept of quality control backward from the production line to include product design. This means that designers and engineers are now part of the quality circle. They are responsible for understanding customer needs and introducing features into the product to reflect these needs. Their work product is then passed on to the next phase, production, where workers take over responsibility for quality control on the production line.

QFD was implemented at NEC, the computer manufacturer, in 1987 when the company was given the task of designing a new 32-bit microprocessor. The company formed a design team that created six complex grids correlating consumer demands to design specifications and hardware details for each of the new microprocessor's functions. In so doing, they identified problems with certain designs and anticipated problems in meeting customer needs. QFD enabled the design team to come up with a superbly designed product. Because of QFD, NEC's design team went from making an average of four errors on a 16-bit chip to turning out the 32-bit microprocessor without a single flaw.

The combination of quality circles and QFD present a challenge to corporate America. Having just begun to accept the concept of quality circles, are they now ready to also adopt its logical extension, QFD?

Questions: How does the operation of quality circles differ from quality-control procedures traditionally used in American industry? Why do quality circles represent adaptive control whereas traditional methods represent after-the-fact control? In what ways is QFD an extension of quality circles?

Sources: "No. 1—and Trying Harder," *Business Week/Quality*, October 25, 1991, pp. 20–24; Susumu Watanable, "The Japanese Quality Control Circle: Why it Works," *International Labor Review, 130*(1991), pp. 57–80.

process can be measured by the number and profitability of the products introduced.

When Gordon McGovern became president of Campbell in 1980, his primary goal was to energize the company into becoming a more diversified packaged-foods firm through new-product development. Over 300 new products were introduced in the first five years of McGovern's reign. New-product introductions were so fast-paced that inadequate cost control and research preceded many of the launches. There were some big winners such as the Le Menu line of premium frozen dinners, but there were too many losers. By 1985 McGovern recognized the need to exert tighter control over the new-product development process to improve profitability. He admitted that "brand managers became so involved in looking at new products that they ignored the base businesses."[32] Tighter control meant moderating the rate of new-product introductions and putting more emphasis on improving the productivity of existing products.

A possible consequence of a lack of control over new product introductions is **unplanned cannibalization,** *which occurs when a new brand unexpectedly draws sales from an existing brand.* The similarity of the design of General Motors cars led to a serious cannibalization problem in recent years. As we have seen in Chapter 21, the company tried to integrate the design process across its divisions to reduce costs, but the result was a number of look-alike models. When Chevrolet introduced models such as the Corsica and Beretta, sales came largely from other Chevrolet models such as the Cavalier and Celebrity rather than from competitors.[33] Better control over new-product development might have led Chevrolet's management to more sharply differentiate its cars or to stagger the introduction of new models in different model years.

Product cannibalization can also be planned. **Planned cannibalization** *results when new technologies create new product improvements that might compete with older products in the company's line.* General Foods introduced Maxim freeze-dried coffee knowing it would cannibalize sales of Instant Maxwell House, but if it did not introduce the product, it would have lost customers to Nestlé's Tasters' Choice (also a freeze-dried brand). It was better to have customers switch from one of the company's brands to another than lose them to another company.

An irony of GM being subjected to unplanned cannibalization is that it was one of the originators of the notion of planned cannibalization. The original idea in having various GM divisions competing with each other was to have a customer stay with GM cars for life by trading up from one division to another. Planned cannibalization was a means of retaining customer loyalty as long as there were sufficient differences between divisions. When these differences started to blur, planned cannibalization turned into unplanned cannibalization.

PRODUCT DELETIONS

Given the emphasis on new-product development, many firms tend to ignore the other side of the coin, product deletions. New products are more glamorous, more fun to work on, and more closely linked to profitability than existing ones. Product deletions tend to be associated with failure. Few managers want to make a career of wielding the axe on existing products. Also, companies rarely reward managers for sound decisions to eliminate existing products; they reward them for introducing successful new products.

Figure 23.6 presents a systematic approach to product deletions. Take the example of Chase & Sanborne, at one time a leading coffee brand marketed by Standard Brands (now part of RJR Nabisco). In evaluating the brand, the first step is to determine if it is meeting sales, profitability, and market-share objectives. If so, the product is retained. Since Chase & Sanborne's sales and market share were sliding, the next question was the brand's future growth potential. If a brand has growth potential, the company will change the marketing strategy to try to revitalize it. Chase & Sanborne had little growth potential, because most former buyers pre-

FIGURE 23.6

A Product Deletion Model

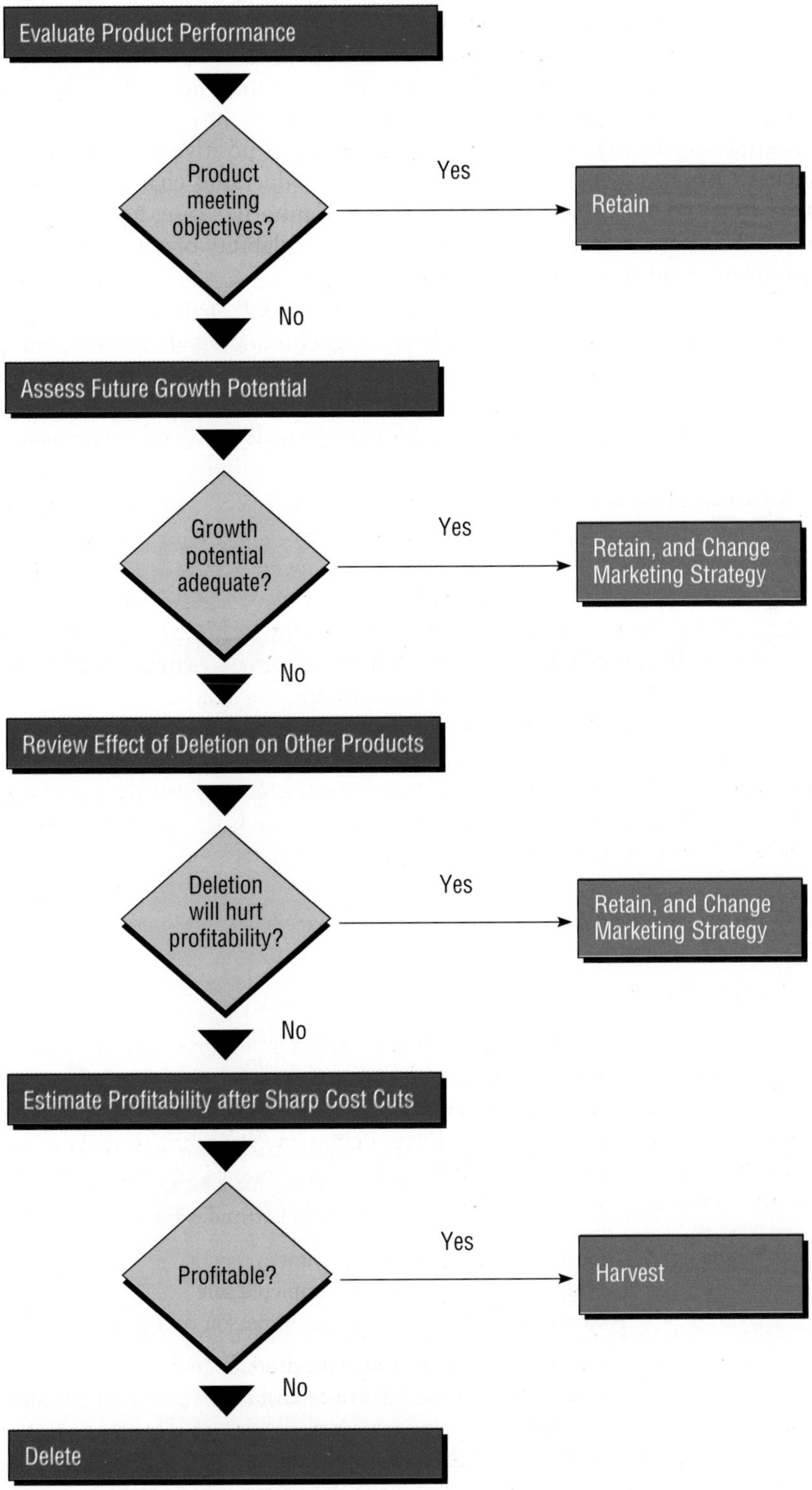

ferred newer freeze-dried and premium coffees and were unlikely to switch back to the brand.

Given a lack of growth potential, the next question is whether deleting a brand would have a negative impact on other coffee brands in the line. If so, deletion might actually decrease profits despite the brand's poor performance. For example, a buyer of steel plate might not deal with a company unless it offers various qualities of plate. High-quality steel plate may be a loss item because of the expense of processing it, yet the seller must maintain it in the line to satisfy customers. Although it may not be profitable, the product has a positive impact on the line. In such a case, the company would retain the product and change its marketing strategy to try to increase its sales. In Chase & Sanborne's case, however, customers did not link purchase of one coffee brand to availability of another, so deleting the product would not harm the company.

The final decision in Figure 23.6 is whether to harvest or delete the product. If a product still has a small but loyal following, eliminating advertising and sales-promotional expenses and minimizing other costs could make the product profitable. If such a harvesting strategy is unlikely to produce profits, the product should be deleted. Chase & Sanborne did have a small group of loyal consumers, so Standard Brands decided to harvest it, with the possibility of deleting it should market share shrink further.

TABLE 23.2

Criteria for Evaluating Components of the Marketing Mix

MARKETING MIX COMPONENT	CRITERIA
Product	Sales Market share Contribution to profit Net profit
Distribution	Cost of on-time delivery Amount of time to process an order Amount of time to deliver an order
Sales Promotion	Cost of coupon redemption Cost of attracting customer to store with in-store promotions
Advertising	Cost of reaching a target customer Cost of creating brand awareness for a target customer Cost of creating favorable brand attitudes for a target customer
Personal Selling	Cost of acquiring a new account Number of sales calls per completed sale Contribution to margin of a salesperson or a sales branch
Price	Evaluation of price relative to product quality Evaluation of price relative to customer's perceived product value Evaluation of adequacy of trade discounts to win trade support

THE MARKETING MIX

In previous chapters, we discussed the evaluation of various components of the marketing mix—the product, distribution, sales promotions, advertising, personal selling, and price. Some of the criteria we discussed for evaluating these strategies are summarized in Table 23.2.

Many of these criteria reflect measures of marketing productivity based on cost *inputs* and performance *outputs*. For example, distribution performance could be measured by the cost (input) of on-time delivery (output), or by the amount of time it takes (input) to deliver an order (output). Similarly, sales-promotional effectiveness could be measured by the cost to the company of an average coupon redemption or by the cost of attracting customers through in-store promotions. These measures give the manager some insight into the effectiveness of the marketing strategy.

THE MARKETING AUDIT

A **marketing audit** *is the evaluation of marketing performance through a comprehensive, periodic, and independent review of a company's or SBU's marketing operations.* It is a comprehensive review, because it should evaluate every aspect of marketing performance. It is a periodic review, because frequent changes in the environment mean that an audit should be an ongoing process. It is an independent review, because it should be conducted by a team outside of marketing (a team of marketing auditors) with no vested interest in the results.

Table 23.3 shows that there are two components to a marketing audit: a strategic and a product component. In the strategic component, the auditors assess the firm's or SBU's strategic planning capabilities and the effectiveness of the firm in responding to environmental change. Key questions asked in a strategic marketing audit are listed in the top of the table—for example, whether the firm has adequately anticipated environmental changes and competitive actions in its planning. Usually, these questions are framed in a longer checklist than that in Table 23.3, but the questions in the table indicate the environmental focus of the strategic marketing audit.

In Westinghouse's case, a marketing audit might review the future prospects for factory automation, competitive threats from large producers of automated equipment such as General Electric, satisfaction with existing systems among large customers such as General Motors, and the potential threat of foreign competition on the company's business. The auditors will also consider Westinghouse's efficiency in producing and marketing their machines, and the company's adaptability to produce custom-made systems.

In the product marketing component of the audit, the focus is on the company's or SBU's ability to exploit specific opportunities through development of an effective marketing mix. The key factors that auditors will evaluate in their review are listed in the bottom of Table 23.3—for example, whether the firm is effective in identifying customer needs and in marketing a product to specific segments. Auditors will also review management's effectiveness in developing the marketing mix for individual products based on the criteria listed in Table 23.2.

TAKE CORRECTIVE ACTION

The last step in the evaluation and control process is taking corrective action if needed. We have referred to corrective actions at various points in our discus-

TABLE 23.3

Key Questions in a Marketing Audit

THE STRATEGIC MARKETING AUDIT

1. Are the firm's business mission and corporate objectives clearly stated?
2. Has the company established a reasonable organizational and planning framework based on customer needs?
3. Is there an environmental scanning system in place capable of identifying marketing opportunity?
4. How has the company adjusted to key changes in demographics, technology, the economy, and legal and regulatory requirements?
5. Has the company effectively anticipated competition?
6. Is product quality satisfying customer needs?
7. Is the firm sufficiently conscious of cost-cutting opportunities?
8. Are there adequate criteria for reviewing potential acquisitions?
9. Has the firm been effective in applying its research and development resources to pursue opportunities?
10. Has the firm adequately exploited opportunities through new-product development?

THE PRODUCT MARKETING AUDIT

1. Have the needs of current and potential customers been adequately identified?
2. Have the major market segments been defined?
3. Have products been effectively positioned to these segments?
4. What is the profitability of each product?
5. What is the profitability of each product line?
6. Does the company have an effective system for new-product introductions?
7. Does it have an effective system for product deletions?
8. Are product, distribution, promotional, and pricing objectives clear for each product and product line?
9. Are expenditures allocated to each component of the marketing mix based on a set of defined criteria?
10. Are the marketing mix components effective in contributing to profits? (See specific marketing mix criteria in Table 23.2.)

sion—Heinz's strategic shift from emphasizing low cost to stressing quality, General Motors massive retrenchment to staunch the tide of losses, and Ford's embrace of statistical process control.

Sometimes corrective actions fail, as in the case of General Motors. The company attempted to control costs in the mid 1980s in the face of decreasing market share by laying off white-collar workers, getting the cooperation of unions in controlling labor costs, and automating many of its plants; however, the ultimate solution eluded the company—making cars that were sufficiently differentiated from each other and that reflected value relative to Japanese imports.

Two types of conditions require corrective action. The first is when objectives are not being met. *The difference between objectives and performance is known as* **performance variance.** For example, if Campbell's return-on-investment goal for new products is 15 percent, and it is actually attaining a 10-percent ROI, the performance variance is 5 percent. In such a case, a company will usually reallocate resources to try to attain the original goals. Campbell might increase advertising for new products, invest more money in concept and product testing, or allocate more funds to coupons and in-store promotions in the first few months after introduction. All three control systems—after-the-fact, steering, and adaptive control—allow for corrective action due to performance variance.

The second condition for corrective action is the need for adjustments in objectives because of changes in environmental conditions. *The difference between the original objective and the new objective is known as* **forecasting variance**. Forecasting variance is particular to an adaptive control system. If Campbell decided that its ROI objectives were too optimistic in an increasingly competitive environment and scaled them back from 15 percent to 12 percent, the forecasting variance would be 3 percent. It would then determine performance variance based on the new ROI objective of 12 percent. Forecasting variance therefore requires corrective action in the form of a change in objectives, whereas performance variance requires corrective action in the form of a change in resource allocations.

If an adaptive control system is in place, a firm will usually require corrective actions as a result of both forecasting and performance variance. In the process of strategic marketing planning, it is rare that a firm has gauged the marketing environment so precisely as to require no change in projections.

Managers should not regard the necessity for corrective action as a failure of the marketing planning process. Corrective action reflects the need to keep a pulse on a constantly changing marketing environment and adapt plans accordingly. Such a process of adaptation suggests that managers are sensitive to customer needs. Ultimately, that is what marketing is all about!

SUMMARY

1. **What is the distinction between strategic control and product-marketing control?**
   Strategic control attempts to ensure that the components of the strategic marketing plan are on target. Product-marketing control attempts to ensure that the components of a product's marketing plan will meet objectives. The strategic dimension of control focuses on evaluating and controlling corporate and business-unit strategies, whereas the product-marketing dimension focuses on controlling the components of the marketing mix.
2. **How do companies control marketing operations?**
   Firms must have a systematic basis for evaluating and controlling marketing operations. The first step is to define criteria for evaluation. The two most widely used profit criteria are contribution to margin and return on investment (ROI). Next, the firm projects cost estimates and revenues in a profit-and-loss (P&L) statement for a product or a business unit. The third step is to establish a marketing organization that is capable of implementing and controlling marketing activities. Next, the firm must develop and implement a plan to achieve the objectives spelled out in the projections. Once the plan is implemented, a control system is established to enable the company to evaluate marketing performance. In the final step, the company determines whether corrective action is necessary.
3. **What is the primary focus of strategic control?**
   The primary focus for control at the corporate and business-unit levels is the product quality of the firm's offerings and the costs of producing and marketing

the product. The relationship between product quality and costs measures marketing productivity. Another area of strategic control is corporate growth. A corporate growth plan requires control over new-product development, market entry, and marketing expenditures if costs are to be kept in line. A third area is to control acquisition strategies by establishing appropriate criteria to evaluate prospective acquisitions.

4. **What is the primary focus of product-marketing control?**
Firms must control marketing performance at the individual product level on several dimensions. First, they must control product additions to ensure that overzealous product managers do not come out with unprofitable new products. Second, firms must have a systematic process for deleting unprofitable products from the line. The third area for evaluation and control is the product's marketing mix. The product's distribution, advertising, personal selling, sales promotion, and pricing strategies must be evaluated. Productivity measures should be established that measure the performance of these strategies relative to their cost.

5. **What types of systems do companies use to implement control processes?**
Firms use after-the-fact, steering, and adaptive systems to implement marketing controls. In an after-the-fact control system, managers wait until the end of the planning period to take corrective action. In a steering control system, corrective action is taken during the planning period by tracking performance and steering it back to the desired objectives if it goes out of control. An adaptive system recognizes that environmental changes over time might require a change in forecasts and objectives as well as a change in strategies. Such a system is more proactive in that it anticipates environmental change, whereas after-the-fact and steering control systems are more reactive in that they deal with changes after they occur.

KEY TERMS

Control (p. 742)
Evaluation (p. 742)
Strategic marketing control (p. 742)
Product marketing control (p. 742)
Quality circles (p. 743)
Productivity (p. 744)
After-the-fact control system (p. 753)
Steering control system (p. 753)
Adaptive control system (p. 754)
Marketing productivity (p. 755)
Statistical process control (p. 758)
Unplanned cannibalization (p. 762)
Planned cannibalization (p. 762)
Marketing audit (p. 765)
Performance variance (p. 766)
Forecasting variance (p. 767)
Assignable fixed costs (p. 770)
Nonassignable fixed costs (p. 770)
Contribution to margin (p. 770)
Profit-and-loss (P&L) statement (p. 770)
Return on investment (ROI) (p. 770)
Net profit (p. 770)

QUESTIONS

1. What were the reasons that Heinz shifted from a focus on cost control to a focus on quality control?
2. In what way was Westinghouse's attempt to bring its operations under control in the 1980s an example of strategic control?
3. What factors led firms to give more attention to control of marketing operations in the 1980s?
4. What are the advantages of using contribution to margin as a criterion of performance rather than return on investment? What are the advantages of using return on investment?
5. What is the distinction between a product-based marketing organization and a market-based organization? How might the development of marketing plans and strategies at Kellogg differ depend-

ing on whether the company is organized on a product or market basis?

6. What are some principles for ensuring effective implementation of the marketing plan? Cite examples demonstrating each of these principles.
7. The two components of marketing productivity defined in Figure 23.4 are lower costs and higher product quality.
   a. Cite examples of companies focusing primarily on cost cutting and companies focusing primarily on product quality to increase productivity.
   b. Are these two approaches mutually exclusive? Explain.
8. Consider the following statement:

   New products ensure future profitability. Therefore, a company should ensure that it comes out with a steady stream of new products every year.

   a. What risks are involved in trying to ensure a steady stream of new products every year?
   b. What was Campbell's experience in emphasizing new-product development? What questions of control are raised by Campbell's experience?
9. Why do most companies pay much more attention to the process of product additions than product deletions? Do you agree with the greater emphasis on additions compared to deletions? Why or why not?
10. In the past, General Motors followed a policy of planned product cannibalization. Now it is plagued with unplanned cannibalization.
    a. What is meant by product cannibalization?
    b. What is the distinction between planned and unplanned cannibalization?
    c. What was General Motors' policy of planned cannibalization? Why is the company now plagued with unplanned cannibalization?
11. What are the differences between after-the-fact, steering, and adaptive control systems? In what sense is an adaptive control system proactive, whereas after-the-fact and steering control systems are reactive? Under what conditions is an adaptive control system most appropriate?

QUESTIONS: YOU ARE THE DECISION MAKER

1. One of the top executives of an electronics company that has found itself losing market share to Japanese competitors made the following statement:

   Contrary to popular belief, one of the reasons our Japanese competitors have a productivity advantage is that they are people oriented, whereas we [American companies] tend to be machine oriented. They reduce costs by motivating their people to work efficiently on a team basis and provide better quality control. We try to reduce costs by replacing people with robots. Overall, human quality control seems to be working better than factory automation as the best road to increasing productivity.

   a. Do you agree or disagree with the executive? Why?
   b. What evidence in this chapter supports your position?
2. Looking back over the last ten years, a former CEO of a firm producing plastics is concerned with America's economic outlook. He says:

   We are slowly losing our manufacturing base as foreign competitors. In particular, the Japanese are undermining domestic companies in the auto, computer, electronics, and small-appliance industries. As a result, we are becoming a service economy as more of our gross national product shifts from manufacturing to services. And I do not see this trend being arrested in the near future. That spells serious trouble for us and our children.

   a. Is the former CEO being overly pessimistic? Why or why not?
   b. Is there any evidence in this chapter that American companies can recapture sales lost to foreign competitors? Explain.

APPENDIX

23 COST AND PROFIT CONCEPTS FOR EVALUATING AND CONTROLLING MARKETING PERFORMANCE

COST CONCEPTS

Costs may be variable or fixed. *Variable costs* vary directly with the amount produced and include costs of labor, raw materials, transportation, order processing, and sales commissions. *Fixed costs* are not determined by the amount produced.

There are two types of fixed costs, assignable and nonassignable. **Assignable fixed costs** *are those that can be associated with the production or distribution of a product and can therefore be assigned to the product.* For example, product advertising is an assignable fixed cost, because advertising expenses do not vary directly with quantity produced yet can be assigned to a particular product. Other assignable fixed costs are the salary of a product manager, sales promotions, retooling costs for a product on the assembly line, and inventory carrying charges.

Nonassignable fixed costs *are those that cannot be directly linked to the production or distribution of a product.* If an auto plant produces many models, the plant and its facilities would be nonassignable since they are not product specific. For the same reason, corporate advertising expenditures, a research and development facility, and salaries of general managers are nonassignable fixed costs.

PROFIT CONCEPTS

The distinction between assignable and nonassignable costs defines the distinction between contribution to margin and return on investment. **Contribution to margin** *is the amount left over after all costs directly related to the product are deducted.* As a result, contribution to margin equals

Total Sales − Variable Costs − Assignable Fixed Costs

The *margin* is defined as nonassignable costs plus profits. Thus, the amount left after deductions for direct product costs is a *contribution* to nonassignable fixed costs and to profits; that is, a contribution to margin.

A **profit-and-loss statement** *is a statement of the actual or projected revenue costs and profits for a product, an SBU, or a company.* An example of a projected profit-and-loss statement for Westinghouse's robotics division in the fifth year after its acquisition is shown in Table 23.4. Projected sales in the fifth year after acquisition are $114 million. Variable costs and assignable fixed costs are estimated at $50.0 million and $34.5 million, respectively, leaving $29.5 million as the contribution to margin. Another frequently cited profitability measure, the contribution as a percentage of sales, is 25.9 percent ($29,500,000 ÷ $114,000,000).

The second most frequently used measure of profitability is **return on investment,** *which is net profit divided by total investment, where* **net profit** *equals*

Total Sales − Variable Costs −
Assignable Fixed Costs − Nonassignable Fixed Costs

To compute net profits for a product or business unit requires the allocation of nonassignable fixed costs to a product or business unit. For example, a portion of the salaries of Westinghouse executives would have to be allocated to the robotics

TABLE 23.4

Profit and Loss Projection for Westinghouse's Robotics Division in Fifth Year after Acquisition (in Millions)

Sales revenue			$114.0
Variable costs		$50.0	
Labor	$22.0		
Raw materials	15.5		
Distribution	10.5		
Sales commissions	2.0		
Assignable fixed costs		34.5	
Assignable Manufacturing costs	28.0		
Product advertising	5.0		
Sales promotions	0.5		
Assignable salaries	1.0		
Contribution to margin[a]			29.5
Nonassignable fixed costs		15.5	
Nonassignable Manufacturing costs	11.0		
Nonassignable salaries	2.0		
Research and development	2.5		
Net profit[b]			14.0

[a] Contribution as a percent of sales is 25.9 percent ($29.5/114.0).
[b] Total investment to buy the robotics division was $107 million. Therefore, projected return on investment in the fifth year is $14 million divided by $107 million, or 13.1 percent.

division. Similarly, a portion of the costs of maintaining Westinghouse's research and development facility and productivity center would have to be allocated to the division. One way to do that might be based on sales. For example, if the robotics division accounts for 7 percent of Westinghouse's total sales, then 7 percent of nonassignable fixed costs would be allocated to the division.

In this example, management projects that $15.5 million of nonassignable costs will be allocated to the robotics division, producing a net profit of $14 million. Since the initial investment in buying the division was $107 million, the return on investment is 13.1 percent ($14,000,000 ÷ $107,000,000).

MARKETING MATHEMATICS

APPENDIX I

The goals of marketing activities are often expressed and discussed in financial terms—net profit, contribution margin, return on investment. Certainly, many marketing decisions, such as adding a new product, changing channels of distribution, adjusting prices of products, or choosing among alternative promotional programs, have a significant financial impact on an organization. Consequently, marketing decision makers must understand certain basic financial concepts. Four areas of financial analysis are examined in this section: financial operating statements (including operating ratios), selected performance ratios, markups, and markdowns. Bear in mind, however, that financial considerations are only one aspect of marketing decision making.

OPERATING STATEMENTS

One of the primary financial statements used by any company is the *operating statement* (which may also be referred to as the *income statement* or the *profit and loss statement*). This document summarizes company sales, cost of goods sold, and expenses incurred during a given time period, usually a monthly, quarterly, or yearly period, although it can be any length. The length is chosen for a particular reason, such as monitoring monthly sales in a region or reporting annual income of the company. The statements may be for the company as a whole or for some operating division, profit center, or even a single product. A typical operating statement is shown in Table 1. The amount of detail in the statement may vary depending on how it is used. Typical uses include determining net income, finding the relationship between sales and the cost of goods sold, analyzing changes in inventory, identifying total expenses and the amounts of expenses by category, and comparing current operating results with past results. Table 1 shows the major sections and some typical subsections and categories included in most statements. Each one of the major sections is examined next.

Sales

The first element of any income statement is *sales*, the total dollar amount the company received for the goods or services it sold during the period. For most companies, the gross sales amount must be adjusted for goods returned by customers. Returns occur for many reasons, including products damaged in transit, errors made in filling customer orders, or perhaps a change in the customer's mind. For goods actually returned for credit, the term *return* is used. If the customer keeps the merchandise but an adjustment is made in its price, the term *allowance* is used. The two amounts are often lumped together, but they may be reported separately if desired. Subtracting total sales returns and allowances from gross sales yields *net sales*, the revenue actually received from sales.

Cost of Goods Sold (CGS)

Often the most complicated part of the operating statement, the *cost of goods sold* (CGS) reflects the amount the company actually spent for the merchandise sold during the period. This section is complicated by the presence of inventory. If a company has no inventory at the beginning of the period (*beginning inventory*) and no inventory at the end of the period (*ending inventory*), then the cost of goods sold is simply *net purchases*.

Net purchases is *gross purchases*, which includes both the actual cost of the merchandise and any additional costs involved with the actual purchase, such as freight costs, less *purchase discounts*.

TABLE 1

Example of a Typical Operating Statement: Ace Analytical Instruments, Inc. Operating Statement for the Year Ended 12/31/92

Gross sales			$20,420
Less: sales returns and allowances			157
Net sales			$20,263
Cost of goods sold:			
Beginning inventory 1/1/92 (at cost)		$ 3,770	
Net purchases:			
Gross purchases	$10,367		
Plus: freight in	628		
Less: purchase discounts	925		
Net purchases		$10,070	
Ending inventory 12/31/92 (at cost)		2,827	
Cost of goods sold (beginning inventory + net purchases − ending inventory)			11,013
Gross margin (net sales − cost of goods sold)			$ 9,259
Expenses:			
Selling expenses:			
Sales salaries and commissions	$ 2,510		
Advertising and promotion	350		
Travel	276		
Total selling expenses		$ 3,136	
Administrative expenses:			
Office salaries	$ 1,256		
Supplies	175		
Miscellaneous	280		
Total administrative expenses		$ 1,711	
General expenses:			
Rent	$ 620		
Utilities	200		
Miscellaneous	150		
Total general expenses		$ 970	
Total expenses			$ 5,817
Net income before taxes (gross margin − total expenses)			$ 3,433

When a company has *inventory* (material pruchased or manufactured for resale, but not yet sold), the cost of goods sold is still net purchases, but now this amount must be adjusted by the net change in inventory during the period. If ending inventory is larger than beginning inventory, this means that some purchases were not sold and are being held in inventory. If ending inventory is smaller than beginning inventory, this means that not only was the total amount of purchases sold, but also some of the beginning inventory was sold as well.

So the cost of goods that were actually sold during a given period is the amount we started with (beginning inventory), plus net purchases for the period, less the amount we had left over at the end of the period (ending inventory).

Gross Margin

Gross margin is the difference between net sales and the cost of goods sold. Gross margin represents the amount available to the company to pay for its other expenses (and profit or loss).

Expenses

Expenses not directly related to purchases are usually categorized as selling expenses, administrative expenses, and general expenses. *Selling expenses* relate directly to the activities involved in selling, such as sales salaries and commissions, advertising, sales promotion, and other miscellaneous selling expenses. *Administrative expenses* usually relate to the operation of offices and the salaries of those people not directly involved in selling. *General expenses* are all those other expenses (sometimes called *overhead expenses*) that are not directly related to selling or administration. Examples include rent, utilities, insurance, depreciation, property taxes, uncollectable accounts, and miscellaneous other expenses.

Net Income before Taxes

Total expenses are subtracted from gross margin to determine net income before taxes. If total expenses exceed gross margin, there is a *net operating loss.* Otherwise, there is a *net profit* from operations from which, in the case of a corporation, both state and federal income taxes must be subtracted to arrive at *net income.*

OPERATING RATIOS

The income statement may be used directly by marketing managers to improve their decision-making abilities. Actual amounts in various categories may be compared with previously forecasted or budgeted amounts. Differences between actual and budgeted amounts may identify activities that warrant further investgation by the manager.

For example, if actual sales are less than budgeted (or forecasted) sales, the problem might be poor forecasting, sales performance below expectations in one or more areas, or unexpected changes in customer demand. Higher than expected customer returns might indicate problems with the product design or package, damage in transit, or poor order-filling procedures. Similarly, higher than expected expense categories might point to inefficient operations. In all cases, the marketing manager must be a good detective to track down the underlying marketing problem.

The manager can be aided in this investigation in several ways. Income statement amounts may be recalculated as percentages of sales and then compared to budgeted percentages, similar percentages from previous periods, and/or percentags reported for similar businesses in trade publications. Table 2 shows the income statement data from Table 1 expressed as percentages of sales. Because many expenses are directly linked to sales and because sales vary each period, converting all amounts to percentages of sales will allow multiple-period data to be compared directly. These percentages are actually simplified *operating ratios.*

Operating statement amounts reflect only cost and revenue amounts. They provide no information concerning the efficiency or the effectiveness of spending. Nor do these amounts identify the type or composition of inventory or purchases.

Notice that changes in income statement amounts may or may not indicate a desirable development. For example, is an increase in selling expense desirable or not? It may reflect rising competition and thus suggest the need to advertise more. Or it may reflect ineffective advertising. The manager must make the determination. Changes in income statement amounts also do not indicate the efficiency or the effectiveness by which expenses are incurred. Improving office efficiency might reduce administrative expense, but improving the efficiency or effectiveness of the salesforce might increase sales commissions (due to increased sales).

Operating ratios express amounts on the income statement as a percentage of sales. The three most important operating ratios are

$$\text{Gross Margin Ratio} = \frac{\text{Gross Margin}}{\text{Net Sales}} = \frac{\$9{,}250}{\$20{,}263} = 45.65\%$$

$$\text{Net Income Ratio} = \frac{\text{Net Income}}{\text{Net Sales}} = \frac{\$3{,}433}{\$20{,}263} = 16.94\%$$

$$\text{Operating Expense Ratio} = \frac{\text{Total Expense}}{\text{Net Sales}} = \frac{\$5{,}817}{\$20{,}263} = 28.71\%$$

PERFORMANCE RATIOS

In addition to investigating changes in income statement amounts, marketing managers might also use *performance ratios* in their financial analysis of company operations.

A discussion of some useful performance ratios follows.

Inventory Turnover. Sometimes called the *stockturn rate*, the *inventory turnover* identifies the number of times an inventory is sold during one year.

TABLE 2

Operating Statement in Percentages: Ace Analytical Instruments, Inc. Operating Statement for the Year Ended 12/31/92

Net sales			100.00%
Cost of goods sold:			
Beginning inventory 1/1/92 (at cost)		18.60%	
Net purchases			
Gross purchases	51.16%		
Plus: freight in	3.10%		
Less: purchase discounts	4.56%		
Net purchases:		49.70%	
Ending inventory 12/31/92 (at cost)		13.95%	
Cost of goods sold (beginning inventory + net purchases − ending inventory)			54.35%
Gross margin (net sales − cost of goods sold)			45.65%
Expenses:			
Selling expenses:			
Sales salaries and commissions	12.39%		
Advertising and promotion	1.73%		
Travel	1.36%		
Total selling expenses		15.48%	
Administrative expenses:			
Office salaries	6.20%		
Supplies	0.86%		
Miscellaneous	1.38%		
Total administrative expenses		8.44%	
General expenses:			
Rent	3.06%		
Utilities	0.99%		
Miscellaneous	0.74%		
Total general expenses		4.79%	
Total expenses			28.71%
Net income before taxes (gross margin − total expenses)			16.94%

$$\text{Inventory Turnover} = \frac{\text{Cost of Goods Sold}}{\text{Average Inventory}} = \frac{\$11{,}013}{(\$3{,}770 + \$2{,}827)/2}$$
$$= 3.3 \text{ times}$$

Whether an inventory turnover rate is too high or too low depends upon the type of industry and management customer service policy. Generally, the higher the turnover number, the better the performance. Higher turnover rates not only mean that sales are being made with a relatively small investment in inventory, but also that the composition of the inventory is more current (and so less likely to become obsolete). However, turnover rates that are too high could foretell shortages and thus reduced customer satisfaction.

Return on Investment (ROI). A measure of the efficiency with which company management can generate sales based upon the amount invested in the company is the *return on investment* (ROI).

$$\text{Return on Investment} = \frac{\text{Net Income}}{\text{Total Investment}}$$

The "Total Investment" amount comes from the balance sheet of the company. (A balance sheet shows the amounts of assets, debt, and net worth of a company at a given point in time.) Total investment may be interpreted as either total assets or net worth (net assets) of the company.

MARKUPS

A *markup* is a dollar amount added to the cost of an item to determine its selling price. As a result:

$$\text{Selling price} = \text{Cost} + \text{Markup}.$$

The amount of the markup must cover all the selling, administrative, and general expenses related to the item, and some additional amount to contribute to profit. Markups are widely used in wholesaling and retailing businesses, although other types of businesses may use them as well.

For ease of use, markups are often expressed as a percentage of either the selling price of the item or its cost. Most consumer goods middlemen use selling price as the basis for the markup.

$$\text{Percentage Markup on Selling Price} = \frac{\text{Dollar Markup}}{\text{Dollar Selling Price}}$$

Cost could also be used as the base for the markup:

$$\text{Percentage Markup on Cost} = \frac{\text{Dollar Markup}}{\text{Dollar Cost}}$$

To better understand markups, consider the following example: The Suitery is a retail clothing store specializing in men's suits. What should be the selling price of its TruFit brand if the suit costs The Suitery $99.90 each and the markup on selling price is 55 percent?

$$\begin{aligned} \text{Selling Price} &= \text{Cost} + \text{Markup} \\ \text{Selling Price} &= \$99.90 + (55\% \times \text{Selling Price}) \\ \text{Selling Price} - (55\% \times \text{Selling Price}) &= \$99.90 \\ \text{Selling Price} &= \$99.90/.45 = \$222.00 \end{aligned}$$

What is the dollar amount of the markup?

$$\text{Selling Price} = \text{Cost} + \$\text{Markup}$$
$$\$\ \text{Markup} = \text{Selling Price} - \text{Cost}$$
$$\$\ \text{Markup} = \$222.00 - \$99.90 = \$122.10$$

or you could determine the dollar amount of the markup as

$$\$\ \text{Markup} = \%\ \text{Markup} \times \text{Price}$$
$$\$\ \text{Markup} = .55 \times \$222.00 = \$122.10$$

Sometimes a retailer might want to set a retail price first, and then determine the markup percentage. Let's consider The Suitery again. The Suitery would like to sell its BestFit brand of suit for a higher price than its TruFit brand ($222.00). The company thinks that customers would be willing to pay $335. If BestFit suits cost The Suitery $134.00 each, what percentage markup on selling price is being received?

$$\text{Percentage Markup on Selling Price} = \frac{\$\ \text{Markup}}{\text{Selling Price}} = \frac{\$335 - \$134}{\$335.} = 60\%$$

Chains of Markups. Each middleman in the channel of distribution generally adds a markup to the selling price of a product, thus creating a chain of markups. Although somewhat more complicated, the basic principle for calculating markups is still the same. Consider this example: the TruFit suits being sold by The Suitery were purchased from Suit City Wholesalers for $99.90 who, in turn, bought them from the manufacturer, Suits-R-US. If Suit City uses a 20 percent markup on its selling price, what was the cost of the suit to Suit City (or the Suits-R-US selling price)?

$$\text{Selling Price} = \text{Cost} + \$\ \text{Markup}$$
$$\$99.90 = \text{Cost} + (.20 \times \$99.90)$$
$$\text{Cost} = \$99.90 - \$19.98 = \$79.92$$

In other words,

Wholesaler's Cost	= $ 79.92	(Manufacturer's Price)
Wholesaler's 20%	= 19.98	(.20 × $99.90)
Retail Cost	= $ 99.90	(Wholesaler's Price)
Retailer's 55%	= 122.10	(.55 × $222.00)
Consumer's Cost	= $222.00	(Retailer's Price)

MARKDOWN RATIOS

A *markdown* is a reduction in the retail selling price of an item. Markdowns are used by retailers as a way of encouraging customers to buy. They are necessitated by such things as style changes, inventory overstock reductions, damage, original markups being too high, or some type of miscalculation. The computation of markdown ratios is not related to the operating statement because the markdown is given to the customer prior to the sale. Operating statement gross revenue is recorded as the actual amount received from the sale after the markdown.

Markdown ratios are an important tool for retailers trying to measure the efficiency of individual departments within the retail company. They are computed for each department and not for each product line. Different department ratios may then be compared to each other and/or over time. The markdown ratio may be calculated as follows:

$$\text{Markdown Ratio} = \frac{\text{Total Markdowns in Dollars}}{\text{Total Net Sales in Dollars}}$$

Assume total markdowns for the Suitery were $50,000 on net sales of $500,000. The markdown ratio would then be 10 percent.

QUESTIONS AND PROBLEMS

1. Define the following based on the income statement:

   a. Net sales
   b. Net purchases
   c. Gross margin
   d. Cost of goods sold.

2. Using the following data, calculate the net income from operations for the Big Zap Electric Supply Co.:

Administrative expense	$ 14,137
Beginning inventory (cost)	25,132
Ending inventory (cost)	21,991
General expense	4,712
Gross sales	169,646
Purchases (net cost)	84,823
Sales returns and allowances	12,566
Selling expense	31,415

3. The shoe department of the Stupendous Sportswear Co. has the following operating data:

Cost of goods sold	$376,842
Gross sales	942,478
Markdowns	62,816
Returns and allowances	57,106
Ending inventory	93,711

   Calculate the markdown ratio for the department.

4. Consider the following income statement:

ABC Company
Income Statement
Year Ended 12/31/92

Sales	$113,097	
Sales returns and allowances	10,178	
Net sales		$102,919
Cost of goods sold		43,811
Gross margin		$ 59,108
Selling and administrative expense	$ 23,909	
Miscellaneous expense	14,622	
Total expenses		$ 38,531
Net income		$ 20,577

   Calculate the following:

   a. Gross margin ratio
   b. Net income ratio
   c. Operating expense ratio

5. The Better Bicycle Co. has net sales of $1,000,000 last year and a gross margin percentage of 24 percent. What must its average inventory be in order to achieve a stockturn rate of 12?

ANSWERS

1. a. Net sales is equal to gross sales minus sales returns and allowances.
   b. Net pruchases is equal to gross purchases minus purchases returns and allowances.
   c. Gross income is a synonym for net sales. Gross margin is net sales minus cost of goods sold.
   d. Cost of goods available for sale is beginning inventory plus net purchases. Cost of goods sold is cost of goods available for sale minus ending inventory.

2. Big Zap Electric Supply Co.
Income Statement
For the Period Ended——

Gross sales		$169,646
Less sales returns and allowances		12,566
Net sales		$157,080
Cost of goods sold:		
Beginning inventory (cost)	$ 25,132	
Purchases (net cost)	84,823	
Cost of goods available for sale	$109,955	
Ending inventory (cost)	21,991	
Cost of goods sold		$ 87,964
Gross margin		$ 69,116
Expenses:		
Selling expense	$ 31,415	
Administrative expense	14,137	
General expense	4,712	
Total expenses		$ 50,264
Net income (before tax)		$ 18,852

3. $\text{Markdown Ratio} = \dfrac{\text{Markdowns}}{\text{Net Sales}} = \dfrac{\$62{,}831}{\$942{,}478 - \$57{,}106} = 8.0\%$

4. a. $\text{Gross Margin Ratio} = \dfrac{\text{Gross Margin}}{\text{Net Sales}} = \dfrac{\$59{,}108}{\$102{,}919} = 57.4\%$

b. $\text{Net Income Ratio} = \dfrac{\text{Net Income}}{\text{Net Sales}} = \dfrac{\$20{,}577}{\$102{,}919} = 20.0\%$

c. $\text{Operating Expense Ratio} = \dfrac{\text{Total Expenses}}{\text{Net Sales}} = \dfrac{\$38{,}531}{\$102{,}919} = 37.4\%$

5. Cost of Goods Sold (CGS) = .76 × $1,000,000 = $760,000

$\text{Stockturn Rate} = \dfrac{\text{CGS}}{\text{Average Inventory}}$

Average Inventory = $760,000/12 = $63,333.

APPENDIX 2

CAREERS IN MARKETING

Students often find themselves attracted to marketing as a career because of the creative challenge it poses. The field is so diverse, however, that selecting a specific career goal presents a dilemma. Marketing is now being used not only for products, but also for services, and not only by for-profit companies, but also by non-profit and government organizations. Overall, an estimated 14.1 million people were employed in marketing, sales, or related areas in 1990. It is projected that jobs in this area will increase by 24% over the next 15 years. Marketing, advertising, and public relations managers held about 427,000 jobs in 1990.

This appendix has been designed to help in the selection of a specialty in marketing. Since career goals represent long-term planning, we will focus on those positions that can lead to the executive suite. The percentage of CEOs from marketing is higher than that of any other group. As competition heats up, companies tend to turn to marketers for leadership.

The positions that will be described as well as the typical career paths are

PRODUCT	Product Manager

PROMOTION	Advertising
	  Account Executive
	  Media Director
	  Creative Director
	Sales Promotion
	  Sales Promotion Manager
	Public Relations
	  Public Relations Manager
	Personal Selling
	  Sales Manager

DISTRIBUTION	Physical Distribution Manager
RETAILING	Merchandise Manager Store Manager Retail Buyer
MARKETING RESEARCH	Project Manager

Of course, the precise titles may differ from company to company, and the levels to reach them may vary by company structure and size.

The one association that covers the entire spectrum of marketing is

American Marketing Association
250 S. Wacker Drive, Suite 200
Chicago, IL 60606
(312) 648-0536

PRODUCT MANAGER

While the position of *product manager* may be found in both the consumer and industrial sectors, producers of consumer products who follow a multi-brand strategy seem to be most in need of product managers. Product managers are the "champions" for the product or brand they are responsible for. They must compete with all of the other product managers for the resources of the company. This generalist position carries with it a high level of responsibility, and many graduates choose product management as a career goal because it may be a fast track into general management.

Sample Job Description

Your marketing career begins with a thorough period of training for about six months including field sales experience, assignments in an advertising agency, and in the marketing services and budget departments. When you begin with a product group, your responsibilities include the full spectrum of product marketing; you help develop the budget and play a significant part in planning and evaluating advertising programs. Your work also involves product development with research and development (R&D) people. You will also be gathering information to effect workable marketing programs for new and existing products, as well as suggesting product ideas and consumer/trade promotion programs. Market research also comes into play as new products, advertising, and promotions are consumer tested. Finally, you must implement marketing decisions and assess their impact on sales, consumer franchises, and profitability. If you perform well, you can expect to be managing your own product about two years after joining a product group. Specific responsibilities are to:

- Gather, analyze, and interpret sales, marketing, and market research data. Write reports on important trends for specific brand/product category and maintain familiarity with general market conditions.
- Assist in the development, organization, coordination, and follow-up on multifaceted marketing assignments. This requires interface with finance, purchasing, graphics, promotion, market research, and sales departments.
- Participate and assist in the development of short- and long-term product marketing programs that identify level of profitability and potential opportunities for the brand.
- Prepare brand reports and update required brand information including forecasts, P&L, and general brand performance.
- Participate in the development of consumer/trade promotions.
- Prepare special reports or participate in special projects as requested by management.

Career Path for Product Manager

Further product managers are hired as *marketing assistants.* The prerequisite may be either an M.B.A. or a bachelor's degree, depending upon the company. They are given detailed tasks covering a variety of functional areas. For example, one assignment may take them into a test market, another into monitoring a promotional program. After a year, or less, they may be promoted to *assistant product manager* and begin to work closely with the product manager in planning and development. In another year or two, they may move up to product manager, usually for a different product or brand than they were involved in as assistant product manager.

Information Sources for Product Manager Careers

Consumer product companies in the Fortune 500, or the top 100 advertisers listed by *Advertising Age* annually are the companies that would be most likely to use the product manager form of organization.

Business publications such as *Business Week*, *Forbes*, and *Fortune* frequently have articles about product management.

ADVERTISING ACCOUNT EXECUTIVE

Advertising account executives are the interface between the agency and the client. They have to interpret the client's objectives to the agency's creative group and then sell the creative group's strategy for meeting those objectives to the client. Once a campaign has been agreed upon, the account executive must coordinate the actions of the media and the production people to implement it.

In large agencies, the account executive may be assigned to a single brand. The account responsibility in smaller agencies may be more diverse and may include new-account solicitation.

This position is very stressful because if the agency loses an account, the account executive's job is often at stake.

Sample Job Description of Assistant Account Executive

A starting position is as an assistant account executive. The major functions of the position include:

- Attaining an understanding of client's business, brand's position in the market, and marketing goals.
- Assisting in brand strategy planning.
- Communicating client needs to all appropriate agency departments.
- Coordinating the creation and implementation of the agency's advertising product with creative, media, and other departments.
- Communicating agency policies, recommendations, or relevant problems to client.
- Production—the production of finished commercials and advertisements.
- Preparing and presenting periodic reports.
- Developing media plans.

Careers in account management can develop from account representative to account supervisor, to management supervisor, ultimately to group account director and on to top management within the agency.

Career Path for Account Executive

Advertising is a difficult field to get into. Because of the glamour associated with the industry, the competition for jobs is intense, allowing compensation for entry-level positions to be on the low side.

The largest agencies are located in New York. They have formal training programs wherein trainees are rotated through all of the departments to give them exposure to everything the agency does. In six months or less the trainee becomes an *assistant account executive* and continues learning the business on the job until such time as an account executive's position opens up.

Smaller agencies may not offer such training. They also do not usually have many openings.

MEDIA DIRECTOR

Advertisers want to make sure that their message is reaching their customers as efficiently as possible. The media department of an advertising agency plans and analyzes purchases of broadcast time and space in print media so as to achieve the client's goal.

The *media director* is responsible for the media department and in that capacity oversees the work of media buyer analysts. He or she may also be involved in corporate level planning.

Career Path for Media Director

Media directors usually start out as *assistant buyers*, receiving on-the-job training in that position. Many menial tasks are involved, including the processing of large quantities of data. A specific type of degree is not as important for this position as relevant quantitative skills. After experience at this level, the next step is to be promoted to *media buyer.*

The media specialist must not be an expert on costs, but must also be able to match the medium with the demographic characteristics that best represent the target market(s). After all of the variables are considered and alternatives weighed, the media buyer must exercise personal judgment based upon experience to produce a proposal that the account executive can present to the client with confidence.

Larger agencies have *associate media directors* who manage smaller groups of media analysts and become involved in more costly media buys that may involve longer time spans.

Information Sources for Media Director

Publications of interest to the media specialist are *Marketing and Media Decisions, Media Decisions*, and *Broadcasting.*

CREATIVE DIRECTOR

The *creative director* manages the creative department of the advertising agency, which includes copywriting and art. Since ideas and strategies are the creative director's forte, there may be a considerable amount of client contact involved, and this may include participation in getting new accounts. The creative director usually starts either as a copywriter or as an artist.

Career Path for Creative Director: Copywriter

The job of the *copywriter* is to take the client's objectives and creatively transform them into words that can be used in the advertisement. These words must be concise, yet effective in creating images in the mind of the reader. Getting an entry-level job as a copywriter means convincing the agency that you possess this talent.

The copywriter is not allowed the luxury of having "writer's block." Deadlines have to be met that may require putting in long hours at times.

Copywriters eventually are given supervisory responsibilities over other copywriters and then follow the path to *associate creative director.*

Career Path for Creative Director: Art Director.

Both agencies and company art departments require *art directors.* Just as the copywriter is responsible for the words in an ad, the art director is responsible for everything that is visual. The two have to work closely together to rightly interpret what the client wants. They usually work with free-lance photographers and illustrators rather than producing art and photography in-house. They also coordinate the activities of production people, printers, typesetters, and so forth.

The art director administers a portion of the budget for each assignment. If the client requires it, he or she may also get involved in package and display design.

The entry level may be as an *assistant art director* who may be doing the layouts, or *mechanicals* (putting the ad components together). An art degree of some sort helps, but you don't have to be able to produce finished art. Visualization is an essential skill, and the ability to communicate this visualization to others is important.

Information Sources for Creative Director Career

The "bible" of the advertising industry is *Advertising Age. AdWeek* is another magazine that has wide readership. The following associations are relevant to people pursuing advertising careers.

American Advertising Federation
1400 K Street NW, Suite 1000
Washington, DC 20005
(202) 898-0089

American Association of Advertising Agencies
666 Third Avenue, 13th Floor
New York, NY 10017
(212) 282-2500

Business/Professional Advertising Association
100 Metroplex Drive
Edison, NJ 08817
(201) 985-4441

International Advertising Association
342 Madison Avenue, 20th Floor
Suite 2000
New York, NY 10017
(212) 557-1133

Women in Advertising and Marketing
11100 Whisperwood Lane
Rockville, MD 20852
(301) 493-5808

SALES PROMOTION MANAGER

When a company is looking for an immediate response, it will spend a larger portion of its promotional budget on sales promotion. It may have a staff group in-house, use an advertising agency, or hire the services of a sales promotion agency. The *sales promotion manager* is someone whose experience lends itself to developing and executing short-term incentives such as sweepstakes, coupons, and premiums to augment the other promotional efforts of the firm. He or she will interface with clients so as to communicate the promotion to the purchaser.

This position is usually found in the area of consumer products. Industrial firms may also get involved in sales promotion, but usually not to the degree of requiring a specialist.

Career Path for Sales Promotion Manager

There are no distinct career paths for a sales promotion manager. Product knowledge is essential, so it is not unusual for them to have some sales experience. This is also a position that *assistant product managers* may go into instead of into product management. A less likely route would be that of *promotion assistant*, since this position does not exist in too many companies. Companies look for someone who has experience not only in promotion, but also in selling and marketing.

PUBLIC RELATIONS MANAGER

The position of *public relations manager* can be an in-house or an agency one. There are agencies that specialize in public relations as well as advertising agencies that offer public relation services for their clients. The public relations manager deals with the company's image rather than with its products. Because the ability to get favorable "press" may depend to a large extent on contacts in the media, journalistic experience is often looked upon favorably for this position.

Public relations managers must communicate with every one in the organization so that they can stay abreast of all activities. If something newsworthy is planned, they have to know about it so that they can obtain media coverage. They may also create newsworthy events to generate publicity. And they often help key executives in preparing for public appearances. Perhaps their most important role, though, is to overcome any negative publicity that may accrue to the company.

Career Path for Public Relations Manager: Company

The entry-level position may be as a researcher or writer for the public relations staff. This is the point at which networks can be developed and contacts made that will provide the ingredients necessary for promotion to *public relations officer* and, ultimately, *director of public relations.*

Career Path for Public Relations Manager: Agency

The starting position in an agency may be as an *assistant account executive* or *staff writer*. These positions are regarded as on-the-job training for public relations.

Information Sources for Public Relations Career

Publications dedicated to the public relations field are the *Public Relations Quarterly* and the *Public Relations Journal.* Other publications of interest are *Communication World*, *Communication Illustrated*, and *PR News*. Relevant associations are

Public Relations Society of America
33 Irving Place, 3rd Floor
New York, NY 10003-2376
(212) 995-2230

International Association of Business Communicators
1 Hallidie Plaza, Suite 600
San Francisco, CA 94102
(415) 433-3400

Marketing Communications Executives International
c/o Strategic Promotions, Inc.
2602 McKinney, Suite 250
Dallas, TX 75204
(214) 871-1016

SALES MANAGER

Any organization of any size that employes salespeople will have a *sales manager.* There is a greater demand for sales managers than for any other key position in marketing. Their responsibilities are significant. They not only have to develop short- and long-range sales goals, but they have to plan strategies for achieving them and control mechanisms for monitoring progress.

In addition, they may have to plan the sales territories so that the coverage required by the company is attained while providing equitable opportunities for the representatives. This may be done geographically, or by product line, or both.

The sales manager must also staff the territories by recruiting and selecting new sales personnel. Training of these new representatives as well as ongoing training of the entire sales force might be delegated to a training specialist in larger firms, but the responsibility is still that of the sales manager.

Other possible areas of involvement for the sales manager are sales compensation and budgeting. They also must evaluate the performance of salespeople. And they frequently represent the company at trade association meetings and trade shows where products are displayed.

In cases where the sales task is delegated to manufacturer's representatives, dealers, or distributors, the sales manager may have to work with these independent sales staffs.

The modern sales manager must be conversant with computers, as a great deal of software has been developed to assist in territory development and management, budget control, and so on.

Since revenues are generated by sales, the sales manager's position is an extremely visible and important one. Moreover the results of his or her efforts are easily quantified.

Career Path for Sales Manager

It is critical that sales managers have experience in sales and marketing, so the entry-level position is usually that of a *sales representative.* What may be frustrating to the college graduate is that sales positions do not always require a degree. Yet as products become more complex and the market more sophisticated, a degree is becoming a threshhold requirement. High-technology firms may require a technical degree in addition to a business degree. Even in the case where completing college is not an entry-level requirement, the graduate will often have a decided edge when it comes to promotion.

There are over 240 separate job descriptions listed under sales in the *Dictionary of Occupational Titles* (4th Ed. 1977, U.S. Department of Labor). A generic description follows:

> ***SALES REPRESENTATIVE***
>
> *Sells products to business and industrial establishments or individual for manufacturer or distributor at sales office, store, showroom, or customer's place of business, utilizing knowledge of product sold; Compiles lists of prospective customers for use as sales leads, based on information from newspapers, business directories, and other sources. Travels throughout assigned territory to call on regular and prospective customers to solicit orders or talks with customer on sales floor or by phone. Displays or demonstrates product using samples or catalog, and emphasizes saleable features. Quotes prices and credit terms and prepares sales contracts for orders obtained. Estimates dates of delivery to customer based on knowledge of own firms' production and delivery schedules. Prepares reports of business transactions and keeps expense accounts.*

Many college students have a negative bias toward sales because they think the objective is to sell a product or service to the consumer, usually as the result of a single call. Encyclopedias and vacuum cleaners are examples of products that have been successfully sold door to door. There is no attempt to develop long-term relationships. These types of salespeople are usually paid a straight commission and are often considered independent contractors rather than employees of the firm.

Other sales positions, however, emphasize call-backs and building long-term relationships. The responsibilities differ markedly by industry and company. Some represent different levels in the channel of distribution: manufacturers selling to wholesalers, wholesalers to retailers, and so on. They emphasize the benefits that the next channel level will receive in terms of profit margins, inventory turnover, and so forth, by including their products in their mix. Assistance may be given in merchandising, display, inventory management, and other areas to reduce the cost of the channel member. A sales representative for a food broker, for example, will check the inventory levels in each store, make sure that the product(s) are displayed properly and adequately on the shelves, put up special displays, and credit merchandise that is being returned.

Sales personnel in the industrial field may be involved in either basic, semi-technical products or very complex technical products. While providing a high level of service is important in both instances, as products become more complex, product knowledge becomes a critical factor. At the extreme, a technical degree may be considered essential.

What is satisfying about a sales position is the ability to work without close supervision and to be measured by the results you produce. It can be a time-intensive occupation, however, and field representatives may find themselves traveling a good portion of the time.

Information Sources for Sales Manager Career

The best generic information source for sales positions is *Sales and Marketing Management* magazine. *Business Marketing* addresses sales management in the industrial area. In addition, every industry has at least one trade journal. These are listed in Standard Rate and Data's *Business Periodical Index*, which most advertising agencies subscribe to. Marketing faculty can obtain old copies from Standard Rate and Data for use in the classroom.

The following associations are relevant to sales managers.

Bureau of Salesmen's National Association
1819 Peachtree Road NE, Suite 210
Atlanta, GA 30309
(404) 351-7355

Direct Marketing Association
11 West 42nd St.
New York, NY 10036-8096
(212) 768-7277

Direct Selling Association
1776 K St. N.W., Suite 600
Washington, DC 20006
(202) 293-5760

National Association for Professional Saleswomen
PO Box 2606
Novato, CA 94948
(415) 898-2606

National Association of Wholesaler-Distributors
1725 K St. N.W., Suite 710
Washington, DC 20006
(202) 872-0885

Sales and Marketing Executives International
Statler Office Tower, No. 458
Cleveland, OH 44115
(216) 771-6650

PHYSICAL DISTRIBUTION MANAGER

Every company is involved in physical distribution, so the position will vary in scope by industry and company size. The *physical distribution manager* manages both people and resources. Because the cost of physical distribution is often a large part of the final cost of the product, the management of this function is becoming increasingly more sophisticated. The larger the firm, the more likely it is to have a professional in charge of physical distribution.

The responsibilities include determining the number, location, and type of warehouses necessary, the method of inventory management, and the appropriate transportation and order-processing methods, as well as interacting with all of the other functions to make sure that they are coordinated with physical distribution.

Career Path for Physical Distribution Manager

Because of the diverse number of career opportunities in this field, a generic career path is impossible to devise. What companies are looking for is someone who may have had some experience in physical distribution. A knowledge of marketing as well as the ability to use computers is increasingly important. Problem-solving abilities as well as financial knowledge are also important.

Information Sources for Physical Distribution Manager Career

Publications that address this area are *Handling and Shipping Management*, *Distribution World Wide*, *Industrial Distribution*, and *Transportation Journal*. Relevant associations are

American Society of Transportation and Logistics
P.O. Box 33095
Louisville, KY 40232

National Council of Physical Distribution Management
2803 Butterfield Road
Oak Brook, IL 60521

MERCHANDISE MANAGER (RETAILING)

The *merchandise manager* is responsible for the activities of all of the buyers within a product area. This includes overseeing the planning of assortments, merchandising, planning promotions, and budgeting. Depending upon the size of the chain, the merchandise manager may report to a *general merchandise manager* who may have the title of *vice-president of marketing*.

Career Path for Merchandise Manager

Employees on this career track begin as *executive trainees*. They are exposed to company policies and procedures as well as how the firm approaches retailing in general. After a relatively short orientation of 16 weeks or less, they are promoted to the position of *assistant buyer*. Working with a buyer, they check deliveries, make sure that merchandise is displayed, communicate price information to the department managers, and distribute promotional material. The buyer may bring them along on buying trips, where they learn about planning merchandise assortments. They will then be promoted to the position of *buyer*, where they will be responsible for administering a rather rigid budget in their merchandise area. They must know what has sold in the past as well as being able to anticipate what will sell in the future. They must be prepared to negotiate with suppliers on quantities, price, and delivery.

Merchandise managers must work with the advertising people and the various departments of the company to make sure that the merchandise moves in a timely manner. Having to mark down prices to move products will result in smaller budgets in the future.

STORE MANAGER (RETAILING)

The other route to the top in retailing is the position of *store manager.* One of the prime responsibilities of this position is in the personnel area, making sure the company has adequate numbers of people, properly trained, and that labor costs are in line. The performance of the store manager is measured by the profit contribution that the store makes, and labor is the cost that the manager has the most control over. He or she must also be sure that the store has the proper amount of inventory and that it is displayed properly.

Providing customer service is an extremely important part of this job, because dissatisfied customers will ultimately reflect on the patronage and profitability of the store. To ensure adequate customer service requires constant interaction with the department managers and sales support groups as well as the corporate officers of the company.

Career Path for Store Manager

After orientation as an executive trainee, the employee aiming for store manager will proceed through sales management positions, where training will be given in supervising sales personnel. He or she may pass through several levels of sales management where wider experience is attained in such areas as display, promotion, and price administration.

Information Sources for Store Manager Career

Many trade journals are product-specific (e.g., publications on furniture or jewelry retailing). In addition, useful publications include *Chain Store Age*, *Stores*, and the *Journal of Retailing.* The association that pertains to store managers is

National Retail Federation
100 W. 31st Street
New York, NY 10011
(212) 244-8780

RETAIL BUYER

Whenever retailing students are asked about their future aspirations, invariably a great number respond that they would like to be buyers. The buying function seems to be the most glamorous aspect of the retail operation. Perhaps to the inexperienced it is a chance to spend a great deal of money in sums that one could never spend for his or her own needs. While the buying job does often present glamorous and exciting moments, few jobs in retailing require more ability and disciplined training. Duties and responsibilities are as follows:

- Most important is the actual purchasing of merchandise. The buyer is faced with the perennial problems of what merchandise to choose and from which vendors, how much of each item to purchase, and the correct timing of delivery to meet with customers' demands.
- After buying arrangements have been worked out, the buyer must price the merchandise to conform with the policies of the store and his or her particular department.
- After goods are received and marked, and come to the selling floor, the placement of goods is often determined by the buyer.

- Depending on the store, the buyer may be involved in the final selection of employees for the department, the supervision of selling, and the arrangement of sales meetings.
- The buyer selects merchandise for promotions, for special displays, and for advertisements. She or he plans fashion shows and any special events that might promote goods.

MARKETING RESEARCH PROJECT MANAGER

The marketing research project manager works with the clients to determine what their information needs are and develops methodology that will efficiently and effectively meet those needs. The project manager has total responsibility for the success of the research project. Based upon information received from the client, a budget is drawn up and a proposal is made. When the research is completed, the account executive presents the results to the client.

The position also entails keeping present clients happy and looking for new customers. At this level the account executive does not engage in any of the research activities personally, but rather acts as a consultant.

Career Path for Marketing Research Project Director

There are a number of entry-level positions that involve gathering data and "number crunching"—jobs such as *field supervision* and *coding and tabulating*. The next level is that of *assistant project director* and *project director*, which are supervisory positions. Communication skills are important because project directors not only have to write reports, but they must also communicate with other research functions and with the client. Competence in statistical analysis as well as knowledge of computer applications is essential.

Qualifications for such a position, besides having proficiency in various research techniques, include excellent analytical and written skills, and an ability to work with people and organize projects. Responsibilities of an assistant or associate usually include most of the following:

- Write proposals for minor research projects.
- Submit budget proposals.
- Prepare research designs, write questionnaires, and create processing plans.
- Supervise data collection.
- Analyze and interpret research results and review these with the supervisor.
- Write final research reports.
- Present findings.

Most of these activities are performed with other members of the research staff. A research associate, however, should be able to head up a research project or be able to execute all elements of the project individually.

Promotion to a research director position usually requires well-developed project management skills. This includes the ability to construct an entire research project, manage personnel well, and lead them in the project. A research director should be knowledgeable in a variety of research designs and analytical techniques.

Depending on the firm, a research director may interact with clients or the managers of the various marketing divisions to suggest and assist in formulating research that will be useful in making marketing decisions. The directors' duties usually include:

- Developing junior staff members.
- Overseeing all major research projects.

- Analyzing research designs.
- Writing and editing reports.
- Ensuring that projects are completed on time and within budget.
- Making certain that research projects satsify the needs of the requesting division or client.

Opportunities for employment in market research can be found in a variety of different firms: advertising agencies, manufacturers, data supply firms, and consulting organizations. Depending on the particular firm, movement from a position in market research to one in marketing management can be readily accomplished.

Information Sources for Marketing Research Career

Publications of interest in this career area are the *Journal of Marketing Research* and *Research Management.* Relevant associations are

Marketing Research Association
111 E. Wacker Drive, Suite 600
Chicago, IL 60601
(312) 644-6610

Marketing Science Institute
1000 Massachusetts Ave.
Cambridge, MA 02138
(617) 491-2060

OVERVIEW OF COMPENSATION

Compensation for the various marketing positions varies geographically and by industry. Below are salary data that are typical of what you will find in the library.

MARKETING, ADVERTISING, AND PUBLIC RELATIONS MANAGERS

Median	$41,400 (1990)
Lowest 10%	20,300 or less
Top 10%	78,500 or more

MANUFACTURER'S SALES REPRESENTATIVES

Median	$31,000 (1990)
Middle 50%	21,600—44,100
Bottom 10%	15,500 or less
Top 10%	59,000 or more

WHOLESALE & RETAIL BUYERS

Median	$25,100 (1990)
Lowest 10%	13,500 or less
Top 10%	46,700 or more

PRODUCT/BRAND MANAGER

Median salary	$53,400 (1990)

Note: The median salaries are the closest estimate of starting salaries.
Source: *Occupational Outlook Handbook,* 1992–1993, U.S. Department of Labor, pp. 48, 223.

WHAT YOU CAN DO WHILE STILL IN SCHOOL

Once you have selected your marketing career, you can tailor your studies and extracurricular activities to position yourself for an entry-level position.

Curriculum

Two skills necessary in all career tracks are oral and written communications. Take elective courses in communications and writing to hone those skills as finely as possible. Also important is the ability to use computers and work with spreadsheets and databases. In addition, those heading toward the quantitative areas such as marketing research should take as many math, computer science, and statistics courses as they can squeeze into their programs.

Employment

Many students work part-time during the school year and summer. Some of the entry-level positions do not require a degree, so they afford a good opportunity for work experience. Marketing research companies often hire students as interviewers, and working with the public is a good background for any marketing career.

Working as a temporary may also be beneficial, as it offers flexible hours plus the chance to observe an organization from the inside.

Organizations

Become part of and active in any student organization that is career-related. The American Marketing Association has student chapters on many campuses. Professional chapters located in every major market welcome students to their meetings. Not only will you benefit from networking with professionals, but you will have a chance to exhibit your leadership abilities, which many employers look for in those they hire for management career tracks.

Campus organizations need help in fund-raising, recruiting new members, and publicity. Campus newspapers and radio stations need help in selling advertising. These all offer opportunities for marketing experience.

Internships and Cooperative Field Experiences

Some schools have cooperative field experience programs where you actually work for a firm in your career field for one or more terms. Others have internship programs that permit you to work for a company part-time. You will have a chance to apply what you've learned in the classroom. In both cases you will be supervised by the faculty and receive academic credit plus job experience. Interns are frequently hired after graduation by the firms that they worked for.

Placement Service

Become acquainted with the people in your placement service as early as possible. Find out what services they offer. For example, they can help you with your resume writing and your interviewing skills, and they have access to a wide range of career-related materials, including brochures and videotapes supplied by organizations who are interested in recruiting at your school. They can also tell you what employers will be conducting campus interviews and when. Some have computer programs to help you in developing career goals.

Testing Services

If you're still at sea as to your career choice, avail yourself of the testing services that many schools provide to reveal your vocational interests, aptitudes, and personality strengths.

Class Projects

Many of your marketing classes will include experiential projects or simulations. Do these as professionally as you can. Make sure that they are typed or reproduced on a word processor or computer. Keep a copy for yourself. These can become an important part of your portfolio to show to prospective employers.

Company Information

It is a good idea to research companies you are interested in. Good sources of information on specific companies are their annual reports and 10K reports required by the Securities and Exchange Commission. Both are probably available in your library. You might also consider doing a computer search on specific companies using your library's on-line search programs.

Outside Reading

Read business publications regularly to be informed about what is happening to companies and industries. *The Wall Street Journal*, *Business Week*, *Advertising Age*, *Fortune*, *Forbes*, and *Marketing News* are recommended.

THE RESUME AND COVER LETTER

Resumes serve two purposes: to get an interview, and to remind the employer of you after the interview. A good resume will not get you the job but a poor resume can eliminate you from consideration. The very best resumes are those that are targeted toward a specific employer and reflect that organization's needs.

Prior to writing the resume, therefore, you should do two things. One is to develop a database of your traits, abilities, and accomplishments. They do not necessarily have to be business related. For example, holding an office in a student organization can show leadership, the ability to set and achieve goals, and the ability to motivate others. The other is to find out as much about the employer as possible. Library research can reveal a lot of information about publicly-held companies. An informational interview with someone who works for the employer can be invaluable.

The two basic types of resumes are the chronological resume and the functional resume. The chronological resume is more traditional and is often preferred by personnel professionals. The functional resume may be a better one, however, for recent graduates who do not have work experience, or whose experience may not be related to the career field they are pursuing.

The chronological resume lists employers and positions held starting with the most recent job. The functional resume shows experience under general headings such as "Leadership," "Sales Experience," "Communication Skills," and so forth.

In either case, recent graduates would do well to show their educational achievements first. Both resumes can be fleshed out by adding subheadings such as "Honors and Awards," "Other Interests and Activities," and so forth. Do not include personal data such as age, sex, or marital status unless you believe including this information will be to your advantage.

Resumes should be kept to one page. Writing a good resume requires thought, so schedule plenty of time and don't get frustrated. Also, remember to use **action** verbs. Describe your activities with proactive words—avoid using passive expressions such as "sales were my responsibility"—instead say "Responsible for sales . . ." Use a terse writing style and avoid personal pronouns. Don't just create "laundry lists"; try to describe as briefly as possible what you've done and what the results were.

Unless you are applying for a creative position (such as an artist), it is best to have your resume look as conservative and professional as possible. Use headings, subheadings, and indentations so that it does not look crowded. Use a good quality white paper.

Every resume that is sent by mail should include a cover letter. You should introduce yourself and explain why you are writing in the first paragraph. The second and third paragraphs should address your qualifications and how they match what the employer is looking for. You should ask for an interview in the final paragraph.

Even if you use a stock resume, you should customize the cover letter for every job you are applying for.

CHRONOLOGICAL RESUME

WHO U. ARE
1234 Anyplace Drive
Anywhere, ST 10160
(817) 123-4567

OBJECTIVE

This is optional. It should relate specifically to the position you are seeking. State the entry level and where you want the job to lead.

EDUCATION

YOUR SCHOOL, DIVISION IF NECESSARY

Degree earned, date you graduated.
Major area of concentration, additional coursework, GPA.
Any prizes, awards or distinctions. Student government, club or athletic activities, professional associations etc. . . .

EMPLOYMENT

FIRST COMPANY/ORGANIZATION, Address

Exact Title, Dates employed.

- what you did that prepares you for your next position
- responsibilities, goals met, etc.
- more detail about what you did

SECOND COMPANY/ORGANIZATION, Address

Exact Title, Dates employed.

- what you did that prepared you position above
- responsibilities, unique achievements
- more detail about what you did

THIRD COMPANY/ORGANIZATION, Address

Exact Title, Dates employed.

- what you did, how you did it
- more responsibilities and unique achievements
- more detail about what you did

ADDITIONAL INFORMATION

Language skills, computer skills, volunteer activities, interests, hobbies, travel—be real!

REFERENCES

Available upon request. (They will be positively glowing!)

Final Note

It is important that you answer the question, "What do I do with a degree in marketing?" While still in school, research the occupations and the industries of interest to you. With good preparation your question at graduation will not be, "Where can I find a job?" but rather, "Which offer should I accept?"

GLOSSARY

Acceptable price range – A price range the customer views as realistic. If the product is priced below this range, quality is suspect. If the product is priced above, the consumer refuses to buy.

Accessories – *See* Installations and accessories.

Adaptation in key markets – A growth strategy where a firm channels resources to a select group of countries.

Adaptive control system – Control that allows for changes in objectives as well as in performance to meet those objectives; requires tracking environmental factors such as competitive intensity, level of customer demand, and technology to determine if objectives are still relevant or need to be changed.

Adaptive strategies – Strategies geared to differing customer needs, cultural norms, trade regulations, economic and political conditions, and competitors on a country-by-country basis.

Administered channel systems – Integration of distributive activities is accomplished through the power of a channel leader rather than through ownership or contractual arrangements.

Advertising – Paid, ongoing, nonpersonal communication from a commercial source such as a manufacturer or retailer. It communicates messages about a product, service, or company that appears in mass media such as television, radio, and magazines.

Advertising exposure – The extent to which a particular ad is seen, read, or heard by a target group.

After-the-fact control – Compares actual product performance at the end of a planning period with expected performance and determines the causes for any deviations in sales results. On this basis, management can institute changes in both marketing objectives and strategies to increase profitability in the next planning period. One shortcoming of this approach is that it corrects for deviations after they occur rather than before.

Approved vendor list – A list of sellers that have been approved by the company.

Assignable fixed costs – Fixed costs that can be associated with the production or distribution of a product and can therefore be assigned to the product.

Atmospherics – In-store decor.

Attitudes – The consumer's tendency to evaluate an object in a favorable or unfavorable way. Attitudes are determined by our needs and perceptions.

Audimeter – Machine attached to a TV set to record the station it is tuned to; used to calculate TV ratings.

Augmented product – Product that includes elements other than the *tangible product*, including delivery, installation, warranties, and service.

Average revenue – Average amount of money received from selling one unit of a product; computed as total revenue divided by quantity. Also equals price.

Backward integration – A type of vertical integration in which the company acquires facilities earlier in the distribution and manufacturing process.

Bait-and-switch pricing – Offering one product at a low price in order to lure customers into the store, where a salesperson tries to influence them to buy a higher-priced item instead.

Barriers to entry – Factors that restrict a company's entry into a market.

Basing-point pricing – The company establishes a location, called a *basing point*, from which transportation charges are added to the list price.

Battle of the brands – The fight for retail shelf space and consumer dollars between controlled and national brands. Controlled brands have a price advantage and national brands have an advertising advantage.

Behavioral segmentation – Identification of consumer groups by differences in behavior (e.g., users versus nonusers or heavy versus light users). Market segments are identified by what consumers do.

Benefit segmentation – Identification of a group of consumers based on similarity in needs. Often marketing opportunities are discovered by analysis of consumers' benefit preferences. Frequently, one or more segments are identified that are not being adequately served by existing brand alternatives.

Bid pricing – Pricing in which organizational buyers send out requests for proposals that invite prospective sellers to bid on a set of specifications developed by the buyer.

Brand – A name or symbol that represents a product.

Brand advertising – Type of advertising which is designed to increase market share of a brand by attracting customers who currently use a competitor's brand, and by maintaining awareness among existing customers.

Brand beliefs – The characteristics we ascribe to a brand.

Brand equity – Refers to the value of a brand name.

Brand evaluations – Our positive or negative evaluations of a brand.

Brand establishment strategy – Creating market position of a new brand by building a distribution network and by establishing awareness and initiating trial among consumers.

Brand image – Represents overall perception of the brand, formed from information about the brand and past experience. The set of beliefs that forms a complete picture of the brand.

Brand leverage – Taking advantage of a strong brand image by introducing related items under the well-known brand name.

Brand loyalty – Commitment to a brand because of past satisfaction as a result of continued usage.

Brand manager – *See* product manager.

Brand reinforcement strategy – To reinforce the brand's position by getting consumers who have tried the brand to repurchase it and by continuing to attract new users.

Brand revival strategy – Requires bringing brands that are being harvested or have been eliminated back to life on the strength of their names.

Branded – The existence of a name or symbol to identify a product, as opposed to no defined name or symbol. Generics, private labels, and commodity products are generally considered to be unbranded.

Break-even analysis – Identifies the point where total revenue equals total cost and profits are zero.

Brokers – People who bring buyers and sellers together. Brokers do not have a formal relationship with either party; they simply serve as an intermediary between the two. Brokers are used primarily by firms which do not need to maintain a permanent sales force.

Bundling pricing – Offering two or more products or services as a single package for a special price.

Business-to-business marketing – The sale of products to firms for use in manufacturing and processing other products or supporting such activities.

Business development – Growth strategy of marketing new products to totally new markets.

Business manager – Manager of a business unit usually responsible for formulating the marketing strategy for that unit.

Business mix – Combination of businesses the firm is in.

Business portfolio analysis – Systematic approach to evaluate the corporation as a mix, or portfolio of businesses, each with a different mission, market, and resources.

Business portfolio strategy – Estimates the revenue potential of each business and allows management to allocate resources to these businesses accordingly.

Buying center – A group of executives providing the different skills necessary to make important decisions in organizational buying. The decision-making unit to select products and vendors in an organization.

Bypass-the-competition strategy – When a company introduces unrelated product lines or enters noncompetitive geographic areas.

Canned sales approach – The salesperson follows a predefined script without regard to the customer's response.

Cannibalization – A switch by a consumer from one of a company's products to another with no net gain in sales. **Unplanned cannibalization** is unexpected and reduces the company's profits. This is most likely to happen if the products are not sufficiently different from one another in the consumer's mind. **Planned cannibalization** occurs when new technologies create new products that might compete with other products in the company's line, so the company prefers to have its customers switch to another of the company's brands rather than to a competitor's brand.

Carrying costs – Costs of tying up capital in inventory, plus some additional costs such as taxes and insurance on inventory.

Case allowance – Type of trade promotion where discounts are given to products sold to retailers depending on how much they buy.

Cash-and-carry wholesalers – Wholesalers that sell from warehouse facilities. Buyers must pay cash and transport their merchandise.

Cash discount – Discount to buyers who pay bills within a specified time.

Casual research objections – Trying to determine cause and effect relationships.

Category manager – *See* Product-line manager.

Cause-related marketing – Involves the firm agreeing to give a fixed amount of money to a chosen charity in return for being able to use the charity's name in promotional ads and events.

Chain stores – Retailers with more than four outlets.

Channel (distribution) system – A group of independent businesses composed of manufacturers, wholesalers, and retailers designed to deliver the right set of products to consumers at the right place and time.

Channel leader – Coordinates the flow of information, product shipments, and payment in a distribution system. Generally, the most powerful member of the system.

Channels of distribution – The networks through which marketing organizations move their products to their customers.

Communications system – System that informs customers of products available and influences them to buy.

Comparative advertising – The naming of a competitive product in the marketer's advertisement. Advertisers use comparative advertising to point out weaknesses in and to create a less favorable attitude toward the competitive brand, thus increasing the likelihood of buying the marketer's brand.

Comparative influence – Influence a membership group exerts in the process of comparing oneself to other members of the group. Provides a basis for comparing one's attitudes and behavior to those of the group.

Competitive advantage – Gained when a company capitalizes on a marketing opportunity by producing a better product, selling it at a lower price, distributing it more widely, providing better services, or offering a wider variety of product options than competing companies.

Competitive analysis – Assessing a competitors' strengths and weaknesses.

Competitive-parity budgeting – Requires setting the promotional budget according to what the competition is doing. One example would be to determine advertising expenditures as a percent of sales for a few key competitors and then use the same percentage to set the budget.

Complex decision making – Associated with a high-involvement purchase that is important to the consumer and entails a significant financial outlay. The buyer is motivated to undertake a process of active search for information and based on this information, alternative brands are evaluated on specific criteria. The cognitive process of evaluation involves consumer perceptions of brand characteristics and development of favorable or unfavorable attitudes toward a brand. The assumption is that consumer perceptions and attitudes will precede and influence behavior.

Concentrated segmentation – Also referred to as a *market niche strategy*, this approach targets a single product to a single market segment. Best suited to a firm with limited resources because it avoids conflicts with major competitors in larger market segments.

Conditioning – The linkage between the brand and a stimulus in the consumer's mind so that just seeing the stimulus will evoke an awareness of the brand.

Consolidated retailing – A strategy of growth through the acquisition of retailers, rather than through store expansion. Many retailers began using this approach as a way of combating "overstoring."

Consolidation centers – A part of the physical distribution system used in the implementation of a just-in-time distribution system. These centers resemble distribution centers, and serve as assembly facilities for different items which are to be delivered to each customer.

Consultative salespeople – Those who take the initiative in defining customer needs and recommending a set of solutions to meet these needs.

Consumer – The final user of a product or service.

Consumer data bases – Demographic and financial information on individual consumers derived from applications for credit, drivers' licenses, or telephone service.

Consumer promotions – Short-term inducements of value to consumers to encourage them to buy a product or service.

Consumer socialization – Process by which people learn to be consumers as they are taught from childhood by their families.

Containerization – A form of intermodal transportation used by shippers in the physical distribution system. Containerization involves putting the product into a container which is in turn loaded onto another form of transport, such as rail.

Continuity – A means of advertising, where the message is dispersed steadily over time.

Contractual systems – Systems where independent manufacturers and intermediaries enter into a contract to coordinate distributive functions that can be performed more efficiently in tandem than separately.

Contribution to margin – Product revenues less costs directly assigned to the product. A measure of product profitability.

Control – Directing or redirecting a company's actions to ensure that they meet objectives.

Convenience goods – Products that consumers purchase frequently with little deliberation or effort.

Convenience stores – Neighborhood food outlets that stay open longer than supermarkets, carry a limited number of high-turnover convenience items, and charge higher prices because of their higher costs of operation.

Convergent acquisition – Strategy of acquiring related businesses.

Cooperative advertising – A type of product-related advertising in which manufacturers and retailers pool resources to promote both the product and the store. Manufacturers offer retailers allowances to advertise the manufacturer's products, permitting retailers to insert the name of the store and, in some cases, details about the retail establishment.

Core product – Characteristics of the product seen as meeting customer needs.

Corporate-brand-names strategy – *See* corporate brand name.

Corporate-image advertising – Advertising which is designed to create and promote a corporate identity. In this way, consumers will know more about the company and its products.

Corporate-issue advertising – Advertising which relays a company's position on a particular issue that is important to consumers.

Corporate brand name – Using the company name as part of the brand, thereby linking the brand name to the company name. An advantage of this strategy is that consumer loyalty can be better cultivated if the consumer can identify which brands belong to the company.

Corporate family name – A brand identification strategy where all of the company's products are included under a corporate umbrella as a family of brands. This strategy works well when the company's product mix is not too diverse, the company has a strong corporate identity, and individual brand identification is difficult.

Corporate growth strategy – Decisions regarding the future of the businesses in which a company currently competes. This is the game plan it will use to exploit marketing opportunities. Corporate strategies usually cover a five-year time span.

Corporate marketing manager – Manager at the headquarters level.

Corporate mission – Statement of what business or businesses the firm should be in.

Corporate-patronage advertising – Type of advertising used to promote the company's offerings. The purpose is to influence consumers, so that they purchase the company's line of products.

Corrective advertising – Advertising in which a company corrects false claims it has made in the past.

Cost advantage – A type of competitive advantage a firm may have which is gained by reducing production or marketing costs below those of competitors and thereby being able to reduce prices or channel the savings into other areas.

Cost-plus pricing – A simple pricing method whereby the firm determines its costs and then adds the desired profit margin. This approach tends to encourage price stability since most competitors will arrive at similar acceptable margins.

Countersegmentation – The grouping together of several segments, and directing a single marketing effort to these segments to reduce costs.

Countertrade – The acceptance, in lieu of currency, of local products that can be resold in the West.

Country-product mix – The decision made by international marketers as to what products will be sold in each country. The ultimate mix is dependent on the overall international strategy chosen by the company.

Coupons – Printed material that offers a discount off the regular price of a brand if presented at the time of purchase.

Cross-cultural influences – Represent the differences in cultural values across countries.

Cross-tabulations – Categorize one variable by another.

Cultural values – An especially important class of beliefs shared by the members of a society about what is desirable or undesirable. Beliefs that some general state of existence is personally and socially worth striving for. Cultural values in the United States include achievement, independence, and youthfulness.

Culture – The implicit beliefs, norms, values, and customs that underlie and govern conduct in a society. The norms, beliefs, and customs learned from society. Culture leads to common patterns of behavior.

Customer orientation – When a firm develops products and strategies directed to meeting customer needs.

Customized marketing – Strategy of offering tailor-made products to meet the needs of individual buyers.

Dealers – Channel members who are granted the right to exclusively sell a company's products in a franchise contract.

Deceptive advertising – Advertising which makes false claims, or is misleading to consumers. The Federal Trade Commission monitors advertising, to ensure that manufacturers and retailers do not indulge in this practice.

Deceptive pricing – Any type of pricing used to deceive customers and take unfair advantage of them. Examples are bait-and-switch pricing, unfair pricing, predatory pricing, price discrimination, and price fixing.

Decision maker – Family member who is responsible for the final selection of a product or service.

Decision support system (DSS) – A computerized facility designed to store and analyze data from diverse sources.

Decoding – Process in which the target audience (1) notices the message (awareness), (2) interprets and evaluates it (comprehension), and (3) retains it in memory (recall).

Delayed-quotation pricing – Industrial pricing method where the risk of cost overruns and imprecise production schedules is passed on to the buyer, because the seller delays quoting a price until delivery.

Delivered pricing – Pricing method where the final price is adjusted to include transportation costs. The seller includes delivery costs in the quoted price, and is responsible for getting the product to the buyer.

Delphi method – Requires experts to make individual forecasts without meeting and to state their reasoning in writing. Forecasts are pooled and sent to participants who are then asked to make a second forecast. A consensus is usually achieved after three or four rounds.

Demand-backward pricing – Pricing set by determining what consumers are willing to pay for an item, then deducting costs to see if the profit margin is adequate.

Demand curve – Curve showing the quantity of a product that customers buy at various price levels.

Demographics – Objective characteristics of consumers, such as age, income, occupation, marital status, location, or education. This information is characteristically used for media planning.

Department stores – Full service stores that offer a broad choice of merchandise.

Depth interviews – Unstructured, personal interviews in which the interviewer attempts to get subjects to talk freely and to express their true feelings. Can be conducted individually or in groups (focus group interviews).

Derived demand – Demand for one product may be determined by the demand for the good the product is used to manufacture, i.e., the demand for industrial goods is derived from the demand for consumer goods.

Descriptive research objectives – Describing and explaining events in the marketplace.

Desk jobber – *See* Drop shipper.

Deterministic models – Predict a particular course of action based on such input variables as consumer characteristics, brand attitudes, consumer needs, etc. Deterministic models attempt to predict behavior in exact or nonprobabilistic terms.

Differentiated segmentation – Strategy in which product offerings are differentiated to meet the needs of particular market segments. A firm using this approach introduces many products within a product category to appeal to a variety of market segments. Separate marketing strategies are needed for each segment. By offering a full line of products, the firm establishes a strong identification with that product category.

Direct derivation method – Requires deriving estimates of primary demand from factors in the marketplace that are directly related to consumer purchases.

Direct marketing channel system – The sale of products directly to consumers, thereby avoiding the use of intermediaries.

Discount – Type of price adjustment, where the seller makes a reduction off of the list price. Discounts serve as an incentive to buy in quantity or during a particular time of the year, to pay in cash, or to handle certain marketing functions.

Discount stores – Stores that offer goods at low prices on a self-service basis. These stores offer a wide variety of product lines but very limited selections within each line.

Discretionary income – Amount of income left after paying for necessities and taxes.

Distribution centers – Centralized distribution facilities that serve broader markets than warehouses. They maintain full product lines, consolidate large shipments from different production points, and usually have computerized order-handling systems.

Distribution system (Channel system) – A group of independent businesses composed of manufacturers, wholesalers, and retailers designed to deliver what the customer wants, when and where the customer wants it. *See also* Channel system.

Distributors – Generally, wholesalers of industrial products. *See also* Wholesalers.

District sales manager – Manager responsible for a particular geographic territory; reports to the divisional sales manager.

Divergent acquisitions – Retail strategy in which the company seeks growth by moving into areas outside of retailing. In this way, retailers can continue to grow even when the retail industry is experiencing a slowdown.

Divisional sales manager – Manager responsible for sales of a total division; often given the title of vice-president of sales.

Downside price elasticity – Price-elasticity changes in response to decreased prices.

Drop shippers – Limited-service wholesalers, also called *desk jobbers,* who take title to the merchandise they sell but do not take physical possession. They obtain orders from wholesalers and retailers and forward these orders to the manufacturer, who then sends the goods directly to the wholesaler or retailer. Used mostly in the distribution of bulky goods that have high transportation costs (e.g., lumber).

Durable goods – Products that are used over time (the most tangible type of product).

Economic infrastructure – A country's transportation, communication, power, distribution and other facilities necessary to sustain economic activity.

Electronic coupons – Coupons delivered from dispensers at the time the customer receives his or her receipt.

Electronic retailing – Process by which customers call up product information through computer terminals in shopping kiosks in various locations and place orders by credit card.

Encirclement strategies – Strategy in which the market leader is challenged on several fronts at the same time or in quick succession.

Encoding – Translating the company's objectives into an advertising or sales promotional strategy that will communicate the appropriate message. The good advertising campaign is one in which the encoding process uses information, symbols, or imagery that successfully communicate the product benefits to the consumer.

Environmental scanning – Collecting and assessing environmental information from diverse sources to judge where future opportunities and threats might lie. Changes that may affect the scope of opportunity include competitive activity, technology, the economy, and social and cultural trends.

Equipment based services – When products play a supportive role in delivering a service, such as ATMs providing banking services.

Eurobranding – The incorporation of several languages on a single package with the same brand name so that it can be introduced to all EC countries.

Evaluation – Refers to determining whether results are on target.

Exchange process – A dynamic process in which a seller requires payment to satisfy a buyer's need for a valued object or service.

Exclusive dealing contract – Formal arrangement in which the seller requires that its buyers carry the company's line of products on an exclusive basis. Such an agreement is illegal if it restrains trade or if smaller buyers are coerced into making the arrangement.

Exclusive distribution – Distribution strategy where manufacturers give intermediaries exclusive territorial rights to sell the product in a specified area. This is most often used when the product requires service, or projects a quality image that could be diluted by a wide distribution channel.

Exclusive sales territories – Exclusive rights to a geographic area offered by manufacturers to wholesalers and retailers to prevent intermediaries from competing with one another. (Franchises are an example.) These contracts are judged on a case-by-case basis to determine whether they restrict competition and violate antitrust rulings.

Expected value method – Tool for determining the best strategy given certain expected trends. Managers are asked to estimate the probability of various scenarios occurring and to predict the sales results as a consequence.

Experimentation – Attempting to control extraneous factors to establish a cause and effect relationship between a marketing stimulus (e.g., advertising) and consumer responses (e.g., intention to buy or sales).

Exploratory research objectives – An objective designed to define a problem so as to guide future research.

Export management companies (EMCs) – Organizations that are similar to export trading companies except that they do not take title to goods and are paid on a commission basis. They serve as the export department for many domestic manufacturers by marketing and distributing their products overseas.

Export trading companies (ETCs) – A domestic merchant, the export trading company buys the firm's merchandise and assumes all responsibility for distribution and marketing abroad. Smaller companies are likely to use ETCs because they reduce their costs and avoid the risk of marketing abroad.

Extinction – The elimination of expected satisfaction with a brand.

Facilitating functions – Activities performed by intermediaries in the distribution channel which help manufacturers obtain information about market conditions, and the effect of marketing mix variables.

Facilitating marketing systems – Systems that provide the means for an exchange process in which there is a transfer of goods from manufacturers to customers, and a reverse transfer of payments from customers to manufacturers.

Factory-outlet stores – A company-owned store that sells excess inventory and defective merchandise at deep discounts.

Factory shipments – Goods a firm sells to retailers and wholesalers.

Failure fees – Charges assessed when products don't live up to sales projections.

Family life cycle – The progression of a family from formation, to child-rearing, to middle age, and finally to retirement.

Feedback – Information received by a company on the impact of its communications on sales; the final stage of the communication process.

Fighting brands – *See* Price brands.

Final consumer – Purchases and consumes the product or service.

Fixed costs – Costs that are constant regardless of the quantity produced.

Flanking strategies – Strategy of challenging the market leader in an area not currently contested; that is, offering customer benefits the leader has overlooked.

Flexible break-even pricing – An offshoot of break-even analysis; price is determined by maximizing the difference between total revenue and total cost across various levels of demand.

Focus-group interviews – Informal marketing research interviews with eight to twelve respondents who are asked to focus on a particular topic in an open-ended discussion guided by a trained moderator.

Follow-the-leader pricing – Pricing strategy whereby the leader in an industry sets prices, and the other competitors use basically the same price structure. This often occurs in industries which are standardized, or where one company is the undisputed leader. Also, this pricing method tends to create stability and deter price wars.

Follow-the-leader strategies – Strategy that copies the leader but also adds some sort of customer benefit. Minimizes the risks of retaliation due to a direct or indirect challenge to the market leader.

Forecasting variance – The difference between the original objective and the new objective that was set due to changes in environmental conditions.

Formula selling approach – Provides information to customers in a step-by-step manner to persuade the customer to buy.

Forward integration – A type of vertical integration in which the company acquires facilities closer to the consumer in the manufacturing and distribution chain.

Four Ps of marketing – Product, promotion, place, and pricing strategies.

Franchise systems – Distribution systems in which a parent company (usually the manufacturer) grants a wholesaler or retailer the right to sell the company's products exclusively in a certain area. One of the fastest-growing forms of distribution, franchised establishments account for about one-third of all retail sales.

Free-on-board (FOB) origin pricing – Geographic price adjustment based on having the buyer take ownership at the point of origin, and not delivery. The buyer is responsible for providing and paying for transportation. The quoted price is lower than it would otherwise be, because the seller does not incur delivery costs.

Free samples – New products offered free as a way to get consumers to try them.

Free-standing inserts – Coupons distributed as inserts in newspapers.

Freight-absorption pricing – Pricing method in which the seller absorbs the total cost of transportation. This type of pricing is used if the freight charges are small, or if they are large enough to provide the seller with a competitive advantage if this pricing method is employed.

Frequency – The average number of times, within a specified time period, that an individual is exposed to the message as a result of the media plan.

Gatekeeper – Person in the purchasing process who controls the flow of information to the buying center.

General-merchandise wholesalers – Full service wholesalers that carry a broad assortment of merchandise but in doing so, sacrifice depth in each product line. They also perform a number of services, like storing and controlling inventory, processing orders and transporting goods.

Generic products – Unbranded products identified by product category only.

Generics – Unbranded products sold with no promotional support.

Geo-demographic analysis – Identifies individual households as targets by analyzing data at the zip code level and linking zip codes to demographic characteristics.

Geographic price adjustments – Companies adjust their prices to reflect differences in transportation costs based on the seller's or buyer's location.

Government agencies – From the marketing perspective, buyers of products and services to implement government services.

Gross rating points (GRPs) – The *total number of exposures* produced by the media schedule, this measurement is determined by the reach times the frequency.

Habit – A connection between stimuli and/or responses that has become virtually automatic through experience, usually resulting in the purchase of the same brand.

Harvest strategy – Involves cutting off most or all promotional support for a brand and relying on sales from loyal buyers for continued profits.

Head-to-head competition – Strategy in which a competitor in the industry challenges the leader.

High-involvement purchases – Purchases that are more important to the consumer, are related to the consumer's self-identity, and involve some risk. It is worth the consumer's time and energies to consider product alternatives more carefully in the high-involvement case. Therefore, a process of complex decision making is more likely to occur when the consumer is involved in the purchase.

Historical analogy – Method used to forecast sales based on past sales results of a similar product.

Horizontal integration – Growth strategy in which a company acquires businesses in the industry within which it is currently operating.

Horizontal price fixing – Competitors within an industry agree to maintain a certain price, thus eliminating price competition and limiting consumer choice.

Hybrid distribution system – A company's use of more than one distribution system.

Hypermarkets – Outlets that are combined food stores and mass merchandisers. They offer all the products of a supermarket as well as a larger variety of nonfood items than superstores or warehouse stores.

Image – An overall perception of an object formed from information and from the consumer's past experiences.

Image oriented change strategy – Strategy to revitalize a brand by using image-oriented advertising.

Image oriented maintenance strategy – Strategy to use imagery to reinforce current advertising campaign.

Inbound telemarketing – Telemarketing facility that enables the company to receive product inquiries from customers. Toll free telephone lines are generally used to ask for further information.

Individual-brand-names strategy – Strategy in which new brands are identified with the company name.

Industrial buyers – Buyers of products and services to be used to further process other products, such as products used in manufacturing, mining, and construction.

Inertia – A passive process of information processing, brand evaluation, and brand choice. The same brand is frequently purchased by inertia to save time and energy.

Information processing – The process of noticing a marketing stimulus, understanding and interpreting it, and then retaining it in memory.

Informational influence – The influence of experts or experienced friends or relatives on consumer brands evaluations.

Information oriented change strategy – Strategy to change consumer perception of a product or service by advertising new features or by providing additional information.

Information oriented maintenance strategy – Strategy to maintain and reinforce existing perceptions of a product or service by using advertising that primarily provides information about a product.

Innovations – Products that are new to both consumers and to a company. Often results in a change in consumption patterns.

Installations and accessories – Industrial goods used in support of the manufacturing process.

Institutional buyers – Buyers of products to be used to provide services (rather than to process products).

Intensity of distribution – The degree of coverage provided by a distribution system.

Intensive distribution – Distributing a product through most retail outlets in an area. Most often used for inexpensive, frequently purchased items. These are low-involvement products. If a store does not have a particular brand, the consumer will buy an alternative.

Intermodal transportation – A means of moving physical goods from the manufacturer to the consumer by utilizing multiple delivery methods, such as air, truck, and rail, and thus allowing a single shipper to more efficiently move a customer's products door-to-door.

International growth strategy – An overall game plan for future growth in international markets based on the opportunities in each country and the company's ability to exploit them.

International marketing – The development of marketing strategies to sell goods abroad and to integrate these strategies across various countries.

Involvement – The importance of the product decision to the consumer.

Irresponsible advertising – Depicts or encourages irresponsible behavior or portrays groups in an irresponsible manner.

Kanban or Just-in-time (JIT) – A Japanese principle that says a company should provide and distribute only what consumers need when they need it.

Keiretsu – A network of Japanese companies that have partial ownership in each other, buy from and sell to each other, share technology, and cooperate to fend off foreign competition.

Learning – In marketing, refers to purchase behavior based on a consumer's past experiences. Purchases based on habit are usually the result of learning.

Length of distribution – The number of different intermediaries that will be used by a distribution system.

Licensing – An offshoot of leveraging where companies sell to other companies the right to use their brand name.

Lifestyles – An individual's mode of living as identified by his or her activities, interests, and opinions.

Limited decision making – Decision making that is not automatic but requires little information search.

Line extensions – Additions to a product line that serve to *deepen* the line.

Line pruning – Reducing the depth of a product line by cutting back on the number of offerings in a particular product category.

Line retrenchment – Reducing the breadth of a product line by cutting back on the diversity of items offered across product categories.

List price – The quoted price that might appear in a catalog or be quoted by a salesperson as the company's official price before discounts. Also referred to as the final selling price.

Logistical functions – Assembling a variety of products, storing them, and providing them in smaller units to customers by sorting them and putting them on the retail shelf.

Low-involvement purchases – Purchases that are less important to the consumer. Identity with the product is low. It may not be worth the consumer's time and effort to search for information about brands and to consider a wide range of alternatives.

Mail-order distributors – Distributors that are the same as mail-order wholesalers except that they sell to industrial buyers. They sell specialized items out of a catalog that can be easily shipped by mail or truck.

Mail-order wholesalers – Limited service wholesalers that sell out of a catalog to small retailers, usually in outlying areas that full-service wholesalers would find too costly to serve.

Manufacturers' agents – Agents that sell a company's product offering in a specific geographic area, often on an exclusive basis. They carry product lines of several noncompeting manufacturers and restrict their activities to selling to wholesalers, retailers, and industrial buyers. They do not take title to the goods they sell and are paid on a commission basis.

Manufacturer's brand – A brand that is both produced and marketed by the manufacturer; also known as *national* or *regional brand.*

Marginal analysis – Principle that as long as the additional revenue gained from the last unit produced (the marginal revenue) is greater than the cost of producing that last unit (the marginal cost), the company should produce it.

Marginal contribution to profit – The contribution made by the last unit produced.

Marginal costs – The changes in total costs that result from producing and marketing additional quantities of a product.

Marginal pricing – Demand oriented pricing method which is based on pricing at the point where marginal revenue equals marginal cost.

Marginal revenue – The change in total revenue obtained by selling additional quantities of a product.

Market – A group of customers who seek similar product benefits.

Market estimation method – Requires estimating the number of buyers in the marketplace and the quantity purchased from past sales data or from surveys.

Market expansion strategy – A marketing strategy which targets existing products to new markets in order to expand the entire product category.

Marketing – All individual and organizational activities directed to identifying and satisfying customer needs and wants.

Marketing advantage – A type of competitive advantage in which a superior marketing strategy is developed that outperforms competing strategies in meeting consumers' needs.

Marketing audit – A periodic and comprehensive review of marketing operations. The marketing audit is designed to (1) identify changes in the environment requiring reassessment of marketing opportunities, (2) evaluate marketing planning and control procedures, and (3) appraise marketing strategy to determine if any changes would increase profitability.

Marketing concept – The philosophy that all marketing strategies must be based on known consumer needs. Marketers must first define the benefits consumers seek from particular products and gear marketing strategies accordingly. Based on a *customer orientation.*

Marketing Information System (MIS) – The system of people, technology, and procedures designed to acquire and generate information from both the marketing environment and the firm. Such information is integrated, analyzed, and communicated to improve marketing planning, execution, and control.

Marketing management process – The mechanism by which the marketing organization interacts with its customers.

Marketing mix – The marketing variables within the control of the marketing manager that are selected to elicit the desired response from the target market. Combination of strategies involving "the four Ps": product, promotion, place, and price.

Marketing plan – The vehicle for developing marketing strategies.

Marketing planning – A function of the product or brand manager that involves developing the product, defining its target market, and formulating marketing strategies.

Marketing productivity – The ratio of marketing performance to the costs involved.

Marketing stimuli – Purchase-related communications designed to influence consumers.

Market niche – Segments of a market that appear to be targets of opportunity.

Market penetration strategy – *See* Penetration pricing strategy.

Market potential – The total demand for a product category in the market.

Market segment – Groups of customers with similar needs and characteristics.

Market segmentation – The process of subdividing a large undefined market into smaller groups of consumers with similar needs, characteristics, or behavior. This enables the marketer to effectively allocate marketing resources to satisfy the needs of a well-defined group of consumers.

Market-segment expansion – Strategy that involves targeting one product to several market segments.

Market share – The amount of sales a brand receives expressed as a percent of total sales generated in the brand's product category.

Market share protection strategy – Competitive strategy used by a market leader wherein the goal is to protect its current share. While the market leader has more to protect, it should find this task easier because it usually has higher margins and, therefore, more resources at its disposal.

Market strategy – The basic approach a company will take in trying to influence customers to buy a product.

Markup – The profit margin realized when a cost plus pricing method is used; it is the percent added to the price after taking into consideration the seller's costs.

Mass marketing – Strategy of offering one basic product without distinguishing among different customer needs and characteristics.

Mass merchandisers – Stores that sell at lower prices than department stores or specialty stores but do not offer the same depth of assortment or service. Their merchandise is often of lower quality also.

Merchandise allowances – Payments by manufacturers to reimburse retailers for in-store support of the product, such as window displays or in-store shelf displays.

Merchandise handling – The component of the physical distribution system which links order processing and shipment. Merchandise handling activities include locating an item in inventory, moving it through the warehouse, and readying it for shipment.

Merchant wholesalers – Independent wholesalers that purchase and take ownership of goods.

Micromarketing – Involves directing marketing strategies toward individual consumers.

Mill supply house – Full-service distributor that sells a wide variety of lines to industrial buyers.

Modified rebuy – Recurring purchase of an industrial product that is less routine than a straight rebuy, requiring some information search and perhaps reevaluation of a straight rebuy because of a new product introduction or a change in technology.

Motivational research – Applications of psychoanalytic theory to marketing.

Motives – The underlying drives that channel and direct behavior toward attaining needs.

Multiple exchanges – The different types of exchanges of resources that nonprofit services must deal with.

Multiple publics – The different groups that nonprofit services market to, including donors as well as clients.

Multiple sourcing – Buying from several vendors so that the risk is spread among them.

Multiple zone pricing – Type of delivered pricing method in which the price within a geographic zone is the same for all buyers, but the price between zones differs.

Multivariate statistical techniques – Techniques designed to examine more than two variables simultaneously.

National account manager – The leader of a national account marketing team, who is responsible for creating a working relationship with the customer, coordinating the activities of other members of a NAM team, and maintaining the relationship.

National account marketing (NAM) team – Selling team composed of a national account manager and other salespeople, who work together to service large clients. NAM teams are usually used in complex industries, when customers need more than just facts about the product.

National/regional brands – Brands that are marketed nationally by the manufacturer. Regional and local brands are sometimes lumped together with national brands to distinguish them from private brands and generics. *See also* Manufacturer's brands.

Needs – Forces directed towards achieving a particular goal. The motive behind purchasing behavior.

Net profit – Sales less variable costs, assignable fixed costs, and nonassignable fixed costs. Net profit is used to determine the return on investment for a particular product or business.

New buy – Purchase of an industrial product (or service) that has not been made before; usually involves extensive information search.

New-product development strategy – A strategy for new products where the new item is targeted to new or existing customers. These strategies apply to completely new-product offerings for the company.

New-product duplications – Products that are known to the market but are new to the company.

Noise in communications – Interference that occurs during the transmission of a message to the consumer. Noise can be competitive communications or misperception of the company's communication.

Nonassignable fixed costs – Fixed costs that cannot be directly linked to the manufacturing of distribution of a product, and are therefore allocated across all products.

Nondurable goods – Products that are consumed in one or a few uses.

Nonprobability sampling – A sample selected primarily according to the researcher's judgment rather than according to the scientific rules of probability sampling; used when representativeness is less important.

Nonstore retailing – Any method of selling to the final customer, which does not involve a store. Examples include catalogs, door-to-door sales, and the home shopping networks on television.

Normative influence – Exerted by a reference group by persuading consumers to conform to its norms.

Objective-task budgeting – This approach develops a promotional budget by specifically defining promotional objectives, determining the tasks required to meet those objectives, and estimating the costs associated with the performance of these tasks.

Odd-even pricing – Sometimes referred to as psychological pricing, odd even pricing is used by manufacturers and retailers in the belief that consumers are more likely to purchase a product if its price ends with an odd number just under a round number (e.g., a price of $2.99 instead of $3.00).

Off-price retailing – Offering brand-name merchandise at deep discounts.

Oligopoly – An industry in which two or three firms dominate and the actions of one firm directly affect those of another.

Opinion leaders – Individuals regarded by a reference group as having expertise and knowledge on a particular subject.

Order getters – Salespeople who search out customers and persuade them to buy the company's products. The focus is on closing the sale, rather than taking an order.

Order processing – Refers to the paperwork required to receive and process customer orders, transmit them to warehouses, fill the order from inventory, prepare a bill, and issue shipping instructions.

Order takers – Salespeople who make an inquiry as to stock levels and product needs, and then take the order. Order takers are product oriented, and have a minimal amount of customer contact.

Organizational buyers – Are those individuals who are responsible for purchasing goods for companies that either use those goods in the products of production and distribution or that resell them.

Outbound telemarketing – Involves trained sales representatives making calls and trying to sell the customer by phone or providing prospective customers with information.

Out-of-stock costs – One type of physical inventory costs, out-of-stock costs indicate the amount of sales lost due to the unavailability of an item at the retail or wholesale level.

Patterned standardization – A compromise between standardized and localized international marketing strategies. This approach requires that the company establish global marketing strategies but leave the implementation of marketing plans to executives in local markets who are aware of national traits and customs.

Payback period – The number of years it takes to recoup investment.

Pegged pricing – Pricing strategy used by companies in an industry without a price leader, to establish price stability by setting prices at, above, or below the industry norm.

Penetration pricing strategy – Pricing strategy of introducing a brand at a low price to induce as many consumers as possible to try it; usually coupled with price deals and coupons. This strategy works best when consumer demand for the product is price elastic.

People-based services – Services which rely only on people in order to be delivered, as distinct from equipment-based services.

People meters – Hand-held devices used to measure which TV shows are being watched by viewers in a household. People meters replaced diaries as the way households recorded when they started and stopped watching TV.

Percent-of-sales budgeting – Technique of setting the promotional budget, which involves determining how much to spend based on a percentage of sales.

Perceptions – The way consumers organize and interpret information about objects like brands and companies.

Perceptual map – A method that seeks to position various brands on a "map" based on the way they are perceived by the consumer. The closer one brand is to another on the map, the more similar it is to the other brand. The basic assumption is that if consumers see two brands as being similar, they behave similarly toward the two brands.

Performance variance – The difference between objectives and performance.

Personality – Consistent and enduring patterns of behavior. Represents a set of consumer characteristics that have been used to describe target segments.

Personal selling – Aspect of the promotional mix which involves face-to-face communication between a sales rep of the company and the consumer. The goal is to sell the product or service to the consumer.

Phantom freight – Type of charge which results from the use of basing point pricing. It is the freight fees charged from the basing point to the delivery city, even if the goods are not actually moved.

Physical distribution – Part of the distribution channel system involving the movement of goods from where they are produced to where they are consumed.

Physical distribution system – A company's combination of order processing, merchandise handling, inventory, storage, and transportation functions. The physical distribution system is the means by which manufacturers get the product to the consumers.

Piggybacking – Intermodal transportation, whereby a loaded truck is put onto a railroad car. Because of the use of two means of distribution, a shipper can provide door-to-door service at a lower cost than with trucking alone.

Place utility – Benefit received by consumers because of the existence of the distribution system, wherein products are available at convenient locations.

Planned cannibalization – *See* cannibalization.

Point-of-purchase displays – Displays for products in the store, such as advertising sign, window display, or end-of-aisle display rack.

Population – The total market under study.

Possession utility – Consumer benefit provided by the distribution system whereby a channel member makes available an assortment of goods for consumer purchase.

Post-purchase dissonance – Doubts as to whether the right decision was made.

Predatory pricing – An attempt to reduce competition by pricing below cost, thus forcing the failure of existing competitors and deterring new entrants into the market. Once competition has decreased, the company can again raise its prices. This action is prohibited by the Sherman Antitrust Act.

Preemptive action – Strategy in which the market leader enters a market to anticipate or discourage competitive entry.

Premiums – Products offered free or at a reduced price as an incentive to buy a promoted brand.

Price brands – Low-priced brands under the manufacturer's control that are sold with minimal advertising and promotional expenditures; also called *fighting brands.*

Price deals – Short-term discounts offered by manufacturers to induce customers to try products they have not bought before or to buy greater amounts of products they are already in the habit of buying.

Price discrimination – Price differences given by sellers to intermediaries or organizational buyers that are not offered equally to the same types of buyers. This action is prohibited by the Clayton Act and the Robinson-Patman Act.

Price dumping – Selling a product below the cost of production to stimulate sales in foreign markets.

Price elasticity – Measured by the percentage change in quantity purchased resulting from a percentage change in price. When the percentage change in quantity is less than the percentage change in price, consumers are relatively price insensitive and demand is inelastic (price elasticity index less than 1). When the percentage change in quantity is greater than the percentage change in price, consumers are relatively sensitive to price changes (price elasticity index greater than 1).

Price fixing – Occurs when competitors agree to maintain fixed price levels to avoid competition based on price. *See also* Horizontal price fixing; Vertical price fixing.

Price leader – Company that tacitly sets a price which every other company in the industry follows. A price leader tends to prevent price wars, because the other companies will not change prices unless the leader does.

Price lining – Introducing various brands in a product line at different prices, thus appealing to consumers with different price elasticities (e.g., the quality-conscious consumer, the average consumer, and the economy-minded consumer).

Price promotions – Short-term discounts offered by manufacturers to induce consumers to try a product.

Primary data – Data originally collected by the marketing organization for its own immediate well-defined purposes. Methods of collecting primary data include survey research and depth interviews.

Primary demand – Demand for a general product category rather than a particular brand.

Private brands – Brands sold under a wholesaler's or retailer's label, usually at a lower price than national brands.

Private warehouse – Warehouse facilities owned by a firm which needs storage facilities on a consistent basis. Because of the fixed maintenance costs, only companies with continual storage needs use private warehouses.

Proactive strategy – Marketing strategy that attempts to anticipate future competitive actions and environmental trends to exploit the resulting market opportunities; an offensive rather than defensive strategy.

Probabilistic models – Sales forecasting models that treat the response of consumers in the marketplace as the outcome of a probabilistic process over time. They attempt to explain brand loyalty and switching behavior based on past purchases.

Probability sampling – Techniques in which every possible sampling unit drawn from a specified population has a known chance of being selected. As a result, the reliability of data from the sample can be estimated (i.e., the sampling error).

Problem solving approach – Requires the salesperson to spend time obtaining an in-depth understanding of the customer and formulating a sales approach accordingly.

Procurement costs – A cost of maintaining physical inventories. These costs are basically the expenses involved in placing reorders, such as processing, order transmitting, and the cost of the product itself.

Product – The features of the item offered and the benefits, both tangible and intangible, that the consumer receives from it. Includes goods, services, and ideas.

Product addition – Represents an extension of an existing product line.

Product advertising – Designed to maintain awareness of a product category among consumers rather than a particular brand. Sometimes sponsored by competitors within an industry, and designed to maintain awareness of a total product category among consumers, as opposed to a particular brand. In such cases, the purpose is to counter an industry-wide drop in demand for the product, rather than a loss in market share for one competitor.

Product category – The generic class to which a brand belongs.

Product concept – A detailed description of the product idea designed to communicate product benefits to consumers.

Product development – Growth strategy of developing new products or extensions of existing product lines, usually directed to existing markets.

Product extensions – Products that are not new to the company but have some new dimension for consumers. There are three types: revisions, additions, and repositionings.

Product Life Cycle (PLC) – The phases a product goes through—introduction, growth, maturity, and decline. Changes are required in marketing strategies to meet changing consumer demand and competitive conditions at each phase. A brand's position on the life cycle directly influences positioning, advertising, pricing, and distribution strategies.

Product line – A line of offerings within a certain product category, frequently having the same name to facilitate identification. *See also entries under* Line.

Product-line brand name – Brand name applied to several products within a product line.

Product-line breadth – The diversity of products in a line, or the range of its items. Broad lines can provide a choice to various segments of the market, but too much breadth can lead to cannibalization because of product overlap.

Product-line depth – The number of different types of brands, sizes, or models within a particular line of products. Deep product lines offer the consumer more choices, but too much depth can lead to cannibalization.

Product-line extensions – New variations of an existing product.

Product-line segmentation – Strategy that involves targeting several products to one market segment.

Product management system – The system within which brand or product managers work.

Product manager (also **Brand manager**) – Person responsible for formulating, implementing, and controlling a given product's marketing mix.

Product-marketing control – Activities which are designed to keep the components of a product's marketing plan on track, in order to meet the product objectives.

Product marketing plan – Defines the marketing strategy (4 Ps) for a given product or service, generally over a one-year period.

Product market unit (PMU) – Set of products aimed at defined markets.

Product mix – All of the products that a business unit or company markets.

Product positioning – The use of advertising and other marketing mix variables to communicate the benefits of the product.

Product prototypes – Preliminary production of a new product.

Product-related services – Services that play a supporting role to tangible products. Examples include warranties, food delivery, and repair service.

Product repositioning – Communicating a new feature of a brand without necessarily changing its physical characteristics.

Product revision – An improvement in an existing product.

Product specifications – Performance requirements set by prospective users of the product (such as lifting capacity for forklift trucks). Usually applies to industrial buyers.

Production goods – Products that are used to manufacture a final product.

Production orientation – Firms focus primarily on production efficiency and product availability with little regard for the needs of consumers.

Productivity – The ratio of output (production output, sales results) to input (manufacturing and marketing costs).

Profit and loss (P&L) statement – A method used to set out a business unit's or product's performance projections, usually for the next one to five years. The P&L statement usually details revenues and expenses to determine net profits.

Profit margin – Net profits as a percent of sales.

Projective techniques – Techniques used for detecting and measuring wants and attitudes not readily discernable through more direct methods. Consists of the presentation of ambiguous materials (e.g., ink blots, untitled pictures, etc.). In interpreting this material, the viewer "projects" tendencies of which he or she may be unaware or may wish to conceal. Diagnostic devices in which interpretation of ambiguous stimuli are taken to reveal something about the observer, based on previous experience and motives, needs, and interests in play at the time.

Promotion – The tactics a company uses to communicate the product's positioning.

Promotional allowances – Price reductions given by the manufacturers to retailers in exchange for advertising the manufacturer's products. Promotional allowances are the foundation for cooperative advertising.

Promotional mix – The combination of strategies that a company uses to communicate its benefits; includes advertising, sales promotions, publicity, and personal selling; a part of the marketing mix.

Prospecting – An important sales function which enables a salesperson to identify new accounts. Sources used include referrals, telemarketing, and mail-in information cards.

Psychoanalytic theory – Stresses the unconscious nature of personality as a result of childhood conflicts.

Psychological set – Consumer's predisposition to react positively or negatively toward a brand, product, or company.

Publicity – A marketing communication which appears in the mass media, and is about a company or product. It is distinguished from advertising in that publicity is not paid for by the company.

Public relations – A form of marketing communications which attempts to influence stockholders, consumers, government officials, and other business people. Public relations is an organized effort to present a positive image of the company and its products.

Public warehouse – Warehouse that provides storage facilities to a firm on a rental basis.

Pull strategies – Promotional strategies directed at end users as a means of stimulating demand. The strategy "pulls" the product through the distribution channel. Examples of pull strategies are couponing and consumer advertising.

Pulsing – A way to advertise in which ads are distributed in a few large burst, as opposed to a steady stream of commercials. Pulsing is commonly used with new products, to gain initial customer awareness.

Push strategies – Promotional strategy (e.g., trade discounts, advertising allowances) directed to channel members. This approach is said to "push" the merchandise from the manufacturer through the channels of distribution.

Qualify prospects – Salespeople qualify potential customers by identifying the best products and screening out poor ones.

Qualitative research – Research that asks consumers to respond to questions in an unstructured manner and is not generally quantifiable.

Quality circles – Groups of autonomous workers who are responsible for their output and are motivated to perform high-quality work based on the recognition that their mistakes will affect the next autonomous work group down the line.

Quantity discounts – Discounts given for volume purchases.

Quota – International trade regulation set by the individual country, which limits the amount of product within a particular category that can be imported.

Rack jobber – Limited-service wholesaler who supplies supermarkets and other retail stores with nonfood items such as housewares and health and beauty aids. The rack jobber owns the goods and the displays (racks) that are supplied and splits the profits with the retailer.

Reach – The number of people or households exposed to one or more of the vehicles in the media plan during a specified time period.

Reactive strategy – Marketing strategies in which the company lets the competition make the major moves before the company responds. This is a defensive strategy.

Rebates – Promotion that allows consumer to recover a portion of the purchase price.

Reciprocity – When two business organizations agree to buy each other's products.

Reference groups – Groups with which an individual identifies such that he or she tends to use the group as a standard for self-evaluation and as a source of personal values and goals. Groups that serve as a reference point for the individual in the formation of beliefs, attitudes, and behavior. Such groups provide consumers with a means of comparing and evaluating their own brand attitudes and purchasing behavior.

Reinforcement – Continued satisfaction with a brand as a result of repeated usage leading to an increased likelihood the brand will be purchased again.

Reliability – Measurement of marketing information that insures unbiased data and thus allows accurate conclusions to be drawn about its implications.

Representativeness – The degree to which a sample of consumers represents the characteristics of a population.

Resellers – Wholesalers and retailers that buy products to resell. They do not process goods but, rather, act as intermediaries for other organizational buyers or for the final consumer.

Retail chains – Retailers with more than four outlets.

Retailers – Members of the distribution system who sell directly to the consumer. The retailer is the final link in the distribution channel, and ensures that products are made available to consumers.

Retailer-sponsored cooperatives – A type of contractual system that integrates the distributive function among smaller retailers. In an effort to protect themselves against the larger chains with greater purchasing power, groups of smaller retailers acquire and operate their own wholesale facilities. This permits them to obtain the quantity discounts available to the chains.

Return on assets – Measure of performance used by retailers, which is equal to stock turnover multiplied by profit margin.

Return on investment (ROI) – Net profits divided by total investment.

Sales agents – Sales agents serve as an extension of the manufacturer's salesforce, particularly in industrial marketing. Sales agents have fuller authority to set prices and terms of sales than manufacturer's agents and at times even assume the manufacturer's total marketing effort by specifying promotional and distribution activities for the product line. They specialize in certain lines of trade and are paid on a commission basis.

Sales branches – A type of wholesale outlet where manufacturer-owned warehouses are designed to handle merchandise and store inventory. Companies use these types of warehouses to sell to large retailers and industrial buyers.

Sales forecast – Estimates demand for an individual brand (selective demand).

Salesforce mix – Combination of different sales methods to service large, medium, and small customers.

Sales orientation – Firms that focus primarily on selling what the company makes as opposed to what the consumer needs.

Sales quota – The expected sales level per territory, per measurement period. Sales quotas are the expression of a territory's volume and profitability objectives.

Sales wave experiment – Preliminary market tests in which the new product is placed in the consumer's home for his or her use. Consumers are given the opportunity to repurchase the new product or competitive products up to six times at reduced prices (six sales waves). Researchers can then better estimate the repurchase rate of the new product.

Scanner data – Collected when checkout clerks record sales by scanning bar codes with a laser.

Scrambled merchandising – Combining food and nonfood items in order to increase profits by allocating shelf space to more profitable nonfood items.

Seasonal discounts – Discounts for buying a product with seasonal demand in the off-season.

Secondary data – Data collected previous to the current study and not designed specifically to meet the firm's immediate research needs. Sources of secondary data include syndicated research services and the government.

Segmenting by consumer characteristics – Strategy in which market segments are identified by consumer characteristics.

Selective demand – Consumer demand for a particular brand within a product category. Companies stimulate selective demand when they try to maintain their current customer base and persuade others to switch brands.

Selective distribution – Most often used for durable goods like small appliances, stereo equipment, and furniture, selective distribution is a compromise between intense and exclusive distribution. The marketer selects a limited number of intermediaries who can provide the desired sales support and service. Because durable goods have higher prices, consumers are more likely to shop around, enabling manufacturers to limit distribution. Selective distribution allows manufacturers more control over the way their products are sold and also decreases the likelihood of price competition between intermediaries.

Selective perception – When consumers perceive the same information differently because they have different needs, motives, and past experiences.

Self-concept (self-image) theory – Holds that individuals have a concept of themselves based on who they think they are (the actual self) and who they would like to be (the ideal self).

Service management system – The equivalent of a product management system for service firms.

Service manager – Manager who develops marketing strategies for a service and has profit responsibility for service performance.

Services – Intangible benefits purchased by consumers that do not involve ownership.

Shopping goods – Those products that consumers are likely to spend more time shopping for. The consumer is involved with the product.

Shrinkage – Theft of merchandise by customers or employees.

Simulated store test – Test in which customers shop in experimental supermarket facilities in which new products are introduced and their purchases are tracked.

Single-source data – Data on an individual consumer's purchases and media exposure from the same source.

Single-zone pricing – Form of delivered pricing method where all buyers pay the same price regardless of where they are located.

Situation analysis – Preliminary evaluation of the market for a product, including identifying the key characteristics of the market, the size of the market, and other products that are likely to compete with the company's brand.

Skimming pricing strategy – A strategic option establishing a high price for a new product entry and "skimming the cream of the market" by aiming at the most price inelastic consumer. Advertising and sales promotion would be limited to specific targets, and distribution would be selective.

Slotting allowances – Direct payments to retailers, generally food chains, for stocking an item.

Slotting fees – A retailer's demand that a manufacturer pay to have a new product stocked.

Social class – A division of society made up of persons possessing certain common social and economic characteristics resulting in equal-status relations with one another and restricting interaction with members of other social classes.

Specialty distributors – Distributors that concentrate on specific lines.

Specialty goods – Products with unique characteristics that consumers make a special effort to search for and buy.

Specialty merchandise wholesalers – Wholesalers that specialize in certain product lines (such as health foods or automotive parts) and carry a deep assortment of alternatives in each line.

Specialty retailing – Retailers that offer limited, specialized lines of merchandise, with a wide assortment within these lines.

Specialty stores – Stores that are small and carry a few product lines in specialty areas. Although these stores do not have a variety of products, they do have a wide assortment within the lines that they carry.

Standardization in key markets – Standardization strategies applied (in international markets) only to markets where opportunity is greatest, particularly if customer needs in these markets is similar.

Standardized strategies – This approach to international marketing assumes that some products have universal appeal. It is thus unnecessary to develop individual marketing strategies on a market-by-market basis. Companies such as Pepsi-Cola, Ford, and Goodyear utilize this strategy. Its advantages over localized strategies are lower unit marketing costs and greater control over local marketing operations.

Statistical process control – Concept of quality control where defects are controlled when they happen instead of after the product is completed. Workers are given responsibility for identifying the defects in their own work, which serves as a motivator to produce quality output.

Status quo strategy – A strategy to avoid competition where the company seeks to keep things in the industry the way they are. This strategy of not rocking the boat can be appealing because it is less expensive than taking on the competition directly.

Steering control system – A method of evaluating marketing performance during the planning period rather than at the end of the period. Performance projected during the period is compared to the performance projected at the beginning of the period. If performance deviates from objectives, corrective action is taken to bring the plan back into control.

Stock turnover rate – Rate at which a store's inventory moves out over a specified time period. Retailers use the stock turnover rate as a measurement of performance.

Store audits – A source of retail sales information for the manufacturer that measures retail sales by subtracting end of period inventory for a product from inventory at the beginning of the period plus shipments. A. C. Nielsen is one organization that conducts audits and supplies information to manufacturers on a syndicated basis.

Straight rebuy – Recurring purchase of industrial products that can be handled on a routine basis; usually involves standardized products and requires little information search.

Strategic Business Units (SBUs) – Division level units within the organization that act as autonomous profit centers. SBU management is responsible for establishing strategic marketing plans. The boundaries of SBUs are generally defined by markets based on homogeneous consumer demand.

Strategic marketing concept – Concept emphasizing the identification of marketing opportunity as a basis for marketing planning; emphasizes marketing's role in developing products and services, as well as its broader and longer-term role in charting a course for corporate growth. Compared to the *marketing concept*, which is based on a customer orientation, the *strategic marketing concept* focuses on both customers and competitors.

Strategic marketing control – An attempt to keep the components of the strategic marketing plan on target and to redirect them if they are not.

Strategic marketing plan – A corporate and SBU-level function that (1) defines the corporate mission, (2) establishes guidelines for long-term corporate growth, (3) guides the development of the firm's overall product mix, and (4) allocates available resources to each of the firm's business units.

Strategic window of opportunity – A term used to describe a situation in which the firm's competencies are at an optimum to exploit marketing opportunities. *See also* Window of competitive opportunity.

Subcultural influences – Involves the values and behavior that distinguish subcultures from society as a whole.

Subcultures – Broad groups of consumers that have similar values that distinguish them from society as a whole.

Subliminal advertising – Advertising that is shown so quickly that consumers can perceive it only at a subconscious level.

Supermarkets – Low cost, high volume food retailer. Supermarkets carry a wide range of products and offer few services. Most supermarkets are part of a national or regional chain.

Superstores – Very large supermarkets that engage in extensive scrambled merchandising. They are at least twice as large as the average supermarket. The goal of a superstore is to provide service and one-stop shopping.

Supplies and services – Products that support the manufacturing process but are not part of it.

Sweepstakes – Allow consumers a chance to win prizes or sums of money simply by submitting their name and address.

Syndicated research – Data collected periodically by firms that sell this research to subscribing companies.

Tangible product – Product attributes representing desired benefits.

Target market (segment) – A group of consumers with similar needs that can be identified and appealed to by a specific product or product line.

Target return on cost – Establishes an objective based on return on total costs at a specified volume level and the price required to move it.

Target return on investment – Establishes a return on investment (ROI) objective and prices to meet it.

Target-return pricing – Pricing method in which the return on investment that a company wants to achieve is stated, and the price is then set based on this target. With this method, demand is not estimated, but instead, price is set relative to expected volume.

Targeting – Selecting one or more segments for marketing efforts.

Tariff – International trade regulation in the form of a tax on imported goods. Tariffs are used to protect domestic industries.

Telemarketing – A sales method whereby the telephone is used to contact existing customers and prospects directly. A telemarketing sales call is significantly less expensive than a face to face contact, and just as effective. Telemarketing is commonly used to sell to smaller clients.

Test marketing – Placing products in company selected markets for a period of time in order to gather pertinent sales information; conducted as part of a complete marketing plan to simulate a national introduction.

Time series analyses – A mathematical growth rate in sales is determined by statistical techniques and projected to future years.

Time utility – Benefit provided by distribution intermediaries, wherein the products are made available to consumers, when they want them.

Total costs – Total costs incurred in producing and marketing a product; the sum of total fixed costs and total variable costs.

Total revenue – Total amount of money received from the sale of a product.

Trade discounts – Discounts given to retailers and wholesalers for performing the marketing functions required to distribute a product.

Trade-in allowance – An adjustment to price which results from trading in a used product. The trade-in allowance is used as a partial payment in the purchase of a new item. Trade-ins are usually durable goods, such as cars.

Trade promotions – Promotions directed toward retailers and wholesalers in order to get them to stock the company's products.
Trade shows – Booths set up by various vendors in one large meeting place to dispense information about their products to prospective customers.
Trademarks – The way a company registers its brand names and symbols to protect them from being duplicated.
Trainship – Combination of rail and ship transportation.
Trait theory – States that personality is composed of a set of measurable traits that describe general response predispositions.
Transactional functions – Function performed by intermediaries in the distribution system, which involves the buying of products and reselling them to customers. The members of the distribution channel who undertake this function also incur the risks of stocking inventory.
Transmission – The process of communicating the message to the audience.
Truck jobbers – Small wholesalers selling directly from their trucks, and specializing in storing and quickly delivering perishable goods.
Tying contracts – The requirement by a manufacturer that a buyer purchase unwanted or less desirable products, in order to obtain the products which are desired. These contracts are illegal when they are in restraint of trade, or cover a significant volume.

Unfair pricing – Pricing practices designed to drive competitors out of business. *See* Predatory pricing; Price discrimination; Price fixing.
Unplanned cannibalization – *See* Cannibalization.
Upside elasticity – Price-elasticity changes in response to increased prices.

Validity – Marketing information that satisfactorily meets the purposes for which it was gathered is said to have validity.
Value-added wholesaling – Improving wholesaling productivity by providing more services and lowering the cost of these services through automation.
Value-based pricing – Method of pricing services based on what the consumer is willing to pay. In other words, it is setting the price at the level the market will bear.
Value pricing – Providing less expensive versions of brand-name products.
Variable costs – Costs that vary directly with the quantity produced.
Variety seeking – Occurs when the consumer tries a variety of brands to create some interest and avoid boredom with low-involvement purchases.
Vendor loyalty – The consistent use of the same vendor as a result of past satisfaction.
Vertical integration – Corporate growth strategy of adding new facilities to existing manufacturing or distribution operations.
Vertically integrated distribution system – Distribution system in which institutions at different levels (e.g., manufacturer, wholesaler, and retailer) combine to distribute goods. Integration requires the management of the system so that common objectives (e.g., adequate inventory, quick delivery) are attained and conflicting ones (e.g., level of discounts, use of company's promotional aids) resolved.
Vertical price fixing – This type of price fixing involves an agreement between manufacturers and retailers that the manufacturers' suggested retail price will actually be charged by the retailer. Once thought of as a means of ensuring manufacturers' profits and legalized by fair trade laws, it is now considered in restraint of trade.
Videotex systems – Two-way (interactive) cable television systems in which the con-

sumer can select information by requesting it through a home computer terminal and can also order merchandise through the terminal.

Warehouse clubs – Type of discounter that offers extremely low prices on a self-service basis, stocking a wide variety of product lines but limited selections within each line. The main differences between warehouse clubs and traditional discount stores are lower prices and a warehouse-like facility.

Warehouse stores – Deep-discount, no-frills outlets that offer food products in cartons straight from the manufacturer and require customers to bag their purchases. These are the food-outlet equivalent of warehouse clubs.

Warranty – Written statement of the manufacturer's commitment to replace or repair a product that is defective or performs poorly.

Wearout – A decrease in the effectiveness of advertising over time because of boredom and familiarity.

Wheel of retailing – The cyclical emergence of new retailers as the existing ones become less price competitive. Innovative retailers come in offering lower prices based on low overhead.

Wholesalers – Organizations that buy and resell merchandise to other businesses. They sell to other wholesalers, retailers, and industrial buyers, but not to the final consumer.

Wholesaler-sponsored voluntary chains – Groups of retailers organized by a wholesaler into an integrated chain operation. Both wholesaler and retailers benefit; costs are reduced because of increased purchasing power and more efficient wholesale operations.

Window of competitive opportunity – The combination of competitive weakness, market attractiveness, and corporate capabilities that allows a firm to establish competitive advantage.

Word-of-mouth communication – Face-to-face, personal communication.

Worldwide adaptation – Global marketing strategy in which different variations of a product are sold in each country. The marketing mix variables, such as advertising, and distribution are adapted to meet the individual needs of each country. This is the most expensive international marketing strategy, but it affords the company the most flexibility.

Worldwide standardization – Global marketing strategy employed by firms which is fairly standardized across countries. This is also known as a world brand strategy, because the underlying assumption is that the band has universal appeal, and is not country specific.

CASES

A new feature of this edition is the video case and accompanying videotape for each chapter. These 23 video cases supplement the information in the text by providing additional insights on the company and industry. They also provide a thought provoking look at specific aspects not otherwise discussed. For example, the case on Federal Express in Chapter 2 provides additional information on Fedex's international strategy which enhances the concepts and examples given within the chapter.

CASE 1

WESTERN CRUISE LINES: UNDERSTANDING THE MARKETING PROCESS

The cruise industry is experiencing strong growth. Growth in the business is driven principally by the North American market, especially the Caribbean, the world's top destination. The U.S. market is estimated to represent nearly 90 percent of the business' passenger traffic, and it has grown from just a few hundred thousand passengers in the 1970s to a record 3.6 million in 1990. Pleasure cruising has become a $5-billion-a-year industry and the total number of Americans taking cruises had increased 600 percent since 1980. Despite this, only 5 percent of Americans have ever taken a cruise, which indicates a huge untapped market.

As demand grows, so does capacity. From 1980 to 1988, 40 new ships had been christened. Twenty-five percent of this new capacity was introduced in 1988 alone. By 1991, more than 80 new cruise ships were on order worldwide. In terms of passenger space, this represents roughly 93,000 new berths since 1980. Not included in these figures is the number of refurbished ships, which adds another 43 liners. By 1990, even the size of the liners has increased dramatically. The largest liner now carries 2,282 passengers, nearly three times the size of the traditional 700 passenger ship.

In the past, cruising was sold as a commodity, with little market planning. Because demand always exceeded supply, marketing was not a part of cruise operators' activities. They just sat around and waited for their boats to fill up. Cruising was directed to a small, affluent segment. As the market became more competitive cruise companies began to turn to marketing to broaden their appeal. Today, the cruise market is broken out into two segments, (1) the long trip segment, which is high on pampering and price, and (2) the short cruise segment, which is considerably less expensive.

Short cruises have allowed companies to appeal to the mass market. The first to do so was Carnival Cruise Lines. Carnival sailed its first ship in 1972, and since then has become the largest U.S. cruise operator. In 1988, it had revenues from sailing operations of about $600 million. Carnival's specialty is the affordable short cruise—three to four days, and seven to eight days. Because this product is different from a traditional cruise and caters to a different market, Carnival has to make this known to consumers if it is to fill berths. To do this, Carnival abandoned the common advertising medium for cruise ships, newspapers, in favor of television. From 1988 to 1991, Carnival spent $60 million on TV commercials. The result: revenues skyrocketed. In 1989 it was estimated that one out of every five cruise goers was on a Carnival ship.

When Western Cruise Lines first entered the west coast market, it took its cue from Carnival. The firm purchased the *SS Azure Seas* for $30 million and spent another $7 million refurbishing it. The ship had a capacity of 300 passengers and a crew of 300 to 500. The *Azure Seas* was designed to take short cruises, departing from Los Angeles.

Filling these cabins was not an easy task for Western Cruise. They began by surveying local travel agents to get an idea of the extent of consumer interest in a three-to-four day cruise. Not surprisingly, Western Cruise ascertained that with any cruise, but particularly with a short cruise, passengers want great food and good service. They also recognized that the key to this quality of service and the key to maintaining it would require paying more attention to the training and welfare of their crew. The people who deliver the range of services that is the cruise product must be happy and motivated in order to do a quality job.

Western also surveyed cruise consumers and found that only 4 percent were aware of *Azure Seas.* This was unacceptably low. In comparison, 90 percent knew of Carnival's *Princess,* and associated it with the TV show, the "*Love Boat.*" Additionally there was no well defined *Azure Seas* customer. Western's consumers included the young and the old, men and women, couples, singles and families. The one common element was that they were mostly from the Los Angeles area. The survey revealed that 70 percent of the passengers were on their first trip and that 70 percent were from L.A.

As a result of lack of awareness Western decided to advertise on TV. Carnival spends $15 million a year on TV commercials and although Western Cruise's budget was not quite as large, they too decided that TV could dramatically improve their brand awareness and that this would lead to increased bookings.

Another marketing strategy that cruise operators began to use were promotions. Carnival initiated much of this by signing Kathy Lee Gifford as its spokesperson. It also ran promotions with a cruise as the prize. Royal Viking, a more upscale cruise line introduced a promotion in the form of a discount based on frequent flier mileage accumulated by the purchaser. Other promotions included tie-ins with local radio stations, where the station's contest winner would sail with a radio celebrity.

In 1989, after becoming part of Admiral Cruises (which combined the former Western and Eastern cruise lines), *Azure Seas* underwent another refurbishment. Its capacity was increased to 740 passengers and it continued to sail on both three and four night cruises. Prices ranged from a low of $505 to a high of $1,095, depending on the duration of the cruise and the size of the cabin.

Later in 1989, Admiral Cruises merged with Royal Caribbean Cruises and their sales forces were combined. Early in 1991, *Azure Seas* was moved to a new home port and began operating services from Florida. As the cruise line industry becomes more competitive, the travel industry is turning to more innovative marketing techniques, such as separately targeting adults over 45 and offering unusual itineraries. The promotional use of Frequent Flier programs tied in with cruises proved to be a very successful way to continue to encourage passenger bookings, and continues to be prevalent. The key to success in today's travel industry will continue to be a well defined marketing identity and marketing planning.

Questions

1. What customer need was Western Cruise Lines trying to meet? How did it meet these needs?
2. What was Western Cruise's marketing mix? Specifically, what was
   - its product (i.e., service) strategy for *Azure Seas?*
   - its pricing strategy?
   - its advertising strategy?
   - its method for distribution?
3. How did Western Cruise Lines' advertising strategy change, and why?

4. Would you label Western Cruise as product, sales, or customer oriented? Why?
5. What characteristics of a service does the *Azure Seas* cruise have? What problems do these characteristics create for the marketer?

References

1. "Creative Cruising," *Incentive*, June 1991, pp. 66–78.
2. "Cruise Ships: Party, Party, Party," *The Economist*, May 4, 1991, p. 71.
3. "Traveler's Comeback," *Advertising Age*, April 22, 1991, p. 31.
4. "How Carnival Stacks the Deck," *Fortune*, January 16, 1989, pp. 109–116.
5. "The Travel Industry Reinvents the Marketing Game," *Marketing Communications*, April 1988, pp. 71–75.

FEDERAL EXPRESS: IDENTIFYING OPPORTUNITIES AND DEVELOPING GROWTH STRATEGIES

CASE 2

In 1970, Fred Smith was selling corporate jets in Little Rock. He was a recent Vietnam vet who had the nagging idea that his dream of starting an overnight delivery service could become a reality. His idea was to establish a hub-and-spoke method of delivery—one central hub for all packages that would be transmitted like spokes to any destination. It also meant that a package from one end of the same town to the other would first have to travel possibly thousands of miles to the hub to get to its destination. The idea earned a "C" as an undergraduate economics paper, but it later proved to be a stroke of genius which created the air courier industry.

Fred Smith tapped a $4 million dollar inheritance and borrowed $80 million dollars to launch Federal Express. He inaugurated the service in the spring of 1973, and lost a million dollars a month for the next two years. Today, however, revenues top $4.6 billion and Fedex handles more than a million packages a day. It is currently the nation's largest overnight letter and package carrier, with 45 percent of the market, competing with UPS, DHL, Airborne and the U.S. postal system. Fedex handles more than a million packages a day, flies 380 planes, operates 31,000 delivery vans, and employs 95,000 people.

The key to Federal Express' success has been its superior ability to define and exercise marketing strategy. As an aggressive and entrepreneurial start-up, Fred Smith and his partners broke new ground in the otherwise stagnant airline industry. Having had experience with airlines, Smith observed, "The big forces in the airplane industry missed the forest for the trees. They were so used to the way they were doing things, they missed the revolution!"

Smith was an astute observer and knew that the United States was relying on the computer industry in many ways for future economic growth. The growing importance of the computer and electronics businesses presented a unique opportunity. Computer manufacturers and similar businesses needed to have their own specialized transportation system to support them and provide a reliable flow of parts and other supplies. This was not unlike the relationship between the railroads who shipped coal to the steel mills and then shipped steel to the automakers. The new twist was that in the competitive computer and electronics industry, customers often needed their shipment in a matter of hours.

Fedex introduced its hub-and-spoke concept which combined pick-up and delivery by truck with the speed of aviation. The key to making this work was the hub in Memphis, linking cities all over the United States. Why ship a package from San Francisco to Los Angeles by sending it to Memphis first? This sounded ludicrous to Smith's early investors, but Smith knew what he was doing. He knew it was impossible to transfer parts from every city to every other city directly. The solution was to gather them centrally and then redistribute them.

In banking, checks were gathered centrally, cleared and then redistributed to the appropriate branches from a central location. Taking a cue from the banks, Smith saw the advantage of this system. Fedex would gather packages at the hub in Memphis, logging them in and then shipping them to their ultimate destinations, all before midnight. Fedex thus implemented their famous "hub-and-spoke" system to be able to provide their customers with quick and reliable delivery because standardized sorting and tracking could be carried out in one location.

Before Fedex came into business consumers were satisfied with "as soon as possible," but Fedex changed this perception by creating a new product which was "overnight" service. The countdown until midnight is the heart of their operations. Packages collected by vans in each city arrive by plane at the end of the day and have to be processed and rerouted to their destination by midnight. With 60 aircraft and 900 people, a total of 120,000 packages could be processed in just four hours.

Marketing this unconventional, new product, required creating broad-based public awareness. Fedex initially marketed its service like a traditional shipping service, going after a narrow target of shipping executives via advertising in trade publications. However, in 1975 Fedex realized that they needed to broaden their target audience to include virtually everyone in business, not just the people who made the shipping decisions. To reach this audience, Federal Express used its first television advertising campaign.

The very first commercials did not reach the right people, or focus on the right consumer needs. People remembered the ads, but did not identify with them. Federal Express then decided to make their shipping concept more appealing to their target audience by portraying their audience. They focused on the white-collar executives who were looking for solutions to their own business problems but who did not really care about the details of loading docks, trucks and planes. Instead, the ads were designed to stress the simplicity, convenience and swiftness of the Fedex service. Delivered by humorous fast-talking executives for whom *yesterday* could not be soon enough, the slogan, "When it absolutely, positively, has to be there overnight" made history.

The television advertising strategy gave Fedex the conspicuous public profile it needed. Most important, sales shot up and the company's growth rate hit 50 percent with sales volume doubling over the next two years. Fedex quickly became a successful enterprise and by 1983 sales topped the $1 billion mark! Their rapid growth meant that Fedex had to define its strategies for the future. This was especially true because competitors duplicated Fedex's hub-and-spoke system, and competition began to intensify, particularly on the basis of pricing.

In 1983, Federal Express established three new divisions to address its future needs. First, in response to the growing use of telefax transmissions, the Electronic Products Division was formed to pioneer international electronic information transmission. They did this with a new product called ZapMail. Second, the International Division was established to extend Federal Express' service network around the world. They already served 80 markets outside the United States, but had an eye on penetrating the lucrative Asian and European markets. Third, the Business Service Center Division was organized to develop the domestic market by introducing retail marketing and new service programs. The company identified four strategic objectives to coordinate their efforts. These were to (1) improve service and differentiate these products, (2) lower prices while enhancing value, (3) get closer to the customer, and (4) improve cash flow and financial returns.

Fedex's entry into the retail market proved very successful. They were able to reach new customers with both existing and new services and achieved significant market expansion. With a real flair for promotion, they opened 60 new service centers in 28 major markets with old fashioned grand openings. They specifically chose service center sites in neighborhoods that were convenient for customers and which fit into the flow of local traffic patterns.

They also began to increase their appeal to customers who wanted to drop-off packages or who wanted to take advantage of a new "hold-at-location" service. This service was developed because Fedex service agents noticed that technical reps and repair servicemen had figured out that they could get parts sooner if they simply let Fedex hold the packages instead of delivering them by the 10:30 deadline. These reps would pick up parts on their way to their service stops. Fedex then began to more aggressively promote the service with a special "Hold Me" campaign complete with point of sale posters displays and a teddy bear give-away. These promotion techniques would become standard practice for rolling out services.

These new tactics not only served new customers in new ways, but also reduced courier expenses for Fedex and allowed them to offer special discounts to drop-off customers. Pricing, location, and convenience were all key components of the success of the retail centers which allowed Fedex to grow through internal development. Federal Express became the first company in the overnight package industry to establish a true retail network.

Internationally, Fedex saw an opportunity to expand its core business, air freight delivery. These days a company's long-term viability often depends on international business potential, so starting in 1985, Fedex decided to become a major force in international deliveries. Growth in the Asian market came from purchasing Tiger International Inc., the world's largest heavy air-cargo carrier, for $880 million. By acquiring the company Fedex gained both the "Flying Tiger" fleet and the proprietary delivery routes which covered most of Asia. This way Fedex would be able to use their own planes for delivery overseas instead of contracting out to other carriers which is both costlier and riskier.

Fedex's attempt to penetrate the Asian market, however, illustrates some of the risks of international strategy. Japan had its own fledgling express air-freight industry to develop and protect, and just before Fedex was to begin its Asian route service in May 1988, the Japanese government erected a roadblock. By restricting Fedex from carrying any package over 70 pounds in or out of Tokyo, the key link in the Oriental routes, Japan significantly limited Fedex's potential business. This resulted in a $1 million a month loss to Fedex for a year.

Another major problem with the International market was that Fedex's rivals already had a significant presence in the European markets. In short, Fedex was late for the party. Companies like DHL and TNT had imitated the Fedex system and were already providing express service in Europe. In fact, while "Fedex it" meant overnight in the U.S., "DHL it" meant overnight in Europe. To make matters worse, Fedex found that it was more difficult to set up its hub-and-spoke system. Local regulators and authorities were not as eager to enable Fedex to fly bigger cargo planes and get exemptions from certain rules which facilitate the operations of hub-and-spoke. An option Fedex can use to expand internationally is partnerships with local companies, or "joint ventures." However, most of these opportunities have already been exploited by rival firms like UPS.

Despite these difficulties, Fedex is not giving up. In Japan, for instance, they are about to introduce a one-day "express freighter" service to the West Coast in the hope that computer manufacturers and other shippers will want to get cargo to the United States faster. The company is still trying in Europe, by beginning to compete with ground service with lower costs. They plan to begin offering a less expensive two-day ground service.

Domestically Fedex is facing increasingly stiff competition from UPS. For example, UPS has been able to match every service innovation to a tee, including the use of hand held computers for drivers. Mounting losses from international efforts combined with the need to tend shop at home may force UPS to retrench somewhat.

Fedex will continue to explore new niches and products in order to promote its growth strategies both at home and abroad. For example, Fedex has very successfully entered into partnership with the burgeoning catalog and mail-order merchandise industry. Fedex still has a key competitive advantage domestically in that it established its reputation as the very first overnight courier.

Questions

1. What was the strategic window of opportunity identified by Fred Smith?
2. What was the original target market for overnight delivery? Why?
3. What was the role of advertising in helping Fedex grow beyond the computer market to the general business market?
4. What was Fedex's growth strategy when it was formed? What is it now?
5. What are Fedex's current plans for the international market? What problems is it facing in this market?

References

1. Daniel Pearl, "Innocents Abroad: Federal Express Finds Its Pioneering Formula Falls Flat," *The Wall Street Journal*, April 15, 1991.
2. "Federal Express: Employees Eliminate Problems Instead of Fighting Fires," *Business Marketing*, February 1990.
3. "Mr. Smith Goes Global," *Business Week*, February 13, 1989.
4. Carl Williams, "The Challenge of Retail Marketing at Federal Express," *The Journal of Business and Industrial Marketing*, Winter, 1987.
5. T.A. Sunderland, "Overnight Success," *Catalog Age*.

CASE 3

ROBERT MONDAVI WINERY, A CASE STUDY IN MARKETING PLANNING

For many families in the Napa Valley and in other wine-making regions throughout the world, wine is more than a product, it is a way of life. This is especially true for the Mondavi family. At the Robert Mondavi Winery, located in Oakville, California, family members are the driving force behind all aspects of creating and marketing their fine wines. The winery's success is the result of dedication, experience, and a commitment to careful marketing planning. The winery's patriarch, Robert Mondavi, has been a sizable force in raising the quality of U.S. wines to worldclass standards. Mondavi's ability to identify market opportunities and introduce innovative new products helped to fuel the wine revolution that has occurred over the past two decades.

This revolution has been the result of a preoccupation with health and fitness. Cocktail hours, which once hosted a variety of hard liquors, now offer an assortment of wines, light beers, and sparkling waters. The dramatic increase in wine sales is evidence of a marketing triumph that has changed the perception of wine from a luxury good to a beverage that can be consumed regularly. In the 1990s consumer purchasing habits are changing once again. While Americans are not drinking more wine than a decade ago (about 2.3 gallons per capita) they are drinking wine of better quality.

In 1988, revenues from fine wines overtook revenues of mass-marketed jug wines for the first time. Another milestone was reached the following year when sales of the California premium wines outsold imported table wines. Not surprisingly, the number of Californian wineries has more than doubled since the early 1980s to well over 700 in 1992. Yet the combination of greater health consciousness and the early 1990s recession has impacted the $13 billion wine industry and all beverages in general. Consumption of alcoholic beverages is currently at an all-time low. The market for California premium wines is flat, as is the market for jug wines. Only the beer and non-alcoholic segments are showing any growth. Some experts predict that sales of wine in California may drop 20 percent as a result of tougher drunk-driving laws and a proposed alcohol tax hike.

The current industry downturn aside, the Robert Mondavi Winery is one vineyard that has prospered from the continuing trend towards premium wines. Before coming to the valley in 1966, Robert Mondavi had 15 years of wine-making experience. He chose Napa Valley because it afforded all the natural conditions needed to make fine wine; an ideal climate, soil and variety of grapes. In the early days of the winery, Mondavi regularly toured Europe to ferret out from master winemakers techniques that he could import to California. For instance, Mondavi was one of the first winemakers in the United States to age his wines in small oak barrels rather than in large cement or redwood tanks.

In later years Robert Mondavi would introduce innovative production techniques so advanced that they attracted the attention of the European wineries. Robert Mondavi's philosophy has always been to excel in everything he does. This philosophy is evident in the winery's selection of a target market. Unlike the Gallo Winery, which advertises heavily, offers numerous products and attempts to penetrate the entire wine drinking market, Mondavi has chosen to employ a niche strategy. According to Michael Mondavi, the company President and Robert's eldest son, "We can't be all things to all people. The goal is to select a specific niche, and then be the best in that niche." Mondavi's niche is the upper 5 percent of the wine-drinking market for which the company produces approximately 2.5 million cases of bottled wine annually. The strategy appears to be paying off. Through 1990, Mondavi has enjoyed annual growth rates of between 10 and 15 percent. The Mondavi Winery is today a $120 million business.

As American consumption behavior changed and health consciousness increased, Mondavi sensed that there was an opportunity for a lighter, more refreshing new white wine. In order to successfully introduce this new product, Mondavi knew he had to alter the deeply embedded attitude about wine being a luxury good. Although the new wine was made from the Sauvignon grapes, Mondavi decided not to call it Sauvignon Blanc since Sauvignon wines had traditionally sold poorly in the United States. They were perceived as too upscale. Instead, he chose the name Fumé Blanc, because he thought it had more appeal. Yet the launch of Fumé Blanc in 1967 was quite risky since white wines accounted for only one fourth of total wines sales in the United States at that time.

Mondavi succeeded in making Fumé Blanc the second best selling wine in California. Mondavi said, "The only mistake I made was in not copyrighting the name." Since Mondavi's introduction of Fumé Blanc in the mid-sixties, many competing wineries have introduced their own versions. Despite heavy competition, the Mondavi Winery is now one of America's 20 largest wineries. The dynamic marketing efforts of the Mondavi Winery have benefited the industry as a whole. White wine sales have risen from 25 percent in 1970 to 53 percent by 1980.

Once the market for white wines began to stabilize and people were more accustomed to matching wines with the different foods they ate, Mondavi decided to pursue an opportunity in the market for dessert wines. He is currently attempting to develop this market by introducing a new dessert wine which he calls Muscato D'Oro. In a taste test, Muscato received the greatest consumer response of all the Mondavi wines. The winery has developed a color brochure that discusses Muscato's association with certain foods and highlights dessert recipes.

What are the reasons for Mondavi's success in the wine industry? Marketing expertise. Because the Mondavi's believe that superior taste and word of mouth sell premium wines, the winery does not advertise. Rather, Mondavi is committed to educating the consumer about wine via three primary marketing tools: a national marketing staff, promotional tie-ins, and regularly scheduled cultural activities at the winery itself.

Mondavi's objective is to effectively educate the top 5 percent of the wine-tasting market and let them influence the remaining 95 percent. He employs a nationwide staff of 54 marketing representatives who host wine tastings and seminars for key wine and foods society groups, as well as restauranteurs and retailers. This gives retail buyers the opportunity to taste the wines and learn more about the products. The Great Chefs of France program is one promotion that attracts people from all over the United States who are interested in learning the latest techniques in French cooking. According to Alex Fabré, the program administrator, "the program teaches the subtleties of the relationship between food and wine . . . it allows the public to realize that Robert Mondavi's wines are of a certain caliber that can be served with these great foods." Yet another promotional tie-in called "Celebrate the Fall Harvest" took place in September and October of 1991. The event, sponsored by Mondavi and Westin Hotels, was held at 43 Westin properties. Hotel guests learned which Mondavi wines go best with certain dishes. The Fall Harvest promotion was designed to give Westin a sophisticated image by linking menu items to specific Mondavi wines. The promotion effectively boosted the hotel chain's wine sales and gave consumers an invaluable education in Mondavi wines.

The third marketing vehicle used by Mondavi is the winery itself. When Robert Mondavi founded the winery, he understood that achieving success required that he first educate the consuming public about wines. Toward this end, Mondavi designed his winery so that it could be used for entertaining and hosting cultural events. Each year over 300,000 people visit the Mondavi vineyards and take the tour of the winery. The winery is also the site of numerous jazz concerts, winemaking demonstrations, cooking classes, wine tastings, and art shows.

Mondavi's wines are higher priced than the competition because they are of higher quality. To maintain a higher base price for its wines, the Mondavi Winery limits its product line, and implements quality controls. The family believes that its pricing strategy works because the quality is long remembered after the price is forgotten. No expense is spared to ensure that the wines produced are of superior quality. Unlike other wineries, which place a limit on the cost of wine production, Mondavi does not specify a target production cost per barrel. The chief winemaker, 32-year-old Tim Mondavi, is afforded the resources and latitude to produce wines of optimum quality. For Tim Mondavi, quality control means keeping a close tab on the status of 10.3 million gallons of wine stored in nearly 150 storage tanks and 13,000 aged barrels.

Evaluation and strict quality control are an essential part of Mondavi's production process. The Mondavi Winery is well known for its advanced laboratory techniques. Once the grapes are crushed, every batch is tested to determine if the fermentation process is occurring on schedule. Also, relative amounts of sugar and acidity are tested daily. Color, aroma, and taste are the standards by which wine experts judge the wine. These factors are also critical to consumer acceptance. Tim Mondavi also works with agricultural engineers at a nearby university to improve the fermentation process of grapes. For the Mondavi Winery, producing better quality wines is an ongoing process.

While many competitors have benefited from the wine revolution, Robert Mondavi remains the marketing leader. As one wine expert said, "Robert Mondavi saw a market opportunity, planned his product carefully, put it in an attractive package, and sold it through a fierce dedication to education, rather than to expensive advertising." Mondavi's compulsion to innovate and promote has not gone unnoticed by his colleagues in the business world. On April 18, 1991, 78-year-old Robert Mondavi was inducted into the National Business Hall of Fame.

Questions

1. Does Robert Mondavi Winery have a marketing plan in introducing new products? If so, what are its components?
2. What strategies are used to market Mondavi wines? Specifically, what strategies are used in lieu of advertising?
3. What is the difference in marketing approach between Gallo and Mondavi?
4. What was the opportunity for introducing Fumé Blanc? What is the market for the product?

References

1. "The National Business Hall of Fame," *Fortune*, March 11, 1991, pp. 98–103.
2. "A Taste for IS and an Ancient Art," *Computerworld*, December 10, 1990, pp. 81–82.
3. "Special Retail Services and Resale Price Maintenance: The California Wine Industry, *Journal of Retailing*, Spring 1990, pp. 101–118.
4. "News for the Nineties: Who'll be Drinking What and Why?," *Restaurant Hospitality*, January 1990, pp. 40, 44.
5. "A Hearty Bunch," *Venture*, April 1989, pp. 41–47.
6. "Catering to America's Sweet Tooth: Dessert Wines Spell Success," *Nation's Restaurant News*, v.22, Sept. 26, 1988, p. 24.
7. "California Wine On the Grapevine," *Economist*, April 23, 1988, pp. 68–69.
8. "Flat Sales Force Winery Changes," *Advertising Age*, March 12, 1984, p. 3.

MITSUBISHI MOTORS: ENVIRONMENTAL FACTORS IMPACTING ON MARKETING DECISIONS

CASE 4

In the 1940s, four out of every five cars in the world were built in the United States. Detroit's largest automakers, Ford, General Motors, and Chrysler were three of the world's best known companies. Japanese carmakers began to gain a foothold in the United States in the early 1970s when oil shortages and higher gasoline prices pressured many Americans to turn to economy cars. Because the Japanese were one of the few countries providing high mileage automobiles, Japan's share of the market grew rapidly. Americans also began demanding quality cars, another opportunity for Japanese automakers. Despite Japan's gains, a quota system existed, limiting the number of Japanese cars that could be imported into the United States.

One of Japan's oldest and largest conglomerates, Mitsubishi, was late in entering the U.S. market. It was not until 1970, after an examination of the U.S. market led to a positive evaluation of the opportunities in this country, that Mitsubishi entered the United States. The company took a cautious approach and signed a marketing agreement with Chrysler.

This arrangement centered on Mitsubishi-built cars being sold in America as Dodges and Plymouths through Chrysler dealerships. At the time, Chrysler needed small, fuel-efficient cars to complement its line. Mitsubishi wanted to gain entrance into the U.S. market. Chrysler bought a 35 percent share of Mitsubishi, in return for franchises to sell Mitsubishi cars under the Chrysler banner for a minimum of ten years. This arrangement worked fine until 1980 when changes in the environment and at Chrysler led Mitsubishi to re-evaluate its relationship with the American automaker.

While Chrysler was experiencing financial hardship and barely escaped bankruptcy, Mitsubishi wanted to further increase its presence in the United States. Mitsubishi and Chrysler decided to modify their agreement. Chrysler would receive financing from Mitsubishi, and in exchange, would sell a minimum of 30,000 Mitsubishi cars through Chrysler dealers. Mitsubishi Motor Sales of America (MMSA) was formed to market these cars.

Mitsubishi's strategy grew directly out of the threats and opportunities of its marketing environment. Because it believed that consumers on the Coasts were more likely to buy Japanese automobiles, Mitsubishi limited distribution to these specific regions. Middle America was left to the Big Three. Mitsubishi also had to plan around import restrictions. A national roll out, for example, was not feasible since the company would not be able to import enough cars to cover expected demand.

Based on expected growth in sales, Mitsubishi determined that it needed its own dealership network. These new dealers would be given four mid-priced models: Mirage, Tredia, Cordia, and Starion. However, Mitsubishi provided no low or high-end cars.

By 1983, Mitsubishi's sales at home were declining. To reverse this trend, Mitsubishi brought in a new president, Toyoo Tate. Tate made a number of changes but the most far reaching, and important to Mitsubishi was the broadening of global partnerships. Tate also took the company public to raise the money needed for expansion. Despite the influx of capital, Mitsubishi's ability to grow was limited by import quotas. Because of its arrangement with Chrysler, Mitsubishi was given a disproportionately low quota of 30,000 vehicles. Consequently, Mitsubishi had difficulty establishing a production base and dealership network in the United States. The import quota has forced Mitsubishi to maintain its alliance with Chrysler in order to get its cars to the public. As a result, in September of 1988, Mitsubishi decided to produce cars jointly with Chrysler in the United States to circumvent quota restrictions. The two companies began operation of Diamond Star, an assembly plant in Bloomington, Illinois. Each company owns 50 percent of the plant and shares equally in the output.

The overwhelming success of Japanese car manufacturers has forced their U.S. counterparts to clean up their act. Detroit has responded to the foreign challenge by focusing on product quality and customer service. Chrysler continues to run ads stressing that "quality is job one." Foreign competition plus a sharp decrease in sales due to the 1990-92 recession has led Detroit to put pressure on the Bush Administration to improve the trade situation with Japan. In late December 1991,

President Bush and 20 top U.S. business executives met with Japanese politicians to get Japan's compliance in reducing the $40 billion dollar trade deficit. A major objective of the trip was to increase auto and autopart sales to Japan.

Mitsubishi recognizes the increasing concerns in the United States with foreign competition. In response, it has developed a strong marketing strategy to maintain competitiveness. The first step was to broaden the product line by adding new models—Galant, Galant Stigma, and the Hyundai made Precis. A corporate headquarters was built in Southern California, near the design center. A research and development facility was built in Detroit, right at the door step of the Big Three. Staff has been expanded and dealerships added in order to handle the projected increase in sales. Finally, Mitsubishi opened 100 new dealerships in 1989, including six in the metro Detroit area. Moving into the Midwest is a major step considering the reluctance of Japanese car makers to compete with Ford, GM, and Chrysler in America's heartland.

Mitsubishi needed to improve its image as a manufacturer of stylish and sporty automobiles. In 1988, an upscale Mirage and a restyled Galant replaced older models. The Tredia was also dropped, thereby completing the makeover of Mitsubishi's line.

But, Mitsubishi did not stop there. It recognized that while consumers want quality, they don't want to compromise on styling. The Diamond Star plant recently began producing the Eclipse, which is priced at $10,000 and offers a sporty look. In keeping with a quality level which consumers have come to expect from Japan, Mitsubishi presented the Galant, a mid-priced sedan.

Because of increased competition, executives at Mitsubishi recognized that they needed to establish a distinct corporate identity in order to survive in the 1990s. The company has relied heavily on advertising to present its new image. The new campaign, "Mitsubishi, the word is getting around," focuses on quality and styling. Mitsubishi introduced its Diamante luxury sedan in May 1991. The introduction of the Diamante is the start of a major new product push as the car manufacturer broadens its scope. In the past two years, Mitsubishi has doubled its number of dealers to 500. Mitsubishi is looking to sell 400,000 automobiles yearly by 1993.

A further sign of Mitsubishi's interest in the U.S. market was its purchase of Value Rent-A-Car in 1990. Mitsubishi hopes to use the car rental company to gain exposure for its many models. The carmaker has also set up its own car financing arm. As the fifth ranked Japanese importer, Mitsubishi is starting to make its own mark, tripling its share of the U.S. car market since 1988. Part of the company's recent success can be traced to increased advertising in 1991 (up 20 percent to $120 million) and the introduction of four new cars that blend high-tech engineering with pleasing shapes and value for the money.

Mitsubishi may soon invest an estimated $300 million in cash starved Chrysler in exchange for a controlling interest in the jointly owned Diamond Star plant. Mitsubishi may also advance $300 million towards the development of a new Chrysler sports car. Although the Mitsubishi-Chrysler partnership has been successful thus far, the arrangement seriously limits Mitsubishi's long-term prospects in the U.S. market. The Japanese automaker could face an unclear future if Chrysler decides to sell its current stake in Mitsubishi, an option being considered by Chrysler's top management to generate much needed capital.

Questions

1. How have each of the key environmental factors-social trends, competition, technology, legal and regulatory factors, the economy-impacted on Mitsubishi's marketing efforts in the United States?

2. What is Mitsubishi's target? Does this target market reflect favorable social trends?
3. How did Mitsubishi's relationship with Chrysler affect its subsequent operations?
4. Which of the factors cited in questions 1 to 3 above would you identify as opportunities? Which would you identify as threats? Why?
5. What actions has Mitsubishi taken to strengthen its position in the American market for the 1990s?

References

1. "Mitsubishi Group Wary of Deeper Ties to Chrysler," *Tokyo Business Today*, July 1991, p. 10.
2. "Mitsubishi Pulls Out all the Stops," *Business Week*, May 6, 1991, pp. 64, 68.
3. "What Sparks Mitsubishi's Drive," *Advertising Age*, May 6, 1991, p. 6.
4. "Mitsubishi Maps Solo Success," *Advertising Age*, July 2, 1990, pp. 3, 33.
5. "Hard Work Ahead," *Automotive Industries*, February 1989, pp. 117–120.
6. "Mitsubishi Is Souping Up Its Image," *Business Week*, February 27, 1989, p. 56.
7. "Japanese Auto Makers Target Midwest," *Wall Street Journal*, December 19, 1988, p. B1.
8. "It's a New Ball Game for Japanese in U.S., Recchia Says," *Automotive News*, March 20, 1988, p. 27.
9. "Mitsubishi Searches for an Image," *Automotive News*, February 1, 1988, p. 31.

CASE 5

FLUOR CORP.: DEVELOPING INTERNATIONAL MARKETING STRATEGIES

Global marketing has become the buzzword of the 1990s. The consensus in business circles is that only those U.S. firms that can compete effectively in the international market will survive long term. This prediction could hold true for a number of reasons. Various cross-country alliances, for one, are being formed, including the alliance of the 12 nation European Community which has begun to remove trade barriers as of December 1992. Many Western and Asian firms will benefit from "EC 1992" because of the lower cost of entry into the European market and the relative ease of access.

Secondly, the U.S. market is saturated. Companies must look to sell their products overseas, in new, untapped markets. Previously unaccessible markets such as the Russian Republic, the Eastern Bloc nations, and Asia are now open to Western products and investment.

Fluor is one company which is taking full advantage of changes in the world market. Based in Irvine, California, Fluor is the largest engineering and construction firm in the United States. Its sales in 1990 were $7.4 billion, up $2.3 billion from 1988. Fluor became an international conglomerate long before globalization became fashionable. The company currently operates in 50 countries on six continents. In the late 1970s, for example, Fluor managed the Aramco Gas Program in Saudi Arabia. The project took four years to complete and employed 25,000 workers, earning Fluor $4 billion in revenues. In 1987 Fluor became involved in an $8 billion project for the Norwegian government to construct a gas pipeline from Norway to Southern Europe.

One might assume that Fluor's products are physical goods. In fact, Fluor's real business is selling services. Its product is the engineering and managerial expertise it offers its customers. Fluor is not alone in selling its services overseas. The exporting of services by American firms is big business; in 1986 American service companies exported $48 billion worth of services abroad. Even though the total U.S. trade balance shows a deficit, service products accounted for a trade surplus estimated at between $23 and $38 billion in 1990. As a major exporter of services, Fluor contributed to this explosion through its many international projects.

While Fluor has indeed flourished in the 1990s, the decade prior was not so kind to the construction giant. In the early 1980s Fluor made all its money building oil refineries and other huge energy related projects. When the price of oil went bust in the mid 1980s, so too did Fluor's revenues. In the three years between 1981 and 1984 its new construction backlog slid from $16 billion to $4 billion. In 1985, Fluor lost $633 million and its survival was in question. To change things around, Fluor's CEO, David Tappan, implemented a strategy of diversification. The company began constructing everything from biotech plants, art museums, paper mills, and prisons. Tappan also reduced the workforce from 27,000 to 17,000 worldwide, and sold off several office buildings and peripheral businesses. These cost cutting tactics earned him the nickname "Ice Man."

Fluor's drive toward diversification was well rewarded. In no time Fluor had landed several large contracts which helped to double revenue and secure $12 billion in backlogs. Fluor even made money, and still does, selecting sites, arranging financing, and even lending directly to some blue-chip clients. When Tappan retired in January 1992, the reins were handed over to Leslie McGraw, Fluor's second in command. McGraw currently has his sights on Europe, where U.S. firms are scrambling to add facilities, and in Canada, where mining is making a comeback. McGraw contends that the global economy is in the early stages of a long-term capital expansion. The end of the Cold War, the lifting of European trade barriers, a strengthening Asia, and the rebuilding of Kuwait all represent opportunities for growth internationally.

As new markets have opened up, Fluor has been quick to move in. Fluor, for instance, was one of the first companies to enter Mainland China. Although China is the world's most populous nation with over 1 billion people, its inhabitants have been prevented by their own government from buying foreign goods. Historically, the Chinese have been wary of Westerners. This fear was exacerbated by the Communists, who took over the country in 1949. The leaders imposed their idea of a Communist economy on the Chinese people and prevented most Westerners from setting up any type of business in China.

In the early 1970s, the Chinese started to become more receptive to American overtures for economic reform. President Nixon's historic visit to China in 1972 helped pave the way for American investment. Fluor started getting involved in China in 1973 when it joined the National Council for U.S.-China Trade, an organization that promotes U.S.-China trade relations. By 1978, Fluor finally set up operations in China, the world's largest consumer market. The company created a management team to develop relations with the Chinese government, an important ingredient for success in a socialist country. Fluor understood from the beginning that its involvement in China would be long term.

Tappan, in an interview shortly before his retirement, discussed three components of Fluor's philosophy regarding its business dealings overseas. First, the company always takes a long-term view when entering a new market. "We're not going in for one project, in and out, fast bucks," said Tappan, "that is the opposite of our philosophy." Second, Fluor looks to transfer technology to build a business enterprise that can be successful by supplementing the technology that already exists in a country. The third rule is to be a good citizen. Fluor works hard to show respect for the cultures and customs of the countries within which it operates.

Doing business in China is not easy for Fluor, or any company for that matter. The Chinese government has an inordinate number of restrictions that complicate business transactions. Since China has a shortage of foreign currency with which to pay Western companies, it often relies on countertrade, paying foreign companies with goods. Although this is not the preferred mode of business for Fluor, it has accepted the practice to stay in China.

Other restrictions affect the way companies operate in China. The Ministry of Trade must approve all projects. Distribution systems are poor in most areas, if they exist at all. Per capita income is approximately $300, hence consumers have little money with which to buy expensive foreign goods. Advertising is strictly regulated. Limits are put on the profits and goods that can be taken out of the country.

In spite of these restrictions, China represents a unique opportunity for Western firms, particularly American companies. Products known the world over are becoming familiar to the Chinese for the first time. For example, in November 1987 Kentucky Fried Chicken, now KFC, opened the first fast-food outlet in China, opposite the tomb of former Chinese leader Mao, in Tiananmen Square, Beijing, and in 1992 McDonald's opened its first outlet. Kodak, Fuji and other Western film manufacturers produce 70 percent of the camera film sold in China. Revlon has a counter in the Friendship department store in Canton, where sales reach $200 a day. Finally, consumer product companies like Unilever and Coca-Cola have introduced their products to eager Chinese consumers.

Although China has opened its doors to the Western world, it is apparent that the current regime is against any major social reforms. In June of 1989, a student-led protest for political reform was crushed when the Chinese army brutally attacked and killed student demonstrators in Tiananmen Square, Beijing. One action taken by many foreign countries was to reconsider current and planned projects in China, primarily for safety and moral reasons. Western companies feared for the welfare of their employees in China, as well as for their investments.

Fluor, at that time, had ten active projects on-going in China. None of them was interrupted by the turmoil in Beijing. Since then the company has signed three new contracts with the Chinese, bringing the total to 55. The business environment for Fluor is better in 1992 than it was three years ago because the Chinese are much more flexible and eager to show that they have not turned the clock back. One problem for both Fluor and China is the difficulty the Chinese have had in securing loans to help pay for projects. The Bush Administration has not restored financing and trade relations at the government level to the position that they were prior to 1989. The United States says that it needs some positive indications from the Chinese that they are going to curb repression. After the tragedy at Tiananmen Square many companies responded in kind, taking a wait-and-see attitude with regards to China. Fortunately, by the early 1990s many foreign firms began doing business again in the world's most populous market.

Questions

1. What opportunities did Fluor see in the Chinese market?
2. What environmental factors affect Fluor's operations in China? Specifically, what are the effects of (a) cultural norms (b) business relations (c) the economic environment (d) trade regulations?

3. Would you describe Fluor's international marketing strategy as adapative, standardized, or somewhere in between? Explain.
4. What do you think were the results of the crackdown on the student movement in June 1989 on Fluor's operations in China?
5. Why are joint ventures with the Chinese government the best mode of marketing operations for Fluor in China?

References

1. "Fluor Corp.: It Banks on a Long-Term Capital Expansion for Global Economies," *Barron's*. October 21, 1991, pp. 51–52.
2. "A Long-Term Look at China," *China Business Review*, May/June 1990, pp. 52–53.
3. "Companies to Watch: Flush Times for Fluor," *Fortune*, November 6, 1989, pp. 113, 116.
4. "Transforming Fluor," *Financial World*, May 30, 1989, pp. 28–29.
5. "Laying the Foundation for the Great Mall of China, *Business Week*, January 25, 1987, pp. 68–69.
6. "The Bright Future of Service Exports," *Fortune*, June 8 1987, pp. 32–36.
7. "After the Frying Pan What?," *Forbes*, March 9, 1987, pp. 60–62.

APPLE COMPUTERS: THE BASIS FOR COMPETITIVE ADVANTAGE

CASE 6

When Steven Jobs and Steven Wozniak made the first Apple computer in 1976, they couldn't possibly have imagined that in five short years they would be heralded as the creators of the multibillion dollar PC market. As the market innovator, Apple enjoyed rapid sales growth from the late 1970s to the early 1980s. Until that time, the company maintained a technological orientation. What was lacking was a cohesive, coherent marketing effort. Apple was able to achieve dramatic success without a strong marketing effort because of limited competition. In 1981, however, IBM entered the arena and Apple quickly lost market share. By 1983, IBM had achieved such market dominance that most smaller competitors were forced to either reposition their products as IBM compatibles, or leave the market.

While IBM maintained its grip on the office market, Apple was busy formulating a marketing counterstrike. Steven Jobs soon realized that although Apple's products were technologically superior, the company lacked the marketing savvy needed to succeed in such a volatile and competitive industry. To fill the marketing void, Steven Jobs, in 1983, recruited PepsiCo's President, John Sculley, to become the President and Chief Executive Officer of Apple. In addition to bringing professional management to a firm widely publicized for its liberal, entrepreneurial culture, Sculley instituted two key changes at Apple. He brought consistency to Apple's product line, and discipline and order to the marketing efforts of the company. Most importantly, under Sculley, Apple evolved from a technology-driven to a marketing-driven organization. The emphasis was on developing a comprehensive line of compatible computers that met the needs of various niche groups.

To bring about this transformation, Sculley formulated detailed marketing strategies that effectively penetrated the desired target markets. Under his guidance, Apple changed its entire product line in 100 days, and increased its advertising budget in 1984 to $85 million. In addition, Apple developed an attention-grabbing promotional campaign to ensure widespread consumer awareness and interest. It was the combination of sound marketing and high quality, innovative products that served as a catalyst for dramatic sales growth. From industry analysis Apple learned that it could strengthen its market position by pursuing a niche strategy in the education, home-user, and desk-top publishing markets. To exploit these opportunities, it was essential that Apple differentiate itself from competitors like IBM. Sculley believed that the combination of effective advertising and personal selling would enable the firm to achieve its goal of differentiation.

Evidence of a well-coordinated marketing strategy was visible throughout all facets of the product introduction process. Advertising created awareness of Apple's PCs, primarily the Apple II and Macintosh, and prompted consumers to go to computer stores. Once consumers were in the stores, they were assisted by extremely knowledgeable sales staffs. Because Apple understood that it was up to the retail sales force to ultimately generate sales, Apple provided product dealers and their sales employees with intensive product training.

The results of Apple's well planned and coordinated marketing efforts are evidenced by the successful introduction of the Apple II and the Macintosh. Although the Apple II received excellent reviews from the press, consumers were still not convinced that such a small machine had so many capabilities. It was Apple's use of innovative advertising that helped to overcome this perception problem and enable the product to generate record sales. TV commercials illustrated the power of the Apple II.

To launch the Macintosh in 1984, Apple used a TV commercial to convey an intense, radical message, that Apple was the IBM alternative. The ad linked the Macintosh to Orwell's "1984," with IBM representing "Big Brother." The ad ran only once, during the Super Bowl, and generated enormous consumer and trade interest. The "1984" commercial was followed by a series of print ads in business magazines which focused on product benefits. The ads emphasized the ease of product usage and the computer's excellent graphics capabilities. The "1984" campaign is credited with generating $100 million in Macintosh revenues.

In addition to using a variety of advertising media to appeal to well-defined target markets, Apple employed other unconventional promotional tactics. To penetrate the education market, Apple gave away hundreds of PCs to elementary and high schools. This strategy was intended to turn current users into future customers. While Apple was utilizing a niche strategy to become the market leader in the education and home-user markets, it also executed a strategy to penetrate an IBM stronghold, the business-user market. John Sculley believed that while a niche strategy was effective for markets with no dominant competitor, it would not be an effective way to penetrate the office market. Since the office market was clearly dominated by IBM, Apple would have to employ a "back door approach" in order to enter this sector. Hence, the creation of the Macintosh Office, which served as the total solution by offering business middle-management communication linkage capabilities and IBM compatibility.

Because IBM was the market leader, it was essential for Apple to refine its marketing efforts in order to successfully launch this new product. Apple did so by redirecting its promotional efforts from advertising to personal selling and publicity. This shift in promotional emphasis was important because the new target market needed to be convinced that the Mac would provide benefits that the IBM PC did not offer.

Apple implemented its "back door approach" (as opposed to its former head-to-head approach) by appealing to "knowledge workers," those who needed a communications tool for graphics but didn't use spreadsheets every day. Apple purposely avoided systems managers who in the past criticized Apple products for being underpowered. Apple responded to the needs of business with a product that could offer current IBM users a better way. The Macintosh Office would serve as the total solution by offering communication linkage capabilities and IBM compatibility. The sales staff, in essence, sought out ordinary individuals in corporations, and touted the computer's graphics and its usefulness in desktop publishing.

By 1990, Apple's share of the $42.3 billion U.S. personal computer market had plunged to 9 percent from 15 percent three years earlier. The slide was a result, in part, of the rising price of the Macintosh. Apple's original customers, schools and small businesses, found it harder to afford new Macs. The company's promise that with a higher price would come technological advances in its products was not being fulfilled. Macintosh was rapidly losing its edge as the inexpensive, easy-to-use personal computer. To help him reverse the trend, Sculley, in early 1990, promoted Michael Spindler, previously the head of Apple Europe, to Chief Operating Officer. Spindler and Sculley decided that the best short-term strategy to bolster sales was to introduce new Macs with lower price tags and more advanced software, and cut prices on older models. The new Mac Classic, for example, was priced at $999.

Besides dropping prices on its products, Apple made a few other changes to bring back its competitive edge. With Spindler's guidance, the company cut costs by tightening budgets and minimizing lavish spending. Marketing planning also became more disciplined. Planning time tables start months earlier now and checking and crosschecking have become the norm.

Apple has also made efforts to patch up relations with dealers who complained about Apple's lackluster promotional efforts and direct selling activities. In 1991 the company began funneling its corporate sales through its local retailers, a move which gives the retailers more credibility with customers. Further, in an effort to better understand the needs of a core user group, educational institutions, the company began surveying schools and colleges to see what they wanted in new software and hardware. Employees are literally dispatched on "camping trips" to universities to pick the brains of students and faculty.

To guarantee long-term growth, Apple is investing heavily in two projects that are part of a permanent revival. One project, called Jaguar, will include extensive video technology and the ability to connect to TVs and VCRs. The second project is a computer that can deal with handwritten information, eliminating the need for keyboards and a mouse.

In what has been called a "180 degree turn in corporate policy," Apple has also begun working directly with outside suppliers and competitors. A new laptop, for example, is being built by a Japanese subcontractor. In late March, 1992, Apple announced a joint venture with the Sharp Corporation. The two firms will develop a computerized electronics product used mainly to store personal information. Apple is also working with the Sony Corporation.

Perhaps the biggest surprise came in 1991. In July of that year, Apple and IBM announced plans to form an alliance that would result in a multitude of cross-licenses, an agreement to launch 2 jointly owned companies, and provisions for sharing facilities and employees. The alliance will have a profound impact on the future direction of personal computing. The joint venture will enable Apple to introduce future versions of Macintosh computers with IBM machines, effectively breaking down the barriers of the corporate marketplace for Apple. IBM, in turn, will benefit from Apple's expertise in proprietary software. The first products to emerge from this alliance will be available to consumers sometime in 1993.

Questions

1. What are Apple's competitive advantages relative to IBM? What are the implications of these advantages for long term growth?
2. In what way did John Sculley change Apple's direction? How did these changes enable Apple to more effectively compete with IBM?
3. What strategy or strategies is Apple using to compete with IBM—head-to-head, flanking, encirclement, follow-the-leader, market niche, bypassing the competition? Explain.
4. How is Apple competing with IBM in the business market? Specifically, what was the "backdoor" strategy? How did Apple use it?

References

1. Deidre Depke, "IBM-Apple Could Be Fearsome," *Business Week*, October 7, 1991, pp. 28–30.
2. Kristi Coale, "Redrawing the Map: Will the IBM/Apple Alliance Shift the Balance of Power?," *Infoworld*, July 22, 1991, pp. 44–46.
3. Barbara Buell, "Apple: New Team, New Strategy," *Business Week*, October 15, 1990, pp. 86–93.
4. Thomas J. Murray, "Special Report: Apple Computer, the New Wave," *Business Month*, December 1988, p. 30.
5. Katherine M. Haffner, "Apple Goes for a Bigger Bite of Corporate America," *Business Week*, August 24, 1987, pp. 74–75.
6. Apple Computer, Inc., 1987 Annual Report.
7. Brenton R. Schender, "Apple Aiming to Revive Growth," *The Wall Street Journal*, June 4, 1986, p. 6.

THE DISNEY CHANNEL: A CASE STUDY IN MARKETING RESEARCH

The Walt Disney Company is one of the best known and well loved American corporations. Its brand names—Mickey Mouse, Donald Duck, Goofy, Bambi, and so forth—are familiar to children around the world. Yet Disney no longer relies solely on cartoon characters and family oriented feature films, such as the 1991 release *Beauty and the Beast*, for its revenues. Disney theme parks, such as the new MGM studio at Orlando's Disney World and the recently opened EuroDisney in France, are accounting for a larger percentage of Disney's profits.

Disney has also entered the retail sector with stores in shopping malls all across America. Touchstone Films, Disney's outlet for movies targeted to adults, is turning out one hit after another. Movies released under the Touchstone label usually star well known comedians such as Bette Midler and Steve Martin, two individuals who don't exactly fit Disney's squeaky clean image. In short, there are many changes taking place at Disney.

Another one of Disney's successes has been its foray into cable TV. The Disney Channel went on the air in April of 1983. Originally, it relied solely on old Disney movies for programming material. After a poor showing, Disney realized that old movies weren't sufficient to attract and maintain viewers in the increasingly competitive premium channel segment of the cable television industry. Disney recognized the need for original programming; the decision was whether to stick with the themes of Disney movies—directed primarily to children—or broaden the programming to attract a wider audience.

Before answering this vital question, Disney needed to conduct primary marketing research. Secondary research was not considered because of the uniqueness of the Disney product and the lack of past data. In 1987, the company employed the research firm ASI to determine what current and potential customers wanted and expected from the Disney Channel.

The first part of the research study involved a phone survey of current subscribers. The survey would provide Disney with quantitative data regarding its target market. It would also give the company an idea of who is watching, who might watch and why. ASI relied on a WATS line to minimize cost and ensure that the survey results were obtained quickly. Respondents were asked questions about what they thought the Disney Channel should be. The overwhelming response was that the channel should be family oriented and not a channel just for children. Armed with this information, the Disney Channel decided to differentiate itself from Nickelodeon, which is mainly geared toward kids.

Through its survey research, Disney also found out about the demographic characteristics of its viewers. Surprisingly, a full 33 percent of Disney subscribers do not have children under 12. By comparison, three years earlier (1984), 25 percent of subscribers did not have children under 12. Thirty-five percent are over the age of 40, up from 27 percent in 1984.

From the same research, Disney also determined the level of satisfaction among its subscribers. Viewers felt that Disney was giving them what they wanted. For example, 94 percent of the people surveyed said that the Disney Channel is as good as they expected it to be, or better. Over 96 percent said that they would continue their subscriptions for at least another six months. A separate survey conducted in 1991 confirmed these findings. Among the pay services, the Disney Channel was rated the highest by respondents in terms of differentiation of programming from other pay services and the overall appeal of programming to subscribers.

Disney managers also wanted to gather qualitative information. They chose to use focus groups to get an idea of what consumers view and how they feel about the Disney Channel. Disney marketers gave ASI information about whom to include in the group and what types of issues to discuss. ASI also used a research method call Preview House, which is a theater setting where participants can view unreleased movies, commercials and TV pilots. Responses are typically given by adjusting dials attached to one's chair. The drawback of this research tool is that the setting is unnatural, therefore the results are not always realistic. ASI also relies upon cable TV for its research. Programming is transmitted to specific homes over vacant cable TV channels. After the show has ended, the telephone operator calls the consumer and asks specific questions about what they have just seen. The advantage of this type of research is that the setting is more familiar so the responses will more accurately reflect the respondents true opinions.

Marketers at the Disney Channel used marketing research to help plan programming as well. One example involves Disney's 1987 introduction of 24-hour broadcasting. Previously, Disney had been broadcasting from 6 a.m. to 1:30 a.m., seven days a week. When it talked to non-subscribers, Disney found that many of them did not work regular daytime hours. In fact, 16 percent of the American labor force works outside of the traditional 9 to 5 time slot. Disney found that 24-hour programming increased the appeal of the Disney Channel. About one-third of cable households that were contemplating adding the Channel said that 24-hour programming would increase the likelihood that they would subscribe. Disney discovered that current consumers would also like to have 24-hour programming. So in 1987, service hours were extended to meet the needs of both current and potential customers.

The Disney Channel uses a form of in-house research to keep track of its customers. The Disney Channel appeals largely to young families who tend to move around a lot. Because of the transient nature of these customers, Disney has a difficult time knowing whether they reorder the channel each time they move. Marketers at Disney use the *Disney Channel Magazine* to help solve this problem. The *Disney Channel Magazine* is a bimonthly publication which, among other things, lists the programming for the channel. It is distributed to 3.5 million channel subscribers. As a result, Disney knows when a customer moves.

Disney can use this information in several ways. For example, it can find out where the subscriber has moved to, and send the household a direct mail packet welcoming them to their new home and reminding them to have the Disney Channel hooked up again. Also, Disney can send the new residents at the old address a direct mail piece describing the benefits of having the Disney Channel.

Disney offers its subscribers 35 percent original programming, the highest of any premium cable channel. Original programming has enabled Disney to achieve a level of flexibility its competitors can't match because competitors must rely on film studios for much of the product they buy. The Disney Channel has, in turn, been highly successful, growing from 3 million subscribers in 1987 to 6.3 million in late 1991. This in an industry which has been in a slump for the past two to three years. HBO lost 300,000 subscribers in 1991, Disney gained 700,000. Much of Disney's success in the 1990s is due to its strategy of gearing its daytime programming to kids, teens and families, and its nighttime programming to adults. During the day Disney airs shows such as *Teen Win Lose or Draw*, *Danger Bay*, and *Kids Incorporated.* At night the channel targets older viewers with specials such as a series titled *Frank Sinatra: A Man and His Music*, which aired in 1991.

Disney has also intensified its marketing efforts during the recent economic downturn. "I don't believe in *not* marketing during a recession," says Disney Channel President John Cooke. Disney has found that the most effective way of demonstrating to nonsubscribers that the Disney Channel runs more than just cartoons is to offer free previews. The overwhelming majority of Disney's subscribers are those who have watched at least two previews. Disney increased its previews in 1992 while other pay services limited them.

According to Disney, one of the company's major hurdles had been getting independent cable operators to lower the price of the Disney Channel to subscribers. While the channel is priced as high as $13 a month in some areas of the country, Disney has maintained a discount pricing strategy that gets many cable operators to lower the channel's price to the $4 to $7 range. According to the cable operators Disney continues to push the envelope on devising new ways to add customers and maximize revenues.

Disney, however, is not alone in its efforts to attempt new marketing strategies. The recession of the early 1990s, the threat of increased regulation and the growing penetration of the VCR has forced many cable networks to offer premiums and rebates to keep and possibly gain new subscribers. Cable networks are increasingly turning to paid advertising as a further means of raising revenues to offset a sluggish market.

In June 1991, John Cooke delivered a speech to the Washington Metropolitan Cable Club urging operators and programmers to be less preoccupied with strategy and competition. Cooke's advice to the cable industry: "Think about the consumer." For the folks at the Disney Channel, learning more about the consumer has always been a top priority. Marketing research plays an integral role in Disney's ongoing quest to better understand what current and potential customers want from the Disney Channel.

Questions

1. Did Disney rely primarily on primary or secondary research in investigating the Disney Channel? Why?
2. Why was survey research conducted for the Disney Channel? How was the survey conducted?
3. Why was qualitative research used? How was it conducted?
4. How does ASI test the appeal of programs for the Disney Channel?
5. What were the objectives in conducting marketing research on the Disney Channel?
6. Did the Disney Channel follow the steps outlined in Figure 7.5 in meeting its research objectives?

References

1. "Pay TV Sees Subscriber Slump Continue into 1991," *Electronic Media*, March 16, 1991, p. 3.
2. "Operators Praise Disney's Flexible Strategy," *Multichannel News*, April 15, 1991, p. 1
3. "Disney Racks Up Subscribers with Previews," *Electronic Media*, March 25, 1991, p. 95.
4. "Programmers, An Open Door for Marketing," *Channels: the Business of Communications*, December 3, 1990, p. 46.
5. *Advertising Age*, September 24, 1987, p. 86.
6. "Disney's Magic, A Turnaround Proves Wishes Can Come True," *Business Week*, March 9, 1987, pp. 62–65.
7. "Disney's Marketing Touch," *Direct Marketing*, January 1987, pp. 50–53.

KAWASAKI: A CASE STUDY IN UNDERSTANDING CONSUMER BEHAVIOR

CASE 8

Motorcycles were first developed at the turn of the century and caught on fast because they were exotic and affordable. In 1910 there were over 100 American motorcycle companies, including Harley Davidson. The appearance of the $500 Model-T Ford in 1913 devastated the industry. Motorcycles made a comeback in the early 1970s with the arrival of peppy, inexpensive, and less complicated bikes from Japan. In 1973 sales in the United States peaked at 1.5 million. But the boom soon faded. In 1990 U.S. sales totaled only 260,000.

For Kawasaki, the fourth largest Japanese manufacturer of motorcycles, the good times stopped rolling in the mid-seventies. Lower economic growth, greater price competition and a maturing of the motorcycle market led to dwindling sales in the United States. Increased government scrutiny of motorcycle safety didn't help bike makers either.

To broaden the market, Japanese motorcycle manufacturers decided to focus on a consumer segment that only a few years before seemed an unlikely target, namely baby boomers. By the late 1980s a growing number of white collar motorcyclists, mainly 45–54 years old, were taking to the streets. Kawasaki asked its advertising agency, Kenyon & Eckhardt, to create a new print campaign that would help motivate the consumer to purchase Kawasaki motorcycles while breaking through the advertising clutter that is so prevalent today. The new campaign was intended to appeal to *all* motorcycle consumers. The difficulty is that Kawasaki marketed two types of motorcycles, a sport model and a custom model. Each appealed to a very different type of consumer. Bike riders include blue collar workers and white collar professionals, and each has a very different lifestyle. In developing an ad campaign, the agency had to be careful to avoid alienating either market segment.

To accomplish this task, Kawasaki's account supervisor Peter Goodwin decided to ask psychologist Renee Fraser, also Kenyon & Eckhardt's research director, to help him gather the information needed for the new campaign. Goodwin understood that the more he knew about the attraction of motorcycles, the more effective the advertising would be at motivating consumers to buy Kawasaki.

Information about motorcycle riders would enable the agency's creative team to determine what motivated these consumers to buy and therefore what images should be emphasized in the advertising. According to senior art director Ron Hicks, information about the consumer helped him to "push the right buttons." "Pushing the right buttons" meant both satisfying motorcycle rider's needs and reassuring current owners that they had made the right purchase decision. The "reassurance" aspect was intended to address cognitive dissonance, which is the post-purchase doubt that consumers experience after making a major purchase.

Renee Fraser learned a great deal about the motorcycle market. She began by checking available databases, which produced considerable demographic information, such as age, sex, income, education, and so forth. While the information was helpful in determining who the average motorcycle rider was, the data provided few clues as to why these people actually rode motorcycles. What was their motivation? What did bike riding offer them?

To answer these questions, Fraser conducted primary research including in-depth interviews, focus groups and field research. Fraser spoke with numerous motorcycle owners. Whether a blue collar worker, doctor, lawyer or engineer, each bike owner expressed a genuine enthusiasm for motorcycles. Fraser concluded that the stereotypical motorcycle owner, a leather jacketed easy rider, was becoming more the exception than the rule.

Fraser also concluded that while motorcycle consumers are a diverse group, they share common traits. Among these are a feeling of independence, the need to be in control and a sense of power and freedom. These people also loved being outdoors . . . in touch with nature and the elements. They enjoyed the thrill and speed of riding and the risks involved. Phrases such as "lone cowboy" and "pioneer" revealed how motorcycle enthusiasts viewed themselves and what motivated them to ride. Fraser commented that "it was almost as if there was a relationship between them and the bike." Riders closely identified themselves with their motorcycles much like cowboys identified with their horses over 100 years ago.

As Fraser assimilated all the available data and began to share it with Kenyon & Eckhardt's account and creative teams, she made additional observations. Fraser noted that motorcycle riders seemed to have an alter-ego. "It's almost like they take off their clothes and they are Superman underneath," said Fraser. It was also surprising, Fraser noted, that motorcycle performance rarely came up during discussions. Most motorcycle riders were concerned with how the bike looked, how they looked to others when riding, and how riding the bike made them feel.

Fraser's research helped the agency identify the psychological needs and values of motorcycle consumers. These needs and values cut across demographic descriptions and are important in determining why consumers purchase. Kenyon & Eckhardt's objective was to develop a campaign that would convince potential users that Kawasaki motorcycles would *best* fulfill their needs.

After gathering all relevant information, the agency developed an ad campaign that was consistent with Fraser's research. The print ad showed a lone motorcycle rider rounding a bend on a deserted country road. The rider is leaning to one side, with his knee almost touching the ground. The position captured the thrill of riding and was mentioned frequently by motorcycle riders in interviews conducted by Fraser. Speed, danger, and contact with the elements were all suggested in the ad. The print ad also instilled a positive image of motorcycle riders and Kawasaki bikes.

The agency's primary goal was to ensure that the ad did indeed cut across demographic boundaries and address the psychological needs common to all motorcycle riders. Hence both the custom and sport models could be advertised simultaneously without alienating any user group. If the agency was successful, the ad would break through the clutter because it "pushed the right buttons" and spoke directly to motorcycle consumers. Therefore, the right people would notice the ad and would receive the right message from the projected image. Ultimately, this was the purpose of the research; to provide information about consumer behavior in order to develop more effective marketing and advertising strategies.

Kawasaki coupled its positioning with a wise pricing strategy. While companies such as Honda were charging the upscale market a premium for the latest technology, Kawasaki held the line on price rises. Consumers flocked to Kawasaki as a result. In 1990, the company sold 400,000 motorcycles in the United States alone.

In the 1990s the market for motorcycles appears promising. Increased traffic jams, rising fuel costs and pollution concerns are all working in Kawasaki's favor. Sales figures reflect these environmental changes. Imports of motorcycles increased for the first time since 1988, up 13.4 percent in 1991. However, U.S. consumers are not as attracted to motorcycles as they were a decade ago. In 1980, 5.6 million motorcycles were registered in the United States. That figure dropped steadily to 4.1 million in 1990. For the first six months of 1991, registration was down 6.6 percent. Nonetheless, sales of motorcycles from Japan and Taiwan are on the rise, up an expected 7.1 percent in 1992. Consumer tastes are changing as well. Small to mid-sized bikes that were popular in the 1980s have lost ground to heavier, more expensive bikes like those sold by Harley Davidson.

The long-term prospects for Kawasaki appear bright. Because of the declining rate of motorcycle accidents, consumer's perception of bikes is improving. Also the heavy spending 45–54 age group will be the fastest growing in the United States until 1996. By marketing motorcycles that appeal to the baby boom generation Kawasaki is on its way to rolling in the good times once again.

Questions

1. What needs does motorcycle riding satisfy? Did Kawasaki appeal to these needs? How?
2. How did the advertising agency, Kenyon & Eckhardt, position Kawasaki? Was this positioning directed to the needs of motorcycle owners? Why or why not?
3. What type of decision making do you think consumers engage in when buying a motorcycle? Why?
4. What type of dissonance might occur when someone buys a Kawasaki? What is the role of advertising in overcoming such dissonance?

References

1. "Misty Eyed over Motorcycles," *Business Week*, October 21, 1991, p. 47.
2. "Playing Chicken with the Japanese," *Business Week*, July 1, 1991, p. 68.
3. "That vroom you Hear is Honda Motorcycles," *Business Week*, September 3, 1990, pp. 74, 76.
4. U.S. Industrial Outlook 1992—Personal Consumer Durables.

CASE 9

SKYFOX: THE NATURE OF INDUSTRIAL MARKETS

Most people don't realize that the majority of the buying and selling done in the United States occurs between one corporation and another, not from manufacturers to final consumer. Companies have special purchasing departments and buying groups that handle business-to-business transactions.

Governments are large purchasers of a variety of goods and services. Military expenditures comprise a large part of a government's budget. Each year nearly $300 billion is spent on defense worldwide. During the 1990s, 7,000 fighter jets alone will be produced. Yet the market is shrinking. After 10 years of almost 4 percent annual increases, led by a massive military buildup by the United States and the former Soviet Union, the world's arms makers face a global contraction in spending of at least 2 percent to 5 percent annually. Since 1985, U.S. spending on the military has dropped 15 percent. The end of the Cold War and a weakened world economy have prompted many governments, including Washington, to curtail spending. In 1982, developing countries spent $61 billion on military hardware. By 1990 that figure had dropped to $41 billion. Experts expect the decline to continue.

Each year, government buyers and military officers from around the world congregate at the Paris Air Show to view the latest aircraft, meet company sales representatives and make purchase decisions. Today, new military aircraft such as the stealthy ATF can cost upwards of $80 million apiece. Additional millions are invested in pilot training, spare parts, and maintenance training for ground personnel.

Because many third world countries simply can't afford the price of today's jet fighters, the prospect of building a sizable air force is quite discouraging. The problem of financing is often coupled with the reality that pilot training can take up to ten years. By the time third-world pilots learned to fly the aircraft, the planes will be outdated.

Several years ago the United States offered Kenya 10 advanced fighter planes to help update its air force. But, it was determined that to train the entire Kenyan air force how to fly and maintain the aircraft would take five years or more. Most developing nations don't see the practicality of purchasing military hardware that require such lengthy training periods.

Russell O'Quinn is a former test pilot who became aware of the military aircraft problem facing third world nations while working for the United Nations. O'Quinn was heading up food airlifts to several famine-plagued areas in Africa when he noticed that these nations had neither the money to purchase expensive jets, nor the airfields or personnel to maintain the planes. What these countries needed, O'Quinn determined, was a realiable jet that was easier to operate than the standard fighter, yet performed on a par with present generation jet trainers, despite lower technology.

O'Quinn immediately thought of the old Lockheed T-33, a standard in jet training aircraft. The T-33's lifespan was virtually unlimited, it was easily maintained and its worldwide reputation was built on reliability. There were actually about 1,100 T-33's still in use. O'Quinn decided that he would redesign and upgrade the T-33 to offer developing nations with limited defense budgets a sophisticated jet trainer at an affordable price.

The new plane O'Quinn developed was named Skyfox. He set up a firm, Skyfox Corporation, to produce and sell the aircraft. O'Quinn financed the construction of the prototype through private funding. The new aircraft, while sharing a 70 percent common structure with the T-33, had a new, sleek aerodynamic design. The T-33's single turbojet was replaced by two externally mounted Garrett TFE-731-3 turbofan engines. This modification resulted in the Skyfox having 60 percent more thrust, better fuel efficiency, and a longer range, resulting from the external placement of the engines. Additionally, the Skyfox cockpit was upgraded to include new Stencil MK3 ejection seats, Canadian Marconi fiber optics instruments and off-the-shelf Collins avionics.

Although O'Quinn was convinced that he had a superb product, selling the Skyfox proved more difficult than designing it. He realized that acceptance of new products by government bureaucracies, especially products costing over $3 million, was not easy. Yet, O'Quinn maintained that the Skyfox was not a completely new product; it was a modification of a well established aircraft, the T-33.

Business consultant Ken Goldsmith, who was familiar with the Skyfox project, pinpointed obstacles O'Quinn would have to overcome in order to successfully market the aircraft abroad. For one, numerous difficulties arise when dealing with foreign government bureaucracies. Numerous individuals are involved in the decision making process, negotiations are often held confidentially and the haggling can be extremely time consuming. Additionally, foreign governments often require that part of the production process take place in the customer's country. This helps retain currency, boost employment and form an industrial base within the developing nation.

After the Skyfox prototype was tested, there was a tremendous amount of publicity generated in both trade and non-trade publications. The attention was due largely to the unique nature of the project. O'Quinn, however, was unable to turn any of this publicity into sales. The only country that showed interest in the Skyfox was Portugal.

O'Quinn began to search for a large firm to buy Skyfox and invest in much needed capital and marketing clout. In 1985, O'Quinn entered into a licensing deal with Boeing, which permitted Boeing to purchase the technology necessary to produce and market the Skyfox. Skyfox Corporation would, in turn, receive monetary compensation. Boeing management felt that the Skyfox could be sold as a multipurpose aircraft, capable of reconnaissance, maritime patrols, electronic simulation and target towing, in addition to its original purpose as a jet fighter.

Boeing also believed that O'Quinn had been correct in his original evaluation of the Skyfox, and that the modifications made to existing T-33s were a cost effective way of extending the aircraft's life by about 20 years. They chose to market the Skyfox as a conversion kit which sold for $3.35 million. The customer could perform the conversion or have Boeing do it for an additional fee.

Boeing marketed the Skyfox by transporting the plane to various airshows and performing demonstration flights for interested customers. By mid-1986, Canada, South Korea, Greece, and Portugal expressed an interest in the Skyfox. The U.S. Air Force/Air National Guard showed interest, and in June of 1989 Boeing submitted a bid to the U.S. Airforce/Navy Primary Aircraft Training Program. Actual orders for Skyfox have not yet materialized. Boeing's official position is that it is still evaluating the project. Skyfox illustrates the difficulties of breaking into the institutional marketplace, even with strong marketing support.

Not surprisingly, shrinking military budgets have prompted many countries to simply upgrade their current fighters to avoid purchasing new ones. Because the air bases of many nations are clogged with military antiques from the 1950s and 1960s, governments are choosing to install computer driven radar and improve weapons in older planes. Nine nations, including Canada, Brazil, Italy, China, and North Korea are revamping their old aircraft. Two companies, LTV in the United States and Smith's Industries in Great Britain, are in the upgrade business as well. In 1991, LTV upgraded Norway's fleet of 15 F-5 fighters at a cost of $2.5 million per plane; nearly $1 million less than the cost of a Skyfox. In short, Skyfox Corporation has plenty of competition.

Jet fighter upgrading poses a new major worry for arms controllers who now have a harder time determining the true air power of third world countries. Most upgrades, which are kept quiet, are not visible from the plane's exterior. This is likely to add a new measure of uncertainty and tension in some international hot spots. Still, in a world arms market that is shrinking fast, upgrading is the only option. It gives countries a substantial boost in air power at a fraction of the cost of buying a new plane. With thousands of older planes just waiting to be upgraded, supply will surely keep up with demand.

Questions

1. The chapter lists a number of characteristics of industrial products. Do these apply to the Skyfox? In what ways?
2. What type of decision process is involved in a decision to buy the Skyfox? Why?
3. What needs is Skyfox meeting? What target does it appeal to?
4. Which criteria in Table 9.3 would be most important to an organizational buyer in the decision to buy the Skyfox? Why?
5. What problems does the company face in introducing the Skyfox that are not typical in introducing consumer goods?

References

1. "Old Warplanes Get Brand New Electronics, Live to Fight Again," *The Wall Street Journal*, September 19, 1991, pp. A1, A8.
2. "As Cold War Ends, Arms Business Finds New Buyers in the Third World," *The Wall Street Journal*, September 19, 1991, p. A8.
3. "Showdown," *Financial World*, September 19, 1989, pp. 62–76.
4. "Aircraft at LeBourget Geared Toward USAF/Navy Buy," *Jet Trainer Aircraft*, June 26, 1989, pp. 67, 71.
5. "Boeing Markets New Acquired Skyfox Twin-Engine Jet Trainer," *Aviation Week and Space Technology*, August 11, 1986, pp. 54–55.
6. "Skyfox Seeks Merger to Fund Production of Jet Trainer Aircraft," *Aviation Week and Space Technology*, January 21, 1989, p. 21.
7. "Skyfox Updates T-33 Trainer Effectively," *Aviation Week and Space Technology*, March 8, 1984, pp. 39, 42, 44, 46.

THE IRVINE COMPANY: THE MEANING OF MARKET SEGMENTATION

CASE 10

Spanning 90,000 acres, the original Irvine Ranch represented some of the most fertile agricultural land in the nation. The land was purchased by James Irvine and his partners in the 1860s for 35 cents an acre. The tract is located south of Los Angeles and runs 22 miles northward along the Pacific Ocean. Today, the original ranch acreage includes the city of Irvine and affluent Newport Beach in Orange County.

Historically, Irvine Ranch was operated as a farm and a ranch. However, in the 1950s the city of Los Angeles began to slowly creep southward, ultimately reaching the northern boundaries of the Irvine property. Orange County became one of the fastest growing suburbs of the United States and as a result, Irvine property was worth more for housing purposes than for agriculture. The Irvine Company wisely decided to enter the housing development business.

Following World War II, there was a mass movement of people to the suburbs, leading to growth without a sense of community structure. What was missing was what Irvine referred to as the "New Town" concept. Since the 1950's, Irvine Company has developed housing communities using this "New Town" concept. This concept was not based on planning homes, but entire communities, including shopping centers, schools, and recreational areas. East Bluff was one of the first neighborhoods Irvine built. Its physical boundaries determined its size and design, but the layout of the development promoted a sense of community. Everyone shared the same schools, shopping center, and recreational facilities.

The Irvine Company pioneered a strategy of market segmentation in the housing industry. In the past, builders treated prospective home buyers as if they had identical needs. Differentiation was limited to the number of bedrooms or the size of the home. Irvine reasoned that families have varying life-cycles which are characterized by different housing needs. As developers, Irvine was prepared to meet the needs of its prospective buyers.

Irvine began by analyzing the housing market and attempting to segment it into separate groups based on needs. Initially, Irvine's management attempted to segment the market based upon consumer life-style. Irvine later realized that while it had accumulated a lot of information about consumers, none of it could be related to housing preferences. Irvine then began to interview consumers in depth, which enabled it to gather demographic data as well as promote its public relations effort.

This demographic data served as the basis for segmenting the market and designing homes which would appeal to several types of buyers. Segmentation also served as the central concept of the planned community. Since Irvine understood that families would prefer to live with families, older people with older people, communities are being designed so that neighbors share similar demographic characteristics.

Woodbridge is one such community. It was built in the late 1980s with a specific target segment in mind, affluent baby boomers. The success or failure of this project will determine the future direction of other marketing efforts. Homes in Woodridge cost between $80,000 and $150,000; however some are priced as high as $300,000.

Market segmentation was the focus of both Irvine's marketing effort and its concept of community. By adopting a segmentation strategy, Irvine was able to meet both its social and marketing goals. Builders designed homes which appealed to the specific needs of given segments. Irvine offered standard one, two and three bedroom houses, but also offered a triplex plan, which enabled first-time buyers to purchase a home that was both affordable and spacious. Irvine also built non-related adult housing, with two separate master bedrooms.

The home development business proceeded smoothly for Irvine until the late 1970s, when rising inflation and a population shift in the United States toward the Sunbelt states, created a tremendous demand for housing in Orange County. Supply couldn't keep up with demand, and home prices rose 25 to 30 percent. Many consumers were priced out of the market, as salaries did not keep pace with housing costs. Additionally, mortgage rates went as high as 20 percent, reflecting a restrictive monetary policy implemented to deal with high inflation.

During this time, some of the houses were sold by lottery, and still others were purchased by speculators. The end result was that many homes remained empty because the consumers in Irvine's target market could not afford these houses. In short, the segmentation strategy that Irvine had perfected, proved totally useless. This unfortunate housing trend ultimately affected Orange County's industrial development as well, since people tend not to work where they cannot afford to live.

The housing boom, high inflation, and interest rates began to stabilize by the mid-eighties. Once again, salaries and housing prices began to resemble more normal conditions. At this time, Irvine was able to return to its segmentation strategy and to its ideas of community development. Irvine refined its strategy even more by encouraging families to remain within the community throughout their lives by purchasing an Irvine home when their needs changed.

Irvine's segmentation strategy would prove effective only until the end of the decade. In the early 1990s, the real estate market in California collapsed as a result of the most severe recession to hit that state since the 1930s. California's housing market began to recover, however, in February 1992. Sales of single-family homes rose 13 percent in that month, the sharpest one-month gain since December 1986.

The Irvine Company is currently developing land at the rate of 700 acres per year. Not surprisingly, the company has recently run into problems with Orange County residents who are resisting further development of the land. However, Irvine is continuing with several new projects. Among them is a joint venture with another developer to turn a 75-acre site into a regional shopping center. The center will offer 750,000 square feet of retail space, and will actually comprise three different centers, each with a unique merchandising theme.

Questions

1. In what way is the Irvine Company different from most other home builders?
2. Where does Irvine fall on the continuum from customized to mass marketing in Figure 10.1?
3. Why are demographics the main criteria for segmenting Irvine's markets? How do consumer needs in housing differ by demographic groups?
4. The chapter cites five criteria in selecting a segment for marketing effort: (1) similarity in customer needs, (2) Failure of competitors to meet these needs, (3) good growth potential, (4) adequate size, and (5) accessability to marketing efforts. Do each of these criteria apply to Irvine's market segments?
5. Why did market segmentation lose its relevance to Irvine in the late 1970s? What dilemma did Irvine face at that point?

References

1. "First Rays of Light in California Economy," *The Christian Science Monitor*, March 27, 1992, p. 3.
2. "Tustin Market Place Blends Three Concepts," *Chain Store Age*, May 1989, pp. 166, 168.
3. "Architects Bring Malls Up to Date," *Chain Store Age*, November 1988, pp. 8A, 10A.
4. "Owning Irvine California Isn't What It Used to Be," *Business Week*, March 9, 1987, pp. 80, 82.
5. "The Land Coup in Orange County," *Fortune*, November 14, 1983, pp. 91–92, 96, 100, 102.

BREW HA! HA!: DEVELOPING NEW PRODUCTS–SAMUEL ADAMS BOSTON LAGER

CASE 11

Samuel Adams is quite simply the best lager brewed in America. Who makes this heady claim? Well, founder Jim Koch (pronounced "cook") does for one. So do over 5,000 beer enthusiasts who judged Sam Adams number one at the Annual Great American Beer Festival—four times since its introduction in 1985. Sam Adams is a European-style lager brewed in small batches—known as "craft" or "microbrewing"—and it is challenging powerful German import beers such as Beck's, St. Pauli Girl and Heineken. How Jim Koch took his business consulting experience and a 100-year-old family recipe to launch a regional, superpremium brand of beer is an exceptional new product success story, featuring skilled product positioning and a "David and Goliath" publicity campaign.

Seven years ago, at the age of 37, Koch quit a $250,000-a-year management consulting job to realize a long-held dream. In 1984 he took personal savings of $100,000 and raised $300,000 from friends and family to launch his new business, the Boston Beer Company. He leased facilities from a Pittsburgh brewery with excess capacity to produce Samuel Adams Boston Lager. After a mere two months of brewing, Koch's suds made a big splash in beer circles by winning first place at the 1985 Great American Beer Festival in Denver!

Today, the Boston Beer Company is the 14th biggest brewery in the United States. While still infinitesimal compared to giants like Anheuser-Busch, Coors, and Miller, the company now sells 2.3 million cases of its unique lager a year. Sales have increased steadily at a rate of over 40 percent annually. Sam Adams is the largest regional craft brewery in the country, and has virtually led the rebirth of the microbrewing industry. When Sam Adams was first introduced in April 1985 only a handful of craft breweries existed. Today 175 are thriving.

The force behind Sam Adams is Jim Koch and he comes from a family of brewers—five generations worth. His father was a brewmaster for several breweries in Cincinnati. His great-great-grandfather once owned a tiny brewery in St. Louis that operated under the shadow of Anheuser-Busch. In 1985, Koch retrieved his great-great-grandfather's recipe from the family attic. The recipe, developed in the mid-1800s, was for an amber colored, thick and spicy lager. This was ideal for Koch's goal to produce a connoisseur's beer with a new twist—a strong American identity.

Koch's analysis of the business he was entering was crucial. Forty-five years ago there were over 600 breweries in the United States. Today there are fewer than 85. Consolidation has been the single most important dynamic in the industry.

Big, powerful breweries bought up the smaller regional producers to gain sales volume and control over market share. In 1985, the industry was so concentrated that the top five brewers had over 94 percent of the U.S. market share. The top three firms—Anheuser-Busch, Miller Brewing, and Coors—alone controlled 80 percent of the market.

Entering the beer market during the eighties was indeed very risky, but Koch had researched the environment and was able to recognize a unique opportunity. He also knew that the failure rate for new microbreweries was more than 40 percent. At the same time he noticed that American beer drinkers, including Yuppies and upscale baby-boomers were increasingly attracted to sophisticated alternatives to the predominantly light and paler American beers. In 1970, imported beer was a negligible part of the U.S. beer consumption, accounting for less than 1 percent of the market. By 1987 their market share had soared to nearly 5 percent.

Koch was convinced that he had spotted a gap in the market, marked by an emerging set of customers with different tastes in beer. What was clearly missing, as Koch saw it, was a great American beer with Old World taste. Given Boston Brewing Company's small size, Koch's strategy was to turn a disadvantage into a competitive advantage in a small, but growing corner of the beer market.

A "craft" beer, Sam Adams was not about to crack the top 10, led by Anheuser-Busch's 72-million barrel production capacity and deep pockets. Sam Adams' first full year's production was only 23,000 barrels. As Koch noted, his sales volume of 6,000 cases a month, represented less than a *minute* of production at Anheuser-Busch. The Boston Brewing company was a start-up without the resources and experience for a national roll-out. Koch instead focused on some very special attributes that made Sam Adams a unique product. They became key parts of Koch's marketing plan.

Koch decided to build awareness of Sam Adams beer by emphasizing that it was fresh and well-brewed. Koch's special lager was brewed with only four ingredients, water, yeast, malt and hops, just like the best German beers. Koch held numerous taste tests at popular Boston nightspots, and won. Koch was also aware that he needed to focus his marketing efforts on a single region. Sam Adams is brewed without stabilizers and cannot withstand the rigors of long distance shipping, so Koch decided to distribute his beer primarily through popular local bars and restaurants. He was very careful not to expand distribution to other cities until Sam Adams' reputation was firmly established.

Koch's lager was priced slightly higher than the leading imported Dutch and German beers. This was also part of Koch's plan to distinguish his newcomer in beer market. At $20 to $25 dollars a case Sam Adams was usually a dollar more than imports and almost double the price of leading domestic brands. This price reinforced the premium image that Koch wanted to convey. Sam Adams was pricey, but it had prestige and cachet and was unique.

To complete his marketing plan, Koch used a brash advertising campaign featuring the slogan, "When we asked for Europe's tired and poor, we didn't mean their beer." Calling it "guerrilla" marketing, he gained notoriety by carefully orchestrating a public brawl. Koch claimed that the products Heineken and Beck's sold in the United States were brewed strictly for export. He also claimed that they contained ingredients called adjuncts that bar them from being sold in Germany under that country's strict "purity" laws.

Koch soon had Sam Adams approved for sale under these same purity laws, making it the first and only American beer to be sold in Germany. By provoking larger competitors like Heineken to defend their reputation Koch popularized his own brand, which generated sales. Taking a cue from the revolutionary patriot on its label, Koch even lobbied and succeeded having the White House place an order. Sam Adams became the only craft beer to be served at White House receptions and aboard Airforce One.

By 1987, Koch was already preparing to expand. Just two years after its introduction, the Boston Beer Company had turned a profit on revenues of $5 million and was in the black. Sam Adams and company were now able to begin raising the funds necessary to build their own brewery. In 1988, the Boston Beer Company finally got its address right. That year an $8 million rehabilitation of a landmark brewery in the Jamaica Plain section of Boston was completed for exclusive production of Samuel Adam Boston Lager.

Sam Adams gained distinction both at home and abroad and Koch continued to expand his marketing efforts. By 1991, the company was able to sell 2.3 million cases in 25 states as well as in Germany and Japan. As brewmaster and CEO, it has always been Koch's philosophy to make his beer as close to the consumer as possible. Therefore, he has chosen to continue brewing small batches in regional locations. In addition to the new brewery, the company rents time at two other breweries in Pittsburgh and Oregon and has opened the Samuel Adams Brew House in downtown Philadelphia. Sam Adams has also been able to extend its product line while keeping its regional character. Today's offerings include eight other recipies—a light beer, four seasonal beers, and two specialty beers.

Expansion abroad was as carefully planned as expansion at home. After turning down dozens of foreign distribution deals, Koch finally agreed in 1989 to export Sam Adams to Japan. Sam Adams is sold in Japan via a cable television home shopping network, and it has been wildly popular—selling at an exorbitant price of 4,300 yen, or about $30 per sixpack. Sam Adams' marketing has been unique if anything!

Koch knew that he had a window of opportunity. He also knew that he had a product that had a taste which was superior to both domestic and foreign beer and, most importantly, that customers liked. The success that followed was the result of a careful marketing plan. Initial analysis of the marketplace revealed an unmet consumer need, a niche where a new beer product could be profitable. The introduction of Sam Adams beer was also singular for its creative and well executed marketing mix.

Questions

1. What category of new product in Figure 11.3 does Sam Adams represent? Why? What are the strategic implications of this categorization.
2. What was Jim Cook's strategy in entering the beer market? Specifically, what was his strategy?
    - -segmentation
    - -distribution
    - -price
    - -advertising
    - -product
3. To what extent does the introduction of Sam Adams meet the five criteria for new product success cited in the chapter? What are the risks of introducing the product?
4. What steps in Figure 11.5 did Jim Cook follow in introducing Sam Adams? Did he follow a sound new product development process?
5. As a regional brewer, how did Jim Cook modify the new product development process cited in Figure 11.5?

References

1. "Portrait of the CEO as Exporter," *Inc.*
2. "Beer Wars, Round Two," *Newsweek.*
3. "Alcoholic Beverages," *Standard & Poor's Industry Survey*, June 27, 1991.
4. "Wooing Jacques and Fritz Six-Pack," *Business Week*, February 4, 1991.
5. "Boston 'Craft' Beer Makes its Way to S.F.," *San Francisco Chronicle*, March 15, 1990.
6. "New Brewery brings Sam Adams Home," *The Boston Globe*, June 25, 1989.
7. "Boston Beer Co. CEO Lays it on the Line," *Forbes*, June 27, 1988.
8. "Sending Coals to Newcastle," *Newsweek*, January 4, 1988.
9. "Boston Brewmaster Meets Rivals Head-On," *The Wall Street Journal*, August 18, 1987.
10. "Faces Behind the Figures—Brewing American," *Forbes*, April 6, 1987.
11. "Brewer in a Froth over Imported Suds," *USA Today*, September 18, 1986.
12. "Boston's Brew Crowned 'America's Best'," *The Boston Herald*, June 3, 1985.
13. "Boston Gets a New Brewer From an Old Family," *Business Week*, March 18, 1985.
14. "Jim Koch Brews Up an Old-Style Beer that Would Make His Great-Great-Granddad Proud," *People Weekly*, November 18, 1985.

CASE 12

CARUSHKA INC.: DEVELOPING PRODUCT LINES AND STRATEGIES

America's adoption of a healthier lifestyle has led not only to a change in eating habits, but also to an increased emphasis on exercise as a part of everyday life. This change in lifestyle has affected many fitness-related industries. Those which have profited include health clubs, health food manufacturers, sporting goods stores, aerobics instruction, weight-loss programs, sports medicine, and sportswear manufacturers. Over $25 billion is spent each year on fitness related activities and merchandise. Shadowing the dramatic growth of the fitness industries is the bodywear business, which includes all types of dancewear and exercise wear.

America has accepted this new lifestyle and in the 1990s bodywear is not only considered proper street attire, but is even regarded as stylish. Witness the body-hugging fashions and growing use of lycra in the latest sportswear. Ric Wanetik, a Marshall Fields' vice president, feels that ". . . people buying this merchandise aren't necessarily doing it to run out and exercise in; they're buying it because it's fashion-smart." Designer Rebecca Moses shares this view: "People like the way they look in workout clothes so they incorporated elements of these designs into their everyday wardrobes." Although more traditional sportswear looks are being added to the bodywear phenomenon, lycra leggings are the essential component. Up until now black has been the outstanding color, but buyers and manufacturers report heavy demand for color. Sassoon is bringing out its first bodywear line and even L. L. Bean has produced a fitness-fashion catalog! A 1991 article in the *New York Times* stated that stretch bodysuits form the "foundation of fashion."

In spite of, or perhaps due to its rapid growth, the bodywear market is extremely unpredictable. Like the sportswear market, whatever is in this season will be out next season. This shift in consumer tastes has resulted in the rapid appearance and disappearance of many bodywear labels and manufacturers. This process is extremely accelerated, since the lifecycle of most bodywear styles lasts approximately three months. In sportswear an established brand name is key. A strong brand name helps to speed customer acceptance of new styles and makes the job of gaining distribution that much easier.

Despite a downturn in the economy that began in 1990, many bodywear makers in the fashion and branded end of the business say they ended 1991 with solid sales gains and expect to see a repeat performance for 1992. Yet while many executives quote increases of 18 to 50 percent for 1991, the projected gains for 1992 are smaller: 8 to 35 percent. Makers credit the upbeat mood to the continuing popularity of stretch Lycra spandex bodywear that doubles as outerwear and to growing acceptance of legwear as a fashion accessory. Another positive factor is the increase in demand during the holiday season. According to Joey Harary, president of Jacques Moret, Inc., "three years ago, Christmas wasn't an important time for bodywear sales. But in the 1990s people lead more active lives and wear more bodywear for exercise or just for hanging out."

The firms which successfully compete in the bodywear industry have a solid product strategy and image. Carushka is a successful bodywear designer who bases her strategy on innovation. Her first leotard was a striped design, an idea she conceived while watching a Gene Kelly movie. Carushka was the first designer to do striped and print bodywear and the first to use cotton instead of synthetics. Carushka views herself as an entrepreneur, a designer willing to risk everything. She considers herself a pioneer and has given her company the motto, "Expect the unexpected."

For the first year and a half Carushka ran her business with just six styles of dancewear. Because of the small size of her business (only 100 stores), Carushka delivered her leotards from the back of her station wagon. Each day she would deliver goods to various accounts and collect payment in cash.

As the business grew, emphasis was placed on quality in terms of materials as well as design. Carushka was careful to meet consumer expectations. Attention was given to small details, such as the placement of seams, which provides a better fit and therefore a better look. Carushka's exercise wear quickly became recognized for its innovative styling, high quality, and tailoring.

In less than two years, Carushka's leotards began to sell and demand increased. Carushka wanted to capitalize on this momentum but realized that she did not have money to advertise. Therefore, she developed an alternative strategy: Carushka began to send celebrities free samples of her bodysuits. The celebrities loved these unusual designs and were repeatedly photographed in them. This media coverage, as well as word-of-mouth promotion, gave Carushka's growing firm the boost it needed.

Carushka became an overnight success. She began to sell heavily to specialty stores but also tripled her sales by selling to department stores, which kept special bodywear sections. At that time Carushka began to broaden her product line in order to satisfy her customers needs for a diversity of styles. She created two lines, one comprised of 120 pieces and the other of 70 pieces. Carushka added even greater breadth by branching out into children's wear and women's casual wear, both of which were moderately successful. She also ventured into men's bodywear at the request of John Travolta, one of the celebrities who first wore her styles. The initial response to the line was positive, with $1 million of merchandise shipped in the first four months. But, men's bodywear never caught on, and Carushka discontinued the line.

Carushka does not believe in test marketing her new concepts. She is an entrepreneur at heart and feels that either the consumer will buy her idea or not. Also, many consumers are reluctant to buy new designs. Additionally, there is the problem of competitors copying Carushka's ideas if she test markets. In the bodywear industry, competitors can copy an idea and bring it to market within six weeks. The companies that look to copy Carushka's styles are largely low-cost, foreign manufacturers. If these companies would market the same styles first, Carushka would lose a lot of her "innovator" sales. The pace of the marketplace is, therefore, a key factor in the long-term success of a firm like Carushka.

Carushka believes that in the long-run, the bodywear market will return to basics. Because of financial problems brought on by a decline in the market, Carushka left the business for one year. Naturally, consumers have a short memory and when the designer re-entered the business in 1987, she had to start from scratch. Carushka began to concentrate on her original customer base, the specialty boutiques, which she feels are more enjoyable to sell to than department stores. Carushka also decided to sell via consumer and retail mail-order catalogs. In 1990, Carushka opened her own retail store in California, which she uses to showcase her clothes.

Carushka still believes in emphasizing a product innovation strategy because, in her opinion, the bodywear category requires it. Her company slogan is still, "Expect the unexpected."

Questions

1. How did Carushka establish her line? How did her strategy change over time?
2. What line extensions did Carushka offer in addition to dance outfits? What were the results?
3. Does Carushka have depth in her product line? Breadth? What is more important for Carushka, depth or breadth? Why?
4. Does the concept of a product life cycle apply to Carushka? Why or why not?
5. Carushka does not test market. Why? Do you agree?

References

1. "Resisting the Recession," *Women's Wear Daily*, December 12, 1991, p. 6.
2. "Producers Serve Up a Variety of Bodywear," *Women's Wear Daily*, May 9, 1991, p. W6.
3. "Bodywear Pace—Heating Up," *Discount Merchandiser*, September 1991, pp. 60–63.
4. "Bodywear Coordinates—High Impact Sales," *Discount Merchandiser*, May 1990, pp. 70–76.
5. "Making Your Fitness Their Business," *Black Enterprise*, September 1991, pp. 82–90.
6. "How Execs Get Fit," *Fortune*, October 22, 1990, pp. 144–152.
7. "Workout Clothes: From the Gym . . . to the Street," *New York Times Magazine*, September 28, 1986, pp. 67–68, 110.
8. "Carushka is Still Shipping, Says Company Won't Close," *Women's Wear Daily*, June 14, 1985, p. 10.
9. "Exercise Wear," *Stores*, June 1987, pp. 13–19.

LAKEWAY RESORT: A CASE STUDY IN SERVICES MARKETING

CASE 13

Today, consumers spend more money on services than on products. By 1990, over 75 percent of the U.S. labor force was employed, directly or indirectly, by the service sector of the economy. Consequently, services now account for over one-half of our gross national product. This major shift in the composition of our economy is primarily the result of demographic changes that have occurred over the past 40 years. These changes include increasing proportions of working women, single-person households, and senior citizens. Moreover, there is greater affluence because of the growing number of dual-income households.

This dramatic growth in the services sector has sparked a significant amount of interest in the marketing of services. Specifically, with the emergence of the service economy, it has become essential for service firms to develop a marketing orientation. More importantly, their marketing efforts have to be flexible and highly sensitive to the changing desires of target markets.

Only by understanding and fulfilling consumers' needs better than anyone else, can these firms sustain a competitive advantage. This is especially true for the resort industry, which has experienced rapid expansion as a result of the growth in discretionary spending. When Lakeway Resort first opened in Austin, Texas, it achieved notable success as a local destination resort which catered to Texas residents. As time passed, however, it was faced with declining occupancy rates and falling revenues. After 25 years of operation, Lakeway began to be perceived as a middle-aged "local Texas resort." Moreover, as it entered the 1980s, Lakeway was further threatened by increasing competition from new resorts and convention centers that were targeting its traditional clientele. The newly remodeled San Antonio Convention Center, Houston's George R. Brown Convention Center, and the 500-room Hyatt Regency Resort (opening in San Antonio in 1993) all represent formidable competition for Lakeway.

The Lakeway Resort was given renewed vitality and a second chance to once again become a leading resort when it was purchased by The Dolce Management Group in 1987. For the Dolce Group, this acquisition was an important part of its corporate strategic plan, which was to position superior conference facilities around the country in areas such as Florida, Texas, New York, and California. In Lakeway, Dolce saw an opportunity for the company to distinguish itself from the local competition and create a nationally recognized conference center for meetings in the state of Texas. Lakeway possessed all of the service offerings needed to establish a "World Class Resort." In addition to the natural beauty of the Texas Hill Country, its offerings included championship golf and tennis facilities, full business conference capabilities, and a wide assortment of lodging.

The new management of Lakeway has a strategic plan for future business success predicated on services marketing. The Dolce Group devised this plan to transform Lakeway into a "World Class Resort." The plan focused on three principle strategies. The first was to invest sufficiently in the property in order to maintain current services and create new services as needed. Second, management had to formulate marketing strategies that would enable Lakeway to re-establish itself in its traditional market, as well as penetrate new target markets. Third, the company had to cultivate a work force that was committed to providing outstanding service to guests.

With the overall strategic plan in place, the Dolce Group began formulating its marketing plan to answer two questions: *Who* would constitute the desired target markets, and *what* marketing efforts would be implemented to attract them. The driving force behind the Lakeway marketing plan was segmenting and selecting specific target markets. The traditional target market was businesses and consumers that reside in Texas. Up until 1987, this Texas base accounted for 87% of Lakeway's business. However, Dolce set out to expand the resort's customer base by pursuing new types of patrons. Thus, Dolce segmented the new target market into four distinct groups: traditional Texas patrons, national businesses, nontraditional businesses, and families. The nontraditional market segment consisted of social, military, reunion, religious, and fraternal groups.

To attract patrons from the new target markets and maintain higher occupancy rates year-round, management has created some very specific marketing strategies, which have proven highly effective. For example, Lakeway created a "kids under 12 eat free" program, as well as a 'summer camp' program in an attempt to attract more families. In addition, according to Andrew J. Dolce, CEO of the Dolce Company, "we are constantly looking at new things to do in terms of expanding the product and expanding the services." A recreation department has been created to provide a wide variety of activities for families and groups. Also, room service has been added to a vast assortment of guest services. The rewards of these improvements have begun to materialize. By 1989, the composition of guests had shifted to 65 percent in-state and 35 percent out-of-state patrons.

In order to achieve the strategic objectives of the new management group, a formal marketing effort and promotional strategy had to be implemented. Two messages were consistently used to appeal to the marketplace. The first message, which was directed at former guests, conveyed the fact that Lakeway was under new ownership and management, and that the facility had been completely upgraded and expanded. The second message, which was directed at new patrons, explained Lakeway's benefits, unique hospitality, and its excellent facilities.

To convey these messages effectively, Lakeway formulated a promotional strategy that was suited to services marketing. Services marketing differs from packaged goods marketing in that what is being sold is an "experience" rather than a tangible good. Lakeway's marketing effort consisted of a combination of personal selling, direct mail, print advertisements, and public relations. Unlike many of its competitors, Lakeway Resort spends only 9 percent of its marketing budget on advertising. Print advertisements are most often placed in trade publications such as *Success Meeting Magazine.* Lakeway chooses to put most of its promotional dollars into direct mail and personal selling efforts, a strategy which has been highly successful. The national direct mail campaign has achieved a response rate of 8 to 10 percent, which is well above the national average of 3 percent.

Lakeway has chosen to employ a highly talented sales staff as the primary force behind its marketing effort. The major responsibilities of the sales team is to bring in new business and negotiate prices and activities for business meetings. Because competition is extremely intense, Lakeway's management makes sure that its sales force is thoroughly aware of the competition's strengths, weaknesses, pricing, service offerings, and overall performance. Competitive information helps Lakeway's sales staff to more effectively discuss the advantages that the resort has over its competitors.

The sales staff is also well aware of the fact that pricing plays an important role in the marketing of a resort. Resort pricing is highly sensitive to the trends in the discretionary spending of the target markets. As a result of poor economic times in Texas, industry room rates dramatically declined in the 1980s as resorts fought for dwindling discretionary dollars. Through the 1990-92 recession, Lakeway has been able to maintain relatively high rates because it has so much to offer as a full destination resort. According to the 1990 Texas Real Estate Investment Guide, occupancy and room rates at Texas resorts are on the rise, and will actually outperform the U.S. average.

Once the marketing plan is implemented and the sales are made, it is up to the service employees to deliver the promises that have been made to the guests. For a resort to be successful, it is vital that a superior level of service be constantly maintained. If it is not, service variability will undoubtedly lead to lost revenues today and in the future. That is why Lakeway takes extreme care to ensure that every customer receives the same high quality treatment.

Lakeway delivers services by means of a company philosophy known as Aggressive Hospitality that the company instills in its entire staff. It is how Lakeway expresses to each customer that it will go the extra mile to ensure that each guest has a pleasant memorable experience at the resort. To reinforce its commitment to superior hospitality, Lakeway gives a monthly "Aggressive Hospitality" award to an employee based upon peer evaluation. The recipient receives recognition in the form of a lapel pin, having his or her name engraved on a wall plaque, and having his or her name inscribed on every employee's paycheck for the entire month.

In the two years since Lakeway has been acquired by the Dolce Group, it has reestablished itself in its regional market, and has begun to successfully penetrate its new target markets. According to Andrew Dolce, one of the biggest challenges for Lakeway is to continue to attract quality people in order to provide superior hospitality that is at the heart of the Lakeway "experience."

Lakeway has a lot to look forward to for the remainder of the decade. According to a financial consulting firm, the resort market will experience 5 percent growth yearly through the mid-1990s, primarily in 4-star and 5-star resorts. There will be steady demand for rooms from senior citizens, overseas travelers, and the business groups market. The states that have showed the greatest gains in resort demand are Nevada, Georgia, and Texas. Since the Lakeway Resort is located in Austin, Texas, it can expect to benefit from the increase in demand.

Questions

1. Do Lakeway's offerings have the attributes of services cited in Chapter 13; namely, intangibility, variability, perishability, and simultaneous production and consumption? Explain.
2. How does Lakeway follow each of the steps in marketing planning for services in Figure 13-3? Specifically?
   a. What opportunities has it identified?
   b. What are its target segments (including its "nontraditional" targets)?
   c. How is Lakeway positioning its service offerings?
   d. What is its marketing mix; particularly its promotional mix and its pricing strategy?
   e. How does it attempt to control service delivery?
3. How does Lakeway's promotional mix differ when compared to a typical consumer packaged good such as paper towels or toothpaste? How does the mix differ for the conference segment versus the vacationer segment?
4. What is meant by Lakeway's Aggressive Hospitality program? Why is such a program particularly important in marketing services?

References

1. "Industry Must Change as Consumers Mature," *National Real Estate Investor*, December, 1990, p. 90.
2. "Resorts: Financial Woes or No?," *Successful Meetings*, January 1990, pp. 49–51.

CASE 14

WHAT MAKES AMOS FAMOUS: THE DEVELOPMENT OF DISTRIBUTION CHANNELS AND STRATEGIES

In 1975, when Wally Amos started the Famous Amos Chocolate Chip Cookie Company, the idea of selling gourmet cookies in a retail bake shop was a novel one. Amos had no previous experience in the food business; he was a former Hollywood talent agent who discovered that he had a knack for making great tasting chocolate chip cookies. When friends told Amos that his cookies were so good he should sell them, he started Famous Amos and set out to make a living. With about $25,000 in start-up capital, he opened one Famous Amos store in California. Significantly, this was the first shop in the world designed exclusively to sell chocolate chip cookies. By 1981, Amos had established a nationwide distribution network, with retail shops and franchises in several countries, including Japan, Australia, and Canada. The cookies were so successful that Famous Amos grossed $7 million in sales in 1981 and $12 million in 1987.

Initially the cookies were sold in the company-owned hot-bake stores and through wholesalers. The fresh cookie batter was prepared in a baking studio, for both hot-bake and wholesale products. There were five kinds of batter for wholesale products and nine for the hot-bake stores. Wally ensured the freshness and quality of his cookies personally, nonetheless smooth distribution was essential for delivering fresh cookies to the customers.

Since Wally never anticipated such strong demand for his cookies, he initially lacked a formal plan for the growth of his business. Instead, retail distribution channels were built up because consumers would go into local stores and ask for the cookies. If the store owner did not carry them, the customers would tell them that they should begin to order them. This consumer "pull-through" of the product is an example of how strong demand can stimulate a retailer to carry a low margin item like cookies. Retailers had commented that the markup was so low that they would not carry the cookies unless the demand level meant faster turnover to offset the lower margins. Based on this kind of pull-through demand, Famous Amos Cookies became well known in the Pacific region. While Amos wanted to expand nationally, he did not have the capital to fund such large scale growth. Rather than raising the capital through debt, he turned to franchising as a means of expanding the hot-bake shops nationwide.

As Ken Wolf, Vice President of Domestic Franchising explains, the firm originally had no intentions to franchise Famous Amos. During the first years of business, Wally Amos received about 100 requests for franchises; when this number reached 1,000, he finally decided to go ahead with the idea. Franchising would let Wally Amos concentrate on cookie development. It would allow the firm to grow quickly, using other people's money to open new stores. However, it was very important for Famous Amos to set guidelines for franchisers to follow to ensure quality. International franchisers, for example, are required to have everything approved by the home office to protect the Famous Amos brand name. At first, the company co-owned the franchised outlets, but this proved to be too risky a strategy. Wally notes that several shops failed because they violated the cardinal rule of retailing: location, location, location. With a good location, such as a shopping mall with 20,000 patrons per day, a franchise may attract 200 to 300 customers a day. There are several drawbacks to franchising, however. A close relationship must be maintained between the franchisee and the firm; if the franchisee does not maintain quality control, the Famous Amos name and product will both suffer.

In addition to franchises, Famous Amos cookies began to be distributed in supermarkets, convenience stores such as 7-Eleven, and specialty shops such as small mom-and-pop stores and gift shops. The firm has a network of 131 wholesalers who, in turn, employ "route men" to deliver cookies to certain stores on a reliable schedule. Rick Royce, a wholesaler, describes the delivery process. Orders are picked up twice a week at the factory and are unloaded at the distributors' premises. Drivers then load the cookies onto trucks and deliver them. Sub-distributors are also used to deliver the cookies to areas that are inaccessible to the main distributor. For example, this may be due to distance or a lack of familiarity with local retailers in a certain area.

Opening new channels of distribution involves the wholesaler making an appointment with local store buyers. These buyers must first be convinced to stock the cookies and then find shelf space for them. Buyers are often reluctant to stock Famous Amos because cookies in general have a low margin and because existing shelf space tends to be dominated by a few manufacturers such as Nabisco, Keebler, Sunshine, and Pepperidge Farm.

Competition in supermarkets is especially fierce. For many years, Nabisco controlled most of the shelf space in supermarkets. Nabisco's control was weakened when competitors pointed out that some of the Nabisco products were slow movers and that their own products could double or triple sales given the same shelf space. Additionally, buyers' reluctance to carry cookies is often overcome by the product's quality and taste. By the mid 1980s, Famous Amos was competing with the leading mass bakers' brands in the supermarkets, and with several gourmet brands, including Unknown Jerome, Mrs. Fields and David's in what were known as "boutique" cookie stores.

With such tough competition, Famous Amos had to be conveniently located and easily identified in order to attract new customers. In supermarkets, Famous Amos cookies are sold in several different sized packages and are located on free-standing display racks, apart from the other cookie products. In convenience stores, Famous Amos cookies are packaged as 2-ounce singles or in 2-ounce bags that are located by the cash register to generate impulse purchases. The firm also introduces new cookie flavors on a regular basis in response to consumer demand. For example, oatmeal-cinnamon raisin cookies and soft cookies were developed to appeal to adult tastes.

Famous Amos' wholesale success is a testimony to its marketing strategy to creating a niche where none had existed before. Famous Amos pursued a unique marketing concept. The firm did not research a market and then develop a product. Instead, they created a product and then built demand.

In addition to cookies, Famous Amos introduced a few new products. These included fresh croissants, ice cream, and waffle cones. Like the cookies, these products can be stored frozen, which means that Famous Amos could utilize its existing distribution channels to deliver the new products along with the cookies. Marketing an ice-cream product will ensure that Famous Amos stores do business all year round, even in the summer when cookie sales are slow.

Part of the brand's success is attributed to Wally Amos' easily recognized face and his Panama hat, which are seen on every package. With his show business background, Wally Amos has proven to be a natural promoter. Although the company does not advertise nationally, Famous Amos receives a great deal of attention through cause-related marketing. These efforts help to build brand recognition. Wally Amos is a supporter and spokesman for several charities, especially for literacy foundations. Amos describes how participating in a literacy campaign in Philadelphia helped him to introduce a new product (ice cream) and increase sales by over 30 percent while furthering a good cause. As a testimony to Wally's marketing flair, his Panama hat and Indian shirt were exhibited in the Smithsonian's Collection of Advertising History.

In spite of Wally Amos' personal appeal and the firm's huge sales, operating Famous Amos has always been difficult and cash flow a problem. Wally admits that he is not a detail person and prefers to handle "people" matters and new ideas. In 1985, with sales of more than $10 million, Amos was losing about $300,000 a year, which he attributed to stiff competition and his own lack of business acumen. When faced with the alternative of filing for bankruptcy or selling his business, he opted for the latter. In 1985, the Bass brothers bought a majority of the stock, and were in turn bought out by an investment group headed by former California Senator John Tunney. Under the new management, the company has finally achieved a healthy cash flow and has opened 10 more hot-bake stores, bringing the U.S. total to 44 stores and international total to 36. Wally Amos retains 8 percent of his stock and is a vice-chairman. In addition to promoting Famous Amos cookies, he has several new projects, including starting a shoe store, writing a book, and developing a pilot series for public television.

Famous Amos cookies continued to pursue new distribution efforts through 1991. In November 1991, Burger King announced that it will sell Famous Amos cookies in its 5,500-outlet restaurant chain. This is Famous Amos' first involvement with a restaurant chain, and the first time a branded cookie will be offered in a restaurant chain on a national level.

Questions

1. Why is distribution a central component of Famous Amos' marketing mix? How did distribution affect the firm's growth?
2. How did Famous Amos pull the product through the channels of distribution?
3. Why does Famous Amos use a multiple channel system? Diagram each type of channel used by Famous Amos (see Figures 14.4 and 14.7).
4. How do the company's advertising and promotional strategies support distribution?

References

1. *Milling and Baking News,* October 15, 1991, p. 1.
2. Michael King, "To Sell or Not to Sell . . . ," *Black Enterprise,* June 1987, pp. 287–289.
3. Judith Dagnoli, "Rich Cookies: Big Marketers Put Dough into Premium Products," *Advertising Age,* March 16, 1987, p. 32.
4. Bill Saporito, "A Smart Cookie at Pepperidge," *Fortune,* December 22, 1986, p. 67.
5. Gail Buchalter, "Happier Cookie," *Forbes,* March 10, 1986, pp. 177–178.
6. "Chocolate Chip Cookies," *Consumer Reports,* February 1985, pp. 69–72.
7. Matthew Heller, "The Great Cookie War," *Madison Avenue,* January 1985, pp. 100–102.

WEST RIDGE MOUNTAINEERING: A CASE STUDY IN RETAILING

CASE 15

Success in the world of retail marketing requires as much in-depth preparation as is needed to scale a mountain. As expert climbers, the founders of West Ridge Mountaineering (WRM) knew first hand that survival within the retail sector would require the right equipment, strong experience, and a will to survive. WRM began as a specialty retail store that catered solely to serious skiers and mountain climbers. Because this target market consisted primarily of experts, West Ridge carried only top-of-the-line climbing hardware, tents, backpacks, and skiing equipment. By carrying only the best quality merchandise, the company quickly developed a cult following. However, after Ed Brekke bought the company from its original owners, he expanded the product offerings as well as the target market. Today, WRM is a Los Angeles retailer specializing in mountaineering and skiing clothing and accessories as well as eqipment.

The first major decision that a retailer makes involves the selection of a product or service that will attract a specific customer base. To keep the specialty appeal, Brekke knew that it was essential for the company to continue to carry top quality, brand name products that were known and requested by customers. Yet, while maintaining this specialty appeal, he was able to add merchandise in various styles and price ranges to attract an even broader customer base. Initially, the company carried sleeping bags within the $100 to $400 price range. To cater to a more diverse target market, Brekke began carrying bags in the $30 to $50 range as well. Broadening the customer base made perfect sense. A poll conducted in 1990 indicates that most Americans consider outdoor recreation an important part of their lives. Over 77 percent of a nationwide sample said outdoor recreation was "very important" to them. In short, there exists today a tremendous market for outdoor leisure equipment. Brekke was able to reach more of these consumers by offering lower-priced products.

While some retailers offer either products or services to customers, the management of West Ridge believes that a retail strategy which offers a combination of both will generate even greater sales. Some of the services which the company provides include ski and binding repair, skiing and climbing equipment rentals, up-to-the-minute ski reports, and published product and sporting information. In addition, West Ridge is the only store in town that offers one-day ski service. By offering this service as well as equipment rentals, the shop has been able to attract a greater number of people into the store. This increase in store traffic has resulted in greater sales of accessory items, such as socks, thermal underwear, and sunglasses.

Display racks are filled with a variety of free brochures and pamphlets which describe the product's attributes, organized hiking and climbing excursions, and instructional programs. Also, the store contains an extensive collection of hiking maps, which are alphabetized and very easy to use. Although the low cost maps and various information pamphlets take up valuable floor space, management continues to offer these services because of their ability to consistently generate store traffic. As Brekke points out, "It's more important to us to have a lot of people in the store than one or two big sales. The results are always better if we have a lot of people in the store, even if sales are down, as opposed to high sales for the day with only a few people. In the long run, we do much better."

The next two major considerations that a retailer must address are store location and layout. In retailing convenience goods, location is the key to survival. However, in marketing specialty goods, location is not as important as some other factors. In the case of West Ridge, Brekke decided upon its present location because the store rent was the most affordable at the time. He believes that specialty retailers have a loyal customer following which will come to the store as long as it is within a reasonable distance. Thus, because West Ridge is a specialty store, its owner avoids paying premium rent for the most convenient location.

From years of experience, Brekke has developed a distinct display philosophy, which dictates that the store never carry back-room stock. If inventory was stocked in the back, employees may be inclined to tell customers that the store was out of stock rather than go back to look for it. Thus, Brekke believes that by displaying all available merchandise on the sales floor where customers can see it, the store will sell more. Having mirrors placed in strategic places is also an important part of an effective store layout. Customers need places to model merchandise in privacy.

Another essential component of retail marketing is having a knowledgeable sales force that can relate well to customers and ultimately sell the products. That is why when Brekke interviews prospective employees, he looks for individuals with personalities that convey enthusiasm, energy, candidness, and trustworthiness. He places importance on this evaluation process because it is the customers who will be relying on the sales force for expert advice. For example, in sporting activities like mountain climbing, where proper clothing and equipment are necessities, their advice could be life-saving. That is why Brekke emphasizes that it is imperative for the sales force to understand the importance of the advice that it gives.

To ensure that the sales force portrays a friendly image and indeed has expert knowledge of the products, Brekke holds regularly scheduled training sessions during which he discusses effective sales strategies with the salespeople. In general, he tells his sales staff to avoid high pressure sales techniques because most customers find them to be a turnoff. Instead, he recommends that they determine what it is that the customer is looking for, and find a product that fits his or her needs. Employees are also encouraged to participate in excursions to gain experience and first-hand knowledge of the products.

Scheduling employees in the most efficient manner is an essential part of retailing because it is the way that a company controls its payroll. In formulating the optimal schedule, a manager must always be sure that there are enough salespeople on the floor at all times. West Ridge compensates both part- and full-time employees on a straight salary basis, although store managers participate in an incentive program that is tied to store sales. The bonus program begins once sales reach a monthly break-even level. By paying part-time employees minimum wage, West Ridge is able to lower its average wage costs.

Keeping costs under control is an integral part of Brekke's buying philosophy. Unlike the original owners, who primarily relied upon preseason purchases, Brekke buys merchandise in smaller quantities and reorders more frequently. Manufacturer's representatives assist retailers in their buying decisions by providing information about which products are moving, and how quickly. Thus, Brekke relies upon these representatives to help identify the optimal order quantity. Keeping close tabs on purchasing has proven to be a real advantage for West Ridge. Brekke is able to minimize his cash outflow as well as fine tune his mid-season inventory levels based upon how quickly particular merchandise is selling.

The best way to overcome the competitive pressures is to employ an effective promotional strategy. West Ridge wants its promotional campaign to remind people about the store, inform them about its product and service offerings, and motivate consumers to visit the store. To do so, at the beginning of the ski season West Ridge places teaser ads in local newspapers and on cable and network TV. The retailer also sends out an in-house newsletter which announces special preseason deals. For example, a ski boot that is regularly priced at $225 would be put on sale for only $99.95. Afterwards, West Ridge runs follow-up ads that focus on special ski packages including skis, poles, and bindings. These ads are strategically placed in skiing magazines and on television during skiing events to more effectively reach the store's target market.

Effective promotion, carefully selected products and services, cost efficient buying, good location, and an experienced sales force are the ingredients for success in specialty retailing. Given the changes in the recreation habits of Americans over the past five years, West Ridge Mountaineering must stay competitive and up to date if it is to succeed long-term.

But, staying competitive may be difficult because of several environmental constraints. The $7 billion ski resort industry ended the 1990-91 season in poor shape. In California, where WRM is located, an ongoing drought limited snowfall and therefore ski activity. The recession has also hurt. A family of four in a major resort can easily spend $200 a day on lift tickets and food alone. The fact is that the number of daily visits to ski hills has been stagnant since 1979, at around 50 million days per year. At least 50 percent of the ski resorts lost money in 1991. That does not bode well for retailers like West Ridge. Despite frequent discount sales of 50 to 70 percent off, ski industry sales in 1991 were running around 600,000, about half of the peak in the 1980s. About 10 percent of retailers and 15 percent of suppliers are expected go out of business.

By its nature, skiing tends to attract 25 to 35-year-olds. As the population of this segment dwindles, so will interest in skiing. According to a 1991 article in *Skiing Trade News*, better service and better value will be the keys to success for ski equipment retailers in the 1990s. Since WRM has a long-standing tradition of service and high quality goods, the retailer is well positioned for long-term stabiity in a declining industry.

While the ski industry has weakened in recent years, rock climbing is growing in popularity, both indoors and outdoors. Over 120 health clubs around the nation now include 70 to 100 foot high man-made walls that climbing enthusiasts can tackle on their lunchbreak or after work. Dubbed "sports climbing," this indoor activity arrived in North America in 1987 and has added to a growing appreciation for rock climbing and outdoor activity in general. Northeast mountains such as Maine's Mount Katahdin are becoming crowded with climbers. Between 1977 and 1987 the number of visitors to federal recreation areas grew by 30 percent. American consumers went to rural forest and water areas 2.7 billion times in 1987, spending $132 billion in the process.

According to the Resources Planning Agency the largest growth in outdoor activity will be in the area of hiking, with the number of trips doubling in the next 50 years. An upturn in this segment is due, in part, to a greater health consciousness among the general population. Because hikers traditionally carry backpacks, equipment, tents, and other accessories, West Ridge Mountaineering will surely benefit from the broad popularity of hiking.

Questions

1. What recent trends in retailing does West Ridge Mountaineering (WRM) reflect?
2. Does WRM have any competitive advantages? If so, what are they?
3. What is WRM's marketing mix? Specifically, explain its
   a. product mix.
   b. service strategy.
   c. in-store decor.

d. advertising strategy.
e. pricing strategy.

4. Why is location a less important factor in the success of WRM compared to a typical retailer?
5. Has WRM done an adequate job in identifying target segments and in positioning its store? Explain.

References

1. "Downhill Bracer," *Forbes*, May 27, 1991, pp. 55–64.
2. "The Future of Fun," *American Forests*, March/April 1991, pp. 21–24, 73–74.
3. "Survey Shows U.S. Keen on Outdoors," *Sporting Goods Business*, October 1990, p. 51.
4. "Go Climb a Rock at the Gym," *Business Week*, November 26, 1990, p. 196.

CASE 16

ARROWHEAD WATER: THE PHYSICAL DISTRIBUTION PROCESS

An explosion has occurred in the bottled water market, due largely to aggressive marketing programs designed to capitalize on the health craze. Bottled water first became popular in the late 1970s, as a result of the growing health and fitness movement. To exploit this growing activity, Perrier began, in 1977, to export bottled water to the United States. Concurrently, its importers launched a $4 million advertising campaign to promote sparkling water as the healthy alternative to alcohol and soft drinks. This marketing effort not only enabled Perrier to become the market leader in the United States, but it also helped to stimulate even greater demand for other types of bottled water.

In the ten years since it began exporting to the United States, Perrier has embarked on a string of acquisitions to further strengthen its position in the marketplace. It acquired companies including Poland Springs, Oasis Water, Calistoga, and Zephyr Hill. Its most aggressive acquisition in that period, however, was the $453 million purchase of the Arrowhead Drinking Water Company from Beatrice Foods in 1987. This action enabled Perrier to double its share of the $1.7 billion bottled water market to 21 percent, and instantly obtain a presence in the nonsparkling water segment.

Arrowhead Drinking Water is based in Monterey, California. The company processes and distributes mountain spring water throughout California, Hawaii, Nevada, and Arizona. The expense of shipping keeps Arrowhead and all other brands regional. The company markets its water via two channels. Nonsparkling and sparkling water products are sold to supermarkets for resale to consumers in 1- and 2.5-gallon containers. In addition, water is delivered in 5-gallon bottles directly to home and office water coolers. Arrowhead attributes its success to superior product quality and efficient distribution.

Arrowhead's beginnings date back to the 1880s, when David Smith built a health spa at Arrowhead Springs so that people could come to bathe and drink the water. Because the water was believed to have restorative qualities, the number of spa visitors quickly grew, as did demand for the drinking water. To meet this rising demand, the company began piping the water down the mountainside. By 1905, Arrowhead began bottling the water in the basement of the spa's hotel, and sending it to customers. In 1917, the company began transporting the water by means of glass-lined railroad cars, in order to geographically broaden its distribution base.

Today, Arrowhead consists of seven springs in the San Bernardino Mountains. Water is gathered from the springs by seven miles of pipeline, and placed into sealed storage reservoirs. Alongside the reservoirs are loading stations, where 64,000-gallon trucks are filled within 25 minutes. Once loaded, the trucks transport the water directly to the bottling plant. Because the trucks operate continuously and provide a means of bringing the water directly to the plant, trucking has proven the most efficient means of transporting the water from its source to the plant.

As soon as the trucks arrive at the bottling plant, the water is tested before being transferred into one of six holding tanks. After the water is put into the tanks, it is ready for filtration. This process yields three types of water: spring, distilled, and fluoridated water. To maximize product freshness, inventory is maintained on a first-in/first-out basis at the bottling plant.

Although the products themselves have not changed much over the years, technology has greatly improved the bottling process. Returned bottles are sanitized and tested before reuse. Because the bottling room is a computer-controlled facility, sanitized bottles can be filled and capped at a capacity of 1,500 bottles an hour, per line. After being filled, the 5-gallon bottles are placed into crates while smaller containers are packed in boxes.

Unitizing is an important component of the distribution process because it plays an enormous part in ensuring distribution efficiency. Unitizing involves designing the truck pallet to safely accommodate the greatest number of bottles. Once packaged, the bottles are unitized so that they can be forklifted from the production line to the warehouse or directly onto a delivery truck in the most efficient manner. Before new products such as Arrowhead's Mountain Spring Sparkling Water can be introduced, unitizing must be addressed to ensure effective distribution.

For Arrowhead, the most important facet of the distribution process is the route sales force. Because satisfying customers is Arrowhead's top priority, the route salespeople represent the backbone of the company. These individuals not only provide physical delivery of the products, but also maintain existing customer relationships, solicit new business, update orders and collect money.

In addition to these responsibilities, the route salesperson is required to manage his or her individual truck inventory, and satisfy customer demand. Inventory management requires the route salesperson to watch while the truck is loaded in the evening, make any daily inventory adjustments in the morning to satisfy last-minute customer requests, and balance the books at the end of the day. Lastly, because deliveries are scheduled on 14-day intervals, it is the responsibility of the route salesperson to ensure that each water delivery is sufficient for a two-week supply.

Another essential component of the distribution process is order processing. Order processing employees assist the route salesperson by answering customer's questions and completing orders via the telephone. In addition, they coordinate the delivery schedules and provide this information to the route salesperson. This support helps the sales force to better service customer needs by providing more efficient distribution.

Warehousing is necessary to ensure that an adequate supply of water is available for retailers. To balance production output with retailer demand, Arrowhead maintains a 3- to 4-day supply of the 1- and 2.5-gallon containers of drinking water and a two-week supply of the sparkling water.

Competition from other water companies and municipal water systems has created the need for strict cost and distribution controls. Because the company provides home and office delivery, selling and delivery costs account for well over 50 percent of total costs. To contain delivery costs, Arrowhead offers a pickup allowance to the grocery trade to provide retailers with an incentive to pick up their orders from the company warehouses. To control capital expenditures, detailed demand forecasts are done for one, five, and ten year periods. This information helps management project how many bottles, crates, and trucks may be needed in the future.

Innovation has also served as a source of increased efficiency and control. To decrease the time taken to load route trucks, the company invented a straddle trailer. By using the trailer, trucks are now loaded in 15 minutes, compared to the 1.5 hours it used to take. This innovation has resulted in time savings for drivers, as well as equipment cost savings for the company. In addition, the company has improved productivity in 5-gallon containers by switching from a 14-pound glass bottle to a 3-pound polycarbonate bottle. As a result of this change, the delivery trucks get much better gas mileage and route salespeople carry one ton less a day.

In 1991, Arrowhead was honored as the number one finisher in Beverage World's annual ranking of the top bottled water brands. Perrier, Arrowhead's parent firm, now lays claim to three of the top seven brands of bottled water. The ongoing growth of the bottled water market has attracted the attention of food companies. In the spring of 1992, Perrier was purchased by Swiss food giant Nestlé, which hopes to capitalize on Perrier's success. By 1995, sales of bottled water are expected to reach $2.4 billion. Arrowhead is well positioned to maintain its market dominance in the West, particularly California, which is the heaviest buyer of bottled water and has the most home delivery.

Questions

1. Arrowhead Drinking Water (ADW) uses two different distribution channels. What are they?
2. How do the various components of ADW's physical distribution system operate; specifically
   a. order processing (see figure 16.3)
   b. merchandise handling and storage (see figure 16.4)
   c. inventory management (see figure 16.5)
   d. transportation
3. Why is physical distribution more important for ADW than for many other companies?
4. What is the role of the route salesperson in the physical distribution system?

References

1. "Best Sellers," *Beverage World*, March 1991, pp. 24–33.
2. "Perrier's Unquenchable U.S. Thirst," *Business Week*, June 29, 1987, p. 46.
3. Beverage Marketing Corporation, 1987 Annual Industry Survey.
4. "Bottled Water Springs Up," *Advertising Age*, September 21, 1987, pp. 24, 83.

CASE 17

SANTA ANITA PARK: DEVELOPING SALES PROMOTIONAL STRATEGIES

Entertainment events do not sell themselves. Rather, they must be sold just like any other product or service. Those that are not effectively promoted will be destined for failure. Saddled with an aging fan base and stagnating attendance rates, the horse racing industry is confronted with a host of betting alternatives, including off-track betting, state lotteries, and riverboat gambling. Over the past two decades, casinos and lotteries have replaced horse racing as the dominant form of gambling in the country. Despite an increase in the number of racing days, the percent of gambling dollars spent on the ponies has dropped from 28 percent in

1974 to 10 percent in 1990. According to Robert Mulcahy, president of the New Jersey Sports and Exposition Authority, "Without a concerted national campaign, horse racing, save for a handful of events of national interest, may cease to exist as an American entertainment form."

In an effort to boost attendance and win over new fans, race track marketers have stepped up the pace of promotional programs; staging family days, creating preferred-gambler clubs, and teaching fans the basics of horse betting. For example, in 1990, the Meadowlands Racetrack made hundreds of patrons owners of a thoroughbred. Fans received an ownership certificate and a free admission pass good any night their horse ran. Turfway Park in Florence, Kentucky created a multifaceted approach to fan education. The track published a beginner's guide to horse racing and even set up a beginner's window.

Although Santa Anita Park, located in Arcadia, California, has been in existence for 50 years, it has not yet developed a patronage base that is strong enough to rely on for long-term survival. According to Michael Williams, director of marketing, "We sell entertainment, and compete against other forms of entertainment. This can be seen in our attendance." For example, if another racetrack is running a sales promotion, or if the Los Angeles Rams have a home game on a day that Santa Anita has races, the park will experience a decline in its attendance level.

In order to strengthen its patronage base and maintain profitability in the future, Santa Anita Park must constantly strive to attract new fans and convince existing patrons to come to the park more often. Thus, its two major marketing objectives are market development and market penetration. To achieve these objectives, the park employs a promotional strategy which consists of heavy advertising, direct selling through its group sales department, and sales promotional techniques.

The sales promotional tools that are used by Santa Anita include discount admission coupons, premium give-aways, entertainment events, and contests. These promotions appear prominently in the park's radio, television, and print advertisements. At Santa Anita, it is the responsibility of the sales promotion manager, Steven Sexton, to create, develop, and implement promotional ideas to boost attendance. Sexton says, "Each promotional tool can be directed at a specific market which currently exists, or at an entirely new group." It is the ability of the promotional tools to be directed at particular market segments that makes them so effective.

Integration of the entire promotional mix is an essential part of the planning process. Before promotional campaigns are launched, the marketing team at Santa Anita meets to discuss the type of promotion to be implemented, which segment it will target, how it will be promoted, when it will be offered, and what the competition is doing. Hollywood Park, a crosstown competitor, offers 1 to 2 *free give-aways* per week. Sexton believes that Hollywood's strategy is not effective because the give-away items are low quality and patrons have come to expect a give-away every time they visit the park.

Sexton feels that for give-aways to induce patrons to visit Santa Anita Park, high quality, useful items have to be offered. Sexton believes that the optimal number of premium give-aways is two per month, because Santa Anita would then have enough time to adequately promote the premium items. In addition, Santa Anita eliminates the possibility of the give-aways becoming part of the total product offering. If they were offered more frequently, people would come to expect them on each visit.

Premiums are used by Santa Anita to achieve market penetration. All leather key and coin holders were offered free to patrons on opening day of Oaktree, horse racing's autumn classic at Santa Anita. People who have already been to the racetrack would most likely be induced to return to receive such give-aways. Experience has shown, however, that new patrons would not be inclined to visit the park merely to get a give-away.

Premiums provide some additional benefits to the park. All premiums are made with the Santa Anita name printed on them. From a promotional perspective, this benefits the racetrack in two ways. First, the items serve as walking billboards for the park. Second, the general public will be able to see the quality items that are given away at Santa Anita. In addition, to better the park's relationship with the community, Santa Anita hires the local PTA to distribute the give-aways at the raceway. This results in a win/win situation because Santa Anita Park gets friendly labor, and the PTA receives a check for the hours worked.

Discount admission coupons are another promotional tool used by Santa Anita. The Park usually offers a 50-cent to 75-cent discount off of the regular $2.25 admission price. The coupons are distributed via newspapers and a direct mail piece which is sent to 200,000 customers. Of the two media, the direct mail piece has a higher number of coupon redemptions. This tool is more effective in achieving market penetration because former patrons are more likely to take advantage of this offering.

Few promotions generate as much excitement as *give-away contests.* This promotion is beneficial to Santa Anita because it is successful in attracting both old and new patrons to the park. In the past, Santa Anita has held a contest aptly named "The Key to the Mint," in which winners were awarded between $10,000 and $25,000 in prize money. Because the amount of prize money was fixed, winners had no influence over the amount of winnings that they would receive. Recently, the marketing group at the park has revised this contest in order to better employ the concept of "fan participation."

Now five winners are chosen to go to the winner's circle after the sixth race, and select a bag filled with money, with the amount of money in the bags ranging from $1,000 to $100,000. This new contest format increases the amount of fan involvement, and provides entertainment to all visiting patrons.

All promotions are analyzed for their effectiveness and profitability. For each promotion, the park calculates the revenues that are generated per patron, based upon the admission price, the parking price, and the average amount of money that was bet. The gross profit per patron is compared to the total cost per patron to determine the level of profitability. In addition, promotions that are offered annually, are compared to see if there has been an increase in attendance and/or profitability from one year to the next.

The demographic composition of the Santa Anita's customers closely parallels that of society. The only difference is that in the horse betting population there are more elderly people and fewer youths. To ensure that the park will maintain a stable level of patronage in the future, it must strive to fortify the youth base. However, this market segment is difficult to attract because the younger set generally do not have a lot of spending money. Also, they have many other alternative activities in which they can be involved.

Entertainment events are a promotional tool which have been successful in attracting the youth, family, and Hispanic market segments. This tool is used by Santa Anita to achieve market expansion by increasing the size and diversity of its patronage base. The events are all held in the infield, which is an area that was specifically designed for picnicking and socializing. Comedy shows have been effective in attracting families and fans between 18 and 25 years old. The park hosted a "Latin Fiesta" day featuring top Latin entertainers, which was successful in attracting more of the Hispanic population to the park.

To better appeal to specific market segments, Santa Anita utilizes marketing research. Demographic research revealed that the Hispanic population is growing rapidly in southern California. For this reason, more promotions are being aimed at the Latin segment. To effectively promote the "Latin Fiesta" day, Santa Anita Park has advertised on Spanish speaking radio and television. In the short run, the park may lose money by featuring costly entertainment events. However, management believes it will pay off in the long run in the form of increased and more diverse patronage.

Even with the increase in promotions, fewer people are visiting Santa Anita than in the past. "Racing used to be recession-proof and inflation-proof," says Clifford Goodrich, CEO of the Los Angeles Turf Club. Between December 26, 1990 and April 22, 1991, there was a 4.5 percent decline in attendance at Santa Anita Park and a 7 percent drop in the amount wagered.

Actually, enthusiasm for horseracing has been on the decline since 1985, when the state's lottery began. Suddenly, there was a legal and easier way to gamble than going to the park. The tracks have fought back, obtaining laws that allow gamblers to bet at their local track on races at other Southern California tracks, as well as allowing some bettors outside the state to bet on California racing. Yet, according to Goodrich, as more "satellite" wagering sights go into operation, attendance at Santa Anita is expected to fall by as much as 25 percent.

In the future, Santa Anita will have to work even harder to convince people that if offers more than just horse racing. The marketers at the racetrack have pioneered infield entertainment and competitors are now mimicking the offering. Through the 1990s the infield will play an even greater role in persuading the folks around Santa Anita that the park provides both horse racing and worthwhile entertainment. Yet technology may render these strategies obsolete. The horseracing industry is already looking into a system that will allow people to place bets from their living rooms as they watch races on a cable channel, with bets and winnings channeled through an account with an authorized bank.

Questions

1. Why are sales promotional tools an essential part of Santa Anita's promotional mix?
2. What sales promotional tools are used by Santa Anita?
3. What specific market segments are Santa Anita's promotions directed to?
4. Are the sales promotional tools used by Santa Anita more likely to fulfill objectives related to market penetration or market development? Explain.
5. What message is Santa Anita trying to convey through its promotional strategy?

References

1. "Racetracks Search Out New Group of Bettors," *The New York Times*, May 28, 1992, p. B6.
2. "Santa Anita Sees Odds in Its Favor," *The New York Times*, May 10, 1991, p. D3.
3. "Incentive Marketing: And They're Off?," *Incentive*, June 1991, pp. 29–31.
4. "Long Shot," *Forbes*, April 16, 1990, pp. 92–93.

CASE 18

CHIAT/DAY: CREATING AN ADVERTISING CAMPAIGN

Chiat/Day is one of the largest U.S. advertising agencies; in 1988 its billings peaked at $314 million. Today its major U.S. accounts include Eveready, American Express, Fox Broadcasting Company, Nissan, National Car Rental, Reebok, and Spy Magazine. Most of the work done for these companies, as well as Chiat/Day's other advertising campaigns, is known for its innovativeness and creativity. Its stunning "1984" campaign for Apple computers was selected as the Commercial of the Decade by *Advertising Age* in 1990.

Further examples of Chiat/Day's talent include the commercials for VeryFine juices, which involve flashes of images, more like an MTV video than a commercial. It also created Reebok's "Lets U.B.U." campaign. Unfortunately, this campaign was too esoteric, and few people understood it. Reebok, after losing its first place spot in the highly competitive athletic shoe market to Nike, had to drop the campaign and create one which was more relevant to the product. Chiat/Day also created the tongue-in-cheek commercials for Nynex Yellow pages, which won several awards. More recently, Chiat/Day's ads featured decathletes Dave Johnson and Dan O'Brien in Reeboks at the 1992 Olympic games.

Chiat/Day has had to face many of the problems associated with the advertising business. First, when it won the Nissan account, it lost the Porsche account. Likewise, it could not be the ad agency for both Nike and Reebok. Companies in general do not like to have their advertising agency creating commercials for one of their major competitors. Conflict of interest questions arise, and one of the accounts almost always moves. Second, Chiat/Day lost its top creative director to Ogilvy and Mather in the late 1980s. Movement of key agency personnel and talent is a fact of life in advertising, but it sometimes hits an agency pretty hard.

Chiat/Day's innovative streak is not limited to its creative side. It was the first U.S. agency to incorporate the idea of account planning into its operations. Originating in Great Britain, account planning involves having a consumer advocate participate at all stages of the campaign development process to make suggestions and give opinions. An account planner helped Chiat/Day win the Porsche of North America account because of the extensive research that was done to understand the Porsche company.

The Porsche account presented some unique advertising problems. In the first place, Chiat/Day had to understand the particular marketing objectives and problems its client faced. Specifically, Porsche is an expensive, high performance car, and the company needed to convince people that they should spend $40,000 to have one when they could fill their transportation needs with a less expensive alternative.

One problem with advertising the Porsche cars was that, unlike creating advertising for a new product, Chiat/Day's creative team had to deal with the entire history and image of the company and the product that had gone before. One advertising executive noted that, "Porsche was not in control of its image." Porsche at once represented technical perfection, excitement, status, and glamour. Was it a sex symbol or a machine? The head of Porsche North America felt that one of Porsche's main advertising problems was that the simple idea that it was a very different kind of car was not being conveyed.

Chiat/Day's creative team soon realized that their mission was to make the advertising live up to the experience of driving a Porsche. They presented two campaigns to their client. The first one, which contained multiple images and more information, failed to capture the essentials of the car and the philosophy of the company behind it. The back-up campaign was a hit with the company. It was more dramatic and a little enigmatic, focusing on the sleek lines of a single car and imparted the commitment of the company to performance.

Advertising can either give information or create a certain feeling to help convince the consumer to buy the product. Consumers use both their logic and their emotions when deciding to buy something as expensive and luxurious as a Porsche. With "high involvement" products like a Porsche, customers may need both kinds of messages to make their purchase decision. Given the many media alternatives, Chiat/Day pros are constantly faced with the dilemma of which combination of print and TV adds to use in a campaign. They are well aware that TV can bring the experience of a product to life with powerful graphics and motion. On the other hand, print ads can carry more information in a more organized way. Print ads also allow the viewer to retain more information.

The difference between emotional and informative advertising became an important dynamic for the design of the campaign to introduce the Macintosh computer from Apple. Apple had several advertising goals to meet at once. Apple was a new company that wanted to change the way people thought about using computers. Apple also wanted to convey that its Macintosh computer was very different from IBM's and much simpler to use.

The resulting campaign involved *both* dramatic and comparative TV ads supported by more detailed print ads. The "Why 1984 Won't Be Like 1984" campaign successfully conveyed the unconventional nature of Apple and its computers. Print ads provided more detailed product information. These advertisements appealed to consumers on a logical level and a psychological level.

The Apple Macintosh campaign was one of the most successful developed at Chiat/Day. But the communications package that they chose was not limited to advertising alone. Chiat/Day also developed an unusual promotion for computers. Computers are a big-ticket item, yet unlike many durable products, consumers cannot try the product before it is purchased. The promotion that Chiat/Day designed involved letting consumers take the Mac home to try it and see if it met their needs. Chiat/Day focused the advertising around the idea of test driving the Mac. The print ads cleverly showed the mouse, then a unique feature on Apple computers, and a hand wearing a driving glove. The copy read "Take Macintosh out for a test drive." Consumers did, in droves!

When Steve Jobs of Apple computer came to Chiat/Day with the idea of letting consumers take the Mac home to try it out, Lee Chow of Chiat/Day immediately thought of a test drive. The concept was good, but Chiat/Day had only one week to come back with complete TV and radio ad mock-ups. Despite the tight time frame, Chiat/Day was able to deliver the ads on schedule. The promotion was tested in Palo Alto, California, and Houston, Texas. It was eventually rolled out on a national basis. All in all, 200,000 Macs were "test driven," and 40 percent of unit sales during the promotion period were attributed to this effort.

Chiat/Day did not limit itself to being just an advertising agency. It has moved effectively into other communications areas as well. It bought Jessica Dee Communications, a public relations agency. Public relations agencies help clients present themselves in a positive way to the public as a whole. The company is usually the focus, not a particular product. Because of the relationship with Chiat/Day, Jessica Dee Communications was able to triple its billings in less than a year. Chiat/Day also bought Bright & Associates, a design and marketing consulting company. Marketing consulting companies provide ideas on marketing strategies and ways to implement them. Through these acquisitions Chiat/Day was able to offer an expanded range of services to its clients.

Chiat/Day also has its own direct marketing unit called Perkins/Butler. This marketing service firm provides clients with ideas on content for direct mail pieces, lists of names to whom they should be sent, and methods to make them as effective as possible. Chiat/Day hired an executive from Wunderman Worldwide, one of the biggest direct mail shops, to head up this new unit. One Chiat/Day client, National Car Rental, immediately signed up with Perkins/Butler. It is expected that other Chiat/Day clients will follow suit.

Chiat/Day has an idea for a sales promotion agency in the works. If it goes through it will become a full service communications company. Chiat/Day also hopes that these marketing communications companies will add cash flows, and help Chiat/Day in the increasingly competitive and difficult advertising business.

Questions

1. What were Porsche's advertising objectives?
2. What were the problems in advertising Porsche?
3. A creative director at Chiat/Day suggests that TV is the best for emotional advertising, whereas print is best for informational advertising. Do you agree? Why or why not?
4. What were Apple's advertising objectives for the Mac?
5. What was Chiat/Day's strategy in advertising the Macintosh? Was it an effective advertising campaign? Why or why not?

References

1. "Ad Review: Nike Leads Way to Super Bowl," *Advertising Age*, January 20, 1992, p. 1.
2. "Chiat/Day Arms AmEx to Fight Back," *Advertising Age*, November 11, 1991, p. 74.
3. "TV Commercial of the Decade–Apple's Bold '1984' Scores on All Fronts," *Advertising Age*, January 1, 1990, p. 12.
4. "1989 Media All-Star," *Marketing & Media Decisions*, December 1989, p. 85.
5. "Apple Drives Off with Unusual Handling," *Advertising Age*, May 2, 1985, p. 18.
6. "Chiat/Day Expands Holdings," *Advertising Age*, February 29, 1988, p. 12; *Advertising Age*, March 30, 1988, p. 34.
7. "New Director Seeks to End Ogilvy Slump," *The New York Times*, November 3, 1989, p. D5.

CASE 19

LIPTON & LAWRY

Personal selling is one of the most important components of the marketing mix. The salesperson has the first contact with the customer (retailer), and is the one who must handle any questions or complaints that customers might have. Salespeople must also deal with a corporate headquarter's staff, which may not fully understand the reality of the marketplace. The salesperson must meet his or her sales objectives, and these are developed by marketers who are not out in the field every day. All in all, the salesperson has a difficult yet important task.

At Lipton & Lawry (L&L), a subsidiary of the Anglo-Dutch company Unilever, the sales force has helped the company grow to what it is today. The company earns sales of $1.3 billion, selling teas, seasonings, spices, and dry soup. Some of these products have captured an 80 percent share of their market. This is due in no small part to L&L's excellent sales force. The L&L sales organization is divided into three regions, and each region is subdivided into districts and then sales units.

L&L salespeople are highly qualified individuals who are well trained and equipped for the job.

When L&L salespeople are first hired, they go through a 27-week training period. During this time they are given information on the company, its products, and its markets. They take part in seminars designed to improve their selling and presentation skills. They also spend a considerable amount of time in the field with other L&L salespeople to get a more realistic idea of what they need to do to be successful. As the training period progresses, the trainees are given more and more responsibilities, until that time when they are ready to receive their own sales assignment.

But training at L&L does not stop after the first six months. Sales meetings are held on a regular basis, at which time sales managers and representatives can discuss any issues or problems that might be causing trouble in the field. At L&L, each sales rep is responsible for selling the company's entire product line, so it is important that he or she be fully aware of what the programs and plans are for each. This can be done through the sales meetings.

One of the ways L&L motivates its salespeople is through a well designed compensation plan. This provides the field people an incentive to sell as much product as they possibly can. L&L uses a compensation plan that is a combination of straight salary and bonuses. Using a straight salary provides security for salespeople and prevents them from suffering financially as a result of sales problems beyond their control. Furthermore, the bonus, which can be as much as 25 percent of the base salary, gives them the incentive to actively sell the product.

Although L&L's sales force has been successful, it must be adaptable. The role of the salesperson is a constantly changing one. As marketing adapts to its environment, so must the sales staff. In an increasingly competitive environment, salespeople, like the ones at L&L, must become partners with their customers if they hope to continue selling to them. Gone are the days when a salesperson simply went into a store and put products on the shelf. A grocery manager has thousands of possible products which he or she could choose to put out on the shelves. It is the L&L salesperson's job to make sure that L&L's product line is prominently included.

To draw attention to a product on the shelf, the L&L sales rep has available to him or her a wide range of point-of-purchase (POP) materials. Displays, posters, specialized shelf tags, and stick-on coupons are but a few of the vehicles used to increase awareness and sales at retail.

In 1988, L&L sales reps began using computers. In the past, the L&L sales rep would keep information regarding display and sales activity on a sales activity sheet that was submitted to the district office at the end of each week. Information regarding product distribution and shelf placement was kept on a separate sheet that the sales rep kept in his or her files. This system of storage was eliminated by L&L in favor of hand-held computers. These computers were made available to every sales rep in the country and proved an effective way of retrieving sales information on a daily basis. The rep could punch in which products were being sold in each store, the number and types of displays present, and the sales made. This information could then be downloaded into a main computer each evening and viewed by sales management the following day. The hand-held computer not only enables sales management to more closely monitor sales activity, it also helps managers to accurately measure the performance of individual sales reps.

The salesperson of today must be willing to work with the retailer if he or she is to receive cooperation. In order to foster this new relationship, salespeople must consider the needs of the retailer, and offer sensible ways to increase the customer's sales and profits.

Questions

1. Is the Lipton & Lawry (L&L) sales rep an order taker, an order getter, or a consultant? Why?
2. Is L&L's sales effort organized by territory, by product, or by customer? What is the rationale behind this organization?
3. What type of compensation plan would you suggest for L&L's salespeople?
4. Could L&L benefit from a telemarketing unit? What would be the role of such a unit?
5. How might L&L management evaluate the effectiveness of its sales effort?

References

1. "Partnership Selling, The Wave of the Future," *Marketing News*, December 19, 1988, p. 17.

CASE 20

YAMAHA MOTORCYCLES: PRICING INFLUENCES

During the early 1980s, Yamaha found itself considering a risky move: marketing a large (1200 cc) high-performance motorcycle, known as the V-MAX, in the United States at a time when a tariff had been imposed on foreign brands having 700 cc or larger engines. The tariff was intended to protect Harley-Davidson's market share, which had slipped from 21.2 percent in 1978 to 12.5 percent in 1983. In the same year Honda, Yamaha and Suzuki had 50.4%, 15.2%, and 11.9% market shares respectively, by way of comparison. In the first year of the tariff, foreign manufacturers' costs increased by about 45 percent, but this percentage was scheduled to fall to 10 percent by 1988. The tariff's sliding scale was designed to give Harley time to complete product-line improvements and implement just-in-time manufacturing techniques, while giving foreign manufacturers a chance to gradually reenter the American motorcycle market.

The tariff affected all foreign motorcycle makers, including Yamaha. Harley's increase in market share came primarily at Honda's expense. Yamaha's market share rose slightly during this three-year period, by less than one percentage point.

In 1986, Harley's market share rose to 19.4 percent and it voluntarily asked the government to lift the tariff a year before it was scheduled to expire. Even with the tariff lifted, Harley believed that an exchange rate favorable to U.S. manufacturers would keep Japanese motorcycle prices high: in an 18-month period the dollar had fallen by more than 50 percent against the yen. For 1986 the market shares for the four other Japanese competitors had shifted to the following split: Honda, 36.9%; Yamaha, 16.1%; Suzuki, 12.0%; and Kawasaki, 11.3%.

In addition to economic factors, Yamaha had to contend with strong competition from both American and Japanese manufacturers. By designing the V-MAX as a powerful "muscle" bike, Yamaha realized that it would be competing head-to-head with Harley Davidson in the United States. Competition from Japanese manufacturers was also steep. In 1981, Honda saturated the Japanese market with so many motorcycles that Yamaha was forced to discount most of its existing models and lost about $300 million in a two-year period. Of the four main Japanese firms, Yamaha suffered the most from recessionary market conditions and the imposition of the tariff. Unlike the other Japanese manufacturers, Yamaha was heavily dependent on motorcycle sales—about 60 percent of its sales came from motorcycles, compared with only 30 percent at Honda and Suzuki. In addition, Yamaha was especially dependent on exports and had to contend with high transportation costs since its production facilities were located primarily in Japan.

The success of the V-MAX was therefore critical to Yamaha's ability to regain market share and become profitable in the motorcycle industry. In deciding whether to go ahead with the design and manufacture of the V-MAX, Yamaha undertook several months of careful market research, including concept and advertising testing, assessing consumer demand and price sensitivity for the new product, and obtaining input from dealers about likely consumer responses to the new product.

Fourteen different focus groups using motorcycle owners as participants were conducted. The participants were shown drawings of different motorcycles and were asked whether they would buy that particular one, and if not, why. Respondents were also shown drawings of the V-MAX and were asked how much they would pay for it and what feelings they got from the motorcycle. Several people offered prices in the range of $4,500 to $5,000, and added that it looked like a very powerful machine. One participant added that it gave him a "Lone Ranger" image, while another stated that if his neighbor saw the V-MAX, he would rush right out to trade in his Honda. All of these comments indicated that there was definitely a market for a high-powered status motorcycle like the V-MAX.

Yamaha's pricing strategy is central to its success. The manager of product planning, Dennis Stefani, states that small, low-priced motorcycles are a part of the product line. This is true in order to provide appeal for new buyers who are looking for features and styling but who are not willing to pay a high price for them. The firm uses a strategy of pricing small motorcycles at the low end in order to get first-time users "hooked" on motorcycle riding. It is assumed that these customers will eventually trade up to larger, more expensive models. Another strategy Yamaha uses is to provide products in different sizes with varying levels of power, so that entire families can ride together.

The issue of pricing was particularly important to Yamaha since the V-MAX had to provide both unique styling and a powerful engine, and the consumer had to be willing to pay more for those qualities. Yamaha realized that offering the V-MAX at the wrong price could greatly impair sales of the new bike—even if consumers were impressed by its other attributes. Yamaha's assistant product manager, John Porter, felt that consumers would not be price-sensitive to the V-MAX: the type of person who would buy the V-MAX will value the fact that it has one of the most powerful engines on the market (135–140 horsepower) and will pay a premium price for it.

Many kinds of costs were included in the price of the V-MAX—research and development, manufacturing, advertising, distribution, and inventory costs. Additional features such as shaft drive and fuel injection also raised its price.

As mentioned, the 1983 tariff and yen-dollar exchange rate also raised the cost to the manufacturer and, ultimately, the price to the consumer. The role of government trade policies and foreign exchange are also critical to price strategy. The 1983 tariff affected the high-priced end of Yamaha's product line and added about 45 percent to the cost of large motorcycles. Yamaha believes that in the long run, the customer loses out as a result of the policy.

With all of those factors in mind, the price for the V-MAX was initially set at $5,299, making it one of the most expensive motorcycles then on the market. Interviews with customers and dealers confirmed that there was a great deal of excitement about the V-MAX and that motorcycle enthusiasts thought that the price was justifiable.

Advertising campaigns were developed to communicate the V-MAX's two most important features: its high-performance engine and its styling reminiscent of the 1950s hot rods. One ad, set in a 1950s hamburger place called Angelo's, shows a V-MAX pulling up to the entrance and creating havoc as many onlookers turn to stare at its unique design. Yamaha dealers also note that just having a V-MAX in their showroom was a kind of advertising; people came in to ask questions about the new product but could be shown models that were more appropriate for their needs.

Yamaha exemplifies the Japanese knack for converting technology and production expertise into products that have worldwide value, and unique customer appeal. By 1988, Japanese motorcycle companies were able to produce an annual 5.78 million motorcycles, which is 23 percent more than in 1987. This boost in output was due to increased production of parts for offshore assembly and increased domestic demand for smaller scooters (50 cc). These factors resulted in a 7 percent increase in output in 1989.

Production and sales remain critical to cost structure and pricing decisions among Japan's motorcycle makers as they faced decreased demand from their principle export market, North America. Two factors contributed to this decrease. First, the 1990–92 recession cut sharply into sales of motorcycles. Second, Harley-Davidson became a more effective competitor due to a successful cost-cutting program. By allowing more cost effective inventory management and production through the implementation of quality control methods, Harley remained viable in a temporarily weak market. Ultimately it allowed them to surpass Yamaha and Honda and become the largest supplier of heavyweight motorcycles in the United States.

In the early 1990s these factors made the motorcycle industry ever more competitive. But, Yamaha is poised to meet competition by generating greater demand in new markets.

Questions

1. Did Yamaha follow the process of price determination in Figure 20.1 in setting prices for its motorcycles? Specify whether and how it followed each step.
2. Does Yamaha follow a price-lining strategy? Explain.
3. What are the cost elements that must be represented in the price?
4. What environmental factors have affected the demand for motorcycles? How did these factors affect price?

References

1. Okubo Toshihiko, "Motorcycle Production Recovers From Slump," *Business Japan*, July 1989, pp. 103–105.
2. Sharon Brady, "Applications: MRP II—School of Hard Knocks," *Software Magazine*, April 1988, pp. 37–44.
3. Beth Bogart, "Harley-Davidson Trades Restrictions for Profits," *Advertising Age*, August 10, 1987, p. S-27.
4. Andrew Tanner, "Create or Die," *Forbes*, April 6, 1987, pp. 52–57.
5. John A. Conway, "Harley Back in Gear," *Forbes*, April 20, 1987, p. 8.
6. Brian S. Moskal, "Reshaping 'Hog Heaven,'" *Industry Week*, February 9, 1987, p. 56.
7. "Yamaha Plays a Different Tune," *The Economist*, November 9, 1985, pp. 96–97.
8. Michael Oneal, "Harley-Davidson: Ready to Hit the Road Again," *Business Week*, July 21, 1986, p. 70.

GREAT MOMENTS IN PRICING: PRICING METHODS AND STRATEGIES

CASE 21

Price may be the most difficult aspect of the marketing mix to determine since it is, to a large extent, set by the marketplace. Of course, producers seek to cover the costs they incur while manufacturing and selling a product; but they must also consider their competitors' prices, the degree to which their product is differentiated from others, the psychological value of the product, the prices of other items in their own product lines, to name a few. According to Barry Tyson, a supplier of aircraft engines at Garret Turbine Co., there is no necessary relationship between what it costs to build a product and the price that is established for it; the difference between the fabrication cost and the selling price is determined by the marketplace.

Most consumers have a perception of what they want to pay for a particular product and they look for a high price-to-value relationship. Determining value is a very subjective process, in which people rely partly on intuition and partly on cues such as brand names and information provided through advertising and promotions.

Assessing consumer perceptions of value for a given product, and therefore a reasonable price, is difficult for a producer because pricing policies are heavily regulated by the government. Producers are prohibited by law from discussing their pricing strategies with competitors and trade associations. In spite of these restrictions, every price structure in the United States probably violates some law. Another reason why pricing is a sensitive subject is that many businessmen don't really know much about pricing. The fashion designer Carushka, for example, admits that she had no idea of how to price her line of clothes during her first year of business, but fortunately made a profit anyway. She realized that her intuitive approach was not necessarily the best one and hired an accounting firm to show her how to complete cost sheets and improve her pricing structure.

The prices producers set for their products should reflect their overall marketing strategy. If a product is highly differentiated from competitive brands and consumer demand is great for that product, a skim-the-cream pricing structure may be appropriate. For example, the Garfield telephone, which is styled after a popular cartoon character, was priced at $50, while regular phones were priced at about $20.

High prices may also be set for products that have inverse demand curve, in which lower prices hurt, rather then stimulate, sales. Perfume and wine are two examples of products for which consumers are willing to pay more and not less. These products are status items often given as gifts. Consumers want to make a statement by their choice of perfume or wine and are therefore willing to pay $200 per ounce for Halston perfume or $50 for a bottle of Robert Mondavi's Opus One wine.

Michael and Timothy Mondavi, of the Robert Mondavi Winery, price their wines at a premium. Mondavi wines are of a higher quality than competitors' brands and consumers remember good quality long after the price is forgotten. Mondavi tries to establish a price that is high but not outrageous. The trade then raises wine prices, which is just another way of saying that the marketplace determines the price.

Many wine experts, such as Jack Davies, the owner of the California-based Schramsberg Winery, believe that premium-priced wines are a segment of the wine industry in which there is sales growth potential, offsetting the overall trend toward flat sales. In 1986, for example, sales of California premium wines—which account for 10 percent of the state's $5.5 billion wine industry—climbed 12 percent for brands priced over $3 per bottle and 17 percent for brands priced over $7 per bottle. In contrast, sales of inexpensive wines (priced below $3 dollars a bottle) fell by about 5 percent. Mr. Davies says that there are many reasons for the growth of this segment, including consumer awareness of drunk driving problems, which has contributed to an emphasis on quality, rather than quantity. In addition, young consumers who drank inexpensive wines during the 1980s now have more disposable income and more sophisticated tastes.

In order to establish a price-value association in the consumer's mind, marketers rely on techniques such as advertising, sales brochures, and information provided by retail dealer. Richard Recchia, a spokesman for Mitsubishi, states that he uses magazine articles and advertisements to help consumers establish a price-value relationship for the firm's premium-priced cars. One ad reads, "Don't tell Mitsubishi it's underpriced," implying that the consumer is getting much more value than he's paying for.

Mitsubishi also makes product design decisions based on how much value a certain feature adds to the entire package. For example, Mitsubishi modified its truck lineup so that additional value was added to its two- and four-wheel drive pickup and sports utility models. The improved Mighty Max and Montero models include features such as a 5-speed manual overdrive transmission, double-wall cargo box, dual outside mirrors, tinted glass, chrome-plated bumpers and an 18-gallon fuel tank.

Value is also enhanced by the establishment of customer satisfaction programs such as Mitsubishi's Diamond Care program, which has three goals: (1) to increase product knowledge on the part of the sales personnel; (2) to institute a more complete pre-delivery inspection process; and (3) to train dealers to follow up on each sale by contacting the consumer after delivery.

Mitsubishi is a good example of how a company can address two or more different consumer markets defined according to differing consumer budgets. By offering low-end models as well as fancier premium cars, Mitsubishi can reach a broader range of customers. Another good example is how Walt Disney offers a range of merchandise that ranges from 25 cents to fit a kid's budget to $400 for a Mickey watch! By pricing each category differently and by keeping the marketing strategies separate, a company can grow into new market segments. This is often called "bracketing" and can also be a very effective competitive tool for pricing relative to your competitors.

Although many consumers believe that higher prices really do signal better quality, some research suggests that price-quality relationships are weak in general and tend to be product-specific. In one study, data were taken from different issues of Consumers' Union's *Buying Guide* which publishes ratings for product characteristics such as convenience, durability and safety. Based on these ratings, different products can be ranked in terms of quality. The *Buying Guide* also lists prices for these products. The researcher analyzed those data for 145 different products, using the ratings as measures of relative quality and the prices as signals to the consumer of brand quality. The researcher found that high price was not usually correlated with high quality; only 27 percent of the best-quality brands were the most expensive, and 36 percent of the best brands had prices below the average price. In addition, the researcher found that frequently purchased items have a weaker price-quality relationship than infrequently purchased, expensive items such as freezers, typewriters and compact stereos among others.

In spite of research that casts doubt on the price quality relationship, many consumers do believe that a high price signals better quality, because most products are not identical. For example, laundry detergents differ in terms of softeners, cold- versus hot-water cleaning strength, amount of bleach, and so on. The average consumer does not know how each one of these attributes contributes to the price of the product. Instead of trying to figure out exactly which product is the best buy, consumers often figure out exactly which product is the best buy, consumers often select familiar brands with names they trust. Aspirin is a product category in which brand names are important, although quality tends to be the same from brand to brand. A study by *Consumer Reports* found that no one brand they tested—including Bayer—performed significantly better than the competition, although the prices differed greatly. For example, Bayer aspirin cost as much as $2.34 for 100 tablets whereas Kroger aspirin cost only $0.38 for 100 tablets.

In contrast to premium-priced products, some goods may be priced below the competitors brands as a part of marketing strategies that are designed to stimulate initial and repeat purchases. They can also be used to build brand awareness. For example, Don Tredennick of Western Cruise Lines stated that he lists his firm's price in brochures as a little lower than the per diem price of his competition. This tactic creates an inducement to select a Western cruise over that of another line.

Another very good example of the strategic value of pricing your product below a competitor is the way Arm & Hammer introduced its new laundry detergent. In the crowded detergent segment, strong brands dominate, Arm & Hammer was innovative enough appeal to the consumer's budget! By selling at a price of 24 cents an ounce compared to Tide's 53 cents an ounce, consumers were enticed just enough by the savings to switch to the new brand. That savings push was just enough to make them try it.

Questions

1. What is the importance of the price-value relationship? Provide an example from the case.
2. What is meant by an inverse demand curve in pricing? Provide an example from the case.
3. Many companies segment their markets by high and low prices. Can you provide an example from the case?
4. Was Mitsubishi practicing price lining? Was West Ridge Mountaineering? Explain.
5. Why did Arm & Hammer introduce its detergent with a penetration strategy?

References

1. Matt DeLorenne, "Mitsubishi Addresses Customer Satisfaction," *Automotive News*, March 17, 1986, pp. 20, 22.
2. Eitan Gerstner, "Do Higher Prices Signal Higher Quality?" *Journal of Marketing Research 22* (May 1985), pp. 209–215.
3. Jean Hamilton, "What Slump? It's a Vintage Year for Premium California Wines," *Business Week*, May 19, 1986, pp. 98, 101.
4. "Is Bayer Better?" *Consumer Reports*, July 1982, pp. 347–349.
5. "Mitsubishi Pushes Value as Part of 1986 Truck Lineup," *Automotive News*, December 2, 1985, pp. 14, 30.
6. Len Strasowski, "Vintner Blends Wine Making and Marketing Savvy," *Advertising Age*, April 7, 1986, pp. S15-16.

CASE 22

PARKER-HANNIFIN: STRATEGIC MARKETING PLANNING

Parker-Hannifin Corporation is the United States' largest producer of a full line of motion control products, including fluid power systems, electro-mechanical controls and related components. The company makes everything from O-rings for the Space Shuttle to automotive parts, but concentrates on fluid-drive (hydraulic) motion control devices. In 1991, sales from Parker's over 100,000 products and services were $2.4 billion. Motion control devices are a vital technology because they serve as the heart and brains of industrial systems; they provide both the power and guidance for an industrial system or device.

The pumps and parts manufactured by Parker are essential components in such products as huge hydroelectric dams and tiny intravenous pump systems. Because of these broad applications, Parker offers more than 800 product lines to over 1,200 diverse markets in the United States and abroad. Parker's customers represent many different industries, including automotive, industrial, aviation, aerospace, marine, and defense.

As a seller of industrial goods, Parker has customers that include both governments and private sector businesses on an international basis. Parker views the world as both a market for its products as well as a prime location for many of its 159 manufacturing facilities. Today, Parker employs over 28,000 people around the world. Parker also has the largest distribution system in the motion control industry, with 4,500 distributors serving more than 258,000 customers around the world.

Because Parker's devices are used by manufacturing companies in their production process, it deals with buyers inside companies rather than with the general public. Consequently, it is directly affected by the ups and downs of these companies. In particular, the decline in the manufacturing sector of the U.S. economy changed the growth strategies used by Parker during the 1980s. In the late 1980s and early 1990s, its growth strategies were further influenced by underlying weaknesses in the U.S. defense industry and lower levels of military spending. An additional factor was the recent restructuring of the European marketplace.

Despite the well-publicized and bemoaned decline in American manufacturing, which directly affects Parker's customers, Parker has managed consistent growth. For most of the 1980s, sales grew at an average annual rate of about 15 percent, and profits per share grew 9.4 percent annually. As measures of its financial stability, until very recently the company had never taken a write-off nor had its debt to equity ratio exceeded 25 percent. Dividends have increased every year for the past 36 years. This stellar performance has been accomplished through Parker's philosophy of growth through diversification.

Since diversification has occurred within Parker's core business, it is better termed a convergent diversification strategy. That is, Parker is spreading its risk by moving into related product markets, instead of relying solely on hydraulic devices. The goal of this strategy is to insulate the company from the risks that result because of shifts in marketplace demand. Optimal diversification allows Parker to invest in a variety of opportunities within its motion control area, which might have previously been disregarded since they were not directly a part of this segment. For example, investment in a small infusion pump with biomedical applications has since generated business with annual growth rates of 25 percent. Before the adoption of this strategy, such an expansion would probably have been overlooked. Basically, a convergent acquisition strategy allows Parker to broaden its product line definition, and therefore increase the number of growth opportunities.

This diversification strategy has served Parker well. For example, from 1984 to 1988, weak demand and a price war in the market for main hydraulic systems left Parker's earnings flat and lowered margins by 33 percent. Additionally, the automotive parts segment of Parker's business was in turmoil, as Parker suffered because of the problems of the domestic auto makers. However, Parker was able to offset these losses with its booming aerospace business. Over the same time period, this segment grew at an annual rate of 20 percent. In addition, profit margins, at 17 percent, were also quite healthy. The net result was a doubling of sales over the five-year time frame. With orders from original equipment manufacturers (OEM's) like Boeing, John Deere, and Caterpillar increasing during that time, Parker captured additional sales growth.

In part, Parker's growth and health today can be attributed to a successful acquisition strategy. In fact, since its founding in 1921, Parker has grown through the acquisition of nearly 90 capital goods companies. Acquisitions made within the past 12 years have accounted for 40 percent of the company's total sales growth. Since 1978, Parker has purchased over 60 of its businesses, each one with the firm's core business area—motion control. From 1984 to 1987 alone, Parker bought 14 companies, moving into new, related areas such as industrial filters and pneumatic components. All of these have been small or single-product companies, which have given Parker the opportunity to broaden its product line.

Parker continued to grow with the purchase of seven new companies in 1988. The company slowed its appetite, however, in 1989 and 1990 to two companies per year and one in 1991. The majority of these recently acquired companies were located in Europe.

Despite this seemingly uncontrolled growth, every potential acquisition had to meet certain requirements. First, Parker only seeks companies that are showing a profit. The company ardently refrains from hostile takeovers. Each acquisition has to contribute to Parker's line of existing products, add a new technology, or increase the firm's market share in a given segment. An important part of Parker's acquisition strategy is that it only considers profitable firms with good management that are willing to stay on. Several examples illustrate the effect of the stringent restrictions on acquisitions imposed by Parker. The recent acquisition of Schrader Bellows allowed Parker to become the market leader in the manufacturing of pneumatic products and automation systems. By buying Finite Filter, Parker extended its current product line to include pneumatic filter products. Finally, with the addition of the Nichols Group, Parker opened the door to the world of fiber optics.

The convergent acquisition strategy has been extremely successful for Parker throughout the 1980s and early 1990s. It helped Parker's 1989 worldwide revenues to exceed $2.5 billion for the first time ever. Parker's success can be attributed to the way in which it actively managed its growth. It sought to diversify risk because of the obvious pitfall of having all of one's eggs in the same basket, particularly as an industrial seller in the manufacturing sector. Parker also recognized the importance of sticking to its core business. By staying within related businesses, it avoided the problems many firms had during the 1980s, when they became huge conglomerates, selling everything under the sun, and eventually lost large sums of money by overextending their expertise and finances.

Furthermore, Parker-Hannifin seems to have weathered the 1990-1992 recession fairly well, given its dependence on the business cycles of the domestic air transportation and industrial markets as well as on the beleaguered defense sector. This is one of the major risks of a closely convergent growth plan. Despite an economy in prolonged recession and very depressed spending on capital assets,

Parker's sales were off only by 3 percent from their 1989 peak. Income from operations, however, fell by nearly half. This prompted some financial restructuring, downsizing of operations and a 9 percent cut in the number of employees.

Profits and shareholder earnings both dropped in 1991, but are expected to cycle back up with an anticipated recovery in the global industrial market. For example, about 45 percent of Parker's aerospace revenues are derived from sales of spare parts. In rough terms, these highly profitable replacement parts account for half of Parker's business. Despite industry-wide budget cuts for *new* equipment, replacement sales to OEM's should remain healthy worldwide and lead the Parker's rebound.

It is the very dynamics behind the U.S. business climate and the reshaping of the European Community that led Parker to emphasize the following in its current five year strategic plan:

- Prioritize financial performance goals
- Provide global product offerings and meet customer specifications, focus on technical and quality standards
- Expand regional marketing and manufacturing
- Provide total customer satisfaction
- Continue strategic acquisitions and emphasize offshore opportunities

The current line-up comprising Parker's mission marks a subtle shift, an adjustment, in its strategy. Parker currently reports that it is focusing on developing close partnerships with distributors to build sales and increase its customer base. Among other major programs, Parker continues to broaden product lines and offers co-op marketing programs to help distributors find new business. For example, Parker has expanded its filter products with new Teflon microfilters and miniature pneumatic filter-regulators. This was in response to the growing need for better filtration systems—driven by environmental concerns. Parker's offering of seal products is emphasizing new designs and compounds to further penetrate the competitive aerospace segment.

Overall, Parker's distributors are viewed as vital links to customers, as they provide service and deliver quality. A new 20,000-square foot "Super Stock" warehouse now enables a current Parker distributor to promptly deliver Parker's fluid-power and fluid-connector products from an extensive inventory. Parker is also developing new distributor networks in Czechoslovakia, rather than direct sales, to develop sales of fluid power and seal products in former East Bloc countries.

Parker continues to be vigilant in its growth strategies, staying within its core businesses yet expanding its global presence. This consists of a primarily European thrust. Despite the weakened economies of Europe, Parker is positioning itself strategically. In 1992, Europe became the largest industrially homogeneous market. For its part, Parker is exhibiting a leadership role by participating in the International Standards Organization, aiding the process of developing and implementing international technical standards for these new markets. For example, reducing the large number of internationally accepted fitting designs reduces manufacturers' cost and increases availability of standard product lines for customers. Parker plans to provide the standard input parts, building upon its superb distribution case.

Because of the successful implementation of its past and present growth strategies, Parker should continue its strong showing through the rest of the 1990s.

Questions

1. What business is Parker in?
2. What is Parker's business mix?

3. What is Parker's growth strategy? What are the risks of such a strategy?
4. What is the purpose of Parker's strategy of optimal diversification?
5. What criteria does Parker use in evaluating potential acquisitions?
6. How is Parker's growth strategy shifting? Why?

References

1. Parker-Hannifin Corporation Annual Report, June 30, 1991.
2. "Parker-Hannifin," *Value Line Investment Survey*, May 15, 1992, p. 1325.
3. "Capital Spending" *Standard & Poor's Industry Surveys*, Vol. 2, April 1992, pp. S15–S17, p. S43.
4. "Guest Commentary: Investment and Hard Work Will Win the Day," *Design News*, July 22, 1991, p. 158.
5. "Products that Cater to Foreign Tastes," *Design News*, July 8, 1991, pp. 90-94.
6. "Streetwalker: Power Plays," *Forbes*, April 15, 1991, p. 148.
7. "Faces Behind the Figures: Cliff Dodger," *Forbes*, January 9, 1989, pp. 322, 324.
8. "Parker-Hannifin Sees Sales Over $2 Billion in this Fiscal Year," *The Wall Street Journal*, April 12, 1998, p. 55.
9. "The Sum of All Parts," *Financial World*, February 23, 1988, pp. 24-25.
10. "The Big Revival in Milltown," *Fortune*, December 7, 1987, pp. 173-176.

HARLEY-DAVIDSON: A STUDY IN EVALUATION AND CONTROL

CASE 23

Nothing quite equals a ride atop the thundering engine and gleaming chrome of a Harley-Davidson motorcycle. Through savvy marketing management the company that makes this American classic has ensured that it is here to stay. With plants in Milwaukee, Wisconsin and York, Pennsylvania, Harley-Davidson, Inc. is the sole manufacturer of motorcycles in the United States today. Harley-Davidson is also an industry success story. The company was on the brink of collapse after a 1981 management buyout and in 1982 they suffered a $25 million loss, which brought them close to bankruptcy. Increasingly stiff Japanese competition from the likes of Honda, Suzuki, Yamaha, and Kawasaki also threatened Harley's survival and almost drove the firm permanently off the road.

Since 1981 the company has made a dramatic comeback, recovering from poor labor relations and plunging market share. Today Harley has regained control of 60 percent of the market share for heavyweight bikes (750 cc and over), which is it's primary market. The key to their success has been management's increased attention to marketing and productivity.

Harley-Davidson was founded in 1903 when William Harley and the Davidson Brothers—William, Walter, and Arthur—built their first three motorcycles in a backyard in Milwaukee. The first motorcycles were crude, but tough. Harley bikes were used as highway patrol bikes starting in 1907 and then as scout and dispatch bikes during both world wars. Indeed, Harley bikes became legendary, and gained status through such Hollywood movie classics as "The Wild One" and "Easy Rider." More importantly, Harley came to be "all-American" symbols of independence and ruggedness. The Harley mystique is unique, conjuring images of tattooed Hells Angels and Easy Riders clad in black leather. Today its image has softened a little, gaining wide appeal among white collar baby boomers. Even celebrities such as Elizabeth Taylor and the late Malcolm Forbes were well-known Harley fans.

Despite Harley-Davidson's long history, loyal customers, and strong reputation, management faced some difficult marketing problems in the early eighties. At this time Japanese manufacturers, especially Honda and Kawasaki, already dominant in Europe, were increasing pressure on the large and lucrative American market. During the 1981 recession Harley was unable to match large discounts being offered by foreign competition.

Japanese manufacturers were also carefully researching the U.S. markets and attempting to sell both the small and large motorcycles that fit consumer needs. As a consequence, for the first time, Harley's sales fell to second place in the super-heavyweight category (850 cc and over). Overall, Harley's market share slipped from 21.2 percent in 1978 to 12.5 percent in 1983. Significant financial losses began to mount and bankruptcy loomed.

In addition, Harley's parent company, AMF—a large leisure conglomerate who acquired Harley in 1969—began winding down the motorcycle manufacturer's operations in the late seventies. This was due to a declining commitment to manufacturing on their part. Specifically, they were cutting back on product design and development. This further aggravated Harley's competitive abilities. In fact, some of the motorcycles that came off of the assembly line were simply leaky and unreliable. It was at this time that a group of Harley-Davidson senior managers, led by Vaughn Beals, persuaded AMF to sell the company to them. According to Beals, who later became chairman, they believed in the product and wanted to do what was right for the company.

The new 13-member owner-management team took over in January 1981, burdened with a bank debt of $70 million. Over the next two years sales continued to fall by roughly 25 percent and in 1982 the firm took its first loss, $25 million, since the Great Depression.

Among the basic problems at Harley-Davidson was a long history of poor industrial relations. In 1973 there had been a 100-day strike at the main plant in Milwaukee. More recently, workers had expressed resentment of management's traditionally distant and unpredictable style. This problem was made worse by the big discounts, as much as 50 percent, that Honda was offering customers for its larger motorcycles. The new management somehow had to convince the heavily unionized work force to accept significant reductions in the cost of producing each unit if they were to stay competitive and increase sales.

The U.S. government was willing to lend Harley-Davidson a helping hand at this time. At the company's request the International Trade Commission levied an unprecedented 45 percent tariff on foreign imports of heavyweight bikes. The government recognized that the motorcycle maker was taking significant steps toward recovery, but that it had also been hurt by Japanese price cuts and the 1981 recession. The five-year tariff would provide protection while the firm rebuilt its competitive strengths. Ultimately, Harley's recovery was so successful that they were able to ask that the tariff be lifted a year ahead of schedule.

When they took over, Beals and his managers went to work with a vengeance. They were keenly aware of the superior manufacturing skills and high productivity of their Japanese rivals. With control of the company in their hands they set out to use the same techniques, and Harley-Davidson became one of the first U.S. companies to imitate Japanese efficiency and quality control systems. The dual objectives were to improve the motivation of Harley-Davidson's employees while at the same time lowering the cost of production.

In the Japanese style, the entire production process was decentralized. The old hierarchical management system was dropped and "area managers" were appointed, each having complete responsibility for their area of manufacturing. Harley-Davidson also implemented the use of another effective Japanese technique, Quality Circles (QCs) which give workers direct responsibility for the output of their area. Voluntary one-hour meetings took place each week on the shop floor. Managers and workers discussed any problems with production, quality, and working conditions.

Specifically, Harley-Davidson was aiming to build motorcycles that were reminiscent of old-style bikes but which were also technically up-to-date. From a marketing point of view they wanted to capitalize on the long tradition behind their motorcycles and on the perception that they made "real" motorcycles. This meant increased engineering efforts to combine the latest in technology and automation with traditional Harley styling. In addition, the motorcycle had to be built for higher reliability and lower maintenance.

To accomplish their manufacturing goals Harley introduced a system called "statistical operator control." This was another concept adapted from the statistical quality control systems widely used by Japanese manufacturers. The premise is that increases in quality and product performance are gained by systematic statistical analysis of components at each stage of the production process. A worker inspects the daily production run, measuring and checking to see if the parts meet the required specifications. How close the parts come to the specifications is tracked as well.

All in all, it was more productive and less expensive to monitor and evaluate the assembly line while parts were being made, and to make adjustments immediately, as opposed to the old method of after-the-fact inspections of the whole bike. In this way, defects or substandard components are weeded out before they even leave the plant. For example, results at the engine and transmission plant in Milwaukee included reduced set-up costs, less scrap, and the manufacture of "truer" and higher quality parts. One of the main benefits of statistical operator control is ongoing improvements in the overall production process, for which the workers themselves have responsibility.

It should be noted that while the focus on productivity and quality at Harley-Davidson was important during these hard times, it had to be accompanied by overall cost cutting as well. At the beginning, in 1982, the new management downsized the manual workforce at both the Milwaukee and York plants by 42 percent from 3,800 to 2,200. In addition, every salaried employee had to take a 9 percent cut in pay. Employees at every level of the firm had to be committed to the survival of the company, so even Beals himself took a pay cut of 12 percent and travelled coach on his frequent trips.

By using QCs and statistical operator control, individual workers were given the power to monitor and improve the performance of their machines and to give feedback on the production process. The men and women who were formerly just operators were specially trained to inspect their equipment by statistically analyzing performance. They were even trained to service the machines themselves. Managers soon noted that as they inspected the shop floors workers were challenging themselves to get tolerances down to the narrowest possible limits. Overall, the employees responded favorably to the new system and Harley gained a hard-won reputation for quality. Chairman Vaughn Beals states, "What we found was that the guys who used to be the problem workers turned out to be the ones who understood this the quickest."

Harley-Davidson's efforts to improve both morale and quality had dramatic, tangible results. By 1986, after five years, productivity was up by 50 percent and defects per unit were down by 70 percent. Its sales were up by 8 percent over 1985 and profits rose by 18 percent. For the first time in six years Harley regained leadership of the super-heavyweight class, at 33 percent market share over Honda's 31 percent. A return to basics put Harley-Davidson back in the black and in 1986 they were able to make an initial public stock offering to help provide additional resources needed to compete with Japanese motorcycle makers.

The improved manufacturing processes at Harley-Davidson has allowed them to compete more effectively with Japanese manufacturers by more closely meeting customer needs. Today, Harley has two specific market segments, motorcycles equipped for long-distance touring and specially fitted custom-factory motorcycles. Changes in manufacturing have allowed Harley-Davidson's assembly line to go from making 250 variations to as many as 1,053. This was accomplished by what workers affectionately refer to as their "jellybean" system, in which several different types of bikes come down the line at the same time. Beals states, "We could tailor-make bikes to any specifications we wanted. Where the Japanese were mass producing bikes by the millions, we could produce small quantities of particular models quickly and profitably. We transformed ourselves into niche marketers." Harley continued to improve this system, by implementing such processes as "Materials as Needed" or MAN in 1988. MAN is their version of Japanese Just-In-Time parts inventory supply and control. This system gives them additional cost savings and manufacturing flexibility.

Harley-Davidson worked hard during the eighties to bring management and workers closer together, which proved to be the key to improving their product and image. They succeeded in again dominating the large bike categories while their Japanese rivals were competing mainly in the smaller bike categories. The overall market size in the United States, however, is shrinking, and Harley's management is preparing for the future by targeting both the Japanese domestic market, where they have gained tremendous popularity, and the growing European market. They are well aware of the internationalization of competition and are poised to continue to be a major player by serving their loyal U.S. customers as well as new international markets.

Questions

1. What problems of control did Harley-Davidson face?
2. What productivity issues are facing Harley-Davidson? How are they addressing these issues?
3. What kind of control does Harley-Davidson's statistical operator control system represent? Why?
4. What evidence is there that Harley-Davidson implemented the quality circles concept?
5. What is the link between Harley-Davidson's productivity improvements and its current marketing strategy?

References

1. "Easy Rider Rides Again," *Tokyo Business Today*, July, 1991, p. 26.
2. "How Harley Outfoxed Japan With Exports," *The New York Times*, August 12, 1990.
3. "Vrooming Back: After Nearly Stalling, Harley-Davidson Finds New Crowd of Riders," *The Wall Street Journal*, August 31, 1990.
4. "Protected Species," *Arena*, Autumn, 1990.

NOTES

CHAPTER 1

1. "After Nearly Stalling, Harley-Davidson Finds New Crowd of Riders," *The Wall Street Journal*, August 31, 1990, A1 and A6.
2. Ibid, p. A1; and "How Harley Outfoxed Japan With Exports," *The New York Times*, August 12, 1990, F5.
3. "Kal Demitros' Campaign Steers Another Turnaround at Harley-Davidson," *Adweek's Marketing Week*, March 5, 1990, 8.
4. "After Nearly Stalling, Harley-Davidson Finds New Crowd of Riders," *The Wall Street Journal*, August 31, 1990, A1 and A6.
5. In 1985 the American Marketing Association formulated the following definition of marketing: "Marketing is the process of planning and executing the conception, pricing, promotion, and distribution of ideas, goods, and services to create exchange that will satisfy individual and organizational objectives." This is an equally acceptable definition as the one in the text, and most of its components will be discussed in this chapter.
6. *The Wall Street Journal*, August 31, 1990, A1.
7. "Now Soft-Drink Makers Brace for the Juice Wars," *The New York Times*, June 2, 1985, F12.
8. "Baking Soda Maker Strikes Again," *The New York Times*, June 16, 1990, 27–28.
9. *The New York Times*, June 16, 1990, 27.
10. Ibid, 28.
11. Ibid.
12. Douglas K. Ramsey, *The Corporate Warriors* (Boston: Houghton Mifflin Co., 1987), 89.
13. Teresa Domzal and Lynette Unger, "Emerging Positioning Strategies in Global Markets," *Journal of Consumer Marketing 4* (Fall 1987): 24.
14. Ibid.
15. "Pepsi, Coke: Art of Deal-Making," *Advertising Age*, February 19, 1990, 45.
16. "Takeovers Are Out, Soap Powder Is In," *Business Week*, May 6, 1991, 83.
17. "Demand Turns New Macintosh Into Rare Apple," *The Wall Street Journal*, November 21, 1990, B1, B5.
18. J. B. McKitterick, "What Is the Marketing Management Concept?" in *The Frontiers of Marketing Thought and Science*, Frank M. Bass, ed., (Chicago: American Marketing Association, 1957).
19. *General Electric Company*, 1952 Annual Report, New York, 21.
20. Michael E. Porter, *Competitive Strategy* (New York: The Free Press, 1980), Ch. 2.
21. "How D&B Organizes for a New-Product Blitz," *Business Week*, November 16, 1981, 87.
22. *Code of Ethics*, American Marketing Association, Chicago Illinois.
23. "Public Interest Groups Achieve Higher Status and Some Permanence," *The Wall Street Journal*, August 27, 1984, 1.
24. John A. Goodman and Larry M. Robinson, "Strategies for Improving the Satisfaction of Business Customers," *Business* (April–June 1982): 40–44. Figure 1.1
25. "The Issues of Corporate Ethics," *Research Alert*, February 5, 1988, 2.
26. John W. Hanley, "Monsanto's Early Warning System," *Harvard Business Review, 59* (November/December 1981): 107–122.
27. "The Green Revolution: McDonald's," *Advertising Age*, May 7, 1990. S-2.

CHAPTER 2

1. "The Picture Brightens," *Barron's*, June 1990, 8.
2. "Kodak Tries to Prepare for Filmless Era Without Inviting Demise of Core Business," *The Wall Street Journal*, April 18, 1991, B1.
3. "Kodak Brand Calls Retreat in the Battery War," *Advertising Age*, October 15, 1990, 3, 69.
4. "Eastman Kodak Co. Has Arduous Struggle to Regain Lost Edge," *The Wall Street Journal*, April 2, 1987, 1.
5. "Aim, Focus and Shoot," *Forbes*, November 26, 1990, 67, 68 and 70.
6. *The Wall Street Journal*, April 18, 1991, B1, B7.
7. *Forbes*, November 26, 1990, 67.
8. Ibid, 67, 70.

9. "Sharply Focused," *Forbes*, December 24, 1990, 53.
10. Derek F. Abell, "Strategic Windows," *Journal of Marketing* 43(July 1978): 21–26.
11. *Advertising Age*, October 15, 1990, 3, 69.
12. Ibid.
13. "Duracell Adds Acid to Battery Zapfest," *Advertising Age*, November 3, 1986, 109.
14. "What's Recharging the Battery Business," *Business Week*, June 23, 1986, 124.
15. "Diet Coke's Formula: Stress Taste, Not Calories," *Advertising Age*, January 1, 1990, 16.
16. "Coca-Cola Discovers What's In a Name," *Marketing & Media Decisions*, Spring 1984, 66.
17. *Advertising Age*, January 1, 1990, 16.
18. "Diet Coke: #2 By '92," *Marketing & Media Decisions*, September 1989, 64.
19. "Playing the Global Game," *Forbes*, January 23, 1989, 90–91.
20. This section is based on "How the Japanese Won the West: Toyota's 20-Year Marketing Plan," *Ad Forum*, March 1985, 42–52.
21. "The Americanization of Honda," *Business Week*, April 25, 1988, 92.

CHAPTER 3

1. "We Had to Change the Playing Field," *Forbes*, February 4, 1991, 82–86.
2. Ibid, 84.
3. "Gillette Sensor: Global Innovation in Technology and Marketing," *Marketing Review*, March 1991, 29.
4. *Forbes*, February 4, 1991, 84.
5. *Marketing Review*, March 1991, 29.
6. "It's One Sharp Ad Campaign, But Where's the Blade?" *Business Week*, March 5, 1990, 30.
7. "With Sensor, Gillette Took Lead in 'Orchestration,' " *Adweek*, June 3, 1991, 18, 20; and *Marketing Review*, March 1991, 29.
8. Glen L. Urban and John R. Hauser, *Design and Marketing of New Products* (Englewood Cliffs, NJ: Prentice-Hall, 1980), 80-84.
9. *Forbes*, February 4, 1991, 84.
10. *Forbes*, February 4, 1991, 83; and *Marketing Review*, March 1991, 16.
11. "Hearts and Minds," *Adweek*, July 1, 1991, 36.
12. *Adweek*, June 3, 1991, 20.
13. "Sensor Turns to Direct Marketing," *Advertising Age*, May 20, 1991, 2.
14. James T. Roth, "Effectiveness of Sales Forecasting Methods," *Industrial Marketing Management* 7(1978): 116.
15. Ibid.
16. *Forbes*, February 4, 1991, 83.
17. "Sensor Sensation," *Advertising Age*, February 5, 1990, 4; and "Gillette Co.," *Advertising Age*, September 26, 1990, 76.

CHAPTER 4

1. "McD's faces U.S. slowdown," *Advertising Age*, May 14, 1990, 1; "An Icon Wakes Up To A Troubled Future," *The New York Times*, May 12, 1991, Business Section, 1.
2. *Advertising Age*, May 14, 1990, 1; and "The Green Revolution: McDonald's," *Advertising Age*, January 29, 1991, 32.
3. "McDonald's Big Mac-Over," *Adweek's Marketing Week*, June 25, 1990, 20.
4. *Advertising Age*, January 29, 1991, 32.
5. "McDonald's Isn't Looking Quite So Juicy Anymore," *Business Week*, August 6, 1990, 30.
6. "McDonald's Big Mac-Over," *Adweek's Marketing Week*, June 25, 1990, 20.
7. "McDonald's to Drop Plastic Foam Boxes . . ." *The Wall Street Journal*, November 2, 1990, A-3.
8. "Low-Fat Burger Being Tested By McDonald's," *The Wall Street Journal*, November 15, 1990, B-1.
9. *Advertising Age*, January 29, 1991, 32.
10. Ibid.
11. "The Green Revolution: P&G gets top marks in AA survey," *Advertising Age*, January 29, 1991, 8.

12. *The New York Times*, May 12, 1991, Business Section, 6.
13. *Adweek's Marketing Week*, June 25, 1990, 21.
14. "The Boomer Report," *Adweek's Marketing Week*, January 22, 1990, 20–27; Andrew P. Garvin, The Boomer Report Newsletter; and "The Baby Boomers Are Richer and Older," *Business Month*, October 1987, 24–28.
15. See also, "Nostalgia makes boomers buy," *Marketing News*, November 26, 1990, 1.
16. "Teens Take Control," *American Demographics*, March 1990, 12; and "The Kids Are Alright," *Mediaweek*, April 15, 1991, 25 and 26.
17. "Targeting Teens," *American Demographics*, February 1985, 25; and "Sexier the Better, Student Body Says," *Advertising Age*, February 5, 1990, S-1.
18. "Teens: The First Global Market," *Sales & Marketing Digest*, March 1990, 4.
19. Ibid.
20. "Getting In Position For The Older Market," *American Demographics*, June 1990, 38.
21. Ibid.
22. Ibid.
23. "P&G's Metamucil plan broadens," *Advertising Age*, January 29, 1991, 32.
24. *Sales and Marketing Management*, April 1987, 29.
25. "Changing Times," *The Wall Street Journal*, March 22, 1991, B-6.
26. "You'll know it's the 21st Century when . . ." *American Demographics*, December 1990, 24.
27. "Changing Times," *The Wall Street Journal*, March 22, 1991, B-6.
28. "Chocolate Makers Tempt Grown-Ups as Market Matures," *Ad Forum*, February 1984, 37–39.
29. "Feeding China's 'Little Emperors'," *Forbes*, August 6, 1990, 84–85.
30. "Panel Sees Change in U.S. Family but Not Jobs," *The New York Times*, January 17, 1986, A-11; "What Is A Working Woman," *American Demographics*, July 1988, 24–27 and 59; and "More Women Work at Traditional Male Jobs," *The New York Times*, November 15, 1982, C-1, C-20.
31. "What Do Women Want?," *Adweek's Marketing Week*, June 25, 1990, 39–42.
32. "Eating Habits Force Changes in Marketing," *Advertising Age*, October 30, 1978, 30, 34 and 65.
33. "Real Men Do Wear Aprons," *Across the Board*, November 1983, 53.
34. "Creating the New Man, Circa 1990," *Adweek*, March 12, 1990, 36–37.
35. *Madison Avenue*, February 1986, 88–90.
36. "Wary Consumers Want More Health Ad Info," *Advertising Age*, December 4, 1989, 12.
37. "Tougher Customers," *Forbes*, December 3, 1990, 40.
38. "Kraft Is Looking For Fat Growth From Fat-Free Foods," *Business Week*, March 26, 1990, 100.
39. *Sales & Marketing Management*, April, 1989, 56; and "Sweat Chic," *Forbes*, September 5, 1988, 96, 101.
40. "Sex, Buys and Advertising," NBC-TV, July 31, 1990.
41. "Canada Dry Directs Its Appeal to 'Couch Potatoes'," *Advertising Age*, June 6, 1988, 70.
42. "National Advertisers Rediscover the Black Market," *Ad Forum*, January 1984, 36; and "Traditional Brand Loyalty," *Advertising Age*, May 18, 1981, S-2.
43. "Afro American Market Opportunities," *Merchandise Discount*, May 1990, 121.
44. U.S. Department of Commerce, Bureau of the Census, Statistical Abstract of the United States, 1990 (Washington, DC: U.S. Government Printing Office), Table No. 730, 452.
45. "Why Big Tobacco Woos Minorities," *Adweek's Marketing Week*, January 29, 1990, 20.
46. "Spanish Spending Power Growing Dramatically, but Consumers Retain Special Characteristics," *Television/Radio Age*, December 1984, A-4.
47. "Reaching the Hispanic Market: A 53 Billion Opportunity," *Listening Post*, June 1984, 3.
48. "Hispanic Supermarkets Are Blossoming," *The Wall Street Journal*, January 23, 1989, B-1.
49. *Fortune*, November 21, 1988, 181.
50. "Asians in the U.S. Get Attention of Marketers," *The New York Times*, January 11, 1990, D-19.
51. "The Art of Reaching Asian Immigrants," *Adweek's Marketing Week*, January 1, 1990, 23.

52. Arnold Mitchell, *Changing Values and Lifestyles* (Menlo Park, CA: SRI International, 1981), 3; and Martha Farnsworth Riche, "Psychographics for the 1990s," *American Demographics*, July 1989, 26.
53. "Anyhow, It Was Nice While It Lasted," *Forbes*, January 12, 1987, 50; and "Get Ready for Shopping at Work," *Fortune*, February 15, 1988, 95–98.
54. "The Innovators," *Fortune*, June 6, 1988, 50–64.
55. "Apple–IBM Pact Is Said To Be Near," *The New York Times*, June 3, 1991, D-1.
56. "Corporate Growth, R&D, and the Gap Between," *Technology Review*, March–April 1978.
57. " 'Shelf-Stable' Foods Seek to Freshen Sales," *The Wall Street Journal*, November 2, 1990, B-1.
58. Statistical Abstracts of the United States, 1991 (Washington, DC: Government Printing Office, 1991), 556.
59. "Penney's 'TV Mall' To Make Its Late, Humbled Debut," *The Wall Street Journal*, February 16, 1988, A-6.
60. "Videotex Markets, Applications, and Systems," *ONLINE*, March 1991, 97–100.
61. "Child Prodigy," *Adweek's Marketing Week*, October 3, 1988, 22–25.
62. *ONLINE*, March 1991, 99.
63. Statistical Abstracts of the United States, 1991 (Washington, DC: Government Printing Office, 1991), 556.
64. "Capturing the Elusive Shopper," *Superbrands*, 1990, 206.
65. "Murjani to Put Shopping for Coca-Cola Apparel at Customers' Fingertips," *Women's Wear Daily*, June 5, 1986, 8.
66. "The Ultimate Sell," *Forbes*, May 13, 1991, 108.
67. "On a Roll, Shoppers' Video Links with Nynex," *Adweek's Marketing Week*, July 2, 1990, 8.
68. *Superbrands*, 1990, 198–206.
69. "Environmental concerns lead some consumers to change buying habits," *Marketing News*, December 24, 1990, 7.
70. "The Greening of Corporate America," *Business Week*, April 23, 1990, 98–99.
71. "The Green Revolution: Procter & Gamble," *Advertising Age*, January 29, 1991, 16.
72. "The Bottom Line on Disposables," Business World supplement to *The New York Times Magazine*, September 23, 1990, 27.
73. "States Mull Rash of Diaper Regulations," *The Wall Street Journal*, June 15, 1990, B-1.
74. "High-Tech has its Impact," *Advertising Age*, July 23, 1990, S-10.
75. "P&G Gets Top Marks in AA Survey," *Advertising Age*, January 29, 1991, 10.
76. "Cola giants take packaging lead," *Advertising Age*, December 17, 1990, 30.
77. Ibid.
78. *Supermarket Shoppers in a Period of Economic Uncertainty* (New York: Yankelovich, Skelly, and White, 1982), 15.
79. " 'Value' strategy to battle recession," *Advertising Age*, January 7, 1991, 1.
80. " 'Value' Brands Head for Shelves," *Adweek's Marketing Week*, October 29, 1990, 6; and "Discount Menu Is Coming to McDonald's As Chain Tries to Win Back Customers," *The Wall Street Journal*, November 12, 1990, B-1.
81. "Firms Change Pitch as Economy Falters," *The Wall Street Journal*, November 9, 1990, B-1.
82. "The Hollow Corporation," *Business Week*, March 3, 1986, 57–59.
83. William L. Wilkie, Dennis L. McNeill, and Michael B. Mazis, "Marketing's 'Scarlet Letter': The Theory and Practice of Corrective Advertising," *Journal of Marketing 48* (Spring 1984).
84. Dorothy Cohen, "Unfairness in Advertising Revisited," *Journal of Marketing 46* (Winter 1982): 73–80.
85. "The Consumer Movement: Whatever Happened?" *The New York Times*, January 23, 1983, A-16.
86. "A Decade of Deregulation?" *Industry Week*, January 7, 1980, 17.
87. "Deregulation Hindsight," *Research Alert*, January 20, 1989, 1.
88. "Coming to Stores Near You: New and Improved Labeling," *The New York Times*, July 6, 1991, A-1.
89. "FTC Warns Agencies; Eyes Tobacco, Cable," *Advertising Age*, March 12, 1990, 6.
90. "FCC Adopts Limits on TV Ads Aimed at Children," *The New York Times*, April 10, 1991, D-7.

CHAPTER 5

1. "P&G in Deal For Czech Soap Maker," *New York Times.* June 20, 1991, D4.
2. "Procter & Gamble is Following Its Nose," *Business Week*, April 22, 1991, 28.
3. "Japan Rises to P&G's No. 3 Market," *Advertising Age*. December 10, 1990, 42.
4. Ibid.
5. Edwin Artzt, "Winning in Japan: Keys to Global Success," *Business Quarterly*, Winter 1989, 12–16.
6. Ibid.
7. Teresa Domzal and Lynette Unger, "Emerging Positioning Strategies in Global Marketing," *Journal of Consumer Marketing, 4* (Fall 1987), 24.
8. Statistical Abstracts of the United States, 1991 (Washington, DC: Government Printing Office, 1991), 804.
9. "Pepsi's New Order: Snack Food, Global Growth and Profit," *Adweek's Marketing Week*, December 17, 1990, 4 and 5.
10. "First Global Kellogg Ad Set for June," *Advertising Age*, April 29, 1991, 47.
11. "Whirlpool Goes Off on a World Tour," *Business Week*, June 3, 1991, 99–100.
12. "General Mills/Nestlé Joint Venture," *Advertising Age*, December 4, 1989, 1, 52; and "Europe Ain't No Bonanza Anymore," *Business Week*, August 6, 1990, 26–28.
13. "The Baby Bells Scramble for Europe," *New York Times*, December 10, 1989, F1, F8, and F9.
14. Ibid, F8.
15. "The Big Japanese Push Into Europe," *Fortune*, July 2, 1990, 94.
16. "The Coming Boom in Europe," *Fortune*, April 10, 1989, 108–114; and "A 'Fortress Europe' in 1992?" *The New York Times*, August 22, 1988, A19.
17. "The First Global Generation," *Adweek's Marketing Week*, February 6, 1989, 18.
18. See: "Going Global," *Marketing*, December 10, 1987, 20.
19. "Feed the World," *Forbes*, October 1, 1990, 111.
20. "Global Approach Seeks Similarities in Markets," *Marketing News*, October 11, 1985, 12.
21. "For Levi's, A Flattering Fit Overseas," *Business Week*, November 5, 1990, 76.
22. "Ad Fads: Global Sales Pitch by Harvard Guru Appears Much Easier in Theory, Marketers Find," *The Wall Street Journal*, May 12, 1988, 4.
23. "Pitfalls Lie Waiting for Unwary Marketers," *Advertising Age*, May 17, 1982, M-9.
24. "Foreign Markets: Not for the Amateur," *Business Marketing*, July 1984, 112.
25. David A. Ricks, *Big Business Blunders* (Homewood, IL, Dow Jones-Irwin, 1983), 84.
26. "Maintaining a Balance of Planning,"*Advertising Age*, May 17, 1982, M-21.
27. "We Are the World," *Superbrands, 1990* (New York: Marketing Insights, 1990), 67.
28. "The Yen to be Yuppy," *Marketing Insights*, Fall 1990, 66.
29. "When in Japan," *Forbes*, March 10, 1986, 153.
30. "Getting in on the Ground Floor," *Fortune*, Fall 1990, Special Issue, 64.
31. *Superbrands 1990*, 65.
32. "Setting Up An Island in the Soviet Storm," *New York Times*, December 30, 1990, 6.
33. "Eastward, Ho! The Pioneers Plunge In," *Business Week*, April 15, 1991, 51.
34. "A New Mass Market Emerges," *Pacific Rim 1990* (New York: Fortune, 1990), 56.
35. "Strauss to Forgo $4 Million in Pay to Take Moscow Post," *New York Times*, July 13, 1991, 3.
36. "Pepsi, Coke: Art of Deal-Making," *Advertising Age*, February 19, 1990, 45.
37. Philip R. Cateora, *International Marketing* (Homewood, IL: Richard D. Irwin, 1983), 61.
38. "America's New Rush to Europe," *Business Week*, March 26, 1990, 49.
39. "America's International Winners," *Fortune*, April 14, 1986, 36.
40. *Business Week*, March 26, 1990, 48–49.
41. *Fortune*, July 2, 1990, 94.
42. "General Motors: What Went Wrong," *Business Week*, March 16, 1987, 105.
43. "Top Patent Winners in the U.S.," *The*

New American Century (New York: Fortune, 1991), 18.
44. Ibid, 18–19.
45. "How to Analyze Political Risk," *Business Marketing*, January 1987, 52–53.
46. *The New American Century*, 23.
47. *Business Week*, March 26, 1990, 48.
48. *Forbes*, October 1, 1990, 114.
49. "U.S./Japan," *Business Week*, July 18, 1988, 50.
50. "Coke, Nestlé Get Together Over Coffee," *Wall Street Journal*, November 30, 1990, B1.
51. "Egypt an Oasis for Soft Drinks," *The New York Times*, August 1, 1978, D1.
52. "New Foreign Products Pour into U.S. Market in Increasing Numbers," *The Wall Street Journal*, November 11, 1982, M-16; and "They Didn't Listen to Anybody," *Forbes*, December 15, 1986, 169.
53. Preston Townley, "Going Global in the 1990s," *Vital Speeches*, July 15, 1990, 592.
54. "Marketing Can Be Global, but Ads Must Remain Cultural," *Marketing News*, July 31, 1987, 26; and "Goodbye Global Ads," *Advertising Age*, November 16, 1987, 22.
55. "Parker Pen," *Advertising Age*, June 2, 1986, 60.
56. "Can Ford Stay On Top?" *Business Week*, September 28, 1987, 80; and "Detroit Pulls Out Stops to Catch Up with World," *Business Week*, June 22, 1981, S-1, S-44.
57. "Even Overseas, Tobacco Has Nowhere to Hide," *Adweek's Marketing Week*, April 1, 1991, 4.
58. Ibid, 5.
59. "Mobil Is Quitting South Africa Blaming 'Foolish' Laws in U.S.," *The New York Times*, April 29, 1989, 1.
60. Rebecca Rolfes, "How Green is Your Market Basket," *Across the Board*, January/February 1990, 49–51.
61. "Eco-Label Plan Grows in Europe," *Advertising Age*, April 20, 1991, 46.
62. "Germans Set P&G's Green Test Agenda," *Advertising Age*, February 11, 1991, 25–26; and "P&G Sets Off Green Powder Keg," *Marketing*, October 12, 1989, 32.
63. Arthur C. Fatt, "The Danger of 'Local' International Advertising," *Journal of Marketing* (January 1967), 60–62.
64. "Multinationals Tackle Global Marketing," *Advertising Age*, June 25, 1984, 50.

CHAPTER 6

1. "Cola Attack," *Forbes*, November 26, 1990, 48.
2. Douglas K. Ramsey, *The Corporate Warriors* (Boston: Houghton Mifflin Co., 1987), 89.
3. "New Coke Gets a New Look, New Chance," *Wall Street Journal*, March 7, 1990, B1 and B8; and "Cola Wars," *Adweek*, March 12, 1990, 6.
4. "Sorry, No Pepsi. How 'Bout a Coke?" *Business Week*, May 27, 1991, 71.
5. *Forbes*, November 26, 1990, 48.
6. "Pepsi Does 'Can-Can' With Coke II," *Advertising Age*, April 30, 1990, 55.
7. "Pepsi Plans Extensive Ad Campaign to Contest Coke's Overseas Dominance," *Wall Street Journal*, April 2, 1990, B1.
8. Michael E. Porter, *Competitive Advantage* (New York: The Free Press, 1985).
9. George Day, *Strategic Market Planning: The Pursuit of Competitive Advantage* (St. Paul: West Publishing Company, 1984), 27–28.
10. "High Stakes at the High Chair," *Marketing & Media Decisions*, October 1986, 67.
11. "How Gallo Crushes the Competition," *Fortune*, September 1, 1986, 28.
12. "The King of Ketchup," *Forbes*, March 21, 1988, 50.
13. "Heinz Ain't Broke But It's Doing a Lot of Fixing," *Business Week*, December 11, 1989, 84–88.
14. "Minnetonka's Revenge," *Forbes*, November 19, 1984, 266, 268.
15. Michael E. Porter, *Competitive Strategy* (New York: The Free Press, 1980), 40.
16. "Flavor by Flavor, Cadbury Builds An Empire of Niches," *Adweek's Marketing Week*, June 18, 1990, 19.
17. Joel E. Ross, "Making Quality a Fundamental Part of Strategy," *Long Range Planning 18*(1985),55; and "America's Quest Can't Be Half-Hearted," *Business Week*, September 28, 1987, 136.
18. "General Motors: What Went Wrong,"

Business Week, March 16, 1987, 105; and "How GM Is Shifting Gears," *Advertising Age*, January 4, 1988, 1.
19. "Japan's Next Push in U.S. Markets," *Fortune*, September 26, 1988, 138; and "Kao Angles Its Way onto the U.S. Stage," *Advertising Age*, April 10, 1989, 54.
20. *Fortune*, September 26, 1988, 138, 140.
21. Michael E. Porter, "How Competitive Forces Shape Strategy," *Harvard Business Review* 57(March–April 1979),137–145; and Porter, *Competitive Advantage*, Chapter 3.
22. "Apple: Fighting Furiously to Stay Number Two," *Marketing & Media Decisions*, November 1984, 54.
23. "A Heartland Industry Takes on the World," *Fortune*, March 12, 1990, 110–112.
24. Ibid, 111.
25. B. Liddell Hart, *Strategy* (New York: Praeger, 1967), 351.
26. See William A. Cohen, "War in the Marketplace," *Business Horizons*, March–April 1986.
27. "Pizza Hut Ads Attack Mac's Test," *Advertising Age*, May 7, 1990, 18; and "Pizza Hut Does McDonald's a Favor With Anti-McPizza Ads," *Advertising Age*, May 14, 1990, 66.
28. "Quaker's Cola War," *Advertising Age*, May 28, 1990, 3 and 62.
29. "Why Folgers Is Getting Creamed Back East," *Fortune*, July 17, 1978, 68-69.
30. "Drip, Drip, Drip. . .Drip,: *Forbes*, April 17, 1989, 196.
31. "Maxwell House, Folgers Clash Over Coffee," *Wall Street Journal*, February 20, 1990, B7.
32. "Colgate, P&G Pack for Road to Russia," *Advertising Age*, March 12, 1990, 56; and "The New, Improved Unilever Aims to Clean Up in the U.S.," *Business Week*, November 27, 1989, 102, 106.
33. "Marketing Warfare," *Marketing Communications*, December 1985, 28.
34. "Colgate's Offensive Heats Up Tartar-Control Toothpaste War," *The Wall Street Journal*, August 20, 1987, 15; and "Colgate Puts the Squeeze on Crest," *Business Week*, August 19, 1985, 40.
35. "P&G Pumps Crest with New Promotion," *Advertising Age*, June 29, 1987, 61.
36. "Bottled Draft Beers Head for Collision as Anheuser Readies Challenge to Miller," *Wall Street Journal*, May 1, 1990, B1.
37. "Forget Satisfying the Consumer—Just Outfox the Other Guy," *Business Week*, October 7, 1985, 58.
38. *Adweek's Marketing Week*, June 18, 1990, 18.
39. "New Product Innovators Find Winning Formulas," *Marketing Communications*, February 1988, 38; and "And Then There Were Two?" *Forbes*, May 19, 1986, 64, 66.
40. "Perrier Plots Comeback," *Fortune*, April 23, 1990, 227; and "Perrier Rivals Refuse to Make Waves," *Advertising Age*, March 12, 1990, 74.
41. "Lever and P&G Wage a Good, Clean Fight," *Sales & Marketing Management*, June 3, 1985, 47–49.
42. "Sparks Fly in Scripto's Battle to Dump Bic as Lighter King," *The Wall Street Journal*, May 2, 1985, 33.

CHAPTER 7

1. "In the Chips," *New York Times*, March 22, 1991, B1 and B2.
2. "Frito's Micro Move," *Advertising Age*, February 12, 1990, 44.
3. *New York Times*, March 22, 1991, B2.
4. "How Frito-Lay Stays in the Chips," *Management Review*, December 1989, 11 and 12.
5. "What the Scanner Knows About You," *Fortune*, December 3, 1990, 51 and 52.
6. *Management Review*, December 1989, 12.
7. "How Software is Making Food Sales a Piece of Cake," *Business Week*, July 2, 1990, 54 and 55.
8. Ibid, 55.
9. David W. Cravens, Gerald W. Hills, and Robert B. Woodruff, *Marketing Decision Making* (Homewood, IL: Richard D. Irwin, 1980), 75-77.
10. "Straws in the Wind," *Financial World* November 3, 1987, 126–128.
11. "Colgate's Next Trick: Controlling the

Chaos," *New York Times*, August 6, 1989, F9.
12. "New Product Excellence at American Express," *Marketing Review*, January/February 1988, 20.
13. "The 'Bloodbath' in Market Research," *Business Week*, February 11, 1991, 72 and 74.
14. "Stouffer's Lean Cuisine Fattens Up Frozen Food Market," *Madison Avenue*, March 1983, 94.
15. "Reading the Consumer's Mind," *Advertising Age*, May 3, 1984, M-16.
16. "Meticulous Planning Pays Dividends at Stouffer's," *Marketing News*, October 28, 1983, 26.
17. *Madison Avenue*, March 1983, 96.
18. *Business Week*, February 11, 1991, 74.
19. Betsy D. Gelb and Gabriel M. Gelb, "New Coke's Fizzle—Lessons for the Rest of Us," *Sloan Management Review* (Fall 1986), 71.
20. "Small Firms Grow Strong on Steady Diet of Data," *Adweek's Marketing Week*, May 16, 1988, 17 and 21.
21. *Business Week*, February 11, 1991, 72.
22. "Matching Face With Image," *Business Marketing*, March 1989, 58.
23. Case obtained from Corning Glass advertisement, 1991.
24. "Using Marketing Research to Explore for Exciting New Product Ideas," *Sales & Marketing Management*, April 4, 1983, 126–130.
25. David A. Aaker and George S. Day, *Marketing Research* (New York: John Wiley & Sons, 1980), 102.
26. "Excuse Me, What's the Pollster's Big Problem?" *Business Week*, February 16, 1987, 108.
27. "Businesses Capitalize on Data from Census," *The New York Times*, March 31, 1980, D1–D2.
28. Communication from *Progressive Grocer* magazine, Research Department, April, 1992.
29. "Powerhouse Tears Down Europe Borders," *Advertising Age*, June 11, 1990, S14–S16.
30. *Starch: Scope, Method, and Use* (Mamaroneck, NY: Starch/INRA/Hooper, 1973), 2.
31. *The 1980 Study of Media and Markets* (New York: Simmons Market Research Bureau, 1980).
32. "Top Worldwide Research Companies," *Advertising Age*, December 5, 1988, S1–S18.
33. *Advertising Age*, July 22, 1985, 58.
34. "Listening, the Old-Fashioned Way," *Forbes*, October 5, 1987, 202, 204.
35. "Dawn of the Computer Age," *Advertising Age*, August 20, 1987, 120, 209.
36. "Big Brother Gets a Job in Market Research," *Business Week*, April 8, 1985, 96.

CHAPTER 8

1. "Gerber to Grow in Europe," *Advertising Age*, March 18, 1991.
2. "Gerber Seeks 'Superbrand' Role," *Advertising Age*, April 9, 1990, 26.
3. "Making Mashed Peas Pay Off," *New York Times*, April 9, 1989, F2.
4. "Gerber Raises New Products," *Advertising Age*, July 30, 1990.
5. "Gerber's High-Energy Baby Marketers," *Adweek's Marketing Week*, May 22, 1989, 21.
6. *Advertising Age*, March 18, 1991.
7. *New York Times*, April 9, 1989, F2.
8. *Adweek's Marketing Week*, May 22, 1989, 23.
9. "Former Customers Are Good Prospects," *The Wall Street Journal*, April 22, 1982, 31.
10. Abraham H. Maslow, "*Motivation and Personality* (New York: Harper & Row, 1954).
11. "In This Taste Test, the Loser is the Taste Test," *Wall Street Journal*, June 3, 1987, 33.
12. "Cadillac Wants to Attract Younger Buyers, but Its 'Old Man' Image Gets in the Way," *The Wall Street Journal*, November 18, 1985, 33.
13. "Marketing Skin Care to Men," *Marketing Communications*, November 1985, 32, 33, and 36.
14. "Lee Maps New Line of Jeans," *Advertising Age*, March 10, 1986, 28.
15. "Agencies Zero in on Segments of the Baby-Boom Generation," *The Wall Street Journal*, June 26, 1986, 33.

16. " 'Inner-Directed' Is Where It's at in New Strategies," *Adweek*, May 26, 1986, 17.
17. "MasterCard Shuns Status," *Advertising Age*, February 24, 1986, 3.
18. Ira Dolich, "Congruence Relationships Between Self Images and Product Brands," *Journal of Marketing Research 6* (February 1969), 80–85; and Edward L. Grubb and Gregg Hupp, "Perception of Self Generalized Stereotypes and Brand Selection," *Journal of Marketing Research 5* (February 1968), 58–63.
19. "Advertisers Put Consumers on the Couch," *The Wall Street Journal*, May 13, 1988, 21.
20. Shirley Young, "The Dynamics of Measuring Unchange," in Russell I. Haley, ed., *Attitude Research in Transition* (Chicago: American Marketing Association, 1972), 72.
21. "Freshman Found Stressing Wealth," *The New York Times*, January 14, 1988, A14.
22. J. Douglas McConnell, "The Economics of Behavioral Factors on the Multi-National Corporation," in Fred C. Allvine, ed., *Combined Proceedings of the American Marketing Association*, Series No. 33 (1971), 265.
23. "Ad Agencies and Big Concerns Debate World Brands' Values," *Wall Street Journal*, June 14, 1984, 33.
24. "6 Myths About Black Consumers," *Adweek's Marketing Week*, May 9, 1991, 18.
25. "The Masculine Dreamscale," *Marketing Communications*, April 1987, 17–18.
26. "The Shifting Power of Influentials in Purchase Decisions," *Ad Forum*, July 1983, 55.
27. "Corona's Unlikely Conquest," *The New York Times*, July 11, 1987, 39, 41; and "Anheuser Beer Arrives without Ads," *Advertising Age*, July 6, 1987, 2.
28. "Auto Makers Set New Ad Strategy to Reach Women," *Advertising Age*, September 23, 1985, 80.
29. Rita Weiskoff, "Current Trends in Children's Advertising," *Journal of Advertising Research 25* (February–March 1985), RC-12–14.

CHAPTER 9

1. "The New IBM," *Business Week*, December 16, 1991, 112–118.
2. "Customers Learn to Cope with the Many Faces of IBM," *InfoWorld*, February 11, 1991, 57–59.
3. "Can John Akers Save IBM?," *Fortune*, July 15, 1991, 40–56.
4. "IBM: As Markets and Technology Change, Can Big Blue Remake Its Culture?," *Business Week*, June 17, 1991, 25–31.
5. "IBM, Apple Deal a Boon for Net Users," *Network World*, July 8, 1991, 1 and 6.
6. *EMI and the CT Scanner (B)* (Boston: Harvard Business School, HBS Case Services, 1983).
7. "The Rise and Fall of EMI," *International Management*, June 1980, 21–25.
8. Rowland T. Moriarty, Jr., and Robert E. Spekman, "An Empirical Investigation of the Information Sources Used During the Industrial Buying Process," *Journal of Marketing Research 21* (May 1984), 137–147.
9. P. J. Robinson, C. W. Faris, and Y. Wind, *Industrial Buying and Creative Marketing* (Boston: Allyn and Bacon, 1968).
10. Peter Lawrence Bubb and David John van Rest, "Loyalty as a Component of the Industrial Buying Decision," *Industrial Marketing Management 3* (1973), 25–32.
11. Anita M. Kennedy, "The Complex Decision to Select a Supplier: A Case Study," *Industrial Marketing Management 12* (1983), 45–56.
12. Yoram Wind, "Industrial Source Loyalty," *Journal of Marketing Research* 7 (November 1970), 450–457.
13. "Crafting 'Win–Win Situations' in Buyer–Supplier Relationships," *Business Marketing*, June 1986, 43.
14. Ronald H. Gorman, "Role Conception and Purchasing Behavior," *Journal of Purchasing* 7 (February 1971), 57.
15. Donald R. Lehmann and John O'Shaughnessy, "Difference in Attribute Importance for Different Industrial Products," *Journal of Marketing 38* (April 1974), 36–42.

16. Christopher P. Puto, Wesley E. Patton III, and Ronald H. King, "Risk Handling Strategies in Industrial Vendor Selection Decisions," *Journal of Marketing 49* (Winter 1985), 89–98.
17. See M. Baker and S. Parkinson, "Information Source Preference in Industrial Adoption Decisions," in Barnett A. Greenberg and Danny N. Bellinger, eds., *Proceedings of the American Marketing Association Educators' Conference*, Series No. 41 (1977), 258–261; and Urban B. Ozanne and Gilbert A. Churchill, Jr., "Five Dimensions of the Industrial Adoption Process," *Journal of Marketing Research 8* (August 1971), 322–328.
18. Moriarty and Spekman, "An Empirical Investigation."
19. Michael P. Peters and M. Venkatesan, "Exploration of Variables Inherent in Adopting an Industrial Product," *Journal of Marketing Research 10* (August 1973), 312–315.
20. Ozanne and Churchill, "Five Dimensions of the Industrial Adoption Process."
21. Charles R. O'Neal, Hans B. Thorelli, and James M. Utterback, "Adoption of Innovation by Industrial Organizations," *Industrial Marketing Management 2* (1973), 235–250.
22. John A. Czepiel, "Decision Group and Firm Characteristics in an Industrial Adoption Decision," in Kenneth L. Bernhardt, ed., *Proceedings of the American Marketing Association Educators' Conference*, Series No. 39 (1976), 340–343.
23. Richard N. Cardozo and James W. Cagley, "Experimental Study of Industrial Buyer Behavior," *Journal of Marketing Research 8* (August 1971), 329–334.
24. Ibid.
25. Rowland T. Moriarty and David J. Reibstein, "Benefit Segmentation in Industrial Markets," *Journal of Business Research 14* (1986), 463–486.
26. John A. Barrett, "Why Major Account Selling Works," *Industrial Marketing Management 15* (1986), 63–73.
27. "Measurex: The Results Company," *Business Marketing*, (November 1985), 64, 66.

CHAPTER 10

1. "Slow Fade," *Marketing & Media Decisions*, October 1990, 64
2. "Sacrificial Brand," *Forbes*, February 6, 1989, 41.
3. "Levi's Dockers Weigh Into Casuals," *Adweek's Marketing Week*, September 24, 1990, 26.
4. "Spike Lee Does A Lot of Things Right," *Business Week*, August 6, 1990, 63.
5. *Marketing & Media Decisions*, October 1990, 64.
6. "100 Leading Advertisers; Levi Strauss & Co.," *Advertising Age*, September 25, 1991, 46.
7. "An Empire of Niches," *Superbrands*, 1991, 18.
8. *Advertising Age*, September 25, 1991, 46; "How Levi Strauss Did An LBO Right," *Fortune*, May 7, 1990, 105; and "For Levi's, A Flattering Fit Overseas," *Business Week*, November 5, 1990, 75–77.
9. *Adweek's Marketing Week*, September 29, 1990, 26.
10. Alan J. Resnik, Peter B.B. Turney, and J. Barry Mason, "Marketers Turn to 'Countersegmentation,'" *Harvard Business Review* 57 (September–October 1979):100–106.
11. "Revamped Tobacco Firm Targets New Consumer Segments," *Marketing News*, July 6, 1984, 8.
12. "Stalking the New Consumer," *Business Week*, August 28, 1989, 55.
13. "Marketing: The New Priority," *Business Week*, November 21, 1983, 95.
14. Spencer L, Hapoienue, "The Rise of Micromarketing," *Journal of Business Strategy*, (November/December 1990), 38–39.
15. "Niche Marketing: What Industrial Marketers Can Learn from Consumer Package Goods," *Business Marketing*, November 1984, 58.
16. "Jean Makers' Task is to Find the Best Fit," *The Wall Street Journal,* July 31, 1986, 6.
17. "Computer Mapping of Demographic Lifestyle Data Locates 'Pockets' of Po-

tential Customers at Microgeographic Level," *Marketing News*, November 27, 1981, Section 2, 16.

18. "Creating the Well-Groomed Child," *New York Times*, July 6, 1991, D1 and D43.
19. "Gatorade for Kids," *Adweek's Marketing Week*, July 15, 1991, 5.
20. "Hispanic Market Profile: Resisting the Winds of Change," *Marketing Communications*, July 1983, 27.
21. "Marketing's New Look," *Business Week*, January 26, 1987, 67; "M'm! M'm! Okay," *Adweek*, October 10, 1988, 22; and "Hungry Man, NFL Team Up: Campbell Suits Up Regional Effort," *Advertising Age*, April 24, 1989, 3.
22. "Mapping Regional Marketing Differences," *Advertising Age*, June 16, 1986, S-32.
23. "Different Folks, Different Strokes," *Fortune*, September 16, 1985, 68.
24. "Ad Agency Finds 5 Global Segments," *Marketing News*, January 8, 1990, 9, 17.
25. Russell L. Ackoff and James R. Emshoff, "Advertising Research at Anheuser-Busch, Inc. (1968–1974)," *Sloan Management Review 16* (Spring 1975), 1–15.
26. "Big, Small Chains Sling Hash for Morning Glory," *Adweek*, March 31, 1986, 20.
27. "Not All Prospects Are Created Equal," *Business Marketing*, May 1986, 54.
28. "New Print Ads for Coors Beer Target Women," *The Wall Street Journal*, June 2, 1987, 33.
29. "A New Stride," *Marketing Insights*, Fall 1991, 113–115, 139.
30. James D. Hlavacek and B. S. Ames, "Segmenting Industrial and High-Tech Markets," *The Journal of Business Strategy*, 41.
31. "Stroh Leverages Strengths With Sundance Sparklers," *Marketing Communications*, February 1988, 44.

CHAPTER 11

1. "The 'Scotch Tape Company' Embraces Home Repair," *Adweek's Marketing Week*, February 5, 1990, 20, 21.
2. Interview with JoAnn Fernandez, July 31, 1991.
3. Ibid.
4. *Adweek's Marketing Week*, February 5, 1990, 20, 21.
5. "The Masters of Innovation," *Business Week*, April 10, 1989, 60.
6. "Boom in Mountain Bikes Revives the U.S. Industry," *The New York Times*, March 30, 1991, A1, D5.
7. "Surprisingly Mixed Returns for Lexus," *Business Week*, January 15, 1990, 21.
8. "Name of the Game: Brand Awareness," *The Wall Street Journal*, February 14, 1991, B1.
9. "ConAgra Expands Healthy Choice," *Advertising Age*, November 19, 1990, 3.
10. "Hot New PCs That Read Your Writing," *Fortune*, February 11, 1991, 113.
11. *New Product Management for the 1980s* (New York: Booz Allen & Hamilton, 1982), 8–10.
12. "A Bright Idea That Clorox Wishes It Never Had," *Business Week*, June 24, 1991, 118.
13. "Inside Nabisco's Cookie Machine," *Adweek's Marketing Week*, March 18, 1991, 22.
14. *Business Week*, May 26, 1988, 88.
15. "Technology Links Will Be Discussed by Apple and IBM," *The New York Times*, June 6, 1991, A1.
16. "Going, Going, Gone," *New York Magazine*, February 18,1991, 19.
17. "How Innovation At P&G Restored Luster To Washed-Up Pert And Made It No. 1," *The Wall Street Journal*, December 6, 1990, B1.
18. "A Culture That Keeps Dishing Up Success," *Business Week*, June 16, 1989, 120.
19. "Hot New PCs That Read Your Writing," *Fortune*, February 11, 1991, 118.
20. "How 3M Manages for Innovation," *Marketing Communications*, November/December 1988, 17, 18.
21. The Binge is Over," *Marketing & Media Decisions*, April 1987, 55.
22. "Frito-Lay's Cooking Again, and Profits are Starting to Pop," *Business Week*, May 22, 1989, 66; and "Frito-Lay: The Binge is Over," *Marketing & Media Decisions*, April 1987, 54–60.
23. "Why Products Fail," *Adweek's Market-*

ing Week, November 5, 1990, 20.

24. "GE Refrigerator Woes Illustrate the Hazards in Changing a Product," *The Wall Street Journal*, May 7, 1990, A1.
25. "Sweet technology, sour marketing," *Forbes*, May 1, 1988, 140.
26. "Going, Going, Gone," *New York Magazine*, February 18, 1991, 19.
27. "Diaper's Failure Shows How Poor Plans, Unexpected Woes Can Kill New Products," *The Wall Street Journal*, October 9, 1990, B1, B4.
28. "Inside Nabisco's Cookie Machine," *Adweek's Marketing Week*, March 18, 1991, 23.
29. "Iced Coffee Next for Coke, Nestlé," *Advertising Age*, May 21, 1990, 4.
30. "How 3M Manages for Innovation," *Marketing Communications*, November/December 1988, 22.
31. "25 Executives to Watch: Richard LeFauve," *The 1990 Business Week 100*, 130.
32. "How Do We Confuse Thee? Let Us Count the Ways," *Forbes*, March 21, 1988, 156.
33. "Don't Do It Like The Big Boys," *Inc.*, April 1990, 116.
34. Eric Von Hippel, "Get New Products from Customers," *Harvard Business Review 60* (March/April 1982), 117–122.
35. "Why Products Fail," *Adweek's Marketing Week*, November 5, 1990, 21.
36. "Forsaking the Black Box: Designers Wrap Products in Visual Metaphors," *The Wall Street Journal*, March 26, 1987, 39.
37. "Surprisingly Mixed Returns for Lexus," *Business Week*, January 15, 1990, 21.
38. "Test Marketing Put to the Test," *S&MM*, March 1987, 67–68.
39. "How Innovation at P&G Restored Luster To Washed-Up Pert and Made it No. 1," *The Wall Street Journal*, December 6, 1990, B6.
40. "Giving Fading Brands a Second Chance," *The Wall Street Journal*, January 24, 1989, 31.
41. "For Want of a Wheel," *Regulation 12* (1988), 7.
42. "Getting Mileage From A Recall," *Business Week*, May 27, 1991, 38.

CHAPTER 12

1. "P&G Changing How Brands Are Managed," *The Wall Street Journal*, July 17, 1991, A3; and "One Brand, One Manager," *Advertising Age*," August 20, 1987, 89–90.
2. Ibid.
3. "P&G Rewrites the Marketing Rules," *Fortune*, November 6, 1989, 34–48.
4. "P&G Makes Changes in the Way It Develops and Sells Its Products," *The Wall Street Journal*, August 11, 1987, A1, A12.
5. *The Wall Street Journal*, July 17, 1991, A3.
6. *Fortune*, November 6, 1980, 42.
7. "Greyhound Dials up a Name Change—More or Less," *Adweek's Marketing Week*, March 5, 1990, 5.
8. "Growing Pains and Gains," *New York Magazine*, March 13, 1989, 22.
9. "Brand Names: The Invisible Assets," *Management Accounting*, November 1990, 41.
10. "What's in a Name? Maybe Plenty, If It's Singer," *Business Week*, October 8, 1990, 95.
11. "Marketers Favor Tales of 2 Brands," *The New York Times*, July 5, 1991.
12. "Branding Strategies," *Small Business Reports*, September 1990, 64
13. "Brand Names Have Cachet in East Bloc," *The Wall Street Journal*, June 27, 1990, B1.
14. "The Selling of the Walkman," *Advertising Age*, March 12, 1982, M37.
15. "Doughboy Pops up for Pillsbury Mixes," *Advertising Age*, May 7, 1990, 65.
16. "How Owens-Corning Turned a Commodity Into a Brand," *Management Review*, December 1986, 11–12.
17. "Package Deals," *New York Magazine*, August 22, 1988, 28.
18. "Romancing the Package," *Adweek's Marketing Week*, January 21, 1991, 10.
19. "Right Package Sets Mood for Image-Driven Brands," *Marketing News*, August 5, 1991, 2.
20. "Package Deals," *New York Magazine*, August 22, 1988, 28.
21. "Folgers Puts Coffee in the Bag," *Advertising Age*, January 21, 1991, 3.

22. "New Coke Packaging Designed in Secret Marathon," *Marketing News*, October 11, 1985, 1, 24.
23. "Sears Gets Serious in Childswear," *Adweek*, July 22, 1991, 8.
24. "More Firms Pledge Guaranteed Service," *The Wall Street Journal*, July 17, 1991, B1.
25. "Dole Wants the Whole Produce Aisle," *Adweek's Marketing Week*, October 22, 1990, 19.
26. "Izod Lacoste Gets Restyled and Repriced," *The Wall Street Journal*, July 17, 1991, B1.
27. "Forget the Ads: Cola Is Cola, Magazine Finds," *The Wall Street Journal*, July 24, 1991, B1.
28. "Branding Strategies," *Small Business Reports*, September 1990, 63.
29. *The New York Times*, October 28, 1988, A1.
30. "A Rose by Any Other Name," *American Demographics*, February 1991, 78.
31. "It's Slim Pickings in Product Name Game," *The Wall Street Journal*, November 29, 1988, B1.
32. "What's in a Name?," *American Demographics*, February 1991, 54.
33. "What's in a Name Brand?" *Money*, February 1974, 41; and "Fragmented Markets Complicate Setting New HBA Product Positions," *Product Marketing*, March 1981, 8.
34. "Managing Brand Equity," *Journal of Advertising Research*, V.30 N.4, August/September 1990, RC-7.
35. "What's in A Name? Less and Less," *Business Week*, July 8, 1991, 67.
36. "Paper Towel Battle: Generic Savings vs. Brand Quality," *The New York Times*, September 1, 1981, D4.
37. Brian F. Harris and Roger A. Strang, "Marketing Strategies in the Age of Generics," *Journal of Marketing*, Fall 1985, 74.
38. "Brand Extensions: The Good, the Bad and the Ugly," *Sloan Management Review 47* (Summer 1990), 54.
39. *New York Magazine*, March 13, 1989, 24.
40. "Sequels for the Shelf," *Newsweek*, July 9, 1990, 42.
41. "Leveraging The Reynolds Name Beyond Aluminum," *Adweek's Marketing Week*, May 21, 1990, 18; and "Brands Can Either Grow Old Gracefully or Become Dinosaurs," *Marketing News*, January 22, 1990, 17.
42. *Newsweek*, July 9, 1990, 43.
43. "L'Oréal Makes Itself Over for the U.S. Market," *Adweek's Marketing Week*, April 22, 1991, 24, 25.
44. "Some Big Ideas From P&G. . .Is Liquid Soap Field Saturated," *The Wall Street Journal*, June 18, 1981, 25.
45. "Reebok responds to Nike," *Advertising Age*, February 20, 1989, 2.
46. "Polaroid and Minolta: More Developments Ahead?" *Business Week*, July 16, 1990, 32.
47. "Alcan Search: New Products," *The New York Times*, May 7, 1986, D1, D6.
48. "Deere Faces Challenge Just When Farmers Are Shopping Again," *The Wall Street Journal*, February 8, 1990, A1.
49. "Winning The War of Battle Creek," *Business Week*, May 13, 1991, 80.
50. "Giving Fading Brands a Second Chance," *The Wall Street Journal*, January 24, 1989, 21.
51. "Mattel Shapes a New Future for Barbie," *The Wall Street Journal*, December 12, 1990, B1.
52. "Dinosaur Brands," *Adweek's Marketing Week*, June 17, 1991, 17.

CHAPTER 13

1. Carl Williams, "The Challenge of Retail Marketing At Federal Express," *The Journal of Business and International Marketing 2*(Winter 1987), 26; and "Mr. Smith Goes Global," *Business Week*, February 13, 1989, 66.
2. "The Challenge of Retail Marketing," 26.
3. Ibid.
4. "Federal Finds Its Pioneering Formula Falls Flat Overseas," *The Wall Street Journal*, April 15, 1991, A8.
5. "The Challenge of Retail Marketing," 26, 27.
6. "Overnight Success," *Catalog Age*, October 1991, 90–92.
7. *The Wall Street Journal*, April 15, 1991, A8.
8. "Baldrige Winner Aims for 100% Satisfaction," *Marketing News*, February 4,

1991, 12; "Federal Express: Employees Eliminate Problems Instead of Fighting Fires," *Business Marketing*, February 1990, 40.
9. "Mr. Smith Goes Global," *Business Week*, February 13, 1989, 67.
10. *The Wall Street Journal*, April 15, 1991, 1.
11. "Presto! The Convenience Industry: Making Life a Little Simpler," *Business Week*, April 27, 1987, 86–94.
12. "The Account That Transformed a Brokerage into a Bank," *Financial & Accounting Systems*, Winter 1991, 8.
13. "AT&T Plays a New Card in Its Financial Strategy," *The Wall Street Journal*, March 30, 1990, B1; "AT&T Crashes The Credit-Card Party," *Business Week*, April 9, 1990, 23; and "Challenging the Credit Card Giants," *Institutional Investor*, August 1990, 51–53.
14. "Beyond 'May I Help You?'" *Business Week*, Quality 1991, 100.
15. "Fidelity's Formula: Technology Keeps Customers Happy," *Wall Street Computer Review*, July 1991, 27–32.
16. "Seafirst Expands Card Delivery Systems," *ABA Banking Journal*, April 1991, 76.
17. "People Express Wants All the Frills It Can Get," *Business Week*, May 12, 1986, 31.
18. "People Express, in Major Strategy Shift, Will Seek to Attract Business Travelers," *The Wall Street Journal*, April 29, 1986.
19. Craig Cina, "Five Steps to Service Excellence," *The Journal of Services Marketing* (Spring 1990),41.
20. "What Customers Really Want," *Fortune*, June 4, 1990, 61.
21. "King Customer," *Business Week*, March 12, 1990, 90.
22. Melinda M. Lele, "How Service Needs Influence Product Strategy," *Sloan Management Review* (Fall 1986),63.
23. "Beyond 'May I Help You?'" *Business Week*, Quality 1991, 100.
24. "McD's Tries Playthings," *Advertising Age*, September 2, 1991, 4.
25. "Accor Goes With the Modified American Plan," *Business Week*, October 1, 1990, 126.
26. "Holiday Inns Thinks Sinatra's a Winner," *Advertising Age*, June 1, 1987, 84.
27. "How Business Tunes into Living Trends to Sell Products," *Christian Science Monitor*, April 22, 1983, 9.
28. *Advertising Age*, June 1, 1987, 84.
29. "Insurers Writing New Healthcare Policy," *Advertising Age*, October 24, 1985, 19–20.
30. "Truck-driving 'Sales Force' Hauls in Extra Customers," *Marketing News*, May 8 1989, 2.
31. "How Carnival Stacks the Decks," *Fortune*, January 16, 1989, 110.
32. "Restaurants Mobilize to Pursue Customers," *The Wall Street Journal*, June 10, 1991, B1.
33. "Federal Express: Employees Eliminate Problems Instead of Fighting Fires," *Business Marketing*, February 1990, 40.
34. Larry Giunipero, William Crittenden, and Vicky Crittenden, "Industrial Marketing in Non-Profit Organizations," *Journal of the Academy of Marketing Science 19* (August 1990), 279.
35. Michael S. Joyce, "Grants and Philosophy: The Foundation Perspective" *The 1978 Longwood Program 10* (Newark DE: University of Delaware, 1978), 5.
36. "Surviving in a Cause-Related World," *Marketing News*, December 18, 1989, 15.
37. James W. Harvey, "Benefit Segmentation for Fund Raisers," *Journal of the Academy of Marketing Science 18* (Winter 1990), 77.
38. Peter B. Barr, Dave Dinesh, and Sammy Amin, "Perceptual Attitudes of a Charitable Organization: An Investigative Approach," *Health Marketing Quarterly 8* (1991), 92.
39. William Lazer and James D. Culley, *Marketing Management*, (Boston: Houghton-Mifflin, 1983), 836.
40. "Non-Profits Revamp List Strategies," *Target Marketing*, February 1991, 32.
41. "Pro Bono Marketing," *Adweek's Marketing Week*, March 25, 1991, 18, 19.
42. "Make My Day," *Creativity*, January 1988, 29.
43. "Advertisers Promote Religion in a Splashy and Secular Style," *The Wall Street Journal*, November 21, 1985, 33.
44. Benson P. Shapiro, "Marketing for Nonprofit Organizations," *Harvard Business Review 51* (September–October 1973), 123–132.

CHAPTER 14

1. "Strategies: Direct Selling Is Alive and Well," *Sales & Marketing Management*, August 1988, 76.
2. "Avon Keeps Ringing, but Wall Street Won't Answer," *The New York Times*, July 15, 1991, 7.
3. "A Troubled Avon Knocks at Several New Doors," *Marketing & Media Decisions*, November 1984, 68.
4. *Sales & Marketing Management*, August 1988, 76.
5. *The New York Times*, July 15, 1991, 7.
6. "Avon's Calling," *Barron's*, February 4, 1991, 14–15.
7. Ibid.
8. "After Many Blunders and Five Takeover Threats, Avon Is Calling on Its Own," *Adweek's Marketing Week*, December 11, 1991, 5.
9. *Barron's*, February 4, 1991, 14–15.
10. Ibid.
11. "Avon Is Calling on New Tactics, FCB," *Advertising Age*, September 2, 1991, 3.
12. "Fast Forward," *Business Month*, February 1989, 25.
13. *Business Month*, February 1989, 25.
14. Ibid, 25–27; "McSweater," *Working Women*, May 1986, 116; "How Benetton Has Streamlined and Branched Out Worldwide in Casual Clothing Market," *International Management*, May 1986, 81; and "Benetton Learns to Darn," *Forbes*, October 3, 1988, 122–126.
15. "Can Dell, CompuAdd Broaden Niches?" *The Wall Street Journal*, February 5, 1990, B4.
16. "Entrepreneur in Short Pants," *Forbes*, March 7, 1988, 85.
17. "Can This Catalog Company Crack the Japanese Marketing Maze?" *Business Week*, March 19, 1990, 60; and "Convenience Stores in Japan Set Sights on Catalog Business," *The Wall Street Journal*, November 30, 1990, A9C.
18. "Compaq's Grip on IBM's Slippery Tail," *Fortune*, February 18, 1985, 76.
19. "New Distribution Channels for Microcomputer Software," *Business*, October–December 1985, 20.
20. "VegiSnax Is Ready to Roll This Spring with Sunkist Signed Up as Distributor," *Adweek's Marketing Week*, February 12, 1990, 35.
21. "Regional Sales Agents Help Cut Rising Staff Costs for Big Firms," *Product Management*, May 1979, 6.
22. "When There's More Than One Route to the Customer," *Sales & Marketing Management*, August 1990, 50.
23. "Distribution: More Art Than Science," *High-Tech Marketing*, June 1986, 30.
24. "Which Approach Is Right for You?" *Business Marketing*, December 1990, 40; "Will Mail-Order Image Stunt Dell Computer's Fast Growth," *Electronic Business*, November 13, 1989, 37–40.
25. Ibid.
26. "For Kodak, Agents Are Their Business Partners," *Agency Sales Magazine*, June 1990, 4–7.
27. "Managing Hybrid Marketing Systems," *Harvard Business Review*, November–December 1990, 146.
28. Ibid, 154.
29. "Ready, Set, Sell—Japan Is Buying," *Fortune*, September 11, 1989, 159.
30. "We're Still Here," *Forbes*, November 1990, 194.
31. "The Revenge of the Little Guy," *Adweek's Marketing Week*, September 17, 1990, 24.
32. Ibid, 27.
33. *Franchising in the U.S. Economy* (Washington DC: U.S. Department of Commerce, 1984).
34. "Adidas Making a Run for Hungarian Franchises," *Advertising Age*, April 9, 1990, 40.
35. "Pepsi Keeps On Going After No.1," *Fortune*, March 11, 1991, 64.
36. *Industrial Marketing*, February 1981, 68.
37. "Myth and Marketing in Japan," *The Wall Street Journal*, April 6, 1989, B1.
38. "They Didn't Listen to Anybody," *Forbes*, December 15, 1986, 169.
39. "Marketing, American-Style," *Forbes*, December 29, 1986, 91.
40. "Franchisers See a Future in East Bloc," *The Wall Street Journal*, June 5, 1990, B1.
41. "Avon's Calling," *Barron's*, February 4, 1991, 15; "Door-to-Door in Guang-

zhou," *The China Business Review*, March–April 1991, 40–41.
42. "Mitsubishi Pulls Out the Stops," *Business Week*, May 6, 1991, 64.
43. This example is based on a communication from Professor Roger A. Kerin, professor of marketing, Southern Methodist University.
44. "Gloria Jean's Leads the Specialty Coffee Stampede," *The New York Times*, August 11, 1991, Business Section, 11.
45. "Flaring Tempers at the Frozen-Yogurt King," *Business Week*, September 10, 1990, 88, 90.
46. Ibid.
47. "Quaker State Switches into a Quick Change Artist," *Business Week*, October 16, 1989, 126.
48. "A Sweet Job with Sour Notes," *The New York Times*, December 1, 1985, F7.
49. Henry Assael, "The Political Role of Trade Associations in Distributive Conflict Resolution," *Journal of Marketing 32* (April 1968), 22–23.
50. "Can Paul Fireman Put the Bounce Back in Reebok," *Business Week*, June 18, 1990, 181.
51. "Managing Hybrid Marketing Systems," *Harvard Business Review*, November–December 1990, 146.
52. "The Importance of Distributor Training at Caterpillar," *Industrial Marketing Management*, 1990, 4–7.
53. "Snapple Enters the Mainstream," *Adweek's Marketing Week*, October 2, 1989, 26.
54. "Why P&G Wants a Mellower Image," *Business Week*, June 7, 1982, 60.
55. *The New York Times*, January 20, 1986, D1.
56. "Masterminding Distribution and Pricing," *Marketing Communication*, September 1984, 25–34.
57. "Can new Macs restore shine to Apple's Future," *Computerworld*, December 24, 1990/January 1, 1991, 22.
58. "A Slow Rebound for Seven-Up," *Business Week*, October 12, 1981, 107.

CHAPTER 15

1. "Patience Called the Turnaround to Sears," *The New York Times*, January 15, 1990, D1; "Will the Big Markdown Get the Big Store Moving Again?," *Business Week*, March 13, 1989, 110.
2. "The Giant Flexes," *Marketing Insights*, Premier Issue, 101.
3. "Sears Battles for Niche in Women's Apparel," *The Wall Street Journal*, May 9, 1990, A1.
4. "Will the Big Markdown Get the Store Moving Again?," *Business Week*, March 13, 1989, 110; "New Policy Challenges Discounters," *The New York Times*, March 2, 1990, D4.
5. "Sears Glitzy Ads Target Affluent Fashion Market," *The Wall Street Journal*, August 15, 1990, B1.
6. "Its Earnings Sagging, Sears Upgrades Line of Women's Apparel," *The Wall Street Journal*, May 3, 1990, A1; "Sears Targets Tots . . ." *The Wall Street Journal*, August 10, 1988, 22.
7. "Big Change Is Expected for Sears," *The New York Times*, January 28, 1991, D1.
8. "At Sears, the More Things Change," *Business Week*, November 12, 1990, 68.
9. Ibid, 66.
10. "Big Change Expected For Sears," *The New York Times*, January 28, 1991, D1; "Sears Says It Will Cut 21,000 Jobs," *The New York Times*, January 4, 1991, D1.
11. "Retailers Face Wild Ride to Recovery," *The Wall Street Journal*, April 9, 1991, B9; "Sears to Close McKids Stores," *Marketing News*, February 18, 1991, 5.
12. "Supermarkets Demand Food Firms' Payments Just to Get on the Shelf," *The Wall Street Journal*, November 1, 1988, 1.
13. Malcolm P. McNair, "Significant Trends and Developments in the Postwar Period," in A. B. Smith, ed., *Competitive Distribution in a Free, High-Level Economy and Its Implications for the University* (Pittsburgh: University of Pittsburgh Press, 1958), 1–25.
14. "The New Retailing Champs," *Fortune*, September 24, 1990. 85.
15. *Business Week*, November 12, 1990, 66.
16. "Coming Together for a Common Market," *Discount Merchandiser*, December 1990, 56.
17. "Discount Clothing Stores, Facing

Squeeze, Aim to Fashion a More Rounded Image," *The Wall Street Journal,* March 15, 1990, B1.
18. "For Toys "Я" Us, Japan Isn't Child's Play," *The Wall Street Journal,* February 7, 1990, B6.
19. "The Evolution of Retailing," *American Demographics,* December 1986, 30.
20. Ibid., 32.
21. "Merchants' Woe: Too Many Stores," *Fortune,* May 13, 1985, 62.
22. "A Tale of Two Companies," *Forbes,* May 27, 1991, 86.
23. "New Shine on a Tarnished Penney," *The New York Times,* April 23, 1989, D4.
24. "Going Shopping in the 1990s," *The Futurist,* December 1983, 15.
25. "Is Wal-Mart Unstoppable?" *Fortune,* May 6, 1991, 54.
26. "Brennan: Ward's Man with a Mission," *Chain Store Age Executive,* May 1987, 206.
27. "The Coming Boom in Europe," *Fortune,* April 10, 1989, 114.
28. "Hard Times? Not for These Stores," *The New York Times,* December 13, 1990, D6.
29. "Inventory of Formats," *Advertising Age,* April 27, 1981, S4, S6.
30. "New Japanese Lesson: Running a 7-11," *The New York Times,* May 9, 1991, D1.
31. "Supermarkets Become Marketing Driven for the 1990s," *Adweek's Marketing Week,* March 19, 1990, 50.
32. "Bigger, Shrewder, and Cheaper Cub Leads Food Stores into the Future," *The Wall Street Journal,* August 26, 1985, 19.
33. "How Much Hype in Hypermarkets?" *Sales & Marketing Management,* April 1988, 51–55.
34. "The Return of the Amazing Colossal Store," *Business Week,* August 22, 1988, 59.
35. "Will American Shoppers Think Big Is Really Better?" *The New York Times,* April 1, 1990, Business Section, 11.
36. "Penney's Catalog Division, Long a Star, Risks Losing Its Luster as Sales Slacken," *The Wall Street Journal,* May 16, 1990, A1.
37. Ibid.
38. "War of the Sales Robots," *Forbes,* January 7, 1991, 294.
39. "Supermarketing Success," *American Demographics,* August 1985, 32.
40. "The Japanese Yen for Non-Store Retailing," *Direct Marketing,* April 1989, 24.
41. "Its Earnings Sagging, Sears Upgrades Line of Women's Apparel," *The Wall Street Journal,* May 3, 1990, 6.
42. "Tandy Seeks a Feminine Edge," *Adweek's Marketing Week,* November 12, 1990, 42.
43. "Is Wal-Mart Unstoppable?" *Fortune,* May 6, 1991, 51.
44. "The New Champs of Retailing," *Fortune,* September 24, 1990, 98.
45. "A Retail Rebel Has the Establishment Quaking," *Business Week,* April 1, 1991, 39.
46. "Wal-Mart's Store of the Future Blends Discount Prices, Department Store Feel," *The Wall Street Journal,* May 17, 1991, B1.
47. Ray O. Werner (ed.), "Legal Developments in Marketing," *Journal of Marketing 43*(Fall 1979),125.
48. "Retailers Adding Touches of Green," *Advertising Age,* December 10, 1990, 58; and "Wal-Mart's Way," *Advertising Age,* February 18, 1991, 3, 48.
49. "Retailers Face Wild Ride to Recovery," *The Wall Street Journal,* April 9, 1991, B1.
50. "Leslie Wexner Pushed Limited's Fast Growth Despite Retailing's Ills," *The Wall Street Journal,* Aug. 15, 1990, 1.
51. "Is Wal-Mart Unstoppable?" *Fortune,* May 6, 1991, 54.
52. Robert D. Buzzell and Marci K. Dow, "Strategic Management Helps Retailers Plan for the Future," *Marketing News,* March 7, 1980, 6.
53. Ibid.
54. "Edward Brennan," *The 1990 Business Week 1000,* 136; "At Sears, the More Things Change," *Business Week,* November 12, 1990, 68.
55. "New Shine on a Tarnished Penney," *The New York Times,* April 23, 1989, 4.
56. "37 Things You Can Do to Keep Your Customers—Or Lose Them," *Progressive Grocer,* June 1973, 59–64.
57. "Ikea's Got 'Em Lining Up," *Fortune,* March 11, 1991, 72.
58. "Wal-Mart Finds New Rivals on Main

Street," *Adweek's Marketing Week*, November 19, 1990, 5.

59. "Retail's Art and Kraft Movement," *Adweek*, April 2, 1990, 26.
60. "Is Wal-Mart Unstoppable?" *Fortune*, May 6, 1991, 52.
61. *Adweek*, April 2, 1990, 26.
62. "At Gap, Clothes Make the Ads as Stars Fade," *The Wall Street Journal*, Aug. 29, 1990, B1.
63. "Will Home Depot Be the Wal-Mart of the 90s," *Business Week*, March 19, 1990, 126.
64. "Wal-Mart's Way," *Advertising Age*, February 18, 1991, 3.
65. "Big City Ambitions at Toys 'Я' Us," *The New York Times*, November 11, 1990, B1.
66. "More Than One Way to Catch a Thief," *Chain Store Age Executive*, April 1982, 39.
67. *The New York Times*, February 24, 1989, A1, D6; and "Minding the Store," *Forbes*, April 7, 1986, 31–32.
68. "New Japanese Lesson: Running a 7-11," *The New York Times*, May 9, 1991, D1.

CHAPTER 16

1. Interview with James Cohune, Public Relations, the McKesson Corp., October 15, 1991; "A Strategic Information System: McKesson Drug Company's Economost," *Planning Review*, September/October 1988, 14–19; "Customer Closeness at Bergen Brunswig," *Computerworld*, February 19, 1990, 69, 75.
2. "The Practice of Making Perfect," *Business Week*, January 14, 1991, 86.
3. "Food Fight," *FW*, January 8, 1991, 40.
4. Interview with James Cohune, McKesson Corp.
5. *Barron's*, October 14, 1985, 32–37.
6. *Business Week*, January 14, 1991, 86.
7. "Behind Wal-Mart's Surge, a Web of Suppliers," *The New York Times*, July 1, 1991, D1; "Wal-Mart Stores Penny Wise," *Business Month*, December 1988, 42.
8. "Bista's rise from jewels to riches," *Asian Finance*, January 1991, 20.
9. "McLane Delivers," *Supermarket Business*, July 1989, 17.
10. "Foremost-McKesson: The Computer Moves Distribution to Center Stage," *Business Week*, December 7, 1981, 115, 118.
11. "Makro's Wholesale Merchandising Machine," *The Discount Merchandiser*, August 1982, 53–54.
12. "Managing Structural Changes in Marketing Channels," *The Journal of Consumer Marketing*, Fall 1990, 37.
13. *FW*, January 8, 1991, 40.
14. " 'Toy Liquidators' Breathes New Life into Over-the-Hill Toys," *Adweek's Marketing Week*, March 19, 1990, 24.
15. "The Practice of Making Perfect," *Business Week*, January 14, 1991, 86; "The Education of Jack Twyman," *Forbes*, March 11, 1985, 75.
16. *FW*, January 8, 1991, 41.
17. *The Journal of Consumer Marketing*, Fall 1990, 38.
18. "Hotline: Value Added, the Key to Distribution Survival," *IS*, November 1985, 58.
19. "Play It Again, Sam," *Forbes*, August 10, 1987, 48.
20. "Just-In-Time Isn't Just for Show—It Sells," *Sales & Marketing Management*, May 1990, 62–63.
21. "Warehousing Success Story in Kansas City," *Material Handling Engineering*, March 1987, 70.
22. "How Toys "R" Us Controls the Game Board," *Business Week*, December 19, 1988, 58.
23. "Toys "R" Us, Big Kids on the Block, Won't Stop Growing," *The Wall Street Journal*, August 11, 1988, 6.
24. Roy D. Shapiro, "Get Leverage from Logistics," *Harvard Business Review 62* (May–June 1984), 124.
25. "Changes in Segmentation, Distribution, Logistics, Demand Analysis Challenge Industrial Marketers," *Marketing News*, June 26, 1981, Sec. 2, 9.
26. "Just-In-Time Isn't Just For Show—It Sells," *Sales & Marketing Management*, May 1990, 64–66.
27. Thomas C. Kinnear and Kenneth L. Bernhardt, *Principles of Marketing* (Glenview, ILL: Scott Foresman and Co., 1986), 402.

28. "Looking for New Fashion Markets, Designers from America Go Global," *New York Times*, November 3, 1991, 20.
29. "Leading-Edge Distribution Strategies," *The Journal of Business Strategy*, November/December 1990, 52.
30. "Is Wal-Mart Unstoppable?" *Fortune*, May 6, 1991, 54.
31. *Smithsonian*, November 1988, 48.
32. "The Remaking of Montgomery Ward," *DM*, September 1989, 19.
33. "Warehouse Site Selection Strategy. Casebook: Lazarus Department Stores," *Distribution*, December 1990, 38, 39.
34. "POS systems finally checking," *Drug Topics*, March 21, 1988, 47.
35. "Spiegel's Small Shipment Innovations," *Distribution*, January 1991, 65.
36. "Danzas Is a Transportation Supermarket," *Global Trade*, August 1990, 38, 39.
37. "Casebook: Beauty for All Seasons," *Distribution*, April 1987, 51.
38. Roy Dale Voorhees and John I. Coppett, "Marketing Logistics Opportunities for the 1990s," *Journal of Business Strategy*, (Fall 1986), 34.
39. "A New Facility," *Handling and Shipping Management*, August 1985, 43–44.
40. "Formica: When a Household Name Becomes an 'Also-Ran'," *New York Times*, August 12, 1990, Business Section, 12.
41. "Competition Stirs Campbell," *Corporate Strategies*, February 1987, 12.
42. "Perrier Sets Slow Pace for U.S. Relaunch," *The Wall Street Journal*, March 7, 1990, B1.
43. "Behind Wal-Mart's Surge, a Web of Suppliers," *The New York Times*, July 1, 1991, D1.
44. Quote of Bernard J. LaLonde in James C. Johnson and Donald J. Wood, *Contemporary Physical Distribution and Logistics* (Tulsa: PennWell Books, 1982), 3.

CHAPTER 17

1. "Burger King Tinkers with 'Break the Rules'," *Advertising Age*, September 10, 1990, 3.
2. "Tempers Are Sizzling over Burger King's New Ads," *Business Week*, February 12, 1990, 33.
3. Ibid.
4. *Advertising Age*, September 10, 1990, 85.
5. "BK Brakes the 'Rules,' " *Advertising Age*, February 21, 1991, 50.
6. "BK Picks Mickey," *Advertising Age*, August 12, 1991, 1, 32.
7. "BK Franchisees Pan Ad Theme," *Advertising Age*, January 29, 1990, 3; "Kidding Around," *Restaurant Business*, June 10, 1991, 100; "Little People, Big Market," *Incentive*, May 1991, 46.
8. *Advertising Age*, February 21, 1991, 1, 50.
9. Ibid.
10. "Amoco, Burger King Team Up in Roadway Cross-Selling Test," *Marketing News*, October 14, 1991, 1, 14.
11. "How Polaroid Flashed Back," *Fortune*, February 16, 1987, 72–76; and "Polaroid Snaps the Customer," *American Demographics*, February 1987, 21–22.
12. "Häagen-Dazs Goes Whole Hog with Ads," *The Wall Street Journal*, April 19, 1990, B8.
13. "Study: Some Promotions Change Consumer Behavior," *Marketing News*, October 15, 1990, 12.
14. Figures based on "Cost of Industrial Sales Calls Reaches $205.40," Labreport (New York: McGraw-Hill Research, 1983), 1–4. Average costs of $205 per sales call and 17 cents per magazine exposure in 1983 were projected to 1991 dollars.
15. "Cadillac Drives Hard with America's Cup," *Advertising Age*, November 19, 1990, 50.
16. "Scoundrel Time at P&G," *Adweek's Marketing Week*, August 19, 1991, 13.
17. *Fortune*, February 16, 1987, 72–76.
18. "Spectra Unites Polaroid's Family," *Advertising Age*, October 6, 1986, 4, 100.
19. "Polaroid Enlarges Ad Budget," *Advertising Age*, February 7, 1987, 76.
20. "Marketing Without Broadcast Media," *Marketing Communications*, January 1987, 31–32.
21. "Bear Essentials," *Marketing & Media Decisions*, March 1990, 71.
22. "Leading Edge Hacks Its Way Back," *Advertising Age*, April 16, 1990, 12.
23. "Cutting Promotions to Fit the Plan," *Sales & Marketing Management*, January 1987, 79–80.
24. "Diet Pepsi Conquers Tulsa with a

Two-Step," *Adweek's Marketing Week*, April 23, 1990, 61.

25. Malcolm A. McNiven, "Plan for More Productive Advertising," *Harvard Business Review 58*(March–April 1980), 131.
26. "Sears Eyes Lower Ad-to-Sales Ratio," *Advertising Age*, December 4, 1978, 3, 8.
27. *Marketing & Media Decisions*, March 1990, 71–73.
28. *Donnelley Marketing Surveys of Promotional Practices*, 1991, and communication from industry sources.
29. "Washday Miracle," *Financial World*, November 3, 1987, 26.
30. Robert Buzzell, John Quelch & Walter Salmon, "The Costly Bargain of Trade Promotion," *Harvard Business Review, 68* (March/April 1990),142.
31. *Marketing Communications*, January 1987, 31–32.
32. "Special Recovery: Tylenol Regains Most of No. 1 Market Share," *The Wall Street Journal*, December 24, 1982, 1.
33. "McDonald's Focus on Promotions in New Ads Faulted by Marketers," *The Wall Street Journal*, May 1, 1989, B4.
34. "Marketing & Media Influencers," *Marketing & Media Decisions*, July 1990, 31.
35. "Turning from Rebates," *Advertising Age*, November 6, 1990, 3, 66.
36. "A Penny Saved Is a Penny Spent," *Advertising Age*, April 2, 1990, 33.
37. "Study: Some Promotions Change Consumer Behavior," *Marketing News*, October 15, 1990, 12.
38. "Global Coupon Use Up; U.K., Belgium Tops in Europe," *Marketing News*, August 5, 1991, 5.
39. "Stealing the Right Shoppers," *Forbes*, July 10, 1989, 104.
40. "Electronic Coupons," *Fortune*, April 23, 1990, 21.
41. "Promotions Get Better Next Time Around," *Adweek*, June 24, 1991, 20.
42. "Waldenbooks' Big-Buyer Lure May Mean War," *The Wall Street Journal*, February 29, 1990, B1.
43. "A Selective Update on Frequent-Shopper Programs," *Adweek's Marketing Week*, July 30, 1990, 27.
44. *Marketing Communications*, April 1986, 47.
45. "Ford Spotlighting Brands, Not Rebates," *Advertising Age*, October 2, 1989, 3.
46. "Marketers Bet Big on Consumer Contests," *The Wall Street Journal*, February 7, 1990, B1.
47. "NBC's 'McMillions' Tops Fall Parade," *Advertising Age*, February 21, 1991, 3.
48. "Supermarket Sweepstakes," *Marketing & Media Decisions*, November 1988, 34.
49. "Bud Puts Stress on Promotions, Trims TV Ads," *The Wall Street Journal*, February 21, 1990, B1, B3.
50. "The Promo Wars," *Business Month*, July 1987, 44–46.
51. "Hitting the Market from Both Sides: With Premiums and Incentives," *Business Marketing*, August 1986, 122–126.
52. "Supermarkets Demand Food Firms' Payment Just to Get on the Shelf," *The Wall Street Journal*, November 1, 1988, 1; and "Grocer 'Fee' Hampers New-Product Launches," *Advertising Age*, August 3, 1987, 1, 60.
53. "Sales Promotion Plays Bigger Role in Brand Support," *Marketing News*, October 15, 1990, 12.
54. "Airborne Sweeps Customers off Their Feet," *Sales & Marketing Management*, July 1986, 80–82.
55. "What Increases Product Knowledge?" *Incentive*, August 1990, 32, 34.
56. Joseph A. Bellizzi and Delilah J. Lipps, "Managerial Guidelines for Trade Show Effectiveness," *Industrial Marketing Management*, 13 (1984), 49–52.
57. Christopher H. Lovelock and John A. Quelch, "Consumer Promotions in Service Marketing," *Business Horizons*, May–June 1983, 66–75.
58. "Banks Add Sweepstakes to Financial Rewards," *Advertising Age*, March 23, 1987, S9.
59. "Free Association," *Advertising Age*, October 23, 1989, 108.
60. *Time*, April 13, 1987.
61. *Advertising Age*, October 23, 1989, 36.

CHAPTER 18

1. "How the Bunny Charged Eveready," *Advertising Age*, April 9, 1991, 20.
2. "Eveready Loses Power in Market," *Advertising Age*, July 11, 1988, 4.

3. Ibid.
4. *Advertising Age*, April 9, 1991, 20.
5. Ibid.
6. "Too Many Think the Bunny Is Duracell's, Not Eveready's," *The Wall Street Journal*, July 31, 1990, B1.
7. "Bunny Back to Battle Duracell," *Advertising Age*, September 17, 1990, 4.
8. *Advertising Age*, April 9, 1991, 20.
9. Ibid.
10. Robert J. Coen, McCann-Erickson Worldwide, "The Insider's Report," June 1991.
11. "P&G Spends $2.28 Billion, Surges to Head of Top 100," *Advertising Age*, September 25, 1991, 21.
12. "Perched between Perrier and Tap," *Forbes*, May 14, 1990, 120.
13. "Corporate Advertising" *Adweek's Marketing Week*, May 20, 1991, 32.
14. "Ford, Chevrolet Raise the Ad Ante in Race for No. 1," *Advertising Age*, September 29, 1990, 3.
15. "Co-Op Advertising: The More Things Change . . ." *Sales & Marketing Management*, May 1990, 94.
16. "How Retailers Are Putting It All Together," *Sales & Marketing Management*, May 1988, 63.
17. "The Sole of a Woman," *Adweek's Marketing Week*, October 7, 1991, 37.
18. "AT&T Has Students' Number," *Advertising Age*, February 5, 1990, S7.
19. *Marketing & Media Decisions*, April 1984, 110–114.
20. "Sara Lee Recipe for Proper Introduction," *Advertising Age*, February 13, 1986, 27.
21. "Wrigley Tries to Be Smoker's Friend," *Advertising Age*, June 18, 1990, 80.
22. "Jeans Genies," *Adweek*, October 14, 1991, 48.
23. "Nonverbal Messages in Ads Gain New Importance," *Adweek*, January 4, 1988, 23.
24. "Chevy Doesn't Miss a Beat," *Adweek*, April 1, 1991, 37.
25. "Humor in U.S. versus U.K. TV Commercials: A Comparison," *Journal of Advertising, 18* (1989), 42.
26. Ibid.
27. "Perrier: Fighting Crisis with Laughter," *Adweek*, March 12, 1990, 12.
28. "Celebrity Pitchmen Are Popular Again," *The Wall Street Journal*, June 25, 1990, B1.
29. Ibid.
30. "Ushering in the Non-Celeb Decade," *Adweek's Marketing Week*, January 14, 1991, 22.
31. "More Car Ads Challenge Rivals Head-On," *The Wall Street Journal*, June 25, 1990, B1.
32. "Lean and Mean: Hardee's Joins Low-Fat Fray," *The Wall Street Journal*, July 15, 1991, B1.
33. "Coke Seeks Tough TV Ad Watchdog," *Advertising Age*, October 8, 1990, 1.
34. "Comparative Advertising Effectiveness," *Journal of Advertising Research, 29* (October/November 1989), 22–37.
35. "What Hidden Sell Is All About," *Life*, March 31, 1958.
36. *New Yorker*, September 21, 1957, 33.
37. See Timothy E. Moore, "Subliminal Advertising: What You See Is What You Get," *Journal of Marketing, 46* (Spring 1982), 38–47.
38. "The Marlboro Man Once Tried to Hop a Train in Hong Kong," *Adweek's Marketing Week*, May 2, 1988, 36
39. "Colgate Axes Global Ads; Thinks Local," *Advertising Age*, November 20, 1990, 1.
40. "TV's Toughest Year Is Just a Preview," *Fortune*, November 19, 1990, 95.
41. Ibid; and "TV Just for Women . . . and Men," *The New York Times*, November 11, 1991, D9.
42. "How Creative Can Cable Advertising Get?" *Madison Avenue*, April 1986, 65.
43. *Forbes*, November 30, 1987, 204; "Orchestrating Your Media Options," *Business Marketing*, April 1990, 46.
44. "Drive Time," *Forbes*, March 19, 1990, 144; and "Hot Spots," *American Demographics*, September 1989, 51.
45. "Radio Is Making a Comeback as an Advertising Vehicle," *Sales & Marketing Digest*, September 1986, 3.
46. "Efficiency Not Enough Anymore," *Advertising Age*, November 26, 1990, S10.
47. "The Last Gasp of Mass Media?" *Forbes*, September 17, 1990, 180.
48. "How Magazines—and a Non-stop Campaign—Made Absolut Number One," *Adweek's Marketing Week*, April 1, 1991, 11
49. *Forbes*, September 17, 1990, 180.
50. "Subaru Targets Women," *Advertising Age*, March 28, 1988, 38.

51. "Colgate-Palmolive Is First to Put Ads on Soviet Busses," *Marketing News*, November 26, 1990, 32
52. "Ads on Rental Videos Prove to Be Less of a Turnoff Than Expected," *The Wall Street Journal*, April 28, 1989, B1.
53. "Push 'M' for Mayo, Sales Pitch Included," *The New York Times*, July 7, 1991, Business Section, 7
54. "What Happened to the Truth?" *Adweek's Marketing Week*, October 28, 1991, 4
55. Ibid.
56. William L. Wilkie, Dennis L. McNeil, and Michael B. Mazis, "Marketing's Scarlet Letter The Theory and Practice of Corrective Advertising," *Journal of Marketing, 48* (Spring 1984), 11.
57. "Just Exactly How Weighty Are the Slogans of Our Times," *Adweek's Marketing Week*, March 26, 1990, 6.
58. "Reebok: If the Shoe Fits," *Adweek*, January 7, 1991, 23.
59. "FCC Tightens Rules on When Kids' TV Show Is Really a Commercial," *Marketing News*, November 26, 1990, 1.
60. "Kids Know 'Old Joe,' " *New York Newsday*, December 11, 1991; and "Camel's Success and Controversy," *The New York Times*, December 12, 1991, D1, D17.
61. "Behind the Wheel of a Quiet Revolution," *Advertising Age*, July 26, 1982, M13.
62. "Blacks Are Found to Be Still Scarce in Advertisements in Major Magazines," *The New York Times*, July 23, 1991, A18.

CHAPTER 19

1. "Money Talks, Xerox Listens," *Business Month*, September 1990, 91.
2. "Xerox's Sales Force Learns a New Game," *Sales & Marketing Management*, July 1, 1985, 48; and "Xerox's Makeover," *Sales & Marketing Management*, June 1987, 68.
3. "Culture Shock at Xerox," *Business Week*, June 22, 1987, 106–110.
4. *Sales & Marketing Management*, July 1, 1985, 49, 50.
5. Ibid, 50.
6. *Business Month*, September 1990, 91, 92.
7. John F. Tanner, Jr., "Leadership Through Quality," *Journal of Personal Selling & Sales Management, 10* (Winter 1990), 49–51.
8. "Building an Integrated Marketing Strategy," *Business Marketing*, August 1987, 52.
9. "Solutions: Duplicating Success," *Adweek*, November 25, 1991, 36, 37.
10. "The Average Cost of a Personal Sales Call by Selected Industries and Geographic Region," *Sales & Marketing Digest*, September 1990, 7.
11. "Hiring & Training," *Sales & Marketing Management*, December 1990, 114, 115.
12. The Myths and Realities of Customer Service," *Electronic Business*, October 7, 1991, 158.
13. "America's Best Sales Forces," *Sales & Marketing Management*, June 1989, 15.
14. Clifton J. Reichard, "Industrial Selling: Beyond Price and Persistence," *Harvard Business Review, 63*(March–April 1985), 127–133.
15. Ibid.
16. "Getting a Leg Up by Using Handhelds," *Datamation*, January 1, 1987, 32.
17. John Barrett, "Why Major Account Selling Works," *Industrial Marketing Management, 15* (1986), 63–73.
18. "America's Best Sales Forces: Six at the Summit," *Sales & Marketing Management*, June 1990, 74.
19. "The Shape of Things to Come," *Sales & Marketing Management*, January 1990, 39.
20. "Ryder Trucks Ahead with Computers," *Marketing Communications*, June 1985, 84.
21. "Reps' Fears of Telemarketing Present Management Hurdle," *Marketing News*, April 25, 1986, 8.
22. "Dow Corning Blends Inquiry Handling with Telemarketing," *Marketing Communications*, June 1985, 87.
23. "Going the Integrated Route," *Business Marketing*, December 1990, 26.
24. "Closing the Loop: Hewlett-Packard's New Lead Management System," *Business Marketing*, October 1987, 74–78.
25. "Send in the Specialists," *Sales & Marketing Management*, April 1991, 47, 48.
26. *Business Marketing*, December 1990, 26.

27. "High Tech Can't Forget Sales Prospecting," *Industrial Marketing*, November 1981, 78.
28. "Sales Lead Management," *Business Marketing*, March 1986, 62.
29. "Crafting 'Win–Win Situations' in Buyer–Supplier Relationships," *Business Marketing*, June 1986, 42.
30. "Putting Customers First," *Business Marketing*, December 1989, 30.
31. "P&G Rolls Out Retailer Sales Teams," *Advertising Age*, May 21, 1990, 18.
32. "Are You Tough Enough to Raise Sales Productivity," *Sales & Marketing Management*, October 1988, 82, 83.
33. "Marketing Assurance," *American Demographics*, November 1990, 42, 43.
34. "An Extra Dose of Recognition," *Business Marketing*, January 1991, 19.
35. "Xerox's Makeover," *Sales & Marketing Management*, June 1987, 68.
36. "Airwick Drops Sales Offices to Increase Sales," *Marketing News*, February 8, 1980, 6.
37. "Apple-Polishing the Dealer," *Sales & Marketing Management*, September 10, 1984, 47.
38. Donald Baier and Robert D. Dugan, "Factors in Sales Success," *Journal of Applied Psychology, 41* (February 1957), 37–40; and Paul J. O'Neill, "Pattern Analysis of Biographical Predictors of Success as an Insurance Salesman," *Journal of Applied Psychology 53* (April 1969), 136–139.
39. John B. Miner, "Personality and Ability Factors in Sales Performance," *Journal of Applied Psychology 46* (February 1962), 6–13; and Thomas W. Harrell, "The Relation of Test Scores to Sales Criteria," *Personnel Psychology 13* (Spring 1960), 65–69.
40. *Sales & Marketing Management's 1985 Survey of Selling Costs*, February 18, 1985, 68.
41. "Burger King Uses A/V 'Their Way'," *Marketing Communications*, April 1986, 91.
42. "Merck's Grand Obsession," *Sales & Marketing Management*, June 1987, 65.
43. "Motivating Willy Loman," *Forbes*, January 30, 1984, 91.
44. Gilbert A. Churchill, Jr., Neil M. Ford, and Orville C. Walker, Jr., "Personal Characteristics of Salespeople and the Attractiveness of Alternative Rewards, *Journal of Business Research* 7 (1979), 25–50.
45. "Bang! Bang! Selling Life Ins. When Bullets Fly," *National Underwriter*, October 22, 1990, 14.
46. "Legislation Blitz Threatens Telemarketers," *Target Marketing*, July 1989, 13.

CHAPTER 20

1. "Management Brief," *The Economist*, August 24, 1991, 61.
2. "Can Apple Go It Alone?" *Forbes*, September 17, 1990, 197.
3. *The Economist*, August 24, 1991, 61.
4. "Apple: New Team, New Strategy," *Business Week*, October 15, 1990, 87.
5. Ibid.
6. "Apple Turns from Revolution to Evolution," *Business Week*, January 23, 1989, 90, 92.
7. *Forbes*, September 17, 1990, 197.
8. "The Second Comeback of Apple," *Business Week*, January 28, 1991, 68.
9. *The Economist*, August 24, 1991, 61.
10. Ibid.
11. *Business Week*, January 28, 1991, 68.
12. Ibid.
13. "Pricing Is Shaping Up As '84's Top Marketing 'Pressure Point'," *Marketing News*, November 11, 1983, 1.
14. "Turning from Rebates," *Advertising Age*, November 15, 1990, 1, 66.
15. "Zenith Is Sticking Its Neck Out in a Cutthroat Market," *Business Week*, August 17, 1987, 72.
16. "Middle-Price Brands Come Under Siege," *The Wall Street Journal*, April 2, 1990, B1.
17. "Deregulating America," *Business Week*, November 28, 1983, 68.
18. "McRisky," *Business Week*, October 21, 1991, 114–122.
19. "Lilly Cuts Price 12% on Major Herbicide to Lift Market Share," *The Wall Street Journal*, December 15, 1982, 10.
20. Thomas Nagle, "Pricing as Creative Marketing," *Business Horizons*, July–August 1983, 15.
21. "Mercedes Finds Out How Much Is Too Much," *Business Week*, January 20, 1992, 92.

22. "Sears' Cudmore Takes 'Trust' Tack," *Advertising Age*, January 29, 1990, 1.
23. "Pride Goeth Before a Fall?" *Forbes*, May 29, 1989, 306.
24. "Busch Fights to Have It All," *Fortune*, January 15, 1990, 81.
25. Louis W. Stern and Adel I. El-Ansery, *Marketing Channels* (Englewood Cliffs, NJ: Prentice-Hall, 1982), 228.
26. "The Trend Is Not Their Friend," *Forbes*, September 16, 1991, 115.
27. "Wal-Mart Puts Its Own Spin on Private Label," *Advertising Age*, December 16, 1991, 26.
28. " 'Value' Brands Head for Shelves," *Adweek's Marketing Week*, October 29, 1990, 6.
29. *Advertising Age*, January 7, 1991, 1, 44.
30. "Ikea Furniture Chain Pleases with Its Prices, Not with Service," *The Wall Street Journal*, September 17, 1991, A1.
31. "The $4,300 TV," *Forbes*, August 22, 1988, 100.
32. "Brands Are Fighting for Their Lives More Than Ever," *Marketing News*, October 29, 1990, 11.
33. "Pricey Ice Cream Is Scooping the Market," *Business Week*, June 30, 1986, 60.
34. "Chocolate Marketers Fatten Sales with Bigger Bars," *Marketing & Media Decisions*, September 1982, 69.
35. *Marketing & Media Decisions*, September 1982, 65.
36. "Doing Unto Compaq As It Did Unto IBM?" *Business Week*, November 19, 1990, 130.
37. "Polaroid, Value Click," *Advertising Age*, November 25, 1991, 33.
38. "Bausch & Lomb: Hardball Pricing Helps It to Regain Its Grip on Contact Lenses," *Business Week*, July 16, 1984, 78.
39. *The Wall Street Journal*, April 2, 1990, B7.
40. Victor E. Grimm, "Some Legal Pitfalls" in *Pricing Practices and Strategies*, edited by Earl L. Bailey (New York: The Conference Board, 1978), 19–23.
41. "Colleges Block Antitrust Charge by Ending Collaboration on Aid," *The New York Times*, May 23, 1991, A1, B13.
42. "Panasonic to Pay Rebates to Avoid Antitrust Charges," *The Wall Street Journal*, January 19, 1989, B1, B6.

CHAPTER 21

1. "Can GM Remodel Itself?," *Fortune*, January 13, 1992, 17.
2. Ibid, 26, 29.
3. "The New Drive to Revive GM," *Fortune*, April 9, 1990, 53.
4. "The U.S. Must Do As GM Has Done," *Fortune*, February 13, 1989, 7.
5. *Advertising Age*, January 4, 1988, 1.
6. "War, Recession, Gas Hikes . . . GM's Turnaround Will Have to Wait," *Business Week*, February 4, 1991, 95.
7. "The Planets May Be Perfectly Aligned for Saturn's Lift-Off," *Business Week*, October 22, 1990, 40.
8. Michael Kublin, "A Guide to Export Pricing," *IM* (May/June 1990), 29–32.
9. Gary W. Bowman and Erwin A. Blackstone, "Low Price Conspiracy: Trade Regulation and the Case of Japanese Electronics," *Atlantic Economic Journal* (December 1990), 59–67.
10. "Software Pricing Strategies," *Computerworld*, January 6, 1986, 53–56.
11. "IBM PS Moves May Cut Prices," *USA Today*, February 10, 1988, 7B.
12. Zarrel V. Lambert, "Perceived Prices as Related to Odd and Even Price Endings," *Journal of Retailing 51*(Fall 1975), 13–22; and Robert M. Schindler, "Consumer Recognition of Increases in Odd and Even Prices" in *Advances in Consumer Research, 11*, edited by Thomas C. Kinnear (Provo, Utah: Association for Consumer Research, 1984), 459–462.
13. "Price and Prejudice," *New York Magazine*, June 12, 1989, 19.
14. Joseph P. Guiltinan, "The Price Bundling of Services: A Normative Framework," *Journal of Marketing, 51*(April 1987), 74–75.
15. Dennis Bartakovich, "Building Competitive Advantage Through Creative Pricing Strategies," *Business Quarterly* (Summer 1990), 45–48.
16. "The Opposites: GE Grows While Westinghouse Shrinks," *Business Week*, January 31, 1977, 62.

CHAPTER 22

1. "From Chuck Wagon to Trail Boss of Marlboro Country," *Business Week*, April 15, 1991, 60–66; and "Beyond Marlboro Country," *Business Week*, August 8, 1988, 54–58.
2. Ibid.
3. "Philip Morris Is Still Hungry," *Forbes*, April 2, 1990, 96–101.
4. *Business Week*, April 15, 1991.
5. *Business Week*, August 8, 1988.
6. "Just Add Billions and Stir," *The Arizona Republic*, Business Section, 1.
7. "Philip Morris Will Buy Suchard's Europe Units," *The New York Times*, June 23, 1990, Business Section, 1.
8. *Business Week*, April 15, 1991.
9. Ibid.
10. "The Mind of Jack Welch," *Fortune*, March 27, 1989, 40.
11. "Welch on Welch," *FW*, April 3, 1990, 62.
12. Theodore Levitt, "Marketing Myopia," *Harvard Business Review, 38*(July–August 1960), 45–56.
13. "Westinghouse Relies on Ruthless Pruning," *The Wall Street Journal*, January 24, 1990, A4.
14. Sidney Schoeffler, Robert D. Buzzell, and Donald F. Heany, "Impact of Strategic Planning on Profit Performance," *Harvard Business Review, 52* (March–April 1974), 137–145.
15. "Zero Base Helps Rationalize Product Strategy," *International Management*, February 1979, 38.
16. "Abbott Labs: Health Care Honcho," *Dun's Business Month*, December 1986, 26.
17. "ConAgra Turns up the Heat in the Kitchen," *Business Week*, September 2, 1991, 58, 59.
18. "Media Colossus," *Business Week*, March 25, 1991, 64.
19. "General Mills Still Needs Its Wheaties," *Business Week*, December 23, 1985, 77.
20. "The Baby Bells Scramble for Europe," *The New York Times*, December 10, 1989, Business Section, 1.
21. "Syntex Tries to Kick a One-Drug Habit," *Business Week*, December 9, 1985, 64.
22. "Warner Lambert: Can R&D Take It to the Top Tier?" *Business Week*, September 24, 1990, 66.
23. "The House That Nolan's Building," *Adweek's Marketing Week*, August 14, 1989, 20–23.
24. "Changing Signals at Radio Shack," *Fortune*, April 29, 1985, 180.
25. *Business Week*, July 1, 1985, 54.

CHAPTER 23

1. "Heinz's New Recipe: Take a Dollop of Dollars. . ." *Business Week*, September 30, 1991, 86–87; and "Heinz Ain't Broke But It's Doing a Lot of Fixing," *Business Week*, December 11, 1989, 129.
2. "Heinz Pushes to Be the Low-Cost Producer," *Fortune*, June 24, 1985, 44.
3. Ibid.
4. "At Heinz, a Bottom-Line Leader," *The New York Times*, May 8, 1988, F1.
5. *Business Week*, December 11, 1989, 129.
6. *Fortune*, June 24, 1985, 46; and *Business Week*, December 11, 1989, 129.
7. *Fortune*, June 24, 1985, 46.
8. "Does Quality Pay?" *CFO*, September 1990, 31.
9. "Reducing the Bile Factor at Heinz," *Fortune*, April 9, 1990, 42.
10. "Cost Cutting: How to Do It Right," *Fortune*, April 9, 1990, 46.
11. *Business Week*, September 30, 1991, 86; and *Business Week*, December 11, 1989, 129.
12. *Business Week*, September 30, 1991, 86.
13. Ibid.
14. *CFO*, September 1990, 27.
15. *Business Week*, March 28, 1988, 47, 50.
16. "Westinghouse Gets a Big Dose of Reality," *Business Week*, February 17, 1992, 110–112.
17. "Chipping Away at Frito Lay," *Business Week*, July 22, 1991, 26.
18. "Cars, Customers & Competition: Lessons for American Managers," *Management Review*, February 1991, 38.
19. "Can James Unruh Recharge Unisys?" *Business Week*, July 20, 1990, 72.
20. "Operation Turnaround," *Business Week*, December 5, 1983, 133; and *Business Week*, March 28, 1988, 50, 52.

21. "You Can Be Sure . . . If It's Danforth," *Nation's Business*, March 1985, 85.
22. "Procter & Gamble's Comeback Plan," *Fortune*, February 4, 1985, 30, 32.
23. *Business Week*, March 28, 1988, 50.
24. Donald W. Jackson, Jr., Lonnie L. Ostrom, and Kenneth R. Evans, *Cost & Management*, July–August 1985, 20.
25. "AT&T: The Making of a Comeback," *Business Week*, January 18, 1988, 56–62.
26. "The New Breed of Strategic Planner," *Business Week*, September 17, 1984, 62–68.
27. "Challenging Global Myths," *Industry Week*, October 7, 1991, 13.
28. "Akers to IBM Employees: Wake Up!" *The Wall Street Journal*, May 29, 1991, B1.
29. Joel E. Ross, "Making Quality a Fundamental Part of Strategy," *Long-Range Planning, 18* (1985), 55; and "America's Quest Can't Be Half-Hearted," *Business Week*, June 8, 1987, 136.
30. "Can Ford Stay on Top?" *Business Week*, September 28, 1987, 84.
31. "Sara Lee: No Fads, No Buyouts, Just Old-Fashioned Growth," *Business Week*, November 14, 1988, 110.
32. "Burned By Mistakes, Campbell Soup Co. Is in Throes of Change," *The Wall Street Journal*, August 14, 1985, 16.
33. "Cannibal Peril for GM Sales," *The New York Times*, October 9, 1987, D5.

ADDITIONAL READINGS

CHAPTER 1

Exchange Processes

- Franklin S. Houston and Jule B. Gassenheimer, "Marketing and Exchange," *Journal of Marketing* (October 1987): 3–18.

The Marketing Environment

- Michael Porter, *Competitive Advantage* (New York: Free Press, 1985).
- Warren J. Keegan, *Global Marketing Management* (Englewood Cliffs, N.J.: Prentice Hall, 1989) Chapter 1.
- Henry Assael, *Consumer Behavior and Marketing Action* (Boston: Kent Publishing Co., 1992) Chapter 1.

Marketing's Relationship to Other Business Functions

- Robert W. Reukert and Orville C. Walker, Jr., "Marketing's Interaction with Other Functional Units: A Conceptual Framework and Empirical Evidence," *Journal of Marketing* (July 1987): 1–19.

The Marketing Concept

- Theodore Levitt, "Marketing Myopia," *Harvard Business Review* (July-August 1960): 45–56.
- Robert J. Keith, "The Marketing Revolution," *Journal of Marketing* (January 1960): 35–38
- Franklin S. Houston, "The Marketing Concept: What It Is and What It Is Not," *Journal of Marketing* (April 1986): 81–87.

The Broader Role of Marketing

- Philip Kotler and Alan R. Andreasen, *Strategic Marketing for Nonprofit Organizations* (Englewood Cliffs, N.J.: Prentice Hall, 1987).
- Leonard L. Berry, "Problems and Strategies in Services Marketing," *Journal of Marketing*, (Spring 1985): 33–46.

CHAPTER 2

- Benson P. Shapiro, "Rejuvenating the Marketing Mix," *Harvard Business Review* (September–October 1985): 28–34.
- H. Igor Ansoff, "Strategies for Diversification," *Harvard Business Review* (September–October 1957): 113–124.
- Daniel H. Gray, "Uses and Misuses of Strategic Planning," *Harvard Business Review* (January–February 1986): 89–96.
- Paul F. Anderson, "Marketing, Strategic Planning, and the Theory of the Firm," *Journal of Marketing* (Spring 1982): 15–26.
- Richard G. Hamermesh, "Making Planning Strategic," *Harvard Business Review* (January–February 1986): 89–96.

CHAPTER 3

Marketing Planning

- Howard Sutton, *The Marketing Plan* (New York: The Conference Board, 1990).
- George S. Day and Liam Fahey, "Valuing Marketing Strategies," *Journal of Marketing* *52*(July 1988): 45–57.
- Francis Buttle, "The Marketing Strategy Worksheet—A Practical Planning Tool," *Long Range Planning* (August 1985): 80–88.
- Thomas V. Bonoma, "Making Your Marketing Strategy Work," *Harvard Business Review*, *62*(March–April 1984): 68–76.

Sales Forecasting

- David M. Georgoff and Robert G. Murdick, "Manager's Guide to Forecasting," *Harvard Business Review 64* (January–February 1986): 110–120.

- F. William Barnett, "Four Steps to Forecast Total Market Demand," *Harvard Business Review 66*(July–August 1988): 28–34.
- E. Jerome Scott and Stephen K. Kaiser, "Forecasting Acceptance of New Industrial Products With Judgment Modeling," *Journal of Marketing 48*(Spring 1984): 54–67.

CHAPTER 4

General

- Philip Kotler, "Megamarketing," *Harvard Business Review* (March–April 1986).

Social Trends

- "The Ageless Market," *American Demographics*, July 1987.
- "Psychographics for the 1990s," *American Demographics*, July 1989, 24–32 and 53–54.
- Joel Garreau, *The Nine Nations of North America* (New York: Avon, 1981).
- "America's Households," *American Demographics*, March 1989, 20–32.

Technology

- Noel Capon and Rashi Glazer, "Marketing and Technology: A Strategic Coalignment," *Journal of Marketing* (July 1987):1–14.
- "Technology in the Year 2000," *Fortune*, July 18, 1988, 92–98.
- "The Good News About U.S. R&D," *Fortune*, February 1, 1988, 48–56.

Ecology

- John W. Hanley, "Monsanto's Early Warning System," *Harvard Business Review* (November–December 1981):107–122.
- "Environmentalism: The New Crusade," *Fortune*, February 12, 1990, 44–52.
- Carl P. Zeithaml and Valerie A. Zeithaml, "Environmental Management," *Journal of Marketing* (Spring 1984):46–53.

Legal

- Louis W. Stern and Thomas L. Eovald, *Legal Aspects of Marketing Strategy: Antitrust and Consumer Protection Issues* (Englewood Cliffs, NJ: Prentice-Hall, 1984).

CHAPTER 5

General

- M. Frank Bradley, "Nature and Significance of International Marketing: A Review," *Journal of Business Research* (June 1987), 205–220.
- Raj Aggarwal, "The Strategic Challenge of the Evolving Global Economy," *Business Horizons* (July/August 1987), 38–44.
- John A Quelch, Robert D. Buzzell, and Eric R. Salama, *The Marketing Challenge of 1992* (Boston: Addison Wesley, 1990).

Global versus Local Strategies

- Theodore Levitt, "The Globalization of Markets," *Harvard Business Review* (May–June 1983), 92–102.
- John A. Quelch and E.J. Hoff, "Customizing Global Marketing," *Harvard Business Review* (May–June 1986), 59–68.
- Subhash C. Jain, "Standardization of International Marketing Strategy," *Journal of Marketing* (January 1989), 70–79.
- Kamran Kashani, "Beware the Pitfalls of Global Marketing," *Harvard Business Review* (September–October 1989), 91–98.

International Environment

- Barbara Mueller, "Reflections of Culture: An Analysis of Japanese and American Advertising Appeals," *Journal of Advertising Research* (June/July 1987).
- James M. Higgins and Timo Santalainen, "Strategies for Europe 1992," *Business Horizons* (July/August 1989), 54–58.
- Thomas W. Shreeve, "Be Prepared for Political Changes Abroad," *Harvard Business Review* (July/August 1984), 111–118.

Market Entry

- Kenichi Ohmae, "The Global Logic of Strategic Alliances," *Harvard Business Review* (March–April 1989), 143–154.
- F. Kingston Berlew, "The Joint Venture—A Way Into Foreign Markets," *Harvard Business Review* (July–August 1984), 48–55.

CHAPTER 6

Competitive Advantage

- Michael E. Porter, "From Competitive Advantage to Corporate Strategy," *Harvard Business Review 65*(May–June 1987), 43–59.
- George S. Day and Robin Wensley, "Assessing Competitive Advantage: A Framework for Diagnosing Competitive Superiority," *Journal of Marketing 52*(April 1988), 1–20.
- Pankaj Ghemawat, "Sustainable Advantage," *Harvard Business Review 64*(September–October 1986), 53–58.

Competitive Strategies

- Philip Kotler and Ravi Singh, "Marketing Warfare in the 1980s," *The Journal of Business Strategy* (Winter 1982).
- Al Reis and Jack Trout, *Marketing Warfare* (New York: McGraw-Hill, 1986).
- Michael E. Porter, "How to Attack the Industry Leader," *Fortune*, April 29, 1985, 153–166.

CHAPTER 7

Marketing Information Systems

- "How Executives Can Shape Their Company's Information Systems," *Harvard Business Review 67* (March–April 1989), 130–134.
- Bernard C. Reimann, "Decision Support Systems: Strategic Management Tools for the Eighties," *Business Horizons* (September/October 1985), 71–77.
- Martin D.J. Buss, "Managing International Information systems," *Harvard Business Review 60* (September–October 1982), 153–162.

Marketing Research

- Robert Ferber, ed. *Handbook of Marketing Research* (New York: McGraw-Hill, 1975).
- Jeffrey Dungee, "Richer Findings from Qualitative Research," *Journal of Advertising Research 26* (August–September 1986), 36–44.
- Keith K. Cox, James B. Higginbotham, and John Burton, "Application of Focus Group Interviews in Marketing," *Journal of Marketing 40* (January 1976).
- Tyzoon T. Tyebjee, "Telephone Survey Methods: The State of the Art," *Journal of Marketing 43* (Summer 1979), 68–77.
- Nicolaos E. Synodinos and Jerry M. Brennan, "Computer Interactive Interviewing in Survey Research," *Psychology and Marketing* (Summer 1988), 117–138.
- Alan G. Sawyer, Parker M. Worthing, and Paul E. Fendak, "The Role of Laboratory Experiments to Test Marketing Strategies," *Journal of Marketing 43* (Summer 1979), 60–67.

CHAPTER 8

Decision Making

- Frances K. McSweeney and Calvin Bierley, "Recent Developments in Classical Conditioning," *Journal of Consumer Research 11* (September 1984), 619–631.
- Michael L. Rothschild and William C. Gadis, "Behavioral Learning Theory: Its Relevance to Marketing and Promotions," *Journal of Marketing 45* (Spring 1981), 70–78.
- Jacob Jacoby and David B. Kyner, "Brand Loyalty vs. Repeat Purchasing Behavior," *Journal of Marketing Research 10* (February 1973), 1–9.
- Girish Punj, "Presearch Decision Making in Consumer Durable Purchases," *Journal of Consumer Marketing 4* (Winter 1987), 71–82.

- Richard L. Celsi and Jerry C. Olson, "The Role of Involvement in Attention and Comprehension Processes," *Journal of Consumer Research 15* (September 1988), 210–224.
- Herbert E. Krugman, "The Impact of Television Advertising: Learning Without Involvement," *Public Opinion Quarterly 29* (Fall 1965), 349–356.
- Richard E. Petty, John T. Cacioppo, and David Schumann, "Central and Peripheral Routes to Advertising Effectiveness: The Moderating Role of Involvement," *Journal of Consumer Research 10* (September 1983), 135–146.
- Michael L. Rothschild and Michael J. Houston, "The Consumer Involvement Matrix: Some Preliminary Findings," in Barnett A. Greenberg and Danny N. Bellenger, *Proceedings of the American Marketing Association Educators' Conference*, Series No. 41(1977), 95–98.

The Psychological Set

- Timothy E. Moore, "Subliminal Advertising: What You See is What You Get," *Journal of Marketing 46* (September 1982), 38–47.
- Mita Sujan and James R. Bettman, "The Effect of Brand Positioning Strategies on Consumers' Brand and Category Perceptions," *Journal of Marketing Research 26* (November 1989), 454–467.
- Jeen-Su Lim, Richard W. Olshavsky, and John Kim, "The Impact of Inferences on Product Evaluations," *Journal of Marketing Research 25* (August 1988), 308–316.
- Richard J. Lutz, "The Role of Attitude Theory in Marketing," in Harold H. Kassarjian and Thomas S. Robertson, eds., *Perspectives in Consumer Behavior* (Glenview, IL: Scott Foresman and Co., 1991).
- Daniel Katz, "The Functional Approach to the Study of Attitudes," *Public Opinion Quarterly 24* (Summer 1960), 163–204.
- Martin Fishbein, "Attitudes and the Prediction of Behavior," in Martin Fishbein, ed., *Readings in Attitude Theory and Measurement* (New York: John Wiley, 1967), 477–492.
- Harold H. Kassarjian and Joel B. Cohen, "Cognitive Dissonance and Consumer Behavior," *California Management Review 8* (Fall 1965), 55–64.
- C. W. Sherif, M. Sherif, and R. W. Nebergall, *Attitude and Attitude Change* (Philadelphia: Saunders, 1965).

Consumer Characteristics

- Harold H. Kassarjian, "Personality and Consumer Behavior: A Review," *Journal of Marketing Research 8* (November 1971), 409–419.
- William D. Wells and Arthur D. Beard, "Personality Theories," in Scott Ward and Thomas S. Robertson, eds., *Consumer Behavior: Theoretical Sources* (Englewood Cliffs, NJ: Prentice-Hall, 1973), 142–199.
- Joseph T. Plummer, "The Concept and Application of Life Style Segmentation." *Journal of Marketing 38* (January 1974), 33–37.
- Arnold Mitchell, *Changing Values and Lifestyles* (Menlo Park, CA: SRI International, 1981).

Environmental Influences

- Joseph F. Hair, Jr., and Rolph E. Anderson, "Culture, Acculturation and Consumer Behavior: An Empirical Study," in Boris W. Becker and Helmut Becker, eds., *Combined Proceedings of the American Marketing Association*, Series No. 34 (1972), 423–428.
- Milton J. Rokeach, "The Role of Values in Public Opinion Research," *Public Opinion Quarterly 32* (Winter 1968), 547–549.
- Richard P. Coleman, "The Continuing Significance of Social Class to Marketing," *Journal of Consumer Research 10* (December 1983), 265–280.
- Joel Garreau, *The Nine Nations of North America* (New York: Avon, 1981).
- Teresa Domzal and Lynette Unger, "Emerging Positioning Strategies in Global Markets," *Journal of Consumer Marketing 4* (Fall 1987).
- Thomas C. O'Guinn et al., "The Cultivation of Consumer Norms," in Thomas K. Srull, ed., *Advances in Consumer Research* Vol. 16 (Provo, UT: Association for Consumer Research, 1989), 779–785.

- Elihu Katz and Paul F. Lazarsfeld, *Personal Influence* (Glencoe, IL: The Free Press, 1955).
- William O. Bearden and Michael J. Etzel, "Reference Group Influence on Product and Brand Purchase Decisions," *Journal of Consumer Research 9* (September 1982), 183–194.
- William O. Bearden, Richard G. Netemeyer, and Jesse E. Teel, "Measurement of Consumer Susceptibility to Interpersonal Influence," *Journal of Consumer Research 15* (March 1989), 473–481.
- Harry L. Davis, "Decision Making Within the Household," *Journal of Consumer Research 2* (March 1976).
- William J. Qualls, "Household Decision Behavior: The Impact of Husbands' and Wives' Sex Role Orientation," *Journal of Consumer Research 14* (September 1987), 264–279.
- George P. Moschis, "The Role of Family Communication in Consumer Socialization of Children and Adolescents," *Journal of Consumer Research 11* (March 1985), 898–913.
- Everett M. Rogers and F. Floyd Shoemaker, *Communications of Innovation* (New York: The Free Press, 1971).

CHAPTER 9

General

- Robert E. Spekman and Wesley J. Johnston, "Relationship Management: Managing the Selling and the Buying Interface," *Journal of Business Research* (December 1986), 519–532.
- Edward F. Fern and James R. Brown, "The Industrial/Consumer Marketing Dichotomy: A Case of Insufficient Justification," *Journal of Marketing 48* (Spring 1984), 68–77.
- Barbara Bund Jackson, "Build Customer Relationships That Last," *Harvard Business Review 63* (November–December 1985), 120–128.
- Stephen T. Parkinson, "Factors Influencing Buyer–Seller Relationships in the Market for High-Technology Products," *Journal of Business Research 13* (1985), 49–60.

Buyer Decision Making

- Jagdish N. Sheth, "A Model of Industrial Buyer Behavior," *Journal of Marketing 37* (October 1973).
- Niras Vyas and Arch G. Woodside, "An Inductive Model of Industrial Supplier Choice Processes," *Journal of Marketing 48* (Winter 1984), 30–45.
- Paul F. Anderson and Terry M. Chambers, "A Reward/Measurement Model of Organizational Buying Behavior," *Journal of Marketing 49* (Spring 1985), 7–23.
- William J. Qualls and Christopher P. Puto, "Organizational Climate and Decision Framing: An Integrated Approach to Analyzing Industrial Buying Decisions," *Journal of Marketing Research 26* (May 1989), 179–192.
- Daniel H. McQuiston, "Novelty, Complexity, and Importance as Causal Determinants of Industrial Buyer Behavior," *Journal of Marketing 53* (April 1989), 66–75.
- Ralph W. Jackson and William M. Pride, "The Use of Approved Vendor Lists," *Industrial Marketing Management* (August 1986), 165–170.

The Buying Center

- Melvin R. Mattson, "How to Determine the Composition and Influence of a Buying Center," *Industrial Marketing Management* (August 1988), 205–214.
- Lowell E. Crow and Jay D. Lindquist, "Impact of Organizational and Buyer Characteristics on the Buying Center," *Industrial Marketing Management* (February 1985), 49–58.
- W. E. Patton III, Christopher P. Puto, and Ronald H. King, "Which Buying Decisions Are Made by Individuals and Not by Groups?" *Industrial Marketing Management* (May 1986), 129–138.
- Donald W. Jackson Jr., Janet E. Keith, and Richard K. Burdick, "Purchasing Agents' Perceptions of Industrial Buying Center Influence: A Situational Approach," *Journal of Marketing 48* (Fall 1984), 75–83.

CHAPTER 10

- Peter R. Dickson and James L. Ginter, "Market Segmentation, Product Differentiation, and Marketing Strategy," *Journal of Marketing 51*(April 1987), 1–10.
- Russell I. Haley, "Benefit Segmentation: Backwards and Forwards," *Journal of Advertising Research 24* (February–March 1984), 19–25.
- Henry Assael and A. Marvin Roscoe, Jr., "Approaches to Market Segmentation Analysis," *Journal of Marketing 40* (October 1976), 67–76.
- Ronald E. Frank, William F. Massy, and Yoram Wind, *Market Segmentation*, (Englewood Cliffs, N.J.: Prentice-Hall, Inc. 1972).
- James F. Engel, Henry F. Fiorillo, and Murray A. Cayley, *Market Segmentation: Concepts and Applications* (New York: Holt, Rinehart and Winston, Inc., 1972).
- Thomas V. Bonoma and Benson P. Shapiro, *Segmenting the Industrial Market* (Lexington, MA: Lexington Books, 1983).
- Peter Doyle and John Saunders, "Market Segmentation and Positioning in Specialized Industrial Markets," *Journal of Marketing 49* (Spring 1985), 24–32.

CHAPTER 11

New Product Definition

- Patrick M. Dunne, "What Really Are New Products," *Journal of Business* (December 1974), 20–25.
- Patrick E. Murphy and Ben M. Enis, "Classifying Products Strategically," *Journal of Marketing 50* (July 1986), 24–42.

New Product Success and Failure

- Peter L. Link, "Keys to New Product Success and Failure," *Industrial Marketing Management* (May 1987), 109–118.
- C. Merle Crawford, "New Product Failure Rates: A Reprise," *Research Management* (July–August 1987), 20–24.

Product Planning and Strategy

- Leigh Lawton and A. Parasuraman, "So You Want Your New Product Planning to be Productive," *Business Horizons* (December 1980), 29–34.
- Marc C. Particelli, "New Product Strategy: How the Pros Do It," *Industrial Marketing* (May 1982).
- Shelby H. McIntyre and Meir Statman, "Managing the Risk of New Product Development," *Business Horizons* (May/June 1982), 51–55.

Idea Generation and Concept Testing

- Eric von Hipple, "Get New Products From Consumers," *Harvard Business Review 60* (March–April 1982), 117–122.
- William M. Moore, "Concept Testing," *Journal of Business Research* (September 1982), 279–294.
- David A. Schwartz, "Concept Testing Can Be Improved—and Here's How to Do It," *Marketing News*, January 6, 1984, 22.

Product Design

- Philip Kotler, "Design: A Powerful but Neglected Marketing Tool," *Journal of Business Strategy* (Fall 1984), 16–21.

Test Marketing

- Steven H. Starr and Glen L. Urban, "The Case of the Test Market Toss Up," *66* (September–October 1988), 10–27.

CHAPTER 12

Product Management

- P.L. Dawes and P.G. Patterson, "The Performance of Industrial and Consumer Product Managers," *Industrial Marketing Management* (February 1988), 73–84.

- Thomas J. Cosse and John E. Swan, "Strategic Marketing Planning by Product Managers—Room for Improvement?," *Journal of Marketing 47* (Summer 1983), 92–102.

The Brand

- Thomas M.S. Hemnes, "How Can You Find a Safe Trademark?," *Harvard Business Review 62* (March–April 1985), 36–72.
- Dorothy Cohen, "Trademark Strategy," *Journal of Marketing 50* (January 1986), 61–74.
- Mark B. Taylor, "Cannibalism in Multibrand Firms," *Journal of Business Strategy* (Spring 1986), 69–75.
- David A. Aaker and Kevin L. Keller, "Consumer Evaluations of Brand Extensions," *Journal of Marketing 54* (January 1990), 27–41.

Product Life Cycle

- George Day, "The Product Life Cycle: Analysis and Applications Issues," *Journal of Marketing 45* (Fall 1981), 60–67.
- John E. Swan and David R. Rink, "Fitting Marketing Strategy to Varying Product Life Cycles," *Business Horizons* (January/February 1982), 72–76.
- Igal Ayal, "International Product Life Cycle: A Reassessment and Product Policy Implications," *Journal of Marketing* (Fall 1981), 91–96.

CHAPTER 13

- Christopher H. Lovelock, *Services Marketing* (Englewood Cliffs, NJ: Prentice-Hall, 1984).
- William H. Davidow and Bro Uttal, *Total Customer Service: The Ultimate Weapon* (Homewood, IL: Dow Jones Irwin, 1988).
- Leonard L. Berry, Edwin F. Lefkowith, and Terry Clark, "In Services, What's In a Name?" *Harvard Business Review 66* (September–October, 1988), 28–30.
- Leonard L. Berry, A. Parasuraman, and Valarie A. Zeithaml, "The Service–Quality Puzzle," *Business Horizons* (September–October 1988), 35–43.
- Theodore Levitt, "Marketing Intangible Products and Product Intangibles," *Harvard Business Review 59* (May–June 1981), 94–102.
- Mary Jo Bitner, Bernard H. Booms, and Mary Stanfield Tetreault, "The Service Encounter: Diagnosing Favorable and Unfavorable Incidents," *Journal of Marketing 54* (January 1990), 71–84.
- Eberhard E. Scheuing and Eugene M. Johnson, "A Proposed Model for New Service Development," *The Journal of Services Marketing* (Spring 1989), 25–34.
- Stephen W. Brown and Teresa A. Swartz, "A Gap Analysis of Professional Service Quality," *Journal of Marketing 53* (April 1989), 92–98.
- Richard B. Chase and David A. Garvin, "The Service Factory," *Harvard Business Review* 67 (July–August 1989), 61–69.
- Betsy D. Gelb, "How Marketers of Intangibles Can Raise the Odds for Consumer Satisfaction," *Journal of Services Marketing* (Summer 1987), 11–17. James L. Heskett, "Lessons in the Service Sector," *Harvard Business Review 65*(March–April 1987), 122–124.
- Doris C. Van Doren, Louse W. Smith, and Ronald J. Biglin, "The Challenge of Professional Services Marketing," *Journal of Consumer Marketing* (Spring 1985), 19–27.

Nonprofit Services

- Philip Kotler and Alan R. Andreasen, *Strategic Marketing for Nonprofit Organizations*, 3rd ed., (Englewood Cliffs, NJ: Prentice-Hall, 1987).
- Christopher H. Lovelock and Charles B. Weinberg, *Marketing for Public and Nonprofit Managers* (New York: John Wiley & Sons, 1984).
- Bonnie S. Gay and Wesley E. Patton, "The Marketing of Altruistic Causes: Understanding Why People Help," *The Journal of Consumer Marketing* (Winter 1989), 19–30.

CHAPTER 14

Distribution Systems

- Louis W. Stern and Adel I. El Ansary, *Marketing Channels*, 3rd ed. (Englewood Cliffs, NJ: Prentice-Hall, 1988).

- Louis W. Stern and Frederick D. Sturdivant, "Customer-Driven Distribution Systems," *Harvard Business Review 65* (July–August 1987), 34–41.
- "Managing Hybrid Distribution Systems," *Harvard Business Review 68* (November–December 1990), 146–157.

Channel Management

- Bruce J. Walker, Janet E. Keith, and Donald W. Jackson, Jr., "The Channel Manager: Now, Soon or Never?" *Academy of Marketing Science* (Summer 1985), 82–96.
- Allan J. Magrath and Kenneth G. Hardy, "Avoiding the Pitfalls in Managing Distribution Channels," *Business Horizons* (September/October 1987), 29–33.

Channel Strategy

- Michael Levy, John Webster, and Roger Kerin, "Formulating Push Marketing Strategies," *Journal of Marketing 47* (Winter 1983), 25–34.
- Alvin A. Achenbaum and F. Kent Mitchel, "Pulling Away from Push Marketing," *Harvard Business Review 65* (May–June 1987), 38–42.

Conflict in Distribution

- Patrick L. Schul, William M. Pride, and Taylor L. Little, "The Impact of Channel Leadership Behavior on Intrachannel Conflict," *Journal of Marketing 47* (Summer 1983), 21–34.
- John E. Robbins, Thomas W. Speh, and Morris L. Mayer, "Retailer's Perceptions of Channel Conflict Issues," *Journal of Retailing* (Winter 1982), 46–67.

CHAPTER 15

Trends in Retailing

- Eleanor G. May, C. William Ress, and Walter J. Salmon, *Future Trends in Retailing* (Cambridge, MA: Marketing Science Institute, 1985).
- Richard V. Sarkissian, "Retail Trends in the 1990s," *Journal of Accountancy* (December 1989), 44–46.

Wheel of Retailing

- Malcolm P. McNair and Eleanor G. May, "The Next Revolution of the Retailing Wheel," *Harvard Business Review 56* (September–October 1978), 81–91.
- Rom J. Markin and Calvin P. Duncan, "The Transformation of Retailing Institutions: Beyond the Wheel of Retailing and Life Cycle Theories," *Journal of Macromarketing 1* (1981), 58–66.
- Ronald Savitt, "The Wheel of Retailing and Retail Product Management," *European Journal of Marketing 18* (1984), 43–54.

Off-Price Retailing

- Jack G. Kaikati, "Don't Discount Off-Price Retailers," *Harvard Business Review 63* (May–June 1985), 85–92.

Nonstore Retailing

- Larry J. Rosenberg and Elizabeth C. Hirschman, "Retailing Without Stores," *Harvard Business Review 58* (May–June 1980), 103–112.
- John D. Tsalikis, "Influence of Catalog vs. Store Shopping and Prior Satisfaction on Perceived Risk," *Journal of the Academy of Marketing Science 14* (Winter 1986), 28–36.

CHAPTER 16

Wholesaling

- J.J. Withey, "Realities of Channel Dynamics: A Wholesaling Example," *Academy of Marketing Science* (Summer 1985), 72–81.
- Arthur Anderson & Co., *Facing the Forces of Change: Beyond Future Trends in Wholesale Distribution* (Washington, D.C.: Distribution Research and Education Foundation, 1987).
- Donald M. Jackson and Michael F. d'Amico, "Products and Markets Served by Distributors and Agents," *Industrial Marketing Management* (February 1989), 27–34.

Physical Distribution

- John T. Mentzer, Roger Gomes, and Robert E. Krapfel, Jr., "Physical Distribution Service: A Fundamental Marketing Concept?," *Journal of the Academy of Marketing Science* (Winter 1989), 53–62.
- Norman E. Hutchinson, *An Integrated Approach to Logistics Management* (Englewood Cliffs, NJ: Prentice Hall, 1987).
- Roy D. Shapiro, "Get Leverage From Logistics," *Harvard Business Review 62* (May–June 1984), 119–126.

Storage and Handling

- James Aaron Cooke, "Here's a High-Tech Warehouse That Works," *Traffic Management* (April 1985).

Inventory Management

- David J. Armstrong, "Sharpening Inventory Management," *Harvard Business Review 63* (November–December 1985), 42–59.
- Hal E. Mather, "The Case for Skimpy Inventories," *Harvard Business Review 62* (January–February 1984), 40–49.

Just-in-Time Systems

- William D. Presutti, Jr., "Just-in-Time Manufacturing and Marketing—Strategic Relationship for Competitive Advantage," *Journal of Business and Industrial Marketing* (Summer 1988), 27–35
- Gary L. Frazier, Robert E. Spekman, and Charles R. O'Neal, "Just-in-Time Exchange Relationships in Industrial Markets," *Journal of Marketing 52* (October 1988), 52–67.

Transportation

- Lewis M. Schneider, "New Era in Transportation Strategy," *Harvard Business Review 63* (March–April 1985), 118–126.
- C.H. White and R.B. Felder, "Turn Your Truck Fleet into a Profit Center," *Harvard Business Review 61* (May–June 1983), 14–17.
- Bagchi T.S. Raghumathan and Edward J. Bardi, "The Implications of Just-in-Time Inventory Policies on Carrier Selection," *The Logistics and Transportation Review* (December 1987), 373–384.

CHAPTER 17

Sales Promotions

- J.F. Engel, M.R. Warshaw, and T.C. Kinnear, *Promotional Strategy* (Homewood IL: Richard D. Irwin, 1988).
- Roger A. Strang, "Sales Promotion—Fast Growth, Faulty Management," *Harvard Business Review 55* (July–August 1976).
- Kenneth G. Hardy, "Key Success Factors for Manufacturers' Sales Promotions in Package Goods," *Journal of Marketing 50* (July 1986), 13–23.
- Sunil Gupta, "Impact of Sales Promotions on When, What, and How Much to Buy," *Journal of Marketing Research 25* (November 1988), 342–355.
- P. Rajan Varadarajan and Anil Menon, "Cause-Related Marketing: A Coalignment of Marketing Strategy and Corporate Philanthropy," *Journal of Marketing 52* (July 1988), 58–74.
- John A. Quelch, "It's Time to Make Trade Promotion More Productive," *Harvard Business Review 61* (May–June 1983), 130–136.

Publicity

- Tom Duncan, *A Study of How Manufacturers and Service Companies Perceive and Use Marketing Public Relations* (Muncie, IN: Ball State University, 1985).
- E. Cameron Williams, "Product Publicity: Low Cost and High Credibility," *Industrial Marketing Management* (November 1988), 355–360.
- Arthur M. Merims, "Marketing's Stepchild: Product Publicity," *Harvard Business Review 51* (November–December 1972).

CHAPTER 18

- Linda L. Golden, "Consumer Reactions to Explicit Brand Comparisons in Advertisements," *Journal of Marketing Research, 16* (November 1979), 517–532.
- William R. Swinyard, "The Interaction Between Comparative Advertising and Copy Claim Variation," *Journal of Marketing Research, 18* (May 1981), 175–186.
- William L. Wilkie and Paul W. Farris, "Comparison Advertising: Problems and Potential," *Journal of Marketing, 39* (October 1975), 7–15.
- Lynette S. Unger and James M. Stearns, "The Use of Fear and Guilt Messages in Television Advertising," in Patrick E. Murphy et al., eds. *Proceedings of the American Marketing Association Educators' Conference*, Series No. 49 (1983), 16–20.
- Brian Sternthal and C. Samuel Craig, "Humor in Advertising," *Journal of Marketing, 37* (October 1973), 12–18.
- Joel Saegert, "Why Marketing Should Quit Giving Subliminal Advertising the Benefit of the Doubt," *Psychology and Marketing* (Summer 1987), 107–120.
- David W. Stewart, "Measures, Methods, and Models in Advertising Research," *Journal of Advertising Research, 29* (June–July 1989), 54–60.
- William L. Wilkie, Dennis L. McNeil, and Michael B. Mazis, "Marketing's Scarlet Letter: The Theory and Practice of Corrective Advertising," *Journal of Marketing, 48* (Spring 1984), 11–31.
- Gary T. Ford and John E. Calfee, "Recent Developments in FTC Policy on Deception," *Journal of Marketing, 50* (July 1986), 82–103.

CHAPTER 19

General

- William J. Stanton, Richard H. Buskirk, and Stanley F. Stasch, *Management of the Sales Force* (Homewood, IL: Richard D. Irwin, 1989).
- C. A. Pederson, M. D. Wright, and B. A. Weitz, *Selling Principles and Methods* (Homewood, IL: Richard D. Irwin, 1986).

The Selling Process

- Theodore Levitt, "After the Sale is Over . . .," *Harvard Business Review, 61* (September–October 1983), 87–93.
- Harvey B. Mackay, "Humanize Your Selling Strategy," *Harvard Business Review, 66* (March–April 1988), 36–47.
- F. Robert Dwyer, Paul H. Schurr, and Sejo Oh, "Developing Buyer–Seller Relationships," *Journal of Marketing, 51* (April 1987), 11–27.

National Accounts Marketing

- John Barrett, "Why Mahor Account Selling Works," *Industrial Marketing Management* (February 1986), 63–74.
- Frank C. Cespedes, Stephen X. Doyle, and Robert J. Freedman, "Teamwork for Today's Selling," *Harvard Business Review, 67* (March–April 1989), 44–59.

Telemarketing

- John I. Coppett and Roy Dale Voorhees, "Telemarketing: Supplement to Field Sales," *Industrial Marketing Management* (August 1985), 213–216.
- Eugene M. Johnson and William J. Meiners, "Selling and Sales Management in Action: Telemarketing—Trends, Issues, and Opportunities," *Journal of Personal Selling and Sales Management* (November 1987), 65–68.

Sales Management

- David M. Szymanski, "Determinants of Selling Effectiveness," *Journal of Marketing, 52* (January 1988), 64–77.
- Douglas N. Behrman and William D. Perreault, Jr., "Measuring the Performance of Industrial Salespersons," *Journal of Business Research* (September 1982), 350–370.
- Stephen X. Doyle and Benson P. Shapiro, "What Counts Most in Motivating Your Sales Force," *Harvard Business Review, 58* (May–June 1980), 133–140.

- Orville C. Walker, Jr., Gilbert A. Churchill, and Neil M. Ford, "Motivation and Performance in Industrial Selling," *Journal of Marketing Research, 14* (May 1977), 156–168.
- Thomas N. Ingram and Danny N. Bellenger, "Motivational Segments in the Sales Force," *California Management Review* (Spring 1982), 81–88.

Ethics

- Joseph A. Bellizzi and Robert E. Hite, "Supervising Unethical Salesforce Behavior," *Journal of Marketing, 53* (April 1989), 36–47.

CHAPTER 20

Pricing Strategies

- Thomas T. Nagle, *The Strategy and Tactics of Pricing* (Englewood Cliffs, NJ: Prentice-Hall, 1987).
- Gerald J. Tellis, "Beyond the Many Faces of Price: An Integration of Pricing Strategies," *Journal of Marketing, 50* (October 1986), 146–160.
- Subhash C. Jain and Michael B. Laric, "A Framework for Strategic Industrial Pricing," *Industrial Marketing Management, 8* (1979), 75–80.
- Saeed Samiee, "Pricing in Marketing Strategies of U.S. and Foreign-Based Companies," *Journal of Business Research* (February 1987), 17–30.
- Suart U. Rich, "Price Leadership in the Paper Industry," *Industrial Marketing Management* (April 1983), 101–104.

Regulatory Aspects

- Louis W. Stern and Thomas L. Eovaldi, *Legal Aspects of Marketing Strategy: Antitrust and Consumer Protection Issues* (Englewood Cliffs, NJ: Prentice-Hall, 1984).

CHAPTER 21

- Thomas T. Nagle, *The Strategy and Tactics of Pricing* (Englewood Cliffs, NJ: Prentice-Hall, 1987).
- Gerard J. Tellis and Gary J. Gaeth, "Best Value, Price-Seeking, and Price," *Journal of Marketing, 54* (April 1990), 34–45.
- Michael H. Morris and Mary L. Joyce, "How Marketers Evaluate Price Sensitivity," *Industrial Marketing Management* (May 1988), 169–176.
- Stuart U. Rich, "Price Leadership in the Paper Industry," *Industrial Marketing Management* (April 1983).
- Gordon A. Wyner, Lois H. Benedetti, and Bart M. Trapp, "Measuring the Quantity and Mix of Product Demand," *Journal of Marketing, 48* (Winter 1984), 101–109.
- Paul D. Boughton, "The Competitive Bidding Process: Beyond Probability Models," *Industrial Marketing Management* (1987), 87–94.
- Kent B. Monroe, *Pricing: Making Profitable Decisions* (New York: McGraw-Hill, 1979).

CHAPTER 22

General

- David A. Aaker, *Strategic Market Management* (New York: John Wiley, 1988).
- Subhash C. Jain, *Marketing Strategy and Planning* (Cincinnati: South-Western Publishing, 1985).
- George S. Day, *Strategic Market Planning* (St. Paul: West Publishing Co., 1984).
- Barton A. Weitz and Robin Wensely (eds.), *Readings in Strategic Marketing: Analysis, Planning, and Implementation* (Hinsdale, IL: Dryden Press, 1988).
- Richard G. Hamermesh, "Making Planning Strategic," *Harvard Business Review, 64* (July–August 1986), 115–120.
- Norman M. Scarborough and Thomas W. Zimmerer, "Strategic Planning for the Small Business," *Business, 37* (April–June 1987), 11–19.

Corporate Mission

- Fred R. David, "How Companies Define Their Missions Statements," *Long Range Planning, 22* (1989), 90–97.

Portfolio Analysis

- Philippe Haspeslagh, "Portfolio Planning: Limits and Uses," *Harvard Business Review, 60* (January–February 1982), 58–73.
- George S. Day, "Diagnosing the Product Portfolio," *Journal of Marketing, 41* (April 1977), 29–38.

Corporate Growth Strategies

- Henry H. Beam, "Strategic Discontinuities: When Being Good May Not Be Enough," *Business Horizons* (July–August 1990), 10–14.
- Christopher K. Bart, "Implementing 'Growth' and 'Harvest' Product Strategies," *California Management Review, 29* (Summer 1987), 139–156.
- David W. Cravens, "Strategic Forces Affecting Marketing Strategy," *Business Horizons, 29* (September–October 1986), 77–86.
- Richard Hamermesh and Steven Silk, "How to Compete in Stagnant Industries," *Harvard Business Review, 57* (September–October 1979), 161–168.

CHAPTER 23

Marketing Control Process

- Bernard J. Jaworski, "Toward a Theory of Marketing Control: Environmental Context Control Types and Consequences," *Journal of Marketing, 52* (July 1988), 23–39.
- Kenneth A. Merchant, "Progressing Toward a Theory of Marketing Control: A Comment," *Journal of Marketing, 52* (July 1988), 40–44.
- Subhash Sharma and Dale D. Achabal, "STEMCOM: An Analytical Model for Marketing Control," *Journal of Marketing, 46* (Spring 1982), 104–113.
- James M. Hulbert and Norman E. Toy, "A Strategic Framework for Marketing Control," *Journal of Marketing, 41* (April 1977), 12–21.

Performance Criteria

- Robin Cooper and Robert S. Kaplan, "Measure Costs Right: Make the Right Decisions," *Harvard Business Review, 66* (September–October 1988), 96–103.
- Michael J. Sandretto, "What Kind of Cost System Do You Need?" *Harvard Business Review, 63* (January–February 1985), 110–118.
- William Bentz and Robert Lusch, "Now You Can Control Your Product's Market Performance," *Management Accounting* (January 1980), 17–25.
- Nigel F. Percy, "The Marketing Budgeting Process: Marketing Management Implications," *Journal of Marketing, 51* (October 1987), 45–59.

Organization

- Robert W. Ruekert, Orville C. Walker, Jr., and Kenneth J. Roering, "The Organization of Marketing Activities: A Contingency Theory of Structure and Performance," *Journal of Marketing, 49* (Winter 1985), 13–25.

Implementation

- Orville C. Walker, Jr., and Robert W. Ruekert, "Marketing's Role in the Implementation of Business Strategies: A Critical Review and Conceptual Framework," *Journal of Marketing, 51* (July 1987), 15–33.
- Rohit Deshpande and Frederick E. Webster, Jr., "Organizational Culture and Marketing: Defining the Research Agenda," *Journal of Marketing, 53* (January 1989), 3–15.

Control Systems

- William J. Bruns, Jr., and W. Warren McFarlan, "Information Technology Puts Power in Control Systems," *Harvard Business Review, 65* (September–October 1987), 89–94.

COMPANY INDEX

Terms in **boldface** refer to key terms.

CREDITS

Chapter 1 Vignette: © Patricia Hinshaw
Exhibit 1.2: Courtesy of Exxon Corporation/McCann-Erickson, Houston
Exhibit 1.3: © Dan Cornish/Esto Photographics, Inc.
Chapter 1 Global box: © Tom Wagner/SABA
Exhibit 1.7: Courtesy of San Diego Zoo

Exhibit 2.1: Copyright © Patricia M. Doty 1992
Chapter 2 Global box: © 1991 Caren Firouz/Black Star
Exhibit 2.7: Courtesy of New United Motor Manufacturing, Inc.

Chapter 3 Vignette: © Susan Lapides 1992
Exhibit 3.1: Courtesy of Prodigy Services Co.
Exhibit 3.3: Courtesy of MCI Communications Corp.
Exhibit 3.4: Copyright © Patricia M. Doty 1992

Exhibit 4.1a: Courtesy of The House of Seagram
Exhibit 4.2: Courtesy of NIKE/Photographer, Dennis Manarchy
Exhibit 4.3: Courtesy of Royal Viking Line
Chapter 4 Global box: Reuters/Bettmann
Exhibit 4.4: Reprint permission granted by Timex Corporation
Exhibit 4.8a: Courtesy of Ocean Spray Cranberries, Inc.
Exhibit 4.8b: Courtesy of A&P
Exhibit 4.9: © 1988 Environmental Defense Fund
Exhibit 4.10: Courtesy of Days Inn of America, Inc.

Chapter 5 Vignette: © Tom Wagner/SABA
Exhibit 5.1a: Courtesy of Chevrolet Motor Division
Exhibit 5.5: Reprinted with special permission of King Features Syndicate
Exhibit 5.7: Courtesy of Aluminum Co. of America
Exhibit 5.8: © Paul Fusco/Magnum Photos

Chapter 6 Vignette: © 1991 Robert Neubecker
Exhibit 6.1c: Apple, the Apple logo, and "The Power to be your Best" are registered trademarks of Apple Computer, Inc.
Exhibit 6.1d: Courtesy of Gerber Products Co.
Exhibit 6.2: Courtesy of AT&T International Long Distance Service
Chapter 6 Global box: COMSTOCK, Inc./Gary Benson

Chapter 7 Vignette: Copyright © Patricia M. Doty 1992
Exhibit 7.1: Copyright © 1992 Reid Horn
Chapter 7 Global box: © Tecmac/Westlight
Exhibit 7.4: © Jon Feingersh 1990/The Stock Market

Exhibit 8.1: Copyright © Patricia M. Doty 1992
Exhibit 8.6b: Courtesy of MasterCard International
Chapter 8 Global box: © Owen Franken/Stock-Boston
Exhibit 8.9a: Reprinted with the permission of Apple Computer, Inc.
Exhibit 8.9b: Courtesy of Chrysler Motors Corporation
Exhibit 8.13: Courtesy of Hart Schaffner & Marx Clothes

Exhibit 9.1: Courtesy of Sonoco Products/Terry Parke, Photographer
Exhibit 9.3: Courtesy of Brock Control Systems Incorporated
Exhibit 9.4: Used with permission of NEC America

Exhibit 10.1: Copyright © Patricia M. Doty 1992
Exhibit 10.3: Courtesy of Campbell Soup Company
Chapter 10 Global box: Copyright © Patricia M. Doty 1992
Exhibit 10.4: Courtesy of Merrill Lynch & Co., Inc.
Exhibit 10.5: Courtesy of E.I. DuPont Company
Exhibit 10.6: © 1992 University Brands

Chapter 11 Vignette: Courtesy of 3M Do-It-Yourself Division
Exhibit 11.1: Courtesy of Cycle Composites, Inc.
Exhibit 11.2: © David Walberg 1991. All Rights Reserved.
Exhibit 11.3: Courtesy of Nabisco Biscuit Company
Chapter 11 Global box: Copyright © Patricia M. Doty 1992
Exhibit 11.4: Source: "Forsaking the Black Box, Designers Wrap Products in Visual Metaphors," *The Wall Street Journal*, March 26, 1987, p. 39; Reprinted by permission of *The Wall Street Journal*, © Dow Jones & Company, Inc. 1987; All Rights Reserved Worldwide.
Exhibit 11.5: AP/Wide World Photos

Exhibit 12.2: Copyright © Patricia M. Doty 1992
Chapter 12 Global box: Michael Grecco © 1991; All Rights Reserved
Exhibit 12.6: Courtesy of Reynolds Metals Company Consumer Products Division

Chapter 13 Vignette: © John Madere
Exhibit 13.2a: Reprinted with the permission of The Prudential Insurance Company of America; All Rights Reserved
Exhibit 13.4: Courtesy of Kentucky Fried Chicken
Chapter 13 Global box: Gordon/REA/SABA
Exhibit 13.5: Courtesy of Shanti Project, San Francisco, Calif.
Exhibit 13.7: Courtesy of The Salvation Army/Brouillard Communications

Chapter 14 Vignette: Copyright © Patricia M. Doty 1992
Exhibit 14.1: Photo: Toscani; Courtesy of Benetton Cosmetics Corporation, New York, N.Y. 10022
Exhibit 14.4: Courtesy of Ace Hardware Corporation
Exhibit 14.5: © Don Smetzer/Tony Stone Worldwide
Exhibit 14.6: Courtesy of Van Cleef & Arpels®.

Chapter 15 Vignette: © 1988 Marc PoKempner
Exhibit 15.1a: Photograph © Art Wolfe
Exhibit 15.1b: Courtesy of Home Shopping Network
Exhibit 15.1c: Copyright © Patricia M. Doty 1992
Exhibit 15.2: Courtesy The Limited, Inc., 1990 Annual Report
Exhibit 15.3: Courtesy of Montgomery Ward & Co.
Exhibit 15.4: Courtesy of Great Atlantic and Pacific Tea Co., Inc.
Exhibit 15.5: © Eli Reichman
Exhibit 15.6: Gordon/REA/SABA
Chapter 15 Global box: © J. Ong/Superstock, Inc.
Exhibit 15.7: © Tom Meyer

Exhibit 16.1: © 1991 Jay Brousseau
Chapter 16 Global box: © J. Ong/Superstock, Inc.
Exhibit 16.2: Reprinted with permission of Compaq Computer Corporation; All Rights Reserved
Exhibit 16.3: Courtesy of W.W. Grainger, Inc.
Exhibit 16.5: Courtesy of Danzas Corporation

Exhibit 18.4b: Courtesy of Sony Corporation of America
Exhibit 18.10: Courtesy of Renault USA, Inc.
Chapter 18 Global box: © Filip Horvat/SABA

Chapter 19 Vignette: Courtesy of Xerox Corporation
Exhibit 19.2: Courtesy of Grid Systems Corporation
Exhibit 19.4: Courtesy of Giltspur, Inc.
Exhibit 19.5: Bob Krist/Black Star

Chapter 20 Vignette: Copyright © Patricia M. Doty 1992
Exhibit 20.2a: Courtesy of Red Devil Company; Ad Agency, Waring & LaRosa, Inc.; Art Director: Howard Title; Copywriter: Bob Murphy
Chapter 20 Global box: Steve Liss/Time Magazine

Chapter 21 Vignette: © 1991 Cindy Lewis; All Rights Reserved

Chapter 22 Vignette: Copyright © Patricia M. Doty 1992
Exhibit 22.2: Copyright © Patricia M. Doty 1992

Chapter 23 Vignette: © Katherine Lambert
Exhibit 23.1: © 1991 Jay Brousseau
Exhibit 23.2: Courtesy of The Procter & Gamble Company

MARKETING Principles & Strategy

Second Edition